Geographica

The Complete Illustrated Atlas of the World

KÖNEMANN

Publisher:	Gordon Cheers
Associate publisher:	Margaret Olds
Managing editors:	Philippa Sandall (text)
	Valerie Marlborough (maps)
Editors:	Scott Forbes
	Sue Grose-Hodge
	Gillian Hewitt
	Siobhan O'Connor
	Sarah Shrubb
	Carolyn Beaumont
	Anna Cheifetz
	Clare Double
	Kate Etherington
	Denise Imwold
	Heather Jackson
Map editors:	Janet Parker
	Fran Church
	Heather Martin
	Marlene Meynert
	Jan Watson
Chief designer:	Clare Forte
Senior designer:	Robert Taylor
Cover design:	Bob Mitchell
Production designers:	Deborah Clarke
	Max Peatman
	James Young
Cartographic manager:	Graham Keane
Senior cartographer:	Andrew Dunlop
Cartographers:	Weimin Gu
	Paul McDonald
	David Morris
	Melissa O'Brien
	Clare Varney
Consultant for water areas:	Tony Davidson
Thematic maps:	John Frith
Contour shading:	John Gittoes
	Oliver Rennert
	Ray Sims
Cartographic coordinator:	James Mills-Hicks
Researchers:	Derek Barton
	Claudia Zipfel
Gazetteer:	Valerie Marlborough
	Heather Jackson
	Janet Parker
	Dee Rogers
	Clare Double
Typesetting:	Dee Rogers
Photo research:	Gordon Cheers
Photo library:	Susan Page
Production manager:	Linda Watchorn
Publishing coordinator:	Sarah Sherlock
Publishing assistant:	Olivia Kleindienst

Published by Random House Australia Pty Ltd
20 Alfred Street, Milsons Point, NSW Australia 2061

First published in 1999

Production: Ursula Schümer
Film separation: Pica Colour Separation, Singapore
Printing and binding: Sing Cheong Printing Co, Ltd, Hong Kong
Printed in Hong Kong China

ISBN 3-8290-3000-2
10 9 8 7 6 5 4 3 2

Page i: Part of the Swiss Alps, showing strata folds.

Pages ii–iii: The European Parliament building in Brussels, Belgium.

Page v: A Parisian sidewalk café, France.

Page xii: Overlooking the principality of Monaco.

Pages xiv–xv: View from Alaka toward the hill of Lykavios in Athens, Greece.

Pages 52–53: An Aboriginal man fishing with spears in wetlands in the Northern Territory, Australia.

Pages 86–87: Scenic Point, Wairarapa, New Zealand.

Pages 98–99: The countryside near Yangshuo in Guangxi Zhuangzu Zizhiqu Province, China.

Pages 106–07: A village on the Sepik River, Papua New Guinea.

Pages 142–43: Terraced hills looking toward the Himalayas, Nepal.

Pages 226–27: A seaside Cornish village, United Kingdom.

Pages 310–11: Rhinoceroses and calves in the waters of the Luangwa River in Zambia, Africa.

Pages 374–75: Grand Canyon, Arizona, USA.

Pages 432–33: Autumn colors in Tierra del Fuego, Argentina.

Pages 462–63: Polar bears in Arctic Siberia.

Pages 472–73: A whale shark in Californian waters.

Consultants and Contributors

GENERAL EDITOR

Professor Ray Hudson BA, PhD, DSc
(University of Bristol), DSc (Honoris Causa, University
of Roskilde); Department of Geography, University of
Durham

CONSULTANTS

Professor Tom McKnight BA, MA, PhD (University
of Wisconsin); Professor Emeritus of Geography,
University of California, Los Angeles

Professor Joan Clemons PhD (University of
Minnesota); Visiting Professor, Graduate School
of Education and Information Studies, University
of California, Los Angeles

Professor John Overton MA, PhD (Cambridge);
Professor, Institute of Development Studies, School
of Global Studies, Massey University

Professor Toru Taniuchi BA, MSc, DSc, (University
of Tokyo); Professor of Human Geography,
University of Tokyo, Japan

Professor Bruce Thom BA, PhD (Louisiana State
University), FIAG; Emeritus Professor of Geography,
University of Sydney, Visiting Professor of Geography,
University of New South Wales,

Professor William Wonders BA (Hons), MA, PhD
(University of Toronto), Fil.Dr.h.c. (Uppsala);
University Professor and Professor Emeritus of
Geography, University of Alberta

CONTRIBUTORS
Part 1 Planet Earth

Professor Bruce Thom BA, PhD (Louisiana State
University), F.I.A.G.

Dr John O'Byrne BSc, PhD (University of Sydney)
Dr Noel de Souza BSc (Hons), MSc., Doctorat de
Specialité (University of Paris)

Dr Ron Horvath BA, MA, PhD (University of
California, Los Angeles)

Dr Scott Mooney BSc (Hons), PhD (University of
New South Wales

Part 2 People and Society

Dr Ron Brunton BA, MA, PhD (La Trobe
University)

Associate Professor Sybil Jack MA, BLitt (Oxon),
DipEd (University of New England)

Dr Ron Horvath BA, MA, PhD (University of
California, Los Angeles)

Tess Rod BA (Hons), MA, BComm

Roger Sandall BA, MA (Columbia University)

Part 3 Regions of the World

Professor Bruce Thom BA, PhD (Louisiana State
University), F.I.A.G.

Roger Sandall BA, MA (Columbia University)

Dr Noel de Souza BSc (Hons), MSc, Doctorat de
Specialité (University of Paris)

Robert Coupe MA, DipEd

CARTOGRAPHIC CONSULTANTS

Henk Brolsma, Associateship in Land Surveying;
Australian Antarctic Division, Tasmania,
Australia
Antarctica

Dr John Cornell BA, PhD (University of London)
*Papua New Guinea, Pacific Islands, Island
Nations and Dependencies*

Tony Davidson
Europe, Russian Federation, former Soviet Republics

Dr Noel de Souza BSc (Hons), MSc, Doctorat de
Specialité (University of Paris)
*India, Sri Lanka, Nepal, Bangladesh, Bhutan,
Pakistan*

Dr Joan Hardjono BA, LittB, PhD (University of New
England); Padjadjaran State University, Bandung,
Indonesia
Indonesia, Malaysia, Singapore

Dr Philip Hirsch BA, PhD
*Thailand, Laos, Myanmar, Cambodia, Vietnam,
Philippines*

Professor Naftali Kadmon BA, MSc, PhD (University
of Wales); Professor Emeritus, The Hebrew University
of Jerusalem, Israel
Israel, Turkey, Iran, Cyprus, Afghanistan

Gerry Leitner
South America, Central America

Dr Zhilin Li BEng, PhD (University of Glasgow)
Assistant Professor, The Hong Kong Polytechnic
University, Hong Kong
China

Professor Tanga Munkhtsetseg; International Relations
Institute, Ulan Bator, Mongolia
Mongolia

Chonghyon Paku MA BSc; Baito-Bunka University,
Tokyo, Japan
Korea

Karen Puklowski NZCD/Survey; Massey University,
New Zealand
New Zealand

Professor Chris Rogerson BSc (Hons), MSc, PhD
(Queens), FSAGS; University of Witwatersrand,
Johannesburg, South Africa
SubSaharan Africa

Dr Nasser Salma PhD (University of Washington,
Seattle); Associate Professor, King Saud University,
Riyadh, Saudi Arabia
*Arabic speaking countries of the Middle East
and Saharan Africa*

Brian Stokes BBus (Tourism), AssDipCart
Australia

Professor Toru Taniuchi BA, MSc, DSc (University
of Tokyo); Professor of Human Geography,
University of Tokyo, Japan
Japan

Glenn Toldi BSc, DipCart&GIS
United States of America, Canada

Lillian Wonders BA, MA
Canada

Contents

Contents

Papua New Guinea • Samoa • Solomon Islands • Tonga • Tuvalu • Vanuatu

Dependencies and Territories: American Samoa, Ashmore and Cartier Islands, Baker and Howland Islands, Christmas Island, Cocos (Keeling) Islands, Cook Islands, Coral Sea Islands, French Polynesia, Guam, Jarvis Island, Johnston Atoll, Kingman Reef, Midway Islands, New Caledonia, Niue, Norfolk Island, Northern Mariana Islands, Palmyra Atoll, Pitcairn Islands, Tokelau, Wake Island, Wallis and Futuna Islands

Afghanistan • Armenia • Azerbaijan • Bahrain • Bangladesh • Bhutan • Brunei • Cambodia • China • Cyprus • Georgia • India • Indonesia • Iran • Iraq • Israel • Japan • Jordan • Kazakhstan • Kuwait • Kyrgyzstan • Laos • Lebanon • Malaysia • Maldives • Mongolia • Myanmar (Burma) • Nepal • North Korea • Oman • Pakistan • Philippines • Qatar • Saudi Arabia • Singapore • South Korea • Sri Lanka • Syria • Taiwan • Tajikistan • Thailand • Turkey • Turkmenistan • United Arab Emirates • Uzbekistan • Vietnam • Yemen

Dependencies and Territories: British Indian Ocean Territory, Paracel Islands, Spratly Islands
Autonomous regions: Gaza Strip, West Bank

Albania • Andorra • Austria • Belarus • Belgium • Bosnia and Herzegovina • Bulgaria • Croatia • Czech Republic • Denmark • Estonia • Finland • France • Germany • Greece • Hungary • Iceland • Ireland • Italy • Latvia • Liechtenstein •

Contents

Contents

Dependencies and Territories: Anguilla, Aruba, Bermuda, British Virgin Islands, Cayman Islands, Greenland, Guadeloupe, Jan Mayen, Martinique, Montserrat, Navassa Island, Netherlands Antilles, Puerto Rico, St Pierre and Miquelon, Turks and Caicos Islands, Virgin Islands of the United States

Argentina • Bolivia • Brazil • Chile • Colombia • Ecuador • Guyana • Paraguay • Peru • Suriname • Uruguay • Venezuela

Dependencies and Territories: Falkland Islands, French Guiana, South Georgia and South Sandwich Islands

Antarctica • Arctic

Dependencies and Territories: Bouvet Island, French Southern and Antarctic Lands, Heard and MacDonald Islands, Peter I Island

PART 4

How This Book Works

Geographica is an authoritative, comprehensive and fully illustrated reference guide to the world. With maps, photographs, illustrations and text, *Geographica* will carry readers on a journey from outer space and Earth's place in the universe to the nations and cities, towns and even villages on the furthermost parts of the globe. An expert team of geographers, historians, anthropologists, astronomers, writers, editors and cartographers have worked together to create this reference.

The early part of the book is organized in topics which are each presented on a double-page spread for easy access to information. The text has been written by leading experts in the field. The very best photographs have been chosen, and illustrations and thematic maps have been specially commissioned to complement the text. Many of the double-page spreads contain a feature box which looks in detail at one aspect of the topic on the spreads.

Geographica then moves on to the core of the book; this contains maps and detailed text on the world's 192 nations which are members of the United Nations and 65 dependencies and overseas territories. The world has been divided into major continents or regions (Oceania, Asia and the Middle East, Europe and the Russian Federation, Africa, North America and Central America, South America, Polar Regions, and Oceans). Each region starts with an introductory essay on the region in general and then moves on to entries for every country, territory or dependency. The country entries feature informative descriptions of the nation and its people, physical features and land use, culture, and economy and resources. Each country entry includes a locator map, the national flag, a locator globe, and a Fact File. Entries for the major nations also include a historical time-line. The entries for the dependencies and territories follow the country entries.

The Fact Files contain a wealth of carefully researched information for quick access to each nation's key indicators, such as form of government, infant mortality, literacy, ethnic diversity, religions, and economy, as well as basic data

MAP TITLE	ALPHA NUMERIC GRID	COUNTRY NAME	MAJOR CITY	LOCATOR GLOBE

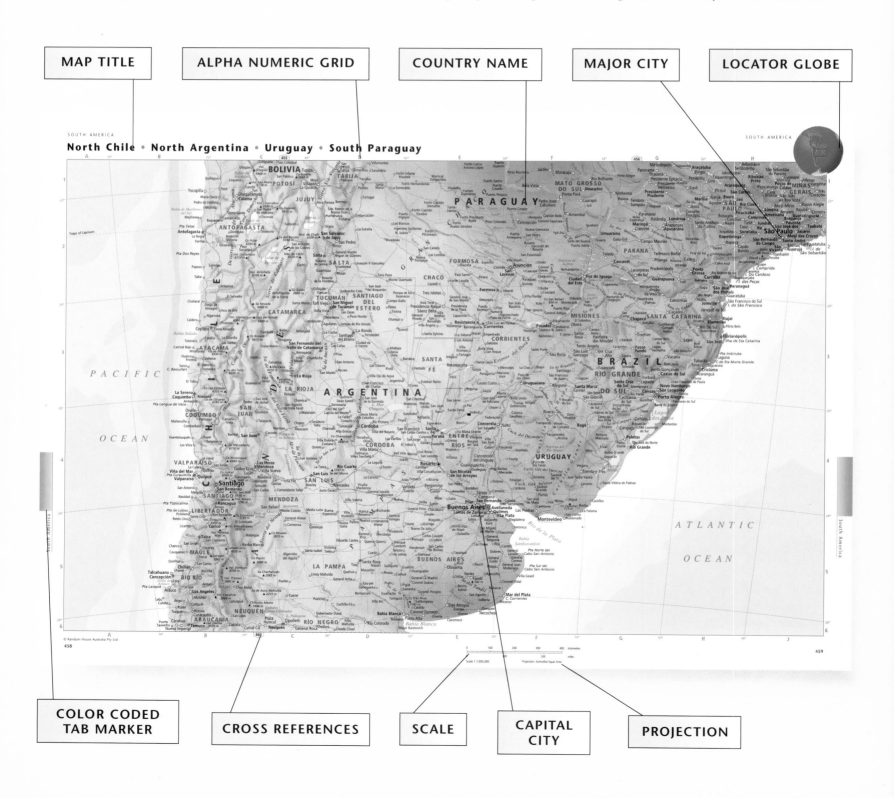

COLOR CODED TAB MARKER	CROSS REFERENCES	SCALE	CAPITAL CITY	PROJECTION

Labels (left column)

- **RUNNING HEAD**
- **COUNTRY NAME**
- **LOCATOR MAP**
- **LOCATOR GLOBE**
- **FLAG**
- **FACT FILE**
- **COLOR CODED TAB MARKER**
- **MAIN ENTRY**

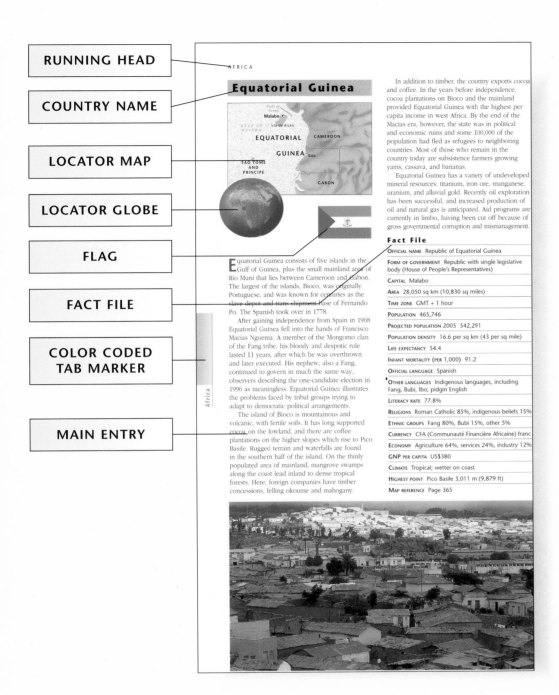

AFRICA

Equatorial Guinea

Malabo
Bight of Biafra
GULF OF GUINEA
Isla de Bioko
EQUATORIAL GUINEA
CAMEROON
Bata
SAO TOME AND PRINCIPE
GABON

Africa

Equatorial Guinea consists of five islands in the Gulf of Guinea, plus the small mainland area of Rio Muni that lies between Cameroon and Gabon. The largest of the islands, Bioco, was originally Portuguese, and was known for centuries as the slave depot and trans-shipment base of Fernando Po. The Spanish took over in 1778.

After gaining independence from Spain in 1968 Equatorial Guinea fell into the hands of Francisco Macias Nguema. A member of the Mongomo clan of the Fang tribe, his bloody and despotic rule lasted 11 years, after which he was overthrown and later executed. His nephew, also a Fang, continued to govern in much the same way, observers describing the one-candidate election in 1996 as meaningless. Equatorial Guinea illustrates the problems faced by tribal groups trying to adapt to democratic political arrangements.

The island of Bioco is mountainous and volcanic, with fertile soils. It has long supported cocoa on the lowland, and there are coffee plantations on the higher slopes which rise to Pico Basile. Rugged terrain and waterfalls are found in the southern half of the island. On the thinly populated area of mainland, mangrove swamps along the coast lead inland to dense tropical forests. Here, foreign companies have timber concessions, felling okoume and mahogany.

In addition to timber, the country exports cocoa and coffee. In the years before independence, cocoa plantations on Bioco and the mainland provided Equatorial Guinea with the highest per capita income in west Africa. By the end of the Macias era, however, the state was in political and economic ruins and some 100,000 of the population had fled as refugees to neighboring countries. Most of those who remain in the country today are subsistence farmers growing yams, cassava, and bananas.

Equatorial Guinea has a variety of undeveloped mineral resources: titanium, iron ore, manganese, uranium, and alluvial gold. Recently oil exploration has been successful, and increased production of oil and natural gas is anticipated. Aid programs are currently in limbo, having been cut off because of gross governmental corruption and mismanagement.

Fact File

OFFICIAL NAME Republic of Equatorial Guinea

FORM OF GOVERNMENT Republic with single legislative body (House of People's Representatives)

CAPITAL Malabo

AREA 28,050 sq km (10,830 sq miles)

TIME ZONE GMT + 1 hour

POPULATION 465,746

PROJECTED POPULATION 2005 542,291

POPULATION DENSITY 16.6 per sq km (43 per sq mile)

LIFE EXPECTANCY 54.4

INFANT MORTALITY (PER 1,000) 91.2

OFFICIAL LANGUAGE Spanish

OTHER LANGUAGES Indigenous languages, including Fang, Bubi, Ibo; pidgin English

LITERACY RATE 77.8%

RELIGIONS Roman Catholic 85%, indigenous beliefs 15%

ETHNIC GROUPS Fang 80%, Bubi 15%, other 5%

CURRENCY CFA (Communauté Financière Africaine) franc

ECONOMY Agriculture 64%, services 24%, industry 12%

GNP PER CAPITA US$380

CLIMATE Tropical; wetter on coast

HIGHEST POINT Pico Basile 3,011 m (9,879 ft)

MAP REFERENCE Page 365

Legend

Boundaries

— — — International border

- - - - - Disputed or undefined border

——— Administrative border

Settlements

Capitals of a depicted administrative division

Budapest		Over 5 million
Sydney	◉	1 million to 5 million
Swansea	⊛ ○	100 000 to 1 million
Kindu	⊛ ○	Under 100 000 (Size of symbol and type indicates the relative importance and population.)
Elorza	⊛ ○	

<u>Canberra</u> National capital

☐ Antarctic research station

Communications

——— Major road

——— Other road

- - - - Railway

Physical features

——— River

Lake, dam or reservoir

Dry/Intermittent lake

Mt Adams ▲ 3751 m Peak (height in meters)

Sea depths

200 meters
2,000 meters
4,000 meters
6,000 meters

Lettering styles

A U S T R A L I A	Country name
T I R O L	Administration name
M O U N T A I N S	Mountain range name
I v o r y C o a s t	Coastal name
V A L L E Y	Valley name
FLORIDA KEYS	Major island group
Comerong Island	Island name
Comerong Point	Point name
Susquehanna	River name
Lake Erie	Lake name
ATLANTIC	Ocean name
TIMOR SEA	Sea name
Small Bay	Bay name

---

including offical name, population, language, currency, and climate. All figures are the latest available and have been drawn from internationally recognized sources such as the *US Bureau of the Census International Database*, *CIA World Factboook*, *United Nations Human Development Report*, *The Statesman's Yearbook*, The *SBS World Guide* (fifth edition), and *World Bank Data Tables*.

Regional maps fall at the end of each section for ease of reference. Physical and political maps for each region are followed by more detailed mapping. Editorial policy on the spelling of place names was decided after researching a wide number of sources. The cartographic and editorial team used the *US Board of Geographic Names* database as a guide, and a team of international cartographic experts consulted on maps for every region. Our editorial policy has been to use English for the names of countries (e.g., France), international bodies of water (e.g., Pacific Ocean, Black Sea), and regional features that cross international borders (e.g., Carpathian Mountains). Local name forms have been used for all other names, but for capital cities and for some major cities and features, the English name is also provided in brackets. These English names are cross-referenced in the gazetteer, which includes all names on the physical and political maps, and the regional maps.

Recent name changes and boundary changes are shown on the maps including, for example, the new territory of Nunavut in Canada. The contour shading used on the maps is based on a combination of altitude and vegetation and provides an idea of how the area would appear from space.

Foreword

Geographica should be seen as a pathway for a journey of each reader's discovery of the world. Our journey commences with the origin of the universe and the birth of Earth, the planet of life. Land, water and the atmosphere provide sustenance for complex evolving life forms, culminating in the arrival of those dominant creatures, humans. Geological history, influenced by ever-changing natural forces, gradually turns into documented human history. Then our journey leads us into an understanding of how Earth has been transformed by the actions of countless millions of humans and their immediate ancestors over the past million years or so.

Geographica is about a world that has, and will continue to be, changed. It is designed to be a substantial reference of world information. Original maps convey a vast amount of place-names and boundaries, many of which have changed with the course of history. Timelines describe events that have influenced how humans relate to their environment and to each other. Fact Files for each country offer readers comprehensive descriptions of national identities as they have emerged in recent times, many of which are still undergoing change. (The breakup of Yugoslavia and the Kosovo conflict is just one illustration of the savagery of change.) A number of essays are used to highlight key characteristics of the way landscapes have evolved and how humans relate to each other. These features are documented by new maps on a world scale and also at national scales.

The journey Geographica offers readers is the exploration of a world often ravaged by war, pestilence, human suffering, and the degradation of the environment. But it is also a world where we can conquer great challenges, discover the unknown, and improve the quality of life of many people through the better use of natural and human resources. The future always holds great uncertainty; yet knowledge of the past and present geographical and historical conditions of our planet can only strengthen our ability to plan for a peaceful and ecologically sustainable world in which we and the generations to come can lead fulfilling lives.

This volume represents the combined efforts of many people. As geographers, cartographers, historians, illustrators and editors we seek to offer our readers a substantial educational experience— a journey into the past and an appreciation of the present as it has evolved.

PROFESSOR BRUCE G. THOM

BA, PhD (Louisiana State University), FIAG

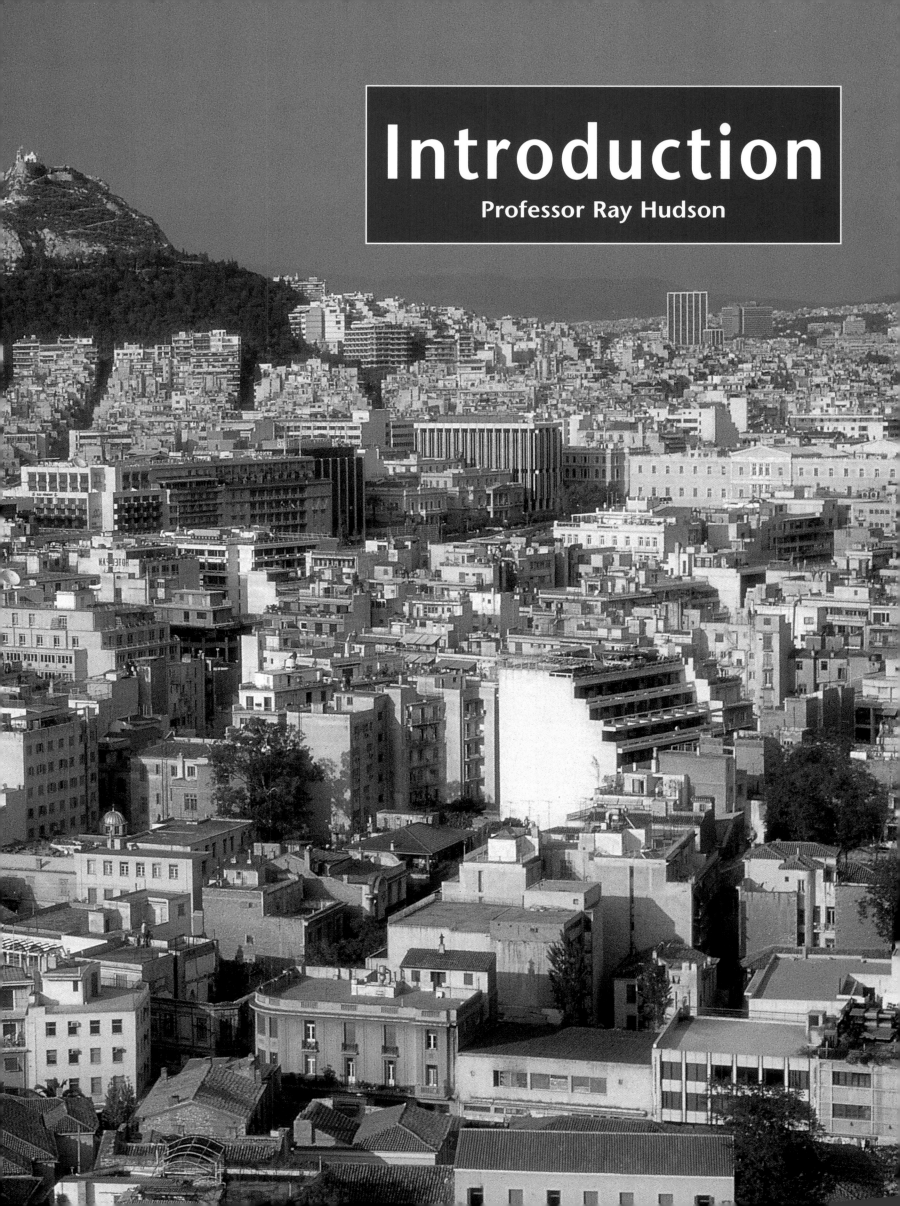

Introduction

Professor Ray Hudson

Europe and the Russian Federation: The Changing Scene

The Mediterranean area is the birthplace of the ancient Greek and Roman civilizations. The Acropolis in Athens (above) shows the ruins of buildings from around 400 BC. Carcassone Castle, France (opposite), is an excellent example of medieval fortification.

If you look at Earth on a globe, the extent of the roughly triangular landmass covered by Europe and the Russian Federation is staggering—an enormous swathe of land extending almost around the world and from around 35° north of the equator to well into the Arctic Circle.

On two and a half sides, this large triangle is bounded by seas and oceans. This gives an initial indication of one of the many problems of defining precisely where the boundaries of Europe and the Russian Federation lie—many of the islands (of which arguably the most significant are those that make up the United Kingdom and the Republic of Ireland) lie off the coasts of Europe and the Federation. Furthermore, some European countries continue to have overseas territories that are colonies or dependencies, legacies of former Empires, and a few have offshore islands that are an integral part of the national state—the Azores and Canary Islands in the Atlantic Ocean, parts of the territories of Portugal and Spain respectively, for example.

There are fairly clear physical boundaries to continental mainland Europe to the west (the Atlantic Ocean), to the north (the Arctic Ocean) and to the south (the Mediterranean Sea), although the southern boundary is less clear-cut around the eastern extremities of the Mediterranean Sea. Turkey, for example, is a member of NATO (the North Atlantic Treaty Organization) but is not generally regarded as a member of Europe.

In the same way, the Russian Federation has clear physical boundaries to the north, east and south, but at its western edge the European landmass slides into the Asian landmass without a precise border. Often the range of the Ural Mountains is taken as the boundary between European Russia to the west and the vast Siberian Plain and Asia to the east. In other respects, however, the boundary between Europe and Asia is more of a political and cultural divide than one that can be defined unambiguously by topography and physical geography.

THE NATURAL ENVIRONMENT

The natural environment of Europe and the Russian Federation is extremely diverse, as variations in latitude, longitude, and altitude combine to produce a great range of climatic and physical conditions and corres-ponding flora and fauna. Some of these environments have offered attractive possibilities for human settlement, influencing early patterns of habitation and also migration; others are harsh and unwelcoming, and have proved difficult to colonize even with the help of developments in contemporary technology.

The legacies of geology offer great opportunities in some parts of Europe and the Russian Federation, which have rich deposits of carboniferous and metallic minerals. Historically, these resources have been critical in influencing the pattern of economic development within these areas.

CLIMATE

Europe and the Russian Federation exhibit a vast latitudinal and longitudinal spread that is reflected in great climatic variation. The landmass extends almost round the globe, from a little more than 20°W at the westernmost tip of Ireland (though the western tip of Greenland is more than 70°W) all the way east (to around 170°E at the tip of the Bering Strait, which separates Asia from Alaska).

From its southernmost point, just below 35°N on the Greek island of Crete (although the Canary Islands lie not far north of the Tropic of Cancer in the Atlantic Ocean, just off the west African coast) Europe stretches northwards, above the Arctic Circle, to North Cape in Norway. Much of Russia also lies well north of the Arctic Circle, extending almost to Alaska. Land in these latitudes is typically tundra, with the soil frozen for much of the year (permafrost) and a very short growing season.

The mean January temperature is below 0°C (32°F) over much of central, eastern and northern Europe and much of the Russian Federation; in inland Siberia it even falls below –50°C (–58°F). Few people live in these harsh environments.

In contrast, much of western and southern Europe has a more temperate climate and support larger populations, though heavy urbanization means that distributions are uneven. The moderation of climatic extremes is especially noticeable in the west of the continent. Here, the effects of the Atlantic Ocean and the Gulf Stream soften the climatic extremes found in the continental interior in areas of eastern Europe and the Russian Federation. Mean July temperatures rarely exceed 30°C (86°F) even in the southernmost parts of Europe, but often exceed 20°C (68°F) over much of the inland continental areas of the Russian Federation. Given the longitudinal extent of Europe and the Russian Federation, the climatic contrast between maritime and inland continental areas is extremely marked.

The climate in the southern areas of Europe, around the Mediterranean Sea is warm temperate, with mild, wet winters and hot, dry summers—the classic Mediterranean climate in which much of European civilization and culture first took root during the classical Greek and Roman periods of history.

This broad climatic pattern generated by latitudinal and longitudinal variation is further complicated by altitudinal variation which adds to the pattern of climatic variation.

LANDFORMS

The landscape of much of the area, and of Europe in particular, is the product of past (but in geological time, fairly recent) periods of orogenesis—when upward movements of the Earth's crust formed mountain ranges—especially during the Alpine period. Major mountain ranges stretch from the Iberian Peninsula through the Massif Central of France, to the French, Swiss, Italian, and Austrian Alps, to the Dynaric Alps and Apennines on either side of the Adriatic Sea in Italy and the former Yugoslavia respectively, and as far east as the Carpathian Alps, mainly in the eastern part of Romania. Most of Europe's major rivers, including the Danube, Rhine, Rhone, Loire and Po, rise in these upland areas and drain to the various seas surrounding the continent.

To the southeast, the Caucasus form a land boundary—on the bridge of land separating the Black Sea and the Caspian Sea, between Armenia and Azerbaijan and Turkey and Iran to their southeast. In the northwest, much of Scandinavia is also mountainous. A large part of these mountainous areas have been glaciated and processes of glaciation are still continuing.

To the north of the main mountain regions, most of Europe and the Russian Federation comprise the north European and Siberian plains. While some major rivers, such as the Ob and Yenisei, drain from the Siberian Plain to the Arctic Ocean, much of the drainage of the plain is to inland seas and lakes. The Volga River, for example, drains into the Caspian Sea, and other rivers drain into the Aral and Black seas. The plains are periodically interrupted by ranges of mountain (such as the Urals) and by lower lying hills, bounded to the south by the hill and mountain ranges of Iran, Afghanistan, China and Mongolia.

In the far east, the Siberian Plain gradually rises in height and eventually gives way to the Verkoyhansk and then the Kolyma Mountains before the Russian Federation finally reaches its eastern boundaries in the Bering Sea and the Sea of Okhotsk.

Much of these plains have been formed by various types of glacial deposits. In the north, much of Finland and southern Scandinavia also exhibit considerable evidence of glacial erosion, as in the numerous lakes of Finland.

VEGETATION

Much of Europe is forested, especially in the higher regions. The natural vegetation of the vast majority of Europe and a fair part of the Russian Federation is a mixture of broad-leafed deciduous and coniferous forest. Deciduous trees are generally more prevalent in the milder and wetter temperate areas with conifers found further north in the colder regions; where the climate becomes too harsh for trees, tundra is dominant.

Around the Mediterranean region, evergreen trees and shrubs are the most common form of vegetation. As rainfall decreases with increasing distance eastwards, however, forested areas give way to steppe grassland. Within the milder temperate and Mediterranean areas, increasing altitude produces the same changes in vegetation as increasing latitude.

ENVIRONMENTAL TRANSFORMATION

While forest is the natural vegetation of much of Europe and Russia, the majority of this, especially in Europe, has been cleared for agriculture and other uses. Manufacturing industry, mining, and the expansion of cities and towns have all dramatically changed the landscape and advances in technology have also allowed us to exploit the resources that offered by the natural environment. Indeed, much of what is often thought of as the natural landscape is in fact a social product—the result of extended interactions between people and the environment. This process of environmental transformation has a very long history—it started when people first began to make the transition from peripatetic hunter-gatherers to become sedentary agriculturalists and farmers, establishing communities and settlements.

It is only in the last two or three hundred years, however, that dramatic technological advances in agriculture, combined with the developments of the Industrial Revolution, have allowed people to radically alter the natural environment in Europe. Irrigation and artificial fertilizers have permitted agriculture to flourish in formerly uncultivable regions, and the gradual process of removing natural vegetation and adding chemicals to the soil has altered the natural balance which had evolved over thousands of years.

While large-scale environmental processes remain beyond human control, the capacity to alter environmental conditions on a local or regional scale and to overcome environmental constraints has increased greatly in moder time, especially in the more wealthy countries. Such transformations have become integral to the development of industrial capitalism in Europe. One spectacular example of this is the reclamation of the Dutch polders and the subsequent development of intensive commercial glasshouse agriculture on this land which used to be part of the sea. Conquering nature was also an important preoccupation, in the communist former USSR (Union of Soviet Socialist Republics), where it was seen as proof of the capacity of state socialism to triumph over a hostile environment for the collective good.

Thus in a whole variety of ways, and for a variety of motives, people have learned to modify their local environments so that they can live more comfortably, so that plants can be cultivated and animals reared.

It is also worth remembering, however, that human efforts to transform the natural environment and improve material living standards in turn have their own impact on the environment. One of the most spectacular—and unwanted—examples of this is the dramatic shrinkage of the inland Aral Sea in Kazakhstan in the Russian Federation. Another is the extensive soil erosion induced by large-scale agriculture in formerly fertile natural grassland transformed to cereal and cotton-growing areas. Manmade disasters can also have a devastating environmental impact—radioactive waste and smoke from the fire at the Chernobyl nuclear reactor, in Ukraine, in 1986,

became established first in Britain and then in Belgium, Germany, France and other continental European countries. This diffusion was an uneven process, however, and many areas of Europe and Russia were virtually untouched by these new developments, remaining locked in a pre-industrial and pre-capitalist world until well into the twentieth century.

The rise of industrial powers within Europe increased the pressure among them to create empires. New colonies would provide European countries with cheap food and raw materials while also creating a new market, beyond the national markets, for the sale of industrial goods made in Europe. In the latter part of the nineteenth century European countries such as Belgium and Germany joined in the race to establish their own foreign empires. At the same time the struggle for supremacy within Europe intensified, as larger modern national states became established. This process of state building often led to people of different nations becoming citizens of the same state. People and places moved between states as national boundaries shifted (for example, Alsace and Lorraine moved between France and Germany on an almost regular basis). This process of economic and territorial competition finally culminated in the appalling destruction of the First World War, and the postwar settlement led to the creation of completely new states in the Baltic and the Balkans as the old Austro-Hungarian Empire was broken up.

There followed a period of deep economic recession and dislocation, part of a wider global slump. This helped produce a resurgence of nationalist sentiment, most infamously in Germany, with the rise of fascism and its concepts of racial supremacy and *lebensraum* (living space), which were used to justify ethnic cleansing and territorial aggrandizement. Other parts of Europe followed a different path—most notably Russia. Here the October 1917 Revolution established a communist government and presaged the emergence of the USSR, dominated by Russia, in 1922. In 1939, the growing ambitions of fascist Germany culminated in the outbreak of the Second World War, leading to further devastation and carnage in Europe.

spread widely over much of Russia and Europe as a result of westerly winds.

In addition, other human activities in the countries of Europe and the Russian Federation are a major contributing force to processes such as global warming which threatens possible climatic change and rising sea levels. Low-lying, coastal areas and those that have been reclaimed from the sea (like the polders of the Netherlands) are particularly vulnerable to such changes.

A CHANGING POLITICAL–ECONOMIC MAP

For much of their history, the lands of Europe and the Russian Federation have been the arena for a succession of migrations and movements of people. As they gradually became settled, people sought to establish the boundaries of their own territories and armed conflict and wars became almost endemic as different groups sought to expand their territory, or to protect it from others seeking to take it from them. Empires were built, then declined within Europe—from the Roman to the Austro-Hungarian.

For several hundred years, this ebb and flow of political fortunes, as an assortment of emperors, kings, queens and princes fought to consolidate and increase their territory, was accompanied by economic stagnation as European economies were predominantly organized around various forms of subsistence agriculture.

THE GROWTH OF EMPIRES

Towards the end of the fifteenth century, a number of European states began to explore the

possibilities of creating empires outside Europe. This added a new dimension to the political struggle between states, and a new source of economic dynamism, as new subtropical and tropical crops and products began to arrive in Europe.

A number of European states sought to establish new empires in the "New World", and there was much competition between the British, Dutch, French, Portuguese, and Spanish. By the nineteenth century, however, Britain had emerged as the dominant power (despite the loss of its colonies in North America). Trade began to allow the accumulation of capital and, in due course, that capital was channelled into economic development within Europe.

The agricultural and industrial revolutions gave considerable impetus to the economies of the leading European states, as industrial capitalism

The Church of Sveti Jovan Bogoslov Kaneo, on the shores of Ohrid Lake, Macedonia (right). Blaenau Ffestiniog in Wales, where the houses are dwarfed by the slate mine workings (above).

AFTER THE SECOND WORLD WAR

The immediate postwar period was to reshape the map of Europe for the next fifty or so years—in ways that had global implications—until the de facto collapse of socialism in Europe in 1989 and the formal break-up of the USSR in 1991. At the end of the Second World War, the USSR occupied most of eastern Europe. The partitioning of Berlin between East and West in 1948 and the creation of two Germanies (the Federal Republic of Germany and the German Democratic Republic) confirmed that postwar Europe would be divided into two ideologically opposed blocs, a capitalist west and communist east. The "Cold War" had descended on Europe.

In 1949 NATO was established as a common defense organization in the west. The USSR developed a series of buffer satellite states between itself and western Europe, and became the center of both economic (COMECON) and defense (the Warsaw Pact) alliances. In these ways, the USSR sought to prevent the spread of capitalism into the east and to limit the ambitions of the USA, with which it vied to become the dominant global power.

There were also significant moves to redraw the political map within western Europe—in large part stimulated by a wish to avoid future European wars—by creating new supranational institutions. Thus in 1951 the European Coal and Steel Community (the ECSC) was established with the signing of the Treaty of Paris by Belgium, France, Germany, Italy, Luxembourg, and the Netherlands. This sought to guarantee the future peace of Europe by inextricably binding together the coal and steel industries of France and Germany, then seen as the key to the capacity to wage war. Plans for a greater degree of political unification and the creation of a common European Defense Force foundered.

In response, the six signatories of the Treaty of Paris then signed the Treaty of Rome (in 1957) creating the European Economic Community (EEC). The aim of the EEC was to promote democratic political systems and economic growth and the free movement of capital and labor within the territory of the member countries. This posed problems for those western European states that had not signed the Treaty of Rome. In 1960 Austria, Denmark, Portugal, Norway, Sweden, Switzerland and the United Kingdom signed the Stockholm Convention, which established the European Free Trade Area (EFTA). This effectively divided western Europe into two free trade areas, EFTA and the EEC. Much of the next thirty or so years witnessed a redefinition of the boundaries between these two groupings.

In the late 1950s and 1960s the countries of the EEC enjoyed sustained high rates of economic growth—so much so that they drew in migrant workers from Mediterranean Europe and north Africa as a way of avoiding labor shortages. Other western European countries began to gaze with envious eyes at the economic growth rates of the six signatories to the Treaty of Rome, and to consider whether their interests would not be better served by joining the EEC. In 1973 Denmark, Ireland, and the UK became members of the EEC, significantly shifting the balance between it and EFTA.

In the 1960s and 1970s, the EEC concluded a series of trade treaties with a number of southern European, Mediterranean and north African states and former colonies in other regions of the developing world. These trade and aid agreements tied these countries closely into the EEC's economy in various ways—as markets for their agricultural produce and migrant workers and as suppliers of technology, especially that needed for industrial development.

Several of the southern European states actively sought full membership of the EEC but failed to meet a key condition for entry to the club—Greece, Portugal and Spain had dictatorial rather than democratic political systems. With a return to democracy in the mid-1970s in these countries, however, the way was clear for full membership—Greece joined the EEC in 1981, Portugal and Spain in 1986. The reunification of the two Germanies in 1990 further enlarged the European Community, while in 1995, Austria, Finland and Sweden also joined. The EEC now had 15 members.

There are strong pressures for further expansion, predominantly south and east, with Cyprus, the Czech Republic, Estonia, Hungary, Poland and Slovenia next in line for entry. Thus former members of COMECON will become members of the European Union following the break-up of the USSR and the emergence of the looser federation of the Commonwealth of Independent States (CIS) in 1991.

This is seen as a way of underwriting capitalism and democracy throughout eastern Europe in the twenty-first century, much as the Mediterranean enlargement of the 1980s was seen as a way of underpinning democracy and ensuring the end of dictatorships in Greece, Portugal and Spain.

At the same time as extending territorially, there have also been processes of deepening integration, leading to a transition from the EEC to the European Union following the 1992 Maastricht Treaty. There have been significant moves to complete the Single European Market and towards Economic and Monetary Union, with eleven of the member states signing up to a common currency (the Euro) from 1 January 1999 (the non-participants are Denmark, Greece, Sweden and the UK).

There has been a complex process of political change throughout Europe since the 1950s, with tendencies towards the creation and collapse of supranational organizations. Of particular significance has been the collapse of the former USSR and, related to this, of the federal Yugoslav Republic. Here, ethnic and religious tensions which had been kept in check for many decades were suddenly released with devastating and tragic consequences. Much of the Balkans and many of the republics in the southeastern European part of the Commonwealth of Independent States erupted into violence as a range of national groups sought to secure their own territorial states. They often pursued this goal using savage military force and ethnic cleansing on a scale not seen in Europe since the horrors of the Holocaust in the 1930s.

At the the beginning of the twenty-first century, as at the start of the twentieth century, much of Europe has again been engulfed in war, centered on the Balkans. Unlike the early years of the last century, however, developments in the global media now ensure that individuals worldwide are kept informed of events in the European arena as televisions broadcast pictures (transmitted iin real time) of the damage wrought by missile attacks and "smart" bombs, and of refugees forced to flee their homes under threat of death.

ECONOMIC DIVERSITY: VARIETIES OF CAPITALISM

With the formal dissolution of the USSR in 1991, the economic landscape was no longer one of competition between capitalism and socialism but rather one of competition between varieties of capitalism found over Europe and the Russian Federation.

One immediate consequence of the collapse of socialism was to increase poverty and inequality within this new shared space. Attempts to establish thriving capitalist economies over much of eastern Europe and Russia and its republics failed initially, as the cultural and institutional requirements for such a change were simply not present. Moreover, the social welfare supports of the former socialist system were swept away.

Economic transition was reasonably smooth in the more economically advanced countries of the former COMECON in which forms of private property ownership had survived in the socialist period or emerged well before 1989 (in the Czech Republic, Hungary and Poland).

Elsewhere, however, economies simply collapsed, while in Russia and several of the other member states of the Commonwealth of Independent States, black markets, gangsterism and criminal capitalism of a sort associated with

the Mafia became the norm. Where economic collapse went hand-in-hand with the devastation of war and forced population movements, problems of poverty, ill-health and death became even more acute.

In contrast, over much of the European Union, economic fortunes have become more assured and lifestyles correspondingly more comfortable. There are differences in the forms of capitalism (for example, Germany, and Sweden remain much more committed to corporatist approaches, the UK to a neo-liberal market approach), but even these differences have been reduced by the need to conform to the criteria for entry to the European Monetary Union. This is not to deny that considerable inequalities remain within the European Union—both at national, regional and local scales and between people—but these are insignificant compared with the situation in much of eastern Europe, Russia and the rest of the CIS.

There are marked variations in population densities within the European Union, with people heavily clustered in urban areas, which typically rely on service-based economies. There are similar variations in output and income per capita and also in the sectoral structure of economies, with the more developed and affluent regions generally relying less upon agriculture and more upon advanced services. National economies vary greatly in size and structure, but the pattern and variation at subnational scales is more complex still.

The scope of welfare state provision has certainly been reduced over much of western Europe, often as a direct response to the need to meet the fiscal and macroeconomic requirements for entry to the European Monetary Union. Nevertheless, the welfare net still remains in place to an extent no longer found over much of the

remainder of Russia and the CIS and parts of southern and eastern Europe.

This provision, along with the perception of more and better job opportunities in the West, has encouraged fears of floods of economic migrants (as opposed to political refugees) from eastern Europe and the Russian Federation (as well as possibly from north Africa). One consequence of this has been concern about both immigration polices into the European Union and

the status of individuals of varied ethnic origins who have lived in Europe for decades, after arriving as temporary migrant workers, but who still lack citizenship rights.

We began with a question—where is Europe? However, more important questions to consider for the future are perhaps who are Europeans now, what does it mean to be European, and what are the rights and responsibilities of each putative European citizen?

The mild climate of Madeira makes these Portuguese islands a popular resort all year round (left). An aerial view of the old city of Salzburg (top) on the south bank of the Salzach River, in Austria. Dubrovnik (above), in Croatia, is another city that retains its Old Town charm; here the Franciscan belltower is featured.

Part 1

Planet Earth

Earth in Space

Humans have always been fascinated by Earth's place in the universe. Earth (above) is just one of many planets, moons, and stars that form our solar system. We still have much to learn about how the solar system formed, and to predict about how it will end. An artist's impression of the surface of Earth (right) shows the land and water that cover its crust.

Ideas on the origin of Earth, other planets, the Sun and stars can be traced to the time of classical Greece. They range from an Earth-centered universe to one where the position of this tiny, life-generating planet is placed in a context of an expanding universe populated by billions of stars, with an unknown number of planets similar in composition and structure to ours.

It was late in the eighteenth century that the great early geologist James Hutton (1726–97), a Scot, captured in a few poignant words the vastness and the immensity of time over which Earth, the Sun, the solar system, the galaxies, and the universe have evolved. He noted that there is "no vestige of a beginning, no prospect of an end." This phrase challenged the established thinking of a very limited time for the creation of the natural world and opened up a new era of geological and cosmological thought.

We live on a planet that is circling a single star of apparently limitless energy. Yet we now know that the engine of nuclear heat driving the Sun has a birth and a stable phase, and, as it runs short of hydrogen fuel, will go through enormous cataclysms. This process will absorb the Sun's dependent planets, and eventually lead to its own slow "death".

Our views of Earth as part of the universe have varied over time. New concepts and theories, such as Einstein's general theory of relativity, have offered scientists different perspectives on the origin of the universe and all matter. New technologies ranging from telescopes to satellites have opened up vast vistas within and beyond our solar system. Now available to scientists are tools to measure the composition and structure of matter racing through space. We understand much better the characteristics of various forces at work, such as those driving the expansion of the universe, the clustering of stars, the condensation of gases, the orbits of planets, and the movement of meteorites.

The big-bang model for the universe is based on a number of observations. It is not speculation. Yet, as a model of how the universe evolved, it has been modified by cosmologists and scientists over time. New observations should lead to further changes as we continue to explore whether there is enough matter and energy in the universe to slow and stop the expansion started 10 billion or 15 billion years ago.

As gases condensed to form stars, there was a distinct tendency for these stars to cluster. The Milky Way Galaxy is an example of a large spiral galaxy or cluster of stars composed of a thin, circular disk surrounding a central bulge. Interestingly, new technologies show that many galaxies, including the Milky Way, have more mass than can readily be seen. There also appears to exist at the core of some galaxies a central powerhouse generating narrow jets of high-energy particles streaming outwards. Only more observations and theorizing will help us understand the significance of these phenomena.

Yet it is the stars themselves which offer so many clues to the origin of the universe and, ultimately, ourselves. They vary widely in size, color, and temperature. Stars are powered by nuclear reactions whereby hydrogen is fused to helium. We now possess knowledge of sequences through which stars may change from one state to another. Our Sun is no exception and can be seen as representative of an average star in the Milky Way Galaxy. It generates light and heat, which are transmitted through space to help transform life on the surface of one of its planets, Earth.

Radiometric dating of ancient rocks on Earth and its moon give some clue as to the age of the solar system—about 5 billion years. Cooling and consolidation under gravity of interstellar gases and dust created the Sun and progressively hardened objects accreted and condensed to form the nine planets and their moons. Early in the period of planet formation, the sweeping up of solar system debris led to bombardment of planet and moon surfaces, a phenomenon dramatically depicted today by photographs of the cratered surface of Earth's moon.

The Sun is the ultimate source of energy for life processes on planet Earth. As the Sun formed, it captured most matter in the Solar system, leaving only 0.1% to form the planets, their moons, asteroids, comets and dust. The Sun possessed sufficient mass needed to generate electromagnetic or radiant energy at various wavelengths. The hot Sun mostly radiates shorter wavelength energy especially at visible wavelengths. There are also large sunspots caused by magnetic storms on the Sun's surface. They can be observed as visible dark patches and as areas of X-ray activity ejecting electrically charged particles, the solar wind. Sunspot activity is not constant but is cyclic in behavior. When these particles meet the Earth's atmosphere dramatic visual displays occur, especially in polar latitudes. Whether sunspots influence the weather is uncertain.

The spinning Earth orbits the Sun, traveling a distance of approximately 150 million km (93 million miles). Energy is received at a more or less constant rate, but is distributed unevenly because of the tilt of Earth's axis, yielding seasonal changes in temperature away from the equator. Yet Earth processes its own heat engine: radioactive processes within its core help generate gases into the atmosphere and drive movements of its crustal plates. The presence of different gases, including water vapor, has provided that vital mixture of substances from which life has evolved, as well as the thin protective envelope high in oxygen and nitrogen which forms the atmosphere.

Thus spaceship Earth, spinning systematically around the Sun, receiving heat, generating gases and driving its crust into mountains, offers various life forms an environment for evolution. Over time these environments change. Ultimately the future of the planet itself is tied to that of its solar system and its Sun.

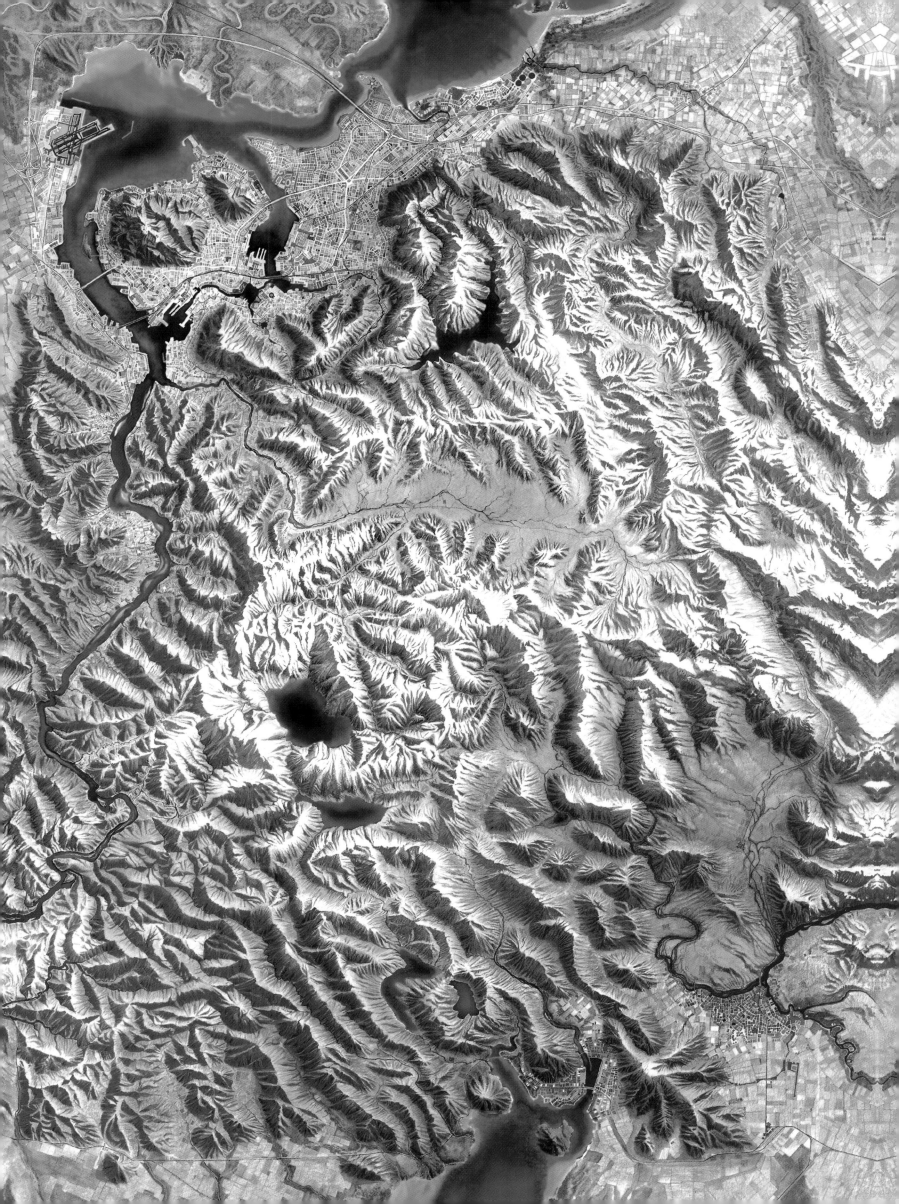

ORIGINS OF THE UNIVERSE

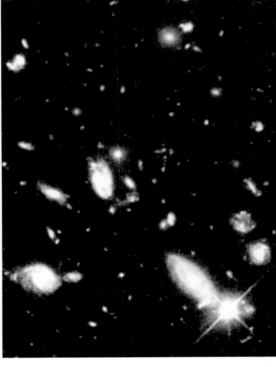

When we look out across the universe, we look back in time. Light traveling from distant galaxies, speeding across 300,000 km (186,000 miles) every second, has taken billions of years to reach Earth. We see the most distant galaxies across billions of light years, as those galaxies were when the universe was younger.

What is the universe really like? The modern view of the origins and future of the universe is based on the idea of a Big Bang that marked the beginning of the ongoing expansion of the universe. The popular view of the Big Bang, however, imagines galaxies flying away from one another out into empty space after a massive explosion. This naturally leads to questions about what happened before the Big Bang, and where it occurred. However, these questions arise from a misunderstanding of the Big Bang concept. Galaxies do not fly away from each other through space; rather, space itself expands, carrying the galaxies with it. The Big Bang was not an explosion *in* space, but an explosion *of* space and time. All of space and time arose in the Big Bang. There was no time before the Big Bang, and all of space was involved.

A brief history of the universe

Ten to fifteen billion years ago, the universe of space and time began, as a hugely hot cauldron of energy governed by physical laws that we do not yet understand. Within a tiny fraction of a second the expansion after the Big Bang had moderated the conditions to a point from which (we believe) our current understanding of physical laws can begin to describe what happened. The universe was expanding and cooling, but there may also have been a brief spurt of dramatic inflation in size—this is critical to understanding today's universe. If this sudden growth spurt *did* occur, then the part of the universe that telescopes can survey today was merely a tiny fraction of the total.

After no more than 10 millionths of a second, the universe had become a sea of high energy radiation—gamma ray photons characteristic of a temperature well over 1 trillion degrees. At such energy, photons can produce a pair of particles, a matter particle and its anti-matter partner, which exist fleetingly before annihilating each other in a flash of gamma ray radiation.

As the universe continued to expand, the photons dropped in energy as the temperature fell. Particle production ended, first for the heavy particles and then for the light ones. Most of the particle and anti-particle pairs were annihilated, leaving only a small residue—the protons, neutrons, and electrons that we see today.

As the temperature dropped further, some of these particles combined to build simple atomic nuclei. Within half an hour this phase was over, and, for the next few hundred thousand years, the universe was an expanding gas of light nuclei and electrons in a sea of photons. It was an opaque fog until continued cooling allowed the atomic nuclei to capture electrons and form atoms of simple elements, mostly hydrogen and helium. Without the free electrons to scatter them, the photons streamed freely through space and the fog cleared.

Matter was then free to respond to the influence of gravity alone. The first generations of individual stars formed from small knots in larger gas clouds that became whole galaxies of stars. The galaxies formed into clusters and superclusters that are still scattered through the universe today.

Are we sure of this picture?

This view of the universe is rather different from earlier versions. Ancient Egyptian cosmology featured the sky goddess Nut arched over Earth, with the Sun god Ra traveling across the sky every day. Greek thinkers removed gods from their cosmology, and constructed their world view largely on philosophical grounds. A more scientific approach to cosmology began to

emerge after Copernicus, in the sixteenth century, discovered that it was the Earth that traveled around the Sun. The current view is the latest step in scientific cosmology, but can we be sure that the modern picture will not also be superseded?

Three important observations form the basis of the Big Bang model. The first emerged early in the twentieth century, when observations revealed the expansion of the universe. This fits into Einstein's theory of General Relativity, which describes the nature of space and time. The second key observation is recent measurements of the abundance of light elements, especially helium, in the universe. These observations agree with the amount that the Big Bang model predicts to have been formed in its first few minutes.

Perhaps the most compelling plank supporting the Big Bang concept was the discovery in 1965 of the cosmic background radiation—an all-pervasive glow coming from all parts of the sky. It is our view of radiation from the era when the universe became transparent. It is the glow of the Big Bang itself, cooled by the universe's expansion.

Recent years have been exciting in cosmology, because new observations have begun to allow us to choose between variations of the basic Big Bang cosmology and some alternative concepts to the Big Bang itself. In particular, the Cosmic Background Explorer (COBE) satellite

After about two minutes the temperature had dropped below 1 billion degrees—low enough for nuclear reactions to build some of the light elements, especially helium.

In its first seconds, the universe was a dynamic soup of gamma ray photons and particles such as protons and electrons, which are the building blocks of atoms.

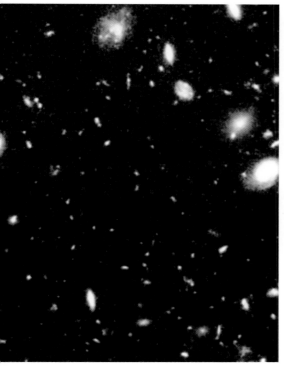

This cluster of yellow, elliptical and spiral galaxies, far left, has a gravitational force so strong that it can bend light—the blue arcs are actually images of one more distant galaxy, not scattered objects at all. Each object in this Hubble Deep Field picture, center, is a distant galaxy. Above: Although rather different in appearance, each of these galaxies harbors an intensely bright quasar.

Gravitational lenses

In recent years astronomers have discovered a new way in which to probe further into the universe and at the same time seek out dark matter nearer home. Einstein's theory of General Relativity predicted that the straight line path of light across the universe is affected by gravity. This was first observed in 1919, when light from stars was observed to be minutely deflected as it passed the Sun.

Recent observations have revealed the gravitational effect of whole galaxies and even clusters of galaxies, which can act as a lens to bend and focus light coming from more distant galaxies. Although the images produced by these gravitational lenses are distorted, they do enable us to study light from galaxies that would otherwise be far beyond the reach of our telescopes.

This gravitational lensing has also been seen—on a smaller scale—when the light of distant stars brightens briefly; this is because of gravitational lensing caused by an intervening object. Knowing this allows us to study the lensing objects that are part of the halo of dark matter believed to encircle our galaxy. What is this dark matter? It seems that gravitational lensing may be able to tell us.

revealed the incredible smoothness of the cosmic background radiation, in all directions, challenging us to explain how the clumpy distribution of galaxies we see today could have had time to develop. Exactly how much time has passed in building this pattern remains uncertain, since astronomers are only now beginning to agree on just how fast the universe is expanding. This is a time of dramatic developments for cosmology.

Will the expansion continue?

Will the universe go on expanding until all the stars have died? The force of gravity governs the fate of the universe, so the question becomes: is there enough matter and energy in the universe to slow and stop the expansion?

In mapping the distribution of matter, it is now clear that there is more matter out there than is apparent. This "dark matter" must surround many galaxies, including the Milky Way, to explain the motions of stars within them. There is more in clusters of galaxies, helping to hold them together. Studies are seeking further evidence of this matter, trying to determine what it is: small dark planets, star-sized bodies, or something less familiar.

Adding all this together, normal forms of matter appear to account for less than 10 percent of the matter needed to halt universal expansion. But many cosmologists think that less than 10 percent is quite close to 100 percent in this instance. Moreover, there are theoretical reasons for thinking the universe may in fact be on that balance point between eternal expansion and ultimate halt and collapse. It may be that most of the matter in the universe is in forms as yet unseen.

The history of the Sun and Earth play only a small part in this picture. Born long after the Big Bang, both will die long before the universe changes much from the way it looks today.

One of the galaxies that formed over 10 billion years ago was the Milky Way. A mere 4.6 billion years ago the Sun was born within it.

Tiny bumps in the density of matter in the early universe grew, under the influence of gravity, to form the galaxies and clusters of galaxies that we see today.

After several hundred thousand years, at a temperature of around 3000°C (5450°F), the electrons were captured by atoms and the universe suddenly became transparent.

GALAXIES

Many people today are city dwellers whose view of the night sky is hindered by the bright lights of the modern world. When we are fortunate enough to look at the night sky from a dark place, we see thousands of stars and the faint starry band of the Milky Way meandering across the sky. We now know that this is an insider's view of the vast collection of more than 100 billion stars we call the Milky Way Galaxy.

A dark sky will also reveal the Andromeda Galaxy, an even larger star system lying beyond the boundaries of the Milky Way. Both are members of the small cluster of galaxies called the Local Group, which lies on the edge of a super-cluster of galaxies. Beyond lies the vast expanse of the universe—countless more distant galaxies.

The Milky Way

In 1785, William Herschel, the astronomer who discovered Uranus, counted stars in various directions across the sky and decided that the Sun lay near the center of a flattened disk of stars. In 1917, Harlow Shapley studied the distribution of globular clusters—clusters of hundreds of thousands of stars—and concluded that they clustered around the center of the galaxy in the direction of the constellation of Sagittarius. Herschel had been deceived by the clouds of dust which are scattered through the Milky Way and which obscure our view of more distant stars.

The modern view reveals the Milky Way to be a large spiral galaxy composed of a thin circular disk surrounding a central bulge, with a halo of stars

and globular clusters. Light would take about 100,000 years to speed across the disk: a distance of 100,000 light years. Traveling as fast as the fastest spacecraft, a trip across the galaxy would take well over a billion years! The Sun lies in the disk, some 28,000 light years from the center, completing an orbit around the central bulge every 240 million years.

Around 95 percent of the visible mass of the galaxy is composed of stars, in particular the vast mass of faint Sun-like stars that contribute the yellowish background glow of the disk and bulge. Despite their vast numbers, the distances between the stars are immense, compared with their sizes. The nearest stars to the Sun are 4.3 light years away (40 trillion km; 25 trillion miles). Traveling on the fastest spacecraft, this trip would take some 60,000 years.

The heart of the galaxy is a mystery being slowly unveiled by observations using radio and infrared telescopes which can pierce the veil of dust which hides it from our eyes. Astronomers suspect that it harbors a black hole with the mass of more than a million suns.

The remaining mass we see in the galaxy is the thin interstellar medium of gas and dust lying between the stars. Most of this is compacted into dense, cold clouds of gas laced with traces of dust.

This spiral galaxy, above, has two prominent arms, showing red patches of ionized hydrogen where stars have formed. A barred spiral galaxy, right, showing the yellow color of old stars at its nucleus, with blue, young stars in its arms.

The Milky Way system originated in a vast condensation of gas, which began to form stars within a billion years of the Big Bang. Early generations of stars in this cloud included those that form the halo of stars and globular clusters surrounding the galaxy. Successive generations of stars had orbits much closer to the thin disk we see today. When the Sun was formed 4.6 billion years ago, the galaxy was already middle aged, and would have looked much as it does today.

New stars are still being born from clouds of gas. While they live, these beacons and their gaseous birthplaces trace out the spiral arms within the background glow of the disk.

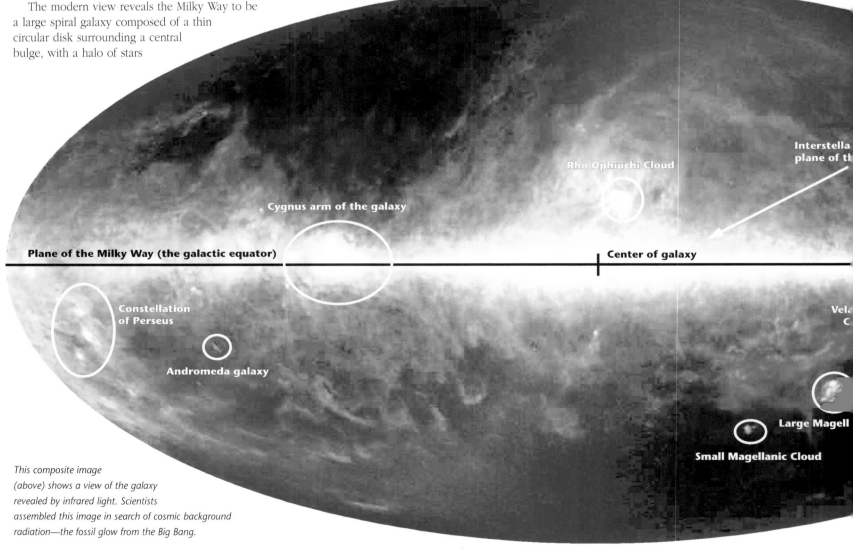

This composite image (above) shows a view of the galaxy revealed by infrared light. Scientists assembled this image in search of cosmic background radiation—the fossil glow from the Big Bang.

Individual stars will live and die, but the Milky Way will probably continue to look much as it does today for billions of years, until stars such as the Sun are long dead.

Other galaxies

The existence of galaxies other than the Milky Way was long suspected, but only became accepted in the 1920s, when Edwin Hubble measured the distance to some nearby galaxies. We classify galaxies according to their overall appearance, since only in the nearest ones can even the brightest stars be discerned individually.

Most familiar are the spiral galaxies like the Milky Way. Photos of these galaxies reveal that they are in beautiful spiral patterns, traced out by bright stars and gas, hiding the fainter background glow of the disk in which they lie. The spiral patterns range from loosely wound S-shapes to arms so tightly

wound that the spiral cannot be discerned. The Milky Way falls midway in this range. Some spirals have a distinct bar across the nucleus from which the spiral arms trail.

Other galaxies show no apparent structure beyond a smooth spherical or elliptical shape. Unlike the spirals, these elliptical galaxies usually lack any significant signs of recent star formation or the gas to promote it. Giants of this class are rare, but are the most massive galaxies known. On the other end of the scale, faint dwarf ellipticals, little larger than a globular star cluster, are probably the most common type of galaxy.

Perhaps a quarter of all galaxies are classified as irregular because they do not fit neatly into either of these categories. They are typically faint, but with a mix of old and young stars, gas, and dust.

Many galaxies, including the Milky Way, show signs of more mass than can readily be seen. Some galaxies hide another enigma—a central powerhouse at their core that generates narrow jets of high-energy particles streaming outward. These active galaxies are believed to be powered by matter swirling around a massive black hole. It may be that many large galaxies have a central black hole with a mass equal to millions of suns, but in most of them, as in the Milky Way, this lies dormant unless brought to life by an inflow of gas.

Clusters of galaxies

Galaxies, like some stars within galaxies, tend to exist in clusters. The Milky Way's Local Group is a small cluster, with 30 or so members, most of them small elliptical or irregular galaxies. The nearest large cluster of galaxies is the Virgo cluster, with some 2,500 members, lying about 60 million light years away. The Virgo cluster is a major component of the Local Supercluster.

Compared with the amount of space between the stars, galaxies in these clusters are relatively close together. As a result of this proximity, they sometimes run into one another, causing cosmic fireworks. The stars within the galaxies almost never collide, but the tenuous interstellar clouds crash together and form new stars, changing the appearance of the galaxy and possibly triggering the nuclear powerhouse into activity.

Some of the bright galaxies of the Virgo cluster, top. Above: This galaxy, Centaurus A, features an unusual obscuring dust cloud and is a powerful source of radio, X- and gamma rays.

Exploring space

Before the telescope, astronomy consisted largely of measuring and predicting the positions of stars and planets observed by eye. In 1609 a revolution began, when Galileo Galilei used a telescope to reveal mountains on the Moon, Jupiter's moons, and countless stars in the Milky Way. Despite these amazing discoveries, however, for the next 250 years astronomy was predominantly devoted to measuring positions and cataloging.

Almost 150 years ago, the first identification of a chemical element in the Sun was made using a spectrograph, which separates sunlight into its component colors. This marked the start of our ability to deduce the composition of the stars. The science of astrophysics was born.

Today, spectrographs are used on optical telescopes hundreds of times the size of Galileo's first instruments. One of these, the Hubble Space Telescope, views the sky from above the distorting effect of Earth's atmosphere. Optical telescopes joined by radio telescopes on the ground and in space can be used to form large radio arrays. Other observatories in space search for sources of infrared and ultraviolet light, X-rays, and gamma rays.

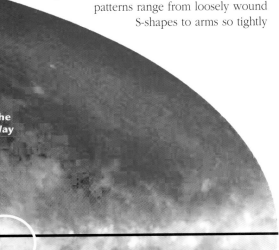

STARS

When we look at the stars in the night sky, it is easy to understand how people in ancient times imagined them to be flickering lights attached to the dark vault of the sky. It was not until 1838 that the first stellar distance was measured and the enormous distances of the stars from Earth and from each other were confirmed.

The first half of the twentieth century saw the development of the physics necessary to understand the composition and structure of the stars and the sources of nuclear energy that power them. As a result, astronomers today have an extensive understanding of the stars and the way they have evolved.

Types of star

While stars vary widely in size, color, and temperature, they are all essentially vast balls of hot gas powered by nuclear reactions deep in their cores. For most of the life of a star, these reactions fuse hydrogen into helium. Late in its life, a star leaves behind this main sequence phase and develops into a giant, converting helium into carbon and heavier elements. In both processes, a small fraction of the matter is converted into energy. The temperatures that are required in a star's core in order to achieve this are measured in tens of millions of degrees.

The main factor determining the characteristics of a main sequence star is its mass—how much matter it contains. Stars range in mass from less than one-tenth of the Sun's mass to perhaps more than 50 times its mass. At the top end of the range are the rare massive stars, which are a few times the size of the Sun but radiate hundreds of thousands of times more energy from their blue–white surfaces. The Sun itself has a slightly yellow color to its 6,000°C (10,800°F) surface. A less massive main sequence star will be somewhat smaller than the Sun, perhaps less than 1 percent as bright, with a cooler, red hue. Red dwarfs of this sort can only be seen from relatively nearby, but are the most common stars in the galaxy.

At the end of their main sequence lifetimes, stars swell to become giants and supergiants. The largest of these are cool red stars, which are more than a thousand times larger and a million times brighter than the Sun. Many of the giants will end their days as white dwarfs only as big as Earth—the faint glowing embers of old stars.

The nearest star

The Sun, which is the only star that we can readily see as anything other than a point of light, is representative of an average star in the Milky Way. Its surface displays a cycle of activity that

This globular cluster—47 Tucanae, above—is an enormous group of stars formed early in the life of the Milky Way galaxy; it contains some of the oldest known stars. One hundred and eighty years ago, the massive star Eta Carinae experienced an outburst which created the lobes of gas now surrounding it, right.

is roughly 11 years long. The most obvious manifestations of the cycle are sunspots, the numbers of which rise and fall during the course of the cycle. Sunspots are often larger than Earth, and are relatively dark in appearance because magnetic effects make them slightly cooler than their surroundings. They are also centers of other activity—powerful solar flares, for instance, which last for a few minutes, glowing brightly and pouring hot gas into space. This gas is channeled by the solar magnetic field and sometimes strikes Earth, causing intense auroral displays near the poles and disrupting radio communication and, sometimes, electrical power systems.

The sudden outburst of a flare punctuates a more general outflow from the Sun's hot outer atmosphere, known as the corona. This solar wind is relatively mild when compared with the massive outflows from certain other stars. While the Sun will lose little mass through the solar wind during the course of its life, larger stars can blow away a sizeable proportion of their mass in this way.

Observations reveal that some other stars have cycles of activity that resemble those of the Sun. Although we are unable to see sunspots on their surfaces, we can detect the slight changes in brightness that accompany changes in activity.

The Sun's magnetism arises from the flow of electrical currents within its outer layers, but most of its material is packed closer to the core, where the energy is generated. In recent

This pillar of gas, left, contains cool hydrogen gas and dust and can incubate new stars. It is a part of the Eagle Nebula, a star-forming region 7,000 light years away. The Trifid Nebula, above, contains hot young stars which cause the gas to emit red light, and cooler gas and dust reflecting blue light.

A star like the Sun takes millions of years to form. It then embarks on the main part of its existence, living for 10 billion years as a stable main sequence star.

As the gas falls in under the force of gravity, it heats up, becoming a protostar, glowing warmly with infrared light through an obscuring cocoon of gas and dust.

Star birth begins deep in a tenuous cloud of interstellar gas and dust. Perhaps triggered by the birth or death of stars nearby, the cloud begins to collapse.

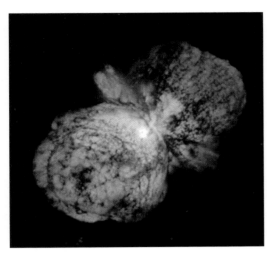

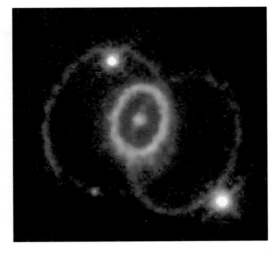

Left: These rings of glowing gas surround an exploded star which was first observed in 1987—a supernova. It is 169,000 light years away in the Large Magellanic Cloud, a nearby galaxy visible from the southern hemisphere.

After a supernova

Massive stars die spectacularly in a supernova explosion. If the remnant after the explosion is less than about three times the mass of the Sun, a neutron star will result. Despite the intense force of gravity, the neutrons making up much of the star refuse to collapse any further than a dense ball 20 km (12 miles) across. Neutron stars are sometimes seen as pulsing sources of radiation—they are then called pulsars.

If the remnant of the star contains more than three solar masses of material, the strength of the gravitational force cannot be resisted, and the collapse produces a black hole. Not even light can escape from within a black hole. Any matter that falls within the boundary of a black hole is lost from view.

The importance of black holes and neutron stars to astronomy lies more in what happens in the intense gravitational field around them than in what is inside them. Gas falls onto black holes or neutron stars with tremendous energy, producing intense radiation. The largest black holes are believed to be millions of times the mass of the Sun, and reside in the nuclei of active galaxies. They are the powerhouses of these beacons that shine across the universe.

years, astronomers have begun to probe beneath the surface of the Sun using a technique called helioseismology. This is helping to clarify our picture of the Sun's structure.

The life of a star

A constant battle takes place between gravity, which is attempting to pull a star inward, and the pressure of hot gas pushing outward. The battle starts when gravity begins to collapse a small part of an interstellar gas cloud. As the cloud falls in, the temperature at its core increases, and eventually hydrogen begins to fuse together to form helium. The collapse slows as the growing pressure of the hot gas resists the gravitational force. Finally the collapse comes to a halt; the protostar has become a stable main sequence star.

A star such as the Sun will remain balanced in this state for around 10 billion years, constantly converting hydrogen to helium at its core and by degrees growing a little bigger and a little brighter. The Sun is currently about halfway through its main sequence phase.

In approximately 5 billion years, after it has circled the center of the galaxy some 20 more times, the Sun will begin to grow quite rapidly. By the time it has doubled in size, the oceans on Earth will have completely boiled away. Eventually, the Sun will become a red giant, perhaps 100 times larger and 1,000 times

brighter than it is at the moment. It will envelop Mercury, Venus, and Earth, evaporating Earth's atmosphere and eventually causing the planet to spiral inward to oblivion.

Cooler, lower-mass stars will follow much the same path, but over spans of time so long that not even the oldest of them has yet had time to complete its sedate main sequence life. In contrast, massive stars consume their nuclear fuel at a prodigious rate and become red giants in a matter of only a few million years.

Once it has become a red giant, the Sun will begin to fuse helium to carbon in its core. However, this new energy source will only delay the inevitable victory of gravity. Within about a billion years the Sun will peel off its outer layers to reveal a white dwarf remnant that will cool slowly, over billions more years.

Stars that begin life larger than about eight times the mass of the Sun will blow away much of their mass during the course of their lives, but will still end up too large to survive as white dwarfs. Instead, they blow up in brilliant supernova explosions, leaving neutron stars or black holes to mark their passing.

The Sun will live on as a white dwarf for billions of years, slowly fading from view, with little or no nuclear fusion to slow the cooling.

After perhaps 1 billion years as a giant, the Sun will eject its outer layers to form a short-lived planetary nebula surrounding the cooling core.

About 10 billion years after it formed, the Sun will run short of hydrogen fuel in its core, but it will actually increase its energy output and swell to become a red giant.

THE SOLAR SYSTEM

Among more than 100 billion stars in the Milky Way Galaxy, one is unique. It is the Sun—the only star that we know has a planetary system, including at least one planet which can support life as we know it. That planet is Earth, of course, although Mars may also be a candidate.

Until recently, the Sun's family was the only planetary system we knew of, but evidence that large planets circle several Sun-like stars is now accumulating. In time, observations may reveal that they also have Earth-sized planets.

The solar system's formation

A little less than 5 billion years ago, the Sun was formed in a cloud of interstellar gas. The infant Sun was surrounded by a cooling disk of gas and dust—the solar nebula—where knots of material were forming, colliding, breaking, and merging. The larger objects, called planetesimals, grew by accreting smaller particles, until a few protoplanets dominated. The protoplanets from the warm inner parts of the disk became the small rocky planets. Further out, in a cooler region where ices of water, ammonia, and methane could condense, the giant planets formed. These planets grew in mass more rapidly, forming deep atmospheres around rocky cores. The giant planets copied the Sun's accretion disk in miniature to create their moons.

As the Sun settled into its present stable state, the pressure of radiation and the gas of the solar wind streaming outward blew away the remains of the solar nebula. The newborn planets swept up the larger debris. In the process they were subjected to an intense bombardment, evidence of which we see in the craters on the rocky surfaces of the inner solar system and the icy surfaces of the moons of the outer solar system.

The solar system today has been largely swept clean of the debris of its formation. It is dominated by the Sun, at its center, which constitutes almost 99.9 percent of the solar system's mass. Most of the remainder is contained in the two giant planets Jupiter and Saturn, while Earth represents less than 0.0003 percent of the Sun's mass.

The region of space inhabited by the planets is a flat plane centered on the Sun and about 15 billion km (just under 10 billion miles) across. This is almost 50 times the span of Earth's orbit. Vast as this sounds, it is only 0.02 percent of the distance to the nearest star! The great void of interplanetary space is sparsely populated by debris orbiting the distant Sun, ranging in size from particles of dust to rocky asteroids and icy comets—these may be tens or even hundreds of kilometers across.

The family of planets

The inner rocky planets and asteroids and Earth's Moon share a common heritage, yet visits by spacecraft have revealed their histories to be quite different. The smaller ones, Mercury and the Moon, are geologically dead worlds retaining little or no atmosphere. Mars has had more geological activity and features Olympus Mons, the solar system's largest volcano. The larger inner planets, Venus and Earth, are similar in size but differ geologically. Both show evidence of volcanic activity, but Earth's activity includes moving plates of rock causing active mountain building; this has not occurred on Venus.

The common thread in the surface histories of the rocky planets is the heavy bombardment they underwent early in their existence. Occasional impacts still occur, as was dramatically illustrated in 1994 when Comet Shoemaker-Levy 9 broke into fragments and crashed into Jupiter.

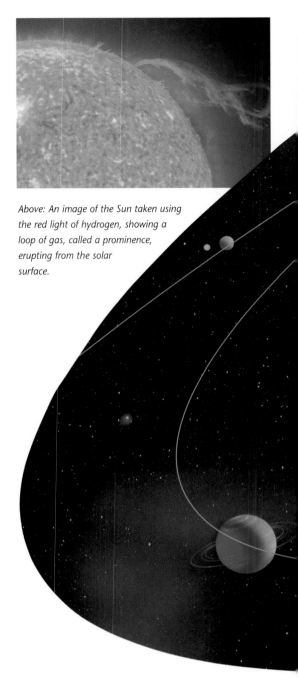

Above: An image of the Sun taken using the red light of hydrogen, showing a loop of gas, called a prominence, erupting from the solar surface.

Of the inner planets, Venus, Earth, and Mars have significant atmospheres, although these are only thin veneers over their rocky surfaces. The atmospheres of Venus and Mars today are mostly carbon dioxide. Earth's atmosphere is unique in having only traces of carbon dioxide in an atmosphere consisting mainly of nitrogen and oxygen. A combination of oceans of liquid water, an active geological history and abundant plant life has stripped the atmosphere of much of its carbon dioxide, and released oxygen.

In stark contrast, the faces presented by the giant outer planets, Jupiter and Saturn, are clouds of ammonia compounds and water in layers riding high in deep atmospheres. These gaseous envelopes are believed to surround a mantle of liquid metallic hydrogen overlying a rocky core. The clouds are split into bands by high-speed winds circulating in regular patterns within the atmosphere. They are punctuated now and then by cyclonic storms, the best known being Jupiter's Great Red Spot, which has survived for at least 300 years.

The asteroid Ida, top, seen by the Galileo spacecraft; a tiny moon can be seen to the right. Comet West displays its tails across the sky, above. Above right: Jupiter, showing the short-lived scars of the impact of Comet Shoemaker-Levy 9. Right: The planets' relative distances from the Sun (see box opposite).

Above: The Sun's family
is comprised of nine major planets and
many smaller moons and asteroids (not to scale).

The smaller, colder giants, Uranus and Neptune, have few atmospheric features, and their blue–green coloring results from methane in the atmosphere. Their atmospheres overlie an icy core of water, methane, ammonia, and rock.

The giant planets all have large moons in orbit around them which were formed in their surrounding nebulae, plus smaller objects that are probably captured asteroids. The largest moons, Jupiter's Ganymede and Saturn's Titan, are larger than the planet Mercury. Most of the moons have thick, icy crusts pitted with craters that date from the heavy bombardment which scarred the inner planets. Distant Pluto and its moon Chiron are much like them, but Pluto's elongated orbit grants it status as a planet. The one exception is Jupiter's large inner moon Io, which has a surface covered in sulfur-rich rock. Io is locked in a gravitational embrace with Jupiter and its neighboring moons, Europa and Ganymede, which causes heating and results in it being the most volcanically active place in the solar system.

All four giant planets have systems of thin rings orbiting over their equators. Saturn's famous rings are by far the most substantial, but none of the rings is solid. They are composed of icy particles that range in size from tiny specks to blocks as large as houses, and their orbits are shepherded by the gravitational influences of nearby moons.

What the future holds

As in the past, the future of the solar system will be dominated by the evolution of the Sun. About 5 billion years from now, the Sun will suddenly increase in size and brightness, ultimately encompassing most of the inner planets, causing their orbits to decay and the planets to spiral into the Sun. The outer planets and their moons will be subjected to 1,000 times the current energy output from the Sun; this will melt icy surfaces and alter their atmospheres. Within a few hundred million years the Sun will decrease in size to become a white dwarf, only feebly illuminating the remains of its family.

Planetary facts

Mercury
Diameter: 4,878 km (3,031 miles)
Average distance from Sun: 0.4 AU*
Known moons: None

Venus
Diameter: 12,104 km (7,521 miles)
Average distance from Sun: 0.7 AU*
Known moons: None

Earth
Diameter: 12,756 km (7,925 miles)
Average distance from Sun: 1.0 AU*
Known moons: 1

Mars
Diameter: 6,787 km (4,217 miles)
Average distance from Sun: 1.5 AU*
Known moons: 2

Jupiter
Diameter: 143,800 km (89,400 miles)
Average distance from Sun: 5.2 AU*
Known moons: 16

Saturn
Diameter: 120,660 km (75,000 miles)
Average distance from Sun: 9.5 AU*
Known moons: 18

Uranus
Diameter: 51,120 km (31,765 miles)
Average distance from Sun: 19.2 AU*
Known moons: 17

Neptune
Diameter: 49,500 km (30,760 miles)
Average distance from Sun: 30.1 AU*
Known moons: 8

Pluto
Diameter: 2,360 km (1,466 miles)
Average distance from Sun: 39.4 AU*
Known moons: 1

*AU stands for astronomical unit: an AU is the average distance between Earth and the Sun— about 150 million km (93 million miles).

PLANET EARTH

With the exception of Pluto, all the planets in the solar system lie in almost the same plane. This reflects their common origin in the disk surrounding the infant Sun. Pluto wanders far from this disk, indicating a history we can only suspect, but clearly one that differs considerably from those of the other planets. Earth is a better-behaved member of the Sun's family but, like the rest of the planets, it has its own particular characteristics and history.

Earth's motion

The orbits of all the planets around the Sun are elliptical, but, like those of most of the planets, Earth's orbit is quite close to circular. The distance between Earth and the Sun varies between 147 and 152 million km (92 and 95 million miles), known as 1.0 AU (astronomical unit). The point of closest approach occurs on 2 January each year, during the southern hemisphere's summer. It is a common misconception that the small change in distance produces the Earth's seasons.

Apart from its revolution around the Sun, Earth also spins around a rotation axis which passes through the north and south geographic poles. Seen from above the north pole, Earth spins on its axis in a counterclockwise direction, and it circles the Sun in the same counterclockwise direction. Most of the other planets and major moons behave in the same way, which again points to their having common origins.

Earth travels around its orbit at 30 km per second (18 miles per second). At this speed, it takes 365.25 days to complete one circuit—that period defines our calendar year. The period of a day is defined by the rotation of Earth on its axis relative to the stars—once every 23 hours and 56 minutes. In that time, however, Earth has also advanced 2.6 million km (1.6 million miles) along its curving orbit, so it has to turn a little further to rotate once relative to the Sun. This takes about 4 extra minutes, and makes the time from midday one day to midday the next exactly 24 hours.

Changing seasons

The Earth's axis is tilted relative to the plane of its orbit by 23.5°. This axis remains pointed in the same orientation relative to the stars as Earth circles the Sun. As a result, Earth's northern hemisphere is tilted more directly toward the Sun in the middle of the calendar year.

From the ground, the Sun then appears higher in the sky and the direct sunlight leads to warmer weather—the northern summer. At the same time, the southern hemisphere has a more oblique view of the Sun, resulting in cooler winter weather. The situation is reversed six months later when Earth is on the opposite side of its orbit.

The direction of Earth's axis is not strictly fixed, but swings around in a circuit lasting 26,000 years. As a result of this precession, our seasons today would seem out of step to the ancient Egyptians, who lived some 5,000 years ago. Their seasons would have differed by around two months from ours, Earth's rotation axis having changed its direction somewhat since that time.

Other effects also operate over periods of tens of thousands of years to slightly change Earth's tilt and how close Earth gets to the Sun. Acting together, these effects produce changes in the amount of heat Earth receives from the Sun, and these changes may significantly affect Earth's climate. There is some evidence that these changes result in periodic ice ages, but the concept remains controversial. Links between the Sun's 11-year sunspot numbers cycle and the Earth's climate also remain speculative.

The largest rocky planet

The Earth is a ball of rock 12,756 km (7,925 miles) in diameter at the equator, but its rotation causes it to be slightly flattened at the poles. It is the largest of the rocky planets in the solar system and, as a result of its bulk, it retains a hot interior; the temperature may reach 6,000°C (10,830°F) at the core—as hot as the surface of the Sun.

Earth's orbit, right: The Earth orbits the Sun in 365.25 days, or one calendar year. It also rotates in slightly less than 24 hours on an axis which is tilted relative to the orbit. This tilt leads to the progression of the seasons each year.

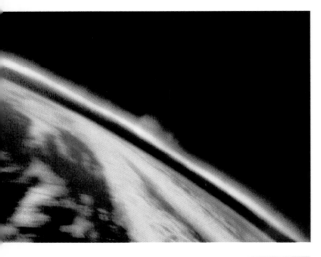

The Earth is surrounded by a protective magnetic envelope called the magnetosphere (in blue and brown, above). Some charged particles from the Sun (red arrows) tend to be channeled down onto the Earth's poles where they cause the air to glow as an aurora, as seen from a space shuttle (top).

Magnetic reversals

When molten lava from a volcano cools and solidifies, it captures the orientation and strength of the Earth's magnetic field at that time and place. This built-in compass needle has proved a powerful tool for studying the gradual drift of Earth's continents. It has also revealed periods, usually spaced by a few hundred thousand years, when Earth's magnetic field has briefly disappeared. Within a geological instant of only about 5,000 years, the field shrinks to zero and then reappears with magnetic north and south swapped. The magnetic imprint of this swapping is found in alternating bands of rocks along mid-oceanic ridges. Each band is made of rocks formed around the same time, and with the same magnetic signature. This provides dramatic confirmation of the picture of continents drifting apart with new crust forming between them. The origin of this change in magnetic directions lies in the electrical dynamo working in Earth's outer core to create the field. How it happens so quickly and why the interval is so irregular remain unknown.

How this change would affect those migratory animals that seem to use the direction of the magnetic field to navigate on their journeys, we do not know. And what if we lost the protective cloak of the Earth's magnetosphere? Cosmic ray particles from the Sun and interstellar space that are normally deflected or trapped by the magnetosphere would reach the surface of Earth. This would cause dramatically higher rates of genetic damage to animals and plants and lead to mutations and perhaps extinctions.

The core is a mix of metallic nickel and iron split into a solid inner core and an outer fluid zone which reaches halfway to the surface. Enclosing the outer core is Earth's mantle. The dense rocks in this zone flow, over geologic time, under the intense heat and pressure. Overlying the mantle, Earth's crust is a skin of lightweight rocks: a mere 60 km (36 miles) deep at its thickest.

Its inner heat makes Earth one of the most seismically active objects within the solar system. On the surface, it causes volcanic activity, and at depth, it drives the separate plates of the crust into motion. This motion—folding the rocks of the crust—creates mountain ranges. At the perimeters of the plates, new crust is created or old crust destroyed. Atmospheric forces such as wind and water flow also act to reshape Earth's surface, by eroding rock and depositing weathered material to form new sedimentary rock strata.

All these processes together act to renew the planet's surface over hundreds of millions of years, removing or altering the ancient impact scarring that can be seen on the surfaces of so many other objects in the solar system. Only a few recent impact craters are visible, providing hints of Earth's turbulent early history.

Earth's atmosphere

Earth is surrounded by a thin atmospheric envelope which tapers off into space and is all but gone 100 km (62 miles) above the surface. This envelope maintains the surface at a higher

Right, top: A total solar eclipse occurs when the Moon passes in front of the Sun and obscures it. As the Sun is finally eclipsed, rays of sunlight filtering through the hills and valleys on the Moon's edge create an effect known as Baily's beads, center. Right, bottom: A lunar eclipse—the Moon darkens as it passes through the Earth's shadow.

temperature than it would otherwise be, permitting oceans of liquid water on the surface. The atmosphere is a unique mixture of nitrogen and oxygen, with only traces of carbon dioxide and other gases, and is certainly not Earth's primeval atmosphere. Oxygen only began to build up when primitive forms of life developed photosynthesis. Oxygen reacts to form ozone, which protects the surface of the planet from intense ultraviolet radiation. Life has crafted the environment of the blue planet to suit itself.

Above the atmosphere lies the protective cocoon of the magnetosphere—the domain of Earth's magnetic field. While most of the particles flowing from the Sun are deflected by the magnetosphere, some become ensnared and are channeled onto the north and south poles, forming the glowing aurorae.

The magnetic field originates in electrical currents within Earth's outer fluid core, and its axis is at a slightly different angle from the planet's rotation axis. As a result, Earth's magnetic and rotation poles are not quite the same, creating a difference between magnetic north, as measured by a compass, and "true" north.

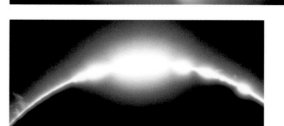

THE MOON

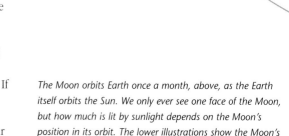

Alight in the darkness of night, the Moon was considered a deity in many ancient cultures and has provided humans with their calendar. The 29¹/₂ days it takes to go through its cycle of phases is close to the length of a month, the word "month" coming from the word "moon."

Galileo's telescopic observations in 1609 of mountains on the Moon played an important part in showing people that the Moon and planets were worlds something like Earth. But the greatest step in this process was the series of six Apollo landings on the Moon between 1969 and 1972. So far, the Moon is the only other world that humans have visited.

Phases of the Moon

The Moon orbits Earth in just under 27¹/₂ days relative to the stars. Earth moves appreciably along its curving path around the Sun in that time, however, so the Moon needs to travel for two more days to get back to the same position relative to the Sun and Earth and complete its cycle of phases. At the same time, the Moon is rotating on its own axis, but the strong gravitational pull of Earth has locked these two

motions together. As a result, the Moon always presents the same familiar face to us on Earth: apart from a little around the edges, we never see the "far side" of the Moon. It also means that a "day" on the Moon is two weeks long!

Half of the Moon is always lit by the Sun, and the amount of that sunny half we can see from Earth depends on where the Moon is in its orbit. If it lies directly sunward of the Earth, the Moon's night side (not the far side) is presented to our view. It appears dark and invisible when it is near the Sun in the sky. This is New Moon. Over the following days the sunlight begins to illuminate one edge of the visible face and the Moon appears as a crescent shape in the twilight sky. The crescent expands through First Quarter and on to Full Moon, when the fully illuminated disk is opposite the Sun in the sky. Over the following two weeks the sunlit portion of the disk shrinks back through Third Quarter towards New Moon.

Solar and lunar eclipses

The Moon's orbit is tilted by just over 5° to the plane of Earth's orbit. As a result, the New Moon usually passes close to the Sun in the sky, but does not cross it.

About twice a year, however, the orbital angles converge—the Sun and Moon line up and the Moon's shadow is cast towards Earth. Sometimes the shadow only just reaches Earth, as a dark spot no more than 270 km (170 miles) across. As Earth turns underneath it, the spot draws a thin line of darkness across the globe.

The Earth-bound observer sited somewhere along the total eclipse track sees the Moon as just big enough to cover the disk of the much larger but more distant Sun. Day turns to night for a few minutes as the solar disk is covered, revealing the faint glow of the surrounding corona. Observers usually find the few minutes of a total solar eclipse a remarkable

The Moon orbits Earth once a month, above, as the Earth itself orbits the Sun. We only ever see one face of the Moon, but how much is lit by sunlight depends on the Moon's position in its orbit. The lower illustrations show the Moon's changing phases as we see them, corresponding to the Moon's position in the upper illustration.

experience, and some have felt compelled to travel around the world, chasing further opportunities to see one.

A wider swath of Earth's surface lies off the track of totality, and sees the Sun only partly eclipsed. Also, about half the time, the shadow falls short of Earth, causing the Moon to appear too small to cover the Sun in the sky; this is called an annular eclipse, and it lacks the darkness and magic of a total eclipse.

When the situation of Earth and the Moon are reversed, the Full Moon can be eclipsed by Earth's shadow. Sky watchers on the whole night side of Earth will see the Moon darken for several hours as it traverses Earth's wide shadow. The effect is somewhat less dramatic than a solar eclipse, but more commonly seen.

The motions of the tides

The most obvious effect of the Moon on Earth is the tides. These alterations in sea level twice a day are caused by the gravitational pull of the Moon on water and on Earth itself.

The water on the side of Earth nearest the Moon feels a stronger force from the Moon than does the center of Earth, which is itself more

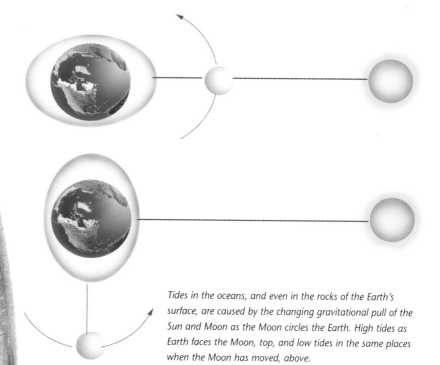

Tides in the oceans, and even in the rocks of the Earth's surface, are caused by the changing gravitational pull of the Sun and Moon as the Moon circles the Earth. High tides as Earth faces the Moon, top, and low tides in the same places when the Moon has moved, above.

strongly attracted than water on the side away from the Moon. This results in water accumulating in two high tides: one on the side of Earth facing the Moon, and one on the far side. In between these regions of high tide are regions of low tide, where the water level is at its lowest. Tide heights vary greatly because of local effects, but they can range as high as 10 m (33 ft) in some locations. Tides of a few centimeters are also raised in the rocky crust of Earth itself.

But tidal forces have even more profound consequences. The Earth's rotation slows by 0.0023 seconds per century. This makes a day now four hours longer than a day was when the first complex life forms arose in Earth's oceans. The same effect on the smaller Moon has already slowed its rotation to make its "day" equal its orbital period. Tidal forces are also causing the Moon to recede from Earth by about 4 cm (1^1/$_2$ in) a year. As a result, solar eclipses will eventually all be annular, because the Moon will be too far away to ever fully cover the Sun's disk.

Lunar history

The origin of the Moon has long been a subject of debate, but current theory imagines a collision over 4 billion years ago between the infant Earth and another planetesimal as large as Mars. Some of the lighter debris then collected in orbit around Earth to become the Moon.

Both Earth and the Moon were subjected to intense bombardment early in their histories, as the solar system was swept clear of most of the debris of its formation. On the Moon, the last stages of this cosmic storm are still recorded in the bright highland areas of the surface, which are covered with impact craters. Other areas suffered large impacts late in the bombardment; these gouged enormous basins in the surface. Many of the basins on the side nearest Earth were soon flooded by dark lava flows from within the Moon. Rocks brought back to Earth by Apollo astronauts reveal that the youngest of these maria (singular mare, Latin for "sea") is over 3 billion years old, despite being marked by relatively few craters.

Since that time, the Moon has cooled to inactivity, with only occasional impacts changing the scene. The last large impact occurred perhaps 100 million years ago, creating the crater Tycho and splashing debris across the surface.

A new generation of spacecraft has recently begun to build on the legacy of the Apollo missions, by studying the Moon again. The most exciting finding from these recent studies has been the apparent discovery of water ice on the Moon's cold crater floors. These crater floors are shielded from the glare of radiation from the Sun, which bombards the rest of the surface unhindered by any atmosphere.

Man on the Moon

Man's first step on the Moon was taken on July 20, 1969, during the US Apollo XI mission, and was watched by millions around the world as it was broadcast live on television.

The excitement this event generated may seem extraordinary now, but man seems to have always dreamt of walking on the Moon.

Since that first landing, when Buzz Aldrin and Neil Armstrong both stepped onto the Moon, there have been six other Apollo Moon missions, all between 1969 and 1972. One was aborted, but on each of the others, two more astronauts walked on the surface of the Moon.

Below: Buzz Aldrin taking a historic step on the Moon, watched by millions of television viewers on July 20 1969.
Bottom: Earthrise—taken from Apollo 11, this picture shows the Earth coming up over the Moon's horizon.

SPACE EXPLORATION

Our view of the solar system and the wider universe has improved dramatically in recent years. The exploration of the solar system by robot probes has revolutionized our perspective on the planets and their moons. Closer to home, telescopes in Earth orbit have studied the universe using ultraviolet, X-ray and gamma-ray radiation which is invisible from the ground. Arrays of radio telescopes, including one in space, probe the radio universe at finer resolution than any single optical telescope can achieve. On the ground, optical astronomers are building a new generation of larger telescopes which will probe the visible universe more deeply than ever before, and scan the infrared radiation coming from the sky to study regions hidden from visible light.

Exploring the solar system

The space age began with the beeping voice of Sputnik 1 circling Earth in 1957. In retrospect, it seems a small step, but Sputnik led to a series of Soviet Luna and American Pioneer and Ranger spacecraft over the next few years; they sped past the Moon or deliberately crashed into it.

The exploration of the planets began with attempts to reach Venus and Mars in the early 1960s. In 1973, the US Mariner 10 spacecraft successfully flew past Venus and then continued to Mercury, where it captured what are still the only close-up images we have of the surface of that planet. The surface of Venus is hidden by perpetual clouds, but in 1975 the Soviet Venera 9 and 10 landers returned images of a rocky, desolate surface. More recently, radar maps of the

surface have been produced by the Pioneer Venus and Magellan spacecraft.

While the Soviets explored Venus, the Americans were visiting Mars. In 1976, the Viking 1 and 2 orbiters arrived to map the surface from space for several years, while their accompanying landers studied two sites on the surface and tested, unsuccessfully, for evidence of life. This exploration of the surface was not resumed for another 21 years until, in 1997, the Mars Pathfinder landed, with its rover Sojourner. The exploration of Mars continues today with renewed vigor.

The exploration of the giant outer planets began in 1972 with the launch of Pioneer 10, followed soon after by Pioneer 11. They returned the first stunning images of Jupiter's colorful clouds and the surfaces of its major moons. Pioneer 11 continued on to a repeat performance at Saturn in 1979. By that time a new generation of explorers, Voyager 1 and 2, had already reached Jupiter. Both journeyed on to Saturn, and Voyager 2 then made a foray to the realms of Uranus and Neptune. All four of these interplanetary explorers are still journeying outward, reaching in different directions towards the edge of the Sun's domain. Meanwhile, the exploration of the giant planets continues, with the Galileo spacecraft surveying Jupiter and Cassini on its way to a rendezvous with Saturn.

While the outer reaches of the solar system were being explored, objects closer to home were also under investigation. Comets, asteroids and the Moon have all recently been explored.

Humans in space

The exploration of the solar system by robot spacecraft has been paralleled by a program of human spaceflight closer to Earth. It began in 1961, four years after Sputnik 1, with the flight of Yuri Gagarin in a Vostok spacecraft. The Soviets continued with the Voskhod and Soyuz programs. After being beaten into orbit, the US rapidly developed the techniques of working in space in the Mercury and Gemini programs, with the ultimate goal of satisfying President Kennedy's challenge of landing a man on the moon before the end of the 1960s.

A lunar landing was the objective of the

The first spacecraft to orbit Earth was Sputnik 1 in 1957. Since then, Skylab and Mir have paved the way for a larger space station to orbit the Earth.

Planetary science spacecraf

PAST MISSIONS

Mariner 9 (1971, NASA)
The first spacecraft to orbit Mars. Carried out detailed photography of the surface and of Phobos and Deimos, Mars' two moons.

Apollo 11, 12, 14, 15, 16, 17 (1969–72, NASA)
Manned landings on the Moon and sample returns.

Pioneer 10 (1973, NASA)
First spacecraft to flyby Jupiter. Now about 10.6 billion km (6.6 billion miles) from the Sun.

Pioneer 11 (1974–79, NASA)
Followed Pioneer 10 in 1974; first probe to study Saturn (1979). Now about 7.6 billion km (4.7 billion miles) from the Sun.

Mariner 10 (1974–75)
Used Venus as a gravity assist to Mercury; returned the first close-up images of the atmosphere of Venus in ultraviolet; made three flybys of Mercury.

Venera 9 (1975, USSR)
Landed on Venus, returned pictures of the surface.

Pioneer Venus (1978, NASA)
An orbiter and four atmospheric probes; made the first high-quality map of the surface of Venus.

Viking 1 (1976, NASA)
Probe in Martian orbit and lander set down on the western slopes of Chryse Planitia; returned images and searched for Martian microorganisms.

Viking 2 (1976, NASA)
Arrived in Martian orbit a month after Viking 1:

Apollo program. It began disastrously with a fire in early 1967 which killed three astronauts. The first piloted mission was Apollo 7 in 1968, followed in rapid succession by Apollo 8, 9, and 10, which tested the equipment needed for the landing. On July 20, 1969, the program reached its culmination, with the landing of the Apollo 11 lunar module Eagle on the dusty floor of the Moon's Sea of Tranquillity. Soon afterward, Neil Armstrong became the first human to set foot on the Moon.

The Apollo program continued through five more successful landings, returning 382 kg (844 lb) of lunar rock and soil, plus photographs and other data which have shaped our current understanding of the history of the Moon.

The 1970s were the in-between years of US manned space activities: between the Apollo program and the advent of the reusable space shuttle. In 1981 the much-delayed space shuttle Columbia was launched for the first time, and a schedule of regular launches has continued since then, but with a break of more than two years after the loss of all seven crew members in the Challenger accident in 1986.

The Soviet human spaceflight program concentrated on learning how to cope with long periods in space aboard the Salyut and Mir space stations. The US program featured

Bottom left: As part of the Pathfinder mission, the unmanned Sojourner rover took X-ray measurements of Martian rocks. Below: The nucleus of Halley's comet, taken by Giotto spacecraft in 1986. Bottom right: astronauts carrying out repairs on the Hubble Space Telescope, 1993.

lander touched down in Utopia Planitia; same tasks as Viking 1, plus seismometer.

Magellan (1989, NASA)
Mapped 98 percent of the surface of Venus at better than 300 m (1,000 ft), and obtained comprehensive gravity-field map for 95 percent of the planet.

ONGOING MISSIONS

Voyager 1 (1977– , NASA)
Flew past Jupiter (1979) and Saturn (1980). At mid-1998, the craft was 10.7 billion km (6.6 billion miles) from Earth.

Voyager 2 (1977– , NASA)
Launched just before Voyager 1, Voyager 2 flew by Jupiter (1979), Saturn (1981), Uranus (1986), and Neptune (1989). At mid-1998, the craft was 8.3 billion km (5 billion miles) from Earth.

Galileo (1989– , NASA)
While in transit to Jupiter, returned the first resolved images of two asteroids (951 Gaspra and 243 Ida), plus pictures of the impact of Comet SL9 on Jupiter (1994). Now in Jupiter orbit. Atmospheric probe has studied Jupiter's upper atmosphere. Mission hampered by antenna problems.

Ulysses (1990– , ESA/NASA)
Launched to investigate the Sun's polar regions. Gravity boost from Jupiter in 1992 took it out of the plane in which the planets orbit and over the Sun's south, then north, poles.

SOHO (1996– , ESA/NASA)
Solar Heliospheric Observatory (for studying the Sun and its structure), in solar orbit 1.5 million km (1 million miles) from Earth.

Pathfinder (1996–7, NASA)
A low-cost planetary discovery mission, consisting of a stationary lander and a surface rover. Operated on Mars for 3 months in 1997 measuring wind and weather, photographing the surface and chemically analyzing rocks.

Mars Surveyor Program (1996– , NASA)
Mars Global Surveyor is the first mission of a 10-year program of robotic exploration of Mars. It entered polar orbit in September 1997 and is mapping surface topography and distribution of minerals, and monitoring global weather.

Cassini (1997– , ESA/NASA)
Consists of an orbiter to study Saturn's clouds and a probe to land on Titan, Saturn's largest moon. Will use gravity to assist flybys of Venus, Earth, and Jupiter before arriving at Saturn in 2004.

NEW MISSION

Stardust (1999– , NASA)
Launched on February 7 1999, Stardust is scheduled to flyby Comet Wild 2 in 2004, collect particles from the comet's tail and return to Earth in 2006.

Skylab in the early 1970s and then lapsed until US astronauts began to visit Mir during the 1990s. The future of long-term human presence in space lies with the international space station.

Exploring the universe

One function of an orbiting space station is to serve as an astronomical observing platform. However, most astronomical observations from within Earth's orbit are performed by unmanned telescope observatories controlled from the ground. The best known is the Hubble Space Telescope (HST), a 2.4 m (95 in) aperture telescope which offers views of unprecedented sharpness in infrared, visible, and ultraviolet light. It orbits at a height of about 600 km (375 miles) above the Earth's surface—well above the blurring effects of Earth's atmosphere.

Equally important is the range of astronomical satellites studying other radiation from space. Satellites such as the International Ultraviolet Explorer (IUE) and the InfraRed Astronomical Satellite (IRAS) have made major contributions in the past. More recently, the Cosmic Background Explorer (COBE) has probed the glow of the Big Bang, while satellites such as BeppoSAX have hunted down elusive sources of energetic gamma-ray bursts. The Japanese Halca satellite is a radio telescope which observes the sky in conjunction with Earth-bound telescopes to create a radio telescope thousands of kilometers across. The Solar Heliospheric Observer (SOHO) observes the Sun from a point 1.5 million km (1 million miles) closer to the Sun than Earth.

Search for life

One of the reasons for exploring the solar system is to search for life beyond Earth. The desolate surfaces of Mercury, Venus, and the Moon are not promising sites. Mars, historically the most popular source of alien neighbors, remains a far more likely candidate after the discoveries of the space age. Although the surface is cold and dry today, evidence indicates it was once warmer and water flowed on it. The Viking landers searched for life in 1976 without success. There is no evidence yet that life ever arose on Mars.

The Galileo mission to Jupiter has enlivened speculation that Europa (right) may have a warm ocean of water under its icy crust. Perhaps life could arise there. The Cassini spacecraft will soon examine Saturn's moon, Titan, and may show whether it has lakes or oceans of carbon compounds where some sort of life might have appeared.

Life elsewhere in the solar system is likely to be primitive, but its discovery may be within reach of interplanetary spacecraft from Earth. The search for life among the stars is far more difficult. Current efforts are directed at listening with radio telescopes for signals from distant civilizations. This project is known as SETI—the Search for Extra-Terrestrial Intelligence.

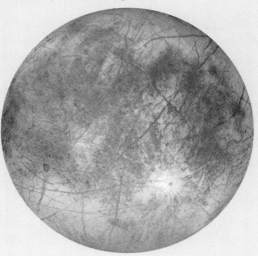

Earth as a biophysical system

The plants and animals we know today—such as this Chinstrap Penguin in Antarctica, above—have evolved over thousands of years to adapt to their surroundings. Opposite: Volcanoes, such as this one in New Zealand, can provide geologists with clues to the puzzle of Earth's history.

There are many factors that make Earth a unique planet. Its atmosphere, oceans, moving plates, escaping gases, diverse life forms, soils, and the presence of humans all contribute to a distinctive biophysical system. Above all else, it is the dynamic, ever-changing ways in which the air, land, and oceans interact that create particular landscapes available for human use and abuse. From the equator to the poles, from mountains to the depths of ocean basins, plants and animals go through their life cycles nurtured by the climates and the nutrients in soils and waters.

Yet what we observe today has not always been present. The world humans inhabit has been transformed not once, but many times since the hard, rocky crusts of continents and the watery masses of oceans first formed, around 4 billion years ago.

Charles Darwin was one of many scientists who conceptualized patterns of evolution. Organisms did not immediately find their place in the world, he proposed; rather, there were countless histories of evolving life for the different plants and animals that have occupied space on land or in the sea over geological time. These patterns of evolution were not uniform. Past life histories show punctuated successions of periods dominated by particular organisms, followed by extensive extinctions of various species. The cause and meaning of such changes are often a mystery and remain to be explained.

It is very difficult to unravel Earth's history. Geologists and paleontologists are like detectives. They are required to piece together fragmentary evidence using their imagination, and their sense of adventure and curiosity, exploring the world and discovering for themselves what has happened in the past. Some geologists, such as Charles Lyell, have had the ability to synthesize masses of information and develop generalized histories from field observations and interpretations. Increasingly, new technologies, including the capacity to calculate accurately the age of rocks using radiometric dating methods, have opened new vistas of thought, allowing the testing of theories such as that of continental drift.

Discoveries of magnetic reversals in rocks on the floor of oceans, the volcanic character of mid-oceanic ridges, and the age of oceanic basalts covered by a veneer of geologically young sediment, have contributed to our understanding of the processes of sea-floor spreading and hence to the development of plate tectonic theory. This was one of the most remarkable scientific advances of the twentieth century. It formalized the grand dreams of those who could see evidence for the validity of continental drift theory in the rock record and in the distribution of plants and animals. Yet, for decades, these geologists and biologists were not able to convince the skeptics, because they had no mechanism to explain the movement of the relatively light continental crust over vast distances.

New technologies in ocean research changed all that; with plate tectonics, it is possible to explain much more satisfactorily the formation of mountains, as well as the distribution of earthquakes, volcanoes and many life forms.

Plants and animals, or biota, occur in particular groups, reflecting their adaptation to each other and to the environment. Interaction of biota with climatic, soil, landform, and other conditions has been the subject of much ecological discovery. Competition and predation are just two of the ways in which species function—on a range of scales from microorganisms in the soil to whales at sea. On land and in the ocean, there are clear regional groupings of biota which contribute to the differences between places. But even these differences are not static—they too are subject to change.

Changes in climate, for instance, whether it be over millions of years or tens of years, require organisms to adjust. On a global scale, it is possible to document periods of Earth cooling and the consequent expansion of ice sheets and falls in sea level. Vast areas of Europe and North America were under 1 km ($^5/_8$ mile) of ice as little as 15,000 years ago. Yet Earth warmed, and the glaciers retreated. Today, these areas are home to millions of people.

Rising sea levels flooded continental shelves and river valleys, creating new habitats for plants and animals; in the fertile deltaic plains of many countries, for instance. Such changes have taken place many times over the past 2 million years, the so-called Quaternary period of Earth's history. Understanding why these and other, smaller-scale climatic fluctuations such as the El Niño phenomenon occur is still the subject of much scientific debate.

Against the background of natural variability in climate, another factor comes into play—the impact of humans disturbing the chemistry of the atmosphere and inducing global warming, or the greenhouse effect.

Plants, animals, and human productivity are highly dependent on the state of soils. Continental rocks are of varied chemical composition; on exposure to the atmosphere, they disintegrate or weather into different mixtures of mineral matter combined with decayed matter from plants and animals. The close inter-relationship between soils and climate, vegetation, landforms, and rock type is well known, and this knowledge has helped us develop crops which can be grown successfully in different soils. Again, however, we are confronted with lands that become transformed as soils are overused and exploited, losing their productive capacity and causing populations to decline and migrate.

Landscapes derived from the changing yet distinctive combinations of these biophysical factors constitute part of the human inheritance. Increasingly, we are recognizing our responsibility towards the management or stewardship of this heritage.

EVOLUTION OF THE EARTH

Earth is believed to have developed, along with the rest of the solar system, some 4,500 to 5,000 million years ago, when whirling dust aggregated to form the Sun and the planets. In the process, Earth may have attracted a primordial gaseous atmosphere around itself. The planet was then dominated by volcanic eruptions pouring out gases, including water vapor, onto its surface.

These gases gave rise to Earth's present atmosphere. As Earth's surface cooled, the water vapor condensed to form oceans. The oxygen content of the atmosphere was built up through photosynthesis by primitive life forms. Earth's plant life, through photosynthesis, gives off oxygen, which is then available to help sustain animals, including humans.

Earth's average density is about 5.5 g/cu cm (3.2 oz/cu in), but this is not uniformly distributed. Earth is formed of concentric layers, the innermost layers having the greatest densities. The density of Earth's crust is only about 2.7 g/cu cm (1.6 oz/cu in), about half its average density; the highest densities (around 12.5 g/cu cm—7.2 oz/cu in) lie at the planet's core, which is believed to consist of iron and nickel, both of which are dense materials.

The surface of Earth

When compared to its diameter, Earth's crust is very thin—only 5 to 40 km (3 to 25 miles). Much of Earth's surface is covered by water bodies, such as oceans, inland seas, lakes, and rivers, and these constitute the hydrosphere. The atmosphere and the hydrosphere together sustain plants and animals, which form the biosphere.

Earth's crust is cool on the surface, with temperatures in most cases not exceeding 30°C (86°F), but its deepest parts have temperatures as high as 1,100°C (2,010°F). The material of which the crust is composed can be divided into light continental material and heavier oceanic material. Light continental material has a density of 2.7 gm/cu cm (1.6 oz/cu in), and is often granitic. Heavier oceanic material has a density of 3.0 gm/cu cm (1.7 oz/cu in), and is mostly basaltic.

The thickness of Earth's crust is very variable; it is much thicker under the continents (an average of 40 km [25 miles]) and much thinner under the oceans (an average of 5 km [3 miles]). The crust is thickest below young, folded mountains such as the Alps and the Himalayas. In places such as these, it can be as thick as 64 km (40 miles).

Below Earth's crust

Below Earth's surface lie the mantle and the core. The mantle is a thick, mostly solid layer. It is about 2,895 km (1,800 miles) thick, with temperatures ranging from 1,100°–3,600°C (2,010°–6,510°F). The upper mantle is about 670 km (420 miles) thick and contains pockets of molten material. In some places, this molten material finds its way to Earth's surface through fractures, causing volcanic eruptions such as those along the mid-oceanic ridges or in isolated hot spots. A feature of the upper mantle is the low-velocity zone, as defined by the decrease in seismic waves penetrating through the Earth. The rock here is near or at its melting

point, and forms material known as "hot slush", which is capable of motion or flow. It is a mobile layer, over which crustal plates can move. In contrast to this, the much thicker lower mantle (2,230 km; 1,385 miles) is entirely solid.

Earth's core is divided into an outer liquid core (2,250 km; 1,400 miles thick) and an inner solid core (1,255 km; 780 miles thick). The outer core has temperatures ranging between 3,600°C (6,510°F) and 4,200°C (7,590°C). Its liquid nature has been deduced from earthquake information.

Earthquakes transmit seismic P- and S-waves. S-waves cannot pass through liquid layers and are therefore deflected from Earth's core. In contrast, P-waves, which can be transmitted through liquids, pass through the liquid outer layer and eventually emerge on the other side of Earth.

Above Earth's surface

Earth's present atmosphere and water make it unique amongst the other planets of the solar system. The atmosphere, however, has undergone many changes in its long history. If Earth still had an atmosphere of primordial gases, that atmosphere would resemble the gaseous mix which occurs elsewhere in the solar system. This mixture contains an abundance of hydrogen and helium, as well as of carbon.

These gases, however, occur in very small amounts in Earth's present atmosphere. It is very likely that those primordial gases were lost from Earth's atmosphere and that a secondary atmosphere developed around the planet from gases emitted by volcanoes and produced by chemical and biological processes.

It is significant that the elements which form Earth's atmosphere are also found in its crust and thus an exchange between the two can take place. For example, carbon occurs in carbon dioxide in the atmosphere and in the oceans, in calcium carbonate in limestones, and in organic compounds in plant and animal life. Both carbon dioxide and oxygen form part of the cyclic process that involves photosynthesis by plants and respiration by animals. Oxygen was actually absent or present only in very small amounts in

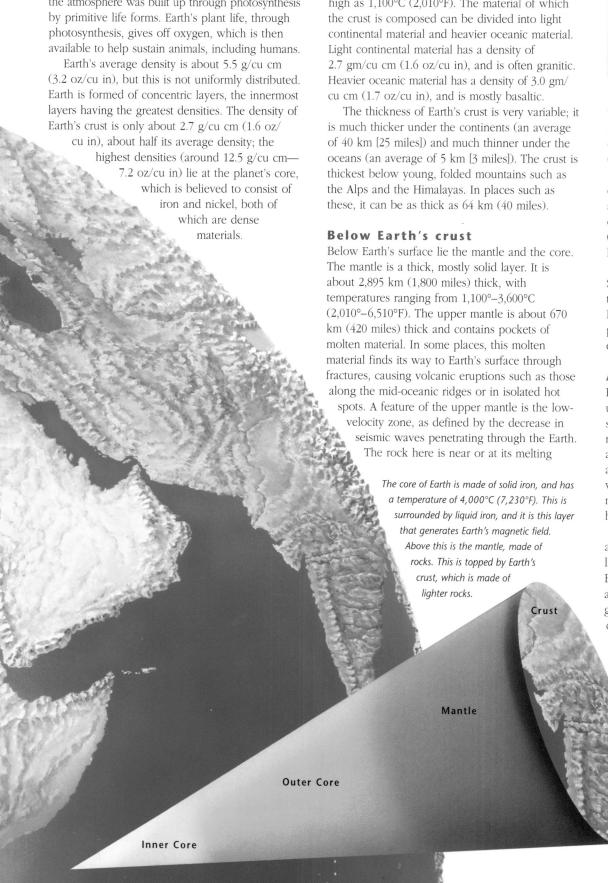

The core of Earth is made of solid iron, and has a temperature of 4,000°C (7,230°F). This is surrounded by liquid iron, and it is this layer that generates Earth's magnetic field. Above this is the mantle, made of rocks. This is topped by Earth's crust, which is made of lighter rocks.

Crust

Mantle

Outer Core

Inner Core

Active volcanoes, such as Volcan de Pacaya, in Guatemala (left) generally occur along fault lines between plates or along mid-oceanic ridges. Molten lava bursts through the Earth's crust and flows downwards, sometimes causing great loss of life and the destruction of entire towns.

Earth's early atmosphere, but became abundant much later. The abundance of plant life that had developed by about 400 million years ago must have boosted oxygen supplies to their current level in Earth's atmosphere. It now seems that oxygen levels which could sustain animal life may possibly have existed as early as some 700 million years ago.

The atmosphere, which rises above Earth's surface to 100 km (60 miles), is mainly made up of nitrogen (78 percent) and oxygen (21 percent), with the remaining 1 percent made up of small quantities of carbon dioxide (0.04 percent), hydrogen, water vapor, and various other gases such as argon. The atmosphere has a layered structure: the densest layers lie close to Earth's surface and the atmosphere becomes more and more rarefied as one moves upwards.

The layer of most concern to us is the troposphere. It is about 12 km (7.5 miles) thick, and contains 75 percent of all the atmospheric gases, including those essential for life. It is within this layer that all our weather occurs. The temperature falls as one rises in this layer.

The stratosphere lies above the troposphere and is about 40 km (25 miles) thick. It contains a narrow layer of ozone molecules. This ozone layer protects life on Earth by shielding it from harmful ultraviolet radiation from the Sun. This ozone layer is under threat from the emission of chemicals produced by human activities—especially chlorofluorocarbons (CFCs), which have been used in aerosol cans and refrigerators. When chlorine is released from CFCs, it rises to the ozone layer and destroys ozone molecules.

In 1985, a large hole (7.7 million square km; 3 million square miles) was discovered in the ozone layer over Antarctica. The depletion of ozone in the area where the hole is has been linked to the increase in skin cancers, especially in Australia. Damage to the ozone layer implies that human impact reaches out 15 to 55 km (9 to 35 miles) into the atmosphere. Worldwide concern about ozone depletion has led to government action; there are now international agreements relating to phasing out the use of CFCs.

Human contribution to Earth's evolution

The changes in the composition of Earth's atmosphere, and the damage to the ozone layer, vividly demonstrate that since the advent of industrialization, humans have had considerable impact on Earth's environment and, as a consequence, on its biosphere. Many of these adverse effects were not foreseen.

It is becoming increasingly clear that human behavior can have far-reaching consequences; not only on our own local environment, but on the entire evolution of Earth. Therefore, all proposed industrial, agricultural, and other developments need to be carefully evaluated in terms of their impact on the environment before they are approved and implemented.

The gaseous mix of the troposphere has also been inadvertently altered by humans, particularly since the acceleration of industrialization in the nineteenth century. The principal change is the increase of carbon dioxide due to emissions from the burning of fossil fuels (coal, natural gas, and petroleum) by factories, power plants, railway engines, and automobiles.

Although carbon dioxide forms only about 0.04 percent of Earth's atmosphere, it is a critical component because, along with the other greenhouse gases, it acts as a blanket, trapping some of the heat of the Earth that would otherwise escape into space.

The emission of carbon dioxide and other gases (methane, nitrous oxide, and ozone) is believed to have caused global warming—the greenhouse effect. Global temperatures have risen by 0.3°C to 0.6°C (32.5°F to 33.1°F) since the mid-nineteenth century and, at the current rate of increase of greenhouse gases, this figure could double by the middle of the twenty-first century. Some predictions place the increase at between 1.5°C (34.7°F) and 5.5°C (41.9°F).

The weather patterns in the world have shown great disturbance in recent decades, according to some observers. This also is being attributed to the greenhouse effect. If global warming continues, it could result in the melting of polar ice sheets and the consequent rising of sea levels, which in turn would seriously threaten low-lying areas, including quite a number of major coastal cities.

The troposphere is the layer of the atmosphere where life exists. The stratosphere is the next layer. The ozone layer, which absorbs most of the Sun's harmful ultraviolet rays, is in the stratosphere. The next layer is the mesosphere. The thermosphere is the outer layer of our atmosphere. Gases are very thin here, and this is where auroras and meteors are seen. The red line shows the decreases and increases in temperature through each layer of the atmosphere.

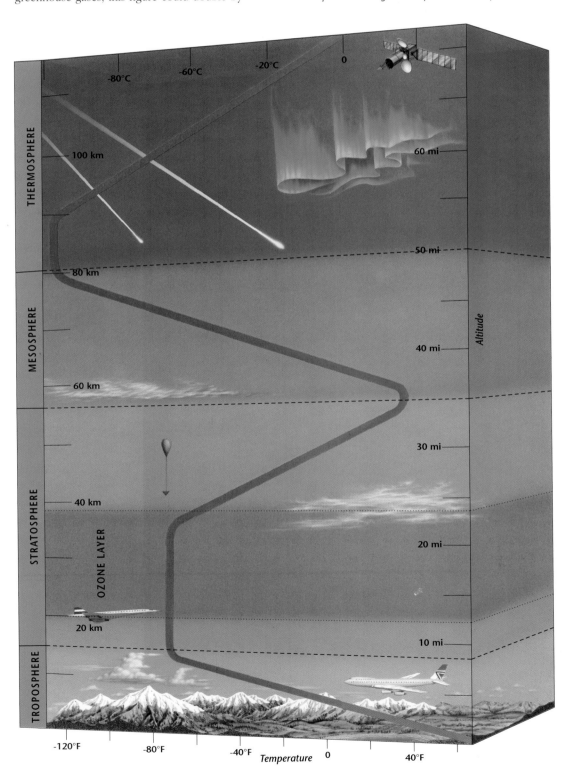

MOVEMENT OF PLATES

Earth is a dynamic planet, and forces within it are continuously active. Continents and oceans have changed in position and shape over time. Earthquakes and other evidence prove that Earth's crust, which is a solid and rigid layer, is broken up into parts called lithospheric or tectonic plates. Plate boundaries coincide with major earthquake zones, many of which also have volcanic chains along them. Seven major plates (Pacific, North American, South American, Eurasian, African, Indo-Australian, and Antarctic), and perhaps twice as many minor plates, have been identified.

Over many millions of years, crustal plates have moved considerably. They have separated (divergent plates), giving rise to oceans, collided (convergent plates), forming the world's highest mountains and the deep oceanic trenches, and slid past each other along fault lines. Thus Earth's crust has spread at divergent plate boundaries and contracted at convergent plate boundaries.

Divergent plate boundaries

In the middle of the Atlantic and Indian oceans, and in the eastern part of the Pacific Ocean, long rifts exist where molten material has risen to form undersea chains of volcanoes. This molten material originates from magma pockets within Earth's upper mantle, and crystallizes as basalt on cooling. These oceanic volcanic chains, called mid-oceanic ridges, form an interlinked system about 60,000 km (37,300 miles) long. In some places, the volcanoes have erupted above the water level, forming islands such as Iceland and the Azores.

Mid-oceanic ridges are not continuous features, but are fractured at several places, with parts being offset by transform faults. Shallow-focus earthquakes, recorded by sensitive instruments, occur frequently along mid-oceanic ridges.

Each time a new series of volcanic eruptions takes place, the existing ridge is split in two and the parts are pushed apart, spreading the sea floor. The corresponding parts of the early ridges are now far apart, on opposite sides of the current mid-oceanic ridge. The separated bands can be identified on the basis of their recorded magnetic directions and age. When the basaltic bands crystallized, Earth's magnetic direction at the time of formation was imprinted in them. Such data proves that Earth's magnetic direction has reversed many times during geological history.

Sea-floor spreading is believed to have produced the Atlantic and Indian oceans, and to have enlarged the Pacific Ocean. Plates move very slowly—on average, only about 2–5 cm (3/4–2 inches) per year—with the spreading of the Atlantic Ocean having taken about 65 million years. Some plates are separating much more quickly—the Nazca and Pacific plates move at about 18 cm (7 inches) per year.

Compared with the continental crust, which is more than 1,000 million years old, most of the oceanic crust (at less than 65 million years old) is geologically very young, the youngest parts being those that lie along the mid-oceanic ridges.

The Red Sea is an example of new sea-floor spreading, whilst the elongated Great Rift Valley in Africa, which extends for more than 2,890 km (1,800 miles), possibly represents new continental rifting and splitting. There are several centers of volcanic eruptions along the Rift Valley; to the north and south of Lake Kivu, for example.

Convergent plate boundaries

Crustal plates may split and diverge on one side, and collide with other plates on the opposite side, giving rise to volcanic chains and oceanic ridges.

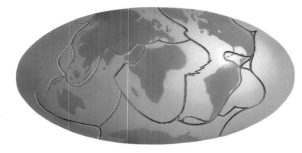

Earth's crust is made up of rigid tectonic plates. Their movement, over millions of years, has determined the structure of our continents and oceans, the formation of mountains and volcanoes, and the distribution of earthquakes.

When plates collide, one plate slides under the other one in a process called subduction, the subducted plate being pushed deep into Earth's mantle. As a result of subduction, collision zones are marked by deep focus earthquakes, such as have occurred in recent times in Japan, Iran and Afghanistan. Subducted plates are dragged deep into the Earth, where they melt. This molten material later rises to form volcanoes.

The deep oceanic trenches lying parallel to the volcanic island arcs, which formed as a result of oceanic-to-oceanic plate collisions, are the deepest features on Earth's surface, ranging from 7,000 to 11,000 m (23,000 to 36,000 ft) deep. The Marianas Trench in the West Pacific is nearly 11,000 m (more than 35,000 ft) deep. There are several trenches in the western Pacific, along the coasts of Japan and the Philippines.

Where continental and oceanic plates collide, the continental plate is crumpled and the oceanic plate buckles downward deep into Earth, where it melts and mixes with the molten material inside the Earth. Lavas from this mixed molten material are lighter in density and color than oceanic basalt. The rock formed is andesite and it is found along a long chain around the Pacific Ocean.

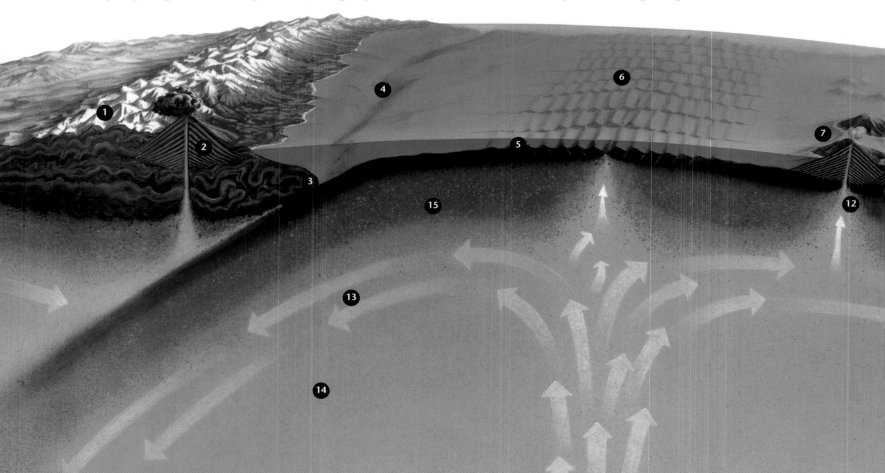

A panoramic view of the Himalayas, the world's highest mountain range (left). The Himalayas are actually made up of three ranges, formed at different times. The koala (below), unique to Australia, may be an animal that became isolated after the break-up of the supercontinent Gondwanaland.

Several plates have collided with the Pacific Plate, giving rise to folded mountain chains, including the Cascade Range in the western USA, and the Andes in South America. This circum-Pacific zone is often referred to as the "Ring of Fire" because of the presence of active volcanoes.

Continent-to-continent plate collisions result in the formation of mountain ranges such as the European Alps and the Himalayas, in Asia. The process gives rise to crustal thickening.

The stupendous Himalayan range arose when the Indo-Australian Plate collided with the Eurasian Plate. The Eurasian Plate rode over the Indian side, pushing up huge sedimentary strata from the then-existing sea into great mountain folds, some of which were thrust towards the south and almost overturned.

Three parallel ranges were formed in successive geological epochs. The southernmost chain is the lowest, ranging from 900 to 1,200 m (2,950 to 3,935 ft) in height, whilst the middle chain rises 2,000 to 4,500 m (6,560 to 14,765 ft).

The chain of highest elevation, lying in the north, has the world's highest peaks (topped by Mount Everest, at 8,848 m [29,028 ft]), which are about 8,500 m (27,885 ft) in height. Its average altitude is 6,000 m (19,685 ft). It adjoins the high Tibetan Plateau, which has an average altitude of 4,000 m (13,125 ft).

Transform fault boundaries

The third type of plate boundary involves two plates sliding past each other along a fault line. There is no collision or separation involved, but earthquakes result from the movement of these plates. The best-known example of this is the San Andreas Fault in California, which has been associated with major earthquakes in San Francisco and Los Angeles. Along that fault line, the Pacific Plate is sliding northwards in relation to the adjacent North American Plate.

Continental drift

It was in 1922 that Alfred Wegener first expounded his theory that the continents had drifted to their present positions. His hypothesis centered on the close jigsaw fit of Africa and South America. The English philosopher and essayist Francis Bacon had drawn attention to this much earlier and, in 1858, so did Snider-Pellegrini, who pointed to the similarities in the characteristics of plant fossils in coal deposits found in both continents.

Wegener marshalled evidence to show that the fit involved the juxtaposition of river valleys, mountain chains, and similar rock formations and mineral deposits. Those rock formations contained similar fossils. Wegener hypothesized that all the continents once formed a single landmass, which he named Pangaea, and which, he claimed, began breaking up in the Carboniferous Period (divided into the Pennsylvanian and Mississipian epochs in the United States) about 300 million years ago. That split first resulted in two continents: a northern one

called Laurasia and a southern one called Gondwanaland. The various supposed parts of the southern continent (South America, Africa, India, Australia, and Antarctica) showed a much better geological fit than did the supposed parts of the northern one.

Wegener's theory was based on the premise that the light continents floated on a denser underlying crust, and that these continents thus drifted to their present positions. The absence of an acceptable mechanism for drifting was used as an argument against Wegener's ideas—it was thought physically impossible that the solid continents could have moved through an underlying rigid, denser layer.

Nevertheless, many scientists were inclined to accept that the continents had moved to their present positions because there was mounting geological evidence, such as that marshalled by Alex du Toit of South Africa, which proved similarities in areas which had been said to have once been joined together.

During the past 50 years, modern technology has provided much new information about the sea floors. In particular, evidence has emerged leading to the acceptance of sea-floor spreading. This, in turn, has led to the development of plate tectonics, which may be considered an update of Wegener's ideas about continental movement. As a result, his main ideas about the original juxtaposition of the continents have now been largely vindicated.

The processes and results of plate movement:
1. Fold mountains 2. Active volcano 3. Subduction zone
4. Subduction trench 5. Spreading sea-floor 6. Mid-oceanic ridge 7. Hot spot island chain (volcanic) 8. Oceanic crust
9. Colliding plates form mountain chain 10. Fold mountains
11. Rift valley 12. Hot spot 13. Magma (convection currents) 14. Asthenosphere
15. Lithosphere

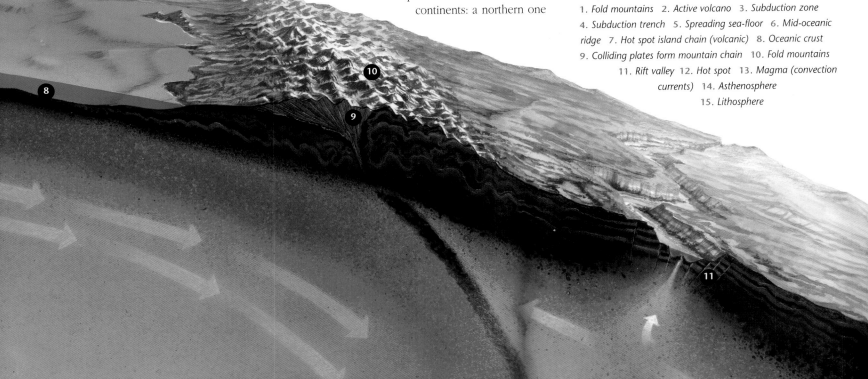

ROCKS

Earth's crust consists of rocks. These rocks combine a variety of minerals that may or may not be crystalline, and which can form in several ways. Igneous rocks are made of crystalline minerals which originate during the cooling of molten material called magma. In contrast, sedimentary rocks result from the compaction or consolidation of loosened minerals, rock fragments, and plant and animal matter. Metamorphic rocks are formed when existing rocks are altered through pressure and temperature—they result either from compaction under pressure or from partial remelting, when new minerals can be formed from crystallization.

Minerals

Minerals are inorganic substances with defined chemical and atomic structures. When magmas cool, minerals crystallize. Each mineral exhibits its own unique crystalline shape. Minerals can also originate in the breakdown of pre-existing minerals, as in the case of clays, or from the reconstitution of existing materials, as in the case of metamorphic rocks.

A common mineral is quartz (an oxide of silica), which occurs as large crystals in some rocks and as sand on sea shores. It is a light-colored mineral. Other light-colored minerals include felspars, which are silicates combining silica, aluminum, potassium, sodium, and calcium. These light-colored minerals are commonly found in rocks of light density, such as granite. Dark-colored silicates, which are combinations of silica, magnesium, and iron (pyroxenes, amphiboles, olivine, and dark micas), predominate in dark-colored rocks such as basalt.

Igneous rocks

When molten material lying deep within Earth's crust cools, minerals form large crystals, because of slow cooling, producing plutonic igneous rocks. The most common plutonic rock is granite, which is also the rock that is most widespread in the continental crust. Granite is light colored and low in density because it contains silica and felspars.

When magma is extruded onto the Earth's surface as lava, faster cooling takes place, resulting in smaller crystals, even glass. The most common volcanic rock is basalt, which is dark colored and dense because of dark-colored minerals such as biotite, pyroxenes, amphiboles, and olivine. The ocean floors are largely made up of basalt.

Large pockets of magma inside the crust give rise to large rock bodies called batholiths, which are mostly made of granite and are often found in great mountain ranges. Smaller igneous intrusions may form in cracks and joints in other rocks. When these intrusions cut through sedimentary strata, they are called dikes; intrusions between the bedding planes of strata are known as sills.

The vapors emanating from igneous intrusions often crystallize in neighboring rocks as valuable minerals—gold, silver, copper, lead, and zinc. Such deposits are found in recent geological formations such as those around the Pacific "Ring of Fire," as well as in more ancient rocks such as those near the Kalgoorlie goldfields of Western Australia. A rare igneous rock called kimberlite, which occurs in pipe-like shapes, contains diamond deposits such as those found in South Africa.

Sedimentary rocks

Sedimentary rocks can be made up of either organic or inorganic particles. Organic sediments are the remains of plants and animals—one example of a sedimentary rock made up of plant remains is coal. Large deposits of limestone are mostly the result of the precipitation of calcium carbonate, but can also be the result of the agglomeration, or clustering, of sea shell fragments and the building of coral reefs. Inorganic sedimentary rocks include those made up of sand (sandstone), clays (shale), or pebbles cemented together (conglomerate).

Sedimentary strata deposited in large basins like the sea sometimes become exposed through vertical uplift, in which case the strata may remain horizontal. When strata are folded in the process of mountain formation, however, they form complex structures such as anticlines (dome-shaped folds) and synclines (basin-shaped folds). Anticlines have often become reservoirs for petroleum, while basin-type structures can often contain artesian water.

Several valuable minerals are found in sedimentary rocks: iron ores; oxides of aluminum (bauxite); and manganese. Coal deposits are sedimentary accumulations of transformed ancient forests. Building materials such as sandstones and materials for producing cement and fertilizers also come from sedimentary rocks.

Metamorphic rocks

When sedimentary rocks are subjected to high pressure they alter to become metamorphic rocks. Thus shale is converted to the more solid slate, sandstone to the very hard rock called quartzite and limestone to the crystallized rock known as marble. The presence of chemical impurities in limestone can result in marbles of a variety of colors and patterns.

When sedimentary and igneous rocks are subjected to high pressure as well

Era	Major geological events	Period	Millions of years ago
CENOZOIC	• Ice age • First humans	Quaternary	
CENOZOIC			1.6
CENOZOIC	• Rockies, Alps and Himalayas begin to form • First hominids	Tertiary	
CENOZOIC			65
MESOZOIC	• First flowering plants • Extinction of giant reptiles	Cretaceous	
MESOZOIC			145
MESOZOIC	• Pangaea splits into Gondwanaland and Laurasia • First birds and mammals	Jurassic	
MESOZOIC			208
MESOZOIC	• First dinosaurs • Supercontinent of Pangaea in existence	Triassic	245
PALEOZOIC	• First amphibians	Permian	288
PALEOZOIC	• Extensive forests which later formed coal deposits	Carboniferous	360
PALEOZOIC		Devonian	408
PALEOZOIC	• First land plants	Silurian	438
PALEOZOIC		Ordovician	508
PALEOZOIC	• Age of the trilobites, the first complex animals, which had hard shells and were marine	Cambrian	570
PRE-CAMBRIAN	• Oldest rocks on Earth's crust identified • First life forms: single cell forms like bacteria and algae • Continents and oceans formed • Extensive sedimentary rocks like iron ore deposits were laid down		4,560

The Grand Canyon, USA (right), with a color-coded strip added (see geological time scale, left) to illustrate the geological history of the area. The diagram shows geological eras from the origin of Earth (4,560 million years ago) until the Cenozoic Era, which began 65 million years ago.

An area of the East Sussex, United Kingdom, coast known as the Seven Sisters (far left) consists primarily of limestone, a sedimentary rock. The banded boulders (left) in the Canadian Rockies, and the Waitomo Caves in the North Island, New Zealand (below), are also limestone; its appearance depends on the depositional environment in which it formed.

as high temperature, partial melting can take place. This partially remelted material gives rise to crystalline metamorphic rocks called schist and gneiss. Gneiss resembles granite in appearance, but it generally has a layered structure. Schists are made of platy minerals, including micas.

Large igneous intrusions often change the rocks into which they intrude to metamorphic rocks through the effects of the heat and the gases that they carry. Batholiths, the largest igneous intrusions, have created metamorphic aureoles in contact zones such as are found in the Alps.

Two important building materials, slate and marble, are metamorphic rocks. Other commercially valuable metamorphic mineral deposits include talc (used for cosmetics) and graphite (used for making pencils).

The rock cycle

In recent years, the concept of the rock cycle has proven useful. It represents the continuous recycling of rock materials and their conversion into different rock types, and helps link the various kinds of rocks found on Earth's surface.

When igneous rocks are exposed on the surface of Earth, they become weathered. Solar radiation, running water, ice, wind, and waves all weather rocks mechanically. Water acidified through the absorption of carbon dioxide and organic acids weathers rocks chemically. Over a long period, mechanical and chemical weathering produces pebbles, sands, and clays, which often consolidate into sedimentary rocks.

When these rocks are then dragged deep into Earth's crust by the process of plate subduction, they enter zones of very high pressure and temperature, resulting in partial melting and producing crystalline metamorphic rocks. If the rocks are carried still deeper into the Earth, however, where the

temperatures are high enough to melt the rocks completely, a new magma is formed. This new magma may either crystallize deep inside Earth and form new plutonic igneous rocks, or be extruded as volcanic lavas.

Where volcanoes have erupted along zones of plate subduction, a rock named andesite has formed from lavas; this rock is a mixture of dark- and light-colored minerals, as it reflects the mixing of light continental and dark oceanic materials.

LANDFORMS

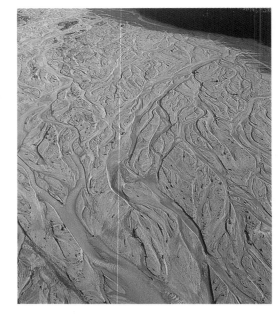

Earth's surface is constantly being transformed by falling rain, glaciers, rivers, underground water, wind, and waves. These constantly erode the land, transporting debris and depositing it elsewhere. The land is moulded into new forms through erosion, and new landforms are also created by the deposition of eroded debris.

Rainfall and water flow in creeks and rivers are the main agents of landform creation in humid areas; glaciers are the most important agents at high latitudes and in mountainous areas of heavy snowfall; and wind is important in arid areas.

Landforms of erosion

Glaciers, rivers, winds, and waves are powerful erosive agents. Glaciers pluck pieces of rock from valley sides, rivers carry rock fragments along in their current, and winds lift and transport particles of dust. Air and water velocities determine the erosive force of winds and rivers, and the rock fragments they carry with them make these agents additionally abrasive.

Rock fragments embedded in glaciers scour rock surfaces on the glacier's floor and sides; sand and gravel in fast-flowing rivers erode their floors and banks; and wind-borne sand blasts rock surfaces, creating intricate structures. Platforms, caves, and cliffs are formed by the action of waves carrying sand, pebbles and boulders and beating them against rocky coasts.

Rivers in mountainous areas flow rapidly because of steep slope gradients. Such streams may be highly erosive, and may cut their channels vertically, producing V-shaped valley profiles.

Glaciers are made of solid ice, and result from the compaction of snow. Some of the longest

The following features are those typically found in glacial areas, showing the close interconnection between current landforms and past glaciers: 1. Cirque basin 2. Hanging valley in a glacial trough 3. Outwash plain from glacial meltwater 4. Terminal moraine of a valley glacier 5. Lateral moraine 6. Medial moraine 7. Ground moraine 8. Arête or sharp-crested ridge 9. Horn or sharp peak

glaciers remaining, at 39 to 73 km (24 to 46 miles) in length, are found in the Karakoram ranges in the Himalayas. Although they generally move very slowly (2 to 3 cm [3/4 to 11/4 inches] per day), glaciers are powerful eroders, and can move 4 to 5 m (13 to 16 1/2 ft) a day.

Glaciers typically create U-shaped valleys called troughs. Glaciers at the head of sloping valleys give rise to basin-shaped features known as cirques. When cirques from two opposing sides meet through erosion, a pass, or col, is formed. Between glacial valleys, sharp ridges, known as arêtes, develop. At the top of glacial mountains, arêtes meet at sharp peaks called horns, such as those on the Matterhorn and Mt Everest.

Where glaciers have disappeared, troughs are exposed, along with tributary glacial valleys, and these form hanging valleys perched above scarps. They often have streams cascading over them as waterfalls, and are often used as sites for the generation of hydroelectric power.

Depending on their velocity, winds can lift loose rock particles or soils. Generally speaking, the wind transports particles which are dry and not protected by plant cover—so wind action is mostly restricted to arid and semiarid regions, and some coastal areas. Strong winds can scoop out hollows in loose, dry soil. This process is known as deflation, and the hollows formed are called blowouts. These can range in diameter from about a meter to a kilometer or more.

When waves approach a coastline made up of headlands and bays, they gather around the headlands and spread out in the bays. Wave energy becomes concentrated on the headlands, where the steady pounding carves platforms and cliffs. In bays, by contrast, wave energy is dissipated, and the waves deposit sand and other detritus. These may also be transported along the shore, depending on the angle of the coast in relation to the direction of the waves.

Rock debris—such as loose, unsupported material and waterlogged soil—tends to move down hill slopes through the action of gravity.

Slow movements known as soil creep are often imperceptible, and are indicated only by the changed position of fixed objects—trees, fences, and houses. The shaking of sloping ground by earthquakes can trigger a more rapid movement of loose materials. Fast movements such as landslides (or snow avalanches) tend to occur after heavy rains (or snowfalls) on steep slopes. In contrast to landslides, slumps are formed when slopes slip in a backward rotation, a phenomenon sometimes found in waterlogged soils.

Transportation and deposition of rock debris

The debris resulting from erosion is transported by glaciers, rivers, winds, and waves. A glacier carries assorted rock debris (boulders, pebbles, or finer materials) on or beneath its solid surface.

As a glacier moves, it plucks rocks from the valley walls, and the rock debris falls along the sides of the glacier to form what are known as lateral moraines. When two glaciers meet and coalesce, two lateral moraines join in the center of the new, larger glacier, forming a medial moraine.

As mountain glaciers reach lower, warmer levels, they melt and drop their debris, which forms terminal moraines. The resulting meltwater carries a fine glacial flour, which may be spread as a vast depositional plain. Rich soils have

An aerial view of a braided river channel showing the build up of sediment on the river bed (far left), and a coastline dramatically eroded by wave action (left). The cirque (below) shows typically steep walls—carved by the movement of glacial ice—and a flat floor.

developed in such plains in both northern Europe and the northern United States.

The amount of rock particle rivers and winds carry is determined by velocity; in general, larger particle sizes need greater velocities. At lower speeds, rivers deposit their sediment load, which then forms fertile alluvial flats and broad alluvial plains. These areas may be periodically inundated by floods. Much of the sediment carried by rivers in flood is deposited at the coast as deltas. Several major rivers carry high sediment loads—the Huang River in China carries more than one and a half million tonnes annually.

Wind

Other landforms result from wind. Strong winds can lift and carry sands, while lighter winds lift and carry silts and clays. High winds rework sand masses into dunes of various types, depending on sand availability and wind direction. Sand dunes in deserts include crescent-shaped barchans, which have gentle windward slopes and abrupt leeward slopes—the crescent's horns point downwind. Silt-sized particles are transported by the wind to form thick, fertile deposits known as loess. Extensive deposits of loess are found on the edges of some deserts and in areas once glaciated (northern China and the Mississippi Valley, for instance).

Waves

Waves tend to approach a beach perpendicularly. The movement of the wave as it runs onto the beach is known as swash; the water, or backwash, then returns to the sea. Swash and backwash move sand along beaches, which contributes to littoral or longshore drift (when waves approach the beach at an angle). Along coastal plains, waves tend to build sand barriers by the shore. Lagoons develop behind these barriers, which are connected to the sea by tidal inlets. These lagoons can later fill with sediment, a stage in the gradual seaward extension of the coastal plain. The sea-level rise, on the other hand, along with storm wave erosion, can drive the sand barriers landward.

During the next several decades, because of global warming, the sea level may rise at rates up to 100 mm (4 inches) per year. This would cause the loss of sand barriers and adjacent lagoons and wetlands, and the loss of some islands on coral reefs.

CLIMATE

Just as weather is the day-to-day condition of the atmosphere, climate consists of the long-term average of weather conditions, including seasonal and year-to-year variability, and extremes. Many distinctive climatic types can be identified. These vary with regard to incoming solar radiation, temperature, wind, precipitation (rainfall and snowfall), evaporation, storms (type, frequency and magnitude), and seasonal patterns.

Solar radiation

Solar radiation (insolation) is received unequally in different parts of Earth. The equatorial belt receives strong solar radiation uniformly throughout the year, whilst places close to the poles, in contrast, have great differences between summer and winter solar radiation; perpetual ice climates exist at the poles. Along the equator, the lands are warm throughout the year, but, in the latitudes further away from the equator, seasonal variations become more discernible, with marked differences in the temperate zone.

General atmospheric circulation

The large amount of heat received at the equator means that air becomes heated and expands, and this air rises and flows towards the poles. Some of this air flows back to the equator in the form of trade winds as part of the Hadley Cell circulation. Flowing from the east, these winds are called easterlies. The subtropical belt (up to about 30° latitude), is the zone of large high-pressure cells from which winds move through more temperate latitudes towards the poles. Cold, dense air from the poles flows, as polar fronts, back through these latitudes towards the equator. These fronts clash with tropical air masses in the temperate

zones, giving give rise to cyclones (low-pressure cells), which bring inclement weather and rainy days. Such weather conditions are more common in the northern hemisphere, where there are extensive landmasses. In the southern hemisphere, in contrast, there are more extensive oceans. In that belt, between 40° latitude and Antarctica, a westerly wind blows eastward along an almost unbroken stretch of seas throughout the year.

Climatic types

Of the several proposed climatic classifications, the best known is that devised by Köppen, who divided climates broadly into five classes: A, B, C, D, and E. The humid climates are A, C, and D, with A being the warmest and lying in the tropics, C being found in the warm temperate regions, and D covering cold climates with regular winter snowfall. Arid climates, both tropical and temperate, are classed as B climates. Ice sheets are represented by E climates.

Humid tropical climates (A)

Type A climates are found between 25°N and 25°S latitudes. These humid tropical climates receive abundant rainfall and have year-round high temperatures, with the areas further away from the equator having hot summers and mild winters.

These areas favor the abundant growth of vegetation, particularly rainforest. This climatic belt has extensive agriculture and often large populations. Heavy rainfall and high temperatures, however, leach soils of their valuable nutrients, which is detrimental for agriculture.

A typical A climate is the tropical monsoon climate that is found in Southeast Asia. It is characterized by a distinct season of heavy rainfall,

Monsoon flooding in Vietnam (above). Monsoons are usually annual events, and deliver 85% of East Asia's annual rainfall, but can also cause devastation to low-lying areas.

preceded and followed by dry months; for example, large parts of India and Southeast Asia receive most of their rain between June and September, while March to May are typically dry months. Along the west coast of India, annual rainfall can be as high as 25,400 to 28,800 mm (9,900 to 1,123 inches).

Desert climates (B)

Deserts are found in subtropical and temperate zones, and are classified by Köppen as B-type climates. Being areas of low rainfall, deserts have either few plants, or only small plants that are particularly well suited to dry environments.

Hot deserts lie in the subtropics—in the belt extending from North Africa (the Sahara Desert) and the Middle East to northwestern India (the Thar Desert)—and in the Central Australian Desert. These deserts have high daily temperature ranges; it can be very hot during the day and quite cool at night. The Gobi Desert, which lies in central Asia, is the best-known cold desert.

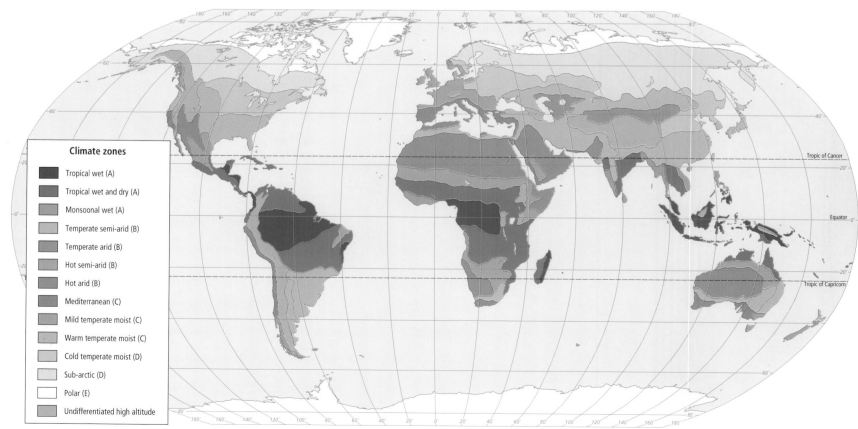

Climate zones

- Tropical wet (A)
- Tropical wet and dry (A)
- Monsoonal wet (A)
- Temperate semi-arid (B)
- Temperate arid (B)
- Hot semi-arid (B)
- Hot arid (B)
- Mediterranean (C)
- Mild temperate moist (C)
- Warm temperate moist (C)
- Cold temperate moist (D)
- Sub-arctic (D)
- Polar (E)
- Undifferentiated high altitude

Projection: Robinson   Equatorial Scale approx 1:110 million

The Valley of the Moon, in the high-altitude Atacama Desert, Chile, said to be the driest desert on Earth (left). Lush mountainous terrain in Bolivia (below). An ice floe, with walrus, in Arctic Siberia (left, below). Productive agricultural land in a temperate zone—southern France (far left, below).

Humid temperate climates (C)

Type C climates lie between latitudes of 25° and 45°. They have marked seasonal variations, with temperature differences between summer and winter being quite large. The Mediterranean climate is a good example of a B climate; summer temperatures can on occasions soar to the mid-40s (110°F) in southern Greece and Italy, while winter temperatures can fall to 10°C (50°F). The Mediterranean climate is characterized by cold, wet winters and hot, dry summers.

The temperate zone close to the tropics (25° to 35° latitudes) is warm. It is now common to find that belt referred to as the subtropics. The subtropical areas lying along the eastern sides of the continents are particularly warm, as they receive the warm easterly tropical winds, and warm ocean currents flow along their coasts. This east coast climate is found in southeast China, eastern Australia and South America.

In contrast, the westerlies in the higher latitudes (35° to 60° latitudes) give rise to a cooler west coast climate. Year-round rainfall and adequate temperatures promote the growth of forests in both east and west coast climates.

Grasslands generally occur in the continental interiors of C climate areas, where annual rainfall is moderate (300 to 400 mm; 12 to 16 in), and water in the soil is not abundant. These areas lie in the rainshadows of major mountain ranges. Seasonal temperature ranges are usually sizeable.

Cold temperate climates (D)

Moving into the temperate zone close to the poles, temperatures fall because there is reduced solar radiation. This is exacerbated by cold polar winds.

Polar winds are easterlies, although their directions can be variable in temperate latitudes. Such type D climates lie between 45° and 65° latitudes, and are only significant in the northern hemisphere—the equivalent belt in the southern hemisphere is mostly covered by the oceans.

The taiga climate is a good example of this climate; lying close to the Arctic polar region, the area is characterized by abundant snowfall and unique woodlands. Temperatures in winter commonly fall to –30°C (–22°F), and in some places can go as low as –40°C (–40°F). During midsummer, however, temperatures can rise to around 15°C (60°F) or higher.

Ice climates (E)

E-type climates are found between 65° and 90° latitudes, the principal examples being Antarctica and Greenland. These ice sheets cover about 10 percent of Earth's surface, and form an essential part of the system which regulates the global atmospheric circulation. These areas are subject to long periods of darkness, and temperatures rise above freezing level for only 2 to 4 months a year.

If global warming reduces the extent of these ice sheets, climatic conditions in the world will alter: ice melting would contribute to rises in sea level, with adverse effects on low-lying areas.

The El Niño phenomenon

Deviations from normal temperature patterns of the waters in the southern Pacific Ocean, between Australia and South America, result in the phenomenon called El Niño. Under normal conditions, eastern trade winds blow across the Pacific. These drive the sun-warmed surface water from the central Pacific to the coast off northern Australia. When clouds form above this area of warm water and move over Indonesia, Papua New Guinea, and Australia, they bring rain with them.

Every two to seven years, however, this pattern is interrupted by the El Niño event. During El Niño, the Pacific Ocean off Australia does not warm as much as it normally does. Instead, it becomes warmer right up to the coast of Peru in South America. At the same time, the easterly trade winds that blow across the Pacific reverse their direction. This causes high-pressure systems to build up to the north of and across the Australian continent, preventing moist tropical air reaching the continent. These conditions in turn result in storms, and in rain falling in the eastern Pacific Ocean and in South America instead of in Australia, Papua New Guinea, and Indonesia, which then suffer drought conditions.

While the effects of El Niño are sometimes weak, at other times they are very strong. During a severe El Niño period, extreme drought conditions prevail, as in 1982–83 and 1997–98. In contrast, heavy rainfall and flooding occurred in parts of North and South America. In 1997, there were severe storms and floods in Mexico and further north along the west coast of the United States.

The converse of the El Niño effect is the La Niña effect, which is an exaggeration of normal conditions. This takes place when trade winds blow strongly and consistently across the Pacific towards Australia. This pushes the warm waters from the central Pacific, off the northern Australian coast, to build up into a mass that is bigger than normal. Thus, much more cloud develops than usual, and this brings considerably more rain to Australia and neighboring countries.

THE WATER CYCLE

Earth, in contrast to all the other planets in the solar system, has an abundant supply of water. Much of this, of course, lies in the oceans and seas (more than 97 percent), and is saline. The polar ice caps lock up slightly more than 2 percent of the remaining water, leaving less than 1 percent of fresh water to sustain life on Earth. Human needs are met by the water from rainfall, rivers, and underground supplies (plus a small amount from desalination plants).

Water falls as rain and snow, and flows as rivers and glaciers before ultimately reaching the sea. It also sinks into the ground to form underground water reservoirs, to emerge as springs or to seep into river water. Fresh supplies of water are continuously needed and nature provides this supply through the water cycle.

How the water cycle works

Solar energy evaporates exposed water from seas, lakes, rivers, and wet soils; the majority of this evaporation takes place over the seas. Water is also released into the atmosphere by plants through photosynthesis. During this process, known as evapotranspiration, water vapor rises into the atmosphere.

Clouds form when air becomes saturated with water vapor. The two major types of cloud formations are a stratified or layered gray cloud called stratus, and a billowing white or dark gray cloud called cumulus. Nimbostratus clouds and cumulonimbus clouds are the cloud types that are associated with rainy weather; nimbostratus clouds will bring steady rain, and cumulonimbus clouds will bring stormy weather.

Precipitation as rain, snow, or hail ensures that water returns to Earth's surface in a fresh form. Some of this rain, however, falls into the seas and is not accessible to humans. When rain falls, it either washes down hill slopes or seeps underground; when snow and hail melt, this water may also sink into the ground.

Rainfall also replenishes river water supplies, as does underground water. Snowfall may consolidate into glaciers and ice sheets which, when they melt, release their water into the ground, into streams, or into the seas.

Water in river courses

Rivers pass through several phases on their journey from hilly and mountainous areas to the seas and oceans. In their early phases—that is, close to their sources in the hills and mountains—they have steep slope gradients and, therefore, move with high velocities. They carry rock fragments and have high erosive force.

In these areas, the energy from these streams provides the potential for hydroelectric development. This potential has been harnessed in many places, such as in the foothills of the Himalayas in Nepal.

On flat plains, rivers tend to wind their way in meandering courses. Here, the water flow has now lost most of its erosive capacity. Massive clay deposits may also give rise to fertile alluvial plains. During times of heavy rainfall, flooding can take place, and this is a serious issue along some of the major rivers of the world, such as the Mississippi in the United States, the Yangtze in China and the Ganges in India.

The Arrigetch peaks and glacier, in Alaska (above). Water is released as steam into the atmosphere from electric power plants (right). A hot water artesian bore (far right).

Human interference in the water cycle

There has been considerable human interference in the water cycle throughout recorded history, but far more so since the beginning of the twentieth century. For centuries, humans have built dams across rivers to store water, which is then used for irrigation, or for domestic or industrial water supply. Dams have also been built to control river flooding, such as across the Huang River in China, and to produce electricity.

The Aswan Dam across the Nile provides arid Egypt with essential water. The two highest dams in the world, more than 300 m (985 ft) in height, have been built across the Vakhsh River in Tajikistan. The dam with by far the largest reservoir capacity—2,700 million cubic meters (3,530 million cubic yards)—is the Owen Falls Dam, across the Nile, in Uganda.

Hydroelectric power is generated in several parts of the world, such as at Itaipu, across the Parana River, in Brazil—this dam can generate

12,600 megawatts of power. The building of dams in areas prone to earthquakes, such as Japan, however, causes great concern because of the potential for serious damage.

Water is necessary for agriculture, industry, and domestic use. Agriculture depends on rainfall, as well as on irrigation from stored water. The provision of water for domestic use—particularly the need for clean drinking water—has become very important with the spread of urbanization. Reservoirs are often built to ensure urban water supplies and water is purified before being channelled to consumers.

The discharge of industrial, agricultural, and domestic effluents into streams and lakes (especially in the twentieth century) has reduced water quality and damaged aquatic life. These effluents include metallic substances. One of the most dramatic examples has been the discharge of mercury into rivers in Japan. This mercury has now entered the food chain through fish, creating serious health problems. The discharge of

Artesian wells

When rain falls, some of it sinks into the ground and is held in the soil—this water is known as ground water. A layer under the ground becomes saturated with this seeped water; the surface of this layer is called the water table. Wells are mostly dug to tap water in the water table. There is another way, however, that water can seep under the ground to form water reservoirs. Some types of rock are porous, and this allows them to hold water; water can move through such permeable rock.

Sandstone is a permeable rock. If a sandstone bed is dipping at an angle, rainwater can penetrate the exposed part of the rock and travel along the stratum into the ground. The water will be retained by the sandstone layer if the rocks above and below it are impermeable. If this water reservoir lies well below the ground, it is held under pressure; if a well is bored to the reservoir, the water will gush out under this pressure. These reservoirs are called artesian wells. The permeable strata that carry the water are called aquifers; the

impermeable layers which lie above and below the aquifers are known as aquicludes.

Artesian waters are important where rainfall is low and water supplies uncertain. Overuse of artesian water can result in the ground sinking, and if the reservoir is close to the sea, excessive removal of water can allow saline water to penetrate the reservoir, reducing water quality.

pesticides has also been detrimental to aquatic life, and excessive use of fertilizers, along with salts released into rivers and lakes by poor land use practices, have also altered the ecological balance.

Changes in air quality brought about by humans have also affected the water cycle. The use of fossil fuels to generate electricity and power transport has resulted in substantial sulfur dioxide and nitrogen oxide emissions. When these gases and water react, sulfuric and nitric acids are produced. These pollutants are present in clouds and fog, and fall with rain and snow as acid rain. A pH value of 5 in water is acidic enough to damage aquatic life.

This acid rain phenomenon is most likely to occur in dense industrial centers such as those in the United States, Canada, and Europe. The problem, however, is not confined to these areas, as winds blow polluting gases over long distances. Acids can become concentrated in still waters and threaten aquatic life. The entire ecology of affected lakes, including the natural food chains, can be very seriously harmed.

The water cycle (below): the sun heats water, which evaporates and rises into the atmosphere as water vapor, only to fall again later as rain and snow. The rain and snow then concentrate in rivers, or flow as ground water to the sea.

OCEANOGRAPHY

Earth is the only planet of the solar system with seas and oceans, and these cover more than 70 percent of its surface. The oceans lie in large and deep basins in Earth's crust. The seas, however, spread to the margins of the continents, drowning their shelves. The melting of the ice sheets following the end of the last ice age (about 15,000 years ago) resulted in a rise in sea levels and thus an increased area covered by seas.

Ocean currents

The waters of the oceans are in constant motion. This motion takes the form of ocean currents. These currents move at an average of 8 km (5 miles) per hour, and redistribute heat energy, thus influencing climate. Winds are the most important originators of ocean currents in the upper layers of the seas: they produce a frictional drag on the water which pushes it along.

As water is a fluid, it is subject to the Coriolis effect (caused by Earth's rotation)—that is, currents tend to move towards the right in the northern hemisphere and towards the left in the southern hemisphere. The resulting deflection is 45° to that of the direction of the wind. In the deeper parts of the oceans, it is water density that produces ocean currents. Water density depends upon two factors: temperature and salinity. The colder the water is, the denser it is; and the higher the salinity, the higher the density. The circulation which results from temperature and salinity difference is referred to as thermo-haline circulation.

There are broadly two types of ocean current: warm currents, which originate in tropical areas; and cold currents, which originate in polar areas. Warm currents are mostly located in the upper 100 m (330 ft) of the seas. Cold currents, on the other hand, are often encountered at greater depths. They move more slowly because of the overlying pressure exerted by surface water. The exchange of heat energy occurs as equatorial currents move towards the poles and polar currents move towards the equator. This exchange moderates Earth's heat patterns, preventing the equatorial belt becoming unbearably hot and the waters in the temperate zone becoming much colder than they are today.

Ocean water temperatures are a major influence on climatic conditions; warm currents bring warmth to the coastlines along which they flow and, likewise, cold currents reduce temperatures in the lands along which they flow.

Warm tropical ocean currents

Winds blowing westward along the equatorial belt generate west-flowing ocean currents called equatorial currents. When water from the equatorial currents piles up against land, the current reverses its direction and flows eastward, resulting in equatorial counter currents.

Equatorial currents turn towards the right in the northern hemisphere and towards the left in the southern hemisphere as a result of the Coriolis

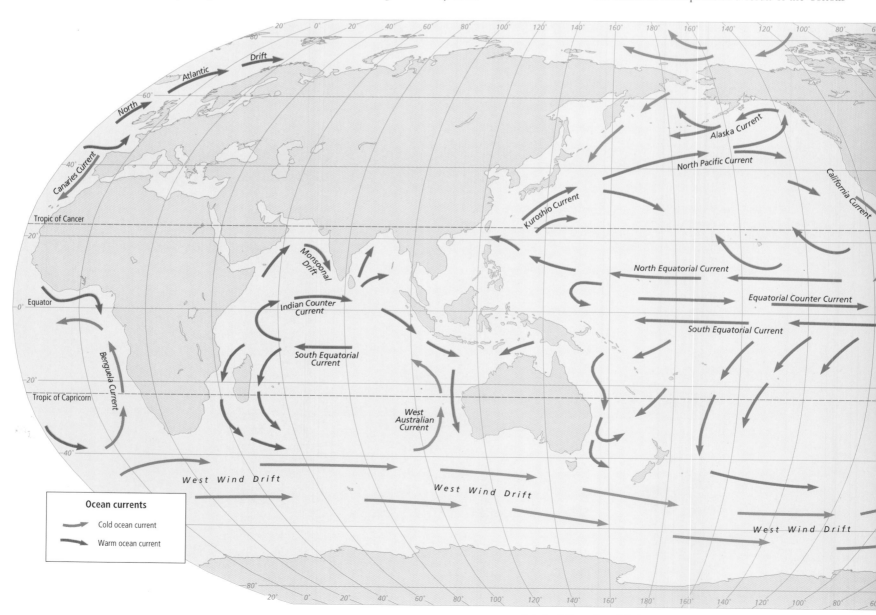

Projection: Robinson   Equatorial Scale approx 1:110 million

A sea whip in the warm waters of the Indian Ocean (far left). Coral islands (left) are at risk if sea levels rise because of the greenhouse effect. Polar bears in Arctic Siberia (below) survive on the ice floes, which are broken off icebergs by strong currents and winds. The southern right whale (far below) feeds off aquatic life that thrives in the nutrient-rich Antarctic waters, which are now threatened by ozone depletion.

effect, and because of that motion, they develop into huge, circular, whorl-like rotating systems. These systems are known as gyres. Gyres rotate in a clockwise direction in the northern hemisphere and an anticlockwise direction in the southern hemisphere.

The distribution of the continental landmasses influences the size and shape of these gyres. There are major gyres in the northern and southern Atlantic and Pacific oceans, and in the southern Indian Ocean. There is also a gyre in the northern Indian Ocean, but it is restricted by the landmasses surrounding it, and so is much smaller.

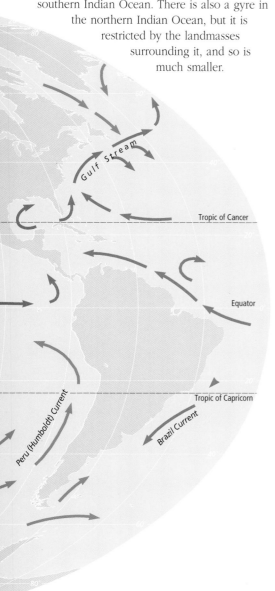

Gyres carry warm equatorial water into the temperate zone. These currents carry about 25 percent of all the heat that moves polewards from the equator. In the North Atlantic, the Gulf Stream or North Atlantic Drift, which flows from the Gulf of Mexico towards Western Europe, warms the seas around those countries, making their climates warmer. Thus London (51°32'N) is warmer than New York, even though New York lies at a much lower latitude (40°43'N), because of this warming effect.

The Japan Current, flowing from Southeast Asia, warms the eastern coasts of China and Japan. The west coast of Japan, on the other hand, is cooled by cold currents originating in northern areas. The magnitude of large ocean currents is demonstrated by the enormous amount of water they can carry—for example, the Gulf Stream carries more than 50 million cubic meters (65.5 million cubic yards) per second.

The build-up of warm waters can have significant effects on climate. For example, tropical cyclones or hurricanes or typhoons develop in the areas of warm water in Southeast Asia. These can have devastating effects on those areas.

Also, temperature changes in the waters of the South Pacific Ocean provide indications of the El Niño and La Niña weather disturbances. The onset of El Niño is heralded by unusually high water temperatures in the central Pacific, with the warm water spreading across to South America.

Cold polar currents

Cold ocean currents originate in polar regions. They flow deep in the oceans and only surface through upwelling—when winds blowing from the land drive warm surface water back out into the ocean. Cold water then rises to the surface.

Two well-known upwelling sites, both on the western sides of continents, are the Humboldt or Peru Current along the coast of South America and the Benguela Current in southern Africa. Their nutrient-laden waters are rich breeding grounds for fish.

Two important cold currents flowing on the eastern sides of continents are the Kamchatka Current, which flows alongside Siberia and Japan, and the Labrador Current, which flows along the east coasts of Canada and the United States.

Icebergs and ice floes

Seas in the polar zones can freeze, forming pack ice that covers the sea surface. If subjected to strong currents or winds, this pack ice can break into pieces, called floes. Ice broken from ice sheets can also be seen floating in the seas as icebergs. Ice floes are mostly less than 5 m (16½ ft) thick—much thinner than icebergs.

Icebergs can be very thick indeed—up to hundreds of meters in thickness—but only about one-sixth of an iceberg floats above water. The rest of it remains submerged or hidden below the water. This makes icebergs a major navigational hazard. There are always likely to be icebergs in the North Atlantic; they originate from the Greenland ice sheet and its glaciers.

The Antarctic zone

The waters around Antarctica flow in an unbroken band around the globe because there are no land areas to obstruct them. The West Wind Drift, as the winds blowing incessantly from the west to the east are called, results in some of the world's most turbulent seas. The seas in latitudes between 40°S and 60°S have been referred to as the "Roaring Forties," the "Furious Fifties," and the "Screaming Sixties."

In the Southern Ocean around Antarctica, between the latitudes 50°S and 60°S, cold currents interact with the warm currents coming from the tropics. The cold, nutrient-rich waters are driven upwards by this convergence, becoming the breeding ground for abundant oceanic life. These waters are thus a vital component of the food chain which depends upon that aquatic life.

PLANTS AND ANIMALS

Earth is about 4,500 million years old. After about 1,000 million years, most of the basic metabolic processes on which modern life depends were in place. The first eukaryote cells (cells that were capable of resisting oxidation) appeared about 1,500 million years ago. After about 4,000 million years, multicellular animals and plants appear in the fossil record. In the past 600 million years, life has exploded into a vast array of forms, but many of the animals and plants we are familiar with are relatively recent arrivals.

To deduce the history of Earth's life forms (collectively known as biota), and the prevailing environmental conditions, scientists primarily rely on physical evidence: the character of rocks or the fossils contained within them. Increasingly, however, biochemical evidence is also used.

The first life forms

Life is defined as a self-contained system of molecules that can duplicate itself from generation to generation. In Earth's early history, the elements that make up the vast majority of living tissues (hydrogen, carbon, oxygen, and nitrogen) were available in some form, and energy was abundant. Also, the concentration of

atmospheric oxygen was low, which probably allowed a period of chemical evolution before the development of life. The earliest life forms may have resembled the bacteria-like organisms that exist today in hot springs associated with volcanic activity.

The first bacteria-like microfossils are dated at 3,500 million years old. Stromatolites, fossilized mats of cyanobacteria (a bacteria secreted by blue–green algae), first appear in the fossil record at about this time. These are the dominant fossils found in rocks older than about 550 million years. Between about 3,500 and 1,500 million years ago, cyanobacteria and blue–green algae were probably the main forms of life. Importantly, they slowly contributed oxygen to the atmosphere.

The build-up of free oxygen, hazardous to most life forms, may have stimulated the development of organisms with more complex cellular organisation (the eukaryotes) about 1,500 million years ago. The eukaryotes could reproduce sexually, thus allowing

Stromatolites in Hamelin Pool, Shark Bay, Western Australia.

evolutionary change. They generated more oxygen and eventually (by about 1,300 million years ago) an ozone shield—this is probably what enabled further biotic evolution.

The earliest fossil record of protozoans, which are animals and so derive their energy from ingesting other organisms, is from about 800 million years ago. By about 680 million years ago, the protozoa were a highly diverse and complex range of multicellular animals—mostly coral- or worm-like life forms.

PROTEROZOIC EON

1,000 mya

2,000 mya

800 mya

EDIACARAN FAUNA

600 mya

680 mya

PROTEROZOIC EON

570 mya

PALAEOZOIC ERA

544 mya

440 mya

245 mya

MESOZOIC ERA

200 mya

MESOZOIC ERA

Invertebrates and vertebrates

During the late Proterozoic or early Paleozoic Era, the principal groups (or phyla) of invertebrates appeared. Trilobites were probably the dominant form of marine life during the Cambrian Period. The seas teemed with a huge diversity of animals, including a group with an elongated support structure, a central nerve cord, and a blood circulatory system—members of the phylum to which humans belong, the Chordata.

A major extinction event ended the Cambrian Period. The Ordovician Period (500 to 435 million years ago) is characterized by another increase in species diversity. The fossil record is dominated by marine invertebrates, but vertebrates also appear. The primitive jawless fish of 485 million years ago are the first ancestors of all advanced life forms: fish, amphibians, reptiles, birds, and mammals. Another major extinction event ended this period.

From ocean to land

The first land plants—probably similar to modern liverworts, hornworts, and mosses—seem to have arisen about 450 million years ago. The move onto land was a significant evolutionary step; life on land was very different, demanding innovation and evolutionary change.

BIG BANG
–14,000 mya

FORMS
0 mya

FIRST
BACTERIA
FOSSILS

3,000 mya

ARCHAEAN EON

CENOZOIC ERA

65 mya

2 mya

The diagram (above) illustrates all the major stages in the evolution of plants and animals, from the first bacteria-like organisms, around 3,500 million years ago (mya), till humans, who first appeared in the late Quaternary Period.

During the Silurian Period (435 to 395 million years ago), algae diversified and all the major fish groups appear. Fossils of vascular plants (with specialized systems for moving nutrients, liquids, and so on) are found at about 430 million years ago. *Cooksonia*, a small moss-like plant common at this time, may have resulted in two distinct lines of evolution, one leading to all other higher plants. Floras of the late Silurian to early Devonian time are very similar worldwide, and may constitute evidence that the supercontinent Pangaea existed then.

During the mid-Devonian Period (395 to 345 million years ago), plants underwent a remarkable diversification, resulting in the development of Devonian "forests," which included giant clubmosses (lepidodendrons) and horsetails (calamites). The fossil record of the amphibians also begins here—animals were moving onto land—and the first fern-like foliage and gymnosperms appeared. The late Devonian was also marked by a mass extinction event.

Fossils from the Carboniferous Period (345 to 280 million years ago) suggest that the clubmoss forests teemed with spiders, scorpions, and centipedes. Amphibians gave rise to the first reptiles about 300 million years ago—vertebrates were no longer dependent on returning to water to reproduce. A trend towards an ice age occurred in the late Carboniferous Period, leading to low-diversity flora dominated by primitive seed ferns.

The Permian Period (280 to 245 million years ago) is dominated by the fossil remains of primitive members of the conifer line. By this period, reptiles with skeletal features characteristic of mammals were present.

The Age of Reptiles

The largest mass extinction event on record marks the end of the Permian Period. During the Mesozoic Era (245 to 65 million years ago), the "Age of Reptiles," flowering plants, dominated by cycads and gymnosperms early on, developed. Birds and mammals also appeared.

During the Triassic Period (245 to 200 million years ago), mammals, lizards, and dinosaurs appear in the fossil record. Some long-established reptiles were replaced by new groups, including the turtles, crocodilians, dinosaurs, and pterosaurs.

Dinosaurs date from early in the Triassic Period. From about 220 million years ago they dominated land habitats—for almost 160 million years. Mammals (initially small, perhaps nocturnal, shrew-like creatures) appear to have arisen from mammal-like reptiles. There was another mass extinction event (about 200 million years ago) in the late Triassic Period. Frogs and toads may have appeared around this time.

Pangaea began to break up during the Jurassic Period (200 to 145 million years ago). Ocean currents and the global climate were altered. The position of the continents and the break-up sequence determined the migration routes available and, therefore, the interrelation or common features of the plants and animals that we now see in the modern world.

Jurassic rocks include Earth's earliest fossils of flies, mosquitoes, wasps, bees, and ants; modern types of marine crustaceans were abundant. It was

also a critical point in the evolution of birds, which evolved either from the dinosaurs or from an earlier group of reptiles. The Archaeopteryx, which existed about 150 million years ago, is perhaps the most famous early bird-like animal.

The early Cretaceous Period (145 to 65 million years ago) had a cosmopolitan flora. The first record of bats appears at this time. From about 80 million years ago, gymnosperms and angiosperms expanded at the expense of cycads and ferns. Mammals were also becoming dominant.

The Cretaceous Period also saw the apparent rise of the monotreme and marsupials and placentals, and the first predatory mammals. The diversification and spread of angiosperms provided the impetus for the co-evolution of animals.

The Age of Mammals

A great extinction event occurred at the end of the Cretaceous Period, causing the demise of the dinosaurs and the loss of about 25 percent of all known animal families. This change marks the beginning of the Cenozoic Era (65 million years ago to the present). This era saw the formation of the famous mountain systems of the world, the movement of the continents to their present positions and a cooling trend that culminated in the ice ages of the Quaternary Period.

After dinosaurs died out, mammals quickly expanded into newly vacated habitats and roles, adapting and diversifying. Eventually, the warm-blooded animals came to dominate, so the Cenozoic Era is often called the "Age of Mammals." Late in the era, humans finally appear.

The Tertiary Period (65 to 1.8 million years ago) saw major new groups developing within pre-established plant families. Grasses appeared (about 50 million years ago), expanding particularly in the Miocene Period.

The development of grasslands resulted eventually in a proliferation of grazing mammals. Hoofed, placental herbivores are first recorded as fossils 85 million years ago. The first horses appeared about 55 million years ago. A similar explosion in small rodents also occurred from about 40 million years ago.

Although birds have been essentially modern since the start of the Cenozoic Era, the first songbirds seem to appear at about 55 million years ago; all the major bird groups of the modern world had evolved by 50 million years ago. At about the same time (mid-Eocene Period), the carnivorous mammals split into two major lines: the dogs and the cats, basically. The first toothed whales are from the Oligocene epoch and the first plankton-feeding whales are from the Miocene.

The first primates seem to date from the end of the Cretaceous Period, though it seems that both monkeys and apes did not separate from earlier groups until the Oligocene epoch. The oldest biped yet found—usually taken as the start of the hominids—is from about 4.4 million years ago.

Nearly 2.5 million years ago, stone tool users—the hallmark of our own genus, Homo—seem to have arisen. Homo erectus, dating from about 1.8 million years ago, migrated from Africa as far as China and Southeast Asia. Our species, Homo sapiens, seems to have evolved in Africa within the past 200,000 years and to have migrated out of that continent only during the past 100,000 years.

EARTH'S BIOSPHERE

The biosphere is the zone where all living organisms on Earth are found. It includes parts of the lithosphere (Earth's crust and mantle), the hydrosphere (all the waters on Earth), and the atmosphere. The term "biosphere" can also refer collectively to all Earth's living organisms.

Imagine a sort of biological spectrum, arranged from the simple to the complex; it would start with subatomic particles, then move through atoms, molecules, compounds, protoplasm, cells, tissues, organs, organ systems, organisms, populations, communities, and ecosystems, to, eventually, the biosphere. Each stage represents another level of organization, and each level implies new attributes and different properties.

"Population" refers to a group of organisms of a particular kind that form a breeding unit. Not all individuals of a kind (or species) can mix—for example, due to geographic isolation—so a population is the functional group that is capable of breeding. A "community" is all the populations of plants, animals, bacteria, and fungi that live in an environment and interact with one another. Populations within a community are linked by their interaction and effects on each other, and by their responses to the environment they share.

"Ecosystem" is a shortening of "ecological system," the concept that the living (biotic) community and the non-living (abiotic) environment are a functioning, integrated system. An ecosystem involves transfer and circulation of materials and energy between living and non-living systems. There is almost infinite variety in the magnitude of ecosystems, from a global ecosystem that encompasses the entire biosphere to the ecosystem of a fallen log or of the underside of a rock, or even of a drop of water.

Environmental conditions influence the distribution of individual organisms. Limiting factors may be physical (such as temperature and moisture availability) or biotic (such as competition, predation, and the presence of suitable food or other resources). A limiting factor is anything that tends to make it more difficult for an organism to grow, live, or reproduce—that makes some aspect of physiology or behavior less efficient and therefore less competitive.

The distribution of organisms is strongly influenced by the fact that each kind can tolerate only a certain set of conditions. For many organisms, distribution is critically associated with, or determined by, relationships with other organisms. A community of organisms is thus likely to include a loose collection of populations with similar environmental requirements, and possibly another, tighter, collection of organisms that are dependent in some way on each other.

Due to genetic variation, individuals within a population have a range of tolerances around their ecological optimum, but beyond a particular tolerance limit, the species is unable to live. Importantly, this spread means a group may be able to cope with environmental change. A species must be able to complete all phases of its life cycle in a given region if it is to persist for a prolonged period, and different species vary in their tolerance of environmental factors.

The major biomes

Communities are strongly linked to their physical environment or habitat; this habitat is also modified by its communities. Since climate, soils, and biotic factors vary around the world, communities are bound to change. Vegetation is often the most visible aspect of communities, so they are often classified on the basis of vegetation. Communities recognized by their vegetation structure are termed "associations" or "formations;" when the definition also implies the consideration of animal communities, the term "biome" is used.

A biome is a grouping of communities or ecosystems that have similar appearances or structures (physiognomy). As physiognomy generally reflects the environment, the environmental characteristics of a specific biome on one continent will be similar to that same biome on any other. Furthermore, widely separated biomes are likely to include unrelated animals with a similar role and possibly similar morphology (form and structure), due to convergent evolution (animals evolving separately, but having similar characteristics).

At the global level, a number of distinctive features are generally recognized. There are several forest biomes, ranging in diversity and ecological complexity from tropical rainforest to the coniferous high-latitude forests of the northern hemisphere. In regions with seasonal contrasts in rainfall, trees become more widely spaced, species less diverse, and savanna grasses more characteristic of grassland areas develop. Other grassland biomes occur in temperate climates. Shrublands are dominated by shortish, scraggly trees or tall bushes, and may have an understorey

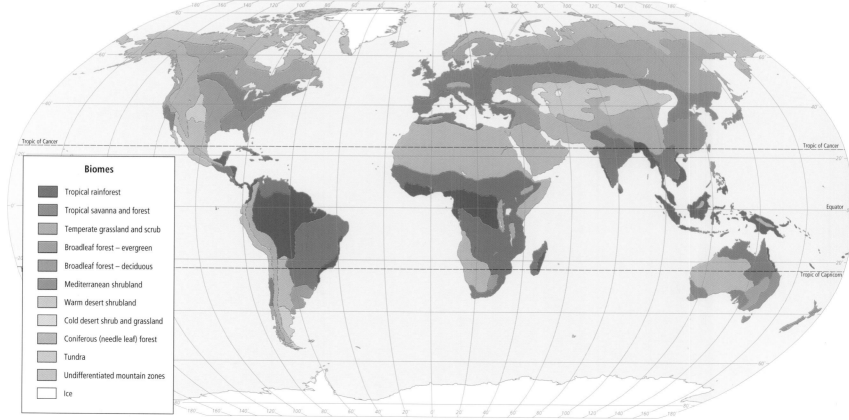

Biomes

- Tropical rainforest
- Tropical savanna and forest
- Temperate grassland and scrub
- Broadleaf forest – evergreen
- Broadleaf forest – deciduous
- Mediterranean shrubland
- Warm desert shrubland
- Cold desert shrub and grassland
- Coniferous (needle leaf) forest
- Tundra
- Undifferentiated mountain zones
- Ice

Tropic of Cancer

Tropic of Cancer

Equator

Tropic of Capricorn

Projection: Robinson   Equatorial Scale approx 1:110 million

These monkeys have adapted to life in the trees in Lombok, Indonesia (left). They find their food there, sleep there, and can move quickly through the branches at considerable heights from the ground. The Weddell seal in Antarctica (below) has few predators, and finds plenty of food in the nutrient-rich waters of the Ross Sea.

A frill-necked lizard from Australia (left) is well adapted to live in its dry environment, and giraffes in Tanzania (above) fill the large herbivore ecological niche of their environment.

of grasses. In drier climates, scrub vegetation may be quite scattered and small in size.

The boundaries of Earth's biomes are rather blurred and maps can only show approximate distributions. Human activity has greatly disturbed natural ecosystems, often leaving mere remnants of once-vast areas of forest or grassland.

Energy in the biosphere

Most life on Earth is supported by the continuous flow of energy from the Sun into the biosphere. A tiny proportion of this radiant energy is used by plants, which are then able to maintain the biomass and the vital processes of the entire biosphere. Energy is eventually converted to heat and lost from the system.

Plants are capable of capturing and storing energy from sunlight. In the process called photosynthesis, plants absorb the radiant energy of the Sun and transform it into the energy of chemical bonds. The energy left after that used for the vital processes of the plant may accumulate as organic matter, and is available for harvest by animals and decomposition by bacteria and fungi.

As only plants can trap solar energy, their productivity determines the energy limits of the entire biosphere, and the total size of all consumer populations, including humans. The amount of this leftover energy is highest in regions with optimum conditions for plant growth.

On land, productivity is controlled primarily by water availability; in aquatic environments, nutrient availability is crucial. The most productive regions are found at the interface between the land and the sea. Generally, terrestrial communities are much more productive than aquatic systems.

The energy stored by plants as organic matter sustains other organisms. This transfer of energy, as food, from plants to herbivores, and from herbivores to carnivores, is a food chain. At each level of a food chain, a large amount of energy is degraded into heat and other forms of non-recoverable energy, so there is a steep decrease in productivity for each step up the sequence of the food chain. Correlated with this is usually a decrease in the number of organisms, and thus a decrease in total biomass.

The ecological niche

An ecological niche is the role that an organism plays in the ecosystem. Whereas habitat is the physical position of the organism, the ecological niche represents its functional position. For example, within grasslands, the kangaroo in Australia occupies the same niche as the bison in North America. They have the same role—large herbivores. Natural selection has often resulted in organisms adapting to their role, which means that the morphology of an animal can often be a good indicator of its niche.

Species vary in the breadth of their niche— some are specialists, others are generalists. Specialists are usually more efficient in the use of resources, due to adaptation, but they are also more vulnerable to change.

Importantly, two species with similar ecological requirements cannot occupy the same niche within an environment. This principle, called competitive exclusion, means that cohabiting organisms either use different resources, behave in such a way that resources are shared, or exist in a variable environment that favors each species alternately. Species that do have similar niches must compete for resources.

Specialization reduces this competition and, given time, adaptation to this new role may result in an altered morphology. Competitive exclusion is thus an extremely important evolutionary force.

The diagram (below) illustrates the food chain in the tundra. At the top of the chain is the wolf, who has no predators. At the bottom is the vegetation. In between are insects, small mammals (such as lemmings, ground squirrels, and Arctic hares) and birds, followed by other larger mammals such as caribou and Arctic foxes.

SOILS

Soil formation is a very complex process. It involves the interaction of climate, type of rock, topography and biota (the total plant and animal life of a region). These factors operate over time, and the amount of time required for soil formation varies substantially from place to place—some soils and their associated weathered products have been forming for millions of years. Soils are formed from weathered materials, usually with the addition of organic matter. The disintegration or weathering of rocks is the result of both physical and chemical processes. Physical weathering breaks rocks down into fragments, while chemical weathering leads to the transformation of rock minerals into products of different composition.

Climate and soils

Weathering products are largely determined by climatic conditions. Mechanical weathering is particularly powerful in drier environments; in hot deserts, the heating of rocks induces expansion and subsequent breakdown of exposed surfaces; freezing has a similar effect. Salt crystallization in crevices mechanically disintegrates rocks. Root growth also leads to mechanical dislodgment.

In wet climates, moisture helps remove particles from exposed rocks, and provides a means by which minerals in those rocks can be attacked chemically to form clay minerals. Pure water is not a significant chemical agent; but the presence of dissolved carbon dioxide and complex organic substances in soil waters generates a chemical environment able to decompose, remove and redeposit rock (clay-rich) materials and salts.

Hot wet climates, plus the opportunity for plants to grow on stable surfaces for long periods of time, leads to extensive decomposition of rocks.

In humid tropical climates, mineral decomposition results in the formation of oxides of aluminum and iron-producing red soils, sometimes cemented into a brick-like substance known as laterite. Such soils are much less fertile than those formed under somewhat drier grassland climates, where organic (or humic) matter and calcium-rich salts accumulate into a nutrient-rich soil capable of growing crops such as wheat and barley.

Rock type and soils

Within one climate area, soil type can vary as a result of the weathering of rocks of different mineral composition. Granites, basalts, quartz-rich sandstones and limestones are common rock types containing distinctive minerals. Chemical decomposition of these rocks over time will yield soils with different types and quantities of clays, varying amounts of precipitated salts, and different degrees of water retention and mobility (due to the existence of pore spaces and the capacity of minerals to absorb moisture).

Similar rock types in contrasting climate zones may also produce different soils. For instance, different rates and intensities of weathering can yield dark, organic-rich soils in grassland areas, underlain by basalt, whereas basalt soils in tropical areas are likely to be red and iron-rich.

Soil processes

The essence of soil formation is the breakdown and mobilization of mineral and organic matter in the presence of water. Living and dead organisms, both microscopic and larger (such as earthworms), assist in this process. The result is the formation of layers, or horizons. Each horizon has distinctive color, grain size (texture), chemical composition, organic matter content and pore space size (porosity). In some soils, binding agents such as organic colloids or iron oxides harden the layers. Over time, these layers may thicken, depending on slope position and the rate of landscape removal or deposition. Ground water movements can lead to precipitation of salts in soil layers, or even on the surface, leading to reduced soil productivity, as in lands bordering the Aral Sea.

Well-structured soils generally display "A," "B" and "C" horizons; A and B horizons are the real soil layers, known as the solum, while the C horizon consists of the weathered parent rock. The A horizon—the exposed soil—is often dark at the top because of the accumulation of organic material. A horizons are subject to leaching (eluviation). Leached material is transported to the B horizon, where it is deposited (illuviation); some B horizons are poor in organic material. Eluviation is assisted by the organic acids produced by decaying vegetation.

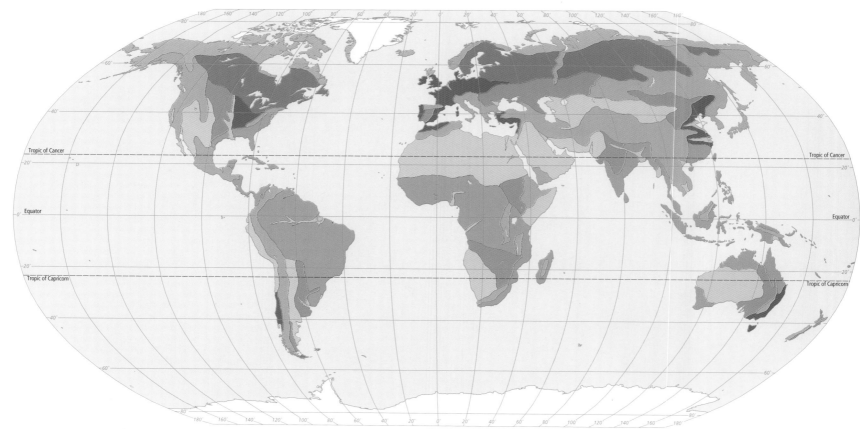

Projection: Robinson   Equatorial Scale approx 1:110 million

Layers of soil are exposed in this weathered escarpment, Australia (far left); parched, eroded ground leaves trees unable to tap into food and water in the soil, Papua New Guinea (left); this plant from the desert of Angola and Namibia has adapted to life in desert soil.

Soil nutrients

Soil texture and composition influence plant growth and therefore the suitability of a soil for agricultural use. Chemical and organic materials form colloids. Colloids are negatively charged, and attract plant nutrients such as calcium, magnesium, and potassium, which are positive ions (or cations). These nutrients are essential to the existence of all life on Earth.

Gray sandy soils of temperate regions are generally acidic; these soils are not rich in plant nutrients such as calcium and potassium, but this can be corrected by adding lime and fertilizers. On the other hand, some dry desert soils, which often contain mineral accumulations such as calcium carbonate and salts, are alkaline. Whilst many such soils have excessive salt levels, some are quite fertile and, irrigated, can be used for agriculture.

Soil types

Many attempts have been made to classify soils. Properties such as color, texture, composition, horizon thickness and porosity are used to define soil types. But even locally there can be considerable variation in soil type, given changes in elevation, slope angle, rock type and vegetation. In mountainous or hilly areas, for example, many different soil types may exist within short distances over a range of altitudes and slope positions.

At the global scale, soil types largely reflect climatic conditions. However, the history of a land surface may also be significant. The "fresh" deposits of recently deglaciated places in North America and Europe contain relatively poorly leached minerals, contrasting markedly with ancient unglaciated tropical plateaus, from which nutrient-rich minerals have long been removed.

Any world map of soil types must be a broad generalization. Iron-rich weathered soils can occur in areas where past climates have had a significant effect (for instance, southwest Western Australia). Alluvial soils, on the other hand, are constantly forming and reforming as new sediments are deposited in flood plains. Yet soils in both areas may be extremely rich in nutrients and thus of great agricultural significance. By way of contrast, the sparsity of moisture and biota in desert regions, or the presence of ice on the ground, will greatly inhibit soil development.

A soil section, showing horizons enriched by organic matter (A1), and leached of humus and minerals (A2). A horizon of accumulation (B) contains mineral matter leached from above. The bedrock (D) is decomposed into a weathered horizon (C).

Soil zones

■	Warm to cool temperate forest soils, moderately to highly leached, moderate to low in mineral bases and organic material, well developed horizons [Alfisols, Gray-brown podzolics].
■	Cool temperate forest soils with highly leached upper profile, acidic accumulation of humus, iron and aluminum in illuvial horizon [Spodosols, Podzols].
■	Grassland soils of subhumid and semiarid areas, often mixed with shrubs, organic rich in upper profile in more moist regions, also rich in mineral bases, fertile [Mollisols, Chernozems, Vertisols].
■	Latosolic soils of tropical and subtropical climates with forest and/or savanna cover; highly to moderately leached profile, low in mineral bases but high in oxides [Ultisols, Oxisols, Red Podzolics, Laterites some relic of past climates].
■	Desert soils of arid areas with little soil profile development and very low organic material but may contain abundant salts [Aridisols].
■	Alluvial soils in all climates especially in deltas, subject to frequent flooding and new deposition of river silt, fertile (only major areas shown), [Entisols].
■	Tundra soils in subpolar areas with permanently frozen subsoils; subject to mass movement on slopes (solifluction) [Inceptisols].
■	Mountainous areas: soils are typically shallow and stony and highly variable in profile and thickness depending on climate and slope position; includes localized areas of fertile soils especially in mountain basins and near volcanoes.
□	Ice sheets

Earth as a home for humans

All humans live by exploiting Earth's natural resources, whether by small-scale fishing in Malawi (above) or employing modern farming techniques to farm cattle in Australia (opposite).

As humans, we dominate our planet. There are very few places where our impact is not felt. Even the atmosphere has now been altered by gases produced by humans, and some of these—such as chloroflurocarbons (CFCs)—are the result of chemical processes alien to natural systems. Many who travel or work at sea are aware of human debris in our waters. Lakes are drying up and are often heavily polluted, as are rivers. Much of the forests and grasslands of Earth have been disturbed. Over the past 200 to 300 years, in particular, we have transformed this planet in ways which at times enhance our welfare, but at others threaten the existence of societies.

As the human race evolved, so did its capacity to utilize natural resources. The mineral uranium was of little use to societies for much of human history, but, from the end of the Second World War, its value as a destructive force and as a source of power has grown immensely. In contrast, the fertile soils of river floodplains and deltas have long been utilized in some areas, and civilizations such as those of Egypt have depended upon their richness. But as a resource, soils need nourishment. Without appropriate care, their ability to maintain the levels of productivity necessary for agriculture will decline. History is full of accounts of battles waged to maintain social structures and population levels in the face of soil degradation. On the other hand, other societies, such as in China, Japan, and Western Europe, have carefully nurtured their soil resources.

For the early humans, the vast forests of Earth were largely avoided. There is some evidence that forests displaced human activities during the period of global warming immediately following the Ice Age in Europe. Progressively, however, forests in tropical, temperate and high latitude areas have been removed or exploited to create new land uses. Today, fires sweep across vast areas of Amazonian and Indonesian rainforests as more timber is removed and land is cleared for cattle grazing and crops.

Marine life has long provided food for humans. Fishing in shallow waters using primitive lines and spears has developed into sophisticated technologies enabling large ships to roam the oceans capturing fish over a vast range of depths. Fears of exploitation and the reduction of stocks to levels at which particular species will not survive have resulted in international agreements on resource use, although the effectiveness of these agreements is in question, with countries such as Japan and Norway still actively hunting whales, for example. Other forms of more sustainable fishing have been developed to feed societies which are heavily dependent upon food from the sea. This includes various forms of aquaculture at sea, in sheltered bays, and on reclaimed land.

Pressures placed on natural resources are closely linked to population growth. One of the most amazing and environmentally significant aspects of the twentieth century has been the rate of increase in population. With nearly 6 billion people alive at the moment and perhaps close to 10 billion by the year 2050, it is no wonder that environmental managers, planners, and scientists are deeply worried about the consequences. Also, population increases are not distributed evenly across the world; it is often in developing countries already suffering from depleted resources that the impacts of many new mouths to feed will be most harshly felt. The effective and equitable distribution of food to those in need will become increasingly important. Unfortunately, major health problems also arise in countries where food supplies are threatened. The impacts of poverty and disease, and the capacity of international aid and economic organizations to support developing countries, create further uncertainties in a world beset with environmental and other problems.

Higher standards of living using available natural resources have been made possible through human inventions, including those designed to increase food production and to resist the ravages of pests and diseases in plants and animals. Many areas of high population have benefited from the so-called "green" revolution, but the ability of pathogens and parasites to undergo genetic change and therefore develop resistance to controls reminds us of the need for constant vigilance and research. Undertaking this research and acting on knowledge gained from other countries remain issues of global concern.

What has changed dramatically in recent years is the ability of individuals and groups to communicate quickly across vast distances. In one sense, space has "shrunk." Geographical isolation—such as that imposed by mountain ranges—no longer impedes the information flow; in the past, such barriers meant that separate languages developed in Papua New Guinea (for instance) in regions which, although physically close, were separated by their inaccessibility. Today, satellite television communications, electronic mail facilitated by fiber optic networks, and 24-hours-a-day business transactions are part of a global economic system which enables information to flow within and between nations.

The ability of societies to respond to natural hazards is another issue of great concern to international aid agencies and governments. Natural hazards may be insidious (droughts) or virtually instantaneous (earthquakes). Great loss of life and property can ensue; the impacts do not respect national economic strength (for example, the number of deaths as a result of tornadoes in the United States). Yet some areas are subject to frequent disasters of a scale which disturbs the economy. Floods in Bangladesh are of this category. Greenhouse-effect-induced rises in the sea level are another more insidious hazard which potentially threatens the futures of coral island nations such as the Maldives in the Indian Ocean.

LAND RESOURCES

Humans meet their principal needs—for water, minerals, and plants—from the land. Inorganic resources include minerals, water, and various elements in soils, whilst organic or biotic resources include plant and animal life. Fossil fuels (coal, petroleum, and natural gas) are of biotic origin. Both mineral and biotic resources are unequally distributed throughout the world—while some countries have abundant plant and water resources, others do not.

The presence or absence of water is often reflected in population densities, with high rainfall areas generally attracting, and being able to support, greater concentrations of people. China, for example, lacks water in its western half, but has a water surplus in its eastern half, and this is reflected in its population distribution.

Mineral resources are also very unevenly distributed. Some countries possess abundant reserves of certain minerals (such as petroleum in the Middle East), and others have gold reserves (Russia and South Africa).

The fact that resources are unequally distributed means that countries must trade what they have for what they need. The highly industrialized countries of Western Europe and Japan, for instance, import raw materials to run their industries. Also, many countries depend upon fossil fuel imports for their energy supplies.

Climate

Climate can be considered a resource because agriculture is so highly dependent on climate. The world's industries and urban centers are mostly located where there is a favorable climate—in areas which have comfortable temperature ranges and adequate rainfall.

Agricultural products can, generally, only be grown economically in suitable climatic conditions. Since the middle of the nineteenth century, plantations in the tropics have produced sugar, tea, coffee, and rubber for international consumption—these areas have been exploited for the production of crops that do not grow elsewhere and are much in demand. Likewise, wheat and other cereals are produced in temperate climates and exported internationally.

Landforms

Human settlement concentrates along river plains and deltas because of fertile soils and available water. In Japan, flat land is prized because of its

A beef cattle feedlot in California, USA (above). This is a method of intensive agriculture; less land is needed per head of cattle, but cattle lead a more restricted existence.

scarcity. In some places, such as in Japan and on the island of Java in Indonesia, hillsides have been terraced for agriculture. In Europe and North America, deposits of sediment, encrusted with ice age glaciations, form fertile plains.

Agriculture

A long-established agricultural practice is "slash-and-burn." This involves clearing a forest patch, then burning to fertilize the soils; cultivation only

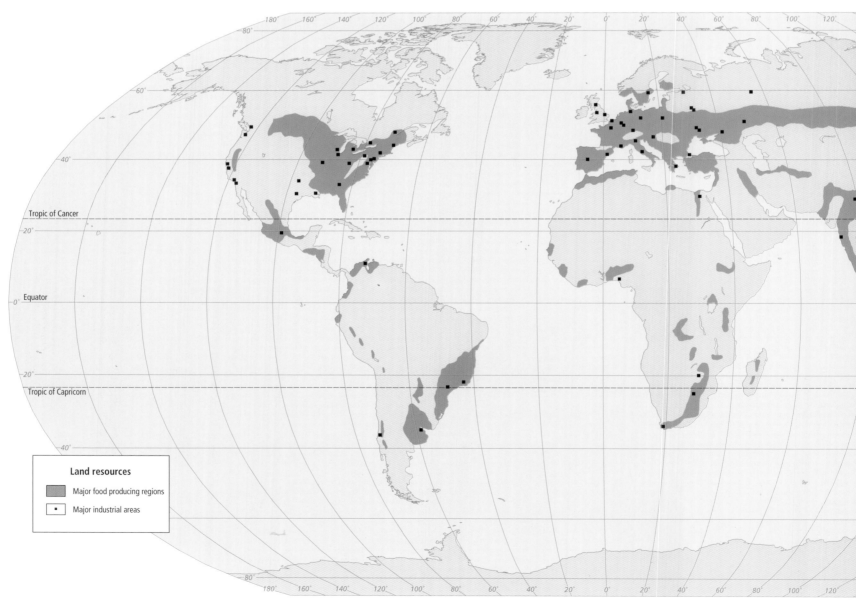

Land resources

- Major food producing regions
- ▪ Major industrial areas

Projection: Robinson   Equatorial Scale approx 1:155 million

Vast wheatfields like these in Saskatchewan, Canada (left) and the "Super Pit" in Kalgoorlie, Australia (below) both show human interference with the environment, and depend on high levels of mechanization. Near Beijing, China (bottom), people still use donkeys to plow—a pre-industrial farming method still used in less developed countries.

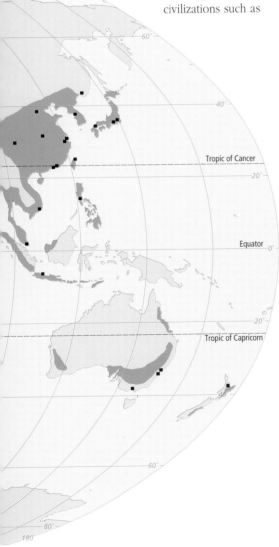

lasts a few seasons as the soils become depleted of nutrients. The exhausted patches are then abandoned and a new patch of forest is cleared. Secondary forests grow in these abandoned sites and, after some years, the reafforested areas can be used again. This rotating system can only support small numbers of people. It is not suitable for the type of food production that is needed for large, or growing, populations.

The development of grain farming, some 10,000 years ago, ensured food production for large populations. It led to sedentary settlements and, ultimately, to some of the great ancient civilizations such as Egypt, northern China, and the Indus Valley. Since the nineteenth century, agriculture has seen the development of mechanization, the use of fertilizers and pesticides, and improved varieties of both plant and animal species. These new developments paralleled the great milestones in industrialization, such as the invention of steam engines, the internal combustion engine, electric power and, more recently, the silicon chip.

The population explosion in several developing countries within the past 50 years greatly increased their demand for food, and it became necessary to increase crop yields per unit of land. This ushered in the so-called Green Revolution, which involved using high-yielding seeds, fertilizers, and pesticides. Although these products increased grain output, the increase has been at some environmental and social cost.

Brazil is a good example of changing uses of the land. Before becoming a colony, its agriculture was of the slash-and-burn type practiced by forest Indians. Colonialism brought in plantation agriculture. The development of coffee plantations boosted Brazil's economy. Great increases in population have placed pressure on its once largely untapped resource, the Amazon rainforest. Large tracts of the Amazon are being transformed by people wishing to establish farms; forests are being burnt down to clear land for agriculture. Large areas are also being cleared to raise beef cattle for export; this also, of course, results in the large-scale loss of forests.

Tropical rainforest clearance cannot easily be reversed. Currently, more than 10 million hectares (24.7 million acres) of forests are being lost each year. These large-scale clearances have adverse effects globally—they accelerate global warming and its effects on climate.

Minerals

Minerals supply the raw materials for several major industries: for the extraction of metals (primarily iron); for fuels such as uranium, coal, and petroleum; and for manufacturing fertilizers and cement. Minerals are valuable resources because they only occur in some places and are finite in nature: once extracted, they cannot be renewed. Minerals are very important for sustaining modern civilization and, as standards of living continue to rise on a global scale, so too does the demand for minerals. In fact, more minerals have been mined in the twentieth century than in all previous centuries. As demand for minerals increases and they become more scarce, their strategic importance to industry—including, especially, the defence industry—also increases, placing even greater strain on already vulnerable finite resources.

The principal metal in demand is iron for making steel; steel forms the basis of much of the world's manufacturing, and every major industrial country produces steel. Other important metals include aluminum, copper, lead, and zinc.

Coal, petroleum, and natural gas provide energy supplies, and, in recent decades, uranium has provided the basis for nuclear energy. Coal is used for electricity generation and in the manufacture of steel. The ever-growing use of automobiles ensures continuing demand for petroleum, while natural gas is being used extensively for heating. Nuclear energy is currently the subject of much controversy because of dangers associated with nuclear power generation, the problems of nuclear waste disposal, and the potential for using nuclear materials from such plants for nuclear weapons.

The greatly increased use of minerals by the developed countries, and the increasing use by newly industrializing countries, has led to concerns about there being adequate mineral supplies for the future. Substitution of new materials for metals and the search for new or renewable energy sources—such as solar power or wind generation—are amongst the developments aimed at conserving our mineral resources.

OCEAN RESOURCES

The oceans, covering more than 70 percent of Earth's surface, are the source of enormous amounts of valuable resources. These broadly fall into two main categories: marine life and minerals. Marine life can be divided into pelagic forms and benthic forms. Pelagic forms move about in the waters—these resources include fish and marine mammals. Benthic forms, which live on the sea floor, include corals, molluscs, and crustaceans. There are also marine plants such as kelp that are harvested and used by humans.

The oceans also contain mineral deposits, including petroleum and gas, and mineral nodules. These resources are more difficult and expensive to obtain, generally, than marine life, but they are of great economic importance.

Within the past 50 years, modern technology has meant that detailed mapping of the oceans has become possible. Recent studies of the oceans, using this technology, have revealed some well-defined physiographic patterns: close to the land lie continental shelves which often end in steep continental slopes; these are followed, further from the shore, by gently sloping features called continental rises, which end in deep ocean basins; and the latter are intersected by mid-oceanic ridges. There are different marine resources commonly found in the different zones where these physiographic features are found.

Many nations, realizing the potential riches of the oceans, have declared resource boundaries under the United Nations' Law of the Sea Convention. Territorial seas are normally set at 12 nautical miles (22 km), whilst exclusive economic zones extend to 200 nautical miles (370 km). These mostly include the resource-rich continental shelves.

Continental shelves, however, can vary in width from 110 to 170 nautical miles (200 to 320 km); the shelves in the Atlantic Ocean and the Gulf of Mexico are exceptional in being up to 260 nautical miles (480 km) wide. A nation can legitimately claim all its adjacent continental shelf, even if that shelf extends beyond 200 nautical miles (370 km), as is the case with the United States and Australia. As a result of this law, some small island nations, such as in those in the South Pacific, have maritime claims that far exceed their land areas.

Fishing

Fishing is the most important resource-gathering activity from the seas. In recent decades, however, overfishing of the seas has reached, in some places, crisis proportions. For example, the North Pacific haddock catch dwindled in 1974 to less than 10 percent of what it had been a decade earlier, and the once highly productive cod fishing industry in Canada, employing an estimated 40,000 people, collapsed in 1992.

Several nations grant licenses to foreign fishing fleets to fish in their waters, and this can exacerbate the situation, as has been the case with the southern bluefin tuna from the waters of Australia, New Zealand, and the Southern Ocean. Overfishing is threatening the very existence of this tuna species; the numbers of this species have fallen, it is estimated, to just 2 to 5 percent of its original population.

Until recently, whales were one of the most threatened species of marine life, but a huge international outcry against whale hunting has resulted in most whaling nations giving up whaling altogether and international agreements for whale protection being enacted. The outcry

Brightly colored fishing boats docked at Nha Trang, Vietnam (above). During the late twentieth century, fishing has been affected by changes in technology, and by ocean pollution.

was generated not only as a result of concern for preservation of whale species, but also because of the horrific nature of the hunting itself.

By the time that whale protection measures were agreed upon, however, several species—including the bowhead, gray and right whale species—had been hunted almost to extinction.

An extensive whale sanctuary in the Southern Ocean now covers the territory of more than 90 percent of the world's whale population. Japan and Norway, however, continue to hunt whales. Japan justifies its whaling operations on the grounds of scientific research, but this explanation is not generally accepted by conservation groups, many of which continue to campaign against all forms of whale hunting.

Coastal fishing

Seas close to shore are usually rich in a wide variety of marine organisms, and have traditionally been fishing grounds for coast-dwelling

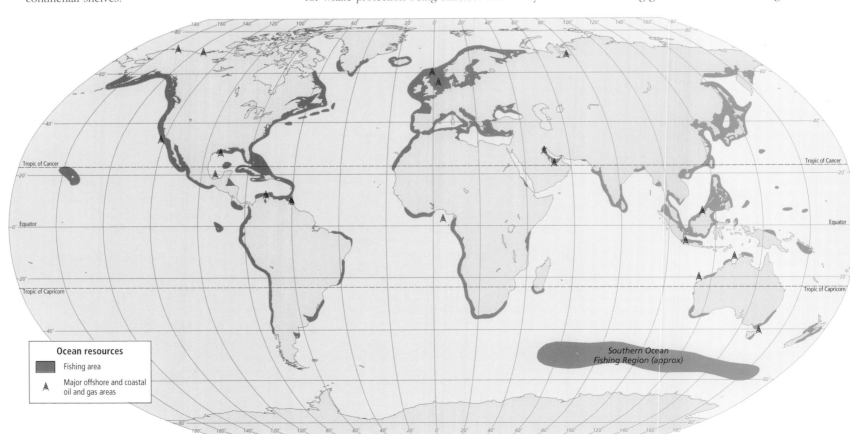

Ocean resources
- Fishing area
- Major offshore and coastal oil and gas areas

Southern Ocean Fishing Region (approx)

Projection: Robinson   Equatorial Scale approx 1:155 million

This busy container port in Singapore (left), and fish farming (of Atlantic salmon in Australia, below), are relatively new commercial uses of ocean resources. Human predation has seriously affected creatures like the humpback whale (bottom), though international agreements aiming to reduce commercial hunting of whales may help to restore numbers.

communities. These are also the areas, not surprisingly, where shellfish farming, aquaculture (fish farming), and salt extraction have, more recently, been widely undertaken.

Kelp, which is rich in potash and iodine, is another product harvested from the seas in coastal areas. It is used for both food and fertilizer.

Fish breeding and shellfish farming, such as oyster breeding, are carried out close to the land. Aquaculture can provide reliable and convenient fish supplies, in contrast to fishing—it is no longer possible to depend upon the ever-dwindling supplies from the seas. Fish farming has been practiced for a long time—the breeding of fish in freshwater lakes in China, for instance, has been carried out for a great many years.

Modern aquaculture is a high-technology industry, as it requires meticulous monitoring of water conditions (such as salinity, oxygen levels, and water temperature) and nutrition. Only a limited number of species—salmon in the Outer Hebrides of Great Britain, for example—are being farmed at present.

In the Inland Sea of Japan, an arm of the sea has been completely cut off by metal nets, thus creating a confined space in which fish can be bred. In Japan particularly, seaweed is another important product of aquaculture.

Coastal countries that do not have sufficient supplies of fresh water can extract fresh water from sea water. However, the capital equipment required to establish these desalination plants is costly. There are several such plants for producing fresh water from salt water in the oil-rich countries bordering the Persian–Arabic Gulf—Kuwait, for instance, has desalination plants.

Continental shelves

These shallow, gently sloping features range in depth between 120 and 180 m (400 to 600 ft). When surface sea water is blown away from the land by offshore winds, colder nutrient-rich water rises to the surface. Where such waters are sunlit—these are known as epipelagic or euphotic zones—they make excellent breeding grounds for the minute marine organisms known as plankton. Plankton are tiny plant (phytoplankton) and animal (zooplankton) organisms that provide nutrition for other larger marine organisms.

Although sunlight can penetrate as far as 1,000 m (3,300 ft) below the ocean surface, photosynthesis can only take place in depths of up to 200 m (660 ft). As a result, phytoplankton can only survive within this shallow layer of ocean water. Small zooplankton feed on the phytoplankton in this layer and they, in turn, are preyed upon by larger organisms such as anchovies and squid. Larger fish such as tuna feed on the smaller marine life, only to be, in turn, consumed by still larger fish. This marine food chain extends even beyond the seas, to the seabirds which are the predators of fish.

The cold and extremely nutrient-rich waters in the continental shelves surrounding Antarctica are the breeding ground for small crustaceans known as krill. Species including seals and whales, as well as penguins, feed on krill.

In recent decades, rich petroleum and natural gas deposits have been discovered in the continental shelves. The petroleum deposits originated from the debris of marine organisms in oxygen-free shelf bottoms millions of years ago. Amongst the well-known deposits that are currently being exploited are those in the North Sea, the Gulf of Mexico, and off the city of Bombay on India's west coast.

Improvements in drilling technology have enabled exploration in ever-deeper seas; drilling for natural gas deposits is currently being carried out at depths of more than 1,700 m (5,600 ft) in the Marlim field, off Brazil.

Ocean basins

The ocean basins are made up of large, flat areas called abyssal plains. These abyssal plains lie at depths of about 4,000 m (15,000 ft). In these dark and cold areas, temperatures are low, perhaps only 4°C (40°F), compared with around 20°C (68°F) at the ocean surface.

These deep ocean basins lack plankton and are, therefore, not rich in marine life. Large parts of these plains, however, are covered with minerals, the most important of which are manganese nodules in the Pacific, Atlantic and southern Indian oceans. These nodules could be exploited at depths of up to 5,000 m (16,500 ft) using technology that has already been developed, but this is currently not economically viable.

The ocean basins are intersected by mid-oceanic ridges, which are formed by volcanic eruptions. The sea water and sediments around them often contain concentrations of zinc, lead, copper, silver, and gold. While these minerals are of considerable economic value and, therefore, importance, no method has yet been devised to extract them economically.

Ocean pollution

The seas have, unfortunately, long been considered convenient dumping grounds for waste—anything from urban sewage to nuclear materials. Chemicals from factories, fertilizers and pesticides from agricultural areas, and oil slicks from ships are also being released, often illegally, into the seas. Ballast water taken on by large ships on one side of the world is released on the other, with all its attendant marine organisms thus finding their way into other environments. The effects of such pollution are quite severe already in some areas, particularly in the semi-enclosed waters of the Mediterranean Sea.

Pollution threatens the existence of marine life, and thus, because marine ecological systems are entwined with land-based ecological systems, it will eventually affect life on land, including human life. There are more immediate effects, too, in some cases: dangerous oil spills such as that from the Exxon Valdez in Alaska threaten the livelihood of the nearby fishing communities who depend on the sea for their economic existence. Fishing communities in the Gulf of Mexico have also experienced this threat following oil spills from offshore petroleum wells.

COMMERCE

The movement of goods and services from place to place has long been a characteristic of human endeavour. The exchange of products, information and ideas within an economic system extends beyond subsistence societies, and into the "global village" of today. The scale of transactions has changed, though—it now ranges from village or tribal bartering to the almost instantaneous transfer of vast sums of money on the international foreign exchange market. The size and bulk of trade also varies with the commodity, and there are great contrasts—camel trains range across deserts and huge bulk carriers roam the oceans.

Trade is the transport and/or communication of commodities from place to place, and is generally measured in terms of the monetary value of the items moved. Until the advent of steam-driven trains and ships and the extensive use of iron and steel for the manufacture of such carriers, the time taken and capacity to move large volumes of materials was limited. These technological limitations helped determine what could be traded, and what could be traded economically.

The volume and scope of trade, the movement of people, and the flow of information increased enormously in the nineteenth century, and continue to do so. The effects of the increasing numbers of roads, cars, and trucks since the Second World War, for example, are so all-encompassing that it is difficult for many people to imagine life without these relatively recent transportation innovations. Add to these changes the enormous advances in electronic communication technology, and it is

easy to see why today's modern suburbanites have become almost completely dependent upon their cars and their electronic communication devices.

The communication of information (ideas, images, audio signals, and written texts), especially as it converges with computer technology to produce information technology (IT), is undergoing another technological revolution. Information technology, combined with cable, satellite, optical fiber, and other technologies, can now transmit digitized information (including money) over cyberspace from one part of the globe to another instantaneously, and with potentially staggering effects. Entire national economic systems can suffer very quickly as a result of currency crises facilitated by the use of such technologies—this happened in parts of Asia during 1997 and 1998.

international trade imbalances

To appreciate the effects of recent changes in transportation and communication technology on trade, it is useful to compare trade between highly industrialized nations (such as the United Kingdom) and other parts of the world in the 1950s with that today.

An international division of labor existed then. Some countries produced manufactured goods in factories, using a highly skilled and well-paid labor force. These goods were traded for primary commodities (coffee and gold, for instance), which were produced by poorly paid and relatively unskilled labor. This unbalanced market system

generated an unequal exchange: wealth accumulated in the industrialized areas, leading to unprecedented levels of development, while the other regions remained underdeveloped, largely because of these trade imbalances. That is, the Western world became richer and the Third World remained underdeveloped and poor.

Recent developments

In the 1960s, manufacturing jobs began to move to selected sites in the so-called developing countries, resulting in deindustrialization in the center, and selective industrialization in the periphery, of the global economy. The textile industry was an early industrial sector to move to the periphery, so some "banana" republics became "pajama" republics. The term "newly industrialized nation" applied to former peripheral nations such as Singapore, South Korea, Taiwan, Mexico, and a dozen or so other countries that were undergoing sustained, rapid growth in manufacturing.

The term "economic tiger" also arose, to describe the performance of some countries in the Pacific Rim. Their economies grew faster than those of the USA or Europe during the 1980s and early 1990s, but as those economies were export-oriented, they suffered greatly as a result of the withdrawal of foreign funds after 1987.

International commerce is led by the wealthy economies; it increasingly involves service industries based on innovation and technology—finance, insurance, transport, marketing and information flow. Trade in raw materials, including those from countries heavily dependent on agriculture or mining, today accounts for little more than 20 percent of total world trade.

Satellite receiving dishes like this one (left) are more common now, as international trade becomes increasingly dependent on satellite communications.

Container ships like the Katie (left) transport all manner of goods worldwide today. Increased freeway traffic (in San Diego, California, US, below) and the pollution it causes are a result of increased technology use in many countries. Simpler forms of transport, such as those that are used in Agra, India (far below), are still used in developing countries.

Manufactured goods are now produced and supplied by a range of developed and developing countries with former closed economies—China, for instance, is becoming more market-oriented and is contributing significantly to world trade.

Multinationals and trade blocs

Another major trend is the spread of multinationals in an ever-widening global process. This is occurring in a number of fields that are engaged in world trade. This process is epitomized by the internationalization of stock markets—they operate around the clock and now even penetrate countries such as Russia.

A further feature of world commerce has been the emergence of powerful trade groups or blocs. These represent collections of countries which, as groups, have accepted rules and regulations that permit a freer exchange of goods and services between the countries in the group. Three main trade blocs are the European Union (EU), the signatories to the North American Free Trade Agreement (NAFTA), and the Association of South-East Asian Nations (ASEAN). The release of a single currency, the Euro, in parts of the EU in 1999 signalled another major development in the concept of trade between and within blocs.

Adverse effects of the global economy

Despite the benefits which have arisen from the growth and development of international trade, there are many areas where market liberalization and the availability of funds for investment and growth have created problems.

The replacement of subsistence agriculture by a limited range of "cash" crops is one. This change has placed many societies at the mercy of declines in commodity prices, or the failure of the crop itself, due to climatic or other factors.

The need for capital has raised debt levels in countries such as Thailand, Mexico, and Indonesia to amounts which, at times of crisis, may induce political and social instability. International funding agencies such as the International Monetary Fund (IMF) and the World Bank, as well as aid agencies operating through the United Nations (UN), have become critical in sustaining these economies in the face of changes in technology and the global marketplace, which they may not have survived or been able to exploit.

"E" stands for "electronic"

Email and e-commerce (electronic mail and electronic commerce) are still quite new to many, but they represent changes in the way business and communication are conducted, worldwide, that will soon affect everyone.

Email allows people to write messages on their computer screens and then, via a phone connection, and for the cost of only a local telephone call, send those messages instantaneously to any person (or group of people) who has the equipment to receive them. It is therefore cheaper (and of, course, faster!) than mailing a letter, cheaper than faxing written material overseas, and cheaper than telephoning overseas. And it is user-friendly—a genuine revolution in communication.

E-commerce means the buying and selling of goods and services via the Internet. It is even newer than email, and has not yet won the acceptance that email has. There are issues—credit card security (the majority of purchases made on the Internet are made by credit card), censorship and copyright, to mention just three—that are as yet unresolved. These issues are particularly difficult as the Internet does not reside in any country; it exists only in "cyberspace", and it is not clear who has jurisdiction to regulate behavior on it, nor how, in practical terms, such regulation could occur effectively. Despite these uncertainties, e-commerce is growing.

The attractions of e-commerce are many: the buyer can, from home, view and compare a range of alternative products; there are web sites that specialize in comparison shopping, so the purchaser can find very low prices for some products; and consumers can buy products that are not available locally at all. The sorts of things that are succeeding in this brave new market range from groceries to clothes, books and compact discs, computers, airplane tickets and shares.

While it is claimed that at present only 1% of commercial activities take place on the Internet, online consumer sales will soon reach $US20 billion, and online commerce between companies will reach $US175 billion. A 1998 US survey found that 46% of commerce-related web sites were currently profitable, and an additional 30% were expected to be within two years. Consumers will determine, as time passes, what sorts of products can be successfully sold this way.

POPULATION AND HEALTH

The growth of the human population in just the last 50 years has been staggering. In 1950, the global population was 2.5 billion, and it is currently 5.5 billion. It is projected that 8.5 billion people will live on the planet in 2025 and perhaps 10 billion people by 2050. If you are 30 years of age or less by the year 2000 and living in a developed country, according to current life expectancy figures, you will probably live through the final exponential surge in the human population—it is estimated that the total number of people may start to decline in the second half of the twenty-first century.

Exponential growth refers to the doubling of a population over a given time period. The growth of the human population is of deep concern, as 5.5 billion people at current levels of resource consumption and waste generation are already causing major environmental problems.

Factors causing population growth

How is the growth in population explained? Demographers and population geographers generally begin explaining world population growth by discussing its two immediate causes: increased fertility and changes in mortality. Fertility refers to the number of children born to women of childbearing age. Mortality refers to various aspects of death, including how long people tend to live (life expectancy) and the causes of death (viruses, cancers, accidents, etc.).

Other factors that play a part in any explanation of population growth include the level of economic development of a given place, the availability of birth control, and the way people in different societies think about children.

Before the Industrial Revolution, the world's population grew slowly or did not grow at all. Although fertility was high in pre-modern societies—women commonly gave birth to between 8 and 12 children—mortality was also high. One out of four children died before reaching its first birthday (infant mortality) and perhaps another one out of five died before reaching 5 years of age (child mortality). Infectious diseases and poor diet were the major causes of high mortality, including infant and child mortality.

Why was the fertility rate so high then? If a family wanted or needed six children, mortality rates alone would require them to have ten or more. Families required the children for agricultural and domestic labor, and as a source of support when a parent grew old—children were the only pension fund available.

The early exponential growth of population resulted from a substantial improvement in the health of populations, especially with respect to control of infectious diseases and the improvement of nutrition, both of which reduced the mortality rate without a corresponding decline in the fertility rate. Infant and child mortality plummeted, and population growth surged.

As economic and social development moved into a more advanced stage, the economic meaning of children also changed. As children began attending school, they were no longer available for labor, and children became an expense rather than an asset. Raising a child today in a developed country may now cost between $US250,000 and $US750,000. Thus, fertility rates have declined with advanced development because of the increased survival rates of children (increased health) and because parents become

economically poorer by having many children (though not necessarily socially poorer) today, as against the past, when children labored for their parents for a substantial portion of their lives.

The advent of modern birth control has also played an important role in the decline of fertility. Most, if not all, developed countries have fertility rates below that required for maintaining current levels of population; immigration is the major factor responsible for continued population growth within developed countries.

Life expectancy—the individual

Looking at changes in health in greater depth, the health of a population has three components: mortality, morbidity (sickness), and disability. Life

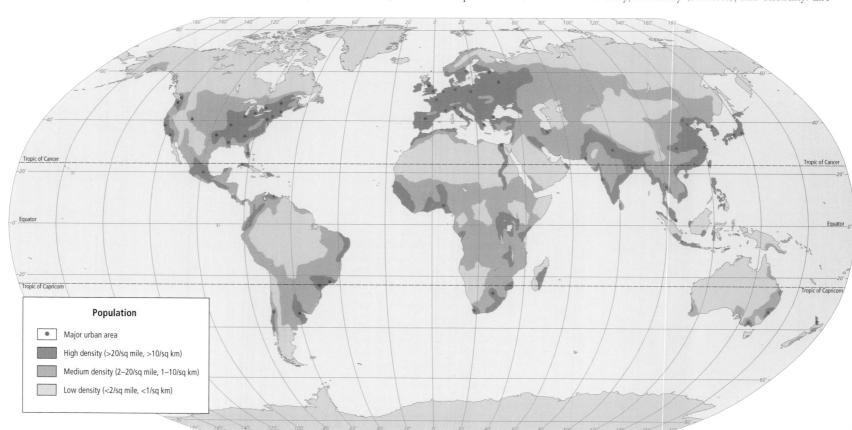

Population

- • Major urban area
- High density (>20/sq mile, >10/sq km)
- Medium density (2–20/sq mile, 1–10/sq km)
- Low density (<2/sq mile, <1/sq km)

Projection: Robinson   Equatorial Scale approx 1:110 million

Exponential population growth occurs when rising prosperity coincides with high fertility rates, as in Bangladesh (above). Communities in Zimbabwe (above right) work to improve their health, while some countries such as India (right) continue to suffer low life expectancy.

expectancy is commonly accepted in demography and development studies as a good general index of the health of a population. In fact, many see life expectancy as the single best index of the development of a nation or population, but it is important to remember that life expectancy specifically measures only the effects of mortality changes; it does not relate to the sickness and disability aspect of human health.

Life expectancy was generally low before the Industrial Revolution. If life expectancy is expressed in terms of years a population as a whole lives, then life expectancy was low (between 45 and 55 years), mainly because of the prevalence of infectious diseases (measles, pneumonia, polio, and malaria, for instance), poor nutrition, lack of family planning, and the like.

Substantial advances in the reduction of a range of infectious diseases, coupled with improvement in nutrition, represent what the United Nations Children's Fund describes in their annual publication *The Progress of Nations* as simply that—the progress of nations. Life expectancy increases by 10 to 15 years because of these improvements to health.

Further increases in life expectancy—when compared with, say, life expectancy in the late 1960s and into the 1970s—are the result of advances in the reduction of death due to degenerative diseases (strokes, cancers, and heart attacks, for example) and the greater emphasis on improving lifestyle—a healthy diet, regular exercise and a reduction in smoking.

For a few nations, life expectancy is slightly more than 81 years at present. At the global scale, life expectancy at birth was 46 years in 1950, 65 years in the late 1990s, and is projected to be 77 years in the year 2050.

Life expectancy—the global view

Considerable regional diversity in the causes of population growth and life expectancy is evident in the late 1990s. Generally speaking, North America, Australia and Europe have high life expectancy and have internal growth rates below population replacement; South America and East and Southeast Asia are not far behind; and Africa south of the Sahara has low life expectancy, but population growth remains explosively high.

Many of the countries in the former communist world are experiencing deterioration in health, and life expectancy is actually declining in some of those nations, including Russia. It is interesting to compare the two most populous nations, China and India. Changes to population growth and life expectancy in China resemble those in other East and Southeast Asian nations, whereas India continues to have a very high growth rate and a moderately low life expectancy.

The future for life expectancy

Is there a limit to life expectancy? This is a most controversial topic about which there is no agreement. Under natural conditions, all life forms have a limit, called senescence: the point where an organism simply wears out. For the human population, senescence was believed to be roughly 85 years; however, a few population

Famine

Famine can be defined as a high degree of lack of food within a population, and it often goes along with widespread mortality. Malnutrition, on the other hand, refers to levels of nourishment that are below those needed to maintain health, and can apply to a whole population or part of a population.

Both are thought to be results of population pressure —the pressure that builds, in developing countries particularly, between the size of the population and the economic resources (especially food) of the country. Falling living standards can be an early sign, in countries with rapidly growing populations, of this pressure. Many societies have suffered famines; in modern times, famine has most often affected societies in Africa.

The links between famine and malnutrition and mortality and fertility now seem not nearly as clear as may previously have been thought. Investigations into mortality in developing countries have found that it is the combination of malnourishment and infectious disease that is responsible for high mortality among infants and children, not simply lack of food.

It seems that populations are able to maintain their rates of fertility despite quite large reductions in nutritional levels—metabolic rates actually appear to readjust.

groups live into the low 90s. Genetic and other medical research, however, may well change the upper limit of life expectancy during the first half of the twenty-first century.

Of course, all of this optimistically assumes that improvements in health will continue. It remains to be seen whether or not the impact of diseases such as AIDS will retard or even reverse the historical improvement in human health, the resistance of some forms of bacteria to antibiotics, in particular, will give rise to deaths from diseases or infections previously thought to be under control, and whether the advances that come through medical research will be affordable to a sizeable proportion of the world's population.

NATURAL HAZARDS

Natural events which cause damage and loss of life are classified as natural hazards. These hazards are generally unpredictable—they strike suddenly and can therefore leave the affected populations traumatized. Natural hazards can result from movements taking place inside the Earth or on its surface, or in its atmosphere.

Movements within the Earth result in volcanic eruptions and earthquakes. Changing weather conditions generate wind storms, cyclones, tornadoes, heavy rainfall, and snowfall, as well as lightning strikes, which can trigger forest fires. River floods and tsunamis can cause loss of life and serious damage to property.

Earthquakes

Plate collision along the Japanese archipelago makes that area vulnerable to earthquakes and to tsunamis generated by earthquakes on the ocean floor. Plates sliding past each other can also cause earthquakes, such as along the San Andreas Fault in California, where earthquakes have occurred in San Francisco and in Los Angeles.

Earthquakes strike suddenly, and if they are of high intensity, buildings can be toppled and life and property lost. The famous San Francisco earthquake of 1906 was devastating to that city and its people—hundreds of buildings were destroyed and the resulting fires swept through the city center, leaving about 3,000 people dead and many thousands more homeless.

An intense earthquake in 1995 toppled and wrecked the tall buildings and infrastructure of Kobe, in Japan, killing more than 6,000 of its inhabitants and injuring more than 35,000 others. The worst scenarios involve earthquakes located close to inhabited areas, notably cities.

On the Richter scale, earthquakes are serious when they exceed a magnitude of 4, cause damage when they exceed 5 and are intensely destructive when they are between 7 and 8.6. Although more than a million earthquakes occur every year, most of these are of low magnitude, and cause no loss of life or damage to property. High-intensity earthquakes, on the other hand, are capable of causing great damage and therefore receive the most publicity, particularly when they are centered on densely populated areas.

Tsunamis

Earthquakes taking place on the sea bed can trigger tsunamis (tidal waves) which, on reaching land, can assume enormous proportions and result in great damage. Such waves may be less than 1 m (3 ft) in height where they begin, in the deep oceans, but they can reach the enormous heights of more than 30 m (100 ft) as they approach land, and they cause devastation to low-lying areas. Worse still, within seconds, more than one such giant tidal wave can strike.

In 1983, a tsunami resulted in the deaths of 30,000 people in Japan. On 17 July 1998, a tsunami struck the northern coast of Papua New Guinea, sweeping over the village of Arop and others nearby, which lay on a low-lying sandy spit; entire villages and their populations were swept away, and it is estimated that the death toll could be as many as 4,000 people.

Volcanoes

Volcanic eruptions are common along certain paths, which are also seismic zones. Here, crustal plates separate and collide. Volcanoes erupt where molten material (magma) accumulates just below

Earth's surface and then rises to the surface. A volcanic explosion ejects ash and superheated steam into the atmosphere and cascades very hot lava along the sides of the volcanic cones. Volcanic eruptions are another natural disaster that can be devastating to life and property.

In AD 79, lava and ash destroyed the ancient city of Pompeii in southern Italy when Mt Vesuvius erupted. Mt Pelée, in Martinique, erupted in 1902, destroying the city of St Pierre and killing most of its inhabitants. Mt Pinatubo, in the Philippines, erupted in 1991, ejecting steam, ash, and lava, and threatened hundreds of thousands of people just 27 km (17 miles) away in Angeles; its ash even blanketed parts of Manila. Volcanic eruptions are also common in Bali and Java (Indonesia).

Volcanic eruptions are rated on the Volcanic Explosivity Index. The Krakatoa eruption of 1883 in Indonesia, one of the most spectacular on record, is rated at 6. No recorded eruption has

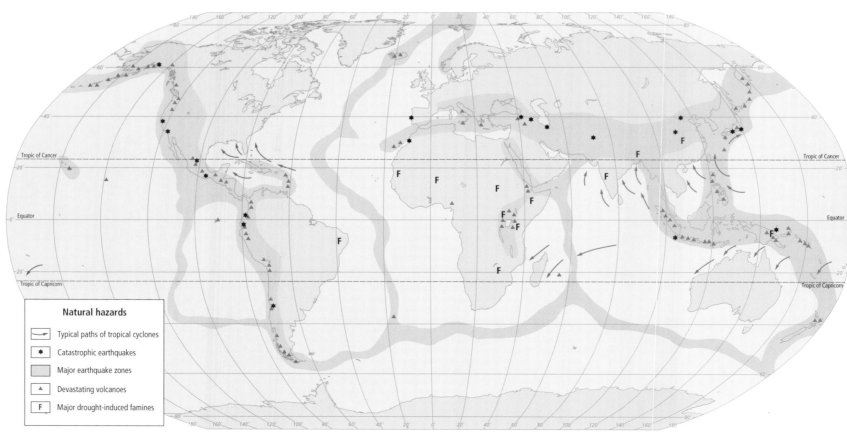

Natural hazards

- ⌐→ Typical paths of tropical cyclones
- ✳ Catastrophic earthquakes
- ▧ Major earthquake zones
- ▲ Devastating volcanoes
- F Major drought-induced famines

Projection: Robinson   Equatorial Scale approx 1:155 million

Wildfires (bushfires, far left) consume large tracts of forest in many countries every year. Often lives are also lost, and millions of dollars worth of property is destroyed. Mt Pinatubo in the Philippines erupted in 1991 (left), causing widespread damage with devastating mud slides which swamped a large area including the town of Lahar (bottom). Drought (below) is a more predictable natural hazard.

reached 8, which is the highest possible rating. The Krakatoa eruption was heard more than 4,500 km (2,800 miles) away; it generated tsunamis, and more than 30,000 people are believed to have perished as a result.

Tropical cyclones and tornadoes

Tropical cyclones, known as typhoons in East Asia and hurricanes in the Caribbean, are also very destructive atmospheric hazards. Tropical cyclones are whirling, low-pressure vortices that can be up to 500 km (310 miles) in diameter and have wind speeds reaching more than 200 km (125 miles) per hour. They can pick up trees, rooftops, light boats, and planes and destroy them. This flying debris is enormously dangerous to people, too.

In coastal areas, large waves, or surges, which sweep the land may be generated, resulting in considerable damage. These cyclones have a calm center, called the "eye" of the cyclone; when the eye passes over an area there is a period of calm, after which the storm returns in all its fury, but with the winds now reversed in direction.

The coastal areas of Southeast and East Asia, the Bay of Bengal, the Pacific Ocean west of Mexico, the Caribbean and Florida, plus island groups of the Pacific Ocean such as Fiji, and northern Australia, are amongst the areas most prone to tropical cyclones.

Cyclones have struck with great fury along the coast of Bangladesh, a small country which mostly consists of the combined deltas of the Ganges and Brahmaputra rivers. That low-lying deltaic area is particularly vulnerable to the surges which cyclones can generate. This has resulted, on several occasions, in considerable loss of life and damage to property.

In contrast to tropical cyclones, tornadoes are small low-pressure cells, not more than 0.5 km (3/10 mile) across. They are, however, very intense, and their wind speeds can exceed 400 km (250 miles) per hour. They thus have the potential to inflict sudden and serious damage. Their vortices become vividly visible as they whip up soil and other debris. The most damaging tornadoes occur in the central parts of the United States, although mini-versions are also found in parts of eastern Australia.

River floods

River floods are a common hazard in floodplains. Spectacular floods, covering thousands of square kilometers, often occur over the immense plains of the major rivers of China, India, and Bangladesh. These areas are often densely populated because of the fertile soils and abundant water supplies.

The Huang River in China flows along a course which is elevated over the surrounding plains; this is because levees have naturally built up on its sides. These levees have been further reinforced by human action. The bursting of the levees in 1887 inundated more than 130,000 sq km (50,000 sq miles) and resulted in a million deaths.

In the case of the Ganges River in India and Bangladesh, the deforestation in the Himalayas has resulted, at times, in water from heavy rainfall and snowmelt rushing onto the vast plains through which the Ganges runs and flooding them. In 1988, 90 percent of Bangladesh lay under water when the Ganges flooded.

Floods regularly bring human and economic disasters to many parts of the world—in 1998 alone, 250 million people were affected by the flooding of the Yangtze River in China—and dams and irrigation networks have been built across many flood-prone rivers in an attempt to mitigate and control flood damage.

Wildfires

Wildfires or bushfires strike when forests are dry. These fires can cause serious damage and result in significant air pollution. The 1997 wildfires in the tropical forests of Sumatra, Indonesia, for instance, released a dense pall of smoke over a large area, including parts of Malaysia and Singapore. These fires were lit by humans clearing land for agriculture or woodchipping. Normally, rains ensure that wildfires are temporary, and restricted to a small area. In Sumatra, however, the prolonged drought, blamed on the El Niño effect, resulted in the uncontrollable spread of the wildfires.

The naturally occurring eucalypt forests of Australia and the eucalypt forest plantations of California are also particularly prone to wildfires, as the volatile oil the eucalypts contain makes them highly flammable. Every year, wildfires wipe out large areas of these forests and damage human settlements or property in the process.

Remote sensing, using satellites and highly sophisticated monitoring techniques, is now being used to track possible natural disasters. It provides data to ground centers about the development of tropical cyclones, the spreading of flood waters from rivers, and the build-up of lava in volcanoes. Such advance warning systems have already helped save lives and limit damage.

Part 2

People and Society

The Changing Scene

Human societies have changed more during the 20th century than during any previous one, but mechanized facilities are not yet available to all—no running water for these Indian women in Varanasi, opposite. Conversely, highly sophisticated cultures developed thousands of years ago without modern conveniences, leaving treasures such as this floor mosaic, above, from Cyprus.

Today's global pattern of peoples and nations rests on a long process of social evolution, going back about 2 million years. It was then that humanity began to clearly distinguish itself as something special on the planet—and unlike the great apes—by physical and mental changes such as a fully upright way of walking, and much bigger brains than the apes possessed. Then, some time in the past 40,000 years, the great evolutionary breakthrough occurred—a fully developed capacity for language, an ability to create new tools for new purposes, and a talent for forward planning. Previously nomadic, hunting wild animals and foraging for seeds and fruits, humans now chose to live a more settled existence. People began to live in regular campsites and used shelters they made themselves. In some places they dug pits for food storage, and had well-built, regularly used fireplaces as far back as 20,000 years ago. Art and religion also appeared, with remarkable cave paintings and evidence of ritual associated with the burial of the dead.

It is thought that *Homo sapiens sapiens* (the technical name for modern humans) originated in Africa. From there waves of migration carried people to every corner of Earth: to distant Australia perhaps 50,000 years ago, to North America across a land bridge (where the Bering Strait is now) perhaps 20,000 years ago. As they moved, they took their languages with them, and when they settled, their languages continued to evolve, many soon becoming mutually unintelligible. Then, around 10,000 years ago came a major development—the rise of agriculture and of permanent settlements. In Turkey and Iraq, in China, and in Mexico, farmers began to grow wheat and barley, or rice, or maize. At around the same time, the first farm animals were domesticated: pigs and cattle, goats and sheep, and llamas in South America.

Permanent farming settlements transformed human life economically, and on this foundation civilizations arose in different parts of the world. In Egypt and Iraq, in China and India, in Mexico and Peru, some towns became cities, with centralized political systems, strong rulers, and monumental buildings. The buildings were often religious temples associated with a class of priests, and in Egypt they were tombs for divine kings, built to preserve their bodies and effects for the afterlife. These social and political developments were accompanied by equally significant developments in science and technology.

The Stone Age, which for millions of years had provided stone implements for hunters, and then stone adzes and reaping blades for the first farmers, came to an end. First bronze was invented, then people found out how to make iron—by 500 BC, iron tools and weapons were spread throughout Europe and Asia. Metals and metallurgical science gave those who had them a huge military advantage over those who did not, as did the wheel, when it appeared around 3,500 BC. Horses harnessed to chariots changed the nature of warfare in ancient times.

War and conquest were normal conditions of life. Other things being equal, victory went to those whose weapons were most advanced. Some dominant cities developed into empires, subjecting other cultures to their rule. The Roman Empire, at its height, included large areas of Europe, North Africa, and the Middle East. By 206 BC, China was united under the Qin Dynasty, while by 1,520 AD the Incas controlled some 2,000 miles (3,330 km) of territory west of the Andes in South America. The military advantages of steel weapons and guns were demonstrated by the easy victories of Cortez over the Aztecs (1521) and Pizarro over the Incas (1533) against vastly greater numbers of ill-equipped Amerindian forces. The consequences of empire were that the knowledge, ideas, religion, technology and language of the dominant civilization were spread far and wide. Trade, both private and state-sponsored, also played a major role in this. The Han Empire in China (206 BC to 220 AD), for instance, traded its silks with the Syrians of the Roman Empire far to the west. Arab trade spread round the Indian Ocean, and by 1200 AD had reached as far east as Java.

The spread of the main world religions has also been of major importance in the last two thousand years. These religions have been responsible for the most enduring examples of the art, literature, and architecture of civilization. A major distinction can be made between proselytizing religions, which actively seek to convert people to their beliefs (such as Chistianity, Islam, and Buddhism) and those which do not, such as Hinduism and Judaism. The world's three major religions are Christianity (33.0%), Islam (19.6%), and Hinduism (12.8%), the first two being derived from early Judaism (0.3%).

In the past 200 years, industrialization has been the biggest force for social change. Beginning in England with textile manufacturing in the 1780s, then progressing to manufacturing based on iron and steel in the nineteenth century, industrialization now combines science with technology in an unending cycle of invention and discovery. What began in Europe has now spread to every country in the world. Industry, which takes raw materials and then turns them into products to be traded, has provided millions of jobs for peasants who would otherwise be tied to the land. But in order to take those jobs they have moved into the cities. Urbanization has created huge concentrations of people in Asia and in South America, and while raising incomes, it has brought social problems too.

Political changes have come thick and fast. The nation-state arose as a political movement in Europe in the nineteenth century, where it superseded an earlier pattern of city-states such as Venice, Antwerp and Amsterdam. After the Second World War it spread through Asia and Africa during the process of decolonization, and since 1989 it has disrupted the domains of the former Soviet Union. Endemic conflicts born of nationalism continue to plague troublespots in Africa, Indo-China, the Balkans, and the Middle East. However, there has been at the same time a balancing move toward large, over-arching international organizations. The European Union steadily moves toward greater political and economic unity. Meanwhile, the United Nations, its resources and abilities increasingly overstretched, its goals more honored in the breach than in the observance, endeavors to keep international peace.

HUMAN EVOLUTION

The oldest primate fossils found in Africa and Asia date from between 45 and 50 million years ago. Around 15 million years ago, Asian and African hominoids (the earliest known ancestors of both humans and apes) diverged. The African hominoids adapted to woodland and savanna habitats and developed the ability to walk on two legs, while the Asian hominoids continued their tree-climbing existence. Although the fossil record is incomplete, a later divergence probably occurred among African hominoids between gorillas and the common ancestors of humans and chimpanzees.

Early hominids

The first hominids (the earliest ancestors of modern human beings not also related to modern great apes) developed about 5 to 6 million years ago. During the earliest phases of their evolution, hominids underwent anatomical changes that resulted in an erect posture, allowing them to walk habitually on two legs. Other changes included the reduction of canine teeth and the development of a comparatively vertical face. Features that are widely accepted as hominid hallmarks, such as a larger brain and the capacity for cultural life (indicated by stone or bone tools), appeared later.

The earliest hominid fossils have been found in southern and eastern Africa. The Olduvai Gorge in the Great Rift Valley of

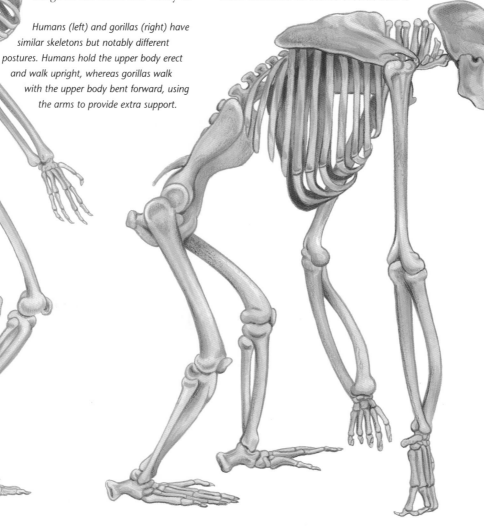

Humans (left) and gorillas (right) have similar skeletons but notably different postures. Humans hold the upper body erect and walk upright, whereas gorillas walk with the upper body bent forward, using the arms to provide extra support.

Tanzania has proved to be a rich source. In the 1930s, the anthropologist Louis Leakey began excavations there, and, in the ensuing years, he and others found a large number of hominid fossils and stone tools. The most famous find occurred in 1959 when his wife Mary uncovered a hominid fossil she called *Zinjanthropus*, believed to be 1,750,000 years old. Most scholars now believe that *Zinjanthropus* is an example of *Australopithecus* (specifically *Australopithecus boisei*), the earliest group of hominids yet found.

Handy man

Other hominid fossils found at Olduvai Gorge were more clearly identifiable as members of our own genus, *Homo*. These hominids were tool users and have been classified as *Homo habilis* ("handy man"). Tools similar to those found at Olduvai have been found at sites elsewhere in Africa and dated at between 1,800,000 and 2,340,000 years old.

Fossils of species that are more recognizably like ourselves have also been found in Africa and dated at about 1.9 million years ago. The best example is a nearly complete 1.6-million-year-old skeleton found in northern Kenya and known as Turkana Boy. The boy died in adolescence, but, had he lived to maturity, he would have been tall (about 1.8 m [6 ft]), with long, slender limbs, and well adapted to living on the open savanna.

Turkana Boy and other similar fossils found in Africa were originally thought to resemble specimens discovered in Java and China. All were classified as *Homo erectus* and it

was believed that *Homo erectus* had evolved in Africa and then migrated to Asia about 1 million years ago. Discoveries in China in the past decade, however, together with the application of more sophisticated dating methods to previously excavated Asian sites, have pushed back the date of the first appearance of early hominids in Asia to about 2 million years ago. Hominid fossils found in Longgupo Cave in Sichuan province in China, dated at around 1.9 million years old, more closely resemble the earlier hominid species *Homo habilis*. This suggests a much earlier migration out of Africa. As a result, some scholars now believe that *Homo erectus* evolved independently in Asia and was not an African species. African hominid fossils of a more modern appearance, such as Turkana Boy, are now classified as a separate species, *Homo ergaster*.

Although there are a number of early hominid sites in Europe, they have yielded few fossils. Sites containing tools have been dated at around 1 million years old, with the earliest being about 1.5 million years old. Until recently, some of these were classified as *Homo erectus* sites. Since this species is now considered to be an Asian evolutionary sideline, however, the fossil record is being reassessed. In 1994, excavations in northern Spain produced numerous simple stone tools and some hominid fossils subsequently classified as a separate species, *Homo heidelbergensis*. This find has been dated at more than 780,000 years old and may provide evidence for the European ancestors of the Neanderthals.

Archaic *Homo sapiens*

The earliest archaeological discoveries made in Europe were fossils of archaic *Homo sapiens*. The fossils were named Neanderthals, after the Neander Valley near Düsseldorf in Germany, where they were first discovered in 1865. This find caused widespread excitement as it was the first discovery of an extinct ancestor of modern humans. Since then, numerous Neanderthal sites have been found throughout Europe and the Middle East. The Neanderthals are generally considered to be a subspecies of *Homo sapiens*, known as *Homo sapiens neanderthalensis*. However, some scholars believe that the Neanderthals' less evolved physical characteristics and less sophisticated technology indicate that they were a separate species, *Homo neanderthalensis*.

The Neanderthals lived in Europe and Western Asia approximately 35,000 to 130,000 years ago, overlapping with the modern human species (*Homo sapiens sapiens*). They had larger brain cases and smaller back teeth than earlier populations, but differed from modern humans in their receding forehead and large, protruding face with front teeth and forward-projecting jaw. The Neanderthals had a relatively short, bulky stature and considerable strength, and showed evidence of complex cultural traits and social organization. For example, they used planning and cooperation to hunt large mammals. They also buried their dead and seem to have had some knowledge of art, demonstrating a capacity for symbolic behavior. Their vocal apparatus and neurological structure provide indirect evidence that they may also have developed speech.

Neanderthals disappear from the archaeological record around 40,000 years ago in the Middle East and about 35,000 years ago in Europe. It may be that they slowly evolved into modern humans, contributing to the gene pool of the present-day inhabitants of Europe and the Middle East. However, many scholars now think that they were gradually overwhelmed and replaced by incoming populations of a more advanced species classified as *Homo sapiens sapiens*, or modern humans.

Out of Africa

The early history of modern humans is still uncertain, as the fossil record is far from complete. Some scholars argue that *Homo sapiens sapiens* developed independently, in a number of different geographical locations. Others consider that what is popularly called the "out of Africa" theory better reflects what is now known about the process of

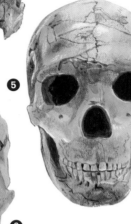

evolution. This proposes that modern human populations are all descended from a single ancestral population that emerged at one location between 150,000 and 100,000 years ago. Increasing archaeological evidence suggests that the place of origin of modern humans was somewhere in Africa. From this homeland, *Homo sapiens sapiens* migrated northward into Europe some 40,000 to 100,000 years ago, and then spread throughout the world, gradually replacing more archaic populations wherever they encountered them.

Human fossil skulls: 1. Australopithecus boisei. 2. Homo habilis. 3. Homo ergaster. 4. Homo erectus. 5. Homo sapiens neanderthalensis. 6. Homo sapiens sapiens. *Note the gradual disappearance of the thick brow ridges, and the growth of the cranium—indicative of increasing brain capacity and intelligence.*

The classification of primate fossils

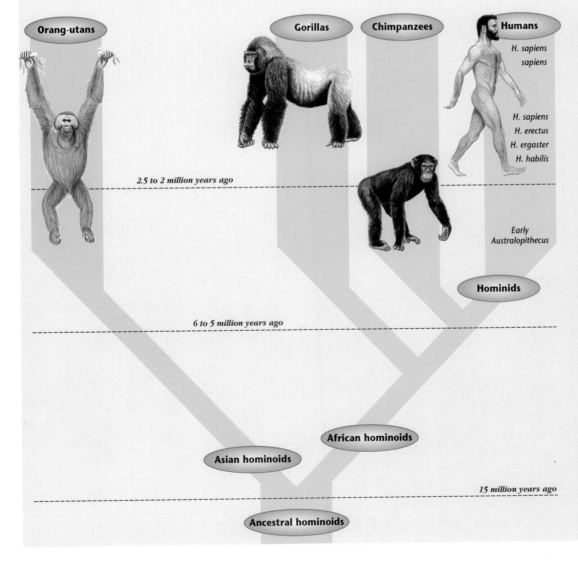

Orang-utans

Gorillas Chimpanzees Humans

H. sapiens sapiens

H. sapiens
H. erectus
H. ergaster
H. habilis

2.5 to 2 million years ago

Early Australopithecus

Hominids

6 to 5 million years ago

African hominoids

Asian hominoids

15 million years ago

Ancestral hominoids

In 1735, the Swedish naturalist Carl Linnaeus caused a public outcry when he classified human beings as part of the animal kingdom. Today, however, his taxonomy—which has been extensively revised and expanded—is the accepted way of classifying all forms of plant and animal life.

The human species, *Homo sapiens sapiens*, belongs to the genus *Homo* (which includes our hominid ancestors) in the family *Hominidae* (which includes the apes). This family is in turn part of the Primate order. The relationship between humans, apes, and early hominid fossils is problematic. Recent studies by molecular biologists have shown that there is a much closer genetic link between humans and the African great apes (especially chimpanzees) than might have been predicted from comparing their anatomies. This has led some taxonomists to place humans, gorillas, and chimpanzees in one family, *Hominidae*, and Asian apes such as the orang-utan in another, *Pongidae*.

The currently accepted classification of hominid fossils establishes a chronology for modern humans from the development of the first australopithecine species (appearing around 5 million years ago), to early *Homo* species such as *Homo habilis* and *Homo erectus* (from around 2 million years ago), through to later *Homo* species (around 1 million years ago) and archaic *Homo sapiens* such as the Neanderthals (about 130,000 years ago). Both the classification and the chronology are likely to be revised as new fossil discoveries are made.

THE FIRST MODERN HUMANS

The success of modern humans, *Homo sapiens sapiens*, in colonizing Earth's landmasses owes much to the evolutionary changes that occurred in the physical form and mental capacity of hominids. Although the basic hominid anatomy changed little, the features that distinguished hominids from other hominoids, such as their erect posture, ability to walk habitually on two legs, vertical face, smaller teeth and enlarged brain, were refined in each successive species and subspecies. By far the most significant change, and the one that signaled the emergence of *Homo sapiens sapiens*, was the progressive enlargement of the brain, which was out of all proportion to changes in body size. In absolute terms, the average brain capacity of modern humans is three times that of the great apes.

Increased brain capacity allowed *Homo sapiens sapiens* to develop greater intelligence and problem-solving capabilities. This led to the appearance of tools as well as speech and language (although full language capacity emerged less than 40,000 years ago). It also enabled modern humans to develop strategies for coping with harsh environments, such as camp fires, clothing, natural food storage facilities, and primitive cooking methods. Further intellectual development resulted in a flourishing cultural life and increased capacity for social organization, which in turn stimulated the growth of civilizations and led to the evolution of modern society.

Making and using tools

Many people believe that it is the presence of tools that distinguishes early humans (*Homo* spp.) from other hominids, but a number of other animals also make and use tools. Chimpanzees, for instance, have demonstrated an ability to make

and use tools for digging for food. More specifically, some scholars have argued that it is the power and complexity of human tool assemblages that distinguishes humans. However, the simplicity of the tool assemblages of archaic humans and certain hunter–gatherers of the recent past makes this explanation inadequate. What *is* unique about human tool making and tool use is that the tools were made for particular purposes. Moreover, they were constantly improved and adapted for new purposes, to the extent that tools eventually pervaded all aspects of human life. This is not the case among chimpanzees.

The first hominid fossils associated with hand-made tools were those of *Homo habilis*, found at Olduvai Gorge in Tanzania, and dated at about 2 million years old. Tools have been found in older East African sites, but without any fossil remains. Although earlier hominid species knew how to make and use tools, it was probably only with the emergence of the genus *Homo* that tools became part of daily life.

The early *Homo habilis* tools were crude, stone hand-axes. Unsurprisingly, stone and some bone tools dominate the archaeological record. Tools made of perishable materials such as wood are found occasionally at waterlogged, frozen, or arid sites, but such finds are rare. From about one million years ago, tool assemblages became more specialized, but it is only in the past 40,000 years that there has been a proliferation of designs.

The simplicity of early tools clearly indicates that hominids obtained their food by foraging and scavenging. The traditional view that the hunting of animals accompanied and influenced the evolutionary development of modern humans has been reassessed in the light of this evidence.

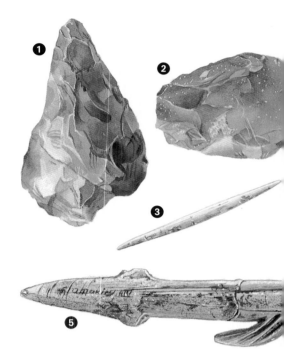

Regular hunting, particularly the killing of large mammals, probably began later. Far more important at this stage in the evolution of modern humans was the development of an ability to plan ahead. Although this would become essential for organizing hunts, it was also required at an earlier stage to enable humans to forage for food and store supplies for lean times.

Art and cooking skills

There seems to have been a watershed in the development of modern humans around 40,000 years ago. This is reflected in a dramatic worldwide

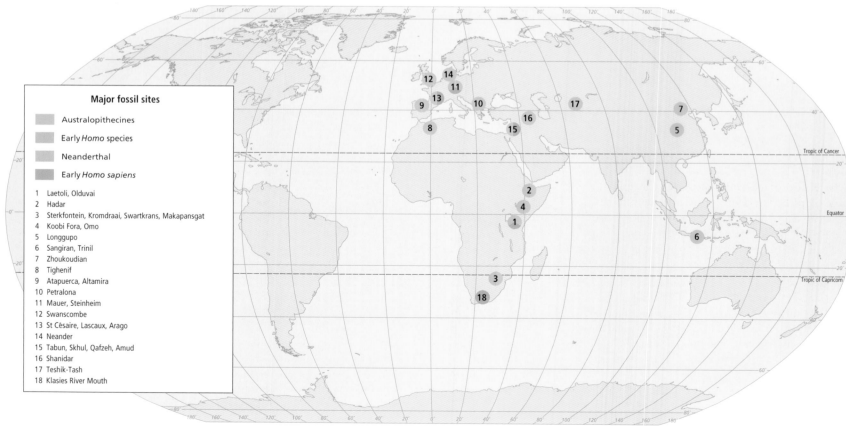

Major fossil sites

- Australopithecines
- Early *Homo* species
- Neanderthal
- Early *Homo sapiens*

1 Laetoli, Olduvai
2 Hadar
3 Sterkfontein, Kromdraai, Swartkrans, Makapansgat
4 Koobi Fora, Omo
5 Longgupo
6 Sangiran, Trinil
7 Zhoukoudian
8 Tighenif
9 Atapuerca, Altamira
10 Petralona
11 Mauer, Steinheim
12 Swanscombe
13 St Cèsaire, Lascaux, Arago
14 Neander
15 Tabun, Skhul, Qafzeh, Amud
16 Shanidar
17 Teshik-Tash
18 Klasies River Mouth

Projection: Robinson   Equatorial Scale approx 1:155 million

Many people believe that the invention and use of tools marked out the early humans from other hominids. The development of human technology is reflected in these tools (below):

1. *Scraper from Swanscombe, England; 300,000–200,000 BP*
2. *Sidescraper from Le Moustier, France; 70,000–35,000 BP*
3. *Bone point from Aurignac, France, 35,000–23,000 BP*
4. *Bifacial stone knife from Solutré, France; 20,000–17,000 BP*
5. *Bone harpoon from Le Morin, France, 16,000–8,000 BP*

❹

change in the archaeological evidence. Not only did tool assemblages become more sophisticated, but art, in the form of jewellery, figurines, paintings, and engravings (often depicting hunting scenes), also become prevalent. The widespread use of raw materials that could only have been obtained from distant sources suggests that trade networks had expanded. Camp sites show evidence of more settled living, including artificial shelters, food storage pits, and well-built, regularly used fireplaces. Burial sites become more elaborate, containing ornaments and other cultural objects. The disposal of the dead clearly involved some form of ritual, reflecting metaphysical concerns and symbolic behavior.

There also appears to have been a "culinary revolution," with stone knives being used to cut up food. This allowed for more thorough cooking, which may in turn have resulted in changes in the cranial structure of humans, as large teeth would no longer have been necessary for tearing raw or partially roasted meat.

These cultural and physical changes occurred during the last ice age, which culminated about 15,000 to 20,000 years ago, when glaciers covered large areas of the world. Successful strategies developed by modern humans to cope with the deteriorating climate gave them a clear advantage over more archaic forms of *Homo sapiens*. Despite the spread of hostile environments during the ice age, *Homo sapiens sapiens* succeeded in colonizing the world far more rapidly and extensively than earlier hominid migrants.

Colonization on the scale undertaken by *Homo sapiens sapiens* required all of the species' new-found technical and social skills. Its success depended not just on tools and an ability to plan ahead, but also on the existence of extensive social structures which could provide the support and cooperation necessary for the completion of long, hazardous journeys into unknown lands.

The art of early hunter–gatherers

Art is widely believed to have originated during the last ice age and appears to have flourished mainly in Europe and the southern hemisphere (southern Africa and Australia). Little has been found at ice-age sites in North Africa, China, or elsewhere in Asia. This does not mean, however, that art did not exist in these areas—it may simply be that the forms of artistic expression were more temporary or that the materials used did not survive.

Ice-age art is linked with major innovations in tool technology, including well-crafted and highly efficient blades, and hafted spears. With the rapid evolution of hunting techniques, obtaining food would no longer have been as difficult and, consequently, more effort could be expended on the development of art, language, and spiritual interests. No record remains of stories, songs, or dances of these pre-literate cultures, nor of artworks made out of perishable materials. The art that has survived can be divided into two main types: moveable objects and rock art.

Moveable objects comprise small figures or decorated weapons made of stone, bone, antler, ivory, or clay, which were sometimes placed in graves to accompany the deceased in the afterlife. Rock art, such as engravings and paintings, is often found in caves. While drawings of human figures have been found, most rock art depicts game animals such as bison, mammoths, deer, and bears, which were important sources of food, clothing, tools, weapons, and ornaments. Outstanding examples of cave art were discovered in the nineteenth century at Altamira in northern Spain and at Lascaux in southwestern France.

This ancient cave painting (above) was found in Rhodes-Matapos National Park in Zimbabwe, Africa. Fertility figures, such as the 20,000-year-old Willendorf Venus from Austria (left), are among the earliest indications of a human concern with rituals and symbols.

HUMAN MIGRATIONS

Recent research undertaken on fossil and genetic evidence suggests that hominids migrated "out of Africa" on many occasions, probably beginning with *Homo erectus*, *Homo habilis*, or the taller and more slender *Homo ergaster* more than 2 million years ago. Changes in the climate may have been a major factor in these early migrations. One theory suggests that between 2 million and 3 million years ago, a widespread drop in temperature led to the replacement of the tropical woodlands in eastern Africa by savanna grassland. This change in vegetation favored the *Homo* species over the australopithecines. With their larger brains, more generalized diets, and greater tool-using ability, the *Homo* species adapted more readily to the open terrain and soon began to roam widely. Initially, they probably followed the land mammals on which they scavenged, as the animals moved north and east following the expansion of the grasslands.

To date, early *Homo* sites have been discovered at several Asian sites in the Republic of Georgia, in China, and on the island of Java in Indonesia. Early humans did not make an appearance in Europe until some time later (around 1 to 1.5 million years ago), and this region remained sparsely populated until 500,000 years ago.

During their migrations, early *Homo* species would have crossed various land bridges that appeared during the recurring ice ages of the past 2 million years. However, to explain the presence of 800,000-year-old stone tools on the Indonesian island of Flores, which would have remained at least 20 km (12 miles) offshore even at the height of the ice ages, scientists have tentatively suggested that *Homo erectus* made use of simple vessels such as bamboo rafts to cross short stretches of sea.

Migrations by modern humans

Compared with the migrations made by archaic populations, the spread of modern humans during the last 100,000 years occurred remarkably rapidly. Furthermore, *Homo sapiens sapiens* ventured much farther than earlier hominids, eventually reaching the Americas and Australia. These more extensive migrations were made possible by this species' greater adaptability and by the exposure of numerous land bridges during the last ice age.

Scientists are still debating when and how the Americas were colonized, although it is generally accepted that hunting groups crossed into Alaska via a land bridge in the Bering Strait. This could have occurred either between 63,000 and 45,000 years ago or between 35,000 and 10,000 years ago. Although some argue that the earlier crossing is more likely because the Alaskan ice sheet would not have been as extensive as during the later period, the earliest reliable dates for archaeological sites in North America are no more than 20,000 years old. Consequently, the more widely held view is that the crossing occurred between 12,000 and 20,000 years ago, with people gradually drifting south down the continent. Recent evidence suggests that Monte Verde in southern Chile may have been settled as early as 12,500 years ago.

The question of whether there was one or more crossings is also unresolved. Some researchers believe that genetic variations among the indigenous peoples of the Americas are so great that they suggest three or four waves of migration. A more recent assessment cautiously suggests that there were no more than two waves—one arriving about 20,000 to 25,000 years ago and the other around 11,300 years ago.

These early settlers were probably of more diverse origins than previously thought, and some may even have arrived by sea rather than across the land bridge.

Debates of a similar nature surround the colonization of Australia. The earliest direct evidence of humans is about 40,000 years old (claims that various artefacts and sites in the Northern Territory date from around 60,000 years ago have not been confirmed). Since some of these sites are in the south of the continent, dates of up to 50–60,000 years ago for the initial arrival of humans from Southeast Asia have been proposed to allow for the settlement of large areas

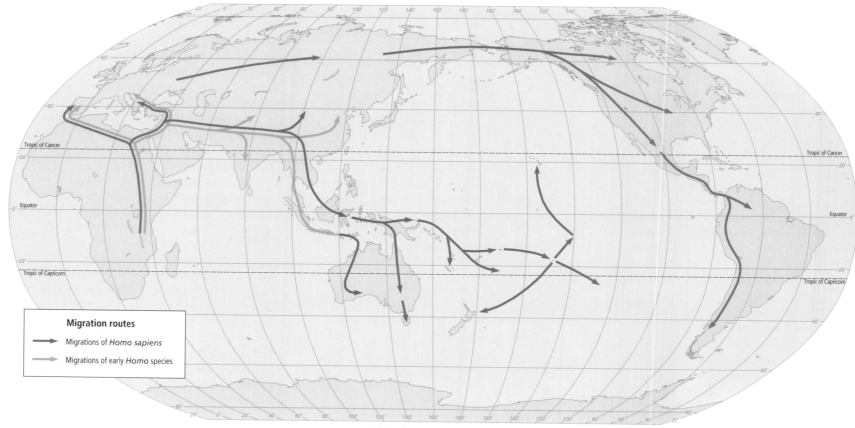

Migration routes

→ Migrations of *Homo sapiens*

→ Migrations of early *Homo* species

Projection: Robinson Equatorial Scale approx 1:155 million

The expansion of African grasslands (left) as a result of climatic changes assisted early migrations. The first people to settle in North America would have had a lifestyle similar to that of present-day Inuit (below). Early Polynesian watercraft may have resembled this canoe from the Solomon Islands (bottom).

of the continent by 40,000 years ago. The absence of Asian fauna in Australia indicates that there must have been a substantial stretch of sea between the two continents for millions of years.

Colonizing the Pacific

The islands along the western rim of the Pacific were probably colonized around the same time as Australia and New Guinea, when sea levels were sufficiently low for them to be linked to the Asian mainland. Of course, *Homo erectus* may also have occupied these islands while they were linked to the mainland during earlier periods of glaciation, but the earliest signs of human occupation in Japan have been dated at around 30,000 years ago. Based on the evidence currently available, it appears that other islands on the western Pacific rim, such as most of the Philippines, were probably occupied 10,000 to 15,000 years later.

By the time European explorers reached the Pacific region in the early sixteenth century, virtually every inhabitable island was populated. Exactly when and how all the islands of the Pacific were first settled, however, is not entirely clear. The archaeological evidence is still meager, and there is considerable speculation about early migrations.

Not long after the Second World War, in an attempt to prove that the population of the Polynesian islands originated in South America, the Norwegian ethnologist and adventurer Thor Heyerdahl and his small crew sailed from the Pacific coast of South America to Polynesia on a balsa raft named *Kon-Tiki*. Although Heyerdahl showed that such a voyage was possible, most scholars still believe that the great bulk of linguistic and botanical evidence suggests that the populations originally came from Southeast Asia rather than South America.

The Pacific Islands are customarily divided into three ethnogeographic areas: Melanesia, Micronesia, and Polynesia. Melanesia includes the

predominantly dark-skinned peoples of New Guinea, the Bismarck Archipelago, the Solomons, Vanuatu, New Caledonia, and Fiji. Micronesia comprises the very small islands and atolls in the northern Pacific, including the Marianas, Carolines, and Marshalls. Polynesia forms a large triangle in the eastern Pacific, from Hawaii in the north, to New Zealand in the south, and Easter Island in the east. Despite these classifications, however, archaeological evidence, linguistic studies, and blood group analyses all suggest similar origins for the people of the three areas. The physical and cultural differences between modern-day peoples may result from the fact that the islands were occupied by successive waves of migrants.

The Lapita people

The earliest dates for settlement of the Pacific Islands in Micronesia and Polynesia go back no further than the second millennium BC. As they moved eastward, these early settlers took with them a well-developed agricultural tradition based

on taro, yams, and pigs. This agricultural tradition was associated with a coarse, finely decorated pottery known as Lapita ware. By studying the distribution of this pottery, archaeologists have been able to trace the movement of this people across the Pacific.

One theory suggests that the Lapita people began to make their way eastward from eastern Indonesia or the Philippines about 4,000 years ago and then spread farther eastward through New Guinea to the southwestern Pacific. It is thought that they may have been forced to keep moving as a result of pressure from incoming groups of rice-growers. As they moved, they gradually developed distinctive Polynesian characteristics, which included complex hierarchical social, political, and religious systems.

The last region of the Pacific to be settled by Polynesians was New Zealand. Colonists probably arrived there by canoe from the Hawaiian islands some time around AD 1,000, although many scholars now favor a date closer to AD 750.

LANGUAGES AND WRITING

As with many other questions about human evolution, there is still no consensus about the origin of speech and language. A number of scholars have suggested that art and language must be closely intertwined because they both require the ability to understand abstract ideas and symbolic concepts and to share these understandings with others as part of a cultural system. According to this theory, fully fledged languages would not have existed before the appearance of art—which first emerged about 40,000 years ago. If this argument is correct, archaic *Homo sapiens* such as the Neanderthals, who coexisted for some time with *Homo sapiens sapiens* and also created primitive art, would have possessed some form of language. Certainly, no one doubts that the Neanderthals were able to communicate with each other, although changes to the brain and facial structure would have meant the linguistic ability of *Homo sapiens sapiens* was markedly superior.

The complexity of human language and speech is dependent on a number of neural and anatomical mechanisms found only in *Homo sapiens sapiens*. These include a vocal tract that permits a wide range of speech sounds, areas of the brain that control and interpret these sounds, and an efficient memory that can use past experiences as a guide to the future. Although scientists believe that earlier hominid species were able to communicate both vocally and by gestures (just as animals do), their use of words, concepts, and sentence construction (syntax) would have been limited. Even chimpanzees can be taught to use words when placed in a human-like environment, yet they never progress beyond the vocabulary or grammatical ability of an average

three-year-old child. Humans alone are able to talk to each other, rather than just transmit words.

Although fully fledged linguistic ability would have been found only among *Homo sapiens sapiens*, it is still possible that language of some sort existed among the first anatomically modern humans in East Africa as early as 130,000 years ago. Some scientists even argue that *Homo habilis* may have been able to communicate vocally, albeit in a much simpler fashion. In other words, early humans may have had speech, but not a complete language.

Further evidence that early hominids were able to communicate verbally has recently emerged from what may at first seem an unlikely source: scientific research into the evolution of dogs. Studies in molecular biology suggest that wolves evolved into domestic animals more than 130,000 years ago, and wolf bones have even been found with 400,000-year-old hominid bones. These facts suggest that the association between humans and canines goes back a very long time. Some scientists now think that the domestication of canines had a profound effect on human evolution. The close association with dogs would have made it less crucial for early hominids to have a keen sense of smell that would alert them to other hominids or animal predators. In turn, this would have allowed the development of the facial and cranial modifications necessary for speech.

Languages of the world

Thousands of languages are spoken in the world today. Populations that share similar cultures and live only a short distance apart may still speak languages that are quite distinct and not readily understood by neighboring populations.

For example, the inhabitants of New Guinea and adjacent islands speak approximately 1,000 different languages, or about one-fifth of the world's total.

At the same time, similarities exist between languages used in different parts of the world, which suggests that they developed from a common source. Scholars group such languages in families on the basis of similarities in vocabulary, sound systems, and grammar. English, for example, is part of the Indo-European family, which includes languages of antiquity, such as Sanskrit and classical Greek, as well as contemporary languages in both Asia and Europe, such as Hindi and Russian. Other geographically dispersed language families are Malayo-Polynesian (also known as

The world's major languages

Language	Speakers (millions)
Mandarin (Chinese)	885
English	322
Spanish	266
Bengali	189
Hindi	182
Portuguese	170
Russian	170
Japanese	125
German	98
Wu (Chinese)	77
Javanese	75.5
Korean	75

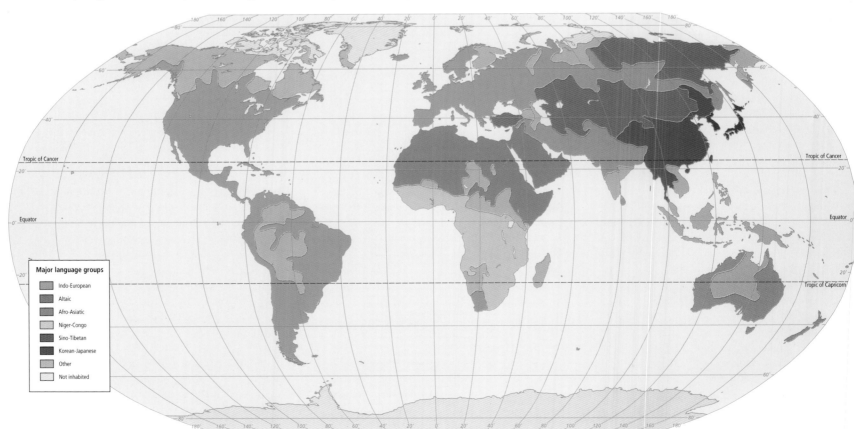

Major language groups
- Indo-European
- Altaic
- Afro-Asiatic
- Niger-Congo
- Sino-Tibetan
- Korean-Japanese
- Other
- Not inhabited

Projection: Robinson   Equatorial Scale approx 1:155 million

As a result of geographical isolation, the Papuan tribes that gather at traditional sing-sing ceremonies (left) may speak many different languages. Egyptian hieroglyphs (bottom) are a form of pictorial writing, whereas the Latin script on this tablet from the Coliseum (below) illustrates alphabetic writing.

Austronesian), which includes Hawaiian, Javanese, and the languages of Madagascar, and Uralic, which includes Finnish, Hungarian, and the Samoyed language of Northern Siberia.

The first languages were disseminated in a number of ways. The most obvious was migration. As they spread out across the globe, early peoples carried their languages into uninhabited territory. Languages would also have spread as a result of contact between different peoples. For example, the invention and adoption of food production would have encouraged agricultural peoples to migrate into territory occupied by hunter–gatherers, who may then have adopted both the cultivation techniques and language of the immigrants.

A third form of language dissemination involves the replacement of an existing language by one spoken by a dominant group. The development of complex societies allowed incoming minorities with some form of centralized organization to dominate larger populations, who, in many cases, subsequently adopted the language of the elite. For example, the adoption of the Chinese language family in southern China in historical times occurred as a result of the military expansion of the Chinese empire.

The origins of writing

Writing is thought to have arisen around 5,000 to 6,000 years ago in Sumeria (southern Mesopotamia), and to have appeared shortly afterward in widely separate parts of the world, including Egypt (3000 BC), the Indus Valley (2500 BC), and China (2000 BC). Writing may have spread from Sumeria to the Indus and probably also to Egypt, but it was almost certainly independently invented in both China and, later, Mesoamerica, where it first appeared in the third century AD. Writing was unknown elsewhere in the Americas, even in the highly developed Inca civilization of the central Andes which flourished in the fifteenth century.

Scholars usually distinguish three broad kinds of writing systems, although in practice some systems combine elements of more than one kind. They are known as logographic, syllabic, and alphabetic writing.

In logographic writing, separate symbols are used to represent single words. This can complicate the representation of even simple statements. Because most of the symbols in logographic writing have, or originally had, a pictorial basis, it is believed that this is the earliest form of writing. Examples of logographic writing include early Sumerian cuneiform, Egyptian hieroglyphs, and modern Chinese characters.

In syllabic writing, symbols represent syllables. Examples of this type include later Sumerian cuneiform and the remarkable Cherokee syllabary developed by a Native American called Sequoyah in Arkansas in the early nineteenth century.

The third, and now most common, form of writing is alphabetic, in which symbols represent units of sound, or phonemes. Widespread alphabetic systems include Arabic, Roman (which is used for English and most other European languages), and Cyrillic (used for Russian and some other Slavic languages).

It has been suggested that these three types of writing reflect an evolutionary progression, from logographic to alphabetic; however, most scholars now regard this view as too simplistic. For instance, in a number of writing systems, logographic elements have been adopted, discarded, and then reintroduced.

The development of writing is closely associated with the rise of hierarchical societies. Literacy contributed to the formation of more complex state structures and bureaucratic institutions. In its early stages, it was often closely linked to religious activities and authorities. In Sumeria, for instance, the recording of economic transactions was controlled by religious officialdom. Writing also arose as a religious practice in Mesoamerica, remaining the preserve of the elite until the Spanish conquest in the sixteenth century.

THE RISE OF AGRICULTURE

Humanity's transition from a mobile life of hunting and gathering to a sedentary farming lifestyle in settled communities was not a sudden "revolution." It took place by degrees, with the dependence on cultivation increasing slowly as selective breeding modified wild plant species. Nevertheless, in terms of the prehistory of modern humans (100,000 years or so), the emergence of full-scale agriculture, which includes the development of both plant cultivation and animal husbandry, was relatively rapid.

It is probable that the cultivation of plants developed independently in a number of different regions, including the Fertile Crescent (a region stretching from present-day central Turkey southeastward through Iraq to the Persian Gulf), China, Mesoamerica (roughly

Foods and their origins

Most agricultural products were native to one part of the world and then spread gradually to other regions. The following list shows the origins of selected foods.

wheat	Fertile Crescent
potatoes	Central Andes
rice	China
corn	Mesoamerica
sugar	New Guinea
coffee	Ethiopia
tea	China
apples	Western Europe
oranges	Southeast Asia
sheep	Fertile Crescent
turkey	Mexico

present-day Mexico and Guatemala), and the Central Andes. Some scholars suggest that food production also originated in other centers such as New Guinea and West Africa.

Plant cultivation first occurred in the Fertile Crescent, where evidence for the domestication of grains such as wheat and barley, and other foods such as pulses and olives, begins to make an appearance in the archaeological record around 11,000 years ago. Flax was also cultivated as a source of fiber for making cloth. Although much of this area was then, as it is now, rocky and rather arid, the fertility of the river floodplains probably encouraged an increasing reliance on cultivation. In the region between the Tigris and Euphrates rivers in present-day Iraq, the development of canal-based irrigation allowed farming centers to flourish. From there, agricultural methods spread throughout the Mediterranean, across the Balkans, and along the Danube River into central Europe. By 7,000 years ago, farming was also firmly established in Egypt's Nile Valley.

Recent archaeological finds have indicated that plant cultivation may have begun in Asia not long after it began in the Fertile Crescent. For example, it is possible that rice was cultivated along the middle Yangtze of central China as early as 9,500 years ago. In northern China, there is evidence that millet and rapeseed were grown around the same time. Farming practices spread along the fertile floodplains of Chinese rivers, where many early sites have been found. At about the same time, local people also began to domesticate animals, including pigs, cattle, sheep, dogs, and chickens.

Food production may have arisen independently in at least two parts of the Americas. One of these

is the Peruvian Andes, where beans were cultivated perhaps as early as 7,000 years ago. At around the same time, people in Mesoamerica also started to grow beans, together with squash and pumpkins. Maize, which became the most important staple, may not have been cultivated until more than a thousand years later. The early archaeological record is sparse in South America, but it appears that plants such as manioc, amaranths, peanuts, potatoes, cotton, and chili peppers were slowly domesticated in different parts of the continent.

Agriculture may have begun earlier in New Guinea. In the island's central highlands, archaeologists have discovered evidence of irrigation ditches in areas of swamp which date from around 9,000 years ago. They remain uncertain about the types of crops grown there, although taro and other native noncereal plants are likely candidates.

The domestication of animals

Although the dog was domesticated somewhat earlier, the process of rearing animals for food—and later for clothing and as draft and pack animals—began at around the same time as plant cultivation. Many animals hunted by humans were unsuitable for breeding as a result of such factors as their diet, growth rate, ability to breed in captivity, or behavioral disposition. Domestication therefore had to proceed by trial and error, and gradually it modified many species.

Some animals, such as the wild pig and the auroch (a large, long-horned wild ox), were distributed over a wide area of Europe and Asia, and were probably domesticated independently in a number of places. Others, such as goats and sheep, were confined largely to the Middle East and western Asia, and were later introduced into Europe.

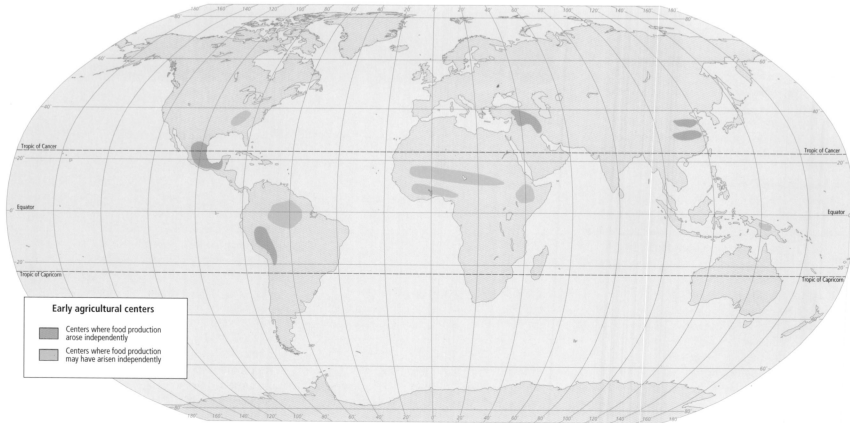

Early agricultural centers

Centers where food production arose independently

Centers where food production may have arisen independently

Projection: Robinson   Equatorial Scale approx 1:155 million

Food production began independently in China when rice was cultivated about 9,000 years ago in the valley of the Yangtze River. From there, rice cultivation spread throughout Southeast Asia, reaching Indonesia (left) about 4,000 years ago. The shift from hunting-gathering to agriculture resulted in the development of new technologies, including animal-driven pulley systems like the one on this well in Egypt (below).

The people of the Andes domesticated llamas for use as pack animals and guinea pigs for food. The earliest evidence for the domestication of cats has been found in Greece. Cats were subsequently domesticated in many areas, usually to protect grain stores from rodents.

Why choose agriculture?

Not all communities switched to agriculture as soon as they came into contact with it. Many early peoples remained dependent on food collecting and hunting, and hunter-gatherer societies continue to exist to this day. These communities may modify their environment—for example, by burning vegetation to encourage growth that attracts game—and some also undertake minimal husbanding of plant resources, such as replanting rootstock cuttings and protecting fruit-bearing trees. But despite this and the fact that they may have often come into contact with people practicing agriculture, they have chosen not to switch to a sedentary lifestyle based on farming.

The reason for this is that subsisting as a hunter-gatherer usually requires less work than subsisting as a farmer. As long as population densities remain low, a food-collecting lifestyle can be more attractive and efficient, and provide a more balanced and diverse diet. In fact, scientists find it hard to explain why certain populations ever became totally dependent on farming. However, once the switch had been made, the demographic and social consequences of an agricultural lifestyle would have made it difficult to reverse the trend.

The consequences of agriculture

Agriculture transformed both human societies and landscapes. The need to make cultivation more efficient encouraged rapid technological innovations. The use of clay, which was already known in pre-agricultural times, became

Despite the attractions of new technologies, many communities, including the San of the Kalahari desert in southwestern Africa, rejected agriculture and continue to follow a hunting-gathering lifestyle to this day (below right).

widespread and people began to make large receptacles for food and water. In turn, these receptacles transformed diets, as grains and pulses could be soaked and boiled, making them easier to eat and digest. Other innovations that emerged in agricultural societies were metalworking, the wheel (which improved the making of pots and stimulated progress in transport), and the use of sails on boats. Small copper objects have been found at early agricultural sites in the Middle East, but extensive metalworking and purification techniques were not developed until a few thousand years later.

Early agricultural societies were based on small village communities. As the range of domesticated plants and animals grew, the village economies became increasingly diverse and food production techniques improved. These developments enabled communities to create surpluses which could be used to support full-time craftspeople. Specialization led to internal barter and to trade with other communities. Items and commodities that were found or produced in only certain localities were traded over considerable distances. Social divisions also increased and, in many areas, complex hierarchies, headed by hereditary leaders, came into existence. In some societies, elite classes emerged who were able to devote their time to religious, cultural, and military pursuits while living off the surplus produced by subordinate groups.

Agriculture and demographics

Some scholars believe that population growth encouraged the adoption of agriculture, while others think that it was agriculture that triggered

an increase in population. Although there is no firm demographic evidence to decide the question, archaeological research suggests that the number and size of settlements usually increased following the appearance of food production in a region.

The rapid expansion of agriculture affected the environment, in some cases quite catastrophically. For example, archaeologists have found that the barren landscape of modern Greece is the result of more than 5,000 years of farming, during which deforestation and land clearance led to the loss of topsoil and severe soil erosion.

EMERGING CIVILIZATIONS

The first civilizations arose on the fertile alluvial basins of major rivers such as the Tigris-Euphrates in Iraq, the Nile in Egypt, the Indus in Pakistan, and the Yellow (Huang Ho) in China. These regions shared many common features, including arid environments that made agricultural communities dependent on irrigation, and readily available supplies of raw materials such as stone, metal, and wood. The Tigris-Euphrates, Nile, and Indus regions were probably linked by trade well before the appearance of the early cities, but Chinese civilization developed in relative isolation.

The first urban societies

Cities emerged in all four regions during the third millennium BC as villages and towns slowly grew into cities with large public buildings and developed specialized and well-organized production and trade, forms of writing, hierarchical social structures, and centralized political systems. This process of evolution varied, although the cultural attributes of emerging cities were similar.

In most cases, cities arose following the emergence of a social elite. As a class or family became dominant, it usually sought to create a power base in one region. This power base attracted immigrants and businesses, resulting in the rapid growth of the urban community. Scholars have suggested various reasons for the emergence of social elites. Some propose that the construction and maintenance

The pyramids at Giza in Egypt (below) were built during the Fourth Dynasty to house the remains of the rulers Khufu, Khafra, and Menkau-re.

of the large-scale irrigation works needed to support a growing population would have required considerable organization and encouraged the development of a managerial class. Others emphasize the role of specialized production and trade in creating a dominant commercial class. Another explanation is the growing influence of warfare: as settlements were overrun by invading peoples, their inhabitants were often forced to become the subjects of their conquerors. It was probably a combination of all these factors that led to the development of the first "upper classes" and the first sophisticated urban societies.

Cradles of civilization

In the region between the Tigris and Euphrates rivers known as Mesopotamia, farming gradually became more productive, canals were built, large temple platforms (called ziggurats) were erected, and the cuneiform script was simplified and standardized. Crafts, such as pottery and metalwork, became more specialized and production more organized, leading to greater social divisions in society. The city-states had their own monarchs, and were often heavily fortified. Their ascendancy came to an end, however, around 2350 BC, when Sargon, a military ruler from Agade in central Mesopotamia, forcibly amalgamated them into the Akkadian empire.

In Egypt, by contrast, it was the unification of the cities and towns of Upper and Lower Egypt at the beginning of the third millennium that caused civilization to flourish, giving rise to a well-developed political and administrative system, writing, and a complex religion. During this period, the massive stone

pyramids of Giza were constructed to preserve the bodies, knowledge, and wealth of the Egyptian kings in the afterlife. The pyramids also symbolized the structure of Egyptian society, with the god-king at the apex, officials in the middle levels, and the mass of the population at the bottom.

The emergence of the Indus civilization was marked by the appearance of distinctive artistic styles in pottery, copper, and bronze (a copper–tin alloy). These objects were traded with nomadic pastoral peoples who, in turn, transported the merchandise into central Asia and along the coast of the Arabian Sea. Around 2400 BC, the different cultural traditions of the Indus merged into one, called Harappa by archaeologists after the first city to be excavated in this region. Harappa culture had writing, a form of centralized control for administration and commerce, and large buildings made out of baked brick. In contrast to other early civilizations, however, Harappan society does not seem to have included a priest-king class, nor did its spread depend on military conquest.

In China, it is likely that villages merged to form states in several areas, but legend and archaeological evidence locate the first civilization, that of the Xia, in the middle and lower valleys of the Yellow River, from about the end of the third millennium BC. Texts written much later suggest that the Xia united a number of groups in a loose confederation. One of these was the Shang, who gained ascendancy in the second millennium BC. They developed an early form of Chinese script and expanded their territory through military campaigns. They were defeated by the Zhou, another Xia confederate, at the end of the second millennium BC.

Culture and trade

The expansion of civilizations was assisted by trade and migration as well as conquest. Trade routes in particular allowed knowledge and practices to be dispersed across sometimes vast distances. They were particularly significant in the expansion of

These bas-reliefs (left), which date from about 500 BC, decorate the walls of the ancient Mesopotamian city of Persepolis. Greek city-states such as Athens (bottom) emerged around 750 BC. At that time, Teotihuacán (below) in Mesoamerica was one of the largest cities in the world.

Chinese culture into Southeast Asia, and in the spread of Egyptian and Middle Eastern traditions as far as North Africa, southern Asia, and Europe.

The first major European civilization emerged in Crete at the end of the third millennium BC. The Minoans, whose powerful navy controlled the Aegean Sea for much of the second millennium BC, constructed large cities centered on elaborate palaces including those at Knossos, Malia, and Phaistos. Later, urban societies also sprang up on the Greek mainland, the most notable being the Mycenean civilization, which came to prominence during the late second millennium BC. Classical Greek civilization emerged during the first millennium BC in a number of self-governing cities such as Athens and Sparta. These urban societies were distinguished by the formal constitutions that directed their political life and by the increasing power held by the male citizenry at the expense of a centralized leadership.

Civilizations also developed independently, but much later, among the agricultural communities of Mesoamerica and the central Andes. Mesoamerican civilizations emerged during the first millennium BC. The most important was that of the Maya, who developed a form of writing around AD 300. The Maya maintained commercial ties to city-states developing elsewhere in the region. One of these, Teotihuacán, in central Mexico, was an important trade center with a population that peaked at more than 100,000 around AD 600. During the same period, several interrelated civilizations existed in the central Andes, with territories that are now in present-day Peru and Bolivia. These societies created monumental buildings and elaborate crafts, but left no evidence of any written languages.

The meaning of "civilization"

In eighteenth-century Europe, "civilization" meant cultural refinement—the opposite of barbarism. Nineteenth-century social philosophers found this meaning too restrictive, so they used the term in the plural sense to refer to large-scale societies. This usage is followed by present-day sociologists and anthropologists.

Human societies can be classified in terms of their size and complexity. Small-scale or tribal societies comprise small bands loosely coordinated by kinship relations. These groups often live together at permanent settlements, although some may be nomadic. Medium-sized communities are usually made up of clusters of villages or small towns united under some form of confederation or chiefdom. In large-scale societies, at least some of the inhabitants live in large urban societies which are linked by a network of social, economic, and cultural ties, and normally unified under a centralized political organization.

Early Mesopotamian artworks such as this ivory carving often include portraits of members of the ruling elite.

THE IMPACT OF CIVILIZATION

The main impetus for rapid progress over the past few thousand years was the development of large-scale urban societies. Their benefits in enriching human experience through technological innovation, scientific knowledge, and diversity in social life appear obvious. Certain consequences of civilization were less benign, however. These include the increasing destructiveness of warfare, the spread of disease, and the life-long bondage imposed on certain classes of people.

Innovation and adaptation

Many thousands of years elapsed between the development of specialized stone and bone tool assemblages and the beginnings of food production. After the adoption of agriculture and a sedentary lifestyle, however, the widespread diffusion of the latest innovations occurred remarkably rapidly. This was partly due to the obvious usefulness of the technology. Many inventions were developed in one location and then rapidly dispersed because of their immediate utility. The wheel, for example, appears to have been invented near the Black Sea around 3400 BC, and within a few hundred years, it was being used throughout Europe and Asia.

Another reason for the exponential growth of technology was that new inventions were rapidly adapted to diverse local needs. For example, shortly after the emergence of the wheel, innovations based on this technology—such as pulleys, water wheels, and windmills—appeared and then spread quickly along ever-expanding trade routes.

Some innovations, however, did not travel as extensively as may be expected. For example, the wheel was probably also invented independently in Mesoamerica, where it was used in children's toys, but it was never adopted for transportation in this region due to the lack of draft animals. Nor did the wheel spread from Mesoamerica to South America, even though the people of the Andes had the Americas' only beast of burden—the llama—and despite the fact that technologies such as metallurgy had already spread northward from the Andes to Mesoamerica.

Technology and warfare

New technologies led to the expansion of production and, consequently, an increase in the size of urban populations. As cities grew in size, conflict over land with neighboring agricultural and pastoral peoples often led to warfare. In turn, this stimulated the manufacture of weaponry.

Early weapons were made of bronze, but by the beginning of the first millennium BC, iron weapons were being widely produced in the Fertile Crescent, and smelting techniques, which produced an early form of steel, were already well understood there. By 500 BC, iron tools and weapons were widespread throughout Europe and Asia. However, ironworking did not appear in the Americas until after the Spanish conquests of the 16th century. The devastating effectiveness of steel weaponry was demonstrated by the Spanish conquest of the Incas. In 1532, the conquistador Pizzaro, with an army of only 168 soldiers, was able to defeat the Inca army of more than

Monuments to royalty, such as the massive temple of Abu Simbel in Egypt (above) built during the reign of Ramses II (1279–1213 BC), reflect both the development of technology and the emergence of complex social hierarchies.

80,000 soldiers and capture their emperor Atahualpa. The Spanish soldiers had chain mail, helmets, steel swords, lances, daggers, and horses, whereas the Inca army was protected by quilted padding, armed with blunt clubs, and traveled on foot.

Science and disease

Although many advances in the domestication of plants and animals and in technology were the result of accidental discoveries or trial and error, written records indicate that early civilizations were making careful observations of natural phenomena. For example, the Maya developed a calendar based on the solar year and lunar month, and could predict eclipses—a feat that required advanced mathematical skills. The Egyptians acquired considerable medical knowledge and surgical skills. Among the sophisticated techniques they developed was the practice of trepanation. This involved the cutting of bone in the skull to relieve pressure on the brain resulting from a skull fracture, or to treat headaches or epilepsy.

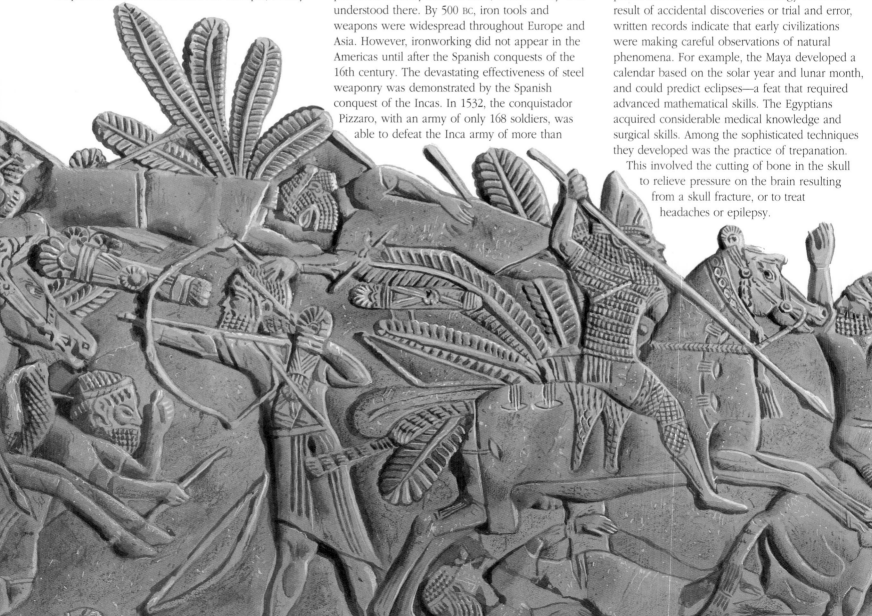

Invented in western Asia, the wheel was rapidly adapted to create devices such as the water wheel (below). As a result of their preference for cooler climates, llamas (left) never spread northward to Mesoamerica. Sophisticated societies such as that of the Maya (bottom) thus remained without pack animals.

A sedentary lifestyle enabled ailing individuals to receive better care than they would receive if they remained nomadic. However, large concentrations of people living in close proximity to domestic animals and (initially, at least) dependent on a relatively limited range of foods created the perfect environment for the spread of disease. When human populations are small and move frequently, the opportunities for parasitic infections to spread are limited. Urban lifestyles, in contrast, with their permanent housing and large refuse dumps, attract disease-carrying vermin and insects, and allow parasites to spread more quickly. Land clearance, irrigation, and the use of natural fertilizers would also have encouraged certain diseases in sedentary communities, particularly where diets were deficient and the population less resilient. Even more significant was the domestication of animals. Today, people associate animals with diseases such as rabies, anthrax, and parasitic worms, but domestic animals were also the original source of infections that are now commonly transmitted by humans, such as smallpox, measles, and influenza.

The spread of disease was encouraged by trade, migration, and conquest. For example, bubonic plague is thought to have been restricted to Asia until it was spread to other parts of the world by traders. When it reached Europe in the mid-fourteenth century, it wiped out one quarter of the population. Diseases carried by conquering armies were often more destructive than their military campaigns. For example, in 1520, the Spaniards under Cortés inadvertently brought smallpox to the Aztecs, causing a massive epidemic that killed more than half the population and led to the demise of the empire.

As civilizations grew and technology spread, warfare, as depicted in this bas-relief from Nineveh in Assyria, became more sophisticated and more commonplace.

Social hierarchies

The increasing division of labor and the steady enhancement of specialized skills in urban communities led to the development of ever-more sophisticated social hierarchies. People directly involved in food production—the commoners—were often obliged to provide tribute payments to a centralized authority. This did not necessarily mean that commoners were physically separated from the elite—in many early cities, they lived in close proximity to each other and even shared in decision-making. But as urban populations increased and relationships became more complex, so the social distinctions became more marked.

In China, for instance, the Shang, and later the Zhou, administered a feudal system of vassal states. Members of the royal clan, and others who assisted the king, were granted fiefdoms over parts of the kingdom. Below these nobles and loyal administrators were the farmers from whose ranks the soldiers were recruited. At the lowest end of the social scale were the slaves, who were usually nomadic pastoralists captured by the ruling elite. This pattern of enslaving captives was common in these evolving nation-states, probably because mass production and large-scale public works provided many uses for slaves in menial occupations.

Domestic horses

Today's domestic horses are descended from wild species native to southern Russia. Horses were first domesticated there around 4000 BC—much later than most other domestic animals—and before long had become the principal means of transportation throughout much of Asia and Europe. Horses transformed warfare, providing formidable military advantages when yoked to battle chariots or ridden. At the same time, however, they transmitted several diseases to humans, including tetanus and the common cold.

Mongolian horses are the only surviving relatives of the species from which all domestic horses are descended.

FROM CITY-STATES TO EMPIRES

There is no doubt that warfare was a part of human experience long before historical records were kept—even the small-scale societies of Melanesia that existed at the time of the first European contact were involved in frequent and violent tribal conflicts. However, the scale, range, and destructiveness of war increased significantly with the development of the first states. High population density, advances in transport and weapons technology, centralized decision-making, and a new fervor among troops willing to die for a powerful leader allowed extensive resources to be mobilized for warfare. This in turn meant that military engagements could take place much farther from home. Whereas war had previously involved only the annexation of adjacent territories from enemies who had either been chased away, killed, or enslaved, now they could lead to the amalgamation of entire societies into larger political units. Furthermore, the subjugated peoples could be forced to pay tribute, thereby increasing the ruler's resources for further campaigns. In this way, empires were born.

The rise of empires greatly enhanced the diffusion of knowledge, ideas, technology, languages, and cultural traditions. It also expanded trade links and imposed administrative and political unity on previously dispersed communities, laying the foundations for future nation-states.

There are three broad reasons why rulers of small city-states and medium-sized kingdoms ventured into empire-building. One was to create alliances that would provide protection against an external threat—the formation of the Chinese Empire is a good example of this. Another reason was to subdue a persistent enemy—this is why Alexander the Great began his conquests. The third was to acquire control over desired commodities, trade routes, and other resources—Roman expansion can be explained in this way. All three reasons influenced most expansionist ambitions, but one tended to be more dominant than the others in the building of individual empires.

The threat from the north

By the third century BC, the Zhou kingdom of northeastern China was breaking up, having been weakened by years of attacks perpetrated by warring tribal peoples to the north and northwest. Following the collapse of the kingdom, wars broke out between rival states and various alliances were formed and severed. Eventually, one of the Zhou vassal states, the Qin (221–206), gained ascendancy and brought the other states under their control. They then set about uniting the states into a single Chinese empire. The principle objective of this policy was to secure Qin territory against the foreign invaders that had plagued the Zhou. To ensure the protection of the empire, the Qin began to construct an enormous physical barrier to invasion by linking defensive structures originally built during the Zhou period. The Great Wall, as this barrier became known, would eventually stretch 3,000 km (1,860 miles) across northern China. The Qin also built an extensive network of highways and canals to improve communications throughout their empire.

Following the death of the First Emperor, the Qin Empire was taken over by the Han in 206 BC. The Han expanded their empire further south beyond the floodplains of the Yellow (Huang Ho) and Yangtze rivers, and also defeated tribes to the west. This helped silk merchants to create a new trade route through central Asia which eventually extended all the way to Europe.

Alexander the Great

The rise of the Persian Empire in the sixth century BC posed a significant threat to Greek city-states such as Athens and Sparta. They responded by forming strategic alliances, which they managed to maintain long enough to defeat the Persians during the following century. However, subsequent disputes between the cities allowed Philip II of Macedon to take advantage of their disunity and unite Greece with Macedonia in 338 BC. In the following year, Philip declared war on Persia to revenge the Persian devastation of Greece, but before the war could begin he was assassinated.

Philip was succeeded by his son, Alexander, who realized his father's plans to crush Greece's formidable enemy. He successfully engaged the Persian army in Turkey and the eastern Mediterranean, moved westward to Egypt where he founded the city of Alexandria, and finally crushed the Persians in a decisive battle at Gaugamela in Mesopotamia in 331 BC. His conquests continued to the Indus River before he turned back, only to die suddenly at the age of 33 in Mesopotamia in 323 BC. Alexander's vast empire was divided up between his generals, and, without a strong leader, it soon disintegrated, although the kingdoms of Egypt, Persia, and Macedonia persisted.

Despite his short reign, Alexander left a long-lasting legacy. His decision to take scholars and scientists on his campaigns ensured that Greek learning, language, and cultural traditions were disseminated widely. He founded a number of Hellenic cities with Greeks and Macedonians, the most notable being Alexandria, which became a renowned center of learning.

Although the Greek city-states had previously established trade centers throughout the northern Mediterranean, they had largely left the southern shore to the Phoenicians. Alexander's conquests extended Hellenistic influence into North Africa and the Middle East. In this way, Alexander imposed a cultural unity on the Mediterranean region which stimulated trade and learning and which later played a significant part in the advancement of the Roman Empire.

The Roman Empire

In the seventh century BC, Rome was one of several small towns in the Tiber Valley that were situated on a strategically important road leading to saltworks at the mouth of the River Tiber. During the following two centuries, Rome gained control of neighboring territories, including the valuable saltworks, and became a potent force in local politics and commerce. Like other Mediterranean cities in that era, Rome was strongly influenced by Greek culture, but it never came under Greek control.

In the fifth century BC, Rome became a republic ruled by a Senate formed by an aristocratic clique. From that time, Rome gradually expanded its territory to encompass the whole of the Italic peninsula—while Alexander was conquering Persia, Rome was winning decisive battles for the control of southern Italy.

Success in southern Italy encouraged the Romans to seize Sicily, which was then under the

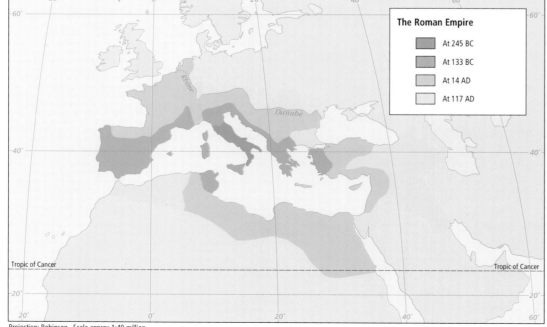

The Roman Empire	
	At 245 BC
	At 133 BC
	At 14 AD
	At 117 AD

Projection: Robinson   Scale approx 1:40 million

This map (left) shows the gradual expansion of the Roman Empire, which reached its greatest extent during the reign of Trajan (AD 98–117). Construction of the Great Wall of China (right) began during the Qin Empire (221–206 BC). Extensive sections of the wall were rebuilt during the fifteenth and sixteenth centuries.

influence of the North African city of Carthage. Over the next 100 years, the Romans fought three major wars—known as the Punic Wars—against Carthage to gain control of the western Mediterranean. By the end of the Third Punic War (146 BC), Carthage had been completely destroyed and Rome had emerged as by far the strongest force in the region. The empire subsequently extended eastward to Greece and the Middle East, where it benefited greatly from Greek advances in art, learning, and technology. Later still, the empire expanded to include large areas of present-day France, Germany, and England, spreading Hellenic culture and Roman political and social institutions across most of Europe.

During the first century BC, the Roman Empire expanded rapidly. Under Pompey, Roman armies seized parts of the Middle East, including Syria (above) in 64 BC; in the west, Julius Caesar (above right) led the conquest of Gaul in 58–50 BC. Both generals subsequently laid claim to the title of emperor. Victory in a short civil war allowed Caesar to begin his reign in 48 BC.

RELIGIONS OF THE WORLD

Religions are a feature of almost all of the world's cultures. They have been the inspiration for much of the world's great art, music, architecture, and literature, but also the source of longstanding disputes and local, regional, and international conflicts.

The tenets and forms of religious belief vary widely. While most religions involve the worship of a deity or deities, supreme beings play only a minor role in some faiths such as Theravada Buddhism. Nor do all religions have practices, core doctrines, and moral codes that are common to every follower. For example, while Hinduism retains a self-identity developed historically through confrontation with other religious traditions such as Buddhism, Islam, and Christianity, it remains extremely diverse internally.

The great majority of the world's religions evolved among particular peoples who had no interest in attracting converts. Few tribal peoples, for instance, would attempt to persuade their neighbors to adopt their religious beliefs and practices. Similarly, some prominent religions such as Hinduism and Judaism make no effort to seek

converts. However, religion is frequently the cause of great social conflict, particularly where two or more proselytizing religions are in competition. Even within religions that have a core doctrine, comparatively minor differences of faith or practice can cause bitter divisions—past tensions between Christian denominations are a good example of this. Frequently, religious conflicts are aggravated by historical factors and by the extent to which religious divisions are overlaid by other divisions, such as language, ethnicity, and class.

World religions

One-third of the world's population identify themselves as Christians, with about half belonging to the Roman Catholic Church. The next largest religious group is Islam, which includes nearly one-fifth of the world's population. These two major faiths are monotheistic—that is, they are based on the belief that there is only one God—and both developed out of Judaism. Hinduism, a non-proselytizing religion followed by almost 13 percent of the world's population, is the third largest faith. Buddhism, which is the third largest proselytizing religion, has approximately 325 million adherents.

Judaism was originally the tribal religion of a people who traced themselves back to Abraham. Abraham is said to have migrated with his clan from the city of Ur in Mesopotamia to Canaan in the eastern Mediterranean. His descendants moved to Egypt, where they were later enslaved, and were

then led back to Canaan by Moses around 1200 BC. Although Judaism has a comparatively small number of contemporary adherents (around 14 million), it is significant both for its role in the development of Christianity and Islam and for its continuing influence on cultural and historical events.

Christianity originated as a movement within Judaism. Fundamental to its doctrine is the belief that Jesus Christ was the Messiah prophesied in the Old Testament. After Christ's crucifixion, Christian doctrines were disseminated throughout the Mediterranean by the apostles and by missionaries, the most prominent of whom was Saint Paul (also known as Saul of Tarsus). Christianity then spread throughout the Roman Empire, first among Jewish communities and then into the general population.

Ethnic religions 4.0%
Sikhism 0.4%
Judaism 0.3%
Christianity 33.0%
Islam 19.6%
Other 4.7%
Buddhism 6.0%
Chinese folk religions 6.2%
Hinduism 12.8%
No religion 13.0%

This pie chart shows the percentages of the world's population belonging to the major religions. Despite their small number, the Jews (above right) have had a major influence on history, culture, and other religions.

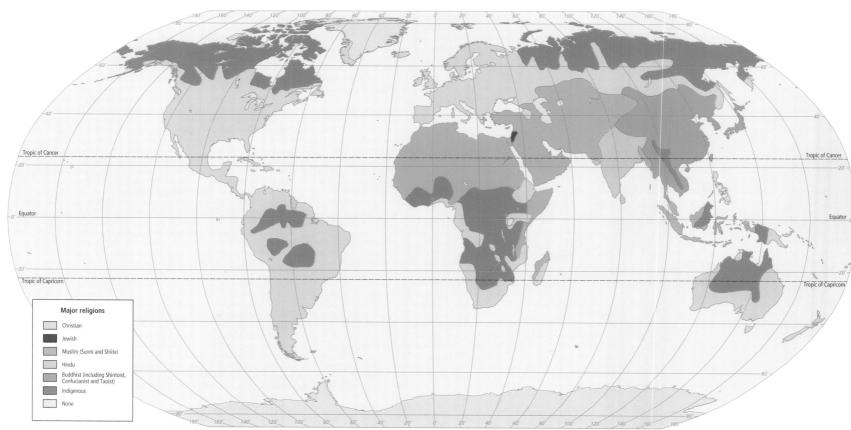

Major religions
- Christian
- Jewish
- Muslim (Sunni and Shiite)
- Hindu
- Buddhist (including Shintoist, Confucianist and Taoist)
- Indigenous
- None

Projection: Robinson   Equatorial Scale approx 1:155 million

Christianity spread rapidly through Europe after the fall of the Roman Empire; churches can be found all over Britain (left). Tibetan Buddhism (below) is based on a tradition called Tantric Buddhism which emerged in India in the seventh century AD. Islam spread to Southeast Asia along trade routes, reaching Malaysia (below left) in the fourteenth century.

Early persecution of Christians by the Romans gave way to tolerance early in the fourth century AD when the Emperor Constantine converted and Christianity became the official state religion. Christianity continued to spread after the fall of the empire in the fifth century, reaching most of Europe by the end of the first millennium. Later, particularly during the era of European expansion in the fifteenth and sixteenth centuries, missionary activity disseminated Christianity to other parts of the world. Over the centuries, theological disputes have resulted in major schisms, out of which have grown the Orthodox, Catholic, Protestant, and other traditions.

Islam was founded early in the seventh century AD by Muhammad, a merchant from the prosperous Arabian city of Mecca. Muhammad had contact with both Jewish and Christian communities, and he came to regard the Judaeo-Christian prophets, including Christ, as forerunners of Islam. After receiving revelations about the worship of one God (Allah), Muhammad began to preach against the polytheistic practices of his home city. Persecution then forced him and his followers to flee to Medina. This migration (Hegira), which took place in AD 622, marks the beginning of the Muslim calendar. By the time of his death in AD 632, Muhammad had become the political and spiritual leader of much of Arabia. After his death, Muslims expanded their territory beyond the Arabian peninsula. At its peak, the Arabic empire stretched from Spain and Morocco in the west to Afghanistan and central Asia in the east, but the Islamic religion was carried even farther into Asia and Africa by Muslim traders.

Eastern deities

Hinduism has its roots in Vedism, the religion of the Indo-European peoples who inhabited northern India during the second millennium BC. The religion's sacred texts are the Vedas which explore humankind's place in the cosmos and describe the roles played by various gods in the functioning of the universe. During the first millennium AD, cults associated with two of these deities, Vishnu and Shiva, spread throughout the continent. Hinduism has a large and faithful following among the diverse peoples of the Indian subcontinent, but it has relatively few adherents elsewhere, except among the descendants of Indian emigrants. This is in part due to its non-proselytizing nature.

Like Christianity and Islam, Buddhism, the third major proselytizing religion, is also based on the religious enlightenment experienced by one man. However, it has much earlier origins. According to tradition, Siddhartha Gautama lived in northeastern India in the sixth century BC, and was reared in the royal household. In his adulthood, Siddhartha is said to have sought enlightenment, which he achieved through a night of meditation, thereby becoming the Buddha or Awakened One. For 45 years he traveled India as an itinerant teacher while formalizing his religious precepts. His teachings spread into southern Asia, where the first Buddhist tradition, the Theravada (meaning "doctrine of the elders"), still prevails in Sri Lanka, Myanmar, Cambodia, Laos, and Thailand. However, it retains few followers in India. Buddhism also spread to the east (Tibet, China, and Japan), where the second tradition, Mahayana (meaning "great vehicle") Buddhism, emerged in the second century BC. A more liberal tradition, Mahayana is said to express greater compassion and social concern than the more aloof Theravada Buddhism.

What is religion?

Scholars have found it extremely difficult to come up with a definition that will allow a clear-cut distinction between religious and non-religious phenomena. In broad terms, religion covers the beliefs and associated practices that focus on the relationship between humans and the supernatural, represented by a god or gods. These beliefs and practices address the ultimate questions of human existence, providing a sense of meaning and purpose to life. Frequently, they also create a feeling of fellowship and community with others who share the same beliefs and practices.

Approached in these terms, religions or religious activity can be found in all, or nearly all, eras and places, although the emphasis placed on religion by particular communities may vary greatly. Scholars have sometimes been surprised to discover that certain tribal or peasant peoples, who might have been assumed to be preoccupied with religion, are in fact relatively indifferent to it.

Religious practices may also have their origins in the need to regulate or control communities. Religion may enforce "taboo" or unacceptable behavior in order to preserve a peaceful and sustainable society.

TRADERS AND TRAVELERS

Humans moved from place to place either individually or in groups long before written records existed. The earliest records show they were impelled by a desire to occupy more fertile areas, by a desire for booty, by an urge to trade, by religious piety which took them on pilgrimages, by a thirst for knowledge, and sometimes by the fear of invasion.

Before the Christian era, Buddhism led monks from the East to travel to India to visit sites where Gautama had been. Nearly 2,000 years later, Ibn Battúta, an Islamic qadi (religious judge), after setting out in AD 1325 to go to Mecca, as all good Mohammedans sought to do, found that he could not rest until he had visited every Muslim state in Asia, Africa, and Europe. Although on his return to Fez, the sultan's court was incredulous at Battúta's stories, they were written down, and in such ways knowledge of the world was spread.

The spread and decline of empires

The growth of empires fostered trade and treaties, both with neighbors and with more distant powers. The Han Empire in China, for example, traded with Phoenicians, Carthaginians, Syrians, and the Roman Empire in silks, iron, furs, glass, and other exotic goods. Merchants also brought back knowledge—in the first century AD, a Greek navigator wrote of the Indian Ocean, where Hindu traders competed with merchants from the Red Sea and Arabs dealing in wax and ivory, rhinoceros horns, tortoiseshell, and palm oil.

However, nomads were always pressing at the frontiers of such empires, seeking to loot and ransack. Loose confederations of "barbarians"—as the civilized empires considered them—hungry for plunder, breached the defences. The Roman

Empire bought their "barbarians" off for a time by settling some on the borders, as confederates, to keep out other tribes, but eventually pressures caused the Empire's defences to tumble. In AD 410, Rome itself was overrun.

The influx of mixed Germanic tribes was precipitated by the driving force of the Huns, who, according to the Goths, were the offspring of witches and evil spirits. No one knows where they originated. From the Carpathian mountains, however, they moved into the Mediterranean region and, by AD 450, under Attila, were poised to crush and drive out the Goths. Then their alliances crumbled, and they disappeared from Europe as quickly as they had come.

Instead, waves of Ostrogoths, Visigoths, Franks, and Saxons arrived and settled in England, France, Spain, Italy, and parts of North Africa, mixing with the local inhabitants, quarrelling amongst themselves and moving on to settle in new areas.

The Arab Empire

While Western Europe was fragmented and trade was declining, in the East, the Byzantine Empire remained the bulwark of Christianity against the rising Arab Empire. Mohammed's followers were spurred on by the idea of jihad, or Holy war, which combined religion with military exploits. After taking Syria and Egypt, they swept along the North African coast, took the Maghrib, and crossed into Spain. They attacked Byzantium by sea and blockaded Constantinople between AD 673 and 678. In the eighth century, the Caliphs of Damascus and Baghdad ruled an empire that stretched from Persia to Morocco.

The Arabs were also starting to dominate Africa by the eighth century. The peoples of the plateau

between the Niger and the Benin had mined and used gold and copper, and later iron, long before Christ. Exotic archaeological finds and the presence of Asian food plants clearly show that trade began early in these areas. Tribal organization became more sophisticated, in order to control and tax trade and the trade routes. By the eighth century, empires such as Ghana had emerged. The Arabs had been pushing their way down the east coast of Africa well before Mohammed. They visited trading posts such as Sofala and dealt with the inland kingdoms, exchanging exotic goods for gold. After AD 700, they began colonizing the coast, establishing settlements such as Mogadishu and Mombasa. They also moved south across the Sahara, and established Arabic kingdoms.

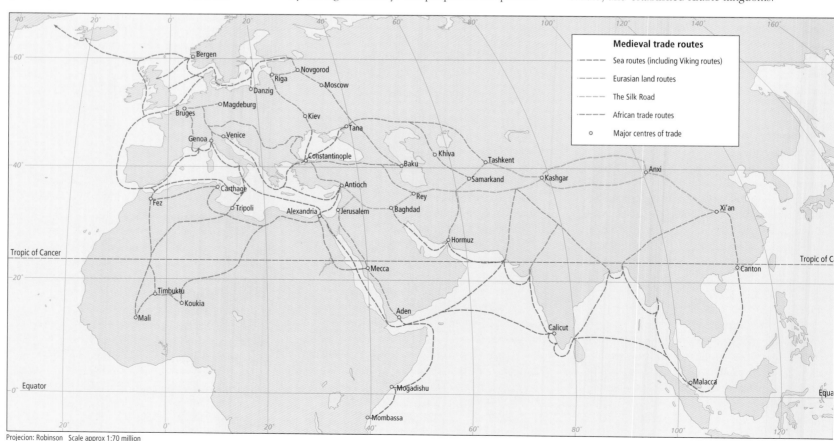

Medieval trade routes

- - - - - Sea routes (including Viking routes)
- - - - - Eurasian land routes
- - - - - The Silk Road
- - - - - African trade routes
- ○ Major centres of trade

Projecion: Robinson Scale approx 1:70 million

Viking graves in Denmark (far left) are a reminder of the early European territorial wars. Khiva (left) was a trading post on the trade route between East and West. Zanzibar (below), an island south of Mombassa, was for many years the center of the slave trade in Africa. Venice today (bottom), is not the major trading power it was in the thirteenth century.

The Arabs next pushed east across the Indian Ocean, carrying Islam to India and overwhelming the Hindu trading colonies of Sumatra, Java, and Borneo, and eventually acquiring a firm footing in Canton and other major Chinese cities.

The Chinese Empire

In the period after the Han, successive empires had been established in China, some ruled by nomad invaders. The Tang had subdued their neighbors and ruled from Korea to the frontiers of Persia. They had also established extensive links with the West. When Canton was sacked in 879, the slaughtered included large numbers of Nestorian Christians, Arabs, Jews, and Zoroastrians.

Western Europe

In the eighth century, driven by population pressure, Vikings settlers from Scandinavia set out along the inland rivers to Constantinople to fight for the Emperor, and by sea in longboats to prey upon the coasts of Northern Europe. Sturdy fighters and skilled sailors, the Vikings explored the western routes via Iceland and Greenland towards the American continent, perhaps even landing there. In time, they settled—in Scotland, Ireland, northern England, and Normandy—and turned to trading.

After the spread of the Arab Empire had been halted in the West by the battle of Poitiers in 732, a new and fragile balance of power saw trade reviving in Western Europe. In 1095, the West felt strong enough to challenge Islam for possession of Jerusalem, and two centuries of Crusades (religious wars) began. The Crusades, however, did not hinder the growing trade in the Mediterranean.

Merchants sought protection behind city walls and, by the twelfth century, fought for the right to govern themselves as independent communities. In Italy, luxury goods brought overland from the mythic Eastern lands of India and Cathay could now be imported from the Near Eastern ports. Genoa, Florence, and Venice became the starting point for travelers and pilgrims going to Jerusalem.

In the north, cities along the great rivers and the Baltic coasts joined in a federation called the Hanse to strengthen their power and regulate trade in the fish and forest products they exported.

Even so, it was the Arabs who could move freely and upon whose knowledge the West relied—few Western merchants traveled to Asia.

The Mongols

Paradoxically, it was the Mongols who reopened the great land trade routes to the West and enabled Western merchants and missionaries to visit the East. The nomads who inhabited the great steppes were united by Genghis Khan in the first part of the thirteenth century into a powerful empire, with its capital at Korokaras. The Mongol hordes provided an extremely effective army, whose tactics left all who faced it outmatched—so much so that that it was seen as an instrument of divine will and punishment. They annexed Russia, ravaged Hungary, overwhelmed China, and set up the Mongol Empire. This empire was ruled in Marco Polo's time by Kublai Khan, whose ambitions stretched to conquering Java and Japan.

In 1258, the Mongols defeated the Turks and took Iraq and Persia. They controlled communications between these centers and enticed or forced skilled workers and traders to live with them.

It was only when the Mongols were eventually converted to Islam and became more sedentary that the Ottoman Turks were able to retake the Arabic Empire and once again cut off Western travelers from land routes to India and China.

Marco Polo

Marco Polo, a thirteenth-century Venetian, is possibly the most famous of early Western travelers. His journey to the Mongol Empire followed a long trading journey that his father and his uncle had made. He learnt Mongolian, and for many years served as an official for the emperor Kublai Khan. His account of his travels, which he dictated while in prison after having been captured by the Genoese, was the major source of Western knowledge of the Far East until the nineteenth century.

EXPLORERS AND SETTLERS

Carrying goods by water may have been cheap in the days of the great empires, but it was fraught with difficulties. Sailing out of sight of land required astronomical and mathematical skills, and sophisticated instruments. The combination of wind, tide, and current with a difficult and rocky shore could be a lethal one.

At the height of the era of world exploration, no one ruled the seas, and pirates were a constant threat. Many of the most honored explorers, such as Vasco da Gama, Alfonso de Albuquerque, and Francis Drake, were also pirates. Seaborne empires such as that of Sri Vijaya had existed before, but during this time, the European empires were unparalleled in their domination of the oceans.

Early explorers
The disruption of overland trade that occurred as a result of the Turks taking Constantinople in 1453 stimulated the search for sea routes to the east. Portugal had long been pushing down the western coast of Africa, albeit slowly, and had established a military hold on that coast which excluded traders from other countries. In 1488, Bartholomew Dias reached the Cape of Good Hope.

Many had sailed west from Europe by this time, and all had been lost. But in 1492, Christopher Columbus found a route and, upon his return, brought the unexpected news of "unknown lands" which were not part of Asia. However, the eastward passage was still of more immediate promise, and in 1497, Vasco da Gama, with the help of an Arab pilot, penetrated the Arab-dominated Indian Ocean.

In an epic voyage that took from 1519 to 1522, Ferdinand Magellan, sailing westward, showed that the world was indeed round. French, Dutch, and English explorers and seafarers were soon blocking the Spanish and Portuguese attempts to monopolize these trading routes.

Southeast Asia
In Asia, trade was the primary objective of exploration. The existing highly developed, wealthy, sophisticated empires were largely invulnerable. However, Portuguese merchants, in well-armed ships, and protected by forts and royal fleets, did succeed in competing with the established Arab merchants.

In 1500, the Portuguese obtained trading rights on the west coast of India. In 1510, they settled in Malacca, the great emporium from which ships went to Borneo, Ternate, Tidore, and Amboina, and eventually to China and Japan. About 1565, the Spanish established an alternative route, with ships regularly crossing the Pacific to the Philippines. As the market for spices became saturated, trade in gold, ivory, silks, Indian cotton textiles, Chinese porcelain, tea, and coffee developed. By 1600, the Dutch and English East India companies had entered the competition, and eventually the Dutch controlled most of the spice trade from Batavia.

For more than two centuries, the costs of governing a distant state restricted colonization. In India, for instance, the British East India Company hesitated to assume direct rule until pushed by French competition. Only in the nineteenth century did direct rule become common.

South and Central America
The discovery of gold, silver, pearls, and industrial raw materials made the Americas attractive to the Europeans. The conquest of the Aztec and Inca

empires enabled Spain to establish its rule from the Caribbean to Mexico, Peru, and Chile, while the Portuguese colonized Brazil. A steady trickle of fortune hunters from Spanish dominions in Europe took over the land and its inhabitants, causing an economic and cultural transformation. Despite the humanitarian protests of missionaries, exploitation of local labor, plus epidemics and diseases brought by the Europeans resulted in up to 95 percent of the indigenous population dying.

African slaves were imported to work the mines whose silver had such profound effects on sixteenth-century Europe. Sugar, cotton, and tobacco production also required intensive labor, and so the slave trade grew. Hides, indigo, cochineal, forest products, dyes, and drugs also

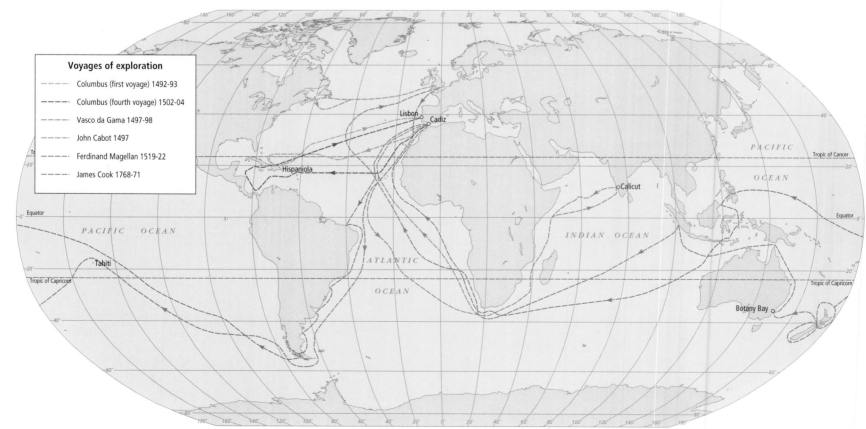

Voyages of exploration
- Columbus (first voyage) 1492-93
- Columbus (fourth voyage) 1502-04
- Vasco da Gama 1497-98
- John Cabot 1497
- Ferdinand Magellan 1519-22
- James Cook 1768-71

Projection: Robinson Equatorial Scale approx 1:110 million

Internal conflicts between groups who consider themselves to be of a separate nation can lead to a state fragmenting into smaller ones, as in the former Yugoslavia (right). Indian Sikhs on parade (below right): the world's largest democracy is home to a wide range of ethnic groups.

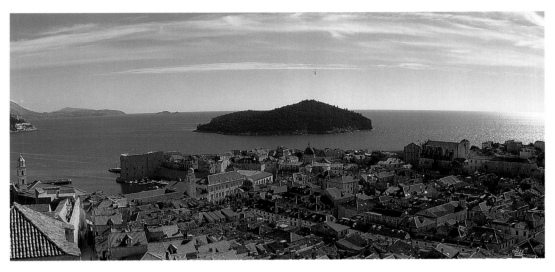

contemporary political map of the world have their origins in two major phases of decolonization.

The first phase unfolded over the half-century following the American War of Independence in 1776. About 100 colonies combined to form the current nation-states in the Americas. Little further decolonization occurred for more than a century, until around the time of the Second World War. Notable exceptions were the British settler colonies of Canada, Australia, and South Africa. The second major phase of decolonization began after the Second World War, when "the winds of change" blew through Africa, South and Southeast Asia, and islands in the Caribbean and the Pacific and Indian Oceans. This resulted in the formation of another approximately 110 nation-states.

Nation-states continued to be created in the 1990s—15 nations were created as a result of the break-up of the Soviet Union in 1991, for example. Eritrea, Slovenia, Croatia, and Macedonia became independent in 1991, as did the Czech Republic, Slovakia, and Namibia in 1994. The final outcome of the break-up of Yugoslavia is still uncertain. Internal ethnic tension in some areas has grown enormously, and ethnic-based nationalist movements continue to emerge. This kind of conflict is currently the most common—of the 89 armed conflicts that occurred between 1989 and 1992, only 3 were between nations.

At the same time, in Europe, where the nation-state first began, the European Union, a supra-

national regional state, continues to transform the European political landscape. Most of Western Europe has now been combined within the European Union, while a number of other European states have applied for admission and await entry. Some commentators see the European Union as the beginning of the end of the territorial nation-state as we have known it; it has undoubtedly changed long-held ideas on what makes a nation.

New European democracies
- New European democracies
- Existing democracies
- International border

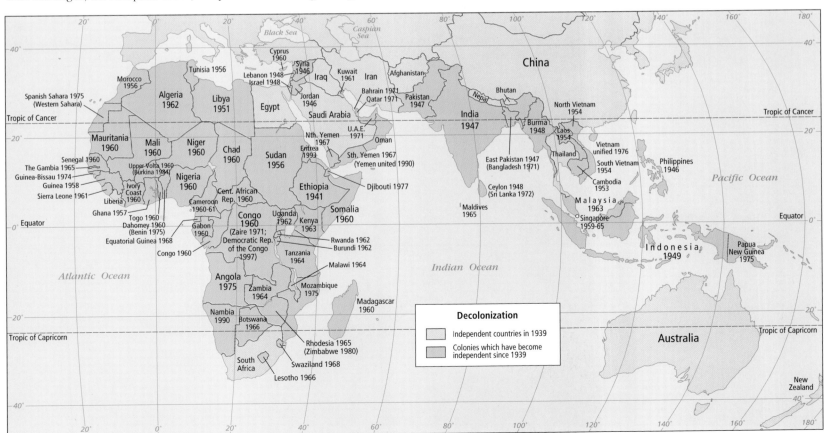

Decolonization
- Independent countries in 1939
- Colonies which have become independent since 1939

INTERNATIONAL ORGANIZATIONS

During the second half of the twentieth century, international organizations, including intergovernmental and nongovernmental bodies, have grown significantly in both number and stature. Today, there are about 500 inter-governmental organizations, such as the United Nations (UN) and the International Monetary Fund (IMF), and approximately 5,000 nongovernmental organizations (NGOs), including the Red Cross and Amnesty International. That represents roughly five times the number that were active at the end of the Second World War.

International organizations form an important part of the social glue that binds the nations and peoples of the world together. They create a set of rules, norms, and procedures—encapsulated in international law, particularly in the form of treaties and conventions signed by nation-states— that define the expected conduct of participants in the international community.

United Nations

The largest and most influential intergovernmental organization is the United Nations. Its predecessor was the League of Nations, which was founded at the end of the First World War, in an attempt to prevent further international conflict. Based in Geneva, the League gradually expanded its membership and became a focus for growing numbers of nongovernmental bodies. However, the refusal of the United States to ratify the League's covenant, and the League's inability to prevent expansion by Germany, Italy, and Japan in the 1930s led to its ceasing operations during the Second World War.

The United Nations (UN) was established in San Francisco in 1946, and now has its headquarters in New York. As with the League of Nations, the main motivation for the creation of the UN was collective security. Half a century later, the membership of the UN has grown to 185, and only a small number of nations (such as Switzerland and Taiwan) and territories (including French Polynesia and the Channel Islands) are not formal member states.

On the world stage, the UN is critically important, but relatively weak and often controversial. At times it has appeared to be an impotent and ineffective institution that more resembles a debating society for the superpowers, their client states, and major power blocs than anything remotely like a "world government."

It is, of course, important to remember that the UN is not a world government, in that its member-states remain independent and sovereign entities. Furthermore, most of the member states clearly have an ambivalent attitude towards the organization. For example, the Norwegians are strong supporters of the UN, but refuse to accept

Refugees in the Sudan (below) and the young Somali girl (left) are likely to receive assistance from international organizations—via UN peacekeeping forces.

UN directives on whaling. The USA frequently seeks UN support for military intervention abroad, but constantly defers payment of its UN dues. Resulting financial difficulties hamper UN operations. Even after the Cold War, when it seemed to have grown enormously in importance and stature, the UN operated on about the same budget as the Tokyo fire department.

During the half-century following the establishment of the UN, other collective issues, including environmental, economic, and legal issues, have been placed under the umbrella of the intergovernmental system. For example, the World Bank and the International Monetary Fund (IMF) have become responsible for managing a wide variety of international economic issues: the IMF coordinates international currency exchange and the balance of international payments, and the World Bank borrows the savings of rich nations and lends them to poor nations under conditions not available on the private capital markets.

Nongovernmental organizations

Nongovernmental organizations (NGOs) are private organizations that are today regarded as legitimate players on the world stage alongside nation-states and intergovernmental organizations. Generally, however, NGOs have significantly less power and far fewer financial resources.

Most NGOs are primarily concerned with the empowerment of marginal and impoverished sectors of the world's population through increasing those people's participation in resolving their own problems. NGOs tend to focus upon specific issues. For example, Greenpeace raises awareness of environmental issues, Planned Parenthood campaigns for reproductive rights and family planning, groups such as the International Federation of the Red Cross and the Red Crescent Societies provide disaster relief, and Médecins Sans Frontières provides medical care.

International organizations and human rights

Human rights is one highly significant area where international organizations have created the emerging rules, norms, and legal instruments that link nations and their citizens together in an embryonic worldwide system. Human rights are the laws, customs, and practices that have evolved to protect people, minorities, groups, and races from oppressive rulers and governments.

Before the Second World War, international human rights issues were restricted to matters such as slavery or armed conflict, and discussions about human rights (and recognition of them) took place mainly within the borders of particular nation-states. A turning point in the history of human rights occurred on December 10, 1948, when the Universal Declaration of Human Rights was adopted by the General Assembly of the UN without a dissenting vote.

Over the next half-century, major advances were made. Most significantly, a series of international covenants was drafted and adopted

A land rights protest in Australia (above). International human rights organizations are increasingly exerting pressure on governments to recognize indigenous peoples' rights.

by the UN and subsequently ratified by individual nation-states. Once ratified by a nation-state, the human rights legislation was usually incorporated within the state's own legal system.

Although the UN has been prominent in human rights legislation, private individuals and nongovernmental organizations such as Amnesty International have frequently provided the political pressure that has persuaded intergovernmental and national agencies to act. Often, though, such action has been taken only reluctantly and retro-spectively. The fact that countless millions of people have suffered (and many still do) terrible violations of their rights as human beings, even since the Declaration of Human Rights, is some-thing of an indictment of the Declaration and of the UN's ability and will to enforce it. Most observers still regard the Declaration of Human Rights as inadequate and in need of enforcement. Its emergence, and the opportunity it created to bring such issues to world attention, are one positive result of the growth in importance of international organizations. While this has certainly produced a world that is better than it was, it is still by no means all that it could be.

Again, the ambivalent attitudes of nation-states to international organizations is a significant factor, affecting their ability to function effectively. For example, when concerns about human rights in Afghanistan were raised by the UN and NGO representatives in 1998, the ruling Taliban militia asked the organizations to leave the country. Yet, when it appeared that Iran may be ready to invade Afghanistan to protect some of its own citizens, the Taliban sought support from the UN to keep Iran out. At the end of the twentieth century, the idea of setting up global governance is still on the world's agenda, but only just.

THE UNITED NATIONS SYSTEM

International Court of Justice   **Secretariat**   **Trusteeship Council**

General Assembly   **Security Council**
Committees   *Peacekeeping Operations*
International Tribunals
Military Staff Committees
Standing Committees

Economic and Social Council (ECOSOC)

UN Programs:

INSTRAW	UN International Research and Training Institute for the Advancement of Women
ITC	International Trade Center
UNCHS	UN Center for Human Habitats
UNCTAD	UN Conference on Trade and Development
UNDCP	UN Drug Control Program
UNDP	UN Development Program
UNEP	UN Environment Program
UNFPA	UN Fund for Population Activities
UNHCF	UN High Commission for Refugees
UNICEF	UN Children's Emergency Fund
UNIFEM	UN Development Fund for Women
UNITAR	UN Institute for Training and Research*
UNU	UN University
WFP	World Food Program
WFC	World Food Council

Functional Commissions

Regional Commissions

Standing Committees

Expert Bodies

Specialized Agencies:

FAO	Food and Agriculture Organization, Rome
ICAO	International Civil Aviation Organization, Montreal
IFAD	International Fund for Agricultural Development, Rome
ILO	International Labor Organization, Geneva
IMF	International Monetary Fund, Washington
IMO	International Maritime Organization, London
ITU	International Telecom-munications Union, Geneva
UNESCO	UN Educational, Scientific, and Cultural Organization, Paris
UNIDO	UN Industrial Development Organization, Vienna
UPU	Universal Postal Union, Berne
WHO	World Health Organization, Geneva
WIPO	World Intellectual Property Organization, Geneva
WMO	World Meteorological Association, Geneva
WTO	World Trade Organization, Geneva*

World Bank Group, Washington

IBRD	International Bank for Reconstruction and Development
IDA	International Development Association
IFC	International Finance Corporation
MIGA	Multilateral Investment Guarantee Agency

* Does not report to ECOSOC

GLOBALIZATION

Globalization refers to a change of scale in human processes and activities which has occurred during the last quarter of a century—one in which the nation-state is giving way, in many fields, to global organizations. Until recently, it was generally felt that human and environmental affairs could and should be conducted at a national level. Nation-states were, in principle at least, sovereign or independent units. Of course, nation-states had relations with one another, and these were referred to as international, as in the terms "international trade" and "international relations." In the 1990s, however, "international" and "internationalization" have been increasingly replaced by "global" and "globalization," as national boundaries have begun to seem less significant in economic, political, cultural, and environmental terms.

The global economy

Transnational corporations—companies that operate in a large number of countries—are the movers and shakers of the modern global economy. Among the firms with operations that are nearly worldwide are Exxon and Royal Dutch Shell in petroleum; McDonalds, Seagrams, Sara Lee, Nabisco and Nestlé in food and beverages; BMW, Ford, Volkswagen, and General Motors in automobiles; and Mitsubishi and Mitsui in banking, manufacturing, and trade.

Although few (if any) companies can be described as truly global at this time—most still focus on certain markets and report to share-holders in their home country—the term "global" is commonly used in business circles to identify a level of operations that many companies hope to attain in the not-too-distant future. This would involve a truly international workforce, share-holders in a number of nation-states, and products that are sold in all markets.

The flow of money from country to country is also encouraging the surge in economic global-ization. National boundaries are no barrier to the movement of funds; thanks to modern telecom-munications and computer technology, funds can now be rapidly transferred to any part of the globe. Such transactions have, it now appears, created a much more volatile and less secure world. In a matter of weeks in the middle of 1997, the Asian economic miracle became the Asian economic meltdown as a result of the massive and rapid withdrawal of global funds.

The phenomenal growth of the Internet has created opportunities for even small companies to operate at a global level. By selling goods via the World Wide Web, a firm can now compete in markets where it could not previously have established a presence, whether for geographical, political, or financial reasons. Governments are struggling to cope with the implications of this for the regulation of trade within their countries. How, for example, do they impose sales taxes on goods or services that are purchased in the virtual market of cyberspace?

Many commentators assert that globalization will transform the world economy in the twenty-first century, leaving no national products, no national corporations, no national industries, and no national economies. To succeed in the global marketplace, countries will have to depend entirely on the skills of their inhabitants, and will have to deal with powerful external forces that could create an ever-widening gulf between skilled, globally aware citizens and a growing unskilled, out-of-touch underclass.

World politics

The globalization of politics has resulted in the decline of the nation-state and the growth of international organizations. Although they remain the principal players on the world political stage, nation-states now appear less independent and less sovereign than they used to. One response to this has been to look to international organizations such as the United Nations to assume some of the roles previously played by nation-states.

Perhaps the most significant political event in the 1990s was the end of the Cold War. During the Cold War (1946–91), most nation-states belonged to one of three geopolitical worlds: the First World, consisting of developed capitalist nations, and dominated by the USA; the Second World, consisting of developed communist nations, and dominated by the Soviet Union; and the Third World, consisting of developing nations that were in theory not aligned with either of the super-powers. The demise of the Cold War brought an end to these divisions, and created a geopolitical situation no longer driven by the rivalry of two opposing superpowers.

Some commentators believe that this has created a vacuum, where no effectively organized power system exists. In the past, when major geopolitical shifts occurred, one dominant power was typically replaced by another: Great Britain (as the United Kingdom then was) replaced Amsterdam, and the USA later replaced the United Kingdom. Globalization has produced a world so complex and integrated that it no longer seems possible for a single nation-state to play the dominant role that these nations once played. The growing emphasis on and allocation of power to international organizations can be seen as an attempt to fill this power vacuum.

The global village

Discussions of the globalization of culture often begin with the expression "global village," a term coined in the 1960s by Marshall McLuhan, an American commentator. He believed that television would replace the printed word as the primary medium of wider social integration, eventually uniting the people of the world through their collective participation in media events. In the 1990s, events such as the Gulf War, the annual Academy Awards, the death of an English princess, and certain sporting competitions were watched on television by people in almost all the world's countries—an audience of between 1 and 2 billion people.

Dealings on the Tokyo Stock Exchange (right) can affect the economy of many other countries; financial centers such as Chicago (below) are experiencing the globalization of trade.

The fact that a rapidly growing number of people are involved in maintaining the global village raises a number of questions. For instance, will globalization mean an inevitable cultural homogenization? Opinion is sharply divided on this question. A great deal of evidence supports the view that a global culture is developing. On the other hand, powerful movements which actively resist this cultural homogenization have also emerged—militant Islamic, Hindu, and Zionist organizations, for example.

One issue that has played a major role in raising awareness of the ways in which we truly are a global community is the environment. The first Earth Day in 1970 marked the beginning of mass awareness of the global significance of environmental issues. Over the next three decades, evidence of the extent of degradation of Earth's natural environment caused by human activity has mounted. This has forced governments and individuals to examine their impact on the natural world, and has encouraged political cooperation at a global level to effect change.

A series of international environmental forums have been held, including Stockholm (1972), the Earth Summit at Rio de Janeiro (1992), and the Population Conference at Cairo (1994). All stressed the worldwide and interconnected nature of the growing environmental crisis. The Earth Summit was attended by an unprecedented 130 heads of state, 1,500 nongovernmental organizations, and 7,000 accredited journalists. However, despite the willingness of many nations to discuss these issues globally, the desire or ability to act locally may be absent.

The slogan "Think globally, act locally" has been widely employed to express the scale shift involved in this transformation of economics, politics, culture, and nature—from what used to be thought local or national concepts to what are now recognized as (or have become) international, global concerns.

Globalization may prove to be the key change in the twenty-first century.

Advertising signs in this village in Peru (below) are an example of the penetration of multi-national corporations into a developing country.

Oceania and Antarctica

Asia and the Middle East

1.8 MILLION BP Hominids of *Homo erectus* species living in Java, Indonesia

Skull of Homo erectus

130,000 BP *Homo neanderthalensis* (Neanderthals) living in western Asia; they have social organization and hunt using strategy and cooperation

1.9 MILLION BP Modern hominids resembling *Homo habilis* living in caves in Sichuan Province, China

800,000 BP *Homo erectus* using simple rafts on Indonesian island of Flores

460,000 BP Earliest known controlled use of fire at Zhoukoudian Cave, China

90,000 BP *Homo sapiens sapiens* present at several sites in Israel

Europe and the Russian Federation

780,000 BP Tool-using hominids living in northern Spain. Classified as *Homo heidelbergensis*, they may have been the ancestors of Neanderthals

130,000 BP Emergence of *Homo neanderthalensis* (Neanderthals); they have social organization and hunt using strategy and cooperation

1.5 MILLION BP Hominids arrive from Africa

500,000 BP Archaic *Homo sapiens* appears in Europe

100,000 BP Neanderthals burying their dead; possibly using burial rituals and decorating graves

Africa

4.0 MILLION BP Earliest recognizable hominid (form of human), *Australopithecus ramidus*, living in southern and eastern Africa

3.0 MILLION BP Hominids living in caves in southern Africa feeding on plants and animals

2.3 MILLION BP Emergence of *Homo habilis* in East Africa, a hominid associated with first use of crude stone tools

1.5 MILLION BP Hominids spread northward, crossing Sahara Desert region at time of abundant vegetation

Skull of Homo ergaster

150,000–100,000 BP Modern humans, *Homo sapiens sapiens*, appear in various parts of Africa and begin to migrate northward

5.0 MILLION BP The southern ape (Australopithecine) family splits into three branches, which will slowly evolve into gorillas, chimpanzees, and humans

3.5 MILLION BP Footprints left at Laetoli, Tanzania, by *Australopithecus afarensis*, a hominid that walks upright

1.9 MILLION BP Hominids of more modern appearance, *Homo ergaster*, appear in Africa, probably evolving from *Homo habilis*

800,000 BP Archaic *Homo sapiens* evolves in Africa

200,000 BP Anatomically modern humans, distinguished by larger brain and use of more sophisticated tools, inhabit a number of cave sites in southern Africa

North and Central America

South America

40,000 BP Rock art appears in Australia; many early works consist of simple patterned engravings etched in rock

30,000 BP Earliest evidence of cremation at Lake Mungo, southeastern Australia

Seafaring groups inhabit the islands east of New Guinea

18,000 BP Rock paintings appear in Arnhem Land, northwestern Australia

Obsidian is traded in the Bismarck Archipelago, Melanesia

8000 BP Land bridge between New Guinea and Australia is submerged

Sharpened kangaroo femur, 12,000 BP

60,000–40,000 BP *Homo sapiens sapiens* enters Australia and New Guinea from Southeast Asia, possibly by raft or canoe—the earliest known seaworthy vessels

35,000 BP Humans hunting wallabies on grasslands of Tasmania, Australia

28,000 BP Buka Island in the Solomons group is colonized

25,000 BP Stone blades and hatchet tools in use in northern Australia and New Guinea

9000 BP Crops including bananas, taro, and sugar-cane cultivated in New Guinea

---

68,000 BP *Homo sapiens sapiens* living in parts of China

Neanderthal skull

20,000 BP Modern humans (*Homo sapiens sapiens*) migrate across Eurasia as far as Siberia

11,000 BP Cultivation of domesticated grains such as wheat and barley in the Fertile Crescent

9500 BP Evidence of rice cultivation in central China

9000 BP Crops including sesame and eggplant are cultivated in the Indus Valley

Pigs domesticated in Anatolia, Turkey

40,000 BP Neanderthals disappear from the fossil record in western Asia

Jomon pot, 12,500–9,500 BP

12,000 BP Dogs domesticated in southwestern Asia

12,500 BP Jomon people of Japan produce the world's first clay vessels

10,000 BP Cattle domesticated in Anatolia, in present-day Turkey

8500 BP Smelting of copper, gold, and lead in south-western Asia

7500 BP Pottery is produced in China

50,000 BP Simple engravings carved on cave walls in eastern Europe

35,000 BP Neanderthals disappear from the fossil record, perhaps displaced by *Homo sapiens sapiens*

Appearance of Cro-Magnon peoples, noted for their use of bone tools and sewn hides

15,000 BP First evidence of use of watercraft in the Mediterranean

14,000 BP Elaborate huts of interlocked mammoth bones built to provide shelter during winter at Mezhirich, Ukraine

8000 BP Permanent farming settlements established in southeastern Europe

Sidescraper tool from France, 70,000–35,000 BP

Austrian fertility figure, 20,000 BP

40,000 BP *Homo sapiens sapiens* arrives from Africa, bringing more sophisticated tools and skills

32,000 BP First cave art appears in southwestern France and northern Spain

15,000–12,000 BP Magdalenian phase, during which most of the best-known cave art is produced, including the galleries of Lascaux, France, and Altamira, Spain

10,500 BP Beginning of colonization of Mediterranean islands, which takes 4,000 years

---

23,000 BP Rock paintings on inland shelters show ceremonial dancers and herds of game animals, including antelope

9000 BP Pottery containers in use in settled areas of the Nile Valley, Egypt

Skull of Homo sapiens sapiens

25,000 BP Paintings on rock slabs made by Stone Age hunter-gatherers in Namibia show animals such as elephants and giraffes

12,000 BP Rock carvings in the Sahara Desert, in present-day Algeria, depict North African aurochs

8000 BP Crops including figs and chufa are cultivated in the Nile Valley, Egypt

---

North American Clovis point tool, c.11,500 BP

12,000 BP Date of earliest reliable evidence of human habitation of North America, found at sites in Alaska

11 000 BP Numerous human settlements appear across present-day United States

Humans hunt mammoths at Clovis, New Mexico

Dogs domesticated

35,000–12,000 BP *Homo sapiens sapiens* enters North America across Bering Strait land bridge between Asia and present-day Alaska, and spreads southward

14,500 BP Disputed date for evidence of human habitation at Meadowcroft Shelter in southwestern Pennsylvania; site includes firepits, stone tools, and plaited basketry

10,000 BP Hunters use trenches to trap and kill bison at Casper, Wyoming

9,000 BP Native peoples of Mesoamerica begin to collect plants more intensively, perhaps beginning domestication

---

12,500 BP Humans inhabiting Monte Verde in southern Chile; evidence includes stone tools, animal skins on poles, and plant remains

12,000 BP Well-organized hunter-gatherers living in the cold high-altitude puna grasslands of modern-day Peru, feeding on plants and vicuñas (a relative of the llama)

8,500 BP Beans and chili peppers cultivated in central Andes

Monte Verde hut, 12,500 BP

25,000 BP Disputed date for evidence of human habitation of eastern South America, including Pedra Furada in Brazil

11,000 BP Humans inhabit Cueva Fell, Tierra del Fuego, southern Chile

10,000 BP Potatoes cultivated in the Andes of present-day Bolivia

Oceania and Antarctica

4000 BC Pig husbandry and vegetable growing (mainly taro) in mainland New Guinea

Forest cleared on the Bismarck Archipelago to increase agricultural production

3600 BC Simple pottery is made on Vanimo coast of northern New Guinea

1500 BC Fiji is settled by Lapita people

Lapita pottery, c.1100 BC

4500–4000 BC People living on High Cliffy Island off Western Australia build stone structures as dwellings or for ceremonial purposes

3500 BC Giant clam-shell adzes in use in Sepik-Ramu basin of New Guinea

2500 BC "Saltwater" people of the Kimberley Coast region of northwestern Australia use fire-hardened spears for fishing

1600 BC Austronesian colonization of New Guinea and the Bismarck Archipelago followed by emergence of Lapita culture, named for its distinctive pottery bearing complex geometric designs

1200 BC Lapita people colonize New Caledonia, Tonga, Samoa

Asia and the Middle East

4200 BC Copper and bronze being worked in Mesopotamia

3500 BC Small cities based on earlier farming communities appear in Sumer, the southern part of Mesopotamia

2400 BC Harappa civilization merges diverse cultures in the Indus Valley; Harappan building methods involve use of bricks and architectural planning

1800 BC Indo-Europeans spread to the Middle East and eastern Mediterranean

1500 BC The Aryans, an Indo-European people, migrate from central Asia to northern India

1290 BC Traditional date for Moses leading the Hebrews from slavery in Egypt back to tribal lands in Canaan (Palestine)

3000 BC Sumerians develop a writing system consisting of pictograms pressed in clay tablets; they also develop the first wheeled vehicles

People from southern Asia (Austronesians) begin expansion south and east into the Philippines, eastern Indonesia, and New Guinea

5000 BC First settlements appear in Mesopotamia, the fertile area between the Tigris and Euphrates rivers

4000 BC Sailing ships in use in Mesopotamia

2200 BC Semites migrate from Arabia to Mesopotamia and found Babylonian and Assyrian kingdoms

1595 BC The Hittites, a powerful Indo-European people from Hattusas in present-day Turkey, sack Babylon; by 1500 BC they control all of Asia Minor

1200 BC Writing system based on pictograms in use in China

2500 BC Rice farming reaches southern China

Europe and the Russian Federation

4000 BC Farming reaches northern Europe

Horses domesticated in the Ukraine; they become the main means of transport throughout Europe and Asia and confer major advantages in battle

Dolmen, large standing stones usually topped by a horizontal stone, are erected in Scandinavia

2500 BC Rise of Minoan civilization—Europe's first—on the island of Crete and in surrounding Aegean region

1800 BC Stone circle at Stonehenge, Wiltshire, England, completed; work may have started as early as 3500 BC

1600–1500 BC Minoan centers destroyed by invaders or earthquakes

Rise of Mycenaean civilization on Greek mainland

Poulnabrone tomb, Ireland, 3000 BC

5000 BC Earliest evidence of burials in Scandinavia

Land bridge between Britain and Europe submerged by rising sea levels

Copper in use in southeastern Europe

1650 BC Writing systems known as Linear A and Linear B in use in Crete and mainland Greece; Linear A is a Minoan script, whereas Linear B constitutes an early form of Mycenaean Greek

1250–1200 BC Mycenean centers destroyed by conflict or earthquakes

Africa

4000 BC People living in central Sudan in loosely organized communities, tending cattle, sheep, and goats as well as continuing to hunt and fish

Copper smelting in Egypt

2650 BC Nile Valley civilization flourishes; pyramids constructed during this period are the most elaborate burial tomb structures to date

2000 BC Kingdom of Kush established in middle Nile Valley

Invention of the water wheel in Egypt

1333–1323 BC Tutankhamun reigns as Pharaoh of Egypt, coming to the throne at age nine and ruling from Memphis near Cairo with the help of regent, Ay

3000 BC Donkeys used for farming in the Nile Valley

First scientific astronomy observations in Egypt and Babylonia

Yams and palm oil domesticated in tropical West Africa

Beginning of Bantu expansion from West Africa into Congo Basin

5000 BC Growth of Nubian settlement in the Nile Valley; agricultural methods begin to spread southward

2200 BC Ducks and geese domesticated in Egypt

1500 BC Trade routes between North Africa and the rest of Africa are disrupted by the spread of the Sahara Desert

Egyptians conquer Kush

1290 BC Rock temples of Abu Simbel built in Egypt by Rameses II

North and Central America

3500 BC Bison hunted on the Great Plains

Beginning of classic period of Northwest Coast culture of Pacific Northwest, characterized by lavish ceremonies and ornate woodwork

Turkeys domesticated in Mesoamerica

1200 BC Olmec civilization spreads throughout much of Mesoamerica; it lasts for 900 years

5000 BC Caribbean islands colonized by people arriving in dugout canoes from the Yucatan Peninsula, present-day Mexico

Plants such as squash, amarinth, chili, and gourds cultivated in Tehuacán Valley, Mesoamerica

Gill-net fishing practiced in Pacific Northwest

2500 BC Squash cultivated in eastern North America, as well as sumpweed, goosefoot, and sunflowers, whose large seeds are stored as winter food

Simple pottery appears in North America

Olmec head

1300 BC People in southeastern North America, in the area known as the lower Mississippi, build major earthworks such as those found at Poverty Point in Louisiana

South America

3500 BC Valdivia culture begins to develop in the Andes (in present-day Ecuador); it is characterized by a complex social culture and village life

Manioc (cassava) and potato cultivated in many parts of the Andes and Amazonia

2500 BC Elaborate temples and mounds constructed in Peruvian highlands

1200 BC Terracing used to increase agricultural output in Andes

3000 BC Cotton grown at Valdivia centers of Ancon and Huaca Prieta in coastal valleys of present-day Peru; mound architecture built at nearby sites such as El Paraiso

Valdivia culture produces incised ceramics at Puerto Horniga

Squash, capsicum, and peppers grown in Peruvian Andes

4000 BC Llamas, alpacas, and guinea pigs domesticated in Peru

1800 BC Huge ceremonial complexes built in coastal valleys of Peru at sites including Casma Valley

1000 BC Settlement of southern Mariana islands of Micronesia

500 BC A distinctive Polynesian culture emerges in islands of southwestern Pacific

Bronze vessel from China

528 BC Buddhism begins under Siddhartha (Gautama Buddha) in Benares, India, and later spreads to Sri Lanka, Myanmar, Laos, Thailand, and other parts of southern Asia

331 BC Alexander the Great conquers the Persian Empire, winning a decisive battle at Gaugamela, Mesopotamia

112 BC Development of the Silk Road as a trading route between China and the West

221–211 BC Shih Huang orders construction of Great Wall of China to protect Qin Empire against nomadic tribes of northern steppes

1020 BC Israelites establish a kingdom in Palestine

400 BC Cast iron in use in China

c.5 BC Birth of Jesus Christ in Bethlehem

800 BC Etruscans settle in central-western Italy between the Arno and Tiber rivers

Phoenician colonies established in Spain, Sardinia, and Sicily

620 BC Roman alphabet, derived from Etruscan, in use

336 BC Alexander the Great succeeds father Philip II as ruler of Macedonia; he soon tightens control of Greek city-states and expands Macedonian Empire into Asia

218–201 BC Hannibal crosses the Alps to invade Italy from the north, beginning the Second Punic War

146 BC Rome emerges victorious from Third Punic War

776 BC The Olympic Games, a combination of religious festival and athletic contest, first held in Delphi and Olympia, Greece

750 BC Rise of Greek city-states including Athens, Corinth, Sparta, and Thebes

Etruscan alphabet in use

Work begins on the Acropolis, Athens

600–400 BC Growth of Celtic warrior societies; major centers include Hunsrück-Eifel region of Germany and Champagne district of France

c.350–322 BC Aristotle writes his major works, advancing the idea that Earth is the center of the universe around which other planets revolve

290 BC Romans take control of central Italy

264–241 BC First Punic War between Rome and Carthage initiates long battle for dominance of Mediterranean

51 BC Julius Caesar conquers Celtic tribes of Gaul as far as the Rhine; he reaches Britain in 55 BC, but Romans do not occupy the country until 43 AD

750 BC Kingdom of Kush-Meroë conquers Egypt and rules until 670 BC

Phoenicians colonize coast of North Africa

Gold sheath from Kush-Meroë Kingdom

480 BC City of Carthage flourishes and holds sway over the western Mediterranean

275 BC The first lighthouse to use reflected light from a fire to warn sea traffic of danger is built at Alexandria in Eygpt

200 BC Paper made from papyrus in use in Egypt

1000 BC Bantu expansion reaches Rift Valley

Kush becomes independent

300 BC African rice is grown in the Niger delta

146 BC Carthage destroyed by Roman army at end of Third Punic War

1000 BC Agriculture, in the form of the cultivation of maize, established in southwestern North America

650 BC Appearance of Zapotec hieroglyphs, the earliest form of Mesoamerican writing

500 BC Adena people of midwestern North America build mounds for ceremonial purposes

Monte Albán, in Mexico's southern highlands, becomes capital city of Zapotec culture; it thrives for about 1,250 years

300 BC Hohokam, Mogollon, and Anasazi peoples inhabit southern North America; the Anasazi occupy villages built beneath overhanging cliffs in and around Chaco Canyon, New Mexico

200 BC In northeastern North America, Hopewell culture begins to take over from Adena; the Hopewell become the region's first farmers

600 BC Team games played with a rubber ball on ball courts in San Lorenzo and La Venta in present-day Mexico; the games may have involved human sacrifices

900 BC Carving of Tello Obelisk, an ornate granite monolith from Chavín de Huántar, one of the most remarkable artefacts of Chavín culture

200 BC Rise of Nasca culture in Peru, noted for its immense geometric figures etched into the ground and only visible from the air; the patterns may mark the sun's passage at solstice

Tello Obelisk, 900 BC

1000 BC The Chavín culture begins to flourish in northern Andes

750 BC Gold mining taking place in central Andes

Oceania and Antarctica

AD 186 One of the world's most violent volcanic eruptions occurs at Mt Taupo, New Zealand, destroying surrounding forests over a radius of 75 km (47 miles)

Fishhook from Marquesas Islands

AD 0 Marquesas Islands colonized

AD 500 Polynesian settlers reach Hawaii and Easter Island

Asia and the Middle East

AD 220 Demise of Han Empire in China

Stone sculpture, Gupta dynasty

AD 527–565 Byzantine Empire (359–1453) reaches its zenith under Justinian I

C. AD 30 Crucifixion of Jesus Christ in Jerusalem

AD 319–450 Gupta dynasty flourishes in India

C. AD 500 Buddhism and Confucianism introduced to Japan from China

AD 622 Followers of Mohammed (570–632), founder of Islam, flee to Medina to escape persecution; this event denotes the start of the Muslim calendar

Europe and the Russian Federation

AD 117 Roman Empire reaches its greatest extent under Trajan; in Britain, the northern boundary is later marked by Hadrian's Wall (built AD 122)

AD 330 Roman Emperor Constantine I converts to Christianity, which subsequently becomes the Empire's official religion

AD 450 Germanic tribes from northern Europe, such as the Angles, Jutes, and Saxons, begin to settle in England

AD 476 Western Roman Empire comes to an end when Romulus Augustus is ousted by Goths

AD 79 The cities of Pompeii and Herculaneum, Italy, are destroyed by the eruption of Mt Vesuvius

AD 140 The Greek astronomer Ptolemy publishes his *Almagest*, an encyclopaedia of scientific information, including his theory that Earth is the center of the universe

AD 443 Attila leads Huns and other barbarian tribes into western Europe; he is turned back in 450 at Châlons by a coalition of Franks and Visigoths led by Aetius

AD 452 Venice founded by refugees from central Europe fleeing the attacks of Attila the Hun

Africa

Pillar at Aksum

C. AD 350 Aksum converts to Christianity; the empire extends inland

C. AD 570 Nubian kingdom converts to Christianity

AD 0–100 Kingdom of Aksum in present-day Ethiopia becomes a major trading center; elaborate temples and palaces are constructed

AD 400–500 Bantu people migrate to southern Africa seeking land for grazing sheep and cattle and planting crops; they soon displace Khoisan hunter-gatherers

AD 600 Arabs begin to colonize North Africa

North and Central America

C. AD 200 Pyramid of the Sun is built at Teotihuacán in eastern Mexico

AD 426 Mayan dynasty of 16 kings founded at Copán in present-day Honduras

Jade ritual offering, Copán dynasty

AD 700 Start of the Pueblo period in southwestern North America; native peoples including Hopi and Zuni live in villages built mainly of adobe

AD 250 Start of the Classic phase of Mayan civilization; growth of Mayan city-states on Yucatan Peninsula (Mexico) and in present-day Guatemala

AD 100 Mayan hieroglyphic writing comes into use

AD 550–800 Mayan civilization reaches its zenith

South America

AD 200–600 Moche civilization of Peru produces highly decorated ceramic pots and murals for public buildings; the Pyramid of the Sun in Moche Valley is the region's largest adobe structure

Moche ear ornament

AD 700 Sicán culture flourishes in the Batán Grande area of Peru's northern coast; the capital city includes 12 adobe pyramids and tombs for leaders

AD 100 Tiwanaku and Wari develop as principal urban centers of southern-central Andes

AD 500 Wari becomes major Andean city with strong administrative structures, large buildings, and highly developed crafts, including ceramics

AD 800 Fishhooks in use along the southeast coast of Australia, similar to those found in New Guinea

AD 900–1000 Polynesians first reach New Zealand islands and settle

Gigantic stone statues are erected on Easter Island

Pitcairn Islands are colonized by Polynesians

Easter Island statue

1300 Chatham Islands, 800 km (500 miles) east of New Zealand, become the last Pacific islands to be colonized by Polynesian settlers

---

AD 868 The first woodblock-printed book, *The Diamond Sutra*, appears in China

1000 Chinese scientists invent gunpowder

1038 Seljuk Turks start Turkish Muslim dynasty; by 1071, it controls Asia Minor

1096–99 First Crusaders temporarily wrest Jerusalem from Arab control

1189 Third Crusade led by Richard I of England and Philippe II of France leads to truce with Arabs

1275–92 Italian merchant Marco Polo resident at court of Mongol emperor Kublai Khan in China

1369 Mongol leader Tamerlane assumes leadership of Samarkand; he later extends his empire into Persia and India

AD 960 Beginning of Song Dynasty in China, which will last until 1279; it adopts Neo-Confucianism as official philosophy

1048 First movable type in use in China, consisting of clay characters in an iron frame

1100 Chinese invent the magnetic compass

1147–49 Second Crusade ends in failure to recapture Holy Land

1192 Yoritomo becomes first Shogun (commander-in-chief) of Japan, initiating the so-called Kamakura period, which is dominated by Samurai and lasts until 1333

1368 After a century of Mongol rule, the Ming dynasty takes power in China, initiating a 300-year period of isolation during which art and culture flourish

---

AD 711 Moors invade Spain, bringing Islamic influence to Europe

AD 800 Charlemagne crowned Holy Roman Emperor in Rome by Pope Leo III

Viking people of Scandinavia begin to explore and plunder the European coastline; they eventually colonize Iceland and parts of Britain and set up trading posts in eastern Europe

1232 Pope Gregory IX establishes the Inquisition, a special court set up at Toulouse, France, to investigate heresies against the Catholic Church

1280 Windmills in use in western Europe

1300 The Renaissance begins in Italy and spreads throughout Europe

1337 Start of the Hundred Years War between England and France

1346 Black Death (bubonic plague) spreads from Asia Minor to Italy and from there to the rest of Europe; 25 percent of the European population die within five years

AD 771 Charlemagne becomes king of the Franks; he soon expands Frankish Empire in western Europe

1066 Norman king William I (Conqueror) invades England and commissions Domesday Book to assess the wealth of the country; population estimated at around 2 million

1326 Gunpowder being used in cannons

AD 800 Rise of the Kingdom of Ghana in West Africa, which lasts until 1050

c.1000 Growth of urban centers in southern Africa; craftworks are traded widely

Rise of kingdoms of Yoruba in present-day Nigeria

Rise of empire of Great Zimbabwe in East Africa, which flourishes until 1400

1100 Different language groups begin to emerge, including the Xhosa and the Zulu

1150 Emergence of Hausa city-states in present-day Nigeria

1300 Emergence of the Benin Empire of Nigeria, West Africa

Construction of royal court at Great Zimbabwe

1340 Empire of Songhai, a strong trading state in present-day Mali, founded on Niger River

AD 900 Trading routes established between East and West Africa as well as across the Sahara

1050 Tokolor people of Senegal, West Africa, become the first group south of the Sahara to follow Islam

1062 Almoravid Muslim sect takes control of Morocco, establishing its capital at Marrakesh

1130 Almohad Muslim sect rises up against corrupt Almoravids, taking control of North Africa and ruling until 1212

1200 Mali Empire, in present-day Ghana, establishes Muslim rule in West Africa; it lasts 200 years

1312–1337 Mali Empire reaches its zenith

1350 Complex irrigation methods in use in East African Rift Valley

---

AD 980 Viking outlaw Erik the Red establishes settlement in Greenland; population of settlement may have reached 5,000, but it is eventually abandoned in 15th century when climate becomes colder

1200 Several tribes, including the Mexica, migrate to the Valley of Mexico, leading to the foundation of Aztec civilization; they begin terracing mountain slopes for food cultivation

1250 Emerald Mound, a huge ceremonial site near Natchez Trace Parkway, Mississippi, in use

c.1300 Drought in southwestern USA forces Anasazi and other native peoples to abandon homelands

AD 800 Native Americans living in present-day Illinois start to abandon hunter-gatherer way of life in favor of agriculture; maize becomes a major crop

Mayan population of Copán Valley reaches 20,000

1000 Viking explorers land on various parts of American coast including Baffin Island, Labrador, and Newfoundland (possibly the place known as Vinland in Norse legends)

Toltecs of Tula (in present-day Hidalgo, Mexico) found an empire which flourishes for next 200 years

1150 Growth of communities in present-day Alabama, Georgia, and Oklahoma; they produce many decorated ceremonial objects

1325 Aztecs establish their capital of Tenochtitlán, which grows into a major city with 250,000 inhabitants; it later becomes Mexico City

---

AD 800 Machu Picchu, a site of religious and symbolic importance for the Inca people, is built in the mountains above the Urubamba Valley in Peru

1200 Cuzco becomes capital of Inca civilization; Inca cultivate mountainous areas with irrigation canals in order to feed a growing population

Inca ceramic plate

AD 725 Tiwanaku becomes a major Moche population center with up to 50,000 inhabitants

AD 850 Chimú people found Chimor Empire and build capital of Chan Chan in the Moche valley; by 1100 it has a population of 8,000

1250 Emergence of Killke style of ceramics in the Cuzco area; this will later become the distinctive style of the Inca civilization

Oceania and Antarctica

c.**1500** Moas hunted to extinction in New Zealand

1400 Traders and fishing vessels from the islands of present-day Indonesia visit the north coast of Australia

Temple city of Nan Madol in use off the island of Temwen, Micronesia; built of stone on artificial islands, it is only accessible by boat

Moa

Asia and the Middle East

1453 Constantinople falls to the Ottoman Turks

1526 Mogul Empire founded when Babar invades Hindustan and conquers all of northern India; for 200 years the empire is well administered, centralized, and prosperous

1543 Shipwrecked Portuguese traders become the first Europeans to visit Japan; they introduce the first firearms to the country

Ottoman Constantinople

1405 Death of Tamerlane

1498 Portuguese sailor Vasco da Gama reaches the Malabar coast in India after sailing round the Cape of Good Hope

1502 Founding of Safavid dynasty in Persia by Ismail, who proclaims himself shah; the dynasty lasts until 1736

1534 Ottoman Turks invade Mesopotamia taking Tabriz and Baghdad

Europe and the Russian Federation

1450 Beginning of Little Ice Age which brings harsh winters, wet summers, and food shortages to Europe for next 400 years

Johannes Gutenberg builds the first printing press

1455 Gutenberg prints the Mazarin Bible at Mainz, Germany

1492 Spanish expel Moors from Granada, their last stronghold in Spain

1538 Flemish geographer Gerardus Mercator uses the name "America" on maps for the first time

1543 Nicholas Copernicus proposes that Earth revolves around the Sun, challenging the traditional Ptolemaic view that the opposite was true

1400 Leprosy eradicated in most parts of Europe due to improved diet and sanitation

1453 End of the Hundred Years War between England and France

1478 Queen Isabella of Spain sets up Spanish Inquisition to investigate heretical activities

1517 Reformation begins when German priest Martin Luther nails 95 theses challenging the power of the Catholic Church to a church door in Wittenberg; the movement soon spreads throughout Europe

1546 Mercator declares that Earth has a magnetic pole

Africa

1415 Portuguese explore North and West African coast in caravels, a new kind of sturdy sailing vessel, capturing Ceuta under Henry the Navigator

1464 Songhai secedes from Mali; in 1468, it captures Timbuktu

1486 Portuguese reach Angola on West African coast

1500 Rise of the Bornu Empire in northern Nigeria following Kanem Empire's demise; it reaches its zenith at end of century

1450 Rise of empires of Congo and Ndongo in central Africa (present-day Congo and Democratic Republic of the Congo)

State of Bono in West Africa becomes an important gold-mining center

1471 Portuguese establish forts on West African coast and begin trading in gold

1488 First Portuguese vessels arrive at the Cape of Good Hope

1517 Ottoman Turks take control of Egypt after defeating the Mamelukes (Muslim slave soldiers) and rule for the next 250 years

1400–1500 Rise of Nyoro kingdom in present-day Uganda

North and Central America

c.**1450** Pueblo farmers of southwestern North America trade with plains-hunters of the north, exchanging corn, cotton goods, and pottery for buffalo meat and hides

1492 Italian seafarer Christopher Columbus reaches the Caribbean and discovers Watling Island, Cuba, and Haiti

1497 John Cabot and son Sebastian explore the east coast of North America

1524 Italian navigator Giovanni da Verrazzano explores northeast coast of North America

1540–42 Spanish explorer Francisco Coronado explores southwestern North America

Aztec mask

Spanish conquer Mayan lands

1500 Aztec Empire at its height

c.**1460** Mississippian Native American societies living along river valleys of eastern North America increasingly dependent on agriculture; they build large earthen mound structures for religious ceremonies

1519 Spanish conquistador Hernán Cortéz meets Aztec ruler Montezuma II at Tenochtitlán, Mexico; two years later, he seizes the city and Montezuma

1539 Spanish explorer Hernando de Soto reaches Florida and travels up the Mississippi River

1400 End of the early Aztec phase sees widespread use of chinampas, swamplands reclaimed for agricultural plantations

1494 Treaty of Tordesillas divides the New World between Spain and Portugal; the treaty is rejected by other European maritime powers

South America

1438 Pachacuti becomes Inca leader and begins expanding empire

1499 Amerigo Vespucci sails from Spain to South America

1516 Spanish explorer Juan Díaz de Solís becomes the first European to land in present-day Argentina; he is killed by Querandi indians

1525 Civil war breaks out in Inca Empire between north led by Atahualpa and south led by his brother Huáscar

1545 Spanish discover silver at Potosí in central Andes, starting a rush to exploit this valuable resource

Gold Inca beaker, 1500s

1400 Rise of Inca Empire known as Tawantinsuyu; Incas develop building techniques of great precision and begin to construct an extensive road system

1450 Incas conquer Chimú state in Peru

1500 Pedro Alvarez Cabral discovers Brazil and claims it for Portugal

1521 Spanish explore northern coast of South America and start a colony in what becomes Venezuela

1532 Spanish conquistador Francisco Pizarro imprisons Inca emperor Atahualpa; despite an enormous ransom being paid, Atahualpa is executed

1568 Spanish sailors visit the Solomon Islands

1595 Spanish sailor Pedro Fernandez de Quiros discovers and names the Marquesas Islands; he has earlier visited the Santa Cruz group

1606 Dutchman Willem Jansz lands on north coast of Australia

Spanish navigator Luis Vaez de Torres sails through the strait that subsequently bears his name without realizing that a continent lies to the south

1616 Dutch sea captain Dirck Hartog lands on the west coast of Australia

Dutch navigators Willem Schouten and Jakob le Maire visit Tonga

1642–43 Dutch navigator Abel Tasman lands on Van Diemen's Land (now Tasmania), claiming possession for the Netherlands; he then discovers the west coast of New Zealand and sights the eastern island islands of Fiji and Tongatapu in the Tongan group

1644 Tasman charts part of the coastline of northern and western Australia

1688 English adventurer William Dampier spends two months on the west coast of Australia

1699 Dampier returns to explore the west coast of Australia; unimpressed, he sails north for New Guinea

---

1568 Akbar, greatest of the Moghuls and grandson of the empire's founder Babar, conquers Chitor in Rajasthan, quells the Rajput princes, and takes control of the region

1580 Unification of Japan under Oda Nobunaga

1600 British East India Company established to develop trade in Asia and challenge the trading empires of the Portuguese and Spanish; similar trading companies subsequently set up by Dutch (1602) and French (1604)

1597 Dutch establish trading post at Batavia (Jakarta) in Dutch East Indies

1603 Tokugawa Shogunate begins rule in Japan, continuing until 1867

1623 At trading center of Ambon, Dutch behead British traders accused of plotting to take over the Dutch fortress; incident creates friction between trading powers

1632–43 Taj Mahal, a white marble mausoleum, built at Agra, India, by Emperor Shah Jehan in memory of his wife Mumtaz Mahal

1639 English colonists settle at Madras in India

1643 First French missionaries arrive in Vietnam

1644 The Manchus, a people from Manchuria, invade China from northwest and establish Qing dynasty, bringing peace and prosperity

1674 Dutch traders help local Muslim leader, Amangkurat I, head of the kingdom of Maturam, Indonesia, to suppress rebellion; in return, Dutch gain possession of parts of central Java

1683 China seizes Formosa (Taiwan)

1569 Mercator produces *Cosmographia*, which includes the first navigational maps of the world

1571 Battle of Lepanto halts maritime expansion of Ottoman Empire

1572 In France, 10 years of religious conflict climax in St Bartholomew's Day Massacre of 2,000 Huguenots (Protestants) in Paris; many Huguenots seek refuge in England

1588 Spanish Armada, Philip II of Spain's invasion force against England, is defeated by Sir Francis Drake in the English Channel

1603 King James VI of Scotland becomes James I of England

1609 Mathematician–astronomer Galileo Galilei improves the recently invented telescope and describes Jupiter's satellites

Johannes Kepler announces his laws of planetary motion

1618 Start of Thirty Years War between Protestant powers—England, Holland, Scandinavia, and German states—and Spain and the Hapsburg Empire

1643 Barometer invented by Italian scientist Evangelista Torricelli

1642–48 English Civil War leads to execution of Charles I

1665 The Great Plague of London takes 70,000 lives between July and October; the following year much of the city is destroyed by a fire lasting from February 2 to 9

1661 Ottoman Turks invade Transylvania and Hungary

1682 Edmund Halley identifies a bright comet and correctly predicts that it will reappear in 1758 and approximately every 77 years thereafter

1675 Greenwich Observatory established by English astronomer Edmund Halley

1699 Under Treaty of Carlowitz, defeated Turks forced to cede most of Balkans to Austrian Hapsburgs

---

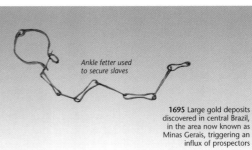

Yoruba sculpture

1591 Morocco defeats Songhai, bringing the empire to an end

1600 Oyo Empire becomes one of the most successful of the Yoruba states after the leader Orompoto uses proceeds of trade to build a large army

1613 Portuguese priest and explorer Pedro Paez discovers the source of the Blue Nile: Lake Tana in Tanzania

1619 First slaves from West Africa shipped to Virginia, North America, by Dutch traders

1626 French establish settlements on Madagascar but island does not become a colony until 1896

1637 French establish military base in Senegal, West Africa

1652 Dutch East India Company establishes garrison at site of modern-day Cape Town

1657 First Dutch settlers take up land grants at Liesbeeck River near Cape Town

First slaves brought to the Cape from India, Indonesia, and West Africa by Dutch

1660 Rise of Bambara kingdoms of Segu and Kaarta on the Niger River; by 1670 they have replaced the Mandingo Empire

1670 Rise of Ashanti Empire in West Africa in modern-day Ghana; by early eighteenth century its rulers are supplying slaves to Dutch and British traders

---

1583 The English found a colony at St Johns, Newfoundland

1584 Sir Walter Raleigh claims Virginia on east coast of North America for England; attempts to form a permanent settlement fail

1605 Port Royal in Nova Scotia becomes the first French settlement in North America

1607 Jamestown, Virginia, becomes first permanent English settlement in North America

1619 The first slaves from West Africa are sold in Virginia, North America, by Dutch traders

1620 The Pilgrim Fathers leave Plymouth, England, and cross the Atlantic to the New World in the *Mayflower*

1624 The Dutch establish a settlement at New Netherlands, North America

1642 The French establish site of Montréal on the St Lawrence seaway

1663 The North American French colonies form a Province by amalgamating as New France, with Québec as the capital

1670 Hudson's Bay Company founded in London by English and French merchants seeking to establish fur trade in the Hudson Bay region of northeastern Canada

1682 Renée La Salle explores the Mississippi River and claims Louisiana for France

---

1553 First settlements of Santiago del Estero and Tucumán in Argentina founded by Spanish arriving from Peru in search of gold and silver

1567 Two million of South American Indian population die from typhoid fever introduced by Spanish soldiers

1573 Córdoba and Mendoza grow as part of trade routes between Chile and Argentina

1580 Spanish colonists establish settlement at Buenos Aires on La Plata estuary

1616 Dutch navigator Willem Schouten sights Cape Horn, the tip of South America

1620 Expansion of silver mining at Potosí, Bolivia

1624 Dutch seize Brazilian territory of Bahia; they later take control of the rich sugar-producing area of Pernambuco (1630–54)

1630 Portuguese begin to import large numbers of slaves from Africa to work on sugar plantations of northeastern Brazil, displacing native populations

Ankle fetter used to secure slaves

1695 Large gold deposits discovered in central Brazil, in the area now known as Minas Gerais, triggering an influx of prospectors

Oceania and Antarctica

1765 British explorer John Byron sails through the Pacific while searching for the "Great South Land," and visits numerous islands including the Gilbert Islands

1788 First Fleet under Captain Arthur Phillip arrives at Botany Bay to found a British penal colony; disappointed with Botany Bay, Phillip establishes the colony at Port Jackson

Captain James Cook, 1728–79

1722 Dutch explorer Jacob Roggeveen explores the Pacific, visiting Samoa and Easter Island as well as Makatea, Bora-Bora, and Maupiti

1766–69 Comte Louis Antoine de Bougainville, scientist and navigator, travels widely throughout the Pacific, visiting Tahiti, the New Hebrides, New Britain, and New Guinea

1770 After visiting Tahiti and New Zealand, English navigator Captain James Cook charts the east coast of Australia and lands at Botany Bay

1793 First free settlers arrive in New South Wales, Australia, from Britain

Asia and the Middle East

1715 Chinese conquer Mongolia and Turkestan

1755 The Nawab of Bengal occupies Calcutta, taking many British prisoners, some of whom die in the "Black Hole," a small room used as a jail; British, led by Robert Clive, retake Calcutta

1761 British capture of Pondicherry marks the end of French colonial power in India

British East India Company coat of arms

1707 Mt Fuji, Japan's biggest volcano, erupts

1730 An earthquake on the island of Hokkaido, Japan, causes the deaths of 137,000 people

1740 British East India Company takes over Mogul land
Dutch and British armies oust Portuguese spice traders and establish ports at Madras, Bombay, and Calcutta

1769 Severe famines in Bengal lead to rural depopulation for more than 20 years

1771 Political crisis of the "Tay Son Rebellion" in Vietnam under which the old Confucian order is threatened by reforms inspired by Western ideas

Europe and the Russian Federation

1707 Act of Union unites Scotland and England as Great Britain

1725 John Harrison, English clockmaker, invents a device for measuring longitude at sea and on land

1755 Lisbon is destroyed by a major earthquake; it is the first earthquake to be studied by scientists

1769 After several years of development, Scotsman James Watt invents the double-acting rotary steam engine which is introduced to textile mills and other factories

1701–14 War of Spanish Succession

1713 Peace of Unsikaupunki ends the Great Northern War between Sweden and Russia; after more than 350 years of allegiance to Sweden, Finland comes under Russian control (until 1721)

1735 Swedish naturalist Carl Linnaeus publishes *Systema Naturae*, a system for classifying plants and animals; his basic hierarchy is still in use

1760 Rise of Amsterdam as world's major economic center

1781 German-born English astronomer Sir William Herschel discovers the planet Uranus; Herschel's studies form the basis of modern astronomy

1789 The French Revolution begins with the storming of the Bastille and lasts for 10 years

Africa

1757 Sultan Muhammad ibn Abd Allah brings peace and stability to Morocco after a period of unrest and economic decline

1779 Sporadic warfare breaks out in south between Dutch and British colonists and indigenous Xhosa people; the conflict lasts for the next 100 years

1787 British set up a colony at Sierra Leone, West Africa

1790 In present-day northern Nigeria, the Islamic Fulani people from Senegal wage a holy war (jihad) against the Hausa kings

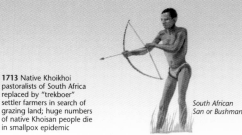

1713 Native Khoikhoi pastoralists of South Africa replaced by "trekboer" settler farmers in search of grazing land; huge numbers of native Khoisan people die in smallpox epidemic

South African San or Bushman

1760 Slaves are traded in increasing numbers in what is now Gabon, West Africa, often in exchange for European goods such as guns, textiles, and rum

1795 British occupy Cape Town, a vital supply post on Britain's expanding trade routes prior to opening of the Suez canal; British settlers arrive in increasing numbers

Scottish explorer Mungo Park reaches the Niger River

North and Central America

1740–48 War between Britain and France over North America

1763 Peace of Paris treaty ending Seven Years War in Europe awards Canada to Britain

1775 Beginning of American War of Independence (to 1783); the following year the 13 American colonies adopt the Declaration of Independence, thereby founding the USA

1787 Delegates at a national constitutional convention—the "Founding Fathers"—create the US Constitution

1789–93 Alexander Mackenzie explores northwestern North America, crossing over the Rockies to reach the Pacific Ocean

1720 Spanish soldiers invade Texas

1752 American scientist and diplomat Benjamin Franklin proves that lightning is an electrical discharge and invents the lightning conductor

1770–72 British adventurer Samuel Hearne explores territories to the northwest of Hudson Bay in northern Canada

1791 Canada is divided into French- and English-speaking territories by the Constitutions Act

1793 Eli Whitney invents the cotton gin, a mechanical threshing machine

South America

1770–80 Improved navigational methods strengthen links between Europe and Latin America, creating opportunities for economic growth

1790 Native people and imported Africans used as slaves on plantations in Brazil; many die from European diseases

1700 Bourbon Spain establishes the Viceroyalty of New Grenada in central and South America; Peru is forced to release control of Guayaquil in modern-day Ecuador

1743 Charles-Marie de la Condamine, a French scientist given the task of measuring a degree of longitude on the equator, takes measurements in Ecuador and then explores the Amazon, bringing back samples of the rubber tree and platinum

1780 Tupac Amaru II leads an unsuccessful revolt by native people against Spanish rule in Peru

1799–1804 German scientist Alexander von Humboldt explores central and South America

1803 British penal settlements founded in Hobart and Port Arthur in Tasmania

1837 Frenchman Lieutenant Jules Dumont d'Urville discovers Joinville Island, off Antarctica

1840 The Treaty of Waitangi gives Britain sovereignty over New Zealand but also gives Maori people sovereignty over their lands (as well as British citizenship), creating conflicting expectations

1861 Thomas Mort builds the first refrigeration unit for the transportation of meat in Sydney, Australia

Gold Rush in New Zealand

1895 Norwegian whaler Henryk Johan Bull becomes the first person to land on the Antarctic continent at what is now Cape Adare

Beginning of severe droughts in Australia which last for the next seven years

1820 Russian naval officer Captain Fabian von Bellingshausen is possibly the first person to see Antarctica

1839–43 British explorers Ross and Crozier map the coast of Antarctica in the *Erebus* and the *Terror*; two volcanoes are later named after the ships

1851 Beginning of the Australian Gold Rush

1868 Transportation of convicted criminals from Britain to Australia ends with the arrival of the last convict ship in Western Australia

1893 New Zealand becomes the first country in the world to give the vote to women

---

1800 British East India Company trading in China; British smuggle opium into China to offset other exports and Opium War breaks out when Chinese object

1842 Treaty of Nanjing ends first Opium War; China cedes Hong Kong to Britain

1850 Failure of monsoon rains in northern India causes famine lasting more than 30 years

1883 Krakatau, Indonesia, erupts, killing 36,000 people; the explosion is heard up to 3,650 km (1,400 miles) away

1894–95 Sino-Japanese War breaks out over Korea—Japan emerges victorious and annexes Formosa (Taiwan)

1880s Indian Nationalist Movement, including Indian National Congress, campaigns for an end to British rule

1815 The largest volcanic eruption ever, at Tambora, Indonesia, kills at least 10,000 people; more than 80,000 later die of starvation and disease resulting from climatic effects of eruption

1857 The Indian Revolt against heavy taxes results in considerable loss of British and Indian lives; it is ruthlessly suppressed

1876 Queen Victoria becomes Empress of India

1887–88 Huang (Yellow) River in China floods, killing up to 2.5 million people

1891 A severe earthquake in Japan kills up to 10,000 people

1804 After conquering much of western Europe, including the Netherlands, Switzerland, and northern Italy, Napoleon crowns himself emperor of France

1834 British mathematician William Babbage invents the "analytical machine," forerunner of the computer

1848 Revolutions occur in various parts of Europe, including Germany, France, Austria, and Italy

1859 Publication of Charles Darwin's *The Origin of Species*, which expounds the theory of natural selection

1871 Unification of Germany under Emperor William I

Charles Darwin, 1809–82

1835 French mathematician Gaspard de Coriolis describes how winds and ocean currents are deflected clockwise around high-pressure systems in northern hemisphere and anti-clockwise in southern hemisphere

Halley's comet reappears, as he had predicted

1850 Karl Marx, a German economist living in London, publishes *The Communist Manifesto*

French physician Louis Pasteur advances a theory that germs cause disease

1861 Italy becomes a single state under King Victor Emmanuel II of Sardinia after Giuseppe Garibaldi and his "red shirts" defeat Bourbon troops

1899 French meteorologist Teisserenc de Bort discovers that temperature stops decreasing at around 10 km (6 miles) above sea level; this leads to discovery of atmospheric layers

1815 Napoleon defeated by British army at Waterloo

---

c.1800 Zulu nation founded in what is now Kwazulu-Natal, South Africa, forcing Shoshangane clan into Swaziland and Mzilikazi clan into Zimbabwe

1853 Scottish explorer and missionary David Livingstone begins his exploration of central Africa

1860 Laborers from India are imported by Natal farmers to work on farms and plantations

1870 Gold and diamonds discovered in South Africa

1884–85 Conference held in Berlin divides up remaining African territories between Germany, France, and Britain

1899 Start of the Second Boer War between British and Afrikaners (Boers)

Gold-mining industry in South Africa employs 110,000 workers; almost 100,000 are African laborers

1861 British occupy Lagos in Nigeria

1871 US journalist Henry Morton Stanley locates Livingstone, who has mapped the river systems of central Africa and traced the source of the Zambeze

1836–38 10,000 Boer (Dutch) settlers unhappy with British rule in the Cape set out on Great Trek to seek new territories in Natal and Orange River region

1858 English explorers John Speke and Richard Burton discover Lake Victoria; Speke later discovers the source of the Nile

1869 The Suez Canal opens, allowing a much reduced voyage time between the Mediterranean Sea and the Indian Ocean

1880–81 British attempts to bring the Boer republics (of Orange Free State and Transvaal) into a federation fail when the Boers defeat the British in the First Boer War

1830–48 France conquers Algeria

1803 Napoleon sells almost 3 million sq km (900,000 sq miles) of southern central North America to the USA in a deal known as the Louisiana Purchase

1813 Mexico declares its independence

1837 Samuel Morse demonstrates the electric telegraph in New York

1861–65 American Civil War between the North and the South caused by disputes over political and economic issues, including the abolition of slavery

1876 Scots-born American Alexander Graham Bell invents the telephone

1886 The transcontinental Canadian Pacific Railway is completed

1804–05 US army officers Meriwether Lewis and William Clark explore the Missouri River, cross the Rocky Mountains, and reach the Pacific Ocean

1824 The Erie Canal opens, creating a navigational route between the Great Lakes and the Atlantic Ocean

1848 As a result of victory over Mexico, the USA gains vast areas of western and southern North America

Discovery of gold in California causes an influx of prospectors in the first Gold Rush

Gold nugget

1867 USA purchases Alaska from Russia

1879 Thomas Edison invents electric lighting

1898 Spanish-American War ends with Cuba becoming independent and the USA gaining Puerto Rico, Guam, and the Philippines

---

1808 Prince John, royal ruler of Portugal, is forced to flee from Portugal and declares Rio de Janiero capital of the worldwide Portuguese Empire; he returns to Portugal in 1821

1824 Simón Bolívar wins a victory over Spanish troops at Ayacucho, Peru, ending Spanish control in South America

1866 San Roque Dam built on the Primero River, Argentina, to supply hydroelectric power and water for irrigation

1879 Population of Gran Chaco region of Argentina grows rapidly as a result of the expansion of the beef industry, with large numbers of immigrants arriving from Europe

1880 Japanese immigrants begin to settle in southeastern Brazil to profit from rapid growth of coffee plantations

1889 Brazil becomes a republic

1816 Argentina declares independence from Spain

1822 Prince John's son Pedro declares Brazil's independence and is crowned Emperor

1830 Argentina lays claim to Islas Malvinas (the Falkland Islands); three years later, Britain occupies the islands

1870 Rubber production soars in the Amazon area of Brazil, attracting migrants from the eastern seaboard and from Europe

1879–83 Pacific War between Chile, Peru, and Bolivia over nitrate deposits results in Chile taking territory in southern Peru

1888 Brazil abolishes slavery: 750,000 people are freed

Oceania and Antarctica

1901–04 British navy captain Robert Scott undertakes the first inland exploration of Antarctica

1907 Englishman Ernest Shackleton, a member of Scott's earlier expedition, reaches the South Magnetic Pole in Antarctica

1914–18 330,000 Australians and 100,000 New Zealanders travel overseas to fight in the First World War

1928 Australian aviator Bert Hinkler arrives at Darwin, Australia, after a 15-day flight from Croydon, England, via Rome, Egypt, India, Malaya, and Java

1939 Australia and New Zealand send troops to support Britain in the Second World War; hundreds of thousands fight in Europe and the Pacific

1947 New Zealand's parliament adopts the Statute of Westminster (1931) which gives it formal independence from the UK

1901 Federation of the six Australian colonies results in the formation of the Commonwealth of Australia

1911 Norwegian explorer Roald Amundsen and his team become the first to reach the South Pole on December 11; just over one month later a British expedition under Captain Scott accomplishes the same feat, but the team perishes on the return journey

1919 Influenza pandemic leaves thousands of Australians dead

First World War digger's hat

1930 The Depression hits Australia and New Zealand

Amy Johnson arrives at Darwin, Australia, having flown solo from London, UK; she fails by only 4 days to beat Hinkler's record

1942 Japanese troops occupy New Guinea

Japanese submarines enter Sydney Harbour, Australia

Asia and the Middle East

1907 France seizes Lao territories east of the Mekong River; formerly under control of Thailand, they include much of present-day Cambodia, Laos, and Vietnam

1934 Mao Ze Dong leads the Long March of the Communist revolutionaries across China

1945 First atomic bombs dropped on Japanese cities of Hiroshima and Nagasaki by USA, bringing the war in the Pacific to an end

1946 Start of war in Indochina between French colonial power and Vietnamese nationalists led by Ho Chi Minh (to 1954)

1900 In Peking (Beijing), the Boxer Rebellion of Chinese nationalists against foreign interests is put down by British and Russian forces

1911 Rebels proclaim Chinese republic under Sun Yat-sen; last Chinese Emperor Pu Yi relinquishes throne during following year

1927–28 Civil War in China between the Communist party and the Kuomintang (Nationalist Party) under Chiang Kai-Shek; Nationalists take Beijing

Mao Ze Dong, 1893–1976

1948 State of Israel proclaimed following partition of Palestine

1947 India gains independence and is partitioned, with Pakistan becoming separate Muslim state

1949 Commu... party takes control of Ch...

Europe and the Russian Federation

1914 Assassination of Archduke Francis-Ferdinand at Sarajevo in Bosnia triggers the First World War between Germany, Austria-Hungary, and the Ottoman Empire on one side, and Britain, France, and Russia on the other; more than 8 million soldiers die

1917 The second Russian Revolution takes place in March and Russian royal family killed; in October, the Bolsheviks seize power

1928 The world's first antibiotic, penicillin, is discovered by Scottish scientist Alexander Fleming

1936–39 Spanish Civil War between Nationalists and Republicans results in General Franco becoming Nationalist head of state of the Falangist (Fascist) government

1945 Second World War ends in Europe (7 May) and the Pacific (2 September); the death toll includes more than 14 million soldiers and about 27 million civilians

1905 Bloody suppression of riots in St Petersburg leads to the first Russian Revolution

1916 German-born physicist Albert Einstein publishes his General Theory of Relativity, which suggests that the universe is expanding

1918–19 Influenza pandemic leaves millions of Europeans dead and kills up to 40 million worldwide

1933 Adolf Hitler becomes Chancellor of Germany; his National Socialist Party ends democratic rule

1939 Germany invades Poland, starting the Second World War

Africa

1907 Mahatma Gandhi campaigns in South Africa for civil rights of ethnic Indian population

1931 South Africa granted independence by Britain as a member of the Commonwealth

1949–50 Racial apartheid becomes the official policy of the National Party government of South Africa

1912 The African National Congress (ANC) founded in South Africa by a small group of educated black Africans seeking political rights

African National Congress flag

1935 Seeking to expand its African territories, Italy invades Ethiopia, capturing Addis Ababa in 1936; Haile Selassie flees until British troops restore him to office during Second World War

1902 Britain emerges victorious from Second Boer War

North and Central America

1903 First successful flights in heavier-than-air machines made by brothers Orville and Wilbur Wright at Kitty Hawk, North Carolina

1917 United States enters First World War

1927 Charles Lindbergh makes the first nonstop solo flight across the Atlantic Ocean from Roosevelt Field, New York, to Le Bourget near Paris

1941 Japanese attack on US naval base at Pearl Harbor, Oahu Island, Hawaii, brings USA into the Second World War; during the war, the USA loses 292,000 troops, Canada 43,000

1948 Universal Declaration of Human Rights adopted by General Assembly of UN in New York; it sets out minimum standards of civil and political rights to which all people are entitled

1902 Mt Pelée, Martinique, erupts, killing 20,000 and burying the town of St Pierre

1906 San Francisco is devastated by a major earthquake measuring 8.3 on the Richter scale

Wright brothers' Flyer III, 1905

1918 Influenza pandemic begins in North America; it eventually kills up to 40 million worldwide

1929 The Wall Street Crash of October 24 causes widespread financial instability; it is followed by the Great Depression which spreads worldwide

1945 Founding charter of United Nations (UN) signed by 51 nations in San Francisco

South America

1930s Huge population growth and urbanization occurs, particularly in Argentina and Uruguay, chiefly as a result of large-scale immigration

1942 Brazil supports Allies in Second World War and sends 25,000 troops to fight in Italy

1946 Juan Perón becomes President of Argentina with backing of both army and labor unions

1914 First World War initially disrupts Latin American trade, but for some countries this is followed by an export-led boom which lasts until the Depression

1932–35 Paraguay defeats Bolivia in war over Chaco region; final settlement negotiated in 1938 awards Chaco territory to Paraguay

1944 A massive earthquake kills 5,000 people in the Andean San Juan province of Argentina

1951 Australia, New Zealand, and the USA sign the ANZUS defence treaty; the signatories agree to offer mutual support in the event of an attack on any of the other parties

Antarctic penguin

1959 Antarctic Treaty bans military activity in Antarctica; signatories also agree to suspend territorial claims

1960 Swiss diver Jacques Piccard and the US navy's Donald Walsh explore the Mariana Trench in the Pacific Ocean to a depth of 11,000 m (36,089 feet)—the lowest known point on the ocean floor

1974 Cyclone Tracy destroys Darwin in northern Australia

1975 Papua New Guinea becomes independent

Thousands of refugees from Vietnam, Laos, and Cambodia, many of them ethnic Chinese, begin to flee to Australia by boat

1979 Scientists discover a hole in the ozone layer above Antarctica

1985 New Zealand's anti-nuclear policy sours relations with traditional allies France and the United States

1996–97 Despite worldwide protests, France concludes a series of nuclear weapon tests on Muraroa Atoll in the South Pacific before agreeing to sign the UN Test Ban Treaty

---

1953 Mt Everest is climbed for the first time by New Zealand explorer Edmund Hillary and Sherpa Tenzing Norgay

1950 Korean War begins when North Korean communist troops invade South Korea; the war lasts until 1953, with US troops fighting on the South Korean side

1957 Vietnam War starts when North Vietnamese (Viet Cong) attack South Vietnamese

1959 China suppresses revolt in Tibet; Tibet's spiritual leader, the Dalai Lama, flees to India

Potala Palace, Tibet

1965 US troops based in South Vietnam committed to aid South Vietnamese forces

1975 Vietnam War ends with the fall of Saigon after the withdrawal of US troops

1976 An earthquake in Tangshan near Beijing, China, kills more than 200,000 people and injures another 150,000

1995 A massive earthquake lasting less than a minute kills 5,000 people in Kobe, Japan, and causes massive disruption to transport and industry

1991 Mt Pinatubo in the Philippines erupts killing 30 people and leaving 10,000 homeless

Following Iraq's occupation of the oil-rich state of Kuwait, US combines with the UK, France, and other allies to defeat Iraq in the Gulf War

---

1961 Russian cosmonaut Yuri Gagarin becomes the first man in space and the first to orbit Earth

Berlin Wall erected by the East German government to stop citizens escaping to the West

1957 The space age starts with the launching by Russia of Sputnik I, a satellite capable of orbiting Earth

Sputnik 1, 1957

1973 A military junta of army colonels siezes power in Greece after overthrowing the elected Government of President Georgios Papadopoulos

1974 Turkish troops invade northern Cyprus following the overthrow of the island's president, Greek Archbishop Makarios; fighting between Greek and Turkish Cypriots results in the creation of a neutral corridor across the island

1984 HIV, the virus that causes AIDS and has already taken the lives of millions worldwide, is identified by Luc Montaigner at the Institut Pasteur, Paris

1989 Collapse of Communism in the Soviet Union and Eastern Europe: Russian leader Mikhail Gorbachev and US President George Bush declare the end of the Cold War, and the Berlin Wall is dismantled

1986 An accident at the Chernobyl nuclear power station in the Ukraine contaminates a huge area and spreads fallout across Europe

Russia launches Mir, an Earth-orbiting space station

1991 Civil War in former Yugoslavia between Croatia and Bosnia; UN sends peacekeeping forces

Collapse of the Soviet Union

1995 Talks at Dayton, Ohio, USA, aimed at ending conflict in Bosnia, lead to a peace agreement; hostilities are gradually halted

---

1956 Egypt closes Suez Canal; British, French, and Israeli troops invade to reopen it but UN intervenes to halt fighting

Independence of Morocco, Tunisia, and Sudan recognized by France

1953 Military coup in Egypt ends monarchy of King Farouk and imposes republic

1960 Massacre of 67 anti-apartheid demonstrators at Sharpeville, Johannesburg, South Africa

1961 South Africa becomes a republic; sanctions imposed by several countries in response to apartheid policies

1962 Nelson Mandela and other members of ANC imprisoned in South Africa

Algerian war of independence ends French rule

1964 Former British colony of Rhodesia (now Zimbabwe) declares independence

1967 Civil war in Nigeria; Biafra secedes until 1970

World's first heart transplant carried out in Cape Town by Dr Christiaan Barnard

1976 Young blacks protesting against compulsory Afrikaans language lessons are gunned down by police at Soweto, Johannesburg, South Africa

1977 Commencement of civil war and famine in Ethiopia, which lead to thousands of deaths

1993 Civil war in Rwanda between Hutu and Tutsi people results in the slaughter of hundreds of thousands of Tutsi

1990 ANC leader Nelson Mandela freed from prison in South Africa; the following year, apartheid is abolished

1994 Global population problems discussed at World Population Conference, Cairo, Egypt

Nelson Mandela elected President in first nonracial, democratic general election in South Africa

---

1961 US President John F. Kennedy backs an invasion of communist Cuba by exiled Cubans but fails to send US troops; Fidel Castro's forces easily repulse the attack at the Bay of Pigs

1963 Assassination of President John F. Kennedy

1968 Martin Luther King and Robert Kennedy assassinated

1969 US astronauts Neil Armstrong and Buzz Aldrin make first landing on the moon from the spaceship *Apollo 11*

1974 US Space probe Mariner 10 sends back the first close-up pictures of the rings surrounding the planets Mercury and Venus

1980 Eruption of Mt St Helens, Washington State, USA—one of the largest in modern times

1981 First flight of the space shuttle *Columbia*

First case of AIDS recognized

1982 A volcanic eruption at El Chichón, Mexico causes the deaths of 3,500 people and blackens the sky for almost two days

1989 US invades Panama

Space shuttle

1955 General strike in Argentina; Perón and wife Eva sent into exile

1960 In Santiago, Chile, 5,000 people are killed by an earthquake

1970 Salvador Allende of Chile becomes the world's first freely elected Marxist president

1973–76 Perón returns to Argentina and is re-elected, but dies in 1974; his third wife Isobel governs until Army chiefs arrest her; thousands subsequently killed by security forces

1973 Allende is deposed in a military coup led by General Augusto Pinochet

1982 Argentina invades Falkland Islands; Britain uses military force to retake the islands by 14 June

1982–83 The century's most severe episode of the El Niño effect: Chile experiences record rainfall

1988 General Pinochet's rule in Chile rejected by large majority in plebiscite

1992 Global environmental problems debated at first Earth Summit in Rio de Janeiro, Brazil

Alberto Fujimori, President of Peru, suspends parliament claiming corruption among government officials; a new constitution is approved in 1993

Part 3

Regions of the World

The Changing Scene

Culture is one way of defining world regions: the Middle East and Central Asia, for example, have a broadly Islamic culture in common (above). North America stretches from Canada (opposite) to Mexico and can be defined by its geographical, as well as its cultural, boundaries.

Geographers, in their attempt to subdivide Earth's land surface into coherent areas, developed the concept of regions. Regions can be delineated within continents or within countries, depending at what scale study is being conducted.

Regions are parts of the world that have a degree of similarity in one or more characteristics, such as climate, physiography, culture, or economy. For example, a Himalayan region can be based on physiography, a Saharan region determined by its desert climate, a Confucian East Asia region determined by a dominant culture, and a European Community region defined by countries linked by economic cooperation. In this book, however, much larger regions have been identified.

Regions, under whatever criteria they are defined, must be geographically contiguous. Countries adjacent to each other often share a major characteristic. Thus, the countries of Southeast Asia have a tropical, humid climate which ensures the growing of tropical crops such as tropical fruits, tea, coffee, and rubber. In contrast, several Middle Eastern countries have arid climates which inhibit large scale agriculture. Southeast Asia and the Middle East can be considered as regions where climate is one of the distinguishing characteristics.

In other cases, culture may be an important criterion for defining a region. The Middle East, besides being climatically different from other parts of Asia, also differs culturally. North America and Central America have considerable cultural and economic differences that justify their being differentiated. This is also true for Africa, as North Africa differing in several aspects from the countries south of the Sahara.

Very often a number of small countries lying close to each other may share one or more characteristics. This is the case with the small island nations of the Pacific. They can then be said to lie within an identifiable region or sub-region. On the other hand, some large countries, such as the Russian Federation, are so large that they have sufficient climatic and cultural diversity within their borders for sub-regions to be usefully identified.

The naming and defining of continents was the first attempt to mark out large regions on the map of the world. Because the continents were named and defined by Europeans, the perspectives used were European. For example, some names came from ancient Greece where the lands lying to its east were named Asia and the lands to its west were called Europe. Because of the European perspective, it became customary to refer to the eastern lands close to Europe as the Near East, the lands lying far to the east as the Far East, and the lands in between these as the Middle East.

Europe and Asia are geographically contiguous, forming the Eurasian landmass, but there are sufficient differences between them for them to be identifiable as two separate continents. This traditional separation is largely based on cultural and historical factors, the lines dividing the two continents being accepted by convention.

Africa, the two American continents, Australia, and Antarctica are easily defined because of their separation from other landmasses. Australia, New Zealand, and several Pacific islands are customarily included in a large region known as Oceania that includes a variety of climates, economies, and cultures. The only factor that gives Oceania its coherence is that these lands form a large cluster in the Central and South Pacific Ocean.

Regions or sub-regions can be identified within most of the world's continents. For instance, the large continent of Asia contains areas with distinctive characteristics that allow them to be considered as regions. Asia can be sub-divided into East Asia, Southeast Asia, South Asia (the Indian subcontinent), West Asia (the Middle East), Central Asia, and North Asia (Siberia). Monsoon Asia (or Asia-Pacific), a larger region, defined on the basis of climate, stretches across East, Southeast, and South Asia. Monsoon Asia is humid, extremely populous, and has extensive agriculture. Central Asia and the Middle East, on the other hand, are more arid, less populated, and have limited scope for agriculture, except where water for irrigation is available.

Europe was within the last half century politically divided into Eastern and Western Europe. This ideological divide resulted in contrasting economic systems, the residual effects of which can still be seen. On economic grounds, Eastern and Western Europe can be considered as sub-regions. Climate can be used to differentiate Mediterranean Europe from lands north of the Alps.

In this book, the continents and regions have been treated in the following order: Oceania, Asia and the Middle East, Europe and the Russian Federation, Africa, North America and Central America, South America, Polar Regions, and Oceans.

Information is provided on each region in a systematic way, recognizing that for some areas and countries data is relatively sparse and incomplete. The descriptions of each country show the differences and similarities, as well as highlighting those factors responsible for natural, economic, and social conditions.

The World: Physical

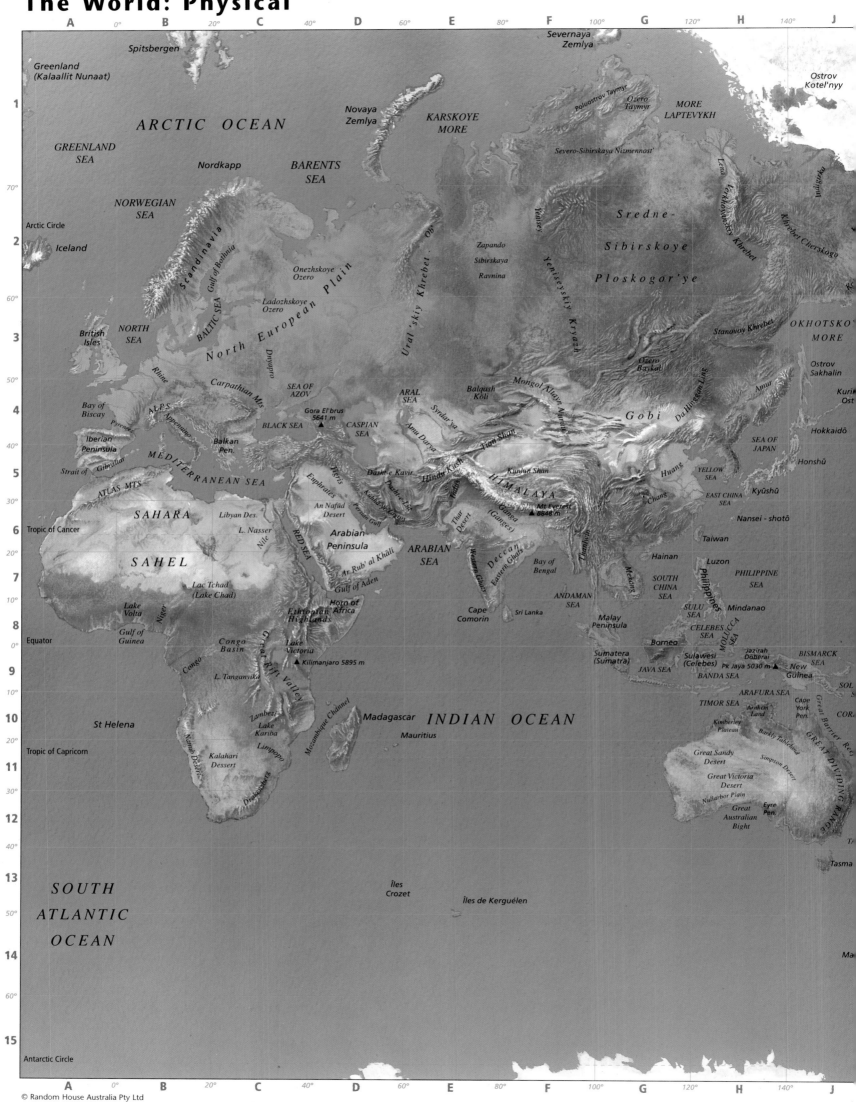

ARCTIC OCEAN

Spitsbergen

Greenland
(Kalaallit Nunaat)

Severnaya
Zemlya

Ostrov
Kotel'nyy

GREENLAND
SEA

Novaya
Zemlya

KARSKOYE
MORE

Poluostrov Taymyr

Ozero
Taymyr

MORE
LAPTEVYKH

Nordkapp

BARENTS
SEA

Severo-Sibirskaya Nizmennost'

NORWEGIAN
SEA

Sredne-

Sibirskoye

Ploskogor'ye

Iceland

Arctic Circle

Scandinavia

Gulf of Bothnia

Onezhskoye
Ozero

Zapando
Sibirskaya
Ravnina

Yenisey

Yeniseyskiy Kryazh

Khrebet Cherskogo

Lena

Verkhoyanskiy Khrebet

British
Isles

NORTH
SEA

BALTIC SEA

Ladozhskoye
Ozero

North European Plain

Ural'skiy Khrebet

Ob

Stanovoy Khrebet

OKHOTSKO
MORE

Rhine

Dnyepr

Carpathian Mts.

SEA OF
AZOV

ARAL
SEA

Balqash
Köli

Mongol Altayn Nuruu

Ozero
Baykal

Da Hinggan Ling

Ostrov
Sakhalin

Bay of
Biscay

ALPS

Apennines

Gora El'brus
5641 m ▲

CASPIAN
SEA

Syrdar'ya

Gobi

Amur

Kuril
Ost

Pyrenees

BLACK SEA

Amu Darya

Tian Shan

Hindu Kush

Kunlun Shan

Huang

SEA OF
JAPAN

Iberian
Peninsula

Balkan
Pen.

Dasht-e Kavir

Indus

HIMALAYA

YELLOW
SEA

Hokkaidō

Strait of Gibraltar

MEDITERRANEAN SEA

Tigris

Dasht-e Lut

Kabul

Persian Gulf

Chang

EAST CHINA
SEA

Honshū

ATLAS MTS

Euphrates

An Nafūd
Desert

Thar
Desert

Ganga
(Ganges)

Mt Everest
▲ 8848 m

Kyūshū

SAHARA

Libyan Des.

Arabian
Peninsula

ARABIAN
SEA

Deccan

Eastern Ghats

Nansei - shotō

Tropic of Cancer

SAHEL

L. Nasser

RED SEA

Ar Rub' al Khāli

Western Ghats

Bay of
Bengal

Brahmaputra

Hainan

Taiwan

Luzon

PHILIPPINE
SEA

Lac Tchad
(Lake Chad)

Nile

Gulf of Aden

Horn of
Africa

ANDAMAN
SEA

SOUTH
CHINA
SEA

Philippines

Lake
Volta

Niger

Ethiopian
Highlands

Cape
Comorin

Sri Lanka

Malay
Peninsula

SULU
SEA

Mindanao

Gulf of
Guinea

Congo
Basin

Great Rift Valley

Lake
Victoria

▲ Kilimanjaro 5895 m

Sumatera
(Sumatra)

Borneo

CELEBES
SEA

Sulawesi
(Celebes)

MOLUCCA
SEA

Jazirah
Doberai

Pk Jaya 5030 m ▲

New
Guinea

BISMARCK
SEA

SOL

Equator

Congo

L. Tanganyika

JAVA SEA

BANDA SEA

ARAFURA SEA

COR

St Helena

Zambezi

Lake
Kariba

Mozambique Channel

Madagascar

Mauritius

INDIAN OCEAN

TIMOR SEA

Arnhem
Land

Cape
York
Pen.

GREAT DIVIDING RANGE

Namib Desert

Linpopo

Kalahari
Dessert

Tropic of Capricorn

Kimberley
Plateau

Great Sandy
Desert

Barkly Tableland

Drakensberg

Great Victoria
Desert

Simpson Desert

Nullarbor Plain

Great
Australian
Bight

Eyre
Pen.

Ta

SOUTH

ATLANTIC

OCEAN

Îles
Crozet

Îles de Kerguélen

Tasma

Ma

Antarctic Circle

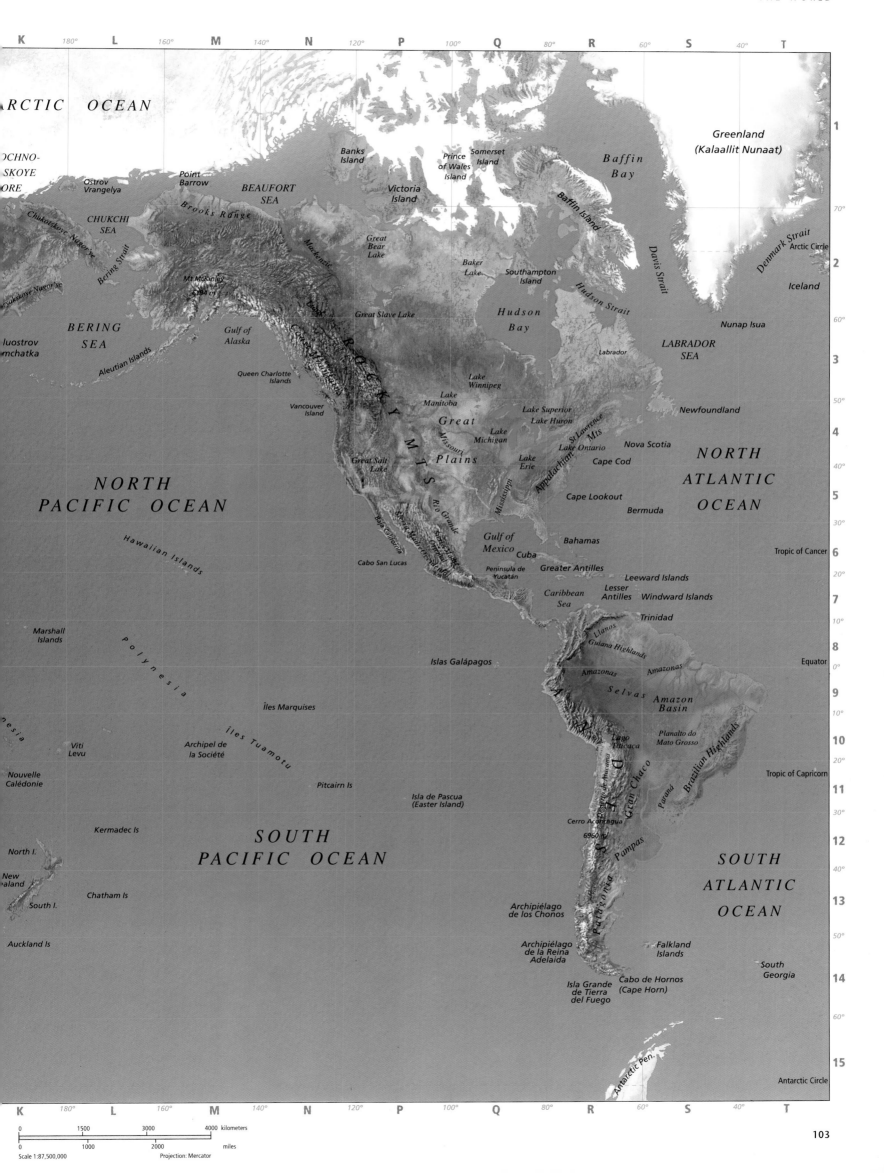

ARCTIC OCEAN

Greenland
(Kalaallit Nunaat)

OCHNO-
SKOYE
ORE

Ostrov
Vrangelya

Point
Barrow

Banks
Island

Prince
of Wales
Island

Somerset
Island

Baffin
Bay

Baffin Island

Denmark Strait

Arctic Circle

Chukotskoye Nagorye

CHUKCHI
SEA

BEAUFORT
SEA

Victoria
Island

Davis Strait

Iceland

ovakeskoye Nagorye

Brooks Range

Mt McKinley
6194 m

Mackenzie

Great
Bear
Lake

Baker
Lake

Southampton
Island

Hudson Strait

Nunap Isua

BERING
SEA

Aleutian Islands

Gulf of
Alaska

Great Slave Lake

Hudson
Bay

Labrador

LABRADOR
SEA

luostrov
mchatka

Queen Charlotte
Islands

ROCKY MTS

Lake Winnipeg

Newfoundland

NORTH

Vancouver
Island

Lake
Manitoba

Great

Lake Superior
Lake Huron

St Lawrence

Nova Scotia

ATLANTIC

NORTH

PACIFIC OCEAN

Great Salt
Lake

Plains

Missouri

Lake
Michigan

Lake
Ontario

Appalachian Mts

Cape Cod

OCEAN

Lake
Erie

Coast Mountains

Hawaiian Islands

Baja California

Rio Grande

Mississippi

Cape Lookout

Bermuda

Sierra Madre Occidental

Gulf of
Mexico

Bahamas

Tropic of Cancer

Cabo San Lucas

Cuba

Peninsula de
Yucatán

Greater Antilles

Leeward Islands

Marshall
Islands

Polynesia

Islas Galápagos

Caribbean
Sea

Lesser
Antilles

Windward Islands

Trinidad

Llanos

Guiana Highlands

Équateur

Îles Marquises

Amazonas

Amazonas

Selvas

Amazon
Basin

Îles Tuamotu

Viti
Levu

Archipel de
la Société

Lago
Titicaca

Planalto do
Mato Grosso

Brazilian Highlands

Nouvelle
Calédonie

Pitcairn Is

Isla de Pascua
(Easter Island)

Desierto de Atacama

Gran Chaco

Paraná

Tropic of Capricorn

Kermadec Is

Cerro Aconcagua
6960 m

Pampas

North I.

SOUTH

ANDES

SOUTH

New
ealand

Chatham Is

PACIFIC OCEAN

Patagonia

ATLANTIC

South I.

OCEAN

Auckland Is

Archipiélago
de los Chonos

Falkland
Islands

Archipiélago
de la Reina
Adelaida

South
Georgia

Cabo de Hornos
(Cape Horn)

Isla Grande
de Tierra
del Fuego

Antarctic Pen.

Antarctic Circle

0   1500   3000   4000 kilometers
0   1000   2000   miles
Scale 1:87,500,000   Projection: Mercator

The World: Political

A · 0° · B · 20° · C · 40° · D · 60° · E · 80° · F · 100° · G · 120° · H · 140° · J

SVALBARD (Nor.)

ARCTIC OCEAN

Novaya Zemlya

Novosibirskiy Ostrova

JAN MAYEN (Nor.)

BARENTS SEA

R U S S I A N

ICELAND

FAEROE IS (Den.)

SWEDEN

FINLAND

NORWAY
Oslo
Helsinki
Stockholm
Tallinn
Riga
ESTONIA

F E D E R A T I O N

OKHOTSKO MORE

DENMARK
København
UNITED KINGDOM
ISLE OF MAN (U.K.)
Dublin
IRELAND
London
Amsterdam
NETH.
Bruxelles BELG.
Luxembourg LUX.
Paris
Bern
CHANNEL ISLANDS (U.K.)
FRANCE

LITHUANIA
Vilnius
Minsk
BELARUS
POLAND
Warszawa
Berlin
GERMANY
Praha
CZECH REP.
SLOVAKIA
Wien Bratislava
AUST. Budapest
SWITZ. LIECH. HUNG.
SLOV. CROAT. ROMANIA
Ljubljana
Zagreb B-H.
Sarajevo YUG.

Moskva

Kyyiv
UKRAINE
MOLDOVA
Chişinău
Bucureşti
Beograd
Sofiya
BULGARIA

Astana

KAZAKHSTAN

Ulaanbaatar

MONGOLIA

Ostrov Sakhalin

Kuril'skiye

PORTUGAL
ANDORRA
Madrid
Lisboa
SPAIN
GIBRALTAR (U.K.)
Madeira (Port.)
Rabat

Roma
ITALY
Tiranë
ALBANIA
MACE.
Skopje
GREECE
Athina
MALTA
Valletta
Tūnis
Alger
TUNISIA
Tarābulus

Sofiya
Ankara
TURKEY
Lefkoşia
CYPRUS
SYRIA
LEBANON
Bayrūt
Dimashq
IRAQ
Yerushalayim ISRAEL
Amman JORDAN
Baghdad

GEORGIA T'bilisi
ARM. AZER.
Yerevan Bakı
TURKMENISTAN
Ashgabat
Tehrān

UZBEKISTAN
Toshkent
Dushanbe
TAJIKISTAN
KYRGYZSTAN
Bishkek

Beijing

P'yŏngyang
NORTH KOREA
SOUTH KOREA Sŏul
JAPAN
Tōkyō

C H I N A

Islas Canarias (Sp.)
MOROCCO
W. SAHARA

ALGERIA
LIBYA
EGYPT
Al Qāhirah

IRAN
Kābol
AFGHANISTAN
Islāmābād

T'ai-pei
TAIWAN

MAURITANIA
Nouakchott
MALI
NIGER
CHAD
SUDAN

Al Manāmah BAHRAIN
Ad Dawhah
QATAR
Abū Zaby
U.A.E.
Masqaṭ
OMAN
Ar Riyāḍ
Al Kuwayt
KUWAIT
SAUDI ARABIA

PAKISTAN
New Delhi
Kathmandu
NEPAL
BHUTAN
Thimphu
BANGLADESH
Dhaka

INDIA

MYANMAR
LAOS
Viangchan Hà Nôi
VIETNAM
Yangon
Krung Thep
THAILAND
CAMBODIA
Phnum Pénh

PHILIPPINES
Manila
GUAM (U.S.A.)
NORTH MARIANA (U.S.

SENEGAL
Dakar
GAMBIA
GUINEA-BISSAU
GUINEA
SIERRA LEONE
Conakry
Bamako
Niamey
Ouagadougou
BURKINA FASO
BENIN
TOGO
GHANA
Freetown
LIBERIA
CÔTE D'IVOIRE
Yamoussoukro
Monrovia
Accra
Lomé
Porto-Novo
NIGERIA
Abuja
Ndjamena

Asmara
ERITREA
Al Khartūm
YEMEN
Şan'a'
Djibouti
DJIBOUTI
ETHIOPIA
Ādīs Ābeba
C.A.R.
Bangui
CAMEROON
Yaoundé

ARABIAN SEA
Suquṭrá (Yemen)

Bay of Bengal

SRI LANKA
Colombo
MALDIVES
Male

MALAYSIA
Bandar Seri Begawan
BRUNEI
Kuala Lumpur
SINGAPORE
Koror
PALAU

MICR

SÃO TOMÉ & PRÍNCIPE
EQ. GUINEA
Malabo
Libreville
GABON
Brazzaville
CONGO
DEM. REP. OF THE CONGO
Kinshasa
Kigali
RWANDA
Bujumbura
BURUNDI
UGANDA
Kampala
KENYA
Nairobi
TANZANIA
Dodoma

Muqdisho
SOMALIA

Chagos Archipelago

BRITISH INDIAN OCEAN TERRITORY (U.K.)

Jakarta

INDONESIA

PAPUA NEW GU
Port Moresby

Luanda
ANGOLA
ZAMBIA
Lusaka
MALAWI
Lilongwe
MOZAMBIQUE
NAMIBIA
BOTSWANA
Windhoek
Gaborone
ZIMBABWE
Harare

Victoria
SEYCHELLES
Moroni
COMOROS
MAYOTTE (Fr.)
Antananarivo
MADAGASCAR
RÉUNION (Fr.)
MAURITIUS
Port Louis

INDIAN OCEAN

COCOS (KEELING) ISLANDS (Aust.)
CHRISTMAS ISLAND (Aust.)
ASHMORE & CARTIER ISLANDS (Aust.)

CORAL ISLAN (Aust

ASCENSION ISLAND (ST HELENA)
ST HELENA (U.K.)

Pretoria
Bloemfontein
Maseru
LESOTHO
SOUTH AFRICA
Cape Town
Mbabane
SWAZILAND
Maputo

AUSTRALIA

Can

TRISTAN DA CUNHA (U.K.)

Île Amsterdam (Fr.)

Tasmania

TA

SOUTH ATLANTIC OCEAN

FRENCH SOUTHERN & ANTARCTIC ISLANDS (Fr.)
Prince Edward Is (S. Africa)
Îles Crozet (Fr.)
Îles de Kerguélen (Fr.)

Mac (A

BOUVET ISLAND (Nor.)

HEARD & McDONALD ISLANDS (Aust.)

SOUTHERN OCEAN

A N T A R C T I C A

Antarctic Circle

A · 0° · B · 20° · C · 40° · D · 60° · E · 80° · F · 100° · G · 120° · H · 140° · J

Scale 1:87,500,000

Projection: Mercator

Oceania

Oceania

Oceania is the name given to a group of islands spread over 8.5 million sq km (3.3 million sq miles) in the Pacific Ocean, the majority of which lie in the southern hemisphere. The islands range in size from the large island continent of Australia, through medium-sized nations such as Papua New Guinea and New Zealand, to much smaller countries, such as Vanuatu and Tonga.

On cultural grounds, the islands can be divided into four groups. The first, Micronesia, lies east of the Philippines and includes the Federated States of Micronesia, Palau, the Marshall Islands, Nauru, and the USA dependencies of Guam and the Northern Mariana Islands. Melanesia, the second group, lies east of Indonesia and Australia, and includes Papua New Guinea, the Solomon Islands, Vanuatu, Fiji, Tonga, Tuvalu, and Samoa and the dependencies of New Caledonia (France) and American Samoa. Polynesia, the third, lies in the center of the Pacific Ocean, and includes Kiribati, French Polynesia, and the dependencies of Niue, the Cook Islands (NZ), the Pitcairn Islands (UK), and Hawaii (part of the USA). The fourth group comprises Australia and New Zealand. Unlike the other groups, these islands have indigenous populations, but the majority of the population are people who have migrated from Europe over the last two centuries. Australian dependencies include Norfolk Island in the Pacific Ocean and the Cocos (Keeling) and Christmas Islands in the Indian Ocean.

Physical features

Physiographically, the islands of Oceania can be classed into four categories. First there is Australia, situated in the middle of the Indo-Australian Plate, where there was no mountain building during the Tertiary geological era. Australia's eastern highlands, the eroded remnants of old mountains, are a series of elevated plateaus; the western half of the country is an ancient eroded plateau linked to the east by vast sedimentary basins.

In the second category are the islands lying along the collision boundaries between crustal plates. In the South Pacific, New Zealand, Papua New Guinea, the Solomon Islands, and Fiji are within the collision zone between the Indo-Australian and the Pacific plates. In the North Pacific, the Mariana Islands lie along the collision boundary of the Eurasian

and Pacific plates. These collisions have produced folded mountain ranges. New Zealand and Papua New Guinea have young mountain ranges, some peaks exceeding 3,000 m (10,000 ft).

The third category includes volcanic islands such as Fiji, which rise from the floor of the Pacific Ocean basin. Much smaller than the countries in the second category, they are mostly made up of high mountains, with some low-lying fringes along the coastlines, including coral reefs.

Finally, there are coral islands and atolls, such as Tuvalu. Atolls form low-lying circular coral reefs which enclose lagoons. The atolls typically develop around submerged volcanic cones. In some places, such as in Guam, coral islands have been raised by crustal movements.

Climate and vegetation

Oceania can be divided into two climatic zones: temperate and tropical. A large part of Australia and all of New Zealand lie in the temperate zone, while most of the island countries of the Pacific are tropical. Persistent trade winds dominate much of Oceania, and tropical cyclones often cause considerable damage.

Large parts of Australia are arid or semiarid. Humid zones are found along most of the east coast and Tasmania, and in part of the northern coast during summer. Most of New Zealand, Papua New Guinea and most of the islands in the Pacific are humid. However, droughts associated with the El Niño phenomenon have been frequent in recent decades in northern Australia and Papua New Guinea.

Rainforests, both tropical and temperate, occur in all the humid regions of Oceania—Australia and the larger and high (mostly volcanic) islands. However, deforestation has taken place in several places, such as parts of eastern Australia, Tasmania, New Zealand, and the Solomon Islands.

The kangaroo, probably Australia's most well known native animal. While some such animals are threatened with extinction, kangaroos are in fact regarded as pests by many.

Isolation has been a major factor in the development of unique species of animals, birds, and plants in the Pacific islands. The spread of human habitation and hunting has seriously affected native animals, especially in Australia—several species are extinct or endangered.

Population

In 1998 the population of Oceania totaled 29.5 million. Australia and New Zealand accounted for 22.1 million people and Papua New Guinea for 4.6 million people. The remaining 2.8 million inhabitants are scattered on many small islands over a large area. Life expectancy for the area as a whole is 71.5 years for males and 76.4 for females. The annual population growth rate averages 1.3 percent but this varies widely, with 1.1 percent for Australia and New Zealand, 4 percent for Papua New Guinea, and 3.6 percent for Melanesia. Rates of urbanization vary widely too, being 85 percent for Australia and New Zealand and 16 percent for Papua New Guinea.

Agriculture

Agriculture in Oceania can be divided into three kinds: labor-intensive subsistence agriculture, which occurs in most of the tropical islands of the Pacific; plantation crops, which are cultivated in the medium-sized tropical islands; and capital-intensive agriculture, which is found in Australia and New Zealand.

Subsistence agriculture in the Pacific islands consists of short-life items such as cassava, taro, yams, breadfruit, and sweet potatoes. Bananas and papayas are the most commonly grown fruits. Coconut palms grow on almost all the islands, and are a source of fresh food. Oil is extracted from the dried coconut meat (copra). Copra is exported from countries such as Vanuatu and Samoa. Cash crops, often a legacy of colonial times, are also important in some of the Pacific nations—sugar in Fiji and cocoa in Vanuatu.

Fishing is important for the majority of Pacific islands, as their economic zones extend to the 200 nautical mile limit—a large area compared to the size of many of the islands. Several islands have granted fishing licenses to Japanese, South Korean, and Taiwanese companies.

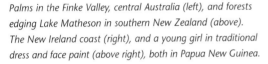

Palms in the Finke Valley, central Australia (left), and forests edging Lake Matheson in southern New Zealand (above). The New Ireland coast (right), and a young girl in traditional dress and face paint (above right), both in Papua New Guinea.

Industrialization

Australia and New Zealand both have modern diversified economies with well-established infrastructures. Australia is particularly well favored as it has rich mineral deposits and energy sources. Manufacturing, including food processing, makes an important contribution to the economy of these two Pacific nations.

In contrast, the other islands of the Pacific are not industrially developed. Papua New Guinea, is rich in minerals such as copper and gold, and has recently dis-covered natural gas fields. There are nickel deposits in New Caledonia and gold in Fiji, both of which are exported rather than used in local industries.

Many islands in the Pacific have few resources; some have insufficient land for their people and a number lack adequate supplies of drinking water. This shortage of natural resources, coupled with poor infrastructures, has impeded industrial development. Industry in most of the islands is limited to food processing.

Tourism has become an important source of revenue for much of Oceania. Australia and New Zealand offer tourists modern amenities and facilities, while the beautiful scenery of tropical Pacific Islands like Fiji, Tahiti, Vanuatu, and the Northern Mariana Islands attract visitors.

Languages

Culturally, Oceania can be divided into two major groups: the predominantly European settlements of Australia and New Zealand, and Melanesia, Polynesia, and Micronesia, which have been long settled by Oceanic peoples. New Caledonia is partially settled by Europeans.

During the colonial era, the entire region came under European influence. This resulted in English and French becoming important languages, depending on the colonial powers (Britain, America, and France). English is the official language of New Zealand, Australia, Papua New Guinea, the Solomon Islands, Vanuatu, and Fiji. French is

spoken in New Caledonia and French Polynesia. On several of the Pacific islands, particularly Papua New Guinea and Vanuatu, pidgin is a common lingua franca.

In Australia, only remnants of the numerous Aboriginal languages that were spoken in the continent before European settlement still exist. Several of these languages are found in the Northern Territory and the northern part of Western Australia (the Kimberleys), where Walmadjeri is becoming a common language among several Aboriginal tribes. In New Zealand, which has a significant Maori population, the Maori language is widely spoken.

Numerous languages are found in Melanesia, Polynesia, and Micronesia. In Papua New Guinea, hundreds of languages are spoken, Austronesian languages being spoken along the coastline and Papuan languages in the highlands. Austronesian languages such as Fijian in Fiji and Tahitian, Tongan, and Samoan in Polynesia are widespread.

Boundary disputes and wars

The whole region was affected by the Japanese invasion during the Second World War, and was the site of many important battles. No significant boundary disputes exist in the region. In recent decades, boundaries have been drawn up for Oceanic economic zones. However, there have been civil disturbances in both Fiji and New Caledonia—the former related to the struggle for a less racially biased government in the years after Fiji became a republic in 1970, the latter related to the wish of some of the people to become independent from France.

Australia

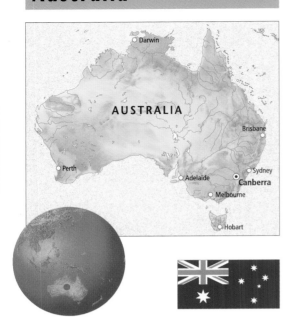

Fact File

OFFICIAL NAME Commonwealth of Australia

FORM OF GOVERNMENT Federal constitutional monarchy with two legislative bodies (Senate and House of Representatives)

CAPITAL Canberra

AREA 7,686,850 sq km (2,967,893 sq miles)

TIME ZONE GMT + 10 hours

POPULATION 18,783,551

PROJECTED POPULATION 2005 19,728,533

POPULATION DENSITY 2.44 per sq km (6.3 per sq mile)

LIFE EXPECTANCY 80.1

INFANT MORTALITY (PER 1,000) 5.1

OFFICIAL LANGUAGE English

OTHER LANGUAGES Indigenous languages, Italian, Greek

LITERACY RATE 99%

RELIGIONS Roman Catholic 27%, Anglican 22%, other Christian 22%, other 12.4%, none 16.6%

ETHNIC GROUPS European 95%, Asian 4%, other (including Aboriginals) 1%

CURRENCY Australian dollar

ECONOMY Services 78%, industry 16%, agriculture 6%

GNP PER CAPITA US$18,720

CLIMATE Hot and arid in center; tropical in north with one wet season (November to March); temperate in southeast and along southern coasts

HIGHEST POINT Mt Kosciuszko 2,229 m (7,313 ft)

MAP REFERENCE Pages 134–35

The Apostles, Port Campbell National Park, Victoria (right). Finke Gorge National Park in the Northern Territory (top right).

Australia is both the world's smallest continental landmass and the sixth-largest country. Most of it consists of low plateaus, and almost one-third is desert. First occupied about 40,000 to 50,000 years ago by peoples from Asia (the ancestors of today's Aboriginals), Australia was visited by Dutch explorers in the seventeenth century, including Abel Tasman in 1642 and 1644, and by the Englishman William Dampier in 1688 and 1699. After being claimed for Britain by Captain James Cook in 1770, a penal colony was established by the British in what is now Sydney in 1788. Some 160,000 convicts arrived before "transportation" from Britain was phased out in the nineteenth century. By then many free settlers had also arrived, and the gold rushes of the 1850s attracted still more people. With both wool and wheat exports providing economic security, the settler population sought greater independence from Britain, and a measure of self-government was granted in 1850. In 1901 the six states formed themselves into the Commonwealth of Australia, and in the 100 years since federation the country has become a successful, prosperous modern democracy. Current concerns include the consequences of economic dependence on Asian markets at a time of recession, demands for the frank acknowledgment of the history of Aboriginal displacement and dispossession, and whether there should be a republican government.

The Western Plateau constitutes the western half of the Australian continent. Made of ancient rocks, the plateau rises near the west coast—the iron-rich Hamersley Range representing its highest elevation in the northwest—and then falls eastward toward the center of the continent. The arid landscape alternates between worn-down ridges and plains, and depressions containing sandy deserts and salt lakes. There is little surface water. The flatness of the plateau is interrupted by the MacDonnell and Musgrave ranges in the center of the continent and the Kimberley and Arnhem Land plateaus in the north. Sheep and cattle are raised on large holdings in parts of this region.

The Central Lowlands forming the Great Artesian Basin, and river systems including the Carpentaria, Eyre, and Murray basins constitute a nearly continuous expanse of lowland that runs north to south. The river systems feed into Lake Eyre, the Bulloo system, or the Darling River. While the Murray Basin is the smallest of the three, its rivers—the Murray and its tributary the Darling—are Australia's longest and most important. Artesian bores make cattle and sheep raising possible through much of the semiarid Central Lowlands.

The Eastern Highlands (known as the Great Dividing Range) and the relatively narrow eastern coastal plain constitute Australia's third main geographic region. This has the greatest relief, the heaviest rainfall, the most abundant and varied vegetation, and the densest human settlement. A notable feature of the eastern marine environment is the Great Barrier Reef. The world's biggest coral reef complex, it lies off the northeast coast, stretching some 2,500 km (1,550 miles) from the Tropic of Capricorn to Papua New Guinea. A major tourist attraction, with over 400 types of coral and 1,500 species of fish, it is now protected as the Great Barrier Reef Marine Park.

The island of Tasmania, to the southeast of mainland Australia, has spectacular mountain wilderness areas and more than 30 percent of the state is protected World Heritage areas, national parks, and reserves.

Australian plant and animal life is distinctive. The most common trees are the gums (*Eucalyptus*) and wattles (*Acacia*). Highly adaptable, *Eucalyptus* varieties range from the tall flooded gum, found on rainforest fringes, to the mallee which grows on dry plains. Most native mammals are marsupials, and include kangaroos, koalas, wombats, and possums. Australia's monotremes—the platypus and the echidna—which lay eggs and suckle their young, are unique. There are also about 400 species of reptile and some 700 species of bird. Australia's vulnerability to introduced plant and animal species was dramatically shown by the spread of prickly pear, which took over vast areas of rural New South Wales and Queensland in the 1920s, and the plagues of rabbits that devastated pastures for a century until the 1960s. Both scourges have been tamed by biological controls.

Once heavily dependent on the pastoral industry—nearly one-third of Australia is still used for grazing sheep—the nation's economy is now diversified, with an important manufacturing sector. Australia is rich in mineral resources, the leading export earners being iron ore from Western Australia and coking coal from Queensland and

Timeline

c.15,000 BP Rock art paintings created in shelters and caves of northwest Australia	**c.13,000 BP** People of robust appearance with thick skulls and large jaws living at Kow Swamp, Murray Valley, Victoria	**1606** Dutch navigator Willem Jansz, first European to set foot in Australia, lands on Cape York Peninsula	**1770** James Cook explores the east coast of Australia and the New Zealand islands, claiming both for Great Britain	**1813** First European crossing of the Blue Mountains, west of Sydney, opens up inland plains to pastoralists	**1851** Gold discoveries first in New South Wales and then Victoria; gold rushes generate wealth and population increase	**1868** Transportation of convicts abolished; last ship lands in Fremantle, WA	**1919** More than 6,000 people die in the worst 'flu epidemic in New South Wales history
c.40,000 BP First Australians arrive in log canoes or sail boats from southeast Asia	**c.25,000 BP** Earliest evidence of cremation, Lake Mungo, New South Wales	**c.6–5000 BC** Dingoes brought to Australia, probably domesticated dogs belonging to people migrating from southeast Asia	**1642** Dutch navigator Abel Tasman lands in Van Diemen's Land (now Tasmania), taking possession for Holland	**1788** First Fleet under Captain Arthur Phillip arrives; penal colony set up in Port Jackson. Aboriginal population c. 750,000	**1829** Charles Sturt explores the Darling River system and later travels inland to disprove the myth of an inland sea	**1855–56** Augustus Charles Gregory makes first west-to-east land crossing of the continent	**1914–18** Australia sends 416,809 troops to fight in First World War; 53,993 killed in battle and 155,133 wounded	**1933** Aboriginal population reduced to 66,000 as a result of suppression and disease

New South Wales, while bauxite is mined in the Northern Territory and Queensland. In recent years Australia has produced more than one-third of the world's diamonds, 14 percent of its lead, and 11 percent of its uranium and zinc. Because commodities account for more than 80 percent of exports, falling commodity prices have severe economic effects: an apparently irreversible decline in world demand for wool has cast a shadow over the pastoral industry. The government has been encouraging increased exports of manufactured goods—cars are being exported to the Gulf States— but international competition is intense. The 1998 Asian economic downturn affected the tourist industry, which was the largest single foreign exchange earner, with 12.8 percent of the total.

STATES

New South Wales • Sydney
Queensland • Brisbane
South Australia • Adelaide
Tasmania • Hobart
Victoria • Melbourne
Western Australia • Perth

TERRITORIES

Australian Capital Territory • Canberra
Northern Territory • Darwin

OVERSEAS TERRITORIES

Ashmore and Cartier Islands
Christmas Island
Cocos (Keeling) Island
Coral Sea Islands
Heard and McDonald Islands
Norfolk Island

1939 Australia's involvement in Second World War dominated by entry of Japanese after Pearl Harbor

1949 Construction of Snowy Mountains hydroelectric scheme, Australia's largest (completed 1972)

1967 Referendum accords citizenship to Aboriginal people for the first time by a vote of 90.8 percent of the population

1974 Cyclone Tracy destroys most of Darwin, Northern Territory

1991–92 Severe drought associated with El Niño climate pattern affects eastern Australia

1993 High Court ruling (Mabo) that Australia was not "empty" when Europeans arrived allows native title claims to proceed

Fiji

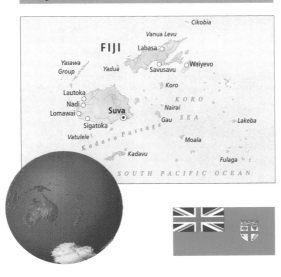

Fiji consists of an archipelago of more than 800 islands and islets, 110 of them inhabited, located about two-thirds of the way from Hawaii to New Zealand. Lying on the air route from Australia to the west coast of the USA, Fiji is well served by flights, and is attracting an increasing number of tourists. Originally inhabited by Melanesian islanders organized into a number of tribes, the islands were visited by Dutch explorers in 1643, and from 1800 attracted growing numbers of traders, along with missionaries who converted the people to Christianity. A period of intense tribal warfare was brought to an end when the paramount chief ceded sovereignty to the British in 1874. Five years later, in 1879, the British began bringing in Indian laborers for the purpose of sugar production; by the time Fiji obtained its independence in 1970 their descendants outnumbered the country's ethnic Fijians.

Racial divisions have been a source of major tension and instability, since for many years the Indian immigrants were treated as second-class citizens, despite their vital role in the sugar industry. A coup in 1987, led by a Fijian army officer against a democratically elected government in which Indians were the majority, led to a new constitution being introduced in

1990. This was racially weighted to ensure permanent indigenous Fijian rule. As a result, large numbers of Indian-Fijians chose to emigrate. The security of land tenure for Indian sugarcane farmers remains a contentious issue.

The main islands are of volcanic origin. About 70 percent of the population live on the two biggest—Viti Levu and Vanua Levu. These have a sharp and rugged relief, rising to Mt Tomanivi on Viti Levu. The islands lie in a cyclone path (Cyclone Kina caused much damage in 1993) and trade winds bring heavy rain to their eastern sides. Dense tropical forest covers the higher slopes. Sugarcane is grown on the fertile coastal plains, sugar exports and tourism being Fiji's main sources of foreign exchange. About 250,000 tourists, many bound for resorts on the smaller coral atolls, visit the islands each year. Fiji has a variety of forest, mineral, and marine resources, and is one of the most developed of the Pacific island economies, producing (as well as sugar) copra, gold, silver, clothing, and timber.

Fact File

OFFICIAL NAME Republic of Fiji

FORM OF GOVERNMENT Republic with two legislative bodies (Senate and House of Representatives)

CAPITAL Suva

AREA 18,270 sq km (7,054 sq miles)

TIME ZONE GMT + 12 hours

POPULATION 812,918

PROJECTED POPULATION 2005 877,594

POPULATION DENSITY 44.5 per sq km (115.2 per sq mile)

LIFE EXPECTANCY 66.6

INFANT MORTALITY (PER 1,000) 16.3

OFFICIAL LANGUAGE English

OTHER LANGUAGES Fijian, Hindustani

LITERACY RATE 91.3%

RELIGIONS Christian 52% (Methodist 37%, Roman Catholic 9%), Hindu 38%, Muslim 8%, other 2%

ETHNIC GROUPS Fijian 49%, Indian 46%, other (including European, other Pacific Islanders, Chinese) 5%

CURRENCY Fiji dollar

ECONOMY Agriculture 67%, services and industry 33%

GNP PER CAPITA US$2,440

CLIMATE Tropical, with wet season November to April

HIGHEST POINT Mt Tomanivi 1,323 m (4,341 ft)

MAP REFERENCE Pages 137, 141

The Parliament House buildings in Suva (below).

Dependencies and Territories

American Samoa

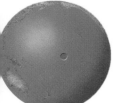

A group of five volcanic islands and two atolls in the South Pacific, about midway between Hawaii and New Zealand, American Samoa has been settled by Polynesian peoples since about 800 BC. The first European contact was made by the Dutch in 1722. British missionaries were active in the region from 1830. In 1872 the USA won exclusive rights from the High Chief to use Pago Pago as a strategic base for the American fleet. Pago Pago has one of the best natural deepwater harbors in the region, sheltered by surrounding mountains from rough seas and high winds. About 90 percent of trade is with the USA, which heavily subsidizes the economy. Tuna fishing, processing, and export are the foundation of private sector economic activity.

Fact File

OFFICIAL NAME Territory of American Samoa

FORM OF GOVERNMENT Unincorporated and unorganized territory of the USA

CAPITAL Pago Pago

AREA 199 sq km (77 sq miles)

TIME ZONE GMT – 11 hours

POPULATION 66,475

LIFE EXPECTANCY 72.9

INFANT MORTALITY (PER 1,000) 18.8

LITERACY RATE 97.3%

CURRENCY US dollar

ECONOMY Fishing 34%, government 33%, other 33%

CLIMATE Tropical; wet season November to April

MAP REFERENCE Pages 136, 141

Ashmore and Cartier Islands

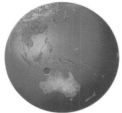

U ninhabited islands in the Indian Ocean north-west of Australia, Ashmore and Cartier Islands are at no point higher than 3 m (10 ft) above sea level. The terrain consists of sand and coral. The islands are surrounded by reefs and shoals that can pose a maritime hazard. The Australian government monitors the state of the Ashmore Reef National Nature Reserve. The Royal Australian Navy and Air Force make visits from time to time.

Fact File

OFFICIAL NAME Territory of Ashmore and Cartier Islands

FORM OF GOVERNMENT External territory of Australia

CAPITAL None; administered from Canberra

AREA 5 sq km (2 sq miles)

TIME ZONE GMT + 8 hours

POPULATION No permanent population

CLIMATE Tropical

MAP REFERENCE Page 134

Baker and Howland Islands

B aker Island is an uninhabited atoll in the North Pacific, midway between Hawaii and Australia.

The terrain consists of a low coral island surrounded by a narrow reef. Climate is equatorial with little rain, constant wind, and burning sun. Used by the US military during the Second World War, it is now mainly a nesting habitat for seabirds and marine wildlife. Howland Island is an uninhabited atoll nearby. Another low coral island surrounded by a narrow reef, it has no fresh water. Entry to Baker and Howland Islands is by special-use permit only.

Fact File

OFFICIAL NAME Baker and Howland Islands

FORM OF GOVERNMENT Unincorporated territory of the USA

CAPITAL None; administered from Washington DC

AREA 3 sq km (1.2 sq miles)

TIME ZONE GMT – 10 hours

POPULATION No permanent population

CLIMATE Hot, dry, and windy

MAP REFERENCE Page 139

Christmas Island

A small island in the Indian Ocean, Christmas Island is about 300 km (200 miles) south of Java. Coastal cliffs rise steeply to a central plateau. Formerly uninhabited, Chinese and Malayan labor was brought in to mine the island's rich phosphate deposits in the 1890s, and from 1900 the people enjoyed something of an economic boom. The mine now operates under strict environmental controls to preserve remaining rainforest. After heavy Australian government investment in infrastructure, a hotel and casino complex was opened in 1993, drawing visitors mainly from Southeast Asia.

Fact File

OFFICIAL NAME Territory of Christmas Island

FORM OF GOVERNMENT External territory of Australia

CAPITAL The Settlement

AREA 135 sq km (52 sq miles)

TIME ZONE GMT + 7 hours

POPULATION 1,906 (1996)

LIFE EXPECTANCY Not available

INFANT MORTALITY (PER 1,000) Not available

LITERACY RATE Not available

CURRENCY Australian dollar

ECONOMY Mining, tourism

CLIMATE Tropical, moderated by trade winds

MAP REFERENCE Page 134

Oceania

Oceania

Cocos (Keeling) Islands

The Cocos (Keeling) Islands are a group of 27 coral atolls in the Indian Ocean midway between Australia and Sri Lanka. When discovered in 1609 by the East India Company's Captain William Keeling they were uninhabited. In 1827 the Scot John Clunies-Ross brought some Malays with him and established a settlement. The inhabited islands today are Home Island, where the Cocos Malays live, and West Island, with a small European community. The group has been administered directly by the Australian government since a referendum in 1984. Coconuts are the sole cash crop, copra and fresh coconuts the major export earners. Though local gardens and fishing make a contribution, additional food and other necessities must come from Australia.

Fact File

OFFICIAL NAME Territory of Cocos (Keeling) Islands

FORM OF GOVERNMENT External territory of Australia

CAPITAL West Island

AREA 14 sq km (5.4 sq miles)

TIME ZONE GMT + 7 hours

POPULATION 655 (1996)

LIFE EXPECTANCY Not available

INFANT MORTALITY (PER 1,000) Not available

LITERACY RATE Not available

CURRENCY Australian dollar

ECONOMY Coconut and copra production

CLIMATE Tropical, moderated by trade winds

MAP REFERENCE Page 134

Cook Islands

About 3,500 km (2,175 miles) northeast of New Zealand, the Cook Islands consist of 24 widely separated coral atolls in the north, and hilly, volcanic islands in the south. The Polynesian inhabitants are believed to have settled the islands around AD 500 to 800. They were visited by the Spanish in 1595; explored by Captain James Cook in 1773 and 1777; Christianized by British missionaries

Pristine waters off the Cook Islands (right). Bora Bora resort and lagoon on the Society Islands (top right). The peaks of Anau and Nunue Bora Bora, French Polynesia (center right). Looking out over the city and bay, Guam (far right).

after 1821; and annexed to New Zealand in 1901. Since independence in 1965 the islands have been self-governing in free association with New Zealand. They have a fully responsible government, with elections every five years to a 25-member parliament, based on full adult suffrage. The climate is tropical with plentiful rainfall. Agriculture provides the economic base, and the main export earners are fruit, copra, and clothing. Marine culture has recently led to the production of black pearls and trochus shell. Financial services are available. New Zealand is both the main trading partner (taking 96 percent of exports) and the source of substantial aid. Tourism is expanding.

Fact File

OFFICIAL NAME Cook Islands

FORM OF GOVERNMENT Self-governing territory of New Zealand

CAPITAL Avarua

AREA 240 sq km (93 sq miles)

TIME ZONE GMT – 10 hours

POPULATION 20,200

LIFE EXPECTANCY 71.1

INFANT MORTALITY (PER 1,000) 24.7

LITERACY RATE Not available

CURRENCY New Zealand dollar

ECONOMY Agriculture, services, industry

CLIMATE Tropical, moderated by trade winds

MAP REFERENCE Pages 136–37, 139

Coral Sea Islands

These uninhabited sandy islands and coral reefs are located in the Coral Sea northeast of Australia's Great Barrier Reef. The numerous small islands and reefs are scattered over a sea area of about 1 million sq km (386,000 sq miles), with Willis Islets the most important. Nowhere more

than 6 m (20 ft) above sea level, the area is an important nesting area for seabirds and turtles. There are no permanent freshwater resources and the islands are occasionally subject to cyclones. Although there are no indigenous inhabitants, three meteorologists are stationed there. Defense is the responsibility of Australia, the islets being regularly visited by the Royal Australian Navy. Australia controls the activities of visitors.

Fact File

OFFICIAL NAME Coral Sea Islands Territory

FORM OF GOVERNMENT External territory of Australia

CAPITAL None; administered from Canberra

AREA 3 sq km (1.2 sq miles)

TIME ZONE GMT + 10 hours

POPULATION No permanent population

CLIMATE Tropical

MAP REFERENCE Page 135

with employment, high wages, and improved infrastructure, and resulted in 70 percent of the population moving to live on Tahiti. Tourism now accounts for 20 percent of the gross domestic product. Cultured pearls are the main export.

Uninhabited Clipperton Island, a coral atoll in the Pacific Ocean west of Mexico, is administered by France from French Polynesia.

source of most fresh water), with steep coastal cliffs and narrow coastal plains in the north, low-rising hills in the center, and mountains in the south. About half its population are Chamorro, of mixed Indonesian, Spanish, and Filipino descent. The island is of great strategic importance to the USA and about one-third of its land is occupied by American naval and airforce facilities. This has resulted in a high standard of living, and there are concerns about the unemployment that is likely to follow the planned closing of four naval installations. As a Pacific tourist destination Guam is second only to Hawaii.

French Polynesia

Fact File

OFFICIAL NAME Territory of French Polynesia

FORM OF GOVERNMENT Overseas territory of France

CAPITAL Papeete

AREA 4,167 sq km (1,609 sq miles)

TIME ZONE GMT – 10 hours

POPULATION 242,073

LIFE EXPECTANCY 72.3

INFANT MORTALITY (PER 1,000) 13.6

LITERACY RATE Not available

CURRENCY CFP (Comptoirs Français du Pacifique) franc

ECONOMY Services 68%, industry 19%, agriculture 13%

CLIMATE Tropical

MAP REFERENCE Page 137

French Polynesia comprises five archipelagoes in the South Pacific, midway between Australia and South America, scattered over an area of ocean as large as Europe. They include the Society Islands (Archipel de la Société), the Marquesas (Îles Marquises), the Tubuai Islands, and the Tuamotus (Archipel des Tuamotu). The Polynesian inhabitants first settled the islands about 2,000 years ago. European contact dates from 1767. The conversion of the islanders to Christianity began in 1797 and after three years of armed resistance the chiefs of Tahiti accepted French colonial control in 1843. The islands send two deputies and a senator to the French Assembly in Paris, and since 1984 have had a local territorial assembly as well. Famous for providing the artist Gauguin with his best-known subjects, French Polynesia has been in the news more recently as a site for French nuclear testing on the atoll of Mururoa. This ceased in 1995. Large military expenditures over the preceding 30 years have provided the islands

Guam

Fact File

OFFICIAL NAME Territory of Guam

FORM OF GOVERNMENT Organized, unincorporated territory of the USA

CAPITAL Agana

AREA 541 sq km (209 sq miles)

TIME ZONE GMT + 10 hours

POPULATION 167,590

LIFE EXPECTANCY 74.3

INFANT MORTALITY (PER 1,000) 15.2

LITERACY RATE 99%

CURRENCY US dollar

ECONOMY Services and tourism 54%, government 40%, other 6%

CLIMATE Tropical, moderated by trade winds; wet season July to October

MAP REFERENCE Page 138

The largest and most southerly of the Mariana Islands in the northwest Pacific, Guam lies about 2,000 km (1,200 miles) due east of Manila in the Philippines. Originally settled by Malay-Filipino peoples around 1500 BC, Guam was mapped by Ferdinand Magellan in 1521, claimed by Spain from 1565, and administered by the USA from 1899 after Spain's defeat in the Spanish-American War. Of volcanic origin, Guam consists of a relatively flat coralline limestone plateau (the

Jarvis Island

Fact File

OFFICIAL NAME Jarvis Island

FORM OF GOVERNMENT Unincorporated territory of the USA

CAPITAL None; administered from Washington DC

AREA 4.5 sq km (1.7 sq miles)

TIME ZONE GMT – 10 hours

POPULATION No permanent population

CLIMATE Hot, dry, and windy

MAP REFERENCE Page 139

An uninhabited island in the South Pacific, Jarvis Island lies about midway between Hawaii and the Cook Islands. A sandy coral islet with a fringing reef, it has a tropical climate with little rain and no fresh water. Guano deposits were worked until late in the nineteenth century, and Millersville settlement on the west of the island was used as a weather station from 1935 until the Second World War. Ground cover consists of sparse bunch grass, prostrate vines, and low-growing shrubs. The island is mainly a nesting place for seabirds and marine wildlife. Entry is by special-use permit only.

Johnston Atoll

Fact File

OFFICIAL NAME Johnston Atoll

FORM OF GOVERNMENT Unincorporated territory of the USA

CAPITAL None; administered from Washington DC

AREA 2.8 sq km (1.1 sq miles)

TIME ZONE GMT – 10 hours

POPULATION No permanent population

ECONOMY US military base

CLIMATE Hot, dry, and windy

MAP REFERENCE Page 139

This remote coral atoll consisting of two islets, Johnston Island and Sand Island, lies in the North Pacific about one-third of the way between Hawaii and the Marshall Islands. The atoll is 5 m (16 ft) above sea level at its highest point and has a dry tropical climate, northeast trade winds ensuring little seasonal temperature variation. Mined during the nineteenth century for its extensive guano deposits, the atoll is now home to approximately 1,200 US military personnel. It was formerly used as a nuclear weapons testing site. The territory is administered by the US Defense Nuclear Agency and managed cooperatively by the DNA and the Fish and Wildlife Service of the US Department of the Interior as part of the National Wildlife Refuge system.

Kingman Reef

A barren triangular-shaped reef in the North Pacific, Kingman Reef is about halfway between Hawaii and American Samoa. No more than 1 m (3 ft) above sea level, and awash most of the time, the reef is a maritime hazard. Although no economic activity takes place and the reef is uninhabited, the deep interior lagoon was used as a halfway station between Hawaii and American Samoa when Pan American Airways used flying boats in the Pacific in 1937 and 1938. While there is no land flora, the reef is rich in marine life. It is administered by the US Navy.

An aerial view of Amadee Island, New Caledonia (right). Historic colonial buildings and ruins on Norfolk Island (top right). Clear blue waters form an inlet on the South Pacific island of Niue (bottom right).

Fact File

OFFICIAL NAME Kingman Reef

FORM OF GOVERNMENT Unincorporated territory of the USA

CAPITAL None; administered from Washington DC

AREA 1 sq km (0.4 sq miles)

TIME ZONE GMT – 10 hours

POPULATION No permanent population

CLIMATE Tropical, moderated by sea breezes

MAP REFERENCE Page 139

Midway Islands

The two Midway Islands constitute part of an atoll in the northern Pacific at the extreme western end of the Hawaiian chain, 1,931 km (1,200 miles) northwest of Hawaii. Their name derives from their position midway along the old shipping route from California to Japan.

The atoll is almost completely flat, and none of the land is higher than 4 m (13 ft) above sea level. During the Second World War it was the scene of a major battle between Japan and the USA, and today it is used as a naval airbase. It is also a wildlife refuge. The islands have no indigenous inhabitants and the population is confined to about 450 US military personnel and civilian contractors. They are serviced by the port of Sand Island, Johnston Atoll.

Fact File

OFFICIAL NAME Midway Islands

FORM OF GOVERNMENT Unincorporated territory of the USA

CAPITAL None; administered from Washington DC

AREA 5.2 sq km (1.9 sq miles)

TIME ZONE GMT – 10 hours

POPULATION No permanent population

ECONOMY US military base

CLIMATE Tropical, moderated by sea breezes

MAP REFERENCE Page 139

New Caledonia

Fact File

OFFICIAL NAME Territory of New Caledonia and Dependencies

FORM OF GOVERNMENT Overseas territory of France

CAPITAL Nouméa

AREA 19,060 sq km (7,359 sq miles)

TIME ZONE GMT + 11 hours

POPULATION 197,361

LIFE EXPECTANCY 75.4

INFANT MORTALITY (PER 1,000) 12.2

LITERACY RATE 93.1%

CURRENCY CFP (Comptoirs Français du Pacifique) franc

ECONOMY Services 40%, agriculture 32%, industry 28%

CLIMATE Tropical, moderated by trade winds

MAP REFERENCE Pages 136, 141

New Caledonia is a group of islands 1,500 km (900 miles) off the northeast coast of Australia. Rich in minerals, and with more than 40 percent of the world's known nickel resources, it is France's largest overseas territory. First populated by indigenous Kanaks (who call the land Kanaky) around 4000 BC, the islands were visited by the Spanish in the sixteenth and seventeenth centuries, were named by Captain James Cook in 1774, and were used as a penal settlement by France between 1853 and 1897. By the end of the nineteenth century French settlers owned more than 90 percent of the land. Dissatisfaction with their situation led to violent resistance from the Kanaks during the 1970s and 1980s, but more recently they have come to accept French rule. The Kanaks now represent only 43 percent of the population, while 37 percent are of European descent. The main island, Grand Terre, consists of coastal plains with a mountainous interior. Only a small amount of land is suitable for cultivation. New Caledonia's prosperity is almost entirely dependent on nickel production, so the economy is at the mercy of varying world demand. Tourism from France, Japan, and Australia is also important.

Niue

Niue is one of the world's biggest coral atolls, lying about 700 km (400 miles) east of Tonga in the South Pacific. The terrain consists of a central limestone plateau with steep cliffs around the coast; the highest point is 68 m (223 ft). The economy is heavily dependent on aid from the New Zealand government. Most of the inhabitants live by subsistence farming. Light industry consists of processing passionfruit, lime oil, honey, and coconut cream. The sale of postage stamps and tourism are also a source of foreign currency. Remittances from family members living overseas supplement domestic income: lack of employment opportunities on the island means that five out of six of the people of Niue live and work in New Zealand.

Fact File

OFFICIAL NAME Niue

FORM OF GOVERNMENT Self-governing territory in free association with New Zealand

CAPITAL Alofi

AREA 260 sq km (100 sq miles)

TIME ZONE GMT – 11 hours

POPULATION 2,321 (1994)

LIFE EXPECTANCY Not available

INFANT MORTALITY (PER 1,000) Not available

LITERACY RATE Not available

CURRENCY New Zealand dollar

ECONOMY Agriculture, industry (food processing, coconuts), services

CLIMATE Tropical, moderated by trade winds

MAP REFERENCE Pages 132, 136

Norfolk Island

Some 1,400 km (850 miles) east of Australia, Norfolk Island is inhabited by descendants of the famous mutineers from HMS *Bounty*. Of volcanic origin, the island was uninhabited when discovered by Captain James Cook in 1774. After serving as a penal settlement in Australia's early history it became a refuge for the entire population of the Pitcairn Islands' *Bounty* mutiny survivors, who were resettled there in 1856. (Some later returned to live on Pitcairn Island.) The present inhabitants speak a mixture of nineteenth century English, Gaelic, and Old Tahitian. They enjoy a degree of autonomy and have rejected proposals to become a part of the Australian state. While there is no income tax, the government raises revenue from customs duty, liquor sales, a public works levy, financial institutions levy, and departure fees. Tourism is the main activity, the island receiving around 30,000 visitors each year.

Fact File

OFFICIAL NAME Territory of Norfolk Island

FORM OF GOVERNMENT External territory of Australia

CAPITAL Kingston

AREA 35 sq km (14 sq miles)

TIME ZONE GMT + 11.5 hours

POPULATION 2,756 (1995)

LIFE EXPECTANCY Not available

INFANT MORTALITY (PER 1,000) Not available

LITERACY RATE Not available

CURRENCY Australian dollar

ECONOMY Tourism, agriculture

CLIMATE Subtropical

MAP REFERENCE Pages 133, 136

Northern Mariana Islands

Fact File

OFFICIAL NAME Commonwealth of the Northern Mariana Islands

FORM OF GOVERNMENT Territory of the USA; commonwealth in political union with the USA

CAPITAL Saipan

AREA 477 sq km (184 sq miles)

TIME ZONE GMT + 10 hours

POPULATION 69,343

LIFE EXPECTANCY 76

INFANT MORTALITY (PER 1,000) 6.5

LITERACY RATE Not available

CURRENCY US dollar

ECONOMY Tourism, industry, agriculture

CLIMATE Tropical, moderated by trade winds

MAP REFERENCE Page 138

These islands are located in the North Pacific about three-quarters of the way between Hawaii and the Philippines. Unlike the nearby Caroline Islands, the Northern Marianas chose not to seek independence in 1987, preferring to remain part of the USA. There are 14 main islands including Saipan, Rota, and Tinian. The southern islands are limestone with level terraces and fringing coral reefs; the northern islands are volcanic, with active volcanoes on Pagan and Agrihan. There is little seasonal variation in the tropical marine climate, as the temperature is moderated by northeast trade winds. The people of the islands belong to a variety of ethnic groups and include Chamorros (mixed Indonesian,

Spanish, and Filipino), Micronesians, Japanese, Chinese, and Koreans. The economy is substantially supported by the USA. Tourism is a fast-growing source of income, employing increasing numbers of the workforce and bringing in most revenue. Cattle ranches produce beef, and small farms produce coconuts, breadfruit, tomatoes, and melons. Industry consists of handicrafts, light manufacturing, and garment production.

Palmyra Atoll

Fact File

OFFICIAL NAME Palmyra Atoll

FORM OF GOVERNMENT Incorporated territory of the USA

CAPITAL None; administered from Washington DC

AREA 12 sq km (4.6 sq miles)

TIME ZONE GMT – 10 hours

POPULATION No permanent population

CLIMATE Tropical

MAP REFERENCE Page 139

A privately owned uninhabited atoll in the northern Pacific, Palmyra Atoll lies about halfway between Hawaii and Samoa. At no point more than 2 m (6 ft) above sea level, the atoll consists of about 50 islets covered with dense vegetation, coconut palms, and balsa-like trees that grow up to 30 m (100 ft) tall. A number of roads and causeways were built during the Second World War, but they are now overgrown and unserviceable, as is the airstrip. In 1990 a Hawaiian property developer took out a 75-year lease from its owners, the Fullard-Leo brothers. There are plans to turn the atoll into a "get away from it all" tourist complex.

Pitcairn Islands

Fact File

OFFICIAL NAME Pitcairn, Henderson, Ducie, and Oeno Islands

FORM OF GOVERNMENT Dependent territory of the United Kingdom

CAPITAL Adamstown

AREA 47 sq km (18 sq miles)

TIME ZONE GMT – 8.5 hours

POPULATION 54 (1995)

LIFE EXPECTANCY Not available

INFANT MORTALITY (PER 1,000) Not available

LITERACY RATE Not available

CURRENCY New Zealand dollar

ECONOMY Fishing, agriculture, services

CLIMATE Tropical, with rainy season from November to March

MAP REFERENCE Page 137

The Pitcairn Islands are located in the southern Pacific about midway between Peru and New Zealand. They have a rugged volcanic formation, cliffs along a rocky coast, and a tropical, hot, and humid climate. The islands are the United Kingdom's most isolated dependency. Uninhabited when they were discovered by Europeans, they were used as a refuge by the mutineers from HMS *Bounty* in 1790, some of whose descendants still live there speaking a dialect that is part-Tahitian, part-English. They exist by fishing and subsistence farming. The fertile valley soils produce fruits and vegetables including citrus, sugarcane, watermelons, bananas, yams, and beans. Barter is an important economic activity. The main source of revenue is the sale of postage stamps and handicrafts to passing ships.

Newly harvested coconuts are piled on a beach in the Pacific Islands (left). Bananas are widely grown on Pacific Islands like Tokelau (above left).

Tokelau

Fact File

OFFICIAL NAME	Tokelau
FORM OF GOVERNMENT	Territory of New Zealand
CAPITAL	None; administrative center on each atoll
AREA	10 sq km (3.9 sq miles)
TIME ZONE	GMT – 11 hours
POPULATION	1,503 (1995)
LIFE EXPECTANCY	Not available
INFANT MORTALITY (PER 1,000)	Not available
LITERACY RATE	Not available
CURRENCY	New Zealand dollar
ECONOMY	Agriculture, industry
CLIMATE	Tropical, moderated by trade winds April to November
MAP REFERENCE	Page 139

Tokelau is a small group of islands in the South Pacific about midway between Hawaii and New Zealand. The islands consist of low coral atolls, no higher than 5 m (16 ft) above sea level, enclosing large lagoons. Lying in the Pacific typhoon belt (a cyclone in 1990 wrecked much of Tokelau's infrastructure), they have a tropical climate moderated by trade winds. There are limited natural resources, subsistence farmers growing coconuts, breadfruit, papaya, and bananas. Small-scale industry produces copra, woodwork, plaited craft goods, stamps, and coins. A tuna cannery is expected to help the economy, and it is hoped that a catamaran link between the atolls will boost tourism. Aid from New Zealand is the main source of revenue and money remitted by relatives in New Zealand is a vital source of domestic income.

Wake Island

Wake Island is located in the North Pacific about two-thirds of the way between Hawaii and the Northern Mariana Islands. It consists of three tiny coral islets linked by causeways around a lagoon. The islets are built on fragments of the rim of an extinct underwater volcano, the lagoon being the former crater. With no indigenous inhabitants or economic activity, the 300 or so US military personnel stationed on Wake Island provide help in the case of emergency landings by aircraft on transpacific flights.

The problem of coral bleaching

Coral reefs constitute one of the Earth's great diverse ecosystems. They are made of limestone formed by millions of tiny marine animals and can only live in tropical seas within a narrow range of physical and chemical conditions. Coral reefs generally form only when winter water temperatures exceed 18°C (64°F) and when light levels are high. Coral is found in the rock record in the form of fossils dating back to the Paleozoic Era. However, although coral has survived this long, it is not immune to the impact of human activities.

In recent years scientists have become interested in the apparent link between the death of large tracts of coral in the Pacific and Caribbean regions and global warming. The greenhouse effect—a result of changes in the amounts of carbon dioxide and other gases in the atmosphere since the industrial revolution— is the cause of this global warming. Satellite data from the US National Oceanographic and Atmospheric Administration show a warming trend in sea-surface temperatures since 1982. In some areas, such as along the Great Barrier Reef in Australia, a combination of higher than usual summer temperatures and the run-off from floods (which reduces salinity) appears to be damaging the coral. As the essential conditions required for the maintenance of a healthy reef system are disrupted, the coral formations turn white.

What will happen to coral reefs in the future? Are the bleaching episodes observed in recent years in so many tropical areas really due to global warming or are there other causes? Predictions that ocean surface temperatures in the tropics may rise by up to 5°C (41°F) in the 21st century are no longer considered fantasy. If this happens, it could greatly disturb even resilient ecosystems, such as coral reefs, and reduce the Earth's biodiversity as well as the ability of societies to live and work in these areas.

Fact File

OFFICIAL NAME	Wake Island
FORM OF GOVERNMENT	Unincorporated territory of the USA
CAPITAL	None; administered from Washington DC
AREA	6.5 sq km (2.5 sq miles)
TIME ZONE	GMT – 10 hours
POPULATION	No permanent population
ECONOMY	US military base
CLIMATE	Tropical
MAP REFERENCE	Page 138

Wallis and Futuna Islands

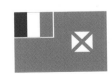

This group comprises three main islands— Futuna, Alofi and Wallis (Uvea)—and 20 islets, located west of Samoa and northeast of Fiji. They are of volcanic origin, with low hills rising to 765 m (2,510 ft) at Mt Singavi. All the main islands have fringing reefs. In the hot wet season from November to April 2,500–3,000 mm (100–120 in) of rain may fall. This rain, combined with deforestation (timber is used locally for fuel), has eroded the terrain of Futuna. The people live by subsistence farming. Exports are negligible and French aid is essential to the islands. First settled perhaps 2,000 years ago, and visited by the Dutch in 1616, the islands became a French protectorate in 1886. In a referendum on independence in 1959 they chose to become a French Overseas Territory. There is no independence movement.

Fact File

OFFICIAL NAME	Territory of the Wallis and Futuna Islands
FORM OF GOVERNMENT	Overseas territory of France
CAPITAL	Mata Utu
AREA	274 sq km (106 sq miles)
TIME ZONE	GMT + 12 hours
POPULATION	15,129
LIFE EXPECTANCY	Not available
INFANT MORTALITY (PER 1,000)	Not available
LITERACY RATE	Not available
CURRENCY	CFP (Comptoirs Français du Pacifique) franc
ECONOMY	Agriculture, fishing
CLIMATE	Tropical, with wet season November to April
MAP REFERENCE	Page 139

Oceania: Physical

Oceania

A 120° B 130° C 140° D 150° E 160°

1

Caroline Islan
Namoluk Ngatik
Mortlock Is Lukunor
Nukuoro

Sonsorol
Pulo Anna
Merir

Tobi
Helen

CELEBES
SEA

Borneo

Kapingamarangi
Atoll

0°

Halmahera
Waigeo

Kep. Togian

MOLUCCA
SEA

Biak

Ninego Group Kaniet Is St Matthias
Group
Manus
Admiralty New Hanover
Islands

Melan

Solomon Islands

Sulawesi
(Celebes)

CERAM SEA

Yapen

BISMARCK
SEA

New Ireland
Nuguria Is
Green Is Buka Tauu Is
New
Britain Bougainville

Nu

Java

2

Buru
Seram

Kai
Besar Kep. Aru

New Guinea

Onto
Java

JAVA
SEA

Kep. Kangean

Selayar

Mt Wilhelm
4509 m

Choiseul
Santa I

Laut
Buton

BANDA
SEA

Kep.
Babar Kep. Tanimbar

Mt Victoria
4038 m

Owen Stanley Range

SOLOMON

Jawa
(Java)

Bali Lombok
Sumbawa

FLORES SEA

Kep.
Sermata

Dolak

Gulf of
Papua

Trobriand Is
Woodlark

New Georgia
Group

Guadalcar

Flores
Timor

Louisiade Arch.

SEA

10°

Sumba

Sawu Roti

ARAFURA SEA

Torres Strait

Prince of C. York
Wales I

Tagula Rossel

Bellona

Rennel

Melville I.

Wessel Is

TIMOR

Cape Londonderry

Joseph
Bonaparte
Gulf

Arnhem
Land

Groote
Eylandt

Gulf
of
Carpentaria

Cape
York

Cape
Melville

Great Barrier Reef

CORAL

Coral Sea
Islands

3

SEA

Kimberley
Plateau

Daly

Victoria

Cape
York
Peninsula

Great Dividing Range

Hinchinbrook
Island

SEA

Lake
Argyle

Tanami

Barkly

Whitsunday Group

Îles
Chesterfield

20°

Great Sandy

Desert

Desert

Tableland

Torilla Pen.

Barrow I.
North West
Cape

Pilbara

Lake
Mackay

Tropic of Capricorn

Hamersley Range

Lake
Disappointment

Hervey Bay

Sandy Cape
Fraser I.

Shark
Bay

Ashburton

Gibson Desert

MacDonnell Ranges

Australia

Great Artesian

4

Mt Augustus
1105 m

863 m
Uluru (Ayers Rock)

Simpson

Basin

Diamantina

Moreton I.
North Stradbroke I.

Murchison

Lake
Carnegie

Desert

Strzelecki

Cooper

Lake Eyre
North

Desert

Great Victoria

Lake Eyre
South

Grey Range

Paroo

Great Dividing Range

30°

Lake
Barlee

Desert

Lake Torrens

Lake
Frome

Darling

Lord Howe I.

Lake
Moore

Nullarbor Plain

Lake
Gairdner

Lake Macfarlane

Lachlan

Cape Hawke

Darling
Range

Eyre
Pen.

Murray

Murrumbidgee

Botany Bay

Great

Cape Leeuwin
Point
d'Entrecasteaux

Cape Pasley

Australian Bight

Spencer Gulf

Jervis Bay

TASMA

5

Kangaroo I.

Encounter Bay

Mt Kosciuszko
2229 m

Great Dividing Range

Cape
Jaffa

Glenelg

Cape Howe

Cape Otway

Bass Strait

Furneaux

40°

King I.

Flinders I.
Group

SEA

Cape Grim

Tasmania

Macquarie
Harbour

Mt Ossa
1617 m

Great
Oyster Bay

South Bruny I.

South East
Cape

6

SOUTHERN OCEAN

50°

7

A 120° B 130° C 140° D 150° E 160°

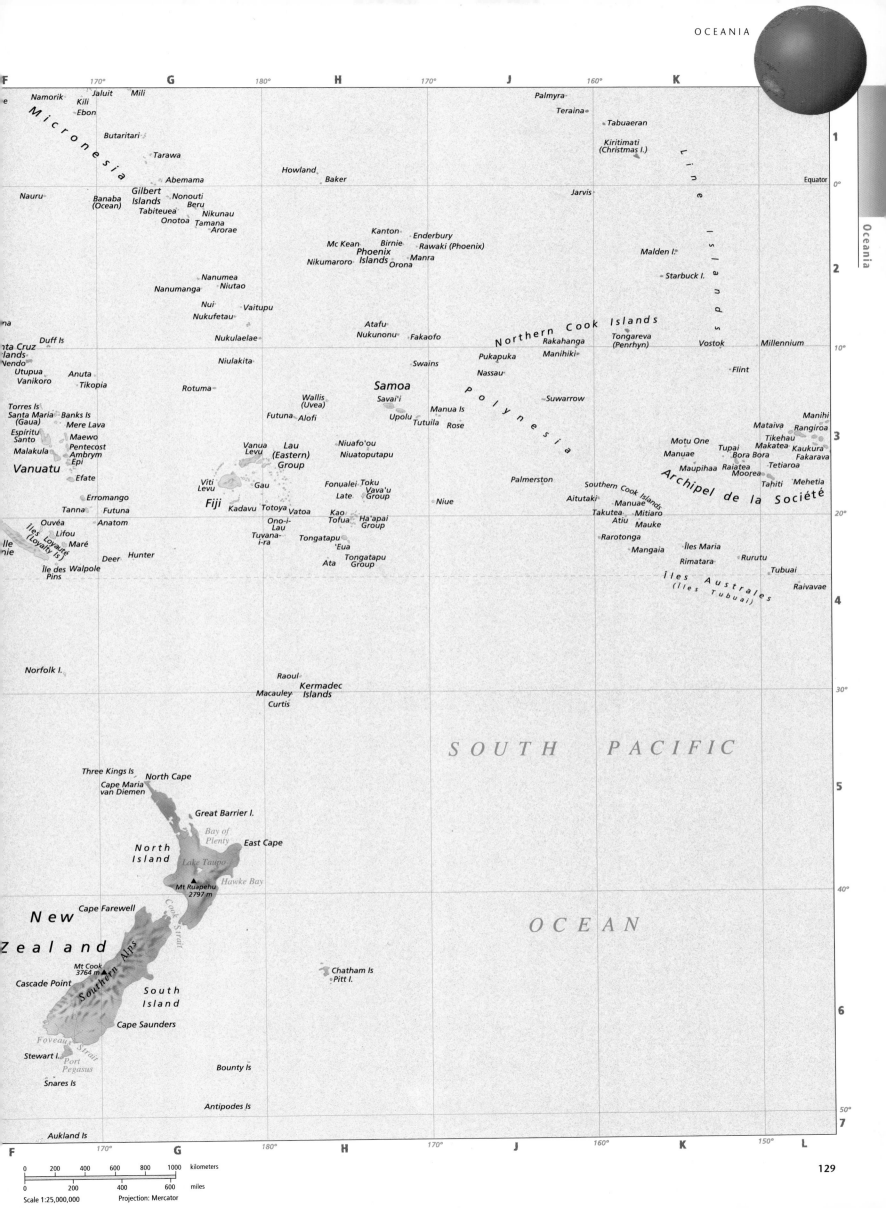

OCEANIA

Micronesia

Namorik Kili Jaluit Mili
Ebon
Butaritari
Tarawa
Abemama
Nauru Banaba Gilbert Nonouti
(Ocean) Islands Beru
Tabiteuea Nikunau
Onotoa Tamana
Arorae

Palmyra
Teraina
Tabuaeran
Kiritimati
(Christmas I.)

Equator

Jarvis

Line Islands

Howland Baker

Kanton
Mc Kean Birnie Enderbury
Phoenix Rawaki (Phoenix)
Nikumaroro Islands Orona
Manra

Malden I.

Starbuck I.

Nanumea Niutao
Nanumanga
Nui Vaitupu
Nukufetau

Atafu
Nukulaelae Nukunonu Fakaofo

Northern Cook Islands
Rakahanga Tongareva Vostok Millennium
(Penrhyn)
Niulakita Pukapuka Manihiki
Swains Nassau
Santa Cruz Samoa Flint
Islands Anuta Savai'i Suwarrow
Vendo Tikopia Rotuma Wallis
Utupua (Uvea) Manua Is
Vanikoro Futuna Alofi Upolu Rose Polynesia
Tutuila
Torres Is
Santa Maria Banks Is Manihi
(Gaua) Mere Lava Vanua Niuafo'ou Mataiva Rangiroa
Espiritu Maewo Levu Lau Niuatoputapu Motu One Tikehau
Santo Pentecost (Eastern) Tupai Makatea Kaukura
Malakula Ambrym Group Viti Gau Fonualei Toku Manuae Bora Bora Raiatea Fakarava
Epi Levu Late Vava'u Maupihaa Tetiaroa
Vanuatu Efate Fiji Kadavu Totoya Vatoa Group Palmerston Moorea
Erromango Kao Niue Southern Cook Islands Tahiti Mehetia
Tanna Futuna Anatom Ono-i- Tofua Ha'apai Aitutaki Manuae Archipel de la Société
Ouvéa Lau Group Takutea Mitiaro
Lifou Tuvana- Mauke
Îles Loyauté Maré i-ra Tongatapu Rarotonga Atiu
(Loyalty Is) 'Eua Mangaia Îles Maria Rurutu
Deer Hunter Ata Tongatapu Rimatara
Île des Walpole Group Îles Australes
Pins (Îles Tubuai) Raivavae
Tubuai

Norfolk I.

Raoul
Macauley Kermadec
Curtis Islands

SOUTH PACIFIC

Three Kings Is North Cape
Cape Maria
van Diemen
Great Barrier I.
Bay of East Cape
North Plenty
Island Lake Taupo
Mt Ruapehu Hawke Bay
2797 m

Cape Farewell

New
Zealand Cook Strait OCEAN
Mt Cook
3764 m Southern Alps
Cascade Point Chatham Is
South Pitt I.
Island

Cape Saunders

Foveaux Strait
Stewart I.
Port
Pegasus
Snares Is Bounty Is

Antipodes Is

F G H J K L

Aukland Is

0 200 400 600 800 1000 kilometers
0 200 400 600 miles
Scale 1:25,000,000 Projection: Mercator

Oceania: Political

Oceania

BRUNEI

MALAYSIA

PHILIPPINES

CELEBES SEA

Sonsorol

Caroline Islan...

Namoluk

Mortlock Is Lukunor Ngatik

PALAU

Tobi

Helen

Nukuoro

MICRONESIA

Kot

Halmahera

Waigeo

Borneo

Kapingamarangi Atoll

Sulawesi (Celebes)

MOLUCCA SEA

Yapen

Ninego Group

New Hanover

JAVA SEA

Buru

INDONESIA

Admiralty Islands

PAPUA

New Ireland Nuguria Is

BANDA SEA

Wewak

BISMARCK SEA

New Britain

Green Is Nukum...

Buka

Tauu Is

Jawa (Java)

Madang

Goroka

NEW

Bougainville

Choiseul

Santa I...

Bali

Kep. Aru

Mount Hagen

Lae

SOLOMON

Honiara

FLORES SEA

Kep. Babar

Kep. Tanimbar

Dolak

Kerema

GUINEA

Trobriand Is

Woodlark

New Georgia Group

Guadalca...

Flores

Timor

ARAFURA SEA

Port Moresby ⊛

SEA

Louisiade Arch.

Bellona

Sumba

Roti

Torres Strait

Tagula

Rossel

Rennel...

TIMOR SEA

Melville I.

Wessel Is

Gulf of Carpentaria

CORAL

ASHMORE AND CARTIER ISLANDS (Aust.)

Darwin ⊛

CORAL SEA ISLANDS (Aust.)

Joseph Bonaparte Gulf

Katherine

Cairns

SEA

Wyndham

NORTHERN

Townsville

Whitsunday Group

Îles Chesterfield

N...

Derby

Halls Creek

Tennant Creek

TERRITORY

Mount Isa

Mackay

CAL...

Broome

Mount Isa

QUEENSLAND

Rockhampton

Port Hedland

Karratha

Barcaldine

Gladstone

Tropic of Capricorn

Newman

WESTERN

AUSTRALIA

Alice Springs

Charleville

Maryborough

Fraser I.

Noosa Heads

Carnarvon

AUSTRALIA

Toowoomba

⊛ Brisbane

Meekatharra

AUSTRALIA

Ballina

Geraldton

Coober Pedy

Grafton

SOUTH

Bourke

Coffs Harbour

Kalgoorlie-Boulder

AUSTRALIA

Tamworth

Lord Howe I. (Aust.)

Perth ⊛

Ceduna

Broken Hill

Port Macquarie

Bunbury

Whyalla

Port Augusta

Dubbo

NEW SOUTH

Orange

Newcastle

Busselton

Esperance

Great Australian Bight

Port Pirie

WALES

Bathurst

⊛ Sydney

Albany

Port Lincoln

Gawler

⊛ Adelaide

Wagga Wagga

Wollongong

Kangaroo I.

Murray Bridge

Albury

A.C.T. ⊛ Canberra

Queanbeyan

VICTORIA

TASMA...

Mount Gambier

Ballarat

⊛ Melbourne

Warrnambool

Geelong

Bass Strait

Furneaux

King I.

Flinders I. Group

Burnie

Devonport

Launceston

SEA

TASMANIA

⊛ Hobart

South Bruny I.

SOUTHERN   OCEAN

© Random House Australia Pty Ltd

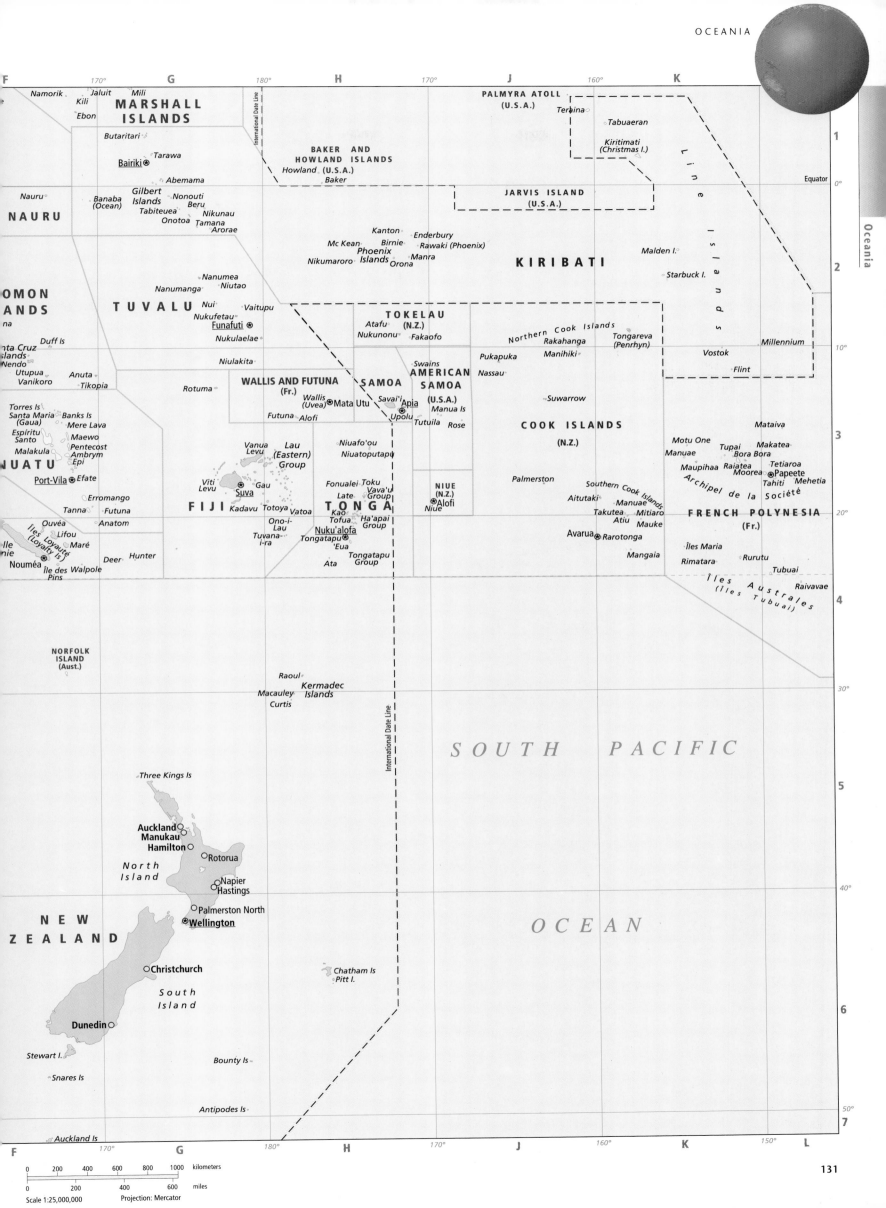

Namorik Jaluit Mili
Kili
Ebon

**MARSHALL
ISLANDS**

Butaritari

Tarawa
Bairiki ⊛
Abemama

PALMYRA ATOLL
(U.S.A.)
Teraina

Tabuaeran

Kiritimati
(Christmas I.)

Equator

Nauru   Banaba   Gilbert   Nonouti
(Ocean)   Islands   Beru
Tabiteuea   Nikunau

NAURU

Onotoa Tamana
Arorae

Kanton
Mc Kean   Birnie   Enderbury
Phoenix   Rawaki (Phoenix)
Islands
Nikumaroro   Manra
Orona

Malden I.

KIRIBATI

Starbuck I.

Nanumea
Nanumanga   Niutao

TUVALU   Nui   Vaitupu
Nukufetau
Funafuti ⊛
Nukulaelae

**TOKELAU
(N.Z.)**
Atafu
Nukunonu   Fakaofo

Northern Cook Islands
Rakahanga   Tongareva
(Penrhyn)

Vostok

Millennium

**OMON
ANDS**

na

Duff Is

nta Cruz
Islands
Vendo
Utupua
Vanikoro   Anuta
Tikopia

Niulakita

Rotuma

**WALLIS AND FUTUNA
(Fr.)**

SAMOA

Swains

**AMERICAN
SAMOA**
(U.S.A.)

Nassau

Pukapuka   Manihiki

Suwarrow

Flint

Mataiva

Torres Is
Santa Maria   Banks Is
(Gaua)
Espíritu   Mere Lava
Santo
Malakula   Maewo
Pentecost
NUATU   Ambrym
Epi

Port-Vila ⊛ Efate

Wallis
(Uvea) ⊛ Mata Utu
Futuna Alofi

Savai'i
⊛ Apia
Upolu   Manua Is
Tutuila   Rose

**COOK ISLANDS
(N.Z.)**

Palmerston

Motu One
Manuae   Tupai   Makatea
Bora Bora
Maupihaa   Raiatea   Tetiaroa
Moorea ⊛ Papeete
Tahiti   Mehetia

Vanua
Levu   Lau
(Eastern)
Group

Niuafo'ou
Niuatoputapu

Archipel de la Société

Erromango
Tanna   Futuna
Anatom

Ouvéa
Îles Loyauté   Lifou
(Loyalty Is)   Maré

Viti
Levu Gau
⊛
Suva

FIJI Kadavu Totoya
Ono-i-
Lau
Tuvana-
i-ra

Fonualei Toku
Late   Vava'u
Group
Kao
Tofua   Ha'apai
Group

TONGA

**NIUE
(N.Z.)**
⊛ Alofi
Niue

Aitutaki
Southern Cook Islands
Takutea   Manuae
Atiu   Mitiaro
Avarua ⊛ Rarotonga   Mauke

**FRENCH POLYNESIA
(Fr.)**

Îles Maria

Rimatara

Rurutu

**NEW
ZEALAND**

Noumea
Deer   Hunter
Île des Walpole
Pins

Vatoa
Nuku'alofa ⊛
Tongatapu
'Eua
Ata   Tongatapu
Group

Mangaia

Tubuai

Raivavae

Îles Australes
(Îles Tubuai)

**NORFOLK
ISLAND
(Aust.)**

Raoul
Macauley   Kermadec
Islands
Curtis

Three Kings Is

Auckland ○
Manukau ○
Hamilton ○
○ Rotorua
**North
Island**

○ Napier
Hastings

○ Palmerston North

⊛ Wellington

Christchurch

**South
Island**

Chatham Is
Pitt I.

S O U T H   P A C I F I C

O C E A N

Dunedin ○

Stewart I.

Snares Is

Bounty Is

Antipodes Is

Auckland Is

0   200   400   600   800   1000   kilometers

0   200   400   600   miles

Scale 1:25,000,000   Projection: Mercator

New Zealand

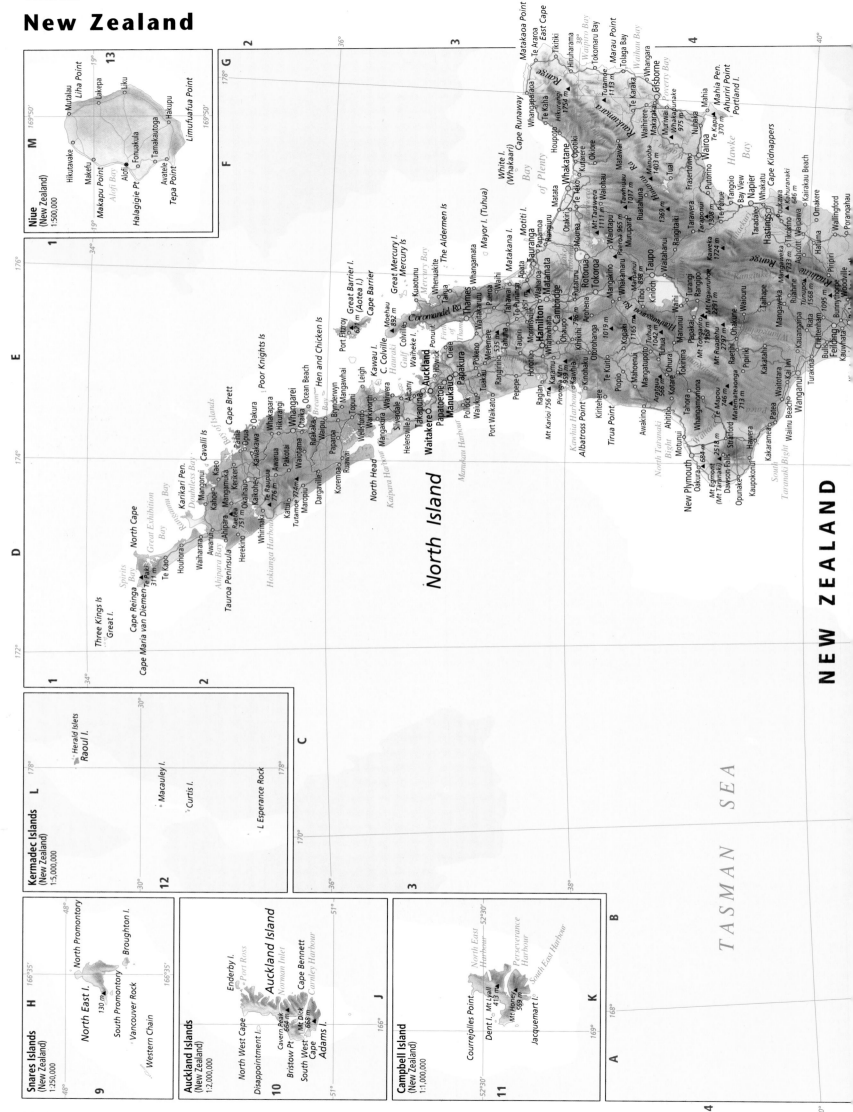

Niue
(New Zealand)
1:500,000

13

Kermadec Islands
(New Zealand)
1:5,000,000

12

Snares Islands
(New Zealand)
1:250,000

9

Auckland Islands
(New Zealand)
1:2,000,000

10

Campbell Island
(New Zealand)
1:1,000,000

11

NEW ZEALAND

North Island

TASMAN SEA

© Random House Australia Pty Ltd

South Island

SOUTH PACIFIC

OCEAN

SOUTHERN ALPS

Stewart Island

Insets

Bounty Islands (New Zealand)
1:400,000

Eastern Group
Western Group
Centre Group

Antipodes Islands (New Zealand)
1:1,000,000

Bollons I.
North Cape
Windward Is.
Leeward I.
Mt Galloway 366 m
Albatross Point
Antipodes Island

Chatham Islands (New Zealand)
1:2,500,000

The Sisters
Cape Young
C. Pattisson
Taupeka Point
Point Munning
Okawa Point
Te Whanga Lagoon
The Forty Fours
Petre Bay
Te Hapuna
Te One
Waitangi
Owenga
Chatham I.
Point Durham
Cape Fournier
Cape L Eveque
Waihola
Mangere I.
Kahuitara Point
Pitt I.
Rangatira I.
Pyramid I.
Pitt Strait

Selected place names

Wainuioru, Greytown, Riversdale, Martinborough, Mt Adams 663 m, Acton Point, Upper Hutt, Lower Hutt, Porirua, Pakuratahi, Wellington, Wairarapa, Mt Ross 981 m, Tuturumuri, Te Kaukau Point (Mungaroa), Turakirae Head, Cape Palliser, Palliser Bay, Cape Jackson, Cape Campbell, Clifford Bay, Cape Stokes 1204 m, Broadmeadows, Picton, Havelock, Blenheim, Tuamarina, Wairau Valley, Seddon, Tapuae-o-Uenuku 2885 m, Clarence, Kekerengu, Mayakau 2610 m, Kaikoura, Kaikoura Peninsula, Spyglass Point, Hawkswood, Cheviot

Motueka, Mapua, Hira, Richmond, Nelson, Wakefield, Mt Richmond 760 m, Belgrove, Ngakawau, Tinangahua, Mt Owen 1875 m, Pinnacle 2131 m, Saint Arnaud, Shingle Peak 2327 m, Mt Franklin 2088 m, Hanmer Springs, Waiau, Motunau Beach, Amberley, Waikari, Scargill, Waipara

Westport, Charleston, Punakaiki, Greymouth, Kumara Junction, Hokitika, Ross, Harihari, Cape Foulwind, Karamea Bight, Karamea, Mt Kendall 1811 m, Aniki, Mt Hutton 1400 m, Murchison, Reefton, Ikamatua, Mt Uriah 1532 m, Aratika, Mt Harata 1373 m, Rotomanu, Stillwater, Kumara, Arthur's Pass, Mt Rolleston 2271 m, Jacksons, Mt Whitcombe 2637 m, Mt Arrowsmith 2795 m, Mt Binser 1859 m, Mt Erys 2195 m, Oxford, Waddington, Eyreton, Kaiapoi, Spenceville, Christchurch, Lyttelton, Sumner, Mt Herbert 917 m, Banks Peninsula, Akaroa, Akaroa Harbour, Diamond Harbour

Franz Joseph Glacier, Fox Glacier, Otorokua Point, Bruce Bay, Lake Moeraki, Okarito Lagoon, Mt Tasman 3497 m, Mt Cook / Aoraki 3764 m, Mt Stevenson 2366 m, Fox Peak 2332 m, Lake Tekapo, The Hunters Hills, Twizel, Omarama, Otematata, Kurow, Mt Mary 2332 m, Mt Pisgah 1643 m, Lake Hawea, Lake Wanaka, Wanaka, Cromwell, Alexandra, Clyde, Roxburgh, Middlemarch, Outram, Mosgiel, Dunedin, Brighton, Otago Peninsula, Port Chalmers, Katiki Point, Shag Point, Waikouaiti, Palmerston, Hampden, Maheno, Oamaru, Pukeuri, Glenavy, Ikawai, Waimate, Makikihi, Pareora, Timaru, Temuka, Pleasant Point, Geraldine, Rangitata, Hinds, Mayfield, Methven, Rakaia, Ashburton, Southbridge, Leeston, Halswell, Tai Tapu

Jackson Bay, Cascade Point, Big Bay, Milford Sound, Milford Sounds, Bligh Sound, George Sound, Caswell Sound, Charles Sound, Doubtful Sound, Breaksea I., Dusky Sound, Resolution I., Mt Aspiring 3027 m, Mt Earnslaw 2819 m, Mt Tutoko 2746 m, Mt Christina 2502 m, Glenorchy, Queenstown, Mt Cardrona 1934 m, Mt Alta 2355 m, Mt Alba 2355 m, Arrowtown, Mt Rosa 1961 m, Kingston, Double Cone 2324 m, Obelisk 1695 m, Mid Dome 1479 m, Jane Peak 2035 m, Garvie Mtns, Nevis, Bannockburn, Gorge Creek, Lawrence, Tapanui, Waipahi, Gore, Mataura, Edendale, Wyndham, Mokoreta 713 m, Quarry Hills, Owaka, Kaka Point, Balclutha, Clinton, Clarksville, Kaitangata, Raes Junction, Clutha, Taieri, Maclennan

Te Anau, Manapouri, Mararoa, Lumsden, Mossburn, Dipton, Riversdale, Benmore, Hedgehope, Winton, Browns, Oreti, Makarewa, Wallacetown, Otautau, Nightcaps, Ohai, Wairio, Wreys Bush, Heddon Bush, Thornbury, Riverton, Colac Bay, Orepuki, Tuatapere, Waiau, Invercargill, Bluff, Awarua, Toetoes Bay, Ruapuke I., Foveaux Strait, Codfish I., Ruggedy Mtns, Mt Anglem 980 m, Halfmoon Bay, Paterson Inlet, Mt Allen 750 m, Owen Head, Pegasus, Port Pegasus, South Cape, Kundy Is.

Solander I. (Hautere), Black Rock Point, Muttonbird (Titi) Is., Centre I., Big South Cape I. (Taukihepa), South West Cape (Taukihepa), The Hump 1067 m, Mt Lyall 1858 m, Mt Solitary 1454 m, Mt Forbes 1305 m, Green Islets, Kakapo Range, Cameron Mtns, Long Burn, Chalky Inlet, Preservation Inlet, Cape Providence, Puysegur Point, Te Waewae Bay, Waiau

Scale

Scale 1:3,500,000   Projection: Conic Equidistant

0   50   100   150   200 kilometers
0   50   100 miles

133

Australia

Christmas Island
(Australia)
1:1,000,000

Cocos (Keeling) Islands
(Australia)
1:1,000,000

Ashmore Reef and Cartier Islet
(Australia)
1:2,000,000

Macquarie Island
(Australia)
1:1,000,000

Heard Island and McDonald Islands
(Australia)
1:2,500,000

PAPUA NEW GUINEA

SOLOMON SEA

CORAL SEA

CORAL SEA ISLANDS (Aust.)

Willis Group
Magdelaine Cays
Chilcott I.
Diamond Is

Louisiade Archipelago

Rennell

°les Chesterfield (New Caledonia)

Normanby I.
Misima I.
Bwagaoia
The Calvados Chain
Samarai
Alotau
Tagula I.
Rossel I.

Gulf of Carpentaria

Cape Wessel
Wessel Is
Nhulunbuy
Cape Arnhem
Cape Shield
Blue Mud Bay
Groote Eylandt
Limmen Bight
Maria I.
Sir Edward Pellew Group
Vanderlin I.
Borroloola
McArthur

Badu I. Moa I.
Torres Strait
Prince of Wales I.
Cape York
Bamaga
Shelburne Bay
Cape Grenville
Weipa
Duyfken Point
Albatross Bay
Portland Roads
Cape Direction
Cape Melville
Princess Charlotte Bay
Cape Flattery

Cape York Peninsula

Coen
Pormpuraaw
Cooktown
Lakeland
Laura
Mossman

Wellesley Is
Mornington I.
Bentinck I.
Wollogorang
Karumba
Normanton
Burketown
Croydon
Georgetown
Forsayth
Einasleigh
Kajabbi
Cloncurry
Camooweal
Mount Isa
Julia Creek
Richmond
Hughenden
Charters Towers

Barkly Tableland
Barkly Homestead Roadhouse

Mareeba
Atherton
Ravenshoe
Cairns
Bartle Frere 1614 m
Innisfail
Tully
Cardwell
Ingham
Hinchinbrook I.
Magnetic I.
Townsville
Ayr

GREAT BARRIER REEF

QUEENSLAND

Middleton
Winton
Boulia
Longreach
Barcaldine
Alpha
Clermont
Emerald
Blackwater
Springsure
Moura
Blackall
Bowen
Proserpine
Whitsunday Group
Mackay
Sarina
Lake Dalrymple
Long I.
Torilla Peninsula
Yeppoon
Rockhampton
Curtis I.
Gladstone
Biloela
Monto
Miriam Vale
Bundaberg
Sandy Cape

Simpson Desert
Bedourie
Birdsville
Bilpa Morea Claypan
Windorah
Betoota
Eromanga
Quilpie
Charleville
Mitchell
Roma
Childers
Hervey Bay
Fraser I.
Maryborough
Gympie
Mundubbera
Murgon
Kingaroy
Noosa Heads
Nambour
Maroochydore
Caloundra
Moreton I.
Caboolture
Ipswich
Brisbane
Nerang
Gold Coast
Coolangatta

Tropic of Capricorn

Strzelecki Desert
Noccundra
Thargomindah
Cunnamulla
St George
Dalby
Toowoomba
Warwick
Stanthorpe
Murwillumbah
Tweed Heads
North Stradbroke I.

Oodnadatta
Lake Eyre North
Lake Eyre South
Marree
Warburton
Cooper Creek
Tibooburra
Hungerford
Barringun
Hebel
Dirranbandi
Goondiwindi
Texas
Tenterfield
Casino
Lismore
Ballina

SOUTH PACIFIC OCEAN

Lake Blanche
Lake Callabonna
Lake Wasby
Grey Range
Bourke
Mungindi
Moree
Warialda
Glen Innes
Grafton

Leigh Creek
Lake Frome
Wilcannia
Cobar
Nyngan
Walgett
Wee Waa
Narrabri
Inverell
Round Mtn 1587 m
Coffs Harbour
Sawtell

St Mary Pk 1168 m
Flinders Ranges
Broken Hill
Coonamble
Coonabarabran
Gilgandra
Tamworth
Nambucca Heads
Kempsey
Port Macquarie

Roxby Downs
Glendambo
Woomera
Port Augusta
Quorn

NEW SOUTH WALES

Menindee
Menindee Lake
Ivanhoe
Narromine
Dubbo
Mt Barrington 1556 m
Gunnedah
Muswellbrook
Taree
Forster

Whyalla
Cowell
Snowtown
Gladstone
Burra
Port Pirie
Peterborough

Lord Howe I. (Aust.)

Hillston
Lake Cargelligo
West Wyalong
Parkes
Orange
Bathurst
Lithgow
Katoomba
Singleton
Maitland
Cessnock
Newcastle
Gosford

Port Wakefield
Gawler
Balranald
Hay
Griffith
Temora
Young
Cowra
Camden
Sydney

Yorke Pen.
Maitland
Adelaide
Murray Bridge
Berri
Renmark
Mildura
Robinvale
Narrandera
Goulburn
Wollongong
Kiama
Nowra

Yorketown
Tailem Bend
Ouyen
Swan Hill
Jerilderie
Canberra
Queanbeyan
JERVIS BAY TERRITORY

Kangaroo I.
Kingscote
Victor Harbor
Lake Alexandrina
Keith
Bordertown
Kerang
Cobram
Albury
Wagga Wagga
AUST. CAPITAL TERRITORY
Batemans Bay

Kingston Southeast
Cape Jaffa
Naracoorte
Nhill
Warracknabeal
Shepparton
Wodonga
Wangaratta
Cooma
Narooma

Millicent
Glenelg
Stawell
Horsham
Echuca
Mt Hotham 1867 m
Mt Kosciuszko 2229 m
Bega
Eden

Mount Gambier
Casterton
Hamilton
Ararat
Mt William 1167 m
Ballarat
Bendigo
VICTORIA
Bairnsdale
Orbost
Cape Howe

Cape Duquesne
Portland
Colac
Melton
Sunbury
Melbourne
Geelong
Moe
Sale
Lakes Entrance

TASMAN SEA

Discovery Bay
Warrnambool
Cape Otway
Rye
Torquay
Morwell
Wonthaggi
Wilsons Promontory

King I.
Currie
Bass Strait
Furneaux Group
Flinders I.
Lady Barron
Cape Barren I.
Eddystone Point

Hunter I.
Robbins I.
Smithton
Stanley
George Town
Scottsdale
St Helens

TASMANIA
Burnie
Devonport
Mt Ossa 1617 m
Queenstown
Launceston
Swansea
Freycinet Pen.

Macquarie Harbour
Lake Gordon
Strahan
Lake Pedder
Bridgewater
Sorell
Hobart
Geeveston
Southport
Port Arthur
South Bruny I.
South East Cape

M
Norfolk I.
Anson Pt
Burnt Pine
Point Ross
Steels Pt
Kingston
Nepean I.
Philip I.
Cascade Bay
Sydney Bay
Ball Bay

Norfolk Island
(Australia)
1:1,000,000

N
Sugarloaf Passage
North Head
Admiralty Is
Mt Malabar 212 m
Mutton Bird I.
East Pt
Lord Howe I.
Mt Lidgbird 777 m
King Pt
Mt Gower 875 m
Balls Pyramid

Lord Howe Island
(Australia)
1:1,000,000

---

0   200   400   600 kilometers
0   100   200   300 miles

Scale 1:12,500,000
Projection: Azimuthal Equal Area

South Pacific

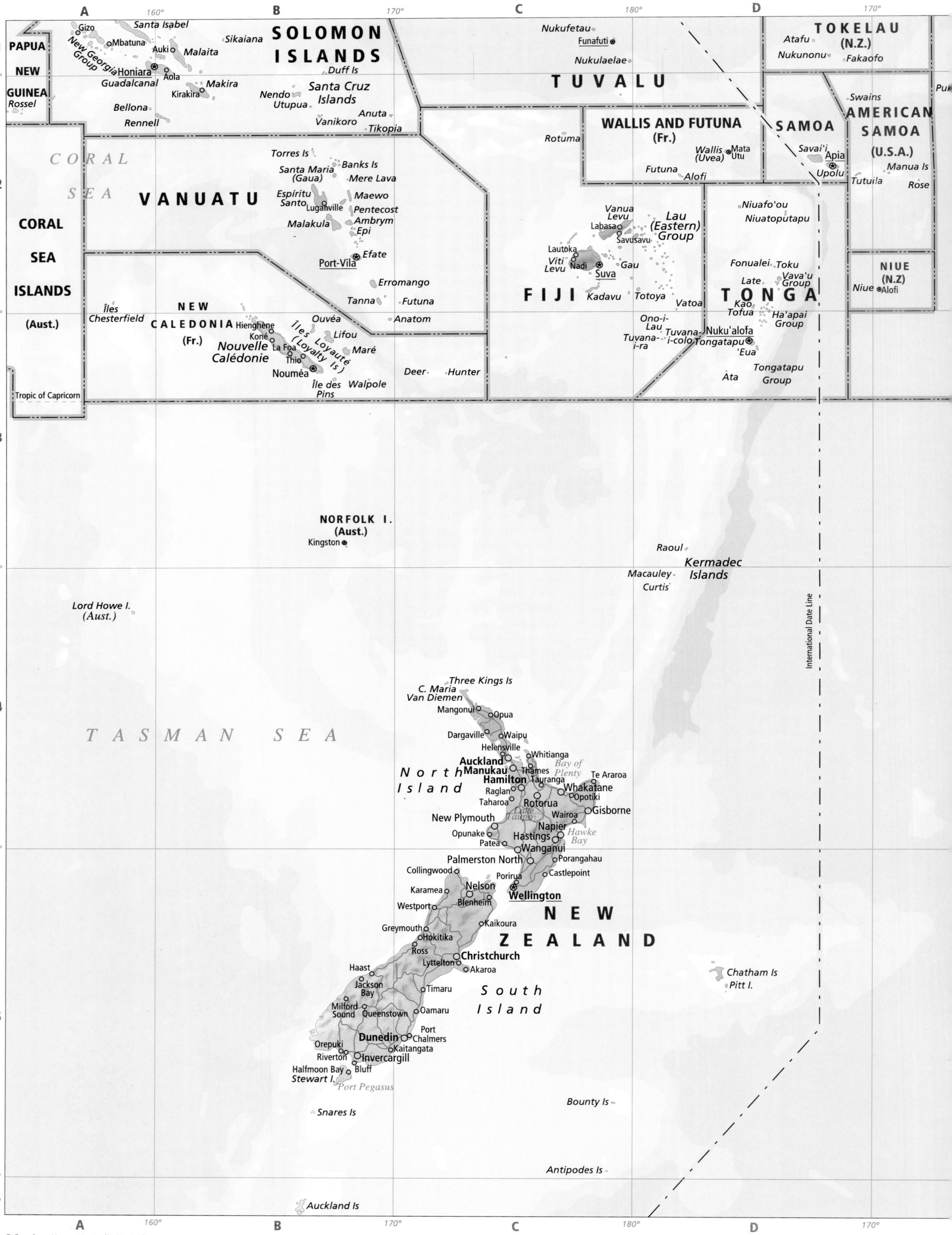

Oceania

| | A | | 160° | | B | | 170° | | C | | 180° | | D | | 170° | |

PAPUA NEW GUINEA
Rossel

Gizo
Santa Isabel
Mbatuna
New Georgia Group
Auki
Malaita
Sikaiana
SOLOMON ISLANDS
Honiara
Aola
Guadalcanal
Kirakira
Makira
Nendo
Santa Cruz Islands
Duff Is
Utupua
Anuta
Bellona
Vanikoro
Tikopia
Rennell

Nukufetau
Funafuti
Nukulaelae
TUVALU

Atafu
TOKELAU (N.Z.)
Nukunonu
Fakaofo

Swains

CORAL SEA

Torres Is
Santa Maria (Gaua)
Banks Is
Mere Lava

WALLIS AND FUTUNA (Fr.)
Rotuma
Wallis (Uvea)
Mata Utu
Futuna
Alofi

SAMOA
Savai'i
Apia
Upolu

AMERICAN SAMOA (U.S.A.)
Manua Is
Tutuila
Rose

CORAL SEA ISLANDS (Aust.)

VANUATU
Espíritu Santo
Maewo
Luganville
Pentecost
Malakula
Ambrym
Epi
Efate
Port-Vila

Vanua Levu
Labasa
Savusavu
Lau (Eastern) Group
Lautoka
Viti Levu
Nadi
Gau
Suva

Niuafo'ou
Niuatoputapu

Fonualei
Toku
Late
Vava'u Group
Kao
Tofua

NIUE (N.Z.)
Niue
Alofi

Îles Chesterfield
NEW CALEDONIA (Fr.)
Hienghène
Koné
Nouvelle Calédonie
La Foa
Thio
Nouméa
Île des Pins

Erromango
Tanna
Futuna
Anatom
Ouvéa
Îles Loyauté (Loyalty Is)
Lifou
Maré
Walpole

FIJI
Kadavu
Totoya
Vatoa
Ono-i-Lau
Tuvana-i-ra
Tuvana-i-colo

TONGA
Ha'apai Group
Nuku'alofa
Tongatapu
'Eua
Ata
Tongatapu Group

Tropic of Capricorn

Deer
Hunter

NORFOLK I. (Aust.)
Kingston

Raoul
Macauley
Curtis
Kermadec Islands

Lord Howe I. (Aust.)

International Date Line

TASMAN SEA

Three Kings Is
C. Maria Van Diemen
Mangonui
Opua
Dargaville
Waipu
Helensville
Whitianga
Auckland
Manukau
Thames
Bay of Plenty
Te Araroa
Hamilton
Tauranga
Whakatane
North Island
Raglan
Rotorua
Opotiki
Taharoa
Lake Taupo
Wairoa
Gisborne
New Plymouth
Napier
Opunake
Hastings
Hawke Bay
Patea
Wanganui
Palmerston North
Porangahau
Collingwood
Porirua
Castlepoint
Karamea
Nelson
Wellington
Westport
Blenheim
NEW ZEALAND
Greymouth
Kaikoura
Hokitika
Ross
Christchurch
Haast
Lyttelton
Akaroa
Jackson Bay
South Island
Timaru
Milford Sound
Queenstown
Oamaru
Chatham Is
Pitt I.
Orepuki
Port Chalmers
Riverton
Dunedin
Kaitangata
Halfmoon Bay
Invercargill
Bluff
Stewart I.
Port Pegasus

Bounty Is

Snares Is

Antipodes Is

Auckland Is

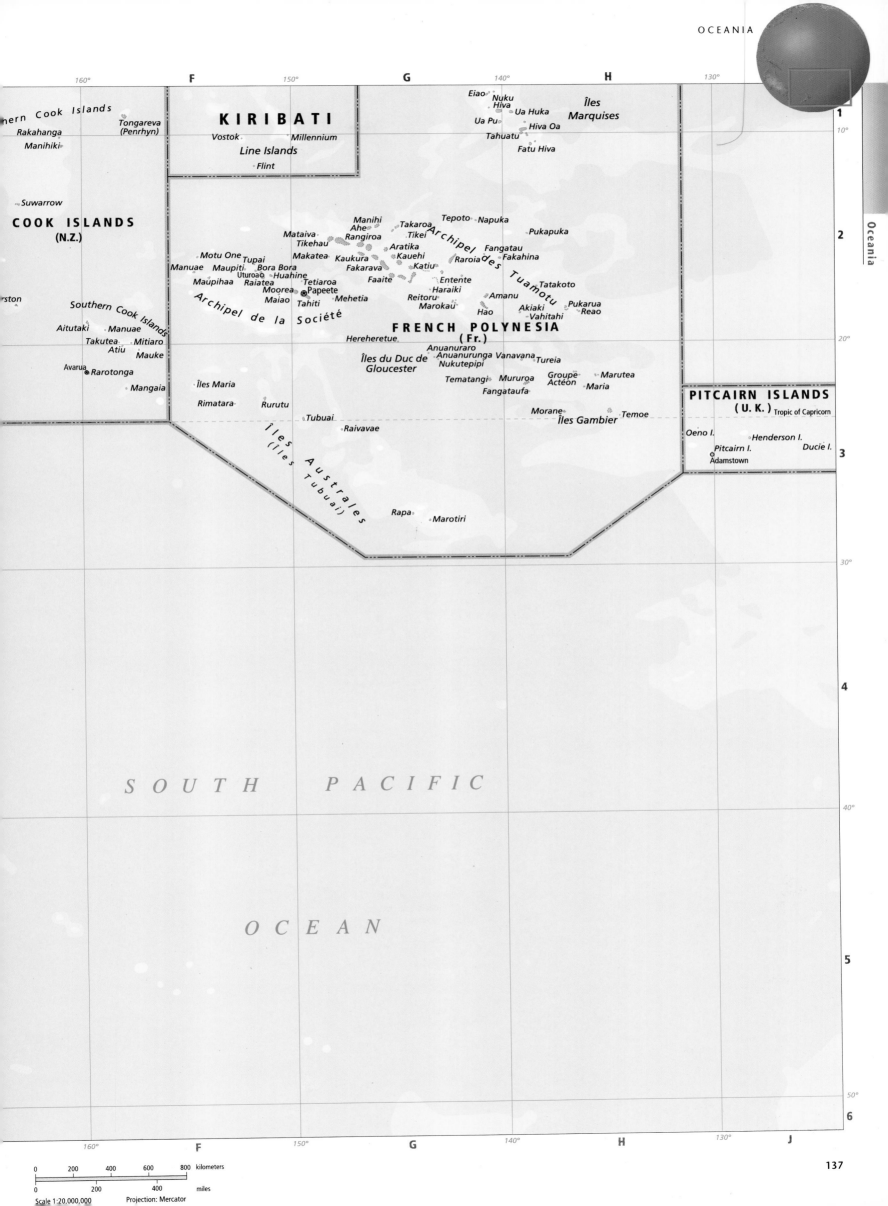

Oceania

160° **F** 150° **G** 140° **H** 130°

1

KIRIBATI

hern Cook Islands
Rakahanga
Manihiki
Tongareva
(Penrhyn)
Vostok · Millennium
Line Islands
· Flint

Eiao · Nuku
Hiva
Ua Pu · Ua Huka
Tahuatu · Hiva Oa
Fatu Hiva
Îles
Marquises

10°

· Suwarrow

2

COOK ISLANDS
(N.Z.)

Motu One Tupai
Manuae Maupiti
Maupihaa Raiatea
Maiao
Tetiaroa
Moorea
Papeete
Tahiti
Mataiva
Tikehau
Makatea
Uturoa
Huahine
Bora Bora
Mehetia

Manihi
Ahe
Rangiroa
Kaukura
Fakarava
Faaite
Aratika
Tikei
Kauehi
Katiu

Tepoto · Napuka
Takaroa
Pukapuka
Fangatau
Raroia
Fakahina
Entente
Haraiki
Reitoru
Marokau
Amanu
Hao
Tatakoto
Pukarua
Reao
Akiaki
Vahitahi

Archipel des Tuamotu

rston

Archipel de la Société

FRENCH POLYNESIA
(Fr.)

Southern Cook Islands
Aitutaki · Manuae
Takutea · Mitiaro
Atiu
Avarua · Mauke
Rarotonga
· Mangaia

· Îles Maria
Rimatara · Rurutu

Hereheretue
Îles du Duc de
Gloucester
Anuanuraro
Anuanurunga Vanavana
Nukutepipi
Tematangi Mururoa
Fangataufa
Tureia
Groupe · Marutea
Actéon
Maria

20°

PITCAIRN ISLANDS
(U. K.) Tropic of Capricorn

Tubuai
Raivavae

Morane
Îles Gambier
Temoe

Oeno I.
Pitcairn I.
Adamstown
Henderson I.
Ducie I.

3

*Îles Australes
(Îles Tubuai)*

Rapa · Marotiri

30°

S O U T H   P A C I F I C

4

40°

O C E A N

5

50°

6

160° **F** 150° **G** 140° **H** 130° **J**

0   200   400   600   800 kilometers
0   200   400   miles
Scale 1:20,000,000   Projection: Mercator

North Pacific

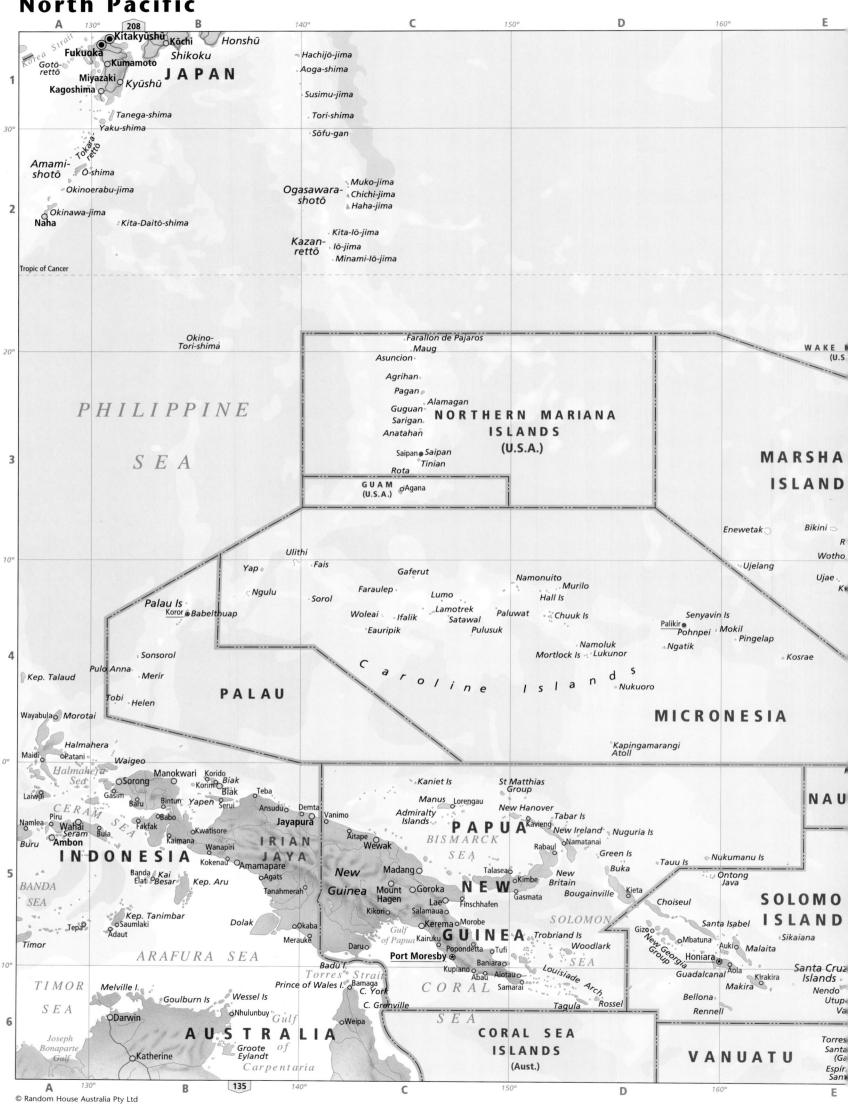

	130°		140°		150°		160°	
A		B		C		D		E

JAPAN

Korea Strait

Kitakyūshū Kōchi *Honshū*
Fukuoka
Gotō-rettō Kumamoto *Shikoku*
Miyazaki *Kyūshū*
Kagoshima

Hachijō-jima
Aoga-shima
Susumu-jima
Tori-shima

Tanega-shima
Yaku-shima

30°

Sōfu-gan

Amami-shotō
Tokara-rettō O-shima
Okinoerabu-jima

Ogasawara-shotō
Muko-jima
Chichi-jima
Haha-jima

Okinawa-jima
Naha
Kita-Daitō-shima

Kita-Iō-jima
Kazan-rettō *Iō-jima*
Minami-lō-jima

Tropic of Cancer

Okino-Tori-shima

20°

Farallon de Pajaros
Maug
Asuncion
Agrihan
Pagan
Guguan Alamagan
Sarigan
Anatahan

**NORTHERN MARIANA
ISLANDS
(U.S.A.)**

WAKE I.
(U.S

**PHILIPPINE

SEA**

Saipan Saipan
Tinian
Rota

3

**MARSHA
ISLAND**

**GUAM
(U.S.A.)** Agana

Enewetak Bikini
R
Wotho

10°

Ulithi
Yap Fais
Ngulu Sorol

Gaferut
Faraulep Namonuito Murilo
Lumo Hall Is
Woleai Lamotrek Ifalik Satawal Paluwat Chuuk Is
Eauripik Pulusuk

Ujelang
Ujae
K

Palau Is Koror Babelthuap

Senyavin Is
Palikir Mokil
Pohnpei Pingelap
Namoluk
Mortlock Is Lukunor Ngatik

Kosrae

4

Sonsorol
Pulo Anna Merir
Kep. Talaud Tobi Helen

PALAU

Caroline Islands

Nukuoro

MICRONESIA

Wayabula Morotai
Halmahera

Kapingamarangi
Atoll

0°

Maidi Patani
*Halmahera
Sea* Waigeo
Manokwari Korido Biak
Laiwui Korim Biak
Gasim Bintun Yapen Serui
Baru Teba
Babo Ansudu Demta
Piru Fakfak Vanimo
Namlea Kwatisore Aitape Wewak
Wahai Kaimana **Jayapura**
Buru Seram Bula Wanapiri

Kaniet Is
Manus St Matthias
Group
Lorengau
**Admiralty
Islands** Tabar Is
Kavieng
New Hanover
New Ireland Nuguria Is
Rabaul Namatanai
Green Is
Tauu Is

NAU

Nukumanu Is

Ambon

INDONESIA

Banda Kai
Elat Besar

Kokenau **IRIAN
JAYA** Amamapare
Agats
Tanahmerah

**CERAM
SEA**

*BISMARCK
SEA*

PAPUA

New
Britain
Talasea Kimbe Bougainville
Gasmata Buka Kieta

Ontong
Java

**SOLOMO
ISLAND**

5

Madang
**New
Guinea** Mount
Hagen Goroka **NEW**
Lae Finschhafen
Kikori Salamaua Morobe
Kerema **GUINEA**
Kairuku
Kupiano Popondetta Tufi
Port Moresby Baniara
Abau Alotau
Samarai

Choiseul

SOLOMON

Santa Isabel

Gizo
New Georgia
Group
Mbatuna Auki Malaita
Honiara Aola
Kirakira
Makira

Santa Cru
Islands
Nendo
Utupe

Kep. Aru

Kep. Tanimbar
Saumlaki
Adaut

Dolak
Okaba
Merauke

Trobriand Is
Woodlark

SEA

Guadalcanal

Bellona

Santa
Sant
(Ga
Espír
San

10°

*BANDA
SEA*

Tepa

Timor

ARAFURA SEA

Badu I.
Torres Strait
Bamaga
Prince of Wales I. C. York
C. Grenville

Daru

Louisiade Arch.
Tagula Rossel

CORAL

Rennell

Torres
Santa
Espir
San

**TIMOR

SEA**

Melville I.
Goulburn Is Wessel Is
Nhulunbuy

Weipa

SEA

**CORAL SEA
ISLANDS
(Aust.)**

VANUATU

6

*Joseph
Bonaparte
Gulf* **Darwin**
Katherine

AUSTRALIA

*Gulf
of*
Groote
Eylandt
Carpentaria

	130°		135	140°		150°		160°	
A		B			C		D		E

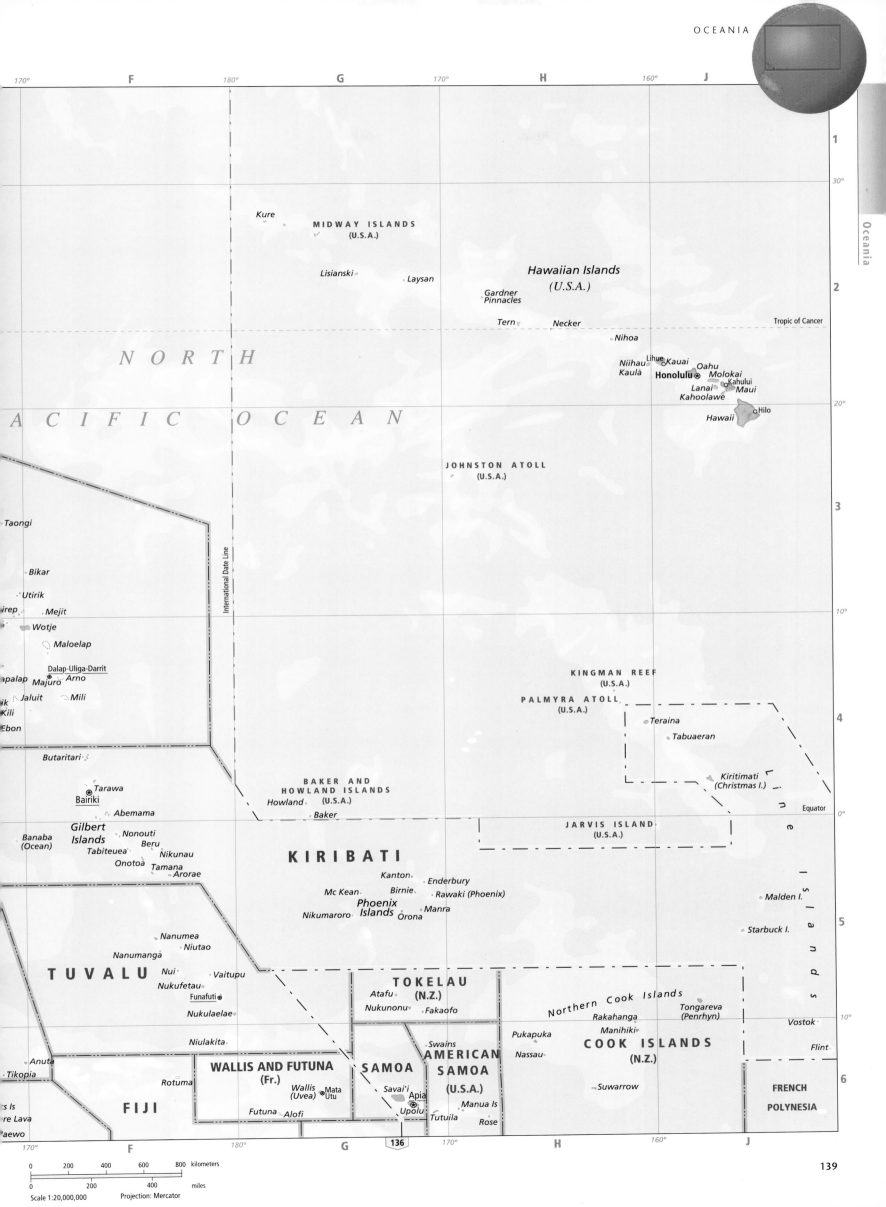

Oceania

170° F 180° G 170° H 160° J

1
30°

Kure
MIDWAY ISLANDS
(U.S.A.)

2
Lisianski • Laysan
Gardner
Pinnacles
Hawaiian Islands
(U.S.A.)

Tern • Necker
Nihoa
Tropic of Cancer

Lihue Kauai
Niihau Oahu
Kaula Honolulu ⊛ Molokai
Kahului
Lanai Maui
Kahoolawe
Hawaii oHilo
20°

N O R T H

A C I F I C   O C E A N

JOHNSTON ATOLL
(U.S.A.)

3

Taongi

Bikar

Utirik
KINGMAN REEF
(U.S.A.)
10°

irep • Mejit
PALMYRA ATOLL
(U.S.A.)
Wotje
Teraina
Maloelap
Tabuaeran

Dalap-Uliga-Darrit
4
apalap Majuro Arno

ik Jaluit • Mili
Kili
Ebon
Kiritimati
(Christmas I.)

Butaritari
Equator

Tarawa
Bairiki
BAKER AND
HOWLAND ISLANDS
Howland
(U.S.A.)
Abemama
Baker
JARVIS ISLAND
(U.S.A.)
0°

Banaba
(Ocean)
Gilbert
Islands
Nonouti
Beru
Tabiteuea
Nikunau
Onotoa Tamana
Arorae
KIRIBATI
Kanton • Enderbury
McKean Birnie
• Rawaki (Phoenix)
Phoenix
Islands
Malden I.
Nikumaroro Orona Manra
5
Starbuck I.

Nanumea
Niutao
Nanumanga
Nui Vaitupu
TUVALU
Nukufetau
Funafuti
TOKELAU
(N.Z.)
Atafu
Nukunonu Fakaofo
Northern Cook Islands
Tongareva
(Penrhyn)
Vostok
Nukulaelae
Rakahanga
Manihiki
Flint
10°

Niulakita
Swains
Pukapuka
COOK ISLANDS
(N.Z.)
Nassau

Anuta
Tikopia
WALLIS AND FUTUNA
(Fr.)
SAMOA
AMERICAN
SAMOA
(U.S.A.)
Suwarrow
FRENCH
6
Rotuma
Wallis
(Uvea) Mata
Utu
Savai'i
Apia
POLYNESIA
FIJI
Futuna Alofi
Upolu
Manua Is
Tutuila
Rose
170° F 180° G 136 170° H 160° J

0 200 400 600 800 kilometers
0 200 400 miles
Scale 1:20,000,000   Projection: Mercator

Papua New Guinea

Scale 1:7,000,000 Projection: Mercator

Islands of the Pacific

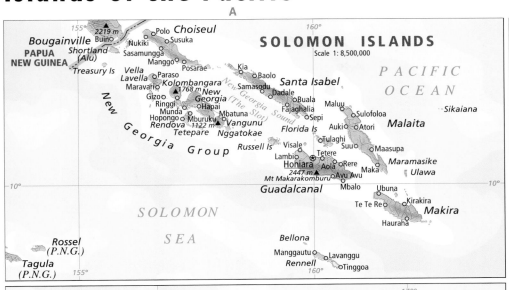

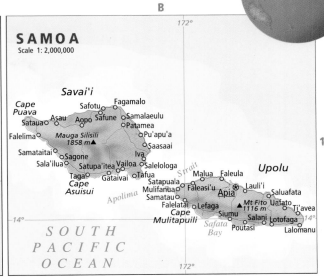

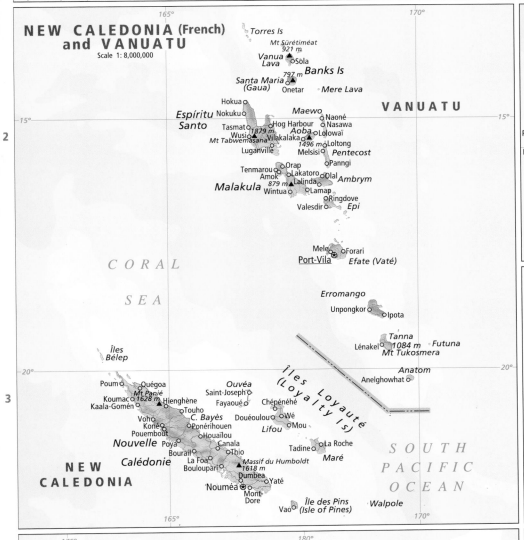

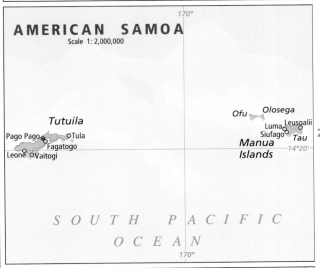

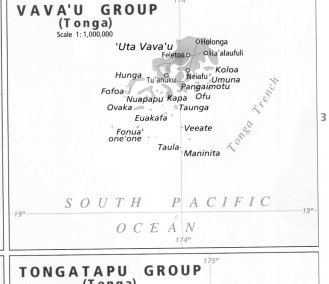

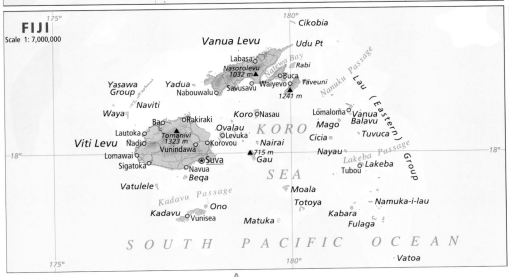

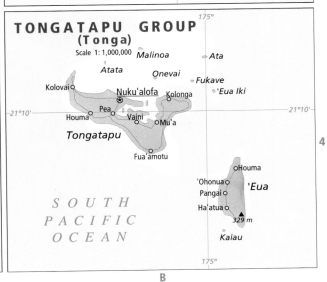

Asia

A sia, the largest continent, covers 43.6 million sq km (16.8 million sq miles), about one-third of the world's land surface. Its western boundaries are the Ural Mountains, the Ural River, the Caspian and Black seas and the Dardanelles Straits, which separate Europe from Asia. The Red Sea and the Suez Canal separate Asia from Africa. Indonesia is the southeasternmost country of Asia.

Asia is traditionally divided into East, Southeast, South, West (Middle East), Central, and North Asia (Siberia, which is part of the Russian Federation). The Middle East and the Russian Federation are discussed in separate sections.

East Asia includes China, Japan, North and South Korea, Taiwan, and Mongolia. Southeast Asia contains the three archipelagic nations of Indonesia, Malaysia and the Philippines; Singapore and Brunei; and the Indochinese nations of Laos, Vietnam, Cambodia, Thailand, and Myanmar (Burma). South Asia includes India, Pakistan, Bangladesh and Sri Lanka; Nepal and Bhutan in the Himalayas; mountainous Afghanistan; and the coral island archipelago of the Maldives. Central Asia includes the former Soviet republics of Kazakhstan, Uzbekistan, Kyrgyzistan, Tajikistan, Turkmenistan, Azerbaijan, and Armenia.

Physical features

Asia is a very geologically active continent. Large areas are covered by mountain and volcanic chains—the world's highest mountain range (the Himalayas), the Indonesian volcanic arc, and the volcanic chains of Japan and the Philippines. Asia also contains some parts of the world's most ancient (Pre-Cambrian) formations, in the Indian and Arabian peninsulas and in Siberia.

Mountain ranges, plateaus, and basins lie within Asia's heartland. The world's highest plateau is in Tibet, averaging 4,000 m (13,000 ft) in altitude, and is bounded to the south by the Himalayas, to

the north by the Kunlun Range, and to the west by the Karakoram Range. Further north, the Tarim and Dzungarian basins lie close to sea level, while the Turfan Depression is 142 m (470 ft) below it.

Numerous streams and 19 major rivers, ranging from 2,500 to 5,500 km (1,500 and 3,400 miles) in length, flow in Asia. These include the Yangtze and Huang rivers in China, the Indus and Ganges rivers of the Indian subcontinent and the Mekong River on the Indochinese Peninsula.

Climate and vegetation

Asia can be broadly divided into a humid monsoon belt, in South, Southeast, and East Asia, and an arid to semiarid zone, in Central Asia.

During summer, the monsoons blow north, toward the continental margins, while in winter they reverse direction and blow toward the south. Some East Asian areas receive rainfall from both monsoons. The Himalayan Range and adjacent mountain ranges concentrate summer rainfall in parts of South and Southeast Asia. Hot, humid climates prevail in South and Southeast Asia while cold climates, with snowfall during winter, are found in more northern parts (the Himalayas and the mountain ranges in Central Asia). The Plateau of Tibet has an extremely cold climate.

Tropical rainforests once covered large parts of South and Southeast Asia, but are now being cleared for agriculture and logging, especially of hardwoods. This threatens the plant and animal diversity of these forests, which is very high.

Broad-leaf evergreen forests cover parts of subtropical East Asia. There are deciduous forests further north in cool, temperate climates, and boreal forests where the winters are cold. The Plateau of Tibet is an almost treeless tundra, with mosses, grasses, lichens, and a few small shrubs.

Grasslands cover areas in the rainshadow belts where rainfall is limited: tropical grasslands in the Deccan Plateau in India and the Khorat Plateau in Thailand, and temperate grasslands (steppes) in the semiarid parts of Central Asia.

Central Asia is predominantly arid to semiarid, with warm summers and winters where the temperature can fall below freezing. The Gobi Desert, the coldest dry desert, lies in this region.

Terraced fields in India (left), a carved entrance in Bali (top), and a curious monkey in Indonesia (above) demonstrate the variety of landform zones and land uses in Asia.

Population

Asia's vast population (3,588.9 million inhabitants, as of 1998, representing some 60 percent of the world's people) is predominantly found in the monsoon belt. The population explosion within the last 50 years (some countries experienced a three-fold increase during this period) is the result of advances in agriculture and improved medical facilities. During this period, life expectancies improved throughout Asia. Life expectancy is currently highest in East Asia (69 years for males and 73 years for females) and lowest in South Asia (61.7 years for males and 62.8 years for females). The high population growth rate has subsided, being currently 1.4 percent overall (0.9 in East Asia to 1.8 in South Asia).

Population indicators for the most developed Asian countries are similar to those for many Western countries: low population growth rates and high life expectancies characterize the more industrialized nations such as Japan and Singapore. High growth rates and much lower life expectancies, however, are found in the least developed countries, such as Bangladesh and Nepal. These characteristics reflect the enormous differences in standards of living between the most and least developed countries in Asia. Urbanization is highest in the most developed areas, but despite having a number of large cities and growing urbanization, Asia still has a low urban population—35 percent.

Industrialization in most Asian countries has, as elsewhere, centered on major urban areas. Labor from rural areas has drifted to urban centers in search of employment. The ensuing urban population explosion has put pressure on infrastructure, and given rise to problems such as the growth of slum dwellings, traffic congestion, and air and water pollution.

Agriculture

A high proportion of Asia's population lives on the alluvial plains of rivers (and their deltas) of the monsoon belt, and is engaged in agriculture.

The monsoon belt is noted for its intensive rice and wheat farming. The population explosion created enormous demand for food. The area under cultivation was expanded through deforestation and by farming marginal areas, such as the borders of deserts, but the Green Revolution was more successful: high-yielding seeds, fertilizers and pesticides often tripled grain yields. However, environmental problems, caused by the chemicals used and by invasions of insects, have raised a number of concerns. In semiarid Central Asia, wheat farming and animal rearing are the main forms of agriculture. With irrigation, cotton is now successfully grown in several places.

Industrialization

By the 1980s, several East Asian countries had developed industrialized economies, largely dependent on imported raw materials, particularly minerals and energy supplies. Manufacturing in Asia ranges from labor-intensive industries such as clothing in the less developed economies to electronics, computers, and motor vehicles in the more developed ones. Japan, the world's second-largest economy, manufactures electronic goods, steel, motor vehicles and ships. Japan's approach has been imitated by South Korea, Taiwan, Hong Kong and Singapore, which have all rapidly industrialized. Thailand, Malaysia, the Philippines, and Indonesia have followed suit.

China and India initially aimed at agricultural and industrial self-sufficiency to support their enormous populations. They possess huge agricultural sectors, but their exports have shifted progressively to industrial products. They have considerable scientific expertise—in nuclear and space technology and satellite launching services (China), and computer programming (India).

The Central Asian nations, following the breakup of the former Soviet Union, are making a slow and painful transition from a state-controlled to a free market economy. There is, as yet, limited industrialization in the countries of Central Asia. Kazakhstan produces metals and chemicals and Azerbaijan, which is rich in petroleum deposits and may establish petroleum-based industries, currently manufactures mining equipment.

The Flaming Cliffs in Mongolia's arid Gobi Desert, Central Asia (above). This Vietnamese woman (below) is carrying wood from her home in the hills to sell.

Languages

Many languages, belonging to several language families, are spoken in Asia. Chinese Mandarin, Cantonese, and Wu are the most widely spoken in East Asia. Japanese is increasingly important. In Southeast Asia, Indonesian and Malaysian predominate, while languages of the Chinese-Tibetan family, such as Burmese and Thai, are spoken in the mainland belt. South Asia has two major language families: Indo-Aryan in the north, of which Hindi and Urdu are the most widespread, and Dravidian, which includes Tamil, in the southern areas. In Central Asia, Ural-Altaic languages, several of which are related to Turkish, are mainly used.

Russian is widely spoken in the former Soviet republics, and of the colonial languages, only English is still important, and continues to spread.

Boundary disputes and wars

Armed conflicts continued after the Second World War in Asia, especially during the decolonization phase. The communist revolution in China resulted in the separation of Taiwan, which China does not accept. Wars resulted in the division of both Korea and Vietnam into two nations: communist North and democratic South. The Vietnam war ended in 1975, when the country reunified. North and South Korea remain technically at war.

Following the division of British India into India and Pakistan in 1947, there was armed conflict over the divided Himalayan state of Jammu and Kashmir; this issue is still unresolved. War between India and Pakistan resulted in 1971 in the creation of the Bangladesh.

Armed conflicts along the disputed boundaries of China have taken place between China and India along the Himalayas, between China and Russia along the Amur River, and between China and Vietnam along their common border.

Indonesia's occupation and then incorporation of the former Portuguese colony of East Timor remains in dispute.

The ownership of the Spratly Islands in the South China Sea is causing tension between China, Malaysia, Philippines, Vietnam, and Taiwan.

Nations

The Middle East

The term "Middle East" applies to the belt of countries in Southwest Asia that lies between Afghanistan and Turkey. It stretches southward to include the Arabian Peninsula. The Middle East is characterized by its arid climate, its petroleum riches, and the prevalence of Islam as its predominant religion. The Middle East forms a strategic belt between the dynamic developing industrial countries of Asia and the long-developed countries of Europe.

The countries of Iran, Iraq, Syria, Turkey, and Cyprus form the northern belt, while toward their south lie Lebanon, Israel, Jordan and the states of the Arabian Peninsula. Saudi Arabia occupies a large part of the peninsula; Oman and Yemen share the southern part of the peninsula and the United Arab Emirates, Bahrain, Qatar, and Kuwait lie along the Arabian (also known as Persian) Gulf.

Afghanistan lies in the area where the Middle East, South Asia, and Central Asia meet. The North African nations of Egypt, Sudan, and Libya are also sometimes considered part of the Middle East, for linguistic and cultural reasons.

Physical features

The collision of the Iranian and Arabian tectonic plates with the Eurasian Plate resulted in the mountain ranges that run from Turkey to Iran. The belt between Turkey and Iran is characterized by elongated mountain ranges such as the Zagros and Alborz ranges in Iran and the Pontic and Taurus mountains in Turkey. These ranges form part of the extensive Alpine-Himalayan Mountain Range System that was formed during the Tertiary geological period. This area is prone to earthquakes, of which there have been several in recent decades. There are plateaus in both Turkey (Anatolian Plateau) and Iran.

In contrast to the geologically active Tertiary mountain belt, the Arabian Plateau is part of an ancient and geologically stable shield.

Jumeura Mosque, Dubai, in the United Arab Emirates (below). Shiraz-style grapevines with clay supports in Iran (right).

Climate and vegetation

The Middle East is predominantly arid to semiarid, except for the areas that adjoin the Mediterranean, Aegean, Black and Caspian seas. The region is characterized by high temperatures, especially in the Arabian, Syrian and Iranian deserts. In contrast, winter temperatures close to freezing point occur in the highlands and snow falls in some of the higher mountainous areas. There are great seasonal temperature differences on the plateaus, as shown by Tehrān and Ankara, which reach temperatures of about 30°C (85°F) in summer and fall as low as freezing point in winter.

The region receives little annual rainfall, except for winter rain in the areas bordering the Mediterranean, and there is a serious shortage of fresh water in the Gulf area. Vegetation in this region is dominated by thorny scrubland.

The Euphrates and Tigris are the largest rivers in the Middle East. Several short rivers flow into the Mediterranean, Black, and Caspian seas.

Population

The population of the region is about 297.4 million (1998). Life expectancies have improved in recent years and now stand at 65.9 years for males and 70.3 years for females. The population growth rate is moderate, at 2.2 percent. Urbanization has been increasing steadily during recent decades and now stands at 66 percent; this reflects the decreasing importance of agriculture and pastoralism in the economies of these countries. In several countries, particularly in the Gulf States, petroleum has indirectly assisted the growth of urbanization as oil-generated revenues have been invested in urban areas and projects.

Agriculture

Because of the arid climate, only a small part of the region can support agriculture. The Euphrates and Tigris Rivers, with their alluvial plains and extensive irrigation, are significant agricultural areas, but their rising salinity levels

constitute a major problem. The region has a great need for irrigation—Syria, for example, has built the Euphrates Dam to irrigate the northeastern part of the country. Israel has also developed areas of intensive irrigation-based agriculture.

Wheat, barley, and rice are the major cereals. Important cash crops include tobacco, sugarcane, cotton, fruits and tea. Dates are a common fruit and are cultivated in oasis areas. Livestock mostly consists of camels, sheep, and goats; herds of goats have been blamed for stripping the ground bare of vegetation, which has resulted in soil erosion and the acceleration of desertification in some areas.

Agriculture based on growing olives, grapes, citrus fruits and apples is found in the Mediterranean coastal areas.

Fishing is important in several places, including the Black and Caspian seas.

Industrialization

Petroleum reserves are the region's most abundant resource. Oil-rich Saudi Arabia, Iran, Iraq, Kuwait, and the United Arab Emirates have economies

The birthplace of Aphrodite in Cyprus (far left). Traditional trading dhows in Doha, Qatar (left), still have a place in this modern capital. Women in the Gaza Strip demonstrate for the release of Palestinian prisoners (below).

predominantly based on petroleum exports, which makes them vulnerable to fluctuations in the price of petroleum. Petroleum prices escalated during the mid to late 1970s, but since then prices have fallen considerably. Oil wealth has facilitated the import of foodstuffs, manufactured goods, and luxury items, and has been also used for military purchases and development.

The hot, arid areas of the region are largely unsuited to the establishment of industries. The lack of fresh water is so severe in the Gulf region that desalinization plants have been set up to produce potable water.

Oil-based electricity is generated in the oil-rich countries, and coal-based electricity is widely used in Turkey. Hydroelectric power is produced in Syria and Turkey.

Industries that use local materials, such as food processing, petroleum refining, and petrochemical industries, have been developed in some places. Some light consumer-based industries, including textiles, footwear, cigarettes, and paper, have also been established.

The countries of the eastern Mediterranean are comparatively more industrialized than the rest of the region, but frequent conflicts with neighboring countries in the area have hampered their ability to maintain production.

the blockade on Iraq has seriously affected the growth of Iraq's economy.

The Kurdish-speaking area, shared by Turkey, Iraq, and Iran, has also been involved in armed conflict, in its attempt to secure independence.

The Turkish conquest of the northern, Turkish-speaking part of Cyprus has strained relations between Greece and Turkey.

These ancient ruins at Buṣrá ash Shām, in Syria (below), remind us how long human civilization has existed in this area. International fast food in Dubai (above).

Nations

Languages

Three language families—the Indo-European, Turkic, and Semitic—are found in the Middle East. The Indo-European languages represented include Persian, Pashto, Kurdish, Armenian, and Baluchi. Turkish and Azerbaijani are Turkic languages, and Arabic and Hebrew are Semitic.

Boundary disputes and wars

The region has experienced several conflicts and wars within the last 50 years. The Israeli-Arab conflict has been the most prominent and is yet to be resolved. Lebanon was drawn into the conflict, which adversely affected its economy.

Iraq's attempt to conquer the Arab-speaking region of southwestern Iran lasted for years, and drained both Iraq and Iran of resources. Iraq's conquest of Kuwait, the subsequent Gulf War and

Afghanistan

Afghanistan is a landlocked country in the central part of South Asia with nearly three-quarters of its territory mountainous. It shares a western frontier with Iran, while Pakistan is across the southeastern border. Once a part of the ancient Persian Empire, Afghanistan was conquered by Alexander the Great in 328 BC. In the seventh century AD it adopted Islam, today the country's dominant religious and cultural force. From 1953 it was closely allied with the former Soviet Union. In 1979 the Soviet government intervened to install a communist faction more to its liking, and though constantly beseiged by mujahideen guerrilla fighters, maintained its military occupation until 1989. After the overthrow of the communist government in 1992 the mujahideen began fighting among themselves along ethnic lines. Twenty years of internal war appeared to have ended in 1998 with the Sunni Muslim Taliban militia, associated with the majority Pashtun, in control of the country. The Taliban has imposed strict Islamic rule.

Geographically, the country's largest area is the thinly populated central highlands. This comprises most of the Hindu Kush, the second highest range in the world, with several peaks over 6,400 m (21,000 ft). The northeast is seismically active. Much of the rest is desert or semidesert, except for a few fertile and heavily populated valleys, among them Herāt in the northwest. Most agriculture

takes place on the northern plains, near the frontiers of Turkmenistan, Uzbekistan, and Tajikistan. The country's main river basins are those of the Amu Darya, Helmand, and Kābol.

Afghanistan is very poor: a list of 192 countries ranked for calorie intake in 1995 placed Afghanistan 191. It depends largely on wheat farming and the raising of sheep and goats. During the Soviet occupation and the subsequent internecine conflict, one-third of the population left the country, 6 million refugees fleeing to Pakistan and Iran. Many have now gone home to an economically devastated land. Millions of people lack food, clothing, housing, and medical care. Though data are shaky, it is likely that the country's most profitable crop is opium, Afghanistan reputedly being the world's second largest producer after Myanmar (Burma), and a major source of hashish.

Fact File

OFFICIAL NAME	Islamic State of Afghanistan
FORM OF GOVERNMENT	Transitional government
CAPITAL	Kābol (Kabul)
AREA	647,500 sq km (250,000 sq miles)
TIME ZONE	GMT + 4.5 hours
POPULATION	25,824,882
PROJECTED POPULATION 2005	30,189,273
POPULATION DENSITY	39.8 per sq km (103 per sq mile)
LIFE EXPECTANCY	47.3
INFANT MORTALITY (PER 1,000)	140.6
OFFICIAL LANGUAGES	Dari (Afghan Persian), Pashto
OTHER LANGUAGES	Uzbek, Turkmen, Indi and Pamiri languages, Dravidian
LITERACY RATE	31.5%
RELIGIONS	Sunni Muslim 84%, Shi'a Muslim 15%, other 1%
ETHNIC GROUPS	Pashtun 38%, Tajik 25%, Hazara 19%, Uzbek 6%, other 12%
CURRENCY	Afghani
ECONOMY	Agriculture 61%, services 25%, industry 14%
GNP PER CAPITA	Est. < US$765
CLIMATE	Mainly semiarid, but arid in southwest and cold in mountains; hot summers and cold winters
HIGHEST POINT	Nowshak 7,485 m (24,557 ft)
MAP REFERENCE	Page 221

Armenia

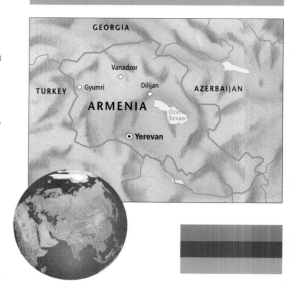

Armenia is a small, mountainous, Christian country, landlocked between hostile Muslim neighbors. To the east is Azerbaijan, and to the west is Turkey, which inflicted genocidal massacres on the Armenian people between 1894 and 1915. The legendary resting place of Noah's Ark after the Flood (its capital supposedly founded by Noah himself), Armenia had already existed as a distinct country for 1,000 years when in the fourth century AD it became the first in the world to make Christianity its state religion. The country has been fought over at various times by Romans, Persians, and Mongols. It became a Soviet Socialist Republic in 1922 and gained its independence from the Soviet Union in 1991. In 1988 there was a devastating earthquake which killed 25,000 people and destroyed power stations and other infrastructure and in the same year conflict began over Nagorno-Karabakh, an internal Azerbaijani area largely populated by Christian Armenians, which is claimed by Armenia.

The mountains of the Lesser Caucasus (Malyy Kavkaz) cover most of the country. The landscape is rugged, and includes extinct volcanoes and high lava plateaus cut with ravines. An active seismic area, the frequency of earthquakes in Armenia indicates that mountain-building is still taking place. Although the city of Ararat is in Armenia, Mt Ararat itself is across the border in Turkey. The centrally located Lake Sevan (Sevana Lich) lies nearly 2,000 m (6,000 ft) above sea level, but its use for hydropower has drained it to a point where drinking water supplies are threatened. Steppe vegetation is the main cover and drought-resistant grasses and sagebrush grow on the lower mountain slopes, where jackals, wildcats, and the occasional leopard are found.

As a Soviet Republic, Armenia developed an industrial sector, supplying machine building tools, textiles, and other manufactured goods to other republics in return for raw materials and energy. It has few natural resources, although formerly lead, copper, and zinc were mined, and there are deposits of gold and bauxite. Agriculture is an important source of income. In irrigated areas around Yerevan, crops include grapes, almonds, figs, and olives, while apples, pears, and cereals are grown on higher ground. Armenia is also known for its quality brandies and wines.

The city of Kābol in Afghanistan, devastated by years of warfare (below left). View over the city of Yerevan in Armenia, with Mt Ararat in the background (above).

Economic decline in the period 1991 to 1994 was a direct result of the ongoing conflict over Nagorno-Karabakh. In retaliation for Armenia's military activities in the region, Turkey and Azerbaijan blockaded pipeline and railroad traffic into the country, causing chronic energy shortages. There have been improvements, but full economic recovery is unlikely before Armenia's conflict with its neighbors is settled.

Fact File

OFFICIAL NAME Republic of Armenia

FORM OF GOVERNMENT Republic with single legislative body (National Assembly)

CAPITAL Yerevan

AREA 29,800 sq km (11,506 sq miles)

TIME ZONE GMT + 4 hours

POPULATION 3,409,234

PROJECTED POPULATION 2005 3,351,982

POPULATION DENSITY 114.4 per sq km (296.2 per sq mile)

LIFE EXPECTANCY 66.6

INFANT MORTALITY (PER 1,000) 41.1

OFFICIAL LANGUAGE Armenian

OTHER LANGUAGE Russian

LITERACY RATE 98.8%

RELIGIONS Armenian Orthodox 94%, other (Russian Orthodox, Muslim, Protestant) 6%

ETHNIC GROUPS Armenian 93%, Azeri 3%, Russian 2%, other (mainly Kurdish) 2%

CURRENCY Dram

ECONOMY Industry 28%, agriculture 27%, services 26%, other 19%

GNP PER CAPITA US$730

CLIMATE Mainly dry, with cold winters and warm summers; cooler in mountains

HIGHEST POINT Aragats Lerr 4,090 m (13,419 ft)

MAP REFERENCE Page 222

Azerbaijan

Oil was being collected from the Caspian Sea near Baku at least 1,000 years ago, when the area was known as "the land of eternal fire" because of burning natural gas flaming out of the ground. Today oil from Baku continues to be the mainstay of the Azerbaijani economy. The home of an independent Azeri state as early as the fourth century BC, the region later fell under the influence of Persia, then in the eleventh century Turkic-speaking people moved in and assumed control. A period of affiliation with the Soviets following the Russian Revolution led to Azerbaijan becoming a member of the Soviet Union in 1936. In 1991 it was one of the first Soviet Republics to declare independence.

Since 1988 there have been troubles with Armenia over the region of Nagorno-Karabakh in southwestern Azerbaijan. This territorial dispute (Armenia now holds 20 percent of the region, most of the people in Nagorno-Karabakh being Christian Armenians) remains a major political problem for the newly independent state.

A range of the Great Caucasus (Bol'shoy Kavkas) running at an angle toward the Caspian Sea separates Russia from Azerbaijan, and reaches almost as far as Baku. South of this range, draining out of the foothills of the Caucasus in Georgia, the

Kura (Kür) River reaches a broad floodplain, some of it lying below sea level. The mountains of the Lesser Caucasus (Malyy Kavkaz) form much of Nagorno-Karabakh in the southwest and also stand between Azerbaijan and its isolated enclave-territory Naxçivan. Although a Naxçivan independence movement exists, this territory, which is surrounded by Iran and Armenia, is regarded by the government as part of the Azerbaijan state.

Dry and subtropical, the lowlands experience mild winters and long, hot summers, and are frequently affected by drought. Plant cover consists of steppe grassland in the drier lowland regions, woods in the mountains, and swamps in the southeast.

Early this century Baku supplied as much as half the world's oil, but production declined steadily during the final years under Soviet control as plant became antiquated and maintenance was neglected. The 1994 ratification of a $7.5 billion deal with a consortium of Western oil companies marked a turning point, and should see a revival in this sector. Baku was the fifth biggest city in Soviet Russia and had a well diversified industrial sector. It is hoped the oil deal will stimulate new production of chemicals, textiles, and electrical goods.

Though Azerbaijan has only a small amount of arable land, it is a major producer of cotton, tobacco, grapes, and other fruit. Sturgeon from the Caspian was an important source of caviar but this industry is threatened by serious water pollution. One hundred years of intensive oil production, plus overuse of toxic defoliants in cotton growing, have taken a severe environmental toll. Azerbaijani scientists consider the Abseron Peninsula, where Baku stands, to be one of the most ecologically devastated areas in the world.

Fact File

OFFICIAL NAME Azerbaijani Republic

FORM OF GOVERNMENT Federal republic with single legislative body (National Assembly)

CAPITAL Baki (Baku)

AREA 86,600 sq km (33,436 sq miles)

TIME ZONE GMT + 4 hours

POPULATION 7,908,224

PROJECTED POPULATION 2005 8,171,979

POPULATION DENSITY 91.3 per sq km (236.5 per sq mile)

LIFE EXPECTANCY 63.1

INFANT MORTALITY (PER 1,000) 82.5

OFFICIAL LANGUAGE Azerbaijani

OTHER LANGUAGES Russian, Armenian

LITERACY RATE 96.3%

RELIGIONS Muslim 93.5%, Russian Orthodox 2.5%, Armenian Orthodox 2%, other 2%

ETHNIC GROUPS Azeri 90%, Dagestani peoples 3%, Russian 2.5%, Armenian 2.5%, other 2%

CURRENCY Manat

ECONOMY Services 42%, agriculture 32%, industry 26%

GNP PER CAPITA US$480

CLIMATE Mainly semiarid

HIGHEST POINT Bazardüzü Dağ 4,466 m (14,652 ft)

MAP REFERENCE Page 222

Bahrain

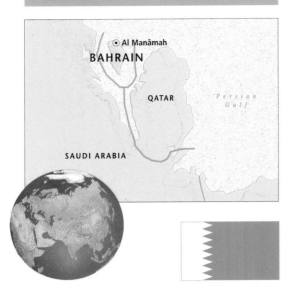

Fact File

OFFICIAL NAME State of Bahrain

FORM OF GOVERNMENT Traditional monarchy

CAPITAL Al Manāmah (Manama)

AREA 620 sq km (239 sq miles)

TIME ZONE GMT + 3 hours

POPULATION 629,090

PROJECTED POPULATION 2005 701,662

POPULATION DENSITY 1,014.6 per sq km
(2,627.8 per sq mile)

LIFE EXPECTANCY 75.3

INFANT MORTALITY (PER 1,000) 14.8

OFFICIAL LANGUAGE Arabic

OTHER LANGUAGES English, Farsi (Persian), Urdu

LITERACY RATE 84%

RELIGIONS Shi'a Muslim 75%, Sunni Muslim 25%

ETHNIC GROUPS Bahraini 63%, Asian 13%, other Arab
10%, Iranian 8%, other 6%

CURRENCY Bahraini dinar

ECONOMY Industry and commerce 85%, agriculture
5%, services 7%, government 3%

GNP PER CAPITA US$7,840

CLIMATE Mainly arid, with mild winters and hot,
humid summers

HIGHEST POINT Jabal ad Dukhān 122 m (400 ft)

MAP REFERENCE Page 220

A cluster of 35 small, low-lying islands in the Persian Gulf, Bahrain is 28 km (17 miles) from the west coast of the Qatar Peninsula. The islands were once the heart of the ancient Dilmun civilization and have been a trading center for over 4,000 years. Bahrain was the first of the Gulf states to export oil, soon after oil was discovered in 1932. A 25 km (16 mile) causeway links the main island to Saudi Arabia.

After the 1970s' collapse of Beirut in Lebanon, previously the region's main commercial center, Bahrain began to provide banking and financial services, at the same time increasing its transport and communication facilities. When the elected assembly was dissolved in 1975 and the country reverted to traditional authoritarian rule, there was growing unrest among the fundamentalist Shi'ite Muslim majority. Encouraged in their resistance by Iran, the Shi'ites resent their low status under Bahrain's Sunni Muslim ruling family. In the opinion of Shi'ite fundamentalists this family is unacceptable for a number of reasons—it belongs to a branch of Islam they regard as oppressive, it is liberal and modernizing in its economic policies, and it is a supporter of US policy. US air bases on Bahrain were vital military assets during the 1990–91 Gulf War.

Consisting of barren rock, sandy plains, and salt marshes, the landscape of Bahrain is low-lying desert for the most part, rising to a low central escarpment. Winters are dry and mild, summers hot and humid. There are no natural freshwater resources. All the country's water needs must be met by groundwater from springs and from desalinated sea water. Imported soil has been used to create several small fertile areas, and domestic agricultural production is capable of meeting local demand for fruit and vegetables. However, the degradation of existing arable land is an environmental concern, along with damage to coastlines, coral reefs, and sea life resulting from spills of oil and oil-tanker discharges.

Waning oil production since the 1970s has forced Bahrain to diversify. Since the opening of the causeway linking the country to Saudi Arabia in 1986 there has been a boom in weekend tourism, visitors pouring in from the Gulf states. Bahrain is now the Arab world's major banking center, and numerous multinational firms with business in the Gulf have offices in the country. Ship repairs are also undertaken in Bahrain. Petroleum production and processing account for 80 percent of export receipts. Natural gas has assumed greater importance, and is used to supply local industries, including an aluminum smelting plant. However, unemployment among the young, especially among the Shi'ite majority, is a cause of social unrest and continuing economic concern.

A spice seller in a Bahrain market (below). Bangladeshi women doing agricultural work (top right). Bus station in Dhaka, Bangladesh (bottom right).

Bangladesh

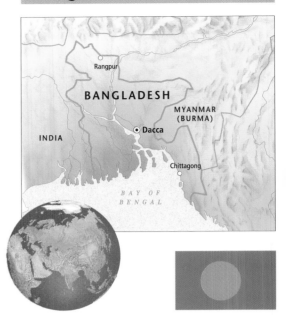

K nown for tropical cyclones and endemic poverty, the small and densely populated country of Bangladesh lies north of the Bay of Bengal. Most of its frontier is with India and it has a short border with Myanmar (Burma) in the southeast. The name Bangladesh means "the land of the Bengalis," a people who have contributed a great deal to Indian history. Once a part of the Mauryan Empire of the fourth century BC, Bengal has been mainly Muslim since the thirteenth century, and during its more recent history its Muslim people have often been ruled by Hindu overlords. At the time of the partition of India in 1947, this situation led to the founding of East Pakistan, the oriental wing of the Muslim state that was set up following independence. In 1971 resentment of the power and privileges of West Pakistan resulted in East Pakistan breaking away and forming the independent state of Bangladesh. Since then its history has been one of political coups, dissolved parliaments, and civil unrest, compounded by natural disasters. In 1991 the worst cyclone in memory killed over 140,000 people.

Asia and the Middle East

industries include textiles, fertilizer, glass, iron and steel, sugar, cement, and aluminum. Fishing is also economically important. However, there are a number of serious impediments to progress. They include frequent cyclones and floods, inefficient state-owned enterprises, a labor force growing (as a consequence of a steady population growth) faster than it can be absorbed by agriculture alone, and delays in developing energy resources such as natural gas.

Fact File

OFFICIAL NAME People's Republic of Bangladesh

FORM OF GOVERNMENT Republic with single legislative body (National Parliament)

CAPITAL Dhaka (Dacca)

AREA 144,000 sq km (55,598 sq miles)

TIME ZONE GMT + 6 hours

POPULATION 129,859,779

PROJECTED POPULATION 2005 142,921,111

POPULATION DENSITY 901.8 per sq km (2,335.7 per sq mile)

LIFE EXPECTANCY 57.1

INFANT MORTALITY (PER 1,000) 95.3

OFFICIAL LANGUAGE Bangla

OTHER LANGUAGE English

LITERACY RATE 37.3%

RELIGIONS Muslim 83%, Hindu 16%, other (mainly Buddhist, Christian) 1%

ETHNIC GROUPS Bengali 98%, Biharis and tribal peoples 2%

CURRENCY Taka

ECONOMY Agriculture 57%, services 33%, industry 10%

GNP PER CAPITA US$240

CLIMATE Tropical, with three seasons: cool, dry winter (October to March); hot, humid summer (March to June); and cool, wet monsoon (June to October)

HIGHEST POINT Mt Keokradong 1,230 m (4,035 ft)

MAP REFERENCE Page 219

Bangladesh is low and flat, its physiography determined by three navigable rivers—the Ganges (Padma), Brahmaputra (Jamuna) and the smaller Meghna. At their confluence they form the biggest delta in the world. The western part of this delta, which is over the border in India, is somewhat higher, and is less subject to flooding. What is called the "active delta" lies in Bangladesh and this region is frequently flooded. During monsoons the water rises up to 6 m (18 ft) above sea level, submerging two-thirds of the country, and the delta's changing channels are hazardous to life, health, and property. However, the floods are also beneficial in that they renew soil fertility with silt, some of it washed down from as far away as Tibet. Whole new islands are formed by alluvial deposition, and the highly fertile silt can yield as many as three rice crops a year. The far south-eastern region of Chittagong has the only high country in Bangladesh, with forested ridges and rubber plantations.

Bangladesh is a major recipient of international aid. Disbursements of aid are currently running at more than 1,000 times the annual value of foreign investment. Despite the efforts of the international community, however, it remains one of the world's poorest and least developed nations. Rice is the main crop in the country's basically agrarian economy, followed by jute, tea, and sugarcane. Bangladesh is the world's largest supplier of high quality jute. About half the crop is exported in its raw form and the rest is processed for export as hessian, sacking, and carpet-backing. A modern paper industry uses bamboo from the hills. Other

Issues in Bangladesh

After 15 years of military rule multi-party politics returned to Bangladesh in 1990, and the country's first woman prime minister, Begum Khaleda Zia, leader of the Bangladesh Nationalist Party (BNP), was elected in 1991. However, factionalism divides the nation and Bangladesh remains politically unstable.

Despite the country's prominent female politicians (the opposition Awami League is also led by a woman), women in Bangladesh face discrimination in health care, education, and employment. In addition, dowry-related violence against women does occur.

Religious divides exist, as elsewhere in the region. Tension between Bangladesh's Hindus and the Muslim majority is a problem, and Buddhist tribes in the southeast are agitating for autonomous rule. Relations with neighboring India are also strained, although in 1996 the countries signed a treaty agreeing to share resources after an Indian dam on the Ganges River reduced irrigation water for Bangladesh.

An exodus of refugees from Myanmar (Burma)—as many as 200,000 by early 1992—also stretched Bangladesh's scarce resources.

International aid finances 90 percent of state capital spending and an economic liberalization program has been introduced.

Bhutan

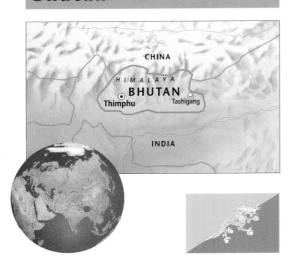

Fact File

OFFICIAL NAME Kingdom of Bhutan

FORM OF GOVERNMENT Monarchy with single legislative body (National Assembly)

CAPITAL Thimphu

AREA 47,000 sq km (18,147 sq miles)

TIME ZONE GMT + 5.5 hours

POPULATION 1,951,965

PROJECTED POPULATION 2005 2,226,481

POPULATION DENSITY 41.5 per sq km (107.5 per sq mile)

LIFE EXPECTANCY 52.8

INFANT MORTALITY (PER 1,000) 109.3

OFFICIAL LANGUAGE Dzongkha

OTHER LANGUAGES Tibetan, Nepalese

LITERACY RATE 41.1%

RELIGIONS Lamaistic Buddhism 75%, Hinduism 25%

ETHNIC GROUPS Bhote (Tibetan) 50%, ethnic Nepalese 35%, indigenous or migrant tribes 15%

CURRENCY Ngultrum

ECONOMY Agriculture 93%, services 5%, industry and commerce 2%

GNP PER CAPITA US$420

CLIMATE Tropical on southern plains; cool winters and hot summers in central valleys; cold winters and cool summers in mountains

HIGHEST POINT Kula Kangri 7,554 m (24,783 ft)

MAP REFERENCE Page 219

A tiny landlocked kingdom nestling in the Himalayas between India and Tibet, Bhutan is difficult to visit, and remains largely closed to the outside world. It is the world's most "rural" country, with less than 6 percent of its population living in towns and over 90 percent dependent on agriculture for a living. Despite its isolation and apparent tranquillity, the country is torn by fierce ethnic tensions which its absolute monarch does little to mitigate. Bhutan's longest-resident ethnic group consists of the Tibetans who probably migrated there 1,000 years ago. Early in the twentieth century, in order to end continual fighting between rival warlords in the area, the British administration in neighboring India established a hereditary monarch in Bhutan, the "Dragon King," in 1907.

The monarch is both head of state and government. Though a modernizer, intent on changing Bhutan's feudal ways, his emphasis on a sense of national identity founded on the language, laws, and dress of his own Drukpa group has stirred up bitter opposition among the resident Hindu Nepalese in southern Bhutan. Many have been deported, and others have fled to refugee camps in southeast Nepal. Dzongkha, which has been proclaimed the official language, is the natural language of only 16 percent of Bhutanese. In 1998 the king announced that in future Bhutan's rulers would have to step down if they received a no-confidence vote from the National Assembly.

There are three main regions distinguished largely by altitude—the Great Himalayas, crowned by huge peaks along the border with Tibet; the slopes and fertile valleys of the Lesser Himalayas, which are divided by the Wong, Sankosh, Tongsa and Manas rivers; and the Duars Plain which opens out toward India from the foothills of the mountains. The central uplands and foothills are cultivated, food staples including maize, wheat, barley, and potatoes. This area supports the bulk of the population. Below this the Duars Plain falls away into broad tracts of semitropical forest, savanna, and bamboo jungle. Forests still cover nearly 75 percent of Bhutan's land area, and timber is exported to India.

Almost all trade is with India. As an export, timber is outweighed in importance by cement. Other revenue-earning activities include a closely supervised and limited tourist industry (visitors are restricted to 4,000 per year), and the sale of stamps. Bhutan has huge hydropower potential but most manufacturing is of the cottage-industry type. Development projects such as road construction rely on Indian migrant labor. Though stabilized at a low level (the economy is one of the world's smallest and poorest) the country's balance of payments is strong, with comfortable reserves.

Brunei

Oil was discovered in the sultanate of Brunei in 1929. By the time it became independent on 1 January 1984 this small country on the north coast of Borneo was already prosperous. Today its oil revenues have made Brunei's sultan perhaps the richest man in the world, and given its people one of the highest per capita incomes in Asia. There is no income tax, the government subsidizes food and housing, and provides free medical care. The downside is that all government employees (two-thirds of the workforce) are banned from political activity, and the Sultan of Brunei rules by decree. Some nongovernmental political groupings have been allowed but the sultan remains firmly in control. There is disquiet among Bruneians over the rising number of resident foreigners, as demand for both skilled and unskilled labor brings contract workers in from outside.

Brunei consists of two semi-enclaves on the northwest coast of Borneo which are bordered by the Malaysian state of Sarawak. They are separated by a few kilometers of coastline where the Limbang River enters Brunei Bay. The topography in both consists of hills bordering a

History

Of India's various civilizations, the earliest developed in the Indus Valley (c.2600 BC) and in the Ganges Valley (c.1500 BC). At this time, the subcontinent was mainly peopled by ethnic Dravidians. It is thought that the Indus civilization succumbed to an invasion of Sanskrit-speaking Aryan peoples who introduced the caste system, a scheme of social division that is fundamental in Indian life. Another important early civilization was the Maurya, which under Ashoka, who reigned from 273 to 232 BC, came to dominate the subcontinent. Later, a succession of Arab, Turkish, and Mongol influences led to the founding in 1526 of the Mogul Empire, which under Akbar (1542–1605) was extended throughout most of northern India and part of the Deccan. It was during the time of Mogul rule that the Taj Mahal was built by Shah Jahan.

The British effectively controlled India from 1805, during the nineteenth century introducing a civil service and a code of law which have profoundly shaped the nation since that time. With the coming of independence in 1947, the division between Hindus and Muslims resulted in the violent and tumultuous partition of the country into India and Pakistan. This first major division to split the country indicates that the most serious rifts within Indian society tend to be religious. In recent years the Sikhs of the Punjab have also been agitating for independence.

Economy

Once essentially rural, India's economy is now a mix of village farming, modern agriculture, handicrafts, a variety of modern industries, and innumerable support services. During the 1980s economic growth allowed a marked increase in real per capita private consumption. Since 1991 production, trade, and investment reforms have provided new opportunities for Indian business and some 200 million middle-class consumers. Among the nation's strengths is a home market of some 900 million, along with a workforce that includes many who are highly skilled, including those trained in high-tech areas such as computer programming. The textile sector is highly efficient. There has been a massive rise in foreign investment as the country has opened up to foreign competition. The downside of this situation is a sizeable budget deficit along with high defense spending (including that for nuclear weapons) because of the longrunning and continuing conflict with Pakistan. Other negative features include an absence of even elementary social services, poor roads, inadequate port facilities, and an antiquated telecommunications system.

Women washing clothes beside the Ganges in Varanasi (left). Drying chilis in Rajasthan (top left). The Taj Mahal (top right).

Fact File

OFFICIAL NAME Republic of India

FORM OF GOVERNMENT Federal republic with two legislative bodies (Council of States and People's Assembly)

CAPITAL New Delhi

AREA 3,287,590 sq km (1,269,338 sq miles)

TIME ZONE GMT + 5.5 hours

POPULATION 999,826,804

PROJECTED POPULATION 2005 1,096,929,474

POPULATION DENSITY 304.1 per sq km (787.7 per sq mile)

LIFE EXPECTANCY 63.4

INFANT MORTALITY (PER 1,000) 60.8

OFFICIAL LANGUAGES Hindi, Bengali, Telugu, Marathi, Tamil, Urdu, Gujarati, Malayalam, Kannada, Oriya, Punjabi, Assamese, Kashmiri, Sindhi, Sanskrit, English

OTHER LANGUAGES Hindustani, about 700 indigenous languages

LITERACY RATE 51.2%

RELIGIONS Hindu 80%, Muslim 14%, Christian 2.4%, Sikh 2%, Buddhist 0.7%, Jain 0.5%, other 0.4%

ETHNIC GROUPS Indo-Aryan 72%, Dravidian 25%, Mongoloid and other 3%

CURRENCY Indian rupee

ECONOMY Agriculture 63%, services 26%, industry 11%

GNP PER CAPITA US$340

CLIMATE Tropical in south, temperate in north; monsoons June to September

HIGHEST POINT Kanchenjunga 8,598 m (28,208 ft)

MAP REFERENCE Pages 216–17, 218–19

STATES AND CAPITALS

Andhra Pradesh • Hyderabad
Arunachal Pradesh • Itanagar
Assam • Dispur
Bihar • Patna
Goa • Panaji
Gujarat • Gandhinagar
Haryana • Chandigarh
Himachal Pradesh • Simla
Jammu and Kashmir • Srinagar (summer) Jammu (winter)
Karnataka • Bangalore
Kerala • Trivandrum
Madhya Pradesh • Bhopal
Maharashtra • Mumbai (Bombay)
Manipur • Imphal
Meghalaya • Shillong
Mizoram • Aizawi
Nagaland • Kohima
Orissa • Bhubaneswar
Punjab • Chandigarh
Rajastan • Jaipur
Sikkim • Gangtok
Tamil Nadu • Madras
Tripura • Agartala
Uttar Pradesh • Lucknow
West Bengal • Calcutta

UNION TERRITORIES

Andaman and Nicobar Islands • Port Blair
Chandigarh • Chandigarh
Dadra and Nagar Haveli • Silvassa
Daman and Diu • Daman
Delhi • Delhi
Lakshadweep • Kavaratti
Pondicherry • Pondicherry

1769 Severe famines in Bengal lead to rural depopulation for more than 20 years

1857 Indian Revolt against heavy taxes results in considerable loss of British and Indian lives. It is ruthlessly suppressed

1876 Queen Victoria becomes Empress of India

1883 Commision into famine recommends building irrigation canals to supply water from Himalayas to grain-producing areas

1943 Severe food shortages in Bengal made worse by the army using scarce supplies results in loss of many lives

1965 Border war with Pakistan over Kashmir

1998 India tests nuclear weapons, followed by Pakistan; tension over Kashmir issue continues

1740 East India Co (founded 1600) takes over Mogul land. Dutch, British establish ports at Madras, Bombay, Calcutta

1800 East India Co trades between Britain, Europe, China. India produces raw materials for British factories

1850 Failure of monsoon rains causes famines in northern India for more than 30 years

1880s Indian Nationalist Movement begins pressure for an end to British rule; violent attacks by extremists

1921 After more than 12 million deaths in 'flu epidemic of 1918–19 India's population surges; by 1921 it passes 250 million

1947 India gains independence. Pakistan becomes a separate Muslim state (East and West). India takes over Kashmir

1971 East Pakistan becomes independent country of Bangladesh; India's population reaches 500 million

1999 Population of India predicted to reach 1 billion

Indonesia

Fact File

OFFICIAL NAME Republic of Indonesia

FORM OF GOVERNMENT Republic with single legislative body (House of Representatives)

CAPITAL Jakarta

AREA 1,919,440 sq km (741,096 sq miles)

TIME ZONE GMT + 7/9 hours

POPULATION 216,108,345

PROJECTED POPULATION 2005 234,875,553

POPULATION DENSITY 112.6 per sq km (291.6 per sq mile)

LIFE EXPECTANCY 62.9

INFANT MORTALITY (PER 1,000) 57.3

OFFICIAL LANGUAGE Bahasa Indonesia

OTHER LANGUAGES English, Dutch, indigenous languages

LITERACY RATE 83.2%

RELIGIONS Muslim 87%, Protestant 6%, Roman Catholic 3%, Hindu 2%, Buddhist 1%, other 1%

ETHNIC GROUPS Javanese 45%, Sundanese 14%, Madurese 7.5%, coastal Malays 7.5%, other 26%

CURRENCY Rupiah

ECONOMY Agriculture 54%, services 38%, industry 8%

GNP PER CAPITA US$980

CLIMATE Tropical, with wet season December to March (except in Moluccas where wet season is June to September)

HIGHEST POINT Puncak Jaya 5,030 m (16,502 ft)

MAP REFERENCE Pages 198–99, 200–01

Geologically, Indonesia is an active volcanic zone, but it was a political volcano which blew up in 1998. After 30 years of solid economic progress, during which a variety of political and ethnic conflicts were militarily contained, the collapse of the economy in 1998 triggered an outbreak of violent protest against the government. A change of leadership followed, and promises of new and more open elections. Nevertheless, long-suppressed class, ethnic, and religious conflicts have been unleashed, and a climate of political instability prevails. The national unity imposed on the numerous Indonesian islands has always been somewhat artificial. Insurrectionary guerrilla groups such as Aceh Merdeka (Free Aceh) in

north Sumatra, for example, have long been at odds with the urban elite in Jakarta.

The 13,677 islands that make up the world's largest archipelago (6,000 of them inhabited) rest on the platform of two continental shelves. The southern chain of islands, from Sumatra in the west to Timor in the southeast, and including Borneo to the north, form part of the Sunda shelf. This is a largely submerged extension of the Asian continent. Eastward, the northern Moluccas and New Guinea rest on the Sahul shelf, which is a northern extension of the Australian continent. Between the Asian and Australian ocean shelves, Sulawesi and the southern Moluccas form the island summits of suboceanic mountain ranges which are flanked by sea trenches 4,500 m (14,800 ft) deep.

All Indonesia's main islands are mountainous: this is an area of great crustal activity. Sumatra, Java, and the Lesser Sunda Islands (Nusa Tengara) form an arc containing 200 volcanoes, many of which are active—Krakatoa (Pulau Rakata) among them.

In Sumatra the Barisan Mountains run the length of the southwest-facing coastline. Along with 10 active volcanoes there are a number of crater lakes, Lake Toba, at an altitude of 900 m (2,953 ft), being one of the more spectacular. Much of Sumatra was once forested but over-cutting of timber in the lowlands means that native forest is now virtually restricted to reserves and national parks. However, isolated mountain forests remain over wide areas. The heavily populated island of Java, next in the island chain, has a long range which contains 50 active volcanoes and 17 that are only recently dormant.

Throughout the archipelago many coasts are lined with mangrove swamps, notably in eastern Sumatra and southern Kalimantan. Several of the islands are of great beauty: tourism, not only to Bali, has been a major activity in recent years.

Indonesia's complex and varied population, and its four major religions—Islam, Hinduism, Christianity, and Buddhism—reflect the country's varied history. Hinduism was the first major religious influence 2,000 years ago, followed by Buddhism in the seventh century AD. Hindu-

Borobudur, the world's largest Buddhist monument, was built in the ninth century BC on the island of Java. Islam is the dominant religion in Indonesia today.

Buddhist religious authority began to decline with the collapse of the Majapahit Empire in the fourteenth century, and the arrival of Arab traders from the west gradually established Islam as the dominant religion.

Under Dutch colonial rule from 1608, the islands were from 1830 subject to a severe extractive regime known as the Culture System. This involved the forced cultivation of commercial crops for export and resulted in a distortion of the traditional economy. Indonesia fell to the Japanese in the Second World War. This additional colonial experience guaranteed that the Indonesians would expect independence after 1945 and not accept the return of the Dutch.

About one-tenth of Indonesia's land area is under permanent cultivation. The majority of the people live by agriculture, growing rice, maize, cassava, and sweet potato. There are also extensive plantations producing rubber, palm oil, sugarcane, coffee, and tea. The last 30 years, however, have seen an intensive state-directed drive toward industrialization, based on diverse and abundant natural resources: oil, natural gas, timber, metals, and coal.

Foreign investment has played in important role in increased industrialization. Prosperity was initially tied to oil exports, but now the economy's growth depends on the continuing expansion of non-oil exports.

East Timor

East Timor, mainly Catholic after 300 years of Portuguese rule, was forcibly incorporated into Indonesia in 1975. Since that time, the Revolutionary Front of Independent East Timor (Fretilin) has continued to fight for independence. Indonesian troops have bombed villages and carried out mass executions of suspected Fretilin sympathizers. The situation is still unresolved.

Iran

Fact File

OFFICIAL NAME Islamic Republic of Iran

FORM OF GOVERNMENT Theocratic republic with single legislative body (Islamic Consultative Assembly)

Capital Tehrān

AREA 1,648,000 sq km (636,293 sq miles)

TIME ZONE GMT + 3.5 hours

POPULATION 70,351,549

PROJECTED POPULATION 2005 80,138,875

POPULATION DENSITY 42.7 per sq km (110.6 per sq mile)

LIFE EXPECTANCY 68.7

INFANT MORTALITY (PER 1,000) 47.0

OFFICIAL LANGUAGE Farsi (Persian)

OTHER LANGUAGES Turkic, Kurdish, Luri, Baloch, Arabic

LITERACY RATE 68.6%

RELIGIONS Shi'a Muslim 89%, Sunni Muslim 10%, other (including Zoroastrian, Jewish, Christian, and Baha'i) 1%

ETHNIC GROUPS Persian 51%, Azerbaijani 24%, Gilaki and Mazandarani 8%, Kurd 7%, Arab 3%, Lur 2%, Baloch 2%, Turkmen 2%, other 1%

CURRENCY Rial

ECONOMY Services 46%, agriculture 33%, industry 21%

GNP PER CAPITA Not available (c. US$766–3,035)

CLIMATE Mainly arid, temperate in far north; cold winters and hot summers

HIGHEST POINT Qolleh-ye Damāvand 5,671 m (18,605 ft)

MAP REFERENCE Pages 220–21, 222

Iran is one of the largest of the Persian Gulf states. It has borders with 10 other states in the region including Afghanistan, Pakistan, and Turkey. Now the home of the world's largest theocracy, and the main center for militant Shia Islam, Persia (as it was formerly known) has seen the rise and fall of a number of civilizations—Medes, Persians, Greeks, and Parthians. In the seventh century it was overrun by an invasion of Arabs who introduced Islam, a religion which under the Safavids in 1502 became the Shi'ite form of the faith which prevails

today. Oil was discovered in 1908. From that time on Persia (retitled in the 1920s by a Shah who adopted the name Iran because it meant "Aryan") became of growing interest to the great powers, and the requirements of international oil companies began to figure in Iranian life.

After the Second World War the Iranians found the corrupt and despotic rule of Shah Reza Khan intolerable, and in 1979 he was overthrown in the first national revolution to be led by Islamic fundamentalists. This event has had profound effects and repercussions throughout the Muslim world. Iran's subsequent support for Islamic radicalism abroad soon produced strained relations with Central Asian, Middle Eastern, and North African nations, as well as the USA. More recently, Iran's economic difficulties and isolation have caused a general relaxation both in the domestic regime and in its external affairs.

The entire central region is dominated by a high, arid plateau (average elevation 1,200 m; 3,937 ft), most of it salt desert, containing the Dasht-e Lūt (Great Sand Desert) and the Dasht-e-Kavīr (Great Salt Desert). Mountain ranges surround the plateau: the volcanic Elburz Range (Reshteh-ye Kūhhā-ye Alborz) along the Caspian Sea; the Khorasan and Baluchestan Ranges in the east and southeast; and the Zagros Mountains (Kūhhā-ye Zāgros) inland from the Persian Gulf. The most productive parts of Iran, and the most heavily populated, lie on its periphery. In the north are the fisheries, tea gardens, and rice fields of the Caspian shore. In Khuzestan to the south there are sugar plantations and oilfields—a prime target of the Iraqis when they invaded in 1980 at the start of the eight-year Iran–Iraq War. Westward lie the wheatfields of Azerbaijan, while to the east are the fruit groves of the oases of Kavir in Kavir (Dasht-e Kavīr) and Lut in Lut Desert (Dasht-e Lūt).

Some 8 percent of Iran's land is arable, and 11 percent of it is forested, mostly in the provinces of Gilan and Mazandaran which border the

Caspian Sea. The province of Tehrān in the north is by far the most densely populated region supporting about 18 percent of the population.

In the years after 1945 Iran's economy became almost totally dependent on oil, and earnings from oil exports still provide 85 percent of its export revenue. But by the end of the war with Iraq (1980–88) production was half the level of 1979. This, combined with the general fall in oil prices, and a surge in imports that began in 1989, has left Iran in severe financial difficulties, and there has been a marked decline in general standards of living. Ideological considerations hamper effective reforms: there is a continuing struggle over how to run a modern economy between the powerful religious leadership on the one hand, and reformist politicians on the other. The mullahs (the Islamic clergy) object to the government using borrowed money and are against the importation of "corrupt" Western technology.

Overall, the Iranian economy is a mix of centrally planned large-scale state enterprise; village agriculture producing wheat, barley, rice, sugar beet, tobacco, and pistachio nuts; and small-scale private trading and service ventures.

Riding a donkey, an Iranian girl leads her cows out to pasture (below). A portion of the facade of the Imam Mosque in Eşfahan, Iran (bottom).

Iraq

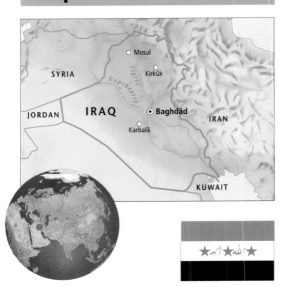

Fact File

OFFICIAL NAME Republic of Iraq

FORM OF GOVERNMENT Republic with single legislative body (National Assembly)

CAPITAL Baghdād

AREA 437,072 sq km (168,753 sq miles)

TIME ZONE GMT + 3 hours

POPULATION 23,871,623

PROJECTED POPULATION 2005 29,366,367

POPULATION DENSITY 54.6 per sq km (141.4 per sq mile)

LIFE EXPECTANCY 68.3

INFANT MORTALITY (PER 1,000) 52.5

OFFICIAL LANGUAGES Arabic, Kurdish

OTHER LANGUAGES Assyrian, Armenian

LITERACY RATE 56.8%

RELIGIONS Muslim 97% (Shi'a 60%–65%, Sunni 32%–37%), Christian or other 3%

ETHNIC GROUPS Arab 75%–80%, Kurdish 15%–20%, other (including Turkoman, Assyrian) 5%

CURRENCY Iraqi dinar

ECONOMY Services 48%, agriculture 30%, industry 22%

GNP PER CAPITA Est. US$766–3,035

CLIMATE Mainly arid, with cold winters and hot summers; winter snows in northern mountains

HIGHEST POINT Kūh-e Hājī Ebrāhīm 3,600 m (11,811 ft)

MAP REFERENCE Page 220

If any country has the right to call itself the cradle of Western civilization it is Iraq. The first city states in the region date from nearly 3500 BC. The land "between the waters" of the Tigris and the Euphrates rivers (the meaning of the old name Mesopotamia) has seen many empires come and go. Babylon defeated its old rival Assyria here in 612 BC, and in the seventh century BC the territory was seized by the Persians; Baghdad became the greatest commercial and cultural center of the Muslim world. The Persians held Iraq until they were conquered by Alexander the Great in 334 BC. Part of the Ottoman Empire from 1534 to 1918, Iraq became independent in 1932.

Modern Iraq has been involved in two major conflicts in the space of 20 years: the First Gulf War between Iraq and Iran, 1980–1988, and the Second Gulf War when it invaded Kuwait, 1990–91.

After the days of the early Mesopotamian empires, the Arab peoples brought Islam to Iraq in the seventh century AD. Like Iran, Iraq has a majority of Shi'ite Muslims. Unlike Iran, the ruling elite in Iraq are Sunni Muslims who fear their own Shi'ites are secretly loyal to Iran. This underlies the tension within Iraqi society. The situation of the Kurds relates to an ethnic rather than a religious division. Distrusted and persecuted in every land in which they live (Turkey, Iran, Iraq, Syria, and Armenia) Iraq's Kurds were assaulted by Baghdad with chemical weapons in the 1980s.

In the far northeast Iraq shares part of the Zagros Mountains (Kūhhā-ye Zāgròs) with Iran. In the west its territory includes a piece of the Syrian Desert. The rest of the country falls into two broad physiographic categories—the lowland desert to the west which makes up nearly 40 percent of the total land area; and the Tigris–Euphrates basin known formerly as Mesopotamia. Here the two rivers flow southeast roughly parallel, before meeting in a vast swamp on their way to the Gulf. In this swamp live communities of Marsh Arabs, Shi'ite Muslims targeted by the leadership in Baghdad after an attempted rebellion following the Second Gulf War. Most Iraqi agricultural activity takes place in the alluvial Tigris–Euphrates plain, where one-third of the farms are irrigated. Vegetables and cereals are the more important crops. In addition to the rice grown in warmer lowland areas, wheat and barley are cultivated in the temperate country near the Zagros Mountains. Exports have fallen sharply, but in better times Iraq's date crop met 80 percent of world demand.

Two wars, followed by international embargoes designed to force acceptance of UN inspection of weapons of mass destruction, have severely damaged the Iraqi economy. It was formerly dominated by the oil sector, but today oil exports are probably no more than 10 percent of their old level. Agricultural development has been hampered by labor shortages, salinization, and the dislocation caused by earlier land reform and collectivization programs. Living standards continue to deteriorate. Shortages are exacerbated by the government's spending of huge sums on both its army and internal security.

Middle East conflict

1964 Iran: Ayatollah Khomeini exiled for criticism of Shah's secular state.
1967 Israel: The Six Day War with Arab states. Israel seizes the Gaza Strip, Sinai, the Golan Heights, and the West Bank of the Jordan River.
1972 Iraq: Nationalization of Western-owned Iraq Petroleum Company.
1973 Egypt and Syria join in attack on Israel and fight 18-day war.
1978 Israel occupies southern Lebanon in response to Palestine Liberation Organization (PLO) attacks.
1979 Israel: Peace Treaty signed with Egypt. Iraq: Saddam Hussein takes over. Iran: Fall of the Shah. Ayatollah Khomeini returns from exile. Iran declared an Islamic Republic.
1980 Iraqi invasion starts Iran–Iraq War.
1981 Egypt: President Anwar Sadat, the first Arab leader to visit Israel, is assassinated.
1986 UN Security Council blames Iraq for war with Iran.
1987 Lebanon: Terry Waite, special envoy, arrives in Beirut to try to secure the release of western hostages and is himself captured.
1988 Iran: US naval ship shoots down Iranian airliner, 290 killed. Iran–Iraq War ends. Iraqi troops use chemical weapons on Kurds.
1990 Iran and Iraq resume diplomatic relations. Iraq invades and annexes Kuwait.
1991 Western allies liberate Kuwait. UN requires Iraq to accept weapons monitoring and to destroy weapons of mass destruction.
1993 Israel: PLO recognizes Israel in return for Palestinian autonomy in Gaza Strip and Jericho.
1994 Iraq recognizes Kuwaiti sovereignty.
1995 Israel: Palestinian autonomy extended to much of West Bank. Prime Minister Rabin assassinated.
1997 UN charges Iraqi officials with blocking weapons inspections. Iran: Mohammed Khatami, more liberal than his predecessors, becomes president.
1998 Iraq: Obstruction of UN weapons inspectors and fears of Iraq's biological weapons program leads to heavy bombing by US and UK.

Israel

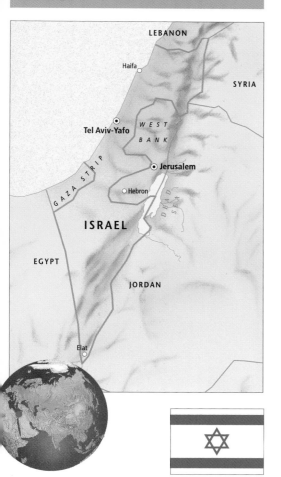

Fact File

OFFICIAL NAME State of Israel

FORM OF GOVERNMENT Republic with single legislative body (Knesset)

CAPITAL Jerusalem

AREA 20,770 sq km (8,019 sq miles)

TIME ZONE GMT + 2 hours

POPULATION 5,749,760

PROJECTED POPULATION 2005 6,303,057

POPULATION DENSITY 276.8 per sq km (717 per sq mile)

LIFE EXPECTANCY 78.6

INFANT MORTALITY (PER 1,000) 7.8

OFFICIAL LANGUAGES Hebrew, Arabic

OTHER LANGUAGES English, French, German, Hungarian, Romanian, Russian, Spanish

LITERACY RATE 95%

RELIGIONS Jewish 82%, Muslim 14%, Druze 2%, Christian 2%

ETHNIC GROUPS Jewish 82%, Arab 17%, other 1%

CURRENCY Shekel

ECONOMY Services 75%, industry 21%, agriculture 4%

GNP PER CAPITA US$15,920

CLIMATE Temperate along coast, hot and dry in south and east

HIGHEST POINT Har Meron 1,208 m (3,963 ft)

MAP REFERENCE Page 225

View across the rooftops of Sāmarrā', Iraq, to the River Tigris (top left). Pilgrims outside the Church of the Holy Sepulchre in Jerusalem, Israel (top right). The Old City of Jerusalem from the Mount of Olives (right).

Created as a Jewish homeland in 1948, Israel is a small country with an illustrious past that involves three of the world's great religions, and an uncertain future. For 50 years, through a succession of wars with hostile Arab neighbors, a secular, democratic political system has managed to constrain strong religious tendencies deeply rooted in the past. Key events in the Jewish history of the region are first, the occupation of the land by the 12 tribes of Israelites 4,000 years ago; second, the scattering (or "diaspora") of the one surviving tribe, the Jews, following a failed revolt against Rome in AD 138; third, the rise of Zionism in the nineteenth century advocating a Jewish homeland in Palestine as a solution to centuries of exile and persecution; fourth, the Holocaust, which reinforced arguments for territorial independence; and fifth, the proclamation of the State of Israel in May 1948, leading to the emigration of many Palestinian Arabs. Since then there has been continual strife between the new state and its neighbors. The subsequent seizure and occupation by Israel of additional territories (see entries for Gaza Strip and West Bank) has been bitterly resisted by their Arab inhabitants. This conflict has intensified as Jewish religious fundamentalists extend their settlements in contested areas.

Geographically, Israel consists of four main regions: the Mediterranean coastal plain of Sharon, irrigated by the Qishon, Soreq, and Sarida rivers; the rolling hills extending from Galilee in the north to Judea in the center; the Jordan–Red Sea section of the Rift Valley running north to south the full length of the eastern frontier from the Golan Heights to the Gulf of Aqaba; and the great southern wedge of desert plateau called the Negev (Ha Negev), which makes up about half of Israel's total land area. With irrigation, the Mediterranean coastal plain is fertile fruit-growing country. In the drier southern stretches its dunes have been stabilized with grass and tamarisk and reclaimed for pasture. The northern hill country around Galilee has good rainfall and a rich black soil weathered from basalt. Here and around Judea, pine, and eucalyptus trees have been planted to fix the soil and hold the water. The Valley of Jezreel ('Emeq Yizre'el), lying between Galilee and Samaria to the south, has deep alluvial soils which are intensively tilled for market gardening. The

Jordan–Western Negev Scheme—the most ambitious of Israel's various irrigation projects—diverts water from the upper Jordan and other sources through a series of culverts and canals south to the Negev. The desert is widely covered with blown sand and loess but tomatoes and grapes grow well when supplied with water.

Israel has the most industrialized economy in the region. Iron is smelted at Haifa and there are steel foundries at Acre. Chemical manufacturing takes place at Haifa and at plants by the Dead Sea. A national electricity grid provides power to widely dispersed towns where factories produce textiles, ceramics, and other products. In the Negev south of Beersheba new settlements mine oil, copper, and phosphates, the factories using potash and salt from the Dead Sea. Israel is largely self-sufficient in food production except for grains. Diamonds, high-technology equipment, and agricultural products are leading exports. About half the government's external debt is owed to the USA, its main source of aid. To earn foreign exchange the government has been targeting high-tech international market niches such as medical scanning equipment. Matters of continuing economic concern include the high level of unemployment following large-scale immigration from the former USSR, and the need to import strategically important raw materials.

Japan

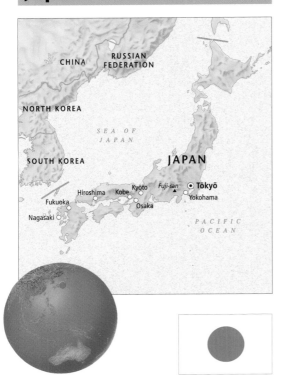

Fact File

Official name Japan

Form of government Constitutional monarchy with two legislative bodies (House of Councillors and House of Representatives)

Capital Tokyo

Area 377,835 sq km (145,882 sq miles)

Time zone GMT + 9 hours

Population 126,182,077

Projected population 2005 127,337,581

Population density 334 per sq km (865 per sq mile)

Life expectancy 80.1

Infant mortality (per 1,000) 4.1

Official language Japanese

Literacy rate 99%

Religions Shinto and Buddhist 84%, other (including Christian 0.7%) 16%

Ethnic groups Japanese 99.4%, other (mostly Korean) 0.6%

Currency Yen

Economy Services 69%, industry 24%, agriculture 7%

GNP per capita US$39,640

Climate Ranges from cold temperate in north to subtropical in south; wet season June to July

Highest point Fuji-san (Mt Fuji) 3,776 m (12,388 ft)

Map reference Pages 208–09

Mainly mountainous, with intensively cultivated coastal plains, the archipelago of Japan lies off the east Asian coast close to Korea and China. By the early 1990s it had become an industrial and trading colossus second only to the USA. But cracks in the country's apparently impregnable economic facade began to appear in 1998 as the yen slid steadily against the dollar. The nation's vast scientific and technological resources, its highly educated personnel, and its substantial trade surpluses, mean that it is better placed than most countries to cope with this and other problems.

History

First populated by migrants from mainland Asia, by the fifth century AD Japan was controlled by a number of clans. During the next 300 years several features of Chinese civilization were introduced, including Buddhism, Chinese script, and methods of administration, while cities modeled on those of the Tang Dynasty were built at Nara (AD 710) and Kyoto (AD 794). Centralized government, however, failed to eventuate and the clan basis of society prevailed. From the twelfth century until the rise of the Tokugawas power was held by rival groups of feudal lords, or shoguns, the emperor becoming a largely symbolic figure. Lasting from 1192 to 1867, the shogun era fostered a ethical code known as *bushido* (the path of the warrior, or samurai) that stressed loyalty, frugality, and courage.

Until 1945 Japan remained unconquered. Two Mongol fleets sent to invade the country were destroyed by typhoons in 1274 and 1281, founding the legend of a *kamikaze* or "divine wind" sent to protect "the land of the Gods." From 1603 a form of semi-centralized feudal rule was imposed by the ruling shogunate, the Tokugawas. Under this family, some 250 *daimyo* (or "great names") ran their own estates watched by state inspectors and a network of spies. Western influence appeared

briefly in 1542, when missionaries arrived from Macao bringing clocks, carpets, guns, and Christianity. The reaction of the Tokugawas was to close the door: from 1639 Japan's citizens were not allowed to travel abroad, and trading contacts were limited to a single Dutch settlement at Nagasaki.

This ended in 1853 when Commodore Perry of the US Navy brought a squadron of warships into Yokohama Harbor, demanding that the country's ports be opened to Western trade. The now weak Tokugawa shogunate collapsed, imperial rule was resumed under the Meiji Restoration, and within 50 years Japan had become westernized and a rising industrial force. Victories in wars with China (1894–95) and Russia (1904–05) led to the seizure of Taiwan and Korea. Expanding imperial ambitions led later to the invasion of China, and eventually, in 1941, to an attack on Hawaii and Japan's entry into the Second World War. Allied victory in 1945 was followed by the introduction of a liberal, US-imposed democratic constitution which has since guided the nation's development.

Physical features and land use

Four large islands, so closely grouped that bridges and a tunnel now connect them, make up 98 percent of Japan's territory. They occupy a

Timeline								
	660 BC Legendary leader Jimmu Tenno is Japan's first emperor and founds imperial dynasty which still holds office today	AD 200 In the Yayoi period (until c.AD 700) rice is grown in irrigated fields and people live in villages protected by moats and wooden palisades	550 Buddhism introduced from China	1281 Mongol conqueror Kublai Khan's invasion plans fail when his fleet is destroyed by a typhoon	1600 Honshu, Shikoku, and Kyushu united under the Tokugawa shogunate which rules for more than 250 years	1730 An earthquake on the island of Hokkaido causes the deaths of 137 000 people		1883 Tsunami kills 30,000 people. Three years later a tsunami occurs off Honshu and kills 28,000 people
4500 BC Islands of Japan inhabited by peoples from Asia. They are later known as Jomon after their pottery	c.1500 BC Rice is introduced from China and cultivated in the islands for the first time	400 BC Wet rice-farming introduced from Korean Peninsula; intensive agriculture enables larger population to survive	300 Large-scale immigration from the Asian continent until around 750 leads to a big increase in population	794 Japanese capital moves from Nara, the eastern end of the Tang Silk Road trade route, to Heian (called later Kyoto) until 1185	1543 Portuguese sailors visit islands of southern Kyushu making Europe aware of the wealth of the Japanese islands	1707 Mt Fuji, Japan's biggest volcano, erupts		1875 Population reaches more than 35 million; Tokyo 1 million by end of the century

highly unstable zone on the earth's crust, and earthquakes and volcanic eruptions are frequent: 140,000 died in the 1923 earthquake which hit Yokohama and part of Tokyo; 6,000 died in the Kobe earthquake of January 1995. Folding and faulting has produced a mosaic of landforms throughout Japan, mountains and hills alternating with small basins and coastal plains. Inland there are several calderas and volcanic cones, the most famous being Fuji-san (3,776 m; 12,388 ft), the highest mountain in Japan, which last erupted in 1707.

Hokkaido, the northernmost of the main islands, is the most rural and traditional. Japan's biggest and most productive farming region, it has a climate similar to the US midwest—which may be why American advisors established wheat farming there in the 1860s. Hokkaido now produces more than half of Japan's cereal needs. Southwest of Hokkaido lies the island of Honshu, where the Japanese Alps provide spectacular scenery. The Kanto Plain where Tokyo stands is the largest of various small alluvial plains, their soils enriched by centuries of careful cultivation. Today the conurbation this plain supports is Japan's most heavily industrialized and densely populated region. From southwestern Honshu across the two southern islands of Shikoku and Kyushu a complex of mountain peaks and undulating uplands stretches down to the Ryukyu Islands (Nansei-Shotō), which includes Okinawa, before extending south toward Taiwan.

Economy

Japan's economy is notable for government–industry cooperation, a motivated population with a strong work ethic, high educational levels and a mastery of high technology. These factors combined with a small defense allocation (1 percent of gross domestic product) have made it the second most powerful economy in the industrialized world. Japan is one of the world's largest and most advanced producers of steel and non-ferrous metallurgy, heavy electrical equipment, construction and mining equipment, motor vehicles and parts, communications and electronic equipment, machine tools, automated production systems, railroad rolling stock, ships, chemicals, textiles, and processed foods. Industry depends heavily on imported raw materials and fuel. The small agricultural sector is highly protected and subsidized; its crop yields are among the world's highest. Self-sufficient in rice, Japan imports about 50 percent of its other grain needs. After decades of spectacular growth, the late 1990s saw a marked contraction. The need for reconstruction remains evident, amid mounting fears of a banking crisis due to bad debts.

The Ginza district in Tokyo, Japan (left). A traditional house in rural Japan (top left). One of the many rock-cut facades in the ancient city of Petra in Jordan (right).

1945 USA drops atomic bombs, destroying Hiroshima and Nagasaki. Second World War ends	1994 Population of Tokyo-Yokohama exceeds 8 million

1923 The Great Kanto earthquake, fires, and tsunamis destroy much of Tokyo-Yokohama and kill more than 140,000 people	1964 Shinkansen high-speed "bullet train" links Tokyo and Kyoto traveling at speeds of 210 km (130 miles) an hour	1995 Earthquake destroys much of Kobe city and kills 6,000 people

Jordan

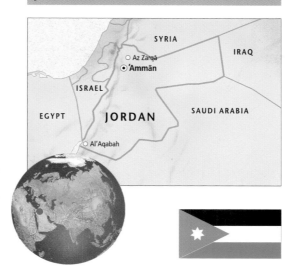

The small Arab kingdom of Jordan, rich in historic associations and sites, lies between Saudi Arabia, Israel, and Syria, and also shares a border with Iraq. It has to deal with Israel on the one hand and with Israel's various Arab antagonists on the other, while accommodating huge numbers of refugees. After the Ottoman Turks were driven out during the First World War the British installed the Hashemite monarchy in 1921. In 1946 Jordan became independent, and King Hussein reigned from 1952 until his death in 1999.

Governing Jordan has not been easy, many problems being connected with the West Bank. In 1967 this area, containing both Jerusalem and much of Jordan's best land, was lost to Israel. With emigré Palestinians using Jordan as a base for guerrilla activities (they were expelled in 1970–71), through two Gulf Wars in which Jordan was sympathetic to its oil supplier Iraq, and with the recent expansion of Israeli settlements in the area, the West Bank became impossible to regain or to administer. In 1988 Jordan ceded it to the PLO.

The Red Sea–Jordan section of the Rift Valley forms the country's western border. It contains the Jordan River valley, the Dead Sea (the lowest point on the earth's surface, at 400 m/1,312 ft below sea level), the Sea of Galilee, and Wadī al Arabah. Parts of the Jordan Valley and the highlands east of the Rift Valley are irrigated, making arable farming possible. Crops include vegetables, olives,

and fruit. Eighty percent of Jordan's land area is desert. In the north it merges with the Syrian Desert and in the south with the deserts of Saudi Arabia. Less than 0.5 percent of the country is forested, mainly in the east. Vegetation ranges from Mediterranean plants in the mountains to grass, sagebrush and shrubs in the steppe country.

Jordan has poor water, oil, and coal supplies. In the late 1970s and early 1980s it received Arab aid and the economy grew at more than 10 percent a year. In the late 1980s reductions in aid and in worker remittances slowed and imports outstripped exports. In 1991 the Second Gulf War overwhelmed the country. Worker remittances stopped, trade contracted, and further refugees arrived, straining resources. Recovery has been uneven. Poverty, debt, and unemployment are continuing problems.

Fact File

OFFICIAL NAME	Hashemite Kingdom of Jordan
FORM OF GOVERNMENT	Constitutional monarchy with two legislative bodies (House of Notables and House of Representatives)
CAPITAL	'Ammān
AREA	89,213 sq km (34,445 sq miles)
TIME ZONE	GMT + 2 hours
POPULATION	4,561,147
PROJECTED POPULATION 2005	5,403,895
POPULATION DENSITY	51.1 per sq km (132.3 per sq mile)
LIFE EXPECTANCY	73.1
INFANT MORTALITY (PER 1,000)	32.7
OFFICIAL LANGUAGE	Arabic
OTHER LANGUAGE	English
LITERACY RATE	85.5%
RELIGIONS	Sunni Muslim 92%, Christian 8%
ETHNIC GROUPS	Arab 98%, Circassian 1%, Armenian 1%
CURRENCY	Jordanian dinar
ECONOMY	Services 64%, industry 26%, agriculture 10%
GNP PER CAPITA	US$1,510
CLIMATE	Mainly arid, but northwest temperate with cool, wet winters and hot, dry summers
HIGHEST POINT	Jabal Ramm 1,754 m (5,755 ft)
MAP REFERENCE	Page 225

Kazakhstan

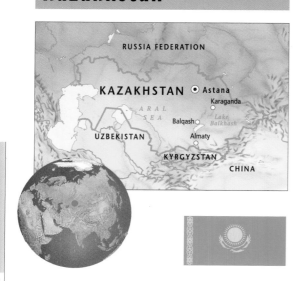

With a land area nearly as large as India, Kazakhstan is an important member of the newly formed Commonwealth of Independent States (CIS). In earlier times, when it was a Soviet Republic, authorities used the region for testing nuclear weapons and for exiling ethnic minorities.

In the 1950s and 1960s when the Soviet "virgin lands" project was underway, vast tracts of pasture were plowed up and sown with wheat or given over to livestock production, and waters from rivers running into the Aral Sea were used in irrigation schemes. As a result, the sea shrank by 70 percent.

During the years of Soviet domination, high levels of immigration from Russia resulted in the Kazakhs being outnumbered. Outmigration of Russians since 1991 and the return of many expatriates has resulted in a Kazak majority once more, but ethnic tensions remain high.

Much of the country is tablelands—the eroded tableland of the east featuring shallow uplands, depressions, and lakes—and there are also several mountains ranges in the east including the Altai Range (Mongol Altayn Nuruu). Running from north to south, steppe country gives way to desert or semidesert, though irrigation schemes have made large areas productive between the Aral Sea and Lake Balkhash (Balqash Köli).

With a climate marked by intense winter cold and extreme summer heat, rainfall is generally low. The lakes in the center of the country are saline, as are the marshes in the west, and in the central region there are few permanent rivers. The grassy steppes of the north are the most naturally fertile part of the country. Though the region has traditionally been associated with livestock rearing (Kazakhstan still supports up to 200,000 nomadic shepherds and herdsmen) the agricultural policies of the Soviet period converted much pasture to grain cultivation. By 1989 the country accounted for 20 percent of the entire cultivated area of the Soviet Union and 12 percent of its grain output.

Other crops grown include fruits, potatoes, vegetables, sugar beet, and cotton. High quality wool is produced, and Kazakhstan supplies meat to surrounding countries. Industry is based mainly on processing raw materials: fuel, metals, textiles, chemicals, and food. Products include rolled metals, agricultural machinery, plastics, clothing, footwear, paper, and cement. Well endowed with oil and gas reserves, the country also has deposits of coal,

iron ore, bauxite, copper, nickel, tungsten, zinc, and silver. In addition, it holds 70 percent of CIS gold reserves. The government has been pursuing a moderate program of reform and privatization— investment incentives have been established, state controls have been lifted, and assets privatized. But government control of key industries remains extensive. Lack of pipeline transportation for oil export hinders a likely source of economic growth.

Environmental problems are extensive and severe. Radioactive or toxic chemical sites associated with weapons development are widespread. The drying up of the Aral Sea has left a crust of chemical pesticides which is periodically blown about in noxious dust storms.

Fact File

OFFICIAL NAME	Republic of Kazakhstan
FORM OF GOVERNMENT	Republic with two legislative bodies (Senate and Majilis)
CAPITAL	Aqmola (Astana)
AREA	2,717,300 sq km (1,049,150 sq miles)
TIME ZONE	GMT + 6 hours
POPULATION	16,824,825
PROJECTED POPULATION 2005	16,903,895
POPULATION DENSITY	6.2 per sq km (16 per sq mile)
LIFE EXPECTANCY	63.4
INFANT MORTALITY (PER 1,000)	58.8
OFFICIAL LANGUAGE	Kazakh
OTHER LANGUAGE	Russian
LITERACY RATE	97.5%
RELIGIONS	Muslim 47%, Russian Orthodox 44%, Protestant 2%, other 7%
ETHNIC GROUPS	Kazak 42%, Russian 37%, Ukrainian 5.3%, German 4.7%, Uzbek 2%, Tatar 2%, other 7%
CURRENCY	Tenge
ECONOMY	Services 43%, industry 31%, agriculture 26%
GNP PER CAPITA	US$1,330
CLIMATE	Mainly arid; cold winters and hot summers; cooler in north
HIGHEST POINT	Khan Tängiri Shyngy 6,995 m (22,949 ft)
MAP REFERENCE	Pages 222–23

Kuwait

The Arab emirate of Kuwait lies in the northwest corner of the Persian Gulf, dwarfed by its neighbors Iraq, Iran, and Saudi Arabia. Beneath its surface lie huge oil reserves. It was settled by wandering Arab peoples in the eighteenth century. When Germany and Turkey were eyeing Kuwait possessively in the nineteenth century it formed a defensive alliance with Great Britain, becoming a British protectorate in 1914. In 1961, when it gained independence, Kuwait was claimed by Iraq.

A constitution was inaugurated by the al-Sabah ruling family in 1962. Whenever the National Assembly has been critical, however, it has been suspended. In 1990, despite Kuwait having lent millions of dollars to Iraq during the Iran–Iraq War of 1980–88, Iraq invaded. The Kuwaitis endured six months of brutality and the destruction of the city of Kuwait before a US-led international coalition expelled the Iraqis in 1991. During the occupation 400,000 residents fled the country—200,000 Palestinian migrant workers not being allowed to return as the Palestinian Liberation Organization had supported Iraq. The destruction of Kuwaiti oil wells by Iraq and deliberate oil-spills in the Gulf have caused environmental costs still difficult to assess.

Kuwait consists of an undulating sandy plateau which rises westward to an elevation of about 300 m (1,000 ft) on the Iraq–Saudi Arabia border. Along the border the plateau is cut to a depth of 45 m (150 ft) by the Wādī al Bāṭin. In the northeast there are a few salt marshes and in the northwest is the Jal az-Zawr escarpment. Vegetation is mostly limited to salt-tolerant plants along the coast, though in modern urban areas green spaces have been produced by irrigating imported soil. The territory of Kuwait also includes nine islands, of which Bubiyan is the largest.

Kuwait owns 10 percent of the world's proven crude oil reserves. Its petroleum sector currently accounts for nearly half of gross domestic product, 90 percent of export revenues, and 70 percent of government income. With the exception of fish, Kuwait depends almost wholly on food imports, though hothouses and hydroponics produce some fruit and vegetables. About 75 percent of potable water must be distilled or imported. The shortage of water constrains industrial activities, which at present include petrochemical production, food processing, desalination, construction materials, and salt. The World Bank has urged the government to push ahead with privatization, including in the oil industry.

Fact File

OFFICIAL NAME State of Kuwait

FORM OF GOVERNMENT Constitutional monarchy with single legislative body (National Assembly)

CAPITAL Al Kuwayt (Kuwait)

AREA 17,820 sq km (6,880 sq miles)

TIME ZONE GMT + 3 hours

POPULATION 1,991,115

PROJECTED POPULATION 2005 2,436,509

POPULATION DENSITY 111.7 per sq km (289.3 per sq mile)

LIFE EXPECTANCY 77.2

INFANT MORTALITY (PER 1,000) 10.3

OFFICIAL LANGUAGE Arabic

OTHER LANGUAGE English

LITERACY RATE 77.8%

RELIGIONS Muslim 85% (Sunni 45%, Shi'a 30%, other 10%), other (including Christian, Hindu, Parsi) 15%

ETHNIC GROUPS Kuwaiti 45%, other Arab 35%, South Asian 9%, Iranian 4%, other 7%

CURRENCY Kuwaiti dinar

ECONOMY Services 90%, industry 9%, agriculture 1%

GNP PER CAPITA US$17,390

CLIMATE Arid, with cool winters and hot, humid summers

HIGHEST POINT Unnamed location 306 m (1,004 ft)

MAP REFERENCE Page 220

Kyrgyzstan

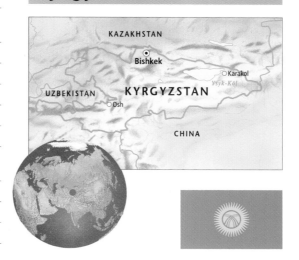

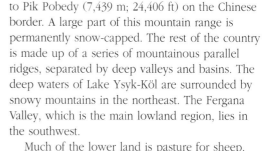

Kyrgyzstan is a small, mountainous, landlocked country in central Asia. China lies over the massive peaks of the Tian Shan Range along its southeast border, Kazakhstan is to the north, and Uzbekistan and Tajikistan are to the southwest. Not only is Kyrgyzstan the least urbanized of all the ex-Soviet republics, its population is growing faster in rural areas than in the towns. Native Kyrgyz are barely a majority and ethnic tension with Uzbeks and other nationals from nearby countries is a feature of everyday life. Fierce clashes between Kyrgyz and Uzbeks took place in the border city of Osh in 1990. Historically, the once nomadic Muslim Kyrgyz pastoralists are descended from refugees of Mongolian and Turkic origin who entered the region in the thirteenth century, escaping from Mongol invaders. For a while in the eighteenth century the region came under Manchu domination, then during the nineteenth century Russia began to colonize the country. Russian immigrants took the best land, settling in the low-lying, fertile areas. For years after the country's incorporation into the Soviet Union in the 1920s, resistance was carried out by local guerrilla groups called *basmachi*. Since independence in 1991, Kyrgyzstan has pursued liberal political and economic policies.

Geographically, Kyrgyzstan is dominated by the western end of the Tian Shan Range, which rises to Pik Pobedy (7,439 m; 24,406 ft) on the Chinese border. A large part of this mountain range is permanently snow-capped. The rest of the country is made up of a series of mountainous parallel ridges, separated by deep valleys and basins. The deep waters of Lake Ysyk-Köl are surrounded by snowy mountains in the northeast. The Fergana Valley, which is the main lowland region, lies in the southwest.

Much of the lower land is pasture for sheep, pigs, cattle, goats, horses, and yaks. Irrigated land is used to produce crops ranging from sugar beet and vegetables to rice, cotton, tobacco, grapes, and mulberry trees (for feeding silkworms). There are major salination problems caused mainly by the excessive irrigation of cotton.

Cotton, wool, and meat are the main agricultural products and exports: one of Kyrgyzstan's strengths is agricultural self-sufficiency. It has small quantities of coal, oil, gas, and the extensive snow-covered ranges ensure great hydropower potential. Energy policy aims at developing these resources in order to make the country less dependent on Russia. After the introduction of market reforms, and a program to control inflation, attention has turned to stimulating growth. This will not be easy: the economy is still dominated by the state and by the mentality of collective farming. Foreign aid plays a major role in the country's budget.

Fact File

OFFICIAL NAME Kyrgyz Republic

FORM OF GOVERNMENT Republic with two legislative bodies (Assembly of People's Representatives and Legislative Assembly)

CAPITAL Bishkek

AREA 198,500 sq km (76,641 sq miles)

TIME ZONE GMT + 6 hours

POPULATION 4,546,055

PROJECTED POPULATION 2005 4,829,120

POPULATION DENSITY 22.9 per sq km (59.3 per sq mile)

LIFE EXPECTANCY 63.6

INFANT MORTALITY (PER 1,000) 75.9

OFFICIAL LANGUAGE Kyrghiz

OTHER LANGUAGE Russian

LITERACY RATE 97%

RELIGIONS Sunni Muslim 70%, Christian (predominantly Russian Orthodox) 30%

ETHNIC GROUPS Kyrghiz 52.5%, Russian 21.5%, Uzbek 13%, Ukrainian 2.5%, German 2.5%, other 8%

CURRENCY Som

ECONOMY Services 41%, agriculture 38%, industry 21%

GNP PER CAPITA US$700

CLIMATE Subtropical in southwest, temperate in valleys, cold and snowy in mountains

HIGHEST POINT Pik Pobedy 7,439 m (24,406 ft)

MAP REFERENCE Page 223

Dome of the Khodja Ahmed Yasavi Mausoleum in Turkestan, Kazakhstan (far left). Women at the market in the town of Osh, Kyrgyzstan (center left). Kuwait City (left).

Laos

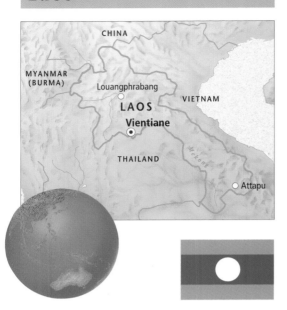

Fact File

OFFICIAL NAME Lao People's Democratic Republic

FORM OF GOVERNMENT Communist state with single legislative body (National Assembly)

CAPITAL Vientiane

AREA 236,800 sq km (91,428 sq miles)

TIME ZONE GMT + 7 hours

POPULATION 5,407,453

PROJECTED POPULATION 2005 6,337,670

POPULATION DENSITY 22.8 per sq km (59 per sq mile)

LIFE EXPECTANCY 54.2

INFANT MORTALITY (PER 1,000) 89.3

OFFICIAL LANGUAGE Lao

OTHER LANGUAGES French, English, indigenous languages

LITERACY RATE 55.8%

RELIGIONS Buddhist 60%, animist and other 40%

ETHNIC GROUPS Lao Loum (lowland) 68%, Lao Theung (upland) 22%, Lao Soung (highland) 9%, ethnic Vietnamese and Chinese 1%

CURRENCY Kip

ECONOMY Agriculture 80%, services and industry 20%

GNP PER CAPITA US$350

CLIMATE Tropical monsoonal, with wet season May to October

HIGHEST POINT Phou Bia 2,818 m (9,245 ft)

MAP REFERENCE Pages 202–03

Novice Buddhist monks in a Laotian monastery (above). A Laotian village (top). Byblos Harbor in Lebanon (right).

Laos is the only landlocked country in Southeast Asia. It also has one of the last official communist regimes, and is the poorest state in the region. Once the home of the fourteenth century kingdom of Lan Xang (the Million Elephant Kingdom), Laos became a French protectorate in 1893. Independent in 1953, it was fought over by royalists, communists, and conservatives from 1964 onward. It was used as a military supply route by the North Vietnamese during the Vietnam War and was heavily bombed with defoliants by the USA during the late 1960s. In 1975 it fell into the hands of the communist Pathet Lao who established a one-party state. Although the leadership has for economic reasons relaxed its doctrinal grip—the 1978 collectivization of agriculture was reversed in 1990—many hill-tribe people, such as the Hmong, remain alienated from the regime. Some continue guerrilla resistance, while others live in exile in Thailand. A new constitution in 1991 confirmed the monopoly of the communist Lao People's Revolutionary Party.

From the mountains in the northwest and the Plateau de Xiangkhoang, the country extends southeast, following the line of the Chaîne Anamitique Range. A number of rivers cross the country westward from this range to the Mekong River which forms the western border, among them the Banghiang, the Noi, and the Theun. The fertile Mekong floodplains in the west provide the only generally cultivable lowland. Despite deforestation and erosion, forest still covers 55 percent of the country.

Most of the Laotian people are engaged in subsistence agriculture. In addition to the staple, rice, other crops grown include maize, vegetables, tobacco, coffee, and cotton. Opium poppies and cannabis are grown illegally: Laos is the world's third-largest opium producer.

The policy of privatization and decentralization that was adopted in 1986 has produced growth averaging an annual 7.5 percent since 1988. Textile and garment manufacture was established, as well as motorcycle assembly. The country's primitive infrastructure is a major handicap to growth. Laos has no railroads, its roads are inadequate, and its telecommunications severely limited. For the foreseeable future the economy will depend heavily on overseas aid.

Lebanon

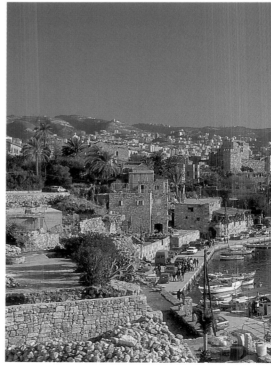

Fact File

OFFICIAL NAME	Republic of Lebanon
FORM OF GOVERNMENT	Republic with single legislative body (National Assembly)
CAPITAL	Beirut
AREA	10,400 sq km (4,015 sq miles)
TIME ZONE	GMT + 2 hours
POPULATION	3,562,699
PROJECTED POPULATION 2005	3,904,380
POPULATION DENSITY	342.5 per sq km (887 per sq mile)
LIFE EXPECTANCY	70.9
INFANT MORTALITY (PER 1,000)	30.5
OFFICIAL LANGUAGES	Arabic, French
OTHER LANGUAGES	Armenian, English
LITERACY RATE	92%
RELIGIONS	Muslim 70%, Christian 30%
ETHNIC GROUPS	Arab 95%, Armenian 4%, other 1%
CURRENCY	Lebanese pound
ECONOMY	Services 60%, industry 28%, agriculture 12%
GNP PER CAPITA	US$2,660
CLIMATE	Temperate, with short mild, wet winters and long, hot, dry summers. In winter rainfall in mountains often turns to snow
HIGHEST POINT	Qurnat as Sawdā' 3,088 m (10,131 ft)
MAP REFERENCE	Page 225

Lebanon, a small country on the eastern shore of the Mediterranean Sea, consists of the region that was once known as the Levant. It has a history that goes back at least 5,000 years. First settled by the Phoenicians around 3000 BC, it saw Alexander the Great (356–323 BC) conquer the Phoenician city of Tyre, and it later became part of the Roman Empire. Early in the seventh century AD Maronite Christians (named after Maro, a Syrian monk who was the sect's founder) settled in northern Lebanon; later, Druze Arabs, who are aligned with Shi'ite Islam, settled in the south of

the country, and Sunni Muslims came to the coastal towns. From the eleventh to the thirteenth century the region was a center of confrontation between Western Christians and Muslims during the Crusades. It then became part of the Muslim Mameluke Empire. In 1516 the Ottoman Turks took control of the country, their rule finally ending with conquest by the British and French during the First World War.

From 1920, following the withdrawal of Turkish forces, a French administration sought to balance the interests of the country's various religious groups. During this period Beirut, which already had a cosmopolitan air, took on a distinctly French flavor. The city became both a center of international commerce and a playground of the rich. The country gained independence in 1946. Deep and persistent tensions between Muslim and various non-Muslim sections of the population led to an outbreak of guerrilla war in 1975. For the next 15 years much of the country was devasted by civil war, and much of its urban infrastructure was destroyed.

From the narrow coastal plain along the Mediterranean, where crops are grown with the aid of irrigation, the land rises eastward to form the Lebanon Mountains (Jabal Lubnān). Running from north to south, these cover about 30 percent of Lebanon's land area. Between the harsh slopes of this range and the Anti-Lebanon Chain (Jabal ash Sharqī) that borders Syria, lies the fertile el Beqaa Valley which is another agricultural area. This is traversed by the River Litani on its journey south, before emptying into the Mediterranean Sea above Şūr (the ancient city of Tyre).

Decades of fighting have left the Lebanese economy in ruins and there is a severe housing shortage. Tourism, which was once an important source of revenue, is beginning to revive with the rebuilding of the once-popular Corniche seafront area at Beirut. Since the decline of industry as a result of the war, agriculture has come to play a more important role: crops include apples, citrus fruits, bananas, carrots, grapes, tomatoes, and olives. Opium poppies and cannabis are illegally produced for export. Traditional areas of activity in the past were banking, food processing, textiles, cement, oil refining, and chemicals. The country now depends heavily on foreign aid.

Beirut

With a population of only 6,000, Beirut was little more than a village in the year 1800. But the nineteenth century saw continuous commercial growth, and by 1850 its population had swelled to 15,000. An ominous development in 1860 also increased Beirut's population: in the nearby mountains there was a massacre of Christians by Druzes (an Islamic sect originating in Syria), with the result that large numbers of Christian refugees entered the city. During the second half of the century a variety of Western missionaries, both Catholic and Protestant, were active, and several major educational institutions (one becoming the highly regarded American University of Beirut) were founded.

In 1926 the Lebanese Republic was established, under French control, and as the city grew rapidly so did its social tensions. Under the terms of a French-brokered unwritten understanding in 1943 the Christians were able to dominate the Muslim population through a fixed 6:5 ratio of parliamentary seats. The Muslims bitterly resented this arrangement. After they had tried for three decades to change the situation, with a serious outbreak of violence between Christians and Muslims in 1958, full-scale civil war erupted in 1975 between numerous armed militias. On the Christian side the major groups consisted of Maronite Christians and Greek Orthodox, along with smaller numbers of Armenians, Greek Catholics, Protestants, and Roman Catholics. On the non-Christian side were the dominant Sunni Muslims, the minority Shi'ites, and the Druzes. As the war extended Beirut became first a divided city, then a city destroying itself. Lebanon had already been destabilized by a deluge of Palestinian refugees following the 1967 Arab–Israeli War, and by a further influx when the Palestinians in Jordan were expelled in 1970. The Palestinians used southern Lebanon as a base for attacks on Israel, and their militias behaved like an occupying army in the area. West Beirut was virtually destroyed in 1982 when Israel launched a full-scale assault on Palestinian Liberation Organization (PLO) bases in the city, action which led to the evacuation of PLO troops and leaders.

While some degree of order existed in East Beirut, West Beirut collapsed into endless anarchic battles between rival factions trying to settle scores. Hostage-taking became common, some captives being held for years on end. In 1986 West Beirut sought Syrian intervention to try to establish order; after a period of intensified fighting the major antagonists accepted the Ta'if Accord in 1989. Since then the level of internal conflict has declined. Syria remains a powerful influence in Lebanese affairs and its forces continue to occupy large areas. It is estimated that about 150,000 people died in the civil war.

Malaysia

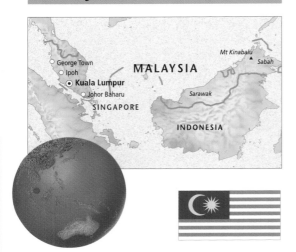

Fact File

OFFICIAL NAME Malaysia

FORM OF GOVERNMENT Federal constitutional monarchy with two legislative bodies (Senate and House of Representatives)

CAPITAL Kuala Lumpur

AREA 329,750 sq km (127,316 sq miles)

TIME ZONE GMT + 8 hours

POPULATION 21,376,066

PROJECTED POPULATION 2005 24,086,817

POPULATION DENSITY 64.8 per sq km (167.8 per sq mile)

LIFE EXPECTANCY 70.7

INFANT MORTALITY (PER 1,000) 21.7

OFFICIAL LANGUAGE Malay (Bahasa Malaysia)

OTHER LANGUAGES English, Chinese languages, Tamil

LITERACY RATE 83%

RELIGIONS Muslim 53%, Buddhist 17.5%, Confucian and Taoist 11.5%, Christian 8.5%, Hindu 7%, other 2.5%

ETHNIC GROUPS Malay 59%, Chinese 32%, Indian 9%

CURRENCY Ringgit (Malaysian dollar)

ECONOMY Agriculture 42%, services 39%, industry 19%

GNP PER CAPITA US$3,890

CLIMATE Tropical, with northeast monsoon October to February and southwest monsoon May to September

HIGHEST POINT Gunung Kinabalu 4,101 m (13,453 ft)

MAP REFERENCE Pages 200–01

Malaysia consists of the southern part of the Malay Peninsula, with Thailand to its north, plus Sarawak and Sabah in northern Borneo. Like Singapore, which lies at the southern tip of the Malay Peninsula, it has had an impressive record of economic growth in recent times.

In the fifteenth century a part of Malaysia was famous as the Kingdom of Malacca (now Melaka), a state that became powerful through its control of local sea routes and shipping. In 1414 the ruler of Malacca adopted Islam, which is the religion of Malaysia today. Seized by the Portuguese as a base for the spice trade in 1511, and held by the Dutch from 1641, Malacca was captured by the British in 1795. The British took control of Singapore in 1819 and in 1867 they established the Straits

Settlements, which consisted of Penang Island (Pinang) in the northeast, Malacca, and Singapore, as a crown colony. During the Second World War Malaysia was occupied by the Japanese. In 1948 it received its independence from the British. A guerrilla war then broke out, led by communists who were sympathetic to the Chinese Revolution. Following the defeat of this insurgency, after a four-year military campaign, the country evolved into the modern state it is today. Ethnic tensions exist, principally between the Malays, who are the most numerous, and the Chinese, who are considerably more prosperous. There were riots between the Malays and Chinese in 1969 with heavy loss of life. The many "affirmative action" provisions that are now in place to help Malays at the expense of Chinese and Indians are strongly resented by the latter groups. There are also a number of unresolved territorial disputes with neighboring states—Sabah in Borneo, for example, being claimed by the Philippines.

Fold mountains aligned on a north–south axis dominate the Malay Peninsula. There are seven or eight distinct chains of mountains, often with exposed granite cores. Climbing to 2,189 m (7,181 ft) at Gunung Tahan, the main range divides the narrow eastern coastal belt from the fertile alluvial plains in the west. To the south lies poorly drained lowland, marked by isolated hills, some of which rise to over 1,060 m (3,500 ft). Several smaller rivers have also contributed to the margin of lowland around the peninsular coasts.

About 2,000 km (1,250 miles) east of the Malay Peninsula, northern Borneo has a mangrove-fringed coastal plain about 65 km (40 miles) wide, rising behind to hill country averaging 300 m (1,000 ft) in height. This ascends through various secondary ranges to the mountainous main interior range. The granite peak of Gunung Kinabalu, the highest mountain in Southeast Asia, rises from the northern end of this range in Sabah, towering

above Kinabalu National Park. Dense rainforest in Sarawak and Sabah support a great diversity of plants and animals.

With a mixture of private enterprise and public management, the Malaysian economy averaged 9 percent annual growth from 1988 to 1995. Poverty is being substantially reduced and real wages are rising. New light industries including electronics are playing an important role in this development: Malaysia is the world's biggest producer of disk drives. Heavy industry has also grown: Malaysia's "national car", the Proton, is now being exported. The traditional mainstays of the economy, however, remain rice, rubber, palm oil, and tin—Malaysia being the world's biggest producer of palm oil and tin. Rice is a problem. Subsistence farming has regularly failed to ensure self-sufficiency in food, and rice production does

Maldives

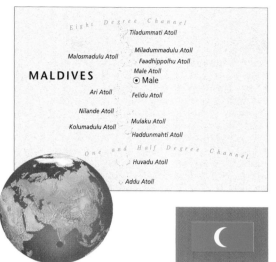

MALDIVES

Eight Degree Channel

Tiladummati Atoll

Malosmadulu Atoll

Miladummadulu Atoll
Faadhippolhu Atoll
Male Atoll
⊙ Male

Ari Atoll   Felidu Atoll

Nilande Atoll

Kolumadulu Atoll   Mulaku Atoll

Haddunmahti Atoll

One and Half Degree Channel

Huvadu Atoll

Addu Atoll

Fact File

OFFICIAL NAME Republic of the Maldives

FORM OF GOVERNMENT Republic with single legislative body (Citizens Council)

CAPITAL Male

AREA 300 sq km (116 sq miles)

TIME ZONE GMT + 5 hours

POPULATION 300,220

PROJECTED POPULATION 2005 364,147

POPULATION DENSITY 1,000.7 per sq km (2,591.8 per sq mile)

LIFE EXPECTANCY 68.3

INFANT MORTALITY (PER 1,000) 38.1

OFFICIAL LANGUAGE Divehi

OTHER LANGUAGES Arabic, English, Hindi

LITERACY RATE 93%

RELIGIONS Predominantly Sunni Muslim

ETHNIC GROUPS Sinhalese, Dravidian, Arab, African

CURRENCY Rufiyaa

ECONOMY Tourism, fishing, manufacturing

GNP PER CAPITA US$990

CLIMATE Tropical, with wet season May to August

HIGHEST POINT Unnamed location on Wilingili 24 m (79 ft)

MAP REFERENCE Page 216

The Maldive Archipelago consists of an 800 km (500 mile) string of nearly 2,000 islands and atolls (202 of them inhabited) southwest of India's southern tip, Cape Comorin. Made up of tiny islets ringed by white sands and clear blue lagoons, they have recently been developed as tourist resorts and receive up to 300,000 visitors each year. Long ago, their first visitors were probably Dravidians from southern India, in around 400 BC. Centuries later, the islands seem to have been taken over by people from Sri Lanka—Divehi, the national language, is a form of Sinhalese. In 1153 the king of the Maldives ordered his subjects to adopt Islam in place of Buddhism: today the people are mainly Sunni Muslims and there are 689 mosques. For the next 800 years the islands were ruled as a Muslim sultanate, though there was a brief period, between 1558 and 1573, of Portuguese control from Goa. The British established a protectorate in 1887, the islands achieved independence in 1965, and the sultan was deposed in 1968. Since then government has been in the hands of a small group of influential families, and by 1995 the president then in office, a wealthy businessman, had survived three attempted coups. Younger political contenders who have tasted democracy abroad are pressing for a more open regime.

The atolls of the Maldives are coral reefs which have grown up around the peaks of a submerged volcanic mountain range. None of them rise more than 1.8 m (6 ft) above sea level. There is concern that if the Greenhouse Effect causes a rise in sea levels, some may be submerged. Adequate rainfall supports a variety of tropical vegetation, and palm and breadfruit trees occur naturally.

Food crops include coconuts, bananas, mangoes, sweet potatoes, and spices. Agriculture plays a role in the economy, though constrained by the small amount of cultivable land, and most staple foods must be imported. In the lagoons and the open sea fish are plentiful. Bonito and tuna are leading exports, fishing being the second leading growth sector of the economy. Manufacturing, consisting mainly of garment production, boat building, and handicrafts, accounts for 15 percent of gross domestic product. Since the 1980s tourism has been the leading growth sector, and now accounts for more than 60 percent of foreign exchange receipts. At present more than 90 percent of tax revenue comes from import duties and tourism-related taxes.

not meet demand. The main industries on the peninsula are rubber and palm oil processing and manufacturing, light industry, electronics, tin mining, smelting, logging, and timber processing. The main activities on Sabah and Sarawak are logging, petroleum production, and the processing of agricultural products. Malaysia exports more tropical timber than any other country, and the tribal people of Sarawak have been campaigning against the scale of logging on their land. The Asian economic downturn in 1998 saw a depreciation of the Malaysian currency and a marked slowing of the economy.

Rice paddies in east Malaysia (top). Street vendor with customers in Malaysia (above). One of the many palm-fringed beaches in the Maldives (right).

Mongolia

Fact File

OFFICIAL NAME Mongolia

FORM OF GOVERNMENT Republic with single legislative body (State Great Hural)

CAPITAL Ulaanbaatar

AREA 1,565,000 sq km (604,247 sq miles)

TIME ZONE GMT + 8 hours

POPULATION 2,617,379

PROJECTED POPULATION 2005 2,834,466

POPULATION DENSITY 1.7 per sq km (4.4 per sq mile)

LIFE EXPECTANCY 61.8

INFANT MORTALITY (PER 1,000) 64.6

OFFICIAL LANGUAGE Khalka Mongol

OTHER LANGUAGES Turkic, Russian, Chinese

LITERACY RATE 82.2%

RELIGIONS Predominantly Tibetan Buddhist with small Muslim minority

ETHNIC GROUPS Mongol 90%, Kazak 4%, Chinese 2%, Russian 2%, other 2%

CURRENCY Tugrik

ECONOMY Mainly agriculture with some industry

GNP PER CAPITA US$310

CLIMATE Cold and arid

HIGHEST POINT Tavan Bogd Uul 4,374 m (14,350 ft)

MAP REFERENCE Pages 300–01

The world's largest and most thinly populated landlocked country, Mongolia has a reputation for isolation. Its deserts, severe climate, and widely scattered population of nomadic pastoralists have tended to shut it off from modern life. Historically, however, it had its hour of glory. In the thirteenth century the Mongol tribes were united under Ghengis Khan (1162–1227), who then established the largest empire yet known, extending from eastern Europe to the Pacific and into northern India. The Mongol Empire collapsed in 1368, after which Mongolia (also known as Outer Mongolia to distinguish it from Inner Mongolia, one of China's Autonomous Regions) fell under Chinese control. Following the Russian Civil War (1918–22) the Chinese were expelled. Today, after 70 years within the Soviet system, the country is trying to remake itself in a more democratic mold.

Mongolia divides into two regions. In the northwest lie the Mongolian Altai Mountains (Mongol Altayn Nuruu), along with the Hangayn and Hentiyn Ranges. Here, high mountains alternate with river valleys and lakes. Pastures support large herds of cattle and sheep, and wheat is cultivated. At the highest levels of the Altai in the northwest boreal forests cover the slopes. The second region is the southern half of the country. This is semidesert steppe changing further south to salt-pans, shallow depressions, and the arid stony wastes of the Gobi Desert.

While more people today live in towns than in the country, Mongolia remains a land of nomadic pastoralists. Herds of goats, sheep, yaks, camels, and horses still provide the base of the traditional economy, and Mongolia has the highest number of livestock per capita in the world. Cattle raising accounts for more than two-thirds of all production. Under the Soviets textiles and food processing were developed, and with aid from the USSR and Comecon mineral deposits such as copper, molybdenum, and coking coal were developed. Mongolia is the world's third biggest producer of fluorspar.

New laws have been passed regulating mining, banking, foreign investment, tourism, and economic planning. Mongolia continues to attract foreign aid, but suffers from the loss of Russian financial support. So far, foreign funds have not been found for the development of Mongolia's considerable oil and gas reserves.

Myanmar (Burma)

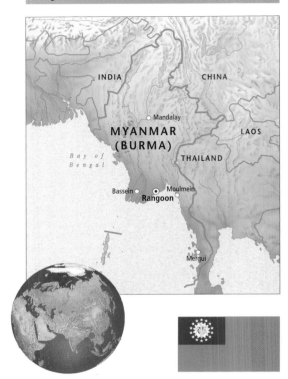

Better known for the name of its Nobel Prize winning opposition leader Aung San Suu Kyi than for that of its prime minister, Myanmar is struggling to overcome 50 years of ethnic strife, one-party socialist government, and military rule. With an ancient literary tradition and style of script going back to the Mon civilization (third century BC), Myanmar was at various times ruled by the eleventh century Tibeto-Burman Dynasty of Anarutha the Great, by the Mongols under Khublai Khan (1287), and by the British, who incorporated the country into its Indian Empire in 1886.

After the country won independence in 1948, General Ne Win's Burmese Socialist Program Party abolished all private enterprise and private trade, nationalized industry, and placed the country under military control. Soon one of the region's richest countries had become an impoverished backwater. For decades, much of the government's energy and 35 percent of its budget has gone into trying to suppress ethnic insurgent movements led by Karens, Shans, Kachins, Mons, and others. To fund their resistance these groups grew opium poppies, a traditional crop, which has led to the country becoming the world's largest opium producer.

On the Bay of Bengal between Bangladesh and Thailand, Myanmar consists of central lowlands, where 75 percent of the people live, enclosed by mountains to the north, bordering China, and west, bordering India, and the Shan Plateau to the east forming a frontier with Laos. The western mountains run southwest along the Indian border and form a series of forested ridges, ending in the Arakan Yoma Range (Pegu Yoma). From the mountains in the north the Irawaddy River flows south 2,100 km (1,300 miles), passing the old city of Mandalay and the capital of Yangon (Rangoon) on its way to the Andaman Sea. While the coast has a wet climate, the inner region, sheltered from the monsoon, has an annual rainfall of less than 1,000 mm (40 in). Here, in narrow valleys, small-scale irrigation supports such crops as rice, sugarcane, cotton, and jute.

Myanmar is rich in natural resources, having fertile soils and good fisheries, along with teak, gems, and natural gas and oil. Recently there has been some liberalization of the economy, notably of small scale enterprise. Twenty-five percent, however, remains under state control, the key industries—in energy, heavy industry, and foreign trade—being 20 military-run enterprises. A recent boom in trade with China has filled the north with Chinese goods and visitors. Economic weaknesses include a shortage of skilled labor, and of trained managers and technicians. Price controls mean that the economy is permeated by the black market. Published estimates of Myanmar's foreign trade are therefore greatly understated.

Fact File

OFFICIAL NAME Union of Myanmar (Burma)

FORM OF GOVERNMENT Military regime; legislative body (People's Assembly) never convened since military takeover in 1988

CAPITAL Yangon (Rangoon)

AREA 678,500 sq km (261,969 sq miles)

TIME ZONE GMT + 6.5 hours

POPULATION 48,081,302

PROJECTED POPULATION 2005 52,697,795

POPULATION DENSITY 70.9 per sq km (183.6 per sq mile)

LIFE EXPECTANCY 54.7

INFANT MORTALITY (PER 1,000) 76.3

OFFICIAL LANGUAGE Burmese

OTHER LANGUAGES Indigenous languages, English

LITERACY RATE 82.7%

RELIGIONS Buddhist 89%, Christian 4% (Baptist 3%, Roman Catholic 1%), Muslim 4%, other 3%

ETHNIC GROUPS Burman 68%, Shan 9%, Karen 7%, Rakhine 4%, Chinese 3%, Mon 2%, other 7%

CURRENCY Kyat

ECONOMY Agriculture 64%, services 27%, industry 9%

GNP PER CAPITA Est. < US$765

CLIMATE Tropical monsoon; dry zone around Mandalay; moderate temperature on Shan Plateau

HIGHEST POINT Hkakabo Razi 5,881 m (19,294 ft)

MAP REFERENCE Pages 202, 205

Buddhist temple ruins at Pagan in Myanmar (bottom left).
A Mongolian musician playing a horsehair fiddle (top left).
Mt Everest and surrounding peaks in Nepal (top right).

Nepal

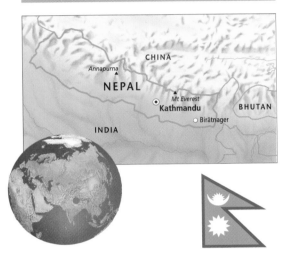

The birthplace of the Buddha c. 568 BC, Nepal is a small landlocked kingdom on the southern slopes of the Himalayas. It is surrounded by India to the west, south, and east, and has a border with China (Tibet) to the north. Tourists coming to trek in the mountains and climb the peaks contribute to national income, but Nepal remains one of the world's poorest countries. Historically, it was influenced both by the Buddhist/Mongol culture of Tibet and by the Hindu/Indian culture of the subcontinent. The present royal family established its rule in 1769. During British colonial rule in India a British resident was installed to provide "guidance" in foreign affairs. In 1959 the country's first elections were held (the Nepali Congress party winning), but in 1960 the king suspended the constitution, and no further elections were held until 1992. In the late 1990s a parliamentary impasse existed: neither the Nepali Congress nor the United Marxist-Leninist (UML) parties had clear majorities enabling them to govern in their own right.

The mountainous heart of Nepal, consisting of the towering Himalayas (including the highest and third-highest peaks in the world, Mt Everest and Kanchenjunga) and the lower Siwalik Range to the south, forms three-quarters of the country. Three main river systems cut the Himalayas, the Karnali (feeding the Ganges), the Gandak, and the Kosi. Kathmandu stands among fruit trees and rice fields typical of Nepal's densely populated uplands. Further south, on the Terai/Ganges Plain, farming settlements grow rice, wheat, maize, sugarcane, and jute which are the country's economic maintstay.

Some 90 percent of Nepalis live by subsistence farming, and many do not live well: more than 40 percent of Nepal's citizens are undernourished. Most industry is concerned with the processing of jute, sugarcane, tobacco, and grain. Recently textile and carpet production has expanded and now provides 85 percent of foreign exchange earnings. The country has limitless hydropower resources. Electricity could be sold to Indian industry south of the border, and various schemes have been proposed, but environmental considerations weigh against them. Restructuring is needed. International aid funds 62 percent of Nepal's development budget and 34 percent of total budgetary expenditure.

Fact File

OFFICIAL NAME Kingdom of Nepal

FORM OF GOVERNMENT Constitutional monarchy with two legislative bodies (National Council and House of Representatives)

CAPITAL Kathmandu

AREA 140,800 sq km (54,363 sq miles)

TIME ZONE GMT + 5.5 hours

POPULATION 24,302,653

PROJECTED POPULATION 2005 28,172,635

POPULATION DENSITY 172.6 per sq km (447 per sq mile)

LIFE EXPECTANCY 58.4

INFANT MORTALITY (PER 1,000) 73.6

OFFICIAL LANGUAGE Nepali

OTHER LANGUAGES Indigenous languages

LITERACY RATE 27%

RELIGIONS Hindu 90%, Buddhist 5%, Muslim 3%, other 2%

ETHNIC GROUPS Newar, Indian, Tibetan, Gurung and many smaller minorities

CURRENCY Nepalese rupee

ECONOMY Agriculture 93%, services 6%, industry 1%

GNP PER CAPITA US$200

CLIMATE Subtropical in south, with wet season July to October; cold and snowy in north, wetter in east

HIGHEST POINT Mt Everest 8,848 m (29,028 ft)

MAP REFERENCE Pages 218–19

North Korea

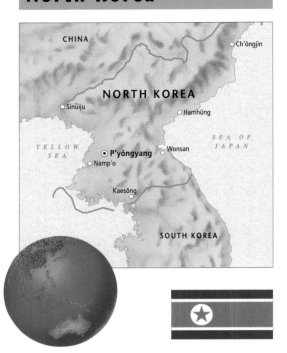

Fact File

OFFICIAL NAME Democratic People's Republic of Korea

FORM OF GOVERNMENT Communist state with single legislative body (Supreme People's Assembly)

CAPITAL P'yongyang

AREA 120,540 sq km (46,540 sq miles)

TIME ZONE GMT + 9 hours

POPULATION 22,337,878

PROJECTED POPULATION 2005 23,348,444

POPULATION DENSITY 185.3 per sq km (480 per sq mile)

LIFE EXPECTANCY 67.5

INFANT MORTALITY (PER 1,000) 35.0

OFFICIAL LANGUAGE Korean

LITERACY RATE 95%

RELIGIONS Buddhist and Confucian 51%, traditional beliefs 45%, Christian 4%

ETHNIC GROUPS Korean 100%

CURRENCY Won

ECONOMY Services and industry 64%, agriculture 36%

GNP PER CAPITA Est. US$7,940

CLIMATE Temperate, with cold, snowy winters and warm, wet summers

HIGHEST POINT Mt Paektu 2,744 m (9,003 ft)

MAP REFERENCE Page 208

North Korea occupies the northern half of the Korean Peninsula. It is separated from South Korea along the ceasefire line that was established at the end of the Korean War (1950–53), roughly along the 38th parallel. After a period as an independent kingdom in the tenth century AD, control of Korea was disputed for hundreds of years between China and Japan, the latter seizing it as a colony in 1910. Following the Second World War it became a separate communist state and after the Korean War it developed into a rigidly closed totalitarian state system. The 50-year-long personal rule of Kim Il Sung ("Great Leader") passed by hereditary succession to his son Kim Jong Il ("Dear Leader")

in 1994. The people of North Korea are classed by the state into three quasi-castes: loyal, wavering, and hostile. Membership of a caste determines whether an individual receives either education or employment. Citizens are subject to arbitrary arrest and execution for criticizing the Korean leaders or listening to foreign broadcasts. Unceasing political indoctrination takes place through the media, the workplace, the military, mass spectacles, and cultural events.

Mountains and rugged hills occupy most of the Korean Peninsula, and dominate its northern half. In the northeast the volcanic peak of Mt Paektu is surrounded by the Kaema Plateau. High forested mountains, cut by river gorges, lie along the border with Manchuria, northeast China. Other mountain chains extend north to south along the east coast. The Yalu River valley in the northwest marks the Korean–Chinese border, while to the southwest the fertile Chaeryŏng and Pyongyang plains are the main areas for agricultural activity. The principal crop is rice, followed by millet and other grains. Fruit and vegetables are grown, and also oilseed rape, flax, and cotton.

The North Korean economy is run according to the Stalinist model. More than 90 percent of operations are controlled by the state, agriculture is totally collectivized, and state-owned industry produces 95 percent of all manufactured goods. Despite over 50 years of complete control by the state, the country is still not self-sufficient in food. The industrial sector produces military weapons, chemicals, minerals (including coal, magnesite, iron ore, graphite, copper, zinc, lead, and precious metals), along with a number of food products and textiles.

During the late 1990s the economy was in crisis: power supplies were unreliable and food shortages were causing famine in the countryside. Flooding in 1995 damaged harvests and led North Korea to seek foreign aid for the first time in decades; aid donors were muted in their response, demanding proof that aid had been properly distributed. North Korea continues to fall farther and farther behind South Korean development and living standards.

The Korean War, 1950–53

Occupied by Japan from 1910 until the Second World War, Korea found itself in 1945 divided between a Soviet-controlled north and an American-controlled south, with a frontier along the 38th parallel. This de facto division of the peninsula was formalized in 1948. In June 1950 heavily armed troops and tanks from the communist People's Republic of North Korea invaded the south, precipitating three years of bitter conflict.

Authorised by a UN resolution, American and South Korean troops, supported by contingents from Britain, Canada, France, and other allies, then fought to reclaim southern territory under the UN flag. Their success soon had the North Koreans in retreat, and American seaborne landings put allied troops far behind the North Korean lines. A crisis then arose when the allied commander, General Douglas MacArthur, neared

Oman

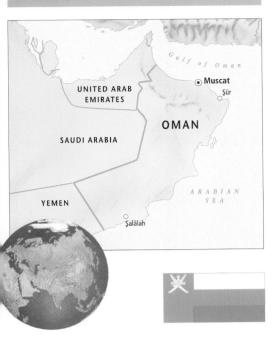

the border of China. Hundreds of thousands of Chinese "volunteers" poured across the Yalu River into North Korea, and drove the allies far into the south once more. A counter-offensive in 1951 pushed the North Koreans and Chinese troops back to the vicinity of the 38th parallel, where an armistice took place in 1953.

After almost 40 years of tension and a series of minor military clashes a non-aggression pact was negotiated between North and South Korea in 1991. While the war resulted in North Korea becoming a rigid Stalinist state, it also ensured decades of US economic and military protection for South Korea.

For some the war is still not over: in October 1998 a 72-year-old South Korean soldier, who escaped from the north after 45 years as a prisoner-of-war, reported that 30 others like him were still being held in North Korean camps.

man is the second largest country in the Arabian Peninsula. Standing on the peninsula's eastern corner, it looks across the Arabian Sea toward Baluchistan and India—in fact Baluchis form a small but significant part of the population. A small, separate, and highly strategic piece of Oman's territory is the tip of the Musandam Peninsula, commanding the entrance to the Strait of Hormuz. The Omani capital of Muscat was a trading center for hundreds of years, dhows sailing to India in one direction and down the African coast to Zanzibar in the other. Zanzibar itself was an Omani conquest, and in the 1960s, when it became part of Tanzania, many Arab Zanzibaris came to Oman. From 1798 Oman had strong ties with the British, and it became a British protectorate. Full independence came in 1971. Sultan Qabus Ibn Sa'id rules his country as an absolute monarch, advised by a *majlis alshura* ("consultative council"), but in the late 1990s the country was moving toward constitutional government. In the late 1960s Oman faced a leftist rebellion in the western province of Dhofur, encouraged and supported by the People's Republic of Yemen across the border. This was defeated in 1975. Since then, with the country enjoying the prosperity of its oil and natural gas (huge additional reserves were discovered in 1991), peace has reigned.

In the north the limestone Hajar Mountains overlook the fertile coastal plain of al-Batinah. Most of Oman's population lives along the alluvial al-Batinah strip, where date gardens stretch for more than 250 km (155 miles). The Jabal Akhdar ridge is the highest part of the Hajar Range, rising to 3,107 m (10,193 ft). Soils in the upland region are poor: herders use the area for running camels, sheep, and goats. Wadis cutting the Jabal Akhdar ridge, underground canals, and wells provide a certain amount of irrigation. North of the Ẕufār (Dhofar) uplands in the southwest the desert meets the sandy wastes of the Saudi Arabian Ar Rub' al Khāli (or "Empty Quarter").

Rural Omanis live by subsistence agriculture, growing dates, limes, bananas, alfalfa, and vegetables. Pastoralists keep camels, cattle, sheep, and goats. The smaller urban population, however,

including a considerable number of guest workers, depends on imported food. The national economy as a whole is dominated by the oil industry: petroleum accounts for nearly 90 percent of export earnings, about 75 percent of government revenues, and roughly 40 percent of gross domestic product. Oman has proved oil reserves of 4 billion barrels, which are equal to 20 year's supply at the present rate of extraction.

Fact File

OFFICIAL NAME	Sultanate of Oman
FORM OF GOVERNMENT	Monarchy with advisory Consultative Council
CAPITAL	Muscat
AREA	212,460 sq km (82,031 sq miles)
TIME ZONE	GMT + 4 hours
POPULATION	2,446,645
PROJECTED POPULATION 2005	2,999,546
POPULATION DENSITY	11.5 per sq km (29.8 per sq mile)
LIFE EXPECTANCY	71.3
INFANT MORTALITY (PER 1,000)	24.7
OFFICIAL LANGUAGE	Arabic
OTHER LANGUAGES	English, Baluchu, Urdu
LITERACY RATE	35%
RELIGIONS	Ibadhi Muslim 75%, Sunni Muslim, Shi'a Muslim and Hindu 25%
ETHNIC GROUPS	Mainly Arab with Baluchi, Indian, Pakistani, Sri Lankan, Bangladeshi, African minorities
CURRENCY	Omani rial
ECONOMY	Agriculture 50%, services 28%, industry 22%
GNP PER CAPITA	US$4,820
CLIMATE	Mainly hot and arid; light rains in south June to September
HIGHEST POINT	Jabal Ash Shām 3,019 m (10,199 ft)
MAP REFERENCE	Pages 220–21

The Gubra Bowl in Oman (top left). A village in the Oman mountains, surrounded by terraced cultivation (below).

Pakistan

Fact File

OFFICIAL NAME Islamic Republic of Pakistan

FORM OF GOVERNMENT Republic with two legislative bodies (Senate and National Assembly)

CAPITAL Islāmābād

AREA 803,940 sq km (310,401 sq miles)

TIME ZONE GMT + 5 hours

POPULATION 138,123,359

PROJECTED POPULATION 2005 156,135,833

POPULATION DENSITY 171.8 per sq km (445 per sq mile)

LIFE EXPECTANCY 59.4

INFANT MORTALITY (PER 1,000) 91.9

OFFICIAL LANGUAGES Urdu, English

OTHER LANGUAGES Punjabi, Sindhi, Urdu, Pashto, Baluchi, Brahvi

LITERACY RATE 37.1%

RELIGIONS Muslim 97% (Sunni 77%, Shi'a 20%), other (Christian, Hindu) 3%

ETHNIC GROUPS Punjabi 60%, Sindhi 14%, Pashtun (Pathan) 9%, other (Baloch and Mohajir) 17%

CURRENCY Pakistani rupee

ECONOMY Agriculture 50%, services 38%, industry 12%

GNP PER CAPITA US$460

CLIMATE Mainly arid; temperate in northwest, cold and snowy in mountains

HIGHEST POINT K2 8,611 m (28,251 ft)

MAP REFERENCE Page 221

Pakistan occupies the valley of the Indus and its tributaries in the northwest of the Indian subcontinent. Its most sensitive political frontiers are with India to the east and Afghanistan to the west. It has shorter borders with Iran and China.

Forming a part of India until 1947, Pakistan shares a history of early civilizations, migrations, and invasions—farmers in the Indus Valley were already using elaborate irrigation works by the second millennium BC. At the time of partition in 1947, Pakistan was two widely separated territories (West and East Pakistan). A dispute over Kashmir has poisoned relations with India since that time.

In 1971 East Pakistan achieved independence as Bangladesh. In that year the populist leader Ali Bhutto assumed power in Pakistan, and in 1973 announced a program of "Islamic socialism" under which banks, insurance companies, heavy industry, and even education were nationalized. Since 1977, when he was overthrown by General Zia ul-Haq (and subsequently executed), military and civilian rule have alternated, accompanied by varying degrees of violence and disorder.

Although 97 percent of Pakistan's population is Muslim, there is a wide range of ethnic groupings, languages, and conflicts. The main linguistic separation is between Iranian languages such as Baluchi and Pashto, and the Indo-Aryan languages of Punjabi, Sindhi, and Urdu. Each of Pakistan's minorities has its own particular concerns. In the northwest of the country the Pathans want to join their kinsmen over the Afghan frontier. The Urdu-speaking Mohajirs migrated in their millions from India at the time of partition and make up the majority of the population in Karachi and Hydera-bad. They resent Punjabi domination and the rule of the old land-owning elite.

The whole of Pakistan is drained by the Indus River. Rising in the Great Highlands of the north it flows southwest, joined by tributaries such as the Jhelum, Chenab, Beas, Ravi, and Sutlej, and forms a fertile and densely populated floodplain in the east of the country before spilling into the Arabian Sea. The waters of this basin feed into one of the largest irrigation systems in the world, the total area being 13 million hectares (32 million acres). Two constructions, one at Tarbela on the Indus, and the other at Mangla on the Jhelum, are among the world's biggest earth- and rock-filled dams. West of the Indus Delta is an ascending landscape of alternating ridges and arid basins, some containing salt marshes like the Hamun-i-Mashkel. In the extreme northwest are the Great Highlands, with the Khyber Pass on the frontier with Afghan-istan to the west and the spectacular peaks of the Karakoram and Pamirs to the east. Along with Nanga Parbat, these include the second highest mountain in the world—K2, Mt Godwin Austen (8,611 m; 28,251 ft) on the border of Tibet.

Irrigation agriculture combined with the new plant varieties that were introduced as part of the "green revolution" during the 1970s produces abundant cotton, wheat, rice, and sugarcane. Fruit and vegetables are also grown widely, while opium poppies and cannabis are illegally cultivated to supply the international drug trade. Despite the fact that approximately half the population work on the land, agriculture now accounts for less than a quarter of the national income.

Karachi is a considerable manufacturing center for the production of textiles, as is Lahore. Other industries produce a wide variety of petroleum products, construction materials, foodstuffs, and paper products. The country has large reserves of unused minerals: copper, bauxite, phosphates, and manganese. However, Pakistan also faces a range of problems. The country's economy is dependent on the highly competitive textile sector, there is a chronic trade deficit and debt burden, and much of the nation's revenue goes into funding massive defense spending on items such as nuclear weaponry and the army.

Philippines

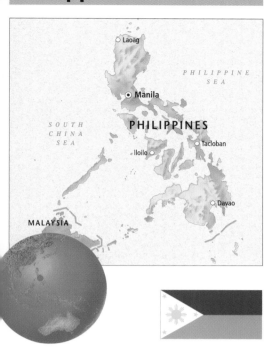

Fact File

OFFICIAL NAME Republic of the Philippines

FORM OF GOVERNMENT Republic with two legislative bodies (Senate and House of Representatives)

CAPITAL Manila

AREA 300,000 sq km (115,830 sq miles)

TIME ZONE GMT + 8 hours

POPULATION 79,345,812

PROJECTED POPULATION 2005 89,055,628

POPULATION DENSITY 264.5 per sq km (685 per sq mile)

LIFE EXPECTANCY 66.6

INFANT MORTALITY (PER 1,000) 33.9

OFFICIAL LANGUAGES Filipino, English

OTHER LANGUAGES About 87 indigenous languages

LITERACY RATE 94.4%

RELIGIONS Roman Catholic 83%, Protestant 9%, Muslim 5%, Buddhist and other 3%

ETHNIC GROUPS Malay 95.5%, Chinese 1.5%, other 3%

CURRENCY Philippine peso

ECONOMY Services 48%, agriculture 42%, industry 10%

GNP PER CAPITA US$1,050

CLIMATE Tropical, with wet season June to November

HIGHEST POINT Mt Apo 2,954 m (9,692 ft)

MAP REFERENCE Page 204

The islands of the Philippines present a combination that is unique in Asia. The people are Malayo-Polynesian; the majority of the population is Roman Catholic; English is the only common language in a country that has 87 native tongues; nearly four centuries of Spanish colonialism have left a flavor of Latin America; and 100 years of US influence (following the Spanish–American War in 1898) mean that the Philippines is also somewhat Americanized.

Long ago, and before the Spaniard explorer Ferdinand Magellan arrived from across the Pacific on his round-the-world voyage in 1521, Islam had reached the southern island of Mindanao. It is still the religion of a substantial minority in that part of the country. The Spanish then imposed whatever unity the archipelago can be said to have (there are 7,107 islands), building haciendas and sugar plantations on its main islands. Administered by the USA from 1898, the Philippines was occupied by the Japanese during the Second World War, was governed by the corrupt and authoritarian Marcos regime from 1965 to 1986, and faced a wide range of insurgencies during the last half of the twentieth century. The first insurgents were communist; more recently they have been members of the Islamic Moro National Liberation Front.

There are three main island groupings within the archipelago of the Philippines: the Luzon group, the Visayan group, and the Mindanao and Sulu Islands. Luzon to the north and Mindanao to the south are the two biggest islands and together they constitute two-thirds of the country's total land area.

Common to all the main islands is a ruggedly mountainous and volcanic topography with narrow coastal belts, a north–south alignment of upland ridges, and rivers that drain toward the north. Lying to the north of Manila Bay, and stretching to the shores of the Lingayan Gulf, is Luzon's heavily populated central plain. This is an important rice-producing area. Beyond hills to the northeast lies the fertile valley of the Cagayan River. Irrigated rice terraces, constructed by the Igorot people, rise tier upon tier up the mountain slopes of northern Luzon. The peninsulas of southeastern Luzon contain a number of volcanoes. The highest peak in the Philippines, Mt Apo (2,954 m; 9,692 ft), is on Mindanao.

Government investment and a range of tax concessions have been used to try to encourage industrial development. Mixing agriculture and light industry, the Philippine economy has been growing at a steady rate in recent years, without approaching the dynamic performance of other countries in the region.

While rice is the Philippines' main food crop, maize is the staple on the islands of Cebu, Leyte, and Negros, reflecting the country's old connection with Spanish America.

The country is well supplied with mineral resources and nickel, tin, copper, zinc and lead are processed in smelting and refining works. The Philippines is also the world's biggest supplier of refractory chrome, and the second biggest user of geothermal power after the USA. Foreign investment turned sluggish as a consequence of the 1998 regional economic slowdown. Persistent weaknesses in the economy include rudimentary infrastructure, power failures due to inadequate generating capacity, low domestic savings rates, and a foreign debt of US$45 billion.

Villagers on a suspension bridge in northern Pakistan (bottom left). The road between Quetta in Pakistan and the border with Iran (top left). A coral reef in the Philippines (below). The "Chocolate Hills" in Bohol in the Philippines (bottom).

179

Qatar

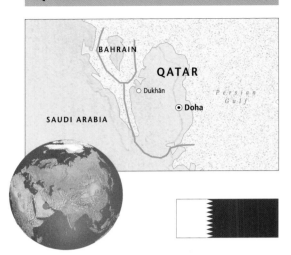

Fact File

OFFICIAL NAME State of Qatar

FORM OF GOVERNMENT Monarchy with Advisory Consultative Council

CAPITAL Ad Dawhah (Doha)

AREA 11,000 sq km (4,247 sq miles)

TIME ZONE GMT + 3 hours

POPULATION 723,542

PROJECTED POPULATION 2005 874,179

POPULATION DENSITY 65.8 per sq km (170.4 per sq mile)

LIFE EXPECTANCY 74.2

INFANT MORTALITY (PER 1,000) 17.3

OFFICIAL LANGUAGE Arabic

OTHER LANGUAGE English

LITERACY RATE 78.9%

RELIGIONS Muslim 95%, other 5%

ETHNIC GROUPS Arab 40%, Pakistani 18%, Indian 18%, Iranian 10%, other 14%

CURRENCY Qatari rial

ECONOMY Services 50%, industry (particularly oil production and refining) 48%, agriculture 2%

GNP PER CAPITA US$11,600

CLIMATE Hot and arid; humid in summer

HIGHEST POINT Qurayn Aba al Bawl 103 m (338 ft)

MAP REFERENCE Page 220

Qatar is a small, wealthy emirate in the Persian Gulf. In 1971 it chose not to join the neighboring United Arab Emirates as a member state, but to go it alone. Recently it has continued to act with independence, signing a security pact with the USA in 1995 involving the stationing of 2,000 US troops, while simultaneously challenging the Gulf Cooperation Council's policy on Iraq. The peninsula it occupies, projecting north from the southern shore of the Persian Gulf near Bahrain, consists of flat and semiarid desert. Most of its population are guest workers from the Indian subcontinent, Iran, and north Africa.

Qatar was ruled for centuries by the Khalifah dynasty. A rift in dynastic affairs opened in 1783, war with Bahrain followed in 1867, and then the British intervened to set up a separate emirate under the al-Thani family. Qatar became a full British

protectorate in 1916. At this time it was occupied by nomadic Bedouin wandering the peninsula with their herds of goats and camels. Oil production, which commenced in 1949, changed everything and now almost 90 percent of the people live in the capital city of Doha or its suburbs. The northern parts of Qatar are dotted with abandoned villages.

A bloodless palace coup in 1995 saw the present emir displace his father, a move that was accepted without fuss. The emir of Qatar rules as an absolute monarch, he occupies the office of prime minister and he appoints his own cabinet. He is advised by a partially elected 30-member *majlis al-shura* (consultative council). From time to time there are calls for democratic reforms from prominent citizens.

The Qatar Peninsula is mainly low-lying except for a few hills in the west of the country at Jabal Dukhān (the Dukhan Heights) and some low cliffs in the northeast. Sandy desert, salt flats, and barren plains cut by shallow wadis (creek beds) occupy 95 percent of its land area. There is little rainfall aside from occasional winter showers. As a result of the shortage of fresh water Qatar is dependent on large-scale desalinization facilities. Summers are usually hot and humid; winter nights can be cool and chilly. Drought-resistant plant life is mainly found in the south. However, by tapping ground-water supplies, Qatar is now able to cultivate most of its own vegetables.

Crude oil production and refining is by far the most important industry. Oil accounts for more than 30 percent of gross domestic product, about 75 percent of export earnings, and 70 percent of government revenues. Reserves of 3.3 billion barrels should ensure continued output at present levels for at least another 25 years. Oil has given Qatar a per capita gross domestic product that is comparable to some of the leading western European industrial economies. Long-term goals include the development of offshore wells and economic diversification.

Saudis at a market wearing traditional dress (below). A view of Singapore's central business district (top right).

Saudi Arabia

Fact File

OFFICIAL NAME Kingdom of Saudi Arabia

FORM OF GOVERNMENT Monarchy with advisory Consultative Council

CAPITAL Ar Riyad (Riyadh)

AREA 1,960,582 sq km (756,981 sq miles)

TIME ZONE GMT + 3 hours

POPULATION 21,504,613

PROJECTED POPULATION 2005 26,336,476

POPULATION DENSITY 11 per sq km (28.4 per sq mile)

LIFE EXPECTANCY 70.6

INFANT MORTALITY (PER 1,000) 38.8

OFFICIAL LANGUAGE Arabic

OTHER LANGUAGE English

LITERACY RATE 61.8%

RELIGIONS Sunni Muslim 85%, Shi'a Muslim 15%

ETHNIC GROUPS Arab 90%, mixed African–Asian 10%

CURRENCY Saudi riyal

ECONOMY Agriculture 49%, services 37%, industry 14%

GNP PER CAPITA US$7,040

CLIMATE Mainly hot and arid; some areas rainless for years

HIGHEST POINT Jabal Sawdā 3,133 m (10,279 ft)

MAP REFERENCE Pages 220–21

Saudi Arabia occupies most of the Arabian Peninsula and covers an area about the size of western Europe. With one-quarter of the world's petroleum reserves, it supplies several major industrial nations with oil. Its role as the custodian of Islam's most holy places, Mecca (Makkah) and Medina (Al Madīnah), is equally important. Aloof from international affairs for many years, Saudis steeled themselves to fight Iraq (which they had earlier supported) in 1990–91. The 500,000 western troops who entered the country (considered a profanation of Muslim land) were seen by Saudis as both necessary and unwelcome. The war highlighted tensions in a society which politically is largely feudal (192 people were beheaded in 1995), yet because of its oil cannot escape the modern world.

Mecca was Muhammad's birthplace (c.570) and Medina the place where Islam was born. In the eighteenth century a severe branch of Islam was adopted by the Sa'ud Bedouin —the Wahhabi Movement—and this, with its austere criminal code, was established by the Saudis throughout their lands early this century. During the 1930s most Saudis were still living traditional desert lives, but this changed when oil was found near Riyadh in 1937. The spending for which the royal family was known in the 1960s and 1970s ended with the drop in oil prices of the 1980s. This is now starting to have social effects. People who were content to live under absolute monarchic rule with prodigious benefits may now be questioning the balance of power. Per capita income fell from $17,000 in 1981 to $10,000 in 1995.

Paralleling the Red Sea, a range of mountains extends northwest to southeast, rising to 3,133 m (10,279 ft) at Jabal Sawdā in the southwest, Saudi Arabia's highest peak. The Asir Highlands in this southwestern corner is the only region with reliable rainfall. Benefiting from the monsoon, the slopes are terraced to grow grain and fruit trees. Further east, separated from the mountains by a wide stretch of basaltic lava, is the high central desert plateau of Najd. The eastern border of this region is a vast arc of sandy desert, broadening into the two dune-wastes of Arabia: An Nafūd in the north, and Ar Rub' al Khāli, or "Empty Quarter" to the south—the world's largest expanse of sand. Some Bedouin nomads still live here as traders and herdsmen. Over 95 percent of Saudi Arabia is arid or semiarid desert.

Petroleum accounts for 75 percent of budget revenue, 35 percent of gross domestic product, and 90 percent of export earnings. Saudi Arabia has the largest reserves of petroleum in the world (26 percent of the proven total), is the largest exporter of petroleum, and backs this up with world-class associated industries. For more than a decade, however, expenditures have outstripped income. The government plans to restrain public spending and encourage non-oil exports. As many as 4 million foreign workers are employed. The 2 million pilgrims who come to visit Mecca each year also contribute to national income.

Singapore

A muddy, mangrove-swampy islet nobody wanted in 1819, Singapore is now a leading Asian city-state with one of the highest standards of living in the world. This was achieved without any resources beyond the skills and commitment of its citizens and the economic vision of its leadership. Standing at the southern extremity of the Malay Peninsula, Singapore was established as a free-trading port and settlement early in the nineteenth century by the English colonial administrator Sir Stamford Raffles. Without customs tariffs or other restrictions it drew numbers of Chinese immigrants, and after the opening of the Suez Canal played a leading role in the growing trade in Malaysian rubber and tin.

After the Second World War, during which it was occupied by the Japanese, it reverted to its former status as a British crown colony. In 1963 it became part of Malaysia, but, after two years, tensions between Chinese Singapore and the Malay leadership in Kuala Lumpur led Malaysia to force the island to go it alone. Under Lee Kuan Yew, prime minister for 31 years until 1990, a strategy of high-tech industrialization enabled the economy to grow at a rate of 7 percent a year. However, freedom of speech is constrained,

political debate limited, and both public behavior and private life (chewing gum is forbidden, and vandalism punished by caning) are watched closely.

Singapore Island is largely low-lying, with a hilly center. With limited natural freshwater resources, water is brought from the Malaysian mainland nearby. Reservoirs on high ground hold water for the city's use. Urban development has accelerated deforestation and swamp and land reclamation: 5 percent of the land is forested, and 4 percent is arable. In addition to the main island of Singapore there are 57 smaller islands lying within its territorial waters, many of them in the Strait of Singapore, which opens from the busy seaway of the Strait of Malacca. Between the main island and the Malaysian mainland is the narrow channel of the Johore Strait. A causeway across this strait links Malaysia to Singapore.

While the foundation of its economic growth was the export of manufactured goods, the government has in recent years promoted Singapore as a financial services and banking center, using the latest information technology. In 1995 this sector led economic growth. Singapore is a world leader in biotechnology. Rising labor costs threaten the country's competitiveness today, but its government hopes to offset this by increasing productivity and improving infrastructure. Despite the reduced growth rate accompanying the Asian economic downturn in 1998 there are plans for major infrastructural development: an additional stage for Changi International Airport, extensions to the mass rapid transit system, and a deep-tunnel sewerage project to dispose of wastes. In applied technology, per capita output, investment, and industrial harmony, Singapore possesses many of the attributes of a large modern country.

Fact File

OFFICIAL NAME	Republic of Singapore
FORM OF GOVERNMENT	Republic with single legislative body (Parliament)
CAPITAL	Singapore
AREA	633 sq km (244 sq miles)
TIME ZONE	GMT + 8 hours
POPULATION	3,531,600
PROJECTED POPULATION 2005	3,725,838
POPULATION DENSITY	5,579.1 per sq km (14,449.8 per sq mile)
LIFE EXPECTANCY	78.8
INFANT MORTALITY (PER 1,000)	3.8
OFFICIAL LANGUAGES	Malay, Chinese, Tamil, English
LITERACY RATE	91%
RELIGIONS	Buddhist and Taoist 56%, Muslim 15%, Christian 19%, Hindu 5%, other 5%
ETHNIC GROUPS	Chinese 76.5%, Malay 15%, Indian 6.5%, other 2%
CURRENCY	Singapore dollar
ECONOMY	Services 70%, industry 29%, agriculture 1%
GNP PER CAPITA	US$26,730
CLIMATE	Tropical
HIGHEST POINT	Bukit Timah 162 m (531 ft)
MAP REFERENCE	Page 200

South Korea

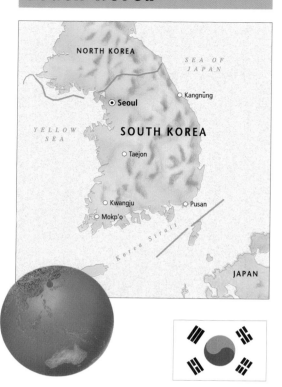

Fact File

OFFICIAL NAME Republic of Korea

FORM OF GOVERNMENT Republic with single legislative body (National Assembly)

CAPITAL Seoul

AREA 98,480 sq km (38,023 sq miles)

TIME ZONE GMT + 9 hours

POPULATION 46,884,800

PROJECTED POPULATION 2005 49,489,750

POPULATION DENSITY 476.1 per sq km (1,223.1 per sq mile)

LIFE EXPECTANCY 74.3

INFANT MORTALITY (PER 1,000) 7.6

OFFICIAL LANGUAGE Korean

OTHER LANGUAGE English

LITERACY RATE 97.9%

RELIGIONS Christianity 21%, Buddhism 24%, Confucianism 1.5%, other 1%, no religion 52.5%

ETHNIC GROUPS Korean 99.9%, Chinese 0.1%

CURRENCY Won

ECONOMY Services 55%, industry 27%, agriculture 18%

GNP PER CAPITA US$9,700

CLIMATE Temperate, with cold winters and hot, wet summers

HIGHEST POINT Halla-san 1,950 m (6,398 ft)

MAP REFERENCE Page 208

South Korea occupies the southern half of the Korean Peninsula. The border between South and North Korea consists of the ceasefire line established at the end of the Korean War (1950–53), roughly corresponding to the original pre-1950 border at the 38th parallel. The kingdom of Korea was dominated by either China or Japan for many centuries and finally annexed by Japan in 1910. After Japan's defeat at the end of the Second World War, Korea was divided between a northern Soviet zone of influence, and a southern zone under US control. These zones soon became separate political entities. In 1950 communist North Korea invaded South Korea, and though the war ended in a stalemate in 1953, bitter hostility between north and south endures to the present day, with covert operations continuing.

In the 40-year period following 1953, both Koreas diverged socially, politically, and economically. South Korea, after a few years under the authoritarian rule of its first president, established constitutional liberalism in the Second Republic of 1960. From then until his assassination in 1979 it was under the elected presidency of General Park Chung Hee, who laid the basis for the economic success of the modern South Korean state with a combination of state planning and free-market incentives.

While questionable practices flourished at the top (two former presidents have been jailed) the country achieved a remarkable record of growth. Only 30 years ago its standard of living was much the same as the poorer countries of Africa. Today its gross domestic product per capita is nine times India's, fourteen times North Korea's, and on a par with some economies of the European Union. Regionally, its technological and scientific prowess is second only to Japan's.

More than 80 percent of South Korea's terrain is mountainous. Along the eastern side of the country the Tabaek-Sanmaek Mountains descend north to southwest. The Han and Naktong Rivers drain from these mountains through low-lying plains—the Han to the northwest, the Naktong to the south. Densely populated and intensively farmed, these plains cover 15 percent of South Korea's total land area. Rice, a staple crop in which the country is almost self-sufficient, is grown on family-owned farms. Other food crops include barley and fruit such as apples, grapes, peaches, nectarines, and plums. Silk and tobacco are produced for the export market. About two-thirds of South Korea is forested. As many as 3,000

Rural scenery in South Korea (below). A broad avenue in Seoul, South Korea (above). The facade of a Hindu temple in Sri Lanka (top right). Tea-pickers on a tea estate in the highlands of Sri Lanka (bottom right).

small islands lie off the west and south coasts, including Cheju which has South Korea's highest peak, the extinct volcano Halla-san at 1,950 m (6,398 ft).

There is little at the high-tech end of modern industry that South Korea does not manufacture and sell. It produces electronic equipment, machinery, ships, and automobiles. Textiles, an early item in its drive for export success, remain significant, along with clothing, food processing, chemicals, and steel. Real gross domestic product grew by an average 10 percent from 1986 to 1991, then tapered off. With the downturn in the Asian economies in 1998 the economy shrank for the first time in years, but the country won IMF praise for acting promptly in order to wipe out billions in bad bank loans and purge companies that were unviable.

Sri Lanka

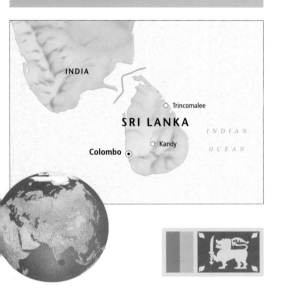

S ri Lanka is a large, scenically dramatic island off India's southeast coast, and was known as Ceylon until 1972. It has a mountainous center, and a string of coral islets called "Adam's Bridge" link it to India in the northwest. Over the last 50 years the country has suffered intermittent strife. For over 1,000 years a minority of Hindu Tamils in the north and a majority of Sinhalese elsewhere have lived side by side. From the sixteenth century successive European nations—the Portuguese, the Dutch, and the British—visited and left their ethnic mark. Britain controlled the whole island from 1815, and brought in large numbers of additional Tamil plantation workers from south India later that century.

When Sri Lanka gained its independence in 1948 the majority Sinhalese stripped 800,000 Tamils of citizenship and the right to vote, and made Sinhala the country's sole official language. From then on there was civil unrest and from 1983 there has been civil war. The Tamil demand for an autonomous northern state has been complicated by separate leftist insurrections by radical Sinhalese seeking to overthrow the government. Sri Lanka has a large number of political parties and movements on the left (including one which is officially Trotskyist)

which have added intransigence to its political life. Civil war and insurgencies have taken at least 50,000 lives.

With high mountains, intermontane plateaus, and steep river gorges, the rugged terrain of the central uplands dominates the island. Much of this higher ground is used for growing tea on large plantations. Falling away to the southwest, the terrain declines toward the sandy coastal lowlands where coconuts are grown (Sri Lanka is the world's fifth-largest producer). Rubber is the third important plantation crop. Overall, 37 percent of the country supports tropical vegetation and open woodland. Though reduced by deforestation, rainforest still covers the wettest areas. The fertile, rice-growing northern plains are bordered to the southeast by the Mahaweli River.

Among Sri Lanka's mineral resources are a variety of precious and semi-precious stones including sapphire, ruby, tourmaline, and topaz. Also mined are graphite, mineral sands, and phosphates. About 43 percent of the workforce is engaged in agriculture, the main subsistence crop being rice—although production falls considerably short of the country's requirements. Fruit,

vegetables, and spices are grown as staples and for export and Sri Lanka is one of the world's main exporters of tea. But today industry, dominated by the manufacture of clothing and expanding in special Export Processing Zones, has overtaken agriculture as the principal source of export earnings. The uncertain economic climate created by civil strife continues to cloud the nation's prospects, deterring tourists and discouraging foreign investment.

Fact File

OFFICIAL NAME Democratic Socialist Republic of Sri Lanka

FORM OF GOVERNMENT Republic with single legislative body (Parliament)

CAPITAL Colombo

AREA 65,610 sq km (25,332 sq miles)

TIME ZONE GMT + 5.5 hours

POPULATION 19,144,875

PROJECTED POPULATION 2005 20,418,172

POPULATION DENSITY 291.8 per sq km (755.8 per sq mile)

LIFE EXPECTANCY 72.7

INFANT MORTALITY (PER 1,000) 16.1

OFFICIAL LANGUAGE Sinhala

OTHER LANGUAGES Tamil, English

LITERACY RATE 90.1%

RELIGIONS Buddhist 69%, Hindu 15%, Christian 8%, Muslim 8%

ETHNIC GROUPS Sinhalese 74%, Tamil 18%, Sri Lankan Moor 7%, other 1%

CURRENCY Sri Lankan rupee

ECONOMY Services 45%, agriculture 43%, industry 12%

GNP PER CAPITA US$700

CLIMATE Tropical; southwest wetter with most rain falling April to June and October to November; northeast drier with most rain falling December to February

HIGHEST POINT Mt Pidurutalagala 2,524 m (8,281 ft)

MAP REFERENCE Page 216–17

Syria

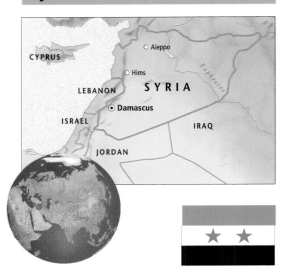

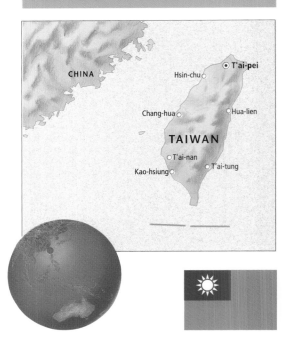

Fact File

OFFICIAL NAME Syrian Arab Republic

FORM OF GOVERNMENT Republic with single legislative body (People's Council)

CAPITAL Damascus (Dimashq)

AREA 185,180 sq km (71,498 sq miles)

TIME ZONE GMT + 2 hours

POPULATION 17,213,871

PROJECTED POPULATION 2005 20,530,413

POPULATION DENSITY 93 per sq km (240.8 per sq mile)

LIFE EXPECTANCY 68.1

INFANT MORTALITY (PER 1,000) 36.4

OFFICIAL LANGUAGE Arabic

OTHER LANGUAGES Kurdish, French, Armenian, Aramaic, Circassian

LITERACY RATE 69.8%

RELIGIONS Sunni Muslim 74%, other Muslim sects 16%, Christian 10%; tiny Jewish communities

ETHNIC GROUPS Arab 90%; Kurdish, Armenian and other 10%

CURRENCY Syrian pound

ECONOMY Services 63%, agriculture 22%, industry 15%

GNP PER CAPITA US$1,120

CLIMATE Temperate, with mild, wet winters and dry, hot summers; arid in interior

HIGHEST POINT Jabal ash Shaykh 2,814 m (9,232 ft)

MAP REFERENCE Pages 200, 225

Syria is in the eastern Mediterranean, with Iraq and Turkey to the east and north and Lebanon, Israel and Jordan to the west and south. Throughout history it has played a key role in the region. Over the years Egyptians, Hittites, Persians, Greeks, and Romans came and went. Converted to Islam when overrun by the Arabs in 634, the Syrians' capital Damascus became a major center during the Umayyad Dynasty. Crusaders seized much of Syria in the twelfth century, but were ousted by the Kurdish general Saladin. Under French control from 1920, Syria became independent in 1946. After various military coups and counter-coups the Ba'ath Party seized power in 1963, and from 1971 party leader Hafez al-Assad has ruled Syria with an iron fist. A member of the minority Alawite religious sect, he has faced resistance from other Muslims, notably the Sunni majority. But in 1992 when the Sunni Moslem Brotherhood rose against Damascus their revolt was crushed, with up to 20,000 deaths. Following the Second Gulf War in 1991 Syria received huge amounts of aid as a result of its unexpected support for the coalition against Iraq.

Syria's Mediterranean coast, well-watered from subterranean sources, is one of the country's most fertile, intensively farmed, and densely populated regions. Inland is the Ghab Depression, a rift valley flanked by two mountain ranges. Here the Orontes ('Āṣī) River flows through gorges and wide valleys. To the south, the Heights of Hermon rise above the eastern slopes of the Anti-Lebanon Range (Jabal ash Sharqī). Snowmelt from the range provides water for Damascus. Inland lies the Syrian Desert (Bādiyat ash Shām), crossed by the Euphrates River (Firat Nehri). Oil was discovered along the Euphrates in the 1980s. Power from the Euphrates barrage produces 70 percent of Syria's electricity.

Under the socialist Ba'ath Party most industry is government controlled. The main industries are textiles, food processing, beverages, tobacco, phosphate rock mining, petroleum, and cement. Oil, textiles, cotton, and agricultural produce are the main exports. The country has many weak government-owned firms and low productivity. Oil production has begun to ebb and unemployment is expected to rise as the more than 60 percent of the population that is under 20 years old enters the labor force. Syria's Gulf War aid windfall of $5 billion has been spent.

Krac des Chevaliers in Syria, a French Crusader castle built in the twelfth century (below). A Taiwanese family in Taipei (right). A yurt in the Pamir region of Tajikistan (far right).

Taiwan

Taiwan is a large island off the coast of China which, with support from the USA, has acted as a de facto independent country for the past 50 years. This is strongly opposed by China, which from the seventeenth century controlled the island and made it a Chinese province in the 1880s. However, Beijing has not had effective control of Taiwan for 100 years. It was ceded to Japan in 1895 (after Japanese victory in the Sino-Japanese War). From 1949 until the present it has been under the Nationalist Kuomintang (KMT), who after being driven from mainland China by the communists in 1949 used Taiwan as their last refuge. Ruling dictatorially over the Taiwanese until 1987, the KMT turned the country into a political, military, and economic fortress.

Seated in the UN as the official representative of China for two decades, Taiwan was displaced in 1971, and still has a marginal status in the international community. Today, after democratic elections, multiple parties are represented in the

National Assembly, and both the president and the prime minister are native-born Taiwanese.

High mountains extending the length of the island occupy the central and eastern parts of Taiwan. The mountains of the Central Range, or Taiwan Shan, are the top of a submerged mountain chain, and rise steeply up from the east coast. Lush vegetation is found through much of the interior—the poor commercial quality of most of the timber having preserved it as forest cover. Rising to altitudes of more than 3,000 m (10,000 ft), the lower slopes support evergreens such as camphor and Chinese cork oak, while further up pine, larch, and cedar dominate. Rice is grown on the well-watered lowlands of the western coastal plain. Other crops include sugarcane, sweet potatoes, tea, bananas, pineapples, and peanuts.

Economically, agriculture is now of less importance than Taiwan's thriving industrial sector. The country as a whole demonstrated an almost unprecedented growth rate of 9 percent annually for three decades until 1996. During this period it was successively the world's biggest producer of television sets, watches, personal computers, and track shoes. Among Taiwan's strengths are its highly educated workforce, many US-trained, with an inside knowledge of the US market. Today the leading exports are electrical machinery, electronic products, textiles, footwear, foodstuffs, and plywood and wood products. With huge dollar reserves, Taiwan has become a major investor in China, Malaysia, and Vietnam. The Asian economic downturn in 1998 has had a steadying effect, but Taiwan is better situated than most to weather the storm. Political relations with China remain cool.

Fact File

OFFICIAL NAME Republic of China

FORM OF GOVERNMENT Republic with two legislative bodies (National Assembly and Legislative Yuan)

CAPITAL T'ai-pei (Taipei)

AREA 35,980 sq km (13,892 sq miles)

TIME ZONE GMT + 8 hours

POPULATION 22,113,250

PROJECTED POPULATION 2005 23,325,314

POPULATION DENSITY 614.6 per sq km (1,591.8 per sq mile)

LIFE EXPECTANCY 77.5

INFANT MORTALITY (PER 1,000) 6.0

OFFICIAL LANGUAGE Mandarin Chinese

OTHER LANGUAGES Taiwanese, Hakka languages

LITERACY RATE Not available

RELIGIONS Buddhist, Confucian, and Taoist 93%; Christian 4.5%; other 2.5%

ETHNIC GROUPS Taiwanese 84%, mainland Chinese 14%, indigenous 2%

CURRENCY New Taiwain dollar

ECONOMY Services 49%, industry 30%, agriculture 21%

GNP PER CAPITA US$10,500

CLIMATE Tropical, with wet season May to September

HIGHEST POINT Yu Shan 3,997 m (13,113 ft)

MAP REFERENCE Page 206

Tajikistan

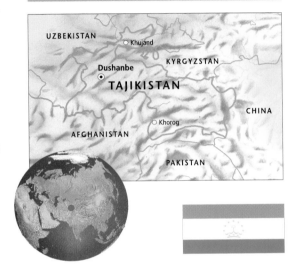

Tajikistan lies between Uzbekistan, Afghanistan, and China on the western slope of the Pamirs. It also shares borders with Kyrgyzstan to the north and Pakistan to the south. The country is an irregular shape because it was carved out of the Soviet Republic of Uzbekistan on Stalin's orders in 1929. This was intended to deal with Tajik resistance to the Soviet regime, but as it left the two Tajik centers of Samarqand and Bukhoro in Uzbekistan, it merely added another grievance. The Tajiks are Persian–Iranian culturally and linguistically, not Turkic–Mongol like many other peoples of Central Asia. Immigration of both Uzbeks and Russians during the Soviet era caused further resentment. Since independence in 1991 ethnic hostility has resulted in a state of near civil war. Tens of thousands have been killed and thousands more have fled to Afghanistan and Kyrgyzstan. Fighting between government and opposition forces goes on, marked by random violence and banditry.

A long finger of territory in the north contains the only fertile agricultural region. This is the western end of the Fergana Valley through which the Syrdar'ya drains northwest toward the Aral Sea. Cotton is the chief crop, though cereals and fruit are also grown. The region has seen the overuse of pesticides on cotton, and the drying up of the distant Aral Sea has been aggravated by water taken for irrigation. Between this valley and one to the south drained by the Vakhsh stand the Turkestan and Gissar Ranges. This substantial physical divide also corresponds to the political divide between the Uzbek communists in the

north and the Islamic secularists in the south. Most of eastern Tajikistan consists of the Pamirs, a part of the Tien Shan Range of western China.

Tajikistan has the second-lowest per capita gross domestic product of any former USSR republic, the fastest growing population, and a low standard of living. Agriculture is the most important sector and cotton the main crop. The country has limited mineral resources, including silver, gold, uranium, and tungsten. Hydropower provides energy for the manufacture of aluminum, cotton textiles and clothing, and for food processing. The economy is weak from years of conflict. Subsidies once provided by the USSR are gone, along with markets—Russia once bought Tajik uranium for its weapons program. Basic subsistence for many people depends on foreign aid. Social instability, plus the continuation in power of Soviet-era politicians and officials, has prevented economic reforms.

Fact File

OFFICIAL NAME Republic of Tajikistan

FORM OF GOVERNMENT Republic with single legislative body (Supreme Assembly)

CAPITAL Dushanbe

AREA 143,100 sq km (55,251 sq miles)

TIME ZONE GMT + 6 hours

POPULATION 6,102,854

PROJECTED POPULATION 2005 6,719,665

POPULATION DENSITY 42.6 per sq km (110.3 per sq mile)

LIFE EXPECTANCY 64.3

INFANT MORTALITY (PER 1,000) 114.8

OFFICIAL LANGUAGE Tajik

OTHER LANGUAGE Russian

LITERACY RATE 96.7%

RELIGIONS Sunni Muslim 80%, Shi'a Muslim 5%, other (including Russian Orthodox) 15%

ETHNIC GROUPS Tajik 65%, Uzbek 25%, Russian 3.5%, other 6.5%

CURRENCY Tajik ruble

ECONOMY Agriculture 43%, services 35%, industry 22%

GNP PER CAPITA US$340

CLIMATE Mild winters and hot summers in valleys and on plains, drier and much colder in mountains

HIGHEST POINT Pik imeni Ismail Samani 7,495 m (24,590 ft)

MAP REFERENCE Page 223

Thailand

Fact File

OFFICIAL NAME Kingdom of Thailand

FORM OF GOVERNMENT Constitutional monarchy with two legislative bodies (Senate and House of Representatives)

CAPITAL Bangkok

AREA 514,000 sq km (198,455 sq miles)

TIME ZONE GMT + 7 hours

POPULATION 60,609,046

PROJECTED POPULATION 2005 63,794,047

POPULATION DENSITY 117.9 per sq km (305.4 per sq mile)

LIFE EXPECTANCY 69.2

INFANT MORTALITY (PER 1,000) 29.5

OFFICIAL LANGUAGE Thai

OTHER LANGUAGES Chinese, Malay, English

LITERACY RATE 93.5%

RELIGIONS Buddhist 95%, Muslim 3.8%, Christian 0.5%, Hindu 0.1%, other 0.6%

ETHNIC GROUPS Thai 75%, Chinese 14%, other 11%

CURRENCY Baht

ECONOMY Agriculture 70%, services 24%, industry 6%

GNP PER CAPITA US$2,740

CLIMATE Tropical, with wet season June to October, cool season November to February, hot season March to May

HIGHEST POINT Doi Inthanon 2,590 m (8,497 ft)

MAP REFERENCE Pages 202–03

Lying between Burma, Laos, and Cambodia, Thailand has a system of "semi-democracy" that has somehow preserved it from the misfortunes of its neighbors. Known as Siam until 1939, it was the home of the Buddhist kingdom of Ayutthaya from the fourteenth to the eighteenth century, during which time the monarch came to be regarded as a sort of god-king, and a bureaucratic administration system was developed. The Chakkri Dynasty was founded in 1782 at Bangkok, and in the late

nineteenth century its representatives ushered Siam into the modern age: treaties with the West were signed, slavery abolished, and study abroad encouraged. The king acquiesced in a bloodless coup which set up a constitutional monarchy in 1932. Since then civilian and military governments have alternated, climaxing in the events of 1992, when violent demonstrations against another general taking over the government led the king to intervene, and the constitution was amended. The prime minister now has to be an elected member of parliament. The military, however, still plays an important part in both political and industrial life.

Thailand can be divided into four regions. To the north there are forested mountain ranges which are the southernmost extension of the Himalayas. The rich intermontane valleys of the Rivers Ping, Yom, Wang, and Nan support intensive agriculture and the forests produce teak and other valuable timbers. The forests provide a home for many hill tribes who live by the shifting cultivation of dry rice and opium poppies. In the northeast lies the Khorat Plateau, a region of poor soils sparsely vegetated with savanna woodlands where crops of rice and cassava are grown. The third region is the central plains—Thailand's rice bowl—with vistas of rice fields, canals, rivers, and villages on stilts. The mountainous southern provinces on the Malay Peninsula are dominated by tropical rainforest. The hills produce tin ore and plantation rubber and the picturesque islands off the west coast draw tourists.

Agriculture is still the main employer, although its economic importance is declining. Rice is the principal crop and Thailand is still one of the world's leading exporters. Other crops include sugar, maize, rubber, manioc, pineapples, and seafoods. Mineral resources include tin ore, lead, tungsten, lignite, gypsum, tantalum, fluorite, and gemstones. Thailand is the world's second largest producer of tungsten, and the third largest tin producer. Tourism is the largest single source of foreign exchange, the development of resorts on the coast along the Andaman Sea having been a major success.

The development of urban manufacturing industry, involving the export of high-technology goods, has been the most significant feature of the economy in recent years. This and the development of the service sector have fueled a

growth rate of 9 percent since 1989. Thailand's domestic savings rate of 35 percent is a leading source of capital, but the country has also received substantial investment from overseas. Beginning in 1997, Thailand was the first country in the region to be affected by a range of problems associated with the Asian economic downturn—a falling currency, rising inflation, and unemployment heading toward 2 million.

Turkey

Fact File

OFFICIAL NAME Republic of Turkey

FORM OF GOVERNMENT Republic with single legislative body (Grand National Assembly of Turkey)

CAPITAL Ankara

AREA 780,580 sq km (301,382 sq miles)

TIME ZONE GMT + 2 hours

POPULATION 65,597,383

PROJECTED POPULATION 2005 71,662,725

POPULATION DENSITY 84 per sq km (217.6 per sq mile)

LIFE EXPECTANCY 73.3

INFANT MORTALITY (PER 1,000) 35.8

OFFICIAL LANGUAGE Turkish

OTHER LANGUAGES Kurdish, Arabic

LITERACY RATE 81.6%

RELIGIONS Muslim 99.8% (mostly Sunni), other 0.2%

ETHNIC GROUPS Turkish 80%, Kurdish 20%

CURRENCY Turkish lira

ECONOMY Agriculture 50%, services 35%, industry 15%

GNP PER CAPITA US$2,780

CLIMATE Temperate, with mild, wet winters and hot, dry summers; arid in the interior

HIGHEST POINT Ağri Daği (Mt Ararat) 5,166 m (16,949 ft)

MAP REFERENCE Page 224

Asia Minor, a large mountainous plateau lying between the Black Sea and the Mediterranean, forms the main part of Turkey. A much smaller part, European Turkey or Thrace, lies across the narrow straits of the Bosphorus and the Dardanelles. Early in the twentieth century Turkey's leader Kemal Ataturk (1881–1938) attempted to create a modern Islamic state that was willing and able to be a part of Europe. At the end of the twentieth century, with Islamic fundamentalism a growing internal force and no end in sight to the repression of the Kurds, his legacy is uncertain. Full integration with Europe still seems remote. Two long-running sources of conflict remain unresolved—Cyprus and the Turkish Kurds. Turkey has occupied the Muslim north of Cyprus since 1974, but their claim is unrecognized internationally. The Kurds in southeastern Turkey are demanding an independent homeland. Opposed by the State, this conflict has resulted in an estimated 19,000 deaths so far.

Historically, Asia Minor or Anatolia was the stage on which some famous scenes have been enacted. The legendary city of Troy stood on the shore of the Aegean. Ephesus and its ruins can still be visited today. Astride the Bosphorus, Constantinople (now Istanbul) was the capital of the Byzantine Empire from the fourth century AD until it fell to the Seljuk Turks in 1071. Later, during the height of its expansion in the sixteenth century, the Empire of the Ottoman Turks spread throughout the Middle East and North Africa, carrying Islam through the Balkans to Vienna. From this time the Ottoman Empire steadily declined (becoming known as "the sick man of Europe") until it was finally dismembered at the end of the First World War. The boundaries of the present Turkish state were set in 1923.

European Turkey has fertile rolling plains surrounded by low mountains. The main feature of the Asian provinces is the largely semiarid Central Anatolian Plateau (1,000 to 2,000 m;

3,300 to 6,600 ft) much of which is used for grazing sheep. On its southern flank the three main ranges of the Taurus Mountains lie inland from the Mediterranean coast. In addition to timber, the uplands provide summer grazing for the flocks of the plateau. The Pontic Mountains stretching west to east along the Black Sea boundary of the plateau are more densely wooded, and have fertile plains. A number of other ranges further east culminate in the volcanic cone of Ağri Daği (Mt Ararat) (5,166 m; 16,949 ft). Important minerals found in the thinly populated eastern regions include chrome, copper, oil, and gold. Tobacco and figs are grown in two fertile valleys that lead westward down from the plateau to the Aegean Sea. Cotton is produced on the deltaic plain near the southern city of Adana.

The Turkish economy combines modern industry and commerce with village agriculture and crafts. Though still of importance, agriculture has been overtaken by manufacturing. A busy industrial sector produces textiles, processed foods, steel, petroleum, construction materials, lumber, and paper, while coal, chromite, and copper are mined. Energy for industry comes in part from oil that is imported, but also from domestic coal and from the country's abundant hydroelectric power.

During the 1980s growth averaged more than 7 percent a year. In 1994 an outbreak of triple-digit inflation led to a period during which public debt, money supply, and the current account deficit were simultaneously out of control. Severe austerity measures and structural reforms were required in order to correct the situation. Shifting political coalitions and economic instability present a challenge for Turkey today.

Landscape near Chiang Mai, in Thailand (top). Two hill tribe women from the mountains of northern Thailand (center left). Ruins of a Thai Buddhist temple (below left). Buildings carved from rock in Cappadocia, Turkey (below).

Turkmenistan

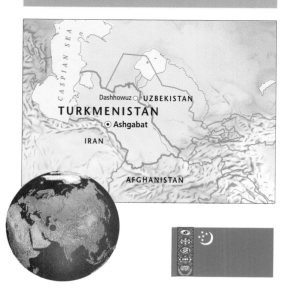

Turkmenistan is in southern Central Asia. From the Caspian Sea it stretches east to Afghanistan, and borders Iran to the south. Kazakhstan and Uzbekistan lie to the north. The Turkmen are probably descended from the same tribes as the Seljuk and Ottoman Turks who conquered what is now Turkey in the eleventh century. Russia annexed Turkmenistan in 1884 and began colonizing it in 1906. In 1924 it became the Turkmen Soviet Socialist Republic. Fierce local resistance to Sovietization continued into the 1930s and there were mass arrests of cultural and religious leaders. Turkmenistan declared its independence in 1991 but little has changed politically. It remains a one-party state and the first secretary of the former Communist Party is now the president, elected with a 99.5 percent share of the vote. The chief difference is that the government can now seek outside capital to develop the country's vast natural gas reserves, and looks to Muslim countries rather than Russia for support.

More than 90 percent of the country is arid, the greater part of it being the Kara Kum Desert. Most of the Kara Kum is made up of the plains of the Krasnovodskoye Plato, but 10 percent consists of huge sand dunes. In the east the Amu Darya River forms part of the Afghanistan border. This river once fed the Aral Sea but from the 1950s much of its water was diverted into the Kara Kum Canal which crosses two-thirds of the country westward to Kizyl-Arvat (Gyzlarbat). This provided irrigation for cotton, but also helped dry up the Aral Sea. To the west of the plateau the land falls to the Caspian shore.

Turkmenistan is poor, despite its natural gas and oil reserves. Half its irrigated land is planted in cotton but industrial development has been limited. Apart from Astrakhan rugs and food processing, industry is largely confined to mining sulfur and salt, and natural gas production. Through 1995 inflation soared, and falling production saw the budget shift from a surplus to a deficit. Since independence in 1991 there have been few changes in economic policy, leading to growing poverty and a shortage of basic foods. Cotton and grain harvests were disastrous in 1996 and desertification remains a serious problem.

Fact File

OFFICIAL NAME	Republic of Turkmenistan
FORM OF GOVERNMENT	Republic with single legislative body (Parliament)
CAPITAL	Ashgabat
AREA	488,100 sq km (188,455 sq miles)
TIME ZONE	GMT + 5 hours
POPULATION	4,366,383
PROJECTED POPULATION 2005	4,791,263
POPULATION DENSITY	9 per sq km (23.3 per sq mile)
LIFE EXPECTANCY	61.1
INFANT MORTALITY (PER 1,000)	73.1
OFFICIAL LANGUAGE	Turkmen
OTHER LANGUAGES	Russian, Uzbek
LITERACY RATE	97.7%
RELIGIONS	Muslim 87%, Eastern Orthodox 11%, other 2%
ETHNIC GROUPS	Turkmen 73.3%, Russian 9.8%, Uzbek 9%, Kazak 2%, other 5.9%
CURRENCY	Manat
ECONOMY	Agriculture 44%, services 36%, industry 20%
GNP PER CAPITA	US$920
CLIMATE	Mainly arid, with cold winters and hot summers
HIGHEST POINT	Ayrybaba 3,139 m (10,298 ft)
MAP REFERENCE	Page 222

United Arab Emirates

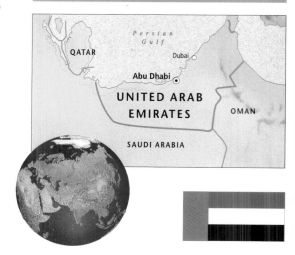

People in the seven small principalities that form the United Arab Emirates lived for centuries as seagoing traders on the shores of the Persian Gulf. When piracy became a nuisance in 1820, Britain entered into truces with the local emirs to end attacks on shipping, and established a protectorate in the region. Soon the principalities were known as the Trucial States. In 1971 they became independent and formed the federation of sheikdoms now known as the United Arab Emirates (UAE). They are situated along the southern coast of the Persian Gulf between the Qatar Peninsula to the west and the Straits of Hormuz, and share borders with Qatar, Saudi Arabia, and Oman.

Abu Dhabi is more than six times the size of all the other states put together, has the biggest population, and is the main oil producer. In the form of federal funds, it contributes to development projects in the poorer states. The port in Dubai is one of the world's largest maritime facilities, and has attracted companies from 58 countries active in the petroleum industry, trading, and financial services. A major economic contribution has been made by expatriates who flocked to the country during the 1970s' oil boom—only 20 percent of UAE citizens are native born. Whether this workforce can now be 'Emiratized' is a concern, as is the growth of Islamic fundamentalism among the young. In world affairs the UAE is a force for moderation in the Arab world. It maintains close links with the UK and USA.

The Gulf coast features saline marshes merging inland with barren desert plains. In the east there is a range of steep mountains. These are an extension of Oman's Hajar Mountains, running northward along the Musandam Peninsula. The sheikhdom of Al-Fujayrah looks out from this peninsula onto the Gulf of Oman, and contains the only highland expanse. Less than 1.2 percent of UAE land is arable, and most vegetation is sparse and scrubby. Virtually all agricultural activity is found in the emirates of Sharjah, Ras al-Khaimana, Ajman, and Fujairah, where oasis date palms grow. Government incentives, however, plus irrigation works, have increased the number of farmers fourfold in recent years. While much food is imported, self-sufficiency in wheat was a target for the year 2000.

Once an impoverished region of small desert sheikhdoms, the UAE has since 1973 been transformed into a modern state with a high

Melon sellers at a market in Turkmenistan (below left).
The Tila Kara Marasa, in Registan Square, Samarqand,
Uzbekistan, built in the seventeenth century (left).

While some of this area supports herders with cattle and sheep, it is today more important for its oil and gas reserves. To the west is the river delta formed where the Syrdar'ya (Oxus) enters the Aral Sea, while the Ustyurt Plateau lies in the extreme northwest. East of the Kyzyl Kum, beyond the capital of Toshkent and the Chatkal Mountains, is a spur jutting into Kyrgyzstan. This contains a large part of the fertile Fergana Basin. Uzbekistan is the world's fourth-largest cotton producer, and the Fergana Valley bears the environmental scars of the fertilizers and pesticides which helped to bring this about.

Although it grows large quantities of cotton, Uzbekistan is unable to produce enough grain for its own needs, importing it from Russia, Kazakhstan, and the USA. A rethinking of the Soviet-style economy has yet to take place.

As well as one of the world's largest gold-mines, at Murantau, Uzbekistan has large deposits of natural gas, petroleum, coal, and uranium. Gas is currently used domestically, but it could become a major export. After 1991 the government tried to strengthen the economy with subsidies and tight price controls. Inflation rose to 1,500 percent at one point and in 1995 food rationing had to be introduced. At present, efforts are being made to tighten monetary policies, expand privatization, and to reduce the state's role in the economy, but so far there have been few serious structural changes.

standard of living. Oil and gas production is the largest economic sector, accounting for 89 percent of export revenue. Though in the short term the fortunes of the economy fluctuate with the price of gas and oil, at the present level of production oil reserves should last more than 100 years. Increased privatization is being encouraged by the government, and service industries are being developed. Although the UAE is much stronger economically than most of the Gulf states, a number of weaknesses remain. While the largest solar-powered water-production plant in the Gulf region is at Taweela, industrial development is likely to be limited by the fact that water will always be in short supply. There is a lack of skilled labor. Most raw materials and foodstuffs have to be imported.

Fact File

OFFICIAL NAME United Arab Emirates

FORM OF GOVERNMENT Federation of Emirates with one advisory body (Federal National Council)

CAPITAL Abu Dhabi

AREA 75,581 sq km (29,182 sq miles)

TIME ZONE GMT + 4 hours

POPULATION 2,344,402

PROJECTED POPULATION 2005 2,610,901

POPULATION DENSITY 31 per sq km (80.3 per sq mile)

LIFE EXPECTANCY 75.2

INFANT MORTALITY (PER 1,000) 14.1

OFFICIAL LANGUAGE Arabic

OTHER LANGUAGES English, Farsi (Persian), Hindi, Urdu

LITERACY RATE 78.6%

RELIGIONS Muslim 96% (Shia 16%); Christian, Hindu, other 4%

ETHNIC GROUPS Emiri 19%, other Arab and Iranian 23%, South Asian 50%, other expatriates 8% (only 20% of population are citizens)

CURRENCY Emirian dirham

ECONOMY Services 57%, industry 38%, agriculture 5%

GNP PER CAPITA US$17,400

CLIMATE Mainly arid; cooler in eastern mountains

HIGHEST POINT Jabal Yibir 1,527 m (5,010 ft)

MAP REFERENCE Pages 220–21

Uzbekistan

Uzbekistan stretches from the shrinking Aral Sea to the heights of the western Pamirs. Its main frontiers are with Kazakhstan to the north and Turkmenistan to the south. The Uzbek people are of Turkic origin and seem to have taken their name from the Mongol Öz Beg Khan (AD 1313–40), who may also have converted them to Islam. In the fifteenth century they moved south into their present land. The Muslim cities of Samarqand and Bukhoro are in Uzbekistan, Bukhoro being a major religious center. Muslims unable to visit Mecca can become hajis by visiting Bukhoro seven times instead. In the former USSR the territory was the Uzbek Soviet Socialist Republic, Uzbek leaders suffering much during Stalin's purges. In 1991 Uzbekistan became independent and is today ruled by the old communist elite as a de facto one-party state. The most populous of the Central Asian republics, Uzbekistan also has the greatest variety of ethnic groups. This is often a source of conflict. The Turkish-speaking Uzbeks clash with the Farsi-speaking Tajiks, and the Meskhetian Turks (deported from Georgia to Central Asia by Stalin) clash with the Uzbeks in the Fergana Valley. Hundreds died during fighting between the latter groups in 1989 and 1990.

The middle region of Uzbekistan consists of the desert plains of the Kyzyl Kum (Peski Kyzylkum).

Fact File

OFFICIAL NAME Republic of Uzbekistan

FORM OF GOVERNMENT Republic with single legislative body (Supreme Assembly)

CAPITAL Toshkent (Tashkent)

AREA 447,400 sq km (172,741 sq miles)

TIME ZONE GMT + 6 hours

POPULATION 24,102,473

PROJECTED POPULATION 2005 26,111,101

POPULATION DENSITY 53.9 per sq km (139.6 per sq mile)

LIFE EXPECTANCY 63.9

INFANT MORTALITY (PER 1,000) 71.6

OFFICIAL LANGUAGE Uzbek

OTHER LANGUAGES Russian, Tajik

LITERACY RATE 97.2%

RELIGIONS Muslim 88% (mostly Sunnis), Eastern Orthodox 9%, other 3%

ETHNIC GROUPS Uzbek 71.5%, Russian 8.3%, Tajik 4.7%, Kazak 4%, Tatar 2.5%, other 9%

CURRENCY Som

ECONOMY Agriculture 43%, services 35%, industry 22%

GNP PER CAPITA US$970

CLIMATE Mainly arid, with cold winters and long, hot summers

HIGHEST POINT Adelunga Toghi 4,299 m (14,105 ft)

MAP REFERENCE Pages 222–23

Indochina

The term Indochina indicates that cultural influences from India and China are intermingled throughout this region. Also once known as French Indochina, it consists of the three states of Vietnam, Laos, and Cambodia, all of which were formerly associated with France in a political group known as the French Union. Despite the fact that the French exercised political control over their countries from the late nineteenth century, the Vietnamese, Cambodian, and Laotian royal houses continued to exercise wide authority. The Japanese occupied Indochina during the Second World War, but interfered little in the existing colonial arrangements; only after 1945 did the military turmoil begin which was to convulse the region.

In 1945, following the withdrawal of the Japanese, the Vietnamese communist nationalist leader Ho Chi Minh proclaimed the Democratic Republic of Vietnam. The returning French attempted to hold their colonial possession together, but soon the protracted guerrilla struggle that became known as the First Indochina War broke out. The forces in the North received support from the Chinese. In 1954 after the siege of Dien Bien Phu, a ceasefire was agreed to by both France and China. This resulted in two independent states: North Vietnam and South Vietnam, which were divided by the 17th parallel.

During the 1960s the attempt of North Vietnamese forces to infiltrate and subvert the southern area led to the Second Indochina War, also know as the Vietnam War. This period saw increasing United States military involvement in the defense of South Vietnam. The US gave strong support to the South Vietnamese government and in 1961 the US commenced sending military advisers.

The US actively entered the Viernam War in 1964. Fighting continued until the Paris ceasefire of 1973, and Saigon was ultimately captured by the North Vietnmese in 1975.

Between 1954 and 1975 about 1,000,000 North Vietnamese soliders, 200,000 South Vietnamese soldiers and 500,000 civilians were killed. Between 1961 and 1975 about 56,500 US soldiers were killed. In 1976 the Socialist Republic of Vietnam was established. This period also saw the rise and fall of the Khmer Rouge regime in Cambodia, and was followed byaa Vietnamese invasion of Cambodia in 1978. Before withdrawing from Cambodia Vietnam installed in power the Communist Khmer People's Revolutionary Party (now the Cambodian People's Party) whose domination of the political system, reinforced by a violent coup in 1997, is a source of widespread discontent.

Today several boundary disputes exist between the three countries of Indochina. In addition to Vietnam's claims to various islands in the South China Sea, sections of the boundary between Cambodia and Vietnam are in dispute, and the maritime boundary between these countries is not defined. A boundary dispute also exists between Laos and Thailand.

Vietnam

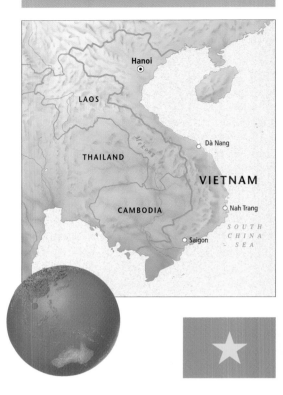

Vietnam is located on the eastern side of the Indochinese Peninsula. A long, narrow strip of country lying between two major river systems, Vietnam bears the scars of one of the longest and most devastating wars of the second half of the twentieth century. Historically, it was for more than a thousand years under Chinese domination, achieving a degree of independence in AD 939. Christian missionary activity began in the seventeenth century and it was a French colony from 1883. During the Second World War a communist-led resistance movement fought the Japanese, and later fought the returning French, defeating them decisively in 1954. The country was divided into two mutually hostile regimes, with a communist government in the north and a

Vietnamese farmers working in the rice fields (below). A fisherman casting his net from a basket boat in Vietnam (top right). Women at a market in Hanoi (above right).

French- and later US-backed government in the south. The north initiated 20 years of insurgency and then full-scale war (the north backed by the USSR, the south by the USA with at one stage 500,000 troops), eventually winning in 1975 and establishing the Socialist Republic of Vietnam.

About 66 percent of Vietnam's land area is dominated by the heavily forested terrain of the Annam Highlands (or Chaîne Annamitique). The crest of this range mostly follows the western border with Laos in the north and Cambodia to the south. At either end of the country are intensively cultivated and densely populated river deltas—the Red River Delta in the north, which is also fed by waters from the valley of the Da, and the Mekong Delta in the south. Both are major rice-growing areas. Rice is the main staple and export crop, Vietnam being the world's third-largest exporter. Other food crops include sweet potato and cassava. On the mountain slopes of the Annam Highlands tea, coffee, and rubber plantations have been established. Most mineral resources are located in the north and include anthracite and lignite. Coal is the main export item and is the principal energy source.

After 10 years during which a typical communist command economy was imposed, along with collectivized agriculture, the government changed direction. In 1986 the more liberal *doi moi* ("renovation") policy was introduced. Investment was welcomed from outside, and during the period 1990 to 1995 real growth averaged more than 8 percent annually. Foreign capital contributed to a boom in commercial construction, and there was strong growth in services and industrial output. Crude oil remains the country's largest single export, now amounting to a quarter of exports overall, slightly more than manufactures. But progress is handicapped by a continuing strong commitment to state direction and bureaucratic controls. Banking reform is needed and administrative and legal barriers delay investment. There is no evidence of a relaxation of the political grip of the Communist Party to match the attempted economic liberalization: in 1991 open anti-communist dissent was made a criminal offence.

Fact File

OFFICIAL NAME Socialist Republic of Vietnam

FORM OF GOVERNMENT Communist state with single legislative body (National Assembly)

CAPITAL Hanoi

AREA 329,560 sq km (127,243 sq miles)

TIME ZONE GMT + 7 hours

POPULATION 77,311,210

PROJECTED POPULATION 2005 83,441,920

POPULATION DENSITY 234.6 per sq km (607.6 per sq mile)

LIFE EXPECTANCY 68.1

INFANT MORTALITY (PER 1,000) 34.8

OFFICIAL LANGUAGE Vietnamese

OTHER LANGUAGES French, Chinese, English, Khmer, indigenous languages

LITERACY RATE 64%

RELIGIONS Buddhist 60%, Roman Catholic 7%, Taoist, Islam and indigenous beliefs 33%

ETHNIC GROUPS Vietnamese 85%–90%, Chinese 3%, other 7–12%

CURRENCY Dong

ECONOMY Agriculture 65%, industry and services 35%

GNP PER CAPITA US$240

CLIMATE Tropical in south, subtropical in north; wet season May to October

HIGHEST POINT Fan Si Pan 3,143 m (10,312 ft)

MAP REFERENCE Page 203

Regional conflicts

1946 Vietnam: Return of French after Second World War. Outbreak of First Indochina War.
1954 Vietnam: Defeat of French at Dien Bien Phu. Division of Vietnam into North supported by USSR and South supported by USA.
1960 Vietnam: Communists in South initiate guerrilla war as Viet Cong.
1961 Vietnam: USA sends "military advisers" to South Vietnam to fight Viet Cong.
1964 US Congress approves war with Vietnam. US bombs Vietnamese sanctuaries in Laos, plus Ho Chi Minh Trail—north–south supply route.
1965 Vietnam: Arrival of first US combat troops. Start of intense US bombing of North which continues until 1968.
1970 Right-wing coup in Cambodia deposes Prince Sihanouk. In exile Sihanouk forms movement backed by communist Khmer Rouge.
1974 Cambodia: Sihanouk and Khmer Rouge capture Phnom Penh. Thousands die as revolutionary programs enforced.
1975 Vietnam: Fall of Saigon. North Vietnamese and Viet Cong take power in South. Laos: Communist Pathet Lao seize power.
1976 Cambodia: Sihanouk resigns—all power held by Pol Pot, leader of the Khmer Rouge.
1978 Vietnam invades Cambodia.
1979 Vietnam captures Phnom Penh. Pol Pot flees, and is held responsible for more than 2 million deaths.
1989 Vietnamese troops leave Cambodia.
1991 Cambodia: Sihanouk again head of state. Flight of Khmer Rouge officials.
1992 Vietnam: Foreign investment permitted; Communist Party monopoly unchanged.
1993 Cambodia: UN-supervised elections. Departure of UN peace mission.
1995 Normalization of US–Vietnam diplomatic relations.
1997 Cambodia: Violent coup restores power to communists under Hun Sen.
1998 Cambodia: Pol Pot dies.

Yemen

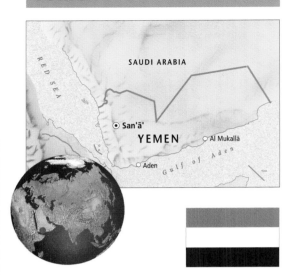

Yemen occupies the southwestern corner of the Arabian Peninsula. Although its people have been Muslim for centuries it has deeply divided political allegiances and was two separate countries until 1990. North Yemen became independent of the Ottoman Empire in 1918, and in 1962 the Yemen Arab Republic (YAR) was proclaimed. The politics of the YAR tended to be conservative and Islamic. South Yemen came under British influence in 1839 and Aden became a vital port on the sea route to India. In 1967 the British withdrew from the region, and in 1969 the People's Democratic Republic of Yemen was proclaimed—the only Marxist state in the Arab world.

Since independence both north and south were mutually hostile but a turning point came with the Soviet collapse in 1989. Having lost USSR support, South Yemen sought political union with the YAR. In 1990 the two countries became the Republic of Yemen. In 1994 an assassination attempt on a northern politician led to civil war and the south's attempted secession. An uneasy peace prevails.

The narrow Red Sea coastal plain of Tihāma, extending south from Saudi Arabia, is generally barren: here, cotton-growing predominates. From the coast the land rises steeply to a comparatively fertile and well-cultivated interior. Around Şan'ā vines are cultivated and a variety of fruit crops are grown. The mountains overlooking Şan'ā rise to Jabal an-Nabi Shu'ayb, the highest point on the Arabian Peninsula. From these heights a number of rivers drain east toward the Ar Rub' al Khālī (Empty Quarter) where they disappear into the sands. Along the coast of the Gulf of Aden a sandy plain rises inland to the rugged Yemen Plateau, which to the north slopes down to the uninhabited wastes of the Rub al-Khali. In this region 10 percent of the mainly rural population are nomadic.

Despite oil and gas reserves, Yemen is weak economically. In the Gulf War of 1990–91 Yemen supported Iraq. As punishment, Saudi Arabia and Kuwait expelled hundreds of thousands of Yemeni workers. Their remittances ceased and they became a huge burden on the economy. The government then abandoned agricultural subsidies and farmers stopped growing food and export crops. Instead they planted a shrub called qat—a stimulant used by Yemenis that has no export value. High inflation and political conflicts make it difficult to implement long-range economic policies and reforms.

Fact File

OFFICIAL NAME Republic of Yemen

FORM OF GOVERNMENT Republic with single legislative body (House of Representatives)

CAPITAL Şan'ā'

AREA 527,970 sq km (203,849 sq miles)

TIME ZONE GMT + 3 hours

POPULATION 16,942,230

PROJECTED POPULATION 2005 20,806,931

POPULATION DENSITY 32.1 per sq km (83.1 per sq mile)

LIFE EXPECTANCY 60

INFANT MORTALITY (PER 1,000) 69.8

OFFICIAL LANGUAGE Arabic

OTHER LANGUAGE English

LITERACY RATE 41.1%

RELIGIONS Muslim: predominantly Sunni in the south, Shi'ite majority in the north

ETHNIC GROUPS Predominantly Arab; small mixed African–Arab and Indian minorities

CURRENCY Yemeni rial

ECONOMY Agriculture 63%, services 26%, industry 11%

GNP PER CAPITA US$260

CLIMATE Mainly arid; humid in southwest and cooler in western highlands; drier in east

HIGHEST POINT Jabal an-Nabi Shu'ayb 3,760 m (12,336 ft)

MAP REFERENCE Page 220

Dependencies and

British Indian Ocean Territory

Otherwise known as the Chagos Islands, and the location of the major US–UK military base of Diego Garcia, the British Indian Ocean Territory is a group of 2,300 islets located about 1,600 km (1,000 miles) from southern India and 600 km (400 miles) south of the Maldives. The islets are coral atolls and once supported a few people who produced copra for export. The islets were bought for $3 million by Britain from Mauritius but have been uninhabited since the copra plantations were closed and the population relocated to Mauritius in 1973.

Fact File

OFFICIAL NAME British Indian Ocean Territory

FORM OF GOVERNMENT Dependent territory of the United Kingdom

CAPITAL None

AREA 60 sq km (23 sq miles)

TIME ZONE GMT + 5 hours

POPULATION No permanent population

ECONOMY Air Force base

CLIMATE Tropical, moderated by trade winds

MAP REFERENCE Page 477

Women herd goats outside a small village near Dhamār in the Central Highlands of Yemen (below). A Yemeni desert town (left). A semi-permanent home on the West Bank, an area still in dispute (top right).

Territories in Asia

Paracel Islands

Fact File

OFFICIAL NAME Paracel Islands

FORM OF GOVERNMENT Disputed territory occupied by China, but claimed by Taiwan and Vietnam

CAPITAL None

AREA Not available

TIME ZONE GMT + 8 hours

POPULATION No permanent population; Chinese garrisons

CLIMATE Tropical. Prone to typhoons

MAP REFERENCE Page 203

Situated in the South China Sea, the Paracel Islands are a collection of coral atolls about one-third of the way from central Vietnam to the northern Philippines. The Chinese have garrisoned the islands and have built port facilities and an airport on Woody Island. They are the center of a regional dispute because oil and natural gas are thought to exist within their territorial waters.

Spratly Islands

The Spratly Islands consist of a collection of reefs, islands, and atolls scattered across a large area of the South China Sea, about two-thirds of the way from southern Vietnam to the southern Philippines. Brunei has made Louisa Reef an exclusive economic zone, but has not publicly claimed the island. The islands are subject to territorial disputes because of their proximity to oil- and gas-producing sedimentary basins.

Fact File

OFFICIAL NAME Spratly Islands

FORM OF GOVERNMENT Disputed territory claimed by China, Taiwan, Vietnam, Malaysia, and the Philippines

CAPITAL None

AREA 5 sq km (1.9 sq miles)

TIME ZONE GMT + 8 hours

POPULATION No permanent population

CLIMATE Tropical. Prone to typhoons

MAP REFERENCE Page 203

Autonomous regions

Gaza Strip

A disputed territory on the Mediterranean with a large permanent exile population of Palestinians, most of whom are descended from those who fled Israel in 1948. Egypt lies to the south and Israel surrounds it to the east and north. As with the West Bank, the Gaza Strip has been in Israeli hands since the Six Days War of 1967. Formally incorporated into Israel in 1973, it has eight Israeli settlements built since 1967. From when Israel assumed control, the Gaza Strip has been the scene of unrest and violence, the town of Gaza witnessing the Palestinian *intifada* ("uprising") in 1987–88. The accord reached between the Palestine Liberation Organization (PLO) and Israel in May 1994 gave self-rule to the Gaza Strip pending "final status" talks to take place in the future. The cycle of violence, involving Palestinian bombings in Israel and Israeli reprisals, makes a resolution of the territory's status difficult to achieve.

Fact File

OFFICIAL NAME Gaza Strip (preferred Palestinian term, Gaza District)

FORM OF GOVERNMENT Disputed by Israel and Palestinian National Authority; interim self-government administered by Palestinian Legislative Council

CAPITAL Gaza

AREA 360 sq km (139 sq miles)

TIME ZONE GMT + 2 hours

POPULATION 1,112,654

LIFE EXPECTANCY 73.4

INFANT MORTALITY (PER 1,000) 22.9

LITERACY RATE Not available

CURRENCY Israeli shekel

ECONOMY Industry 44%, services 36%, agriculture 20%

CLIMATE Temperate. Mild winters; warm, dry summers

MAP REFERENCE Page 225

West Bank

Under a 1947 UN agreement this area on the west bank of the Jordan River was to become Palestinian when the State of Israel was formed. After the 1967 Six Day War Israel had control of a larger area than originally proposed. The building of Israeli settlements since then has been bitterly resented by the more than 95 percent Palestinian Arab population. The area depends on remittances from workers in Israel. Lack of jobs has also led to many working in the Gulf States. But the *intifada* in 1988 reduced the numbers working in Israel, and many West Bank workers were sent home following Palestinian support for Iraq in the Gulf War. Unemployment is about 30 percent. Under a 1993–95 Israeli–PLO declaration certain powers were to be transferred to a Palestinian Legislative Council, but ongoing Palestinian bombings in Israel, Israeli reprisals, and persistent Israeli settlement construction, make a speedy end to strife unlikely.

Fact File

OFFICIAL NAME West Bank

FORM OF GOVERNMENT Disputed by Israel and Palestinian National Authority; interim self-government administered by Palestinian Legislative Council

CAPITAL Jerusalem

AREA 5,860 sq km (2,263 sq miles)

TIME ZONE GMT + 2 hours

POPULATION 1,611,109

LIFE EXPECTANCY 72.8

INFANCY MORTALITY (PER 1,000) 25.2

LITERACY RATE Not available

CURRENCY Israeli shekel, Jordanian dinar

ECONOMY Industry 45%, services 34%, agriculture 21%

CLIMATE Temperate, with cool to mild winters and warm to hot summers

MAP REFERENCE Page 225

Asia and the Middle East: Physical

ATLANTIC OCEAN

Ireland
British Isles

NORWEGIAN SEA

GREENLAND SEA

ARCTIC OCEAN

Arctic Circle

Svalbard

Zemlya Frantsa-Iosifa

Galdhøpiggen 2469 m

Scandinavia

Nordkapp

BARENTS SEA

Novaya Zemlya

Iberian Peninsula

Bay of Biscay

Strait of Gibraltar

Jebel Toubkal 4165 m

Atlas Mountains

Grand Erg Occidental

Pyrenees

Massif Central

Islas Baleares

Mont Blanc 4807 m

TYRRHENIAN SEA

Corse

Sardegna

MEDITERRANEAN SEA

Apennino

ADRIATIC SEA

Dinara

Elbe

Wisła

North

European

Plain

Gulf of Bothnia

BALTIC SEA

Kol'skiy Poluostrov

Beloye More

Ladozhskoye Ozero

Onezhskoye Ozero

Sredne-Russkaya Vozvyshennost'

Dnepr

Rybinskoye Vodokhranilishche

Volga

Ostrov Kolguyev

Ural'skiy Khrebet (Ural Mountains)

Pechora

KARSKOYE MORE

Ostrov Vaygach

Gydanskiy Poluostrov

Poluostrov

SAHARA

Grand Erg Oriental

Sicilia

IONIAN SEA

Hora Hoverla 2061 m

Stara Planina

Carpathian Mts

Dunărea

Dnipro

BLACK SEA

Kryms'kyy Pivostriv (Crimean Peninsula)

Sea of Azov

Caspian Depression

Zapadno

Sibirskaya

Ravnina

Ob'

Irtysh

Yenisey

Tropic of Cancer

Khalīj Surt

MEDITERRANEAN SEA

AEGEAN SEA

Kriti

Anatolia

Toros Dağları

Amanos Dağları

Gora El'brus 5641 m

Bol'shoy Kavkaz

Volga

Mughalzhar Tauy

Aral Sea

Plato Ustyurt

Peski Kyzylkum

Balqash Köli

Mongol Altayn

Tavan Bogd Uul 4374 m

Libyan Desert

Western Desert

Cyprus

Sīnā'

Jabal ash Shaykh 2814 m

Agri Dağrı (Mt Ararat) 5137 m

Ağrı Dağı

Euphrates

Tigris

Reshteh-ye Kūhhā-ye Alborz (Elburz Mts)

Dasht-e Kavīr

Pik Imeni Ismail Samani 7495 m

Tian Shan

Pic Pobedy 7439 m

Tarim Pendi

Tibesti

Eastern Desert

Lake Nasser

Al Hijāz

RED SEA

Bādiyat ash Shām (Syrian Desert)

An Nafūd

Kūhhā-ye Zāgros (Zagros Mountains)

Persian Gulf

Iranian Plateau

Dasht-e Lūt

Helmand

Hindu Kush

K2 8611 m

Kunlun Sha

Qingzang Gaoy (Plateau of Tib

Arabian

Peninsula

Gulf of Oman

Ar Rub'al Khālī

Suleiman Range

Indus

Sutlej

HIMALAY

Nyainqê S

Mt Everest 8848 m

75

Ethiopian Highlands

Gulf of Aden

Thar Desert

Rann of Kachchh

Indo-Gangetic Plain

Vindhya Range

Sātpura Range

Deccan

Ganga

(Ganges)

Mouths of the Ganges

Equator

Lake Albert

Lake Turkana

Lake Victoria

Kirinyaga (Mt Kenya) 5199 m

Great Rift Valley

Suquṭrá

ARABIAN SEA

Godavari

Western Ghats

Eastern Ghats

Bay of Bengal

Kilimanjaro 5895 m

Lake Tanganyika

Cape Comorin

Palk Strait

Sri Lanka

Andam Islan

Nic Isl

INDIAN

OCEAN

Maldives

Comoros

Seychelles

Madagascar

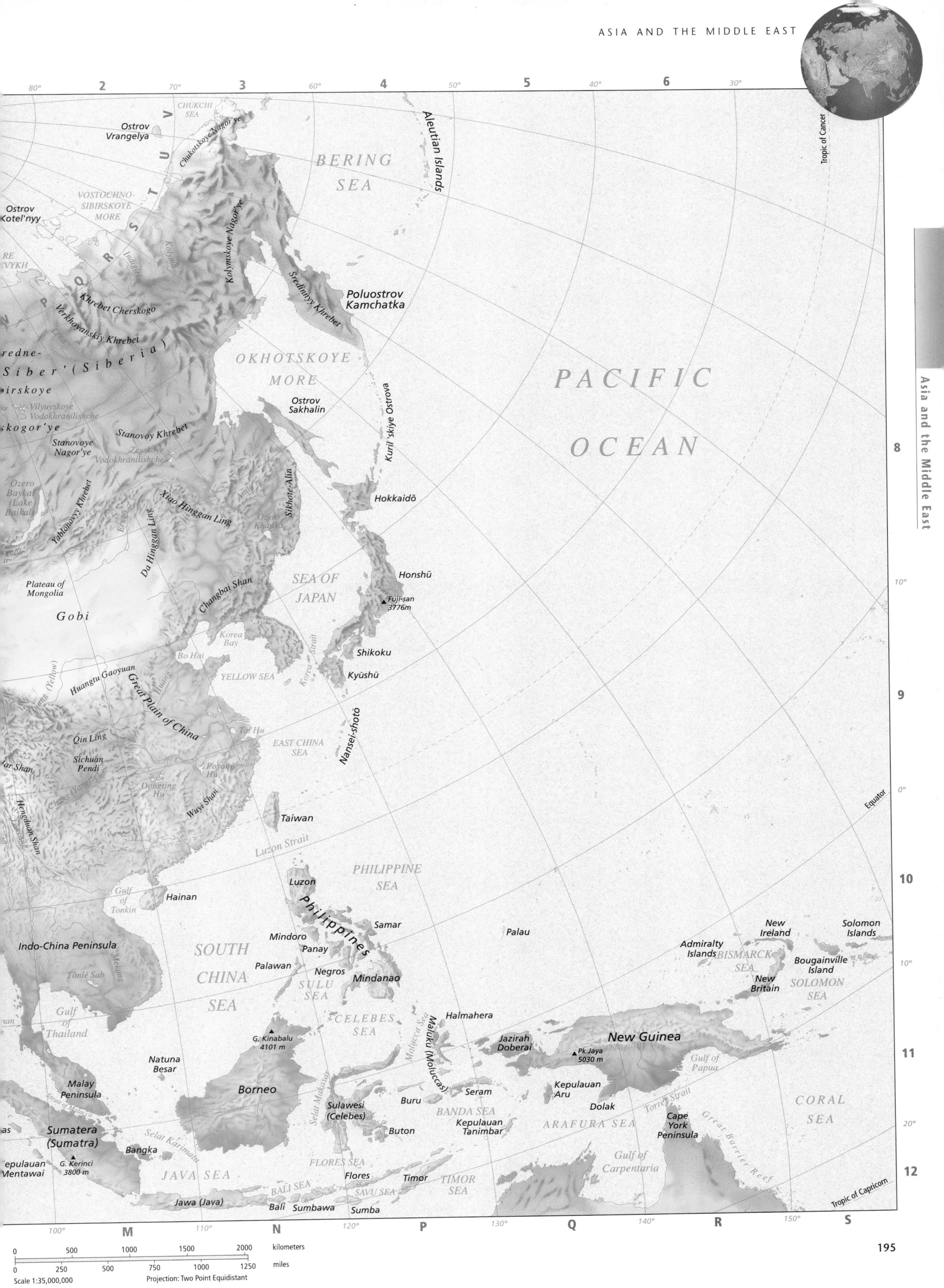

2 3 4 5 6

80° 70° 60° 50° 40° 30°

Tropic of Cancer

CHUKCHI
SEA

Ostrov
Vrangelya

Chukotskoye Nagor'ye

Kolymskoye Nagor'ye

VOSTOCHNO-
SIBIRSKOYE
MORE

Ostrov
Kotel'nyy

RE
VYKH

P

Khrebet Cherskogo

Verkhoyanskiy Khrebet

Sredne-
Siber' (Siberia)
irskoye

skogor'ye

Vilyuyskoye
Vodokhranilishche

Stanovoye
Nagor'ye

Stanovoy Khrebet

Zeyskoye
Vodokhranilishche

Yablonovyy Khrebet

Ozero
Baykal
(Lake
Baikal)

Amur

Xiao Hinggan Ling

Da Hinggan Ling

Changbai Shan

Ozero
Khanka

Sikhote-Alin

Plateau of
Mongolia

Gobi

Huangtu Gaoyuan

Huang

Great Plain of China

Qin Ling

Sichuan
Pendi

Dongting
Hu

Poyang
Hu

Wuyi Shan

Chang Yiang (Yangtze)

Hengduan Shan

ar Shan

Srednyy Khrebet

Poluostrov
Kamchatka

BERING
SEA

Aleutian Islands

OKHOTSKOYE
MORE

Ostrov
Sakhalin

Kuril'skiye Ostrova

PACIFIC

OCEAN

Hokkaidō

Honshū

▲ Fuji-san
3776m

SEA OF
JAPAN

Korea
Bay

Bo Hai

YELLOW SEA

Korea Strait

Shikoku

Kyūshū

Nansei-shotō

EAST CHINA
SEA

Taiwan

Luzon Strait

Hainan

Gulf
of
Tonkin

Indo-China Peninsula

Tônlé Sap

Mekong

Gulf
of
Thailand

an

Malay
Peninsula

Natuna
Besar

Borneo

Selat Makassar

Sumatera
(Sumatra)

▲ G. Kerinci
3800m

Bangka

Selat Karimata

JAVA SEA

epulauan
Mentawai

as

Strait of Malacca

Selat Sunda

Jawa (Java)

Bali

Sumbawa

BALI SEA

SAVU SEA

Sumba

Luzon

Philippines

PHILIPPINE
SEA

Mindoro

Panay

Samar

SOUTH
CHINA
SEA

Palawan

Negros

Mindanao

SULU
SEA

▲ G. Kinabalu
4101 m

CELEBES
SEA

Sulawesi
(Celebes)

Buru

Buton

FLORES SEA

Flores

Timor

Molucca Sea

Maluku (Moluccas)

Halmahera

Jazirah
Doberai

Seram

BANDA SEA

Kepulauan
Tanimbar

TIMOR
SEA

Palau

New
Ireland

Admiralty
Islands

BISMARCK
SEA

New
Britain

New Guinea

▲ Pk Jaya
5030 m

Kepulauan
Aru

Dolak

ARAFURA SEA

Gulf of
Carpentaria

Gulf of
Papua

Torres Strait

Cape
York
Peninsula

Great Barrier Reef

Solomon
Islands

Bougainville
Island

SOLOMON
SEA

CORAL
SEA

Tropic of Capricorn

8

9

0° Equator

10°

10°

11

20°

12

100° 110° 120° 130° 140° 150°

M N P Q R S

0 500 1000 1500 2000 kilometers

0 250 500 750 1000 1250 miles

Scale 1:35,000,000

Projection: Two Point Equidistant

10°

Asia and the Middle East

Asia and the Middle East: Political

80° **2** 70° **3** 60° **4** 50° **5** 40° **6** 30°

Tropic of Ca[ncer]

St Lawrence I.
(U.S.A.)

Ostrov
Vrangelya

MIDWAY ISLANDS
(U.S.A.)

osibirskiye
Ostrova

Anadyr'

BERING
SEA

Aleutian Islands

RATION

Magadan

Petropavlovsk-Kamchatskiy

OKHOTSKOYE
MORE

Yakutsk

PACIFIC

OCEAN

Ozero
Baykal

Chita

Ulan-Ude

Blagoveshchensk

Komsomol'sk-na-Amure

Yuzhno-Sakhalinsk

Khabarovsk

Ostrov
Sakhalin

Kuril'skiye Ostrova

8

Jiamusi

Asahikawa
Hokkaidō

WAKE ISLAND
(U.S.A.)

Ulaanbaatar

Qiqihar Harbin Jixi

Sapporo
Hakodate
Aomori
Akita

Mudanjiang

Vladivostok

NGOLIA

Changchun Jilin

Ch'ŏngjin

Yamagata Fukushima
Honshū

10°

Siping Liaoyuan

Sea of
Japan

Tōkyō Yokohama

MARSHALL
ISLANDS

Shenyang Fushun

NORTH
KOREA

Kyōto Ōsaka

Anshan

P'yŏngyang

Kōbe
Shikoku

Zhangjiakou

Dalian

Sŏul

Hiroshima

Inch'ŏn

JAPAN

Beijing Tangshan

Pusan

Shijiazhuang Tianjin

SOUTH
KOREA Taegu

Kitakyūshū

Shizuishan

Jinan Qingdao

Fukuoka

Kumamoto
Kyūshū

Taiyuan Yuci

Kagoshima

ng
vei Xinxiang Xintai
g Zhengzhou Kaifeng

Lanzhou Luoyang

Nantong

Xi'an Xuchang Hefei

Nanjing
Shanghai

Nansei-shotō
(Japan)

NORTHERN
MARIANA ISLANDS
(U.S.A.)

9

Wuhan Wuhu

Ningbo

Huangshi Hangzhou

Nanchong

Nanchang

Wenzhou

Chengdu

GUAM (U.S.A.)

Equator

Chongqing Changsha

Fuzhou

T'ai-pei

Neijiang Luzhou Hengyang

T'ai-chung

0°

Zunyi Zixing

Xiamen

Chia-i TAIWAN

Dali Huaihua

Shaoguan

Kao-hsiung

MICRONESIA

kyinā Guilin

Guangzhou Dongguan

Liuzhou Foshan Juilong

Nanning Zhuhai

Xianggang (Hong Kong)

Hà Nôi Zhanjiang

Luzon PHILIPPINES

10

lay Hải Phòng

Baguio

MAR *Hainan*
Dao

Angeles Quezon City
Manila Lucena

PALAU

New Ireland

Bougainville

LAOS

SOUTH
CHINA
SEA

Mindoro

Tacloban

New
Britain SOLOMON
ISLANDS

Viangchan

Đà Nang

Bago Cebu

10°

THAILAND

Negros

PAPUA NEW GUINEA

Moulmein

VIETNAM

Palawan

Cagayan de Oro

Thep CAMBODIA

Mindanao Davao

on Buri Phnum Pénh

Zamboanga

Jayapura

Thanh Phố
Hồ Chí Minh

Kota
Kinabalu

CELEBES
SEA

Halmahera

New Guinea

Gulf of
Thailand

Bandar Seri BRUNEI
Begawan

Manado

11

Kota Baharu Kuala
Town Terengganu

Kalimantan Samarinda

Ipoh Kuala Lumpur

Balikpapan

Ambon *Seram*

Seremban Singapore

Sulawesi

Pekanbaru SINGAPORE

Pontianak

ARAFURA SEA

CORAL SEA ISLANDS (Aust.)

Padang

Banjarmasin

Jambi

INDONESIA

20°

Sumatera
Palembang

Ujungpandang

Gulf of
Carpentaria

Bandarlampung

Flores

Melville I.

Semarang *Madura*
Jakarta *Jawa* Surabaya *Sumbawa*

Sumba Timor

12

Bandung Yogyakarta Malang *Bali* *Lombok*

AUSTRALIA

100° **M** 110° **N** 120° **P** 130° **Q** 140° **R** 150° **S**

0   500   1000   1500   2000 kilometers
0   250   500   750   1000   1250 miles

Scale 1:35,000,000   Projection: Two Point Equidistant

East Indonesia

PHILIPPINES

BRUNEI

LABUAN

SABAH

MALAYSIA

SARAWAK

BORNEO

KALIMANTAN

TIMUR

KALIMANTAN

TENGAH

KALIMANTAN

SELATAN

CELEBES

SEA

SULAWESI

UTARA

Manado

Gorontalo

Kep. Togian

SULAWESI

TENGAH

Palu

SULAWESI

(CELEBES)

SULAWESI

SELATAN

Parepare

Ujungpandang
(Makassar)

MOLUCCA

SEA

P. Halmahera

Ternate

P. Buru

SULAWESI

TENGGARA

Kendari

BANDA

SEA

INDONESIA

JAVA SEA

Kep. Masalembu

P. Madura

Kep. Kangean

BALI SEA

FLORES SEA

Jawa
(Java)

Bali

Lombok

Sumbawa

NUSA TENGGARA BARAT

Flores

NUSA TENGGARA TIMUR

SAVU SEA

Sumba

P. Sawu

Roti

Kupang

Timor

TIMOR
TIMUR

Dili

TIMOR

SEA

INDIAN OCEAN

E   132°   F   136°   G   140°

1

4°

PACIFIC

OCEAN

HALMAHERA
SEA

2

rotai
angeo
Berebere
la

Akelamo
Dorolemo
Watam

Buli

Equator   0°

P. Waigeo

Rabia

Warmandi

Selat Dampier

Koor

Tg Manundi   P. Supiori

Mega   Ambuaki   Kaironi   Korido   Korim
G. Kwoka   Mubrani   Manokwari   P. Biak
3000 m   Sajam   Tg Memori   Biak   Tg Wararisbari

Sorong   Germakolo   Rawas   G. Mebo   Number   Tg D'Urville
Tg Dadi   Gasim   2940 m   P. Numfor   Teba
P. Salawati   Oransbari   P. Num

Atkri   Seget   Baru   Ransiki   Serui   *Selat Yapen*   Danau   Sarmi
Tamulol   Robooksibia   P. Yapen   Rombebai   Maffin
P. Misool   Tomu   P. Rumberpon   Pamdai   Betaf   Ansudu
CERAM SEA   Inanwatan   P. Waar   Tg Ranbausawa   *Tel.*   Kaptiau   Demta
Tg Sabra   *Tel.*   *Waropen*   Depapre   Jayapura
(LUCCAS)   Kokas   Babo   *Tel. Berau*   G. Dom   *PEG. VAN REES*   *WEST*
Wahai   Tanisapata   Rufrufua   Fakfak   Siembra   *Tel. Bintuni*   Kwatisore   Nabire   *IRIAN JAYA*   1430 m   *Tariku*   Krau   *SEPIK*
Bulao   Vanimo
Amahai   Haya   Bemu   Tg Marsimang   G. Angemuk   Leitre
P. Seram   Kilwo   P. Karas   Kaimana   *Danau*   Wandai   3962 m   Ossima   Sissano
Urung   Mirobia   *Yamur*   G. Ubia   Wamena   Imonda   Aitape
Tg Tongerai   *Tel.*   4234 m   *Torricelli Mts*
Kep. Gorong   *Kamrau*   Enarotali   Pk Jaya   Pk Trikora   Amanab
Tg Papisoi   P. Adi   5030 m   4730 m   Pk Yamin   Green River
Kep. Watubela   Tembagapura   4595 m   Pk Mandala
Aiduna   Wanapiri   *Peg.*   *Peg.*   4700 m   *EAST*
Uta   Kokenau   *Jayawijaya*   New   *SEPIK*   Guinea
MALUKU   *Maoke*   *SEPIK*   Kubkain
Amamapare   Telefomin
Agats   Tabubil
Kep. Kai   Tg Borang
P. Kai Besar   Ningerum
P. Kai   Banda Elat   Dobo   Tanahmerah   Rumginae
Kecil   Dosi   Kiunga
Tg Weduar   *Kep. Aru*   *Lake*
Tg Ngoni   *Murray*
Tg Laru Mat   Tg De Jongs   Mapi   Aiambak
Tg Waarlangier   Tafermaar   *WESTERN*
ep. Damar   Tg Ngabordamlu
Kep. Tanimbar   Watmuri   P. Dolak
P. Yamdena   Pembre   Duru
Tepa   Batkes   Kimaan   Okaba   Goe
Latdalam   Saumlaki   Wamal   Kumbe   Serki
Adaut   Kladar   Buk
Sermata   *Kep. Babar*   Eliase   P. Komoran   Merauke   Morehead
Tg Vals   Bula   Mari
Boigu I.

ARAFURA SEA

Torres Strait

Badu I.
Moa I.
Thursday I.
Prince of Wales I.
Bamaga

Dundas Strait   Cape Wessel
C. Van Diemen   *Wessel*
Cobourg   C. Cockburn   *Is*
Pen.   Goulburn Is
Bathurst I.   Melville I.   C. Keith   *Howard*   *Melville Bay*
Van Diemen Gulf   C. Hotham   *Island*   *AUSTRALIA*
Beagle Gulf   Nhulunbuy
Darwin

E   132°   **134**   F   136°   G   140°   H

0   100   200   300   400   kilometers
0   100   200   miles

Scale 1:7,000,000   Projection: Mercator

140

West Indonesia • Malaysia • Singapore

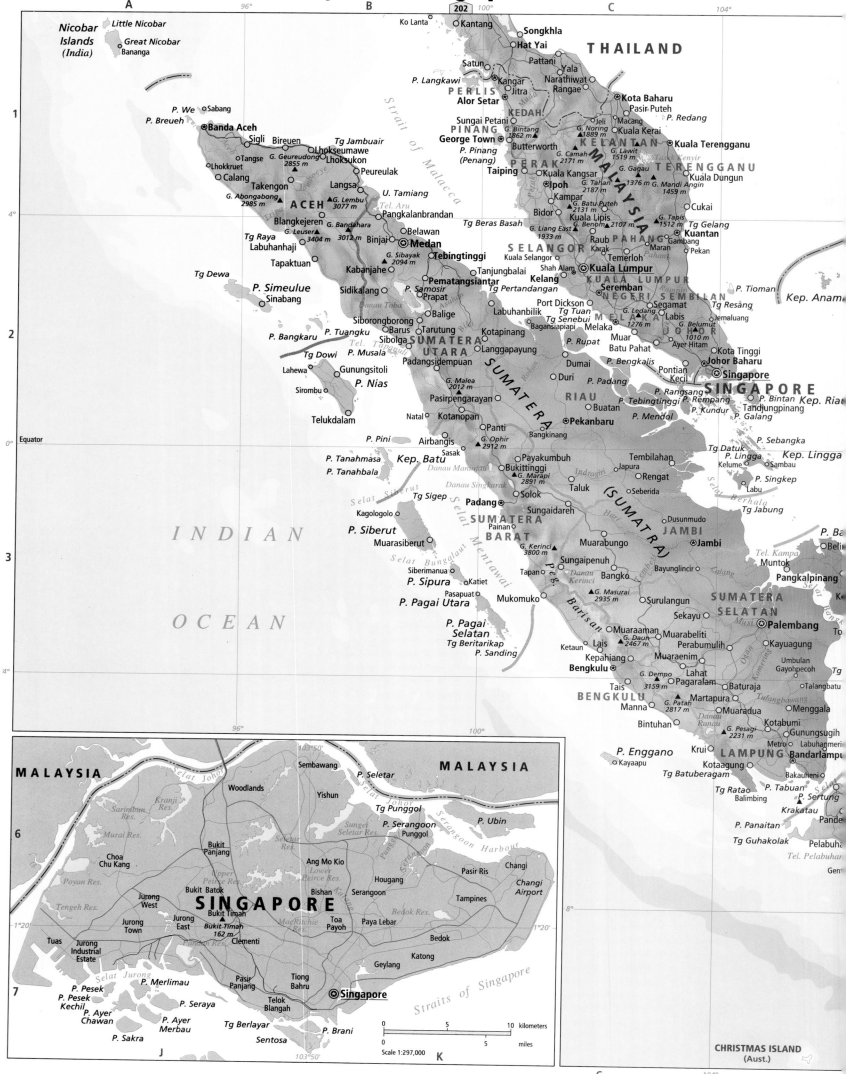

SOUTH CHINA SEA

P. Natuna
Besar

P. Lagong

~. Midai
P. Subi Besar   P. Subi
P. Panjang
P. Serasan
Selat Serasan
Tg Mungguresak
Tg Datu   Tel. Datu
Paloh   Sematan   Tg Sipang
Tg Po

Tg Gunung   Pemangkat   G. Niut
Sambas   1701 m
Singkawang

Tg Bangkai   Mempawah   Ngabang
Sanggau
Pontianak
KALIMANTAN BARAT
Tg Putus   Kertamulia
Nangapinoh   G. Saran
1758 m
P. Padangtikar
P. Maya   Telukbatang   G. Sebayan
Sukadana   1377 m
Sandai
Kep. Karimata   Nangatayap
Tg Bawang   Ketapang
P. Belitung   Kendawangan
rikat   Tanjungpandan   P. Bawal
Manggar   Sukaraja
balong   Dendang   Pangkalanbuun
Kumai
Tg Sambar   Tg Keluang

INDONESIA

JAVA SEA

ARTA RAYA   Kep. Karimunjawa
arta
Pamanukan
Subang   Indramayu   JAWA TENGAH   Tg Bugel
umi   Purwakarta   Cirebon   Keling   G. Muria   Tg Benda
Cianjur   Bandung   Pekalongan   Jepara   1602 m   Rembang
Tegal   Kudus   Blora   Tuban
Garut   G. Careme   Semarang
3078 m   Salatiga   Surabaya
Tasikmalaya   Ciamis   Purwokerto   G. Slamet   Wonosobo   Surakarta (Solo)   Gresik
barang   Cilacap   3418 m   Magelang   Madiun   Pamekasan
Tg Garut   Yogyakarta   G. Lawu   Kediri   Pasuruan
JAWA BARAT   Tel. Penanjung   Ponorogo   3265 m   Probolinggo
Parangtritis   G. Liman   Malang
YOGYAKARTA   2561 m   Kepanjen   G. Semeru   Jember
JAWA (JAVA)   Pacitan   Blitar   3676 m   Banyuwangi
JAWA TIMUR   P. Nusa
Barung

SARAWAK
MALAYSIA

BORNEO

KALIMANTAN TIMUR

KALIMANTAN TENGAH

KALIMANTAN SELATAN

P. Balambangan   P. Banggi
Kudat   P. Malawali
Langkon   Kanibongan   P. Jambongan
Tuaran   G. Kinabalu   Lingkabau   Sandakan
Kota Kinabalu   4101 m   SABAH
Kuala Penyu   Sukau
LABUAN   Telupid   Lamag
Victoria   G. Trus Madi   Lahad Datu
BRUNEI   Beaufort   2649 m   Kunak   Tapul Group
Muara   Pinangah   Tawitawi I.
Bandar Seri   Sapulut   Kalabakan
Begawan   G. Pagon   Tawau   P. Timbun Mata
Tg Baram   1850 m   P. Sebatik   Sibutu I.
Lutong   G. Mulu   G. Harun   Semporna   Sibutu Group
Miri   2371 m   2160 m   Longbawan
Long Teru   G. Murud   G. Basakan   P. Mandul
Batu   2438 m   1372 m   Sesayap
Tg Payong   Niah   Tangung   Tarakan
Tg Kidurong   Mantadau
Bintulu   Long Murum   Nyurang   Tanjungselor
Mukah   Tatau   Kejaman   G. Bakayan   Tanjungredeb
Tg Sirik   1599 m   Tg Batu
P. Bruit   Rumah   G. Kemal   Tintang   P. Maratua
Sibu   Kulit   2053 m   G. Guguang
Tg Datu   Sarikei   Julau   Song   Kapit   Longnawan   2467 m   Barung
Sematan   Saratok   Baleh   Pulai   Tg Arus
Debak   Pelawanbesar   G. Dako
G. Lawit   G. Menyapa   2304 m
Bau   1767 m   G. Kerihun   G. Liangpran   2000 m   Sepasu   Tolitoli
Kuching   1980 m   2240 m   Tg Mangkalihat   Tinabogan
Bandar Sri Aman   Putussibau   Kembangjanggut   G. Ogoamas   Tg Dampelas
(Simanggang)   Danau Luar   2565 m
Sintang   Danau Sentarum   Longiram   Danau   Bontang   Sigenti   Equator
Melintang   Danau   Tg Manimbaya   Kasimbar
Purukcahu   Semayang   SULAWESI
Danau   TENGAH
G. Raya   Jempang   Tawaeli
2278 m   Kualakurun   Samarinda   Donggala   Toboli
Tumbangsamba   Benangin   Palu   Parigi
Memala   Muarapayang   G. Lumut   Pakuli   Sedoa
Palangkaraya   1233 m   Balikpapan   Poso
Sampit   Pendang   SULAWESI   Taripa
Semuda   Kualakapuas   Kupangnunding   G. Serempaka   (CELEBES)
Sukaraja   Tanahgrogot   1380 m   Teluk
Pangkalanbuun   Amuntai   Tel. Adang   Tomini
Kumai   Pulangpisau   Jangeru   Mamuju   G. Kambuno
Tg Sambar   Rantau   G. Besar   2950 m   Wotu
Semuda   1892 m   G. Gandadiwata   Peg. Quarles
Banjarmasin   Kotabaru   3074 m   Rantepao
Martapura   P. Sebuku   Tg Kai   Makale   G. Rantekombola
Pagatan   P. Laut   3455 m
Batakan   Kintap   Semaras   Majene   Polewali
Tg Malatayur   Tg Layar   SULAWESI SELATAN   Siwa
Tg Puting   Tel. Pamukan   Parepare   Singkang
Tg Selatan   Maros   Watampone   Bone
Kep. Masalembu   Ujungpandang   Sinjai
(Makassar)   G. Lompobatang
Kep. Kangean   2876 m   Bira
P. Madura   P. Selayar   S e l a t   S e l a y a r
Bangkalan   Benteng
Bangkalan   BALI SEA   P. Tanahjampea
Tuban   P. Kalao
Ketapang   P. Selayar
Gresik
Pamekasan   FLORES SEA
Situbondo
Bondowoso   Bali   G. Tambora
Pasuruan   3088 m   2821 m   Tg Besi
G. Argopuro   G. Raung   Reo
Probolinggo   3332 m   Singaraja   G. Rinjani   Sumbawa   Bima   P. Komodo
Negara   3142 m   3726 m   Besar   Dompu   Ruteng
G. Agung   Mataram   Sumbawa   Raba   G. Ranakah
Denpasar   Selong   Plampang   2382 m   P. Rinca
P. Nusa   Praya   Flores
P. Nusa   Penida   Lombok   Sumbawa   Tg Sasar
Barung   NUSA TENGGARA BARAT   Waingapu
G. Wanggamet
Waikabubak   1225 m
Sumba   Baing
NUSA TENGGARA TIMUR

Peg. Iran
Peg. Hose
Peg. Muller
Peg. Schwaner
Kapuas
Peg. Meratus
Peg. Sambaliung
Tel. Sukadana
Selat Karimata
Tel. Sukadana
Tel. Kumai
Tel. Sampit
Kahayan
Barito
Selat Laut
Tel. Pamukan
Selat Makasar
Selat Mandar
Teluk Bone
Bali

Scale 1:7,000,000
Projection: Mercator

0   100   200   300   400   kilometers
0   100   200   miles

Thailand • Laos • Cambodia • Vietnam

E | F | G

CHINA

Gejiu
Wenshan
Malipo
Pingguo
Binyang
Wuming
Guiping
Teng Xian
Yunan
Sihui
Guangzhou
(Canton)
Boluo
Huizhou
Haifeng
Jingxi
Tiandeng
Litang
Guigang
Deqing
Zhaoqing
Foshan
Dongguan
Huidong
Jiazi
Hà Giang
Daxin Fusui
Taiping
Heng Xian
Rong Xian
Cenxi
Yunfu
Zhaoqing
Shunde
Taiping
Lufeng
Jieshi Wan
Bắc Quang
2419 m
Longzhou
Lingshan
Yulin
Luoding
Xinxing
Kaiping
Jiangmen
Zhong-
Danshui Shanwei
Fan Si Pan
3143 m
Nà Hang
Pingxiang
Banli
GUANGDONG
Gaozhou
Yangchun
Enping
Taishan
shan
Shenzhen
Zhuhai
Zhong-
shan
Jiulong
(Kowloon)
Tuầ'n Giáo
Yên Bái
Đoan Hùng
Ningming
Qinzhou
Zhanghuang
Bobai
Maoming
Yangjiang
Pingsha
Dongping
Shangchuan Dao
Macao
Xianggang (Hong Kong)
Sơn La
2985 m
Phú Thọ
Việt Trì
1312 m
Hepu
Lianjiang
Huazhou
Dianbai
Shapa
Guangzhou
XIANGGANG
(HONG KONG)
Hòa Bình
Hà Đông
Cẩm Phả
Beihai
Weizhou
Dao
Zhanjiang
Anpu
Suixi
Wuchuan
Hồng Gai
Haikang
Donghai Dao
Ninh Bình
Longmen
Thanh Hóa
Sầm Sơn
Qiongzhou Haixia
Xiuying
Haikou
Xinying
Chengmai
Wenchang

Gulf of Tonkin

Philippines

A   116°   B   120°   C   124°   D

PHILIPPINE SEA

SOUTH CHINA SEA

PHILIPPINES

Batan Is
Basco

Babuyan Is

Babuyan Channel

Mayraira Pt
Bangui
Bacarra
Laoag
Batac   Mt Sicapoo 2048 m
Badoc
Vigan
Narvacan
Candon
Cervantes

Abulog   Palaui I.   C. Engaño
Agbulu   Aparri
Alcala   Gonzaga
Cabugao   Tuao
Bangued   Tuguegarao
Tabuk
Lubuagan
Bontoc   Ilagan   Palanan Pt
Banaue
Santiago   Cauayan   *Luzon*
Bagabag
Tarigtig Pt

Magat   *Cagayan*   *Sierra Madre*

San Fernando
Bauang   Mt Pulog 2934 m
Bolinao   **Baguio**
Cabauyan I.   *Lingayen Gulf*   **Dagupan**   C. San Ildefonso
Agno   Villasis
Lingayen
San Carlos
High Peak 2037 m   San Jose   Baler   *Baler Bay*
Iba   **Tarlac**   **Cabanatuan**
Botolan   Capas   Gapan   *Dingalan Bay*
Mt Pinatubo 1759 m   **Angeles**
San Fernando   **Malolos**
Olongapo   **Quezon**
Balanga   **City**   Infanta   *Polillo Is*
Bagac   ⊡ **Manila**   *Lamon Bay*
Mariveles   Santa Cruz   *Calagua Is*
Muntinglupa   Labo   Daet
Nasugbu   Calamba   Mt Labo 1544 m   San Miguel
Calatagan   **San Pablo**   Calauag   Tinambac   Viga
Lipa   **Lucena**   Sipocot   Lagonoy   *Catanduanes I.*
Lobo   **Batangas**   Santa Cruz   **Naga**   Nabua   Virac
Lubang Is   *Tayabas Bay*   Boac   Pili   *Lagonoy Gulf*
Golo I.   C. Calavite   Calapan   Marinduque I.   San Andres   Tabaco   Batan I.
Paluan   San Francisco   **Legaspi**   Rapu Rapu I.
Mamburao   Mt Halcon 2587 m   *Naujan*   Donsol   Sorsogon
Mindoro   Pinamalayan   Burias I.   Bulan   Matnog
Sablayan   Bongabong   Sibuyan I.   Ticao I.   Catarman
Calintaan   Mt Baco 2488 m   Romblon   Masbate I.   Allen   Mt Capotoan 850 m
San Jose   Tablas I.   Mandaon   Masbate   **Calbayog**
Bulalacao   Mt Guitinguitin 2050 m   Balud   Placer   Catbalogan   **Samar**
Busuanga   (San Pedro)   *Asid Gulf*   Biliran I.   Taft   Borongan
Coron   Busuanga I.   Nabas   Pulanduta Pt.   Naval   Carigara   Llorente
Semirara Is   Pucio Pt   Kalibo   *VISAYAN SEA*   San Remigio   **Tacloban**   Guiuan
Culion I.   Coron I.   Culasi   Daanbantayan   Ormoc   *Leyte*   Homonhon I.
Nelyan Pt   Tibiao   Sara   Bantayan   *Leyte Gulf*   Desolation Pt
El Nido   Linapacan I.   Bugasong   Passi   Cadiz   Camotes Is   Baybay   Dinagat I.
Iloc I.   **Roxas**   Bantayan   Sogod   Loreto
Batas I.   **Silay**   **Ormoc**   Hilongos   Siargao I.
Maytiguid I.   Panay   **Iloilo**   San Carlos   **Mandaue**   Maasin   Dapa
Taytay   San Jose   Miagao   **Bacolod**   Danao   **Cebu**   Pintuyan   Bucas Grande I.
Cuyo Is   **Bago**   **Toledo**   ⊙ **Lapu-Lapu**   Cantilan
Dumaran I.   Anini-y   Kabankalan   Bohol   Guindulman   Surigao
Bacao   *Panay Gulf*   Cebu I.   Dalaguete   Tagbilaran   Diuta Pt   Tandag
Imuruan Bay   Sipalay   Cauayan   Santander   *L. Mainit*   Mt Hilonghilong 2012 m
Boayan I.   Hinoba-an   Dumaguete   Camiguin I.   **Butuan**
Caruray   *Negros*   Santa Catalina   Siquijor I.   Balingoan   **Bayugan**
Ulugan Bay   Roxas   Cleopatra Needle 1593 m   *Tolong Bay*   Siaton   Balingasag   Salvacion
Anepahan   Bacungan   Siaton   Dapitan   El Salvador   **Gingoog**   Lianga
Long Pt   **Puerto Princesa**   Dipolog   Oroquieta   **Cagayan de Oro**   Hinatuan
Victoria Peak 1709 m   Panagtaran Pt   Sindangan   Mt Jimenez   Sanco Pt
Quezon   **Palawan**   Panganuran   Lugait   Bislig
Aborlan   Liloy   Ozamiz   **Iligan**   Malaybalay   *Mindanao*
Rasa I.   Siocon   Marawi   Valencia   Cateel
Mt Mantalingajan 2073 m   Ipil   **Pagadian**   Kabasalan   Kalatungan Mts 2865 m   Monkeyo   Baganga
Brooke's Point   Tungawan   Margosatubig   *Lake Lanao*   Malabang   Kibawe   **Tagum**
Rio Tuba   San Antonio Bay   Sibuco   Parang   Mabini
C. Buliluyan   Olutlanga I.   **Cotabato**   Midsayap   Mt Apo 2954 m   Samal I.
Pandanan I.   Bolong   Pikit   ⊙ **Davao**
Bugsuk I.   **Zamboanga**   Sacol I.   *Moro Gulf*   Kidapawan   Mati
Balabac I.   Isabela   Linao Pt   Tacurong   Lamigan Pt
Balabac   Lamitan   Basilan I.   Lebak   Norala   Digos   *Davao Gulf*
Maluso   1011 m   Surallah   Koronadal   C. San Augustin
Patikul   Kiamba   Mt Matutum 2295 m   Malita
P. Balambangan   Jolo   Jolo I.   **General Santos**
P. Banggi   Tapul I.   (Dadiangas)
P. Malawali   Tapul Group   Glan
Kudat   Siasi   Batulaki
P. Jambongan   Tawitawi I.   *Sarangani Is*
Tuaran   Langkon   Kaniongan   *Sulu Archipelago*
G. Kinabalu 4101 m   Lingkabau   Sibutu I.   *CELEBES SEA*
Kota Kinabalu   **Sandakan**   Sibutu Group
SABAH   Lamag   Sukau
Telupid   Lahad Datu
G. Trus Madi 2649 m   Geme
MALAYSIA   Kunak   *Kep. Talaud*
Pinangah   P. Timbun Mata   Beo
Kuala Penyu   Tel. Darvel   P. Sebatik   Mangaran
Victoria   Beaufort   Semporna   Tahuna   P. Sangihe
Brunei Bay   Kalabakan   Tawau
Bandar Seri   G. Murud 2438 m   G. Harun 2160 m
Begawan   Longbawan   P. Mandul
BRUNEI   G. Basakan 1372 m   **INDONESIA**
Sesayap

SULU SEA

Palawan Passage   *Island Bay*   *Honda Bay*

kilometers   0   100   200   300   400
miles   0   100   200

Scale 1:7,000,000   Projection: Mercator

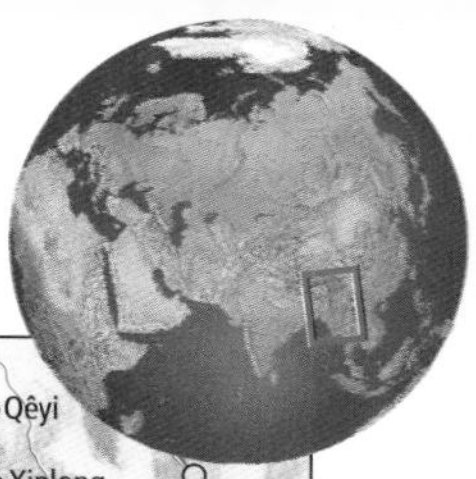

Myanmar · Bangladesh · Bhutan

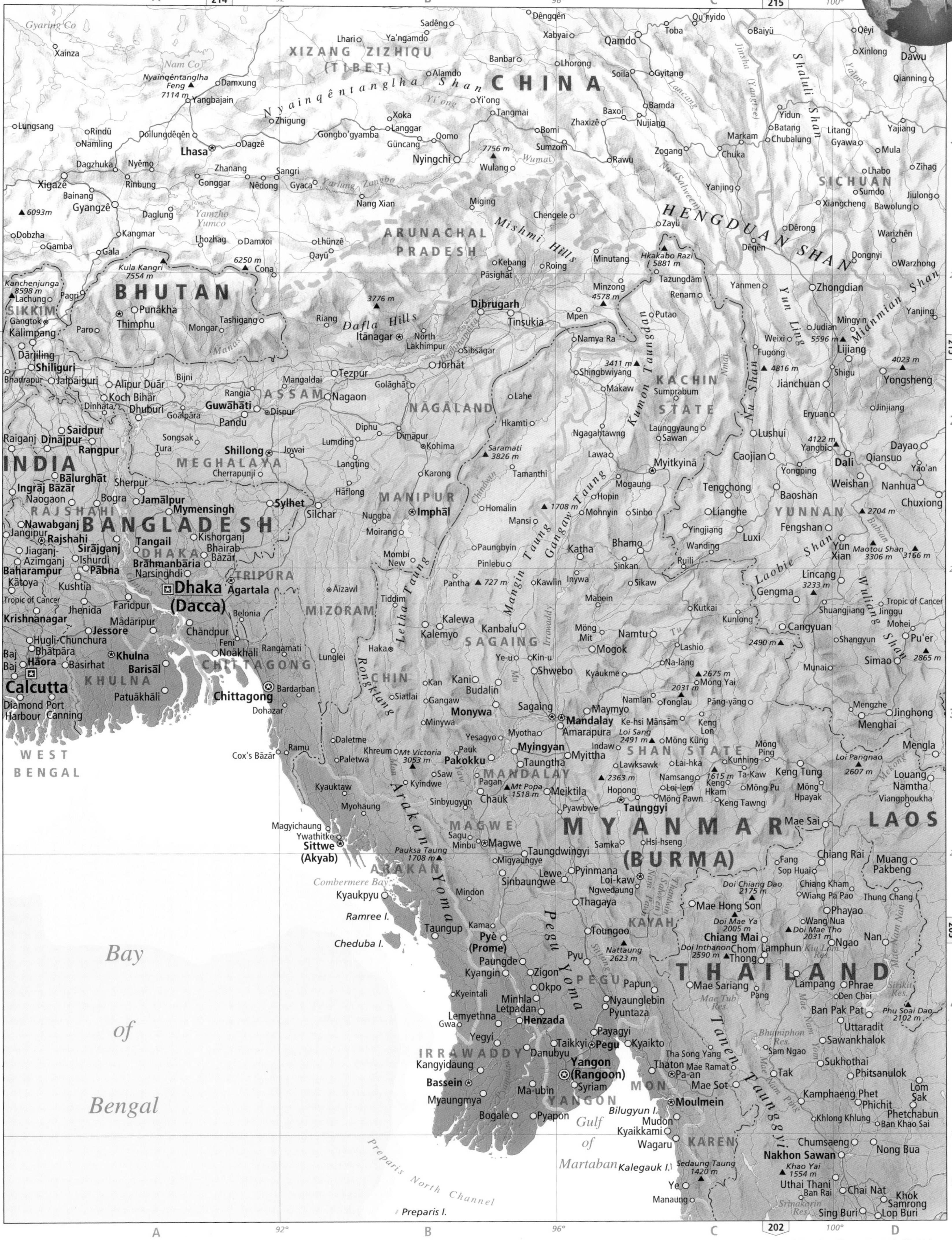

CHINA

XIZANG ZIZHIQU (TIBET)

Nyainqêntanglha Shan

Nam Co

Gyaring Co

Lhasa

Xigazê

Kanchenjunga 8598 m

BHUTAN

Kula Kangri 7554 m

Thimphu

Punākha

Paro

SIKKIM

Gangtok

Kālimpang

Dārjiling

ARUNACHAL PRADESH

Mishmi Hills

Hkakabo Razi 5881 m

HENGDUAN SHAN

SICHUAN

Dibrugarh

Tinsukia

ASSAM

Guwāhāti

Shillong

MEGHALAYA

NĀGĀLAND

Saramati 3826 m

KACHIN STATE

Myitkyinā

YUNNAN

Dali

INDIA

Rangpur

Dinājpur

Saidpur

RAJSHAHI

BANGLADESH

DHAKA

Dhaka (Dacca)

MANIPUR

Imphāl

Mangin Taung

Gangaw Taung

Bhamo

Ruili

Lincang

Tropic of Cancer

TRIPURA

Agartala

MIZORAM

CHIN

SAGAING

Shwebo

Mandalay

Monywa

SHAN STATE

Lashio

Kēng Tung

Calcutta

KHULNA

Khulna

Barisāl

CHITTAGONG

Chittagong

Cox's Bāzār

ARAKAN YOMA

Mt Victoria 3053 m

Pakokku

Pagan

Mt Popa 1518 m

Meiktila

MANDALAY

Taunggyi

LAOS

Mae Sai

WEST BENGAL

Sittwe (Akyab)

ARAKAN

MAGWE

Magwe

Minbu

MYANMAR (BURMA)

Chiang Rai

Chiang Mai

Bay

of

Bengal

Ramree I.

Cheduba I.

Taungup

Pyè (Prome)

PEGU YOMA

Toungoo

KAYAH

THAILAND

Lampang

IRRAWADDY

Henzada

PEGU

Pegu

Yangon (Rangoon)

Bassein

MON

Moulmein

YANGON

Gulf of Martaban

KAREN

TANEN TAUNGGYI

Nakhon Sawan

Preparis North Channel

Preparis I.

© Random House Australia Pty Ltd

Scale 1:7,000,000   Projection: Mercator

0 100 200 300 400 kilometers

0 100 200 miles

205

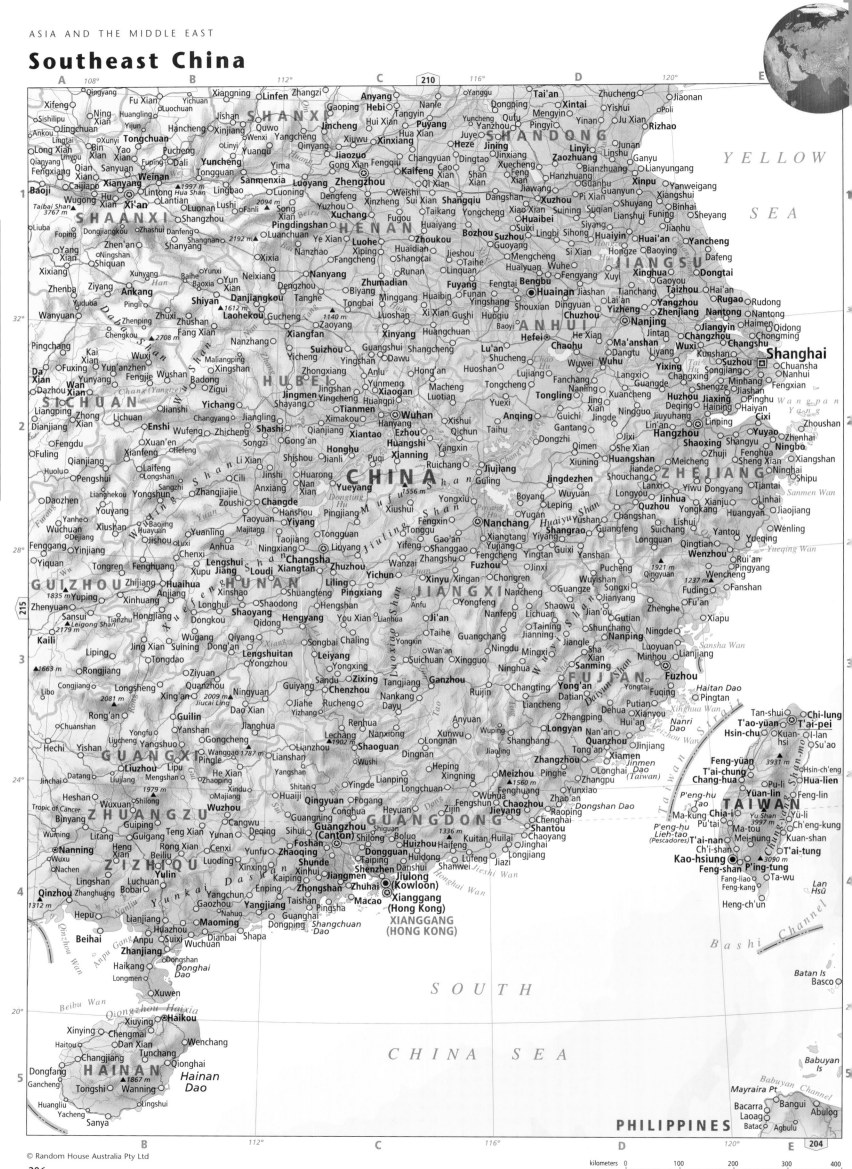

210

A   108°   B   112°   C   116°   D   120°   E

YELLOW

SEA

SHANXI

SHANDONG

SHAANXI

HENAN

JIANGSU

1

32°

SICHUAN

HUBEI

ANHUI

Shanghai

2

CHINA

ZHEJIANG

28°

GUIZHOU

HUNAN

JIANGXI

FUJIAN

TAIWAN

3

24°

GUANGXI

ZHUANGZU

ZIZHIQU

GUANGDONG

Tropic of Cancer

XIANGGANG
(HONG KONG)

4

SOUTH

20°

HAINAN
Hainan
Dao

CHINA SEA

PHILIPPINES

5

A   B   112°   C   116°   D   120°   E   204

kilometers 0   100   200   300   400

miles 0   100   200

Scale 1:7,000,000   Projection: Equidistant Conic

Xianggang (Hong Kong) and Guangdong, China

Asia and the Middle East

206

A · 113°30' · B · 114° · 206 · C · 114°30' · D

Hengshi
Fogang
Shuitou
Quingyun Shan
Lantian
Xinfengjiang
Shuiku
Dong
Heyuan
Baibu
Huangtang
1

Longshan
Tangtang
Liuxihe
Reservoir
Lütian
Longmen
Pingling
Buqian
Guzhu

Gaoqiao
Longtan
Minle
Liangkou
Zuotan
Shajing
Longhua
Luofu Shan

Aotou
Beixia
Wenquan
Yonghan
Xiniuwei
Juzi
23°30'
Jiuhe

Qigan
Conghua
Mazha
Yangcun
Guanyinge
Lantang

Huacheng
Lianglong
Tropic of Cancer
Tuiguang
Shengang
Taipingchang
Lapu Zeng
Zhengguo
Xiaolou
Shiguan
1281 m
Luofu Shan
Futian
Henghe
Ping'an
Baitang
Taimei
Dalan
Lianhua Shan
Andun

Zhuliao
Zhongluotan
Jiufo
Fuhe
Zhongxin
Zengcheng
Zhucun
Changning
Huzhen
Xiangshui
Xinzuotang
Ruhu
Hengli
2

Jianggao
Jiahe
Longyandong
Lianhe
Luogang
Yonghe
Ningxi
Yayag
Xiancun
Shitan
Tiechang
Longhua
Boluo
Dong

Shahe
Shipai
Nangang
Xintang
Zhongtang
Tangxia
Masi
Qishi
GUANGDONG
Huizhou
Pingtan
Xin'an
Duozhu

Guangzhou
(Canton)
Huangpu
Mayong
Dongguan
Chashan
Qiaotou
Chengjiang
Hai'an Shan
Renshan
Jilong

Dashi
Xinzao
Shilou
Daojiao
Baima
Liaobu
Changping
Lilin
Zhenlong
Xinxu
23°

Shatou
Panyu
(Shiqiao)
Wangniudun
Houjie
Dalang
Huangjiang
Sima
CHINA
Danshui
Xiayong
Pinghai

Shawan
Yuwotou
Huangge
Baihao
Jinjuling
Songmushan
Zhangmutou
Qingxi
Pingdio
Dajiang
Longgang
Honghai
Wan

Lanhe
Dagang
Taiping
Humen
Changan
Songgang
Gongming
Guanlan
Tiantangwei
Tangtouxia
Fonggang
Pingshan
Aotou

Rongqi
Guizhou
Tanzhou
Langwang
Nansha
Wanqingsha
Beizha
Shajing
Shiyan
591 m
Longhua
Pinghu
Henggang
Kuiyong
Daya
Wan

Dongfeng
Fusha
Gangkou
Minzhong
Hu
Wan
Fuyong
Buji
Yantian
Dashuikeng
Maliaohe

Tanbei
Zhangjiabian
Hengmen
Dao
Xin'an
Baoan
Nantou
Shenzhen
Shatoujiao
(Sha Tau Kok)
Crooked Island
Tai Pang Wan
Sanmen
Dao

Shaxi
Zhongshan
Nanlang
Shekou
Hau Hoi
Wan
Lo Wu
Sheung
Shui
Sam A Tsuen
Tap Mun
Chau
Hoi Ha
22°30'

Dayong
Huancheng
Cuihengcun
Qi'ao
Dao
Zhujiang
San Tin
Yuen
Long
573 m
Fanling
Tai Po
Shek Uk Shan
Tai Long
Tai Long Wan

Banfu
Qi'ao
Neilingding
Dao
Tuen
Mun
Shek Kong
957 m
Tai Mo Shan
Sai Kung
482 m
Pak Tam Chung

Shenwan
Xiaojia
Tangjia
Lung Kwu Tan
Sham
Tseng
Tsuen
Wan
Sha
Tin
Kau Sai
Chau
Basalt
Island

Sanxiang
Kou
Chek Lap
Kok
Ma Wan
Chung
Xianggang
(Hong Kong)
Jiulong
(Kowloon)
Tai Po Tsai
Clear Water Bay

Tanzhou
Zhuhai
Qianshan
Dai Yue Shan
(Lantau Island)
Hong Kong
Island
Chai Wan
Wong Chuk
Hang
XIANGGANG
(HONG KONG)
4

Baijiao
Nanping
Wanzai
Tai O
935 m
Shek Pik
Pui O
Wan
Cheung
Chau
351 m
Tong O
Pok Liu Chau
(Lamma Island)
Po Toi

Doumen
Macao
Niutou
Dao
Wailingding
Dao
Dangan
Dao

Xiaolin
Modao
Wan
Guishan
Dao
Zhiwan
Dao
Dangan
Liedao
22°

Sanzao
Sanzao
Dao
Tianxin
Jiu'ao
Dao
Wanshan
Qundao
Dawanshan
Dao
Beijian
Dao
SOUTH CHINA SEA

Gaolan
Dao

5

A · 113°30' · B · 114° · C · 114°30' · D · 115° · E

0 · 25 · 50 · kilometers
0 · 20 · miles
Scale 1:900,000
Projection: Equidistant Conic

Japan • Korea

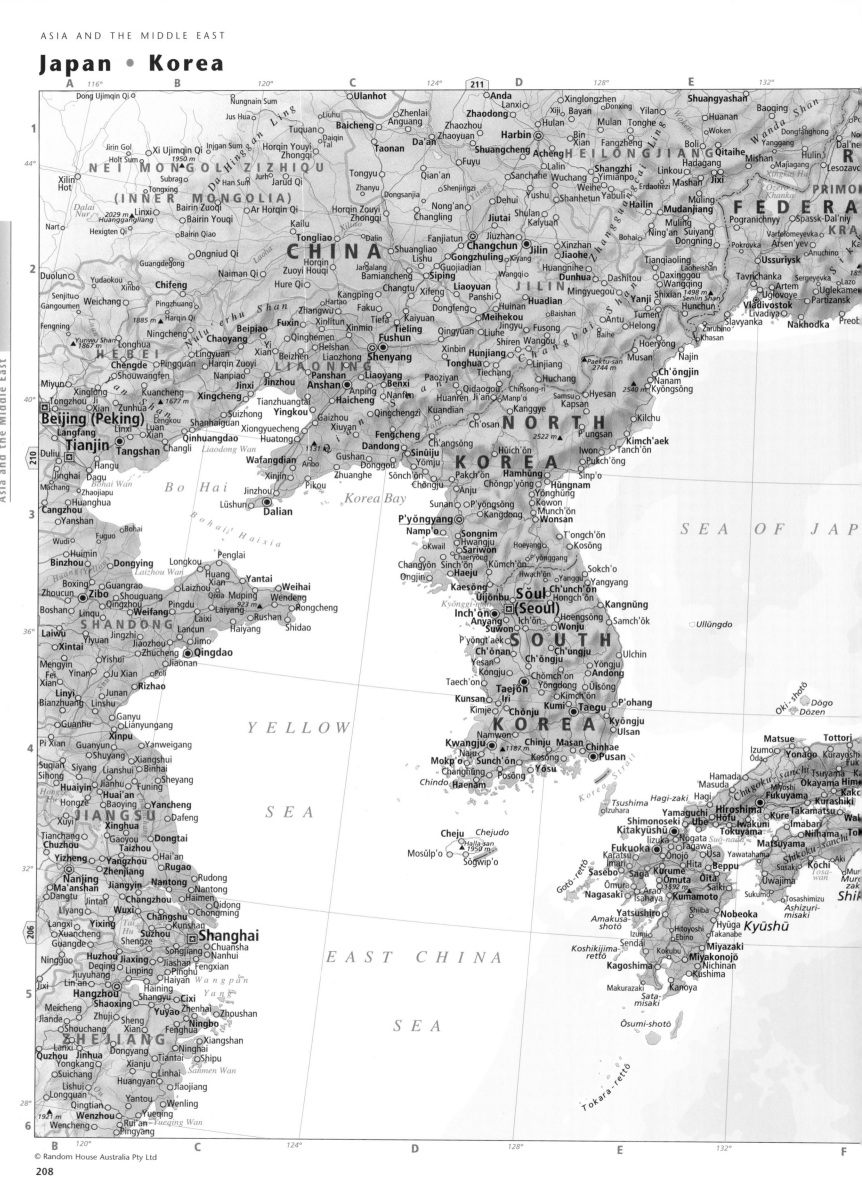

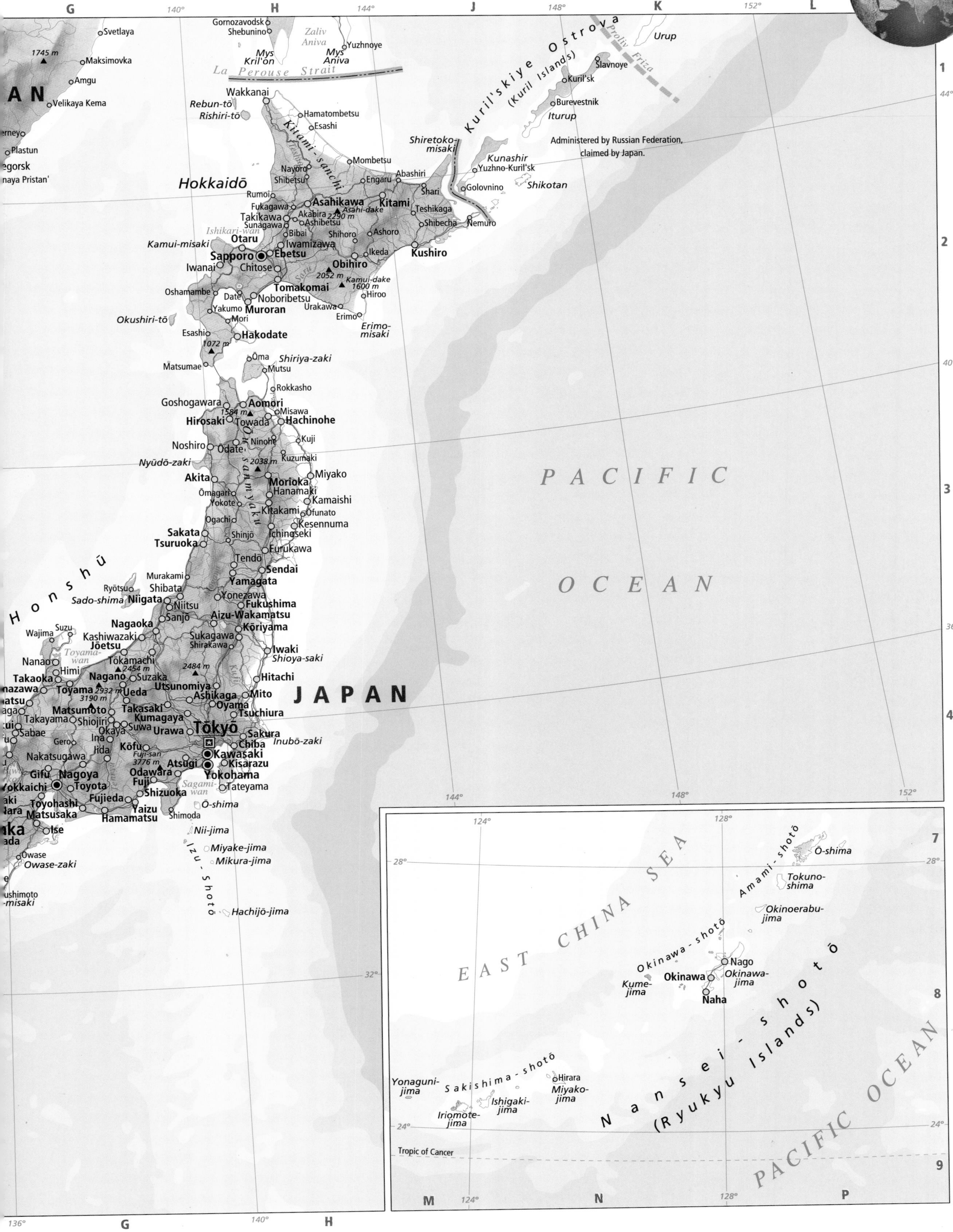

G 140° H 144° J 148° K 152° L

Svetlaya
1745 m
Maksimovka
Amgu
Velikaya Kema
erneyo
Plastun
egorsk
naya Pristan'

Gornozavodsk
Shebunino
Yuzhnoye
Zaliv Aniva
Mys Kril'on
Mys Aniva
La Perouse Strait
Wakkanai
Rebun-tō
Rishiri-tō
Hamatombetsu
Esashi
Kitami-sanchi

Kuril'skiye Ostrova
(Kuril Islands)
Proliv Friza
Urup
Slavnoye
Kuril'sk
Burevestnik
Iturup

Hokkaidō
Nayoro
Shibetsu
Mombetsu
Engaru
Abashiri
Shiretoko-misaki
Kunashir
Yuzhno-Kuril'sk
Golovnino
Shikotan

Administered by Russian Federation,
claimed by Japan.

Rumoi
Asahikawa
Kitami
Takikawa
Akabira 2290 m Asahi-dake
Fukagawa
Sunagawa
Ashibetsu
Ashoro
Shibecha
Teshikaga
Shari
44°
Bibai
Shihoro
Ishikari-wan
Otaru
Kamui-misaki
Iwamizawa
Ikeda
Kushiro
Sapporo
Ebetsu
Obihiro
Iwanai
Chitose
2052 m
Kamui-dake
Oshamambe
Tomakomai
Date
Noboribetsu
Hiroo
Okushiri-tō
Yakumo
Muroran
Urakawa
1600 m
Mori
Erimo
Esashi
Hakodate
Erimo-misaki
1072 m
Matsumae
Ōma
Shiriya-zaki
Mutsu
Rokkasho
40°
Goshogawara
Aomori
Misawa
1584 m
Hirosaki
Towada
Hachinohe
Noshiro
Ninohe
Kuji
Ōu-sanmyaku
Odate
2038 m
Kuzumaki
Akita
Morioka
Miyako
Ōmagari
Hanamaki
Yokote
Kamaishi
Sakata
Ogachi
Kitakami
Ōfunato
Tsuruoka
Shinjō
Ichinoseki
Kesennuma
Tendō
Furukawa
Murakami
Yamagata
Sendai
Ryōtsu
Shibata
Sado-shima
Niigata
Yonezawa
Fukushima
Nagaoka
Niitsu
Aizu-Wakamatsu
Sanjo
Kōriyama
Kashiwazaki
Sukagawa
Iwaki
Jōetsu
Shirakawa
Shioya-saki
Tokamachi
2454 m
Takaoka
Himi
Suzaka
2484 m
Hitachi
Nanao
Nagano
Suzu
Wajima
Toyama 2932 Ueda
3190 m
Utsunomiya
Mito
Matsumoto
Ashikaga
Takayama
Shiojiri
Takasaki
Oyama
Tsuchiura
Okaya
Kumagaya
Ina
Suwa
Sakura
Nakatsugawa
Kōfu
Urawa
Tōkyō
Chiba
Fuji-san
Inubō-zaki
Gifu
Nagoya
3776 m
Atsugi
Kawasaki
Kisarazu
okkaichi
Toyota
Odawara
Yokohama
ara
Fuji
Tateyama
Matsusaka
Fujieda
Shizuoka
Sagami-wan
Ise
Yaizu
Hamamatsu
Shimoda
Ō-shima
Owase
Nii-jima
Owase-zaki
Miyake-jima
ushimoto
Mikura-jima
misaki
Izu-shotō
Hachijō-jima

Honshū

JAPAN

PACIFIC

OCEAN

36°

52°

144° 148° 152°

124° 128°

28° Ō-shima 28°
EAST CHINA SEA
Amami-shotō
Tokuno-shima
Okinoerabu-jima
Nago
Okinawa
Okinawa-jima
Kume-jima
Naha
Nansei-shotō
(Ryukyu Islands)
32°
Yonaguni-jima
Sakishima-shotō
Hirara
Miyako-jima
Iriomote-jima
Ishigaki-jima
24° 24°
Tropic of Cancer
PACIFIC OCEAN

M 124° N 128° P

7

8

9

G 136° G 140° H

0 100 200 300 400 kilometers
0 100 200 miles
Scale 1:7,000,000
Projection: Equidistant Conic

Asia and the Middle East

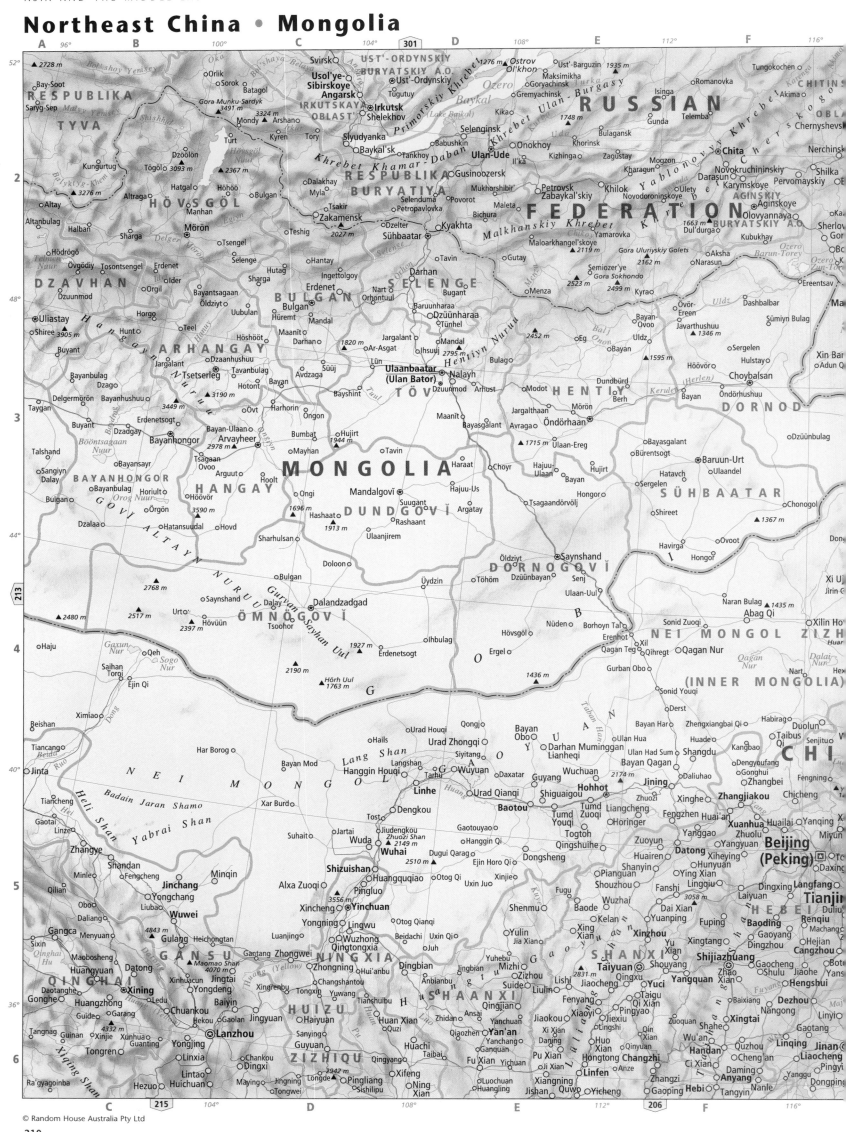

301

Asia and the Middle East

SEA OF JAPAN

YELLOW SEA

Bo Hai

Korea Bay

NORTH KOREA

SOUTH KOREA

JAPAN

HEILONGJIANG

JILIN

LIAONING

AMURSKAYA OBLAST'

KHABAROVSKIY KRAY

YEVREYSKAYA AVTONOMNAYA OBLAST'

PRIMORSKIY KRAY

208

Scale 1:7,000,000
Projection: Equidistant Conic

0   100   200   300   400 kilometers
0   100   200 miles

Northwest China • East Kazakhstan • Mongolia

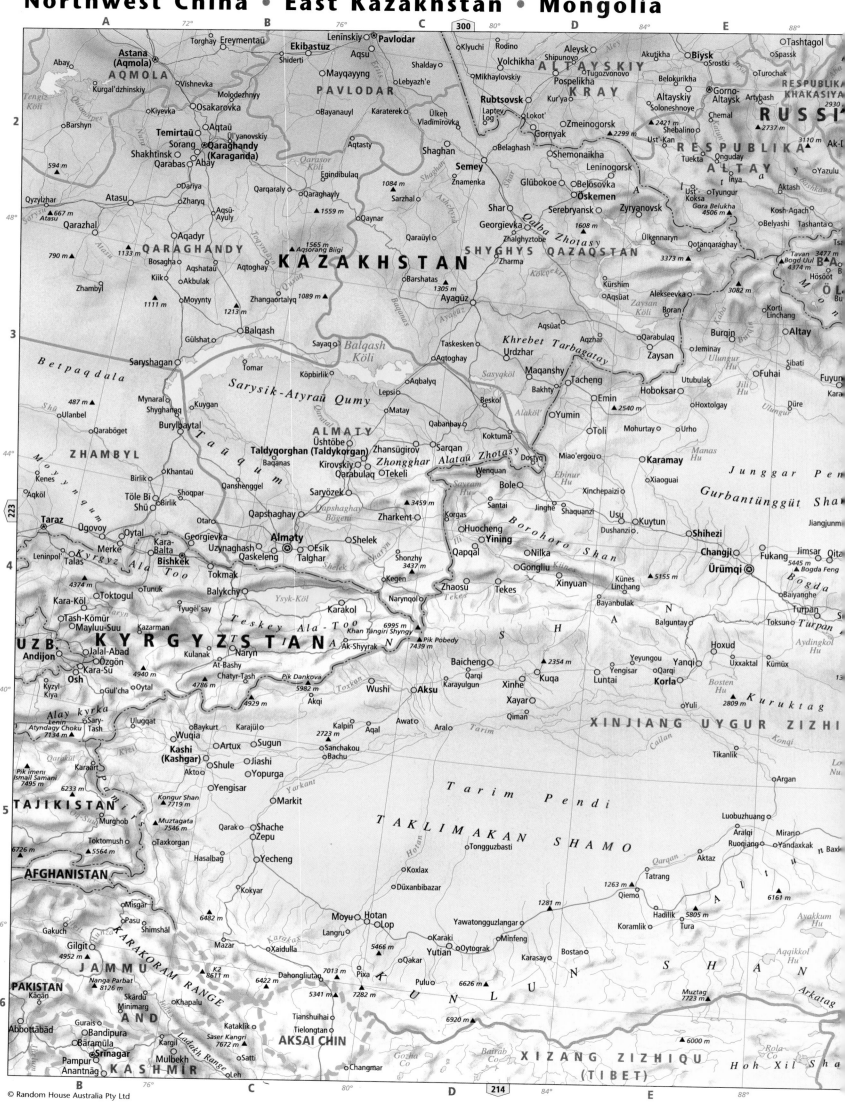

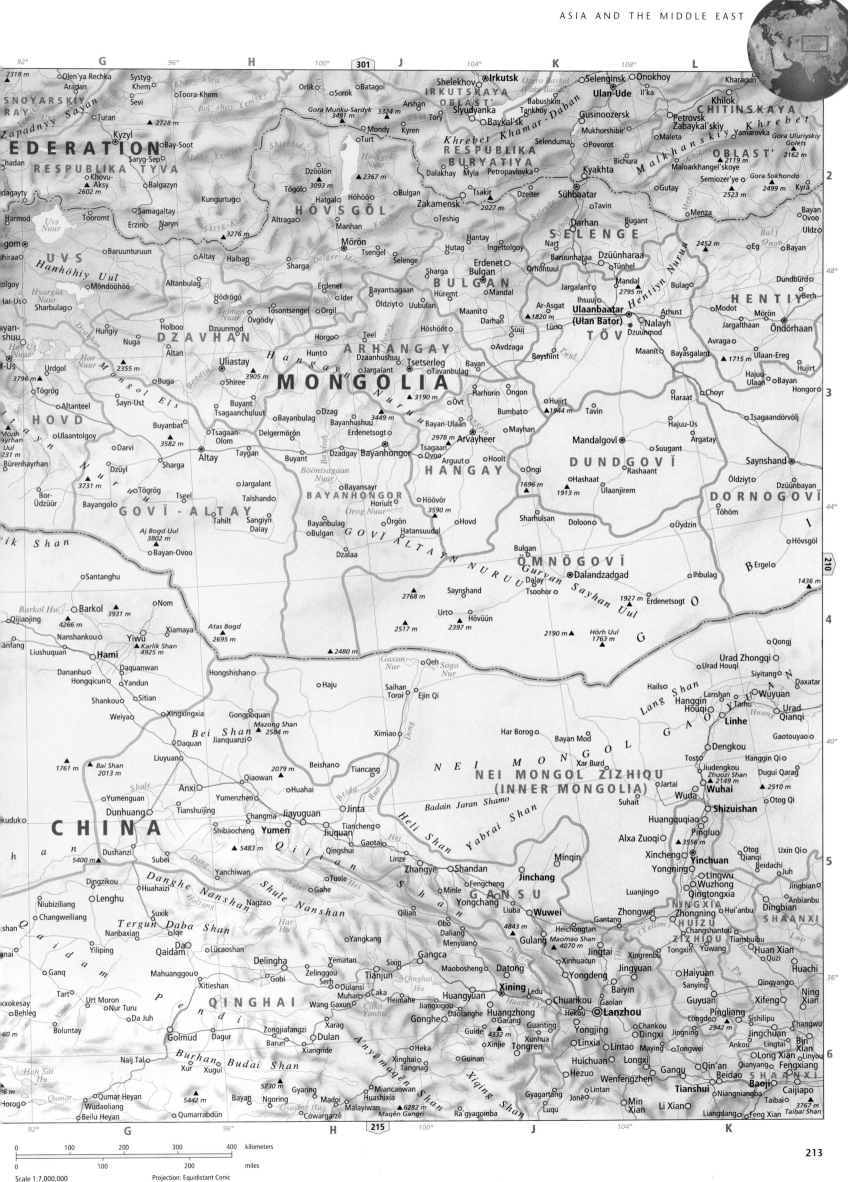

0   100   200   300   400   kilometers

0   100   200   miles

Scale 1:7,000,000   Projection: Equidistant Conic

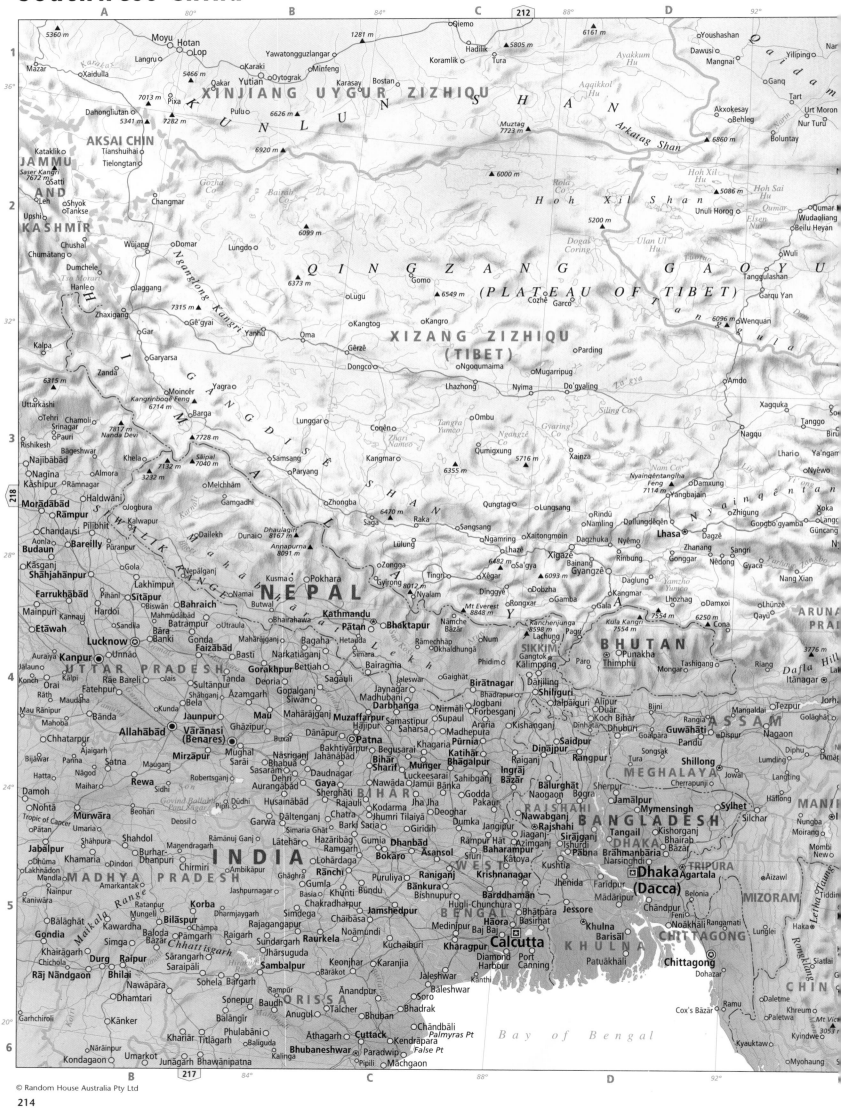

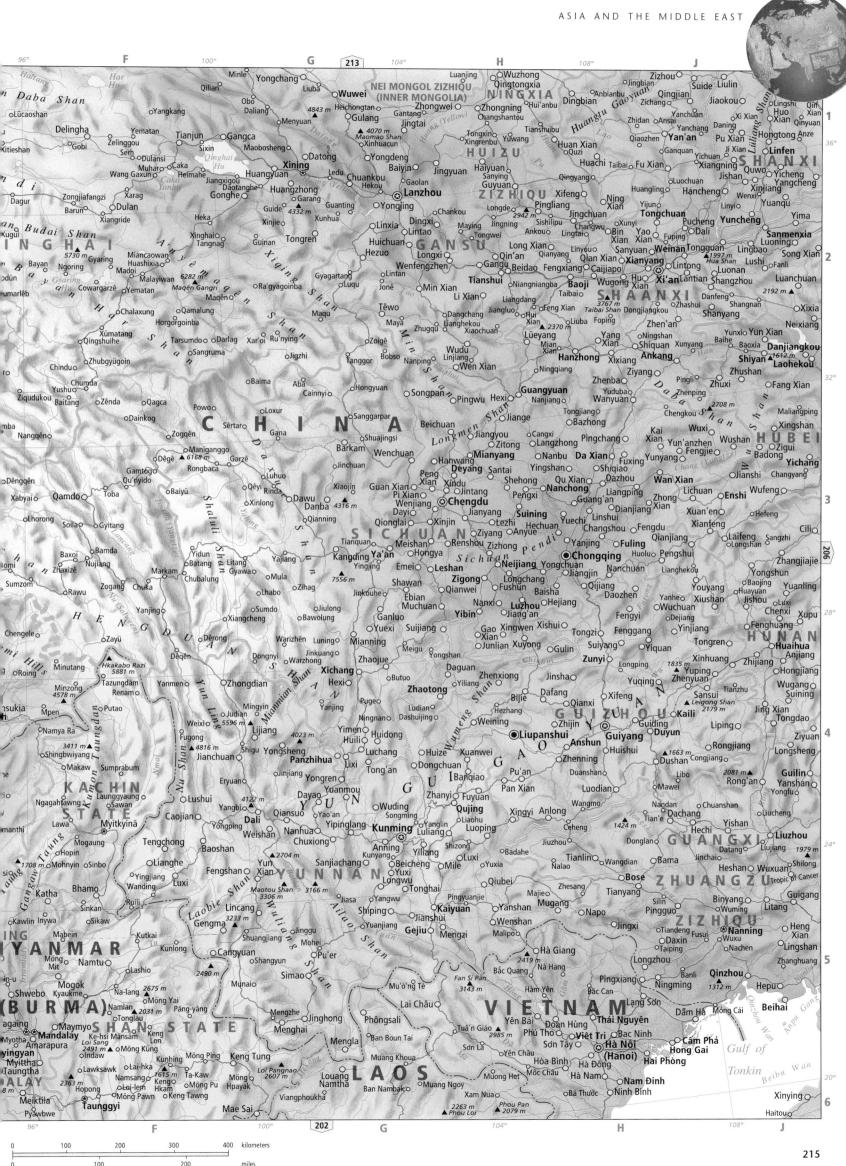

Asia and the Middle East

215

Scale 1:7,000,000   Projection: Equidistant Conic

0   100   200   300   400 kilometers

0   100   200 miles

South India • Sri Lanka

A 68° **B** 72° **C** 76° **D** 80°

218

GUJARĀT

Rānāvāv • Porbandar • Bāntva • Kutiyana • Keshod • Junāgadh • Amreli • Māngrol • Gīr Hills • Kundla • Mahuva • Verāval • Kodīnar • Diu • Una • Delvāda

Bhāvnagar • Bharūch • Rājpīpla • Barwāni • Julwānia • Dediāpāda • Shāhāda • Surat • Navsāri • Bilimora • Vyāra • Vānsada • Valsād • Dharampur • Māndvi • Nandurbār • Shirpur • Burhānpur • Khargon • Harisāl • Multai • Pāndhurna • Gondia • Bhandāra

Seoni

MADHYA PRADESH

DAMĀN AND DIU • DAMĀN AND DIU • Daman

DĀDRA AND NAGAR HAVELI

Dhule • Jālgaon • Bhusāwal • Malkāpur • Akot • Achalpur • Amrāvati • Warud • Kāmthi • Nāgpur • Bori • Umred

Nāsik • Manmād • Satāna • Malegaon • Ajanta • Buldāna • Pārola • Mangrūl Pir • Dārwha • Wardha • Hinganghāt • Warora • Chandrapur

Deolāli • Aurangābād • Bhokardan • Kalamnūr • Jagtiāl • Karimnagar

Bhiwandi • Thāne • Ulhāsnagar • Amarnāth • Kalyān
Mumbai (Bombay) • Pimpri-Chinchwad • Kirkee • Pune • Bhor • Bārāmati • Satāra • Karād • Sāngli • Kolhāpur • Ichalkaranji • Rājapur

ARABIAN SEA

MAHĀRĀSHTRA

INDIA

Gevrai • Parbhani • Nānded • Ahmadnagar • Bīr • Parli • Ahmadpur • Nizāmābād

Yermala • Lātūr • Udgir • Diglūr • Sirsilla • Siddipet • Venkatāp

Bārsi • Osmānābād • Bidar • Zahirābād • Dudada • Waran

Tembhurni • Taljāpur • Homnābād • Sadāseopet • Secunderābād • Hyderābād

Daund • Nira • Murud • Dāpoli • Guhāgar • Mhāsvad • Sāngola • Solāpur • Akalkot • Chincholi • Gulbarga • Vikārābād • Korangal • Suriapet

ANDHRA PRADESH

Ratnāgiri • Hatkamba • Nagaj • Dudhani • Seram • Mahbūbnagar

Tikota • Bijāpur • Shāhpur • Yādgir • Nāgarjuna Sāgar

Miraj • Jamkhandi • Tālikota • Raichūr • Emmiganūru • Kurnool • Mārkāpur • Darsi • Chilak

Mālvan • Chikodi • Mudhol • Bāgalkot • Sindhnūr • Ādoni • Nandyāl • Kanigiri • Giddalūr

Sāvantvādi • Nipāni • Hukeri • Yargatti • Kushtagi • Ālūr • Proddatūr • Kandukūr • Kāvali • Duttalūru

Vengurla • Belgaum • Nargund • Gadag-Betgeri • Hospet • Guntakal • Allagadda

Panaji • Dandeli • Hubli • Bellary • Cuddapah • 1105 m • Muttukūru • Gūdūr

GOA • Mārmagao • Kārwār • Hāveri • Rānibennur • Kalyāndrug • Anantapur • Tadpatri • Kadiri • Durgarājupatnam • Nāyudu

Ankola • Sirsi • Harihar • Dāvangere • Pāvagada • Penukonda • Hindupur • Madanapalle • Tirupati

Kumta • Hirekerūr • Holalkere • Hiriyūr • Sira • Gauribidanūr • Chintāmani • Chittoor • Thir • Arkonam

Bhatkal • Channagiri • Shimoga • Bhadrāvati • Tiptūr • Tumkūr • Kolār • Bangalore • Gudiyattam • Vellore • Ch (Ma)

KARNĀTAKA • WESTERN GHATS • EASTERN GHATS

Coondapoor • Koppa • Kārkal • Chikmagalūr • Hassan • Channapatna • Kolār Gold Fields • Kānchipuram

Udipi • Saklespur • Mandya • Krishnagiri • Tiruvannāmalai

Mangalore • Bantvāl • Puttūr • Kushālnagar • Mysore • Malavalli • Javādi Hills

Kāsaragod • Hosdrug • Nanjangud • Chāmrājnagar • 1514 m

Cannanore • Mahe • Udagamandalam • Salem • Attūr • Neyveli • Cud

TAMIL NĀDU • PONDICHERRY

Lakshadweep Is (Laccadive Is) • Amindivi Is • Chetlat I. • Kiltān I. • Kadamatt I. • Agatti I. • Āndrott I. • Kavaratti I.

PONDICHERRY • Badagara • Erode • Nāmakkal • Perambalūr • Chid

LAKSHADWEEP • Manjeri • Mettuppālaiyam • Turaiyūr

Kozhikode (Calicut) • Ponnāni • Coimbatore • Tiruppur • Tiruchchirāppalli • Kumba • PONDIC

Suheli I. • Kalpeni I. • Shoranur • Pollachi • Kiranūr • Thanjāvūr

Cannanore Is • Palghāt • Trichūr • Vālpārai • Pudukkottai

KERALA • Munnar • Dindigul • Nattam • Kāraikkudi

Angamāli • Allinagaram • Melūr • Sivaganga • Palk

Kochi (Cochin) • Kottayam • Madurai • Tondi • Jaffna • Chāva

Alleppey • Rājapālaiyam • Aruppukkottai • Rāmanāthapuram

Kāyankulam • Kadaiyanallur • Sankarankovil • Sattūr • Medawa • Anurād

Kollam (Quilon) • Punalur • Tirunelveli • Tuticorin • Vilātikkulam • Mannar I.

Nedumangād • Palayankottai • Mannar I. • Talai

Thiruvananthapuram (Trivandrum) • Melapalawam

Neyyāttinkara • Nāgercoil • Tisaiyānvilai • Gulf of Mannar

Cape Comorin • Kanniyākumāri • Medawa

ANDHRA PRADESH

12°

16°

20°

1 • 2 • 3

Maldives inset (left):

B 72° **C**

Eight Degree Channel

Tiladummati Atoll

Miladummadulu Atoll

Malosmadulu Atoll • Faadhippolhu Atoll

MALDIVES • Male Atoll • Male

Ari Atoll

Felidu Atoll

Nilande Atoll

Kolumadulu Atoll • Mulaku Atoll

Haddunmahti Atoll

Huvadu Atoll

Equator 0°

Addu Atoll

5 • 6 • 7

B 72° **C**

Maldives inset (right / lower):

72°

12° • Chetlat I. • Kilttān I. • Kadamatt I.

8°

Eight Degree Channel

Tiladummati Atoll

MALDIVES

Miladummadulu Atoll

Malosmadulu Atoll • Faadhippolhu Atoll

INDIAN

Male Atoll • Male

4° • Ari Atoll

C 72° **D** 76°

Nine Degree Channel

Minicoy I.

One and Half Degree Channel

INDIAN

Sri Lanka eastern labels:
Chilaw • Kuru • Negombo • Colombo • Dehiwala-Mount Lavinia • Sri Jayawardanapura-Kotte • Moratuwa • Kalutara • Puttalam Lagoon

E | 84° | F | 88° | 219 | G | 92° | H

Chhattisgarh
Pāmgarh   Jhārsuguda   Jhārsuguda   Keōnjhar   Soro   Bāleshwar   Kyauktaw   Sinbyugyun
Baloda   Sārangarh   Bārākot   Keōnjhar   Myohaung   Sagu   Minbu   Magwe
Saraipāli   Bargarh   Ānandpur   Bhadrak   Magyichaung   Ywathitke   Migyaungye   Taungdwingyi
ur Bāzār   Sohela   Sambalpur   Rampūr   Tālcher   Bhuban   Sittwe   Pauksa Taung   MYANMAR
Nawāpāra   Sonepur   Baudh   Ānugul   Āthagarh   Jājapur   Kendrāpara   Palmyras Pt   (Akyab)   1708 m
Dhamtari   Balāngir   Phulabāni   Cuttack   False Pt   Oyster I.   ARAKAN (BURMA)
    Titlāgarh   Baligu   Kalinga   Paradwip   Combermere Bay   Kyaukpyu   Mindon   Kama   PEGU
Khariār   Khallikot   Āsika   Māchgaon   Ramree I.   Pyè
Junāgarh   Bhawānipatna   Baliguda   Chatrapur   Konārak   Taungup   (Prome)
Umarkot   Puri   Cheduba I.   Kyangin   Paungde   Zigon
    ORISSA   Brahmapur   Chatrapur   1076 m   Okpo
agaon   Pāppadāhāndi   Gunupur   Kyeintali   Minhla
anpal   Jagdalpur   Parlākimidi   Henzada   Letpadan
    Jaypur   Palkonda   Narasannapeta   Gwa   Yegyi   Lemyethna
ndul   Mālkāngiri   Srikākulam   Kangyidaung   Danubyu
    Anakāpalle   Vizianagaram   IRRAWADDY   Ma-ubin
ru   Krishnadēvipeta   Waltair   Bassein   Myaungmya
    Vishākhapatnam   Bogale
    Tuni
    Rājahmundry   GHATS
egūdem   Kākināda
mavaram   Yanam   PONDICHERRY
    Pālakollu
    Narasapur
chilīpatnam
Chirāla

Bay

of

Bengal

Preparis North Channel

Preparis I.

Preparis South Channel

Great Coco I.   Little Coco I.
Coco Channel
Landfall I.   C. Price

North   Saddle Peak
Andaman   738 m
    Pahlāgaon

Middle
Andaman

South
Andaman   Port Blair
    Rutland I.
    ANDAMAN AND
Duncan Passage   NICOBAR ISLANDS
Nachuge   Little
    Andaman
    Andaman Is

Ten Degree Channel

Car Nicobar I.   Kakana

Andaman and Nicobar Islands (India)

Tarasa Dwip I.   Camorta I.
    Misha
Nicobar Is

Sombrero Channel
Little Nicobar

Bananga
Great Nicobar

Trincomalee
Mutur

RI

NKA
Batticaloa
lagata   Amparai
Senanayake   Pottuvil
Samudra
Wellawaya
pe

Hambantota
Head

O   C   E   A   N

E | 84° | F | 88° | G | 92° | H

0   100   200   300   400   kilometers
0   100   200   miles
Scale 1:7,000,000   Projection: Equidistant Conic

20°

2

214

16°

3

12°

4

8°

5

4°

6

Asia and the Middle East

North India • Pakistan • Nepal

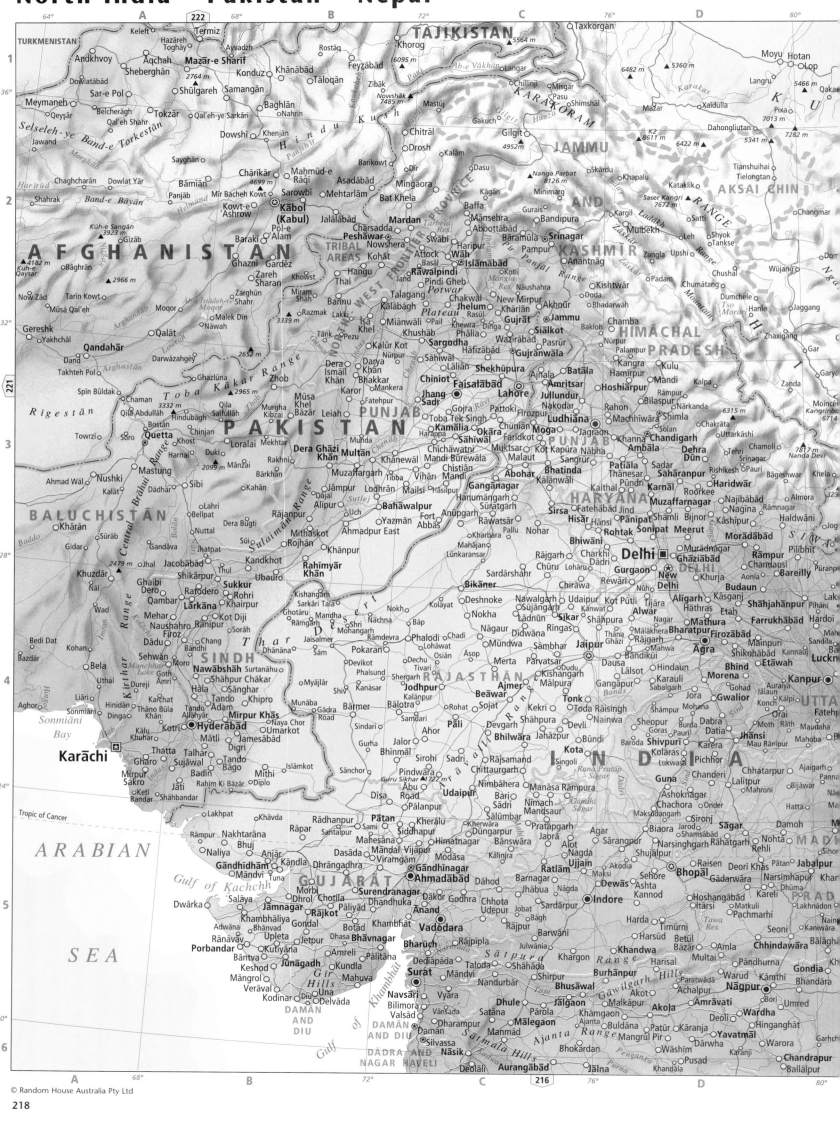

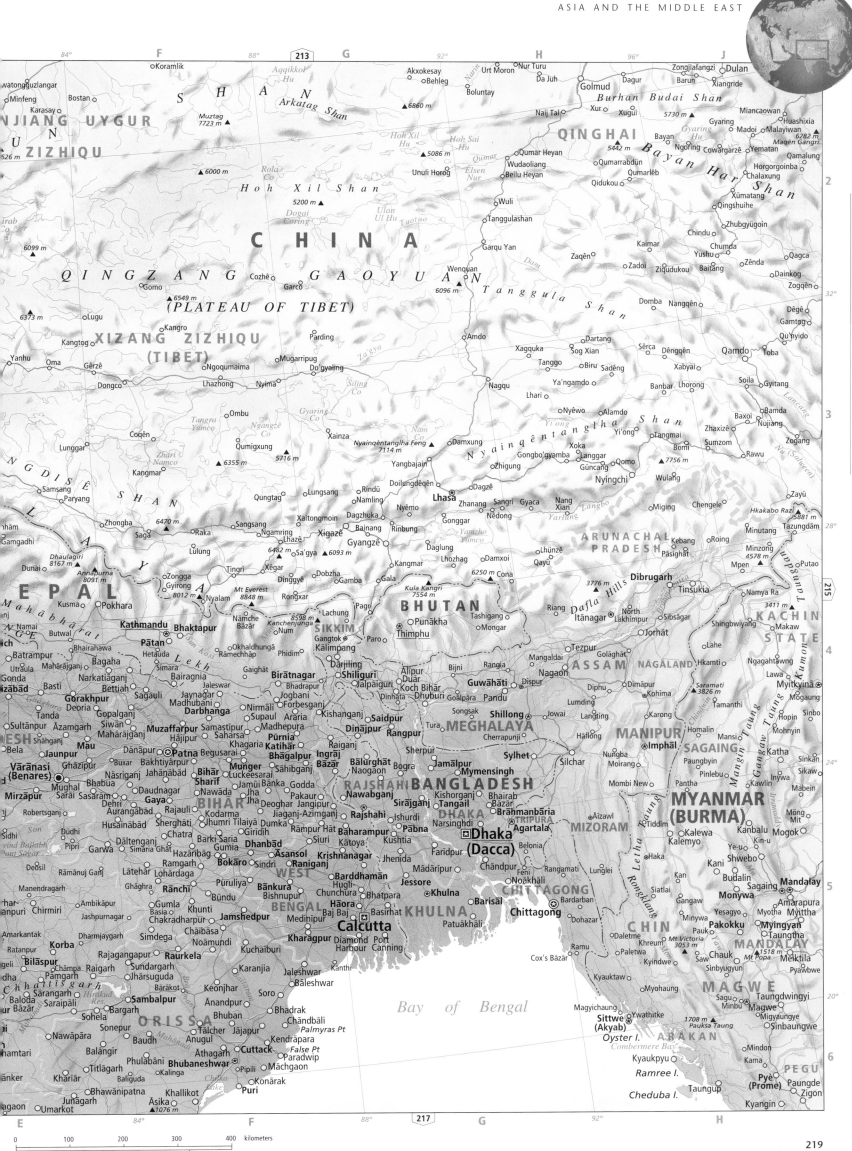

0   100   200   300   400 kilometers
0   100   200 miles
Scale 1:7,000,000   Projection: Equidistant Conic

Middle East

MEDITERRANEAN SEA

CYPRUS

LEBANON

ISRAEL

SYRIA

IRAQ

JORDAN

EGYPT

SAUDI ARABIA

KUWAIT

BAHRAIN

QATAR

RED SEA

SUDAN

Nubian Desert

ERITREA

ETHIOPIA

DJIBOUTI

YEMEN

CASPIAN

Persian Gulf

Gulf of Aden

Ar Rub' al Khālī

An Nafūd

Bādiyat ash Shām (Syrian Desert)

Selected place names:
Anamur, Silifke, İskenderun, Antakya (Antioch), Kilis, Akçakale, Cizre, Al Qāmishlī, Orūmīyeh (Urmia), Benāb, Mīāneh, Bandar-e Anzalī, Rasht, Lefkosia (Nicosia), Al Lādhiqīyah (Latakia), Manbij, Halab (Aleppo), Ar Raqqah, Al Ḥasakah, Dahūk, Heydarābād, Marāgheh, Zanjān, Sakht-Sar, Tonekābon, Ammochostos (Famagusta), Larnaka, Ḥamāh, Ma'arrat an Nu'mān, Dayr az Zawr, Al Mawṣil (Mosul), Rawāndūz, Arbīl, Takāb, Divān Darreh, Abhar, Hashtgerd, Karaj, Tehrān (Teheran)

Ḥimṣ (Homs), Al Qaryatayn, Al Mayādīn, Abū Kamāl, Ash Sharqāṭ, Kirkūk, As Sulaymānīyah, Ṭūz Khurmātū, Sanandaj, Kabūdarāhang, Qazvīn

Dimashq (Damascus), As Suwaydā', At Tanf, Ar Ramādī, Baghdād, Karbalā', An Najaf, Al Kūfah, Al Ḥillah, Kermānshāh, Hamadān, Malāyer, Arāk, Qom

Bayrūt (Beirut), Ṣaydā (Sidon), Ṣūr (Tyre), Hefa (Haifa), Irbid, Dar'ā, Amman, Yerushalayim (Jerusalem), Al Karak, IRAQ, An Nāṣirīyah, Al Başrah (Basra), KUWAIT, Al Kuwayt (Kuwait)

Al Iskandarīya (Alexandria), Al Qāhirah (Cairo), Al Jīzah, Banī Suwayf, Al Minyā, Asyūṭ, Sūhāj, Qinā, Al Uqṣur (Luxor), Aswān

Tabūk, Al Wajh, Al 'Ulā, Ḥā'il, Buraydah, 'Unayzah, Al Madīnah (Medina), Ar Riyāḍ (Riyadh), Ad Dammām (Dhahran), Al Manāmah, Ad Dawḥah (Doha)

Jiddah (Jedda), Makkah (Mecca), Aṭ Ṭā'if, Al Qunfudhah, Abhā, Khamīs Mushayṭ, Najrān, Ṣa'dah, Şan'ā', Al Ḥudaydah, Ta'izz, 'Adan (Aden)

Būr Sūdān (Port Sudan), 'Aṭbara, Kassalā, Asmara, Wad Medanī, Al Qaḍārif, Bahir Dar, Gonder, ETHIOPIA, Djibouti

G · 60° · H · 65° · 222 · J · 70° · K · 75° · L

TURKMENISTAN

Mashhad · Bayramaly · Mary · Jolotan' · Mazār-e Sharif · Konduz · Tāloqān · Nowshāk 7485 m · Mastūj · Gakuch · Gilgit · K2 8611 m · Saser Kangri 7672 m · Kataklik

Āndkhvoy · Sheberghān · Baghlān · Nahrin · Hindu Kush · Chitrāl · Kalam · Skārdu · Nanga Parbat · JAMMU

Qūchān · Esfarāyen · Dāvarzan · Dushak · Tejen · Sandykgachy · Tashkepri · Dowlatābād · Sar-e Pol · Dowshī · Barikowt · Mingãora · Kāghãn · Mānsehra · Bāramūla · Srinagar · Anantnāg · Leh · Tankse · Chushal

Bojnūrd · Gonbad-e Qābūs · Babadurmaz

Sabsevār · Neyshābūr · Tagtabazar · Qeyşãr · Meymaneh · Chārikār · Sārowbī · Chārsadda · Mardan · Abbottābād · AND KASHMIR

Kāshmar · Torbat-e Ḥeydarīyeh · Ţayyebāt · Asadābād · Bālā Morghāb · Bāmiān · Kābol (Kabul) · Jalālābād · Peshāwar · Wāh · Islāmābād · Rāwalpindi · Jammu · Nūrpur · Kangra · Kulu

Ferdows · Shūrāb · Ghūriān · HERĀT · Shahrak · Chaghchārān · Panjāb · Barakī · Hangu · Kohāt · Pindi Gheb · Jhelum · Wazirābād · Mandi · Rāmpur

Bajestān · Deyhūk · Mandel · Shindand · Baghrān · Zarghūn Shahr · Miram Shāh · Razmak · Ţānk · Talagang · Miānwāli · Sargodha · Gujrānwāla · Amritsar · Shimla

Bāyāzīyeh · Posht-e Bādām · Anār Darreh · Farāh 2560 m · Delārām · Now Zād · Mūsá Qal'eh · Gereshk · Nāwah · Khushāb · Shekhūpura · Lahore · Ludhiāna · Chandigarh · Dehra Dūn

AFGHANISTAN · Qalāt · Darwāzagēy · Ghazlūna · Dera Ismaīl Khān · Karor · Chiniot · Faisalābād · Moga · Ambāla · Sahāranpur · Karnāl

Kūh-e Nāy Band 2992 m · Nāy Band · Sar Bisheh · QANDAHĀR · Toba Kākar Range · Zhob · Leiah · Multan · Gojra · Okāra · Sāhiwāl · Abohar · Sirsa · Meerut · Ghāziābād · Delhi · New Delhi

Dasht-e Lūt · Zābol · Lūţak · Dasht-e Mārgow · Takhteh Pol · Spin Būldak · Chaman · Bostān · Khost · Bārkhan · Rājanpur · Bahāwalpur · Anūpgarh · Rājgarh · Chūru · Rewari · Bikāner · Sīkar · Alwar

Kermān · Noşratābād · Deh Shū · Rūdbār · Rīgestān · Helmand · Quetta · Mastung · Sibi · Dādhar · Bellpat · Ahmadpur East · Khānpur · Lūnkaransar · Deshnoke · Nāgaur · Dīdwāna · Jaipur

Zāhedān · Saindak · Dālbandin · 3007 m · Nushki · Kalāt · Nokh · Nāchna · Bāp · Merta · Nāinwa

Kāhnūj · Bam · Shūr-e Gaz · Mirjāveh · Khārān · Nok Kundi · Gandāva · Jhatpat · Shikārpur · Sukkur · Rohri · Phalodi · Mūndwa · Parvatsar · Ajmer · Tonk · Būndi · Kota

Khāsh · Kārvāndar · Khuzdar · Jhal · Khairpur · Jaisalmer · Lohāwat · Jodhpur · Beāwar · Devli

Sarāvān · Esfandak · Nāl · Wad · Moro · Dādu · Sānghar · Bārmer · Bālotra · Pāli · Devgarh · Bhilwāra

Tūrānshahr · Bampūr · Panjgūr · Bazdar · Bela · Kohān · Nawābshāh · Munāba · Gadra Road · Gurha · Jalor · Sirohi · Udaipur · Chittaurgarh

Nikshahr · Rāsk · Bāhū Kalāt · Polāno · Pidarak · Turbat · Hoshāb · Uthal · Liāri · Kotri · Hyderābād · Tando Adam · Mirpur Khās · Digri · Bhīnmal · Sānchor · Abu Road · Mandsaur · INDIA

Bandar-e 'Abbās · Mīnāb · Jāsk · Sadich · Ḥūmedān · Chābahar · Jiwani · Gwādar · Pasni · Ormāra · Sonmiāni Bay · Gharo · Thatta · Badin · Khāvda · Rāpar · Pālanpur · Dūngarpur · Banswāra · Jaora · Ujjain

Strait of Hormuz · Jabal Yibir 1527 m · Al Khasab · Gulf of Oman · Gwatar Bay · Karāchi · Mirpur Sakro · Jāti · Lakhpat · Nakhtarāna · Bhuj · Mahesāna · Gāndhinagar · Ratlām · Dewās · Indore

Şuḩār · Al Khābūrah · Gulf of Kachchh · Naliya · Mundra · Morbī · Dhrāngadhra · Dākor · Jhābua · Khargon

Masqat (Muscat) · 'Ibrī · Ḥarah · Al Hajar · Dwārka · Jāmnagar · Surendranagar · Pāliyād · Anand · Vadodara · Rājpipla · Barwāni · Julwānia

Jabal ash Shām 3019 m · Ibrā · Nizwā · Şūr · Ra's al Ḥadd · Sālāya · Rājkot · Gondal · Bhāvnagar · Bhārūch · Bhusāwal

Al Kāmil · Porbandar · Bāntva · Gīr Hills · Amreli · Surat · Navsari · Dhule · Jālgaon

OMAN · Dawwah · Jazīrat Maşīrah · Mangrol · Veraval · Kodinar · Diu · Mahuva · Valsād · Daman · Silvassa · Nāsik · Malegaon · Aurangābād

Khalūfo · Mānmād · Deolāli · Sārmala Hills · Ahmadnagar · Gevrai

Haymā' · Jiddat al Ḥarāsīs · Khalīj Maşīrah · Bhiwandi · Thāne · Ulhāsnagar · Pune · Daund · Bārsi

Ra's al Madrakah · Mumbai (Bombay) · Murud · Bhor · Bārāmati · Pandharpur

Ghubbat Şawqirah · Dāpoli · Guhāgar · Sātāra · Nāgaj

ARABIAN SEA · Ratnāgiri · Hatkamba · Karād · Sāngli · Kolhāpur · Miraj · Ichalkaranji · Belgaum

Jazā'ir Khurīyā Murīyā (Kuria Muria Is) · Rājapur · Mālvan · Sāvantvādi · Dandeli

Ḥāsik · Ra's Naws · Şadḥ · Mirbāţ · Panaji · Marmagao · WESTERN GHATS · Kārwār · Ankola · Kumta · Bhatkal

Laccadive Is

221

Scale 1:10,000,000 · Projection: Equidistant Conic
0 100 200 300 400 kilometers
0 100 200 miles

Asia and the Middle East

Kazakhstan • Republics of Central Asia

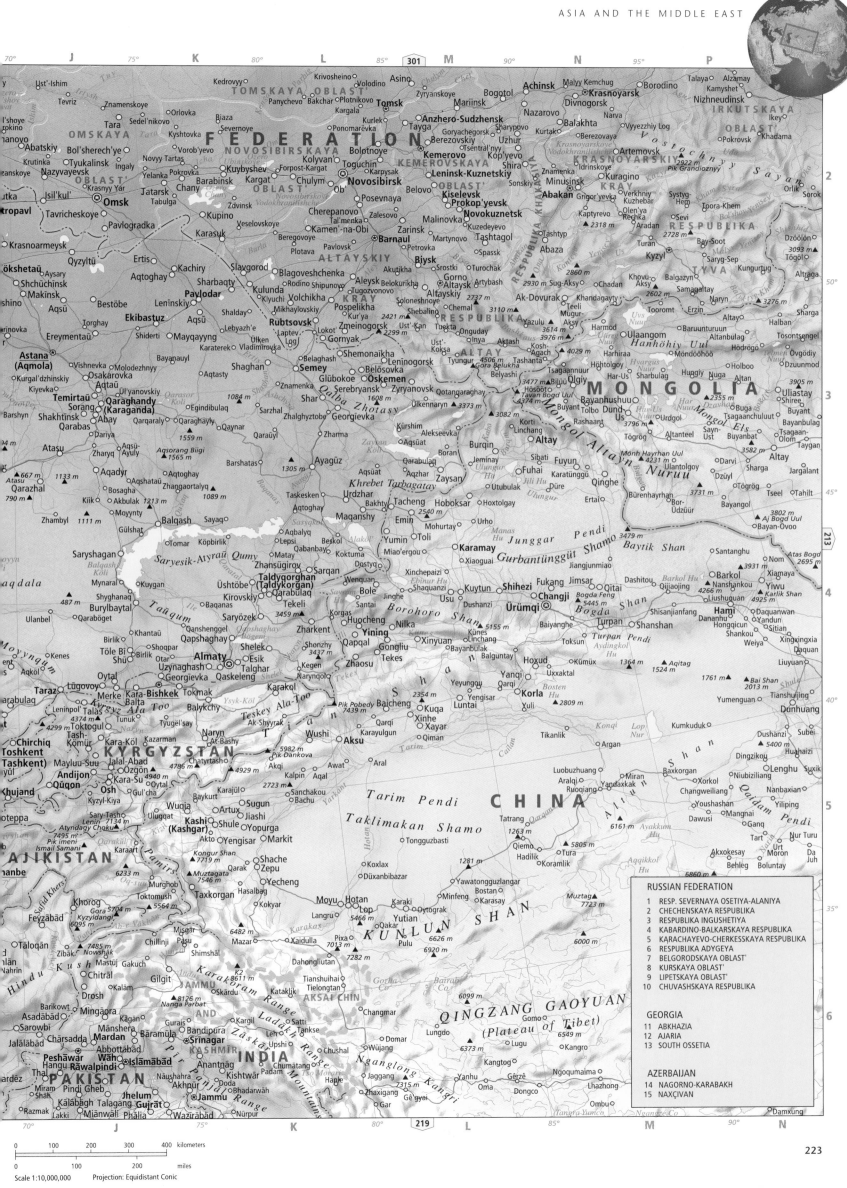

213

219

RUSSIAN FEDERATION
1 RESP. SEVERNAYA OSETIYA-ALANIYA
2 CHECHENSKAYA RESPUBLIKA
3 RESPUBLIKA INGUSHETIYA
4 KABARDINO-BALKARSKAYA RESPUBLIKA
5 KARACHAYEVO-CHERKESSKAYA RESPUBLIKA
6 RESPUBLIKA ADYGEYA
7 BELGORODSKAYA OBLAST'
8 KURSKAYA OBLAST'
9 LIPETSKAYA OBLAST'
10 CHUVASHSKAYA RESPUBLIKA

GEORGIA
11 ABKHAZIA
12 AJARIA
13 SOUTH OSSETIA

AZERBAIJAN
14 NAGORNO-KARABAKH
15 NAXÇIVAN

0   100   200   300   400 kilometers
0   100   200 miles
Scale 1:10,000,000   Projection: Equidistant Conic

223

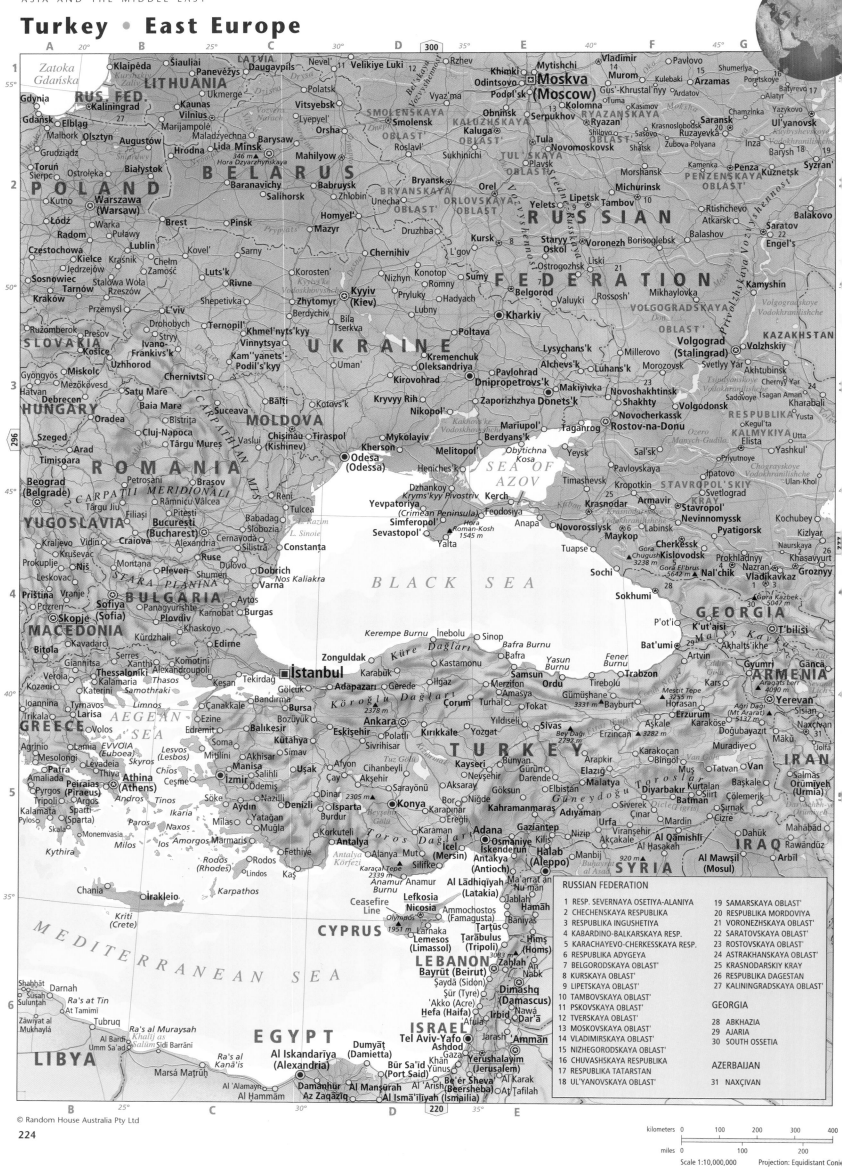

Zatoka
Gdańska

RUS. FED.
Klaipėda Šiauliai
LITHUANIA
Kaliningrad
Panevėžys **LATVIA**
Daugavpils Nevel' Velikiye Luki Rzhev Vladimir Pavlovo Shumerlya
Gdynia
Gdańsk Elbląg
Ukmerge
Kaunas Vilnius
Marijampolė
Polatsk
Vitsyebsk
Lyepyel'
Odintsovo Moskva Mytishchi Murom Kulebaki Arzamas Poretskoye
Podol'sk (Moscow) Gus-Khrustal'nyy Ardatov Alatyr Batyrevo

POLAND BELARUS RUSSIAN FEDERATION

UKRAINE

ROMANIA

BULGARIA

BLACK SEA

TURKEY

MEDITERRANEAN SEA

kilometers 0 100 200 300 400
miles 0 100 200 300
Scale 1:10,000,000 Projection: Equidistant Conic

RUSSIAN FEDERATION	
1 RESP. SEVERNAYA OSETIYA-ALANIYA	19 SAMARSKAYA OBLAST'
2 CHECHENSKAYA RESPUBLIKA	20 RESPUBLIKA MORDOVIYA
3 RESPUBLIKA INGUSHETIYA	21 VORONEZHSKAYA OBLAST'
4 KABARDINO-BALKARSKAYA RESP.	22 SARATOVSKAYA OBLAST'
5 KARACHAYEVO-CHERKESSKAYA RESP.	23 ROSTOVSKAYA OBLAST'
6 RESPUBLIKA ADYGEYA	24 ASTRAKHANSKAYA OBLAST'
7 BELGORODSKAYA OBLAST'	25 KRASNODARSKIY KRAY
8 KURSKAYA OBLAST'	26 RESPUBLIKA DAGESTAN
9 LIPETSKAYA OBLAST'	27 KALININGRADSKAYA OBLAST'
10 TAMBOVSKAYA OBLAST'	
11 PSKOVSKAYA OBLAST'	GEORGIA
12 TVERSKAYA OBLAST'	
13 MOSKOVSKAYA OBLAST'	28 ABKHAZIA
14 VLADIMIRSKAYA OBLAST'	29 AJARIA
15 NIZHEGORODSKAYA OBLAST'	30 SOUTH OSSETIA
16 CHUVASHSKAYA RESPUBLIKA	
17 RESPUBLIKA TATARSTAN	AZERBAIJAN
18 UL'YANOVSKAYA OBLAST'	31 NAXÇIVAN

East Mediterranean

A B 32° 34° 224 C ADANA 36° D 38° E

TURKEY

Kızılot
Güzelbağ ANTALYA
Okurcalar
Ermenek
Mut
Mağara
Erdemli
Tuzla
Yumurtalık
Kilis Elbeyli
İçEL
Yemişli
Qatmah A'zāz Jawbán Bayk Manbij
Alanya İçEL
(Coracesium)
Belen
Kargıcak
Silifke
Taşucu
İskenderun
Kırıkhan
Afrin
A'zāz
As Safirah
Dayr Hafir
Gazipaşa
Anamur
Aydıncık
Büyükeceli
İnekum Burnu
Hınzır Burnu
Kale
Reyhanlı
Hamam
Ürmā aş Şughrā
Halab (Aleppo)
Dibsi Faraj
'Ayn 'Īsá
Bozyazı
Anamur Burnu
Samandağı
Antakya (Antioch)
IDLIB
As Safirah
Sabkhat al Jabbūl
Maskanah
Ath Thawrah

SYRIA

AR RAQQA

Buhayrat al Asad

Hammām

KARAMAN

225

Scale 1:3,500,000
Projection: Equidistant Conic

0   50   100   200 kilometers
0   50   100 miles

Europe and the Russian Federatio

Covering 10.5 million sq km (4 million sq miles), Europe is the second smallest continent in the world. It is part of the Eurasian landmass and its conventional separation from Asia is therefore more cultural than physical. The Ural Mountains and Ural River, the Caspian and Red seas, and the Dardanelles Straits separate Europe from Asia and, to the south, the Mediterranean Sea separates it from Africa.

The countries of Europe can be divided into three groups: Western Europe, Eastern Europe (most countries of which came under the influence of the former Soviet Union), and the countries that emerged from the break-up of the former Soviet Union. Each of these groups can be distinguished by the history of its political systems.

Western Europe includes Andorra, Austria, Belgium, Denmark, Finland, France, Germany, Greece, Iceland, Ireland, Italy, Liechtenstein, Luxembourg, Malta, Monaco, the Netherlands, Norway, Portugal, San Marino, Spain, Sweden, Switzerland, the United Kingdom and Vatican City. There are also several dependencies: Guernsey, Jersey, the Isle of Man, and Gibraltar are dependencies of the United Kingdom, the Faeroe Islands of Denmark and Svalbard of Norway.

The nations of Eastern Europe are Poland, Hungary, the Czech Republic, Slovakia, Bulgaria, Romania, Slovenia, Croatia, Bosnia and Herzegovina, Macedonia, Yugoslavia and Albania. Yugoslavia currently consists of Serbia and Montenegro.

When the former Soviet Union broke up, several new nations emerged in Europe and Asia; the European nations consist of the Russian Federation, Ukraine, Belarus, Latvia, Lithuania, Estonia, and Moldova.

During the last 500 years, Europe has exerted a strong influence on the rest of the world through colonialism. Several Western European countries were colonial powers and their languages have become international; European sciences, laws, and arts have spread around the globe. European

A valley (with vineyards) in Switzerland (below), and a beech forest in Germany (right), both in Western Europe.

companies developed commercial agriculture, mining, and manufacturing in their colonies. The colonial powers promoted European migration to the Americas, Australia, and New Zealand—Europeans are now the dominant people there. Many Europeans also migrated to South Africa.

Physical features
The elongated Tertiary Period mountain chain that stretches between the Alps in France and the Carpathians in Romania, rising 3,000 to 4,500 m (10,000 to 15,000 ft), is a prominent feature in Europe. In contrast, there are geologically old and worn-down mountains in Scandinavia and northern Britain. Glacial carving, including sharp-peaked mountains (such as the Matterhorn) and flat-bottomed and steep-sided glacial valleys as in Switzerland, is found in most European mountainous areas. Along the Scandinavian coasts there are fiords, which are glacial valleys drowned by the sea. There are extensive plains in Central and Eastern Europe and France. Europe is well watered by a large number of rivers—the Volga, the Danube, the Rhône, and the Rhine. Many of these rivers are navigable far inland and are interconnected in places by canals.

Climate and vegetation
Although much of Europe can be described as humid temperate, significant climatic differences exist within its borders. The climates of Western Europe are moderated by the Atlantic Ocean, which is warmed by the waters of the Gulf Stream.

In contrast, the winter temperatures in continental Russia are below freezing.

The northernmost parts of Europe are treeless, with very cold winters and mild summers. Further south is the taiga, with broad-leaf deciduous and needle-leaf coniferous trees covering large tracts of land, particularly in Russia.

Cool, humid temperate climates stretch along the coast of the Atlantic Ocean between northern Spain and Norway, including Iceland. This area is characterized by mixed forests, but most of the original trees have been cleared. Some forests, like the Black Forest, have been harmed by acid rain.

Further inland, Central and Eastern Europe experience more extreme temperature ranges. There is a semiarid belt in the south, and forests are found in the wetter and higher areas. The drier regions with less reliable rainfall, such as the Ukraine and southwestern Russia, are characterized by extensive steppes of short grasses.

The southern Mediterranean belt experiences hot, dry summers and cool, wet winters. Forests and scrub cover large areas.

Population
The population of Europe at present (excluding the Russian Federation) totals 701 million. The relatively high standards of living in most European nations are reflected in life expectancies of 68.3 years for males and 77 years for females. Population numbers are stable, with a near zero growth rate. The Russian Federation has 147.2 million people; its life expectancies are 58 years for males and 75 years for females.

There has been significant urbanization in Europe since the nineteenth century, and this accelerated following the Second World War. Currently 74 percent of the population lives in cities and towns (84 percent in northern Europe and 65 percent in southern Europe); the figure for the Russian Federation is 76 percent.

Agriculture
Europe has a well-developed agricultural economy based on a wide range of food and animal products. Farming is more advanced in Western Europe, in terms of technology and organization, than in the former communist countries of Eastern Europe, which experimented with collectivized agriculture for several decades. Farm size varies considerably, but pressure to create larger farm units is changing the agricultural landscape.

Within Europe's cool, humid zone, mixed farming (grain growing and livestock rearing) is widespread. Wheat, barley, and rye are the main grains, and sheep and cattle the main livestock. Dairy farming is important in some of the cool countries such as the Netherlands and Denmark. Apples and pears are significant fruits.

Southern Europe, with its warm, dry summers and mild winters is suited to growing grapes, citrus fruits, and olives. Irrigation is extensively used in parts of the Mediterranean areas; for growing rice, for example.

There is extensive fishing in the Atlantic Ocean and in both the Mediterranean and Black Seas.

Hungary

A landlocked, central European country, Hungary shares borders with Yugoslavia to the south, Croatia and Slovenia to the southwest, Austria to the west, Slovakia to the north, Ukraine to the northeast and Romania to the southeast. Modern Hungary had its beginnings in the eighth century AD, when the area was settled by the Magyars, nomadic tribes from the central Volga. Their kingdom thrived and expanded. In the sixteenth century the Turks seized the central part of Hungary and the northern and western sections of the country accepted Austrian Hapsburg rule rather than submit to Turkish domination. In 1699 the Turks were driven out and the entire country came under Hapsburg rule. Continuing unrest and the defeat of Austria by the Prussians in 1866 culminated in the establishment of Austria–Hungary as a dual monarchy in 1867. The defeat of Austria–Hungary in 1918 was followed by the establishment of the Hungarian nation, but with two-thirds of its former territory and almost 60 percent of its former population ceded to surrounding states. In the Second World War Hungary sided with Germany against the Soviet Union and was finally occupied by Soviet forces as they pushed southward in 1945. In 1948 communists, with Soviet support, again seized control, beginning 42 years of Soviet domination. A popular anti-communist uprising in 1956 was brutally suppressed by the Soviet Union. As the Soviet Union began to collapse a new constitution in 1989 set the scene for Hungary's first multi-party elections in 1990.

Hungary is drained by two southward-flowing rivers, the Danube and the Tisza. These two rivers traverse the Great Hungarian Plain, which occupies most of the eastern part of the country and more than half the total land area. West of the Danube a line of hills and mountains runs northeast from Lake Balaton, which covers an area of 370 sq km (140 sq miles), to the Slovakian border, where it joins the Carpathian Mountains. Northwest of these hills the Little Hungarian Plain extends to the westward-flowing Danube, which here

The dome of a church on the island of Thíra, in Greece (bottom left). The city of Athens, Greece (top left). Looking across the Danube in Budapest, Hungary (right).

separates Hungary from Slovakia. While most of the low-lying areas have long been cleared of trees, some of the forested areas still survive in the hills and mountains.

Most of the two plains areas are fertile agricultural country, although there are dry sandy expanses, as well as marshlands that are home to a rich variety of waterbirds. More than 70 percent of Hungary's agricultural land is devoted to crops, the most important of which are maize, wheat, sugar beet, and sunflowers. Of the rest, more than four-fifths are meadows and pasturelands and the rest are orchards and vineyards. Pigs and poultry are the most extensively farmed livestock.

Except for natural gas, bauxite, and lignite—a low quality coal that provides much of the country's energy—Hungary is poorly endowed with mineral resources. It imports most of the raw materials for its now largely privatized industries, among which iron and steel production, and the manufacture of fertilizers, pharmaceuticals, and cement are prominent. Most of these industries are located in the north and are centered mainly around the capital, Budapest, and Miskolc, which is the second-largest city and is situated in the far northeast. Aluminum, using local bauxite, is manufactured north of Lake Balaton.

Hungarians enjoy a reasonable standard of living by the standards of former communist countries, though it still compares unfavorably with that in most Western countries. Pollution of air, soil, and water is a major problem and almost half the population lives in seriously affected areas.

Fact File

OFFICIAL NAME Republic of Hungary

FORM OF GOVERNMENT Republic with single legislative body (National Assembly)

CAPITAL Budapest

AREA 93,030 sq km (35,919 sq miles)

TIME ZONE GMT + 1 hour

POPULATION 10,186,372

PROJECTED POPULATION 2005 10,084,830

POPULATION DENSITY 109.5 per sq km (283.6 per sq mile)

LIFE EXPECTANCY 71.2

INFANT MORTALITY (PER 1,000) 9.5

OFFICIAL LANGUAGE Hungarian

OTHER LANGUAGE Romany

LITERACY RATE 99%

RELIGIONS Roman Catholic 67.5%, Calvinist 20%, Lutheran 5%, other 7.5%

ETHNIC GROUPS Hungarian 89.9%, Gypsy 4%, German 2.6%, Serb 2%, Slovak 0.8%, Romanian 0.7%

CURRENCY Forint

ECONOMY Services 48%, industry 31%, agriculture 21%

GNP PER CAPITA US$4,120

CLIMATE Temperate; cold, wet winters and warm summers

HIGHEST POINT Mt Kekes 1,014 m (3,327 ft)

MAP REFERENCE Pages 289, 294, 296

Iceland

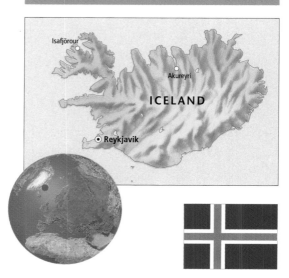

Fact File

OFFICIAL NAME Republic of Iceland

FORM OF GOVERNMENT Republic with single legislative body (Parliament)

CAPITAL Reykjavík

AREA 103,000 sq km (39,768 sq miles)

TIME ZONE GMT

POPULATION 272,512

PROJECTED POPULATION 2005 281,653

POPULATION DENSITY 2.7 per sq km (6.9 per sq mile)

LIFE EXPECTANCY 79

INFANT MORTALITY (PER 1,000) 5.2

OFFICIAL LANGUAGE Icelandic

LITERACY RATE 99%

RELIGIONS Evangelical Lutheran 96%; other Protestant and Roman Catholic 3%; none 1%

ETHNIC GROUPS Icelandic 97%; others including Danish, American, British, Norwegian, German 3%

CURRENCY Króna

ECONOMY Services 61%, industry 35%, agriculture 4%

GNP PER CAPITA US$24,950

CLIMATE Cool temperate, with cool, windy winters and mild, wet summers

HIGHEST POINT Hvannadalshnukur 2,119 m (6,952 ft)

MAP REFERENCE Page 284

True to its name, the island of Iceland, in the north Atlantic Ocean, has one-tenth of its total area covered in icefields and glaciers. The human occupation of this island, which lies just south of the Arctic Circle, dates back to the late ninth century AD when Norwegian Vikings settled there. In the thirteenth century the Icelanders submitted to Norwegian rule and a century and a half later, when the Norwegian and Danish monarchies were combined, they came under Danish control. In 1918 Iceland was granted its independence, but still owed allegiance to the Danish monarch. In 1944, as the result of a referendum, Iceland chose to become a republic. In 1972, because of its economic dependence on the surrounding seas, Iceland, without consultation with other nations,

more than quadrupled the extent of its territorial waters from 12 to 50 nautical miles. Three years later it extended them to 200 nautical miles, a provocative move that brought condemnation, particularly from Britain, and gave rise to serious aggression at sea between Icelandic and British fishing vessels. Britain was later granted some degree of access to the disputed waters.

In addition to icefields and glaciers, Iceland's spectacularly rugged and volcanic landscape includes hot springs, sulphur beds, geysers, lava fields, deep rocky canyons, and plummeting waterfalls. There are numerous small freshwater lakes and 200 volcanoes, many of which are active. Earth tremors, and occasionally larger quakes, are a frequent feature.

The interior of the island consists mainly of an elevated plateau of basalt, interspersed with occasional high peaks. There are small areas of forest and very little arable land. In the north, however, there are extensive grasslands where a small number of sheep, cattle, and horses can graze. More than 90 percent of the population lives in towns and cities around the coast, mainly in the southwest corner near Reykjavík.

Deep-sea fishing is the backbone of Iceland's economy, with fish and associated products constituting more than two-thirds of the country's exports. Apart from fish processing, aluminum smelting from imported bauxite and cement manufacture are growing industries. All of Iceland's domestic and industrial electricity needs are met by locally generated power from hydroelectric or geothermal plants. About one in four Icelanders is employed in manufacturing and processing industries. Iceland attracts about 150,000 tourists a year, more than half its permanent population, making tourism an important income-earner.

The people of Iceland enjoy a very high standard of living. Their economy is robust but is susceptible to variations in international fish prices. The country's free health-care system has contributed to a life expectancy that is among the highest in the world.

Crofts and a patchwork of fields on one of the Aran Islands in Ireland (below). A cobbled shopping street in Dublin, Ireland (top right). A unionist mural in Belfast, Northern Ireland (bottom right).

Ireland

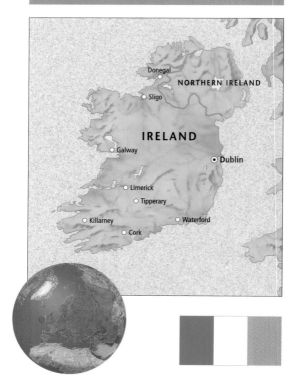

Situated in the northern Atlantic Ocean and separated from the British mainland to the east by the Irish Sea, the Republic of Ireland covers more than three-quarters of the island of Ireland. The northeast corner comprises the six counties that form Northern Ireland, which is part of the United Kingdom. In the fourth century BC, Gaelic-speaking invaders conquered the island and established a Celtic civilization. Tradition has it that St Patrick brought Christianity to Ireland in AD 432, and to this day Catholicism remains the dominant religion. From the eighth century AD Viking raiders attacked the coasts and settled some coastal regions, but they were finally repulsed in 1014. During the twelfth century, the pope, Adrian IV, ceded the entire island to the English crown, but another five centuries were to pass before local opposition was finally subjugated.

From 1846 to 1851 disease destroyed the Irish staple crop, potatoes, leading to famine and more than a million deaths. Roughly half the population emigrated at this time, mainly to the USA.

Although the Irish were granted a degree of autonomy in the eighteenth century, opposition to British rule festered throughout the nineteenth century, leading to the unsuccessful Easter rebellion of 1916 and the eventual granting of home rule to most of the island, as the Irish Free State, in 1921. In 1949 the Republic of Ireland was declared and formal ties with the British crown were severed. Today Ireland is a parliamentary democracy, with a popularly elected president as head of state and two houses of parliament.

Most of the landscape consists of a low-lying limestone plain, with undulating hills and areas of fertile soils. Small lakes and peat bogs abound throughout the countryside. Mountain ranges run along much of the coast, creating, especially in the southwest, some of Europe's most spectacular coastal scenery. The most significant ranges are the Wicklow Mountains in the southeast and Macgillicuddy's Reeks in the far southwest. The Shannon, the country's longest river, rises in the Iron Mountains not far from the Northern Ireland border. It drains the central plain and flows through a number of Ireland's largest lakes.

Traditionally an agricultural country, Ireland now relies mainly on manufacturing and processing industries for its present, relatively healthy, economic strength. The country joined the European Community in 1973. Four in ten members of the population live in urban areas. Clothing, pharmaceuticals, and the manufacture of heavy machinery contribute largely to Ireland's export earnings and tourism is also significant. More than 3 million people visit Ireland every year. About one in eight workers is still involved in agriculture, mainly in livestock raising and dairying, but also in cultivating crops such as potatoes, barley, and wheat. The country has reserves of natural gas, oil and peat.

Fact File

OFFICIAL NAME	Ireland
FORM OF GOVERNMENT	Republic with two legislative bodies (Senate and House of Representatives)
CAPITAL	Dublin
AREA	70,280 sq km (27,135 sq miles)
TIME ZONE	GMT
POPULATION	3,632,944
PROJECTED POPULATION 2005	3,727,595
POPULATION DENSITY	51.7 per sq km (133.9 per sq mile)
LIFE EXPECTANCY	76.4
INFANT MORTALITY (PER 1,000)	5.9
OFFICIAL LANGUAGES	Irish Gaelic, English
LITERACY RATE	99%
RELIGIONS	Roman Catholic 93%, Anglican 3%, other 4%
ETHNIC GROUPS	Celtic 94%, English minority
CURRENCY	Irish pound
ECONOMY	Industry 54%, services 36%, agriculture 10%
GNP PER CAPITA	US$14,710
CLIMATE	Temperate, with cool, wet winters and mild summers; wetter in the west
HIGHEST POINT	Carrauntoohil 1,041 m (3,415 ft)
MAP REFERENCE	Pages 303, 309

The Troubles in Northern Ireland

Ever since Britain's granting of independence to the Irish Free State in 1921, Northern Ireland has been a troubled province, a place where terrorism and sectarian strife have been the norm. The arrangements for the government of Northern Ireland created bitter resentment among its minority Catholic population. Northern Ireland was granted self-government, with its own parliament in Belfast, but maintaining strong links with the British government in London. The government ruled blatantly in favor of the Protestant majority, excluding Catholics from positions of authority or influence. Catholics moved in great numbers from the country to Belfast and other cities in order to find work, almost invariably in menial jobs in shipbuilding, textile, and other industries.

The Irish Republican Army (IRA), which had used guerrilla tactics against the British during Ireland's struggle for independence, became a threat to the stability of Northern Ireland, carrying out sporadic attacks on Protestant targets. When, in 1949, the Irish Free State, as Ireland was then called, left the British Commonwealth and became the Republic of Ireland, battle lines became marked. The IRA began to campaign aggressively for Northern Ireland to be absorbed into the republic and the breaking of ties with Britain, but for the next two decades it made little progress in the face of Northern Ireland's largely apathetic Catholic population.

However, as discrimination, especially in housing and employment, continued in Northern Ireland, Catholics grew increasingly militant, and in the late 1960s waged a widespread campaign for increased civil rights. Their demonstrations provoked counter-demonstrations by militant Protestants and a 30-year period of violent sectarian clashes was launched. The situation was aggravated by the arrival of British troops, ostensibly to maintain the peace. They were soon perceived by Catholics to be acting in the interests of the Protestants, especially after 1972, when they opened fire on Catholic demonstrators in Londonderry, killing 13 of them. In March 1972, in the wake of this incident, the British

government suspended the parliament in Belfast and instituted direct rule for the province from London, a move that antagonized people on both sides of the struggle.

The desire of one section of the IRA to abandon violence led to a split in 1969. A wing of the IRA—the Provisionals, or Provos—consisting mainly of younger members, remained committed to terrorism and during the 1970s and 1980s carried out repeated bombings, murders, and kidnappings of both civilians and British army personnel, not only in Ireland, but also on the British mainland. Protestants in Northern Ireland responded in kind. From the early 1970s until the mid-1990s more than 3,000 people died in the conflict, and many more were wounded. The most prominent victim was Earl Mountbatten, who was assassinated in the Irish Republic in 1979. Northern Ireland towns and cities were divided into Catholic and Protestant zones, and an atmosphere of fear and distrust prevailed.

Any possibility of a negotiated peace was thwarted by the determination of successive British governments not to recognize or to have discussions with the IRA. This situation changed in 1994, when the Provisional IRA suspended its terrorist campaign and talks, at first in secret, but later open, were held in London. The talks broke down in 1996 when the Provisional IRA revoked its cease-fire and continued its attacks. However, over the following years, new overtures were made and new talks, brokered with the help of the USA, have brought hopes for a lasting peace.

Italy

Fact file

OFFICIAL NAME Italian Republic

FORM OF GOVERNMENT Republic with two legislative bodies (Senate and Chamber of Deputies)

CAPITAL Rome

AREA 301,230 sq km (116,305 sq miles)

TIME ZONE GMT + 1 hour

POPULATION 56,735,130

PROJECTED POPULATION 2005 56,253,452

POPULATION DENSITY 188.3 per sq km (487.7 per sq mile)

LIFE EXPECTANCY 78.5

INFANT MORTALITY (PER 1,000) 6.3

OFFICIAL LANGUAGE Italian

OTHER LANGUAGES German, French, Greek, Albanian

LITERACY RATE 98.1%

RELIGIONS Roman Catholic 98%, other 2%

ETHNIC GROUPS Italian, 94%; German–Italian, French–Italian, Slovene–Italian and Albanian–Italian communities 6%

CURRENCY Lira

ECONOMY Services 71%, industry 20%, agriculture 9%

GNP PER CAPITA US$19,020

CLIMATE Temperate; north has cool, wet winters and warm, dry summers; south has mild winters and hot, dry summers

HIGHEST POINT Mont Blanc 4,807 m (15,771 ft)

MAP REFERENCE Pages 294–95

Situated in southern central Europe, the Italian mainland consists of a long peninsula that juts out into the Mediterranean Sea. Shaped roughly like a long, high-heeled boot, this land mass is bordered to the north by Switzerland and Austria, to the west by France, and to the east by Slovenia. At the southwestern tip of the peninsula, the narrow Strait of Messina separates the toe of the boot from the large Italian island of Sicily, while further west in the Mediterranean, separated from the mainland by the Tyrrhenian Sea and sitting just south of the French island of Corsica, is the island of Sardinia, also part of Italy. About 70 other small islands, scattered mainly around the coasts of Sicily and Sardinia and off the western coast of the mainland, make up the rest of present-day Italy. The peninsula's eastern coastline is washed by the waters of the Adriatic Sea, across which lies the coast of Croatia.

History

Italy's capital, Rome, situated in central western Italy, was for 800 years, from about 400 BC, the hub of the mighty Roman Empire. At the height of their powers in the first and second centuries AD the Romans controlled the whole of the Italian Peninsula and vast swathes of Europe. Their empire stretched as far as Britain in the north, the Iberian Peninsula in the west, into Egypt in North Africa and eastward as far as the Persian Gulf. Italy became Christianized after the conversion of the Roman Emperor Constantine in AD 313. The sacking of Rome by the Visigoths in AD 410 precipitated a series of subsequent invasions which resulted, over the centuries, in the fragmentation of Italy into a number of states ruled by different powers. For some time all of Italy came under the control of the eastern Roman Empire, based in Constantinople. The Franks, under Charlemagne, gained control of much of northern Italy at the end of the eighth century AD, and in the eleventh century the Normans invaded Sicily, which led to the creation of a kingdom based around the southern city of Naples.

In the later Middle Ages there emerged, in central and northern Italy, a number of powerful city-states, the most notable being Florence, Venice, Pisa and Genoa. From the fourteenth century, these states, especially Florence, promoted a great cultural revival which saw a blossoming of artistic, musical, literary, and scientific activity. This revival, which gradually spread through most of Europe, is now known as the Renaissance.

France, Spain, and Austria vied for domination of different parts of Italy between the fifteenth and the eighteenth centuries. Most of Italy fell to Napoleon's armies in 1796–97, but after Napoleon's downfall in 1815 Italy was again fragmented, with Austria the dominant power in the north. A series of uprisings during the 1820s and 1830s gave rise

to the movement known as the Risorgimento (resurrection), which eventually led to the total unification of Italy and the installation of Victor Emmanuel II, the King of Sardinia, as King of Italy in 1861. During the next half-century Italy acquired a number of overseas territories, including Eritrea, part of Somalia, and some Greek islands.

Although officially allied to Germany, Italy at first remained neutral in the First World War and later joined the Allied side. In 1919 Benito Mussolini, a former socialist, founded the Fascist Party as a bulwark against communism. In 1922 he seized power, setting up a dictatorship. Embarking on a policy of foreign conquest, Italy invaded Ethiopia in 1935. Fascist Italy joined the side of Nazi Germany in the Second World War but in 1943 it was invaded by Allied troops and subsequently declared war on its former German ally. Dismissed from the Italian government, Mussolini was installed by Germany as head of a puppet government in northern Italy but he was captured and executed by partisans in 1945.

After the war, Italy was stripped of its foreign territories. A referendum in 1946 resulted in the abolition of the monarchy and the establishment of a democratic republic. Since then, government in Italy has been wracked by instability as changing allegiances and coalitions have created a succession of short-lived governments. In 1993 a referendum approved a plan to simplify Italy's complex electoral system. Since 1994 three-quarters of the members of Italy's two houses of parliament have been elected by a simple majority of votes, while the rest are elected by proportional representation. The president, whose duties are largely ceremonial, is elected for a seven-year term. Both houses are elected for a maximum of five years.

Timeline

	6th century BC Under rule of Etruscan kings Rome grows from village to wealthy city	476 Germanic leader Odoacer defeats last Roman Emperor; ends dominance of western sector of Roman Empire	962 Otto the Great crowned Emperor of the Holy Roman Empire	c.1300 Renaissance begins. Interest flourishes in arts, sciences, and literature as well as philosophy, politics, and religion	1519 King Charles I of Spain becomes Holy Roman Emperor. Siezes much of Italy including Rome and Milan from France	1796 Napole Bonaparte invac north Italy, setting independent republi Interest in Itali independence gro

| 900 BC Etruscan civilization founded between Arno and Tiber Rivers by people arriving from the east; lasts till c.200 BC | | 568 BC Langobardi (Lombards) seize much of northern Italy from Roman Empire | AD 79 Mt Vesuvius near Naples erupts, buries city of Pompeii in lava and ash, and Herculaneum under mud | 800 Pope Leo III crowns Charlemagne Emperor of the Romans | 1000 Rise of city states such as Florence, Venice, Genoa, and Pisa which have strong commercial and cultural identities | 1345 Black Death, bubonic plague, kills more than one-quarter of the population | 1663 Volcano Mt Etna erupts destroying much of the town of Catania, northeast Sicily |

The rooftops of Florence, including the cathedral, seen from Piazzale Michelangelo (below). Fishing boats in the harbor of Camogli in Liguria, northern Italy (above). One of the many palaces on the Grand Canal in Venice (right).

Physical features and land use

Most of Italy is mountainous, with a central range, the Appenines, sweeping down the length of the peninsula and extending into Sicily, where the volcanic, and still active, peak of Mount Etna soars to a height of 3,323 m (10,902 ft) above sea level. Further north, near Naples, the active Mount Vesuvius offers evidence of the volcanic origins of Italy's mountains. The Appenines, which are rich in limestone, reach heights of almost 3,000 m (10,000 ft) in the Gran Sasso Range, east of Rome. The slopes of the Appenines are covered with thin soils, which in some places provide reasonable pasture. In the valleys there are some extensive

stretches of arable land. At the far northwestern tip of the Italian peninsula the Appenines merge with the Alps, which are generally higher than the Appenines and which arch right across the north of Italy, forming natural boundaries with the countries of Switzerland, Austria, and France. In the southern extremities of the Alps are a series of large, spectacular lakes, which include the much visited Lago Maggiore, Lago di Como, and Lago di Garda. These lakes and the rivers that feed into them are the source of the hydroelectricity which supplies about half the electricity needs of industrialized northern Italy.

In the northeast of the country, enclosed by the Alps to the north and the west and the Appenines to the south, and stretching in the east as far as the Adriatic coast, is the country's largest lowland region, known as the Plain of Lombardy. Drained by the River Po, which flows from west to east across the widest part of the country, this area is the most fertile, as well as the most heavily industrialized and populous part of Italy. About two-fifths of Italy's crops are grown here. Agriculture is also extensive on the coastal plains on each side of the Appenines. Farms are mainly small. Crops include potatoes, wheat, maize, olives, and other vegetables as well as a wide range of citrus and stone fruits. Italy produces more wine than any other country and there are extensive vine-yards, most particularly in the Chianti region in Tuscany. Sheep, pigs, and cattle are the principal livestock.

Industry, commerce, and culture

Apart from marble in the south, for which it is famous, and some oil deposits in Sicily, Italy is not well endowed with mineral resources and imports most of the energy needed by its highly developed industrial sector. This is concentrated overwhelmingly in the north of the country— although Naples, Bari, and Taranto in the south and Rome in the center have a certain amount of heavy industry—and is based around such cities as Milan, Turin, and Genoa. The building of cars, aircraft, and other transport equipment are major industries, as are tool, textile, clothing, and chemical manufacture.

Italy's manufacturing sector, which was heavily subsidized by the state, developed largely in the half-century since the Second World War, before which the economy was based predominantly on agriculture. It now employs about a fifth of the country's workforce. Tourism is an important source of income, with about 30 million people visiting Italy every year.

There is a great divide in Italy between the high living standards of the industrialized, affluent north and the much lower living standards of the largely undeveloped south, especially in Calabria in the far south. In the south unemployment is chronically high, investment is hard to attract, poverty is widespread, and crime for many people offers the best means of survival.

REGIONS

**Abruzzi • Basilicata • Calabria
Campania • Emilia-Romagna
Friuli-Venezia Giulia • Lazio • Liguria
Lombardy • Marche • Molise
Piedmont • Puglia • Sardinia
Sicily • Trentino-Alto Adige • Tuscany
Umbria • Valle d'Aosta • Veneto**

1814 Napoleon defeated by European powers; under Congress of Vienna most of Italy returns to Austrian rule

1858 French troops help Kingdom of Sardinia to push back Austrian troops, regaining most of northern Italy

1860 Garibaldi's redshirts regain contol of Sicily; eventually they take all southern Italy, including Naples

1861 King Victor Emmanuel announces Kingdom of Italy. To include entire peninsula except Rome, Venice, and San Marino

1908 Earthquake in Messina, Sicily, kills 120,000 people

1915 Italy joins Allies in First World War

1922 Mussolini becomes leader and the Fascist movement grows

1939 Start of Second World War; Italy enters on Germany's side nine months later, soon after the fall of France, in June 1940

1940 Italy's forces defeated in Eritrea, Ethiopia, and Greece; Mussolini overthrown, but reinstalled by Germans; Allies retake Italy (1943)

1943 Allies invade Italy; Italian prime minister signs armistice with Allies; Italy declares war on Germany

1946 First free elections held since 1930s after Humbert III takes up the Italian throne; Italians vote to establish a Republic

1960s Rapid postwar industrialization brings prosperity to northern cities but the south remains largely agricultural and poor

1980 Earthquake in southern Italy kills more than 4,500 and leaves 400,000 homeless

Latvia

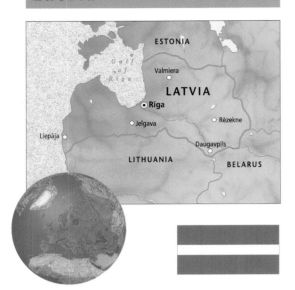

Fact File

OFFICIAL NAME Republic of Latvia

FORM OF GOVERNMENT Republic with single legislative body (Parliament)

CAPITAL Riga

AREA 64,100 sq km (24,749 sq miles)

TIME ZONE GMT + 3 hours

POPULATION 2,353,874

PROJECTED POPULATION 2005 2,221,761

POPULATION DENSITY 36.7 per sq km (95.1 per sq mile)

LIFE EXPECTANCY 67.3

INFANT MORTALITY (PER 1,000) 17.2

OFFICIAL LANGUAGE Lettish

OTHER LANGUAGES Lithuanian, Russian

LITERACY RATE 99%

RELIGIONS Mainly Lutheran with Russian Orthodox and Roman Catholic minorities

ETHNIC GROUPS Latvian 51.8%, Russian 33.8%, Belarusian 4.5%, Ukrainian 3.4%, Polish 2.3%, other 4.2%

CURRENCY Lats

ECONOMY Services 43%, industry 41%, agriculture 16%

GNP PER CAPITA US$2,270

CLIMATE Temperate. Cold, wet winters and mild summers

HIGHEST POINT Gaizinkalns 312 m (1,024 ft)

MAP REFERENCE Page 287

Latvia lies between its sister Baltic republics of Estonia, to the north, and Lithuania, to the south, its coastline along the Baltic Sea indented by the Gulf of Riga. To the east and southeast respectively it shares borders with the Russian Federation and Belarus. Like Estonia and Lithuania, Latvia has for most of its history been controlled by foreign powers. For more than 1,000 years, its inhabitants, the Letts, have been ruled successively by Germans, Poles, Swedes, and finally Russians. In 1991 Latvia declared its independence from the Soviet Union. It is now a multi-party parliamentary democracy with an elected president as its head of state. Since independence, the Communist Party of Latvia has been banned.

The rooftops of a town in Latvia (right). More than two-thirds of the Latvian population are urbanized.

The country is mostly flat with hillier land in the east. There are large areas of bogs and swamps and about 40 percent of the land is woodland or forest, in which oak and pine predominate. Small farms account for most agriculture, which is mainly dairy farming and cattle raising. Some grain and vegetable crops are also grown. Forestry and fishing, which were important in earlier times, have enjoyed a resurgence in recent years.

Latvia is the most heavily industrialized of the Baltic republics. It has few mineral resources and imports the raw materials needed for its industries —the manufacture of electrical goods, shipbuilding, and train and vehicle making. It relies on its former ruler for energy supplies and much of the Russian Federation's oil and gas exports pass through the Latvian port of Venspils. Air and water pollution from industrial wastes is a matter of concern.

Latvia's economy was severely affected in 1995 by bank failures and financial scandals and its dependence on Russia limits its development. Latvians have a reasonable standard of living, although discrepancies in wealth are marked.

Liechtenstein

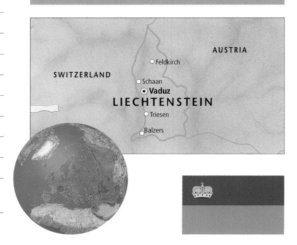

This small central European country sits high in the Alps. To the west the Rhine River forms a border with Switzerland, with which Liechtenstein has political ties and whose currency it shares. Austria lies to the east and south. The country takes its name from the Austrian Liechtenstein family which, in 1699 and 1713, acquired two fiefdoms and formed them into the principality. It later came under French and then German influence. In 1866 it achieved independence, and two years later declared itself permanently neutral, a position it has since maintained. In all subsequent European wars, Liechtenstein has remained unmolested. Its head of state is an hereditary monarch who appoints a government on the recommendation of an elected parliament. Elections are held every four years and there is universal adult suffrage, although women have had the vote only since 1984.

The Rhine is the source of Liechtenstein's agricultural strength. Its floodplain, once marshy, has been drained and reclaimed for agricultural and pastoral use. The capital sits on a plateau overlooking the undulating expanses of the Rhine Valley. The slopes of the Rhatikon alpine range

rise to impressive peaks in the south. From the southern highlands, the Samina River flows northward through the center of the country. Thick forests—of beech, maple, and ash—cover much of the mountain region.

The main agricultural industries are cattle, sheep, and pig raising, and some vegetables and cereal crops are grown. There is little heavy industry but prominent among light industries are textile and ceramic goods and the manufacture of electronic equipment. There are no mineral resources, and Liechtenstein imports all its fuel and raw materials. A major source of revenue is the sale of postage stamps. More than half the country's residents are foreign nationals, largely attracted by the country's low rates of taxation and its banking laws, which ensure great secrecy.

Fact File

OFFICIAL NAME Principality of Liechtenstein

FORM OF GOVERNMENT Constitutional monarchy with single legislative house (Parliament)

CAPITAL Vaduz

AREA 160 sq km (62 sq miles)

TIME ZONE GMT + 1 hour

POPULATION 32,057

PROJECTED POPULATION 2005 33,981

POPULATION DENSITY 200.4 per sq km (519 per sq mile)

LIFE EXPECTANCY 78.1

INFANT MORTALITY (PER 1,000) 5.2

OFFICIAL LANGUAGE German

LITERACY RATE 99%

RELIGIONS Roman Catholic 87.3%, Protestant 8.3%, other 4.4%

ETHNIC GROUPS Alemannic 95%, Italian and other 5%

CURRENCY Swiss franc

ECONOMY Services 50%; industry, trade and building 48%; agriculture, fishing and forestry 2%

GNP PER CAPITA US$33,000

CLIMATE Temperate, with cold, wet winters and mild, humid summers

HIGHEST POINT Grauspitz 2,599 m (8,527 ft)

MAP REFERENCE Page 288

Lithuania

The largest of the Baltic states, Lithuania has borders with Latvia to the north, Belarus to the east and southeast, Poland to the south, and the Russian Federation to the southwest. The Baltic Sea lies to its west. In the thirteenth century, Lithuania was united under a Christian king, in the sixteenth century it merged with Poland, then in 1795 it came under Russian control. Occupied by Germany in the First World War, Lithuania became independent in 1918. It became part of the Soviet Union in 1940 and was then invaded by Germany. When Soviet armies arrived in 1944, over 200,000 people, more than three-quarters of them Jews, had perished. In 1991 the country declared its independence from the Soviet Union. It is now a multi-party democracy with a president as head of state and a prime minister as head of government.

Most of Lithuania consists of a relatively fertile plain with extensive marshlands and forests. Many marshes have been reclaimed for growing cereal and vegetable crops. Sand dunes predominate along the Baltic coast and there is a range of hills dotted with more than 3,000 lakes in the southeast. Numerous rivers traverse the landscape.

Machine manufacturing, petroleum refining, shipbuilding, and food processing are some of Lithuania's key industries, but they have resulted in soil and groundwater contamination. The country has few natural resources and depends on Russia for oil and most of the raw materials needed for its industries. The main forms of agriculture are dairy farming and pig and cattle raising. Continuing dependence on Russia and a high rate of inflation are among factors that make Lithuania the least prosperous of the Baltic states.

Fact File

OFFICIAL NAME Republic of Lithuania

FORM OF GOVERNMENT Republic with single legislative body (Parliament)

CAPITAL Vilnius

AREA 65,200 sq km (25,174 sq miles)

TIME ZONE GMT + 3 hours

POPULATION 3,584,966

PROJECTED POPULATION 2005 3,526,180

POPULATION DENSITY 55 per sq km (142.4 per sq mile)

LIFE EXPECTANCY 69

INFANT MORTALITY (PER 1,000) 14.7

OFFICIAL LANGUAGE Lithuanian

OTHER LANGUAGES Russian, Polish

LITERACY RATE 98.4%

RELIGIONS Roman Catholic 90%; Russian Orthodox, Muslim and Protestant minorities 10%

ETHNIC GROUPS Lithuanian 80.1%, Russian 8.6%, Polish 7.7%, Belarusian 1.5%, other 2.1%

CURRENCY Litas

ECONOMY Industry 42%, services 40%, agriculture 18%

GNP PER CAPITA US$1,900

CLIMATE Temperate. Cold winters and mild summers

HIGHEST POINT Mt Juozapine 292 m (958 ft)

MAP REFERENCE Pages 287, 289

Luxembourg

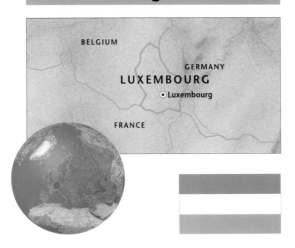

The Grand Duchy of Luxembourg is one of the smallest countries in Europe. Situated in northern Europe, it shares borders with Belgium to the west and France to the south. Three connecting rivers—the Our, Sûre, and the Moselle—separate it from Germany to the east. Part of the Holy Roman Empire since the tenth century AD, Luxembourg became an independent duchy in 1354, one of hundreds of such states in medieval Europe. It is the only one to survive today as an independent nation. Throughout the intervening centuries, Luxembourg has come under Austrian, Spanish, French, and Dutch rule. In 1830 part of the duchy was taken over by Belgium when that country split from the Netherlands. Luxembourg separated from the Netherlands in 1890. Germany occupied Luxembourg during both world wars and annexed it in 1942. After the Second World War it became a founder member of NATO and in 1957 joined the European Economic Community. It has been a keen advocate of European cooperation and was the first country, in 1991, to ratify the Maastricht Treaty. Luxembourg is a constitutional monarchy, with the Grand Duke as head of state, and a prime minister as head of an elected 21-member Council of State.

The northern part of Luxembourg is called the Oesling. Covering about one-third of the country's total area, it is part of the densely forested Ardennes mountain range. Numerous river valleys dissect this northern region and deer and wild boar abound. It is a rugged, picturesque area but has poor soils. In contrast, the southern two-thirds, known as the Gutland or Bon Pays (meaning good land), consists of plains and undulating hills covered with rich soils and extensive pastureland.

Iron ore deposits in the south of the country contributed to the development of a thriving iron and steel industry. These deposits are now less abundant and industries such as food processing, chemical manufacturing and tyre making now rival steel in importance. A growing service sector, especially in banking, has become increasingly central to the country's prosperity. The Gutland area is still strongly agricultural. Wheat, barley, potatoes, and grapes are the principal crops and more than 5 million cattle and 6 million pigs are raised. The people of Luxembourg are among the most affluent in Europe. Unemployment is low and salaries, especially among urban workers, are high.

Fact File

OFFICIAL NAME Grand Duchy of Luxembourg

FORM OF GOVERNMENT Constitutional monarchy with single legislative body (Chamber of Deputies)

CAPITAL Luxembourg

AREA 2,586 sq km (998 sq miles)

TIME ZONE GMT + 1 hour

POPULATION 429,080

PROJECTED POPULATION 2005 445,932

POPULATION DENSITY 165.9 per sq km (429.7 per sq mile)

LIFE EXPECTANCY 77.7

INFANT MORTALITY (PER 1,000) 5.0

OFFICIAL LANGUAGE Letzeburgish

OTHER LANGUAGES French, German

LITERACY RATE 99%

RELIGIONS Roman Catholic 97%, Protestant and Jewish 3%

ETHNIC GROUPS Luxembourger (French and German) 70%; Portuguese, Belgian and Italian minorities 30%

CURRENCY Luxembourg franc

ECONOMY Services 77%, industry 19%, agriculture 4%

GNP PER CAPITA US$41,210

CLIMATE Temperate, with cool winters and mild summers

HIGHEST POINT Burgplatz 559 m (1,834 ft)

MAP REFERENCE Page 291

Macedonia

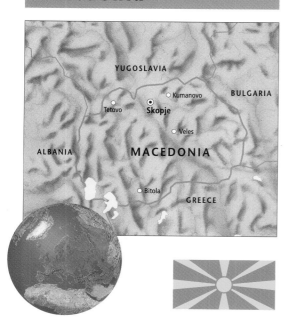

This small, landlocked Balkan country in south-eastern Europe is bordered by Yugoslavia to the north, Bulgaria to the east, Greece to the south, and Albania to the west. During the third century BC Macedonia was the heart of the Greek Empire. It later became a Roman province, but from the fourth century AD it was invaded numerous times. In the fourteenth century it came under Ottoman control. As the Ottoman Empire declined in the nineteenth century, Bulgaria, Greece, and Serbia contended for control of Macedonia and by the First World War it had been divided between them. Present-day Macedonia is essentially the region that was in Serbian hands at the end of the First World War. Macedonia was then incorporated into the Kingdom of Serbs, Croats, and Slovenes, which in 1929 became the Republic of Yugoslavia. In 1946 it became an autonomous republic within Yugoslavia. In 1991 Macedonia withdrew from Yugoslavia and it is now a multi-party democracy, governed by a legislative body with 120 elected members and a directly elected president. Tensions with neighbors remain high. Macedonia is also the name of a Greek province, over which Greece claims the former Yugoslav state has territorial ambitions.

Macedonia is largely isolated from its neighbors by mountains. Mountain ranges separate it from Greece in the south and the Korab Mountains in the west lie along the Albanian border. Much of the country is a plateau more than 2,000 m (6,500 ft) above sea level. The River Vadar rises in the northwest. It flows north, almost to the Yugoslavian border, then continues on a southeasterly course through the center of the country and into Greece.

One-quarter of the land is used for agriculture. Crops include cereals, fruits, vegetables, and cotton, and sheep and cattle are raised extensively. The country is self-sufficient in food and, thanks to its coal resources, in energy. Manufacturing industries have suffered since independence, partly because of trade embargoes imposed by Greece. Macedonia is the least developed of the former Yugoslav republics and is suffering a declining standard of living.

Fact File

OFFICIAL NAME	Former Yugoslav Republic of Macedonia
FORM OF GOVERNMENT	Republic with single legislative body (Assembly)
CAPITAL	Skopje
AREA	25,333 sq km (9,781 sq miles)
TIME ZONE	GMT + 1 hour
POPULATION	2,022,604
PROJECTED POPULATION 2005	2,086,849
POPULATION DENSITY	79.8 per sq km (206.8 per sq mile)
LIFE EXPECTANCY	73.1
INFANT MORTALITY (PER 1,000)	18.7
OFFICIAL LANGUAGE	Macedonian
OTHER LANGUAGES	Albanian, Turkish, Serbian, Croatian
LITERACY RATE	94.0%
RELIGIONS	Eastern Orthodox 67%, Muslim 30%, other 3%
ETHNIC GROUPS	Macedonian 65%, Albanian 22%, Turkish 4%, Serb 2%, Gypsy 3%, other 4%
CURRENCY	Denar
ECONOMY	Services and agriculture 60%; manufacturing and mining 40%
GNP PER CAPITA	US$860
CLIMATE	Temperate, with cold winters and hot summers
HIGHEST POINT	Mt Korab 2,753 m (9,032 ft)
MAP REFERENCE	Pages 296–97, 298

Malta

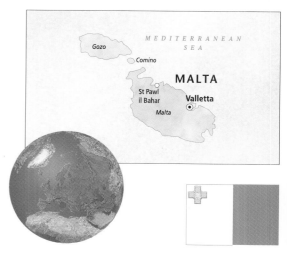

The Republic of Malta consists of an archipelago of three inhabited islands—Malta, Gozo, and Comino—and three tiny uninhabited islands, which are little more than rocky outcrops. They are situated in the center of the Mediterranean Sea 93 km (58 miles) south of Sicily. Malta, the largest and most populous of the islands, contains the capital, Valletta, the country's fifth largest city, picturesquely situated on a promontory between two harbors, and the four larger cities of Birkirkara, Qormi, Hamrun, and Sliema. Successive civilizations have recognized the importance of Malta's position and the advantages of its many harbors. It was occupied successively by the Phoenicians, the Greeks, and the Romans. In the ninth century AD, when it was part of the Byzantine Empire, it was conquered by Arabs but fell two centuries later to Sicily and then, in 1282, to Spain. In 1530 the Spanish king gave Malta to the Knights of St John, a religious order, which built and fortified the town of Valletta and occupied the island of Malta until it was seized by Napoleon in 1798. Britain took the island in 1800 and held it until 1947, when the country was granted self-government as a parliamentary democracy. In 1964, Malta gained full independence. Relations with Britain and other Western nations have often been strained, largely because of Malta's close links with Libya in northern Africa.

The three inhabited islands are mostly flat—although the island of Malta is undulating in places—with spectacular rocky coastlines. There is little natural vegetation and there are no forests or major rivers. Low rainfall, poor drainage, a limestone base and a hot climate all contribute to the paucity of the islands' shallow soils, which, however, support a range of cereal and vegetable crops as well as substantial vineyards.

Apart from limestone for building, Malta has virtually no mineral resources and is heavily dependent on imported materials. It has no natural sources of energy and produces only one-fifth of its population's food needs. Tourism is the mainstay of the economy. Every year about a million visitors, mainly from the United Kingdom, arrive to enjoy its beaches, its historic towns, and its rugged scenery. Ship repairs and clothing and textile manufacture are other significant industries. The average income is low by Western standards and Maltese residents are among the least affluent of Western Europeans.

The town of Ohrid on the shore of Lake Ohrid in southwestern Macedonia (bottom left). One of Malta's megalithic temples, built more than 5,000 years ago (left). The harbor front in Valletta, the capital of Malta (below left).

Fact File

OFFICIAL NAME Republic of Malta

FORM OF GOVERNMENT Republic with single legislative body (House of Representatives)

CAPITAL Valletta

AREA 320 sq km (124 sq miles)

TIME ZONE GMT + 1 hour

POPULATION 381,603

PROJECTED POPULATION 2005 389,772

POPULATION DENSITY 1,192.5 per sq km (3,088.6 per sq mile)

LIFE EXPECTANCY 77.8

INFANT MORTALITY (PER 1,000) 7.4

OFFICIAL LANGUAGES Maltese, English

LITERACY RATE 86%

RELIGIONS Roman Catholic 98%, other 2%

ETHNIC GROUPS Mixed Arab, Sicilian, French, Spanish, Italian and English

CURRENCY Maltese lira

ECONOMY Government 37%, services 30%, manufacturing 27%, construction 4%, agriculture 2%

GNP PER CAPITA US$7,200

CLIMATE Temperate, with mild, wet winters and hot, dry summers

HIGHEST POINT Dingli Cliffs 245 m (804 ft)

MAP REFERENCE Pages 361, 362

Moldova

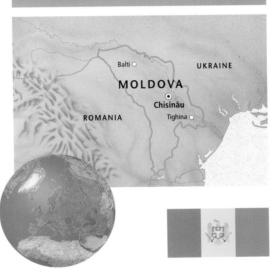

Moldova is a small, landlocked country in southeastern Europe, near the northern shores of the Black Sea. To the west the Prut River separates Moldova from Romania. Otherwise, it is completely enclosed by Ukrainian territory. Bessarabia—the section between the Prut and Dniester rivers—which comprises almost all of present-day Moldova, was under Ottoman rule until 1812, when it passed to Russian control. With the collapse of the Russian Empire after the First World War, Bessarabia merged in 1918 with Romania, with which it is ethnically and linguistically almost identical. The part of Moldova east of the Dniester remained under Russian control. As a result of the Nazi–Soviet Pact of 1940 Romania was forced to cede Bessarabia. Most of it was combined with a narrow strip of the Ukraine east of the Dniester to form the new state of Moldova. The remaining parts were incorporated into Ukraine.

After the Second World War, Moldova became a Soviet republic and systematic attempts were made to suppress all links with Romania. Large numbers of ethnic Romanians were forcibly removed to other countries in the Soviet Union, and Russian and Ukrainian immigration was fostered. Independence came in 1991, as the Soviet Union crumbled, but tensions between the predominantly Russian population in the region lying to the east of the Dniester, who wished to declare a separate republic, and the ethnic

Romanians, who sought closer ties, and even reunification, with Romania, resulted in violent clashes. In 1992, a joint Russian–Moldovan peacekeeping force was instituted to help restore order, although ethnic tensions persist. In 1994 a constitution was adopted, defining the country as a democratic republic.

Most of the countryside of Moldova is low-lying but hilly steppe country. It is eroded by rivers and the landscape is cut by numerous deep valleys and gorges. Thick forests grow on many of the hillsides and most of the country is covered with thick, black, fertile soils. This fertile land, combined with a temperate climate, short winters and high summer rainfall, made Moldova one of the foremost producers of food in the former Soviet Union.

Agriculture remains the main element in the Moldovan economy. Vegetables, sunflower seeds, tobacco, wheat, and maize are the principal crops, as well as grapes, which contribute to a thriving winemaking and exporting industry. Cattle and pig raising are also widespread.

The country has minimal reserves of mineral resources and depends upon Russian imports for all its oil, gas, and coal supplies. Electricity, too, is mainly imported and power shortages occur quite frequently. Industries include machine manufacturing and food processing.

Fact File

OFFICIAL NAME Republic of Moldova

FORM OF GOVERNMENT Republic with single legislative body (Parliament)

CAPITAL Chisinau

AREA 33,700 sq km (13,012 sq miles)

TIME ZONE GMT + 3 hours

POPULATION 4,460,838

PROJECTED POPULATION 2005 4,522,745

POPULATION DENSITY 132.4 per sq km (342.9 per sq mile)

LIFE EXPECTANCY 64.4

INFANT MORTALITY (PER 1,000) 43.5

OFFICIAL LANGUAGE Moldovan

OTHER LANGUAGES Russian, Gagauz (Turkish dialect)

LITERACY RATE 98.9%

RELIGIONS Eastern Orthodox 98.5%, Jewish 1.5%

ETHNIC GROUPS Moldovan/Romanian 64.5%, Ukrainian 13.8%, Russian 13%, Gagauz 3.5%, Jewish 1.5%, Bulgarian 2%, other 1.7%

CURRENCY Leu

ECONOMY Services 46%, agriculture 34%, industry 20%

GNP PER CAPITA US$920

CLIMATE Temperate, with mild winters and warm summers

HIGHEST POINT Mt Balaneshty 430 m (1,411 ft)

MAP REFERENCE Page 296

Monaco

Netherlands

Monaco, the world's smallest independent nation after the Vatican City, sits on the Mediterranean coast in the far southeast corner of France. Except for its coastline, it is completely surrounded by French territory. In the thirteenth century the Genoese built a fortress there and in 1297 members of the Grimaldi family of Genoa established themselves as rulers. Grimaldi princes retained control for almost 500 years, until 1792, when an uprising deposed the reigning prince and declared the state a republic. France annexed Monaco the following year, but in 1815, after the Congress of Vienna, it was placed under the protection of Sardinia. France annexed most of Monaco, including Menton, in 1848. In 1861, the Grimaldis were restored as rulers of less than half their former territory, governing under French protection. In 1911 democratic government was introduced by Prince Albert of Monaco. An 18-member National Council is elected every five years, but the head of government is selected by the monarch from a list drawn up by the French government. The present monarch, Prince Rainier III, is a descendant of the Grimaldis. He achieved fame in 1956 for his much-publicized marriage to the American film actress Grace Kelly.

Occupying the lower slopes of the Maritime Alps, Monaco is hilly and rugged. It is densely populated, mainly by foreign nationals. In the southwest is the industrial district of Fontvieille,

which consists partly of land reclaimed from the sea. Further east is the old town of Monaco-Ville, where the royal palace is situated. La Condamine, the banking, commercial, and fashionable residential center, overlooks a sheltered harbor. Northeast of La Condamine is Monte Carlo, with its casino, luxury hotels, and apartment blocks.

Apart from pharmaceutical, food processing, and other light industries in Fontvieille, Monaco thrives on its attractions as a tourist haven. The major drawcard is the state-run casino, from which the citizens of Monaco are banned. Until 1962, Monaco's status as a tax haven attracted many wealthy French businesses. The people of Monaco still pay no income tax, but foreigners now do, though at quite favorable rates.

Fact File

OFFICIAL NAME Principality of Monaco

FORM OF GOVERNMENT Constitutional monarchy with single legislative body (National Council)

CAPITAL Monaco

AREA 1.9 sq km (0.7 sq miles)

TIME ZONE GMT + 1 hour

POPULATION 32,149

PROJECTED POPULATION 2005 32,610

POPULATION DENSITY 16,920.5 per sq km (43,824.1 per sq mile)

LIFE EXPECTANCY 78.6

INFANT MORTALITY (PER 1,000) 6.5

OFFICIAL LANGUAGE French

OTHER LANGUAGES Italian, English, Monégasque

LITERACY RATE 99%

RELIGIONS Roman Catholic 95%, other 5%

ETHNIC GROUPS French 47%, Monégasque 16%, Italian 16%, other 21%

CURRENCY French franc

ECONOMY Tourism and services 90%, industry 10%

GNP PER CAPITA US$18,000

CLIMATE Temperate, with mild, wet winters and hot, dry summers

HIGHEST POINT Mt Agel 140 m (459 ft)

MAP REFERENCE Page 291

Situated in northwestern Europe, with a western and northern coastline on the North Sea, the Netherlands is bordered by Germany to its east and Belgium to its south. About half the area of this low-lying nation is below sea level and the country is saved from inundation only by a series of coastal dikes and sand dunes, heavily planted with marram grass to prevent erosion, and a complex network of canals and waterways, into which excess water is pumped from low-lying areas and then carried to the rivers that flow to the coast. For centuries the Dutch have been engaged in battle with the sea, and have gradually reclaimed huge amounts of land from it. In the last century more than 3,000 sq km (1,000 sq miles) of land were added. The most spectacular reclamation was the Zuiderzee project that began in 1920 and was completed almost 50 years later.

In the first century BC the Germanic peoples of the Low Countries, which include present-day Belgium and Luxembourg, were colonized by Roman armies. From the fifth century AD the region came under the successive control of Frankish, Burgundian, Austrian, and finally, in the fifteenth century, Spanish rulers. In 1568, William of Orange, outraged by Spain's suppression of a

Monaco, looking out over the Mediterranean Sea (left). Spreading fields of bulbs in the Netherlands (below). Houses and houseboats along one of Amsterdam's canals (top right).

spreading Protestant movement, led a revolt. In 1581 the seven northern provinces of the Low Countries declared their independence as the United Provinces of the Netherlands.

This set the scene for the consolidation and expansion of Dutch power throughout the seventeenth century. Trading posts and colonies were established in the East Indies (now Indonesia), the Caribbean (the Antilles), Africa, and South and North America. This period also saw the emergence of the Netherlands as a great maritime nation and a blossoming of Dutch art, literature, and scientific achievements.

The French, under Napoleon, invaded in 1794. After the defeat of France, the Congress of Vienna united the Netherlands, Belgium, and Luxembourg under a Dutch monarch in 1814. Belgium declared itself independent in 1831 and Luxembourg was granted autonomy in 1848. In 1848 a new constitution was introduced reducing the power of the monarch and investing greater authority in the Estates-General, as the parliament is still called. This laid the groundwork for the later emergence of a parliamentary democracy under a monarch with strictly formalized and limited powers.

The Netherlands remained neutral in the First World War and its neutrality was respected by both sides. In the Second World War it was overrun by Nazi forces in 1940. Its East Indies colonies were invaded by Japan. At the end of the war, the Netherlands began an armed conflict with rebel forces in its East Indies colony. It finally granted them independence, as the Republic of Indonesia, in 1949. Suriname, in South America, became independent in 1975, leaving the Antilles and Aruba as the Netherlands' only overseas territories.

After the Second World War the Netherlands joined the NATO alliance and became a founder member of the European Economic Community, later the European Union. In 1992 the Treaty on European Union, the Maastricht Treaty, was signed in the southern Dutch city of Maastricht.

Physical features and land use

Almost all of the Netherlands is flat and much of the landscape is covered by small farming plots, intensively cultivated and surrounded by ditches or canals. Dotting the landscape are windmills which for centuries have been used to drain the land. These are now largely picturesque as they have been supplanted by motor pumps. Much of this land is dedicated to horticulture, especially the growing of tulips and other bulb plants, often in tandem with vegetable produce.

Cattle farming and dairying, the country's main forms of agriculture, are strongest in the northwest, in the provinces of Nord Holland and Friesland, on either side of the Ijsselmeer, the area of the Zuiderzee project. The Ijsselmeer is an expanse of fresh water, separated by a dike, 32 km (20 miles) long, from the salt water of the Waddenzee. This lies between the northwest coast and a succession of accumulations of sand, which are known as the West Frisian Islands.

Further south, near the coast, is a succession of densely populated urban areas that include Amsterdam and the other major Dutch cities, including Rotterdam, one of the world's largest ports. Just south of this urban conglomeration, the major rivers that flow into the Netherlands—among them the Rhine from Germany and the Schelde and the Meuse from Belgium—share a common delta area. The only relief from flat land is in the far southeast, where a range of hills rises in places to about 100 m (300 ft).

Industry and commerce

Concentrated in the heavily populated urban southwest, manufacturing industry employs about one in five members of the workforce. Food processing, chemical and electrical machinery manufacture, metal and engineering products, and petroleum refining are major industries. Natural gas is the country's principal natural resource, and there are extensive reserves in the north.

Most Dutch people enjoy an affluent lifestyle, although some groups of immigrants on the fringes of the cities live in conspicuous poverty. Social services are well developed and the country has one of the best state-funded health-care systems in the world.

Fact File

OFFICIAL NAME Kingdom of the Netherlands

FORM OF GOVERNMENT Constitutional monarchy with two legislative bodies (First Chamber and Second Chamber)

CAPITAL Amsterdam; The Hague is the seat of government

AREA 37,330 sq km (14,413 sq miles)

TIME ZONE GMT + 1 hour

POPULATION 15,807,641

PROJECTED POPULATION 2005 16,143,653

POPULATION DENSITY 423.5 per sq km (1,096.8 per sq mile)

LIFE EXPECTANCY 78.2

INFANT MORTALITY (PER 1,000) 5.1

OFFICIAL LANGUAGE Dutch

OTHER LANGUAGES Arabic, Turkish, English

LITERACY RATE 99%

RELIGIONS Roman Catholic 34%, Protestant 25%, Muslim 3%, other 2%, unaffiliated 36%

ETHNIC GROUPS Dutch 96%; Moroccan, Turkish, and other 4%

CURRENCY Netherlands guilder

ECONOMY Services 79%, industry 17%, agriculture 4%

GNP PER CAPITA US$24,000

CLIMATE Temperate, with cool winters and mild summers

HIGHEST POINT Mt Vaalserberg 321 m (1,053 ft)

MAP REFERENCE Page 288

OVERSEAS TERRITORIES

Aruba
Netherlands Antilles

Norway

Fact File

OFFICIAL NAME Kingdom of Norway

FORM OF GOVERNMENT Constitutional monarchy with single legislative body (Parliament)

CAPITAL Oslo

AREA 324,220 sq km (125,181 sq miles)

TIME ZONE GMT + 1 hour

POPULATION 4,438,547

PROJECTED POPULATION 2005 4,523,798

POPULATION DENSITY 13.7 per sq km (35.5 per sq mile)

LIFE EXPECTANCY 78.4

INFANT MORTALITY (PER 1,000) 5.0

OFFICIAL LANGUAGE Norwegian

OTHER LANGUAGES Lapp, Finnish

LITERACY RATE 99%

RELIGIONS Evangelical Lutheran 94%; Baptist, Pentecostalist, Methodist and Roman Catholic 6%

ETHNIC GROUPS Germanic (Nordic, Alpine, Baltic) 97%, others include Lapp minority 3%

CURRENCY Norwegian krone

ECONOMY Services 61%, industry 36%, agriculture 3%

GNP PER CAPITA US$31,250

CLIMATE Cold in north and inland, temperate and wet on coast

HIGHEST POINT Glittertind 2,472 m (8,110 ft)

MAP REFERENCE Pages 284–85, 286

Houses built along the banks of a small fiord in Norway (right). The Norwegian city of Bergen (center right). High plateau country, dotted with tiny lakes, in Norway (top). The rooftops of Gdansk in northern Poland, a major port and birthplace of the trade union Solidarity (far right).

Norway's long, narrow landmass wraps around the western part of Sweden and the north of Finland and shares a land border with the northwest tip of the Russian Federation. Its rugged western coastline is washed by the North Sea in the south and the Norwegian Sea further north. Its northern tip juts into the Arctic Ocean, making it the most northerly part of Europe. To the south the Skagerrak Strait separates it from the northern tip of Denmark. Like the Swedes and Danes, modern Norwegians are descendents of the Vikings, Teutonic peoples who settled the area and who, from the ninth to the eleventh centuries AD, raided and conquered lands to the north, east, and west. In the fourteenth century, Denmark, Sweden, and Norway came under Danish rule. Although Sweden became independent in the sixteenth century, Norwegians remained subject to the Danes. In 1815, at the end of the Napoleonic Wars, in which Denmark sided with France, control of Norway was transferred to the Swedish crown. The modern Norwegian state dates from 1905, when the country declared its independence. Norway remained neutral in the First World War and was not attacked. However, Nazi forces invaded in 1940 and, despite spirited resistance, subdued the country. Norway joined the NATO alliance in 1949, and in the early 1990s attempted to join the European Union, a move that was thwarted when the option was defeated at a referendum. Norway is a parliamentary democracy with a monarch as the titular head of state.

Norway's more than 21,000 km (13,000 miles) of coast is punctuated by deep fiords. Most of the country consists of mountains with deep valleys formed by ancient glaciers. There are also vast areas of high plateaus. More than one-quarter of the land surface is forested, mainly with conifers, and there are many lakes. The population is centered in the lowlands on the southern coasts

OVERSEAS TERRITORIES

Bouvet Island
Jan Mayen
Peter Island
Svalbard

and in the southeast. Only a tiny proportion of the land area is suitable for cultivation and agriculture is limited mainly to areas around lakes.

Norway has large oil and gas reserves in the North Sea and produces more oil and gas than any other European country. Its electricity, produced mainly from hydroelectric plants, is used largely to power industry. Key industries include pulp and paper manufacture, shipbuilding, and aluminum production. Fishing and fish farming are also major industries and farmed salmon is a major export.

Poland

Situated in northern central Europe, Poland has a northern coastline on the Baltic Sea and land borders with seven countries. To the west, the Oder River forms part of the border with Germany, while to the southwest the Sudeten Mountains separate it from the Czech Republic. The Carpathian Mountains form a natural boundary with Slovakia in the south. Ukraine and Belarus lie to the east, Lithuania is to the northeast and a part of the Russian Federation is adjacent to the northern coastline.

In the seventh and eighth centuries AD, Slavic peoples from the south—known as Polanie, or plain-dwellers—occupied most of Poland. In the tenth century their king was converted to Christianity, beginning a Catholic tradition that has survived to the present, despite attempts to suppress it by post-war communist governments. Over the next two centuries, invaders from Prussia divided up the country, which was reunited in the fourteenth century. Poland retained its independence and at times extended its power during the next two centuries, but again came under Prussian and Austrian control in the late eighteenth century. The nation regained its

independence in 1918 with the defeat of Austria–Germany in the First World War. Early in the Second World War, Poland was overrun by Germany and then Russia, which divided the country between them until June 1941, when the Germans took full control. After the war Poland's borders shifted to the west, as part of what was formerly Germany was ceded to Poland, and as the Soviets were given control of substantial territories in the east. Under these arrangements Poland suffered a net loss of both territory and population. From then until 1989 Poland was effectively a vassal state of the Soviet Union.

Growing civil unrest during the 1980s focused on a series of strikes in a range of industries, organized by the trade union Solidarity. In 1989 the besieged government capitulated and allowed Solidarity to contest the government elections, which it won decisively. The first entirely free elections were held in 1991. Poland is now a democratic republic with a directly elected president and a multi-party system.

Except for the mountain ranges in the south and southwest, most of Poland is low-lying, forming part of the North European Plain. The landscape is drained by numerous rivers, the most significant of which is the Vistula, which rises in the Carpathian Mountains and flows through the center of the country, through Warsaw, and to the Baltic Sea near the industrial city of Gdansk. Most of this plain is fertile, covered with rich loess soil which supports a range of cereal and vegetable crops, in which Poland is almost self-sufficient, and livestock, the most important of which are cattle and pigs. In the northeast the country is more undulating, and much of northern Poland is dotted with extensive lakes. Towards the Baltic coast a range of hills, known as the Baltic Heights, slope down to a sandy coastal plain.

Agriculture, which once employed more than half of Poland's workforce, still accounts for just over a quarter of it. The post-war years saw a rapid expansion of heavy industries, which now include shipbuilding, based in Gdansk, and steel and cement manufacture, based around the mining centers in the south. Many industrial activities rely on Poland's rich coal reserves, and coal is used to

generate more than half the country's electricity. Reliance on this form of fuel has resulted in serious air pollution and acid rain. Other mineral resources include natural gas, iron ore, and salt, on which important chemical industries are based.

Poland has been more successful than many former communist states in converting to a privatized economy. While many Poles have prospered from a growing number of entre-preneurial opportunities, however, others have seen their incomes seriously lowered. Unemployment remains comparatively high.

Fact File

OFFICIAL NAME	Republic of Poland
FORM OF GOVERNMENT	Republic with two legislative bodies (Senate and Parliament or Sejm)
CAPITAL	Warsaw
AREA	312,683 sq km (120,727 sq miles)
TIME ZONE	GMT + 1 hour
POPULATION	38,608,929
PROJECTED POPULATION 2005	39,257,669
POPULATION DENSITY	123.5 per sq km (319.8 per sq mile)
LIFE EXPECTANCY	73.1
INFANT MORTALITY (PER 1,000)	12.8
OFFICIAL LANGUAGE	Polish
LITERACY RATE	99%
RELIGIONS	Roman Catholic 95%; others include Eastern Orthodox, Protestant 5%
ETHNIC GROUPS	Polish 97.6%, German 1.3%, Ukrainian 0.6%, Belarusian 0.5%
CURRENCY	Zloty
ECONOMY	Services 40%, industry 32%, agriculture 28%
GNP PER CAPITA	US$2,790
CLIMATE	Temperate, with cold winters and warm, wet summers
HIGHEST POINT	Rysy 2,499 m (8,199 ft)
MAP REFERENCE	Page 289

Portugal

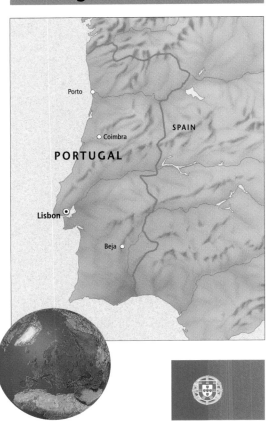

Fact File

OFFICIAL NAME Portuguese Republic

FORM OF GOVERNMENT Republic with single legislative body (Assembly of the Republic)

CAPITAL Lisbon

AREA 92,080 sq km (35,552 sq miles)

TIME ZONE GMT + 1 hour

POPULATION 9,918,040

PROJECTED POPULATION 2005 9,792,757

POPULATION DENSITY 107.7 per sq km (279 per sq mile)

LIFE EXPECTANCY 75.9

INFANT MORTALITY (PER 1,000) 6.7

OFFICIAL LANGUAGE Portuguese

LITERACY RATE 89.6%

RELIGIONS Roman Catholic 97%, Protestant 1%, other 2%

ETHNIC GROUPS Portuguese 98%, African immigrants from former colonies 2%

CURRENCY Escudo

ECONOMY Services 61%, industry 26%, agriculture 13%

GNP PER CAPITA US$9,740

CLIMATE Temperate; cool and rainy in north, warm and dry in south

HIGHEST POINT Ponta de Pico in the Azores 2,351 m (7,713 ft); Serra de Estrela on the mainland, 1,993 m (6,539 ft)

MAP REFERENCE Page 292

Farm buildings at the foot of Mt Giestoso in Minho Province, Portugal (right). The Transylvanian Alps in Romania (top right). The village of Ponte da Lima, surrounded by terraced fields, in Andrao, Portugal (bottom right).

Situated at the western edge of the Iberian Peninsula, Portugal is shaped somewhat like a long, narrow rectangle. It has a long Atlantic coastline bordering its western edge, and a much shorter one at its southern extremity. Spain surrounds it on the other two sides. From the second century BC until the fifth century AD, Portugal was part of the Roman Empire. As the empire collapsed the territory suffered a series of invasions—by Germanic tribes, Visigoths, and, in the eighth century, by Muslim Moors from northern Africa. The Moors were finally expelled by Christian invaders from Burgundy during the twelfth century and a Burgundian line of monarchs was established. An abortive Castilian attempt to seize the crown in the fourteenth century saw a new dynasty installed under John of Aviz, who reigned as John I. His son, Prince Henry the Navigator, encouraged widespread exploration and the establishment of a vast empire, with colonies in Africa, South America, India, and Southeast Asia. The invasion of Portugal by the Spanish in 1581, even though they were expelled 60 years later, heralded the decline in Portugal's influence. A French invasion in 1807 was reversed three years later when the British expelled the invaders in 1811.

During the nineteenth century widespread poverty and growing resentment at the power of the monarchy culminated in the 1910 revolution, in which the monarchy was overthrown. An army coup in 1926 installed Olivier Salazar as a right-wing dictator. He remained in power until 1968,

but his successor, Marcello Caetano, was overthrown by a left-wing army coup in 1974, which eventually led to democratic elections in 1976. Portugal is now a democratic republic, with a popularly elected president as head of state.

Portugal is divided fairly evenly into its wetter northern and more arid southern regions by the River Tagus. This river flows west into the country from Spain and then takes a southwesterly course toward the Atlantic, entering it at Lisbon. Highland forested areas dominate the north. The highest mountains are in the far north, especially in the east. Here, the landscape is characterized by high plateaus, punctuated by deep gorges and river valleys, which gradually descend to the western coastal plain. In these mountains are thick forests of both conifers and deciduous trees. South of the Douro River the landscape becomes less rugged and the slopes more gentle until they reach the plain around the Tagus. South of the Tagus, the country is mainly flat or undulating. In the Tagus Valley and further south are forests of cork oaks, the bark of which is used to produce wine corks. In the Algarve, in the far south, a range of hills runs across the country from the Spanish border to its southwestern tip.

Portugal has two self-governing regions in the Atlantic: the nine volcanic islands that constitute the Azores and the volcanic archipelago of two inhabited and two groups of uninhabited islets that make up Madeira. In 1987, Portugal signed a treaty to return its last territory, Macau, to China in 1999.

By western European standards Portugal is still a highly rural society, with agriculture and fishing still employing a significant number of the country's workforce. Many farms, especially the smaller ones that predominate in the north, continue to use traditional methods. Cereals and vegetables are widely cultivated, and wine production, especially port wine from the Douro Valley, is the major agricultural activity. Manufacturing is growing in importance, much of it concerned with processing the country's agricultural products. Paper and cork manufacture, and textiles and footwear, are among the significant industries. Tourism, especially in the warm, southern Algarve region, has greatly expanded in recent years, leading to rapid building development and considerable attendant environmental degradation.

Portuguese products

Portugal is famous for two products, cork and port. Before modern plastics were invented, cork had no equal as a strong, lightweight, buoyant, impermeable, and elastic material. It is the bark of the cork oak, found in Portugal, Spain and the Mediterranean. Cork was formerly used for lifebelts and floats on fishing nets, and is only slowly being replaced as a stopper for wine bottles by plastics. Portugal produces more cork than the rest of the world combined.

The bark is first harvested when the tree is about 20 years old, supplies being taken at subsequent 10-year intervals. The cork is removed by making cuts in the bark using an curved knife. The pieces are soaked in water, scraped, washed, and dried.

Port is a dark red, full-bodied fortified wine named after the town of Oporto, from which it has been exported for many years. No one variety of grape is used. The wine's distinctiveness comes from the climate and soil of the mountainous Alto Douro region of north Portugal, and from the methods of cultivation and wine-making used in its production. British capital contributed to the port industry, and the UK was for many years the main destination for the finished product.

Romania

Except for its Black Sea coast, Romania is land-locked—by Ukraine to the north, Moldova to the northeast, Hungary to the west, Yugoslavia to the southwest, and Bulgaria to the south. From the sixth century AD the country was often invaded. From the ninth to the eleventh centuries Magyars occupied part of Transylvania and between the fourteenth and sixteenth centuries Walachia, Moldova, and Transylvania formed part of the Ottoman Empire. At the end of the First World War, Bessarabia—most of present-day Moldova—Transylvania and Bukovina were restored to Romania. Much of this land was lost during the Second World War when Romania, which sided with Nazi Germany, came under Soviet control. During Ceausescu's oppressive regime, beginning in 1967, Romania distanced itself from the Soviets. In 1989 a popular uprising saw Ceausescu arrested and executed. Romania is now ruled by an elected parliament headed by a president.

The Carpathian Mountains curve through the center of the country, dividing the timbered uplands of Transylvania from the Danube Plain. The southern part of the range, the Transylvanian Alps, contains the highest peaks and the most rugged scenery. The fertile eastern plain is crossed by many tributaries of the Danube. To the east, around the Danube Delta, the landscape is marshy and dotted with numerous lakes and lagoons.

There has been a shift toward heavy industries since the 1970s but agriculture is still economically important. Maize, wheat, vegetables, and grapes for wine are the main crops and sheep and pigs the main livestock. Romania is rich in coal, natural gas, iron ore, and petroleum. Most of the raw materials for the country's industries are imported. Prominent industries include chemical and metal processing and machine manufacturing. Lumbering has depleted much of the country's forest and industry has caused widespread pollution. Moves to a market economy have been slow and Romania's standard of living remains relatively low.

Fact File

OFFICIAL NAME	Romania
FORM OF GOVERNMENT	Republic with two legislative bodies (Senate and House of Deputies)
CAPITAL	Bucharest
AREA	237,500 sq km (91,699 sq miles)
TIME ZONE	GMT + 2 hours
POPULATION	22,334,312
PROJECTED POPULATION 2005	22,304,366
POPULATION DENSITY	94 per sq km (243.5 per sq mile)
LIFE EXPECTANCY	70.8
INFANT MORTALITY (PER 1,000)	18.1
OFFICIAL LANGUAGE	Romanian
OTHER LANGUAGES	Hungarian, German
LITERACY RATE	96.9%
RELIGIONS	Romanian Orthodox 87%, Roman Catholic 5%, Protestant 5%, other 3%
ETHNIC GROUPS	Romanian 89.1%, Hungarian 8.9%, other 2%
CURRENCY	Leu
ECONOMY	Industry 38%, services 34%, agriculture 28%
GNP PER CAPITA	US$1,480
CLIMATE	Temperate; cold winters and warm, wet summers; cooler in Carpathian Mountains
HIGHEST POINT	Moldoveanu 2,544 m (8,346 ft)
MAP REFERENCE	Page 296

Europe and the Russian Federation

Russian Federation

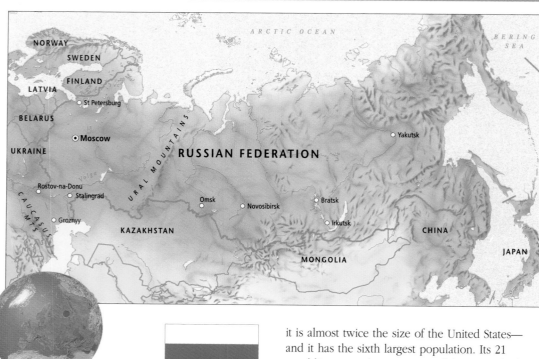

Fact file

OFFICIAL NAME Russian Federation

FORM OF GOVERNMENT Federal republic with two legislative bodies (Federation Council and State Duma)

CAPITAL Moscow

AREA 17,075,200 sq km (6,592,735 sq miles)

TIME ZONE GMT + 3–12 hours

POPULATION 146,393,569

PROJECTED POPULATION 2005 144,263,571

POPULATION DENSITY 8.6 per sq km (22.3 per sq mile)

LIFE EXPECTANCY 65.1

INFANT MORTALITY (PER 1,000) 23.0

OFFICIAL LANGUAGE Russian

OTHER LANGUAGES More than 100 minority languages

LITERACY RATE 98.7%

RELIGIONS Russian Orthodox 27%; Muslim, Jewish, Roman Catholic and other minorities 73%

ETHNIC GROUPS Russian 81.5%, Tatar 3.8%, Ukrainian 3%, Chuvash 1.2%, Bashkir 0.9%, Belarusian 0.8%, Moldovan 0.7%, other 8.1%

CURRENCY Ruble

ECONOMY Industry 27%, agriculture 15%, education and culture 11%, other 47%

GNP PER CAPITA US$2,240

CLIMATE Warm and dry in far south; cold temperate (long, cold winters and short, mild summers) in most inland areas; polar in far north

HIGHEST POINT Mt Elbrus 5,633 m (18,481 ft)

MAP REFERENCE Pages 299, 300–01

Sprawling across the easternmost part of northern Europe and occupying the whole of northern Asia, the Russian Federation, often called simply Russia, is the largest country in the world—

it is almost twice the size of the United States— and it has the sixth largest population. Its 21 republics cover three-quarters of the area of what was for almost 70 years (until it collapsed in 1991) the Union of Soviet Socialist Republics.

The Russian Federation has long coastlines along the Arctic Ocean in the north and along the Pacific Ocean in the east. Its southeastern coastline is on the Sea of Japan and north of this the Kamchatka Peninsula encloses the Sea of Okhotsk. In its far southwestern corner there is a short stretch of coast along the Caspian Sea; a little further north, it briefly borders the Black Sea; and in the northwest, near St Petersburg, it touches on the eastern tip of the Gulf of Finland. Its mainland has borders with 12 other countries. In the far southeast it borders the northeast tip of North Korea. In the south it borders China in two places: to the east and the west of its long border with Mongolia. The western half of its southern border is with the former Soviet republic of Kazakhstan. To the west of the Caspian Sea are Azerbaijan and Georgia, and north of the Black Sea are Ukraine, Belarus, Latvia, and Estonia. Northeast of the Gulf of Finland is a border with Finland and at its very northwest tip the Russian Federation borders on a tiny part of Norway. Further west, tucked in between Lithuania and Poland, and with a coast on the Baltic Sea, is another small area of Russian territory, centered on the coastal city of Kaliningrad.

History

Until the sixth century AD, almost all of what is now Russia was inhabited only by nomadic tribes of Finnic and Slavic origin. In the sixth century peoples from what are now Iran and Turkey settled the part of southwestern Russia between the Carpathian Mountains and the Volga River, establishing a capital on the Caspian Sea. They in turn were overrun by Viking invaders and traders who spread southward along river routes from the Baltic Sea. One tradition has it that modern Russia dates back to the establishment of a dynasty by the Viking Rurik at Novgorod in AD 862. Soon after, however, the center of power moved farther southwest, to Kiev in present-day Ukraine, and a unified confederation, known as Kievan Rus,

emerged. In the tenth century the leader Vladimir was converted to Christianity. Over the next two centuries a Russian culture, based on the traditions of Orthodox Christianity, developed, but in the thirteenth century Kievan Rus fell to invaders from Mongolia and the confederation broke down into a number of dukedoms, under Mongol domination. The Muscovite dukes emerged as the most powerful, mainly through their role as tribute collectors for the Mongols. Opposition to Mongol rule gathered strength during the fourteenth century and in the fifteenth century the Muscovite Duke Ivan III finally expelled the Mongols. His grandson, Ivan IV, known as "The Terrible," was the first to declare himself "Tsar of all the Russians." Under his oppressive rule, which lasted from 1533 to 1584, the power of princes and landowners (known as "boyars") was broken and the Muscovite state spread eastward across the Urals and into what is now Siberia.

After Ivan's death, a series of internal disputes culminated in Polish invasion in 1609 and, after the ousting of the Poles in 1612, the emergence of the first Romanov tsar, Mikhail, in 1613. Under his grandson, Peter I (known as "The Great"), who ruled from 1696 to 1725, the country was renamed "Russia," and a new capital was established at St Petersburg. Territories along the Baltic were acquired from Sweden, and western European ideas, technology, and styles of dress and other fashions were embraced. During the eighteenth and nineteenth centuries Russia extended its borders south and east into Asia.

The defeat of Napoleon's invading armies, in 1812, confirmed Russia's status as a great power, but the country remained socially and industrially backward in comparison with Western Europe.

A feudal system, under which peasants were bonded to landlords, remained until 1861, when Tsar Alexander II abolished serfdom. Alexander's political and social reforms earned him powerful enemies and led to his assassination in 1881. The oppressive rule of his successor, Alexander III, spawned the formation of the Marxist Russian Social Democratic Party in 1898, under the leadership of Vladimir Ilich Ulyanov, who called himself Lenin. Civil unrest intensified following Russia's defeat in its war with Japan in 1904–05, forcing Tsar Nicholas II to establish a parliament, known as the Duma, elected by a very limited suffrage, and to institute some civil liberty reforms.

These reforms, however, failed to stem the revolutionary tide, which was further strengthened by the reverses and heavy loss of life in the First World War. In February 1917, rioting and strikes broke out in the capital, St Petersburg, there was a massive defection of Russian troops, and Tsar Nicholas II abdicated, leading to the decisive revolution of October 1917, in which the All-Russian Communist Party emerged as the ruling force, with Lenin as dictatorial leader. Four years of civil war ensued, until the communists fully took control. In December 1922, Russia, with Moscow as capital, became the dominant power in the newly formed Union of Soviet Socialist Republics, having seized Georgia, Armenia, and Azerbaijan and established its ascendancy in Ukraine and central Asia.

Following Lenin's death in 1924, there was a bitter factional struggle for power. By 1929 Josef Stalin was the undisputed leader and remained in power until he died in 1953. Under his regime, agriculture was collectivized, industry expanded, and brutal labor camps were established in Siberia

for those suspected of espousing dissident ideas. Political rivals and enemies, whether real or imagined, were routinely eliminated in a series of ruthless purges. In one purge in 1929–30, hundreds of thousands of peasants who opposed farm collectivization were either murdered or sent away to remote, desolate parts of the country. Farm collectivization led to immense agricultural disruption and resulted in famine in the early 1930s in which many thousands of people died.

Russia, and the rest of the Soviet Union, suffered terribly during the Second World War. At first allied with Germany, the Soviet Union, in 1939 and 1940, seized territory in Poland and Romania, and annexed the Baltic republics of

Estonia, Latvia, and Lithuania. In 1941, Hitler's troops suddenly invaded the Soviet Union, and in the occupation and struggles that ensued in the following four years, an estimated 20 million Soviet citizens were killed.

At the end of the war, the regions that were occupied by Soviet forces—most of Eastern Europe—came under Soviet domination. This gave rise to a 40-year period of international tension as the Soviet Union and the United States assumed the mantles of mutually distrustful, competing superpowers, each building up an arsenal of ever more potentially destructive nuclear weapons. During the premiership of Stalin's successor, Nikita Khrushchev, the Soviet Union and its satellites

St Petersburg, once the capital of Russia, seen from across the misty Neva River (left). Shoppers in Arbat Street, a prosperous part of Moscow (top). Fishing through a hole in the ice, using large nets, in Siberia (above).

Most of Russia's agriculture is concentrated in the south of the plain, as the harsh climates further north are not conducive to the growing of crops or to the raising of livestock. Less than one-tenth of Russia is under cultivation. Cereals are the main crops, although in most years the country produces only about half the grain it requires. The rest has to be imported. Livestock raising, most commonly cattle and dairy farming, is also based mainly in the west.

To the east of the Ural Mountains, the Siberian Plain is largely desolate, treeless, and flat. Central Siberia, to the east of the Yenisey River, is a region of plateaus that range from between 450 and 900 m (1,500 and 3,000 ft) in height and rise in the south to a series of mountain ranges that border Mongolia and China. Lowlands flank these plateaus to the north and east. East of the Lena River the country rises again toward the rugged and mountainous east coast. South of the Bering Sea, the Kamchatka Peninsula and the Kuril Islands form part of the Pacific "Ring of Fire." This is an area of considerable geothermal activity and there are about 30 active volcanoes.

The landscape of northern Russia is mainly arctic tundra—a treeless expanse which remains frozen throughout the year. Tundra vegetation consists of sedges, grasses, mosses, lichens, and ground-hugging plants. Further south, and in the southwest, the landscape varies between tracts of semidesert and expanses of forest, largely conifers, known as the taiga.

A group of Russian women at a festival wearing traditional costume (above left). The gilded domes and turrets of Pushkin Palace in Moscow (right). A river winding through fertile farming country (below).

entered into a defense treaty, the Warsaw Pact, to oppose the Western NATO alliance. Nuclear war seemed a real danger in 1962, when a Soviet attempt to place nuclear weapons on Cuba was met by a United States blockade. Khrushchev's humiliating backdown in this crisis, as well as a serious rift between Russia and communist China, led to his being removed from office the next year and his replacement by Leonid Brezhnev.

The Brezhnev era lasted until 1982 and during this time, Soviet–Western relations fluctuated. Periods of relaxation, which became known as "détente," alternated with times of renewed suspicion and hostility. Despite this, and despite the USSR's invasions of Czechoslovakia in 1968 and Afghanistan in December 1979, genuine agreements about arms reduction were achieved. During the brief premierships of Brezhnev's two immediate successors, East–West relations soured again. However, in 1985, the accession to the leadership of Mikhail Gorbachev led to an era of greater trust as well as to a less dictatorial and more open style of political leadership, and the first tentative moves toward a loosening of government controls over the economy. The terms *glasnost,* meaning "openness" and *perestroika,* meaning "restructuring" were used widely at this time, in reference to Gorbachev's reforms.

Growing social unrest, deteriorating economic conditions, and a resurgence of nationalism in a number of Soviet republics created immense strains in the Soviet Union. An attempted coup by communist conservatives took place in 1991 but was put down, largely through the heroic opposition of Boris Yeltsin, who emerged as the de facto leader of the country, enjoying widespread popular support.

Against Gorbachev's wishes, the Soviet Union was officially dissolved in December 1991 and replaced by the Commonwealth of Independent States (see box on facing page). Gorbachev then resigned as president and Yeltsin assumed control. Yeltsin's leadership was confirmed in a national referendum that was held in 1993 and, despite a poor economic situation and widespread hardship, as well as serious misgivings about his health, Yeltsin was re-elected president in 1996. In the parliamentary, or Duma, elections, however, conservative nationalists, some of them stridently anti-Western, received widespread support.

A new constitution, adopted in 1993, established a two-chambered Federal Assembly, headed by a prime minister, who is appointed by the president. The president is popularly elected for a five-year term and has considerable independent powers, including the right to dissolve parliament.

Physical features and land use

Stretching all the way from the Arctic Ocean in the north to the border with Kazakhstan in the south, the Ural Mountains separate European Russia in the west from the vast Siberian Plain to the east. European Russia, where most of the population lives and where the bulk of Russian industry and agriculture is located, consists mainly of a huge fertile plain, the East Europe Plain, which has an average elevation of 170 m (550 ft) but rises to a maximum of 400 m (1,300 ft). In the far southwest, the Caucasus Mountains form a natural boundary with Georgia and Azerbaijan, and there are upland areas in the far north near the border with Finland. In the western part of the plain are the Valdai Hills, in which the Volga and Dnieper Rivers have their source.

Timeline		AD 300 Spread of peoples including Huns, Goths, and Magyars into forests west of the Ural Mountains	AD 830 Scandinavian merchants establish new base in the Volga region, close to present-day Ryazan		1237 Russia becomes part of Mongol Empire until late 1400s, extending the empire's boundaries to Arctic, Baltic and Pacific	1547 Ivan IV, known as "the Terrible," is crowned Tsar and takes the title for all Russia	1613 Romanovs become the Tsarist family, ruling until the murder of Nicholas II in 1918	1703 Peter the Great opens Russia to Western ideas. Builds St Petersburg on the Baltic Sea, making it the capital in 1712
20,000 BP Huts made from mammoth bones covered in animal skins at Mezhirich in Ukraine region	4000 BC Horses domesticated on the steppes, first mainly as draft animals but later (2000 BC) as fast transport in warfare		AD 770 Germanic traders and soldiers from Baltic move into Volga region previously occupied by Finnic and Slavic groups	AD 882 Scandinavian groups capture Kiev; Russia takes its name from Kievan Rus, term given by Slavic groups to the Black Sea area	1318 Mongols appoint Yuri of Moscow Crown Prince; he makes Moscow an important center and later the capital of Russia	1697 First recorded eruption of Klyuchevskaya Volcano in Kamchatka, Siberia		1725 Catherine the Great becomes Empress. Encourages Western ideas in arts and education. Most Russians impoverishe

Industry, commerce, and culture

Russia, and especially Siberia, has abundant mineral resources. These contributed greatly to the country's rapid transformation during the Soviet period from a predominantly agricultural economy to one that was heavily industrialized. These mineral resources underpin the federation's present reliance on heavy industry and provide important mining exports. They include coal, petroleum, natural gas, iron ore, bauxite, copper, lead, zinc, and gold and other precious metals. Steelmaking, the manufacture of agricultural machinery, chemicals, textiles, and food processing are among the principal industries, centered on such large cities to the west of the Urals as Moscow, St Petersburg, Novgorod, and Volgograd, but also in a number of cities in Siberia such as Yekaterinburg and Novosibirsk.

The country's move toward a market economy has been fraught with difficulties and has been accompanied by a marked increase in social and financial inequalities as a new class of rich entrepreneurs has emerged. The majority of Russians live in relative poverty, victims of steeply rising prices and severe shortages of food and other basic consumer items. Corruption and crime have also increased significantly and a number of the leaders of organized crime are among the richest citizens in the nation. These conditions were aggravated by a virtual collapse of the Russian economy in 1998 and continuing political uncertainty based on serious doubts, unallayed by official reassurances, about the capacity of the president, Boris Yeltsin, who suffers chronic ill health. There are strong movements within the country for a return to centralized control of the economy and for a more aggressive nationalistic approach to relations with the West.

Russia has contributed much to literature, music, and the performing arts, especially in the nineteenth century. Writers such as Turgenev prepared the way for other giants of literature like Tolstoy and Dostoyevsky. Among composers, Tchaikovsky and Stravinsky established Russia's place in musical history. The Imperial Russian Ballet was founded in 1735, and Russian ballet has become internationally renowned for its choreography and dancers like Pavlova and Nureyev.

The Commonwealth of Independent States

The Commonwealth of Independent States is a loose confederation of twelve former Soviet republics that was formed after the breakdown of the Soviet Union in 1991. The idea for the formation of the commonwealth was agreed to at a meeting of Russian president Boris Yeltsin and the presidents of Belarus and Ukraine in Minsk, in Belarus, in early December 1991 and was ratified at Alma-Ata in Kazakhstan by 11 of the former Soviet republics on 21 December. Georgia and the three Baltic states of Estonia, Latvia, and Lithuania declined to join, although Georgia has since become a member. Not surprisingly, Russia assumed the status of dominant member of the group, taking control of all former Soviet embassies and consulates and occupying the former Soviet Union's seat on the United Nations Security Council. Minsk was designated as the administrative center of the new commonwealth, which was much more an alliance than a state entity. According to the agreement, the political independence of each state was guaranteed in return for a commitment to certain forms of economic and defence cooperation.

The commonwealth remains a tenuous confederation and there are many areas of dispute between its constituent members. There is a natural suspicion that the Russian Federation seeks to impose its political will on the other members, and this was in no way diminished in 1996 when the Russian parliament, or Duma, passed a non-binding resolution in favor of reinstating the former Soviet Union. Difficult economic conditions throughout the former Soviet Union have led to increasing support, especially in Belarus, for a return to the previous status quo.

| 1773–74 The Peasants Revolt sweeps across Russia from the Urals to the Volga but is put down by troops | 1890 Migration of large numbers of people from eastern Russia to Siberia and Asia lasts for around 10 years | 1917 Revolution puts Bolsheviks in power after storming of the Winter Palace, at St Petersburg | 1918 Tsar Nicholas II and family are shot, allegedly at the hands of the Bolsheviks; Moscow again capital of Russia | 1928 First Five-Year Plan introduced to further centralize the economy and increase industrial and agricultural production | 1935 Great Purge by Stalin's secret police takes many lives; millions starve in a famine partly caused by farm collectivization | 1956 Bezymianny Volcano in Kamchatka, Siberia, erupts leaving ash 50 cm (20 in) deep 10 km (6 miles) from volcano | 1985 Gorbachev heads Communist Party; pursues policies of *perestroika* ("economic restructuring") and *glasnost* ("openness") |
| 1812 Napoleon's invasion of Russia defeated. Most of the 500,000 French forces die or are captured | 1891 Construction of the Trans-Siberian Railroad from Moscow to Vladivostok begins. Not completed until 1916 | 1914 Germany declares war on Russia and for three years Russia sides with Allies | 1918-20 Communists victorious in a civil war with the anti-communist White Russians | 1924 Stalin leader of one of four factions that run party | 1929 Stalin becomes undisputed leader and rules USSR for more than 20 years | 1941 Russia sides with Allies in Second World War after Germany invades USSR and is defeated in the Battle of Stalingrad (1943) | 1986 Chernobyl nuclear reactor in Ukraine explodes; cancers from radiation kill up to 40,000 worldwide |

San Marino

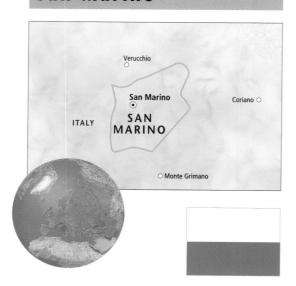

Completely surrounded by Italian territory, most of the tiny state of San Marino sits on the slopes of Mount Titano in the Appenine Mountains, 20 km (12 miles) inland from the city of Rimini on the Adriatic coast of northern Italy. The republic takes its name from St Marinus who, so legend has it, arrived there with a group of followers in the fourth century AD and established a settlement. This makes it arguably the world's oldest surviving republic. Records of its existence can be traced back to the twelfth century. It became one of the many mini-states on the Italian peninsula and was accorded papal recognition in 1631. The Sanmarinesi, as its inhabitants are known, offered refuge to Giuseppe Garibaldi when he passed through in 1849, pursued by his enemies. However, when the newly unified state of Italy was declared in 1861 the Sanmarinesi declined to join. San Marino fought with Italy in the First World War. In the Second World War it began by supporting Fascist Italy but later changed sides and was invaded by Germany. San Marino is a democratic republic with elections held every five years.

This picturesque little country is centered on the fortified medieval town of San Marino, where most of the population lives. On the lower slopes, beneath the rugged limestone peak, are thick forests, expanses of pastureland and a string of ancient villages. Almost one-fifth of the land is used for agriculture. Cereals, olives, and vines are cultivated and sheep and goats are raised. Cheeses and wine are its principal agricultural products.

Since 1862 San Marino has had a friendship and cooperation treaty with Italy. It also shares its currency and enjoys a standard of living roughly equivalent to that of its neighbor. About one in five of Sanmarinesi workers are in the tourism industry, which caters for more than 2 million visitors each year, although many do not stay overnight. Winemaking, textiles, and ceramics are siginificant industries. Even more significant is the sale of the country's distinctive postage stamps, which are sought by collectors and account for up to 10 percent of the country's revenues.

Fact File

OFFICIAL NAME Republic of San Marino

FORM OF GOVERNMENT Republic with single legislative body (Great and General Council)

CAPITAL San Marino

AREA 60 sq km (23 sq miles)

TIME ZONE GMT + 1 hour

POPULATION 25,061

PROJECTED POPULATION 2005 25,864

POPULATION DENSITY 417.7 per sq km (1,081.81 per sq mile)

LIFE EXPECTANCY 81.5

INFANT MORTALITY (PER 1,000) 5.4

OFFICIAL LANGUAGE Italian

LITERACY RATE 99%

RELIGIONS Roman Catholic 95%, other 5%

ETHNIC GROUPS Sanmarinesi 87.1%, Italian 12.4%, other 0.5%

CURRENCY Italian lira

ECONOMY Services 58%, industry 40%, agriculture 2%

GNP PER CAPITA US$15,000

CLIMATE Temperate, with mild winters and warm summers

HIGHEST POINT Monte Titano 739 m (2,425 ft)

MAP REFERENCE Page 294

Slovakia

This small central European country is bordered by Poland to the north, the Czech Republic to the northwest, Austria to the west, Hungary to the south, and Ukraine to the east. It is the smaller, less populous, and less industrially developed part of the former state of Czechoslovakia, which split peacefully in 1993 to form the two separate nations of Slovakia and the Czech Republic.

Ethnically distinct from their former compatriots, the Slovaks had lived for ten centuries under continuous Hungarian domination when, in 1918, they merged with the Czechs to form a new, independent nation. At the beginning of the Second World War, Czechoslovakia was invaded by Germany and the Germans installed a pro-Fascist government in Slovakia. Soviet troops restored the pre-war status quo in 1945 and communists seized power in 1948, making the country effectively a Soviet satellite. In 1968 Soviet forces invaded to put down an attempt to establish democracy under the leadership of Czechoslovakia's First Secretary, Alexander Dubcek, a Slovak. Twenty-one years later a revival of nationalism and a weakened Soviet Union led to a successful declaration of independence and the establishment of democratic government. Since its separation from the Czech Republic, Slovakia has been

governed by a single-chamber parliament, whose 150 members, or deputies, are elected for a four-year term.

Except for lowland areas in the south and southeast, most of the country is ruggedly mountainous, with extensive forests and tracts of pastureland. In the north of the country the high Carpathian Mountains extend along the Polish border, and further south, the Tatra Mountains, an offshoot of the Carpathians and the Slovakian Ore Mountains, run parallel across the center of the country. Ski resorts in the Tatra Mountains attract large numbers of tourists. The Danube, which forms part of the border with Hungary, flows through an extensive fertile plain. Here, and in the lowland area further to the east, most of Slovakia's agriculture, which employs more than one-tenth of the workforce, is centered. Wheat and potatoes are the principal crops, and sheep, cattle, and pigs are widely raised.

Slovakia is poorly endowed with mineral resources. There are significant deposits of lignite, but most of it is poor in quality. Industries, which employ about one in three workers, are centered mainly around the cities of Bratislava in the southwest and Kosice in the southeast. Significant industries are iron and steelmaking, and car and clothing manufacture. The move from a centrally controlled to a privatized market economy has proceeded fitfully, and the country has suffered economically from the loss of subsidies that it used to receive from the Czech Republic.

Fact File

OFFICIAL NAME Slovak Republic

FORM OF GOVERNMENT Republic with single legislative body (National Parliament)

CAPITAL Bratislava

AREA 48,845 sq km (18,859 sq miles)

TIME ZONE GMT + 1 hour

POPULATION 5,396,193

PROJECTED POPULATION 2005 5,509,202

POPULATION DENSITY 110.5 per sq km (286.2 per sq mile)

LIFE EXPECTANCY 73.5

INFANT MORTALITY (PER 1,000) 9.5

OFFICIAL LANGUAGE Slovak

OTHER LANGUAGE Hungarian

LITERACY RATE 99%

RELIGIONS Roman Catholic 60.3%, Protestant 8.4%, Orthodox 4.1%, other 27.2%

ETHNIC GROUPS Slovak 85.7%, Hungarian 10.7%, others include Gypsy, Czech 3.6%

CURRENCY Koruna

ECONOMY Services 44%, industry 44%, agriculture 12%

GNP PER CAPITA US$2,950

CLIMATE Temperate, with cold winters and warm, wet summers

HIGHEST POINT Gerlachovka 2,655 m (8,711 ft)

MAP REFERENCE Page 289

A crenellated building in San Marino (far left). The city of Trecin in Slovakia (left). Lake Bled in Slovenia (top right).

Slovenia

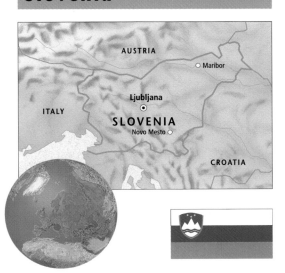

This former Yugoslav republic shares borders with Italy to the west, Austria to the north, Hungary to the east, and Croatia to the south. The port of Koper on Slovenia's short coastline on the Gulf of Venice is an important transit point for products from Austria and much of central Europe. First settled by Slavic peoples in the sixth century AD, Slovenia became a Hungarian province in the eleventh century. Austria gained control of the region in the sixteenth century, and Slovenia was later absorbed into the Austro-Hungarian Empire. At the end of the First World War it became part of the Kingdom of the Croats, Serbs, and Slovenes, which in 1929 became Yugoslavia. Like the rest of Yugoslavia, it was occupied by Axis powers during the Second World War. In 1991 it became the first Yugoslav republic to declare its independence. This prompted a military response from the Yugoslav army, which, however, withdrew its forces after a 10-day conflict. According to its constitution of 1991, Slovenia is a democratic republic with a directly elected president and prime minister as head of the government.

Slovenia is mountainous, with the highest and most spectacular regions in the Slovenian Alps near the border with Austria in the northwest. Almost half the land is densely forested. There are areas of lowland in the west near the coast and much of the center and east of the country consists of undulating plains. The most fertile region is in the east, where the Drava River flows southward across the Pannonian Plain into Croatia.

Slovenia's tourist industry, based on its alpine scenery and its coastal beaches, remains important, although it has been adversely affected by conflicts in the region. Almost half the workforce is employed in mining and manufacturing industries. Metallurgy and heavy machine manufacture, including trucks and cars, are prominent among these. Textile manufacture is also widespread. The main mineral resource is coal and there are large mercury deposits in the northwest. Dairy farming and pig raising are the main agricultural activities. Slovenia's nuclear power plant, which supplies one-third of the country's electricity, is a cause of some international tension, especially with Austria.

Fact File

OFFICIAL NAME Republic of Slovenia

FORM OF GOVERNMENT Republic with two legislative bodies (National Assembly and National Council)

CAPITAL Ljubljana

AREA 20,256 sq km (7,821 sq miles)

TIME ZONE GMT + 1 hour

POPULATION 1,970,570

PROJECTED POPULATION 2005 1,977,517

POPULATION DENSITY 97.3 per sq km (252 per sq mile)

LIFE EXPECTANCY 75.4

INFANT MORTALITY (PER 1,000) 5.3

OFFICIAL LANGUAGE Slovenian

OTHER LANGUAGES Serbian, Croatian

LITERACY RATE 96%

RELIGIONS Roman Catholic 96%, Muslim 1%, other 3%

ETHNIC GROUPS Slovene 91%, Croatian 3%, Serbian 2%, Muslim 1%, other 3%

CURRENCY Tolar

ECONOMY Services 52%, industry 46%, agriculture 2%

GNP PER CAPITA US$2,950

CLIMATE Temperate, with colder winters and hotter summers inland

HIGHEST POINT Mt Triglav 2,864 m (9,396 ft)

MAP REFERENCE Page 294

Spain

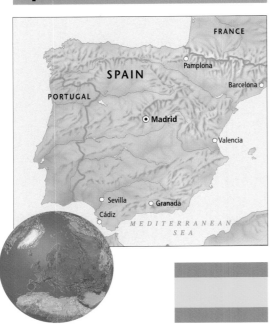

Fact File

OFFICIAL NAME Kingdom of Spain

FORM OF GOVERNMENT Constitutional monarchy with two legislative bodies (Senate and Congress of Deputies)

CAPITAL Madrid

AREA 504,750 sq km (194,884 sq miles)

TIME ZONE GMT + 1 hour

POPULATION 39,167,744

PROJECTED POPULATION 2005 39,334,191

POPULATION DENSITY 77.6 per sq km (201 per sq mile)

LIFE EXPECTANCY 77.7

INFANT MORTALITY (PER 1,000) 6.4

OFFICIAL LANGUAGE Spanish (Castillian)

OTHER LANGUAGES Catalan, Galician, Basque

LITERACY RATE 97.1%

RELIGIONS Roman Catholic 99%, other 1%

ETHNIC GROUPS Ethnically homogenous, but divided into the following cultural/linguistic groups: Spanish 73%, Catalan 17%, Galician 7%, Basque 2%, Gypsy 1%

CURRENCY Peseta

ECONOMY Services 68%, industry 21%, agriculture 11%

GNP PER CAPITA US$13,580

CLIMATE Temperate, with mild, wet winters and hot, dry summers; cooler and wetter in northwest

HIGHEST POINT Mulhacén 3,478 m (11,411 ft)

MAP REFERENCE Pages 292–93

Spain occupies the bulk of the Iberian Peninsula at the southwestern tip of Europe. It shares land borders with Portugal to the west, France to the north, and the tiny principality of Andorra, perched high in the Pyrenees on the border with France. To the west and south, Spain has short stretches of coastline along the Atlantic Ocean and to the north, a long coast on the Bay of Biscay. Its southern tip is separated from Morocco by the narrow Strait of Gibraltar and its southeastern and eastern coastlines are on the western edge of the Mediterranean Sea.

The Iberian Peninsula had already experienced a long history of human habitation when, at the end of the third century BC, the Romans subdued the Celts, Iberians, and Basques who lived there. The region remained a Roman colony until the Visigoths invaded early in the fifth century AD. Over the next three centuries the region became Christianized, but in AD 711 an invasion from Morocco in the south established what would become a flourishing Islamic civilization that lasted for six centuries. In the ninth century Christian invaders from the north gained control of Catalonia in the northeast, thus beginning a process of slow reconquest that would, by the early thirteenth century, see the Moors only retaining control of Granada in the south.

The marriage of Ferdinand II of Aragon and Isabella I of Castile in 1469 brought together the two most powerful states on the peninsula, and in 1492, when the Moors were finally expelled from Granada, Spain became a unified country under Catholic rule. Thus began a century of Spanish exploration and conquest in which Spain acquired colonies in Central and South America, as well as the Philippines in Southeast Asia. The Spanish also conquered a large part of Western Europe, including Portugal, the Netherlands, Austria, and part of Italy.

The beginning of Spain's decline from being a dominant power in the world to a state of secondary importance can be traced to 1588, when Philip II sent his mighty armada of 130 ships in an abortive attempt to invade Protestant England. This defeat by the English spelled the end of Spain's maritime dominance. By 1714 Spain had lost all its European possessions and by 1826 it had been forced to surrender all its American colonies except Cuba and Puerto Rico.

A small farm in the province of Navarra (below). Fertile countryside in Catalonia (right).

Timeline

10,000 BC Images of bison painted on the walls of a deep cave at Altamira, northern Spain, probably used for ceremonies	**3200 BC** Larger communities develop around southern and southwestern Spain and Portugal, such as Los Millares, Almeria	**1000 BC** Phoenician traders from eastern Mediterranean begin to colonize southern and eastern coasts of Spain	**218 BC** After defeat of Carthaginians in the Second Punic War, Spain slowly becomes part of the Roman Empire	**AD 711** Moors invade from North Africa bringing Muslim religion and building palaces and mosques		**1469** Marriage of Ferdinand of Aragon and Isabella of Castile brings together both kingdoms—almost all of modern Spain

780,000 BP Stone tools used by hominids in northern Spain; classified as *Homo heidelbergensis*	**280,000 BP** Caves inhabited by *Homo Sapiens* at Atapuerca, Burgos, northern Spain, as well as Torralba and Ambrona	**5500 BC** Sheep and wheat used by early farmers along the western Mediterranean	**3000 BC** Iberian people, including Gauls and Basques, move in from the north to found towns on Iberian Peninsula	**400 BC** Carthaginians of North Africa take over much of Spain	**AD 476** Romans rename peninsula Hispania; lose control to Germanic tribes who occupy whole territory by 573	**962–1212** Christian push back Moors; Moors confined to Granada	**1492** Columbus sails on first voyage in the service of Ferdinand and Isabella; Spanish take last Moorish stronghold, Granada

French revolutionary forces invaded Spain in 1794. They were defeated in 1814 and the Spanish Bourbon monarchy was restored. During the nineteenth and much of the twentieth century Spain has been destabilized by political turmoil and a series of military revolts and wars. Quarrels about the succession to the crown led to the removal of Isabella II from the throne in 1868, the declaration of a republic in 1873, and a military uprising in 1874 that restored the monarchy. In 1898 Spain and the United States fought a war at the end of which a defeated Spain was forced to cede its colonies of Cuba, Puerto Rico, and the Philippines to its adversary.

Spain remained neutral in both world wars, but was wracked by a bitter civil war from 1936 to 1939. Universal adult suffrage was introduced in 1931 and in 1936 the election of a Republican government with socialist leanings prompted an army officer, Francisco Franco, to lead a revolt against the government. With the support of right-wing Spanish forces and of Fascist Italy and Nazi Germany, and after the loss of 750,000 Spanish lives, Franco's forces were eventually victorious and Franco was installed as head of state. His dictatorial regime lasted until his death in 1975. Almost immediately the monarchy was restored and in June 1977 the first parliamentary elections since 1936 were held. In December 1978 a referendum approved a new constitution in which Spain was declared a parliamentary democracy with a monarch as head of state. There are two houses of parliament, both elected by universal adult suffrage for maximum terms of four years.

Physical features and land use

More than half Spain's land area is occupied by a central plateau, the Meseta, which has an average elevation of 700 m (2,300 ft). Much of the Meseta is harsh and barren. It is surrounded by mountain ranges to the north, northeast, south, and southwest, and is traversed by a low mountain range, the Sistema Central. The plateau is drained by three rivers—the Douro to the north of the Sistema Central, and the Tagus and Guadiana to its south—all of these rivers flow westward to the Atlantic.

In the far northeast of the country, between the Sistema Ibérico, a range that fringes the Meseta on the northeast and the Pyrenees to the north, is an extensive lowland area through which the Ebro River, which rises in the Basque country, flows south to the Mediterranean. In the southwest of Spain, beyond the Sierra Morena Range at the Meseta's southwestern edge, the Guadalquivir River drains another extensive low-lying region. In the far southeast is a coastal range, the Sistema Pinibético, which contains the snow-covered peaks of the Sierra Nevada, including the country's highest mountain, Mulhacén.

The Ramblas in Barcelona (above). Storks are among the many bird species found in southern Spain (right).

About one-tenth of Spain is heavily forested. Most of the forests are in the north and northwest, where the weather is wetter and more humid than in the center and south. Beech and oak predominate. Despite the fact that much of the country is arid and covered with low-growing scrub and water is a scarce resource, crops are widely grown. The most productive areas are in the north of the country, especially in the valley of the Ebro. There are significant crops of cereals, vegetables, fruits, and olives.

Spain is one of Europe's main producers of wine and there are 1.5 million hectares (3.7 million acres) of vineyards, mainly in the south and east. About one-fifth of Spain is pastureland, though cattle and dairying are largely confined to the north and pig farming to the southwest. Sheep are widespread on the Meseta, while goats graze in many of the more barren regions.

Industry and commerce

Although Spain has a wide range of mineral resources, it is not rich in any of them and imports the oil and gas needed to fuel its industries. These industries are concentrated towards the north, mainly around the major cities of Madrid and Barcelona. Spain is a major manufacturer of motor vehicles and a number of multinational companies have car manufacturing plants in parts of northern and central Spain. Steelmaking and shipbuilding are among the most significant heavy industries. There are important shipyards at Barcelona, on the Mediterranean coast, La Coruña in the far northwest, and Cadiz in the southwest. Chemical manufacture and fishing are also major industries. Spain has one of the world's largest fishing fleets,

although its activities have been curtailed in recent years by European Union restrictions in response to serious fish stock depletions. About one in ten of Spain's workers are employed in the tourist industry.

While Spain is still a predominantly Catholic country, the influence of the Church has waned in recent years. This is reflected in the fact that Spain has one of the lowest birth-rates in Europe, even though divorce is still relatively rare. Although most Spaniards enjoy a reasonably high standard of living, unemployment during the 1990s has been alarmingly high.

REGIONS

**Baleares • Basque Country
Canary Islands • Cantabria
Castilla-La Mancha • Castilla Y León
Catalonia • Ceuta and Melilla
Extremadura • Galicia • La Rioja
Madrid • Murcia • Navarra • Valencia**

1516 King Charles I, grandson of Ferdinand and Isabella, is first Hapsburg to rule Spain; becomes Holy Roman Emperor in 1519	**1808** French invade Spain; Spanish resistance grows, French expelled in Peninsular War (1814)	**1931** King Alfonso XIII flees after elections show preference for a republic; Spain briefly a democracy—deep political divisions	**1960s** Rapid industrialization, expansion of economy and growth in tourist resort development along Mediterranean	**1973** Basque separatists (ETA) assassinate Prime Minister Carrero Blanco in Madrid	**1976** Government under Prime Minister Suarez liberalizes politics, permits new parties to participate in elections (1977)	**1986** Prime Minister González embarks on more economic development; Spain joins European Community (EC)
1556 Charles's son becomes King Philip II; height of Spanish Empire in Americas, Europe, and Africa	**1820** Spanish troops refuse to sail to reconquer American colonies; revolt spreads, crushed with help of French troops	**1860** Population begins to decline for almost a century due to emigration	**1936–38** Spanish Civil War; victorious Nationalists under Franco enter Madrid in 1939	**1970** Population grows following industrialization. More than 1 million immigrants in 10 years, almost half illegal	**1975** On the death of Franco, Spain adopts political reform agenda despite accession of Juan Carlos (grandson of Alfonso XIII) as king	**1980** The 2.5 million Basque people of northern Spain are granted limited autonomy	**1995** Population more than 39 million; Spain lifts passport controls with EC nations

Europe and the Russian Federation

Sweden

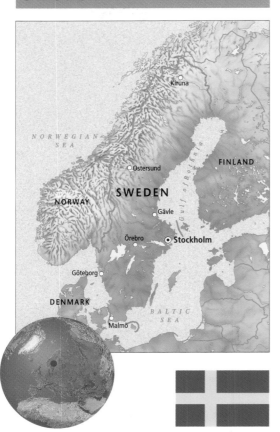

Fact File

OFFICIAL NAME Kingdom of Sweden

FORM OF GOVERNMENT Constitutional monarchy with single legislative body (Parliament, Riksdag)

CAPITAL Stockholm

AREA 449,964 sq km (173,731 sq miles)

TIME ZONE GMT + 1 hour

POPULATION 8,911,296

PROJECTED POPULATION 2005 9,051,287

POPULATION DENSITY 19.8 per sq km (51.3 per sq mile)

LIFE EXPECTANCY 79.3

INFANT MORTALITY (PER 1,000) 3.9

OFFICIAL LANGUAGE Swedish

OTHER LANGUAGES Lapp, Finnish

LITERACY RATE 99%

RELIGIONS Evangelical Lutheran 94%, Roman Catholic 1.5%, Pentecostal 1%, other 3.5%

ETHNIC GROUPS Swedish 91%, others include Lapp, Finnish, Yugoslav, Danish, Norwegian, Greek, Turkish 9%

CURRENCY Swedish krona

ECONOMY Services 69%, industry 28%, agriculture 3%

GNP PER CAPITA US$23,750

CLIMATE Temperate in the south, with cold winters and mild summers; subpolar in the north, with severe winters

HIGHEST POINT Kebnekaise 2,111 m (6,926 ft)

MAP REFERENCE Pages 284–85

A Swedish city in winter (top right). Rows of holiday chalets and small boats in Sweden (right). Early summer foliage in a birch forest (center right).

The fourth largest country in Europe, Sweden shares the Scandinavian Peninsula with Norway, which sits between it and the North Atlantic Ocean. To the northeast Sweden shares a border with Finland, and its eastern coastline is separated from the west coast of Finland by the Gulf of Bothnia. Its southern shores are washed by the Baltic Sea, and south of the land border with Norway the Kattegat Strait divides it from the northern tip of Denmark. Close to Sweden's southeast tip are Gotland and Öland, the largest of many islands dotted around the Swedish coastline.

By the seventh century AD, Teutonic tribes from the south had occupied much of central Sweden, and between the ninth and the eleventh centuries Swedes took part in Viking raids deep into Russia and south to the Black Sea. Over the following five centuries Sweden and Denmark vied for Scandinavian supremacy. Both Sweden and Norway came under the Danish crown in 1397, but 50 years later the Swedes rebelled and elected their own king. The accession to the Swedish throne in 1523 of Gustav I ended Danish claims to all but the south of Sweden. During the next 200 years Sweden became one of the most powerful states in Europe, annexing parts of Estonia, Finland, and Poland, driving the Danes out of southern Sweden, and playing a crucial role in curbing Hapsburg expansion in northern Europe. At the beginning of the eighteenth century, however, a coalition of Russia, Poland, and Denmark forced Sweden to relinquish its Baltic possessions.

At the end of the Napoleonic wars, in 1815, Norway was ceded to Sweden, a union that lasted until 1905. In the mid-nineteenth century the beginnings of parliamentary democracy were introduced in Sweden with the establishment of a two-chamber parliament, although suffrage was limited largely to landowners and industrialists. Universal adult suffrage was introduced in 1919.

Sweden remained neutral in both the First and the Second World Wars. Following the Second World War it tried unsuccessfully to form a military alliance with Denmark and Norway. When these nations joined NATO Sweden did not follow, fearing closer ties with the West might damage its relations with the Soviet Union, and give it an excuse to absorb Finland into the Soviet bloc. Since then, although maintaining a high level of

defence preparedness, it has kept its distance from NATO and maintained its reputation for neutrality, for playing an active role in international affairs, and as a negotiator in international disputes.

During the 1960s and early 1970s, the Social Democrats, who had laid the foundations of a welfare state since 1932, held the majority of seats in the Riksdag and were able to govern alone. They then inaugurated the more radical socialist policies which came to define modern Swedish politics. Welfare services were extended, and "the Swedish Way" was seen by socialists as a model for the rest of Europe. After 1982 Olof Palme's government introduced what it called a middle way between capitalism and communism, with

Scandinavia

Today the term Scandinavia is often understood to refer only to Norway and Sweden, which both occupy the Scandinavian Peninsula, and the more southerly peninsula and islands that make up Denmark. Many people, however, would also include Finland, Iceland, and the Faeroe Islands, which are possessions of Denmark. These countries are also collectively referred to as the Nordic countries, or Norden.

Culturally, geographically, and geologically, the countries of Scandinavia have much in common and the whole region forms a distinctive part of Europe. All of them lie close to the Arctic Circle and share a cold, moist, and often harsh climate, which is mitigated in parts of Scandinavia by the effect of the Gulf Stream. All five countries have a high degree of ethnic and religious homogeneity. Lutheran is the overwhelmingly predominant religion in every part of Scandinavia. The languages of four of the countries are closely related, but Finnish is entirely different and is more closely related to the Estonian language. Historical links are also very strong and during the fifteenth century the countries were united under Danish rule. For five centuries, until 1809, Finland was under Swedish control and Swedish was the language of its ruling classes. For almost a century, until 1905, Norway was ruled by Sweden, and Iceland only gained its independence as late as 1944, after almost five and half centuries of Danish rule and domination.

Greenland has, since the early eighteenth century, been part of Denmark. Situated to the west of Iceland, it is ethnically distinct and geographically closer to North America. Although it was granted home rule in 1979 its inhabitants are still Danish citizens and Denmark still controls Greenland's foreign affairs.

Despite climatic difficulties, Scandinavian economies have traditionally depended heavily on agriculture and fishing. The improvements in agricultural techniques and technologies that flowed from the Industrial Revolution were slow to be implemented in Scandinavia and until late in the nineteenth century the region remained economically stagnant. In recent years, however, there have been significant technological innovations and increasing industrialization and Scandinavians now enjoy some of the highest standards of living in Europe.

annual levies on profits and wages which went into "wage-earner funds" used to buy stock in private firms for the benefit of labor. Palme was assassinated in mysterious circumstances in Stockholm in 1986. By then the economic costs of the welfare state were becoming evident. The country had almost zero economic growth, and was becoming less competitive in world markets.

From the late 1970s domestic policy discussion has been less along socialist/capitalist lines and more concerned with ecological issues. Sweden has taken the lead in a number of environmental debates, and has been the venue of influential conferences devoted to such matters as global warming and greenhouse gases. An application for EC membership was lodged in 1992. In 1995 it was admitted to the European Union. Sweden is a constitutional monarchy with a single-chamber parliament that is elected every three years.

Physical features and land use

Northeastern Sweden is a region of low plateaus that drop away to a coastal plain along the Gulf of Bothnia, but rise to the Kjölen Mountains along the Norwegian border. Most of the country's more than 95,000 lakes are in this mountainous region. Shaped by ancient glaciers, many of the lakes are in the upper valleys of the numerous rivers that flow east to the Gulf of Bothnia. They are the source of most of Sweden's hydroelectricity, which is gradually replacing nuclear energy as the main means of power generation. The mountains are heavily forested. Despite extensive land clearing for agriculture in the south, well over half the country remains forested, with spruce, pine and birch among the most prominent trees.

Central Sweden is a lowland area that stretches between Stockholm in the east and the country's second largest city, Göteborg, in the southwest. Four large lakes—the only remnants of a strait that once joined the Baltic to the Kattegat Strait—cover much of this region, the most heavily populated part of the country. The rich soils around these lakes support much of Sweden's agricultural produce, which includes cereals and vegetables and fodder crops for large herds of cattle. Dairy farming is the main form of agriculture, and Sweden is self-sufficient in dairy products.

South of the lakes is a low, largely infertile plateau and further south, stretching to the tip of the peninsula and across to the island of Gotland, is a rich plain—the most intensively cultivated part of the country. Significant areas of woodland still survive here, dotted between stretches of farming and grazing land.

Although it lacks oil and coal reserves, Sweden is rich in mineral resources, most of which are concentrated in the northeast. These include iron ore, zinc, lead, copper, and silver, and almost one-sixth of the world's known reserves of uranium.

Industry, commerce, and culture

Sweden's vast forests are the basis for timber and paper manufacturing industries that form almost one-fifth of the country's exports. Machines, cars, trucks, aircraft, and chemical and electrical goods and communication equipment are among the chief manufacturing industries, based in the central region and Malmö in the southwest.

Apart from the Saami people (Lapps) in the far north of the country, Sweden is ethnically and culturally quite homogeneous. Despite there being a relatively high rate of unemployment, its citizens enjoy one of the highest standards of living in Europe and an extensive range of government-provided social services. Sweden also boasts one of Europe's highest rates of female participation throughout its workforce.

PROVINCES

Älvsborg • Blekinge • Gävleborg
Göteborg and Bohus • Gotland
Halland • Jämtland • Jönköping
Kalmar • Kopparberg • Kristianstad
Kronoberg • Malmöhus • Norrbotten
Örebro • Östergötland • Skaraborg
Södermanland • Stockholm • Uppsala
Värmland • Västerbotten
Västernorrland • Västmanland

Switzerland

Fact File

OFFICIAL NAME Swiss Confederation

FORM OF GOVERNMENT Federal republic with two legislative bodies (Council of States and National Council)

CAPITAL Bern

AREA 41,290 sq km (15,942 sq miles)

TIME ZONE GMT + 1 hour

POPULATION 7,275,467

PROJECTED POPULATION 2005 7,351,686

POPULATION DENSITY 176.2 per sq km (456.4 per sq mile)

LIFE EXPECTANCY 79

INFANT MORTALITY (PER 1,000) 4.9

OFFICIAL LANGUAGES German, French, Italian

OTHER LANGUAGES Spanish, Romansch

LITERACY RATE 99%

RELIGIONS Roman Catholic 48%, Protestant 44%, other 8%

ETHNIC GROUPS German 65%, French 18%, Italian 10%, Romansch 1%, other 6%

CURRENCY Swiss franc

ECONOMY Services 64%, industry 30%, agriculture 6%

GNP PER CAPITA US$40,630

CLIMATE Temperate, varying with altitude; generally cold winters and warm, wet summers

HIGHEST POINT Dufourspitze 4,634 m (15,203 ft)

MAP REFERENCE Pages 288, 291, 294

A landlocked country in central Europe, Switzerland shares borders with Italy to its south and southeast, France to its west, Germany to its north, and Austria and Liechtenstein to its east. This small nation has enjoyed a generally peaceful independence for more than 450 years, despite the conflicts that have often raged around it. Modern Switzerland dates back to the late thirteenth century when three German districts, or cantons, combined to form a federation. A century later, other cantons had joined the federation, which survived as a unit, despite linguistic differences and often intense and violent conflicts

between Catholics and emerging Protestant groups. Although part of the Holy Roman Empire, and effectively under Hapsburg domination, the Swiss cantons remained neutral during the Thirty Years War of 1618–48, at the end of which they were formally granted independence. In 1798 French revolutionary armies invaded Switzerland and declared it to be a centralized Helvetic Republic, named after Helvetia, the Roman province that had existed there in ancient times. In 1815, after the defeat of Napoleon, the Congress of Vienna declared Switzerland to be independent once more, as well as permanently neutral, and added two more cantons—Valais and the previously separate republic of Geneva.

The country has maintained this military neutrality ever since and its stance has been respected by its neighbors throughout numerous conflicts, including the First and Second World Wars. Religious tensions flared briefly in 1847, when the Catholic cantons seceded. The following year, however, a new constitution, inspired by that of the United States, re-established the former federation and defined Switzerland as a republic with a strong central government but with considerable powers still vested in individual cantons. In 1874 a new constitution was adopted which essentially confirmed this division of power. Switzerland's central government, which controls foreign policy, railway and postal services, and the mint, consists of a an elected bicameral parliament, with a president, elected by the parliament for a one-year term. Women were granted the vote only in 1971.

Physical features and land use

Mountains dominate the Swiss landscape making it Europe's most mountainous country. They cover seven-tenths of the land area. The rest of the country consists of an elevated central plateau on which the majority of the population lives and which is the center of the country's agricultural, industrial, and economic activity. This area is

bordered by a number of large lakes and drained by the River Aare, which rises in Lake Neuchâtel and flows northward into the Rhine, which constitutes Switzerland's border with Germany and part of Austria. Lake Neuchâtel is overlooked by the lightly wooded Jura Mountains, which separate Switzerland from France. More than half of Switzerland is covered by the peaks and glaciers of the Alps, which sweep across the south of the country. The most spectacular sections are in the Pennine Alps along the southwestern frontier with Italy. Both the Rhône and the Rhine rivers rise in this alpine region and drain it in opposite directions, flowing respectively through the two largest lakes in the country, which are Lake Geneva in the far southwest, and Lake Constance in the far northeast.

About one-quarter of Switzerland consists of forests, which are found mainly in the valleys and on the lower slopes. Cypresses and figs are prominent among the tree species. About one-tenth of the land is arable. Crop cultivation is concentrated in the area immediately to the east and southeast of the Jura and in the valleys of the Rhône and Rhine rivers. Wheat, potatoes, and sugar beet are the main crops. The principal agricultural activity, however, is dairy farming, although pig raising is also significant. Switzerland produces less than half its food needs.

Switzerland is not well endowed with mineral resources. Most of the country's electricity is generated by hydropower, but a significant amount is provided by the country's five nuclear power plants. A sixth nuclear plant was planned but was cancelled in the aftermath of the Chernobyl disaster in Ukraine in 1986.

Industry, commerce, and culture

Switzerland has for centuries been a world leader in the production of precision instruments such as clocks and watches. Other industries which are vital to the country's prosperity include heavy engineering, textile manufacture, clothing, chemicals and food processing. Swiss chocolate, sought after the world over because of its high quality, is also a major contributor to the national economy. Tourism, centered mainly on the Alps, attracts more than 12 million visitors annually.

Banking is highly developed and is one of the country's key industries. Switzerland attracts almost half the world's foreign investment capital and is the base of numerous multinational companies.

Although the country is divided geographically among its predominantly German-, Italian- and French-speaking populations, Switzerland is now a unified nation and its people have a strong sense of common purpose. This is attributable in large measure to Switzerland's status as one of the world's most stable and prosperous countries, with a very high per capita income.

Ukraine

Ukraine, formerly part of the USSR, has a southern coastline on the Black Sea and on the almost landlocked Sea of Azov. Surrounding it are seven other countries. From southeast across its northern border to southwest, they are the Russian Federation, Belarus, Poland, Slovakia, Hungary, Romania, and Moldova. The Ukrainian capital, Kiev, has existed since the ninth century AD, when a Viking tribe established a center there. A century later it was a powerful force in eastern Europe. It was overrun by Mongols in the thirteenth century and then came under Polish control. In the seventeenth century the eastern part of Ukraine fell to the Russians, who eventually absorbed the whole of the country into their empire. Despite attempts to establish a separate state after the 1917 Revolution, invading Soviet armies subdued Ukraine in 1920. During the 1930s more than 3 million Ukrainians perished in a famine and another 6 million died in the Nazi occupation during the Second World War. After the war, part of western Ukraine that was under Polish occupation was returned, as was the Crimea, and Ukraine assumed its present boundaries, under Soviet domination.

Ukraine declared its independence in 1991 as the Soviet Union began to break up, although it still retains close ties with Russia. It is now a democratic republic, with a directly elected president as head of state.

Formerly referred to as "the granary of the Soviet Union," most of Ukraine consists of fertile black-soil plains that produce an abundance of wheat and other cereal grains as well as vegetables, fruits, and fodder crops. Much of the country's agricultural output remains affected by the widespread contamination caused by the nuclear accident at Chernobyl, near the Belarus border, in 1986.

There are mountainous areas in the southwest, where the Carpathian Mountains sweep down from Poland, and in the Crimean Peninsula in the far south. The Dnieper River flows through the heart of the country and empties into the Black

The Jungfrau Mountain in Switzerland's Bernese Oberland (left). An alpine vegetable farm in Switzerland (top). Yalta and the crowded promenade on the Sea of Azov, Ukraine (right).

Sea. In its northern plain there are large stretches of marshland and many forest-rimmed lakes. In the south, bordering the Black Sea, much of the landscape is a semiarid, treeless plain.

Coal is Ukraine's most abundant and heavily exploited mineral resource. There are also significant reserves of natural gas, uranium, and oil, though the latter remains largely unexploited. Steel production, machine building, engineering, and chemical processing are the main industries. These industries are centered around the large cities and the coalfields in the east of the country. In the post-Soviet era, the Ukrainian economy has suffered periods of extremely high inflation and growth has been hampered by a largely conservative legislature that has resisted many attempts at reform. There is widespread poverty, exacerbated by a declining health-care system.

Fact File

OFFICIAL NAME	Ukraine
FORM OF GOVERNMENT	Republic with single legislative body (Supreme Council)
CAPITAL	Kiev
AREA	603,700 sq km (233,089 sq miles)
TIME ZONE	GMT + 3 hours
POPULATION	49,811,174
PROJECTED POPULATION 2005	48,308,739
POPULATION DENSITY	82.5 per sq km (213.7 per sq mile)
LIFE EXPECTANCY	65.9
INFANT MORTALITY (PER 1,000)	21.7
OFFICIAL LANGUAGE	Ukrainian
OTHER LANGUAGES	Russian, Romanian, Hungarian, Polish
LITERACY RATE	98.8%
RELIGIONS	Predominantly Christian (Ukrainian Orthodox, Ukrainian Autocephalus Orthodox, Roman Catholic); small Protestant, Jewish and Muslim minorities
ETHNIC GROUPS	Ukrainian 73%, Russian 22%, other 5%
CURRENCY	Hryvna
ECONOMY	Services 46%, industry 33%, agriculture 21%
GNP PER CAPITA	US$1,630
CLIMATE	Temperate, with cold winters and mild summers; warmer on Black Sea coast
HIGHEST POINT	Hora Hoverla 2,061 m (6,762 ft)
MAP REFERENCE	Pages 289, 298

United Kingdom

Fact File

OFFICIAL NAME United Kingdom of Great Britain and Northern Ireland

FORM OF GOVERNMENT Constitutional monarchy with two legislative houses (House of Lords and House of Commons)

CAPITAL London

AREA 244,820 sq km (94,525 sq miles)

TIME ZONE GMT

POPULATION 57,832,824

PROJECTED POPULATION 2005 58,135,972

POPULATION DENSITY 236.2 per sq km (611.8 per sq mile)

LIFE EXPECTANCY 77.6

INFANT MORTALITY (PER 1,000) 5.8

OFFICIAL LANGUAGE English

OTHER LANGUAGES Welsh, Scots Gaelic; Chinese, Gujarati, Bengali, Punjabi, Urdu, Hindi, Arabic, Turkish, Greek, Spanish, Japanese

LITERACY RATE 99%

RELIGIONS Anglican 63%, Roman Catholic 14%, Presbyterian 4%, Methodist 3%, Muslim 3%, other 13%

ETHNIC GROUPS English 81.5%, Scottish 9.6%, Irish 2.4%, Welsh 1.9%, Northern Irish 1.8%, other 2.8%

CURRENCY Pound sterling

ECONOMY Services 78%, industry 20%, agriculture 2%

GNP PER CAPITA US$18,700

CLIMATE Temperate, with cool winters and mild summers; generally wetter and warmer in the west, and cooler in the north

HIGHEST POINT Ben Nevis 1,343 m (4,406 ft)

MAP REFERENCE Pages 302–03

L ying just north of the westernmost edge of continental Europe, the United Kingdom consists of the large island of Great Britain, the far northeast corner of the island of Ireland, which sits across the Irish Sea to the west, and several hundred small islands scattered around the British coast. The United Kingdom is separated by the English Channel from the north coast of France which, at its nearest point, is no more than 32 km (20 miles) away, and a rail tunnel under the Channel now links England and France. England, in the south and southwest, occupies the greatest part of the island. Scotland is to the north, and Wales in the west juts out into the Irish Sea. The long eastern coast of Great Britain faces the North Sea; its western coastline is on the Atlantic Ocean and the Irish Sea.

History

Thanks partly to the natural protection offered by surrounding waters, but also to its maritime supremacy in certain periods of history and to a degree of good fortune in others, Britain is unique among major European nations in that it has escaped foreign invasion for almost 1,000 years. When William, Duke of Normandy led his successful invasion in 1066, this was the culmination of a long series of incursions that the island kingdom had suffered since the first invasion—the Romans in the first century AD.

Within 60 years of their arrival in Britain in AD 55, the Romans had established control over England and Wales and later introduced Christianity. When they finally withdrew at the beginning of the fifth century, the Britons eventually fell prey to Germanic tribes from Scandinavia and the Low Countries. By the eighth century most of Britain, except the far west and the north, had succumbed and the country was divided into a number of Anglo-Saxon kingdoms.

Viking attacks from Norway and Denmark occurred during the course of the eighth and ninth centuries, with Danish invaders controlling much of north and northeast England by the late ninth century. United under the kings of Wessex by the middle of the tenth century, England again fell to Danish control early in the eleventh century. When Edward the Confessor came to the throne in 1042, he presided over a unified, but fractious, kingdom. On his death in 1066, both his brother-in-law, Harold, and his cousin, William of Normandy, claimed the throne. William was victorious at the Battle of Hastings and was crowned on Christmas Day 1066.

The feudal system of government developed by William gave significant power to the nobles. Under Henry II, the first Plantagenet king, power became more centralized in the crown. This, and increasing civil unrest during the reign of John, led to a revolt by nobles, who in 1215 forced the king to sign the Magna Carta, a document limiting royal power and enshrining basic civil rights. This in turn gave rise to the development of a more consultative style of government, and, by the late thirteenth century, to the establishment of a House of Commons with powers to raise taxes.

Under Edward I (1272–1307) Wales was brought under English control, much of Ireland was subjugated, and a portion of Scotland was conquered. In 1314, however, at the Battle of

Bannockburn, the English were driven out of Scotland. Between 1338 and 1453, in a series of devastating wars, known as the Hundred Years War, England lost all its French territories. This led to a further 30 years of civil war, known as the Wars of the Roses, which culminated in the accession to the throne of Henry VII, the first of the Tudor monarchs, in 1485.

The Tudor dynasty lasted until 1603, and during this time, especially during the reign of Elizabeth I (1558–1603), England became a leading power in the world, enjoying a golden age in which colonies were established in North America, British navigators sailed to remote corners of the globe, and there was a notable flowering of English theatre. During the reign of Elizabeth's father, Henry VIII, Protestantism, in the form of the Church of England, had been established in England.

When Elizabeth died without an heir, James VI of Scotland, the first Stuart king, succeeded her, combining the two kingdoms and reigning as James I of England. Attempts by his son, Charles I, to curb the powers of parliament led to the outbreak of civil war in 1642. With the victory of the parliamentary armies, led by Oliver Cromwell, in 1646, the monarchy was abolished and a commonwealth, virtually a military dictatorship, set up under Cromwell. The Commonwealth did not long survive the death of Cromwell and in 1660 Charles II was installed as king. When, however, his brother, the Catholic James II, attempted to restore Catholic domination, he was ousted and his Protestant daughter, Mary, and her Dutch husband, William of Orange, accepted the crown in 1689. In the same year, parliament enacted legislation barring Catholics from the

throne. In 1690, at the Battle of the Boyne, their armies defeated a Catholic uprising in Ireland. In 1707 an Act of Union, between the Scottish and English parliaments, formally joined the two countries. Scottish rebellions against British rule were finally put down in 1746, when Charles Edward Stuart (Bonnie Prince Charlie) was defeated in the Battle of Culloden.

Under the Hanoverian monarchs, the first of whom, George I, accepted the throne in 1814 as King of Great Britain and Ireland, greater power devolved to the parliament. In 1721, Sir Hugh Walpole became the first prime minister to head a ministry that exercised executive power with the sanction of parliament. The eighteenth century, too, was a period of great expansion of British power that saw the acquisitions of British colonies in India and Canada and the exploration and colonization of Australia. A major setback was the loss of the American colonies in 1776. The military defeat of Irish rebels in 1798 led to an Act of Union that formally joined the two countries in 1801. Defeat of Bonaparte at Waterloo in 1815 confirmed Britain as the world's leading power.

The nineteenth century was a time of further expansion and consolidation of Britain's influence and power. By the end of Queen Victoria's 64-year reign in 1901, Britain's colonies extended throughout much of the world, including large parts of Africa, although by then Australia, New Zealand, and Canada had gained their independence and demands for Irish independence were growing. During the century a number of Reform Bills brought in significant democratic reforms and the Industrial Revolution resulted in increasing industrialization, urban growth, and a slowly rising standard of living.

Three-quarters of a million British soldiers were killed during the First World War, which also left the country considerably weakened economically. This situation was exacerbated by the Great Depression. After a protracted and bitter struggle, Ireland, with the exception of the provinces of Northern Ireland, became independent in 1922 and British troops faced growing unrest in India and in parts of the Middle East. Following the Second World War, in which British cities, especially London, were subjected to sustained German bombardment from the air, Britain endured almost a decade of austerity.

India gained its independence in 1947, and in 1956 Britain suffered a humiliating defeat in its

armed attempt to prevent Egypt's nationalization of the Suez Canal. In 1982, Britain was again at war, this time against Argentina, which attempted to seize the Falkland Islands. In a two-week conflict, Britain repulsed the Argentines with the loss of 255 British lives. In recent years, bitter violence between Catholics and Protestants in Northern Ireland has been a major preoccupation of British governments. Since 1995, however, there have been developments, including the intervention of the United States, that augur well for a peaceful resolution of this conflict.

Britain, as a member of the European Union and a signatory of the Maastricht Treaty, is a significant force in Europe as it moves closer to

The Cuckmere River meanders through pastureland in England (left). The Giant's Causeway, a promontory of hexagonal basalt columns, in County Antrim, Northern Ireland (top). Ebbw Valley British Steel tinplate mill in the town of Ebbw Vale, south Wales (above).

political and economic integration. It is one of the world's most stable multi-party democracies, in spite of ongoing debate about the role and viability of the monarchy and of its unelected, and largely hereditary, upper house of parliament, the House of Lords, which is in the process of reform. Power resides in the House of Commons, which is elected by universal adult suffrage for terms of five years.

Physical features and land use

The United Kingdom has a considerable variety of landscapes, ranging from craggy mountain ranges and tranquil upland lakes in the north, to gently rolling hills and green plains that are characteristic of the south and southeast.

Scotland is the most mountainous part of the country. Mainland Scotland has three main regions: the Highlands in the north, the Southern Uplands near the border with England, and in between the flatter, though often hilly, Central Lowlands. It also has several groups of offshore islands: the Shetlands in the far north, the Orkneys, off the northeastern tip of the mainland, and the Inner and Outer Hebrides off the northwestern coast. The most rugged country is in the north, where two granite ranges, the North West Highlands and the Grampians, dominate the scene. In the northwest the mountains are cut by deep glaciated valleys and the coastline is rocky and deeply indented. South and east of the Great Glen, which contains the famous Loch Ness, are the Grampians, where Britain's highest peaks are found. Here, the country is generally less harsh, and there are stretches of sheep-grazing land and forested slopes where there are herds of deer. East of the Grampians is a rich agricultural lowland area that stretches in an arc from near Inverness around to Aberdeen.

Scotland's two largest cities, Glasgow and Edinburgh, lie in the Central Lowlands, the most populous region and Scotland's industrial heart. The Central Lowlands contain several ranges of undulating hills and are drained by the eastward-flowing Tay and Forth rivers and the westward-flowing Clyde. The area east of Edinburgh is prime country, both for stock raising and crop cultivation. The Southern Uplands, gentler and less lofty than their northern counterparts, are characterized by hills, moorlands, and picturesque valleys, and in the valley of the Tweed and its tributaries are large areas of sheltered farmland. The Cheviot Hills in the south form a natural border with England.

Beginning just south of the Cheviot Hills, and running southward as far as north Derbyshire, are the Pennine Mountains, a predominantly limestone range of hills, plateaus, expanses of moorlands, and soft, green valleys, which are often referred to

CONSTITUENT COUNTRIES

England • London
Scotland • Edinburgh

CONSTITUENT REGION

Northern Ireland • Belfast

PRINCIPALITY

Wales • Cardiff

OVERSEAS TERRITORIES

Anguilla
Bermuda
British Indian Ocean Territory
British Virgin Islands
Cayman Islands
Falkland Islands
Gibraltar
Guernsey
Isle of Man
Jersey
Montserrat
Pitcairn Islands
St Helena
South Georgia and the South Sandwich islands
Turks and Caicos islands

A coastal village in Scotland (top). A tile-hung house in a village in southern England (center). Scotney Castle in Kent, southeastern England (right). Heathland on the rugged Pembrokeshire coast of Wales (top right.)

Timeline

	4000 BC Tribes from various parts of Europe arrive; they farm and live in villages, burying their dead in earth mounds	**43 BC–AD 446** Roman occupation of Britain brings wealth, military skills, and Christianity; Hadrian's Wall built AD 120	**1066** Norman invasion. William I's Domesday Book assesses Britain's wealth and estimates population about 2 million	**1300** Population reaches 5 million after expanding rapidly as a result of more efficient farming methods	**1536** Parliament formally makes Wales part of English territory	**1664–66** Great Plague kills more than 75,000 of London's population of around 450,000, then spreads to other parts of the country	**1801** Act of Union extended to join Ireland to United Kingdom
200,000 BC Hominids living in southeastern Britain use stone tools and hunt animals	**12,000 BC** Paleolithic hunters carve mammal bones at Cresswell Crags, Derbyshire; one shows a dancing man, others, animal heads	**3300 BC** Construction of a large stone circle begins: Stonehenge completed 1800 BC	**AD 410** Anglo-Saxons settle in south England destroying remains of Roman culture; later, Danish Vikings settle in north and east	**1489** Enclosure of common land forces many people off the land, causing rebellions and rural depopulation	**1500** Little ice age of cold winters and wet summers (which continues until 1700) causes crop failures across the country	**1707** Act of Union between England and Scotland creates United Kingdom of Great Britain	**1750** Use of iron grows rapidly; machines for spinning and weaving invented in late 1700s, accelerating Industrial Revolution

as the Dales. West of the Pennines, and separated from it by the valley of the Eden, are the Cumbrian Mountains, a region of craggy peaks with many lakes. This is England's famous Lake District. To the east of the Pennines are the elevated expanses of the North York Moors.

South of the Pennines, beginning around the fertile valleys of the Trent and Avon rivers, the countryside becomes flatter and gently undulating, reaching its lowest point in the marshy fen country north of Cambridge. Numerous ranges of hills provide relief from the generally rolling country-side. The most notable hills are the Cotswolds, in the central southwest, where England's longest river, the Thames, begins its course eastward across the country, passing through London, and out to the North Sea.

Wales, which juts out into the Irish Sea to the west of England, is more mountainous, its center dominated by the Cambrian Mountains, in which the Severn, Britain's second longest river, rises. Mount Snowdon, in Snowdonia, a large national park in northern Wales, rises to 1,085 m (3,559 ft) and is the highest peak in England and Wales.

Northern Ireland is flat for the most part, but to the north of Belfast is the Antrim Plateau, whose basalt cliffs provide some of the country's most arresting coastal scenery.

Industry, commerce, agriculture, and culture

Crop cultivation in Britain is concentrated mainly in the east and southeast of the country. Wheat is the principal crop, though potatoes and fruits are widely cultivated. Pasturelands are more common in the west and southwest, where sheep and cattle raising and dairy farming predominate. Although the United Kingdom exports much of its produce, it still imports about one-third of its food needs.

The United Kingdom has traditionally relied on coal for its energy resources, and there are still adequate reserves. However, the replacement of most coal-fired power stations with gas-powered facilities in recent years has resulted in the near closure of the coalmining industry. The country also has a number of nuclear power stations which are a continuing subject of controversy. Oil and gas reserves in the North Sea are a major source of revenue, and have helped to make the country self-sufficient in energy.

Manufacturing was once the mainstay of the British economy, with a large proportion of heavy industry centered on industrial cities in the Midlands such as Birmingham, Manchester, and Liverpool. Food processing, machinery, and textile manufacture are still among the principal manu-facturing industries. Motor vehicle and aircraft manufacture are long-established core industries, although much of the motor vehicle industry is now owned by foreign companies. Most of the

raw materials needed to supply Britain's industries have to be imported from other countries.

Apart from the ethnic and cultural minorities found in Wales and Scotland, Britain's population is relatively homogeneous. Since the 1950s, how-ever, large numbers of immigrants from former British colonies in the Caribbean, Asia (especially India and Pakistan), and Africa have changed the racial composition, most notably in inner-city areas, where the majority of ethnic minorities have congregated. Despite certain tensions, these immigrants are now generally accepted as an integral, if still relatively disadvantaged, part of British society. Britain's economy is one of the most developed in Western Europe and its people enjoy a high standard of living, although there are considerable variations in levels of affluence. Universal free school education and health systems are maintained by the state, although some social services and the value of pensions, including those for the elderly, have been sharply cut back in recent years.

The European Union

On 1 January 1999 eleven European countries adopted a new and common currency—the euro. This momentous step marked the climax of a movement for closer European integration which had begun in 1957. In March of that year Belgium, France, the Federal Republic of Germany, Italy, Luxembourg, and the Nether-lands signed a treaty which proposed the gradual integration of their economies in the European Economic Community (EEC or EC). They planned to gradually eliminate restrictive quotas and import duties between member nations in order to allow the free movement of persons and capital within their common boundaries. It was hoped that the larger market that resulted would promote greater productivity and higher standards of living for all.

The success of the Community led to a number of additional countries seeking member-ship. Others, however, objected to the surrender of sovereignty that was entailed: at first Britain, along with the Scandinavian nations, Switzerland, Austria, and Portugal, formed their own free-trade area (known as the outer seven) instead. Nor were the policies of the EEC uniformly successful: the Common Agricultural Policy, for example, led to the overproduction of butter, wine, and sugar in member countries. However, although national referenda on membership and treaty ratification have not been without a degree of controversy, most of the countries in Europe have now decided that the benefits of being a member of the EEC outweigh the costs, and by 1997 all of the following states belonged: Austria, Belgium, Denmark, Finland, France, Germany, Greece, Ireland, Italy, Luxembourg, the Nether-lands, Portugal, Spain, Sweden, and the UK.

With the ratification of the Maastricht Treaty, which prepared the way for monetary union and the euro, the EEC and its associated bodies became formally known as the European Union (EU). An important feature of monetary union has been the establishment of an independent Euro-pean Central Bank (ECB). This bank has as its main goal "price stability," a term meaning inflation of less than 2 percent per year. At present the UK, Denmark, and Sweden have decided not to adopt the euro, while Greece is unable to satisfy the economic criteria for monetary union and the new currency.

1825 World's first public railway opens between Stockton and Darlington, starting a worldwide boom in railway construction

1837 Queen Victoria crowned. Rule lasts until 1901, coincides with period of great wealth and growth of British Empire

1845–46 Potato crop failure causes Great Famine in Ireland; millions die or emigrate to England, USA, Canada, Australia

1901 The population of Britain reaches 42 million after rapid population growth in the second half of the nineteenth century

1914–18 First World War against Germany causes the loss of more than 900,000 British Empire lives

1920 Northern Ireland separates from the rest of Ireland and remains part of the United Kingdom; the Irish Free State (southern Ireland) is set up in 1921

1930s Unemployment rises to 3 million; some relief provided by economic progress in manufacturing industries

1939–45 Cities across Britain bombed during Second World War—widespread damage and the loss of thousands of lives

1945 Churchill loses election to Labour Party's Attlee who begins a program of reconstruction, reform, and nationalization

1957 Extensive postwar migration from Commonwealth regions such as Pakistan, India, and West Indies

1967 Britain fails to join the EC; membership not achieved until 1973; sterling devalued

1975 Offshore North Sea oilfields begin operation, boosting the UK economy; Britain becomes self-sufficient in oil

1994 Passenger train services through the fixed-link railway tunnel under the English Channel link France and the UK

Europe and the Russian Federation

Vatican City

Occupying a hill in the city of Rome on the western bank of the Tiber, and including as well the pope's residence at Castel Gandolfo, southeast of Rome, and ten churches throughout Rome, Vatican City is the world's smallest state, and probably its most homogeneous. Its population is 100 percent Catholic, and it is the home of the pope, the spiritual head of the Roman Catholic Church, and several hundred clergy and Catholic lay people, all employees of the Vatican.

Vatican City is all that remains of the former Papal States, which from the fourteenth to the nineteenth centuries expanded from a palace on the present site to cover an area of almost 45,000 sq km (17,000 sq miles). During the Risorgimento ("resurrection"), which resulted in the unification of Italy in the 1860s, most of this area was absorbed into the new Italian state. From 1870 until 1929, neither the Church nor successive Italian governments recognized each other's sovereignty over the area, which the Church refused to relinquish to the state. In 1929, however, Pope Leo XI and Mussolini concluded an

agreement—the Lateran Treaty—under which the independence of the Vatican City State, and the pope's temporal sovereignty over it, was recognized in return for the Church's recognition of the kingdom of Italy. Under this treaty, Catholicism was also recognized as the state religion of Italy. This provision, along with a number of other privileges enjoyed by the Church in Italy, was removed under a subsequent Church–state agreement, known as a "concordat," signed in 1984. Vatican City, which now has diplomatic relations with more than 100 countries, has the pope as head of state, while responsibility for administration of the area is vested in a Commission of Cardinals. The roles of secretary of state, chief of staff, and foreign minister are filled by senior members of the clergy.

Surrounded by medieval walls, Vatican City contains the huge St Peter's Basilica, built between 1506 and 1626 by a number of architects, including Michelangelo and Bernini. Pilgrims come to visit the basilica in vast numbers throughout the year, but particularly to celebrate Christmas and Easter. Visitors also come to see the richly endowed Vatican Museums, which include the renowned Sistine Chapel (the personal chapel of the popes) in the Vatican Palace. Parklands cover most of Vatican City.

Vatican City has its own radio station, publishes a daily newspaper, and issues its own stamps and coins. It also has an army—the 100-strong Swiss Guard—which is responsible for maintaining security. Vatican state finances depend on voluntary contributions, interest on extensive investments, and on the income derived from millions of tourists.

Fact File

OFFICIAL NAME	Vatican City State (Holy See)
FORM OF GOVERNMENT	Monarchical–sacerdotal state with single legislative body (Pontifical Commission)
CAPITAL	Vatican City
AREA	0.44 sq km (0.16 sq miles)
TIME ZONE	GMT + 1 hour
POPULATION	1,000
PROJECTED POPULATION 2005	Not available
POPULATION DENSITY	2,272.7 per sq km (5,886.3 per sq mile)
LIFE EXPECTANCY	Not available
INFANT MORTALITY (PER 1,000)	Not available
OFFICIAL LANGUAGES	Italian, Latin
LITERACY RATE	Not available
RELIGION	Roman Catholic
ETHNIC GROUPS	Predominantly Italian; some Swiss
CURRENCY	Vatican lira
ECONOMY	Services 100%
GNP PER CAPITA	Not available
CLIMATE	Temperate, with mild winters and hot summers
HIGHEST POINT	Unnamed location 75 m (246 ft)
MAP REFERENCE	Page 295

St Peter's Square in Vatican City, seen from the roof of the basilica (left). An old stone bridge spans a river in Montenegro, Yugoslavia (top right).

Yugoslavia

At its southwestern edge, the "rump" republic of Yugoslavia has a toehold on the Adriatic Sea. Otherwise it is landlocked, sharing borders with seven countries. Moving from the west around to south clockwise, these are Bosnia and Herzegovina, Croatia, Hungary, Romania, Bulgaria, Macedonia, and Albania. Yugoslavia now comprises the republics of Serbia and Montenegro—all that remains of the former federation of Yugoslavia after four of its six constituent republics seceded in the early 1990s. Yugoslavia came into existence in December 1918 as a combination of formerly separate Balkan states, most of which had been under Austro-Hungarian control. Serbia had become independent in 1878, bringing to an end five centuries of almost continuous Ottoman rule. The new country was originally called the Kingdom of Serbs, Croats, and Slovenes, but in 1929 the name Yugoslavia was adopted. During the Second World War Yugoslavia was invaded by Germany and the country was further devastated by civil war. More than a million Yugoslavs perished during this time. At the end of the war, a communist government, led by a Croat, Josip Broz, better known as Marshal Tito, came to power, but remained independent of the Soviet Union. After Tito died in 1980 ethnic tensions began to assert themselves, and in 1991 Croatia and Slovenia seceded, leading to four years of bitter ethnic-based conflict between Serbia and its neighbors. Ethnic conflict still simmers. A constitution adopted in 1992 decreed that democratic elections for the presidency and for two houses of parliament be held every five years.

In 1999, Serbia forced most of the population of the southern province of Kosovo—Muslim Albanians—to leave. Conflict continued between guerrilla forces of the Kosovo Liberation Army (KLO) and Serb forces as a meeting of NATO nations decided to launch air strikes against major administrative and industrial targets in

Serbia. Most of the NATO strikes were aimed at bridges and buildings in the Serb capital of Belgrade, with strikes also affecting the Serb city of Novi Sad and the Kosovo capital of Pristina. Russia, which opposed the NATO air strikes, held talks with Serb President Slobodan Milosevic, as well as US President Clinton, in an attempt to resolve the conflict.

Serbia and Montenegro are largely mountainous. The heavily forested Balkan Mountains, with their rocky peaks, separate Serbia from Bulgaria and Romania and stretch across much of southern and central Serbia and into Bosnia and Herzegovina. Much of Montenegro, in the southwest, is covered by the bare limestone ridges of the Dinaric Alps, which run from Slovenia south into Albania. In the north of the country, and covering most of the province of Vojvodina, is the fertile Pannonian Plain. A number of rivers, including the Sava, the Tisza and the Danube traverse this plain, which extends northwest into Croatia and Hungary.

Agricultural produce is centered on the northern plain, which supports substantial crops of wheat, maize, and vegetables as well as livestock and poultry. Agriculture in Montenegro is based mainly on the raising of sheep and goats. Yugoslavia has considerable reserves of coal and petroleum and is largely self-sufficient in fuel. Most of these resources are in the northern province of Vojvodina and the troubled southern region of Kosovo. Mining and heavy machine manufacture are major contributors to the country's economy, which, however, remains seriously destabilized by years of warfare and the consequent disruption of trade links.

Fact File

OFFICIAL NAME Federal Republic of Yugoslavia

FORM OF GOVERNMENT Federal republic with two legislative bodies (Chamber of Republics and Chamber of Citizens)

CAPITAL Belgrade

AREA 102,350 sq km (39,517 sq miles)

TIME ZONE GMT + 1 hour

POPULATION 10,526,478

PROJECTED POPULATION 2005 10,626,538

POPULATION DENSITY 102.8 per sq km (266.2 per sq mile)

LIFE EXPECTANCY 73.5

INFANT MORTALITY (PER 1,000) 16.5

OFFICIAL LANGUAGE Serbian

OTHER LANGUAGE Albanian

LITERACY RATE 93%

RELIGIONS Eastern Orthodox 65%, Muslim 19%, Roman Catholic 4%, Protestant 1%, other 11%

ETHNIC GROUPS Serbian 63%, Albanian 14%, Montenegrin 6%, Hungarian 4%, other 13%

CURRENCY Yugoslav dinar

ECONOMY Services and agriculture 60%, industry 40%

GNP PER CAPITA US$1,500

CLIMATE Temperate, with cold winters and hot summers

HIGHEST POINT Daravica 2,656 m (8,714 ft)

The Balkans

The Balkans is the collective name for the countries that occupy the Balkan Peninsula, the easternmost of the three peninsulas that jut southward into the Mediterranean Sea. It comprises the countries of Greece, Bulgaria, Romania, Moldova, Albania, Macedonia, Yugoslavia, Bosnia and Herzegovina, Croatia, and Slovenia. The word Balkan emerged in the nineteenth century. It was the Turkish name for a mountain range in Bulgaria and at first was applied to the land that lay to the south of this range. At various times since, it has had different meanings. Since the First World War, which was sparked by the assassination of the heir to the Austro-Hungarian Empire in Sarajevo, in Bosnia, the region has often been referred to as "the powder keg of Europe," and has had strong connotations of violence and ethnic conflict. In more recent times that phrase has acquired new significance and the term Balkan is increasingly used to refer specifically to those countries that formerly constituted the state of Yugoslavia.

The present troubles in the Balkans can be traced back to the reawakening of long-dormant nationalist sentiments as the formerly powerful Turkish Empire declined during the nineteenth century. This led to the formation of a number of nation states, some of which were, until the end of the First World War, under Austro-Hungarian domination. Many of these states were formed with scant regard to the ethnic, religious, or linguistic homogeneity of their populations. Thus significant populations of Muslim Albanians were incorporated into predominantly Christian Serbia and Macedonia and large numbers of Serbs, the most widely dispersed of the Balkan peoples, lived in Croatia and Bosnia, which is now called Bosnia and Herzegovina.

The explosive potential of this situation was largely contained after the formation of the federated state of Yugoslavia, in which Serbians were dominant, and during the Second World War, in which all Balkan countries suffered grievously. Ethnic tensions remained suppressed during the regime of the strong communist leader Marshal Tito after the Second World War. During this period, cold war politics dominated Europe, and Yugoslavia adopted relatively liberal socialist policies independently of the Soviet Union. Albania and Romania also pursued their own, albeit more oppressive, socialist agendas, but like Yugoslavia, refused to bow to Soviet domination. Greece remained non-communist, but only after a bitter civil war, which saw the communists finally defeated in 1949.

The death of Tito in 1980 and the later disintegration of communist regimes in Eastern Europe set the scene for the breakdown of Yugoslavia into its component republics. A series of civil wars followed, as Serb minorities in Croatia and Bosnia and Herzegovina fought, with Serbian support, for the extension of Serbian territories. An uneasy truce was brokered in 1995, only after the deployment of United Nations forces. In 1998, simmering resentment by ethnic Albanians in the southern Yugoslav province of Kosovo erupted again into bloody warfare and led to brutal massacres by Yugoslav forces.

Dependencies in Europe

Faeroe Islands

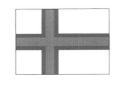 

The Faeroes are an archipelago of 22 islands in the north Atlantic Ocean, between Scotland and Iceland, eighteen of which are inhabited. Although they are part of Danish territory, the Faeroes have, since 1948, enjoyed a high degree of autonomy. They have their own parliament, which is elected for four-year terms. In the eleventh century these islands came under Norwegian control, but when, in the fourteenth century, the crowns of Norway and Denmark combined, Denmark became the dominant power. Since 1709 the islands have been administered solely by Denmark.

The Faeroes, formed from volcanic lava, are rocky, with spectacular cliffs along the coasts. Sheep raising has been the economic mainstay, though recently fishing has supplanted it in importance. Despite international criticism, the Faeroese maintain a vigorous whaling industry.

Fact file

OFFICIAL NAME Faeroe Islands

FORM OF GOVERNMENT Self-governing overseas administrative division of Denmark

CAPITAL Torshavn

AREA 1,400 sq km (541 sq miles)

TIME ZONE GMT

POPULATION 41,059

LIFE EXPECTANCY 78.6

INFANT MORTALITY (PER 1,000) 10.3

LITERACY RATE Not available

CURRENCY Danish krone

ECONOMY Mainly fishing; some agriculture, light industry, and services

CLIMATE Mild winters, cool summers; foggy and windy

MAP REFERENCE Page 302

Gibraltar

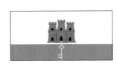 

Jutting into the Strait of Gibraltar at the southwest tip of Spain, Gibraltar sits at the entrance to the Mediterranean Sea. Spain's capture of Gibraltar in 1462 ended seven centuries of Moorish rule. Seized by the British and Dutch in 1704, it was ceded to Britain in 1713 and, despite subsequent Spanish attempts to take it back, it has remained in British hands ever since. Spain and Britain still dispute possession of "The Rock," and there is strong support for independence among the inhabitants. Gibraltar has its own elected parliament and is virtually autonomous. Britain maintained a military garrison there until 1991, when it handed over control to the local regiment.

Gibraltar consists of a high rocky mountain, joined to the Spanish mainland by a sandy plain. Tourism, served by an airport on the peninsula, is an important contributor to Gibraltar's economy.

Fact file

OFFICIAL NAME Gibraltar

FORM OF GOVERNMENT Self-governing dependent territory of the United Kingdom

CAPITAL Gibraltar

AREA 6.5 sq km (2.5 sq miles)

TIME ZONE GMT + 1 hour

POPULATION 29,165

LIFE EXPECTANCY 78.7

INFANT MORTALITY (PER 1,000) 8.4

LITERACY RATE Not available

CURRENCY Gibraltar pound

ECONOMY Financial services, tourism, manufacturing, horticulture

CLIMATE Temperate; mild winters and warm summers

MAP REFERENCE Page 292

Guernsey

Guernsey, the second largest of the Channel Islands, lies in the English Channel, 50 km (30 miles) to the west of France. Though it is a British dependency, it is effectively self-governing, and administers all the other Channel Islands bar Jersey. Picturesque scenery, a gentle climate, and the relaxed lifestyle of its inhabitants make tourism an economic mainstay. Market gardening is also important and the island is famed for its distinctive cattle. Immigration is strictly controlled.

Fact File

OFFICIAL NAME Bailiwick of Guernsey

FORM OF GOVERNMENT British crown dependency

CAPITAL St Peter Port

AREA 63 sq km (24 sq miles)

TIME ZONE GMT

POPULATION 65,386

LIFE EXPECTANCY 78.7

INFANT MORTALITY (PER 1,000) 8.4

LITERACY RATE Not available

CURRENCY Guernsey pound

ECONOMY Financial services, tourism, manufacturing, horticulture

CLIMATE Temperate; mild winters and cool summers

MAP REFERENCE Page 304

Europe and the Russian Federation

Jersey

Svalbard

 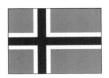

Jersey, the largest and most populous of the Channel Islands, lies in the English Channel, 20 km (12 miles) from the west coast of the Cherbourg Peninsula in northern France. Said to be the sunniest part of the British Isles, it is noted for its superb beaches. These account for the booming tourist industry, which, along with financial services, has in recent years supplanted agriculture as the mainstay of the economy.

Jersey is a dependency of the British crown, but it has its own legislature and a tax regime that is entirely independent and whose low rates attract many foreign businesses. Jersey cattle are among the most important exports and flower cultivation is also a significant income earner.

Fact File

OFFICIAL NAME	Bailiwick of Jersey
FORM OF GOVERNMENT	British crown dependency
CAPITAL	St Helier
AREA	117 sq km (45 sq miles)
TIME ZONE	GMT
POPULATION	89,721
LIFE EXPECTANCY	78.8
INFANT MORTALITY (PER 1,000)	2.8
LITERACY RATE	Not available
CURRENCY	Jersey pound
ECONOMY	Financial services, agriculture, tourism
CLIMATE	Temperate; mild winters and cool summers
MAP REFERENCE	Page 290

Situated in the Arctic Ocean about 650 km (400 miles) north of Norway, Svalbard consists of nine bleak, rocky, and icy islands. From Viking times until the sixteenth century, these islands remained unknown. Recently they have served as a base for Arctic explorers. Svalbard's coal reserves have been mined by a number of nations, under Norway's supervision. Now, only Norway and Russia mine the much depleted deposits.

Vegetation on the islands is restricted to mosses, lichens, and a few hardy, low-growing plants.There is an expanding tourist industry. Visitors are attracted mainly by the many migratory birds that come to the islands.

Fact File

OFFICIAL NAME	Svalbard
FORM OF GOVERNMENT	Territory of Norway
CAPITAL	Longyearbyen
AREA	62,049 sq km (23,957 sq miles)
TIME ZONE	GMT + 1 hour
POPULATION	2,864 (1996)
LIFE EXPECTANCY	Not available
INFANT MORTALITY (PER 1,000)	Not available
LITERACY RATE	Not available
CURRENCY	Norwegian krone
ECONOMY	Mainly coal mining, some tourism
CLIMATE	Polar, moderated by Gulf Stream ocean current; cold winters and cool summers
MAP REFERENCE	Page 300

The Isle of Man

The Isle of Man is situated in the Irish Sea between the west coast of England and Northern Ireland, and just south of Galloway in Scotland. At its southern tip is a tiny uninhabited island, the Calf of Man, which is a nature reserve. Two regions of uplands in the center of the main island are divided by a valley extending from Douglas, on the east coast, to Peel, on the west.

The Isle of Man is a dependency of the British crown, but has its own legislature, legal system, and taxation system. Traditionally agriculture and fishing have been the island's main source of income, but it now depends mainly on tourism and financial and business services. Although English is the main language, the local Gaelic language—known as Manx—is still widely spoken and is taught in schools.

Fact File

OFFICIAL NAME	Isle of Man
FORM OF GOVERNMENT	British crown dependency
CAPITAL	Douglas
AREA	588 sq km (227 sq miles)
TIME ZONE	GMT
POPULATION	75,686
LIFE EXPECTANCY	77.8
INFANT MORTALITY (PER 1,000)	2.5
LITERACY RATE	Not available
CURRENCY	Manx pound
ECONOMY	Services 72%, industry 22%, transport and communication 6%
CLIMATE	Temperate; cool, wet winters and mild summers
MAP REFERENCE	Page 306

A seaside town on the Isle of Man (center). A skidoo and sleds on Svalbard (top). St Peter Port, in Guernsey (left).

The Channel Islands

The Channel Islands lie in the English Channel between 15 and 50 km (10 and 30 miles) off the coast of Normandy in northern France. As well as the two largest islands of Jersey and Guernsey, there are the smaller islands of Sark and Alderney and a number of even smaller islands. In all, the Channel Islands cover an area of only 200 sq km (80 sq miles).

Since the Norman invasion of England in 1066, these islands have been dependencies of the British crown and are the only part of the Duchy of Normandy to have been retained by Britain after 1204. During the Second World War they were the only region of Britain to be occupied by German troops.

Both Jersey and Guernsey have separate legislatures and their own taxation systems, independent of Britain. While English is the most widely spoken language, French is also common and it is the official language of the Jersey legislature. The majority of the place names on Jersey are French.

Especially during the summer, both English and French tourists flock to these islands, and tourism, along with financial services, is now the mainstay of the islands' economies. Tourism on Jersey employs a large number of Portuguese nationals. The residents of the Channel Islands enjoy a high standard of living, maintained in part by strictly enforced residential controls.

Europe and the Russian Federation: Physical

NORWEGIAN SEA

No

Iceland
Hekla 1491 m ▲
Hvannadalshnúkur 2119 m ▲

Arctic Circle

Vesterålen
Haltī 1328 m ▲

Lofoten
Kebnekaise 2111 m ▲

Scandinavia

Galdhøpiggen 2469 m ▲

Faeroe Islands

Shetland Islands

Rockall

Gulf of Bothnia

Hebrides
Cape Wrath
Orkney Islands

ATLANTIC OCEAN

British Isles

Ben Nevis 1343 m ▲ Grampian Mountains

Gotland

Gulf of Riga

Öland

Gaizi

NORTH SEA

Jylland

Skagerrak

Kattegat

Vänern

BALTIC SEA

Lough Neagh

IRISH SEA

Carrauntoohil 1041 m ▲
Mizen Head

Snowdon 1085 m ▲

Pennines

Bornholm

Nemuna

Severn

Trent

Ostfriesische Inseln

St George's Channel

CELTIC SEA

Thames

Oder

Elbe

Harz

North E

Land's End

English Channel

Strait of Dover

Botrange 694 m ▲

Ardennes

Meuse

Rhein (Rhine)

Weser

Erzgebirge

Sudety

Wisła

Channel Islands

Seine

Marne

Mosel

Taunus

Praděd 1492 m ▲

Warta

Bug

Cabo Fisterra

Bay of Biscay

Loire

Cher

Loire

Saône

Vosges

Jura

Schwarzwald

Rhein

Bodensee

Donau

Inn

Zugspitze 2962 m ▲

Gerlachovský Štit 2655 m ▲

CAR

H

Hove 206

Massif Central

Matterhorn 4478 m ▲

Großglockner 3797 m ▲

Duna

Cordillera Cantábrica

Minho

Garonne

Mont Blanc 4807 m ▲

Monte Rosa 4634 m ▲

A L P S

Dolomiti

Triglav 2863 m ▲

Balaton

Drava

Plain of Hungary

Moldov 25

PYRENEES

Cévennes

Po

Sava

Dinara

CARPAT

Iberian

Duero

Ebro

Pico de Aneto 3404 m ▲

Golfe du Lion

LIGURIAN SEA

APPENNINO

ADRIATIC SEA

2522 m ▲

S

Peninsula

Tajo

Corse

Musala 2925 m ▲

Cabo de São Vicente

Sierra Morena

Guadiana

Júcar

Golfo de Valencia

Islas Baleares

Menorca

Korab 2764 m ▲

Guadalquivir

Eivissa

Mallorca

Sardegna

Strait of Bonifacio

TYRRHENIAN SEA

Strait of Otranto

Golfo di Taranto

Pindos

Oros Olymp 2917 m ▲

Golfo de Cádiz

Sierra Nevada
Mulhacén 3481 m ▲

Strait of Gibraltar

MEDITERRANEAN

Strait of Sicily

Sicilia

Monte Etna 3323 m ▲

IONIAN SEA

Ionioi Nisoi

Peloponni

ATLAS MOUNTAINS

Jebel Toubkal 4165 m ▲

Cap Bon

Jabal ash Sha'nabī 1544 m ▲

Malta

SEA

Shaţţ al Jarīd

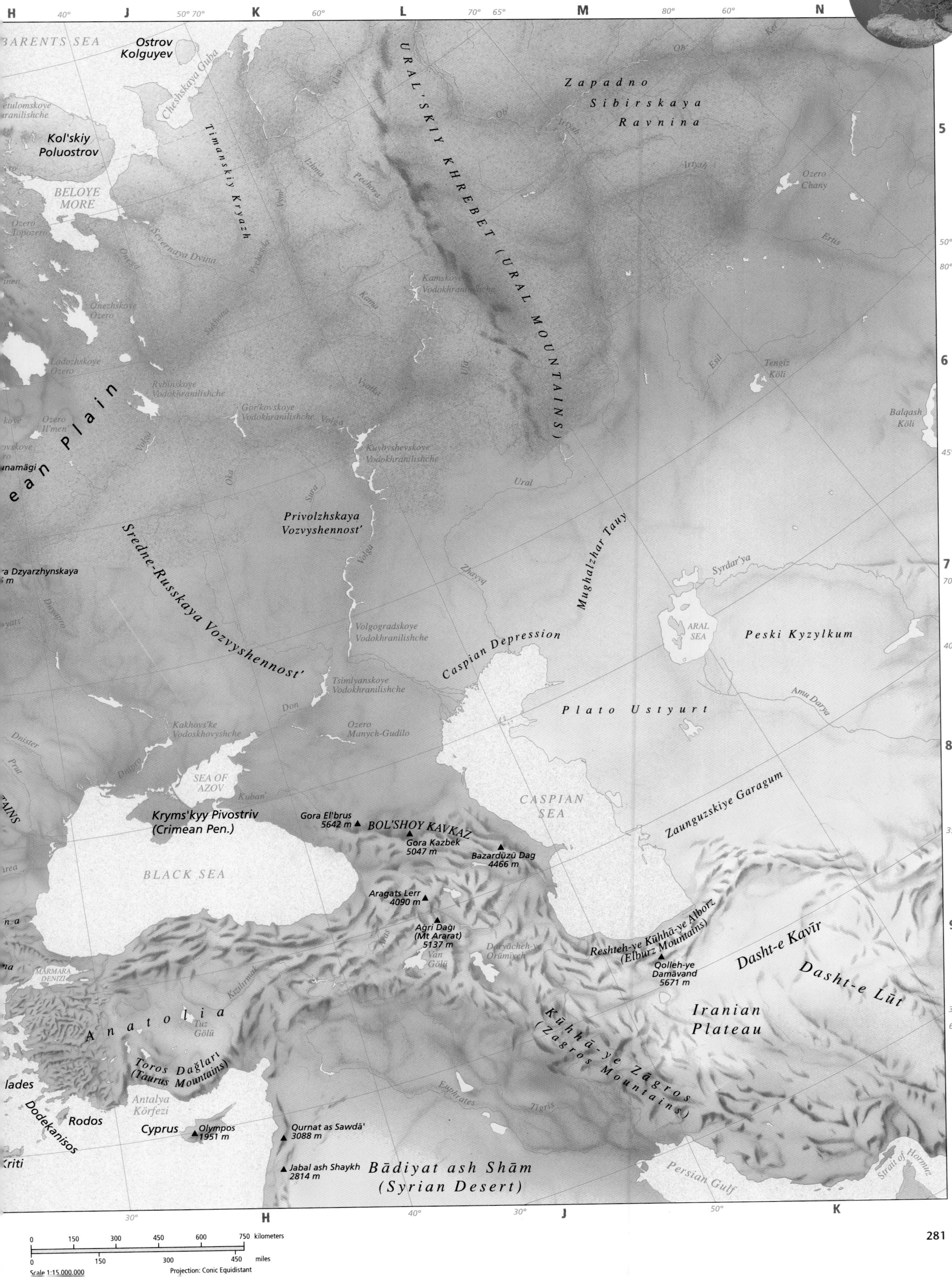

H J K L M N

40° 50° 70° 60° 70° 65° 80° 60°

BARENTS SEA

Ostrov
Kolguyev

Kol'skiy
Poluostrov

BELOYE
MORE

Chëshskaya Guba

Timanskiy Kryazh

URAL'SKIY KHREBET (URAL MOUNTAINS)

Zapadno
Sibirskaya
Ravnina

Ob'

Ob'

Irtysh

Ozero
Chany

Ertis

5

50°
80°

Severnaya Dvina

Pechora

Izhma

Kamskoye
Vodokhranilishche

Kama

Esil

Tengiz
Köli

Balqash
Köli

6

Ozero
Topozero

Onezhskoye
Ozero

Ladozhskoye
Ozero

Rybinskoye
Vodokhranilishche

Gor'kovskoye
Vodokhranilishche

Vyatka

Volga

Ural

45°

Privolzhskaya
Vozvyshennost'

Kuybyshevskoye
Vodokhranilishche

Mughalzhar Tauy

Syrdar'ya

7

70°

Dzyarzhynskaya

Sredne-Russkaya Vozvyshennost'

Volga

Zhayyq

Volgogradskoye
Vodokhranilishche

Caspian Depression

ARAL
SEA

Peski Kyzylkum

40°

Desna

Don

Tsimlyanskoye
Vodokhranilishche

Plato Ustyurt

Amu Darya

8

Dnister

Prut

Kakhovs'ke
Vodoskhovyshche

Ozero
Manych-Gudilo

CASPIAN
SEA

Zaunguzskiye Garagum

SEA OF
AZOV

Kuban'

Kryms'kyy Pivostriv
(Crimean Pen.)

Gora El'brus
5642 m ▲

BOL'SHOY KAVKAZ

35°

BLACK SEA

Gora Kazbek
5047 m ▲

Bazardüzü Dag
4466 m ▲

Aragats Lerr
4090 m ▲

Reshteh-ye Kühhä-ye Alborz
(Elburz Mountains)

Dasht-e Kavīr

Dasht-e Lūt

9

MARMARA
DENIZI

Agri Dağı
(Mt Ararat)
5137 m ▲

Van
Gölü

Daryācheh-ye
Orümiyeh

Qolleh-ye
Damävand
5671 m ▲

Kızılırmak

Aras

30°
60°

Anatolia

Tuz
Gölü

Kühhä-ye Zägros
(Zagros Mountains)

Iranian
Plateau

Toros Dağları
(Taurus Mountains)

Antalya
Körfezi

Euphrates

Tigris

lades

Dodekanisos

Rodos

Cyprus

Olympos
▲ 1951 m

Qurnat as Sawdā'
▲ 3088 m

Persian Gulf

Strait of Hormuz

10

Kriti

Jabal ash Shaykh
▲ 2814 m

Bādiyat ash Shām
(Syrian Desert)

30° 40° 30° 50°

H J K

0 150 300 450 600 750 kilometers

0 150 300 450 miles

Scale 1:15.000.000   Projection: Conic Equidistant

Europe and the Russian Federation: Political

40° J 50° 70° K 60° L 70° 65° M 80° 60° N

Arctic Circle

RUSSIAN FEDERATION

KAZAKHSTAN

UZBEKISTAN

TURKMENISTAN

Kolpashevo
Anzhero-Sudzhensk
Nizhnevartovsk
Tomsk
Kemerovo
Surgut
Leninsk-Kuznetskiy
Novosibirsk
Barnaul
Biysk
Igrim
Nar'yan Mar
Inta
Nyagan'
Pechora
Murmansk
Monchegorsk
Apatity
Kandalaksha
Mezen'
Ukhta
Tatarsk
Severodvinsk
Arkhangel'sk
Kem'
Serov
Nazyvayevsk
Omsk
Ishim
Syktyvkar
Tyumen'
Rubtsovsk
Medvezh'yegorsk
Kotlas
Solikamsk
Berezniki
Nizhniy Tagil
Kurgan
Petrozavodsk
Yekaterinburg
Perm'
Kamensk-Ural'skiy
Pervoural'sk
Vyatka
Chelyabinsk
Votkinsk
Zlatoust
Sankt-Peterburg
Vologda
Izhevsk
Sarapul
Kolpino
Cherepovets
Naberezhnyye
Chelny
Ufa
Magnitogorsk
Novgorod
Rybinsk
Yaroslavl'
Kostroma
Cheboksary
Kazan'
Ivanovo
Al'met'yevsk
Sterlitamak
kov
Tver'
Nizhniy
Novgorod
Salavat
Sergiyev Posad
Murom
Arzamas
Dimitrovgrad
Orsk
Velikie Luki
Moskva
Ul'yanovsk
Samara
Orenburg
Obninsk
Kolomna
Tol'yatti
Novokuybyshevsk
Smolensk
Ryazan'
Saransk
Syzran'
Sol'-Iletsk
ebsk
Kaluga
Penza
ilyow
Tula
Novomoskovsk
nsk
Tambov
Balakovo
ARUS
Bryansk
Lipetsk
Saratov
Engel's
avichy
Orel
Homyel'
Kursk
azyr
Voronezh
Chernihiv
Belgorod
Sumy
Volzhskiy
Kyyiv
Volograd
hytomyr
Kharkiv
Poltava
UKRAINE
Kremenchuk
Luhans'k
tsya
Dniprodzerzhyns'k
Astrakhan'
Kirovohrad
Donets'k
Kryvyy Rih
Zaporizhzhya
Makiyivka
vtsi
Taganrog
Rostov-na-Donu
Bălţi
Mykolayiv
Melitopol'
Mariupol'
MOLDOVA
Kherson
Krasnodar
Stavropol'
i
Chisinău
Odesa
Armavir
Makhachkala
Simferopol'
Novorossiysk
Cherkessk
Groznyy
IA
Maykop
Nal'chik
Vladikavkaz
CASPIAN
SEA
alaţi
Sevastopol'
Sochi
Braila
cureşti
GEORGIA
Constanţa
BLACK SEA
AZERBAIJAN
se
Varna
ARMENIA
AFGHANISTAN
IA
Burgas
ra Zagora

TURKEY

IRAN

Rodos

SYRIA

IRAQ

CYPRUS

kleio

Triti

LEBANON

ISRAEL   JORDAN   SAUDI ARABIA

KUWAIT

OMAN

U.A.E.

30° H 40° 30° J 50° K

5
50°
80°
6
45°
70°
7
40°
8
35°
9
30°
60°
10

283

Scale 1:15,000,000

0   150   300   450   600   750 kilometers
0   150   300   450 miles

Projection: Conic Equidistant

North Scandinavia • Iceland

GREENLAND SEA

Arctic Circle

Straumnes Hornbjarg Rifstangi Fontur
Unaðsdalur Siglufjörður Kópasker Raufarhöfn
Suðureyri Ísafjörður Hraun Ólafsfjörður Húsavík Bakkaflói
Bíldudalur Munaðarnes Hofsós Grenivík Vopnafjörður Kollumúli
Vatneyri Glama Hólmavík Dalvík Borgarfjörður
920 m Blönduós Akureyri Grímsstaðir Karlfell
Bjargtangar Reykhólar Hvammstangi Bergstaðir 1052 m
Breiðafjörður Herðubreið Egilsstaðir Seyðisfjörður
Stykkishólmur Búðardalur Myri 1682 m
Hellissandur Hofsjökull Fáskrúðsfjörður
Búðir Bárðarbunga Breiðdalsvík
Borgarnes 2000 m 1248 m Djúpivogur
Faxaflói Svíanúkar Vatnajökull
Akranes 1719 m Stokksnes
Reykjavík Laki Hvannadalshnúkur Höfn
Sandgerði Hafnarfjörður 818 m 2119 m Kálfafellsstaður
Hafnir Hella Hekla
Grindavík Þorlákshöfn 1491 m Fagurhólsmýri
Hvolsvöllur
Mýrdalsjökull
Skógar 1450 m Langholt
Dyrhólaey Vík

ICELAND

ATLANTIC OCEAN

NORWEGIAN SEA

Arctic Circle

Europe and the Russian Federation

B A R E N T S   S E A

FINNMARK

Nordkapp
Ingøya Magerøya Honningsvåg Mehamn Gamvik
Rolvsøya Havøysund Kjøllefjord Berlevåg
Kvaløya Kåfjord Repvåg Skjånes Bätskapp
Hammerfest Olderfjord 578 m Hopseidet Båtsfjord
Seiland ▲1075 m Ifjord 668 m Stangenestind 724 m
Saraby Kalak 637 m Vardø
Nyvoll Børselv Rustefjelbma Varangerhalvøya
Alta Lakselv Storfjordbotn Tana
Skoganvarre 1139 m Rastegai'sa 1067 m Grasbakken
Nuvvus Vetsikko Nesseby Vadsø
Valjok Utsjoki Bugøyfjord Varangerfjorden
Karasjok Jomppala Neiden Grense Jakobselv
Karigasniemi 443 m Bjørnevatn

Poluostrov Rybachiy
Pummanki 299 m
Kirkenes Linakhamari Ostrov Kil'din
Svanvik Pechenga Port-Vladimir
Nikel 637 m Zapolyarnyy Polyarnyy
Gora Kuorpukas Severomorsk Teriberka
Nyrud Prirechnyy Murmansk Tumannyy 375 m
Gora Kuchin-Tundra ▲578 m Kola Kharlovka Vostochnaya
Murmashi Litsa Varzino
Magnetity Kil'dinstroy Mys Svyatoy Nos

MURMANSKAYA

Verkhnetulomskiy Taybola
Verkhnetulomskove Vodokhranilishche Pulozero Gremikha
Lovozero Gora Balkon-Myl'k 340 m
Gora Ionn-N'yugoayv ▲714 m Gora Chiltal'd 907 m Olenegorsk Revda
Gora Elgoras Kanevka
997 m

OBLAST'

Gora Ebruchorr 1115 m Monchegorsk Kirovsk
Girvas Yena Upoloksha Apatity
Kovdor Afrikanda Krasnoshchel'ye
Zasheyek Ozero Umbozero
Tulppio Tuntsa Polyarnyye Zori Kapustnoye

RUSSIAN

Kandalaksha
Sorsatunturi 629 m 622 m Beloye More Kolvitsa Pustaya Guba
Kuolayarvi Alakurtti Por'ya Guba
Zelenoborskiy Umba Kuzreka
Zarechensk Kovda Olenitsa Varzuga
Vuoriyarvi Kuzomen' Kashkarantsy
Khetolambina Chavan'ga Tetrino

Arctic Circle

Chupa Keret'
Zasheyek Sonostrov
Gora Nuorunen ▲577 m Loukhi

BELOYE MORE (WHITE SEA)

Gridino
Sosnovyy Ostrov Oleniy
Ambarnyy Engozero Undukša
Kesten'ga Nil'maguba Sig
Sofporog Letniy Navolok
Tungozero Karelakša Letnyaya Zolotitsa
Tukhkala Kuzema Lopshen'ga
Kuzema Pushlakhta

FEDERATION

Voynitsa Kalevala Kepa Yuma
Shombozero Kem' Rabocheostrovsk
Kentozero Borovoy Solovetskiye Ostrova
Voknavolok Yushkozero Pushnoy Kreml'
Ladvozero Belomorsk Poluostrov
Kostomuksha 277 m Letnerechenskiy Nizhmozero
Virma Lyamtsa
Luvozero Sumskiy Posad Ostrov Myagostrov
Idel' Kolezhma Kyanda

RESPUBLIKA

Kuivajärvi Ledmozero Rugozero Kochkoma Virandozero Vorzogory
Tiksha Vacha Nadvoitsy Unezhma
Muyezerskiy Vorenzha Kusha Nimen'ga
Segezha Polga ARKHANGEL'SKAYA

KARELIYA

Rovkuly Yemel'yanovka Popov Porog Urosozero
Rebolly Voloma Peninga 398 m Stantsiya Sumerichi OBLAST'
Kimovaara Padany Yevgora Vorozhgora
Tulos 290 m Sel'ga Masel'gskaya Ogorelyshi
Sukkozero Medvezh'yegorsk Pindushi
417 m Gimoly Povenets Lobskoye
Lendery Yustozero Pyal'ma
Padany Chelmuzhi
Proletarka Porosozero Guba Kazhma Unitsa
Kuolismaa Sovdozero Sopokha Velikaya
Kondopoga Kurgenitsy

FINLAND

LAPPIN LÄÄNI

Palojärvi 632 m Noarvaš 531 m
Menesjärvi Ivalo Raja-Jooseppi
Viipustunturit 599 m Törmänen
Saariselkä Sokosti 718 m Vuotso
Pokka Raattama 807 m Pallastunturi
Muonio Tepasto Pomovaara 424 m
Särkijärvi Sirkka Lokka Tanhua Petkula
Kangosjärvi Kittilä Rajala Tulppio
Kiistala Ylläsjärvi Tepsa Sodankylä Martti
Kihlanki Kaukonen Vaalajärvi Aska Savukoski
Kolari Kurtakko Lohiniva Saija
Sieppijärvi Unari Pelkosenniemi Salla
Meltaus Pyhätunturi 540 m Ahvenselkä
Konttajärvi Kemijärvi Kursu
Pello Vikajärvi Joutsijärvi Gora Rokhmoyva 657 m
Raanujärvi Misi Hautajärvi
Meltosjärvi Mellakoski Rovaniemi Pirttikoski
Övertorneå Käylä
Ylitornio Muurola Pera Posio Juuma Ruka
Hedenäset Varejoki Koivu Portimo Posio
Korpikä Arpela Tervola Ranua Mäntyjärvi Kuusamo Kärpänkylä
Karungi Puukkokumpu Kuha Kuloharju Kuolio
Tornio Keminmaa Yli-Kärppä Kelankylä Sarajärvi Murtovaara
Kemi Simo Oijärvi Rytinki Taivalkoski
Kuivaniemi Pudasjärvi Tyrävaara Hossa
Pohjois-Ii Olhava Yli-Ii Metsäkylä Peranka
Hailuoto Haukipudas Kipina Livo Pintamo Juntusranta
Hailuoto Kiiminki Siivikko Puhos Näljänkä
Oulu Ylikiiminki Hetekylä Joukokylä 384 m
Kempele Juorkuna Vuokki

OULUN LÄÄNI

Keskikylä Muhos Utajärvi Suomussalmi Ala-Vuokki
Liminka Puokio Hyrynsalmi Kuivajärvi
Ruukki Kylmälä Vaala Kotila Moisiovaara
Paavola Rantsila Kivesjärvi Ristijärvi Luvozero
Raahe Saloinen Säräisniemi Kontiomäki Lentiira
Pyhäjoki Vihanti Pulkkila Hietapera
Kalajoki Oulainen Piippola Sotkamo Kiekinkoski
Alavieska Karhukangas Kestilä Vuokatti Rovkuly
Ylivieska Pyhäntä Tuhkakylä Kuhmo
Himanka Nivala Kärsämäki Nissilä Sukeva Maanselkä
Kälviä Haapajärvi Vieremä Jyrkkä Valtimo Naarva Koli
Kannus Pyhäjärvi Koirakoski Nurmes Hattuselkonen Jaakonvaara
Kalvia Toholampi Reisjärvi Kiuruvesi Iisalmi Rautavaara Savikylä Nurmijärvi
Kronoby Ullava Lestijärvi Pielavesi Lapinlahti Juuka Lieksa
Ytteresse Veteli Kaustinen Muurasjärvi Vaaraslahti Juminen Uimaharju
Evijärvi Perho Pihtipudas Siilinjärvi Ahmovaara 347 m Hattuvaara
Kortesjärvi Kivijärvi Keitele Talluskylä Toivala Höytiäinen Kuusjärvi
Lapua Kauhava Kyyjärvi Vesanto Tervo Juankoski Luikonlahti Ilomantsi
Alajärvi Soini Karstula Konginkangas Kuopio Kontiolahti Kovero
Alavus Töysä Ähtäri Saarijärvi Istunmäki Suonenjoki Outokumpu Liperi Girvas
Pylkönmäki Hytölä Tuusniemi Joensuu Lindozero
Karvio Pyhäselkä Tolvajarvi

ITA-SUOMEN LÄÄNI

LÄNSI-SUOMEN LÄÄNI

Bottenviken
Perämeri
of Bothnia

0   50   100   200 kilometers
0   50   100 miles
Scale 1:3,500,000
Projection: Equidistant Conic

287   299
300

South Scandinavia • Baltic States

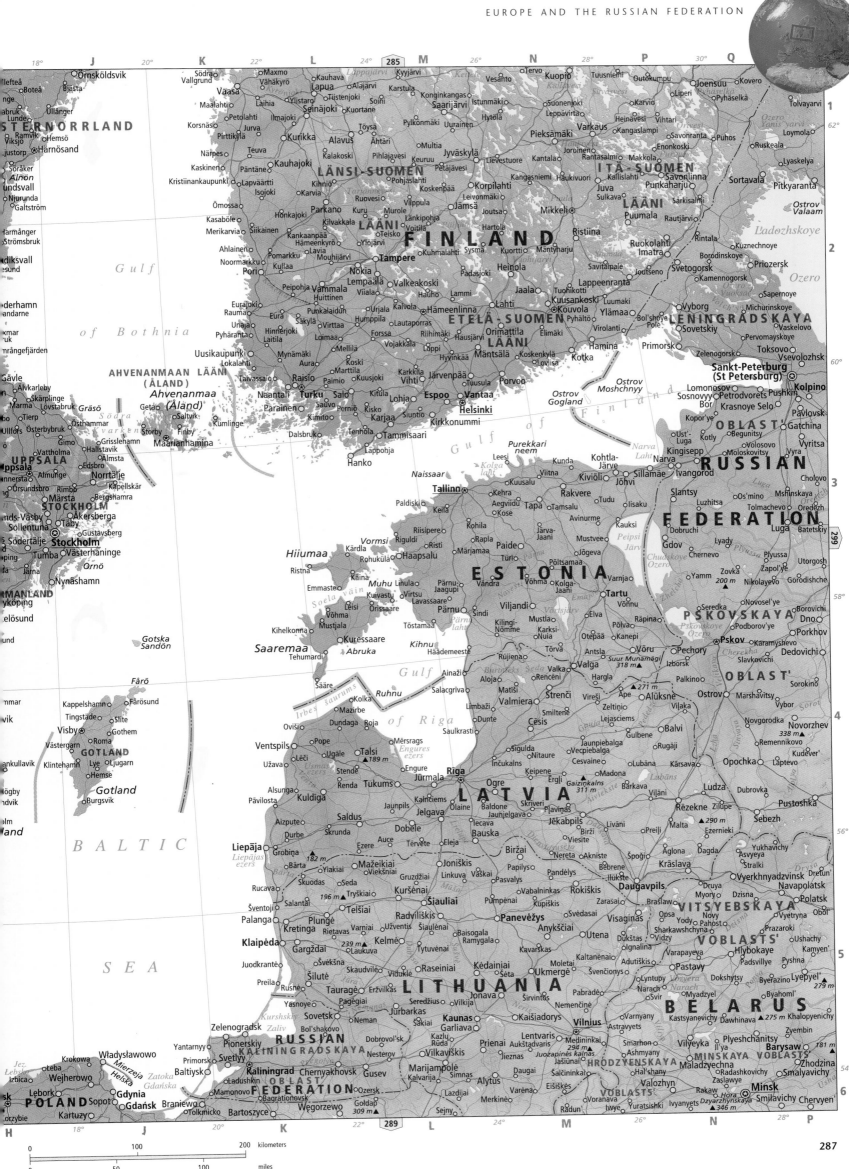

Europe and the Russian Federation

285

289

299

0   100   200 kilometers
0   50   100 miles
Scale 1:3,500,000
Projection: Equidistant Conic

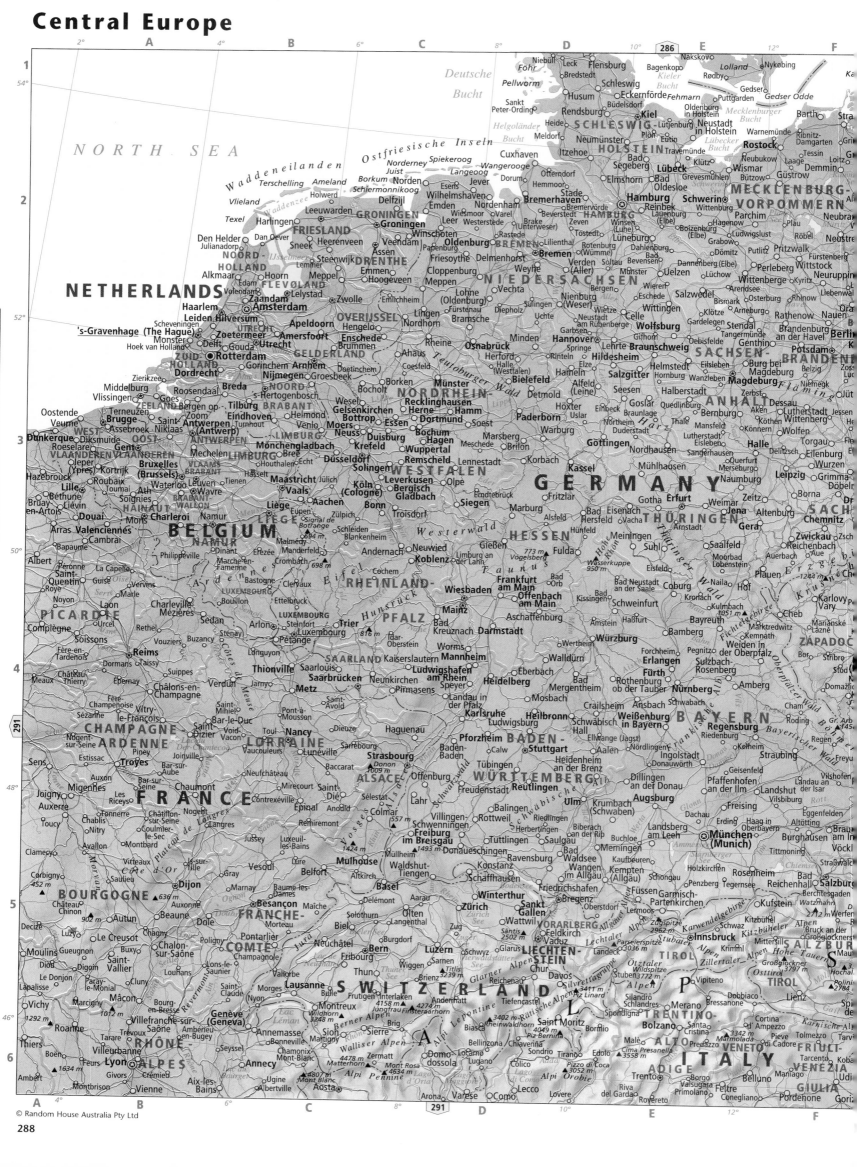

286

291

291

Europe and the Russian Federation

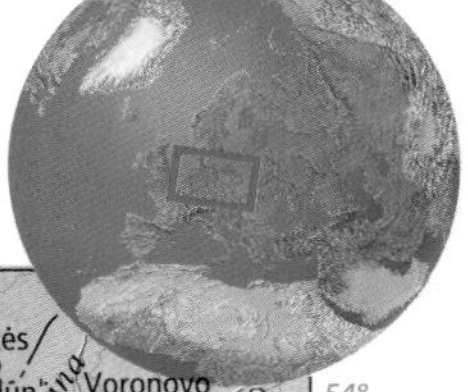

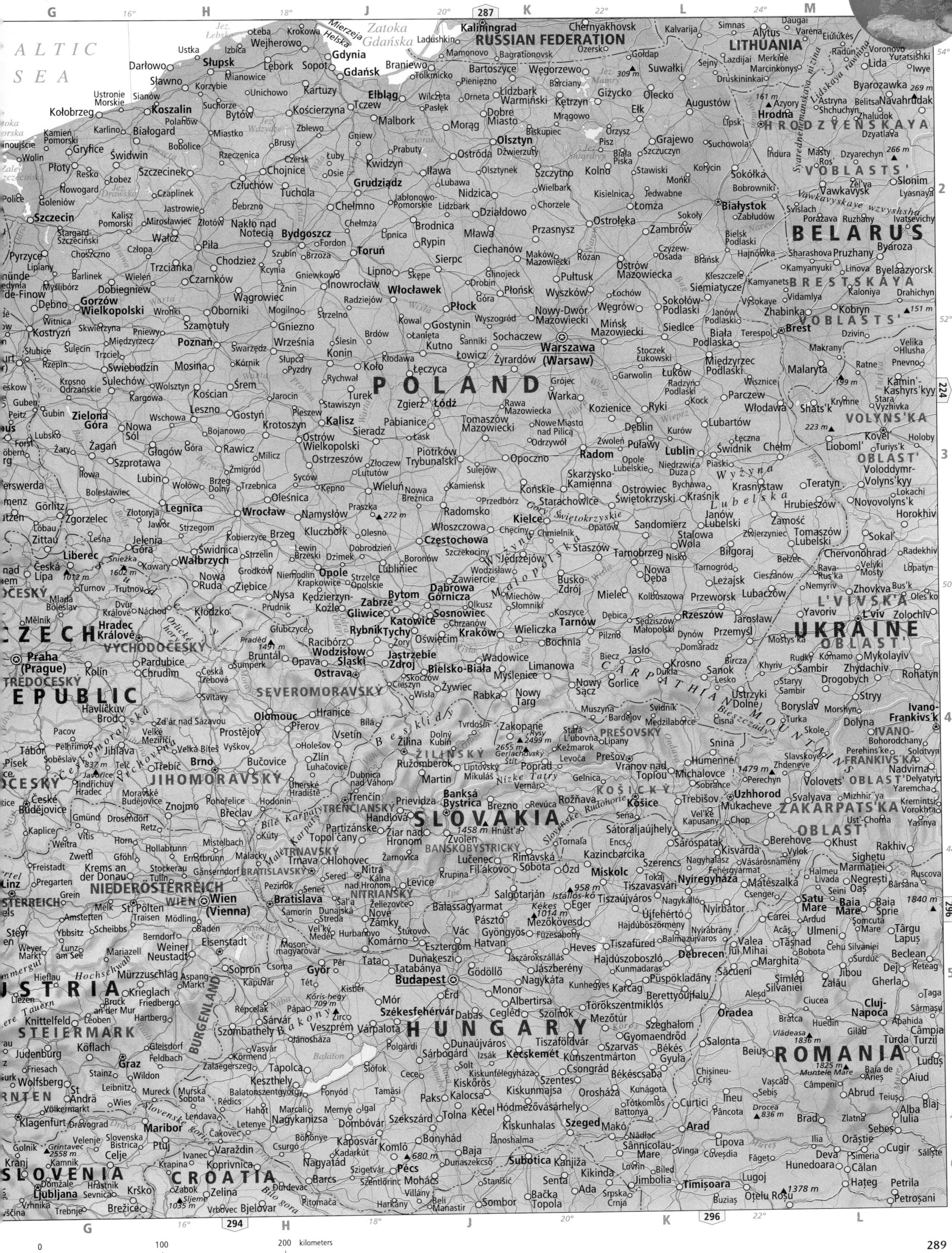

BALTIC SEA

RUSSIAN FEDERATION

LITHUANIA

BELARUS

HRODZYENSKAYA VOBLASTS'

BRESTSKAYA VOBLASTS'

POLAND

UKRAINE

VOLYNS'KA OBLAST'

L'VIVS'KA OBLAST'

ZAKARPATS'KA OBLAST'

CZECH REPUBLIC

VYCHODOCESKY

STREDOCESKY

JIHOMORAVSKY

SLOVAKIA

ZILINSKY

PRESOVSKY

KOSICKY

TRENCIANSKY

BANSKOBYSTRICKY

NITRIANSKY

TRNAVSKY

BRATISLAVSKY

AUSTRIA

NIEDERÖSTERREICH

WIEN (Vienna)

STEIERMARK

KÄRNTEN

HUNGARY

ROMANIA

SLOVENIA

CROATIA

Major cities: Kaliningrad, Gdynia, Gdańsk, Słupsk, Koszalin, Szczecin, Elbląg, Olsztyn, Białystok, Bydgoszcz, Toruń, Grudziądz, Poznań, Gniezno, Włocławek, Płock, Warszawa (Warsaw), Łódź, Kalisz, Zielona Góra, Wrocław, Legnica, Wałbrzych, Opole, Częstochowa, Kielce, Radom, Lublin, Chełm, Katowice, Kraków, Tarnów, Rzeszów, Przemyśl, L'viv, Praha (Prague), Brno, Bratislava, Wien (Vienna), Budapest, Graz, Maribor, Ljubljana, Cluj-Napoca, Oradea, Debrecen, Miskolc, Nyíregyháza, Satu Mare, Baia Mare, Arad, Timişoara

Scale 1:3,500,000
Projection: Equidistant Conic

0   100   200 kilometers
0   50   100 miles

France · Switzerland

Spain • Portugal

Europe and the Russian Federation

A · 12° · B · 10° · C · 8° · D · 6° · E

ATLANTIC

OCEAN

Cabo Ortegal
Punta da Estaca de Bares
Ortigueira
Cabo Prior
Ferrol
Viveiro
Ribadeo
Luarca
Cabo Vidio
Cabo de Peñas
Costa Verde
Avilés
Gijón
Ribadesella
A Coruña
Pontedeume
Mondoñedo
Vegadeo
Navia
Salas
Oviedo
Malpica
Carballo
Villalba
Baamonde
Pico de Bobia 1201 m
Xistral 1036 m
Mieres
Langreo
Covadonga
Picos de Europa 2648 m
Vimianzo
Guitiriz
Meira
A Fonsagrada
Pajares
Mampodre 2190 m
Peña Prieta 2536 m
Cabo Touriñán
Cée
Ordes
Melide
Lugo
Sarriá
Becerreá
Villablino 2417 m
Miravalles 1969 m
Catoute 2117 m
Cistierna
Fisterra
Santiago de Compostela
GALICIA
Cabo Fisterra
Noia
Padrón
A Estrada
Lalín
Chantada
Monforte
Faro 1187 m
Quiroga
Ponferrada
Astorga
El Teleno 2185 m
León
Mansilla de las Mulas
Santa Eugenia
Villagarcía de Arousa
Cerdedo
Ourense
Puebla de Trives
CASTILLA Y LEÓN
Pontevedra
A Cañiza
Sierra de la Cabrera
La Bañeza
Villada
Illa de Ons
Marín
Avión 1351 m
Cabeza de Manzaneda 1778 m
A Gudiña
Puebla de Sanabria
Benavente
Villalpando
Sahagún
Illas Cíes
Vigo
Tui
Peneda 1373 m
Verín
Bragança
Villadangos
Medina de Rioseco
Baiona
A Guardia
Ponte da Barca
Viana do Castelo
Serra do Larouco 1525 m
Chaves
Rebordelo
Alcañices
Embalse de Ricobayo
Tiedra
Valla
VIANA DO CASTELO
Braga
Boticas
Valpaços
Mirandela
Miranda do Douro
Zamora
Toro
Tordesillas
Duero
Póvoa de Varzim
BRAGA
Guimarães
VILA REAL
BRAGANÇA
Fermoselle
Corrales
Alaejos
Medina del Campo
Olmed
PORTO
Penafiel
Vila Real
Marão 1415 m
Torre de Moncorvo
Mogadouro
Trabanca
Embalse de Almendra
Cañizal
Olmedo
Porto
Lamego
Montemuro 1381 m
Moimenta da Beira
Marofa 976 m
Ledesma
Vitigudino
Arévalo
São João da Madeira
São Pedro do Sul
Celorico da Beira
Pinhel
Lumbrales
Barbadillo
Peñaranda de Bracamonte
Sanchidrián
Ovar
AVEIRO
VISEU
Viseu
Vilar Formoso
Ciudad Rodrigo
El Cabaco
Vecinos
Fresno Alhándiga
Ávila
Aveiro
Albergaria-a-Velha
Guarda
1075 m
1730 m
Peña de Francia
Guijuelo
Ibiza 2315 m
Serrota 2294 m
Mira
Águeda
GUARDA
Ciudad Rodrigo
Béjar
El Barco de Ávila
Piedrahita
Almanzor
Gredos
Sierra de Gredos
Cabo Mondego
Figueira da Foz
COIMBRA
Coimbra
da Estrela 1993 m
Covilhã
Embalse de Gabriel y Galán
Arenas de San Pedro
2592 m
Tiétar
Maqu
Góis
Fundão
Peñamacor
Moraleja
Plasencia
Coria
Jarandilla de la Vera
Navalmoral de la Mata
Talavera la Reina
Pombal
Pontão
CASTELO BRANCO
Cabeço Rainha 1084 m
Segura
Coria
Bohonal
La Nava de Ricomalillo
Navahermos
Leiria
Batalha
Fátima
Tomar
Torres Novas
Abrantes
Alpalhão
Valencia de Alcántara
Aliseda
Cáceres
Trujillo
Guadalupe
Montes de To
Nazaré
LEIRIA
São Mamede 1027 m
Alcántara
Brozas
Peniche
Rio Maior
Óbidos
SANTARÉM
Santarém
Almeirim
Portalegre
Alburquerque
Zorita
Herrera del Duque
Cabo Carvoeiro
Torres Vedras
Vila Franca de Xira
Coruche
Alter do Chão
PORTALEGRE
La Roca de la Sierra
Miajadas
Navalvillar de Pela
Talarrubias
Piedra
Barragem de Montargil
Vimieiro
Estremoz
Elvas
Mérida
Villanueva de la Serena
LISBOA
Sintra
Cascais
Amadora
Vendas Novas
Arraiolos
Redondo
Ossa 653 m
Badajoz
Olivenza
EXTREMADURA
Cabeza del Buey
Almadén
Puertol
Lisboa (Lisbon)
Almada
Setúbal
Barragem de Marinhão
Montemor-o-Novo
Évora
Alor 610 m
Almendralejo
Castuera
Santa Eufemia
Cabo Espichel
Baía de Setúbal
SETÚBAL
Grândola
Torrão
Mourão
Portel
Barcarrota
Santa Marta
Villanueva del Fresno
Zafra
Campillo de Llerena
Villanueva de Córdoba
Carden
Santiago do Cacém
325 m
Ferreira do Alentejo
Vidigueira
Moura
Barrancos
Fregenal de la Sierra
Fuente de Cantos
Llerena
Azuaga
Fuente Obejuna
Espiel
Sines
Cercal
Beja
Serpa
Rosal de la Frontera
Cortegana
Tentudía 1104 m
Monesterio
Cazalla de la Sierra
Erillas 896 m
Montoro
Santa Luzia
BEJA
Sierra de Aracena
Odemira
Castro Verde
Almodóvar
Mértola
Puebla de Guzmán
El Ronquillo
Lora del Río
Palma del Río
Odeceixe
Aljezur
Mú
577 m
Alcoutim
Gibraleón
Valverde del Camino
Carmona
Écija
Aguila
Fóia 902 m
Algarve
FARO
Castro Marim
Huelva
Bollullos par del Condado
Sevilla
Alcalá de Guadaira
Puente-Genil
Estepa
Lucena
Vila do Bispo
Portimão
Loulé
Faro
Tavira
Ayamonte
Mazagón
El Rocío
Utrera
Morón de la Frontera
Campillos
Ante
Cabo de São Vicente
Sagres
Lagos
Golfo de Cádiz
Torre de la Higuera
Lebrija
Villamartín
Ronda
Ponta de Sagres
Cabo de Santa Maria
Sanlúcar de Barrameda
Jeréz de la Frontera
Arcos de la Frontera
Algodonales
Ronda
Costa de la Luz
El Puerto de Santa Maria
Cádiz
San Fernando
Medina Sidonia
Jimena de la Frontera
Estepona
M
Chiclana de la Frontera
Vejer de la Frontera
La Línea de la Concepción
Ubrique
Marbella
Coín
Fuengiro
Barbate de Franco
Algeciras
Gibraltar
GIBRALTAR (U.K.)
Serranía de Ronda
Punta Marroquí o de Tarifa
Tarifa
Strait of Gibraltar
Punta Almina
Ceuta (Sp.)
Cap Spartel
Tanger (Tangier)
Ksar es Sghir 838 m
Tetouan (Tetuán)
Asilah
MOROCCO

42°
40°
38°
36°

FRANCE

MIDI-PYRÉNÉES

AQUITAINE

Mimizan, Sabres, Labrit, Houeillès, Aiguillon, Castelsarrasin, Caussade, Naucelle, Najac, Carmaux, Millau, Gangeo, Uzès, Avignon

Morcenx, Roquefort, Nérac, Agen, Condom, Montech, Montauban, Albi, Camarès, Le Caylar, Sommières, Nîmes, PROVENCE-ALPES-CÔTE-D'AZUR

Castets, Mont-de-Marsan, Aire-sur-l'Adour, Riscle, Auch, Gimont, Colomiers, Toulouse, Castres, Saint-Pons-de-Thomières, Bédarieux, Lodève, Gignac, Montpellier, Arles, Aix-en-Provence

Dax, Hagetmau, Garlin, Lombez, Muret, Carbonne, Carcassonne, Narbonne, Béziers, Agde, Cap d'Agde, Martigues, Marseille

Bayonne, Pau, Tarbes, Pamiers, Foix, LANGUEDOC-ROUSSILLON, Perpignan

Biarritz, Donostia-San Sebastián, Bilbao, Vitoria-Gasteiz, Pamplona, NAVARRA

PAÍS VASCO

Logroño, LA RIOJA, ARAGÓN

Zaragoza, Huesca, Lleida, CATALUÑA, Barcelona, Girona

Soria, Calatayud, Teruel, Castelló de la Plana, VALENCIA, Valencia

Cuenca, Albacete, Alicante, Elche, Murcia, MURCIA, Cartagena

Granada, Almería, ANDALUCÍA

SPAIN

CASTILLA-LA MANCHA

ANDORRA, Andorra la Vella

ISLAS BALEARES (Balearic Islands)

Menorca, Ciudadela, Mahón
Mallorca, Palma de Mallorca, Inca, Manacor
Eivissa (Ibiza), Formentera

Costa Brava, Costa Daurada, Costa del Azahar, Costa Blanca

Golfo de Valencia

Golfe du Lion

MEDITERRANEAN SEA

ALGERIA

Alger (Algiers), Tizi Ouzou, Blida, Médéa, Dellys, Azazga

Mostaganem, Arzew, Oran, Relizane, Chlef, Tiaret, Sidi Ali

Cap des Trois Fourches, Isla del Alborán

Scale 1:3 500 000
Projection: Equidistant Conic

0 — 100 — 200 kilometers
0 — 50 — 100 miles

Italy • Austria

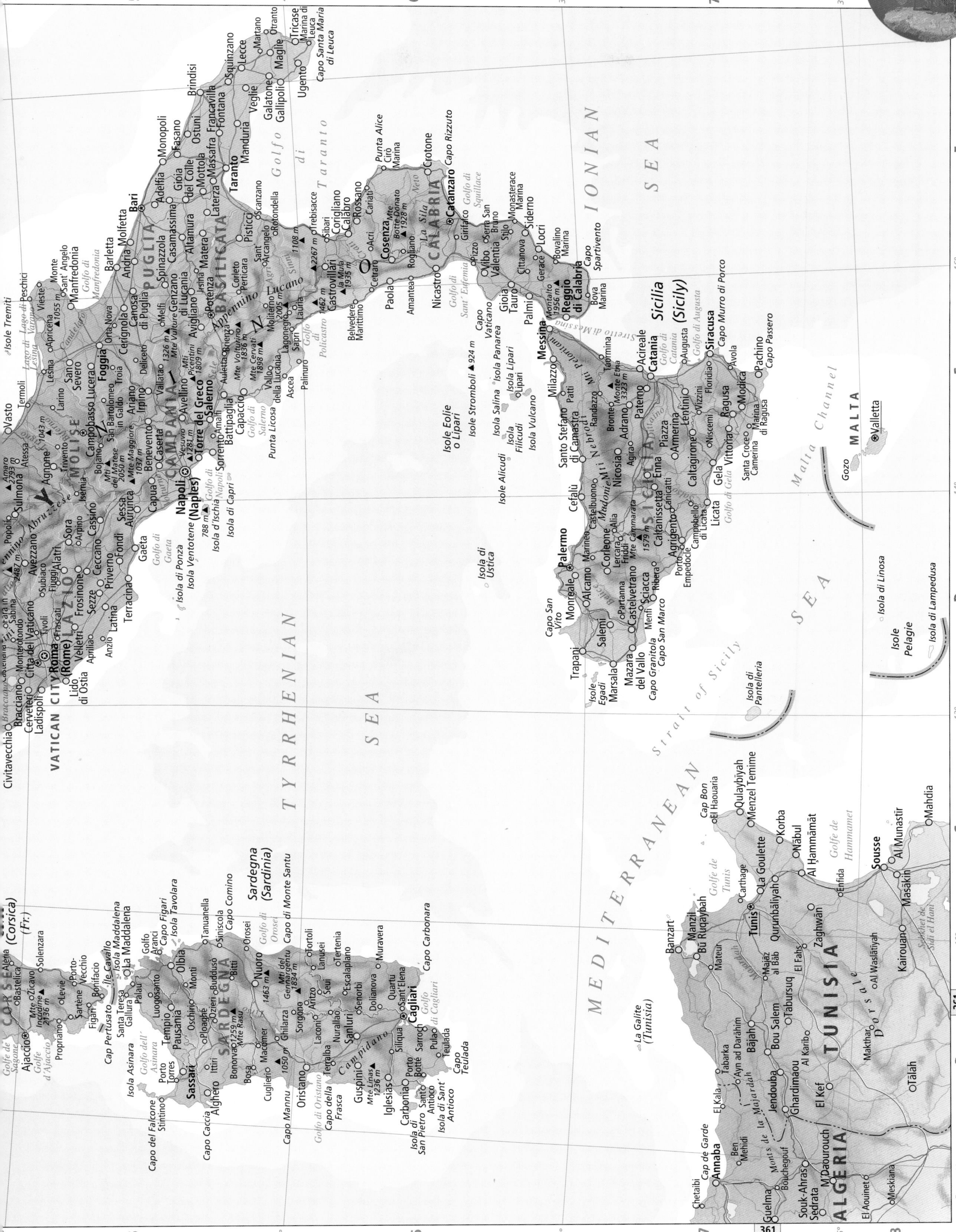

ITALY

LAZIO
MOLISE
ABRUZZO
CAMPANIA
PUGLIA
BASILICATA
CALABRIA
MOLISE

VATICAN CITY
Roma (Rome)
Napoli (Naples)
Bari
Taranto
Foggia
Salerno
Torre del Greco
Benevento
Avellino
Cosenza
Catanzaro
Reggio di Calabria
Messina

Appennino Lucano
Appennino Abruzzese

Sicilia (Sicily)
SICILIA
Palermo
Catania
Siracusa
Marsala
Trapani
Agrigento
Caltanissetta
Enna
Ragusa
Gela
Monte Etna 3323 m
Stretto di Messina

Sardegna (Sardinia)
SARDEGNA
Cagliari
Sassari
Oristano
Nuoro
Olbia
Alghero
Mti del Gennargentu 1834 m
Campidano

CORSE (Corsica) (Fr.)
Ajaccio

Isole Eolie o Lipari
Isola Stromboli ▲ 924 m
Isola Vulcano
Isola di Pantelleria
Isola di Linosa
Isola di Lampedusa
Isole Pelagie
Isola di Ustica
Isola di Ponza

MALTA
Valletta
Gozo
Malta Channel

TUNISIA
Tunis
Sousse
Bizerte
Kairouan
Al Hammāmāt
Golfe de Hammamet
Golfe de Tunis

ALGERIA
Annaba
Souk-Ahras
Guelma

TYRRHENIAN SEA
IONIAN SEA
MEDITERRANEAN SEA
Golfo di Taranto
Strait of Sicily
Strait of Sicily
Malta Channel

Scale 1:3,500,000
Projection: Equidistant Conic

0   100   200 kilometers
0   50   100 miles

361

Southeast Europe

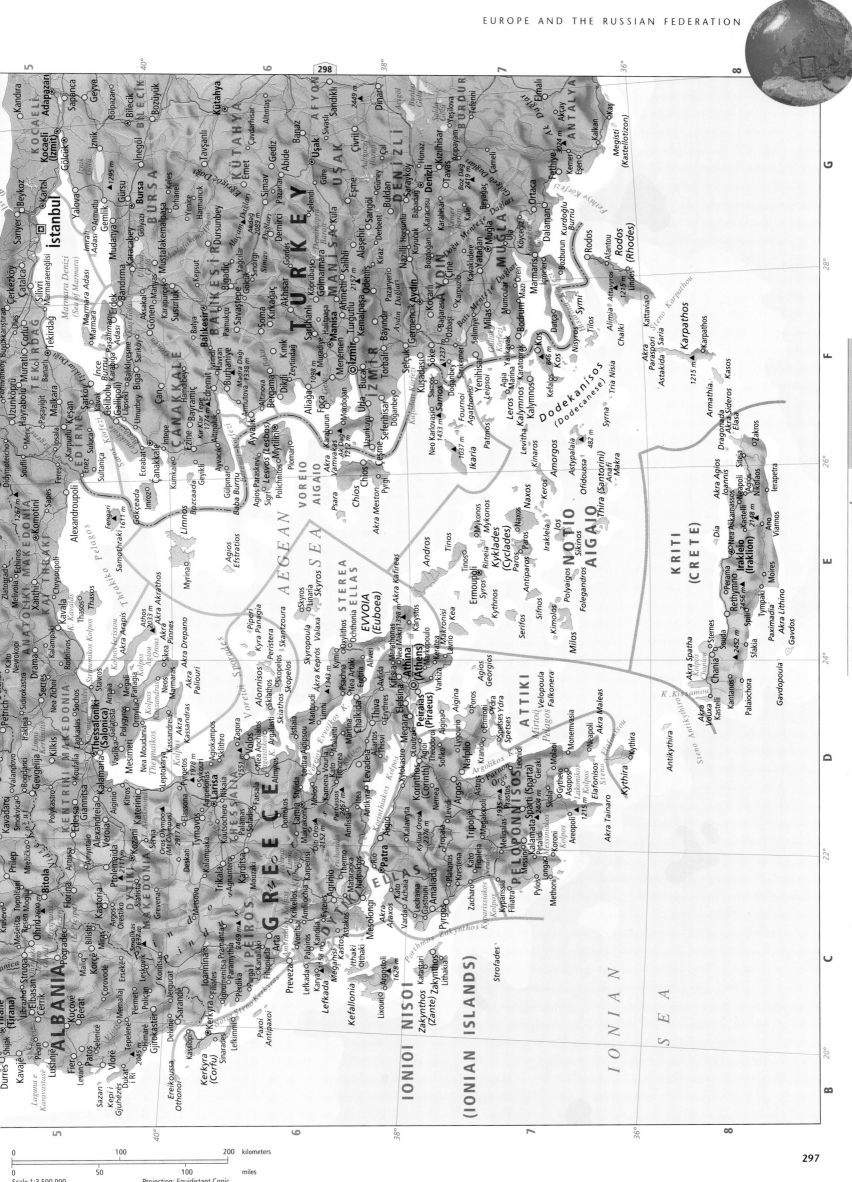

298

0	100	200 kilometers
0	50	100 miles

Scale 1:3,500,000
Projection: Equidistant Conic

East Europe • Turkey

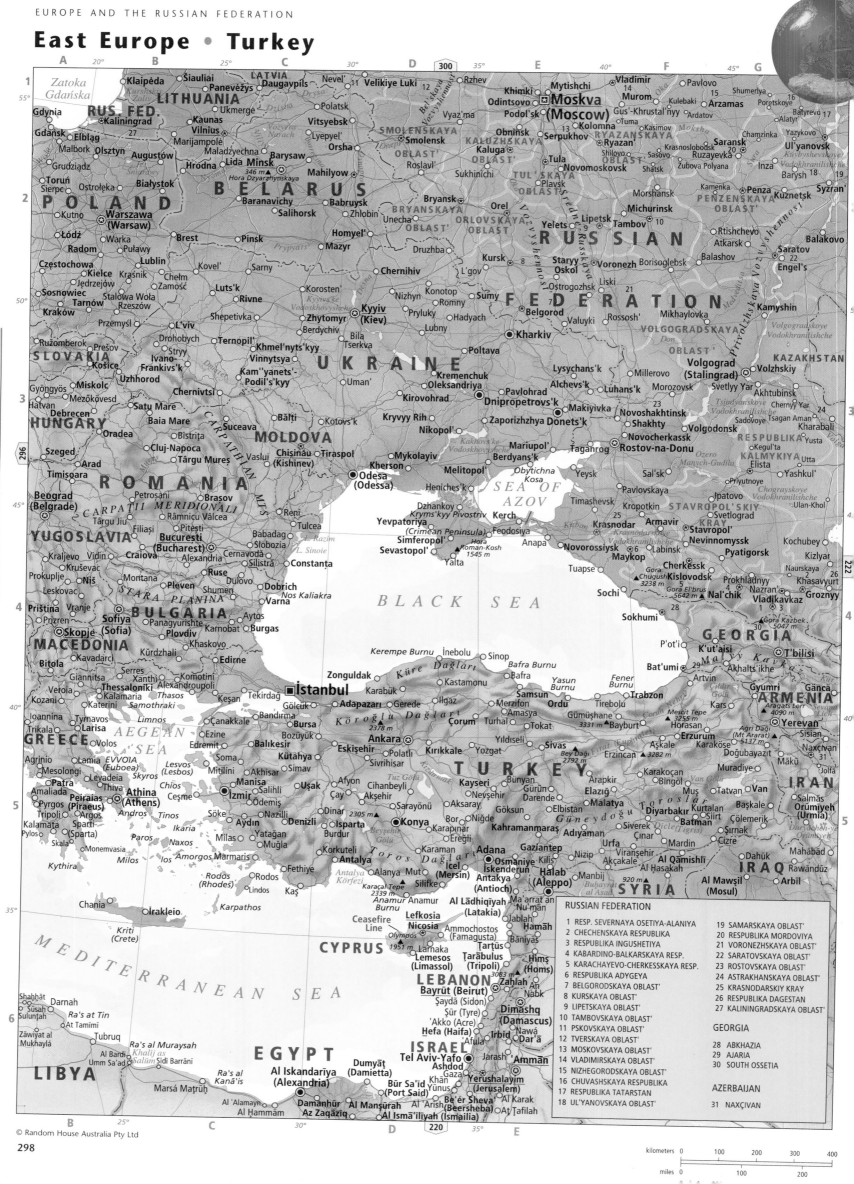

© Random House Australia Pty Ltd

298

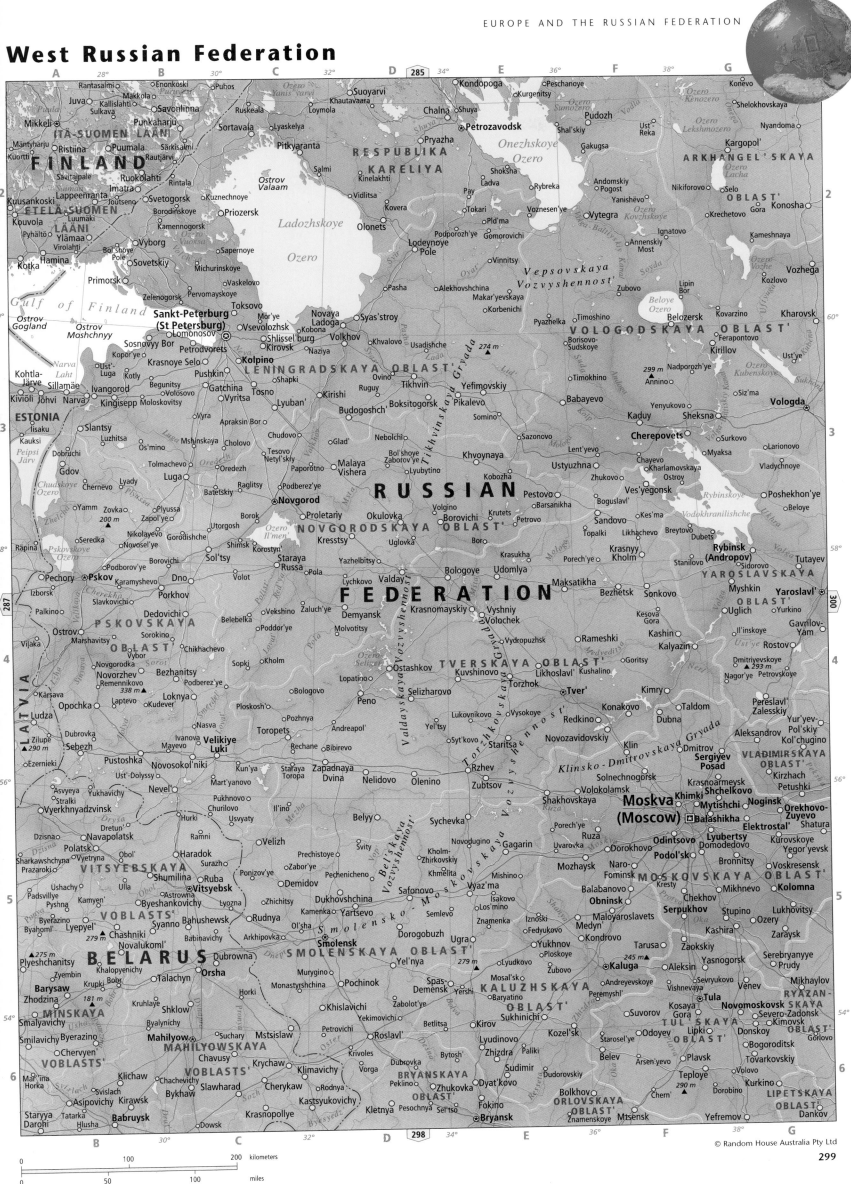

West Russian Federation

Europe and the Russian Federation

Russian Federation and Surrounding Countries

90° 170° 180° **1** 170° **2** 160° 70° **3** 410 60°

Q R S T U V W **1** X 80° **2** 160° 70° **3** 410 60°

160°
170°

U.S.A.

Point Hope
Cape Lisburne
Wainwright
Seward Peninsula
Nome Norton Sound
Kotlik
Scammon Bay
Bethel
Togiak
Dillingham
Bristol Bay
Alaska Peninsula
Unimak Island

CHUKCHI SEA

Ostrov Vrangelya
Ushakovskoye

Mys Shelagskiy
Pevek
Uľtin
Chukotskiy Poluostrov
Mys Chukotskiy
St Lawrence Island
Nunivak Island
Cape Newenham

VOSTOCHNO-SIBIRSKOYE
MORE

Bilibino
Chukotskoye Nagor'ye
Ugol'nyye Kopi
Anadyr'

BERING

Aleutian Islands

170°
4

Novosibirskiye Ostrova
Ostrov Faddeyevskiy Ostrov Novaya Sibir'
Ostrov Kotel'nyy

Mys Shelagskiy
Cherskiy
Ostrova Medvezh'i
Ostrov Ayon
Mys Kovalskiy

Anadyrskoye Ploskogor'ye
Gora Belaya 1359 m

Mys Olyutorskiy

SEA

Rat Islands
Near Islands
Andreanof Islands

50°
180°

Lyakhovskiye Ostrova
Ostrov Bol'shoy Lyakhovskiy

Gora Pobeda 3147 m

172 m
Koryakskoye Nagor'ye

Ostrov Karaginskiy
Mys Ozernoy

Ostrov Beringa
Ostrov Mednyy
Komandorskiye Ostrova

170°
5

LAPTEVYKH
MORE

Ostrov Bol'shoy Begichev
Yanskiy Zaliv

Yano-Indigirskaya Nizmennost'

Khrebet Kular

RESPUBLIKA SAKHA

Khrebet Cherskogo
Verkhoyansk

Gora Volna 1585 m
Ust'-Nera 2341 m

Zaliv Shelikhova

Sredinnyy Khrebet

Ust'-Kamchatsk
4750 m Klyuchevskaya Sopka

Kronotskiy Zaliv
Petropavlovsk-Kamchatskiy
Yelizovo

PACIFIC

Nizmennost'
Tiksi
Siktyakh

Verkhoyanskiy Khrebet 2389 m

Khonuu
Omsukchan
Sinegor'ye
Susuman

Magadan
Mys Tolstoy

Poluostrov Kamchatka
Mys Lopatka
Ostrov Paramushir
Ostrov Onekotan
Ostrov Shiashkotan

Zhilinda
Udachnyy

Olenek
Muna

Khrebet Suntar Khayata
Khandyga

Poluostrov Koni
Okhotsk

OKHOTSKOYE MORE

Ostrov Simushir

160°
40°

Vilyuy Sangar
FEDERATION
Yakutsk
Nyurba
Mirnyy

Prilenskoye Plato
Olekminsk
Lensk

Aldan
Dikimdya
Aldanskoye Nagor'ye

Khrebet Dzhugdzhur
Ayan
Mys Yelizavety
Okha

(SEA OF OKHOTSK)

Ostrov Urup
Ostrov Iturup

Administered by Russian Federation, claimed by Japan.

OCEAN

Ust'-Ilim'sk
Kirensk
Ust'-Kut
Bodaybo

Chul'man
Gora Golets Skalistyy 2412 m
Stanovoy Khrebet

Shantarskiye Ostrova
Mys Yelizavety
Okha

Nogliki

Ostrov Sakhalin

Kuril'skiye Ostrova (Kuril Islands)

Bratskoye Vodokhranilishche
Severobaykal'sk

Stanovoye Nagor'ye
Neryungri
Tynda

Zeya Vodokhranilishche
Zeya
Magdagachi

Nikolayevsk-na-Amure

Poronaysk
Mys Terpeniya

Zima
Usol'ye-Sibirskoye
Ozero Baykal (Lake Baikal)

Taksimo

Skovorodino
Shimanovsk 1490 m
Belogorsk
Chegdomyn
Komsomol'sk-na-Amure
Amursk

Vanino
Mys Aniva
Yuzhno-Sakhalinsk
Tatarskiy proliv

RESPUBLIKA
BURYATIYA
Chita

Ulan-Ude
Khilok
Sherlovaya Gora
Borzya

Zeya
Berezovyy
Svobodnyy
Blagoveshchensk
Obluch'ye
Bikin

Khabarovsk

Svetlaya

Sikhote-Alin'

Kitami

150°
6

Darhan
Erdenet
Ulaanbaatar (Ulan Bator)

Choybalsan
Yakeshi
Manzhouli
Hulun Nur

Nenjiang
Xiao Hinggan Ling
Yichun
Hegang
Jiamusi
Jixi

Dal'negorsk
Ussuriysk
Vladivostok

Wakkanai
Asahikawa
Otaru
Sapporo
Muroran
Hokkaidō
JAPAN
Hachinohe
Aomori
Morioka

RUSSIAN FEDERATION
1 RESPUBLIKA DAGESTAN
2 RESPUBLIKA INGUSHETIYA
3 CHECHENSKAYA RESPUBLIKA
4 RESP. SEVERNAYA OSETIYA-ALANIYA
5 KABARDINO-BALKARSKAYA RESPUBLIKA
6 KARACHAYEVO-CHERKESSKAYA RESPUBLIKA
7 RESPUBLIKA ADYGEYA
8 RESPUBLIKA KALMYKIYA
9 RESPUBLIKA MORDOVIYA
10 CHUVASHSKAYA RESPUBLIKA
11 RESPUBLIKA TATARSTAN
12 RESPUBLIKA MARIY EL
13 UDMURTSKAYA RESPUBLIKA
14 RESPUBLIKA BASHKORTOSTAN

Kyra
Darhan
Erdenet
Arvayheer
nhongor

Choybalsan
Baruun-Urt

Qiqihar
Anda
Harbin
Mudanjiang

Baicheng
Jilin
Changchun
Tongliao

Akita
Sendai

GEORGIA
15 ABKHAZIA
16 AJARIA
17 SOUTH OSSETIA

Mandalgovi
Saynshand
Dalandzadgad

Xi Ujimqin Qi
Erenhot

Chifeng
Fushun
Shenyang
Anshan

Kangye
Sinŭiju
Hŭngnam
P'yŏngyang

Ch'ŏngjin

NORTH KOREA

Niigata
Toyama
Nagoya
TOKYO
Yokohama

SEA OF
JAPAN

AZERBAIJAN
18 NAGORNO-KARABAKH
19 NAXÇIVAN

30°
140°

Linhe
Hohhot
Baotou
Datong

Zhangjiakou
Bayan Har
Duolun

Beijing (Peking)
Tianjin
Dalian
Bohai Wan

Haeju
Sŏul (Seoul)
SOUTH KOREA
Taejŏn
Andong

Matsue
Kyōto
Osaka
Hiroshima
Kōchi
Shikoku

7

CHINA

213 **M** 110° **N** 120° **P** 208 130° **Q** 30° 140° **R**

0 200 400 600 800 kilometers
0 200 400 miles
Scale 1:20,000,000
Projection: Equidistant Conic

301

The British Isles

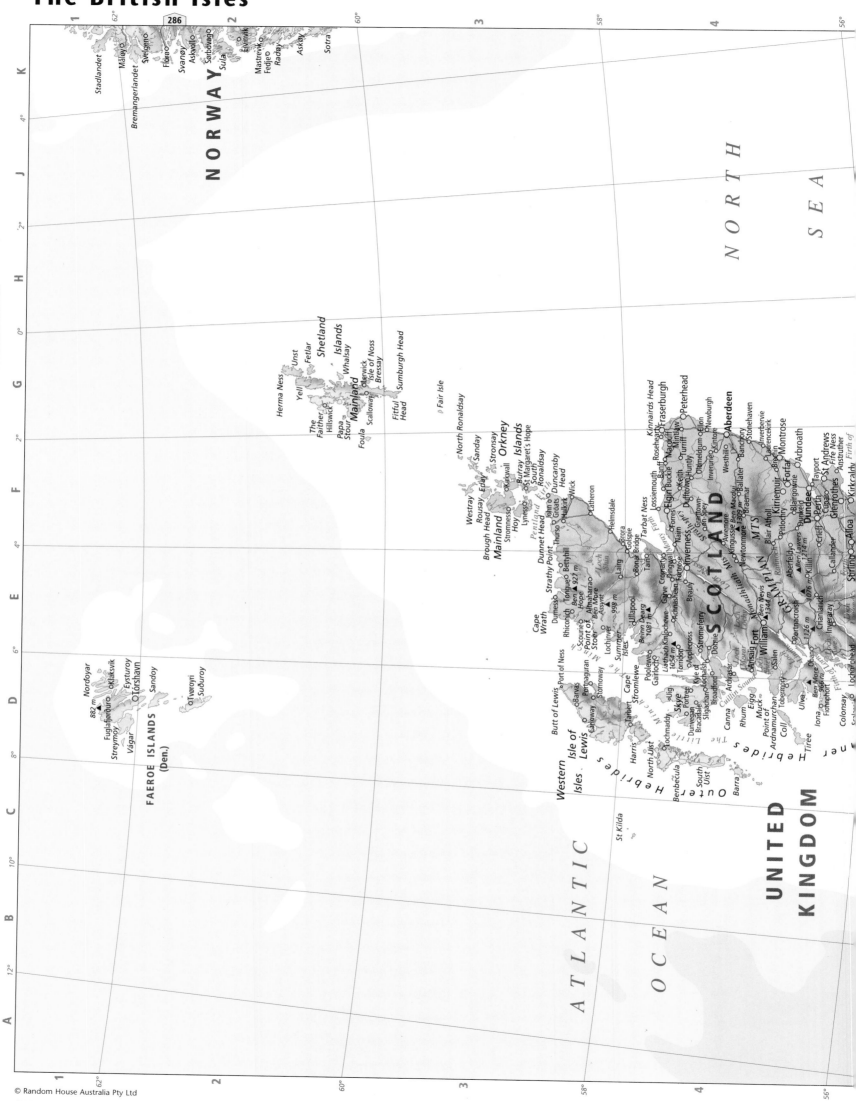

286

NORWAY

Stadlandet
Måløy
Bremangerlandet
Svelgen
Florø
Askvoll
Svanøy
Sørbøvåg
Sula
Mastrevik
Fedje
Radøy
Askøy
Sotra

NORTH SEA

Herma Ness
Unst
Yell
Fetlar
The Faither
Hillswick
Papa Stour
Foula
Shetland Islands
Whalsay
Scalloway
Lerwick
Isle of Noss
Bressay
Mainland
Fitful Head
Sumburgh Head

Fair Isle

North Ronaldsay
Westray
Sanday
Rousay
Eday
Stronsay
Orkney Islands
Brough Head
Strommess
Kirkwall
South Ronaldsay
Mainland
Hoy
Burray
St Margaret's Hope
Lynness
Duncansby Head
Dunnet Head
John o' Groats
Pentland Firth
Cape Wrath
Strathy Point
Rhiconich
Tongue
Durness
Bettyhill
Halkirk
Wick
Ben A 927 m
Scourie
Point of Stoer
Ben Hope
Catherton
Loch Shin
Thurso
Laxford
Helmsdale
Ben More Assynt 998 m
Altnaharra
Lairg
Brora
Lochinver
Ben Dearg 1081 m
Golspie
Bonar Bridge
Ullapool
Taín
Dornoch
Cromarty
Tarbat Ness
Summer Isles
Beinn Dearg
Dingwall
Forres
Kinnairds Head
Poolewe
Liathach
Kinlochewe
Beauly
Nairn
Loch Ness
Elgin
Rosehearty
Fraserburgh
Gairloch
Torridon
Achnasheen
Inverness
Grantown
Cullen
Buckie
Banff
Macduff
Turriff
Peterhead
Applecross
Kyle of Lochalsh
Strathcarron
Dornie
Strome Ferry
Aviemore
Keith
Dufftown
Huntly
Ellon
Newburgh
Broadford
Kingussie
Ben Macdui 1309 m
Rhum
Portree
Dunvegan
Sligachan
Lochalsh
Carrbridge
Cairngorm
Kintore
Westhill
Aberdeen
Skye
Cuillin Hills
Invergarry
Spean Bridge
Newtonmore
Braemar
Ballater
Banchory
Stonehaven
Canna
Ardvasar
Mallaig
SCOTLAND
GRAMPIAN MTS
Inverurie
Laurencekirk
Inverbervie
Eigg
Point of Ardnamurchan
Arisaig
Fort William
Ben Nevis 1344 m
Ben Lawers 1214 m
Blair Atholl
Pitlochry
Muck
Salen
Glen Spey
Kirriemuir
Brechin
Montrose
Tobermory
1126 m
Aberfeldy
Dunkeld
Blairgowrie
Forfar
Arbroath
Coll
Ulva
Oban
Cranlarich
Killin
Crieff
Perth
Dundee
Tiree
Iona
Ben More 966 m
Dalmally
Callander
Glenrothes
St Andrews
Fife Ness
Colonsay
Inveraray
Stirling
Alloa
Crail
Anstruther
Tayport
Cupar
Firth of
Kirkcaldy

ATLANTIC OCEAN

St Kilda

Nordoyar
882 m
Fuglafjørður
Eysturoy
Klaksvik
Streymoy
Vágar
Tórshavn
Sandoy
Svínoy
Tvøroyri
Suðuroy
FAEROE ISLANDS (Den.)

Butt of Lewis
Port of Ness
Barvas
Stornoway
Cape Stromlewe
Uig
Western Isles
Isle of Lewis
Tarbert
Harris
Lochmaddy
North Uist
Benbecula
South Uist
Barra
Outer Hebrides
The Minch
Little Minch
Inner Hebrides

UNITED KINGDOM

© Random House Australia Pty Ltd

302

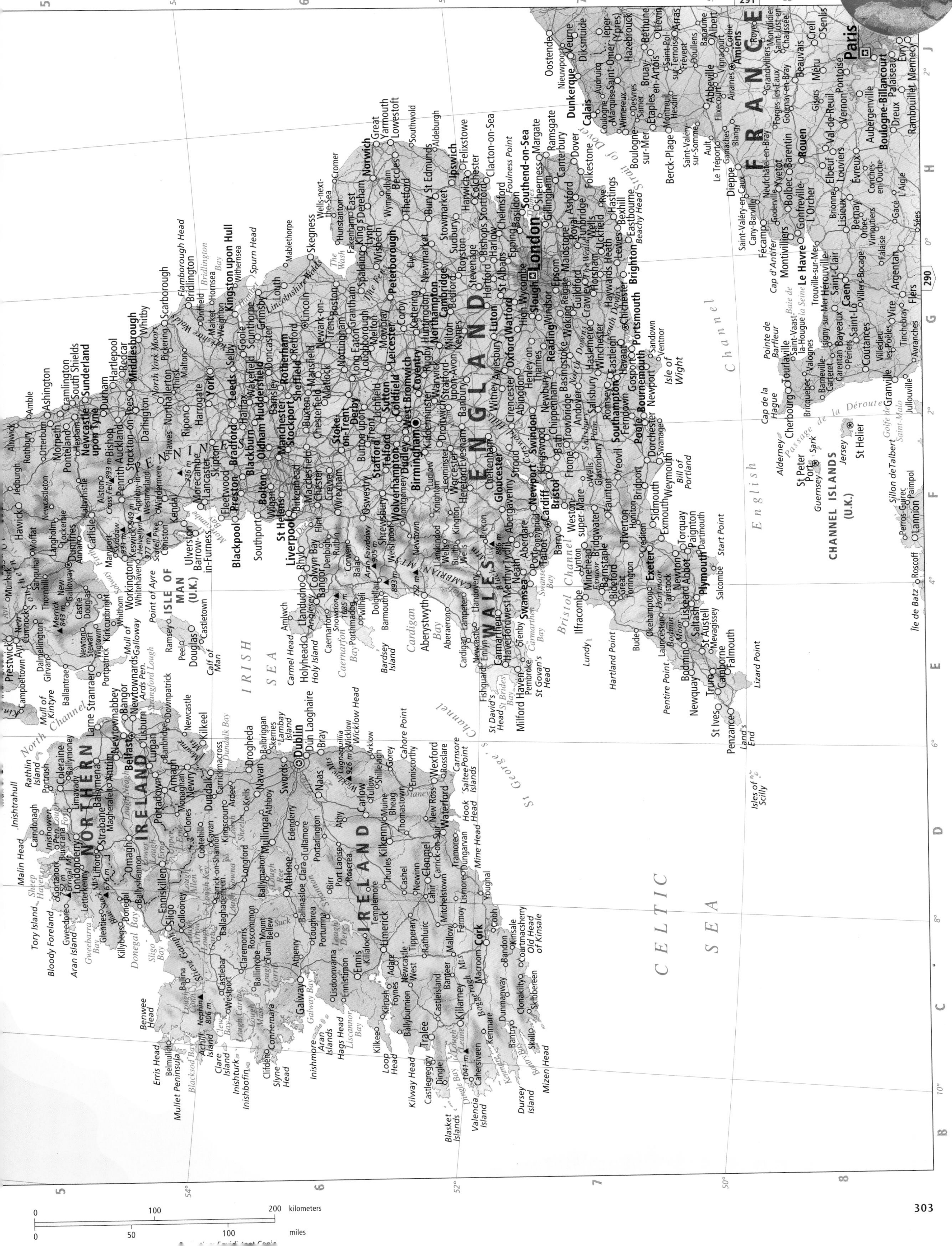

FRANCE

ENGLAND

WALES

NORTHERN IRELAND

IRELAND

ISLE OF MAN (U.K.)

CHANNEL ISLANDS (U.K.)

IRISH SEA

CELTIC SEA

North Channel

St George's Channel

English Channel

Bristol Channel

Strait of Dover

PENNINE

CAMBRIAN MTS

Paris

London

Dublin

Cardiff

Belfast

Europe and the Russian Federation

| 0 | 100 | 200 | kilometers |

| 0 | 50 | 100 | miles |

South England • Wales

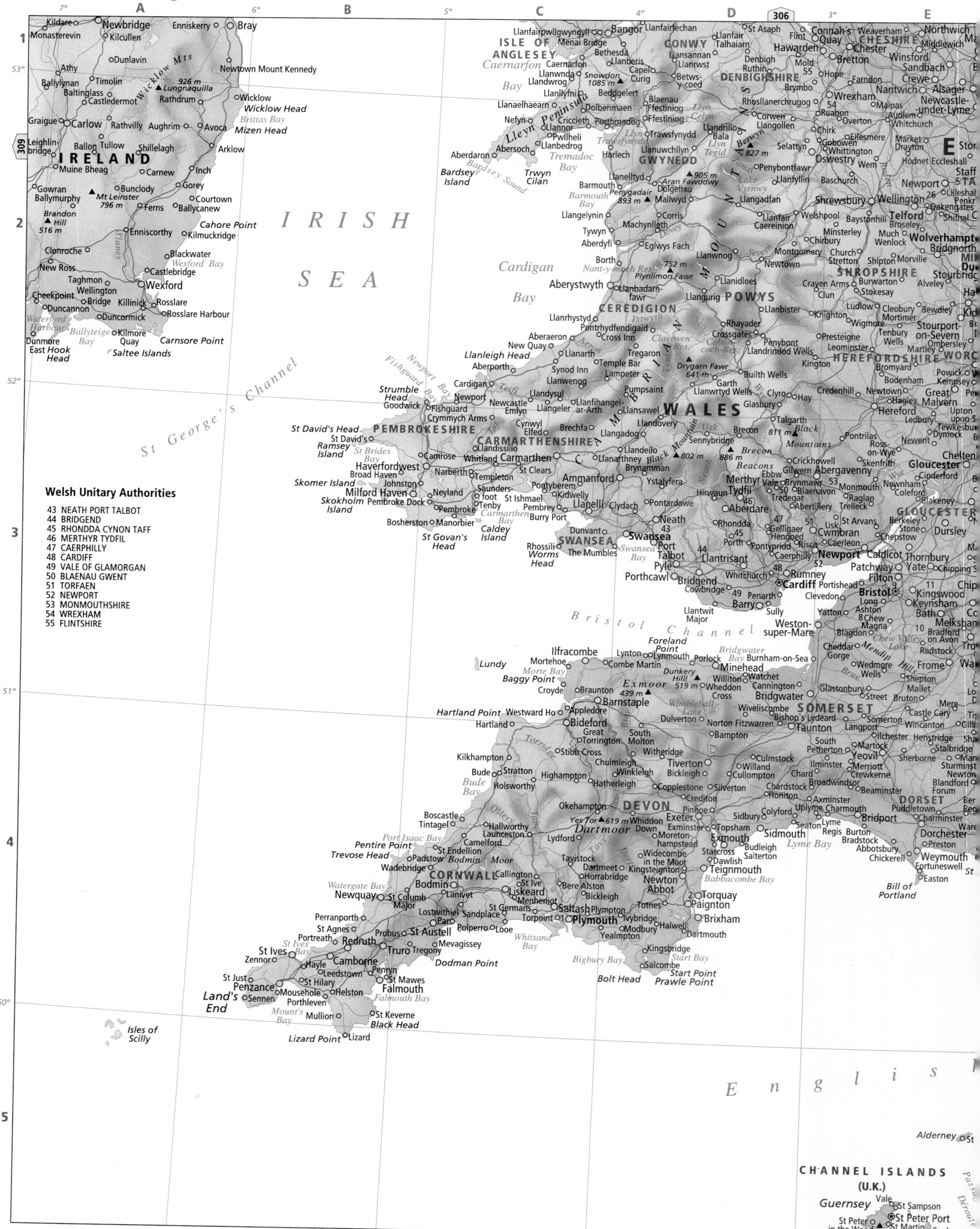

Europe and the Russian Federation

Welsh Unitary Authorities

43 NEATH PORT TALBOT
44 BRIDGEND
45 RHONDDA CYNON TAFF
46 MERTHYR TYDFIL
47 CAERPHILLY
48 CARDIFF
49 VALE OF GLAMORGAN
50 BLAENAU GWENT
51 TORFAEN
52 NEWPORT
53 MONMOUTHSHIRE
54 WREXHAM
55 FLINTSHIRE

IRISH SEA

IRELAND

St George's Channel

Cardigan Bay

WALES

PEMBROKESHIRE

CARMARTHENSHIRE

CEREDIGION

POWYS

GWYNEDD

CONWY

DENBIGHSHIRE

SHROPSHIRE

HEREFORDSHIRE

SWANSEA

Bristol Channel

CORNWALL

DEVON

SOMERSET

DORSET

Land's End

Isles of Scilly

Lizard Point

CHANNEL ISLANDS (U.K.)

Guernsey

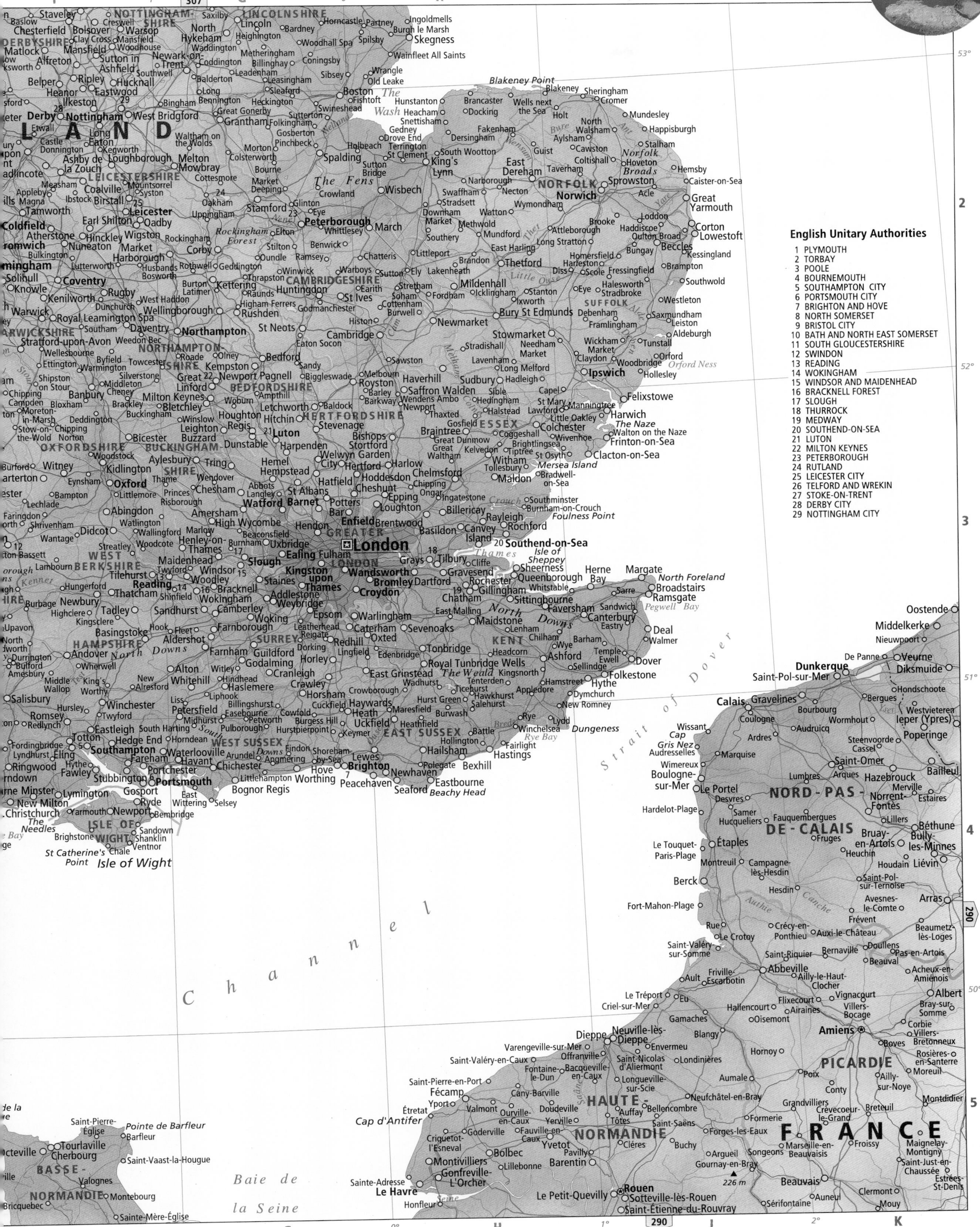

English Unitary Authorities

1 PLYMOUTH
2 TORBAY
3 POOLE
4 BOURNEMOUTH
5 SOUTHAMPTON CITY
6 PORTSMOUTH CITY
7 BRIGHTON AND HOVE
8 NORTH SOMERSET
9 BRISTOL CITY
10 BATH AND NORTH EAST SOMERSET
11 SOUTH GLOUCESTERSHIRE
12 SWINDON
13 READING
14 WOKINGHAM
15 WINDSOR AND MAIDENHEAD
16 BRACKNELL FOREST
17 SLOUGH
18 THURROCK
19 MEDWAY
20 SOUTHEND-ON-SEA
21 LUTON
22 MILTON KEYNES
23 PETERBOROUGH
24 RUTLAND
25 LEICESTER CITY
26 TELFORD AND WREKIN
27 STOKE-ON-TRENT
28 DERBY CITY
29 NOTTINGHAM CITY

Europe and the Russian Federation

Scale 1:1 500 000

Projection: Equidistant Conic

kilometers
0   50   100

miles
0   25   50

North England

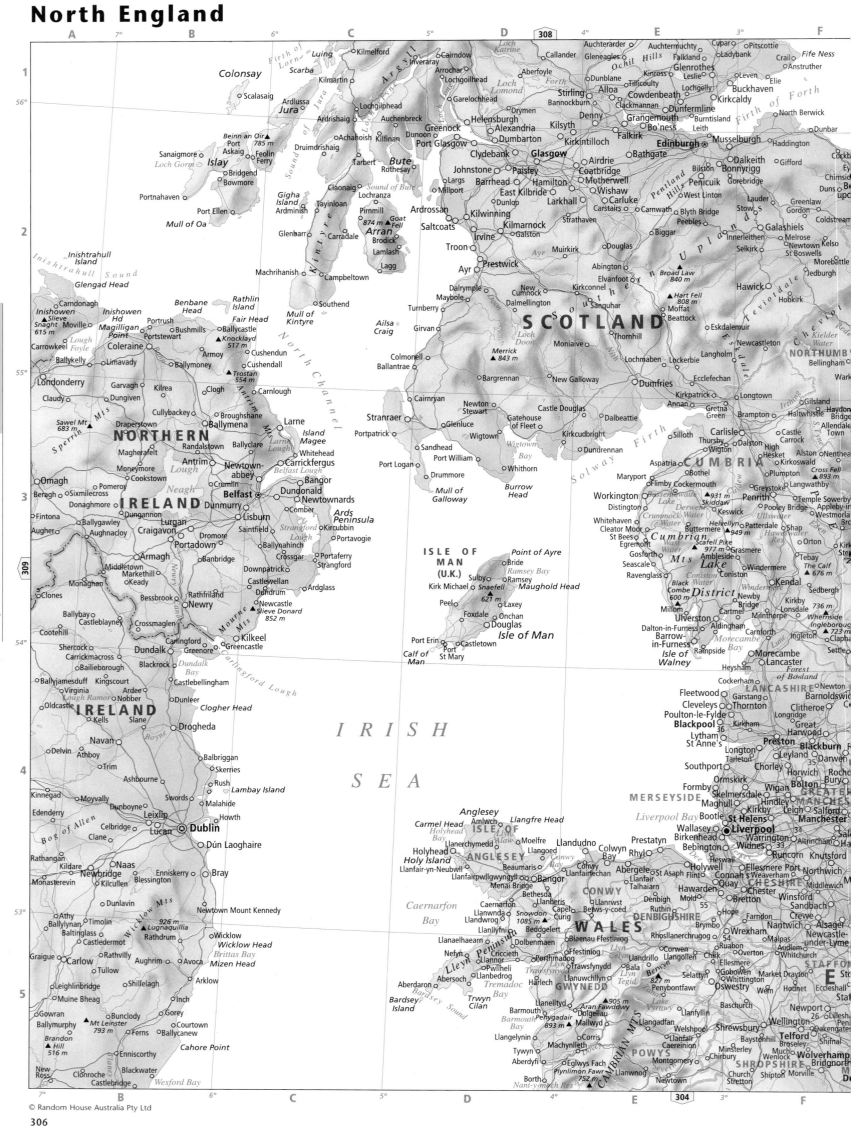

G   1°   H   0°   J   1°   K   2°   L   3°

1

56°

English Unitary Authorities

23 PETERBOROUGH
24 RUTLAND
25 LEICESTER CITY
26 TELFORD AND WREKIN
27 STOKE-ON-TRENT
28 DERBY CITY
29 NOTTINGHAM CITY
30 NORTH EAST LINCOLNSHIRE
31 KINGSTON UPON HULL
32 NORTH LINCOLNSHIRE
33 HALTON
34 WARRINGTON
35 BLACKBURN WITH DARWEN
36 BLACKPOOL
37 YORK CITY
38 DARLINGTON
39 HARTLEPOOL
40 STOCKTON-ON-TEES
41 MIDDLESBROUGH
42 REDCAR AND CLEVELAND

2

Welsh Unitary Authorities

54 WREXHAM
55 FLINTSHIRE

oly Island
ndisfarne

Bamburgh
rd North Sunderland
Beadnell Bay

Embleton

Boulmer
Lesbury

Ample
ongframlington

Longhorsley

ington Lynemouth
Newbiggin-by-the-sea
ngton Blyth
Cramlington
teland Whitley Bay
Gosforth Tynemouth
astle North South Shields
Shields
Tyne Gateshead **TYNE & WEAR**
ey Washington **Sunderland**
Chester Houghton-le-Spring
le-Street
AM Durham Peterlee
ingham Crook
vmoor Trimdon **Hartlepool**
pp Ferryhill 39 *Tees Bay*
nd Shildon Billingham
Newton **Middlesbrough** Redcar
Aycliffe Stockton 42 Saltburn-by-the-Sea
on-Tees 40 Thornaby Loftus
arlington 38 on Tees Guisborough Sandsend
Yarm Castleton Whitby
Scotch Corner Crathorne Stokesley Sleights
Catterick *Cleveland Hills* Egton Robin Hood's
Bay
NORTH Bedale Leeming Bar *North York* Hackness
Middleham Thirsk Rosedale *Moors*
ham Abbey
YORKSHIRE Topcliffe Kirkbymoorside Wrelton Scalby
ey Ripon Coxwold Helmsley Pickering Seamer Scarborough
Boroughbridge Easingwold Malton *Filey Head*
rnside Ripley Stillington Norton *Yorkshire* Filey
aresborough Haxby North Bempton Hunmanby
arrogate Grimston Flamborough
Otley Wetherby Fridaythorpe Wharram *Flamborough Head*
hley Horsforth **York** Stamford le Street Langtoft **Bridlington**
Shipley Tadcaster Bridge Driffield *Bridlington*
al Pudsey Garforth Pocklington *Bay*
ewsbury **Leeds** Holme upon Brandesburton Skipsea
SHIRE Morley Castleford Spalding Moor Market
fiield Wakefield Bubwith Weighton **Beverley** Hornsea
elthham Darton South Selby *Holderness* Leven
Barnsley Elmsall Howden South Cave 31 Bilton Tunstall
SOUTH YORKSHIRE Hatfield Snaith Brough Anlaby Withernsea
Chapeltown Doncaster Goole **Kingston**
pp Rossington Winterton **upon Hull**
Sheffield Rotherham Bawtry Thorne Barton- Patrington
Maltby Crowle upon-Humber Easington
Mosbrough Anston Epworth 32 Scunthorpe *Humber* *Spurn Head*
el-en- Dronfield Blyth Kirton Brigg Immingham
Frith Staveley Retford in Lindsey Caistor **Grimsby**
Baslow Creswell Worksop 30 **Cleethorpes**
Chesterfield Bolsover Blyton Tetney
DERBYSHIRE Clay Cross Gainsborough North
Matlock Warsop Market Somercotes
rslow Alfreton Mansfield North Rasen Manby Mablethorpe
irksworth Sutton **NOTTINGHAM** Hykeham Dunholme Maltby Sutton on Sea
in Ashfield Woodhouse Waddington **Louth** le Marsh Alford
Belper Hucknall Southwell Coddington **Lincoln** *Lincolnshire* Ingoldmells
Heanor SHIRE Metheringham Horncastle Burgh le Marsh
railsford Ripley Newark- Balderton Billinghay Woodhall Spa Partney **Skegness**
rne Ilkeston Eastwood on-Trent Long Leadenham Spilsby Wainfleet All Saints
Derby Nottingham Bingham Bennington Sleaford Coningsby
Etwall 29 Long West Bridgford Heckington Sibsey Wrangle
Castle Eaton Great Gonerby Swineshead Old Leake *Blakeney Point* Blakeney Sheringham
Donnington Waltham on **Grantham** **Boston** *The* Brancaster Wells next Cromer
pp the Wolds Folkingham Benwick *Wash* Hunstanton the Sea Holt Mundesley
ent Swadlincote Ashby de Loughborough Melton Morton Pinchbeck Gedney Heacham Docking North Happisburgh
la Zouch Mowbray Colsterworth Bourne Spalding Drove End Dersingham Fakenham Walsham
Appleby Coalville Cottesmore Holbeach Terrington Guist Aylsham Coltishall Hoveton Hemsby
Birstall Syston Oakham Market St Clement South Wootton Cawston *Norfolk* Stalham
Ibstock **LEICESTERSHIRE** 24 Deeping King's Narborough East *Broads* Caister-on-Sea
Measham Mountsorrel 24 **Stamford** *The Fens* Lynn Swaffham Necton Dereham Taverham Sprowston
hills Atherstone Earl Wigston Rockingham Crowland Wisbech Stradsett **NORFOLK** Acle Great
Sutton Shilton Hinckley Oadby Uppingham Glinton Swaffham **Norwich** Yarmouth
Coldfield Nuneaton Wigston 23 Eye Downham Watton Wymondham Corton
ich Bulkington Market **Peterborough** Nene Market Methwold Brooke Long Oulton Broad Lowestoft
Birmingham Harborough Corby Whittlesey March Southery Mundford Attleborough Stratton Beccles
LAND Oundle *Rockingham* Stilton **CAMBRIDGESHIRE** Littleport East Harling Homersfield Bungay Kessingland
Forest Chatteris

NORTH
SEA

55°

54°

53°

3

4

5

0   50   100 kilometers
0   25   50 miles

Scale 1:1,500,000
Projection: Equidistant Conic

Scotland

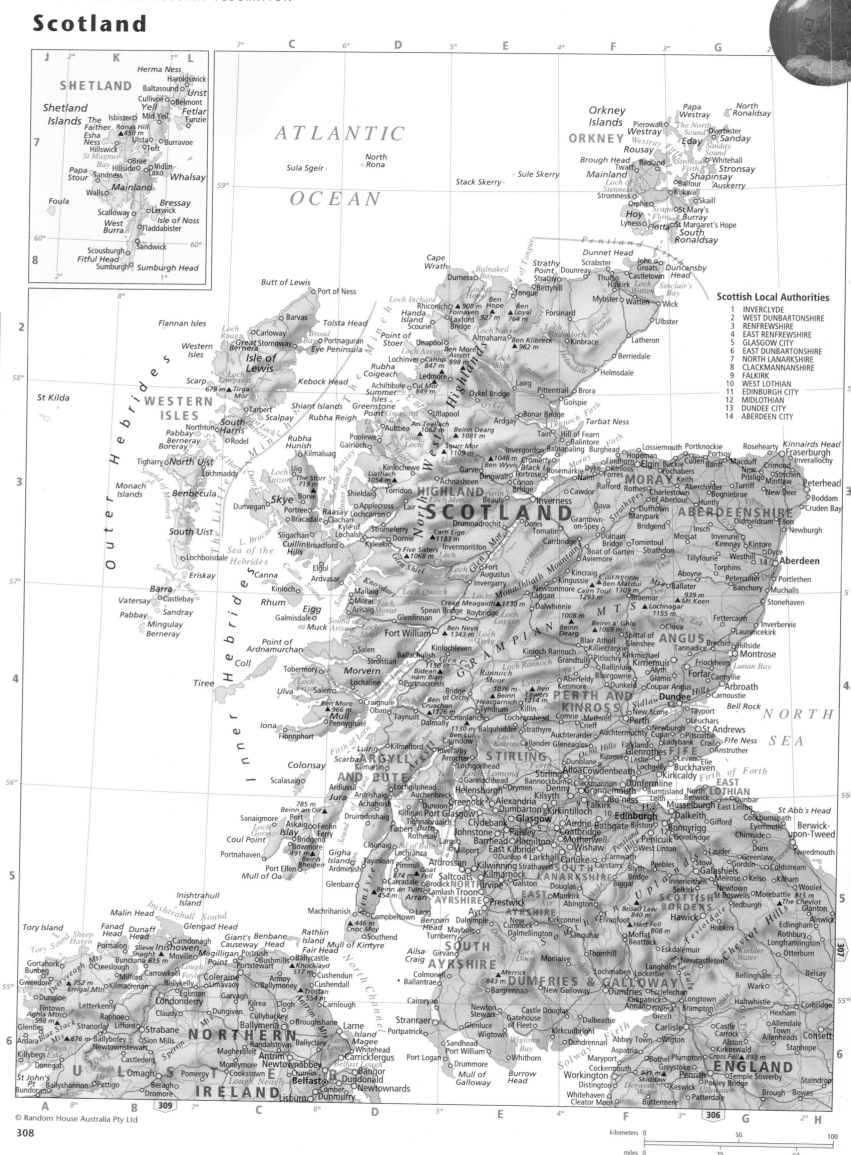

Scottish Local Authorities

1. INVERCLYDE
2. WEST DUNBARTONSHIRE
3. RENFREWSHIRE
4. EAST RENFREWSHIRE
5. GLASGOW CITY
6. EAST DUNBARTONSHIRE
7. NORTH LANARKSHIRE
8. CLACKMANNANSHIRE
9. FALKIRK
10. WEST LOTHIAN
11. EDINBURGH CITY
12. MIDLOTHIAN
13. DUNDEE CITY
14. ABERDEEN CITY

kilometers 0   50   100

miles 0   25   50

Scale 1:2,000,000

Projection: Equidistant Conic

Ireland

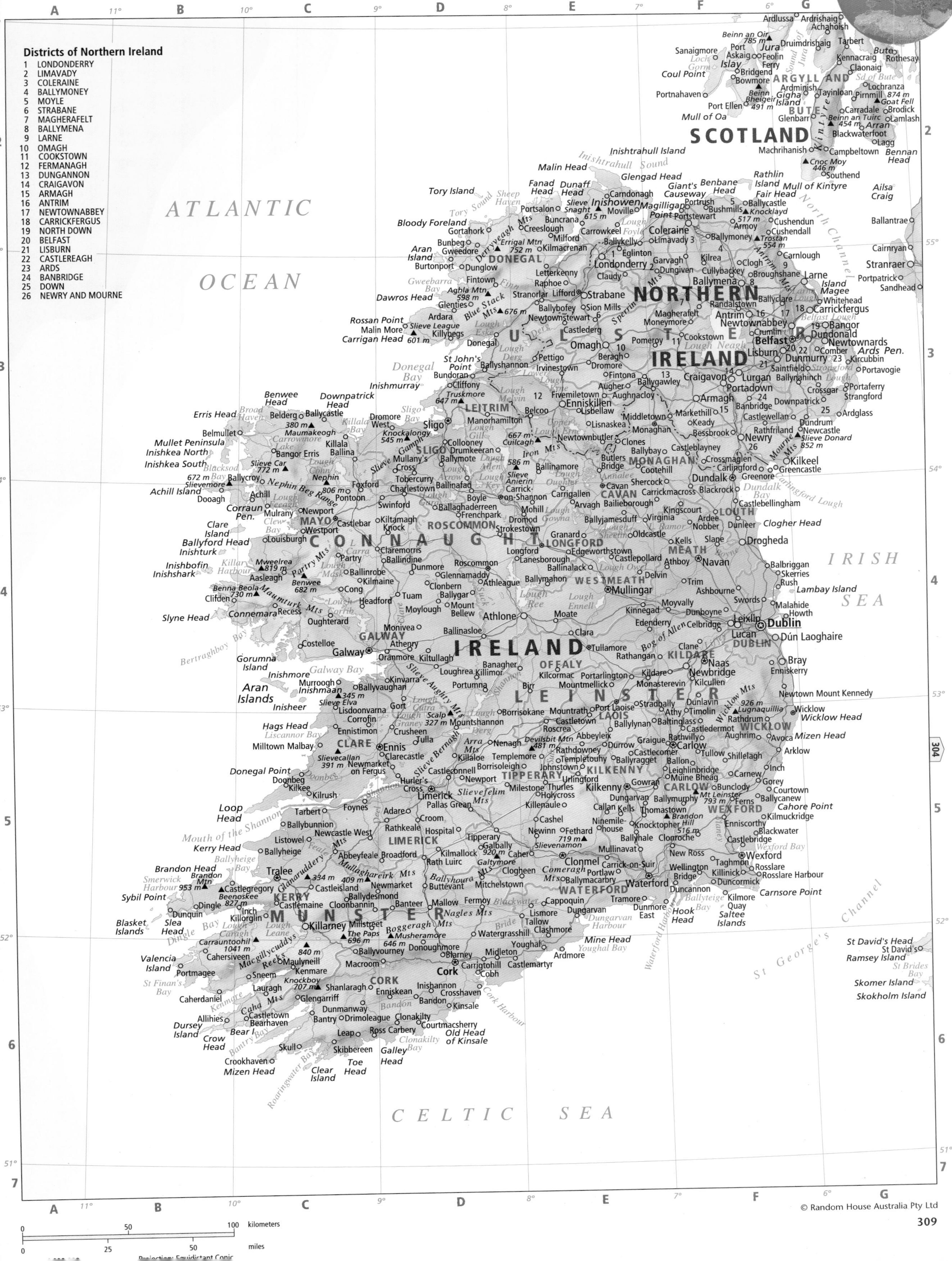

Districts of Northern Ireland

1 LONDONDERRY
2 LIMAVADY
3 COLERAINE
4 BALLYMONEY
5 MOYLE
6 STRABANE
7 MAGHERAFELT
8 BALLYMENA
9 LARNE
10 OMAGH
11 COOKSTOWN
12 FERMANAGH
13 DUNGANNON
14 CRAIGAVON
15 ARMAGH
16 ANTRIM
17 NEWTOWNABBEY
18 CARRICKFERGUS
19 NORTH DOWN
20 BELFAST
21 LISBURN
22 CASTLEREAGH
23 ARDS
24 BANBRIDGE
25 DOWN
26 NEWRY AND MOURNE

ATLANTIC OCEAN

SCOTLAND

ARGYLL AND BUTE

NORTHERN IRELAND

ULSTER

CONNAUGHT

DONEGAL

LEITRIM

SLIGO

MAYO

ROSCOMMON

LONGFORD

CAVAN

MONAGHAN

LOUTH

MEATH

WESTMEATH

GALWAY

IRELAND

LEINSTER

OFFALY

KILDARE

DUBLIN

WICKLOW

LAOIS

CLARE

TIPPERARY

KILKENNY

CARLOW

WEXFORD

LIMERICK

KERRY

MUNSTER

CORK

WATERFORD

IRISH SEA

CELTIC SEA

St George's Channel

Dublin

Cork

Galway

Limerick

Belfast

Londonderry

© Random House Australia Pty Ltd

309

Europe and the Russian Federation

kilometers
0   50   100

miles
0   25   50

Projection: Equidistant Conic

of the Ogooué River. The wooded basin of this large watercourse dominates Gabon, 60 percent of the country's land area being drained by its tributaries. These flow down from the African central plateau and the borders of Equatorial Guinea and Cameroon to the north, and from Congo to the east and south.

Before the development of oil and manganese in the early 1970s, valuable timbers were one of the country's main exports. These included Gabon mahogany, ebony, and walnut. Even today, as much as two-thirds of Gabon's total land area consists of untouched rainforest, but the completion in 1986 of the Trans-Gabon Railway from the port of Owendo to the interior town of Massoukou is likely to lead to further exploitation of timber resources.

Gabon has considerable mineral resources. It has about one-quarter of the world's known reserves of manganese, and is the world's fourth biggest manganese producer. France imports most of its uranium from Gabon. Oil currently accounts for 50 percent of gross domestic product. This figure, when combined with Gabon's small population, gives a distorted picture of the country's per capita earnings, disguising the fact that more than half the country's people still make their living by subsistence farming. A wide gap separates rural people from the urban élite and the country faces economic problems.

Fact File

OFFICIAL NAME Gabonese Republic

FORM OF GOVERNMENT Republic with single legislative body (National Assembly)

CAPITAL Libreville

AREA 267,670 sq km (103,347 sq miles)

TIME ZONE GMT + 1 hour

POPULATION 1,225,853

PROJECTED POPULATION 2005 1,340,781

POPULATION DENSITY 4.6 per sq km (11.9 per sq mile)

LIFE EXPECTANCY 57

INFANT MORTALITY (PER 1,000) 83.1

OFFICIAL LANGUAGE French

OTHER LANGUAGES Indigenous languages (including Fang, Myene, Bateke, Bapounou/Eschira, Bandjabi)

LITERACY RATE 62.6%

RELIGIONS Christian 94%, Muslim 3%, other 3%

ETHNIC GROUPS Mainly Bantu tribes (including Fang, Eshira, Bapounou, Bateke) 92%, foreign Africans and Europeans 8%

CURRENCY CFA (Communauté Financière Africaine) franc

ECONOMY Agriculture 65%, industry and commerce 30%, services 5%

GNP PER CAPITA US$3,490

CLIMATE Tropical, with dry season mid-May to mid-September

HIGHEST POINT Mt Iboundji 1,575 m (5,167 ft)

MAP REFERENCE Page 368

Traders at the goat and donkey market in Lalibela, in northern Ethiopia (left). Fishing boats and fishermen at a beach in Gambia (top right).

Gambia

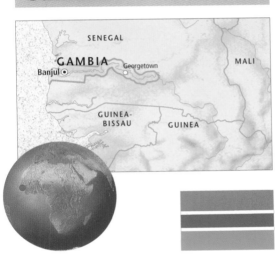

S̶urrounded on nearly all sides by Senegal, Gambia is Africa's smallest independent state. Once a part of the Mali Empire, it became a British colony in 1816 and has been independent since 1965. Following independence it was governed for almost 30 years by Sir Dawda Jawara and the People's Progressive Party. A military coup displaced him in 1994. The country has been notably stable otherwise, though resentment of the dominant Mandinka exists among minority tribal groups such as the Fula and Wolof.

A subtropical climate and a sunny dry season has enabled Gambia to expand tourism in recent years but the conflict between tourist life and the main religion, Islam, has made this controversial. In 1982 Gambia joined its neighbor, Senegal, in a union named the Senegambian Federation. This proved unsuccessful and was dissolved in 1989.

The Gambia River and its estuary are navigable for some 200 km (125 miles), allowing ships of up to 3,000 tonnes to reach Georgetown. Consisting of a riverine plain running inland 275 km (170 miles) from the estuary, Gambia's countryside is low and undulating, the land beside the river varying from swamp to savanna. Although rice is grown in the swamps and on the river floodplain, not enough is produced to meet domestic needs. Millet, sorghum, and cassava are grown on higher ground. On the

upper river, a dam provides irrigation.

Gambia has unmined deposits of minerals such as ilmenite, rutile, and zircon. The economy has a limited agricultural base, three-quarters of the population growing crops and raising livestock. Peanuts are the main cash crop, providing more than 75 percent of export earnings, and peanut processing is important industrially. Palm kernels are also exported. Because Banjul is the best harbor on the west African coast, much Senegalese produce passes through Gambia, and re-export forms one-third of economic activity.

Fact File

OFFICIAL NAME Republic of the Gambia

FORM OF GOVERNMENT Republic with single legislative body (House of Representatives)

CAPITAL Banjul

AREA 11,300 sq km (4,363 sq miles)

TIME ZONE GMT

POPULATION 1,336,320

PROJECTED POPULATION 2005 1,616,322

POPULATION DENSITY 118.2 per sq km (306.1 per sq mile)

LIFE EXPECTANCY 54.4

INFANT MORTALITY (PER 1,000) 75.3

OFFICIAL LANGUAGE English

OTHER LANGUAGES Indigenous languages (including Madinka, Wolof, Fula), Arabic

LITERACY RATE 37.2%

RELIGIONS Muslim 90%, Christian 9%, indigenous beliefs 1%

ETHNIC GROUPS Indigenous 99% (including Mandinka 42%, Fula 18%, Wolof 16%, Jola 10%, Serahuli 9%), non-Gambian 1%

CURRENCY Dalasi

ECONOMY Agriculture 75%; industry, commerce, and services 19%; government 6%

GNP PER CAPITA US$320

CLIMATE Tropical, with wet season June to November

HIGHEST POINT Unnamed location 53 m (174 ft)

MAP REFERENCE Page 364

Africa

Ghana

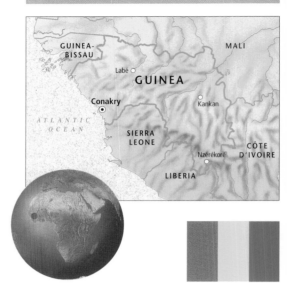

Ghana was once known as the Gold Coast. A well-known source of gold in west Africa for a thousand years, the nation's modern name comes from the Ghana Empire of the eighth to the twelfth centuries. The Ashanti people established themselves in the seventeenth century, selling slaves to Portuguese, British, Dutch and Danish traders. Under British control from 1874, Ghana became the first tropical African colony to win independence in 1956. Soon after this it became a Soviet-style one-party state.

After 1966, Ghana was wracked by military coups for 15 years before Flight-Lieutenant Jerry Rawlings took control in 1981. An election in 1996 returned Rawlings to power once more. Although government pressure is often brought to bear, vigorous political debate takes place in a relatively free media, and despite economic troubles Ghana still has twice the per capita output of the poorer countries in west Africa.

Geographically, the country is formed by the basin of the Volta Rivers. A large area flooded by the Akosombo Dam is now Lake Volta, the world's largest artificial lake. This provides hydroelectric power for smelting alumina into aluminum, and for use in the towns, mines, and industries of the Takoradi-Kumasi-Tema triangle. In the north there is savanna country. In earlier days the southern part of the country was covered by dense tropical forest. Much of this has been cleared for agriculture, especially for growing cocoa, which from 1924 until the present day has usually been the leading export.

Like other west African countries, Ghana has few natural harbors. Its coast consists mainly of mangrove swamps, with lagoons toward the mouth of the River Volta. The rivers are home to crocodile, manatee, and hippopotamus. The wildlife of the northern savanna includes lion, leopard, hyena, and antelope.

Ghana is well endowed with natural resources—gold, timber, industrial diamonds, bauxite, manganese, fish, and rubber. In 1995, largely as a result of increased gold, timber, and cocoa production, overall economic growth was about 5 percent. Although the economy is based on subsistence agriculture, Ghana is not self-sufficient in food. President Rawlings' efforts

to reverse the statist policies of his predecessors continue, but face a number of obstacles. Public sector wage increases, and various peace-keeping missions, both internal and external, have strained the budget and led to inflationary deficit financing. Corruption is a continuing obstacle to growth.

Fact File

OFFICIAL NAME	Republic of Ghana
FORM OF GOVERNMENT	Republic with single legislative body (Parliament)
CAPITAL	Accra
AREA	238,540 sq km (92,100 sq miles)
TIME ZONE	GMT
POPULATION	18,887,626
PROJECTED POPULATION 2005	21,128,132
POPULATION DENSITY	79.2 per sq km (205.1 per sq mile)
LIFE EXPECTANCY	57.1
INFANT MORTALITY (PER 1,000)	76.2
OFFICIAL LANGUAGE	English
OTHER LANGUAGES	Indigenous languages, including Akan, Mole-Dagbani, Ewe
LITERACY RATE	63.4%
RELIGIONS	Indigenous beliefs 38%, Muslim 30%, Christian 24%, other 8%
ETHNIC GROUPS	Indigenous 99.8% (including Akan 44%, Moshi-Dagomba 16%, Ewe 13%, Ga 8%), European and other 0.2%
CURRENCY	Cedi
ECONOMY	Agriculture 58%, services 31%, industry 11%
GNP PER CAPITA	US$390
CLIMATE	Tropical: warm and arid on southeast coast; hot and humid in southwest; hot and arid in north
HIGHEST POINT	Mt Afadjato 880 m (2,887 ft)
MAP REFERENCE	Page 364

Guinea

Guinea is on the African Atlantic coast to the north of Sierra Leone and Liberia. A slave-trading center from the fifteenth century, it became the colony of French Guinea in 1890. After achieving independence in 1958 it was for 25 years a one-party Marxist dictatorship under Ahmed Sékou Touré. A member of the Malinke tribe, he centralized and nationalized, attempted to enforce the use of local languages in the place of French, and paid large numbers of state informers to monitor village and family life. Guinea now ranks last or near last on most international social development scales. Women face many disadvantages, including the practice of genital mutilation, which is widespread.

In the past 15 years governmental efforts at reform have led to a number of improvements, and in 1995 Guinea's first multi-party elections took place. The country has had to bear the additional burden of several hundred thousand refugees who have fled from the civil wars in Liberia and Sierra Leone. Many of these people are now returning home.

Africa

From mangrove swamps and lagoons along the coast, the land rises through densely forested foothills to the Fouta Djalon Highlands in the east. These highlands—from which the Gambia, Senegal, and Niger Rivers flow north and north-east—form a barrier between the coast and the grassland and savanna woodland of the Upper Niger Plains. Typical wildlife on the savanna includes lion and leopard, while crocodile and hippopotamus are found in the rivers.

The 80 percent of the workforce who live by agriculture are spread fairly evenly through the countryside. Those who live on the wet Atlantic coastal plain, much of which has been cleared for farming, cultivate bananas, palm oil, pineapples, and rice. Cattle are raised by nomadic herders in the interior.

Guinea possesses more than 25 percent of the world's reserves of high-grade bauxite, and three large bauxite mines contribute about 80 percent of the country's export revenue. Since it opened in 1984, the Aredor diamond mine has also been extremely profitable. Good soil and high yields give the country a prospect of self-sufficiency in food but the years of stifling state controls that were imposed by Touré have made market reforms difficult to implement, and infrastructures are few and much in need of modernizing. Corruption and harassment obstruct business growth. Aside from the bauxite industry, there is little foreign investment.

Fact File

OFFICIAL NAME Republic of Guinea

FORM OF GOVERNMENT Republic with single legislative body (People's National Assembly)

CAPITAL Conakry

AREA 245,860 sq km (94,926 sq miles)

TIME ZONE GMT

POPULATION 7,538,953

PROJECTED POPULATION 2005 8,396,806

POPULATION DENSITY 30.7 per sq km (79.5 per sq mile)

LIFE EXPECTANCY 46.5

INFANT MORTALITY (PER 1,000) 126.3

OFFICIAL LANGUAGE French

OTHER LANGUAGES Indigenous languages

LITERACY RATE 34.8%

RELIGIONS Muslim 85%, Christian 8%, indigenous beliefs 7%

ETHNIC GROUPS Peuhl 40%, Malinke 30%, Soussou 20%, smaller tribes 10%

CURRENCY Guinean franc

ECONOMY Agriculture 80%, industry and commerce 11%, services 9%

GNP PER CAPITA US$550

CLIMATE Tropical, with wet season May to November

HIGHEST POINT Mt Nimba 1,752 m (5,748 ft)

MAP REFERENCE Page 364

The large, covered market in Kumasi, central Ghana (far left). A public voodoo ritual in eastern Ghana (left). Children from rural Guinea (top right).

Guinea-Bissau

Guinea-Bissau is a small west African state between Guinea and Senegal. A large part of the country consists of mangrove swamps, estuaries, and islands, and it is both poor and underdeveloped. After the French and British used the area as a slave-trading station in the seventeenth and eighteenth centuries, Portugal named it Portuguese Guinea and claimed it as a colony in 1879. Independence, achieved in 1974, came following 12 years of guerrilla war.

One-party rule plus attempted coups and assassinations marked the next 17 years. Moves toward multi-party democracy, designed to allow for ethnic divisons and inequalities, began in 1990. The contrast between the limited opportunities available to the 99 percent of the population which is African, and the privileges of the tiny Afro-Portuguese elite, is a major cause of tension. The existence of the opposition Democratic Front was made legal in 1991. Women face significant disad-vantages and female genital mutilation is widespread.

Three main waterways—the Geba, Corubal, and Cacheu Rivers—mark the landscape. These wander across the plains toward broad estuaries and mangrove swamps on the coast. Here, the seasonal rainfall is especially heavy. Rice, the staple food, is grown on the floodplains and in the swamps, as well as on the offshore islands of the Arquipélago dos Bijagós, but not enough is produced to make the country self-sufficient. An area of upland savanna lies toward the border with Guinea in the southeast.

Mineral resources include phosphates, bauxite, and offshore oil but their development has been hampered by political instability, state controls, and (in the case of oil) disputes with Guinea and Senegal. Agriculture and fishing employ 90 percent of the workforce. Cashew nuts, peanuts, and palm kernels are the main exports. Economic reforms featuring monetary stability and private sector growth have been undertaken but progress is being hampered by the burden of foreign debt and the many cultural and institutional constraints.

Fact File

OFFICIAL NAME Republic of Guinea-Bissau

FORM OF GOVERNMENT Republic with single legislative body (National People's Assembly)

CAPITAL Bissau

AREA 36,120 sq km (13,946 sq miles)

TIME ZONE GMT

POPULATION 1,234,555

PROJECTED POPULATION 2005 1,415,330

POPULATION DENSITY 34.2 per sq km (88.5 per sq mile)

LIFE EXPECTANCY 49.6

INFANT MORTALITY (PER 1,000) 109.5

OFFICIAL LANGUAGE Portuguese

OTHER LANGUAGES Indigenous languages

LITERACY RATE 53.9%

RELIGIONS Indigenous beliefs 65%, Muslim 30%, Christian 5%

ETHNIC GROUPS Indigenous 99% (inclduing Balanta 30%, Fula 20%, Manjaca 14%, Mandinga 13%, Papel 7%), European and mixed 1%

CURRENCY CFA (Communauté Financière Africaine) franc

ECONOMY Agriculture 90%, industry and services 10%

GNP PER CAPITA US$250

CLIMATE Tropical, with wet season June to November

HIGHEST POINT Unnamed location in northeast 300 m (984 ft)

MAP REFERENCE Page 364

Africa

331

Kenya

Zebras in the Masai Mara National Reserve in Kenya (above). A Masai woman in traditional dress (top right). A village in the Maluti Mountains foothills in Lesotho (bottom right).

Fact File

OFFICIAL NAME Republic of Kenya

FORM OF GOVERNMENT Republic with single legislative body (National Assembly)

CAPITAL Nairobi

AREA 582,650 sq km (224,961 sq miles)

TIME ZONE GMT + 3 hours

POPULATION 28,808,658

PROJECTED POPULATION 2005 31,156,521

POPULATION DENSITY 49.4 per sq km (128 per sq mile)

LIFE EXPECTANCY 47

INFANT MORTALITY (PER 1,000) 59.1

OFFICIAL LANGUAGES English, Swahili

OTHER LANGUAGES Indigenous languages

LITERACY RATE 77%

RELIGIONS Protestant 38%, Roman Catholic 28%, indigenous beliefs 26%, other 8%

ETHNIC GROUPS Kikuyu 22%, Luhya 14%, Luo 13%, Kalenjin 12%, Kamba 11%, Kisii 6%, Meru 6%, other 16% (including Asian, European, Arab 1%)

CURRENCY Kenya shilling

ECONOMY Agriculture 80%, services 12%, industry 8%

GNP PER CAPITA US$280

CLIMATE Coastal regions tropical, with wet seasons April to May and October to November; inland plateau cooler and drier

HIGHEST POINT Mt Kenya 5,199 m (17,057 ft)

MAP REFERENCE Pages 368–69

Kenya, in east Africa, is where humankind may have originated: remains of humans and pre-humans found in the Olduvai Gorge go back several million years. By the tenth century AD Arabs had settled along the coast, and in the nineteenth century both Britain and Germany became interested in the region. In 1920 Kenya became a British colony, the pleasant climate in the highlands attracting English immigrants who displaced Kikuyu farmers and took their land.

After the Second World War, widespread resentment at this expropriation erupted in the violent Mau Mau rebellion which lasted eight years. Independence came in 1963. Since then, control of the state and its resources has been contested by political parties allied with particular tribes, the domination of the Kikuyu (in recent years under President Daniel Arap Moi) yielding to a trial of multi-party democracy in 1991.

The Kenya Highlands consist of a fertile plateau formed by volcanoes and lava flows. The highlands are divided in two by the Rift Valley, the Eastern Highlands falling away toward the densely populated plain near Lake Victoria, the Western Highlands descending to the valleys of the Tana and Galana Rivers as they cross the Nyika Plain to the north of Mombasa. The populous and fertile coastal belt is fringed by mangrove swamps, coral reefs, and groups of small islands. In the sparsely populated north toward Lake Turkana desert conditions prevail. Kenya's wildlife, consisting of the full range of African fauna, can be seen in the country's several large national parks, and has made it a leading destination for tourists for many years.

By African standards, Kenya has a stable and productive economy. It has a broad and highly successful agricultural base, with cash crops such as coffee and tea. It also has east Africa's largest and most diversified manufacturing sector, producing small-scale consumer goods such as plastics, furniture, batteries, textiles, and soap. But the country also has one of the world's highest rates of population growth: between 1988 and 2000 it is expected to experience an 82 percent increase in population, a figure exceeded only by Haiti.

This continuous increase in the number of its citizens is accompanied by deforestation, lack of drinking water, and infrastructural breakdown. Floods have destroyed roads, bridges, and telecommunications. Crime, including the murder of visitors and ethnic massacres, has caused a steep decline in tourist numbers.

Lesotho

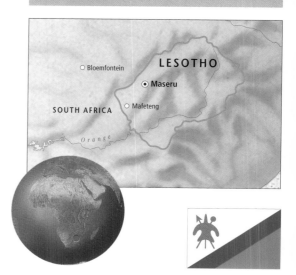

Lesotho is a small landlocked country entirely surrounded by South Africa. Formerly the British Protectorate of Basutoland, it is the only country in the world where all the land is higher than 1,000 m (3,300 ft). About two-thirds of the terrain is mountainous, and at higher altitudes it often snows throughout the winter. As the head of a fragile constitutional monarchy, the king of Lesotho has no executive or legislative powers: traditionally, he could be elected or deposed by a majority vote of the College of Chiefs. Proposals to unite Lesotho with post-apartheid South Africa have been resisted by members of the population who feel an independent state will better defend their cultural heritage.

A high mountainous plateau declining from east to west, Lesotho's highest ridges were formed on basaltic lavas. Treeless, with steep valleys, the wet highlands are soft and boggy in summer and frozen in winter. Numerous river valleys and gorges dissect the plateau, among them the River Orange. To the northwest the border of the country is defined by the Caledon River. This is flanked by a 30 to 65 km (18 to 40 mile) strip of fertile land which supports most of Lesotho's farmers and provides the bulk of its agriculturally useful land. Subsistence crops include maize, sorghum, wheat, and beans. Sheep and goats are kept for wool and mohair on the high plateau.

Lesotho is without important natural resources other than water. Hopes are held for the future of a major hydroelectric facility, the Highlands Water Scheme, which will sell water to South Africa and become a major employer and revenue earner. The scheme will supply all of Lesotho's energy requirements. In scattered hamlets, cottage industry produces woven mohair rugs. Manufacturing based on farm products consists of milling, canning, and the preparation of leather and jute. Roughly 60 percent of Lesotho's male wage earners work across the border in South Africa, mostly as laborers in mines. The wages they send back provide some 45 percent of domestic income.

Fact File

OFFICIAL NAME Kingdom of Lesotho

FORM OF GOVERNMENT Constitutional monarchy with two legislative houses (Senate and National Assembly)

CAPITAL Maseru

AREA 30,350 sq km (11,718 sq miles)

TIME ZONE GMT + 2 hours

POPULATION 2,128,950

PROJECTED POPULATION 2005 2,327,735

POPULATION DENSITY 70.2 per sq km (181.8 per sq mile)

LIFE EXPECTANCY 53

INFANT MORTALITY (PER 1,000) 77.6

OFFICIAL LANGUAGES Sesotho, English

OTHER LANGUAGES Zulu, Afrikaans, French, Xhosa

LITERACY RATE 70.5%

RELIGIONS Christian 80%, indigenous beliefs 20%

ETHNIC GROUPS Sotho 99.7%, European and Asian 0.3%

CURRENCY Loti

ECONOMY Agriculture 75%, services and industry 25%

GNP PER CAPITA US$770

CLIMATE Temperate, with cool, dry winters and hot, wet summers

HIGHEST POINT Thabana-Ntlenyana 3,482 m (11,424 ft)

MAP REFERENCE Page 371

Liberia

Settled by freed slaves after 1822, and a republic since 1847, the west African state of Liberia has always been a socially divided country. The coastal settlements of ex-slaves from America formed an élite with a Christian faith and an American colonial lifestyle. They had little in common with the long-established tribal peoples of the interior. During the long rule of the coastal Americo-Liberian élite the country was politically stable. It also made economic progress, the activities of the Firestone Rubber Company turning Liberia into a major rubber producer.

This ended in 1980 with a coup led by Master Sergeant Samuel Doe (a Krahn). When Doe was ousted by forces led by members of the Gio tribe in 1990, civil war began. Massacres and atrocities have marked succeeding years; famine threatens several regions; some 750,000 refugees have fled the country; organized economic life is at a standstill; and the rule of law has ended.

Liberia has three major geographic regions. Like its neighbors, it has a narrow sandy coastal strip of lagoons and mangrove swamps. Inland from the Atlantic Ocean are rolling hills, covered in tropical rainforest, which rise to a plateau. This ascends to form a mountainous belt along the Guinean border. Most of the plateau region is grassland or forest—forests cover 39 percent of the land area. Only 1 percent of the country is arable.

Until the outbreak of civil war Liberia had been a producer and exporter of iron ore, rubber, timber, and coffee. Industries included rubber processing, food processing, construction materials, furniture making, palm oil processing, and diamond mining. Rice was the main staple, but some food was imported. The catch from coastal fisheries was supplemented by inland fish farms.

By the end of the 1990s war had destroyed much of the Liberian economy, especially the infrastructure in and around Monrovia. The business classes fled, taking with them their capital and expertise. With the collapse of the urban commercial part of the economy, many people have reverted to subsistence farming.

Fact File

OFFICIAL NAME Republic of Liberia

FORM OF GOVERNMENT Republic with single transitional legislative body (Transitional Legislative Assembly)

CAPITAL Monrovia

AREA 111,370 sq km (43,000 sq miles)

TIME ZONE GMT

POPULATION 2,923,725

PROJECTED POPULATION 2005 3,749,894

POPULATION DENSITY 26.3 per sq km (68 per sq mile)

LIFE EXPECTANCY 59.9

INFANT MORTALITY (PER 1,000) 100.6

OFFICIAL LANGUAGE English

OTHER LANGUAGES Indigenous languages

LITERACY RATE 39.5%

RELIGIONS Indigenous beliefs 70%, Muslim 20%, Christian 10%

ETHNIC GROUPS Indigenous tribes 95% (including Kpelle, Bassa, Gio, Kru, Grebo, Mano, Krahn, Gola, Gbandi, Loma, Kissi, Vai, Bella), Americo-Liberian (descendants of repatriated slaves) 5%

CURRENCY Liberian dollar

ECONOMY Agriculture 70%, services 25%, industry 5%

GNP PER CAPITA US$487

CLIMATE Tropical, with wet season May to September

HIGHEST POINT Mt Wuteve 1,380 m (4,528 ft)

MAP REFERENCE Page 364

Africa

Libya

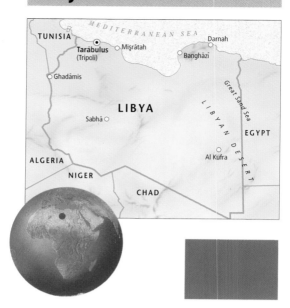

Fact File

OFFICIAL NAME Socialist People's Libyan Arab Jamahiriya

FORM OF GOVERNMENT Republic with single legislative body (General People's Congress)

CAPITAL Tarābulus (Tripoli)

AREA 1,759,540 sq km (679,358 sq miles)

TIME ZONE GMT + 2 hours

POPULATION 5,903,128

PROJECTED POPULATION 2005 7,315,326

POPULATION DENSITY 3.4 per sq km (8.8 per sq mile)

LIFE EXPECTANCY 65.8

INFANT MORTALITY (PER 1,000) 54.0

OFFICIAL LANGUAGE Arabic

OTHER LANGUAGES Italian, English

LITERACY RATE 75.0%

RELIGIONS Sunni Muslim 97%, other 3%

ETHNIC GROUPS Berber and Arab 97%; other (including Greek, Maltese, Italian, Egyptian, Pakistani, Turkish, Indian, Tunisian) 3%

CURRENCY Libyan dinar

ECONOMY Services 51%, industry 32%, agriculture 17%

GNP PER CAPITA Not available (c. US$766–3,035)

CLIMATE Mainly arid; temperate along coast

HIGHEST POINT Bikubiti 2,285 m (7,497 ft)

MAP REFERENCE Page 362

First settled by the Greeks, and once part of the empire of Alexander the Great, Libya was ruled by the Romans for 500 years. Tourists visiting the country today are shown the ruins of an impressive 2,000-year-old Roman theater at Leptis Magna. Later, in AD 642, the region was conquered by the Arabs, and later still became part of the Ottoman Empire. It was occupied by Italy in 1911, and the years 1938 to 1939 saw Mussolini bring in 30,000 Italians to farm the Jefra Plain. Libya became independent in 1951. Since 1969, when he seized power, it has been a one-party socialist state ruled dictatorially by Colonel Muammar al Gaddafi.

The arid Saharan Plateau takes up 93 percent of Libya's land area. The great expanse of the Sahara gives way to a fertile coastal strip along the Mediterranean, where the majority of the population lives, though only 1 percent of the total land area is arable. Tripoli stands on the Jefra Plain, Libya's most productive farming area. Cereals, especially barley, are a major crop. Sorghum is grown in the Fezzan to the south; wheat, tobacco, and olives are produced in the north; dates and figs are cultivated at a few scattered oases in the desert. Predominantly low-lying, the desert terrain rises southward to Bikubiti in the Tibesti Range on the border with Chad. The country is without lakes or perennial rivers, and artesian wells supply nearly two-thirds of its water requirements.

Oil provides almost all export earnings and about one-third of gross domestic product. Though Libya's per capita gross domestic product is usually Africa's highest, the people suffer from periodic shortages of basic goods and foodstuffs caused by import restrictions and inefficient resource allocation.

The largely state-controlled industrial sector (almost all the oil companies were nationalized in 1973 and the state has a controlling interest in all new ventures) suffers from overstaffing and other constraints. However, oil revenues have enabled important state initiatives to be undertaken: the government has planted millions of trees, and the Great Manmade River Project, being built to bring water from large aquifers under the Sahara to the coastal cities, is one of the world's largest water development projects.

Madagascar

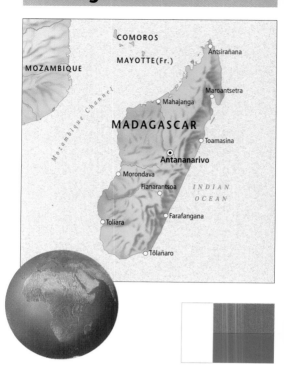

Larger than France, Madagascar is the world's fourth largest island. Located off the southeast coast of Africa, it contrasts sharply with the African mainland in its wildlife, people, culture, language, and history. In the center and the east live the Merina or Hova people who migrated to the island from the islands now known as Indonesia about 2,000 years ago. By the nineteenth century the Merinas, with their capital in Tanarive, ruled much of the country. In 1896 the island became a French colony. It won independence from France in 1960, following a bloody insurrection. From 1975 it was run as a one-party socialist state associated with the Soviet Union. Since 1991, following deepening poverty, riots, and mass demonstrations, there have been attempts to introduce multi-party democracy.

To the east the land drops precipitously to the Indian Ocean through forests dissected by rushing

Antananarivo, the capital of Madagascar (below). A street scene in Toliara, Madagascar (left). Lake Malawi (Lake Nyasa), near Chilumba, looking toward Mozambique (top right).

streams. Inland lies the mountainous central plateau, accounting for 60 percent of the island's total area, and rising in several places above 2,500 m (8,200 ft). Various geological eras are represented in the island's rugged topography, which features steep faulting, volcanic outcrops, and deep-cut valleys. On the western slopes of the plateau the land falls away more gently to broad and fertile plains. In the central highlands both the landscape and agriculture have a south Asian character, rice farming being combined with raising cattle and pigs. Land usage is more African in style on the east coast and in the northern highlands, with fallow-farming of food crops such as cassava and maize, and the cultivation of coffee, sugar, and spices for export.

Separated from the African mainland for over 50 million years, Madagascar developed its own distinctive wildlife: three-quarters of the flora and fauna are found nowhere else. The island is known for its 28 species of lemur—dainty, large-eyed primates—and for the tenrec, a small, spiny, insect-eating mammal. Many of the island's 1,000 or so orchid species are endemic, and it is home to half the world's chameleon species.

Among the poorest countries in the world, Madagascar is not self-sufficient in food. The main staples are rice and cassava, but production is failing to keep pace with an annual population growth rate of around 3 percent. Additional problems derive from past government initiatives. When collective farming was introduced in 1975 it resulted in falling production and widespread resentment. Since 1993 corruption and political instability have accompanied economic confusion and a decay in the infrastructure.

Fact File

OFFICIAL NAME Republic of Madagascar

FORM OF GOVERNMENT Republic with two legislative bodies (Senate and National Assembly)

CAPITAL Antananarivo

AREA 587,040 sq km (226,656 sq miles)

TIME ZONE GMT + 3 hours

POPULATION 14,873,387

PROJECTED POPULATION 2005 17,558,869

POPULATION DENSITY 25.3 per sq km (65.5 per sq mile)

LIFE EXPECTANCY 53.2

INFANT MORTALITY (PER 1,000) 89.1

OFFICIAL LANGUAGES Malagasy, French

LITERACY RATE 83%

RELIGIONS Indigenous beliefs 52%, Christian 41%, Muslim 7%

ETHNIC GROUPS Chiefly Malayo-Indonesian inland (including Merina, Betsileo, Betsimisaraka) and mixed African, Arab, Malayo-Indonesian on coasts (including Tsimihety, Sakalava) 99%; other 1%

CURRENCY Malagasy franc

ECONOMY Agriculture 81%, services 13%, industry 6%

GNP PER CAPITA US$230

CLIMATE Tropical in coastal regions; temperate inland (wet season November to April); arid in south

HIGHEST POINT Maromokotro 2,876 m (9,436 ft)

MAP REFERENCE Page 372

Malawi

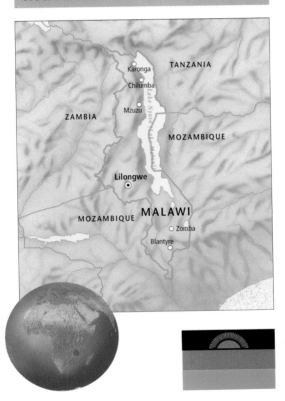

Malawi is a hilly and in places mountainous country at the southern end of Africa's Rift Valley, one-fifth of it consisting of Lake Malawi (Lake Nyasa). The lake contains 500 fish species which support a sizeable fishing industry. Most of the country's people are descended from the Bantu who settled the area centuries ago. Arab slave-trading was suppressed by the incoming British in 1887–89, and in 1907 the country became the British Protectorate of Nyasaland. Independence in 1964 put Dr Hastings Banda in charge and he ruled dictatorially for 30 years. Cumulative difficulties, including drought and crop failures, some 800,000 refugees from Mozambique, and resentment at the apparent assassination of political opponents, led to Dr Banda's removal and Malawi's first multi-party elections in 1994.

At the southern end of Lake Malawi (Lake Nyasa) the Shire River runs through a deep, swampy valley flanked by mountains to the east. Most of the population live in this southern region, growing maize as the main food crop and cultivating cash crops such as peanuts and sugarcane. The western central plateau rises northward to the Nyika Uplands, where rainfall is highest. In the Shire Highlands to the south, tea and tobacco are grown on large estates. Savanna grassland in the valleys gives way to open woodland, much of which has been cleared for cultivation. Wildlife is largely confined to reserves.

Agriculture provides more than 90 percent of exports. Reserves of bauxite and uranium exist, but not in commercially usable quantities. Hydro-electricity supplies only about 3 percent of total energy use—most needs are met from fuelwood, which is resulting in continued deforestation. The economy depends heavily on foreign aid.

Fact File

OFFICIAL NAME Republic of Malawi

FORM OF GOVERNMENT Republic with single legislative body (National Assembly)

CAPITAL Lilongwe

AREA 118,480 sq km (45,745 sq miles)

TIME ZONE GMT + 2 hours

POPULATION 9,888,601

PROJECTED POPULATION 2005 10,469,217

POPULATION DENSITY 83.4 per sq km (216 per sq mile)

LIFE EXPECTANCY 33.7

INFANT MORTALITY (PER 1,000) 136.9

OFFICIAL LANGUAGES Chichewa, English

OTHER LANGUAGES Indigenous languages

LITERACY RATE 55.8%

RELIGIONS Protestant 55%, Roman Catholic 20%, Muslim 20%, indigenous beliefs 5%

ETHNIC GROUPS Indigenous tribes: Malavi (including Chewa, Nyanja, Tumbuke, Tonga) 58%, Lomwe 18%, Yao 13%, Ngoni 7%; Asian and European 4%

CURRENCY Kwacha

ECONOMY Agriculture 79%, services 16%, industry 5%

GNP PER CAPITA US$170

CLIMATE Tropical, with wet season November to April

HIGHEST POINT Mt Mulanje 3,001 m (9,846 ft)

MAP REFERENCE Page 369

Mali

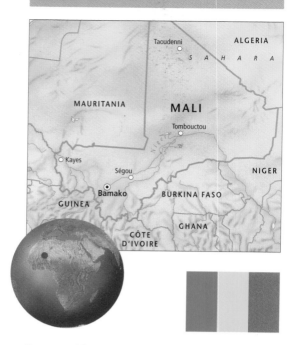

Fact File

OFFICIAL NAME Republic of Mali

FORM OF GOVERNMENT Republic with single legislative body (National Assembly)

CAPITAL Bamako

AREA 1,240,000 sq km (478,764 sq miles)

TIME ZONE GMT

POPULATION 10,429,124

PROJECTED POPULATION 2005 12,536,227

POPULATION DENSITY 8.4 per sq km (21.8 per sq mile)

LIFE EXPECTANCY 47.5

INFANT MORTALITY (PER 1,000) 119.4

OFFICIAL LANGUAGE French

OTHER LANGUAGES Bambara and other indigenous languages

LITERACY RATE 29.3%

RELIGIONS Muslim 90%, indigenous beliefs 9%, Christian 1%

ETHNIC GROUPS Mande 50%, Peul 17%, Voltaic 12%, Songhai 6%, Tuareg and Moor 10%, other 5%

CURRENCY CFA (Communauté Financière Africaine) franc

ECONOMY Agriculture 85%, services 13%, industry 2%

GNP PER CAPITA US$250

CLIMATE Subtropical in south and southwest; arid in north

HIGHEST POINT Hombori Tondo 1,155 m (3,789 ft)

MAP REFERENCE Pages 361, 364–65

Mali is a landlocked west African country, watered by the River Niger in the south and with vast stretches of the Sahara Desert lying to the north. It derives its name from the Malinke or Mandingo people whose empire flourished between the eighth and fourteenth centuries. Later it was a center of trade and Islamic scholarship, based on the city of Timbuktu (now Tombouctou). At the end of the nineteenth century it became a colony of French West Africa, achieving independence in 1960. For the next 30 years the country was ruled by either civilian or military

dictators. Demonstrations in 1991 in which about 100 people died were followed by the overthrow of the regime, and free elections were held for the first time in 1992.

There is a major ethnic division between the black African majority in the south, and the minority of Arab Tuareg nomads in the north. Violent Tuareg guerrilla activity in northern Mali ended with a peace pact in 1995.

Mali's flat landscape consists mainly of plains and sandstone plateaus. The need for water is the main concern. The northern and virtually rainless Saharan plains are inhabited almost entirely by Tuareg nomads. The semiarid center—the Sahel—has in recent years suffered from devastating droughts. Such arable land as exists is found in the south, along the Senegal and Niger Rivers, the latter spreading out to form an inland delta before turning southward on its way to the border of Niger. These rivers provide water for stock and for irrigation. Rice is grown on irrigated land; millet, cotton, and pea-nuts grow elsewhere. Away from the rivers southern Mali is mostly savanna country where mahogany, kapok, and baobab trees grow, these being replaced further north by palms and scrub. Animal life includes lion, antelope, jackal, and hyena.

Some 80 percent of the labor force works in agriculture and fishing—dried fish is exported to Burkina Faso, Côte d'Ivoire, and Ghana. With 65 percent of its land either desert or semidesert, however, and industry limited mainly to a single gold mine, salt production, and small-scale textiles and shoes, Mali is extremely poor. As well as gold there are phosphates, uranium, bauxite, manganese, and copper but development is hampered by poor transport facilities and the fact that the country is landlocked. With expenditures almost double its revenues, Mali is a major recipient of foreign aid.

Mauritania

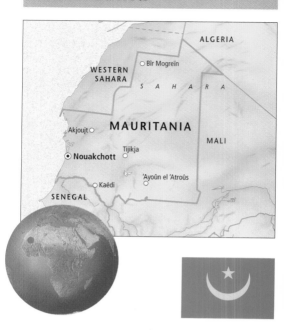

Most of Mauritania consists of the wastes of the western Sahara Desert. Islam in the region dates from the Almoravid Empire of the twelfth century. Later, it was conquered by Arab bidan or "white" Moors (*Maure* in French, meaning Moor), nomads who subjugated and enslaved the black Africans of the south, producing a people of mixed Arab and African descent known as *harratin* or "black" Moors. Deep social tensions between the dominant "white" Moors, the "black" Moors, and the subordinate 30 percent of black African farmers in the south lie at the heart of Mauritanian politics. Slavery in Mauritania was not officially abolished until 1970, and it is estimated that tens of

thousands of *harratin* still live as slaves. France entered the region early in the nineteenth century and established a protectorate in 1903. Independence came in 1960.

Inland from the low-lying coastal plains of the Atlantic seaboard there are low plateaus—a tableland broken by occasional hills and scarps. The Saharan Desert to the north, which forms 47 percent of Mauritania's total land area, rises to the isolated peak of Kediet Ijill. In the southern third of the country there is just enough rain to support Sahelian thornbush and grasses. After rain, cattle herders drive their herds from the Senegal River through these grasslands, in good years the livestock outnumbering the general population five to one. During the 1980s the whole area suffered severely from drought and the nomadic population, which had numbered three-quarters of the national population, fell to less than one-third, many nomads abandoning rural life entirely for the towns.

Farmers near the Senegal River grow millet, sorghum, beans, peanuts, and rice, using the late-summer river floods for irrigation. A hydroelectric project on the river is intended to provide water for the irrigated cultivation of rice, cotton, and sugarcane, but drought has also driven many subsistence farmers from the land. Off the coast, cooled by the Canaries current, lie some of the richest fishing grounds in the world. Although about 100,000 tonnes of fish are landed annually, the potential catch is estimated at about 600,000 tonnes. Exploitation by foreign fishing boats threatens this source of revenue.

Fact File

OFFICIAL NAME	Islamic Republic of Mauritania
FORM OF GOVERNMENT	Republic with two legislative bodies (Senate and National Assembly)
CAPITAL	Nouakchott
AREA	1,030,700 sq km (397,953 sq miles)
TIME ZONE	GMT
POPULATION	2,581,738
PROJECTED POPULATION 2005	3,088,823
POPULATION DENSITY	2.5 per sq km (6.5 per sq mile)
LIFE EXPECTANCY	50.5
INFANT MORTALITY (PER 1,000)	76.5
OFFICIAL LANGUAGES	French, Hasaniya Arabic
OTHER LANGUAGES	Indigenous languages, Arabic
LITERACY RATE	36.9%
RELIGIONS	Muslim 99%, other 1%
ETHNIC GROUPS	"Black" Moors 40%, "White" Moors 30%, African 30%
CURRENCY	Ouguiya
ECONOMY	Agriculture 70%, services 22%, industry 8%
GNP PER CAPITA	US$460
CLIMATE	Mainly arid, with wet season in far south (May to September)
HIGHEST POINT	Kediet Ijill 915 m (3,002 ft)
MAP REFERENCE	Pages 360, 364

The city of Tombouctou, in Mali, following a dust storm (left). Women agricultural workers walking beside a field of sugarcane in Mauritius (top right).

Mauritius

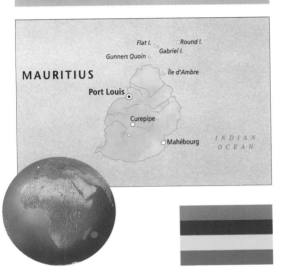

F amous as the home of the now-extinct flightless bird, the dodo, the Republic of Mauritius consists of one large and several smaller islands 800 km (500 miles) east of Madagascar. Mauritius was uninhabited when visited by the Portuguese and the Dutch between the fifteenth and seventeenth centuries. It was first settled by the French, after 1715, who brought African slaves for the sugar plantations. In 1810 it was taken over by the British, who brought in numerous indentured laborers from India. These colonial origins produced two distinct communities, one Afro-French Creole (27 percent), the other English-speaking and Indian (73 percent), who compete for influence and power. Independence within the British Commonwealth was granted in 1968 and Mauritius became a republic in 1992. Despite occasional unrest, the country has a record of political stability and economic growth.

Fringed with coral reefs, the main island rises from coastal plains on its north and east to a plateau surrounded by rugged peaks—the remains of a giant volcano. The climate is tropical, but moderated by rain-bearing winds from the southeast. Sugarcane is grown on 90 percent of the cultivated land, and accounts, with derivatives such as molasses, for 40 percent of export earnings. A by-product of the sugar industry, the cane-waste called bagasse, has been used to fuel power stations. Fast-flowing rivers descending from the plateau are used to produce hydroelectric power.

Industrial diversification (textile and garment manufacture now accounts for 44 percent of export revenue) and the development of a tourist industry (up to half a million visitors per year) have enabled Mauritius to transcend the low income agricultural economy that existed at the time of independence. Since 1968 annual economic growth most years has been about 5 percent, life expectancy has been increasing and the infrastructure has improved.

Fact File

OFFICIAL NAME	Republic of Mauritius
FORM OF GOVERNMENT	Republic with single legislative body (Legislative Assembly)
CAPITAL	Port Louis
AREA	1,860 sq km (718 sq miles)
TIME ZONE	GMT + 4 hours
POPULATION	1,182,212
PROJECTED POPULATION 2005	1,265,011
POPULATION DENSITY	635.6 per sq km (1,646.2 per sq mile)
LIFE EXPECTANCY	71.1
INFANT MORTALITY (PER 1,000)	16.2
OFFICIAL LANGUAGE	English
OTHER LANGUAGES	Creole, French, Hindi, Urdu, Bojpoori, Hakka
LITERACY RATE	82.4%
RELIGIONS	Hindu 52%, Roman Catholic 26%, Protestant 2.3%, Muslim 16.6%, other 3.1%
ETHNIC GROUPS	Indo-Mauritian 68%, Creole 27%, Sino-Mauritian 3%, Franco-Mauritian 2%
CURRENCY	Mauritian rupee
ECONOMY	Services 51%, agriculture 27%, industry 22%
GNP PER CAPITA	US$3,380
CLIMATE	Tropical, moderated by trade winds
HIGHEST POINT	Piton de la Petite Rivière Noire 828 m (2,717 ft)
MAP REFERENCE	Pages 372, 373

Morocco

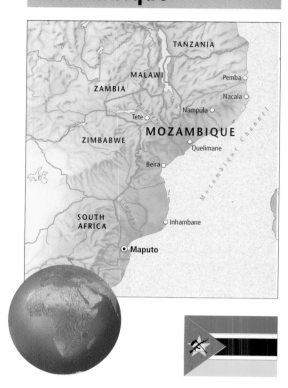

Morocco's earliest inhabitants were the Berbers, who still live in the country today. At one time under Carthaginian rule, and then a part of the Roman Empire, the Berbers were overrun by Arabs in the seventh century AD and converted to Islam. The country's name derives from the Arabic *Maghreb-el-aksa* ("the farthest west"), and because of the protective barrier of the Atlas Mountains, Morocco has always been less a part of the Arab world than the other north African states. Under political pressure from Spain and France during the nineteenth century, Morocco became a French protectorate in 1912. About 35 percent of the people live in the highlands and are Berber-speaking, while the Arab majority live in the lowlands.

Under the rule of King Hassan II since 1961, Morocco has followed generally pro-Western policies. The king's popularity at home owes a good deal to Morocco's disputed territorial claim to the phosphate-rich resources of Western Sahara across the southern border. A costly armed struggle with the Polisario Front guerrilla movement of Western Sahara led to a cease-fire in 1991, by which time 170,000 of the native-born Sahrawis of the region had become refugees in Algeria. Sovereignty is still unresolved.

More than one-third of Morocco is mountainous. Three parallel ranges of the Atlas Mountains run southwest to northeast, where a plateau reaches toward the Algerian border. Most of the people living in the mountains are peasant cultivators and nomadic herders. Modern economic development is found mainly on the Atlantic plains and the plateaus—the fertile Moulouyan, Rharb, Sous, and High (Haut) Atlas plains constituting virtually all of Morocco's cultivable land. In the Rharb and Rif regions extensive areas are covered with cork oak, while on the northern slopes there are forests of evergreen oak and cedar. Wildlife includes Cuvier's gazelle, the Barbary macaque, and the mouflon (a wild sheep), while desert animals such as the fennec fox live in the south.

A gold seller in Morocco (right). Old-style houses in Fès, Morocco (far right). Sand dunes in Namib-Naukluft Park in Namibia (above right).

In 1995 Morocco suffered its worst drought in 30 years. This seriously affected agriculture, which produces about one-third of Morocco's exports and employs about half the workforce. Irrigation is essential over most of the country, the chief crops being barley and wheat, along with citrus fruit, potatoes, and other vegetables. Dates are grown in desert oases. The country's natural resources are still largely undeveloped. It has coal, iron ore, and zinc, along with the world's largest reserves of phosphates. Debt servicing, unemployment, the high rate of population increase, and the unresolved territorial claim to Western Sahara are all long-term problems.

Fact File

OFFICIAL NAME Kingdom of Morocco

FORM OF GOVERNMENT Constitutional monarchy with single legislative body (Chamber of Representatives)

CAPITAL Rabat

AREA 446,550 sq km (172,413 sq miles)

TIME ZONE GMT + 1 hour

POPULATION 29,661,636

PROJECTED POPULATION 2005 32,923,967

POPULATION DENSITY 66.4 per sq km (172 per sq mile)

LIFE EXPECTANCY 68.9

INFANT MORTALITY (PER 1,000) 11.0

OFFICIAL LANGUAGE Arabic

OTHER LANGUAGES Berber languages, French

LITERACY RATE 42.1%

RELIGIONS Muslim 98.7%, Christian 1.1%, Jewish 0.2%

ETHNIC GROUPS Arab–Berber 99.1%, other 0.7%, Jewish 0.2%

CURRENCY Moroccan dirham

ECONOMY Agriculture 46%, services 30%, industry 24%

GNP PER CAPITA US$1,110

CLIMATE Temperate along northern coast, arid in south, cooler in mountains

HIGHEST POINT Jebel Toubkal 4,165 m (13,665 ft)

MAP REFERENCE Pages 360–61

Mozambique

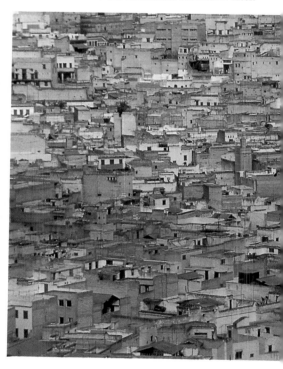

Lying on the southeast coast of Africa facing Madagascar, Mozambique is divided in two by the Zambeze River. This division is also found in its social and political life: people in the north support the Renamo party, while south of the river they support Frelimo. Visited by Vasco da Gama in 1498 and colonized by Portuguese in search of gold, Mozambique remained a slave-trading center until the 1850s.

A long war of liberation against Portugal led to independence in 1975 and brought the Marxist Frelimo to power. Frelimo's one-party regime was then challenged by a guerilla movement, Renamo, supported by South Africa. The ensuing civil war, aggravated by famine, led to nearly 1 million deaths. By 1989 Mozambique was world's poorest country. That year Frelimo renounced Marxism. At multi-party elections in 1994 it won by a narrow majority.

A considerable amount of rain falls in the north: south of the Zambeze conditions are much drier.

North of Maputo, the only natural harbor, is a wide coastal plain where there are coconut, sugar, and sisal plantations, and smallholders grow maize and peanuts. Inland, the terrain rises to the high veld.

Economically, Mozambique faces a huge task of reconstruction and the government is trying to redistribute to peasants large areas of land that were seized by the state. Agricultural output is only 75 percent of its 1981 level and grain is imported. Industry is operating at less than half capacity. There are substantial agricultural, hydropower and petroleum resources, and deposits of coal, copper and bauxite but these are largely undeveloped.

Fact File

OFFICIAL NAME Republic of Mozambique

FORM OF GOVERNMENT Republic with single legislative body (Assembly of the Republic)

CAPITAL Maputo

AREA 801,590 sq km (309,494 sq miles)

TIME ZONE GMT + 2 hours

POPULATION 19,124,335

PROJECTED POPULATION 2005 22,155,576

POPULATION DENSITY 23.9 per sq km (61.8 per sq mile)

LIFE EXPECTANCY 45.9

INFANT MORTALITY (PER 1,000) 117.6

OFFICIAL LANGUAGE Portuguese

OTHER LANGUAGES Indigenous languages

LITERACY RATE 39.5%

RELIGIONS Indigenous beliefs 55%, Christian 30%, Muslim 15%

ETHNIC GROUPS Indigenous tribes (including Shangaan, Chokwe, Manyika, Sena, Makua) 99.7%, other 0.3%

CURRENCY Metical

ECONOMY Agriculture 85%, services 8%, industry 7%

GNP PER CAPITA US$80

CLIMATE Mainly tropical: wet season December to March

HIGHEST POINT Monte Binga 2,436 m (7,992 ft)

MAP REFERENCE Pages 369, 371

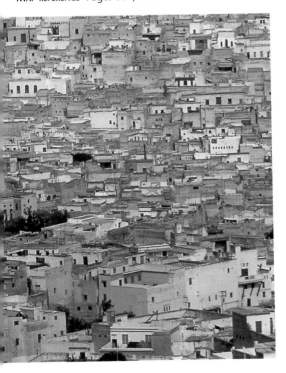

Namibia

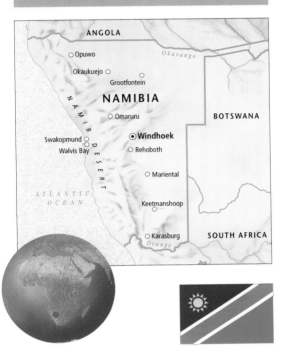

A large, arid country in southwest Africa, Namibia was born of the European scramble for colonies in the nineteenth century. The German connection with the area (formerly South West Africa) began with the arrival of missionaries in the 1840s. Namibia was a German protectorate from 1884; the scene of a brutal German punitive action in 1904 in which the Herero were decimated and scattered; under South African control for many years; and endured 23 years of a bitter anti-colonial war that began in 1966. In 1989 an election gave the guerrilla movement SWAPO (the South West African People's Organization) victory at the polls, and in 1990 came independence.

The virtually uninhabited sand dunes of the Namib Desert fringe the country's south Atlantic coastline. A major escarpment inland separates the desert from a north–south range of mountains which includes the Tsaris Mountains, Aûas Mountains, and Mt Erongo. The interior plateau, which occupies the eastern part of the country, has an average elevation of 1,500 m (5,000 ft) and is covered with the dry scrub grassland typical of the Kalahari Desert. Largely rainless, the coast is often shrouded in fog. Here, welwitschia plants, some of them up to 2,000 years old, live by absorbing moisture from the fog that rolls in from the sea. Namibia's

wildlife is typical of southern Africa, with Etosha National Park providing sanctuary for baboon, antelope, elephant, giraffe, zebra, and lion.

Namibia's natural resources include diamonds, copper, uranium (world's fifth largest producer), gold, lead (world's second largest producer), tin, lithium, cadmium, zinc, vanadium, and natural gas, and there are thought to be deposits of oil, coal, and iron ore. Mining accounts for 25 percent of gross domestic product, this sector relying on the expertise of Namibia's small white population. More than half its African peoples depend on agriculture for a livelihood, working poor soils in an unfavorable climate. Livestock farmers produce beef and mutton. About half the country's food is imported, mainly from South Africa.

Fact File

OFFICIAL NAME Republic of Namibia

FORM OF GOVERNMENT Republic with two legislative bodies (National Council and National Assembly)

CAPITAL Windhoek

AREA 825,418 sq km (318,694 sq miles)

TIME ZONE GMT + 2 hours

POPULATION 1,648,270

PROJECTED POPULATION 2005 1,798,625

POPULATION DENSITY 2 per sq km (5.2 per sq mile)

LIFE EXPECTANCY 41.3

INFANT MORTALITY (PER 1,000) 65.9

OFFICIAL LANGUAGE English

OTHER LANGUAGES Afrikaans, German, indigenous languages

LITERACY RATE 40%

RELIGIONS Christian 85% (Lutheran at least 50%, other Christian denominations 35%), indigenous beliefs 15%

ETHNIC GROUPS Indigenous tribes 86% (including Ovambo 50%, Kavangos 9%, Herero 7%, Damara 7%), mixed indigenous–European 7.4%, European 6.6%

CURRENCY Namibian dollar

ECONOMY Agriculture 60%, industry and commerce 19%, services 8%, government 7%, mining 6%

GNP PER CAPITA US$2,000

CLIMATE Mainly arid, with higher rainfall inland

HIGHEST POINT Brandberg 2,573 m (8,439 ft)

MAP REFERENCE Page 370

Africa

Niger

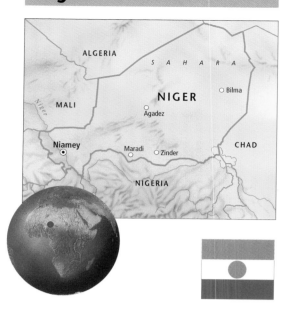

Niger is two-thirds desert, which may seem strange for a country that is named after a great river (the name "Niger" comes from the Tuareg word *n'eghirren*, for flowing water), but the River Niger only cuts across the extreme southwest of this large, landlocked country. Elsewhere, there is an arid landscape of stony basins, drifting sands, and a northern highland that forms part of the mountain chain stretching from Algeria to Chad.

The home of the Sokoto Empire of the Fulani in the nineteenth century, the region became part of French West Africa in 1922, and received independence in 1960. Then followed three decades of dictatorial civilian and military rule. Despite the holding of multi-party elections in 1993, continuing unrest caused by Tuareg rebels in the north and power struggles within the government led to the reimposition of military rule in 1996.

Niger's central geographic feature is the Massif de l'Aïr. In these mountains, which rise out of the Saharan plains to jagged peaks up to 1,900 m (6,230 ft) high, there is sometimes sufficient rain for thorny scrub to grow. Formerly nomads grazed their camels, horses, cattle, and goats in this area, but devastating droughts in 1973 and 1983 destroyed their livelihood. To the east and west of the Massif de l'Aïr are the Saharan Desert plains of Ténéré du Tafassasset and the Western Talk. Sand and sandy soil cover most of the desert plains to the north and east, an area which is virtually rainless and, aside from small numbers of people living at the occasional palm-fringed oasis, uninhabited. Plant life includes kapok and baobab trees. Buffalo, antelope, lion, hippopotamus, and crocodiles are found in Niger but their survival today is more a matter of chance than good management.

With its gross domestic product growth barely matching the growth of its population, Niger is one of the most impoverished countries in Africa. More than 95 percent of its people earn a living from farming and trading. Where the Niger River crosses the country in the far southwest there are fertile arable soils: crops include yams, cassava, and maize, and rice in areas where the river floods. On the drier land toward Lake Chad (Lac Tchad) millet and sorghum are grown. The drought that has affected extensive areas of the Sahel has reduced Niger from self-sufficiency to being an importer of food. Tin and tungsten are mined, and there are reserves of iron ore, manganese, and molybdenum. During the 1970s, when prices were high, uranium became the main source of revenue, and it continues to be the country's most valuable export. Between 1983 and 1990, however, revenues fell by 50 percent. At present the government of Niger relies on aid for both operating expenses and for public investment.

Fact File

OFFICIAL NAME	Republic of Niger
FORM OF GOVERNMENT	Republic with single legislative body (National Assembly)
CAPITAL	Niamey
AREA	1,267,000 sq km (489,189 sq miles)
TIME ZONE	GMT + 1 hour
POPULATION	9,962,242
PROJECTED POPULATION 2005	11,864,407
POPULATION DENSITY	7.9 per sq km (20.5 per sq mile)
LIFE EXPECTANCY	42
INFANT MORTALITY (PER 1,000)	112.8
OFFICIAL LANGUAGE	French
OTHER LANGUAGES	Hausa, Djerma, Fulani
LITERACY RATE	13.1%
RELIGIONS	Muslim 80%, Christian and indigenous beliefs 20%
ETHNIC GROUPS	Hausa 56%, Djerma 22%, Fula 8.5%, Tuareg 8%, Beri Beri 4.3%, other (including 4,000 French expatriates) 1.2%
CURRENCY	CFA (Communauté Financière Africaine) franc
ECONOMY	Agriculture 87%, services 10%, industry 3%
GNP PER CAPITA	US$220
CLIMATE	Mainly arid; tropical in south, with wet season June to October
HIGHEST POINT	Mt Gréboun 1,994 m (6,540 ft)
MAP REFERENCE	Pages 361, 362, 365

Nigeria

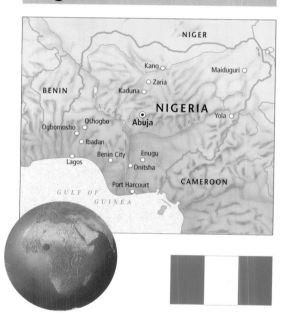

With the continent's largest population, huge oil revenues, and a territory that is four times the size of the United Kingdom, Nigeria is one of Africa's most important nations. It also ranks as one of the most corrupt countries in the world, and a place where tensions between the main tribal groups are close to breaking point.

Such tensions are not new to the region: regional and ethnic conflict go back to the days of Nigeria's ancient city-states. The life of the Yoruba people centered on the city of Ife, while the Hausa kingdom was in the north. The kingdom of Benin, well known for its portrait bronzes of past rulers, was in the west, and a number of communities of Ibo lived in the southeast. Bringing all these peoples together to form a single nation has proved difficult: since independence, in 1960, there has been a series of military dictatorships, and only 10 years of elected government. An unsuccessful attempt to secede by the Ibo in 1967 (who set up an independent state named Biafra) failed in 1970, following a bitter civil war in which thousands of people died. Today, an uneasy peace prevails under military rule.

Africa

Women drawing water from a deep well in Niger (far left). Wooded countryside turned to desert in Niger as a result of drought (left). Donkeys are used to transport produce in a village in Nigeria (below).

Agricultural production has failed to keep pace with population growth, and Nigeria is now a food importer. There are fundamental imbalances in the economy that result in chronic inflation and a steadily depreciating currency. Investors are wary because of political instability and corruption at the highest levels of government. Domestic and international debts prevent an agreement with the IMF on debt relief.

Fact File

OFFICIAL NAME Federal Republic of Nigeria

FORM OF GOVERNMENT Military regime

CAPITAL Abuja

AREA 923,770 sq km (356,668 sq miles)

TIME ZONE GMT + 1 hour

POPULATION 113,828,587

PROJECTED POPULATION 2005 133,974,486

POPULATION DENSITY 123.2 per sq km (319 per sq mile)

LIFE EXPECTANCY 53.3

INFANT MORTALITY (PER 1,000) 89.5

OFFICIAL LANGUAGES English

OTHER LANGUAGES French, Hausa, Yoruba, Ibo, Fulani

LITERACY RATE 55.6%

RELIGIONS Muslim 50%, Christian 40%, indigenous beliefs 10%

ETHNIC GROUPS About 250 indigenous groups: the largest of which are Hausa, Fulani, Yoruba, Ibo 68%; Kanuri, Edo, Tiv, Ibidio, Nupe 25%; other 7%

CURRENCY Naira

ECONOMY Services 51%, agriculture 45%, industry 4%

GNP PER CAPITA US$260

CLIMATE Tropical in south, with wet season April to October; arid in north

HIGHEST POINT Chappal Waddi 2,419 m (7,936 ft)

MAP REFERENCE Page 365

Physical features and land use

Nigeria's coast on the west African Gulf of Guinea consists of long, sandy beaches, and mangrove swamps where its rivers flow into the sea. The mouth of the Niger forms an immense delta, threaded with thousands of creeks and lagoons, with Port Harcourt on one of the main channels. Upstream it divides, the Benue (Bénoué) River leading east into Cameroon, the Niger heading northwest toward Benin. These two large rivers provide transport, by boat, for cargo and people. High rainfall on the coast and in the river valleys enables yams, cassava, maize, and vegetables to be grown and on floodland alongside the rivers rice is cultivated.

In the rainy forested belt to the north the hills gradually rise to the semiarid central savanna plateau, and then to the Jos Plateau, reaching 1,780 m (5,840 ft) at Share Hill. Up the Benue (Bénoué) River to the east the land rises to the wooded slopes of the Adamaoua Massif and the Cameroon highlands. From these hill-slope areas come such products as cocoa, rubber, hardwoods, and palm oil. North of the Jos Plateau the savanna becomes dry, in many places degenerating into arid Sahelian scrub, where both herds and herders have difficulty surviving. Around Lake Chad (Lac Tchad) the typical vegetation is hardy acacia and doum palms.

Together, the river systems of the Niger and the Benue (Bénoué) drain 60 percent of Nigeria's total land area. Though much reduced by clearing for cultivation, the Nigerian rainforests still produce mahogany and iriko. Wildlife includes elephant, chimpanzee, and the red river hog.

People and culture

In addition to the Yoruba, Fulani, Hausa, and Ibo, Nigeria has 245 much smaller ethnic groups. Not only are they divided along lines of ethnicity, language, and regional dialect, there is also a major religious division. The north of the country is largely Islamic (the religion of the Hausa and Fulani) while the south is for the most part Christian, combined with indigenous African beliefs. Outbreaks of communal violence in the north sometimes occur as a result of clashes between Islamic fundamentalists and missionary Christians. Despite widespread Christian proselytizing there is evidence that Islamic influence is gradually growing in the south.

Although 54 percent of the labor force works in agriculture, and many rural people are subsistence farmers, Nigerians have also lived in cities for centuries. This contrasts with many other parts of Africa. Long before European commercial expansion into the region, places such as Benin, Kano, Ibadan, and Ife were administrative and trading centers with sizeable populations. As in other parts of west Africa, women in the non-Islamic Nigerian cultures play a prominent role in commercial life.

Economy and resources

Nigeria is rich in natural resources and these are the basis of its economic strength. They include tin, columbite, iron ore, coal, limestone, lead, zinc, and natural gas. By far the most important, however, is oil: Nigeria is OPEC's fourth largest producer, with oil providing 80 percent of government revenue and 90 percent of export earnings overall. This has led to what many consider over-dependence on a single commodity. In addition it has provided a limitless source of independent wealth for the political elite.

Rwanda

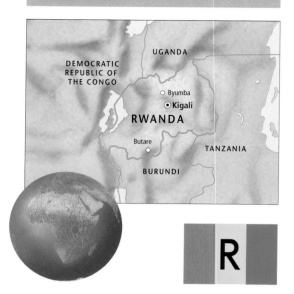

Fact File

OFFICIAL NAME Republic of Rwanda

FORM OF GOVERNMENT Republic with transitional legislative body (National Assembly)

CAPITAL Kigali

AREA 26,340 sq km (10,170 sq miles)

TIME ZONE GMT + 2 hours

POPULATION 8,154,933

PROJECTED POPULATION 2005 9,135,398

POPULATION DENSITY 309.6 per sq km (801.9 per sq mile)

LIFE EXPECTANCY 41.3

INFANT MORTALITY (PER 1,000) 112.9

OFFICIAL LANGUAGES French, Kinyarwanda

OTHER LANGUAGE Kiswahili

LITERACY RATE 59.2%

RELIGIONS Roman Catholic 65%, Protestant 9%, Muslim 1%, indigenous beliefs and other 25%

ETHNIC GROUPS Hutu 80%, Tutsi 19%, Twa (Pygmy) 1%

CURRENCY Rwandan franc

ECONOMY Agriculture 93%, services 5%, industry 2%

GNP PER CAPITA US$180

CLIMATE Tropical, with two wet seasons (October to December and March to May)

HIGHEST POINT Karisimbi 4,507 m (14,783 ft)

MAP REFERENCE Page 369

A small landlocked country in central Africa, Rwanda shares much of its social history with Burundi, across its southern border. In the fifteenth and sixteenth centuries a tall cattle-herding people, named Tutsi, probably from Sudan, came to the region and formed a small feudal aristocracy that dominated the more numerous Hutu farmers who had settled in the area some time before them. Since then, the Hutu people have endured the situation with resentment. In recent times, beginning with a Hutu revolt in 1959 (independence from Belgium coming in 1962), there have been decades of ethnic strife and intermittent violence, with hundreds of thousands of deaths occurring on

both sides. This culminated in the massacre of half a million Tutsi (and also some moderate Hutu) by Hutu in 1994, waves of refugees spilling out into the Democratic Republic of Congo, Burundi, Tanzania, and Uganda. An uneasy peace followed.

Rwanda is the most densely populated country in Africa. Almost 30 percent of the land is arable, steep slopes are intensively cultivated, and terracing and contour plowing are used in order to keep erosion to a minimum. Lake Kivu and a part of the southward-flowing Ruzizi River form the western boundary of the country. From here the land rises steeply to the mountains, part of the Rift Valley, which constitute the Nile–Congo divide. To the north are the mountains, and several volcanoes, of the Mufumbiro Range. These include one of the last refuges of the mountain gorilla. From the heights of the eastern rim of the Rift Valley a plateau slopes eastward toward the Tanzanian border, the River Kagera marshes, and a number of lakes.

During peacetime, Rwanda's production of coffee and tea constituted 80 to 90 percent of total exports. Pyrethrum and sugarcane are other cash crops, cassava, maize, bananas, sorghum, and vegetables being crops grown for food. In keeping with their status as one-time nomadic herders, the Tutsi people keep cattle. The Hutu generally keep sheep and goats. Arable land is overused and deforestation and soil erosion are widespread. Natural resources include gold, tin, tungsten, and natural gas, but they are undeveloped because of infrastructure and transport difficulties. Political and ethnic disorders have affected the economy which suffers from infrastructural damage, lack of maintenance, looting, and the widespread destruction of property and crops. Recovery of production to earlier levels will take time.

A crater lake in Volcanoes National Park, Rwanda (below). The endangered mountain gorilla still survives in the highlands of Rwanda (right). Women removing small fish from a fishing net in Senegal (top right).

São Tomé and Príncipe

São Tomé and Príncipe are two islands lying off the coast of Gabon in the Gulf of Guinea. They were occupied in the 1520s by the Portuguese, who used slaves as laborers on the sugar plantations. The population now consists mainly of the Afro-Portuguese descendants of these first immigrants, plus contract laborers brought from Mozambique and Cape Verde to work on cocoa plantations in the nineteenth century. Following independence in 1975, a one-party Marxist regime was imposed. For a time the islands were allied to the Soviet bloc and Russian and Cuban military advisors were brought in.

At a referendum in 1990, however, 72 percent of the people voted in favor of democratic government. Now the main concern of the government is to rebuild the country's relationship with Portugal and to secure beneficial working relationships with the EU and the USA.

An extinct volcano, São Tomé is the largest and most populous of the two main islands, some 440 km (273 miles) off the coast of Gabon. Low lying in the northeast and the southwest, it rises to Pico de São Tomé in the volcanic highlands. The island of Príncipe lies about 150 km (100 miles) to the northeast. As well as the two main islands there are also a number of rocky islets—Caroco, Pedras, Tinhosas, and Rôlas. On both São Tomé and Príncipe, streams drain to the sea from mountainous interiors, up to 70 percent of which are densely forested. The climate is hot and humid, moderated to a certain extent by the cold Benguela current that flows up Africa's western shore.

Following independence in 1975 the cocoa plantations which formed the foundation of the country's economy deteriorated as a result of mismanagement aggravated by drought. By 1987 the production of cocoa had fallen to 3,500 tonnes from an annual output of 9,000 tonnes prior to 1975. While there has been some economic recovery in recent years, São Tomé and Príncipe have had serious balance of payments problems. During the 1980s agriculture diversified into palm oil, pepper, and coffee but since then production has faltered. Deforestation and soil erosion are an increasing cause for concern. Today, São Tomé imports 90 percent of its food, all its fuel and most manufactured goods.

Fact File

OFFICIAL NAME Democratic Republic of São Tomé and Príncipe

FORM OF GOVERNMENT Republic with single legislative body (National People's Assembly)

CAPITAL São Tomé

AREA 960 sq km (371 sq miles)

TIME ZONE GMT

POPULATION 154,878

PROJECTED POPULATION 2005 187,394

POPULATION DENSITY 161.3 per sq km (417.8 per sq mile)

LIFE EXPECTANCY 64.7

INFANT MORTALITY (PER 1,000) 52.9

OFFICIAL LANGUAGE Portuguese

OTHER LANGUAGES Various creoles

LITERACY RATE 67%

RELIGIONS Roman Catholic 80%, Protestant and other 20%

ETHNIC GROUPS Predominantly mixed African–Portuguese, with various African minorities

CURRENCY Dobra

ECONOMY Mainly agriculture and fishing

GNP PER CAPITA US$350

CLIMATE Tropical, with wet season October to May

HIGHEST POINT Pico de São Tomé 2,024 m (6,640 ft)

MAP REFERENCE Pages 365, 373

Senegal

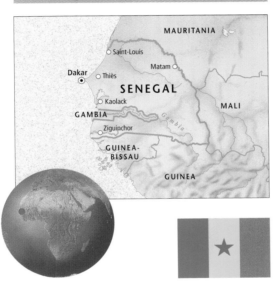

Dakar, the capital of Senegal, lies on the westernmost point of west Africa and in the seventeenth and eighteenth centuries it was a major slave-trading base. French colonial control of Senegal was established during the suppression of the slave trade in the nineteenth century. As the administrative center of the huge region of French West Africa, an effective road network was established in Dakar, plus extensive port facilities and a large civil service.

Independence from France came in 1960. Despite being a de facto one-party state for the next 10 years, Senegal avoided military and dictatorial rule, and has recently liberalized its economic and political life. The country's most serious problem is continuing armed revolt in the oil-rich southern province of Casamance, south of Gambia, a region that differs ethnically, economically, and geographically from the north.

Senegal is split by the near-enclave of Gambia and the Gambia River. To the north the land is drier, with sand dunes along the coast. Inland there are plains, savanna, and semidesert, where Fulani cattle-herders eke out an existence. South of Dakar and Cape Vert it is wetter and more fertile, with coastal mangrove swamps and forest inland. Sorghum is grown in the rainier areas of savanna bushland, while south of Gambia rice is cultivated on the floodplain of the Casamance River—the most fertile part of the country.

Peanuts have long been the foundation of Senegal's economy and are grown on half the cultivated land. Efforts are being made to diversify, and sugarcane, millet, cotton, and rice are now cultivated. Other than the recently developed oil fields in Casamance, with the promise of more offshore, natural resources are few. Though its arrangements are democratic, Senegal's ruling party has been in power since the 1950s, creating a network of patronage through the civil service, the judiciary, and the state-owned industries. Senegal receives a considerable amount of foreign aid.

Fact File

OFFICIAL NAME Republic of Senegal

FORM OF GOVERNMENT Republic with single legislative body (National Assembly)

CAPITAL Dakar

AREA 196,190 sq km (75,749 sq miles)

TIME ZONE GMT

POPULATION 9,051,930

PROJECTED POPULATION 2005 12,235,259

POPULATION DENSITY 51.2 per sq km (132.6 per sq mile)

LIFE EXPECTANCY 57.8

INFANT MORTALITY (PER 1,000) 59.8

OFFICIAL LANGUAGE French

OTHER LANGUAGES Wolof, Pulaar, Diola, Mandingo

LITERACY RATE 32.1%

RELIGIONS Muslim 92%, indigenous beliefs 6%, Christian 2% (mainly Roman Catholic)

ETHNIC GROUPS Wolof 36%, Fulani 17%, Serer 17%, Toucouleur 9%, Diola 9%, Mandingo 9%, European and Lebanese 1%, other 2%

CURRENCY CFA (Communauté Financière Africaine) franc

ECONOMY Agriculture 81%, services 13%, industry 6%

GNP PER CAPITA US$600

CLIMATE Tropical, with wet season June to October

HIGHEST POINT Unnamed location in southeast 581 m (1,906 ft)

MAP REFERENCE Page 364

Seychelles

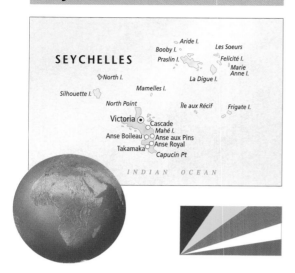

Fact File

OFFICIAL NAME Republic of Seychelles

FORM OF GOVERNMENT Republic with single legislative body (People's Assembly)

CAPITAL Victoria

AREA 455 sq km (176 sq miles)

TIME ZONE GMT + 4 hours

POPULATION 79,164

PROJECTED POPULATION 2005 82,044

POPULATION DENSITY 174 per sq km (450 per sq mile)

LIFE EXPECTANCY 71

INFANT MORTALITY (PER 1,000) 16.5

OFFICIAL LANGUAGES English, French, Creole

LITERACY RATE 88%

RELIGIONS Roman Catholic 90%, Anglican 8%, other 2%

ETHNIC GROUPS Seychellois (mixture of Asian, African, European) 93.8%, Malagasy 3.1%, Chinese 1.6%, British 1.5%

CURRENCY Seychelles rupee

ECONOMY Services 80%, agriculture 10%, industry 10%

GNP PER CAPITA US$6,620

CLIMATE Tropical, with wet season December to May

HIGHEST POINT Morne Seychellois 905 m (2,969 ft)

MAP REFERENCE Pages 372, 373

The Seychelles are a group of 4 large and 36 small granite islands, plus a scattering of about 65 coralline islands, in the Indian Ocean northeast of Madagascar. Some 98 percent of the population live on the four main islands, the great majority on tropical and mountainous Mahé. Uninhabited when occupied by the French in 1742, the Seychelles were ceded to the British at the time of the Napoleonic Wars, and became a crown colony in 1903. After independence in 1976 the islands were ruled for 15 years as a one-party socialist state, North Korean military advisors being hired to guard against attempted coups. The first open elections were held in 1993 and the previous government party won a new term in office.

The granite islands consist of a mountainous central spine—sometimes consisting of bare, eroded rock—surrounded by a flat coastal strip with dense tropical vegetation. In the areas cleared

for farming, vanilla, tobacco, tea, cinnamon and coconuts (for copra) are grown for export, along with food crops such as cassava, sweet potatoes, and bananas. Most food, however, is imported. The outer coralline islands are flat, waterless, and sparsely inhabited, having a total population of only 400. Short droughts periodically occur; though catchments collect some rainwater, there are no natural sources of supply. The Seychelles lie outside the cyclone belt, which is important for an economy depending on tourism.

The island's only natural resources are fish, copra, and cinnamon trees, which in earlier times provided a bare subsistence. Since independence in 1976, however, with the vigorous promotion of the tourist industry, per capita output has increased sevenfold. In recent years foreign investment has been encouraged in order to upgrade hotels and other services. Visitors find many attractions—the unique wildlife includes a rare giant land turtle and the colorful green sea turtle found on the coral reefs. The country's vulnerability in relying so heavily on tourism was shown during the Gulf War, when visitor numbers dropped sharply. The government is moving to reduce over-dependence on this sector by promoting farming, fishing, and small-scale manufacturing, including furniture-making, coconut-fiber rope-making, printing, and the re-export of petroleum products.

Sierra Leone

Sierra Leone's capital, Freetown, was so named when the British government settled freed slaves there in 1787. Once the freed-slave settlers became a ruling class over the Africans already living in the country, deep social divisions opened. Many settlers, and foreign missionaries, were killed in a war with the indigenous Mende in 1898.

Once a British crown colony, and independent from 1961, Sierra Leone's recent history has been marked by military coups, ethnic factionalism, and violence. Since 1992, civil war has raged in the east and the south, thousands of lives have been lost, and thousands of farms have been abandoned in the country's main grain growing areas. Liberian troops have been involved, and Libyan weapons. Child soldiers have been used by both sides.

Unlike most of west Africa, Sierra Leone is mountainous near the sea. These mountains are volcanic, and run southeast of Freetown on the Atlantic forming a thickly wooded peninsula (the Sierra Leone, or Lion Range). The peninsula interrupts a swampy coastal plain, stretching north and south, dominated by mangrove forests. Rolling savanna uplands to the north, known as the Bolilands, were once the scene of government efforts to introduce large-scale mechanized rice cultivation. Rice is also grown in the seasonally flooded riverine grasslands of the southeast, and in the swamps near Port Loko. Inland, to the northeast, the land rises to the Loma Mountains and the Tingi Hills. Rainfall on the coast is extremely high. The soils are heavily leached and weathered.

Subsistence farming dominates the agricultural sector, which employs about two-thirds of the population. Rice is the staple food crop and along with palm oil it is produced throughout Sierra Leone, except in the drier north. There, in the savanna, peanuts and cattle herding predominate. The country has substantial mineral resources, and the mining of diamonds, bauxite, and rutile or titanium ore provides essential hard currency. The economy is currently almost at a standstill because infrastructure has collapsed through neglect and both the mining and agricultural sectors have been disrupted by civil war.

Fact File

OFFICIAL NAME Republic of Sierra Leone

FORM OF GOVERNMENT Republic with single legislative body (House of Representatives)

CAPITAL Freetown

AREA 71,740 sq km (27,699 sq miles)

TIME ZONE GMT

POPULATION 5,296,651

PROJECTED POPULATION 2005 6,415,757

POPULATION DENSITY 73.8 per sq km (191.1 per sq mile)

LIFE EXPECTANCY 49.1

INFANT MORTALITY (PER 1,000) 126.2

OFFICIAL LANGUAGE English

OTHER LANGUAGES Krio, Mende, Temne

LITERACY RATE 30.3%

RELIGIONS Muslim 60%, indigenous beliefs 30%, Christian 10%

ETHNIC GROUPS 13 indigenous tribes 99%, other 1%

CURRENCY Leone

ECONOMY Agriculture 70%, services 17%, industry 13%

GNP PER CAPITA US$180

CLIMATE Tropical, with wet season April to November

HIGHEST POINT Loma Mansa 1,948 m (6,391 ft)

MAP REFERENCE Page 364

Somalia

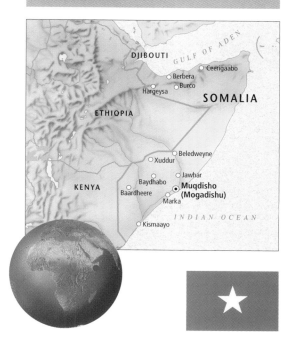

Somalia, a coastal state on the Horn of Africa, is in one respect unlike any other African country. It is the only place where the whole population feels that they are "one people"—Somali—and because of this ethnic homogeneity it has the makings of a nation state. Briefly under the control of Egypt from 1875, the region became a British protectorate in 1885. In 1889 Italy took control of the eastern coast, and from then on the country was divided into British Somaliland in the north and Italian Somaliland in the south and east. It has been independent since 1960.

The history of the people of Somalia since independence has been one of repression (under the Soviet-aligned Siyad Barre), military adventure (the invasion of the Ethiopian Ogaden), and civil war. When in 1992 an estimated 2,000 people a day were dying from war and starvation, the United Nations intervened, but its troops were unable to stop the military and civil unrest and withdrew. Anarchy and banditry now prevail. In the absence of any central authority, and without a functioning

government in Muqdisho, the northern area once known as British Somaliland seceded and proclaimed itself an independent state. Centered on the city of Hargeysa, it calls itself the Somaliland Republic. It has not been recognised internationally.

Along the northern shore facing the Gulf of Aden lies the semiarid Guban coastal plain. Behind this is a range of mountains, the Ogo Highlands, running eastward from Ethiopia to the point of the Horn itself. South of the highlands is the Haud Plateau, and beyond this the land slopes down toward the Indian Ocean. Much of Somalia has semidesert thornbush and dry savanna cover. Only in the better watered south is there enough rainfall to support meager forests and grassland. Arable farming takes place between the Rivers Jubba and Shabeelle in the south. The Shabeelle, blocked by dunes, provides water for irrigation. Bananas from this area are a major export, mainly to Italy. Rival clans fight over this important resource; some plantation work is done by women and children in slave-labor conditions guarded by armed militia.

Nomadic pastoralists form much of the population in the north. Searching for grass and water, they wander with their herds across the state boundaries between southern Djibouti, the Ogaden, and northeast Kenya. Livestock accounts for 40 percent of gross domestic product and 65 percent of export earnings. In the south, in addition to the export crop of bananas, food crops of sugar, sorghum, and maize are grown. A small industrial sector is based on the processing of food products, but the prevailing disorder has caused many facilities to be shut down.

Fact File

OFFICIAL NAME Somali Democratic Republic

FORM OF GOVERNMENT Republic; no effective central government exists at the present time

CAPITAL Muqdisho (Mogadishu)

AREA 637,660 sq km (246,200 sq miles)

TIME ZONE GMT + 3 hours

POPULATION 7,140,643

PROJECTED POPULATION 2005 8,795,258

POPULATION DENSITY 11.2 per sq km (29 per sq mile)

LIFE EXPECTANCY 46.2

INFANT MORTALITY (PER 1,000) 125.8

OFFICIAL LANGUAGE Somali

OTHER LANGUAGES Arabic, Italian, English

LITERACY RATE 24%

RELIGIONS Sunni Muslim with tiny Christian minority

ETHNIC GROUPS Somali 85%, remainder mainly Bantu with small Arab, Asian, and European minorities 15%

CURRENCY Somali shilling

ECONOMY Agriculture 76%, services 16%, industry 8%

GNP PER CAPITA Est. < US$765

CLIMATE Mainly hot and arid, with higher rainfall in the south

HIGHEST POINT Mt Shimbiris 2,416 m (7,927 ft)

MAP REFERENCE Page 367

The Seychelles nut tree (Coco de Mer) is widespread on those islands (center left). Looking toward Silhouette Island in the Seychelles (top left). A group of Somali villagers (left).

South Africa

Along the west coast, north of Cape Town, the cold Benguela current inhibits rainfall, producing the desert of the Namib. In the northeast there is dry savanna bushland. On the Mozambique border the best-known of South Africa's eight wildlife reserves, Kruger National Park, contains lions, leopards, giraffes, elephants, and hippopotamuses.

People and culture

First inhabited by San, or Bushmen, southern Africa was in the fifteenth century occupied by a wave of cattle-keeping, grain-growing Bantu peoples from the north—their modern descendants being groups such as the Xhosa and the Zulu. Then in 1652 and 1688 two groups of settlers arrived from Europe—the first Dutch, the second French Huguenot, both firmly Protestant in their faith—and established a colony in the south at Cape Town. They became known as Boers (farmers) and later as Afrikaners (after their language, Afrikaans). The British established themselves on the Cape in 1806. Over the years a population of mixed Afro-European descent emerged who became known as "Cape Coloreds." In the nineteenth century laborers from India were brought in by the British, creating yet another large and distinct ethnic community. There are also a small number of Malays.

After 1948, under the ruling Afrikaners, apartheid (apartness) laws were drafted defining how each community should associate, where each should live, whether they could intermarry, and what work they could do. The entire population was to be organized in a hierarchy of privilege, with whites at the top and blacks at the bottom. Africans were to be confined to a series of internal Black States called "homelands," which were in practice mere labor pools, since the only way people could find

Occupying the southernmost tip of the African continent, South Africa comprises a central plateau or veld, bordered to the south and east by the Drakensberg Mountains and to the north by the countries of Namibia, Botswana, Zimbabwe and Mozambique. The Independent State of Lesotho is contained within South Africa's borders. European settlement in the seventeenth century culminated in white minority rule, and a controversial policy of racial segregation was officially implemented in 1948. After 50 years of deepening crisis and international isolation as a result of its racial policies, South Africa changed course in 1990, held democratic elections in 1994, and under a new government rejoined the international community. Always the economic powerhouse of southern Africa, it is now free from sanctions and able to renew normal trading relations. The abandonment of apartheid, and the freeing of long-term political prisoner (and then president) Nelson Mandela, have had an uplifting effect on national morale and provided a chance for a fresh start. Problems currently facing the nation include discrepancies between the educational level and skills of blacks and whites; vastly different income levels; increasing

unemployment; high urban crime rates; and the ongoing conflict between Zulu groups and the ruling party, the African National Congress.

Physical features and land use

South Africa has three main geographic regions. First, there is the vast African plateau of the interior. This slopes gradually north and west to form part of the semiarid and sparsely populated Kalahari basin, while to the east it rises to elevations of 2,000 m (6,500 ft). Second, the Great Escarpment, varying in height, structure, and steepness, forms a rim around the entire plateau from the mountains of the Transvaal Drakensberg in the northeast to Namibia in the northwest. Its highest peaks are in the Drakensberg along the Lesotho border. The third region consists of the narrow, fertile strips of land along the peripheral coastal plains.

Agricultural products include maize (a staple for many African farmers); apples, pears, stone fruit, grapes, and wine from Eastern Cape Province; wheat from Western Cape Province; and sugarcane from coastal KwaZulu-Natal. On the grasslands of the plateau large-scale pastoralism produces wool, mohair, skins, and meat. South Africa is geologically ancient—only a few superficial strata are less than 600 million years old. In the 1880s rocks of the Witwatersrand were found to contain gold and diamonds, and since then gold and diamond mining has been the basis of South Africa's national wealth.

Timeline							
	25,000 BP Rock paintings on shelters show ceremonial dancers and animals, like antelope, which were hunted for food	4–500 AD Bantu people arrive from East Africa to find grazing for sheep and cattle and to plant crops. Displace Khoisan hunter-gatherers	1100 Different language groups emerge, such as the Xhosa and the Zulu	1615 British settlement at Table Bay lasts only a few years	1652 Dutch East India Co. garrison at site of Cape Town supplies Dutch fleet; settlers granted land at Liesbeek River in 1657	1713 Khoikhoi pastoralists displaced by "trekboer" settlers in search of grazing land; numerous San people die of smallpox
3 MYA Cave-dwelling Australopithecines in what is now Cape Province and Gauteng, kill animals for meat and eat plants	120,000 BP "Modern" humans inhabit cave near Port Elizabeth; they eat shellfish, tortoises, and bird's eggs	c.2000 BC Kalahari San (bushmen) inhabit the Kalahari Desert herding animals	c.1000 Urban centers established; bone and ivory crafts; products traded between groups	1488 First Portuguese vessels arrive at the Cape of Good Hope	1657 First slaves brought to the Cape from India, Indonesia, and West Africa as agricultural labor and to act as herders	1795–1802 British occupy Cape, a vital trade route supply post prior to opening of Suez Canal; more British settlers arrive

employment was by leaving home and traveling to the South African mines. The impracticality, unreality, and injustice of the system aroused widespread international condemnation. The misery it created led to ongoing violent resistance.

Economy and resources

Although both the Bantu and the first Europeans to colonize South Africa were farming people, and agriculture formed the foundation of the economy for hundreds of years, during the nineteenth century gold and diamonds were the attractions that drew a new wave of settlers. Today, gold and precious stones still make up half the country's total exports, and over the last 100 years almost half the world's gold has come from South African mines. Other important minerals include asbestos, nickel, vanadium, and uranium (which can

sometimes be found in old gold mines). In addition, South Africa is the world's largest producer of manganese, platinum, and chromium.

Energy conservation is a vital concern to the country as no petroleum deposits have yet been found. During the long period of South Africa's isolation and of trade boycotts, the state corporation Sasol extracted oil from coal. Though this is a expensive process, extensive deposits of coal make this a feasible supplementary supply. Many white South Africans enjoy a standard of living that is equal to the highest in the world. The challenge for the government in the next century will be to provide the circumstances and conditions in which less privileged social groups can have a share of the wealth. This will not be an easy task: at present there are jobs for less than 5 percent of the 300,000 workers who enter the labor force each year.

Fact File

OFFICIAL NAME Republic of South Africa

FORM OF GOVERNMENT Republic with two legislative bodies (Senate and National Assembly)

CAPITAL Pretoria (administrative); Cape Town (legislative); Bloemfontein (judicial)

AREA 1,219,912 sq km (471,008 sq miles)

TIME ZONE GMT + 2 hours

POPULATION 43,426,386

PROJECTED POPULATION 2005 46,220,919

POPULATION DENSITY 35.6 per sq km (92.2 per sq mile)

LIFE EXPECTANCY 54.8

INFANT MORTALITY (PER 1,000) 52

OFFICIAL LANGUAGES Afrikaans, English, Ndebele, Pedi, Sotho, Swazi, Tsonga, Tswana, Venda, Xhosa, Zulu

OTHER LANGUAGES Indigenous languages, Hindi, Urdu, Gujarati, Tamil

LITERACY RATE 81.4%

RELIGIONS Christian (most Europeans and people of mixed origin and about 60% of Africans) 68%, Hindu (60% of Indians) 2%, Muslim 2%, indigenous beliefs 28%

ETHNIC GROUPS Indigenous 75.2%, European 13.6%, mixed 8.6%, Indian 2.6%

CURRENCY Rand

ECONOMY Services 62%, industry 24%, agriculture 14%

GNP PER CAPITA US$3,160

CLIMATE Mainly semiarid; subtropical on southeast coast

HIGHEST POINT Thabana-Ntlenyana 3,482 m (11,424 ft)

MAP REFERENCE Pages 370–71

High-rise buildings in Pretoria (far left). An elephant browsing in Kruger National Park (below left). The Hexrivier Pass (left). The seaside town of Muizenberg (below).

PROVINCES

Eastern Cape • Free State • Gauteng • KwaZulu-Natal • Mpumalanga • Northern Province • Northern Cape • North West • Western Cape

c.1800 Zulu nation founded in today's KwaZulu-Natal, forcing Shoshangane clan into Swaziland and Mzilikazi clan into Zimbabwe

1836–38 10,000 Boer settlers unhappy with British rule in Cape set out on Great Trek to seek new land in Natal and Orange River areas

1870 Gold rush in the Kimberley area and discovery of diamonds transform the economic base from agriculture to mining

1899 Gold-mining industry employs 110,000 workers; almost 100,000 are African laborers

1912 The African National Congress (ANC) founded by group of black Africans interested in obtaining political rights

1948 National Party passes law restricting parliamentary representation to whites; "apartheid" official in 1950

1962 Nelson Mandela and other leading members of the ANC are imprisoned

1990 Mandela freed; apartheid abolished (1991); population 37 million (76% black, 13% white, 9% mixed race, 2% Asian)

1860 Laborers from India are imported by Natal farmers to work on farms and plantations

1880–81 British fail to bring Boer republics (Orange Free State, Transvaal) into federation—British defeat in First Boer War

1899–1902 British defeat the Boers (Afrikaners) in Second Boer War

1931 South Africa granted independence by Britain as a member of the Commonwealth

1961 South Africa leaves Commonwealth and becomes a Republic, without asking non-whites

1976 Black African protest over compulsory Afrikaans language lessons results in violence and the loss of 600 lives

1994 Mandela elected president in first non-racial general election—pronounces the new South Africa a "Rainbow Republic"

Sudan

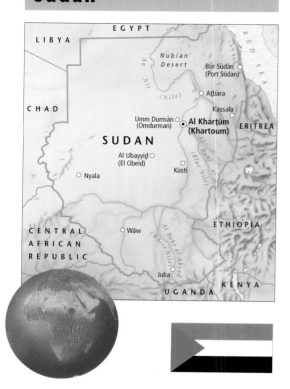

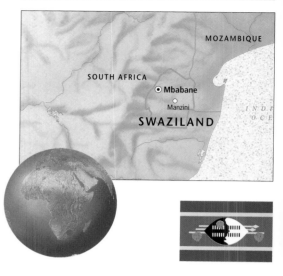

Swaziland

South of Egypt, Sudan is Africa's largest country, and the pathway to the headwaters of the Nile. (An Nīl). It is also one of Africa's most divided countries. Known in Ancient Egypt as Nubia, its northern region came under Islamic Arab control in the fourteenth century, and Egyptian and British rule in the nineteenth. With some 570 distinct ethnic groups and over 100 languages, it has been difficult to form Sudan into a modern state.

Since achieving independence from Egypt and Britain in 1956, Sudan has seen military rule, coups, and civil conflict for all but 10 of the next 40 years. The main cause is the determination of the Muslim north to impose Arab and Islamic values on the varied African, animist, and Christian peoples of the south. Strict sharia (Muslim) law has been proclaimed but is widely ignored. At present the government is conducting a "war of annihilation" against the 1.5 million Nuba people. Over half a million people have died in the past 12 years, the miseries of the ethnic Africans being compounded by famine, displacement, and the enslavement of women and children. One task of relief workers has been to purchase the freedom of slaves.

In northern Sudan the rocky Sahara Desert stretches westward to become a waste of sand dunes, the land rising to 3,071 m (10,075 ft) at the Darfur Massif toward the border with Chad. In the east the Red Sea Mountains rise 2,000 m (6,500 ft) above a narrow coastal plain. Most people live near the south–north flowing Nile (An Nīl), a river that divides into two streams at Khartoum. From here the source of the Blue Nile (Al Bahr al Azraq) can be traced southeast to the Ethiopian border and Lake Tana. The White Nile (Al Bahr al Abyad) runs southwards into the vast marshland of the Sudd (where dense, floating vegetation makes navigation difficult), then further upstream to Uganda and its headwaters in Lake Albert.

Crumbling pyramids in the desert at Meroë in the Sudan (right). A typical kraal (village) in Swaziland (top right). A boy poling a dugout canoe in Tanzania (top, far right).

About two-thirds of Sudan's workforce are farmers. There is a heavy emphasis on growing cotton, at the expense of food crops, as it accounts for 24 percent of export revenue. Food crops include sorghum (the staple) along with millet, wheat, barley, and peanuts. Declining rainfall and huge displacements of the rural population as a result of war have played havoc with production in recent years. The socialist government is resisting reform: in 1990 the IMF declared Sudan noncooperative because of nonpayment of debts. At present aid comes mainly from Iran. Natural resources include copper, chromium ore, zinc, tungsten, mica, silver, and gold. Some gold is mined.

Fact File

OFFICIAL NAME	Republic of the Sudan
FORM OF GOVERNMENT	Military regime with single transitional legislative body (Provisional National Assembly)
CAPITAL	Al Kharţūm (Khartoum)
AREA	2,505,810 sq km (967,493 sq miles)
TIME ZONE	GMT + 2 hours
POPULATION	34,475,690
PROJECTED POPULATION 2005	40,899,171
POPULATION DENSITY	13.8 per sq km (35.7 per sq mile)
LIFE EXPECTANCY	56.4
INFANT MORTALITY (PER 1,000)	70.9
OFFICIAL LANGUAGE	Arabic
OTHER LANGUAGES	Nubian, Ta Bedawie, English, indigenous languages
LITERACY RATE	44.8%
RELIGIONS	Sunni Muslim 70%, indigenous beliefs 25%, Christian 5%
ETHNIC GROUPS	African 52%, Arab 39%, Beja 6%, other 3%
CURRENCY	Sudanese pound
ECONOMY	Agriculture 65%, services 31%, industry 4%
GNP PER CAPITA	US$423
CLIMATE	North mainly arid; south tropical, with wet season April to October
HIGHEST POINT	Mt Kinyeti 3,187 m (10,456 ft)
MAP REFERENCE	Pages 362–63, 366–67

Swaziland is a tiny landlocked kingdom almost surrounded by South Africa. Across its eastern border it is about 130 km (80 miles) from the Indian Ocean and the Mozambique port of Maputo. Enjoying relative stability and prosperity, popular among South African tourists for its wildlife reserves, mountain scenery, and casinos, the kingdom's hereditary Bantu monarchy is now being pressed to modernize and accept constitutional reforms including democracy and political opposition.

The country owes its autonomy to events in the mid-nineteenth century. The Swazi were then facing Zulu expansion, as well as pressure from Boer farmers. They sought and received British protection, and from 1906 Swaziland was administered by the high commissioner for Basutoland (now Lesotho), Bechuanaland (now Botswana), and Swaziland. Full independence came in 1968.

The landscape descends in three steps from west to east. The high veld in the west is mountainous with a temperate climate, and supports grasslands, and plantations of pine and eucalyptus. Mixed farming takes place in the middle veld, the most populous area, where black Swazi subsistence farmers grow maize, sorghum, and peanuts. Cash crops such as sugarcane, citrus fruits, and tobacco are produced by white-run

agribusinesses and by Swazi on resettlement schemes. Livestock are raised on the low veld.

Swaziland's economy is relatively diversified and buoyant: during the 1980s it grew at a rate of 4.5 percent a year. Relaxed investment rules have ensured a supply of development capital, and project aid has been forthcoming from a number of donors. Sugar and forestry products are the main earners of hard currency, and are produced by white residents on large plantations. The country has small deposits of gold and diamonds. Mining was once important, but is now in decline. The high-grade iron ore deposits were depleted by 1978 and health concerns have cut the demand for asbestos. Remittances from workers in South Africa provide up to 20 percent of household income. The main threat to the Swazi way of life comes from land pressure due to high population growth. Family planning is being promoted.

Fact File

OFFICIAL NAME Kingdom of Swaziland

FORM OF GOVERNMENT Monarchy with two legislative bodies (Senate and House of Assembly)

CAPITAL Mbabane

AREA 17,360 sq km (6,703 sq miles)

TIME ZONE GMT + 2 hours

POPULATION 985,335

PROJECTED POPULATION 2005 1,101,082

POPULATION DENSITY 56.8 per sq km (147 per sq mile)

LIFE EXPECTANCY 57.3

INFANT MORTALITY (PER 1,000) 101.9

OFFICIAL LANGUAGES English, Swazi

OTHER LANGUAGES Indigenous languages

LITERACY RATE 75.2%

RELIGIONS Christian 60%, indigenous beliefs 40%

ETHNIC GROUPS Indigenous 97%, European 3%

CURRENCY Lilangeni

ECONOMY Agriculture 60%, industry and services 40%

GNP PER CAPITA US$1,170

CLIMATE Temperate, with wet season November to March

HIGHEST POINT Emlembe Peak 1,862 m (6,109 ft)

MAP REFERENCE Page 371

Tanzania

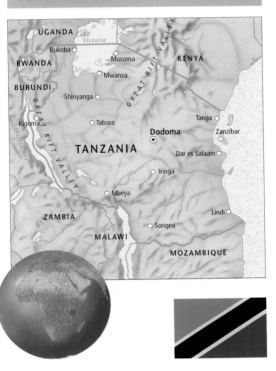

With Africa's highest mountain (Kilimanjaro), and Serengeti National Park, Tanzania is well known to the outside world. It also the home of some of East Africa's most ancient human remains, those found at Olduvai Gorge dating back 2 million years. From the eighth century AD onward, the country's coastal region was subject to Islamic influence from Arab traders who dealt in slaves and ivory. In the nineteenth century both British and German settlers arrived.

Tanzania won independence from England in 1961, becoming a de facto one-party state under Julius Nyerere, whose version of African socialism prevailed until he retired in 1985. Opposition parties were allowed in 1992. An uprising by pro-Tanzanian forces violently incorporated the Muslim island of Zanzibar in 1964: unreconciled Islamic interests on the island represent a potential flashpoint.

From the coast, Tanzania stretches across a plateau averaging about 1,000 m (3,000 ft) to the Rift Valley Lakes of Malawi (Lake Nyasa) and Tanganyika. The eastern Rift Valley, with the alkaline Lake Natron, and Lakes Eyasi and Manyara, divides the Northern Highlands. These are dominated by Mt Kilimanjaro near the Kenyan border. The Southern Highlands overlook Lake Malawi (Lake

Nyasa). Semiarid conditions in the north and tsetse fly in the west–central areas mean that people mainly live on the country's margins. Attempts to farm the savanna woodland have failed.

Though repressive, Nyerere's government achieved relatively high levels of education and welfare, but the economy languished as a result of falling commodity prices abroad and inefficient and corrupt state corporations at home. Over 80 percent of the workforce live off the land, producing cash crops such as coffee, tea, sisal, cotton, and pyrethrum, along with food crops of maize, wheat, cassava, and bananas. Since 1985 there has been some liberalization of the market, along with an effort to boost tourism and a substantial increase in gold production. Reforms have increased private sector growth and investment.

Fact File

OFFICIAL NAME United Republic of Tanzania

FORM OF GOVERNMENT Republic with single legislative body (National Assembly)

CAPITAL Dodoma

AREA 945,090 sq km (364,899 sq miles)

TIME ZONE GMT + 3 hours

POPULATION 31,270,820

PROJECTED POPULATION 2005 35,686,963

POPULATION DENSITY 33.1 per sq km (85.7 per sq mile)

LIFE EXPECTANCY 46.2

INFANT MORTALITY (PER 1,000) 95.3

OFFICIAL LANGUAGES Swahili, English

OTHER LANGUAGES Arabic, indigenous languages

LITERACY RATE 66.8%

RELIGIONS Mainland: Christian 45%, Muslim 35%, indigenous beliefs 20%; Zanzibar: Muslim 99%, other 1%

ETHNIC GROUPS Indigenous 99%, other 1%

CURRENCY Tanzanian shilling

ECONOMY Agriculture 85%, services 10%, industry 5%

GNP PER CAPITA US$120

CLIMATE Mainly tropical; hot and humid along coast, drier inland, cooler in mountains

HIGHEST POINT Mt Kilimanjaro 5,895 m (19,340 ft)

MAP REFERENCE Page 369

Africa

Togo

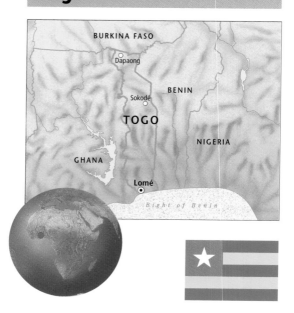

Togo is a small west African country squeezed between Ghana and Benin. It was colonized by Germany in 1884, later becoming French Togoland. It became independent in 1960. A deep social division exists between the Kabye people in the north and the majority Ewe of the south. The Ewe are generally better educated, and live in the more developed part of the country, but have no say in government. This is run by Africa's longest serving president, General Eyadema, a Kabye who has held this position since his coup in 1967. The first multi-party elections took place in 1993.

Most people live on the coast and the adjacent plains. Inland a mountain chain crosses the country north to south. The far northwest is mainly granite tableland. Roads connect the northern savanna with the railhead of Blitta, and the phosphate mining area with its port of Kpeme. The River Oti crosses in the northwest between Burkina Faso and Ghana; the River Mono drains south into the Gulf of Guinea. About a quarter of the land is arable. The most fertile land—28 percent of the country—is forested; here slash-and-burn cultivation occurs.

Togo depends on subsistence agriculture. Food crops include yams, cassava, maize, beans, rice, and sorghum. The main export crops are coffee, cocoa, and cotton, which together generate about 30 percent of earnings. Cattle, sheep, and pigs are raised in the north. The annual fish catch is about 14,000 tonnes. Togo is normally self-sufficient in food, though drought has recently cut productivity, and the deforestation caused by slash-and-burn agriculture is causing concern. Phosphate mining is the most important industrial activity.

Fact File

OFFICIAL NAME Republic of Togo

FORM OF GOVERNMENT Republic with single legislative body (National Assembly)

CAPITAL Lomé

AREA 56,790 sq km (21,927 sq miles)

TIME ZONE GMT

POPULATION 5,081,413

PROJECTED POPULATION 2005 6,254,894

POPULATION DENSITY 89.5 per sq km (231.8 per sq mile)

LIFE EXPECTANCY 59.3

INFANT MORTALITY (PER 1,000) 77.6

OFFICIAL LANGUAGE French

OTHER LANGUAGES Ewe, Mina, Dagomba, Kabye

LITERACY RATE 50.4%

RELIGIONS Indigenous beliefs 70%, Christian 20%, Muslim 10%

ETHNIC GROUPS Indigenous (Ewe, Mina, and Kabye largest of 37 tribes) 99%, European and Syrian–Lebanese 1%

CURRENCY CFA (Communauté Financière Africaine) franc

ECONOMY Agriculture 68%, services 28%, industry 4%

GNP PER CAPITA US$310

CLIMATE Tropical, with wet seasons Mar to July and Oct to Nov; semiarid in north, with wet season Apr to July

HIGHEST POINT Pic Baumann 986 m (3,235 ft)

MAP REFERENCE Page 364

Tunisia

Tunisia has a long history. Located in north Africa, across from Sicily, it was founded by Phoenician sailors 3,000 years ago, became famous as the Carthage of Queen Dido, and fell to the Romans in 146 BC. Arab conquest brought Islam to the region in the seventh century AD.

In modern times control of Tunisia was disputed by Italy, England, and France before it became a French protectorate in 1883. Ruled since independence in 1956 as a de facto one-party state, Tunisia held its first multi-party elections in 1994 (the government claiming 99.9 percent of the vote). Tunisia is a relatively prosperous country, strongly influenced by French and European culture, with a record of modest but steady economic growth. While Islamic fundamentalism is on the rise, women are treated with greater equality in Tunisia than elsewhere in the Arab world.

The eastern end of the Atlas Mountains juts across the border from Algeria in the north. A mountainous plateau called the Dorsale extends northeast, sloping down to the coastal plains. Parallel to the Mediterranean Sea in the extreme northwest, the Kroumirie Mountains, covered with cork oaks, shelter the fertile valley of the Majardah River as it flows down from the Dorsale. Harnessed for hydroelectric power, this enters the sea near Tūnis across broad alluvial lowlands used for growing a wide variety of crops, some extensively irrigated: wheat and barley, olives, sugar beet, citrus fruits, grapes, and vegetables. South of the mountains a dry expanse of plateau-steppe gives way to a series of salt lakes, the largest, Shaṭṭ al Jarīd, extending halfway across the country. The large remaining area to the south is desert.

Tunisia has a diverse economy. Agriculture is the main employer, but in recent years it has declined in importance as an revenue earner relative to mineral and petroleum exports. Most industrial production is based on agricultural and mining products. Real growth averaged 4.2 percent from 1991 to 1995, with moderate inflation. Growth in tourism has been a key factor.

Traditional houses in Togo (left). Workmen taking a break in Tunisia (above left). The Ruwenzoris in western Uganda, Africa's highest range of mountains (right).

Africa

Since the 1960s Tunisia has been a popular destination for European tourists, drawn by winter sunshine, beaches, and Roman remains. In recent times there have been almost 2 million visitors per year, with tourism employing 200,000 people, but the activities of Islamic militants have had a dampening effect.

Fact File

OFFICIAL NAME Republic of Tunisia

FORM OF GOVERNMENT Republic with single legislative body (Chamber of Deputies)

CAPITAL Tūnis

AREA 163,610 sq km (63,170 sq miles)

TIME ZONE GMT + 1 hour

POPULATION 9,513,603

PROJECTED POPULATION 2005 10,302,595

POPULATION DENSITY 58.5 per sq km (151.5 per sq mile)

LIFE EXPECTANCY 73.4

INFANT MORTALITY (PER 1,000) 31.4

OFFICIAL LANGUAGE Arabic

OTHER LANGUAGE French

LITERACY RATE 65.2%

RELIGIONS Muslim 98%, Christian 1%, Jewish 1%

ETHNIC GROUPS Arab–Berber 98%, European 1%, Jewish 1%

CURRENCY Dinar

ECONOMY Agriculture 48%, services 42%, industry 10%

GNP PER CAPITA US$1,820

CLIMATE Temperate in north, with mild, rainy winters and hot, dry summers; desert in south

HIGHEST POINT Jabal ash Sha'nabī 1,544 m (5,065 ft)

MAP REFERENCE Page 361

Uganda

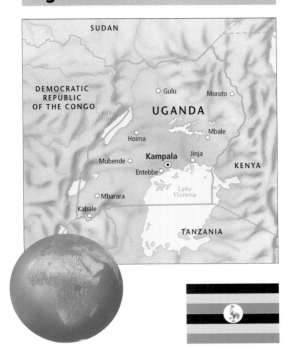

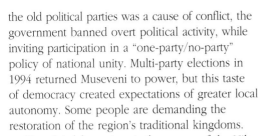

Extending north from Africa's largest body of water, Lake Victoria, the east African state of Uganda is a country of lakes and marshland. With a mild climate and varied resources—from fertile soil to freshwater fish to copper—it was once called "the pearl of Africa." After independence in 1962, however, its people suffered two decades of civil war, military coups, atrocities, and massacres, the worst period being the ten years under Idi Amin. It is estimated that between 1966 and Yoweri Museveni's takeover in 1986 more than half a million Ugandan inhabitants were killed.

The Museveni regime has overseen a return to peace and prosperity. Because the tribal basis of the old political parties was a cause of conflict, the government banned overt political activity, while inviting participation in a "one-party/no-party" policy of national unity. Multi-party elections in 1994 returned Museveni to power, but this taste of democracy created expectations of greater local autonomy. Some people are demanding the restoration of the region's traditional kingdoms.

Uganda's lake system is the source of the Nile. The pattern of lakes originates in the tilting and faulting of the Rift Valley, with the Ruwenzori Range on the western side of the country and the extinct volcano of Mt Elgon to the east. North of the lakes lies a savanna of trees and grassland, where farmers grow millet and sorghum for food, with cotton and tobacco as cash crops. Certain areas where cattle herding is impossible because of tsetse fly have been designated wildlife parks. Desert nomads live in arid Karamoja still further north. Coffee, tea, and sugarcane are grown in the south, which is the most fertile region and has the highest rainfall. This is the most densely settled part of the country, and is where the industrial center of Jinja is located, not far from Kampala, near the large Owen Falls hydroelectric plant.

Agriculture is the basis of the economy, with coffee the main export. Since 1986 the government has been engaged in raising producer prices for export crops, increasing prices for petroleum products (all oil must be imported), and raising civil service wages. Railways are being rebuilt. With the return of prosperity and public order, Indo-Ugandan entrepreneurs (expelled by the Obote and Amin regimes) are beginning to return from exile. The mining of gold and cobalt in the Ruwenzori region is also expected to resume.

Fact File

OFFICIAL NAME Republic of Uganda

FORM OF GOVERNMENT Republic with single legislative body (National Assembly)

CAPITAL Kampala

AREA 236,040 sq km (91,135 sq miles)

TIME ZONE GMT + 3 hours

POPULATION 21,470,864

PROJECTED POPULATION 2005 24,157,273

POPULATION DENSITY 91 per sq km (235.6 per sq mile)

LIFE EXPECTANCY 38.6

INFANT MORTALITY (PER 1,000) 96.5

OFFICIAL LANGUAGE English

OTHER LANGUAGES Luganda, Swahili, Bantu and Nilotic languages

LITERACY RATE 61.1%

RELIGIONS Roman Catholic 33%, Protestant 33%, indigenous beliefs 18%, Muslim 16%

ETHNIC GROUPS Indigenous tribal groups 99% (mainly Ganda, Teso, Nkole, Nyoro, Soga), other 1%

CURRENCY Ugandan shilling

ECONOMY Agriculture 86%, services 10%, industry 4%

GNP PER CAPITA US$240

CLIMATE Tropical, with two wet seasons March to May and September to November; semiarid in northeast

HIGHEST POINT Mt Stanley 5,110 m (16,765 ft)

MAP REFERENCE Page 366

Zambia

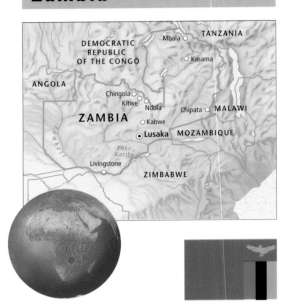

Fact File

OFFICIAL NAME	Republic of Zambia
FORM OF GOVERNMENT	Republic with single legislative body (National Assembly)
CAPITAL	Lusaka
AREA	752,610 sq km (290,583 sq miles)
TIME ZONE	GMT + 2 hours
POPULATION	9,663,535
PROJECTED POPULATION 2005	10,972,136
POPULATION DENSITY	12.8 per sq km (33.1 per sq mile)
LIFE EXPECTANCY	37
INFANT MORTALITY (PER 1,000)	91.9
OFFICIAL LANGUAGE	English
OTHER LANGUAGES	About 70 indigenous languages including Bemba, Kaonda, Lozi, Lunda, Luvale, Nyanja, Tonga
LITERACY RATE	76.6%
RELIGIONS	Protestant 84%, Hindu 35%, Roman Catholic 26%, other including Muslim, indigenous beliefs 5%
ETHNIC GROUPS	Indigenous 98.7%, European 1.1%, other 0.2%
CURRENCY	Kwacha
ECONOMY	Agriculture 82%, services 10%, industry 8%
GNP PER CAPITA	US$400
CLIMATE	Tropical, with three seasons: cool and dry May to August, hot and dry August to November, wet December to April
HIGHEST POINT	Mafinga Hills 2,301 m (7,549 ft)
MAP REFERENCE	Pages 368–69, 370–71

Zambia is a landlocked country in south-central Africa. It stretches from Victoria Falls in the south to Lake Tanganyika in the north, and is one of the world's major copper producers. Ancestral branches of the Zambian Tonga first entered the area in the eighth century AD, but other African groups now living there are more recent arrivals—the Ngoni and Kololo came as fugitives from Zulu aggression in 1835. Formerly a British colony, and once known as Northern Rhodesia, Zambia became independent in 1964. From that year it was ruled for more than a quarter of a century by President Kaunda, who nationalized commerce and industry and built a one-party socialist state. In 1991, economic decline and political agitation led to Zambia's first free elections. Kaunda was defeated, but recovery from his economic and political legacy may take time.

A wide expanse of high plateau broken by scattered mountains and valleys, Zambia is drained by the Zambeze in the west and south, where the river forms a boundary with Zimbabwe and Namibia. Below Victoria Falls the Zambeze is dammed at the Kariba Gorge to form one of the largest artificial lakes in the world, Lake Kariba. Power from the Lake Kariba hydroelectric station is shared with Zimbabwe. Another major river, the Luangwa, runs southwest from the Malawi border down a broad rift valley to join the Zambeze at the frontier of Mozambique.

Compared with its neighbors, Zambia has a high ratio of urban dwellers who are dependent on the rural sector for food. Commercial farming of maize in the central districts, and other food crops such as sorghum and rice, is proving insufficient to meet their needs. This situation has been aggravated both by drought and the phasing out of agricultural subsidies.

Zambia is dependent on copper production, which accounts for over 80 percent of export earnings. Production is down, however, and so are world copper prices, which is intensifying the

difficulties caused by high inflation and shrinking internal food supplies. In the post-Kaunda years there has been some attempt at privatization and budgetary reform, but this has produced little improvement. In 1995 four of Zambia's 20 banks failed. Most export earnings go toward paying off the 7 billion dollar external debt—itself a product to some extent of bureaucratic misuse of funds.

African wildlife

Nowhere on earth is there anything to equal the variety of African wildlife, much of it still to be seen in a natural setting. There are 90 species of hoofed mammal alone, including a huge variety of antelope, from the giant eland to the swift impala. Africa has the world's fastest animal, the cheetah, and also the world's largest land animal, the African elephant. In the giraffe it has the tallest animal in the world, while Africa's chimpanzees and gorillas represent families of primates closer to *Homo sapiens* than any others.

The future welfare of African wildlife is a major international concern. Today, many animals only survive in the many national parks throughout the continent, the oldest and best-known being Kruger National Park in South Africa. Kenya's parks include the 20,000 sq km (8,000 sq mile) expanse of Tsavo, one of the biggest. Tanzania's Serengeti National Park has unrivaled herds of antelope and the migratory movements of wildebeest amid lions, leopards, and other predators—not to mention crocodiles in the rivers—provide a glimpse of life on the grasslands of east Africa as it has been for thousands of years.

Only one large African mammal is known to have become extinct in historical times: this is an antelope called the blaubok. However, there were so few white rhinoceros at the end of the nineteenth century that they were thought to be extinct. Then a few were discovered in the South African province of Natal, and as a result of careful protection in South African national parks their numbers had grown to 6,375 by 1994. Outside South Africa very few white rhinoceros have survived: there may be no more than 80 in Kenya. A number of other animals are endangered, including the critically endangered mountain gorillas found in the Democratic Republic of the Congo, Uganda, and Rwanda.

In the early twentieth century professional hunters from Europe and America depleted numbers of animals such as lion, rhino, and buffalo. Today, the main threat comes from Africans themselves. Pastoral people kill wildlife because antelope compete for grassland with their cattle. Many mountain gorillas died during the civil wars in Rwanda in the 1990s. Most killing in Kenya and Tanzania is done by poachers seeking decorative skins, ivory, and rhino horn. A 2 kg (4 lb) rhino horn sells for up to US$122,000 in Asia, where in powdered form it is valued as an aphrodisiac. It is estimated that in the last two decades 40,000 rhinos have been killed for their horns.

The management of wild animal populations is not easy. After policies designed to ensure the survival of elephants were followed in Tsavo National Park, herds grew until there are now too many elephants for the land to support. This is damaging the habitat of other native species.

Africa

The Round House, one of the Great Ruins in Zimbabwe, built by Bantu peoples (left). Zimbabwean dancers in masks and traditional dress (above). The massive Victoria Falls on the Zambeze River in Zimbabwe (below).

Zimbabwe

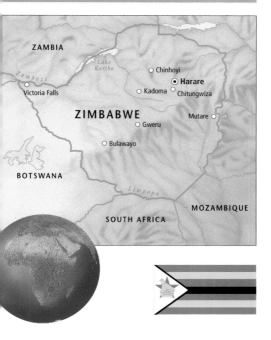

Zimbabwe is a landlocked country south of Zambia. Zimbabwe means "house of the chief" in the Shona language and refers to what are known as the Great Ruins, built by Bantu peoples in the country's south and thought to date from the ninth century AD. The country's two main tribes today, the minority Ndebele (popularly known as Matabele) and the majority Shona, arrived as nineteenth-century fugitives from the warlike expansion of the Zulus under King Shaka.

British settlement began in the 1890s, and there were 280,000 whites in the country in 1965 when their leader, Ian Smith, declared independence from the UK. African guerrilla action to overthrow Smith led to black majority rule in 1980. Since then the government has been led by Robert Mugabe, a Shona. Though he renounced Marxism–Leninism in 1991, and market reforms are on the agenda, during the 1990s Zimbabwe has edged closer to being a de facto one-party state.

Some 25 percent of the country consists of a broad mountainous ridge known as the high veld, which crosses the country southwest to northeast. On the northeastern Mozambique border this climbs to the peak of Inyangani. The rolling plateaus of the middle veld fall gently away north and south of this central upland, reaching the riverine low veld regions near the Limpopo River in the south and the Zambeze in the north. On the northern border the Zambeze plunges over Victoria Falls into a number of gorges. The falls, with Lake Kariba further downriver, along with several national parks, are among Zimbabwe's principal tourist attractions. Almost 40 percent of electricity needs are met by hydroelectric power, much of it from the Kariba Dam facility shared with Zambia.

Zimbabwe's near self-sufficiency in food is a by-product of the trade boycotts and economic isolation imposed on the white minority regime of Ian Smith after 1965. This forced both agriculture and manufacturing to diversify. African farms are still mainly small-scale subsistence operations, growing maize, cassava, and wheat. Large-scale white-owned enterprises produce most of the cash crops such as tobacco, cotton, and sugarcane, and earn much of agriculture's 35 percent share of national export revenue. Zimbabwe's mineral resources include coal, chromium, asbestos, gold, nickel, copper, iron, vanadium, lithium, tin, and platinum. Mining employs only 5 percent of the workforce, but minerals and metals account for about 40 percent of exports.

Fact File

OFFICIAL NAME Republic of Zimbabwe

FORM OF GOVERNMENT Republic with single legislative body (Parliament)

CAPITAL Harare

AREA 390,580 sq km (150,803 sq miles)

TIME ZONE GMT + 2 hours

POPULATION 11,163,160

PROJECTED POPULATION 2005 11,703,270

POPULATION DENSITY 28.6 per sq km (74 per sq mile)

LIFE EXPECTANCY 58

INFANT MORTALITY (PER 1,000) 61.2

OFFICIAL LANGUAGE English

OTHER LANGUAGES Shona, Ndebele

LITERACY RATE 84.7%

RELIGIONS Mixed Christian–indigenous beliefs 50%, Christian 25%, indigenous beliefs 24%, Muslim and other 1%

ETHNIC GROUPS Indigenous 98% (Shona 71%, Ndebele 16%, other 11%), European 1%, other 1%

CURRENCY Zimbabwean dollar

ECONOMY Agriculture 65%, services 29%, industry 6%

GNP PER CAPITA US$540

CLIMATE Tropical, moderated by altitude; wet season November to March

HIGHEST POINT Inyangani 2,592 m (8,504 ft)

MAP REFERENCE Page 371

Africa

Dependencies in Africa

Mayotte

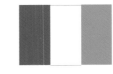

Fact File

OFFICIAL NAME Territorial Collectivity of Mayotte

FORM OF GOVERNMENT Territorial collectivity of France

CAPITAL Mamoudzou

AREA 375 sq km (145 sq miles)

TIME ZONE GMT + 3 hours

POPULATION 112,863

LIFE EXPECTANCY 60

INFANT MORTALITY (PER 1,000) 69.1

LITERACY RATE Not available

CURRENCY French franc

ECONOMY Mainly agriculture and fishing

CLIMATE Tropical, with wet season November to May

MAP REFERENCE Page 372

Mayotte is a small island at the northern end of the Mozambique Channel, 34 km (21 miles) long, between Madagascar and the mainland. It is the easternmost of the four large islands of the Comoros group (a group first visited by Europeans ships in the sixteenth century) and was the first to be ceded to France in 1841. When, in the 1974 referendum, the other islands chose to become the Republic of the Comoros, Mayotte decided to become a territorial collectivity of France. Volcanic in origin, Mayotte rises to 660 m (2,165 ft) at its highest point. The people are of African, Arab, and Madagascan descent. Agricultural products include coconuts, cocoa, and spices.

Réunion

Réunion is the largest of the Mascarene Islands which lie southwest of Mauritius and east of Madagascar. A fertile plain surrounds Réunion's rugged and mountainous interior. One of two volcanic peaks, Piton des Neiges rises to 3,069 m (10,069 ft) and is sporadically active. Plentiful rainfall comes with the winter trade winds. On the intensively cultivated lowlands there are large sugarcane plantations which provide 75 percent of exports and are the island's only significant industry. Vanilla, perfume oils, and tea also produce revenue, while vegetables and maize are grown for local consumption. Tourism is growing, but unemployment is high. The population is divided over continued association with France, which uses Réunion as its main military base in the area.

The small, uninhabited islands of Bassas da India, Europa, Glorieuses, Île Juan de Nova, and Tromelin are associated dependencies.

Fact File

OFFICIAL NAME Department of Réunion

FORM OF GOVERNMENT Overseas department of France

CAPITAL Saint-Denis

AREA 2,510 sq km (969 sq miles)

TIME ZONE GMT + 4 hours

POPULATION 717,723

LIFE EXPECTANCY 75.7

INFANT MORTALITY (PER 1,000) 6.9

LITERACY RATE 78.6%

CURRENCY French franc

ECONOMY Services 49%, agriculture 30%, industry 21%

CLIMATE Tropical; cool and dry May to November, hot and rainy November to April

MAP REFERENCE Page 373

St Helena

The island of St Helena lies about 1,950 km (1,200 miles) off the west coast of Africa. Together with Tristan da Cunha and Ascension Island, it is a British crown colony, and is Britain's main dependency in the South Atlantic. The crater rim of an extinct volcano, St Helena is marked by gorges and valleys, has many freshwater springs, and rises to an elevation of 824 m (2,703 ft).

Discovered by the Portuguese in 1502 and first visited by the English in 1588, St Helena was granted to the British East India Company in 1659. It was Napoleon's place of exile from 1815 to 1821. Today, the island's main activities are fishing, livestock raising, and the sale of handicrafts, but it depends on aid from the UK. Tristan da Cunha, 2,000 km (1,243 miles) to the south, has a farming community. Ascension Island, a military base and communications center, has no resident population.

Fact File

OFFICIAL NAME St Helena

FORM OF GOVERNMENT Dependent territory of the United Kingdom

CAPITAL Jamestown

AREA 410 sq km (158 sq miles)

TIME ZONE GMT

POPULATION 7,145

LIFE EXPECTANCY 75.9

INFANT MORTALITY (PER 1,000) 28

LITERACY RATE 97.3%

CURRENCY St Helenian pound

ECONOMY Mainly fishing and agriculture

CLIMATE Tropical, moderated by trade winds

MAP REFERENCE Page 373

Africa

Western Sahara

Fact File

OFFICIAL NAME Western Sahara

FORM OF GOVERNMENT Territory disputed by Morocco and Polisario Front independence movement

CAPITAL None

AREA 266,000 sq km (102,703 sq miles)

TIME ZONE GMT

POPULATION 239,333

LIFE EXPECTANCY 49.1

INFANT MORTALITY (PER 1,000) 136.7

CURRENCY Moroccan dirham

ECONOMY Agriculture 50%; fishing 25%, mining 25%

CLIMATE Mainly hot and arid

MAP REFERENCE Page 360

A bay and a small village in Réunion (bottom left). Pico de Teide on the island of Tenerife in the Canary Islands (top). A village with a view of the Atlantic in Madeira (above).

Western Sahara is a former Spanish possession. South of Morocco (and more than half the size of Morocco itself) it consists of the desert country lying between Mauritania and the Atlantic coast. The terrain is largely flat, with large areas of rock and sand, rising to low mountains in the northeast and the south. Possessing the world's largest known deposits of phosphate rock, it is a contested region of uncertain sovereignty, though since 1975 it has been occupied and administered by Morocco. Most of the indigenous people are Sahrawis, a mixture of Berber and Arab. Since 1983 a war has been waged on their behalf by the Polisario Front (Popular Front for the Liberation of the Saguia el Hamra and Rio de Oro) and by 1991 more than 170,000 Sahrawi refugees had fled the country and were living in camps in Algeria. Guerrilla activities continue, despite a United Nations-monitored ceasefire in 1991. Trade and other activities are controlled by the Moroccan government and most food for the urban population must be imported. Western Sahara's standard of living is well below that of Morocco.

Autonomous communities

The municipalities of Ceuta and Melilla on the Moroccan coast, and the Canary Islands, off southern Morocco, are autonomous communities of Spain. The islands of Madeira, to the north of the Canary Islands, constitute an autonomous region of Portugal.

Ceuta and Melilla

In 1912 the Sultan of Morocco signed a treaty with France making Morocco a French protectorate. At the same time the French, recognizing Spanish interests in the region, gave Spain several enclaves along the Moroccan coast. Two of these enclaves remain under Spanish administration—Ceuta and Melilla.

The high promontory of Jebel Musa at Ceuta, on the African side of the Strait of Gibraltar, stands opposite Gibraltar on the northern side. Legend has it that Jebel Musa and the Rock of Gibraltar were the two "Pillars of Hercules", set there by Hercules to commemorate his travels and achievements. Today, Ceuta is a military station and seaport with a population of about 75,000.

Canary Islands

The Canary Islands, grouped off southern Morocco, are an autonomous community of Spain. There are seven large islands and numerous smaller islands, the nearest of which are within 100 km (60 miles) of the African coast. The "inshore" islands of Lanzarote and Fuerteventura are low lying. The more mountainous outer islands of Gran Canaria and Tenerife include the volcanic cone of Pico de Teide (3,718 m; 12,198 ft).

With a subtropical climate and fertile soils, the islands support farming and fruit growing, and such industries as food and fish processing, boat building, and crafts.

Once known as the Fortunate Islands, the Spanish took control of the Canaries in 1479, subjugating the original Guanche and Canario inhabitants. Today, the islands' mild climate makes them a major tourist destination year round. They are divided into two provinces: Las Palmas de Gran Canaria, and Santa Cruz de Tenerife.

Madeira

Madeira is the largest of a group of volcanic islands forming an autonomous region of Portugal. A tourist destination, they are situated 550 km (340 miles) from the coast of Morocco, and 900 km (560 miles) southwest of Lisbon. The two islands of Madeira and Porto Santo are inhabited, unlike the barren islets of the Desertas and Selvagens. Madeira is 55 km (34 miles) long and 19 km (12 miles) wide, has deep ravines and rugged mountains, contains the group's capital, Funchal, and rises to Pico Ruivo (1,862 m; 6,109 ft) in the middle of the island. It was once heavily forested, but settlers cleared the uplands for plantation use. Produce includes wine (madeira), sugar, and bananas.

Africa

Africa: Physical

ATLANTIC OCEAN

NORTH SEA

Scandinavia

BALTIC SEA

British Isles

North European Plain

E u r o p e

Channel Is.

Pyrenees

Iberian Peninsula

Golfo de Cádiz

Madeira

Islas Canarias (Canary Islands)
La Palma
Hierro
Lanzarote
3718 m
Pico de Teide
Gran Canaria

Rás Nouâdhibou

Cap Vert

Tropic of Cancer

CASPIAN SEA

BLACK SEA

Stara Planina

Plain of Hungary

Alps

Appennino

Corse (Corsica)

Sardegna (Sardinia)
Mallorca

TYRRHENIAN SEA

IONIAN SEA

Sicilia (Sicily) ▲ 3323 m Mte Etna

326 m

MEDITERRANEAN SEA

ALPES

Kythira ▲ 2452 m

Kriti (Crete)

Rodos (Rhodes)

AEGEAN SEA

▲ 3088 m

Atlas Saharien

Atlas

Jebel Toubkal ▲ 4165 m

Haut Atlas

H a m a d a

Plateau du Tademaït

Libyan Plateau

Khalīj Surt

Golfe de Gabès

A H A G G A R

Hoggar
Tahat 2918 m

▲ 2022 m Monts Bagzane

S A H A R A

Libyan Desert

Jabal Zaltan

▲ 1200 m Qârat as Sab'ah

Tarso Emissi ▲ 3376 m

▲ 3088 m

Aoukâr

Sahel

Niger

Sénégal

Fouta Djalon
1948 m ▲ Loma Mansa

Lac de Guiers

Lake Volta

Bénoué

Hosére Vokre 2049 m ▲

Massif de l'Adamaoua

Persian Gulf

Gulf of Oman

▲ 4547 m

▲ 4811 m

▲ 4434 m

Bādiyat ash Shām (Syrian Desert)

Al Taysīyah

Arabian Peninsula

Ar Rub' al Khālī

▲ 2580 m Jabal al Lawz

▲ 2637 m
▲ 1977 m Jabal Hamātah

RED SEA

Lake Nasser

Nubian Desert

Nile

Ẓufār

Ra's Naws

Ghubbat al Qamar

Suqutrā (Socotra)

Raas Caseyr

Raas Xaafuun

Gulf of Aden

Aden

▲ 3133 m Jabal Saudā

▲ 3760 m Jabal an Nabī Shu'ayb

Shimbiris ▲ 2416 m

▲ 3018 m Soira

▲ 2780 m

Tana Hāyk' (Lake Tana) ▲ 4620 m Ras Dashen Terara

Ethiopian Highlands

Eritrea

East Africa

INDIAN

OCEAN

ATLANTIC

OCEAN

Madagascar

Mozambique Channel

Congo
Basin

Great Rift Valley

Great Rift Valley
Mont Miton

Kalahari
Desert

Namib Desert

Drakensberg

Equator
Tropic of Capricorn
Tropic of Capricorn

Sihouette I. Mahé I.
Platte I.
Coetivy I.
Amirante
Isles
Alphonse I.
Providence I.
Farquhar
Group
Aldabra Is
Assumption I.
Tanjona Bobaomby
(Cap d'Ambre)
Helodrano
Antongila
2876 m
Maromokotro
Tanjona
Vohimena

Réunion

Pemba I.
Mafia I.
Cabo Delgado
Rovuma
Lago Niassa
3001 m
Mt Mulanje
2436 m
Monte Binga
1788 m
Zambezi
Lake Malawi
Lago de
Cahora Bassa
2960 m
Lake
Tanganyika
Lake
Victoria
Lake
Kariba
Ilha do
Bazaruto
Cabo de Santa Maria

Kirinyaga
(Mt Kenya)
Kilimanjaro
5895 m
Stanley
4507 m
Karisimbi
Lualaba
Congo
Kwango
Kasai
L. Mai-Ndombe
Cuanza
Cunene
Okavango
Limpopo
Vaal
Orange
3482 m
Thabana-
Ntlenyana
2504 m
Kompasberg
Great Karoo
Cape of
Good Hope
Walvis Bay
Lüderitz Bay
2573 m
Brandberg
2620 m
Moco
980 m
Mont Iboundji
Ponta das
Palmeirinhas
Ponta Albina
São Tomé
Annobón

St Helena

Ascension

Tristan da Cunha

Prince Edward I.
Iles Crozet
Iles de Kerguélen
Heard I.

Africa

0   400   800   1200 kilometers
0 200 400 600 miles
Scale 1:30 000 000   Projection: Azimuthal Equal Area

Africa: Political

7
10°
8
20°
9
30°
10
40°
11
50°
80°

N

SEYCHELLES
Victoria
Silhouette I. Mahé I.
Amirante Platte I.
Isles
Alphonse I. Coetivy I.
Providence I.
Farquhar
Group

MAURITIUS
Port Louis
Tropic of Capricorn

Saint-Denis
REUNION (Fr.)

Antsirañana
Sambava
Soanierana-Ivongo
Toamasina
Antananarivo
Fianarantsoa
Vangaindrano

M

Íles de Kerguélen (Fr.)

HEARD AND MACDONALD IS (Aust.)

70°

Kismaayo
Aldabra Is
Assumption I.
COMOROS
Moroni
MAYOTTE (Fr.)
Dzaoudzi
Antsohihy
Mahajanga
Tsiroanomandidy
Morondava
Toliara

MADAGASCAR

Tôlañaro

L

60°

Mombasa
Pemba Island
Zanzibar
Dar es Salaam
Mafia I.
Garissa
Nacala
Nampula

Mtwara
Lindi
Quelimane
Ilha do Bazaruto
Inhambane

INDIAN

OCEAN

50°

Nairobi
Moshi
Tanga
Dodoma
TANZANIA
Iringa
Songea
Lichinga
Beira
Chimoio

Mozambique Channel

K

Kampala
Kigali
RWANDA
BURUNDI
Bujumbura
Tabora
Mbeya
MALAWI
Mpika
Lilongwe
Blantyre
ZIMBABWE
Gweru
Maputo
SWAZILAND
Durban

MOZAMBIQUE

40°

Goma
Bukavu
Kindu
Mansa
Kasama
Lusaka
Harare
Bulawayo
Thohoyandou
Chókuè
Mbabane
Maseru
LESOTHO
East London

J

DEMOCRATIC
REPUBLIC
OF THE CONGO
Kalemie
Kolwezi
ZAMBIA
Chingola
Luanshya
Kariba
Pretoria
Johannesburg
SOUTH
Bloemfontein
Port Elizabeth

30°

Kinshasa
Lodja
Kananga
Mbuji-Mayi
Kamina
Solwezi
Dilolo
Mongu
Francistown
Mauu
BOTSWANA
Gaborone
Mahalapye
Klerksdorp
Upington
De Aar
AFRICA
Beaufort West
Mossel Bay

H

Luena
Saurimo
Uíge
Menongue
Rundu
Tsumeb
Otjiwarongo
Windhoek
Keetmanshoop

20°

GABON
Port-Gentil
Brazzaville
Pointe-Noire
Tchibanga
Mouila
ANGOLA
Luanda
Benguela
Huambo
Lubango
Namibe
NAMIBIA
Oshakati
Swakopmund
Cape Town

São Tomé
Annobón (Eq. Guinea)

G

ATLANTIC

OCEAN

10°

ASCENSION ISLAND (ST HELENA)

ST HELENA (U.K.)

Prince Edward I. (S. Africa)

Íles de Crozet (Fr.)

F

0°

E

10°

D

20°

C

30°

TRISTAN DA CUNHA (St Helena)

B

Tropic of Capricorn

A

40°

0 400 800 1200 kilometers
0 200 400 600 miles
Scale 1:30,000,000   Projection: Azimuthal Equal Area

Africa

Azores
(Port.)

Corvo

Flores

Graciosa
São Jorge Terceira
Faial Horta Praia da Vitória
Madalena Angra do Heroísmo
Pico

São Miguel
Ponta Delgada Povoação

Santa Maria

ATLANTIC

OCEAN

Madeira
(Port.)
Funchal Ilhas
Desertas

Ilhas Selvagens
(Port.)

Islas Canarias
(Canary Islands)
(Sp.)
Alegranza
Lanzarote Graciosa
Santa Cruz
de la Palma Arrecife
La Palma Santa Cruz de Tenerife
Tenerife Fuerteventura Puerto del Rosario
Gomera Pico de Teide
3718 m
Hierro Las Palmas de
Gran Canaria Gran Canaria Tarfaya

El Aaiún
(Laâyoune)

ATLANTIC

OCEAN

Tropic of Cancer

PORTU

Leiria

Por
Lisboa
(Lisbon)
Grândola
Odemira
Lagos
Sagres Faro

Ra
Mohammedia
Casablanca
Azemmour Berrechid Be
El Jadida Settat
Khourib
Youssoufia Kasb
Safi Beni M
Chemaia El Kelaa des S
Marrakech (Marrakesh)
Essaouira Ounara
Imi-n-Tanoute Hau
Cap Rhir MOROCCO
Agadir Ouarzazate
Taroudannt
Oulad
Teima Anti Atlas
Tafraoute Foum
Tiznit Tata
Sidi Ifni Bou Izakarn Akka
Guelmim

Jebel Ouarkziz Ham

Tan-Tan Tisgui-Remz

Tindouf

Hagunia

Semara

Bu Craa Tifariti

Aïn Ben Tili

E

Guelta Zemmur Bîr Mogrein

WESTERN
SAHARA
(occupied by Morocco)
Sebkhet Oumm ed
Drôus Telli TIRIS
ZEMMOUR
Sebkhet Oumm El Hank
ed Drôus Guebli
Sebkhet
Ti-n-Bessaïs

Ad Dakhla Bir Enzarán S
Punta Durnford El Aargub

Ausert Fdérik
Zouérat
Aguenit

Cabo Barbas

Tichla Zug
Tmeimichât Choûm
Sebkhet
Chemchâm
Nouâdhibou Ouadane
Ouadane
Râs Nouâdhibou ADRAR
Azeffâl Atâr
Chinguetti

DAKHLET
NOUÂDHIBOU INCHIRI Oujeft HOD
Akjoujt ECH

Râs Timirist MAURITANIA
Nouâmghâr TAGANT Tichît CHARG

Sebkha
Narhamcha
Jreïda Tidjikja

Nouakchott A o u k â r
Moudjéria
TRARZA Oualâta

Ponta do Sol
Santo Antão
Porto Novo
Mindelo
São Vicente Pedra Lume Sal
São Nicolau Vila da Ribeira Brava
Boa Vista
Sal Rei
Curral Velho

CAPE VERDE

São Tiago Maio
Tarrafal Porto Inglês
Brava Fogo Praia

MEDITERRANEAN SEA

SPAIN

Fuenlabrada
Plasencia
Montes de Toledo
Mérida
Puertollano
Ciudad Real
Córdoba
Andújar
Écija
Granada
de la
Ubrique
Vélez-Málaga
Marbella
Algeciras
Gibraltar **GIBRALTAR** (U.K.)
Ceuta (Sp.)
Tetouan (Tetuán)
Al Hoceima
Chefchaouene
el Kebir
el-Arba-Rharb
Kacem
sset
Fès
Taza
Moyen Atlas
Midelt
Er Rachidia
Erfoud
el-Ziz
ro
Taouz
Abadla

Ocaña
Toledo
Utiel
Sagunto
Valencia
Villarrobledo
Albacete
Almansa
Hellín
Alicante
Murcia
Elche
Cartagena
Jaén
Linares
Valdepeñas
Guadix
Málaga
Adra
Cabo de Gata
Almería
Nador
Oujda
Taourirt
Jerada
Sebdou
Marhoum
Guercif
Ain Beni Mathar
Boulemane
Missour
Tendrara
Plaine de Tamlelt
Bouârfa
Figuig
Béchar
Taghit
Hamaguir
Boudenib
Meridja
Beni-Ounif
Beni-Abbes
Kerzaz
Timmoudi
Tabelbala
Ksabi

Mallorca
Alcúdia
Mahón
Menorca
Palma de Mallorca
Manacor
Eivissa (Ibiza)
Eivissa
Formentera
Islas Baleares (Balearic Islands) (Sp.)

Alger (Algiers)
Dellys
Tipasa
Ténès
Blida
Médéa
Chlef
Théniet el Had
Berrouaghia
Ksar el Boukhari
Aïn el Hadjel
Mostaganem
Oran
Mascara
Relizane
Mehdia
Sougueur
Ksar Chellala
Sidi Ali
Ain Defla
Sidi Bel Abbès
Aïn Temouchant
Ghazaouet
Tlemcen
Saïda
Aïn Deheb
Télagh
Frenda
Charef
Djelfa
Laghouat
Aflou
El Bayadh
Mecheria
Naama
Aïn Sefra
El Abiodh Sidi Cheikh
Berriane
Ghardaïa
Tadjrouna
Tilrhemt
Guerara
Zelfana
El Alia
Messaad
Sidi Khaled
Ouled Djellal
Biskra
Sidi Okba
Zeribet el Oued

Tizi Ouzou
Larba
Akbou
Sétif
Bordj Bou Arreridj
M'Sila
Bou Saâda
Bejaïa
Ijjel
Mila
Constantine
Batna
Barika
Khenchela
Souk Ahras
Guelma
El Eulma
Oum el Bouaghi
Chéria
El Qaşrayn
Feriana
Redeyef
Gafsa
El Meghaïer
Touggourt
El Oued
Djamaa
Guemar
Dzioua
Hassi Messaoud
Ouargla
Haoud el Hamra
Hassi Bel Guebbour
Bordj Omar Driss
I-n-Amenas
Edjeleh
Illizi
Tarat

Skikda
Annaba
El Hadjar
Jendouba
Tabursuq
Bâjah
Qulaybîyah
Nâbul
Zaghwân
Sousse
Kairouan
Al Munastîr
Mahdia
Al Jamm
Ksour Essaf
Sfax
Maharès
Sidi Bou Zid
Talah
Sbeïtla
Al Qaşrayn
TUNISIA
Qâbis
Medenine
Jarjis
Ra's Ajdîr
Zuwârah
Ţarābulus (Tripoli)
Al 'Azīzīyah
Tarhūnah
Gharyān
Mizdah
Banī Walīd

ITALY
Iglesias
Cagliari
Sant' Antioco
Sardegna (Sardinia)
Palermo
Cefalù
Messina
Milazzo
Trapani
Marsala
Caltanissetta
Agrigento
Gela
Catania
Siracusa
Ragusa
Modica
Vittória
Sicilia (Sicily)
Mte. Etna 3323 m
MALTA
Gozo
Valletta
Isola di Lampedusa (Italy)
Isola di Pantelleria (Italy)
Gozo

LIBYA
Ghadāmis
Dirj
Ash Shuwayrif
Al Hamādah al Hamrā'
Sīnāwin
Nālūt
Az Zintān
Jabal Nafūsah
Adh Dhahibāt
Lorzot
Ramādah
Tijī
Jādū
Yafran
Az Zāwiyah
Al Khums
Zlīṭan
Al Qaşābāt
Banzart

ALGERIA

Grand Erg Occidental
Grand Erg Oriental
El Goléa
Hassi Inifel
El Homr
Timimoun
Plateau du Tademaït
Plateau du Tinrhert
Adrar
Sbaa
I-n-Belbel
Reggane
Sebkha Reggane
Aoulef
In-Salah
Foggaret ez Zoua
Akabli
Plaine du Tidikelt
Sebkha Mekerrhane
Sebkha Azzel Matti
Arak
Adrar N'Ahnet
Monts du Mouydir
Amguid
Zarzaïtine
Ohanet
Erg Issaouane
El Adeb Larache
Tarat
Djanet
Zaouatallaz
Al 'Uwaynāt
Ghāt
Tassili n'Ajjer

Er Raoui
Erg er Raoui
Chech
Tanezrouft
Asedjrad
H o g g a r
Abalessa
Silet
Tamanrasset
I-n-Eker
Idelès
I-n-Amguel
Tefedest
In-Guezzam

MALI
Taoudenni
Hamada el Haricha
El Khnâchîch
Tanezrouft Tan-Ahenet
Bordj Mokhtar
Tessalit
Boughessa
Ti-n-Zaouâtene
Aguelhok
Timétrine
KIDAL
Kidal
Ti-n-Essako
Anéfis
I-n-Tebezas
Almoustarat
GAO
Araouane
Ti-n-Aguelhaj
Bamba
Téméra
TOMBOUCTOU

NIGER
Madama
Plateau du Djado
Djado
Chirfa
Ténéré du Tafassâsset
Séguédine
Aney
Dirkou
Bilma
Massif de l'Aïr
Iferouâne
Sidaouet
Arlit
AGADEZ
Fachi
Timia
Akrérèb
Aouderas
Teguidda-n-Tessoumt
Ingal
Agadez
Tassara
Falaise de Tiguidit
Assamakka
I-n-Guezzam
TAHOUA
ZINDER
DIFFA
Grand Erg de Bilma
Tassili du Hoggar
Plateau du Manguéni

Golfe de Tunis
Carthage
Tūnis
Golfe de Hammamet
Strait of Sicily
Golfe de Gabès
Houmet Essouk
Jazīrat Jarbah
Shatt al Jarid
Chott Melrhir
Chott el Jarid

Sahara
Plateaux
Hauts
Atlas
Sahariens

Oued Chair
Oued Guir
Oued Ziz

361

Scale 1:9,000,000   Projection: Azimuthal Equal Area

0 100 200 300 400 kilometers
0 100 200 miles

Libya • Egypt • North Sudan • North Chad

A   10°   B   15°   295   C   20°   297   D   25°   E

TYRRHENIAN SEA

Iglesias
Cagliari
Sant' Antioco
Sibari
Paola   Cosenza   1723 m
Crotone
Capo Sta Maria di Leuca
Kerkyra (Corfu)
Ioannina
Trikala
Larisa
Çanakkale
Ezine   Çan   Balıkesir
Susurluk
Edremit
Burhaniye   Soma
Dursunbey
Bigadiç
Kırkağaç   Akhisar   Sima
Manisa

ITALY
Trapani   Palermo
Marsala
Mazara del Vallo   Cefalù   Milazzo
Messina
Reggio di Calabria
Siderno
Ionian   SEA
GREECE
Lefkada
Mesolongi
Karditsa
Volos
Menemen   Bornova
Salihli
Urla   Alaşehir
Çeşme   İzmir   Demiş

Manzil Bū
Ruqaybah   Banzart
Golfo di Sant'Eufemia
Capo Rizzuto
Catania
Mte Etna 3323 m
Catanzaro
Kefallonia
Zakynthos (Zante)
Patra   Korinthos
Peiraias (Piraeus)
Athina (Athens)
Pyrgos
Tripoli
Andros   Aydın
Söke   Nazilli
Muğla

Bou Salem
Bâjah
Carthage
Tunis
Qulaybiyah   Nâbul
Agrigento
Caltanissetta
Gela   Ragusa
Vittoria   Modica
Siracusa
Kyparissia
Kalamata   Sparti
Skala
Tinos
Samos
Ikaria
Syros
Paros   Naxos
Amorgos
Kos   Marmaris
Rodos
Fethiye

Jendouba
Tabursuq
Zaghwān
Nâbul
Golfe de Hammamet
MALTA
Gozo   Valletta
Milos   Ios
Kythira
Rodos (Rhodes)
Karpathos

Tālah
Dorsale
Sousse
Jabal ash Sha'nabī   1544 m
Al Qaşrayn
Sbeïtla
Masākin   Al Munastir
Mahdia   Al Jamm
Ksour Essaf
Isola di Pantelleria (Italy)
Isola di Lampedusa (Italy)
Kriti (Crete)
Chania   Irakleio (Iraklion)
2452 m
Akra Lithino

Feriana
Gafsa
Sidi Bou Zid
Maharès
Sfax

MEDITERRANEAN   SEA

Al Metlaoui
Al Hāmmah
Qibīlī
Qābis
Dūz
Golfe de Gabès
Medenine   Humeit Essouk
Jazīrat Jarbah
Ra's al Hilāl
Ra's al   Shahhāt   Darnah
Jarjis
TUNISIA
Bin Qirdān
Ra's Ajdīr
Zuwārah
Ţarābulus (Tripoli)
Tūkrah   Al Bayḑā   Sūsah   Ra's at Tīn
Al Marj   Suluntah   At Tamimi
Tubruq
Ra's al Muraysah

Ţaţāwin
Az Zāwiyah
Al 'Azīziyah   Al Qaşabāt
Al Khums   Zlitan
Banghāzī   Al Abyār
Zāwiyat al Mukhaylā
Al Bardī
Sīdī Barrānī
Ra's al Kanā'is

Adh Dhahibat
Lorzot
Ramādah   Tiji
Yafran   Gharyān
Tarhūnah
Mişrātah
Qaminis   Sulūq   Zāwiyat Masūs
Umm Sa'ad
Khalīj as Salūm

Al Burmah
Nālūt
Az Zintān   Mizdah
Banī Walīd
Qaryat al Qaddāhiyah
Bu'ayrāt al Hasūn
Ajdābiyā
Marsá Maţrūh
Al 'Alamayn
Al Har

Bordj Messouda
Sīnāwin
Jādū
Khalīj Surt
Surt
As Sultan   Sultan
Marsá al Burayqah
Libyan   Plateau

Ghadāmis
Dirj
An Nawfaliyah
As Sidrah
Al 'Uqaylah
Libyan   Plateau
Qattara Depression

Zarzaïtine
I-n-Amenas
Ash Shuwayrif
Abū Nujaym
Al Jaghbūb
Qārah

Al Hamādah al Hamrā'
Jabal Waddān   671 m
Mabrūk
Marādah
Awjilah   Jālū
Siwah
Al Bawīţi

Edjeleh
'Uwaynāt Wanin
Sūknah   Hūn
Waddān

Adīrī   Birāk
Tamanhint
Samnū
Al Fuqahā'
Jabal Zaltan
Qārat as Sab'ah   1200 m
LIBYA
Al Farāfirah

Tarat
Awbārī
Sabhā
Zillah
Western Desert

Al 'Uwaynāt
Ghaddūwah
Tmassah
Zawilah
Murzuq   Tarāghin
Wāw al Kabīr
Tāzirbū

Ghāt
Şahrā' Awbārī
Al Qaţrūn
Zighan

Djanet
Şahrā' Murzuq
Tajarhī   Al Wigh
Şahrā' Rabyānah
467 m

Tropic of Cancer
ALGERIA
Sarīr Tibesti
Al Jawf   Al Khufrah
Hadabat al Jilf al Kabīr

Plateau du Manguéni
Jabal Arkanū   1435 m
Jabal Al 'Uwaynāt   1893 m
Al 'Uwaynāt
Jabal Kissū   1712 m

Madama
Bikubiti   2285 m

Ténéré du Tafassâsset
Plateau du Djado
Aozou
Kamal
Tarso Emissi   3376 m
SAHARA

Djado
Chirfa
Pic Toussidé   3315 m
Bardaï
Yebbi-Souma
Yebbi-Bou
Zouar
Tibesti

AGADEZ
EGYPT

NIGER
Séguédine
Emi Koussi   3415 m
Gouro

Aney
Dirkou
Bilma
Ouanga Kébir
Ouanga Sérir

CHAD
BORKOU-ENNEDI-TIBESTI
SHAMĀL DĀRFŪR

Fachi
Grand Erg de Bilma
Borkou
Faya-Largeau
Dépression du Mourdi
Ennedi

DIFFA
Fada
Basso   1450 m

ZINDER
Erg du Djourab

A   B   15°   C   20°   366   D   25°   E

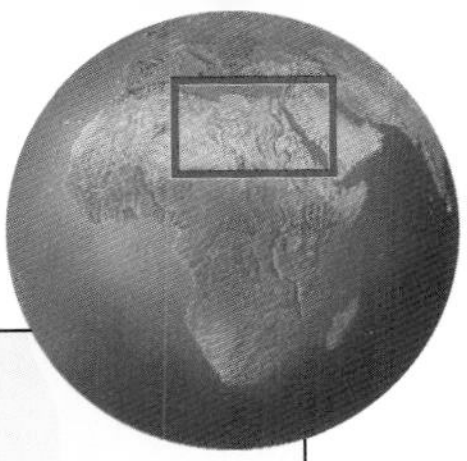

224

TURKEY

Ankara · Kırıkkale · Yozgat · Sivas · Zara · Erzincan · Malazgirt · Doğubayazıt · Makü · Sisian · Goris · Masallı · Lankaran
Polatlı · Kèskin · Yıldızeli · Hafik · 2792 m · 3282 m · Varto · Patnos · Naxçıvan · Khvoy · Marand · Meshgin Shahr · Astara

CASPIAN SEA

Konya · Kayseri · Malatya · Diyarbakır · Batman · Van · Tabrīz · Ardabīl · Rasht · Now Shahr

IRAN

Tehrān (Teheran) · Karaj · Qazvīn · Zanjān · Hamadān · Qom · Kāshān

Adana · Gaziantep · Halab (Aleppo) · Al Qāmishlī · Al Mawşil (Mosul) · Arbīl · As Sulaymānīyah · Kirkūk · Sanandaj

SYRIA

Al Lādhiqīyah (Latakia) · Tarţūs · Ḩamāh · Ar Raqqah · Dayr az Zawr · Sāmarrā · Baghdād · Kermānshāh · Khorramābād

LEBANON · Bayrūt (Beirut) · Dimashq (Damascus)

ISRAEL · Tel Aviv-Yafo · Yerushalayim (Jerusalem)

IRAQ

Al Ḩillah · Karbalā · An Najaf · Al Başrah (Basra) · Abādān

Al Qāhirah (Cairo)

JORDAN · Amman · Al 'Aqabah · Badiyat ash Shām (Syrian Desert)

KUWAIT · Al Kuwayt (Kuwait)

Persian Gulf

SAUDI ARABIA

An Nafūd · Jabal Shammar · Ḩā'il · Buraydah · At Ţaysīyah · Ad Dahnā'

Tabūk · Al Wajh · Al Madīnah (Medina) · Ar Riyāḍ (Riyadh) · Al Hufūf

Red Sea

Jiddah (Jedda) · Makkah (Mecca) · Aţ Ţā'if

Tropic of Cancer

Aswān · Nubian Desert · AL BAḨR AL AḨMAR · Būr Sūdān (Port Sudan)

SUDAN · ERITREA · YEMEN · Abhā · Khamīs Mushayţ · Najrān · Ar Rub' al Khālī

0 100 200 300 400 kilometers
0 100 200 miles
Scale 1:9,000,000   Projection: Azimuthal Equal Area

363

West Africa

Scale 1:9,000,000
Projection: Azimuthal Equal Area

0   100   200   300   400 kilometers

0   100   200 miles

Sudan • Ethiopia • Somalia

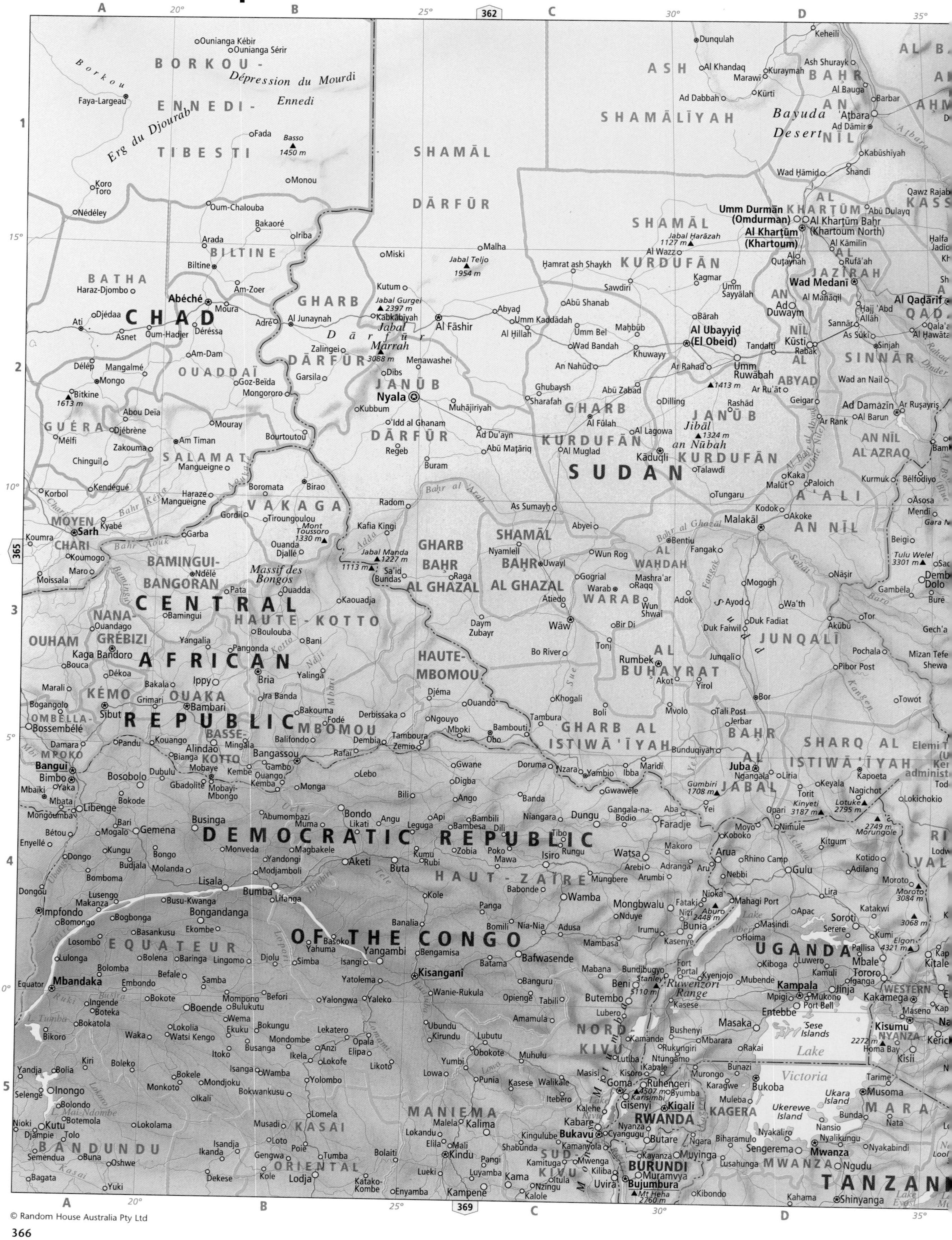

Map labels (north-western / central portion shown):

Chad / Borkou–Ennedi–Tibesti region
Ounianga Kébir, Ounianga Sérir, Fada, Basso 1450 m, Monou, Oum-Chalouba, Faya-Largeau, Koro Toro, Nédéley, Bakaoré, Arada, Iriba, Biltine, Am-Zoer, Miski, Haraz-Djombo, Batha, Abéché, Moura, Am-Zoer, Djédaa, Ati, Asnet, Oum-Hadjer, Déréssa, Mangalmé, Am-Dam, Délép, Mongo, Bitkine 1613 m, Abou Deïa, Goz-Beïda, Mongororo, Guéra, Mélfi, Mouray, Zakouma, Chinguil, Salamat, Mangueigne, Korbol, Kendégué, Haraze Mangueigne, Boromata, Birao, Moyen-Chari, Koumra, Kyabé, Garba, Sarh, Koumogo, Gordil, Tiroungoulou, Mont Toussoro 1330 m, Ouanda Djallé

Central African Republic
Maro, Moissala, Ndélé, Bamingui-Bangoran, Massif des Bongos, Jabal Manda 1227 m, Sa'id Bundas, Nana-Grébizi, Ouandago, Yangalia, Bouloua, Pangonda, Bani, Kaga Bandoro, Bouca, Dékoa, Marali, Bakala, Ippy, Bria, Yalinga, Central African Republic, Kémo, Ouaka, Grimari, Bambari, Ira Banda, Bakouma, Derbissaka, Sibut, Damara, Bossembélé, Basse-Kotto, Mbomou, Fodé, Ngouyo, Zemio, Djéma, Haute-Mbomou, Bangui, Bimbo, Mbaïki, Mobaye, Kembe, Gambo, Ouango, Bangassou, Rafaï, Lebo, Gwane, Doruma, Nzara, Yambio, Ibba, Maridi

Democratic Republic of the Congo
Mongoumba, Bétou, Mogalo, Kungu, Libenge, Bosobolo, Dubulu, Gbadolite, Mobayi-Mbongo, Monga, Bili, Ango, Banda, Gwadolite, Bondo, Abumombazi, Muma, Likati, Bambesa, Dili, Niangara, Dungu, Faradje, Mongbwalu, Businga, Magbakele, Yandongi, Modjamboli, Aketi, Buta, Angu, Leguga, Api, Poko, Isiro, Rungu, Watsa, Makoro, Arua, Lisala, Bumba, Lifanga, Kole, Babonde, Wamba, Mungbere, Nebbi, Gulu, Impfondo, Makanza, Busu-Kwanga, Bongandanga, Banalia, Panga, Nduye, Bunia, Mahagi Port, Soroti, Bomongo, Bogbonga, Basankusu, Ekombe, Demokratic Republic, Haut-Zaïre, Bomili, Nia-Nia, Adusa, Irumu, Kasenye, Serere, Equateur, Bolenge, Baringa, Lingomo, Djolu, Yahuma, Isangi, Yangambi, Bengamisa, Batama, Banguru, Opienge, Tabili, Butembo, Lubero, Masindi, Hoima, Mbandaka, Equator, Embondo, Bokote, Befori, Yalongwa, Yaleko, Kisangani, Wanie-Rukula, Beni, Ruwenzori Range 5110 m, Fort Portal, Kasese, Bikoro, Ingende, Boteka, Bokatola, Boende, Wema, Ekulu, Mondombe, Ubundu, Kirundu, Lubutu, Amamula, Lutunguru, Kamande, Kyenjojo, Mubende, Kampala, Entebbe, Port Bell, Waka, Lokolia, Watsi Kengo, Busanga, Ikela, Likoti, Obokote, Muhulu, Kisoro, Kabale, Masaka, Mbarara, Bushenyi, Western, Nyanza, Kisumu, Kiri, Boleko, Bokele, Isanga, Wamba, Lowa, Punia, Kasese, Walikale, Itebero, Bunazi, Lake Victoria, Homa Bay, Kisii, Yandja, Bolia, Monkoto, Mondjoku, Yolombo, Goma, Ruhengeri, Byumba, Bukoba, Musoma, Selenge, Bolondo, Botembela, Lomela, Lodja, Musadi, Kasai, Lokandu, Kalima, Goma, Gisenyi, Kigali, Karagwe, Muleba, Ukara Island, Mara, Nioki, Kutu, Djampie, Tolo, Isandja, Gengwa, Poïé, Tumba, Bolaiti, Kabare, Bukavu, Cyangugu, Butare, Rwanda, Kagera, Ukerewe Island, Nyalikungu, Nyakabindi, Bagata, Bandundu, Oshwe, Dekese, Kole, Lueki, Pangi, Kindu, Sud-Kivu, Burundi, Bujumbura, Mwanza, Yuki, Kataka-Kombe, Enyamba, Kampene, Oriental, Lukashi, Uvira, Muramvya, Mt Heha 2760 m, Kibondo, Kahama, Shinyanga, Tanzania

Sudan / Darfur / Kurdufan region
Ash Shamālīyah, Dunqulah, Keheili, Al Khandaq, Kuraymah, Ash Shurayk, Bahr an Nīl, Al Bauga, Barbar, Ad Dabbah, Kūrti, Marawi, Shamal, Bayuda Desert, 'Atbara, Ad Dāmir, Kabūshīyah, Darfur, Shamāl, Wad Hāmid, Shandi, Qawz Rajab, Kassala, Umm Durmān (Omdurman), Al Khartūm Bahri (Khartoum North), Al Khartūm (Khartoum), Al Kāmilin, Jabal Harāzah 1127 m, Al Wazz, Qutaynah, Rufā'ah, Wad Medanī, Al Mahaqil, Al Qadārif, Jazīrah, Kurdufān, Shamāl Kurdufān, Malha, Jabal Teljo 1954 m, Kutum, Al Fāshir, Abyaq, Umm Kaddādah, Abū Shanab, Sawdiri, Kagmar, Umm Sayyālah, Ad Duwaym, Al Obeid (Al Ubayyid / El Obeid), Tandalti, Kūsti, Rabak, Sinjah, Sinnār, Jabal Gurgei 2397 m, Kabkābīyah, Al Junaynah, Adré, Zalingei, Dārfūr, Jabal Marrah 3088 m, Menawashei, Dibs, Janūb Dārfūr, Nyala, Muhājiriyah, Idd al Ghanam, Ad Du'ayn, Abū Matāriq, Regeb, Buram, Al Hillah, Wad Bandah, Khuwayy, An Nahūd, Ghubaysh, Abū Zabad, Sharafah, Umm Bel, Mahbūb, Bārah, Ar Rahad, Umm Ruwābah, Ar Ru'āt, Dilling, Rashād, Jibāl an Nūbah 1324 m, Al Fūlah, Al Lagowa, Al Muglad, Kādugli, Talawdi, Kaka, Malūt, Paloich, Kurmuk, Bēlfodiyo, An Nīl, Al Azraq, Ad Damāzin, Ar Rusayris, Ar Rank, Al Barun, Wad an Nail, Abyei, Bentiu, Fangak, Kodok, Akoke, Asosa, Mendi, Gara, As Sumayh, Bahr al Ghazal, Nyamlell, Wun Rog, Malakāl, Beigio, Tulu Welel 3301 m, Gharb Bahr al Ghazal, Raga, Uwayl, Gogrial, Mashra'ar Raqq, Adok, Ayod, Wa'th, Nāsir, Gambēla, Dembi, Dolo, Warab, Wun Shwai, Tonj, Rumbek, Junqalī, Akūbo, Tor, Gech'a, Mizan Tefe, Shewa, Daym Zubayr, Wāw, Bir Di, Duk Faiwil, Duk Fadiat, Pochala, Pibor Post, Bo River, Akot, Yirol, Al Buhayrat, Khogali, Boli, Mvolo, Tali Post, Jerbar, Towot, Gharb al Istiwā'īyah, Ouando, Obo, Bambouti, Tambura, Bir Di, Bunduqiyah, Bahr al Jabal, Sharq al Istiwā'īyah, Juba, Ngangala, Liria, Kapoeta, Lokichokio, Gumbiri 1708 m, Torit, Keyala, Nagichot, Lotuke 2795 m, Gwawele, Yei, Opari, Kinyeti 3187 m, Moyo, Koboko, Nimule, Morungole 2749 m, Kitgum, Kotido, Adilang, Rhino Camp, Nioka, Aru, Adranga, Arumbi, Moroto 3084 m, Katakwi, Elgon 4321 m, Pallisa, Mbale, Tororo, Iganga, Jinja, Kamuli, Luwero, Kiboga, Sese Islands, Kakamega, Maseno, Maseno

Map scale references: 362, 365, 369

SAUDI ARABIA

OMAN

YEMEN

ERITREA

ETHIOPIA

SOMALIA

DJIBOUTI

KENYA

RED SEA

Gulf of Aden

INDIAN OCEAN

Al Qunfudhah · An Nimāş · Hamdah · Sanāw · Thamarit · Hadbaram · Ḩāsik · Ra's Naws

Al Khawsh · Khaybara · Mar'ayt · Ḩāsik · Mirbāţ · Ra's Mirbāţ

Dīts · Banī Thawr · Ar Rub' al Khālī · Al Qa'āmiyāt · Şalālah · Ra's Sājir

3133 m · Jabal Sawdā' · Khamīs Mushayţ · Rakhyūt · Damqawt

Al Birk · Abhā · Najrān · Z̧ufār · Ghubbat al Qamar

Al Qaḩmah · Ad Darb · Zahrān · Wuday'ah · Al Ghaydah

Ash Shuqayq · Jīzān · Saywūn · Shibām · Al Hawţah · Ma'rib · Jabal Mahrāt

Ra's aţ Ţarfā · Ḩaraḑ · Ḩūth · Khamr · Ramlat as Sab'atayn · Ḩaḑramawt · Al Mahrah · Sayḩūt · Ra's Fartak

Jazā'ir Farasān · Hajjah · Amrān · Raydah · Manākhah · Ḩarīb · Bayḩān al Qişāb · 'Atāq · Ash Shiḩr

Dahlak Archipelago · Az Zuhrah · Şan'ā' · Al Mukallā · Ash Shiḩr

Keren · Kelamet · Az Zaydīyah · Dhamār · Al Ţawţah · Ra's al Kalb

Massawa · Al Ḩudaydah · Bājil · Yarīm · Al Bayḑā' · Balḩāf

Asmara · Dek'emhāre · Al Marāwi'ah · Ibb · Qa'ţabah · 2513 m · Lawdar · Al 'Irqah

Ādī Ugrī · Al Fāzah · Zabīd · Hays · Aḑ Ḑāli' · Al Ḩumayshah · Suquţrá (Socotra) (Yemen)

Adwa · Adigrat · Jazīrat al Hanīsh al Kabīr · Mawshij · Ta'izz · 3227 m · Māwiyah · Shaqrā' · Qulansīyah · Qāḑub · Hadiboh · 1503 m

Aksum · Wik'ro · Al Mukhā · Dhubāb · Laḩij · Zinjibār · 'Abd al Kūrī (Yemen)

Ras Dashen Terara · Āmba Alāgē · Afrēra Terara · Assab · Khōr 'Angar · At Turbah · Ash Shaykh 'Uthmān

Gonder · Maych'ew · Korem · Musa 'Alī Terara · Little Aden · 'Adan (Aden)

Ādīs Zemen · Bāti · Tadjoura · Ras Bir · Raas Caluula · Raas Caseyr

Debre Tabor · Desē · DJIBOUTI · Obock · Geesaley · Caluula · Hodda · Tooxin

Guna Terara · Kembolcha · Djibouti · Sâylac · Qandala · Boosaaso · Bargaal · Raas Binna

Amba Farit · Debre Werk' · Dikhil · Ali Sabieh · Ceel Gaal · Lasqoray · Ceel Gaal · Hurdiyo · Raas Xaafuun

Debre Sina · Ayelu Terara · Boorama · Lughaye · Karin · Xiis · Maydh · Shimbiris · Ceerigaabo · Iskushuban · Xaafuun

Gebre Guracha · Fichē · Jeldesa · Bullaxaar · Berbera · SANAAG · Buraan · Qardho · Bandarbeyla

Ādīs Ābeba (Addis Ababa) · Dirē Dawa · Mandheera · WOQOOYI GALBEED · SOMALIA · BARI · Dhuudo · Raas Macbar

Ak'ak'ī Besek'a · Jijiga · Hargeysa · Bandar Wanaag · Oodweyne · Garadag · Rass Dhuudo

Debre Zeyit · Āsbe Teferi · Harēr · TOGDHEER · Xudun · NUGAAL · Eyl · Raas Gabbac

Nazrēt · Awārē · Durukhsi · Caynabo · Laascaanood · Garoowe · Kalis · Qooriga Neegro

ETHIOPIA · Daga Medo · Tukayel · Domo · Raas Cabaad

Asela · K'ech'a Terara · Degeh Bur · Bircot · Danot · Bacaadweyn · Jirriiban · Garacad

Robē · Megalo · Gedlegubē · Geladī · Beyra · MUDUG · Gaalkacyo

Shashemenē · Goba · Ginir · El Fud · Uarandab · Werdēr · Daborow · Iidaan

Āwasa · Denan · K'ebrī Dehar · K'orahē · Godinlabe

Yirga 'Alem · Dīla · Godē · El Kerē · Sina Dhaqa · Dhuusamarreeb · Hobyo

Kibre Mengist · Buddi · Mustahīl · GALGUDUUD

Agere Maryam · Negēlē · Hargele · Godere · Beledweyne · Ceelbuur · Xarardheere

Yābēlo · Chumba · Melka Guba · Yeed · Ted Ceidaar · Dabole · Derri · Bud Bud · Mereeg

Mega · El Lēh · Amino · Dolo Odo · Xuddur · Maxaas · Muqaakoori · Buulobarde

Moyalē · Mandera · Waajid · Tayeeglow · HIIRAAN

Takabba · Luuq · BAKOOL · Garbahaarrey · Mahadday Weyne · SHABEELLAHA DHEXE

Bute Helu · Baydhabo · Buurhakaba · Jawhar · Warshiikh

Buna · El Wak · Diinsoor · Wanlaweyn · Afgooye · Warshiikh

GEDO · BAY · Awdheegle · Muqdisho (Mogadishu) · BANAADIR

Marsabit · Baardheere · Marka

Wajir · Faafxadhuun · Tarbaj · Bu'aale · Baraawe

Mado Gashi · Dif · JUBBADA DHEXE · SHABEELLAHA HOOSE

Habaswein · Afmadow · Jilib · Makungo

NORTH-EASTERN · JUBBADA HOOSE · Kamsuuma · Jamaame

Meru · Garba Tula · Garissa · Bura · Kismaayo

Kirinyaga (Mt Kenya) 5199 m · Buur Gaabo · Kaambooni

Embu · Holao

KENYA · Nairobi · Kitui · Machakos · COAST · Garsen · Lamu · Ras Shaka

Makindu · Namanga · Ungama Bay · Galana

Kilimanjaro 5895 m · Voi · Malindi · Kilifi · Moshi

Scale 1:9 000 000
Projection: Azimuthal Equal Area

0   100   200   300   400 kilometers
0   100   200 miles

367

Central Africa • East Africa

AFRICA

ETHIOPIA

SUDAN

GHARB AL ISTIWĀ'IYAH

BAHR AL JABAL

SHARQ AL ISTIWĀ'IYAH

Elemi Triangle (under Kenyan administration)

RIFT EASTERN

Lake Turkana

SOMALIA

GEDO

JUBBADA DHEXE

NORTH-

EASTERN

JUBBADA HOOSE

UGANDA

VALLEY

KENYA

Kampala

Lake Victoria

Sese Islands

WESTERN NYANZA

Nairobi

CENTRAL

COAST

NORD KIVU

RWANDA

Kigali

BURUNDI

Bujumbura

SUD KIVU

MANIEMA

UBLIC

KAGERA

MARA

MWANZA

Mwanza

SHINYANGA

ARUSHA

Arusha

KILIMANJARO

Moshi

Mombasa

Pemba I.

Zanzibar I.
Zanzibar

KIGOMA

Kigoma

TABORA

Tabora

SINGIDA

DODOMA

Dodoma

TANGA

Tanga

Dar es Salaam

TANZANIA

INDIAN

RUKWA

IRINGA

Iringa

MBEYA

Mbeya

MOROGORO

PWANI

Mafia I.

OCEAN

LINDI

Lindi

NORTHERN

RUVUMA

MTWARA

Mtwara

COMOROS
Njazidja (Grande Comore)
Moroni
Mitsamiouli
Kartala 2361 m
Fomboni
Mwali (Mohéli)

Kasama

ZAMBIA

LUAPULA

Mansa

Lubumbashi

COPPER-
BELT

Kitwe
Ndola
Luanshya

CENTRAL

EASTERN

NIASSA

Lichinga

CABO
DELGADO

Pemba

MALAWI

Lilongwe

Blantyre

MOZAMBIQUE

Lusaka

LUSAKA

TETE

Tete

SOUTHERN

ZAMBÉZIA

NAMPULA

Nampula

Nacala

ZIMBABWE

MASHONALAND
CENTRAL

MASHONALAND
WEST

0   100   200   300   400 kilometers

0   100   200 miles

Scale 1:9,000,000
Projection: Azimuthal Equal Area

	A	10°		B	15°	368	C	20°		D

ATLANTIC OCEAN

Africa

Tropic of Capricorn

© Random House Australia Pty Ltd

Cabo de Santa Marta
Chongoroi
Lucira
Quilengues
Caluquembe
Chicomba
Camucuio
Caitou
Lola
Dinde
Kuvango
Dongo
Cuchi
1729 m
Longa
Menongue
Cangamba
Sessa
Lumbala
N'guimbo
Mumbeji
Lukulu
Bentiaba
Bibala
Munhino
Lubango
Quipungo
Matala
Cassinga
Cuito Cuanavale
Baixo Longa
Nankova
Calunga
Ninda
Kalabo
Mongu
Namibe
Humpata
Chibia
HUILA
ANGOLA
Cuvelai
Caiundo
Mavinga
Neriquinha
Rivungu
Shangombo
Senanga
WESTE
Ponta Albina
Tombua
Virei
Chiange
Chibemba
Quiteve
CUNENE
Humbe
Nehone
Bondo
Mavengue
Bambangando
Luiana
Luana
Pediva
Mucope
Xangongo
CUANDO
CUBANGO
Baía dos Tigres
Iona
Oncócua
Cahama
Naulila
Ondjiva
Cuangar
Calai
Dirico
Katima Mu
Kongola
CAPRI
Foz do Cunene
Cunene
Baynes
Mts
2074 m
Chitado
Ruacana
Ombalantu
Oshakati
Ondangwa
Namacunde
Oshikango
OHANGWENA
Nkurenkuru
Rundu
Okavango
Bagani
Muhembo
Seronga
Sangwali
Humba
Ongandjera
OSHANA
OSHIKOTO
OKAVANGO
Okavango
Delta
Gumare
NGAMILAN
Cape Fria
Opuwo
OMUSATI
Maun
Rocky Pt
KUNENE
Namutoni
Okaukuejo
Tsumeb
Grootfontein
Tsumkwe
Sehithwa
Nhabe
Sesfontein
Kamanjab
Otavi
OTJOZONDJUPA
Xhur
Khorixas
Outjo
Okaputa
Palgrave Pt
Otjiwarongo
Okakarara
Ghanzi
BOTS
Kalkfeld
Sukses
GHANZI
Brandberg
2573 m
Uis
NAMIBIA
Erongo
2350 m
Omaruru
Hochfeld
OMAHEKE
Steinhausen
Usakos
Okazize
Okahandja
Hentiesbaai
ERONGO
Ebony
Karibib
Windhoek
Buitepos
Gobabis
Xanagas
Tshootsha
Swakopmund
Witvlei
Dordabis
2479 m
Kalahari
Walvis Bay
KHOMAS
Rehoboth
Gross Ums
Ncojane
Sandwich Bay
Nauchas
Auas Mts
Tsumis Park
Hoachanas
Aminuis
Lehututu
Kang
Tsetseng
KWEN
Narib
Stampriet
Aranos
Hukuntsi
Tshane
Motokwe
Takatokwane
St Francis Bay
HARDAP
Mariental
Gochas
KGALAGADI
Kokong
SOUTHE
Dolphin Head
Maltahöhe
Gibeon
Desert
Werda
Jwaneng
Hottentots Bay
Helmeringhausen
Brukkaros
1586 m
Tses
Koës
Terra
Firma
Tosca
Luderitz Bay
Berseba
Bethanie
Morokweng
Tosca
Diaz Pt
Lüderitz
Aus
Keetmanshoop
Bokspits
Tshabong
NOR
Elizabeth Bay
Sandverhaar
Seeheim
Schroffenstein
2202 m
Tsineng
Vrybu
KARAS
Holoog
Hotazel
WES
Cape Dernberg
Rosh Pinah
Grünau
Kanus
Karasburg
Kuruman
Gakarosa
1855 m
Oranjemund
Ariamsvlei
Warmbad
Onseepkans
Kakamas
Keimoes
Upington
Postmasburg
Lime
Acres
Warren
Barkly
West
Alexander Bay
Wreck Point
Orange
Griquatown
Kim
Steinkopf
Pofadder
Kenhardt
Marydale
Prieska
Douglas
Port Nolloth
Nababiep
Kleinsee
Springbok
Granaatboskolk
Garies
Brandvlei
Van Wyksvlei
Vosburg
Britstown
Cole
NORTHERN CAPE
De Aar
Bitterfontein
Sakrivier
Carnarvon
Vredendal
Calvinia
Williston
Victoria West
Richm
Lamberts Bay
Vanrhynsdorp
Fraserburg
Loxton
Murraysburg
Kompas
250
Saint Helena
Bay
Clanwilliam
SOUTH AFRICA
Cape Columbine
Vredenburg
Citrusdal
Sutherland
Beaufort West
Graaff-Reinet
Aberdeen
So
Piketberg
WESTERN
CAPE
Saldanha
Porterville
Ceres
Laingsburg
Prince Albert
Willowmore
17
Malmesbury
Touws River
2152 m
Calitzdorp
Atlantis
Paarl
2252 m
Ladismith
Dysselsdorp
Uite
Bellville
Worcester
Oudtshoorn
George
Knysna
Kwa Nob
Cape Town
Stellenbosch
Swellendam
Mossel Bay
Cape George
Jeffrey's Bay
Nyanga
Strand
Cape Seal
Cape of Good Hope
False
Bay
Hermanus
Port Beaufort
Danger Pt
Bredasdorp
Quoin Pt
Cape Agulhas

MOXICO
Cangombe
N O R T H
Lumbala
Chiume
CUANDO
CUBANGO
W E S T E
N a m i b
D e s e r t
Tsaris Mts
Hunsberge
K A L A H A R I
Desert
GHANZI

Grid references

E 30° F 35° G 40° H

Row 1

Mkushi · Chipata · Mchinji · CENTRAL · Salima · Massangulo · Maúa · Namuno · Namapa · Memba · Baía de Memba

EASTERN · Lilongwe · MALAWI · Mandimba · Muite · Mutali · Meconta · Minguri · Nacala

Kabwe · Petauke · Katete · Cassacatiza · Nyimba · Chofombo · Furancungo · Ulongwé · Ntcheu · Mangochi · Cuamba · NIASSA · MOZAMBIQUE · Mecuburi · Monapo · Mossuril

Lubungu · CENTRAL · Kachalola · Fingoè · Bene · Dedza · Balaka · Machinga · Malema · Ribáuè · Muecate · Moçambique

Mumbwa · Chisamba · Rufunsa · Zambue · TETE · Cazula · SOUTHERN · Zomba · Chiradzulu · Namuli 2419 m ▲ · Gurúè · Erregó · Naiopué · Gilé · Chalaua · Angoche

Lusaka · LUSAKA · Chongwe · Luangwa · Zumbo · Lago de Cahora Bassa · Songo · Mt Mulanje 3001 m ▲ · Molumbo · Alto Molócuè · NAMPULA · Mogincual · Quinga

Other labels

ZAMBIA · Kabwe · Mazabuka · Kafue · Chirundu · Màgoè · Mucumbura · Cataxa · Tete · Blantyre · Mulanje · Chikwawa · Milange · Lugela · Mugeba · Mulevala · Nova Nabúri · Moma

UTHERN · Choma · Kalomo · Zimba · Maamba · Monze · Pemba · Kariba · Karoi · MASHONALAND · Guruve · Mungari · Nhamalabue · Morrumbala · Namacurra

Livingstone · Kariba · Mhangura · CENTRAL · Mount Darwin · Centenary · Bindura · Shamva · MASHONALAND EAST · Guro · Vila de Sena · Caia · Namidobe · Quelimane

Kafue · MASHONALAND WEST · Chinhoyi · Zave · Concession · Murewa · Chiramba · Changara · Bandar · Mopeia · Marromeu · ZAMBÉZIA

Msuna · Kamativi · ZIMBABWE · Harare · Chitungwiza · MANICA · Catandica · Maringué · Chinde

MATABELELAND · Gokwe · Chakari · Chegutu · Kadoma · Marondera · Rusape · Inyangani 2592 m · Gorongosa · Serra de Gorongosa ▲ 1862 m · SOFALA · Ponta Lipobane

MIDLANDS · Kwekwe · Chivhu · Nyanga · Chimoio · Nhamatanda · Dondo

NORTH · Ngamo · Nkayi · Redcliff · Empress Mine · Gweru · Lalapansi · Mvuma · Buhera · Cashel · Mutare · Nhamatanda · Buzi · Sofala · Beira

MATABELELAND · Nyamandhlovu · Bulawayo · Mashava · Fort Rixon · Shurugwi · Gutu · Chimanimani · Monte Binga ▲ 2436 m · Dombe · Espungabera

Tutume · Sebina · Esigodini · Mbalabala · Filabusi · Zvishavane · MASVINGO · Masvingo · Chiping · Zaka · Hacufera · Chitobe · Divinhe · Machanga

NORTHEAST · Plumtree · Kezi · Gwanda · West Nicholson · Mbizi · Mwenezi · Chiredzi · Save · Jofane · Nova Mambone · Bartolomeu Dias

Francistown · MATABELELAND SOUTH · Bobonong · Tuli · Mazunga · Massangena · Mabote · Mapinhane · Vilanculos · Ilha do Bazaruto

Mmadinare · Serule · Beitbridge · Pafuri · Machaila · Sango · Chicualacuala · INHAMBANE

Selebi Phikwe · Messina · Alldays · Mapai · Chigubo · Nhachengue · Funhalouro

Palapye · Tom Burke · Vivo · Mara · Louis Trichardt · Giyani · GAZA · Massinga · Ponta da Barra Falsa

Mochudi · NORTHERN PROVINCE · Thohoyandou · Phalaborwa · Mabalane · Morrumbene · Homoíne · Panda · Ponta da Barra · Inhambane

orone · Selokwe · Sefophe · Pietersburg · Tzaneen · Lebowakgomo · Massingir · Chókuè · Inharrime · Quissico

tswa · Ellisras · Thabazimbi · Nylstroom · Warmbad · Marble Hall · Mapulanguene · Macia · Chidenguele

Sun City · Siyabuswa · MPUMALANGA · MAPUTO · Magude · Magude · Xai-Xai

ustenburg · Pretoria · Mamelodi · Newington · Tshokwane · Moamba · Marracuene

Tembisa · Krugersdorp · GAUTENG · Johannesburg · Barberton · Nelspruit · Matola · Maputo

Soweto · Germiston · Evaton · Heidelburg · Bethal · Ermelo · Manzini · Mhlume · Siteki · Cabo de Santa Maria

arletonville · Vanderbijlpark · Vereeniging · Standerton · SWAZILAND · Big Bend · Bela Vista

Klerksdorp · Sasolburg · Volksrust · Piet Retief · Hlatikulu · Lavumisa · Catuane

Kroonstad · Madadeni · Vryheid · Ubombo

Welkom · Newcastle · Ozizweni · Ulundi · Lake St Lucia

Virginia · Bethlehem · Harrismith · Dundee · Empangeni · Richards Bay

Phuthaditjhaba · Ladysmith · KWAZULU-NATAL · Richards Bay

ontein · Maseru · Teyateyaneng · Mokhotlong · Greytown · Sundumbili

Thabana Ntlenyana 3482 m ▲ · Pietermaritzburg · Stanger

Roma · Kwa Mashu · Umlazi · Durban

LESOTHO · Mafeteng · Umzinto · Isipingo · Amanzimtoti

Mohale's Hoek · Quthing · Kokstad · Marburg · Scottburgh

STERN CAPE · Barkly East · Elliot · Tsolo · Uvongo · Port Shepstone

Molteno · Umtata · Port St Johns

Queenstown · Coffee Bay

Butterworth

William's Town · Stutterheim · East London · Mdantsane

Zwelitsha · Grahamstown

Port Alfred

Ocean / regional labels

INDIAN OCEAN

Mozambique Channel

MADAGASCAR · Morondava · Bassas da India (Réunion) · Île Europa (Réunion)

Tambohorano · Maintirano · Reharaka · Masoarivo · Belo Tsiribihina · Tanjona Tsiribihina · Andranopasy · Manja · Morombe · Tanjona Ankaboa · TOLIARA · Ankazoabo ▲ 1348 m · Mahaboboka · Manombo Atsimo · Sakaraha · Andranovory · Longobory · Toliara · Betioky · Soamanonga · Fotadrevo · Ejeda · Itampolo · Ampanihy · Androka · Beloha · Tanjona Vohimena

372

Scale

0 100 200 300 400 kilometers

0 100 200 miles

Madagascar

SEYCHELLES

Praslin I.
Silhouette I.
La Digue I.
Victoria
Mahé I.

Amirante
Isles

Platte I.

Alphonse I.

Coetivy I.

Agalega Is
(Mauritius)

St Pierre I.
Providence I.

Aldabra
Is
Cosmoledo
Group
Assumption I.
Astove I.
Farquhar
Group

Kilifi
Mombasa

Wete
Pemba I.
Chake Chake

Mafia I.

TANZANIA
Mtwara
Quionga
Cabo Delgado
Palma
CABO DELGADO
Mocimboa da Praia
Diaca
Chai
Mucojo
Muaguide
Quissanga
Baía de Pemba
Pemba
Lúrio
MOZAMBIQUE
Memba
Baía de Memba
Minguri
Mogapo
Nacala
Mossuril
Moçambique
NAMPULA
Mogincual
Quinga

COMOROS
Mitsamiouli
Njazidja
(Grande Comore) Moroni
Kartala
2361 m
Fomboni
Mwali
(Mohéli)
Nzwani
(Anjouan)
Moutsamoudou
Domoni
MAYOTTE
(Fr.)
Mamoudzou Dzaoudzi

Îles Glorieuses
(Réunion)
Tanjona Bobaomby
(Cap d'Ambre)
Andranovondronina
Ramena
Ambohitra
1475 m
Antsiranana
Bobasakoa
Anivorano Avaratra
Ampisikinana
Nosy Bé
Ambilobe
Iharaña
Lohatanjona Angadoka
ANTSIRANANA
1785 m
Ampanefena
Ambanja
Maromokotro
Marovato
2876 m
Doany
Sambava
Bealanana
Analalava
Ampahana
Lohatanjona Maromony
Antsohihy
Andapa
Antalaha

INDIAN

Mahajanga
Katsepy
Befandriana Avaratra
Leanja
Mahalevona
Ampanavoana
Vinanivao
Ambalakida
Boriziny
Maroantsetra
Mandritsara
Tanjona Masoala
Tanjona Vilanandro
Mitsinjo
Marovoay
Mampikony
Mananara
Avaratra
Tromelin I.
(Réunion)
Ambohipaky
Soalala
Manarantsandry
1301 m
Helodrano
Antongila
Madirovalo
Ambato Boeny
Besalampy
Sitampiky
Tsaratanana
TOAMASINA
Manompana
Mahabe
Maevatanana
Andilamena
Soanierana-Ivongo
Île Juan de Nova
(Réunion)
MAHAJANGA
Ikahavo
847 m
Kandreho
Betrandraka
Vavatenina
Fenoarivo Atsinanana
Tambohorano
Andriamena
Amparafaravola
Mahavelona
Morafenobe
Ambatomainty
Vatoloha
1575 m
Ambatondrazaka
Maintirano
Beravina
Ankazobe
Andilanatoby
Didy
Toamasina
Reharaka
Antsalova
ANTANANARIVO
Fanandrana
Ambohidratrimo
Maroseranana
Masoarivo
Miarinarivo
Moramanga
Ampasimanolotra
Tsiroanomandidy
Antananarivo
MADAGASCAR
Miandrivazo
Ambatolampy
Anosibe an'Ala
Vatomandry
Belo Tsiribihina
Antanambao
Tanjona Tsiribihina
Antsirabe
Manampotsy
2119 m
Ibinty
Mahanoro
Morondava
Malaimbandy
2254 m
Fandriana
Marolambo
Mahabo
Ambato-
finandrahana
Ambositra
Amborompotsy
2052 m
Vohitrandriana
Andranopasy
Mandabe
Ikalamavony
Ambohimahasoa
Manja
Mananjary
Morombe
Beroroha
Fianarantsoa
Ifanadiana
Tanjona
Ankaboa
Ambalavao
FIANARANTSOA
Ampasimanjeva
TOLIARA
Zazafotsy
Ikongo
Vohilava
Ankazoabo
Boby
Ihosy
2658 m
Manakara
Satrokala
Ivohibe
Vohipeno
Mahaboboka
1348 m
Ranohira
Vondrozo
Manombo Atsimo
Sakaraha
Farafangana
Tropic of Capricorn
Andranovory
1824 m
Lopary
Toliara
Bezaha
Ranomena
Vangaindrano
Tongobory
Benenitra
Midongy Atsimo
Betioky
Belamoty
Ivakoany
Manambondro
Soamanonga
1637 m
Manankoliva
Befotaka
Fotadrevo
Beraketa
Ejeda
Bekily
Imanombo
Manantenina
Itampolo
Tranoroa
Tranomaro
Ampanihy
Antanimora Atsimo
Androka
Tôlañaro
Beloha
Tsiombe
Ambovombe
Tanjona
Vohimena
Betanty
Ambosary

MOZAMBIQUE
OCEAN

MAURITIUS
Port Louis
Curepipe
Mahébourg
Saint-
Denis
RÉUNION
Saint-
Paul
(Fr.)
Saint-
Pierre

Mascarene Islands
Tropic of Capricorn

Africa

© Random House Australia Pty Ltd

kilometers 0 100 200 300 400
miles 0 100 200

Island Nations and Dependencies

RÉUNION
(France)
Scale 1:1,500,000

INDIAN OCEAN

Pte des Galets
Le Port
La Possession
Saint-Denis
Sainte-Marie
Sainte-Suzanne
Bagatelle
Saint-André
Saint-Paul
Saint-Gilles-les Bains
Salazie
Hell-Bourg
Bras-Panon
Pte des Aigrettes
Trois Bassins
▲2401 m
Le Piton Rouge
Piton des Neiges
▲3069 m
Saint-Benoît
Sainte-Rose
Saint-Leu
Les Makes
Cilaos
La Plaine des Cafres
Pte Rouge
Bois-Blanc
Les Avirons
Le Riviere
▲2632 m
Piton de la Fournaise
Saint-Louis
Pte de la Table
Saint-Pierre
Le Tampon
Takamaka
Pte du Parc
Saint-Joseph
Langevin
Saint-Philippe

RODRIGUES
(Mauritius)
Scale 1:500,000

INDIAN OCEAN

Pte aux Cornes
Port Mathurin
Pte Coton
Pte du Diable
Mt Limon
396 m
Rodrigues
Topaze Bay
Gombrani I.
Crab I.
Pierrot I.

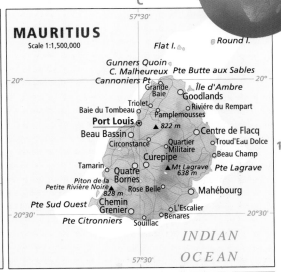

MAURITIUS
Scale 1:1,500,000

Flat I.
Round I.
Gunners Quoin
C. Malheureux
Pte Butte aux Sables
Cannoniers Pt
Grande Baie
Goodlands
Triolet
Île d'Ambre
Baie du Tombeau
Rivière du Rempart
▲822 m
Pamplemousses
Port Louis
Centre de Flacq
Beau Bassin
Quartier Militaire
Troud'Eau Dolce
Circonstance
Beau Champ
Tamarin
Curepipe
Quatre Bornes
▲Mt Lagrave
638 m
Pte Lagrave
Piton de la Riviere Noire
Rose Belle
Mahébourg
Petite Rivière Noire
828 m
L'Escalier
Pte Sud Ouest
Chemin Grenier
Benares
Pte Citronniers
Souillac
INDIAN OCEAN

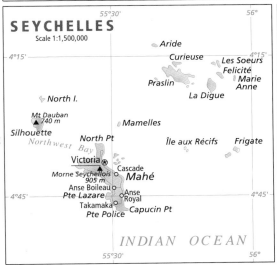

SEYCHELLES
Scale 1:1,500,000

Aride
Curieuse
Les Soeurs
Felicité
Praslin
Marie Anne
La Digue
North I.
Mt Dauban
▲740 m
Silhouette
Mamelles
Northwest Bay
Île aux Récifs
Frigate
North Pt
Victoria
Cascade
Morne Seychellois
▲905 m
Mahé
Anse Boileau
Anse Royal
Pte Lazare
Takamaka
Capucin Pt
Pte Police
INDIAN OCEAN

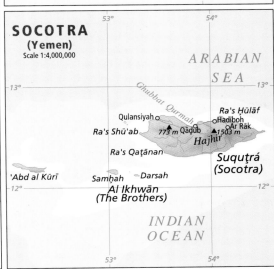

SOCOTRA
(Yemen)
Scale 1:4,000,000

ARABIAN SEA

Ghubbat Qurmah
Ra's Hūlāf
Qulansiyah
Hadiboh
Ra's Shū'ab
773 m
Qāḍūb
Ar Rāk
1503 m
Hajhir
Suquṭrá
(Socotra)
Ra's Qaṭānan
'Abd al Kūrī
Samhah
Darsah
Al Ikhwān
(The Brothers)
INDIAN OCEAN

TRISTAN DA CUNHA
(St Helena)
Scale 1:750,000

ATLANTIC OCEAN

Rookery Pt
Edinburgh
Anchorstock Pt
Queen Mary's Peak
▲2060 m
Sandy Pt
Tristan da Cunha
Stonyhill Pt
Seal Bay
West Pt
Inaccessible I.
East Pt
▲561 m
Stoltenhoff I.
Middle I.
Nightingale I.

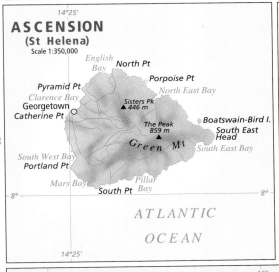

ASCENSION
(St Helena)
Scale 1:350,000

English Bay
North Pt
Porpoise Pt
Pyramid Pt
North East Bay
Clarence Bay
Sisters Pk
▲446 m
Georgetown
Catherine Pt
The Peak
859 m
Boatswain-Bird I.
Green Mt
South East Head
South West Bay
South East Bay
Portland Pt
Mars Bay
Pillar Bay
South Pt
ATLANTIC OCEAN

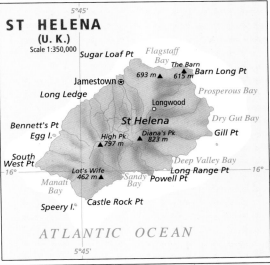

ST HELENA
(U.K.)
Scale 1:350,000

Sugar Loaf Pt
Flagstaff Bay
The Barn
693 m ▲
Barn Long Pt
615 m ▲
Jamestown
Long Ledge
Longwood
Prosperous Bay
Bennett's Pt
St Helena
Dry Gut Bay
Egg I.
High Pk
▲797 m
Diana's Pk
▲823 m
Gill Pt
South West Pt
Long Range Pt
Manati Bay
Lot's Wife
462 m ▲
Sandy Bay
Powell Pt
Deep Valley Bay
Speery I.
Castle Rock Pt
ATLANTIC OCEAN

MADEIRA
(Portugal)
Scale 1:2,000,000

Porto Santo
517 m ▲
Ilhéu de Ferro
Porto Santo
Ilhéu de Baixo
Porto Moniz
São Vicente
Santana
Pto do Pargo
Faial
Pta de São Lourenço
Calheta
Pico Ruivo de Santana
▲1862 m
Machico
Ribeira Brava
Santa Cruz
Câmara de Lobos
Madeira
Funchal
Deserta Grande
Ilhas Desertas
Ilhéu do Bugio
ATLANTIC OCEAN

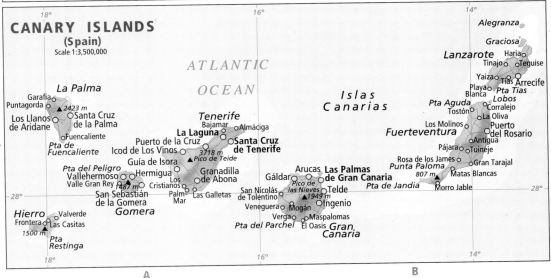

CANARY ISLANDS
(Spain)
Scale 1:3,500,000

ATLANTIC OCEAN

La Palma
Garafia
Puntagorda
▲2423 m
Los Llanos de Aridane
Santa Cruz de la Palma
Fuencaliente
Pta de Fuencaliente
Tenerife
Bajamar
Almáciga
La Laguna
Santa Cruz de Tenerife
Puerto de la Cruz
Icod de Los Vinos
▲3718 m
Pico de Teide
Guía de Isora
Granadilla de Abona
Hermigua
Los
▲1487 m
Cristianos
Vallehermoso
Valle Gran Rey
Gáldar
Arucas
Las Palmas de Gran Canaria
San Sebastián de la Gomera
Palm Mar
San Nicolás de Tolentino
▲1949 m
Telde
Gomera
Las Galletas
Ingenio
Hierro
Veneguera
Mogán
Maspalomas
El Oasis
Frontera
Valverde
Las Casitas
Pta del Parchel
Verga
Gran Canaria
1500 m
Pta Restinga

Islas Canarias
Alegranza
Graciosa
Lanzarote
Haria
Tinajo
Teguise
Yaiza
Tías
Arrecife
Playa Blanca
Pta Tias
Lobos
Pta Aguda
Corralejo
Tostón
La Oliva
Los Molinos
Puerto del Rosario
Fuerteventura
Pájara
Antigua
Tuineje
Rosa de los James
Gran Tarajal
Punta Paloma
807 m ▲
Matas Blancas
Pta de Jandia
Morro Jable

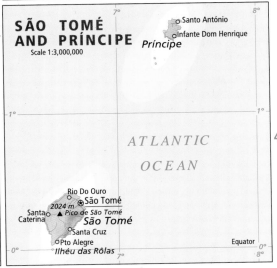

SÃO TOMÉ AND PRÍNCIPE
Scale 1:3,000,000

Santo António
Infante Dom Henrique
Príncipe
ATLANTIC OCEAN
Rio Do Ouro
São Tomé
2024 m
Santa Caterina
Pico de São Tomé
São Tomé
Santa Cruz
Pto Alegre
Ilhéu das Rôlas
Equator

Africa

North and Central America

Juventud lies off the southwest coast. Less mountainous than the other islands in the Greater Antilles group, Cuba nevertheless has three distinct ranges—the Oriental (Sierra Maestra), the Central, and the Occidental (Sierra de los Organos). These cover roughly 25 percent of the territory east to west. The remaining 75 percent of Cuba's surface area consists of lowlands and basins. On the more fertile soils sugar plantations, rice fields, coffee plantations, and tobacco fields are found; livestock is run on the central savanna. Cuba's irregular coastline is lined with mangroves, beaches, and coral reefs. Despite deforestation the island still has considerable areas of woodland, ranging from tropical near-jungle to pines growing in upland areas. Cuba has a mostly hot climate and experiences heavy seasonal rainfall and periodic hurricanes.

Sugarcane remains the country's main cash crop, as it has for more than 100 years. Cuba is the world's third-largest sugar producer, and sugar represents almost 50 percent by value of the country's exports. Other crops are tobacco, rice, potatoes, tubers, citrus fruit, and coffee. There are also extensive timber resources, including mahogany and cedar. Cuba has the world's fourth-largest nickel deposits, and production is rising as a result of a joint venture with a Canadian company.

Its situation as one of the world's few remaining communist states has left Cuba isolated and with few trading partners. In addition, because the government has been unwilling to hold multi-party elections, the country has been subject to a severe embargo imposed by the USA. Poor sugar harvests, insufficient funds to pay for fuel, and mounting deficits, have added to the country's difficulties in recent times.

Fact File

OFFICIAL NAME Republic of Cuba

FORM OF GOVERNMENT Communist state with single legislative body (National Assembly of People's Power)

CAPITAL Havana

AREA 110,860 sq km (42,803 sq miles)

TIME ZONE GMT – 5 hours

POPULATION 11,088,829

PROJECTED POPULATION 2005 11,313,934

POPULATION DENSITY 100 per sq km (259 per sq mile)

LIFE EXPECTANCY 75.5

INFANT MORTALITY (PER 1,000) 8.9

OFFICIAL LANGUAGE Spanish

LITERACY RATE 95.4%

RELIGIONS Roman Catholic 40%, Protestant and African Spiritist 10%, non-religious 50%

ETHNIC GROUPS Mixed African–European 51%, European 37%, African 11%, Chinese 1%

CURRENCY Cuban peso

ECONOMY Services 48%, industry 29%, agriculture 23%

GNP PER CAPITA Est. US$766–3,035

CLIMATE Tropical, moderated by trade winds; wet season May to October

HIGHEST POINT Pico Turquino 1,974 m (6,476 ft)

MAP REFERENCE Pages 428–29

Dominica

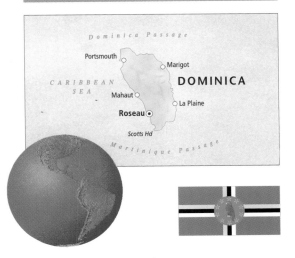

Fought over for years by the English and the French, the Caribbean island of Dominica was mainly occupied by the British after 1759. Locally it is known as the "nature island" because of its extensive forests and wildlife. It is unusual in still having a community of about 3,000 Carib Indians, whose fierce ancestors, protected by the forests in the interior, held off European colonization for 250 years. In the eighteenth century African slaves were brought to the island as labor and their descendants form the majority of the population today. Independence came to Dominica in 1978. Soon after, it was devastated by a series of hurricanes, while two coup attempts complicated its political life. Today, in free elections, power is contested between three parties in a stable democracy.

The most mountainous of the Lesser Antilles, Dominica is a volcanic island with fertile soils and the second largest boiling lake in the world. A high ridge forms the backbone of the island, from which several rivers flow to an indented coastline. There are many vents and hot springs. The rich volcanic soil supports dense tropical vegetation over 41 percent of Dominica's surface; only 9 percent of the land is arable. The climate is warm and humid, with a risk of hurricanes during the rainy season from June to October. During 1995 hurricanes ruined 90 percent of the banana crop.

The wildlife to be seen in the Morne Trois Pitons National Park is an important tourist attraction.

Dominica's only mineral resource is pumice and it has to import all its energy. There is hydro-electric potential in the rivers of the interior. Bananas, citrus fruits, and coconuts are the main cash crops—bananas accounting for 48 percent of exports, and coconut-based soaps 25 percent. Other exports include bay oil and vegetables. The country has to import much of its food and is depending on the development of luxury tourism for economic growth. Ecotourism is increasing, with visitors coming to view rare indigenous birds and volcanic sulphur pools. The lack of an airport able to take jetliners makes the country less accessible than its neighbors for mass-market tourism.

Fact File

OFFICIAL NAME Commonwealth of Dominica

FORM OF GOVERNMENT Parliamentary state with single legislative body (House of Assembly)

CAPITAL Roseau

AREA 750 sq km (290 sq miles)

TIME ZONE GMT – 4 hours

POPULATION 64,881

PROJECTED POPULATION 2005 60,761

POPULATION DENSITY 86.5 per sq km (224 per sq mile)

LIFE EXPECTANCY 78

INFANT MORTALITY (PER 1,000) 8.8

OFFICIAL LANGUAGE English

OTHER LANGUAGE French Creole

LITERACY RATE 94%

RELIGIONS Roman Catholic 77%, Protestant 15%, other 6%, none 2%

ETHNIC GROUPS African 92%, mixed 6%, indigenous 1.5%, European 0.5%

CURRENCY East Caribbean dollar

ECONOMY Services 55%, agriculture 25%, industry 20%

GNP PER CAPITA US$2,990

CLIMATE Tropical, moderated by trade winds

HIGHEST POINT Morne Diablatins 1,447 m (4,747 ft)

MAP REFERENCE Page 427

Dominican Republic

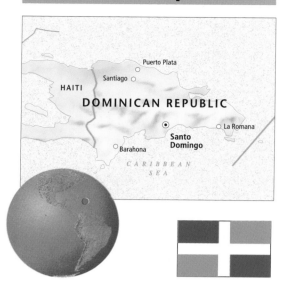

The second largest Caribbean nation in both area and population, the Dominican Republic occupies the eastern two-thirds of the island of Hispaniola. The island was visited by Christopher Columbus in 1492 and in 1496 his brother founded the city of Santo Domingo on its southern coast—the oldest Spanish city in the Americas. It was first colonized by Spain but the development of its sugar industry resulted from a period of French control. The country won independence in 1844 and since that time it has been ruled by a series of dictators with only short intervals of democracy. A bitter civil war in 1965 brought the intervention of the USA, which has kept a watch on Dominican affairs since then. Civil unrest continues.

With a mountainous landscape, including the highest point in the West Indies, Pico Duarte, the Dominican Republic contains three considerable ranges—the Cordillera Septentrional in the north, the massive Cordillera Central, and the southern Sierra de Bahoruco. Between these ranges, and to the east, lie fertile valleys and lowlands. These include the Cibao Valley in the north, the Vega Real, and the coastal plains where sugar plantations are found. Because of the mountainous terrain there are wide variations in temperature and rainfall. Low-lying areas in the south and east support a dry savanna vegetation suitable for livestock raising. The Dominican Republic also has the

lowest point in the West Indies—Lake Enriquillo, 44 m (144 ft) below sea level. The lake bisects the mountains in the southwest.

While still heavily dependent on its traditional agricultural base, in recent years the economy has been supplemented by industrial growth (making use of a vast hydroelectric potential), and a large increase in tourism. The Dominican Republic has good beaches, and a hotel capacity of 30,000 rooms, the highest in the Caribbean. Sugar is still the leading agricultural export, followed by coffee, cocoa, tobacco, and fruit. Nickel and gold mining are increasing in economic importance. Subsistence farming provides most of the rural population with its livelihood, the staple crops being rice and corn. State-owned sugar plantations provide another source of employment. Illegal narcotics also play a part in the economy; the country is a transshipment point for drugs bound for the USA.

Fact File

OFFICIAL NAME	Dominican Republic
FORM OF GOVERNMENT	Republic with two legislative bodies (Senate and Chamber of Deputies)
CAPITAL	Santo Domingo
AREA	48,730 sq km (18,815 sq miles)
TIME ZONE	GMT – 4 hours
POPULATION	8,129,734
PROJECTED POPULATION 2005	8,936,667
POPULATION DENSITY	166.8 per sq km (432 per sq mile)
LIFE EXPECTANCY	70.1
INFANT MORTALITY (PER 1,000)	42.5
OFFICIAL LANGUAGE	Spanish
OTHER LANGUAGE	French Creole
LITERACY RATE	81.5%
RELIGIONS	Roman Catholic 95%, other 5%
ETHNIC GROUPS	Mixed African–European 73%, European 16%, African 11%
CURRENCY	Peso
ECONOMY	Agriculture 46%, services 38%, industry 16%
GNP PER CAPITA	US$1,460
CLIMATE	Tropical, with wet season May to November
HIGHEST POINT	Pico Duarte 3,175 m (10,416 ft)
MAP REFERENCE	Page 429

El Salvador

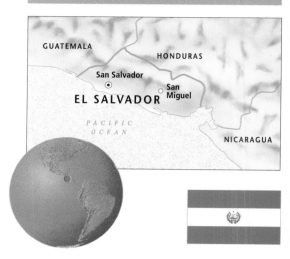

El Salvador is the smallest, most densely populated country in Central America, and the only one without a coast on the Caribbean. It is in a seismic zone and has some 20 volcanoes, several of which are active. Once the home of the Pipil Indians and later a part of the Mexican Empire, the country won full independence in 1841 and established itself as the Republic of El Salvador in 1859. Over 100 years of civil strife and military rule followed.

From the 1880s about 75 percent of the land has been in the hands of 14 families, who farm huge plantations producing coffee, tobacco, and sugar. The potential for conflict between this landed oligarchy and the rural poor has been present since that time and in the 1970s left-wing disillusionment with the electoral process led to the formation of a number of guerrilla groups. Between 1979 and 1991 civil war raged, with the loss of 75,000 lives, and many people emigrated. The political and economic effects of this conflict are still evident.

Behind El Salvador's narrow Pacific coastal plain rises a volcanic range. Inland is a rich and fertile central plain, occupying 25 percent of the country's total land area. The urban and rural population in this area accounts for 60 percent of the country's total, and produces 90 percent of El Salvador's coffee and tobacco, along with most of its sugar and corn. Further inland still, along the frontier with Honduras, are mountain ranges. Once forested and unpopulated, they now draw poor farmers desperate for land.

El Salvador's economy has few strengths other than a large amount of cheap labor. Damage from the civil war is estimated at $2 billion and cotton and sugar cultivation declined significantly during the conflict. Coffee contributes about 90 percent of exports. Foreign aid remains important, much coming from the USA. Manufacturing is based on food and beverage processing, while other industries are textiles, clothing, petroleum products, and cement. The civil war brought tourism to a standstill but peace has resulted in visitors returning to the Pacific beach resorts of El Salvador's Costa del Sol.

El Salvador contains about 20 volcanoes, some still active. Izalco Volcano, El Salvador, seen from lush forest (left). Grenada is volcanic in origin and bisected by a mountain ridge; the coastal capital of St Georges, sheltered by hills (above right).

Fact File

OFFICIAL NAME Republic of El Salvador

FORM OF GOVERNMENT Republic with single legislative body (Legislative Assembly)

CAPITAL San Salvador

AREA 21,040 sq km (8,123 sq miles)

TIME ZONE GMT – 6 hours

POPULATION 5,839,079

PROJECTED POPULATION 2005 6,382,909

POPULATION DENSITY 277.5 per sq km (718.7 per sq mile)

LIFE EXPECTANCY 70

INFANT MORTALITY (PER 1,000) 28.4

OFFICIAL LANGUAGE Spanish

OTHER LANGUAGE Nahua

LITERACY RATE 70.9%

RELIGIONS Roman Catholic 75%, Protestant and other 25%

ETHNIC GROUPS Mixed indigenous–European 94%, indigenous 5%, European 1%

CURRENCY Colón

ECONOMY Services 70%, industry 22%, agriculture 8%

GNP PER CAPITA US$1,610

CLIMATE Tropical, with wet season May to October; cooler in mountains

HIGHEST POINT Cerro El Pittal 2,730 m (8,957 ft)

MAP REFERENCE Page 428

Grenada

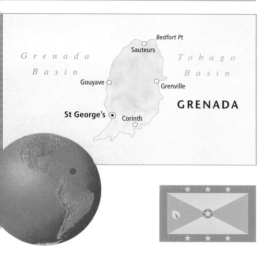

The state of Grenada consists of the island of Grenada, lying off the coast of Venezuela not far from Trinidad, and two small islands of the Southern Grenadines—Carriacou and Petite Martinique. The islands were visited by Columbus in 1498 but the original Carib Indian inhabitants fought off all invaders until French settlers arrived in the 1650s. Grenada then became a typical sugar-producing Caribbean island, with plantations worked by slaves brought from Africa. British since 1762, it has English as an official language, though some Grenadans still speak a French patois. It won independence in 1974 and in 1979 the country became communist after a bloodless coup. When the coup leader was murdered by fellow Marxists in 1983, the USA, with support from a number of other Caribbean countries,

intervened to restore democratic elections. Since then power has been contested, and has alternated between several different political parties. Economic recovery from the events of 1983 has been slow.

The most southerly of the Windward Islands, the main island of Grenada is volcanic in origin and has fertile soils. A forested mountain ridge runs north–south, cut by rivers, and there are a number of lakes, including the Grand Etang at an elevation of 530 m (1,739 ft). The western coastline is precipitous; the southern coastal landscape of beaches is gentler and includes some natural harbors. In recent years the government has become interested in developing ecotourism but protection of key environmental sites remains a concern. Large resort projects have resulted in serious beach erosion.

Grenada is known in the Caribbean as "the spice island," and is the world's leading producer of nutmeg and mace, its main crop. Other exports include cocoa and bananas, but attempts to diversify the economy from an agricultural base have so far been unsuccessful. The farming practised by the rural population is mostly small scale, with the exception of a few cooperatives. The small manufacturing sector is based on food-processing and makes products such as chocolate, sugar, alcoholic beverages, and jam. Garments and furniture are also produced, mainly for export to Trinidad and Tobago. After the political crisis of 1979 to 1983 tourism largely ceased, but it is gradually recovering.

Fact File

OFFICIAL NAME Grenada

FORM OF GOVERNMENT Constitutional monarchy with two legislative houses (Senate and House of Representatives)

CAPITAL St Georges

AREA 340 sq km (131 sq miles)

TIME ZONE GMT – 4 hours

POPULATION 97,008

PROJECTED POPULATION 2005 104,434

POPULATION DENSITY 285.3 per sq km (738.9 per sq mile)

LIFE EXPECTANCY 71.6

INFANT MORTALITY (PER 1,000) 11.1

OFFICIAL LANGUAGE English

OTHER LANGUAGE French patois

LITERACY RATE 98%

RELIGIONS Roman Catholic 64%, Protestant (including Anglican, Seventh Day Adventist, Pentecostal) 27%, other 9%

ETHNIC GROUPS African 84%, mixed 12%, East Indian 3%, European 1%

CURRENCY East Caribbean dollar

ECONOMY Services 65%, agriculture 20%, industry 15%

GNP PER CAPITA US$2,980

CLIMATE Tropical, moderated by trade winds

HIGHEST POINT Mt Saint Catherine 840 m (2,756 ft)

MAP REFERENCE Page 427

Guatemala

Fact File

OFFICIAL NAME Republic of Guatemala

FORM OF GOVERNMENT Republic with single legislative body (Congress of the Republic)

CAPITAL Guatemala

AREA 108,890 sq km (42,042 sq miles)

TIME ZONE GMT – 6 hours

POPULATION 12,335,580

PROJECTED POPULATION 2005 14,423,051

POPULATION DENSITY 113.3 per sq km (293.4 per sq mile)

LIFE EXPECTANCY 66.5

INFANT MORTALITY (PER 1,000) 46.2

OFFICIAL LANGUAGE Spanish

OTHER LANGUAGES Indigenous languages

LITERACY RATE 55.7%

RELIGIONS Roman Catholic 75%, Protestant 25%; some traditional Mayan beliefs

ETHNIC GROUPS Mixed indigenous–European 56%, indigenous 44%

CURRENCY Quetzal

ECONOMY Agriculture 50%, services 38%, industry 12%

GNP PER CAPITA US$1,340

CLIMATE Tropical, but cooler in highlands

HIGHEST POINT Volcan Tajumulco 4,220 m (13,845 ft)

MAP REFERENCE Page 428

Guatemala lies just south of Mexico, and is the most populous of the Central American states. It was once part of the home of the Mayan civilization which reached its peak about AD 300–900. It has numerous volcanoes, including Tajumulco, the highest peak in Central America. In 1523 the region was overrun by Spanish conquistadors. As elsewhere in Central and South America, the newly arrived Spanish established large agricultural estates worked by Amerindian laborers, setting the social and economic pattern for 300 years. After becoming a republic in 1839, Guatemala has had a history of dictatorship, coups d'état, and guerrilla insurgency. Profound social divisions exist between the Amerindian majority, and an elite of mixed Spanish and Amerindian ancestry (called Ladinos) who run the government. Guatemala has had

One of the ruined temples of Tikal, the great Mayan religious center in Guatemala (above). The Sunday market in Chichi, Guatemala (right). An aerial view of Tegucigalpa, the capital of Honduras (far right).

civilian rule since 1985. In 1996 a United Nations mediated accord was signed by President Alvaro Arzu and the members of the URNG guerrilla movement which it is hoped will bring an end to 36 years of armed struggle.

Two large mountain ranges cross the heart of the country. In the north are the older and more eroded Altos Cuchumatanes. To the south the geologically younger Sierra Madre Range includes 33 volcanoes, of which three are still active. Soil enriched with volcanic ash washed down from the Sierra Madre has created a narrow but fertile plain on the Pacific coast. This has been used for agriculture on a commercial scale only since the 1950s, when malaria was first brought under control and access roads were built. Now cattle and cotton are more important than this region's traditional banana crop. On the lower mountain slopes, up to about 1,500 m (5,000 ft), most of the country's highest quality coffee is grown. In the north of Guatemala the highlands fall away to the large, flat, forested Peten Tableland, where many ancient Mayan ruins are found, and to the plains along the Gulf of Honduras.

Guatemala's economy is largely agricultural. Coffee is the main crop and chief export, other exports being sugar, bananas, cardamom, and beef. From the forests, now reduced to about 40 percent of the country's land area, come timber and chicle, the gum used for chewing gum. The country has few mineral or energy reserves, apart from small amounts of petroleum, and until recently guerrilla activity has hindered access to the wells. Industries include sugar refining, furniture, chemicals, metals, rubber, textiles and clothing, and tourism. Tourism, largely comprising visits to the Maya ruins, revived after the military activities of the 1980s, but fell into decline again in 1994 and 1995 following attacks on foreigners. From 1990 the economy has shown mild but consistent growth though, given the extreme disparity of wealth, the government faces many difficulties in implementing its program of modernization and the alleviation of poverty.

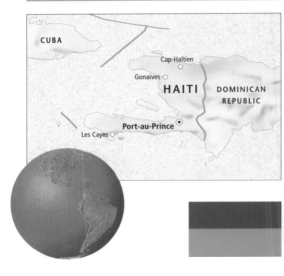

Haiti

Haiti lies in the Caribbean, east of Cuba. It is the western third of the island of Hispaniola, the Dominican Republic occupying the remainder. Visited by Columbus in 1492, it was used by the Spanish for sugarcane cultivation and was ceded to France in 1697. In the aftermath of the French Revolution it was the scene of a slave rebellion which led to the establishment, in 1804, of the world's first black republic. Since then the country has endured almost two centuries of instability, violence, dictatorship, military rule, and endemic poverty. Today, Haiti is the poorest country in the western hemisphere. Under the brutal regime of the Duvalier family, between 1957 and 1986, it became a police state enforced by a private militia called the Tontons Macoute. Recent years have seen faltering steps toward electoral democracy and modest civil service reforms, but political killings are still occurring under an apparently corrupt and ineffective judicial system.

Two peninsulas enclose the central plain of the Artibonite River, and the bight of the Golfe de la Gonâve beyond. Some 75 percent of Haiti's terrain is mountainous, the Massif du Nord providing the range which forms the northern peninsula, before extending east into the Dominican Republic where it becomes Hispaniola's Cordillera Central. The southern peninsula contains the Massif de la Hotte at its western end, and the Massif de la Selle in the east. The fertile lowland areas are densely populated, the largest of these being the Plaine du Nord. On the plains the major crop is sugarcane, coffee plantations being found on the higher land. The majority of the population is engaged in subsistence farming, growing cassava, bananas, and corn. Haiti's environmental problems are severe: one-third of its soil is seriously eroded, and extensive deforestation has occurred in the course of charcoal production.

Haiti is without strategic resources and, during a period of economic sanctions imposed to put pressure on the government in 1991, it was forced to find clandestine sources of oil. In addition to sugar refining, light industry includes flour and and cement and the manufacture of textiles, shoes, and cooking utensils. The country's location, history, and culture proved attractive to tourists in the 1960s and 1970s, despite the repressive regime, but widespread crime has affected the industry in recent years.

Fact File

OFFICIAL NAME Republic of Haiti

FORM OF GOVERNMENT Republic with two legislative bodies (Senate and Chamber of Deputies)

CAPITAL Port-au-Prince

AREA 27,750 sq km (10,714 sq miles)

TIME ZONE GMT – 5 hours

POPULATION 6,884,264

PROJECTED POPULATION 2005 7,583,777

POPULATION DENSITY 248.1 per sq km (642.6 per sq mile)

LIFE EXPECTANCY 51.7

INFANT MORTALITY (PER 1,000) 97.6

OFFICIAL LANGUAGE French

OTHER LANGUAGE French Creole

LITERACY RATE 44.1%

RELIGIONS Roman Catholic 80% (most of whom also practice Voodoo), Protestant 16% (Baptist 10%, Pentecostal 4%, Adventist 1%, other 1%), other 4%

ETHNIC GROUPS African 95%, mixed African–European 5%

CURRENCY Gourd

ECONOMY Agriculture 50%, services 44%, industry 6%

GNP PER CAPITA US$250

CLIMATE Mainly tropical; semiarid in eastern mountains; wet seasons April to June and August to November

HIGHEST POINT Pic de la Selle 2,680 m (8,792 ft)

MAP REFERENCE Page 429

Honduras

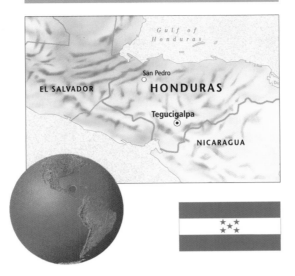

Honduras is the second largest of the Central American countries. Its mountainous mass lies across the isthmus north of Nicaragua, with Guatemala to the west and El Salvador to the southwest. The Caribbean shoreline runs eastward from the Guatemalan border to the flat and almost uninhabited Mosquito Coast. In the west are the historic ruins of Copan, a site of the ancient Maya civilization which ended long before the Spaniards arrived in 1522. Gold first drew the Spanish to Honduras and when they discovered it in the west they founded Tegucigalpa in 1524. The Honduran mountains are highly metalliferous and silver is still an important export. Independent from Spain since 1821, the country has had decades of military rule with only the occasional elected government. The challenge for the present administration is to reduce the role of the military in political and economic life.

At least 75 percent of Honduras is mountainous. From the central highlands several river valleys run northwest to the coast, where the plains along the Caribbean shore broaden toward the east. The lower valleys have been reclaimed and the forests have been replaced by banana plantations. On the Pacific side there is a short stretch of coast in the Gulf of Fonseca. The adjacent lowlands are used for growing cotton. Rainforest in the northeast provides sanctuary for a great variety of wildlife.

The original "banana republic," Honduras was the world's leading exporter during the 1920s and 1930s. Bananas still account for nearly a quarter of all exports but coffee is now the largest earner. The country depends heavily on the USA for trade: 53 percent of its exports and 50 percent of its imports are with the US. Most the workforce are farmers, many of them at a subsistence level: food staples are corn, beans, and rice. Small-scale manufactures include furniture, textiles, footwear, chemicals, and cement. Subject to an International Monetary Fund (IMF) restructuring program in the 1990s, Honduras has faced difficulties, with its already poor people subject to sharp tax rises. In 1998, Hurricane Mitch killed more than 9,000 people in Central America, and devastated crops and left thousands homeless.

Fact File

OFFICIAL NAME Republic of Honduras

FORM OF GOVERNMENT Republic with single legislative body (National Congress)

CAPITAL Tegucigalpa

AREA 112,090 sq km (43,278 sq miles)

TIME ZONE GMT – 6 hours

POPULATION 5,997,327

PROJECTED POPULATION 2005 6,750,160

POPULATION DENSITY 53.5 per sq km (138.6 per sq mile)

LIFE EXPECTANCY 64.7

INFANT MORTALITY (PER 1,000) 40.8

OFFICIAL LANGUAGE Spanish

OTHER LANGUAGES Indigenous languages, English Creole

LITERACY RATE 72%

RELIGIONS Roman Catholic 97%, Protestant 3%

ETHNIC GROUPS Mixed indigenous–European 90%, indigenous 7%, African 2%, European 1%

CURRENCY Lempira

ECONOMY Agriculture 60%, services 24%, industry 16%

GNP PER CAPITA US$600

CLIMATE Tropical on plains, cooler in mountains

HIGHEST POINT Cerro Las Minas 2,849 m (9,347 ft)

MAP REFERENCE Page 428

Jamaica

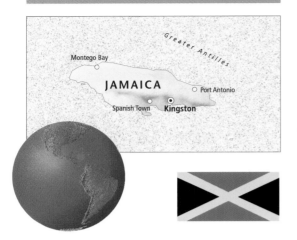

The Caribbean island of Jamaica lies 144 km (98 miles) south of Cuba and southwest of Haiti. Mountainous in the interior, it is the most populous of the English-speaking Caribbean islands. Arawak Indians were its first inhabitants. Columbus visited in 1494 and a slave-based sugar producing plantation society was established by the British after they seized the island in 1655. It won independence from Britain in 1962. An important contributor to world music, Jamaica is the home of reggae, a style originating in Kingston's tough urban environment. Also from Jamaica come the Rastafarians, followers of the one-time Emperor of Ethiopia. In September 1988 Jamaica was devastated by the fiercest hurricane to strike the island this century, causing widespread loss of life and leaving 20 percent of the people homeless.

In the northwest of the island is a limestone area of steep ridges and isolated basins, pitted with sink-holes. This "cockpit country" once gave refuge to escaped slaves. In the east the land rises to become the densely forested Blue Mountains. In the west the River Black is navigable upstream for about 30 km (19 miles). Sugar plantations dominate the densely populated and extensively cultivated lowland coastal fringe. Seasonal rains fall most heavily on the northeastern mountain slopes—still covered in the rainforest once found all over the island. In the rainshadow of the mountains, the southern lowlands support only savanna scrub.

Bauxite has been mined since 1952. Most of it is exported as ore, and about one-fifth as alumina, making Jamaica the world's third-largest producer. This accounts for more than 50 percent of exports. Tourism and bauxite production are Jamaica's two main industries, and comprise almost two-thirds of foreign earnings. Other export industries include printing, textiles and food processing, along with rum distilling and sugar production. In agriculture, sugarcane and bananas are the main cash crops, along with coffee, cocoa, and fruit. In recent years the government has removed most price controls and privatized state enterprises. Unemployment remains high. Jamaica's medium-term prospects depend largely on its ability to attract foreign capital and limit speculation against the Jamaican dollar.

Fact File

OFFICIAL NAME Jamaica

FORM OF GOVERNMENT Constitutional monarchy with two legislative bodies (Senate and House of Representatives)

CAPITAL Kingston

AREA 10,990 sq km (4,243 sq miles)

TIME ZONE GMT – 5 hours

POPULATION 2,652,443

PROJECTED POPULATION 2005 2,763,836

POPULATION DENSITY 241.4 per sq km (625.2 per sq mile)

LIFE EXPECTANCY 75.6

INFANT MORTALITY (PER 1,000) 13.9

OFFICIAL LANGUAGE English

OTHER LANGUAGE Creole

LITERACY RATE 84.4%

RELIGIONS Protestant (mainly Anglican, Presbyterian–Congregational, Baptist, Methodist) 70%, Roman Catholic 7–8%, other including Rastafari 22–23%

ETHNIC GROUPS African 76.5%, mixed African–European 15%, East Indian and mixed African–East Indian 3%, European 3%, Chinese and mixed African–Chinese 1%, other 1.5%

CURRENCY Jamaican dollar

ECONOMY Services 63%, agriculture 25%, industry 12%

GNP PER CAPITA US$1,510

CLIMATE Tropical; cooler inland

HIGHEST POINT Blue Mountain Peak 2,256 m (7,402 ft)

MAP REFERENCE Page 429

Mexico

The story of Mexico is the story of Central American civilization itself. For thousands of years people have lived in the central valley, and when the Spanish arrived under Cortés in 1519 the population of the Aztec Empire may have numbered 15 million. The pattern of settlement established by Spain in Mexico, with large estates worked by Indians, was followed in many other Central and South American countries. Although most Mexicans are Roman Catholics, the relation of Church and state has not always been easy, governments often viewing the Church's power as a challenge to their own. Mexico possesses major petroleum resources, is industrializing rapidly, and includes many traditional Indian cultures among its people, from the Tarahumara in the northwest to the Maya of Quintana Roo.

Physical features and land use

The northern and less-populated part of Mexico consists of the basin-and-range country of the Mesa Central. In this region desert scrub is the main plant cover, with grasses, shrubs, and succulents on higher ground. Cattle ranching is notable in this region. The land reaches heights of 2,400 m (7,900 ft) around Mexico City. South of the city three major peaks—Citlaltepetl, Popacatepetl, and Ixtaccihuatl—of the Sierra Volcanica Transversal reach elevations of around 5,500 m (18,000 ft). An active earthquake zone, this is the most densely settled part of the country.

East of the Mesa Central the land falls steeply from the Sierra Madre Oriental to a broad coastal plain on the Gulf of Mexico fringed with swamps, lagoons, and sandbars. Further south is the isthmus of Tehuantepec, a neck of rainforested land dividing the mountains of the Sierra del Sur from the highlands rising toward the Guatemalan

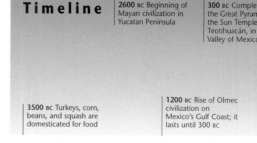

Timeline

2600 BC Beginning of Mayan civilization in Yucatan Peninsula

300 BC Completion of the Great Pyramid of the Sun Temple at Teotihuacán, in the Valley of Mexico

3500 BC Turkeys, corn, beans, and squash are domesticated for food

1200 BC Rise of Olmec civilization on Mexico's Gulf Coast; it lasts until 300 BC

Economy and resources

Agriculture occupies around a quarter of the population, many farmers living by growing maize, beans, and squash. The main export crops are coffee, cotton, and sugarcane. Some meat is exported from the north, while fish exports include tuna, anchovies, sardines, and shrimp. About one-fifth of Mexico is forested, producing hardwood and chicle, the base for chewing gum.

Mexico is one of the largest oil exporters outside OPEC, most oil coming from the Gulf of Mexico. Petrochemicals provide most of the country's export earnings and are the chief energy source. Mexico is the world's leading producer of silver. Only about 20 percent of the country's mineral reserves have so far been exploited. There are also sizeable deposits of coal and uranium. Hydroelectricity contributes 34 percent of all power used.

Although the economy is diverse, with food-processing, textiles, forestry, and tourism making a contribution, it has been through a series of crises beginning with devaluation in 1994. Economic activity contracted by 7 percent in 1995 and more than 1 million Mexicans lost their jobs. The health of the banking sector, investor confidence, drug-linked corruption, and the shaky grip of the ruling elite on power are matters of continuing concern.

Port Antonio on the northeast coast of Jamaica (below left). The Mayan Pyramid of the Magician, Uxmal, Mexico (above). A market scene in Mexico (right).

border. The Yucatan Peninsula to the east is a limestone plain lying only a little above sea level, marked by natural wells and sinkholes. Petroleum discoveries in the 1970s in Tabasco and Campeche, in the northwest Yucatan, have made Mexico one of the world's biggest oil producers.

The Mesa Central ends just as abruptly on its western frontier, falling from the pine-forested heights of the Sierra Madre Occidental to a narrow coastal strip extending north to the Californian border. In the far northwest is the long narrow, dry, mountain-spined peninsula of Baja California.

Contrasts in altitude and latitude produce wide climatic variations, from the coasts, where temperatures are uniformly high, to the temperate land which prevails over much of the Mesa Central. Above 2,000 m (6,000 ft) lies what is known as the cold land, while on the higher slopes of the snow-capped volcanic cones is the frozen land where temperatures are usually below 10°C (50°F).

People and culture

Most Mexicans are descendants of the Amerindian peoples who lived in the region at the time of the Spanish conquest, and of the Spanish colonists. The Aztecs were one of a number of developed cultures in the region. Their capital, Tenochtitlan, featured monumental architecture in the form of pyramids, and their society was strongly hierarchic, with slaves at the bottom and an emperor at the top. Art, sculpture, and poetry were advanced and they had a form of writing. Aztec religious practices involved the annual sacrifice (and eating) of large numbers of slaves, prisoners, and captives

taken in war. The Maya in Yucatan were another major culture in the region but by the time the Spanish arrived the empire had already collapsed. Only their majestic stone monuments in the jungle remained, with settlements of corn-cultivating Mayan subsistence farmers nearby.

The Spanish brought Christianity and a system of large scale estates using poorly paid (or unpaid) Amerindian labor. Colonial control was exercised by a form of serfdom under which Amerindians paid either tribute or labor in return for conversion to Christianity. This system was abolished in 1829. In 1810 the independence struggle began, in 1822 Mexico declared itself a republic and in 1836 Spain formally recognized the country's independence. A century of political chaos climaxed with the violent Mexican Revolution of 1910 to 1921.

Since 1929 Mexico has been dominated by one party, the PRI, which has ruled until recently in a corporatist and authoritarian fashion. There is widespread dissatisfaction with the political process and with the unsolved 1994 murders of two high-profile reformers within the ruling party. A peasant revolt in Chiapas in 1994 dramatized the problem of rural poverty and the poor understanding of Mexico's urban élite of the world beyond the cities.

Fact File

OFFICIAL NAME	United Mexican States
FORM OF GOVERNMENT	Federal republic with two legislative chambers (Senate and Chamber of Deputies)
CAPITAL	Mexico City
AREA	1,972,550 sq km (761,602 sq miles)
TIME ZONE	GMT – 6/8 hours
POPULATION	100,294,036
PROJECTED POPULATION 2005	110,573,561
POPULATION DENSITY	50.8 per sq km (131.6 per sq mile)
LIFE EXPECTANCY	72
INFANT MORTALITY (PER 1,000)	24.6
OFFICIAL LANGUAGE	Spanish
OTHER LANGUAGES	Indigenous languages
LITERACY RATE	89.2%
RELIGIONS	Roman Catholic 93%, Protestant 4%, other 3%
ETHNIC GROUPS	Mixed indigenous–European (mainly Spanish) 60%, indigenous 30%, European 9%, other 1%
CURRENCY	Mexican peso
ECONOMY	Services 57%, agriculture 23%, industry 20%
GNP PER CAPITA	US$3,320
CLIMATE	Tropical in south and on coastal lowlands; cooler and drier in central plateau and mountains
HIGHEST POINT	Vol Citaltepetl (Pico de Orizaba) 5,700 m (18,701 ft)
MAP REFERENCE	Pages 430–31

MAP REFERENCE Pages 430–31

1000 Rise of Toltec Empire based in Tula, present-day Hidalgo, to the north of the Valley of Mexico; lasts around 200 years	1325 Aztecs establish their capital of Teotihuacán, a city housing 100,000–300,000 people	1629 Floods kill 30,000 people in Mexico City; new drainage systems constructed	1836 Mexico's independence is formally recognized by Spain	1847–48 US troops capture Mexico City in Mexican–American War until treaty grants large amounts of territory to USA	1910–20 Mexican revolution; Madero overthrows Diaz government in 1911	1934 Government begins major land reforms; in 1938 all foreign-owned oil company assets taken over by government	1985 Two earthquakes occur in south-central Mexico, including Mexico City, killing more than 10,000 people
AD 325 Mayan civilization flourishes during its classic period (which lasts until 925); fine stone buildings with hieroglyphics	1519 Spanish explorer Cortés expelled by Aztec Emperor Montezuma from Tenochtitlan; Cortés destroys city in 1520	1521 Spanish rebuild Tenochtitlan and it becomes new Spanish capital, Mexico City	1810 Hidalgo y Costilla calls for rebellion against Spain; Hidalgo executed in 1811	1876 Diaz becomes dictator; expands economy by building railways, developing industries, encouraging foreign investment	1917 New Constitution adopted	1970s Massive oil deposits discovered in the Gulf of Mexico	1997 Paramilitary groups in Acteal massacre 45 Indian villagers

North and Central America

Nicaragua

The largest republic in the Central American isthmus, Nicaragua is also the least populated. The western half, including Lake Nicaragua, the largest lake in Central America, was settled by the Spanish in the sixteenth century, and the Caribbean shore was for two centuries the British protectorate of Mosquito Coast (Costa de Miskitos). Becoming independent from Spain in 1821, Nicaragua then experienced much instability. The 45-year right-wing rule of the Somoza family ended in 1979, being overthrown by the Marxist Sandinistas. Their left-wing rule provoked a US-backed insurgency known as the "contras." In free elections held in 1996 a right-of-center party defeated the Sandinistas. In rural areas, however, violence continues.

Nicaragua's broad plain on the Caribbean side leads to a coastal region of lagoons, beaches, and river deltas. Rainfall here is heavy and the tropical wildlife includes crocodile and jaguar. Inland, toward the east, there are mountain ranges broken by basins and fertile valleys. In the west and south a broad depression containing Lakes Managua and Nicaragua runs from the Gulf of Fonseca, on the Pacific Coast, to the mouth of the San Juan del Norte River, on the Caribbean. Before the Panama Canal was built this was an important route across the isthmus. This is a region of cotton growing. Overlooking the lakes are 40 volcanoes, among them the active Momotombo. An earthquake destroyed most of Managua in 1972.

Nicaragua is still reorganizing its economy—at one point under the Sandinistas inflation reached 3,000 percent. Large-scale confiscation of estates took place under the Sandinistas but the peasants to whom land was given have not always been able to live off their allotments, and some land has been resold. Coffee and cotton are the major export crops. Staples grown by the many subsistence farmers include maize, rice, and beans. Mineral production is led by silver and gold, followed by tungsten, lead, and zinc. Falling prices for most of Nicaragua's export commodities, the loss of aid, and the impact of IMF policies reduced the nation's income in 1993 to close to Haiti's—the poorest in the Americas. There is a huge foreign debt. Conditions peculiar to Nicaragua include Sandinista "land reforms" in which luxury properties were seized and given to the movement's leaders and "privatized" state operations that are union-controlled. More than 50 percent of agricultural and industrial firms are state-owned.

Fact File

OFFICIAL NAME	Republic of Nicaragua
FORM OF GOVERNMENT	Republic with single legislative body (National Assembly)
CAPITAL	Managua
AREA	129,494 sq km (49,998 sq miles)
TIME ZONE	GMT – 6 hours
POPULATION	4,717,132
PROJECTED POPULATION 2005	5,521,705
POPULATION DENSITY	36.4 per sq km (94.3 per sq mile)
LIFE EXPECTANCY	67.1
INFANT MORTALITY (PER 1,000)	40.5
OFFICIAL LANGUAGE	Spanish
OTHER LANGUAGES	Indigenous languages, English
LITERACY RATE	65.3%
RELIGIONS	Roman Catholic 95%, Protestant 5%
ETHNIC GROUPS	Mixed indigenous–European 69%, European 17%, African 9%, indigenous 5%
CURRENCY	Córdoba
ECONOMY	Agriculture 47%, services 37%, industry 16%
GNP PER CAPITA	US$380
CLIMATE	Tropical in lowlands, cooler in highlands; wet season May to January
HIGHEST POINT	Pico Mogoton 2,107 m (6,913 ft)
MAP REFERENCE	Page 428

Nicaraguan children outside their thatched home on the island of Omotepe, with the volcano of Concepción in the background (left). A cargo ship heading east through the Gatun locks on the Panama Canal (right). The port of San Juan del Sur on the west coast of Nicaragua (far right).

Panama

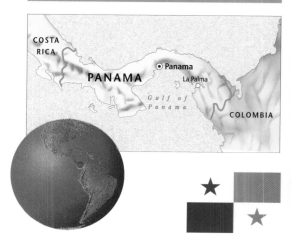

Panama joins two oceans and two continents. With Costa Rica to the west and Colombia to the east, it forms a narrow neck of land connecting Central to South America, while the Panama Canal links the Atlantic Ocean to the Pacific. The first proposal for a canal was made by the Spanish in the early sixteenth century. Later, at the time of the Californian Gold Rush, the USA began to press for action. In 1881 work began on a design prepared by de Lesseps, who was the builder of the Suez Canal, but malaria and yellow fever killed so many workers on the project that it had to be abandoned. Control of these diseases was one of the achievements of the later American builders, who eventually completed the canal in 1914.

Part of Colombia until 1903, Panama has been closely linked with the USA since the construction of the canal gave the latter rights over a 16 km (10 mile) wide Canal Zone. These rights run out in the year 2000. A major upheaval took place in Panama during 1989 when the USA invaded and removed the country's self-proclaimed "maximum leader" General Manuel Noriega in order that he face drug charges in Miami. Electoral democracy was restored in the country, and Noriega was jailed, but the laundering of large amounts of drug money in association with cartels in neighboring Colombia continues to be a problem.

The 3,000 m (9,850 ft) tall mountains of the Serrania de Tabasara (Cordillera Central) run west of the canal along the isthmus, and are separated from the southern Peninsula de Azuera by a long stretch of plain. East of the canal two more ranges of mountains form arcs running parallel to the Pacific and Caribbean coasts. Most of the country, however, including 750 offshore islands, lies below 700 m (2,300 ft) and swelters in tropical heat and high humidity. Rainforests are extensive, and those of the Darien National Park, with their abundant wildlife, are among the wildest areas left in the whole of the Americas. Most Panamanians live within 20 km (12 miles) of the Canal Zone, a quarter of them in the capital itself.

Panama's economy is based on services, and is heavily weighted toward banking, commerce, and tourism. The country has the largest open-registry merchant fleet in the world. Along with the export of bananas (43 percent of total exports) and shrimp (11 percent), plus income derived from the USA's military installation, Panama has the highest standard of living in Central America. However,

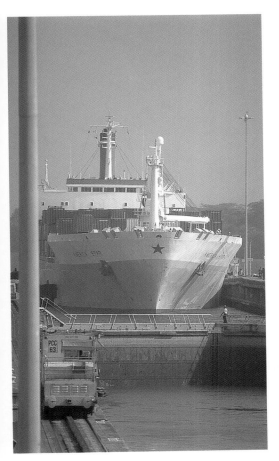

the country's commercial debt is also one of the highest in the world in per capita terms, and during the mid-1990s the country experienced an economic slow-down. Despite the presence of a degree of nationalist fervor, with the termination of the US Canal Zone, approximately 75 percent of Panamanians now favor a continuing US presence in the country to help preserve stability.

Fact File

OFFICIAL NAME Republic of Panama

FORM OF GOVERNMENT Republic with single legislative body (Legislative Assembly)

CAPITAL Panama

AREA 78,200 sq km (30,193 sq miles)

TIME ZONE GMT – 5 hours

POPULATION 2,778,526

PROJECTED POPULATION 2005 3,030,173

POPULATION DENSITY 35.5 per sq km (92 per sq mile)

LIFE EXPECTANCY 74.7

INFANT MORTALITY (PER 1,000) 23.4

OFFICIAL LANGUAGE Spanish

OTHER LANGUAGE English

LITERACY RATE 90.5%

RELIGIONS Roman Catholic 85%, Protestant 15%

ETHNIC GROUPS Mixed indigenous–European 70%, African 14%, European 10%, indigenous 6%

CURRENCY Balboa

ECONOMY Services 60%, agriculture 27%, industry 13%

GNP PER CAPITA US$2,750

CLIMATE Tropical, with long wet season May to January

HIGHEST POINT Volcán Barú 3,475 m (11,401 ft)

MAP REFERENCE Page 429

St Kitts and Nevis

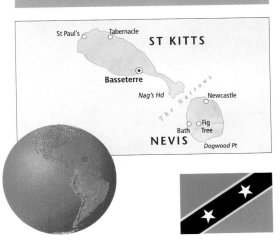

St Kitts and Nevis is a federation of two Caribbean islands in the Leeward Islands group. Each is well-watered and has a mountain of volcanic origin rising to about 1,000 m (3,300 ft). Once inhabited by Carib and Arawak Indians, St Kitts and Nevis were, in 1623 and 1628, the first West Indian islands to be colonized by Britain. Ownership of the islands was disputed with the French until 1783. In 1983 the country became fully independent from Britain.

As on other Caribbean islands, African slaves were imported as labor for sugar and cotton plantations, this ceasing with the abolition of slavery in 1834. Most islanders today are descended from former slaves. The growing and processing of sugarcane remains important, though falling prices have hurt local industry in recent years. The government intends to revitalize this sector. Tourism and export-oriented manufacturing are of growing significance, in addition to manufactured products including machinery, food, electronics, clothing, footwear, and beverages. The main cash crops are sugarcane on St Kitts, cotton and coconuts on

Nevis. Staple foods include rice, yams, vegetables, and bananas, but most food is imported.

Nevis claims it is starved of funds by its partner and is dissatisfied with its place in the federation. In 1996 Nevis announced its intention of seeking independence from St Kitts. Nevis has the constitutional right to secede if two-thirds of the elected legislators approve and two-thirds of voters endorse it through a referendum.

Fact File

OFFICIAL NAME Federation of St Kitts and Nevis

FORM OF GOVERNMENT Constitutional monarchy with single legislative body (House of Assembly)

CAPITAL Basseterre

AREA 269 sq km (104 sq miles)

TIME ZONE GMT – 4 hours

POPULATION 42,838

PROJECTED POPULATION 2005 46,750

POPULATION DENSITY 159.2 per sq km (412.3 per sq mile)

LIFE EXPECTANCY 67.9

INFANT MORTALITY (PER 1,000) 17.4

OFFICIAL LANGUAGE English

OTHER LANGUAGE English Creole

LITERACY RATE 90%

RELIGIONS Anglican 36%, Methodist 32.5%, Roman Catholic 11%, Pentecostal 5.5%, Baptist 4%, other 11%

ETHNIC GROUPS African 94.5%, mixed African–European 3%, European 1%, other 1.5%

CURRENCY East Caribbean dollar

ECONOMY Services 69%, industry and agriculture 31%

GNP PER CAPITA US$5,170

CLIMATE Tropical, moderated by sea breezes

HIGHEST POINT Mt Misery 1,156 m (3,793 ft)

MAP REFERENCE Page 427

St Lucia

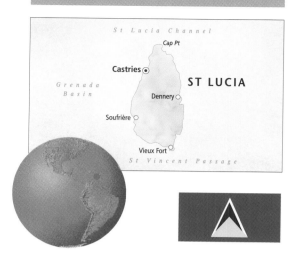

Fact File

OFFICIAL NAME St Lucia

FORM OF GOVERNMENT Constitutional monarchy with two legislative bodies (Senate and House of Assembly)

CAPITAL Castries

AREA 620 sq km (239 sq miles)

TIME ZONE GMT – 4 hours

POPULATION 154,020

PROJECTED POPULATION 2005 164,413

POPULATION DENSITY 248.4 per sq km (643.4 per sq mile)

LIFE EXPECTANCY 71.8

INFANT MORTALITY (PER 1,000) 16.6

OFFICIAL LANGUAGE English

OTHER LANGUAGE French Creole

LITERACY RATE 82%

RELIGIONS Roman Catholic 90%, Protestant 7%, Anglican 3%

ETHNIC GROUPS African 90.5%, mixed 5.5%, East Indian 3%, European 1%

CURRENCY East Caribbean dollar

ECONOMY Services 65%, agriculture 26%, industry 9%

GNP PER CAPITA US$3,370

CLIMATE Tropical, moderated by trade winds; wet season May to August, dry season January to April

HIGHEST POINT Mt Gimie 950 m (3,117 ft)

MAP REFERENCE PAGE 427

An island in the Caribbean, St Lucia is one of the prettiest of the Windward Group of the Lesser Antilles. Tropical beaches and typical Caribbean towns like Soufrière have long drawn tourists to the island, who also come to see its varied plant and animal life. Once inhabited by Arawak and Carib Indians, St Lucia was wrangled over between France and Britain before finally being ceded to Britain in 1814. As elsewhere in the Caribbean, African slaves were imported to work sugar plantations until slavery was abolished in 1834. Most of the population are descended from slaves, though some are from South Asia. Internally self-governing from 1967, St Lucia has been fully independent since 1979.

The main features of the island are its forested mountains stretching north to south, cut by river valleys, and rising to Mt Gimie. In the southwest lies the Qualibou, an area with 18 lava domes and 7 craters. In the west, marking the entrance to Jalousie Plantation harbor, are the spectacular twin Pitons, two peaks rising steeply from the sea to a height of about 800 m (2,625 ft). The climate is tropical, with annual rainfall varying from 1,500 mm (59 in) in the lowlands to 3,500 mm (137 in) in mountainous areas.

While not poor, St Lucia still depends heavily on bananas (60 percent of export income), a crop which is easily ruined by hurricanes and disease. Bananas are also a source of political tension: in recent years the USA has pushed for the abolition of the preferential treatment the EU accords banana imports from the Caribbean. The people of St Lucia have strongly objected to this. Other agricultural exports are coconuts, coconut oil, and cocoa. Clothing is the second largest export, and the free port of Vieux Fort has attracted modern light industry. Grande Cul de Sac Bay in the south is one of the deepest tanker ports in the region and is used for the transshipment of oil.

St Vincent and the Grenadines

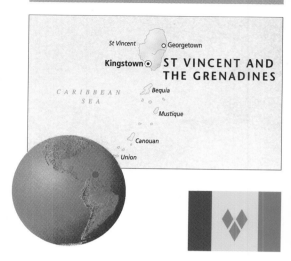

The mountainous, volcanic Caribbean island of St Vincent has 89 percent of the country's total land area and 95 percent of the population, the rest consisting of the islands of the Northern Grenadines—Bequia, Mustique, Canouan, and Union. St Vincent was visited by Columbus in 1498 but the fierce resistance of the Amerindian Caribs meant that settlement was slow. A long dispute with France (the French often being supported by the Caribs) finally led to it becoming a British colony in 1783. As St Vincent and the Grenadines the country became self-governing in 1969 and independent in 1979.

St Vincent is dominated by a north–south spur of densely forested mountains, cut east to west by numerous short, fast-running rivers and streams. In the north, volcanic Mt Soufrière is still very active. It caused serious damage in 1891 and in 1902 it killed 2,000 people. The 1979 eruption, which was followed by a hurricane the next year, devastated agriculture and caused a major setback in tourism.

The Northern Grenadines are coralline islets, extending south of St Vincent toward Grenada, some of them with picturesque names, such as All Awash Island and The Pillories. The tropical climate is moderated by steady trade winds.

Agriculture, led by banana production, is the foundation of the country's economy, most of it small-scale or subsistence farming on the lower mountain slopes or terraces. Other crops exported include arrowroot starch used to make medicines, and paper for computer printers. Tourism is of growing importance, with visitors drawn to the clear, clean waters of Mustique and Bequia. Attempts to develop various industries have so far had little success: unemployment stands at about 35 to 40 percent.

Fact File

OFFICIAL NAME St Vincent and the Grenadines

FORM OF GOVERNMENT Constitutional monarchy with single legislative body (House of Assembly)

CAPITAL Kingstown

AREA 340 sq km (131 sq miles)

TIME ZONE GMT – 4 hours

POPULATION 120,519

PROJECTED POPULATION 2005 125,501

POPULATION DENSITY 354.5 per sq km (918 per sq mile)

LIFE EXPECTANCY 73.8

INFANT MORTALITY (PER 1,000) 15.2

OFFICIAL LANGUAGE English

OTHER LANGUAGE French Creole

LITERACY RATE 82%

RELIGIONS Anglican 42%, Methodist 21%, Roman Catholic 12%, other 25%

ETHNIC GROUPS African 82%, mixed 14%, European, East Indian, indigenous 4%

CURRENCY East Caribbean dollar

ECONOMY Agriculture 50%, services 30%, industry 20%

GNP PER CAPITA US$2,280

CLIMATE Tropical, with wet season May to November

HIGHEST POINT Mt Soufrière 1,234 m (4,048 ft)

MAP REFERENCE Page 427

The spires of the Pitons tower above a small village on the southwest coast of St Lucia (top left). Kingstown Harbor on the island of St Vincent (left). A bay on the north coast of Trinidad (above). A view of one of Tobago's many bays (above right).

Trinidad and Tobago

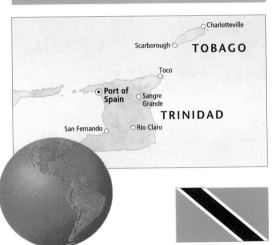

Trinidad is a square-shaped Caribbean island at the south end of the Windward Island chain, only 11 km (7 miles) off the coast of Venezuela. Along with Tobago it is the most prosperous island in the West Indies, oil and asphalt forming the basis of its wealth. It was visited by Columbus in 1498 and then held by the Spanish for three centuries before becoming a British possession after it was seized in 1797. The island's sugar plantations were initially worked by African slaves, and then after the abolition of slavery in 1834 East Indian and Chinese labor was imported. Today, in rural districts, some villages are mainly Afro-Trinidadian, some mainly Asian. Since gaining independence in 1962, Trinidad has been vexed by racial and ethnic complications, notably "Black Power" in 1970 and an attempted coup by black Muslim extremists in 1990. In 1995 the first prime minister from the Asian community was sworn in.

Unlike the Caribbean islands to the north, Trinidad is geologically an extension of South America across the Gulf of Paria. It is traversed by three mountain ranges (northern, central and southern) with El Cerro del Aripo in the Northern Range, and is drained by the Caroni, Ortoire and Oropuche Rivers. The Caroni Swamp is notable for the immense variety of its butterflies. The rest of the island is mostly low-lying, fringed with mangrove swamps.

Tobago Island is a detached piece of the Northern Range, with volcanic uplands, that lies 34 km (21 miles) to the northeast of Trinidad. Tourism is concentrated on Tobago, which is renowned for its wildlife.

The strength of Trinidad's economy is its oil sector, and its large petroleum reserves. But living standards have fallen since the boom years of 1973 to 1982 and the country's prospects depend to a great extent on the success of efforts toward diversification and on economic reforms. The floating of the exchange rate, capital market liberalization, and the partial privatization of such state operations as the main airline are among recent government initiatives.

Fact File

OFFICIAL NAME Republic of Trinidad and Tobago

FORM OF GOVERNMENT Republic with two legislative bodies (Senate and House of Representatives)

CAPITAL Port of Spain

AREA 5,130 sq km (1,981 sq miles)

TIME ZONE GMT – 4 hours

POPULATION 1,102,096

PROJECTED POPULATION 2005 1,032,684

POPULATION DENSITY 214.8 per sq km (556.3 per sq mile)

LIFE EXPECTANCY 70.7

INFANT MORTALITY (PER 1,000) 18.6

OFFICIAL LANGUAGE English

OTHER LANGUAGES Hindi, French, Spanish

LITERACY RATE 97.9%

RELIGIONS Roman Catholic 32%, Hindu 24.5%, Anglican 14.5%, other Protestant 14%, Muslim 6%, other 9%

ETHNIC GROUPS African 43%, East Indian 40%, mixed 14%, European 1%, Chinese 1%, other 1%

CURRENCY Trinidad and Tobago dollar

ECONOMY Services 73%, industry 15%, agriculture 12%

GNP PER CAPITA US$3,770

CLIMATE Tropical, with wet season June to December

HIGHEST POINT El Cerro del Aripo 940 m (3,084 ft)

MAP REFERENCE Page 427

North and Central America

395

United States of America

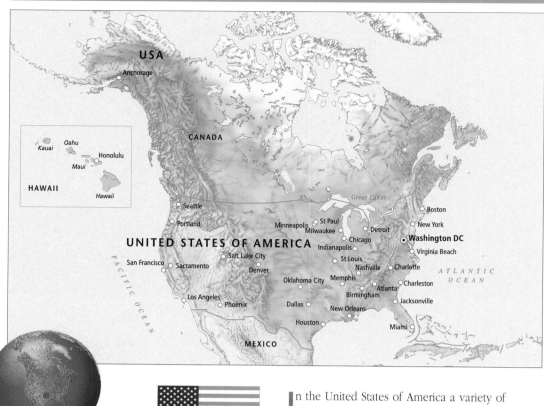

Fact File

OFFICIAL NAME United States of America

FORM OF GOVERNMENT Federal republic with two legislative bodies (Senate and House of Representatives)

CAPITAL Washington DC

AREA 9,372,610 sq km (3,618,765 sq miles)

TIME ZONE GMT – 5/11 hours

POPULATION 272,639,608

PROJECTED POPULATION 2005 286,291,020

POPULATION DENSITY 29.1 per sq km (75.4 per sq mile)

LIFE EXPECTANCY 76.2

INFANT MORTALITY (PER 1,000) 6.3

OFFICIAL LANGUAGE English

OTHER LANGUAGES Spanish, German, French, Italian, Chinese, indigenous languages

LITERACY RATE 99%

RELIGIONS Protestant 56%, Roman Catholic 28%, Jewish 2%, other 4%, none 10%

ETHNIC GROUPS European 83.5%, African 12.5%, Asian 3%, Native American 1%

CURRENCY US dollar

ECONOMY Services 79%, industry 18%, agriculture 3%

GNP PER CAPITA US$26,980

CLIMATE Varied: eastern states are temperate, with warm summers and snowy winters in north and subtropical conditions in south; southwest is arid and semiarid; west coast is temperate but warmer in California and wetter in the Pacific Northwest; Hawaii is mainly tropical; Alaska is mainly polar but cooler and wetter on south coast

HIGHEST POINT Mt McKinley 6,194 m (20,321 ft)

MAP REFERENCE Pages 418–19, 420–21, 422–23, 424–25, 426

In the United States of America a variety of peoples, united by a shared belief in social and economic freedom, have built the most prosperous and powerful nation on earth. Abundant resources, a climate and soils ensuring plentiful food supplies, and an open society rewarding individual energy and initiative, were all advantages from the beginning. In addition, huge oceans on both eastern and western coasts isolated America from the troubles of Europe and Asia, and its relations with Mexico to the south and Canada to the north were generally benign. Starting with these favorable conditions, and guided by the ideals of democracy and freedom, the United States of America—in this respect unique among nations—successfully invented itself according to its own political and social ideals.

The most serious danger to its existence was self-inflicted. From 1861 to 1865 the US was wracked by a civil war in which the implications of universal human liberty were played out in a struggle between slave-owners in the south of the country and slave-liberators in the north, but the nation survived. Later, in the face of widespread domestic opposition, the US entered the First World War in 1917, its military strength leading to Germany's defeat. Even more decisive was its role in the Second World War between 1941 and 1945, in alliance with Great Britain and the Soviet Union, when its industrial power and military might ensured victory over both Germany and Japan. After 1945, challenged for superpower supremacy by the Soviets, it engaged in a protracted trial of strength known as the Cold War. This ended in 1989 with the collapse of the USSR and its communist allies, leaving America stronger politically and economically than ever before.

The economy, already the most powerful, diverse, and technologically advanced in the world, continues to grow. But US prosperity is combined with a variety of problems: drug addiction; crime; long-term unemployment for some sectors of the population; racial tensions; air and water pollution in some areas from automotive and industrial wastes; traffic congestion approaching "gridlock" in major cities; and rising medical costs. All these side-effects appear to be the price of modernity on the American model. It is a price that most other developed countries have been prepared to pay, however, in order to establish high-tech, high-energy industrial societies.

Physical features and land use

Mainland United States can be divided into three major physical regions. The eastern part consists of the range of the Appalachian Mountains and the coastal plain that runs along the Atlantic Ocean. The broad basin of the Mississippi and Missouri Rivers comprises the central section. The western region is composed of mountain ranges, desert landscapes, and the land along the Pacific coast. In addition, there are two outlying sections of the country—Alaska and Hawaii.

In eastern North America the Appalachians, a band of sedimentary mountains and plateaus which are still widely forested, extend from northern Alabama to the Gulf of St Lawrence. They consist of a number of parallel ranges, including the Blue Ridge Mountains in Virginia and the Great Smoky Mountains along the North Carolina–Tennessee border. For a long time these ranges constituted a barrier to inland settlement. In New York State the valley of the Mohawk River divides the mountains of the Appalachians from the Adirondacks, which are a southern extension of the ancient granite mass of the Canadian Shield. Traveling up this valley, from east to west, the early settlers were able to find a way through the range that led on to the land bordering the Great Lakes and the Ohio country beyond.

The original vegetation on these mountains was broadleaf deciduous forest of oak, ash, beech, and maple, grading into yellow birch, hemlock, and pine toward the north. During the eighteenth and nineteenth centuries much of this forest area was cleared for farming, but declining agriculture in New England and the abandonment of farmland has brought widespread regeneration of tree growth. Flying across eastern America, much of the landscape still gives the impression of continuous woodland.

The coastal plain to the southeast through the Carolinas and Georgia is generally low-lying, and includes many areas of swamp. Nearly 1,700 km (more than 1,000 miles) of barrier islands and sandbars run parallel to the shore and are popular seaside resort areas for the inland population, despite being exposed to occasional hurricanes.

To the west of the Appalachian Range lies the enormous continental drainage basin of the Mississippi–Missouri system. This basin is about 2,500 km (1,500 miles) wide, extending south from the Canadian border to the Gulf of Mexico. At its northern limit there are the hills along Lake Superior, a vestige of the Canadian Shield. What are called the Central Lowlands of this drainage basin are bounded on the east by the low plateaus of Kentucky and Tennessee. To the west of the Mississippi lie vast areas planted in wheat, and eventually grasslands, as the Great Plains reach 1,500 km (900 miles) across to the foothills of the Rocky Mountains.

Once the home of such tribes as the Mandan, the Omaha, and the Kansa Indians (settled farmers near the Missouri River), and the nomadic Blackfoot, Crow, and Arapaho further west, most of the plains had been taken by incoming ranchers and farmers by the end of the nineteenth century. Former range land was planted in wheat and maize. These crops were hugely productive at first, but overcropping and dry years led to severe soil deterioration in the first decades of the twentieth century. This reached a climax in the disasters of the 1930s, when a large part of the region became a "dustbowl." Although diversification of grain crops, contour plowing, and widespread irrigation have helped to restore agricultural productivity, some areas are still highly sensitive to climatic variation, especially where the original terrain was semidesert. Combined with fluctuations in grain prices, agriculture remains a risky business in a region where much of the land is marginal.

The mountain ranges of the western Cordillera, as it extends south from Canada, are divided by a number of high plateaus and deep valleys. There are two main systems, to the west and the east. The northern and central Rocky Mountains are the eastern arm facing out across the Great Plains, with the Grand Tetons forming spectacular ridges in Wyoming. The southern Rockies of Colorado and New Mexico—the remains of an ancient granite plateau—are also weathered into a series of striking peaks. In Colorado there are more than 1,000 mountains of 3,000 m (10,000 ft) or more. As with the mountains on the east of the continent, the Rockies were a major obstacle for westward-heading settlers. One major route lay through the

A desert landscape in Arches National Park, Utah (left). Fall colors in northern Maine (top). Juneau, in Alaska, lies on the Inside Passage, a marine waterway that runs through the vast Tongass National Forest (above).

Wyoming Basin, a rangeland where bison once grazed, and where yesterday's pioneer trails have become interstate highways.

On the lower slopes of the Rockies grow a mixture of piñon pines and juniper scrub, with ponderosa pine, spruce, and fir at higher altitudes. Wildlife includes elk, deer, moose, mountain sheep, bear, and a variety of smaller animals. National Parks such as Yellowstone and Grand Teton provide an opportunity to see these animals in dramatic natural settings, and draw millions of visitors to the region every year.

High plateaus, rocky ranges, and desert basins extend westward across the states of Utah, Arizona, and Nevada, seamed in many places by vast, abrupt canyons, of which the Grand Canyon of the Colorado River is the most spectacular. On the Pacific side of these plateaus is the western branch of the cordillera. This forms a chain of mountains consisting of the Sierra Nevada in the south and the Cascade Range to the north. Stretching from Washington through Oregon to Lassen Peak in California, the Cascades include several large volcanoes, Mt Saint Helens erupting violently in 1980. The Sierra Nevada faces out over the fertile Central Valley of California, with its fruit and vegetable growing, viticulture, cotton, other crops, and livestock. In the early days long dry summers made farming difficult in the Central Valley. Meltwater from the snows of the Sierra Nevada, much of it diverted in lengthy canals, now provides summer irrigation.

Beyond the Central Valley on its western side rise the comparatively low Coast Ranges, running parallel to the Pacific shore all the way from the Mexican border to Canada. Together, the Coast Ranges, the Cascades, and the Sierra Nevada, all serve to keep precipitation away from the interior plateaus and create its arid landscape. East of the Cascade Range in the Pacific Northwest lies the Columbia Basin. Here, the meltwaters of ancient glaciers have cut deep gorges in the land. In western Washington the most spectacular trees consist of Douglas fir, western hemlock, and Sitka spruce, some almost as tall as the giant redwoods of northern California. The wealth of the US Northwest was originally based on timber from the huge conifers that covered the Cascade Range.

The two non-contiguous parts of the US have very different physical landscapes. The expansive state of Alaska is a mixture of massive glaciated mountains and broad river valleys, with a vegetation cover that varies from dense forest to sparse tundra. For much of the year, large areas of Alaska are covered in snow. The Hawaiian islands mostly consist of the tops of prominent volcanoes which protrude above the sea, with a host of distinctive plants nurtured by the tropical climate.

History and settlement

The first peoples to settle North America probably crossed from Siberia to Alaska during the ice ages between 10,000 and 30,000 years ago. It is thought they became the ancestors of the many Indian tribes living in North America when the first Europeans arrived. Their cultures varied widely, from the Iroquois who lived in bark lodges in the east, to the cliff-dwelling Pueblo peoples of the west, to the salmon-fishing and whale-hunting Northwest Coast Indians of Washington State and British Columbia, who lived in large timber houses. Plains Indians such as the Sioux or the Comanche are sometimes depicted hunting bison on horseback, but this was only possible after horses had been introduced by incoming European settlers from the fifteenth century onward.

The oldest authenticated European settlement in North America was made by Norse Vikings at the northern tip of the island of Newfoundland about AD 1000, but it was occupied for only a short time. The first successful English settlement was at Jamestown, Virginia, in 1607. Not long after this a party of religious dissenters, the so-called Pilgrim Fathers, arrived in 1620 to found the first of the New England colonies at Plymouth. Joined by other migrants later, this became part of the large Massachusetts Bay colony.

A Dutch colony on Manhattan Island (founded in 1624) was captured by the British in 1664, who changed its name from New Amsterdam to New York. The Quaker William Penn founded one of the more successful of the early English colonies in 1682. Part of Pennsylvania later split off to become Delaware; North and South Carolina were established in 1663; Georgia, originally designed as a philanthropic alternative to a debtor's prison, in 1732. The defeat of the French, which ended the Seven Years War in 1763, brought huge territorial accessions to England: all of France's Canadian territories, the land west of the Mississippi River, plus Louisiana and Florida. The settlers throughout these areas became directly subject to the British Crown, and when London sought to recoup the huge expenses of the war (about £101,500,500) by imposing taxes, the cry of "No taxation without representation" was raised in Boston, and resistance to England began. When the American War of Independence broke out in 1776 George Washington commanded the troops, and when it was won and the first elections were held in 1788 he became the inaugural president. In the aftermath, tens of thousands of "loyalists" moved north to Canada.

The British government had forbidden westward expansion beyond the mountains of the Appalachians. After independence, however, this took place with a rush. Indian tribes were quickly dispossessed from the area and exiled, their land taken for farms, and throughout the nineteenth century there was a series of wars in the region to crush resistance. The last armed Indian defiance collapsed with the Ghost Dance Uprising of 1890. But by far the most serious crisis for the new nation was the American Civil War of 1861 to 1865. This was both a clash of ideals (liberty versus servitude) and of ways of life (the industrializing, modern north versus the old agrarian south). Led by the eloquent commonsense of Abraham Lincoln, the northern forces of the Union defeated the southern armies of the Confederacy, but the legacy of bitterness lasted for many decades.

Meanwhile, westward expansion proceeded apace. Pioneers followed trails explored by men such as Lewis and Clark. Railroads spanned the

Timeline					
	3500 BC Native Americans hunt bison; by 2500 BC squash, goosefoot, and sunflowers (seeds used as winter food) cultivated	**300 BC** Hohokam, Mogollon, and Anasazi people inhabit the south and southwest; Anasazi build villages at Chaco, New Mexico	**AD 700** Start of Pueblo period in southwest; Native Americans of Hopi, Zuni, and other tribes live in villages built mainly of adobe	**1492** Columbus reaches America while searching for route to Orient; later, French and English establish fur trading posts in Canada	**1584** Sir Walter Raleigh claims Virginia for England, but no permanent settlement created until founding of Jamestown in 1607
35,000–12,000 BP Modern humans *Homo sapiens sapiens* migrate to North America across Bering Strait land bridge and spread south	**13,000 BP** Settlements appear from south of Canadian border to Mexico; stone spearpoints in use in New Mexico	**1000 BC** The Adena in eastern North America build ceremonial mounds; agriculture established in southwest	**200 BC** Hopewell culture takes over from Adena; Hopewell become first farmers in eastern North America (until AD 500)	**790** Vikings explore coasts of Europe and North America for the next 100 years, forming settlements in Greenland and Iceland	**1539** Hernando de Soto reaches Florida and travels up the Mississippi; following year Coronado explores southwest **1619** First slaves shipped from West Africa to USA

continent, coal and iron were discovered and used, and new cities such as Pittsburgh and Chicago grew up in the interior. European migrants pouring in through the ports of Boston, Philadelphia, and New York substantially changed the nation's ethnic composition. Manufacturing cities, which were big markets in their own right, developed along the shores of the Great Lakes, while the mechanized farming of the Midwestern "corn belt" turned it into the granary of much of the Western world.

The history of California differed from that of the rest of the country in many ways, in that it was a part of Spanish conquest rather than of English settlement. The small, semi-nomadic hunting and seed-gathering Indian cultures of the area were little affected by the spread northward of Spanish forts and missions from New Spain (Mexico) in the 1760s. But by the middle of the nineteenth century pressures from land-hungry pioneers moving in from the eastern states were irresistible: by the end of the century the whole of the southwest, including Texas, had been either ceded, purchased, or annexed. Since then the Pacific Coast economy has passed through various stages, from gold-prospecting and lumbering, through agriculture, the expansion of the aircraft industry after the Second World War, to the highest of high-tech today in Silicon Valley south of San Francisco Bay.

Once independence was established by the beginning of the nineteenth century, the US kept Europe at arm's length, and the Monroe Doctrine

warned Europe that the representatives of the old empires—Spanish, Portuguese, and British—were not to intervene in the Americas any more. Isolationism was the other side of this doctrine: the US had no wish to be entangled in Europe's troubles. But as the US developed into a major global power this disengagement was no longer possible. In two world wars in the twentieth century American military intervention was decisive, and with the onset of the Cold War, designed to contain the Soviet Union after 1945, it was prepared to intervene wherever it saw the need. However, subsequent action in Korea from 1950 to 1953, and in Vietnam from 1964 to 1975, both with heavy loss of US lives, has made the nation less enthusiastic about overseas military

commitments and the risks and casualties of policing trouble-spots (Haiti, Somalia, the Persian Gulf) are often unpopular at home. Generally the American mood is inward-looking, more concerned with domestic than with foreign affairs.

People and culture

The US is a prosperous, industrial, capitalistic democracy, in which anyone with training and skills who is prepared to assimilate can usually find a place. It is the most open multicultural society on earth, which is the main reason why there are so many people from other countries wanting to live here. In addition to its huge numbers of legal immigrants (the US still has the highest legal immigration level of any country in

Rugged country in Great Basin National Park in Nevada (left). One of California's numerous vineyards (right). The famous Empire State Building in New York City (far right). Undulating farming country in Idaho (below).

| 1804 Lewis and Clark explore the Missouri River then cross Rocky Mts and reach the Pacific near mouth of Columbia River | 1848 California gold rush. Within two years 90,000 people from San Francisco, the east, and overseas travel to diggings | 1869 World's first transcontinental railroad is completed when the Union Pacific line and Central Pacific line link up | 1917 USA enters First World War on the side of Allies | 1929 Wall Street Crash ruins many investors and affects industry and farming; millions lose jobs in Depression | 1941 USA joins Allies in Second World War after Japan bombs Pearl Harbor; war ends 1945 after USA drops atomic bombs on Japan | 1992 Hurricane Andrew strikes Florida and Louisiana causing $25 billion damage and the loss of more than 50 lives |

| 1776 USA founded, with American colonies adopting Declaration of Independence. Population 3 million | 1805 The Louisiana Purchase acquires a large area of south from France, almost doubling the land area of the USA | 1861–65 Civil War between southern (Confederate) and northern (Union) states; all slaves freed in Confederate states | 1908 Ford launches Model T, a mass market automobile. It transforms US industry and economy; 15.5 million sold in 19 years | 1920 More Americans now living in industrial cities than on the land; women are given the vote in all elections | 1936 Boulder Dam on Colorado River completed impounding Lake Mead; renamed Hoover Dam (1947) | 1969 Apollo 11 mission opens a new chapter in space exploration by landing three astronauts on Moon |

Navajo Indians in Monument Valley, Arizona (left). Chapel of the Alto Vista, on the eastern side of Aruba (top right). Islands of the Great Sound in Bermuda (bottom right).

the world) illegal entry is estimated to bring in up to one million people a year.

The descendants of the original Native American inhabitants are a small but not insignificant element of the population. People arriving from overseas were at first mainly English, and with those of Scots and Irish descent dominated all other arrivals from the other side of the Atlantic until the middle of the nineteenth century. During this period the only other major ethnic group to arrive were African slaves imported to work the plantations in the South. After the Civil War, however, mass immigration was encouraged, and a flood of migrants arrived from Italy, Scandinavia, Germany, the Balkans, and various troubled parts of Eastern Europe, including Russia. Many were Jews fleeing poverty and pogroms. In the 60 years up until 1920, 30 million people arrived, radically changing the ethnic composition of the country. Although there were national concentrations in specific neighborhoods (such as Little Italy in New York) the ideal of assimilation ensured that by the middle of the 20th century most new arrivals, or their children, had come to share the benefits of other citizens. More recently there has been an influx of Japanese, Chinese, Filipinos, Cubans, Vienamese, Koreans, and large numbers of Mexicans and Central Americans. In some places, Puerto Rican, Cuban, and Mexican groups provide a strongly Hispanic cultural orientation.

One group of long-term residents did not enjoy full participation in American life. These were the African–Americans descended from the slaves, who became increasingly concentrated in the cities. Long after the Civil War systematic discrimination barred them from jobs, and from equal access to housing, commercial premises, public facilities, and education—even forcing them to sit at the back of the bus in the old slave states. As a result of agitation and affirmative action, the second half of the twentieth century saw the legal rights of African–Americans secured. What remains, however, are inequalities which law alone seems unable to resolve. In the cities, many African–Americans remain part of an underclass plagued by unemployment, drug addiction, crime, and unstable family life.

Economy and resources

The US economy is the largest among the industrial nations, possessing an invaluable combination of skilled and unskilled labor and natural resources. Internationally, it is the most powerful, diverse, and scientifically advanced. With the early application of research and technology, agriculture developed into a highly mechanized industry for food production and processing, with a distinct zonal pattern across the country. Dairy farming predominates in a broad belt from New England to Minnesota. Further west, where the climate is drier, wheat is grown. The corn (maize) belt, highly productive land which was once prairie and forest, consists of the maize-growing eastern and central states from Ohio to Nebraska. Maize is mainly used for feeding to cattle and pigs. In the warmer southern states where cotton and tobacco were grown—the old "cotton belt"—a variety of other crops are now also cultivated, from vegetables to fruit and peanuts. There has

been a strong tendency for farming to move from small to large-scale operations and from labor-intensive to mechanized. Although agriculture's share of gross domestic product is only 2 percent, the US remains a leading producer of meat, dairy foods, soy beans, maize, oats, wheat, barley, cotton, sugar, and forest products.

Despite 20 years of strong competition from Japan and various other Asian economies, the giant US economy remained resurgent throughout the 1990s. One reason for its success may be the greater flexibility of US capitalist enterprise when compared with either Asia or Western Europe. A labor market responsive to changing demands is another factor, and over the last 20 years there has been a huge shift in employment from manufacturing to services. US unemployment remains today one of the lowest in all the major industrialized states. But the main reason for the health of the economy is probably its dynamic technological inventiveness. In every field, US firms are at or near the frontier of technological advance. This is especially so in computers, medical equipment, and aerospace. The advantages of this onrush of technology are obvious. But there are major social costs as well. What is called a two-tier labor market has evolved in which those at the bottom lack enough skills and education to compete, failing to get pay rises, health insurance cover, and other benefits.

Despite the economy's basic good health, marked by low inflation and low unemployment, debate continues on how a number of its continuing problems should be addressed. These include low rates of saving, inadequate investment in infrastructure, the rising medical costs of an ageing population, large budget and trade deficits, and the stagnation of family income in the lower economic groups.

STATES

Alabama • Montgomery	Minnesota • St Paul	Oregon • Salem
Alaska • Juneau	Mississippi • Jackson	Pennsylvania • Harrisburg
Arizona • Phoenix	Missouri • Jefferson City	Rhode Island • Providence
Arkansas • Little Rock	Montana • Helena	South Carolina • Columbia
California • Sacramento	Nebraska • Lincoln	South Dakota • Pierre
Colorado • Denver	Nevada • Carson City	Tennessee • Nashville
Connecticut • Hartford	New Hampshire • Concord	Texas • Austin
Delaware • Dover	New Jersey • Trenton	Utah • Salt Lake City
District of Columbia • Washington DC	New Mexico • Santa Fe	Vermont • Montpelier
Florida • Tallahassee	New York • Albany	Virginia • Richmond
Georgia • Atlanta	North Carolina • Raleigh	Washington • Olympia
Hawaii • Honolulu	North Dakota • Bismarck	West Virginia • Charleston
Idaho • Boise	Ohio • Columbus	Wisconsin • Madison
Illinois • Springfield	Oklahoma • Oklahoma City	Wyoming • Cheyenne
Indiana • Indianapolis		
Iowa • Des Moines		
Kansas • Topeka		
Kentucky • Frankfort		
Louisiana • Baton Rouge		
Maine • Augusta		
Maryland • Annapolis		
Massachusetts • Boston		
Michigan • Lansing		

OVERSEAS TERRITORIES

American Samoa	Navassa Island
Baker and Howland Islands	Northern Mariana Islands
Guam	Palmyra Atoll
Jarvis Island	Puerto Rico
Johnston Atoll	Virgin Islands of the US
Kingman Reef	Wake Island
Midway Islands	

Dependencies and territories

Anguilla

Anguilla's name comes from the Spanish *anguil* meaning "eel." The country is a long, thin, scrub-covered coral atoll in the Caribbean, north of St Kitts and Nevis. First colonized by Britain in 1690, its status as a UK dependent territory was formalized in 1980. While the governor is a crown appointee, a local assembly manages internal matters. Anguilla has few natural resources and depends heavily on tourism, offshore banking, lobster fishing, and overseas remittances. Drawn by a subtropical climate tempered by trade winds, tourists have multiplied in recent years, this reflecting the generally healthy economic conditions in both the USA and the UK. As a result, annual growth has averaged about 7 percent. The offshore finance sector was strengthened by comprehensive legislation enacted in 1994.

Fact File

OFFICIAL NAME Anguilla

FORM OF GOVERNMENT Dependent territory of the United Kingdom

CAPITAL The Valley

AREA 91 sq km (35 sq miles)

TIME ZONE GMT – 4 hours

POPULATION 11,510

LIFE EXPECTANCY 77.7

INFANT MORTALITY (PER 1,000) 18.7

LITERACY RATE 80%

CURRENCY East Caribbean dollar

ECONOMY Services 65%, construction 18%, transportation and utilities 10%, manufacturing 3%, agriculture 4%

CLIMATE Tropical, moderated by trade winds

MAP REFERENCE Page 427

Aruba

Aruba is most unusual among the islands of the Caribbean in that it has a 1 percent unemployment rate, numerous unfilled employment vacancies, and a high gross domestic product. A flat, limestone island lying off the Venezuelan coast at the mouth of the Gulf of Venezuela, Aruba is barren on its eastern side and more lush on the west. It was once a part of the Netherlands Antilles, but is now a separate but autonomous part of the Dutch realm. The population is mainly of African, European, and Asian descent.

Closed in 1985, the oil refinery on the island was reopened in 1993. This is a major source of employment and foreign exchange earnings and has greatly spurred economic growth. Tourism is extensive on the western side of the island, known as the Turquoise Coast, and its rapid development has seen an expansion of other activities.

Fact File

OFFICIAL NAME Aruba

FORM OF GOVERNMENT Self-governing part of the Kingdom of the Netherlands

CAPITAL Oranjestad

AREA 193 sq km (74 sq miles)

TIME ZONE GMT – 4 hours

POPULATION 68,675

LIFE EXPECTANCY 77

INFANT MORTALITY (PER 1,000) 7.8

LITERACY RATE Not available

CURRENCY Aruban florin

ECONOMY Tourism, financial services

CLIMATE Tropical

MAP REFERENCE Page 427

Bermuda

Bermuda is an island in the Atlantic Ocean 900 km (560 miles) off the coast of South Carolina, USA. It has one of the highest per capita incomes in the world, its balmy location and lush vegetation drawing tourists and its financial services offering tax-haven advantages. Bermuda also has one of the world's biggest flag-of-convenience fleets. The largest of some 360 low-lying coral islands which have grown atop ancient submarine volcanoes, it was discovered by the Spaniard Juan Bermudez in 1503, was later taken over by the British, and has a tradition of self-government going back to its first parliament in 1620. Its people are mainly descendants of former African slaves or British or Portuguese settlers. A move for full independence was rejected by 73 percent of voters in 1995, partly for fear of scaring away foreign business. With 90 percent of tourists coming from the US, links with that country are strong.

Fact File

OFFICIAL NAME Bermuda

FORM OF GOVERNMENT Dependent territory of the United Kingdom

CAPITAL Hamilton

AREA 50 sq km (19 sq miles)

TIME ZONE GMT – 4 hours

POPULATION 63,503

LIFE EXPECTANCY 75

INFANT MORTALITY (PER 1,000) 13.2

LITERACY RATE Not available

CURRENCY Bermudian dollar

ECONOMY Clerical 25%, services 29%, laborers 21%, professional and technical 13%, administrative 10%, agriculture 2%

CLIMATE Subtropical; windy in winter

MAP REFERENCE Page 476

North and Central America

Greenland

Greenland is nearly 50 times the size of its "mother country," Denmark, yet it has only 1 percent as much population. It is the biggest island in the world and about 85 percent of its land area is covered by an ice-cap with an average depth of 1,500 m (5,000 ft). Though there are a few sandy and clay plains in the ice-free areas of the island, settlement is confined to the rocky coasts.

It was named "Greenland" by the Viking Erik the Red during the tenth century, in the hope that the name would attract other adventurous Norsemen as settlers. The island became a Danish colony in 1721, an integral part of Denmark in 1973, and received full internal self-government in 1981. Most Greenlanders today are of mixed Inuit and Danish descent, and sometimes live uneasily between these two worlds. The social cost of this divide can be heavy; in the towns alcoholism, venereal disease, and suicide are high.

Greenland's economic prospects are somewhat limited in that it is now almost completely dependent on fishing and fish processing. These constitute 95 percent of all exports, and there is the added problem of falling catches of shrimp—in recent years the Arctic fishing industry has contracted. Though it has a certain amount of mineral resources, the last lead and zinc mine was closed in 1990. There is some ship building and also potential for the development of adventure tourism. One problem is the large role of the public sector, which accounts for two-thirds of total employment. About half of government revenue comes from Danish government grants.

Fact File

OFFICIAL NAME Greenland

FORM OF GOVERNMENT Self-governing overseas administrative division of Denmark

CAPITAL Nuuk (Godthab)

AREA 2,175,600 sq km (839,999 sq miles)

TIME ZONE GMT – 1/4 hours

POPULATION 59,827

LIFE EXPECTANCY 70.1

INFANT MORTALITY (PER 1,000) 20.1

LITERACY RATE Not available

CURRENCY Danish krone

ECONOMY Fishing

CLIMATE Polar, with bitterly cold winters and cool to cold summers

MAP REFERENCE Page 411

Most of Greenland is covered by a thick ice cap. Ice floes are visible in the water surrounding the town of Narsaruaq (above left). The French Island of Martinique in the eastern Caribbean (above right).

British Virgin Islands

East of Puerto Rico in the Caribbean, the British Virgin Islands are the most northerly of the Lesser Antilles. There are four low-lying islands—Tortola, Anegada, Virgin Gorda, and Jost Van Dyke—and 36 coral islets and cays. Most are the peaks of a submerged mountain chain, and they share a subtropical climate moderated by trade winds. With the exception of Anegada, which is flat, the landscape is hilly, with sandy beaches and coral reefs around the coasts. Visited by Columbus in 1493, the British Virgin Islands were for 200 years pirate bases used by the English and the Dutch, until Tortola was annexed by the British in 1672. Today, they are a British dependency enjoying a large measure of self-government, and highly dependent on the tourism which produces some 45 percent of national income. International business makes use of offshore services, incorporation fees generating substantial revenues. Livestock raising is agriculturally important. Soil fertility is low and much food must be imported.

Fact File

OFFICIAL NAME British Virgin Islands

FORM OF GOVERNMENT Dependent territory of the United Kingdom

CAPITAL Road Town

AREA 150 sq km (58 sq miles)

TIME ZONE GMT – 4 hours

POPULATION 13,732

LIFE EXPECTANCY 72.9

INFANT MORTALITY (PER 1,000) 18.7

LITERACY RATE 98.2%

CURRENCY US dollar

ECONOMY Tourism, agriculture

CLIMATE Subtropical, moderated by trade winds

MAP REFERENCE Page 427

Cayman Islands

The largest of Britain's dependencies in the Caribbean, the Cayman Islands consist of three low-lying coral islands south of Cuba and 300 km (186 miles) west of Jamaica. Until the 1960s the main occupations were farming and fishing. Today the islands are one of the world's biggest offshore financial centers, offering a confidential tax haven to some 35,000 companies and several hundred banks. Tourism is also a mainstay, accounting for 70 percent of gross domestic product and 75 percent of foreign currency earnings. Tourism is aimed at the luxury end of the market and caters mainly to visitors from North America. The Cayman Islands were uninhabited when first discovered by Europeans. Most residents today are of mixed Afro-European descent, while an immigrant Jamaican labor force makes up about one-fifth of the population.

Fact File

OFFICIAL NAME Cayman Islands

FORM OF GOVERNMENT Dependent territory of the United Kingdom

CAPITAL George Town

AREA 260 sq km (100 sq miles)

TIME ZONE GMT – 5 hours

POPULATION 39,335

LIFE EXPECTANCY 77.1

INFANT MORTALITY (PER 1,000) 8.4

LITERACY RATE Not available

CURRENCY Caymanian dollar

ECONOMY Services 20%, clerical 20%, construction 13%, finance and investment 10%, directors and business managers 10%, other 27%

CLIMATE Tropical, with cool, dry winters and warm, wet summers

MAP REFERENCE Page 429

Guadeloupe

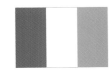

Guadeloupe consists of seven Caribbean islands in the Lesser Antilles, to the southeast of Puerto Rico. The biggest is the high, volcanic Basse-Terre (the active volcano of La Soufrière is the highest point in the Lesser Antilles) lying alongside the slightly smaller flat limestone island of Grande-Terre. A narrow sea channel separates the two. Arawak and Carib Indians were the original inhabitants. The first European settlers to arrive were the French, in 1635. Although there has been considerable agitation for independence, no vote in favor of it has succeeded, and the country is still governed by France—on which it is entirely dependent for subsidies and imported food. Tourism is important, most visitors coming from the USA. Sugar production is being phased out; bananas now supply about 50 percent of export earnings and the cultivation of other crops such as aubergines and flowers is being encouraged.

Fact File

OFFICIAL NAME Department of Guadeloupe

FORM OF GOVERNMENT Overseas department of France

CAPITAL Basse-Terre

AREA 1,780 sq km (687 sq miles)

TIME ZONE GMT – 4 hours

POPULATION 420,943

LIFE EXPECTANCY 78

INFANT MORTALITY (PER 1,000) 8.5

LITERACY RATE 90%

CURRENCY French franc

ECONOMY Services 65%, industry 20%, agriculture 15%

CLIMATE Subtropical, moderated by trade winds

MAP REFERENCE Page 427

Jan Mayen

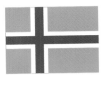

The mountainous island of Jan Mayen lies in the Arctic Ocean about 900 km (560 miles) west of Norway. It is volcanic, with the mighty active Beerenberg volcano rising 2,400 m (7,874 ft) straight out of the surf. From its ice-cap some 15 glaciers descend into the sea. Once an important base for Arctic whaling, Jan Mayen's only resources today are rich fishing grounds. These were the subject of a long dispute with Greenland over fishing rights, and possible oil and gas

deposits. Mediated by the International Court of Justice, the two parties reached a compromise on this issue in 1993. The island's birdlife is spectacular and includes millions of fulmar, petrel, kittiwake, little auk, guillemot, and puffin.

Fact File

OFFICIAL NAME Jan Mayen

FORM OF GOVERNMENT Territory of Norway

CAPITAL None

AREA 373 sq km (144 sq miles)

TIME ZONE GMT – 1 hour

POPULATION No permanent population

ECONOMY Radio and meteorological stations

CLIMATE Polar: cold, windy, and foggy

MAP REFERENCE Page 485

Martinique

Christopher Columbus described Martinique as "the most beautiful country in the world" when he laid eyes on it in 1493. This island in the eastern Caribbean was colonized by France in 1635 and has been French ever since. It consists of three groups of volcanic hills and the intervening lowlands, and is dominated by the dormant volcano Mt Pelée. Mt Pelée is famous for the eruption of 1902, when it killed all the inhabitants of the town of St-Pierre except one prisoner, who was saved by the thickness of his prison cell. The economy is based on sugarcane, bananas, tourism, and light industry, the export of bananas being of growing importance. Most sugarcane is used for making rum. The majority of the workforce is in the service sector and administration, tourism having become more important than agricultural exports as a source of foreign exchange.

Fact File

OFFICIAL NAME Department of Martinique

FORM OF GOVERNMENT Overseas department of France

CAPITAL Fort-de-France

AREA 1,100 sq km (425 sq miles)

TIME ZONE GMT – 4 hours

POPULATION 411,539

LIFE EXPECTANCY 79.3

INFANT MORTALITY (PER 1,000) 6.8

LITERACY RATE 92.8%

CURRENCY French franc

ECONOMY Services 73%, industry 17%, agriculture 10%

CLIMATE Tropical, moderated by trade winds; wet season June to October

MAP REFERENCE Page 427

The colonial legacy

The Caribbean contains many small island states and a significant number of dependencies. This diversity in status is the legacy of centuries of engagement with colonial powers. After Columbus discovered the area at the end of the fifteenth century, Spain took possession of many islands, but Great Britain, France and the Netherlands also claimed, fought over and exploited the Caribbean. From the end of the fifteenth century to the middle of the eighteenth century the indigenous people were nearly wiped out and replaced by a much larger population of Europeans and African slaves, imported to work in the sugar, tobacco and coffee plantations that dominated the local economies. The Caribbean has long served as an important trading route between North and South Americas and to Europe and the East.

The result is a diversity of economic, social and political interests. Some islands have retained their colonial status while others chose independence. The mixture of races (Carib, African and European) and cultures has created national identities marked by different peoples, languages, customs and political systems.

Montserrat

Montserrat is a Caribbean island with seven active volcanoes. In 1995 deep ash from one of them destroyed numerous crops and forced the evacuation of the capital, Plymouth. Montserrat was colonized in 1632 by the British, who at first brought in Irish settlers. (Together with its lush green foliage, this is why it is locally known as "the Emerald Isle.") Later, the island's sugar plantations were worked by African slaves. It has been a self-governing UK dependent territory since 1960. Tourism provides a quarter of the national income, other support coming from the export of electronic components which are assembled on the island, plastic bags, clothing, rum, hot peppers, live plants, and cattle. Data processing facilities and offshore banking are available.

Fact File

OFFICIAL NAME Montserrat

FORM OF GOVERNMENT Dependent territory of the United Kingdom

CAPITAL Plymouth

AREA 100 sq km (39 sq miles)

TIME ZONE GMT – 4 hours

POPULATION 4,000 (after volcanic eruption led to evacuation; formerly 12,853)

LIFE EXPECTANCY 75.6

INFANT MORTALITY (PER 1,000) 12

LITERACY RATE Not available

CURRENCY EC dollar

ECONOMY Tourism, industry, agriculture

CLIMATE Tropical

MAP REFERENCE Page 427

Navassa Island

Navassa Island is an uninhabited rocky outcrop in the Caribbean halfway between Cuba and Haiti. It is strategically located for the USA, since it is 160 km (100 miles) south of the Guantanamo Bay (Bahía de Guantánamo) naval base. The island is administered by the US Coast Guard. The surface is mostly exposed rock but it has dense stands of fig-like trees, cacti, and enough grass to support herds of goats. Its principal resource is guano.

Fact File

OFFICIAL NAME Navassa Island

FORM OF GOVERNMENT Unincorporated territory of the United States

CAPITAL None

AREA 5.2 sq km (2 sq miles)

TIME ZONE GMT – 5 hours

POPULATION No permanent population

CLIMATE Tropical, moderated by sea breezes

MAP REFERENCE Page 429

The oceanfront in old San Juan, Puerto Rico (below). Mud and lava from the 1995 volcanic eruption on Montserrat (bottom). The Virgin Islands of the United States (above right).

Netherlands Antilles

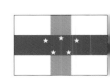

The Netherlands Antilles consist of two very different island groups in two parts of the Caribbean. Curaçao and Bonaire are located off the coast of Venezuela, and while they may once have made money from the well-known orange liqueur, today 98 percent of their income comes from petroleum—either processed for products or for transshipment facilities. The other group, which lies east of the Virgin Islands, consists of the three islands of Saba, St Eustasius, and part of St Maarten. The people are largely of African and European descent, the original inhabitants having been killed in the sixteenth century by Spanish settlers. All told, the islands have a high per capita income and a well-developed infrastructure in comparison with others in the region. Nearly all consumer and capital goods are imported from the USA and Venezuela. Crops grown include aloes, sorghum, peanuts, vegetables, and tropical fruit, but poor soils and limited water make agriculture difficult.

Fact File

OFFICIAL NAME Netherlands Antilles

FORM OF GOVERNMENT Self-governing part of the Kingdom of the Netherlands

CAPITAL Willemstad

AREA 960 sq km (371 sq miles)

TIME ZONE GMT – 4 hours

POPULATION 215,139

LIFE EXPECTANCY 77.4

INFANT MORTALITY (PER 1,000) 8.5

CURRENCY Netherlands Antillean guilder

ECONOMY Tourism, offshore finance

CLIMATE Tropical, moderated by trade winds

MAP REFERENCE Page 427

Puerto Rico

Fact File

OFFICIAL NAME Commonwealth of Puerto Rico

FORM OF GOVERNMENT Commonwealth associated with the United States

CAPITAL San Juan

AREA 9,104 sq km (3,515 sq miles)

TIME ZONE GMT – 4 hours

POPULATION 3,890,353

LIFE EXPECTANCY 75.2

INFANT MORTALITY (PER 1,000) 10.5

LITERACY RATE 87.8%

CURRENCY US dollar

ECONOMY Government 22%, manufacturing 17%, trade 20%, construction 6%, communications and transportation 5%, other 30%

CLIMATE Tropical, moderated by sea breezes

MAP REFERENCE Page 427

Puerto Rico is a large Caribbean island east of the Dominican Republic. Ceded by Spain to the USA in 1898, its citizens enjoy a number of privileges as a result of their American connection (for example, Puerto Ricans have full US citizenship, pay no federal taxes, and have free access to the US). In 1993 the population once more voted to continue their self-governing commonwealth status and forgo becoming either the 51st state of the USA or independent. Mountainous, with a narrow coastal plain, the little flat ground available for agriculture is used for growing sugarcane, coffee, bananas, and tobacco. Today, Puerto Rico's economy is essentially modern and industrialized. Tax relief and cheap labor have brought many businesses to the island and tourism is growing. Industries include petrochemicals, pharmaceuticals (the island produces over 90 percent of all US

tranquillizers), and electronics. The standard of living in Puerto Rico is the highest in Latin America (outside the island tax havens), and is rising.

St Pierre and Miquelon

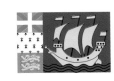 

St Pierre and Miquelon are islands in the North Atlantic Ocean, south of Newfoundland. They are cold and wet and have little vegetation. Surrounded by some of the world's richest fishing grounds, the islands were settled by French fishermen in the seventeenth century. Since then the inhabitants have earned a living from fishing and by servicing the foreign trawler fleets that operate off the coast. A dispute between Canada and France over fishing and mineral rights was settled in 1992. Since the French subsidize the islands, and their economy has been declining, the authorities are now trying to diversify by developing port facilities and encouraging tourism.

Fact File

OFFICIAL NAME Territorial collectivity of St Pierre and Miquelon

FORM OF GOVERNMENT Territorial collectivity of France

CAPITAL St-Pierre

AREA 242 sq km (93 sq miles)

TIME ZONE GMT – 4 hours

POPULATION 6,966

LIFE EXPECTANCY 77.1

INFANT MORTALITY (PER 1,000) 8.1

LITERACY RATE 99%

CURRENCY French franc

ECONOMY Mainly fishing and fish processing

CLIMATE Cold, wet, and foggy

MAP REFERENCE Page 417

Turks and Caicos Islands

The Turks and Caicos Islands are a group of 30 islands, 8 of them inhabited, north of Hispaniola. They are composed of low, flat, scrub-covered limestone, with areas of marsh and swamp. There is little land for agriculture, though cassava, maize, citrus fruits, and beans are grown on Caicos by subsistence farmers. Today, the islands' economy is mainly based on tourism, fishing, and offshore

financial services. Nearly all consumer and capital goods are imported. The islands have been British since 1766, and a crown colony since 1973.

Fact File

OFFICIAL NAME Turks and Caicos Islands

FORM OF GOVERNMENT Dependent territory of the United Kingdom

CAPITAL Grand Turk

AREA 430 sq km (166 sq miles)

TIME ZONE GMT – 5 hours

POPULATION 15,192

LIFE EXPECTANCY 75.5

INFANT MORTALITY (PER 1,000) 12.4

LITERACY RATE Not available

CURRENCY US dollar

ECONOMY Fishing, tourism, agriculture

CLIMATE Tropical, moderated by trade winds

MAP REFERENCE Page 429

Virgin Islands of the United States

The US Virgin Islands consist of 68 hilly volcanic islands east of Puerto Rico in the Caribbean. They are on a key shipping lane and were bought from Denmark by the USA in 1917 to protect the approaches to the Panama Canal. They contain, on St Croix, one of the world's largest oil refineries but tourism is still the main economic activity, accounting for over 70 percent of the island's gross domestic product and 70 percent of employment. Manufacturing includes textiles, pharmaceuticals, electronics, and watch assembly. Business and financial services are also of growing importance. Agriculture is limited, most food being imported.

Fact File

OFFICIAL NAME Virgin Islands of the United States

FORM OF GOVERNMENT Unincorporated territory of the United States

CAPITAL Charlotte Amalie

AREA 352 sq km (136 sq miles)

TIME ZONE GMT + 7 hours

POPULATION 119,555

LIFE EXPECTANCY 78.5

INFANT MORTALITY (PER 1,000) 9.4

LITERACY RATE Not available

CURRENCY US dollar

ECONOMY Tourism, light industry, agriculture

CLIMATE Subtropical; wet season May to November

MAP REFERENCE Page 427

North and Central America: Physical

North and Central America

GREENLAND SEA

Denmark Strait

GREENLAND
(KALAALLIT NUNAAT)
(Den.)

Arctic Circle

LABRADOR SEA

Newfoundland

Labrador

Île d'Anticosti

Davis Strait

Baffin Bay

Péninsule d'Ungava

Bylot Island

Baffin Island

Prince Charles Island

Southampton I.

Coats I.

Mansel I.

Hudson Bay

Belcher Islands

Akimiski Island

Peary Land

WANDEL SEA

ARCTIC OCEAN

Ellesmere Island

Devon Island

Bathurst Island

Prince of Wales I.

King William Island

Baker Lake

CANADIAN SHIELD

Prince Patrick I.

Melville Island

Victoria Island

Contwoyto Lake

Dubawnt Lake

Kasba Lake

Reindeer Lake

Southern Indian Lake

L. Winnipeg

Lake Winnipegosis

L. Manitoba

Lake of the Woods

BEAUFORT SEA

Banks Island

Great Bear Lake

Lac la Martre

Great Slave Lake

Lake Athabasca

Lake Claire

Lesser Slave Lake

Wollaston Lake

Peter Pond Lake

Highrock Lake

Ostrov Vrangelya

CHUKCHI SEA

Brooks Range

Mackenzie Mountains

Mackenzie

North Saskatchewan

South Saskatchewan

Red Deer

Fort Peck

ROCKY MO

Gre

Arctic Circle

Bering Strait

Norton Sound

Alaska Range

▲ Mt Logan 5959 m

Coast Mountains

Columbia Basin

Columbia

BERING SEA

St. Lawrence Island

Iliamna Lake

Mt Foraker 5304 m
Mt McKinley 6194 m ▲

Gulf of Alaska

Baranof I.

Prince of Wales I.

Graham Island

Moresby Island

Vancouver Island

Range

Bristol Bay

Aleutian Range

Kodiak Island

Afognak I.

Umnak I.

Unalaska I.

Unimak I.

Aleutian Islands

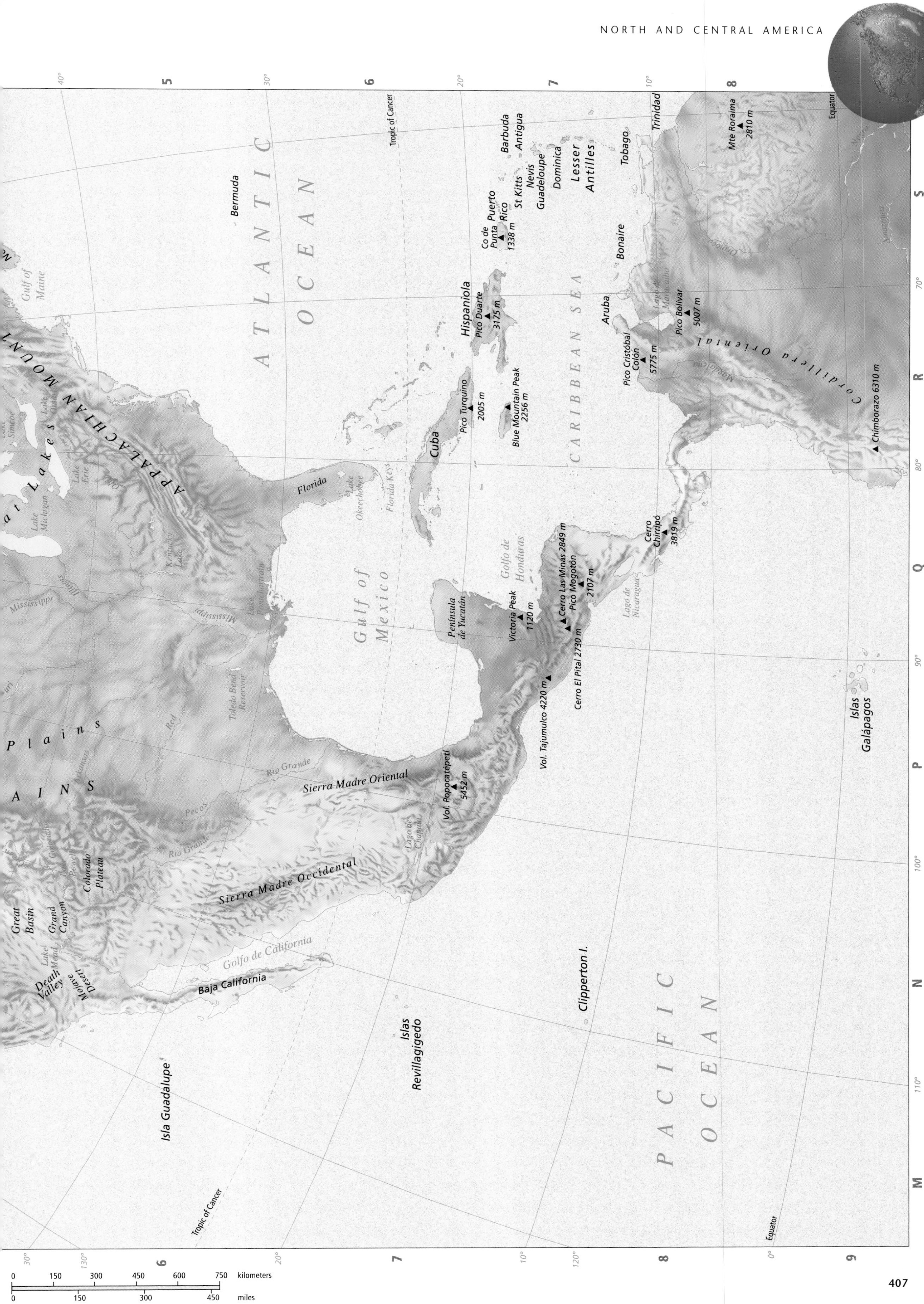

ATLANTIC OCEAN

Bermuda

Gulf of Maine

Lake Simcoe

Lake Ontario

Lakes

Lake Michigan

Lake Erie

Lake Huron

Kentucky Lake

Mississippi

Illinois

Lake Pontchartrain

Toledo Bend Reservoir

Red

Arkansas

Rio Grande

Pecos

Rio Grande

Lago de Chapala

Missouri

Plains

AINS

APPALACHIAN MOUNTAIN

Florida

Lake Okeechobee

Florida Keys

Cuba

Pico Turquino 2005 m

Blue Mountain Peak 2256 m

Hispaniola

Pico Duarte 3175 m

Co de Punta 1338 m

Puerto Rico

Barbuda

Antigua

St Kitts

Nevis

Guadeloupe

Dominica

Lesser Antilles

Tobago

Trinidad

Mte Roraima 2810 m

Nevis

Orinoco

Equator

CARIBBEAN SEA

Aruba

Bonaire

Lago de Maracaibo

Pico Cristóbal Colón 5775 m

Pico Bolívar 5007 m

Cordillera Oriental

Cordillera

Chimborazo 6310 m

Medellín

Gulf of Mexico

Golfo de Honduras

Península de Yucatán

Victoria Peak 1120 m

Cerro Las Minas 2849 m

Pico Mogotón 2107 m

Cerro El Pital 2730 m

Vol. Tajumulco 4220 m

Cerro Chirripó 3819 m

Lago de Nicaragua

Sierra Madre Oriental

Vol. Popocatépetl 5452 m

Sierra Madre Occidental

Great Basin

Grand Canyon

Lake Mead

Colorado Plateau

Colorado

Powell

Death Valley

Mojave Desert

Golfo de California

Baja California

Isla Guadalupe

Islas Revillagigedo

Clipperton I.

Islas Galápagos

PACIFIC OCEAN

Tropic of Cancer

Tropic of Cancer

Equator

40°

30°

130°

120°

110°

100°

90°

80°

70°

10°

20°

30°

20°

10°

0°

0   150   300   450   600   750   kilometers

0   150   300   450   miles

North and Central America: Political

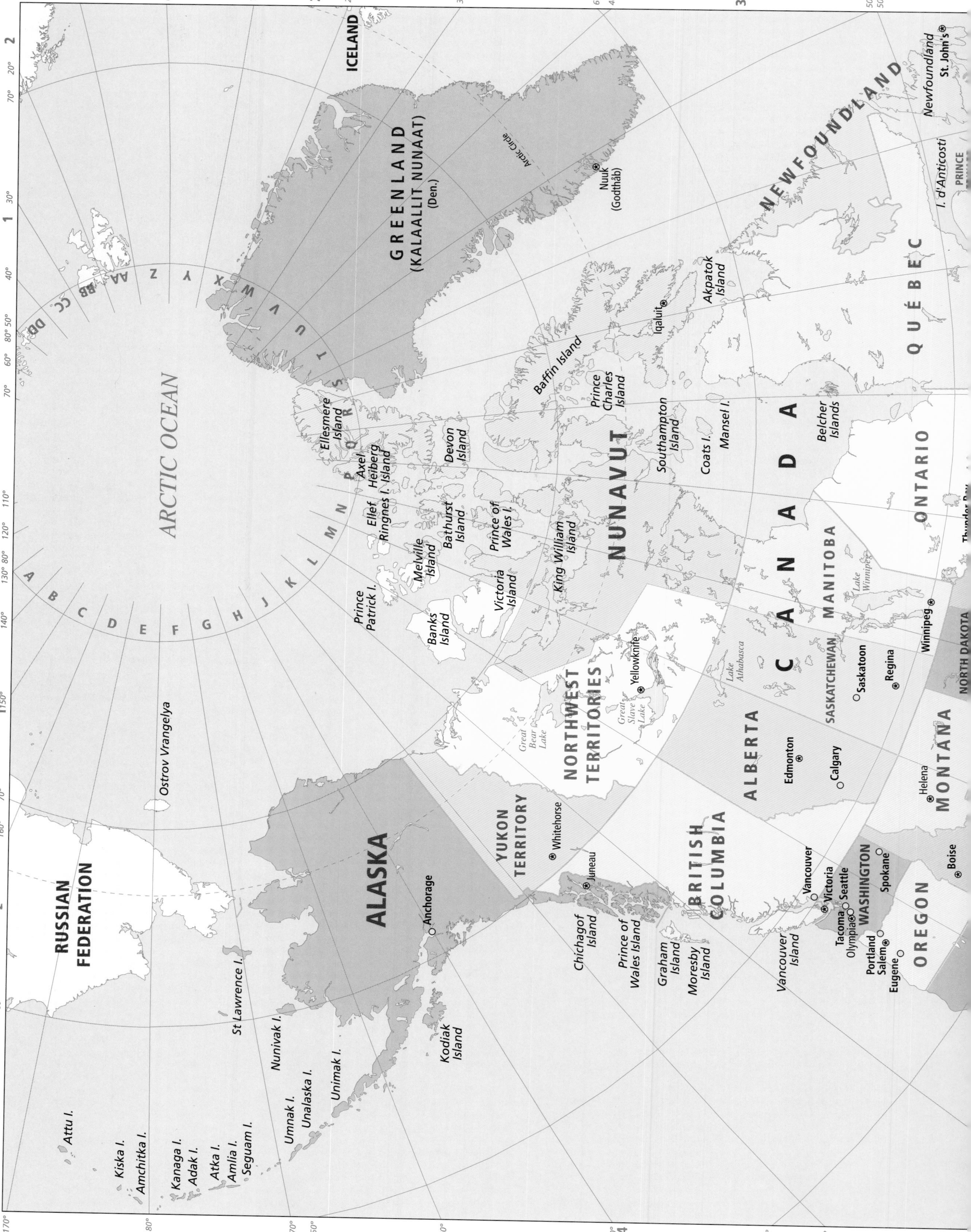

Native/Central America

ICELAND

GREENLAND
(KALAALLIT NUNAAT)
(Den.)

Arctic Circle

Nuuk
(Godthåb)

NEWFOUNDLAND

Newfoundland

St John's

I. d'Anticosti

PRINCE

QUÉBEC

ARCTIC OCEAN

Ellesmere
Island

Axel
Heiberg
Island

Devon
Island

Baffin Island

Prince
Charles
Island

Iqaluit

Akpatok
Island

Elef
Ringnes I.

Prince
Patrick I.

Melville
Island

Bathurst
Island

Prince of
Wales I.

King William
Island

Southampton
Island

Mansel I.

Coats I.

NUNAVUT

Belcher
Islands

Banks
Island

Victoria
Island

CANADA

ONTARIO

Ostrov Vrangelya

Great
Bear
Lake

Yellowknife

NORTHWEST
TERRITORIES

Great
Slave
Lake

Lake
Athabasca

ALBERTA

SASKATCHEWAN

MANITOBA

Lake
Winnipeg

Winnipeg

Thunder Bay

RUSSIAN
FEDERATION

ALASKA

YUKON
TERRITORY

Whitehorse

Edmonton

Calgary

Saskatoon

Regina

NORTH DAKOTA

Anchorage

Juneau

BRITISH
COLUMBIA

Helena

MONTANA

Boise

Attu I.

St Lawrence I.

Nunivak I.

Unimak I.

Kodiak
Island

Chichagof
Island

Prince of
Wales Island

Graham
Island

Moresby
Island

Vancouver
Island

Vancouver

Victoria

Seattle

Tacoma
Olympia

WASHINGTON

Spokane

Portland

Salem

Eugene

OREGON

Kiska I.

Amchitka I.

Kanaga I.
Adak I.

Atka I.
Amlia I.
Seguam I.

Umnak I.

Unalaska I.

PACIFIC OCEAN

ATLANTIC OCEAN

CARIBBEAN SEA

UNITED STATES OF AMERICA

MEXICO

CANADA

WASHINGTON

OREGON

CALIFORNIA
Fresno
Bakersfield
Anaheim
Long Beach
Los Angeles
San Diego
Mexicali
Ensenada

UTAH
Lake City

COLORADO
Denver
Pueblo

NEW MEXICO
Santa Fe
Albuquerque

ARIZONA
Phoenix
Mesa
Tucson

NEVADA
Las Vegas

Cheyenne

NEBRASKA
Lincoln

KANSAS
Topeka

IOWA
Des Moines
Davenport

WISCONSIN
Madison
Milwaukee

MINNESOTA

ILLINOIS
Chicago
Springfield

INDIANA
Indianapolis

MISSOURI
Jefferson City
St Louis

OKLAHOMA
Oklahoma City

ARKANSAS
Little Rock

LOUISIANA
Baton Rouge
New Orleans

TEXAS
Amarillo
Lubbock
El Paso
Fort Worth
Dallas
Shreveport
Austin
San Antonio
Houston
Corpus Christi

OHIO
Columbus
Lansing
Detroit

MICHIGAN

Toronto
Hamilton
Buffalo

NEW YORK
New York
Albany

PENNSYLVANIA
Harrisburg

VERMONT
Montpelier

NEW HAMPSHIRE
Concord

MAINE
Augusta

MASSACHUSETTS
Boston

CONNECTICUT
Hartford

RHODE ISLAND
Providence

NEW JERSEY
Trenton

DELAWARE
Dover

MARYLAND
Annapolis
Washington D.C.

W.VIRGINIA
Charleston

VIRGINIA
Richmond
Virginia Beach

KENTUCKY
Frankfort
Louisville

TENNESSEE
Nashville
Memphis
Chattanooga

NORTH CAROLINA
Raleigh
Charlotte

SOUTH CAROLINA
Columbia
Charleston

GEORGIA
Atlanta
Columbus

ALABAMA
Birmingham
Montgomery

MISSISSIPPI
Jackson

FLORIDA
Tallahassee
Jacksonville
Orlando
Tampa
St Petersburg
Fort Lauderdale
Miami

Savannah
Mobile

BERMUDA (U.K.)

BAHAMAS
Nassau

CUBA
La Habana (Havana)
Pinar del Rio
Matanzas
Cienfuegos
Santiago de Cuba
Bayamo

TURKS AND CAICOS ISLANDS (U.K.)

CAYMAN ISLANDS (U.K.)

JAMAICA
Kingston

HAITI
Port-au-Prince

DOMINICAN REPUBLIC
Santo Domingo

PUERTO RICO (U.S.A.)

VIRGIN ISLANDS (U.K.)
VIRGIN ISLANDS (U.S.A.)

ANGUILLA (U.K.)

ST KITTS AND NEVIS
Basseterre

ANTIGUA AND BARBUDA
St Johns

MONTSERRAT (U.K.)

GUADELOUPE (Fr.)

DOMINICA
Roseau

MARTINIQUE (Fr.)

ST LUCIA
Castries

BARBADOS
Bridgetown

ST VINCENT AND THE GRENADINES

GRENADA
St George's

TRINIDAD AND TOBAGO
Port of Spain

NETHERLANDS ANTILLES (Neth.)

ARUBA (Neth.)

MEXICO
Tijuana
Hermosillo
Chihuahua
La Paz
Culiacán
Monterrey
Nuevo Laredo
Matamoros
San Luis Potosí
Tampico
León
Guadalajara
Querétaro
Morelia
México
Cuernavaca
Puebla de Zaragoza
Acapulco
Coatzacoalcos
Tuxtla Gutiérrez
Mérida
Campeche

BELIZE
Belmopan

GUATEMALA
Guatemala

EL SALVADOR
San Salvador

HONDURAS
Tegucigalpa

NICARAGUA
Managua

COSTA RICA
San José

PANAMA
Panamá

Isla de Coiba

Islas Galápagos (Ecu.)

VENEZUELA

COLOMBIA

ECUADOR

PERU

BRAZIL

GUYANA

Islas Revillagigedo (Mex.)

Isla Guadalupe (Mex.)

Tropic of Cancer

Equator

Lake Ontario

Lake Erie

```
0    150   300   450   600   750   kilometers
0    150      300      450   miles
Scale 1:15,000,000    Projection: Conic Equidistant
```

North Canada • Alaska • Greenland

RUSSIAN
FEDERATION
Chukotskiy
Poluostrov

Koryakskoye Nagor'ye
Mys Navarin
Anadyr'
Ugol'nyye Kopi
Iul'tin
C. Lisburne
Ostrov
Vrangelya
Ushakovskoye

Arctic Circle
Anadyrskiy Zaliv
Mys Chukotskiy
St Lawrence I.

CHUKCHI SEA

BERING SEA

St Matthew I.
St Lawrence I.

Bering Strait
Point Hope

BEAUFORT SEA

Nunivak I.
St Michael
Scammon Bay
Kotlik
Nome
Kotzebue
Seward Peninsula

Wainwright
Pt Barrow
Barrow
Nuiqsut

Prince Patrick I.

C. Newenham
Togiako
Bethel
Tanunak

Kuskokwim Bay

Brooks Range
Umiat
Sagwon
Deadhorse
Kaktovik

C. Prince Alfred

McClure Strait

Banks Island

Passage Point

Norton Sound
Huslia
Shungnak
Olnyat

Herschel I.
Mackenzie Bay

Sachs Harbour

Prince Albert Peninsula

U. S. A.

Bristol Bay
Dillingham
Kuskokwim Mountains
Kuskokwim
Ruby
Galena
Koyukuk
Tanana
Fort Yukon
Chalkyitsik
Mt Greenough
2207 m

C. Bathurst

Holman

Victoria Island

Alaska Pen.
Aleutian Range
Togiako

ALASKA
Mt McKinley
6194 m
Cantwell
Fairbanks
Delta Junction
Old Crow
Aklavik
Inuvik
Tuktoyaktuk
C. Parry

Amundsen Gulf
Cape Baring

Dolphin and Union Strait
Wollaston Peninsula

Paulatuk

Camp

Afognak I.
Kodiak
Kodiak I.

Shelikof Strait

Kenai
Homer
Seward
Palmer
Chugach Mountains
Cordova
ANCHORAGE
Glennallen
Alaska Range
Tok
Beaver Creek
Snag
Koidern
Dawson
Mayo

Fort McPherson
Tsiigehtchic

Good Hope

Fort Good Hope

Norman Wells
Tulita

Déline

Franklin Mountains

Colville Lake

Kugluktuk

Coronation Gulf

Gulf of Alaska

Mt Logan
5959 m
Burwash Landing
Kluane
Haines Junction
Carmacks
Pelly Crossing
Faro
Ross River

Ogilvie Mountains

YUKON TERRITORY

Selwyn Mountains

Mackenzie Mountains

Reele Peak
2972 m

NORTHWEST

Great Bear Lake

Bathurst Inlet

Yakutato
Carcross
Whitehorse
Haines

Teslin
Watson Lake

Wrigley

TERRITORIES

Contwoyto Lake

Lac de Gras

Skagway
Atlin
Cassiar
Dease Lake

Liard River

Fort Simpson

Rae Lakes
Edzoo
Rae

Aylmer Lake

PACIFIC

Juneau
Sitka
Petersburg
Wrangell

Mezzah Peak
2164 m
Telegraph Creek

Liard River
Toad River
Summit Lake
Fort Nelson

Fort Providence

Great Slave Lake

Yellowknife

Lutselk'e

C A

OCEAN

Ketchikan

Alexander Archipelago

Coast Mountains
Ware
Trutch

Kakisa
Hay River

CANADA

C. Knox
Graham I.
Queen Charlotte Is
Moresby I.

Stewart
Prince Rupert
Hazelton
New Hazelton
Terrace
Kitimat
Kemano

Cassiar Mountains

Fort St John
Hudsons Hope
Mackenzie
Chetwynd
Dawson Creek

Fort Smith

Fort Fitzgerald

Rainbow Lake
High Level

Carcajou
Fort Vermilion

Peace River

Fort Chipewyan

Lake Athabasca

Stony Rapids

Black

Houston
Burns Lake
Ootsa Lake
Vanderhoof

Manning

843 m
Birch Mts

Fort MacKay

C. Scott
Port Hardy

Bella Coola
Bella Bella

Rivers Inlet

ROCKY

Spirit River
Hythe
Grande Prairie

Peace River
Atikameg
Slave Lake
Faust

Fort McMurray

La Loche

Wollaston Lake

Reindeer Lake

Southend

Vancouver Island

Kelsey Bay
Campbell River
Nanaimo
Tofino

Mt Waddington
4016 m
Hanceville
Williams Lake
Quesnel
McBride

Prince George

Whitecourt
Hinton
Edson

Assiniboine
ALBERTA

Conklin

Churchill Lake

La Ronge

SASKATCHEWAN

Cache Creek
Kamloops

Valemount
Mt Columbia
3747 m
Jasper
Wetaskiwin
Leduc

Athabasca
Westlock

Waskesiu
Prince Albert

C. Flattery
Victoria
Burnaby
Vancouver

Golden
Kelowna
Penticton

Clearwater
Red Deer
Didsbury
Ponoka

Edmonton
Vegreville
Vermilion
Pierceland
Cold Lake

North Battleford
Unity
Biggar

Melfort
Wynyard

C. Disappointment
Olympia
Tacoma
Seattle

Mt Olympus
2424 m

WASHINGTON

U. S. A.

Cranbrook
Kamloops
Cardston
Magrath
Lethbridge

Calgary
Drumheller
Medicine Hat
Claresholm

Hanna
Cereal
Kindersley
Rosetown
Davidson
Watrous

Swift Current

Moose Jaw

Melville
Yorkton

Saskatoon

Regina

L 88° L 86° M 84° N 82° P 80° Q 78° R 76° S 410 74° T

Mansel I.

Péninsule d´Ungava

Lac Nantais

Akulivik

1

60°

Mosquito Bay

Rivière de Povungnituk

Puvirnituq

Kogaluk

Lac Payne

Arnaud

Povungnituk Bay

410

Ottawa
Is

2

Lac La
Potherie

Hudson

Rivière aux Feuilles

Inukjuak

58°

Bay

Lac Minto

3

Sleeper Is

King George
Islands

Nastapoka

Islands

Nastapoka

Lac à l'Eau
Claire

Lac
Guillaume-
Delisle

56°

Sanikiluaq

Lac d'Iberville

Lac
Bienville

Belcher Is

4

Fort
Severn

Sainsbury Pt   Merry I.

Kujjuaraapik

Grande Rivière de la Baleine

Severn

Shagamu

Kanaaupscow

Winisko

C. Henrietta
Maria

Long I.

Lac
Burton

Réservoir de
La Grande Deux

Réservoir de
La Grande Trois

54°

Peawanuck

Pte
Louis-XIV

Winisk

Sutton Ridges

Shamattawa

Sutton

Lac de la
Corvette

Radisson

5

rout

Ekwan

James

Chisasibi

Lac
Duncan

La Grande Rivière

Castor

Lac
Sakami

Réservoir
Opinaca

QUÉBEC

Kasabonika

Bay

North
Twin I.

Winiskisis Channel

Webequie

Akimiski I.

South
Twin I.

Nouveau-Comptoir
(Wemindji)

Eastmain

52°

Attawapiskat

C. Duncan

Attawapiskat

Missisa
Lake

Kapiskau

Charlton I.

Eastmain

Lansdowne
House

Fort
Albany

Baie de
Rupert

Rivière de Rupert

Lac
Mesgouez

6

ONTARIO

Albany

Waskaganish

Lac
Mistassini

Marten
Falls

Hannah
Bay

Ogoki

Moosonee

Moose
Factory

Nottaway

Lac Evans

Mistassini

Ogoki
Res.

Ogoki

Kesagami
Lake

Hurricana

50°

Caribou
Lake

Chibougamau

Chapais

Lac au
Goéland

7

ay

Auden

Aroland

Nakina

Fraserdale

Lac
Matagami

Matagami

Desmaraisville

Lake

Bell

Miquelon

Nipigon

Gerladton

Hearst   Mattice

Réservoir
Gouin

Jellicoe   Longlac   Caramat

Joguès

Lowther

Opasatika

Kapuskasing

Smooth Rock Falls

Normétal

Beattyville

Beardmore

Hillsport

Moonbeam

Driftwood

La Sarre

Long
Lake

Hornepayne

Cochrane

Iroquois
Falls

Authier

Villemontel

Senneterre

Langlade

Oskélanéo

Nipigon

Manitouwadge

Oba

Porquis
Junction

Matheson

Amos

Barraute

Forsythe

Red
Rock

Terrace
Bay

Fire River

Elsas

Timmins

Ramore

Duparquet

Malartic   Val-d'Or

Parent

St Ignace I.

Marathon

Peterbell

White River

Rouyn-Noranda

K 88° L 86° M 84° N 421 82° P 80° Q 78° R 76° S

0   100   200 kilometers

0   50   100 miles

Projection: Albers Equal Area

North and Central America

East Canada

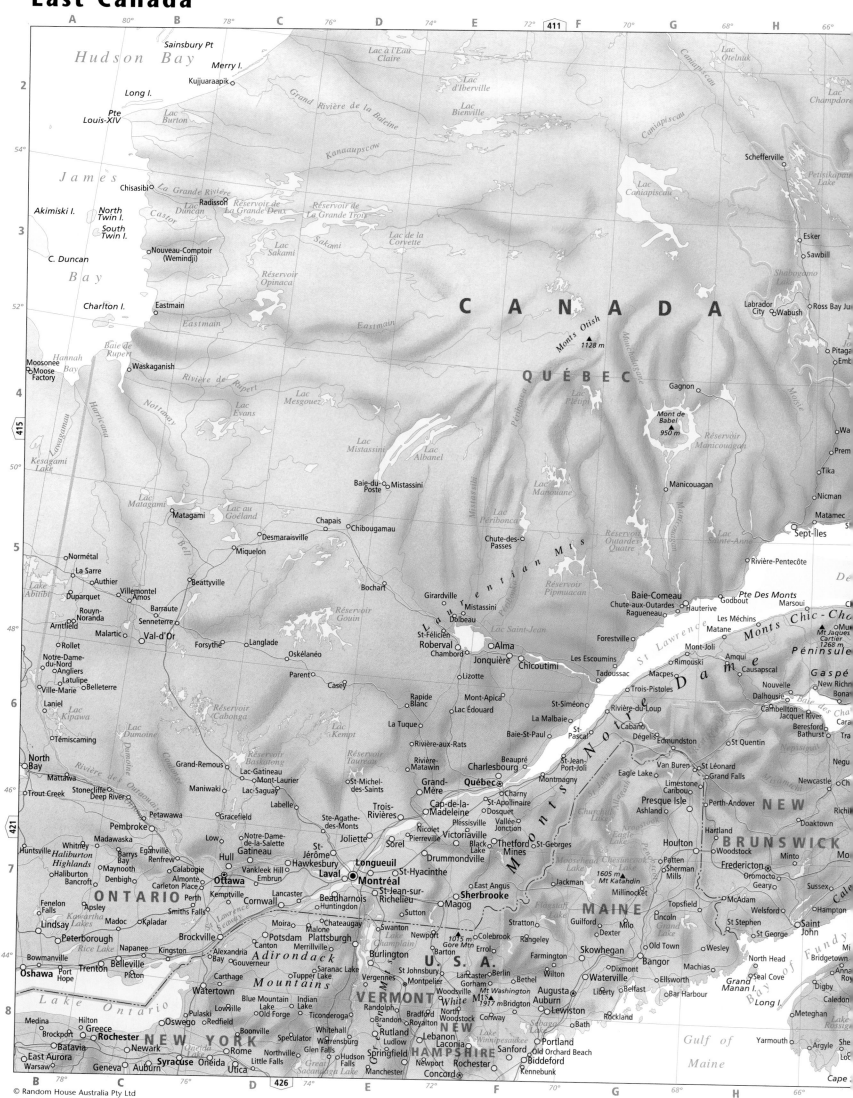

Hudson Bay

Sainsbury Pt
Merry I.
Kujjuaraapik
Long I.
Pte Louis-XIV

James
Bay

Akimiski I.
North Twin I.
South Twin I.
C. Duncan
Bay

Lac Otelnuk
Lac à l'Eau Claire
Lac d'Iberville
Lac Bienville
Lac Champdore

Chisasibi
Radisson
Réservoir de La Grande Deux
Réservoir de La Grande Trois
Caniapiscau
Lac Caniapiscau
Schefferville
Petisikapau Lake
Esker
Sawbill

Lac Burton
Lac Duncan
Castor
Grand Rivière de la Baleine
Kanaaupscow

CANADA

Nouveau-Comptoir (Wemindji)
Lac Sakami
Réservoir Opinaca
Sakami
Lac de la Corvette
Ross Bay Ju
Labrador City
Wabush
Shabogamo Lake

Eastmain
Eastmain
Eastmain
Esker

Baie de Rupert
Moosonee
Moose Factory
Waskaganish
Rivière de Rupert
QUÉBEC
Monts Otish ▲ 1128 m
Gagnon

Hannah Bay
Charlton I.
Hurricana
Lac Mesgouez
Lac Evans
Lac Plétipi
Mont de Babel ▲ 950 m
Réservoir Manicouagan
Wa
Prem

Kesagami Lake
Lac Matagami
Lac Mistassini
Lac Albanel
Mistassini
Tika
Nicman

Baie-du-Poste
Mistassini
Lac Manouane
Manicouagan
Matamec
Sept-Îles

Matagami
Lac au Goéland
Chapais
Chibougamau
Lac Péribonca
Réservoir Pipmuacan
Lac Sainte-Anne

Desmaraisville
Miquelon
Chute-des-Passes
Réservoir Outardes Quatre
Rivière-Pentecôte
De

Normétal
La Sarre
Authier
Beattyville
Bochart
Girardville
Mistassini
Laurentian Mts
Baie-Comeau
Pte Des Monts
Godbout
Marsoui

Duparquet
Villemontel
Amos
Barraute
Dolbeau
Chute-aux-Outardes
Ragueneau
Hauterive
Les Méchins
Monts Chic-Cho

Rouyn-Noranda
Senneterre
Réservoir Gouin
St-Félicien
Lac Saint-Jean
Forestville
Mont-Joli
Rimouski
Amqui
Causapscal
Mt Jaques Cartier ▲ 1268 m
Péninsule

Arntfield
Malartic
Val-d'Or
Forsythe
Langlade
Oskélanéo
Roberval
Chambord
Alma
Les Escoumins
Trois-Pistoles
Macpes
Nouvelle
New Richm
Gaspé
Bona

Notre-Dame-du-Nord
Angliers
Latulipe
Parent
Jonquière
Chicoutimi
Lizotte
Tadoussac
Rivière-du-Loup
St Lawrence
Cabano
Dalhousie
Cambellton
Jacquet River
Beresford
Bathurst
Cara

Ville-Marie
Belleterre
Casey
Rapide Blanc
Mont-Apica
Lac Édouard
St-Siméon
La Malbaie
St-Pascal
Dégelis
Edmundston
St Quentin
Tra

Laniel
Lac Kipawa
Réservoir Cabonga
La Tuque
Baie-St-Paul
Monts Notre Dame
Cabano
Newcastle

Témiscaming
Lac Dumoine
Réservoir Baskatong
Lac Kempt
Rivière-aux-Rats
Beaupré
Charlesbourg
St-Jean-Port-Joli
Eagle Lake
Van Buren
St Léonard
Grand Falls

North Bay
Mattawa
Rivière des Outaouais
Grand-Remous
Lac-Gatineau
Réservoir Taureau
Rivière-Matawin
Québec
Montmagny
Limestone
Caribou
Presque Isle
Perth-Andover
NEW

Trout Creek
Stonecliffe
Deep River
Petawawa
Maniwaki
Mont-Laurier
Lac-Saguay
St-Michel-des-Saints
Grand-Mère
Charny
St-Apollinaire
Dosquet
Ashland
Presque Isle
Hartland
Doaktown
BRUNSWICK

Huntsville
Whitney
Madawaska
Barrys Bay
Eganville
Low
Notre-Dame-de-la-Salette
Gatineau
Labelle
Ste-Agathe-des-Monts
Trois-Rivières
Nicolet
Victoriaville
Plessisville
Vallée Jonction
Thetford Mines
St-Georges
Houlton
Woodstock
Fredericton
Minto

Haliburton Highlands
Renfrew
Maynooth
Denbigh
Gracefield
Joliette
Sorel
Pierreville
Black Lake
Patten
Sherman Mills
Oromocto
Geary
Sussex

Haliburton
Bancroft
Calabogie
Almonte
Carleton Place
Hull
Hawkesbury
St-Jérôme
Longueuil
Laval
St-Hyacinthe
Drummondville
Jackman
Mt Katahdin ▲ 1605 m
Millinocket
McAdam
Welsford
Hampton

ONTARIO
Fenelon Falls
Apsley
Perth
Smiths Falls
Kemptville
Embrun
Lancaster
Montréal
St-Jean-sur-Richelieu
Sherbrooke
East Angus
Stratton
MAINE
Topsfield
Lincoln
St Stephen
Saint John

Lindsay
Madoc
Kaladar
Ottawa
Cornwall
Beauharnois
Huntingdon
Sutton
Magog
Guilford
Dexter
Old Town
Wesley
St George

Peterborough
Napanee
Kingston
Alexandria Bay
Moira
Chateaugay
Swanton
Newport
Colebrook
Rangeley
Farmington
Skowhegan
Bangor
North Head
Bridgetown

Bowmanville
Port Hope
Trenton
Belleville
Picton
Brockville
Potsdam
Plattsburgh
Merrillville
Barton
Errol
Stratton
Waterville
Dixmont
Ellsworth
Seal Cove
Digby

Oshawa
Rice Lake
Gouverneur
Saranac Lake
Burlington
St Johnsbury
Montpelier
Gorham
Augusta
Liberty
Belfast
Bar Harbour
Meteghan

Lake Ontario
Medina
Hilton
Greece
Brockport
Batavia
East Aurora
Warsaw
Rochester
Newark
Syracuse
Geneva
Auburn
Oneida
Utica
NEW YORK
Watertown
Carthage
Lowville
Pulaski
Oswego
Redfield
Boonville
Rome
Little Falls
Northville
Adirondack Mountains
Blue Mountain Lake
Old Forge
Indian Lake
Speculator
Warrensburg
Whitehall
Ticonderoga
Rutland
Glen Falls
Hudson Falls
Ludlow
VERMONT
Vergennes
Woodsville
Mt Washington ▲ 1917 m
White Mts
Randolph
Bradford
North Royalton
Conway
NEW HAMPSHIRE
Bethel
Wilton
Waterville
Auburn
Lewiston
Sanford
Old Orchard Beach
Biddeford
Rennebunk
Lebanon
Laconia
Newport
Rochester
Concord
Manchester
Springfield
Portland
Bath
Rockland
Gulf of Maine
Yarmouth
Argyle
Cape

Lake Champlain
Gore Mtn 1015 m
Lake Winnipesaukee
Sebago Lake
Grand Manan I.
Long I.
Bay of Fundy

LABRADOR
SEA

Kogaluk

Tunungayualok Island

Davis Inlet

Mistastin Lake

Hopedale

C. Makkovik

Snegamook Lake

Nipishish Lake

Kanairiktok

C. Harrison
C. Turley

Mt Benedict
829 m

Holton

Groswater Bay

Double Mer

Humber

C. Porcupine

Grady Harbour

Labrador

Grand Lake

Lake Melville

Cartwright

Separation Point

Batteau

Happy Valley - Goose Bay

Churchill

Mealy Mts

Comfort Bight

Square Islands

Port Hope Simpson

Table Head

Belle Isle

Little Mecatina

Red Bay

C. Bauld
L'Anse aux Meadows

Rivière-St-Paul

Blanc-Sablon

Forteaux

St Anthony

Main Brook

Strait of Belle Isle

Hare Bay

St-Augustin

Brig Bay

Groais I.

Grey Is

Hare Bay

St John I.

Northern

Engle

Bell I.

Port aux Choix

Mutton Bay

Hawkes Bay

Williamsport

Horse Is

White Bay

St-Jean

Baie-Johan Beetz

Lac Musquaro

Daniel's Harbour

Peninsula

C. St John

La Scie

Fogo

Fogo I.

Havre-St-Pierre

Natashquan

Kegaska

Gethsémani

Baie Verte

Notre Dame Bay

Pointe-Parent

Sally's Cove

Westport

Musgrave Harbour

oit de Jacques - Cartier

Rocky Harbour

Grose Morne
806 m

Hampden

Springdale

Cape Freels

Gander Bay

Wesleyville

Île d'Anticosti

Mt 674 m
St Gregory

Deer Lake

Sandy Lake

Grand Falls-Windsor

Badger

Gander

Bonavista Bay

Chicotte

Pte de l'Est

Corner Brook

Buchans

Grand Lake

Gambo

Bonavista

uedo

Lewis Hills
815 m

Glover I.

Red Indian Lake

Summerville

Grates Cove

des-iers de Gaspé achois

Lourdes

Stephenville

Victoria Lake

Meelpaeg Lake

Newfoundland

Musgravetown

Clarenville

Gulf of

Cape St George

St George's Bay

Middle Ridge

Goobies

Trinity Bay

Pouch Cove

St Lawrence

C. Anguille

St Alban's

Milltown

Carbonear

Conception Bay

St John's

u I.

C. Ray

Rose Blanche

Burgeo

Harbour Breton

Bay Roberts

Mount Pearl

Bay Bulls

Channel-Port aux Basques

Hermitage Bay

Fortune Bay

Garnish

Placentia Bay

Avalon Peninsula

Placentia

Ferryland

Cap aux Meules

Grand-Entrée

Îles de la Madeleine

Miqeulon

Grand Bank

Fortune

Marystown

Branch

Trepassey

Cape Race

North Cape

Havre-Aubert

Cape North

ST PIERRE AND MIQUELON
(Fr.)

St Pierre

St Lawrence

C. St Mary's

St Mary's Bay

Cape Pine

PRINCE EDWARD

Cape North

Ingonish

ISLAND

Chéticamp

Summerside

St Peters

East Pt

Elmira

Margaree Forks

New Waterford

Glace Bay

Charlottetown

Inverness

Montague

Port Hood

Whycocomagh

Main-à-Dieu

Sydney

Cape George

Bras d'Or Lake

Cape Breton

mherst

Oxford

Tatamagouche

New Glasgow

Port Hawkesbury

Fourchu

Isle Madam

Island

ATLANTIC

equid Mts

Stellarton

Monastery

Arichat

sboro

Truro

Bolyston

Aspen

Canso

St Marys

Tor Bay

SCOTIA

Musquodoboit Harbour

Sheet Harbour

OCEAN

alifax

Dartmouth

aster any enburg

Sambro

Northwest United States

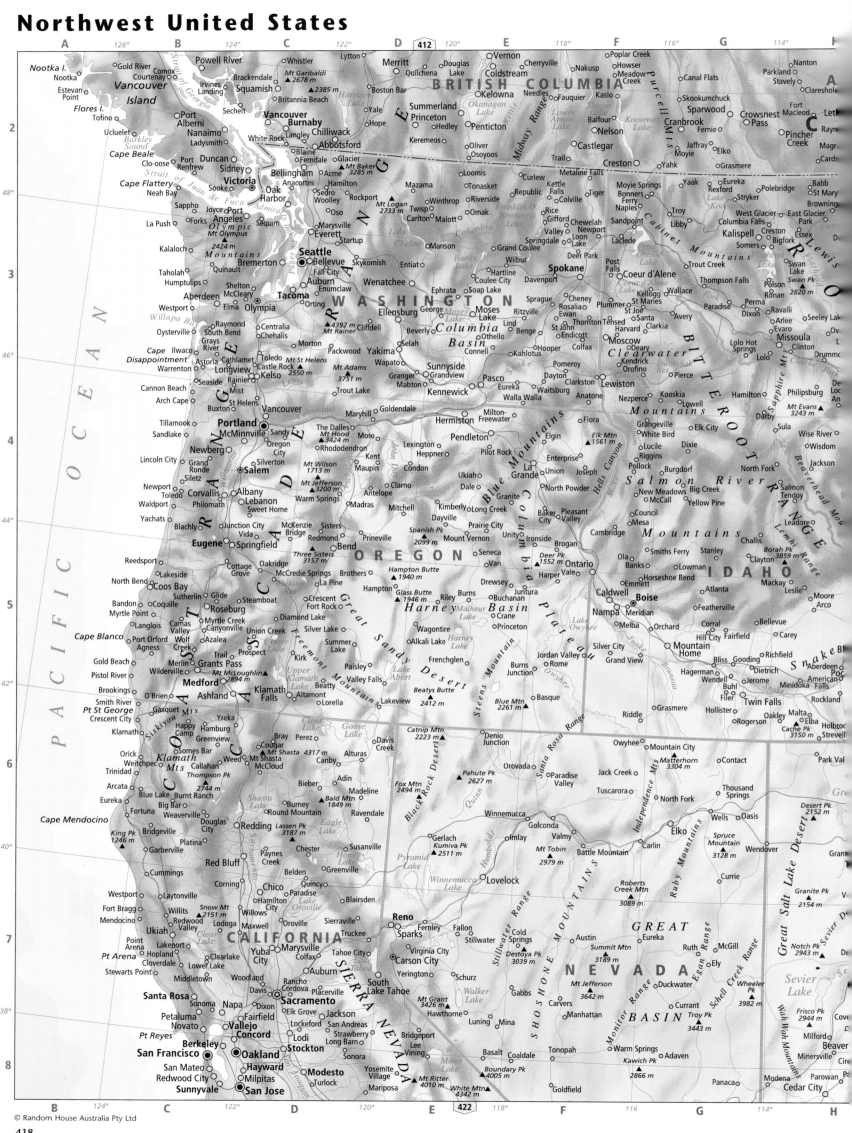

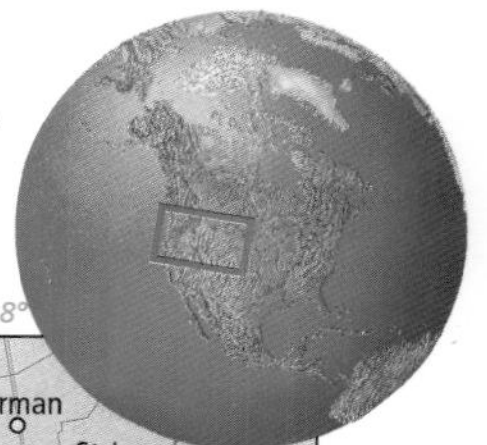

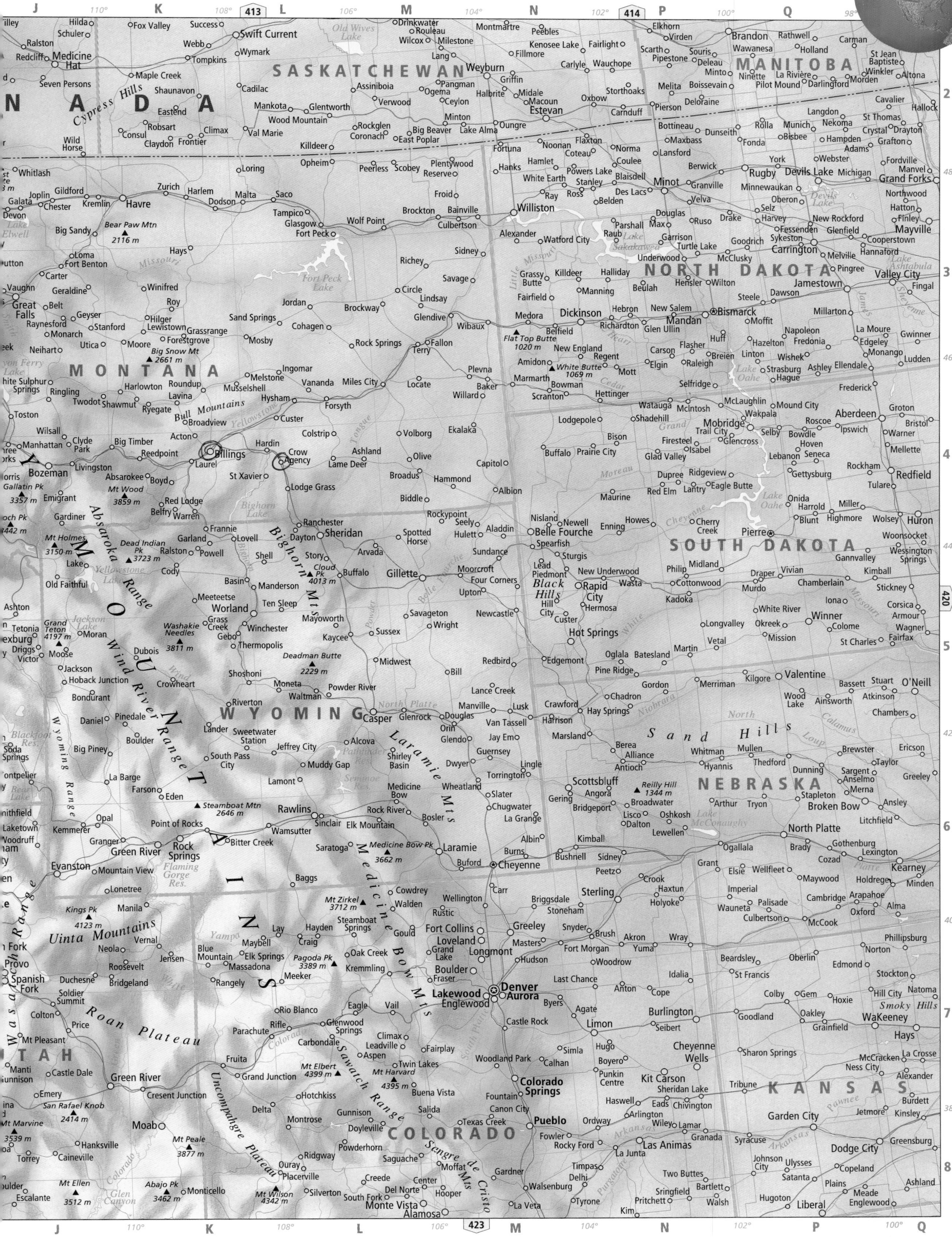

413 414

J 110° K 108° L 106° M 104° N 102° P 100° Q 98°

CANADA

SASKATCHEWAN

MANITOBA

MONTANA

NORTH DAKOTA

SOUTH DAKOTA

WYOMING

NEBRASKA

Black Hills

Sand Hills

Uinta Mountains

Wasatch Range

Wind River Range

MOUNTAINS

Medicine Bow Mts

Laramie Mts

UTAH

COLORADO

KANSAS

Roan Plateau

Uncompahgre Plateau

Sangre de Cristo Mts

Sawatch Range

Mt Elbert 4399 m
Mt Harvard 4395 m
Grand Teton 4197 m
Gallatin Pk 3357 m
Cloud Pk 4013 m
Kings Pk 4123 m
Mt Holmes 3150 m
Dead Indian Pk 3723 m
Bear Paw Mtn 2116 m
Big Snow Mt 2661 m
Mt Wood 3859 m
Mt Zirkel 3712 m
Pagoda Pk 3389 m
Steamboat Mtn 2646 m
Deadman Butte 2229 m
Medicine Bow Pk 3662 m
Reilly Hill 1344 m
White Butte 1069 m
Flat Top Butte 1020 m
Mt Peale 3877 m
Mt Ellen 3512 m
Abajo Pk 3462 m
Mt Wilson 4342 m
Mt Marvine 3539 m
San Rafael Knob 2414 m
Washakie Needles 3811 m

Denver Aurora Lakewood Englewood
Cheyenne
Bismarck Mandan
Pierre
Colorado Springs
Pueblo
Rapid City
Billings
Bozeman

Scale 1:5 000 000 Projection: Albers Equal Area

0   100   200 kilometers
0   50   100 miles

419

Central United States

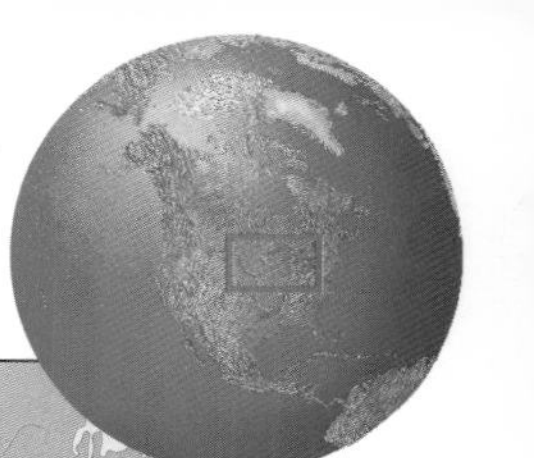

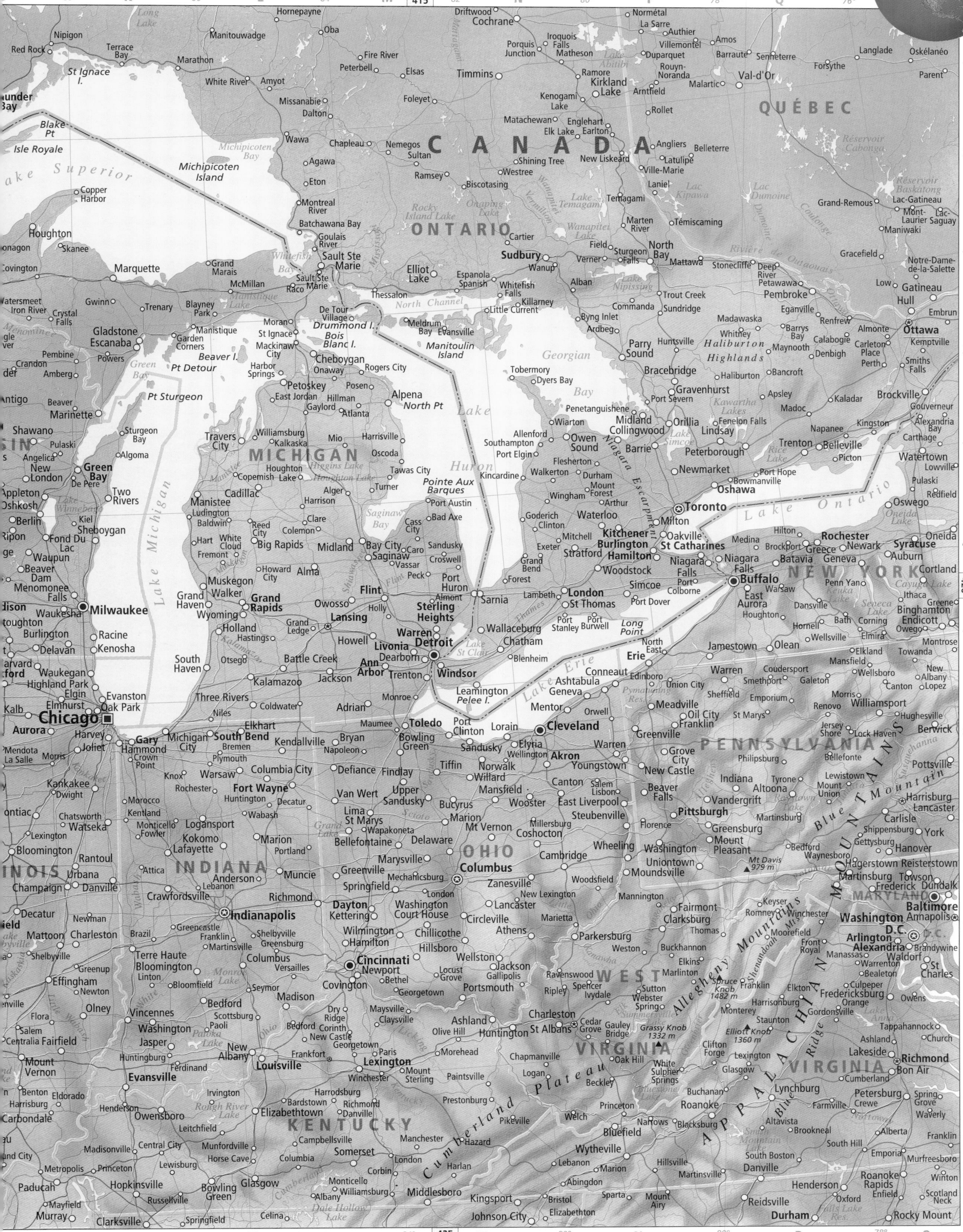

QUÉBEC

CANADA

ONTARIO

Lake Superior

Lake Huron

Lake Michigan

Lake Erie

Lake Ontario

Georgian Bay

MICHIGAN

WISCONSIN

ILLINOIS

INDIANA

OHIO

PENNSYLVANIA

NEW YORK

WEST VIRGINIA

VIRGINIA

KENTUCKY

MARYLAND

Chicago

Milwaukee

Green Bay

Detroit

Toronto

Buffalo

Cleveland

Columbus

Cincinnati

Indianapolis

Pittsburgh

Ottawa

Sudbury

Washington D.C.

Baltimore

Richmond

Louisville

Lexington

APPALACHIAN MOUNTAINS

Blue Ridge Mountain

Allegheny Mountains

Cumberland Plateau

Mt Davis 979 m

Spruce Knob 1482 m

Grassy Knob 1332 m

Elliott Knob 1360 m

Scale 1:5 000 000 Projection: Albers Equal Area

0 100 200 kilometers

0 50 100 miles

Southwest United States

States / Regions: UTAH · COLORADO · KANSAS · ARIZONA · NEW MEXICO · TEXAS · SONORA · CHIHUAHUA · COAHUILA · MEXICO

Mountains / Features: Uinta Mountains · Roan Plateau · ROCKY MOUNTAINS · Medicine Bow · Sawatch Range · San Juan Mtns · Sangre de Cristo Mts · Uncompahgre Plateau · Monument Valley · Glen Canyon · Painted Desert · Zuni Mountains · Sacramento Mountains · Gila Mts · Theodore Roosevelt Lake · Elephant Butte Res · LLANO ESTACADO · GREAT PLAINS · Edwards Plateau · Stockton Plateau · Davis Mts · Sierra Vieja · Llano de los Caballos Mesteños · Lake Powell · Smoky Hills

Major cities: Denver · Aurora · Lakewood · Englewood · Colorado Springs · Pueblo · Santa Fe · Albuquerque · Amarillo · Lubbock · El Paso · Ciudad Juárez · Tucson · Las Cruces · Roswell · Odessa · Midland · Hermosillo · Chihuahua · Ciudad Acuña · Del Rio

Selected elevations:
Kings Pk 4123 m · Mt Zirkel 3712 m · Pagoda Pk 3389 m · Mt Elbert 4399 m · Mt Harvard 4395 m · San Rafael Knob 2414 m · Mt Marvine 3539 m · Mt Ellen 3512 m · Mt Peale 3877 m · Abajo Pk 3462 m · Mt Wilson 4342 m · Hesperus Mtn 4033 m · Wheeler Pk 4011 m · Blanca Pk 4372 m · Mt Taylor 3445 m · South Baldy 3287 m · Baldy Pk 3476 m · Mazatzal Pk 2409 m · Rose Pk 2678 m · Pelona Mtn 2810 m · Whitewater Baldy 3321 m · Mt Turnbull 2524 m · Mt Graham 3265 m · Ladron Pk 2797 m · Salinas Pk 2730 m · Capitan Pk 3073 m · Chiricahua Pk 2986 m · Animas Pk 2597 m · Sierra Blanca 2101 m · Victoria Pk 1960 m · Mt Livermore 2555 m · Sierra Vieja 1971 m · Cathedral Mtn 2091 m · Chinati Pk 2353 m · Santiago Pk 1988 m · Emory Pk 2385 m · Picacho del Centinela 2896 m · Pico de Johnson 1063 m · Humphreys Pk 3851 m · boquivari Pk 2356 m

North and Central America

Scale 1:5 000 000   Projection: Albers Equal Area

0   100   200 kilometers
0   50   100 miles

Southeast United States

H · 88° · J · 86° · K · 84° · 421 · L · 82° · M · 80° · N · 78°

KENTUCKY

Girardeau · Central City · Munfordville · Campbellsville · Manchester · Hazard · Wytheville · South Boston · South Hill · Murfreesboro — 1

Mound City · Madisonville · Lewisburg · Somerset · London · Corbin · Harlan · Lebanon · Marion · Hillsville · Martinsville · Danville · Oxford · Henderson · Enfield · Roanoke Rapids · Scotland Neck · Winton

Metropolis · Princeton · Hopkinsville · Bowling Green · Glasgow · Monticello · Middlesboro · Kingsport · Abingdon · Bristol · Sparta · Boone · North Wilkesboro · Mount Airy · Reidsville · **Winston-Salem** · **Durham** · **Raleigh** · Wilson · Goldsboro · Williamston · Washington · Greenville — 426, 36°

Paducah · Murray · Russellville · Bowling Green · Albany · Williamsburg · La Follette · Johnson City · Greeneville · Elizabethton · North Wilkesboro · **High Point** · **Greensboro** · Lexington · Salisbury · Statesville · Kannapolis · Concord · Lexington · Sanford · Smithfield · Kinston · New Bern

Martin · Paris · Clarksville · Springfield · Gallatin · Lebanon · Cookeville · Morristown · Jefferson City · Newport · Asheville · Rutherfordton · Statesville · Salisbury · Concord · **Charlotte** · Monroe · Fayetteville · Clinton · Jacksonville

McKenzie · yersburg · Hendersonville · **Nashville** · Dickson · Fairview · Murfreesboro · Sparta · Crossville · Harriman · Oak Ridge · **Knoxville** · Maryville · Great Smoky Mts · Mt Guyot 2018 m · Hickory · Morganton · Gastonia · Raeford · Lumberton · Elizabethtown · Wallace

TENNESSEE · Waverly · Mt Mitchell 2037 m · Bryson City · **NORTH CAROLINA** — 2

Milan · Brownsville · Lexington · Columbia · Lewisburg · Shelbyville · Manchester · Dayton · Athens · Sweetwater · Cleveland · Hendersonville · Franklin · Inman · **Charlotte** · Rockingham · Hamlet · Laurinburg · Burgaw · Holly Ridge

Jackson · Waynesboro · Lawrenceburg · Tullahoma · Winchester · Red Bank · **Chattanooga** · Blairsville · Brasstown Bald 1458 m · Gaffney · Spartanburg · Rock Hill · Cheraw · Bethune · Dillon · Chadbourn · Whiteville · Wilmington — Onslow Bay

Bolivar · Selmer · Pulaski · Fayetteville · Stevenson · Dalton · Ellijay · Cleveland · Murphy · Taylors · Jonesboro · Chester · Lancaster · Kershaw · Florence · Mullins · Southport · Shallotte · Long Beach

Corinth · Florence · Huntsville · Guntersville Lake · Fort Payne · La Fayette · Calhoun · Jasper · Clemson · Greenville · Whitmire · Great Falls · Camden · Marion · Loris · Conway · Smith I. · Long Beach — 34°

New Albany · Booneville · Sheffield · Decatur · Scottsboro · Arab · Albertville · Cedartown · Marietta · Gainesville · Royston · Abbeville · Anderson · Laurens · Newberry · Saluda · Batesburg · Columbia · Sumter · Lake City · Myrtle Beach

Tupelo · Amory · Winfield · Cullman · Boaz · Gadsden · Roswell · Winder · Athens · Elberton · Greenwood · **SOUTH** · North Augusta · Orangeburg · St Stephen · Georgetown · Long Bay

Birmingham · Bessemer · **Atlanta** · Covington · Farmington · Madison · Thomson · Augusta · New Ellenton · Denmark · Bamberg · Moncks Corner · Summerville — 3

CAROLINA · Columbia · Lake Marion · Manning

PPI · Macon · Starkville · Tuscaloosa · Aliceville · Woodstock · Alabaster · Sylacauga · Alexander City · La Grange · Newnan · Senoia · Griffin · Forsyth · Monticello · Eatonton · Wrens · Waynesboro · Allendale · Walterboro · Mount Pleasant

Louisville · Columbus · Reform · Leeds · Talladega · Columbiana · Clanton · Carrollton · Thomaston · Roberta · Milledgeville · Wadley · Sylvania · Hampton · Jacksonboro · Charleston

Philadelphia · Greensboro · Eutaw · **ALABAMA** · Centreville · Maplesville · Prattville · Auburn · Opelika · Thomaston · Fort Valley · Warner Robins · Dublin · Swainsboro · Twin City · Estill · Beaufort

Meridian · Demopolis · Linden · Selma · Montgomery · Phenix City · **GEORGIA** · **Macon** · Perry · Statesboro · Tillman · Hardeeville · Hilton Head Island — 32°

Newton · Quitman · Butler · Camden · Union Springs · Eufaula · Cusseta · **Columbus** · Americus · Hawkinsville · Eastman · Vidalia · Lyons · Claxton · Richmond Hill · Savannah

Dixons Mills · Glenville · Troy · Abbeville · Rochelle · McRae · Baxley · Glennville · Ludowici · Ossabaw I.

Thomasville · Awin · Greenville · Luverne · Cordele · Fitzgerald · Douglas · Surrency · Jesup · Riceboro · St Catherines I.

Coffeeville · Grove Hill · Brantley · Eufaula · Dawson · Sylvester · Ocilla · Tifton · Alma · Hortense · Darien · Sapelo I. · **ATLANTIC** — 4

Waynesboro · Monroeville · Georgiana · Elba · Enterprise · Headland · Arlington · Colquitt · Albany · Moultrie · Adel · Pearson · Waycross · Blackshear · Brunswick · St Simons I.

Jackson · Evergreen · Andalusia · Opp · Dothan · Blakely · Camilla · Lakeland · Homerville · Woodbine · Cumberland I.

Frisco City · Onycha · Bainbridge · Thomasville · Barney · Valdosta · Kingsland · Fernandina Beach

Mount Vernon · Atmore · Brewton · De Funiak Springs · Bonifay · Cairo · Quitman · Fargo · Yulee

Bay Minette · **Mobile** · Milton · Crestview · Marianna · Quincy · Greenville · Jasper · Macclenny · Baldwin · **Jacksonville** — 30°

Ocean Springs · Pensacola · Valparaiso · Freeport · Blountstown · Bristol · **Tallahassee** · Madison · Live Oak · Lake City · Jacksonville Beach

Biloxi · Pascagoula · Warrington · Fort Walton Beach · Panama City · Saint Marks · Perry · Mayo · Branford · Green Cove Springs · St Augustine · **OCEAN**

Horn I. · Dauphin I. · Gulf Shores · West Bay · Wewahitchka · Apalachee Bay · Steinhatchee · High Springs · Alachua · Palatka

Chandeleur Sound · Port St Joe · Carrabelle · Deadman Bay · Gainesville · Bunnell · Ormond Beach

Chandeleur Is · St Joseph Point · Dog I. · St George I. · Cross City · Chiefland · Williston · Ocala · Crescent Lake · Daytona Beach — 5

phur · Venice · East Bay · Cedar Key · Waccasassa Bay · Lake George · Durnellon · Eustis · Deltona · New Smyrna Beach

FLORIDA · Leesburg · Sanford · Orlando · Titusville · Cape Canaveral

Floral City · Spring Hill · Brooksville · Dade City · Haines City · Kissimmee · Merritt Island — 28°

Tampa · **Clearwater** · Largo · **St Petersburg** · Lakeland · Lake Wales · Holopaw · Melbourne · Palm Bay

Tampa Bay · Bartow · Wauchula · Avon Park · Yeehaw Junction · Vero Beach

Bradenton · Gardner · Sebring · Fort Pierce — 6

Sarasota · Myakka City · Arcadia · Brighton · Okeechobee · Stuart · Hobe Sound · Grand Bahama Island

Venice · North Port · Lake Okeechobee · Freeport

Port Charlotte · La Belle · Clewiston · **West Palm Beach** · Palm Beach · Northwest Providence Channel

Knob I. · Fort Myers · Belle Glade · Delray Beach · Boca Raton · **MEXICO** · Cape Coral · Immokalee · Sunniland · Plantation — 26°

Sanibel I. · Naples · Ochopee · Carol City · **Fort Lauderdale** · **Hollywood** · Bimini Islands

Cape Romano · **Hialeah** · Coral Gables · **Miami** · South Miami · Cutler Ridge · Homestead · **BAHAMAS**

Ten Thousand Is · Florida City — 7

Flamingo · Key Largo · Florida Bay · Marathon · Florida Keys · Straits of Florida

Key West

H · 88° · J · 86° · K · 84° · L · 82° · M · 80° · N

0 · 100 · 200 kilometers
0 · 50 · 100 miles

Northeast United States

Scale 1:5 000 000 Projection: Albers Equal Area

East Caribbean • North Venezuela

A 72° B 68° C 64° D 60°

Tropic of Cancer

ATLANTIC

OCEAN

1

TURKS AND
CAICOS ISLANDS
(U.K.)
Caicos
Islands   Turks Islands
Cockburn
Harbour   Grand Turk

20°

LEEWARD ISLANDS

Cabo
Isabela
Cap-
Haïtien   Puerto Plata
Monte Cristi   Cabrera
Fort Liberté   Moca
Santiago   San Francisco de Macorís
Hinche   La Vega   Bahía Escocesa
HAITI   DOMINICAN   Bahía de Samaná
Comendador 3175 m   Pico Duarte   Monte Plata
San Juan   Bonao   Hato Mayor   El Seibo   Cabo
Jimani   REPUBLIC   Engaño
Neiba   San Pedro de Macorís   Aguadilla   Arecibo   San Juan
Port-au-Prince   Azua   San   La Romana   Mayagüez   Cerro de Punta   Carolina   Road
Barahona   Cristóbal   Santo Domingo   1338 m   Caguas   Town
Pedernales   Punta   San Germán   Ponce   Guayama   St Croix   Charlotte
Salinas   Isla Saona   PUERTO RICO   Amalie
Cabo   (U.S.A.)   VIRGIN   Frederiksted
Beata   ISLANDS
HISPANIOLA   (U.S.A.)

VIRGIN
ISLANDS
(U.K.)   Anegada

ANGUILLA
(U.K.)
The Valley
Marigot   St Martin (Guad.)
St Maarten (Neth.)
Philipsburg
Saba   Barbuda   Codrington   ANTIGUA AND
St Eustatius   BARBUDA
Basseterre   St John's   Antigua
ST KITTS   Redonda
AND NEVIS   Plymouth   Passage
MONTSERRAT   GUADELOUPE
(U.K.)   (Fr.)
Sainte-Rose   Pointe-à-Pitre
Basse-Terre   Guadeloupe
Dominica Passage
Portsmouth   Morne
Diablotin
DOMINICA   1447 m
Roseau   La Plaine
Martinique Passage
Montagne Pelée   Sainte-Marie
1397 m   Le Lamentin
Fort-de-France
MARTINIQUE   St Lucia Channel
(Fr.)
Castries
ST LUCIA   Micoud
Vieux Fort
St Vincent Passage
Soufrière
1234 m
ST VINCENT AND   Georgetown
THE GRENADINES   Kingstown

16°

GREATER   ANTILLES

CARIBBEAN

SEA

6°

LESSER
ANTILLES

WINDWARD ISLANDS

BARBADOS
Speightstown
Bridgetown

3

ARUBA   LESSER   ANTILLES
(Neth.)
Pta Gallinas   Oranjestad   Curaçao   Bonaire
Puerto Estrella   Willemstad   Kralendijk
Península   C. San Román   Pen. de   NETHERLANDS
de Guajira   Paraguaná   ANTILLES
Carrizal   Los Taques   Pueblo Nuevo   (Neth.)   La Orchila   La Blanquilla
Paraguaipoa   Punto Fijo   Puerto   The Grenadines
Golfo de Venezuela   Cumarebo   Grenville   GRENADA
San Juan de los Cayos   St George's
Campo   Maracaibo   Coro   Piritu   Isla de   Tobago
Mara   Casigua   Pedregal   Margarita   Charlotteville
Santa   Dabajuro   Churuguara   La Asunción   Scarborough
Rita   Cabimas   Mene   San Felipe   Catia   Porlamar   Carúpano   Galera Pt   TRINIDAD
de Mauroa   Baragua   Puerto   La Mar   Caracas   Río Caribe   Güiria   AND TOBAGO
Lagunillas   Cerro El Cerrón   Carora   Cabello   Petare   La Asunción   Pen. de   Arima   Sangre Grande
1990 m   Valencia   Maracay   Baruta   C. Codera   Paria   Port of   Trinidad
Barranquitas   Barquisimeto   Yaritagua   Los Teques   Higuerote   San Fernando   Spain   Rio Claro
Lago   Mene   El Tocuyo   La Victoria   Puerto la Cruz   San Fernando   Galeota Pt
de Maracaibo   Grande   Acarigua   San Juan   Barcelona   Cumaná
San Carlos del Zulia   Valera   Guanare   de los Morros   San Antonio   Aragua de   Caripe   Caripito   Boca de la Serpiente
Betijoque   Trujillo   Nueva Florida   Tinaco   de Tamanaco   Barcelona   Maturín
El Vigía   Boconó   San Carlos   El Pao   Zaraza   Anaco   Cantaura
Mérida   Barinas   Guanarito   Ortiz   El Sombrero   El Tigre   San José de Guanipa   Tucupita
Pico Bolívar   Obispos   El Baúl   Chaguaramas   Valle de la   El Chaparro   Barrancas   Boca Araguao
5007 m   Pascua
Tovar   Pedraza La Vieja   Camaguán   Las Mercedes   Santa María   Pariaguán   El Toro   Waini Pt
Calabozo   de Ipire   San José   Morawhanna
San Antonio   Achaguas   Puerto Miranda   de Guanipa   Ciudad Guayana   Mabaruma
de Caparo   Puerto de Nutrias   San Mauricio   Boca del Pao   Soledad   Puerto   El Palmar   La Horqueta   Port Kaituma
Guasdualito   San Fernando de Apure   Cabruta   Ordaz   El Pao   San José   Baramanni
Palmarito   Mantecal   Caicara de Orinoco   Ciudad   Ciudad Piar   Upata   de Amacuro
VENEZUELA   Maripa   Bolívar   Serranía de Imataca
Arauquita   Arauca   Co Turagua   Ciudad Piar   El Miamo   Matthews Ridge
1839 m   Embalse   Guasipati
Tame   Guasdualito   La Urbana   Las Lajitas   Las Trincheras   de Guri   El Callao   Tumeremo
Puerto Rondón   Elorza   Mapire   San Pedro   El Dorado
1320 m   La Paragua   de Las Bocas

GUYANA

COLOMBIA
Cravo Norte
Puerto Nuevo   Parguaza   Tumereng   Peter's Mine
Puerto Carreño   Keweigek   Issano

60°

8°

12°

4

5

B 68° C 64° D 60° E

© Random House Australia Pty Ltd

North and Central America

kilometers
0 100 200 300 400
miles
0 100 200
Projection: Lambert Conformal Conic

Rio de Janeiro, in Brazil (below left). The Igaçu Falls, from the Brazilian side (above). Mountains in the Torres del Paine National Park, Chile (below right).

of the Xingu, Araguaia, and Tocantins Rivers, small groups of Indians such as the Tapirapé survive in forest refuges. Gold prospectors have driven off or killed those Yanomami Indians in Roraima State who have stood in their way.

Economy and resources

Traditional rural activities continue to be important, the rural sector employing 29 percent of the labor force. Brazil is the world's largest producer of coffee and Brazilian livestock numbers are among the world's largest—mainly cattle and pigs—but trends show a steadily falling agricultural contribution to gross domestic product. Industry is increasing in importance, particularly manufacturing, with 90 percent of power coming from hydroelectric schemes. Despite some development of domestic sources, gasoline is still imported. Brazil attempted to substitute ethanol made from sugar for gasoline during the 1980s but falling oil prices made this uneconomical.

With South America's largest gross domestic product, Brazil has the potential to play a leading international role. Yet it must still be considered a developing country as it does not have a fully modern economy. Some difficulties have arisen from heavy state borrowing for unproductive projects; others stem from runaway inflation in the 1980s. Fiscal reforms are difficult to carry through politically—many need constitutional amendments. However, these problems are being addressed (consumer prices rose by 23 percent in 1995 compared with more than 1,000 per cent in 1994) and investor confidence is returning.

1960 Capital moves from Rio de Janeiro to Brasilia, a new city built in the highlands of the interior	**1982** Itaipú Dam on Paraná River, one of the world's largest, completed, provides hydroelectric power for growing industries	**1992** Brazil hosts UN summit on global environmental issues, particularly global warming and greenhouse gas emissions
1973 Trans-Amazon Highway links remote western areas to the rest of the country	**1975** Population reaches 108 million (rising from 53 million in 1950)	**1998** Clearing of rainforest in Roraima attracts international attention—attempts are made to halt the process

Chile

Chile lies between the Andes and the sea. It stretches 4,350 km (2,700 miles) along South America's Pacific coast, yet is never more than 180 km (110 miles) wide. In the fifteenth century, the Incas from Peru tried but failed to subjugate its Araucanian Indian population. This was gradually achieved by the Spanish, against strong resistance, after their arrival in the sixteenth century. The Spanish established mining in the north and huge estates in the Central Valley; by the nineteenth century produce was being exported to California, Australia and elsewhere. Today, fruit and vegetables remain important exports, along with wine.

The Atacama Desert (Desierto de Atacama), in the north, has one of the lowest rainfalls in the world. In the nineteenth century it was the world's main source of nitrate for fertilizer, an export which underwrote Chile's early economic development. Santiago and the port of Valparaíso form an urban cluster midway along the length of the country. Santiago lies in a sheltered, temperate valley between a coastal range of mountains to the west and the high Andes in the interior. This fertile 800 km (500 mile) valley is where Chile's main vineyards are located, and where 60 percent of the population live. It is also where most manufacturing industry is located. Volcanoes, active and inactive, mark the length of the Chilean Andes to the east. In the southern third of the country the coastal range disintegrates into a maze of islands, archipelagoes, and fiords.

In 1970 President Allende nationalized the copper industry and other large enterprises, raised wages, and fixed prices. By 1973 inflation had reached 850 percent. Fearing a Cubanization of

Chile, the political right under General Pinochet staged a coup and ruled for the next 17 years. During that time, over 2,000 political opponents "disappeared." Economically, the coup's effects were more positive. The regime restored economic liberalism and dismantled state controls. Democracy was restored at a general election in 1989.

After two decades of political turmoil, Chile is now one of the more economically progressive of South America's democracies. It is the world's leading supplier of copper, and high copper prices remain vital to the nation's economic health. Growth in gross domestic product averaged more than 6 percent annually from 1991 to 1995, and in recent years an estimated 1 million Chileans have ceased to be classed as poor.

Fact File

OFFICIAL NAME	Republic of Chile
FORM OF GOVERNMENT	Republic with two legislative bodies (High Assembly and Chamber of Deputies)
CAPITAL	Santiago
AREA	756,950 sq km (292,258 sq miles)
TIME ZONE	GMT – 4 hours
POPULATION	14,839,304
PROJECTED POPULATION 2005	15,716,337
POPULATION DENSITY	19.6 per sq km (50.8 per sq mile)
LIFE EXPECTANCY	75.2
INFANT MORTALITY (PER 1,000)	12.4
OFFICIAL LANGUAGE	Spanish
LITERACY RATE	95%
RELIGIONS	Roman Catholic 89%, Protestant 11%
ETHNIC GROUPS	European and mixed indigenous–European 93%, indigenous 5%, other 2%
CURRENCY	Chilean peso
ECONOMY	Services 63%, agriculture 19%, industry 18%
GNP PER CAPITA	US$4,160
CLIMATE	Arid in north, cold and wet in far south, temperate elsewhere
HIGHEST POINT	Ojos del Salado 6,880 m (22,572 ft)
MAP REFERENCE	Pages 458, 460

Colombia

Fact File

OFFICIAL NAME Republic of Colombia

FORM OF GOVERNMENT Republic with two legislative bodies (Senate and House of Representatives)

CAPITAL Bogotá

AREA 1,138,910 sq km (439,733 sq miles)

TIME ZONE GMT – 5 hours

POPULATION 39,309,422

PROJECTED POPULATION 2005 43,662,177

POPULATION DENSITY 34.5 per sq km (89.4 per sq mile)

LIFE EXPECTANCY 70.5

INFANT MORTALITY (PER 1,000) 24.3

OFFICIAL LANGUAGE Spanish

LITERACY RATE 91.1%

RELIGIONS Roman Catholic 95%; Protestant, Jewish, other 5%

ETHNIC GROUPS Mixed indigenous–European 58%, European 20%, mixed European–African 14%, African 4%, mixed indigenous–African 3%, indigenous 1%

CURRENCY Colombian peso

ECONOMY Services 46%, agriculture 30%, industry 24%

GNP PER CAPITA US$1,910

CLIMATE Tropical along coast and on plains, cool to sometimes cold in highlands

HIGHEST POINT Nevado del Huila 5,750 m (18,865 ft)

MAP REFERENCE Pages 450–51

Ecuador

Visited by Christopher Columbus in 1499 and named after him, Colombia straddles the South American continent south of the isthmus of Panama. Once the home of the Chibcha Indians, the country came under Spanish control in 1544, after which it became their chief source of gold. Colombia achieved independence in 1819. From that time on the political and economic fortunes of the country have been contested by the anti-clerical free-trading Liberals and the Conservatives, upholders of protectionism and the Church. While Colombia is notorious for its drug cartels and exports of cocaine, it has a diversified and stable economy that has, for 25 years, shown Latin America's most consistent record of growth.

The country can be divided into three regions. The hot, wet Pacific lowlands run south from the Panamanian border; to the north they merge into drier lowlands along the Caribbean. The cities that face the Caribbean—Barranquilla, Santa Marta, and Cartagena—are tourist resorts. Inland, the parallel Andean ranges running north from the Ecuadorian border define the second region, the high valleys of the Cauca and Magdalena Rivers. This is where most people live. The third region comprises the foothills east of the Andes, where the land falls away into the forested basins of the Amazon (Amazonas) and Orinoco Rivers. This region amounts to almost two-thirds of Colombia's area but only a few cattle ranchers and Indians live here.

With Latin America's largest proven reserves of coal, Colombia is the region's biggest coal exporter. Some 80 percent of the world's emeralds also come from here. Coffee, however, remains the biggest legitimate revenue-earning export. Since 1990 growth in gross domestic product has averaged 4 percent annually, led by expanding construction and financial service industries, and inflows of foreign capital. Nevertheless, earnings from processed cocaine probably exceed all others. Problems include a poverty index of 40 percent, and a continuing political crisis related to allegations of drug connections at high levels.

Riverboats in Puerto Colombia, Colombia (below). Pigs for sale at the market at Otavalo, Ecuador (bottom). The volcano Cotopaxi in Ecuador (above right). A view of one of the Galapagos Islands (bottom right).

Ecuador is the smallest of the Andean republics, taking its name from the equator which divides it in half. Quito was briefly an Inca city before being conquered by the Spanish in the 1530s. The city is ringed by volcanoes, including Cotopaxi (5,896 m; 19,344 ft), the world's highest active volcano. The groups of Indians that form 25 percent of the population are pressing for recognition as distinct nationalities within the state.

Ecuador's agriculture is based on the coastal plains. Bananas, coffee, and cocoa are the main crops. Most production is on haciendas—huge estates established during the early years of Spanish occupation. Inland, among the Andes, are valleys where livestock is raised. The eastern slopes of the Andes give way to forested upland and the border with Peru. This region is so little known that hostilities between Peru and Ecuador in 1995 arose partly from uncertainty as to where the frontier should be. Petroleum and natural gas from this area are piped over the Andes to the Pacific port of Esmeraldas.

Ecuador grows more bananas than any other country in the world. Until overtaken by petroleum

and natural gas, bananas were its biggest export earner, and access to markets in the USA and the EU is a continuing concern. The highland Indians survive through subsistence farming, growing maize and potatoes. Recent economic reforms have helped control inflation and increased foreign investment. Growth has been uneven, however, because manufacturing is handicapped by a shortage of electricity.

Ecuador owns the Galapagos Islands, home to many unique species of animal, such as the giant tortoise. These islands are a popular ecotourism destination, with visitor numbers limited to 40,000 a year so as to protect the fragile ecosystem.

Fact File

OFFICIAL NAME Republic of Ecuador

FORM OF GOVERNMENT Republic with single legislative body (National Congress)

CAPITAL Quito

AREA 283,560 sq km (109,483 sq miles)

TIME ZONE GMT – 5 hours

POPULATION 12,562,496

PROJECTED POPULATION 2005 13,837,829

POPULATION DENSITY 44.3 per sq km (114.7 per sq mile)

LIFE EXPECTANCY 72.2

INFANT MORTALITY (PER 1,000) 30.7

OFFICIAL LANGUAGE Spanish

OTHER LANGUAGES Indigenous languages, particularly Quechua

LITERACY RATE 89.6%

RELIGIONS Roman Catholic 95%, other 5%

ETHNIC GROUPS Indigenous–European 55%, indigenous 25%, Spanish 10%, African 10%

CURRENCY Sucre

ECONOMY Services 42%, agriculture 39%, industry 19%

GNP PER CAPITA US$1,390

CLIMATE Tropical on coast and plains, cooler in highlands

HIGHEST POINT Chimborazo 6,310 m (20,702 ft)

MAP REFERENCE Page 450

Guyana

Guyana means "the land of many waters." In 1616 it was settled by the Dutch, who built dikes, reclaimed coastal land, and planted sugarcane. When the indigenous people refused to work in the sugar plantations, the Dutch, and later the British, imported slaves from Africa and indentured labor from India. The contrast between the communities descended from these two immigrant groups defines Guyanese political life. Beginning in 1953, and sharpened by independence in 1970, a struggle for dominance continues between the Afro-Guyanese and the numerically superior Indo-Guyanese. Some 95 percent of the people live on the coastal strip, and there is concern about flooding because of poor dike maintenance. The savannas, river valleys, and forested plateaus of the interior are largely unpopulated. There are, however, settlements of two neglected minorities in the forests—blacks descended from escaped slaves; and Carib, Warrau, and Arawak Amerindians.

Numerous rivers, including the country's main river, the Essequibo, flow down from the mountains in the west through tropical forests inhabited by a rich assortment of wildlife, including sloth, jaguar, tapir, and capybara. There is diamond dredging in many of the rivers, and in 1995 there was a major cyanide spill at the Omai gold mine near the Essequibo. The effects of mining activities on the wildlife is of major concern to conservationists.

The mining of high-quality bauxite and sugar production accounts for 80 percent of exports. Other resources include gold, diamonds, uranium, manganese, oil, copper, and molybdenum. Under successive governments, state ownership and government controls have stunted development and made adaptation to market fluctuations difficult. The bauxite industry remains a state monopoly. Recent deregulation has, however, shown benefits. Though weak infrastructure hampers tourist development, the spectacular scenery and wildlife of the interior is attracting visitors.

Fact File

OFFICIAL NAME Cooperative Republic of Guyana

FORM OF GOVERNMENT Republic with single legislative body (National Assembly)

CAPITAL Georgetown

AREA 214,970 sq km (83,000 sq miles)

TIME ZONE GMT – 3 hours

POPULATION 705,156

PROJECTED POPULATION 2005 708,582

POPULATION DENSITY 3.3 per sq km (8.5 per sq mile)

LIFE EXPECTANCY 61.8

INFANT MORTALITY (PER 1,000) 48.6

OFFICIAL LANGUAGE English

OTHER LANGUAGES Amerindian languages, Hindi, Urdu

LITERACY RATE 97.9%

RELIGIONS Protestant 34%, Hindu 34%, Roman Catholic 18%, Muslim 9%, other 5%

ETHNIC GROUPS East Indian 51%, African and mixed indigenous–African 43%, indigenous 4%, European and Chinese 2%

CURRENCY Guyana dollar

ECONOMY Industry 44%, agriculture 34%, services 22%

GNP PER CAPITA US$590

CLIMATE Tropical with two rainy seasons (May to mid-August, mid-November to mid-January)

HIGHEST POINT Mt Roraima 2,810 m (9,219 ft)

MAP REFERENCE Page 451

Paraguay

Fact File

OFFICIAL NAME Republic of Paraguay

FORM OF GOVERNMENT Republic with two legislative bodies (Senate and Chamber of Deputies)

CAPITAL Asunción

AREA 406,750 sq km (157,046 sq miles)

TIME ZONE GMT – 4 hours

POPULATION 5,434,095

PROJECTED POPULATION 2005 6,340,163

POPULATION DENSITY 13.4 per sq km (34.7 per sq mile)

LIFE EXPECTANCY 72.4

INFANT MORTALITY (PER 1,000) 36.4

OFFICIAL LANGUAGE Spanish

OTHER LANGUAGE Guaraní

LITERACY RATE 91.9%

RELIGIONS Roman Catholic 90%; other (including Mennonite, Baptist and Anglican) 10%

ETHNIC GROUPS Mixed indigenous–European 95%; indigenous, European, Asian, African 5%

CURRENCY Guaraní

ECONOMY Agriculture 49%, services 30%, industry 21%

GNP PER CAPITA US$1,690

CLIMATE Subtropical; wet in east, semiarid in west

HIGHEST POINT Cerro San Rafael 850 m (2,789 ft)

MAP REFERENCE Pages 455, 458–59

A small landlocked country, Paraguay was originally the home of the Guaraní Indians. It was settled by the Spaniards in 1537 who hoped to use the Guaraní as laborers on their big estates. The strong influence of the Jesuits, however, largely prevented the exploitation of the indigenous people by settlers that occurred elsewhere in South America under Spanish Catholic rule, and a socially benign intermix took place. Today, 95 percent of the population are of combined Indian and Spanish descent.

Fully independent since 1813, Paraguay is best known in modern times for the severe regime imposed by General Stroessner between 1954 and

1989. Assuming power after a period of chronic upheaval—six presidents in six years and revolts that had left thousands dead—he brought economic and political stability, and greatly improved the national infrastructure. This was at the price of considerable repression, and the huge hydroelectric projects that were built on the Paraná River incurred sizeable foreign debts.

Across the plains, south of Asunción, the Paraná becomes a highway to the sea. Paraguay has some 3,100 km (1,900 miles) of navigable waterways, the most important being the Paraguay River which bisects the country north to south. To the west of Paraguay are the marshy, insect-infested plains of the Gran Chaco, but as the land rises toward the Bolivian border the Chaco changes to semidesert scrub. East of the river the land rises to a plateau forested with tropical hardwoods.

The economy of Paraguay has long been based on agriculture, and large numbers of people still live by means of subsistence farming. Cattle raising and the production of meat products remain the leading agricultural activity but cash crops such as cotton, soybeans, and timber are of increasing importance as a source of export income. Moreover, Paraguay's excess electricity capacity enables it to export power to Brazil.

The informal sector of the economy is also important. Small enterprises and street vendors flourish by importing and re-exporting consumer goods such as electronic devices, alcoholic beverages, and perfumes. While tourism is poorly developed, day-trippers pour in from Brazil and Argentina to buy these goods.

Peru

Humans have been living in Peru for about 10,000 years, and by 3,000 years ago Peruvian civilization had emerged, featuring irrigation agriculture, fine pottery, and expertly woven textiles of striking design. The Incas, one of the many tribes that inhabited the highlands of Peru, established a great empire in the thirteenth century that extended from Ecuador south to central Chile. Accomplished engineers, the Incas built an extensive network of roads and bridges, and many fine cities. The most famous of these is Machu Picchu, high above the Urubamba Valley. The Spanish came to Peru in 1532, lured by stories of a "kingdom of gold" and rapidly destroyed Inca civilization.

Recently Peru has experienced serious political trouble. Deep social divisions gave rise in 1980 to

Indians dancing at a festival in Peru (below left). A rural settlement near Cuzco, Peru (top left). A civic building in Paramaribo, Suriname (above).

the movement known as Sendero Luminoso, or Shining Path, a Maoist guerrilla group. By 1990 its activities had resulted in the loss of 23,000 lives—most of them members of its own constituency, the Indians and mixed Spanish–Indians of the Andes—along with damage to the economy in the order of US$20 billion. In recent years the government has been able to bring about greater stability.

Some 40 percent of Peru's population live on its arid coastal plain, which merges in the south with the rainless Atacama Desert of northern

Fact File

OFFICIAL NAME Republic of Peru

FORM OF GOVERNMENT Republic with single legislative body (Congress)

CAPITAL Lima

AREA 1,285,220 sq km (496,223 sq miles)

TIME ZONE GMT – 5 hours

POPULATION 26,625,121

PROJECTED POPULATION 2005 29,658,649

POPULATION DENSITY 20.7 per sq km (53.7 per sq mile)

LIFE EXPECTANCY 70.4

INFANT MORTALITY (PER 1,000) 41.4

OFFICIAL LANGUAGES Spanish, Quechua

OTHER LANGUAGE Aymara

LITERACY RATE 88.3%

RELIGIONS Roman Catholic 90%; others, including Anglican and Methodist 10%

ETHNIC GROUPS Indigenous 45%, mixed indigenous–European 37%, European 15%; others (mainly African, Japanese, Chinese) 3%

CURRENCY Nuevo sol

ECONOMY Services 53%, agriculture 35%, industry 12%

GNP PER CAPITA US$2,310

CLIMATE Tropical in east, arid along coast, cold on high mountains

HIGHEST POINT Nev. Huascarán 6,768 m (22,204 ft)

MAP REFERENCE Pages 450, 454–56

Chile. Numerous rivers crossing the plain from the Andes have made fertile valleys where cotton, rice, and sugarcane are grown. Inland, in the valleys of two high ranges of the Andean Sierra, the western and the eastern Cordilleras, about 50 percent of the people live, most of them Indians practicing subsistence agriculture. East of the Andes the land falls away into the almost uninhabited region of the Amazon Basin. Here, the Ucayali and Marañón Rivers flow through rainforest to Iquitos, the most inland navigable port on the Amazon River.

Peru's economy depends heavily on copper and petroleum exports. Agriculture is limited by the lack of arable land. Fishing for anchovies and sardines has been historically important in the cool Humboldt current offshore, but periodic warming of the ocean from the El Niño effect reduces the catch, as has occurred several times in recent years. In 1992 it fell by 30 percent.

The ruins of Machu Picchu are an incomparable spectacle for tourists, but poor facilities and guerrilla activities have discouraged visitors. Battered by hyperinflation, which reached 7,480 percent in 1990, Peru has recently undergone a series of economic reforms guided by the IMF and the World Bank. By 1995 inflation had been reduced to 11 percent, while growth in gross domestic product for that year was about 7 percent.

Suriname

Formerly known as Dutch Guiana, Suriname is a small country on the northeastern coast of South America. In 1667 two colonial powers exchanged territory: the Dutch gave the British New Amsterdam, which became New York. In return the British gave Suriname to the Dutch. From the Low Countries the new proprietors brought their dike-building skills to reclaim a narrow coastal strip, and soon sugar plantations took the place of marshes and mangrove swamps. At first African slaves were imported to do the work; later labor was brought from India, China, and Java, and these three immigrant groups have determined both the ethnic composition of the country and its political fate.

Since 1954 Suriname has had the status of an equal partner in the "Tripartite Kingdom of the Netherlands." This has benefited those who have

---

fled the continual military coups and civil disturbance in Suriname, using their Dutch citizenship to enter the Netherlands in large numbers. As was the case in nearby Guyana, escaped African slaves established isolated settlements in the hinterland. Guerrilla uprisings in both 1986 and 1994 have made the descendants of these people an urban political force.

Inland of the cultivated coastal strip lies a zone of sandy savanna, and south of this a vast area of dense forest begins (92 percent of the nation's total land area). Suriname has the world's highest ratio of forested country and it is still virtually untouched as timber is not among the nation's exports. The forests stretch inland to the Guiana Highlands, which are an extension of the Tumucumaque mountain range in northeastern Brazil. Over time, weathered soils have been washed from the uplands down to the alluvial valleys below, providing the foundation of the thriving bauxite industry.

Bauxite accounts for 15 percent of Suriname's gross domestic product and more than 65 percent of export earnings. Other exports include shrimp, fish, rice, bananas, citrus fruits, and coconuts. For most people rice is the staple food, supplemented by tropical fruits and vegetables.

Both ethnic conflict and economic crises have damaged the country's prospects for some years, although the campaign by guerrillas against the urban political elite seems for the present to have faded. Inflation was running at 600 percent in 1994. The resumption of economic aid by the Netherlands has led to a greater confidence in Suriname's economy, but substantial progress is unlikely without major economic reform.

Fact File

OFFICIAL NAME Republic of Suriname

FORM OF GOVERNMENT Republic with single legislative body (National Assembly)

CAPITAL Paramaribo

AREA 163,270 sq km (63,038 sq miles)

TIME ZONE GMT – 3 hours

POPULATION 431,156

PROJECTED POPULATION 2005 445,506

POPULATION DENSITY 2.6 per sq km (6.7 per sq mile)

LIFE EXPECTANCY 70.9

INFANT MORTALITY (PER 1,000) 26.5

OFFICIAL LANGUAGE Dutch

OTHER LANGUAGES English, Sranang Tongo (Surinamese), Hindi, Javanese, Chinese

LITERACY RATE 92.7%

RELIGIONS Hindu 27.4%, Muslim 19.6%, Roman Catholic 22.8%, Protestant 25.2%, indigenous 5%

ETHNIC GROUPS Hindustani (East Indian) 37%, mixed European–African 31%, Javanese 15%, African 10%, Amerindian 3%, Chinese 2%, European 1%, other 1%

CURRENCY Suriname guilder

GNP PER CAPITA US$880

CLIMATE Tropical: hot and wet year-round

HIGHEST POINT Julianatop 1,230 m (4,035 ft)

MAP REFERENCE Page 452

Uruguay

Fact File

OFFICIAL NAME Eastern Republic of Uruguay

FORM OF GOVERNMENT Republic with two legislative bodies (Senate and Chamber of Deputies)

CAPITAL Montevideo

AREA 176,220 sq km (68,038 sq miles)

TIME ZONE GMT – 3 hours

POPULATION 3,308,583

PROJECTED POPULATION 2005 3,458,798

POPULATION DENSITY 18.8 per sq km (48.7 per sq mile)

LIFE EXPECTANCY 75.8

INFANT MORTALITY (PER 1,000) 13.5

OFFICIAL LANGUAGE Spanish

LITERACY RATE 97.1%

RELIGIONS Roman Catholic 66%, Protestant 2%, Jewish 2%, unaffiliated 30%

ETHNIC GROUPS European 88%, mixed indigenous–European 8%, African 4%

CURRENCY Uruguayan peso

ECONOMY Services 67%, industry 18%, agriculture 15%

GNP PER CAPITA US$5,170

CLIMATE Temperate, with warm summers and mild winters

HIGHEST POINT Cerro Catedral 513 m (1,683 ft)

MAP REFERENCE Page 459

Uruguay, the second-smallest country in South America, lies northeast of Argentina on the estuary of the River Plate (Río de la Plata). Controlled for 150 years alternately by the Portuguese and the Spanish, Uruguay finally gained independence in 1828, after which came 40 years of civil war. When peace was secured, waves of immigrants flocked to Uruguay from Spain and Italy, the cattle industry and meat exports expanded, investment poured in, and the country prospered. It may even have prospered too much: many benefits and welfare provisions were introduced in the days of prosperity which in

poorer times have proved difficult to pay for. An urban guerrilla movement known as the Tupamaros paralyzed the cities during the 1960s, provoking a repressive military crackdown and dictatorship. Democracy was restored in 1984.

Most of Uruguay is temperate and mild: it never snows and frosts are rare, though the pampero, a wind coming off the pampas to the south, can be cold and violent. Most of the country is covered with rich grasslands, a continuation of the Argentine pampas, where cattle and sheep are raised. Although 90 percent of Uruguay's land is suitable for cultivation, only some 10 percent is currently used for agriculture, but this is enough to ensure that the country is largely self-sufficient in food. Uruguay's main river is the Negro, flowing east–west across the center of the country. On either side of the Negro the land rises to a plateau that marks the southern limits of the Brazilian Highlands. Water from the uplands feeds down the Negro into a large artificial lake, Lake Rincón del Bonete, which is used for hydroelectric power.

Uruguay's rural economy is based on sheep and cattle raising, and its industries are mainly based on animal products: meat processing, leather, and wool and textile manufacturing. The country is the second largest wool exporter in the world. But Uruguay is not rich in other resources: it has no petroleum or minerals except for agate, amethyst, gold deposits, and small quantities of iron ore. It is entirely dependent on imported oil. The ample supplies of hydroelectricity that are available help to offset this disadvantage, and only governmental regulatory constraints prevent industrial expansion.

Uruguay is at present undergoing a program of modernization, the most prominent issue being the privatization of the extremely large state sector (25 percent of the country's employees are currently civil servants) inherited from its more prosperous past. Tourism is booming, consisting mainly of visitors to Montevideo.

A view of Caracas, the capital of Venezuela (below). The mizzen mast of Great Britain *on the harbor foreshore of Stanley in the Falkland Islands (top right).*

Venezuela

Venezuela is on the north coast of South America. When the first Spaniards arrived in 1499 they named it "New Venice" because the Indian stilt houses built in the water of Lake Maracaibo reminded them of the Italian city. The famous liberator Simon Bolivar was a Venezuelan general, the military campaign he led resulting in the country becoming independent in 1821. For the next century Venezuela's economy was largely based on agriculture, but in the 1920s it took a new direction with the development of a petroleum industry. In the last 80 years great wealth (unevenly shared) followed by industrialization have produced one of Latin America's most urbanized societies. Out of every 20 Venezuelans, 17 are city-dwellers, and migration from the countryside has left much of the interior depopulated.

Confident that oil revenues would never end, the Venezuelan government expanded the economic role of the state, even buying hotels. Falling oil prices in the early 1980s produced a fiscal crisis, and in 1991 a program of cutbacks and austerity measures triggered street riots in

which hundreds died. Two attempted coups took place during 1992. Since that time there has been a concerted effort to achieve economic diversification and to cut back the state sector.

The hot lowlands surrounding Lake Maracaibo in the far northwest comprise one of the areas of greatest population density. In this region abundant electricity from oil-fired generators provides power for light industry: food processing, pharmaceuticals, electrical equipment, and machinery. A spur of the northern Andes divides the Maracaibo Basin from the drainage system of the Orinoco to the east. Here are the lowland plains of the Llanos, savanna country used for cattle grazing. Much of the Llanos floods during the summer rains, especially in the west, though it is dry for the rest of the year. To the south is the vast granite plateau of the Guiana Highlands, and the highest waterfall in the world—Angel Falls (979 m; 3,212 ft).

Despite fluctuations in oil prices, petroleum continues to provide over 70 percent of Venezuela's export earnings and 45 percent of government revenue. Other minerals exported include iron ore, gold, and diamonds. The main cash crops are coffee, sugarcane, and tobacco; food crops include bananas, sorghum, and maize. Only 5 percent of arable land is cultivated, and agriculture supplies little more than 70 percent of the country's needs. During the 1990s, economic reforms proposed by the IMF have been resisted as "economic totalitarianism" by the populist president, who has responded to economic rationalism by defending exchange controls and other regulatory measures.

Fact File

OFFICIAL NAME Republic of Venezuela

FORM OF GOVERNMENT Federal republic with two legislative bodies (Senate and Chamber of Deputies)

CAPITAL Caracas

AREA 912,050 sq km (352,142 sq miles)

TIME ZONE GMT – 4 hours

POPULATION 23,203,466

PROJECTED POPULATION 2005 25,504,115

POPULATION DENSITY 25.4 per sq km (65.8 per sq mile)

LIFE EXPECTANCY 73

INFANT MORTALITY (PER 1,000) 26.5

OFFICIAL LANGUAGE Spanish

OTHER LANGUAGES Indigenous languages

LITERACY RATE 91%

RELIGIONS Roman Catholic 96%, Protestant 2%, other 2%

ETHNIC GROUPS Mixed indigenous–European 67%, European 21%, African 10%, indigenous 2%

CURRENCY Bolívar

ECONOMY Services 63%, industry 25%, agriculture 12%

GNP PER CAPITA US$3,020

CLIMATE Tropical, with dry season December–April; cooler in highlands

HIGHEST POINT Pico Bolívar 5,007 m (16,427 ft)

MAP REFERENCE Pages 450–51

Dependencies in South America

Falkland Islands

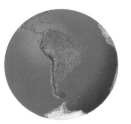

The Falkland Islands are in the South Atlantic. They were named for Lord Falkland, a seventeenth-century British Navy official. Lying 772 km (480 miles) northeast of Cape Horn, they consist of a hilly archipelago where rain falls on average 180 days a year. The area is known for the diversity of the bird life. East Falkland and West Falkland are the two main islands and there are about 200 islets. Most people are employed in sheep farming. Efforts to establish a fishing industry have failed. Sovereignty of the islands is disputed between the United Kingdom and Argentina, which in 1982 invaded, unsuccessfully, in an assertion of its claim. The resulting conflict lasted for 3 months. In 1995 the UK and Argentina launched a joint oil exploration program.

Fact File

OFFICIAL NAME Colony of the Falkland Islands

FORM OF GOVERNMENT Dependent territory of the UK

CAPITAL Stanley

AREA 12,170 sq km (4,699 sq miles)

TIME ZONE GMT – 4 hours

POPULATION 2,607 (1996)

CURRENCY Falkland Islands pound

ECONOMY Agriculture 95%, services and industry 5%

CLIMATE Cold, wet, and windy

MAP REFERENCE Page 460

French Guiana

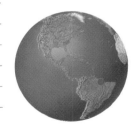

Located along the northeast coast, French Guiana has a narrow coastal plain and a largely unpopulated, forested hinterland. Brazil lies across its southern and eastern borders. After the French Revolution one of the islands became the French penal colony of Devil's Island (Île du Diable). Now French Guiana is the site of the European Space Agency's rocket base. Sugarcane plantations influenced its development; today, cash crops such as bananas and sugarcane grow on the coast, and the main exports are fish and fish products. It depends on France for its economic viability.

Fact File

OFFICIAL NAME Department of Guiana

FORM OF GOVERNMENT Overseas department of France

CAPITAL Cayenne

AREA 91,000 sq km (35,135 sq miles)

TIME ZONE GMT – 3 hours

POPULATION 167,982

LIFE EXPECTANCY 76.6

INFANT MORTALITY (PER 1,000) 12.9

LITERACY RATE 83%

CURRENCY French franc

ECONOMY Services 61%, industry 21%, agriculture 18%

CLIMATE Tropical with two wet seasons (Dec and June)

MAP REFERENCE Page 452

South Georgia and South Sandwich Islands

South Georgia is a barren island in the South Atlantic 1,300 km (800 miles) southeast of the Falklands. Annexed by Captain Cook in 1775, the harbor of Grytviken was long used as a whaling base. Until the 1940s it had a population of up to 800 employed in the whaling industry. Its wildlife is now attracting increasing numbers of ecotourists.

The South Sandwich Islands are six uninhabited volcanic cones to the southeast of South Georgia.

Fact File

OFFICIAL NAME South Georgia and the South Sandwich Islands

FORM OF GOVERNMENT Dependent territory of the UK

CAPITAL None; Grytviken is garrison town

AREA 4,066 sq km (1,570 sq miles)

TIME ZONE GMT – 4 hours

POPULATION No permanent population

ECONOMY Military base and biological station only

CLIMATE Cold, wet, and windy

MAP REFERENCE Pages 461, 476

South America

South America: Physical

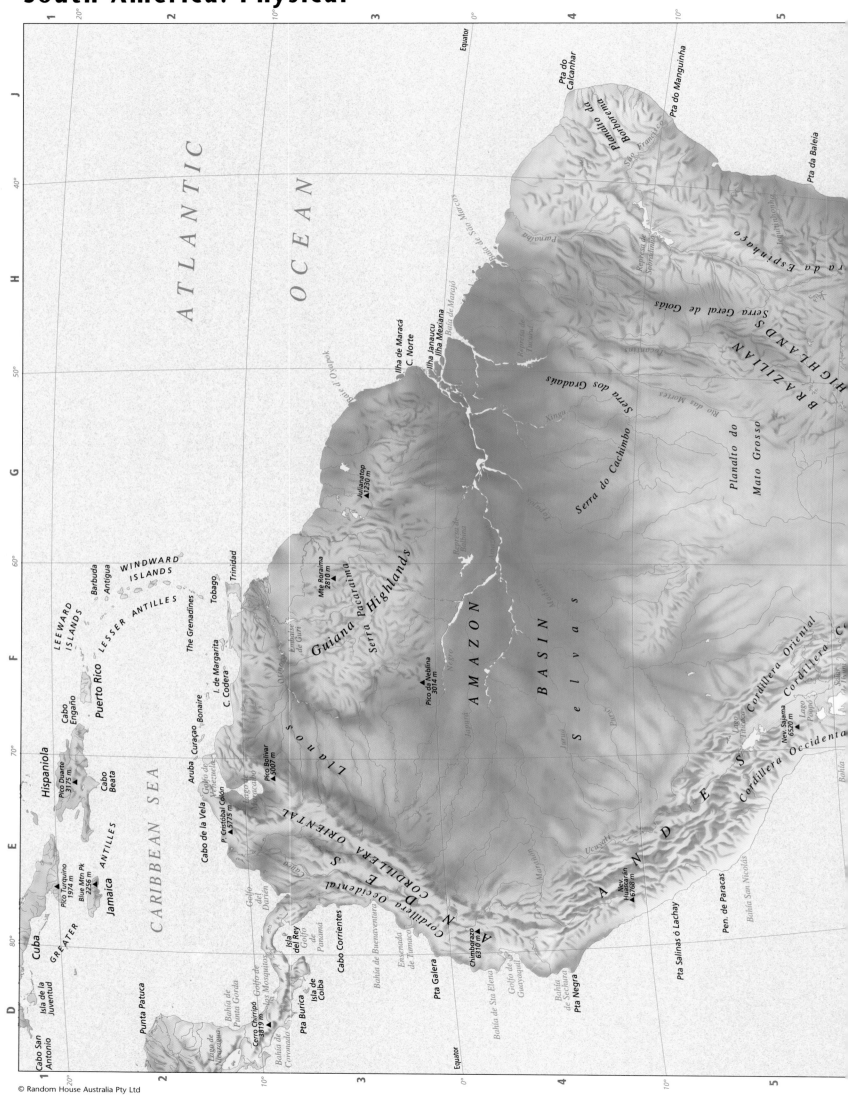

SOUTH AMERICA

ATLANTIC

OCEAN

CARIBBEAN SEA

AMAZON BASIN

Selvas

ANDES

Guiana Highlands

BRAZILIAN HIGHLANDS

Serra Pacaraima

Cordillera Occidental

Cordillera Oriental

Planalto do Mato Grosso

Serra do Cachimbo

Serra dos Gradaús

Serra Geral de Goiás

Planalto do Borborema

WINDWARD ISLANDS

LEEWARD ISLANDS

LESSER ANTILLES

GREATER ANTILLES

Hispaniola

Cuba

Jamaica

Puerto Rico

Barbuda

Antigua

Tobago

Trinidad

The Grenadines

I. de Margarita

Aruba

Curaçao

Bonaire

Pta do Calcanhar

Pta do Manguinha

Pta da Baleia

Pico Duarte 3175 m

Pico Turquino 1974 m

Blue Mtn Pk 2256 m

Cabo San Antonio

Isla de la Juventud

Punta Patuca

Cabo Engaño

Cabo Beata

Cerro Chirripó 3819 m

Pta Burica

Isla de Coiba

Cabo Corrientes

Pta Galera

Isla del Rey

Golfo de Panama

Golfo del Darién

Bahía de Buenaventura

Ensenada de Tumaco

Bahía de Sta Elena

Golfo de Guayaquil

Bahía de Sechura

Pta Negra

Pen. de Paracas

Pta Salinas ó Lachay

Bahía San Nicolás

Golfo de los Mosquitos

Bahía de Punta Gorda

Lago de Nicaragua

Bahía de Coronado

Lago de Maracaibo

Golfo de Venezuela

Cabo de la Vela

C. Codera

Cristóbal Colón 5775 m

Pico Bolívar 5007 m

Llanos

Orinoco

Embalse de Guri

Cauca

Magdalena

Cordillera Occidental

Cordillera Oriental

CORDILLERA OCCIDENTAL

CORDILLERA ORIENTAL

Chimborazo 6310 m

Nev. Huascarán 6768 m

Nev. Sajama 6520 m

Lago Titicaca

Lago Poopó

Mte Roraima 2810 m

Pico da Neblina 3014 m

Julianatop 1230 m

Baie d'Oyapok

Ilha de Maracá

C. Norte

Ilha Janaucu

Ilha Mexiana

Baía de Marajó

Baía de São Marcos

Represa de Sobradinho

São Francisco

Parnaíba

Tocantins

Represa de Tucuruí

Xingu

Rio das Mortes

Tapajós

Madeira

Juruá

Purus

Ucayali

Marañón

Napo

Japurá

Negro

Equator

© Random House Australia Pty Ltd

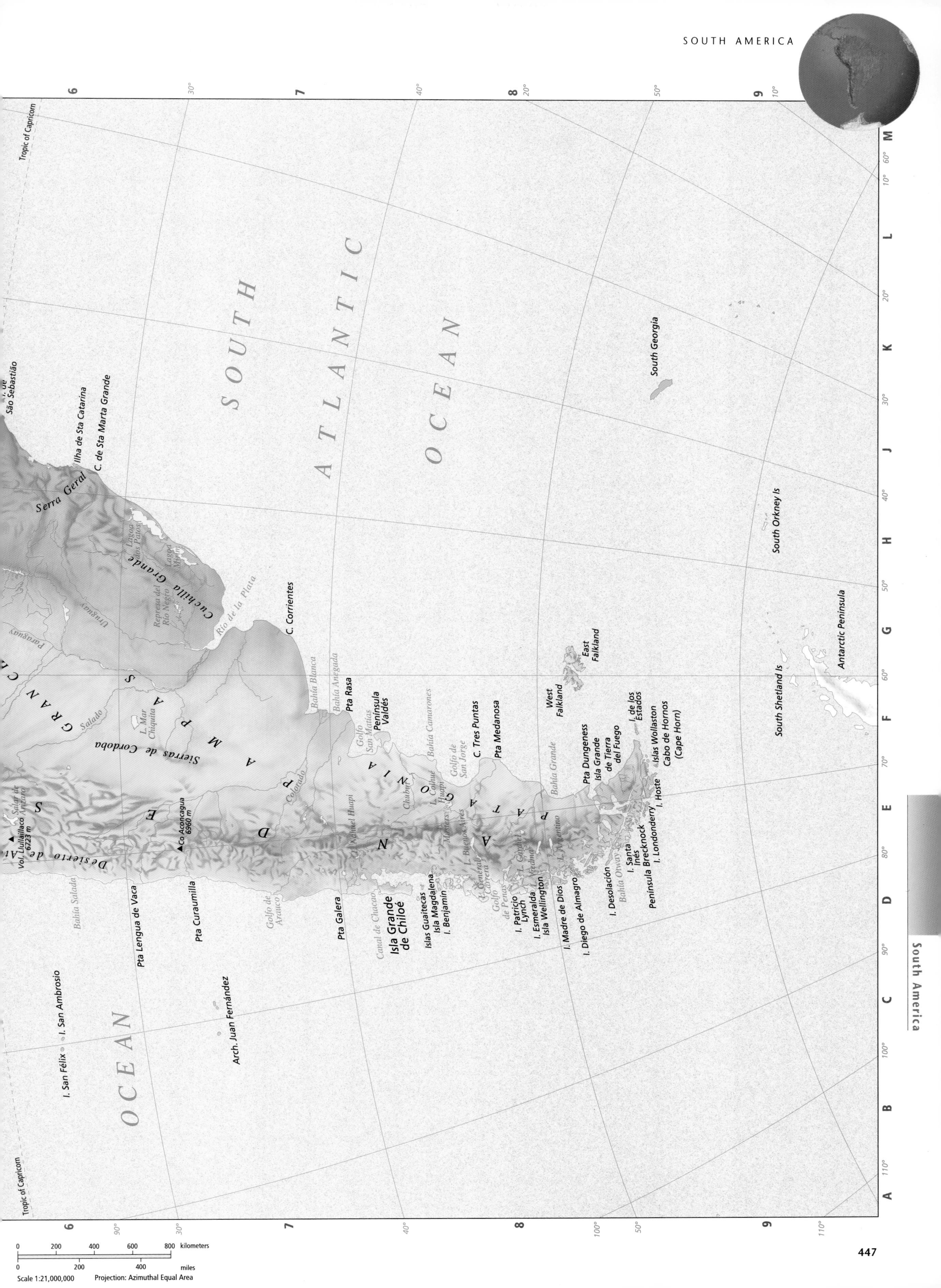

S O U T H

A T L A N T I C

O C E A N

South Georgia

South Orkney Is

South Shetland Is

Antarctic Peninsula

Serra Geral

C. de Sta Marta Grande

Ilha de Sta Catarina

São Sebastião

Lagoa dos Patos

Lagoa Mirim

Cuchilla Grande

Uruguay

Paraguay

Represa del Río Negro

Río de la Plata

C. Corrientes

Bahía Blanca

Bahía Anegada

Pta Rasa

Golfo San Matías

Península Valdés

Bahía Camarones

Golfo de San Jorge

C. Tres Puntas

Pta Medanosa

Golfo San Jorge

I. Cohue Huapi

Chubut

Colorado

Negro

Manuel Huapi

Sierras de Córdoba

L. Mar Chiquita

Salado

G R A N C H

S A L A D O

P A M P A S

D E S E R T O

Vol. Llullaillaco 6723 m

Salar de Atacama

Co Aconcagua 6960 m

Bahía Salada

Pta Lengua de Vaca

Pta Curaumilla

Arch. Juan Fernández

I. San Félix

I. San Ambrosio

Desierto de At...

Golfo de Arauco

Pta Galera

Canal de Chacao

Isla Grande de Chiloé

Islas Guaitecas

Isla Magdalena

I. Benjamín

Golfo de Penas

G. Corcovado

Is. Guardián

L. General Carrera

I. Patricio Lynch

I. Esmeralda

Isla Wellington

I. Madre de Dios

I. Diego de Almagro

I. Desolación

Bahía Onway

Santa Inés

Peninsula Brecknock

I. Londonderry

I. Hoste

Islas Wollaston

Cabo de Hornos (Cape Horn)

I. de los Estados

Isla Grande de Tierra del Fuego

Pta Dungeness

Bahía Grande

West Falkland

East Falkland

L. Argentino

L. Viedma

L. Buenos Aires

P A T A G O N I A

O C E A N

Tropic of Capricorn

Tropic of Capricorn

0   200   400   600   800   kilometers

0   200   400   miles

Scale 1:21,000,000   Projection: Azimuthal Equal Area

447

South America: Political

ATLANTIC OCEAN

CARIBBEAN SEA

Countries and regions:
VENEZUELA, COLOMBIA, ECUADOR, PERU, BOLIVIA, BRAZIL, GUYANA, SURINAME, FRENCH GUIANA (Fr.), TRINIDAD AND TOBAGO

CUBA, CAYMAN ISLANDS (U.K.), JAMAICA, HAITI, DOMINICAN REPUBLIC, PUERTO RICO (U.S.A.), VIRGIN ISLANDS (U.S.A.), VIRGIN ISLANDS (U.K.), ANGUILLA (U.K.), ST KITTS AND NEVIS, ANTIGUA AND BARBUDA, MONTSERRAT (U.K.), GUADELOUPE (Fr.), DOMINICA, MARTINIQUE (Fr.), ST LUCIA, ST VINCENT AND THE GRENADINES, The Grenadines, BARBADOS, GRENADA

NETHERLANDS ANTILLES (Neth.), ARUBA (Neth.)

PANAMA, COSTA RICA, NICARAGUA, HONDURAS

Cities and places:
Natal, João Pessoa, Recife, Caruaru, Garanhuns, Arapiraca, Maceió, Campina Grande, Aracaju, Mossoró, Juazeiro do Norte, Paulo Afonso, Salvador, Alagoinhas, Fortaleza, Ilhéus, Canavieiras, Itabuna, Jequié, Sobral, Caxias, Teresina, Floriano, Picos, Parnaíba, São Luís, Senhor do Bonfim, Feira de Santana, Bacabal, Imperatriz, Tocantinópolis, Carolina, Bom Jesus da Lapa, Vitória da Conquista, São Francisco, Grão Mogol, Teófilo Otoni, Governador Valadares, Bragança, Castanhal, Abaetetuba, Araguaína, Barreiras, São Félix do Xingu, Santa Maria das Barreiras, Anápolis, Brasília, Montes Claros, Patos de Minas, Belo Horizonte, Uberaba, Uberlândia, Belém, Cametá, Pôrto de Moz, Santarém, Altamira, Gurupi, Itaberaí, Goiânia, Araguari, Macapá, Calçoene, Cayenne, St-Laurent du Maroni, Georgetown, New Amsterdam, Paramaribo, Linden, Óbidos, Parintins, Itaituba, Marabá, Ituiutaba, São José do Rio Preto, Cuiabá, Rondonópolis, Jataí, Coxim, Corumbá, Campo Grande, Cáceres, Manaus, Manicoré, Humaitá, Lábrea, Bôca do Acre, Pôrto Velho, Ariquemes, Pimenta Bueno, Rio Branco, Costa Marques, Guajará-Mirim, Guayaramerin, Boa Vista, Normandia, Tefé, Benjamin Constant, Leticia, Cruzeiro do Sul, Eirunepé, Xapuri, Plácido de Castro, Riberalta, Trinidad, Santa Cruz, Montero, Puerto Maldonado, La Paz, Cochabamba, Punata, Sucre, Potosí, Oruro, Huanuni, Camirí, Boca de Puerto, Iquitos, Pucallpa, Cerro de Pasco, La Oroya, Huancayo, Ayacucho, Cuzco, Juliaca, Arequipa, Tacna, Arica, Iquique, Lima, Callao, Ica, Pisco, Nazca, Marcona, Mollendo, Ilo, Sicuani, Cajamarca, Moyobamba, Yurimaguas, Chimbote, Trujillo, Chiclayo, Piura, Sullana, Talara, Bayovar, Guayaquil, Machala, Loja, Cuenca, Riobamba, Ambato, Quito, Ibarra, Tulcán, Pasto, Popayán, Mocoa, Florencia, Cali, Armenia, Ibagué, Bogotá, Villavicencio, San José del Guaviare, Mitú, Puerto Inírida, Puerto Ayacucho, São Gabriel da Cachoeira, Pereira, Manizales, Quibdó, Medellín, Tunja, Yopal, Bucaramanga, Cúcuta, San Cristóbal, Barinas, San Fernando de Apure, Sincelejo, Montería, Valledupar, Santa Marta, Barranquilla, Cartagena, Maracaibo, Cabimas, Coro, Valencia, Caracas, Willemstad, Maturín, Cumaná, Barcelona, Ciudad Bolívar, Ciudad Guayana, Tucupita, La Asunción, Port of Spain, I. de Margarita, Trinidad, Tobago

ATLANTIC OCEAN, Equator

Golfo de Guayaquil, B. de Buenaventura, Isla del Rey, Golfo de Panamá, Isla de Coiba, Gulf of Panama

Baía de Marajó, Ilha de Marajó, Ilha Januari, Ilha Mexiana, Baía de São Marcos, Ilha de Maracá

Map Labels

Grid References (top): 6 · 30° · 7 · 40° · 8 · 20° · 50° · 9 · 10° · 60° · M · L · K · J · H · G · F · E · D · C · B · A

Tropic of Capricorn

I. San Félix · I. San Ambrosio

Arch. Juan Fernández

OCEAN

SOUTH ATLANTIC OCEAN

Janeiro
Santos
Itanhaém
Ponta Grossa
Curitiba
Joinville
Itajaí
Chapecó
Lajes
Passo Fundo
Caxias do Sul
Laguna
Porto Alegre
Rio Grande
Cruz Alta
Santa Maria
Bagé
Pelotas
Obérá
Uruguaiana
Rivera
Salto
Treinta-y-Tres
Concordia
Paraná
Santa Fe
Rosario
San Nicolas
de los Arroyos
Zárate
Junín
Buenos Aires
La Plata
Las Piedras
Montevideo
URUGUAY
Río de la Plata
Mar del Plata

Asunción
San Lorenzo
Formosa
Posadas
Corrientes
Resistencia
Presidencia Roque
Sáenz Peña
Goya
Reconquista
Rafaela
San Francisco
Córdoba
Villa María
Río Cuarto
San Luis
Mercedes
Venado
Tuerto
Olavarría
Tandil
Tres Arroyos
Necochea
Punta Alta
Bahía Blanca
Santa Rosa
Bahía Blanca
Río Colorado
San Antonio Oeste
Carmen De Patagones
Viedma
Golfo San Matías
Sierra Grande
Puerto Madryn
Rawson
Trelew
Golfo de San Jorge
Comodoro Rivadavia
Caleta Olivia
Pico Truncado
Bahía Grande

Salta
Tafí Viejo
San Miguel
de Tucumán
La Banda
Santiago
del Estero
La Rioja
San Fernando del
Valle de Catamarca
Copiapó
La Serena
Coquimbo
Ovalle
San Juan
Mendoza
San Luis
Santiago
San Bernardo
San Rafael
Rancagua
Curicó
Talca
Chillán
Talcahuano
Concepción
Arauco
Los Angeles
Curacautín
Temuco
Zapala
Neuquén
San Martín
De Los Andes
San Carlos
de Bariloche
Esquel
Valdivia
Osorno
Puerto Montt
Castro
Coihaique
Golfo
de Penas
Islas Guaitecas
Isla Magdalena
I. Benjamín
I. Patricio
Lynch
I. Esmeralda
Isla Wellington
I. Madre de Dios
I. Diego de Almagro
I. Desolación
Puerto Natales
Punta Arenas
I. Santa Inés
Río Gallegos
Isla Grande
de Tierra
del Fuego
Río Grande
Ushuaia
I. de los Estados
I. Londonderry
Islas Wollaston

Viña del Mar
Valparaíso

ARGENTINA
CHILE

FALKLAND ISLANDS (U.K.)
West Falkland
East Falkland
Stanley

SOUTH GEORGIA AND SOUTH SANDWICH ISLANDS (U.K.)
South Georgia
South Sandwich Islands

South Orkney Islands (U.K.)

South Shetland Islands (U.K.)

Antarctic Peninsula

Tropic of Capricorn

Grid References (bottom): 6 · 90° · 30° · 7 · 30° · 40° · 8 · 50° · 9 · 110° · 100° · 90° · 80° · 70° · 60° · 50° · 110°

0   200   400   600   800 kilometers

0   200   400 miles

Scale 1:21,000,000   Projection: Azimuthal Equal Area

Colombia • Venezuela • Ecuador • Guyana • Northwest Brazil

A   82°   B   78°   429   C   74°   D

CARIBBEAN SEA

Cabo de la Vela

Santo Domingo • Laguna de Perlas
Juigalpa • Bluefields
Acoyapa

NICARAGUA
Lago de Nicaragua • Punta Gorda
Bahía de Punta Gorda
San Carlos • San Juan del Norte

429

Vol. Miravalles ▲ 2028 m
Altamira • Río Frío • Guápiles
Puerto Jesús • Puerto Limón
Alajuela Heredia • Bribri
San José **Cartago**
COSTA RICA Parrita
B. de Coronado Dominical
Ciudad Cortés • Volcán • Volcán Barú ▲ 3475 m
La Concepción Boquete
Puerto Armuelles • David
Península de Osa Pta Burica
Golfo de Chiriquí Santiago • Soná • Río de Jesús • Atalaya
Isla de Coiba Pedasí
Cordillera Central Antón
Penonomé
PANAMÁ **San Miguelito**
Panamá
Chimán

Golfo de Panamá

Portobelo • El Porvenir *Arch. de San Blás*
Colón • Palenque • Ailigandi
Coclé del Norte
La Chorrera
San Francisco • Aguadulce
Parita • Chitré
Las Tablas
Península de Azuero
Pta Mala
Tonosí
Pta Mariato

San Miguel • La Palma
Isla del Rey El Real
I. San José Garachiné
Jaqué

Puerto Obaldía
Acandí
Riosucio
Palo de las Letras
▲ 3960 m
Dabeiba • Paramillo
Antioquia • Anzá
Yarumal

Cartagena Turbaco • Piviay
Arjona • Calamar
Sincé • Sincelejo
Lorica • Cereté
Sahagún
Montería Puerto Rey
Ciénaga de Oro • Caucasia
Tierralta • Planeta Rica
Cáceres • Zaragoza
Turbo
Chigorodó

Golfo de Morrosquillo
Tolú
El Carmen de Bolívar
Plato
Mompós
Magangué
Sucre
El Banco
Tamalameque
La Gloria

Santa Marta
Barranquilla
Puerto Colombia • Baranoa
Sabanalarga **Soledad**
P. Cristóbal Colón ▲ 5775 m
Ciénaga Barrancas
Valledupar
Fundación
El Difícil
Chiriguaná • La Jagua de Ibirico
Casigua
Ocaña • La Fría
Simití • Sardinata
Cáchira • Pedraza
Encontrados

Cabo de la Vela
Carrizal
Ríohacha Maicao
Carraipía • Uribia
Barrancas
Maracaibo
Valledupar
Villanueva • Campo
Machiques • Cabi

Sierra de Perijá

Golfo del Darién

Golfo de Urabá

Serr. de Abibe

Cauca

Serr. de San Jerónimo

Cúcuta
Pamplona
Chinácota
San An
Bucaramanga
Cubará
Barrancabermeja Zapatoca
Floridablanca
Amalfi • Segovia • San Gil
Puerto Berrío
Socorro • El Cocuy
Sierra Nevada del Cocuy ▲ 5493 m
Belén • Paz de Río

Bello **Medellín**
Itagüí **Envigado**
Cocorná
Santa Bárbara • Sonsón
Quibdó Bolívar
Andes • Aguadas
Salamina
Manizales Líbano
Pereira Armero
Nev. del Ruiz ▲ 5399 m
Cartago **Armenia**
Sevilla
Ibagué
Tuluá Saldaña
Buga • Chaparral

Nuquí
Cabo Corrientes
El Valle
Istmina
Bajo Baudó
Pta Charambirá

Buenaventura
B. de Buenaventura
Yumbo
Cali • **Palmira**
Naya • Puerto Tejada
Pta Coco ▲ 5750 m
Nev. de Huila **Neiva**
Santander
Popayán
Co Munchique ▲ 3012 m
Volcán Puracé ▲ 4646 m
Mosquera • Guapí
La Plata • Gigante
Garzón

Chiquinquirá • Ubate
Duitama **Sogamoso**
Chocontá **Tunja** Pore
Zipaquirá • Yopal
Facatativá ▲ 4560 m • Maní
Soacha **Bogotá**
Fusagasugá **Villavicencio**
Agua de Dios • Puerto López
Cerro Nevado
San Martín
Granada • Pavón
COLOMBIA
Campoalegre
Chafurray
Colombia • Baraya
Aipe
San Vicente del Caguán
Altamira
Pitalito
Florencia
Calamar

Puerto La Concordia
San José del Guav
Guayabero

Tres Esquinas
Mesa de Iguaje
Macayari
Cerro Cumare 720 m
Macujer

B PACIFIC
3
OCEAN

Ensenada de Tumaco
Tumaco Barbacoas
Sotomayor
La Unión
La Cruz
Pasto
Mocoa

Patía
Cordillera Occidental
Cordillera Central
Serr. de la Macarena

San Lorenzo
El Divisó
Valdez
Esmeraldas
Punta Galera • Muisné
Cabo de San Francisco
Rosa Zárate
Otavalo
Ibarra
Cayambe *Volcán Cayambe* ▲ 5790 m
Santo Domingo de los Colorados
Quito ▲ 5704 m
Machachi *Vol. Antisana*
Vol. Cotopaxi ▲ 5897 m
Baeza
Equator
Bahía de Caráquez
B. de Caráquez Chone
B. de Manta Rocafuerte **Quevedo**
Manta Montecristi
Portoviejo • Santa Ana
Latacunga
Tena
Jipijapa • Balzar
Zapotal *Chimborazo* ▲ 6310 m
Ambato Puyo
Guaranda **Riobamba**
Pajón • Babahoyo
Vol. Sangay ▲ 5230 m
Santa Lucía
B. de Sta Elena
Salinas **Guayaquil** **Durán**
Santa Elena
Playas • Naranjal
Alausí • Macas

Sandoná
Túquerres
Tulcán
Ipiales
San Gabriel
ECUADOR
Villano
Montalvo

Puerto Asís
Hacha
La Tagua
Puerto Leguízamo
Santa Rita
Macayari
La Chorrera
Co Maine Hanari 860 m
Araracuara

Lago Agrio
Cuyabeno
Puerto Francisco de Orellana
Pantoja
Santa María
Arica
Pamar
El Encanto
Arica

Napo
Curaray
Río Tigre
Ayuy
Santa María de Nanay

Puerto Tunigrama
Andoas
Morona
Santa Clotilde
Puca Urco
Pebas

Cuenca Cañar
Azogues
Gualaceo
Girón
Golfo de Guayaquil
Isla Puná
Machala
Zaruma
Santa Rosa
Tumbes • Piñas
Zorritos
Canoas • Saraguro
Mánca • Zamora
Catacocha
Loja
Sullana Las Lomas
Tambo Grande
La Huaca **Piura** Chulucanas
Paita
Catacaos • Castilla
Lobitos • Suyo
Talara
Pta Pariñas Macará • Cariamanga
Negritos

Intuto
Mazán
Francisco de Orellana
Iquitos
Omaguas
Tamshiyaco
Nauta

PERU

Zamora
Cord. del Cóndor
Gualaquiza
Borja
Orellana
San Ignacio

Concordia
Barranca
Cahuapanas
Lagunas
Requena
Palmeiras do Javari
Brasil

Marañón
Amazonas
Río Javari

© Random House Australia Pty Ltd

A   82°   B   78°   C   454   74°   D

South America

BARBADOS

70° E 66° 427 F 62° G

ARUBA (Neth.) NETHERLANDS ANTILLES (Neth.)

Oranjestad
Román
Pen. de Paraguaná
Pueblo Nuevo Willemstad Kralendijk
aques
to Fijo
bajuro Curaçao Bonaire
LESSER ANTILLES
La Orchila
La Blanquilla
The Grenadines
Grenville
St George's GRENADA

Puerto Cumarebo
Coro Píritu
Pedregal Jacura
Baragua Churuguara
San Juan de los Cayos
La Tortuga
Isla de Margarita
La Asunción
Porlamar
Tobago Charlotteville
Scarborough

Serro El Cerron 1990 m
San Felipe Puerto Cabello Catia La Mar Caracas
C. Codera
Higuerote
Pen. de Paria
Carúpano Río Caribe Güiria
Galera Pt
Arima Sangre Grande
TRINIDAD AND TOBAGO

arora
Valencia Maracay Petare Baruta
La Victoria Los Teques
Puerto la Cruz
Cumaná
Caripe Caripito
Port of Spain
San Fernando
Trinidad
Rio Claro Galeota Pt

Barquisimeto Yaritagua
El Tocuyo San Carlos Tinaco
Acarigua El Pao
San Juan de los Morros Ortiz
Barcelona
Aragua de Barcelona
Anaco Cantaura
Maturín
Golfo de Paria
Boca de la Serpiente

Trujillo Boconó
Guanare Nueva Florida
El Sombrero Calabozo
San Antonio de Tamanaco Zaraza
El Chaparro El Tigre
San José de Guanipa
Tucupita
Boca Grande

Barinas Obispos
Guanarito
Las Mercedes El Baúl
Chaguaramas
Valle de la Pascua
Santa María de Ipire
Pariaguán
Barrancas
Boca Araguao

Puerto de Nutrias
San Mauricio
El Toro
San José de Amacuro

Camaguán Puerto Miranda
San Fernando de Apure
Boca del Pao
Soledad
Ciudad Guayana
Puerto Ordaz Upata
El Palmar
La Horqueta
Waini Pt
Morawhanna
Mabaruma

Palmarito Mantecal
Achaguas
Parmana Cabruta
Mapire
Ciudad Bolívar
El Pao
El Miamo
Port Kaituma
Baramanni

alito
Elorza
Caicara de Orinoco
Ciudad Piar
Guasipati
Matthews Ridge

La Urbana
Las Lajitas Las Trincheras
Co Turagua 1839 m
La Paragua
San Pedro de las Bocas
El Callao
Tumeremo
Marlborough
Charity Anna Regina

Cravo Norte
1320 m
Mariposa
El Dorado
Suddie
Spring Garden

Parguaza
VENEZUELA
Puerto Páez Puerto Carreño
Sa de Parguaza
La Paragua
Georgetown
Parika Enmore
Mahaicony

Puerto Nuevo
Casuarito
Puerto Ayacucho
Sierra Guanay
Co Yavi 2285 m
San Juan
Co Guaiquinima 2100 m
Auyantepui 2585 m
Luepa
La Gran Sabana
Pakaraima
Tumureng
Peter's Mine
Keweigek
Kangaruma
Tumatumari
Mahdia
Linden Mara
New Amsterdam
Corriverton Paradise
Nieuw Nickerie

Samariapo
Arabelo
Rejunya
Equeipa
Uacauyén
Mte Roraima 2810 m
Arabopó
GUYANA
Issano
Malali
Kwakwani Epira
Oltuni Orealla
Apoera

José de Ocuné
Mituas Arrecifal
Puerto Inírida
San Antonio
Co Marahuaca 2579 m
Co Duida 2404 m
La Esmeralda
Maihiá
Santa Elena de Uairén
Orinduik
Tepequém
Normandia
Maipuri Landing
Annai Apoteri
Yupukarri
Kabalebo stuwmeer
Lacie

Vichada
Sucuaro
San Fernando de Atabapo
Uaicás
Sa Tepequém
Lethem
Dadanawa
Aishalton

Co Guasacaví 668 m
Co Canapiare 692 m
Tomo
Capibara
Boca Mavaca
Orinoco
Serra do Mucajaí
Kahuku Mts
Isherton
CLAIMED BY SURINAME

San Carlos
Serra de Unturán
Serra Curupira
Caracaraí
Biloku
Kamoa Mts
Serra Acaraí

lutica
Cucuí
Pico Tamacuari 2340 m
RORAIMA
734 m
Serra Iricoumé
502 m
452

Iauareté
Içana
Taraquá
Pico Padauari 2755 m
Pico da Neblina 3014 m
Uberlândia
PARÁ

São Gabriel da Cachoeira
São José
Tapurucuara
Catrimani
Equator

Tonantins Jutaí
Fonte Boa
Uarini
Ilha Grande
Boiaçu
Faro
Nhamundá

BRAZIL

Santa Clara Tarapacá
Santo Antônio do Içá
Alvarães Tefé
AMAZONAS
Barcelos
Carvoeiro Moura
Novo Airão
Santa Maria
Balbina
Urucará
Urucurituba Parintins
Barreirinha

Leticia Tabatinga
Benjamin Constant
São Paulo de Olivença Amaturá
Maraã
Manaus
Manacapuru Anamã
Itacoatiara
Silves
Ariaú
Maués
Sapucaia

La Pedrera
Vila Bittencourt
Mamori
Japurá
Juruá
Badajós
Codajás Anori
Careiro
Autazes
Ilha Tupinambarana
Novo Olinda do Norte

Carauari
Jutaí
Coari
Beruri
Axinim Canumã
Borba
Laranjal
Cantagalo
Vila Nova

Itaboca
Arumã
São Pedro
Novo Aripuanã
Lua Nova

E 66° F 455 62° G 58° H

0 100 200 300 400 kilometers
0 100 200 miles
Scale 1:7,000,000
Projection: Azimuthal Equal Area

Northeast Brazil • Suriname • French Guiana

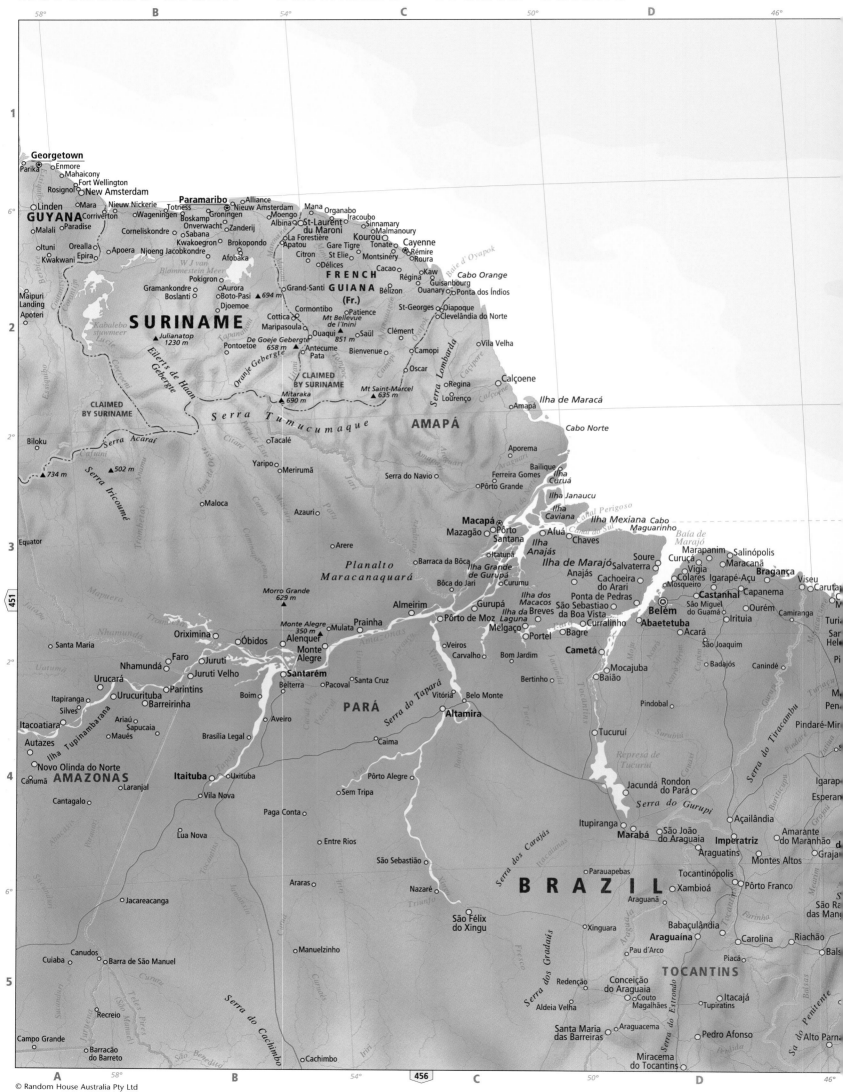

B 58° 54° **C** 50° **D** 46°

1

Georgetown
Parika○ ○Enmore
○Mahaicony
Fort Wellington
○New Amsterdam
Rosignol

6° **Paramaribo** ○Alliance
Linden○ ○Mara Nieuw Nickerie Totness Nieuw Amsterdam Mana Organabo
GUYANA Corriverton Wageningen Groningen Albina Iracoubo
Malali○ ○Sabana Boskamp Onverwacht Zanderij St-Laurent Sinnamary
Paradise Corneliskondre Kwakoegron Brokopondo du Maroni Malmanoury
Iltuni○ Orealla○ Apoera Njoeng Jacobkondre Afobaka La Forestière Kourou
Kwakwani Epira○ Pokigron Apatou Gare Tigre Tonate
Citron St Elie Montsinéry Cayenne
Gramankondre Aurora Grand-Santi Cacao Rémire
Boslanti Boto-Pasi ○694 m **FRENCH** Régina Roura
SURIName Djoemoe Cormontibo **GUIANA** Kaw
Cottica Patience **(Fr.)** Bélizon Guisanbourg
Julianatop▲ Maripasoula Mt Bellevue St-Georges Ouanary Ponta dos Índios
1230 m De Goeje Gebergte de l'Inini Oiapoque
Pontoetoe 658 m▲ Ouaqui 851 m▲ Clevelândia do Norte
Antecume Saül Clément
Pata Camopi
CLAIMED Bienvenue Vila Velha
BY SURINAME Oscar
CLAIMED Mitaraka Mt Saint-Marcel Regina
BY SURINAME ▲690 m ▲635 m Loução Calçoene
Biloku○ Serra Tumucumaque **AMAPÁ** Amapá Ilha de Maracá

2° Serra Acaraí Tacalé Cabo Norte
▲734 m ▲502 m Yaripo○ Merirumã Aporema
Serra do Navio Bailique
Ferreira Gomes Ilha
Maloca Pôrto Grande Curuá

3 Equator Azauri Ilha Janaucu
Arere Ilha
Planalto Caviana Cabo
Maracanaquará Barraca da Bôca Ilha Mexiana Maguarinho Baía de
Macapá Ilha Grande Marajó
Morro Grande Mazagão Pôrto de Gurupá Curumu Marapanim Salinópolis
629 m▲ Santana Afuá Chaves Soure Curuçá
Monte Alegre Almeirim Gurupá **Ilha de Marajó** Salvaterra Vigia Maracanã **Bragança**
350 m▲ Mulata Prainha Pôrto de Moz Ilha dos Anajás Colares Igarapé-Açu Viseu
Oriximiná Óbidos Macacos São Sebastião Cachoeira Mosqueiro
Santa Maria Alenquer Melgaço da Boa Vista do Arari **Castanhal** Capanema
Faro Juruti Monte Ilha da Breves Ponta de Pedras **Belém** São Miguel Ourém
Nhamundá Alegre **Santarém** Laguna Curralinho do Guamá Irituia
Urucará Juruti Velho Belterra Pacoval Portel **Abaetetuba** Acará
Itapiranga Urucurituba Parintins Boim Veiros Bagre **Cametá** São Joaquim
Silves Ariaú Santa Cruz Carvalho Bom Jardim Mocajuba Badajós Canindé
Itacoatiara Sapucaia Aveiro Bertinho Baião
Autazes Maués Brasília Legal Caima Pindobal
Ilha Tupinambarana Serra do Tapará Vitória Belo Monte
Novo Olinda do Norte **PARÁ** **Altamira** Tucuruí
AMAZONAS **Itaituba** Uxituba Jacundá Rondon
Canumã Laranjal Vila Nova Pôrto Alegre do Pará
Cantagalo Sem Tripa Itupiranga Açailândia
Paga Conta Represa de
Lua Nova Tucuruí **Marabá** São João Amarante
Entre Rios do Araguaia **Imperatriz** do Maranhão
São Sebastião Araguatins
Araras Parauapebas Montes Altos
Jacareacanga Nazaré **BRAZIL** Tocantinópolis Pôrto Franco
Xambioá
São Félix Araguanã
do Xingu Xinguara Babaçulândia Carolina
Manuelzinho **Araguaína** Riachão
Pau d'Arco
Canudos Piaçá
Cuiabá Barra de São Manuel **TOCANTINS** Itacajá
Recreio Redenção Conceição Tupiratins
do Araguaia Couto
Campo Grande Aldeia Velha Magalhães
Santa Maria Araguacema Pedro Afonso
Barracão das Barreiras
do Barreto Cachimbo Miracema
do Tocantins

A 58° **B** 54° **456** **C** 50° **D** 46°

F 38° G 34° H

1

6°

ATLANTIC

OCEAN

2°

2

Equator 3

2°

Baía de São Marcos
Ilha de São Luís
Baía de São José

São Luís Primeira Cruz
Icatu Barreirinhas
Axixá Tutóia Luís Correia Camocim Acaraú
Urbano Santos Araioses Parnaíba Granja
São Bernardo Buriti dos Lopes Amontada Paracuru
Itapecuru- Brejo Luzilândia Pôrto Coreaú Massapê Itapipoca São Gonçalo do Amarante
Mirim Chapadinha Buriti Tianguá Carlré Sobral Caucaia Fortaleza
Miguel Alves Piracuruca São Benedito Maranguape Aquiraz
Peritoró Barras Piripiri Ipu Santa Canindé Cascavel
Codó União Pedro II Quitéria Baturité
Caxias Campo Maior Ipueiras Tamboril Aracati
RANHÃO Dom Pedro Timon Altos Crateús Boa Quixadá Russas Areia Branca São Bento
Teresina Castelo Viagem Morada do Norte Ponta do
Presidente do Piauí Quixeramobim Nova Mossoró Macau Calcanhar
Dutra Alto Longá CEARÁ Senador Pompeu Açu Parazinho Touros
Parnarama São Miguel Mombaça Solonópole Apodi Cabo de São Roque
Buriti Bravo Novo Parnarama do Tapuio Tauá Jaguaribe Lajes
Colinas Palmeirais Sambito Acopiara Açude RIO GRANDE DO NORTE Natal
São João Amarante Valença Orós Icó
dos Patos do Piauí Iguatu Currais Novos Santa Cruz São José de Mipibu
Floriano Saboeiro Caicó Acari Cuité
Jerumenha Oeiras Picos Sousa Parelhas Canguaretama
Bertolínia Campos Sales Pombal Patos PARAÍBA Guarabira
PIAUÍ Jaicós Boa Esperança Crato Juazeiro do Norte Cajàzeiras Baía de Traição
Flores do Araripina Chapada Milagres Teixeira São João Santa Rita Cabedelo
Eliseu Piauí Simplício Mendes Exu Conceição do Cariri Campina Grande João Pessoa
Martins Canto do Buriti Paulistana Ouricurí Salgueiro Flores Sumé Timbaúba
São João Parnamirim Serra Sertânia Limoeiro Carpina Goiana
Cristino Castro do Piauí Afrânio Cabrobó Talhada Ibimirim Pesqueira Caruaru Paulista
Santa Maria Floresta Arcoverde Belo Jardim Jaboatão Olinda
Petrolina da Boa Vista Belém de São Francisco Santana PERNAMBUCO Gravatá Recife
Juazeiro Curaçá Chorrochó Inajá do Ipanema Escada
Caracol São Raimundo Paulo Afonso Garanhuns Palmares
Nonato Santana Barreiros
do Ipanema União dos Palmares

1

4

6°

5

E 42° F 457 38° G 34° H

0 100 200 300 400 kilometres
0 100 200 miles
Scale 1:7,000,00 Projection: Azimuthal Equal Area

South America

453

Bolivia • Peru • Southwest Brazil • North Paraguay

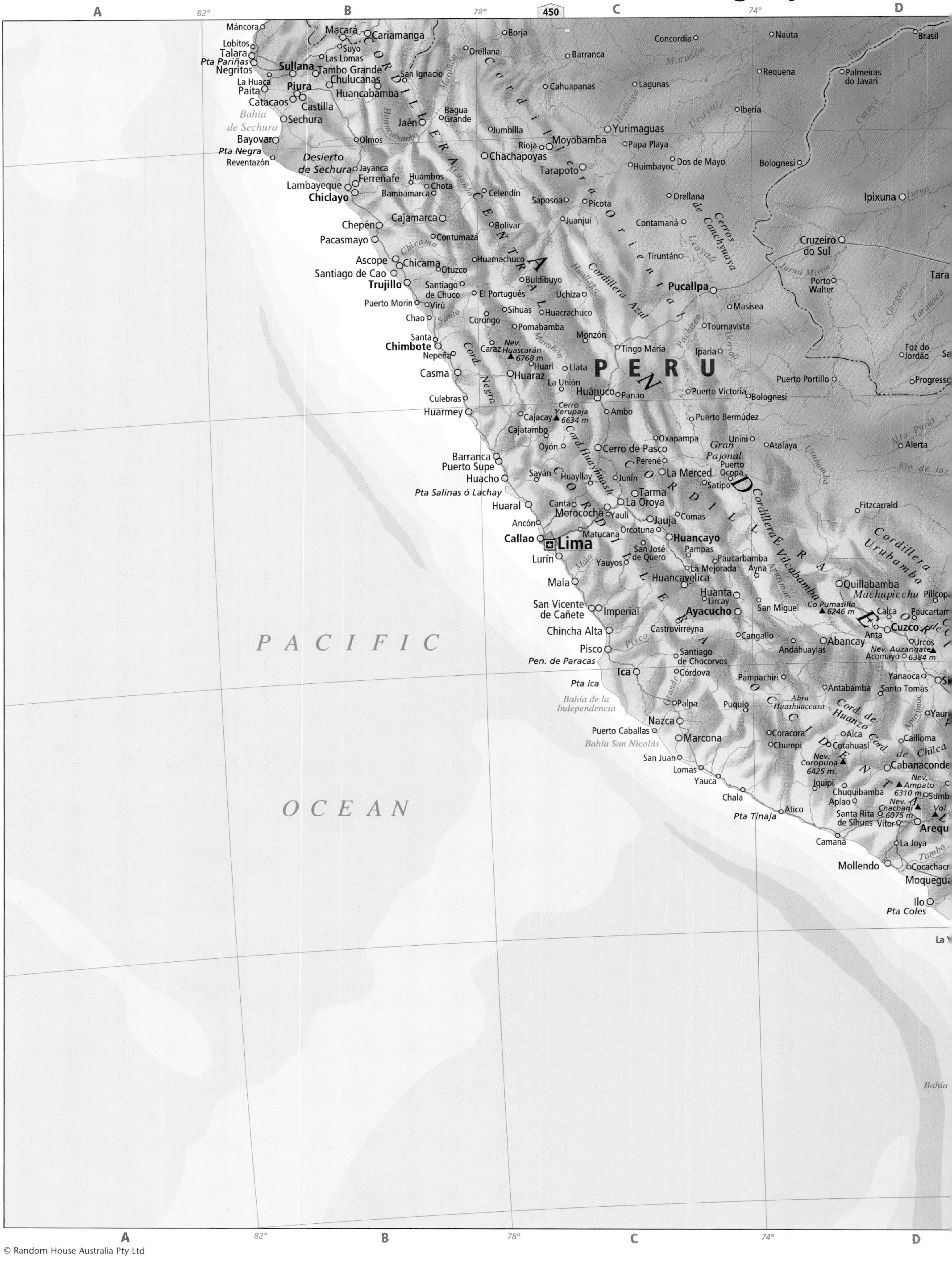

A
B
C
D
450
82°
78°
74°
6°
10°
14°
18°
1
2
3
4
5
Máncora
Lobitos
Talara
Pta Pariñas
Negritos
Sullana
La Huaca
Paita
Piura
Catacaos
Castilla
Sechura
Bahía de Sechura
Bayovar
Pta Negra
Reventazón
Macará
Cariamanga
Suyo
Las Lomas
Tambo Grande
Chulucanas
San Ignacio
Huancabamba
Jaén
Bagua Grande
Olmos
Desierto de Sechura
Jayanca
Lambayeque
Ferreñafe
Chiclayo
Huambos
Chota
Bambamarca
Cajamarca
Chepén
Pacasmayo
Contumazá
Ascope
Chicama
Santiago de Cao
Otuzco
Trujillo
Santiago de Chuco
Puerto Morin
Virú
Chao
Santa
Chimbote
Nepeña
Casma
Culebras
Huarmey
Barranca
Puerto Supe
Huacho
Pta Salinas ó Lachay
Huaral
Ancón
Callao
Lima
Lurín
Mala
San Vicente de Cañete
Imperial
Chincha Alta
Pisco
Pen. de Paracas
Ica
Pta Ica
Bahía de la Independencia
Nazca
Puerto Caballas
Bahía San Nicolás
Marcona
San Juan
Lomas
Yauca
Chala
Pta Tinaja
Atico
Camaná
Mollendo
Cocachacra
Moquegua
La Joya
Ilo
Pta Coles
Borja
Orellana
Barranca
Concordia
Nauta
Brasil
Requena
Palmeiras do Javari
Cahuapanas
Lagunas
Iberia
Yurimaguas
Jumbilla
Rioja
Moyobamba
Papa Playa
Chachapoyas
Tarapoto
Huimbayoc
Dos de Mayo
Bolognesi
Celendín
Saposoa
Picota
Orellana
Ipixuna
Bolívar
Juanjuí
Contamaná
Cruzeiro do Sul
Huamachuco
Tiruntán
Buldibuyo
Pucallpa
Porto Walter
Tara
El Portugués
Uchiza
Masisea
Sihuas
Huacrachuco
Corongo
Pomabamba
Tournavista
Monzón
Caraz
Nev. Huascarán 6768 m
Huari
Tingo María
Iparia
Foz do Jordão
Huaraz
Llata
PERU
La Unión
Huánuco
Panao
Puerto Victoria
Bolognesi
Puerto Portillo
Progresso
Cajacay
Cerro Yerupaja 6634 m
Ambo
Puerto Bermúdez
Cajatambo
Oxapampa
Unini
Atalaya
Alerta
Oyón
Cerro de Pasco
Gran Pajonal
Perené
Puerto Ocopa
La Merced
Sayán
Huayllay
Junín
Satipo
Tarma
La Oroya
Canta
Morococha
Yauli
Jauja
Comas
Fitzcarrald
Orcotuna
Matucana
Huancayo
San José de Quero
Pampas
Paucarbamba
Yauyos
La Mejorada
Ayna
Huancavelica
Quillabamba
Machupicchu
Pillcop
Huanta
Lircay
Ayacucho
San Miguel
Co Pumasillo 6246 m
Calca
Paucartam
Anta
Cuzco
Castrovirreyna
Cangallo
Abancay
Andahuaylas
Urcos
Nev. Auzangate 6384 m
Acomayo
Santiago de Chocorvos
Córdova
Pampachiri
Yanaoca
Antabamba
Santo Tomás
Palpa
Puquio
Abra Huashuaccasa
Yauri
Coracora
Chumpi
Alca
Cotahuasi
Cailloma
Nev. Coropuna 6425 m
Cabanaconde
Iquipi
Chuquibamba
Aplao
Nev. Ampato 6310 m
Nev. Chachani 6075 m
Vol.
Santa Rita de Sihuas
Vitor
Arequ
La Y
Bahía
CORDILLERA OCCIDENTAL
Cordillera Central
Cordillera Oriental
Cordillera Azul
Cerros de Canchyuaya
Cordillera Vilcabamba
Cordillera Urubamba
Cord. Negra
Cord. Huayhuash
Cord. de Huanzo
Cord. de Chilca
ANDES
CORDILLERA
Marañón
Ucayali
Huallaga
Huancabamba
Chicama
Santa
Mala
Pisco
Grande
Apurímac
Urubamba
Pachitea
Juruá
Juruá Mirim
Javari
Curuçá
Gregório
Tarauacá
Alto Purús
Río de las
Tambo
PACIFIC
OCEAN

E · 66° · F · 451 · 62° · G · 58°

1

Benjamin Constant

Jutaí · Carauari

Itaboca · Arumã · Borba · Laranjal · Cantagalo · Vila Nova

São Pedro

Tauariá · Novo Aripuanã · Lua Nova

São Romão · Tapauá · Manicoré

AMAZONAS · Constância dos Baetas · Canumã

Eirunepé · Canutama · Caranapatuba · PARÁ

Gaviãozinho · Mutum · Jacareacanga

6°

Bôca do Moaco · Mamoriá · Lábrea · Humaitá · Cuiaba · Canudos

Pauini · São Bento · Calama · Castanho · Barra de São Manuel

Guajarraã · **BRAZIL**

Vera Cruz · Recreio

2

Manuel Urbano · Bom Jardim · Campo Grande · Barracão do Barreto

Pôrto Alegre · Bôca do Acre · Pôrto Velho · Aripuanã

ACRE · Floriano Peixoto · Jaciparaná · Caritianas

Sena Madureira · Pôrto Acre · Bom Comércio · Manoa · Abunã · São Sebastião · Alta Floresta

Agostinho · Rio Branco · Nuevo Mundo · Ariquemes · Nova Vida · Porto dos Gaúchos

Canamari · Plácido de Castro · Cachuela Esperanza · Jaru · Serra do Norte

Xapuri · Palmares · Humaitá · Guayaramerín · Guajará-Mirim · Antuerpia · Presidente Médici · José Bonifácio

Brasiléia · Cobija · Riberalta · Serra dos Pacaás Novos · **RONDÔNIA** · Pimenta Bueno

10°

San Miguelito · Puerto Rico · Concepción · Cautário · Vilhena · **MATO GROSSO**

PANDO · Sena · Tres Mapajos · Santa Rosa · Costa Marques · Nambiquara · Utiariti

Lucerna · Asunción · El Perú · Mayo Mayo · El Mojar · Pedras Negras · Colorado do Oeste · Ponte de Pedra

Chive · Fortaleza Bolívar · Cavinas · Puerto Siles · Mategua · Santa Isabel

Astillero · Guarayos · Exaltación · San Ramón · Magdalena · Puerto Villazón · Piso Firme · Parecis

Puerto Maldonado · José Agustín Palacios · Baures · Puerto Alegre

Santo Domingo · Anchopaya · **BENI** · Lago de San Luis · El Carmen · Puerto Alegre

Limbani · Sandia · Reyes · Santa Rosa · Holanda · Puerto Saucedo · Nortelândia · Diamantino

Palomani 5999 m · Rurrenabaque · San Borja · Perseverancia · La Esperanza · Puerto Frey · Mato Grosso · Nobres

14°

Apolo · Chevejécure · San Javier · El Pensamiento · Barra do Bugres · Rosário Oeste · Arruda

Anánea · Trinidad · San Antonio · Puerto Frey · Rio Branco · Araputanga

LA PAZ · Chuma · Mapiri · San Ignacio · San Andrés · La Unión · Chapada dos Guimarães

Nev. Illampu · Tipuani · Santa Ana · San Lorenzo · Loreto · Pontes-e-Lacerda · Pôrto Esperidião · Várzea Grande · Cuiabá

Achacachi 6400 m · Coroico · San Miguel de Huachi · Puerto Márquez · Limoquije · Los Cusis · Nossa Senhora do Livramento

Huarina · Irupana · San Pablo · Ascención · La Unión · Poconé · Santo Antônio do Leverger

BOLIVIA · Concepción · Santa Rosa de la Roca · Cáceres · Pirizal

La Paz · El Puente · San Ignacio · Cambará · Barão de Melgaço

Viacha · Todos Santos · Puerto Mamoré · La Estrella · San Ramón · Las Petas · Joselândia

Nev. Illimani 6460 m · Inquisivi · San Pedro · San Miguel · San Matías · Rio Alegre

Berenguela · Luribay · **COCHABAMBA** · Puerto Grether · San Rafael · Pôrto Jofre

18°

Corocoro · Colquiri · Quillacollo · Cochabamba · San Carlos · Pozo del Tigre · El Cerro · San José de Chiquitos

Calacoto · Cliza · Punata · Warnes · Santa Cruz · Roboré · Santo Corazón · Amolar · Promissão

General Lagos · Tomás Barrón · Caracollo · Capinota · Totora · Comarapa · Terevinto · Pampa Grande · **SANTA CRUZ** · Puerto Isabel · Paiaguás

Sajama · Oruro · Tacopaya · Villa Viscarra · Mizque · Pojo · Samaipata · San José de Chiquitos · Puerto Suárez · Nhecolândia

6520 m · Nev. Sajama · Machacamarca · Aiquile · Vallegrande · Florida · Fortín Suárez Arana · Tucavaca · Corumbá

Vol. Guallatiri 6060 m · Huanuni · Uncia · Quiroga · Cabezas · Pantanal do Rio Negro

Cosapa · Corque · Andamarca · Colquechaca · Huari · Masavi · Fortín Ravelo · Fortín Paredes

Camiña · Sabaya · **ORURO** · Challapata · Ravelo · Sucre · Tarabuco · Lagunillas · Mayor Pablo Lagerenza · Puerto Suárez · Bodoquena

Vol. Isluga 5530 m · Huachacalla · Sacaca · Sopachuy · Padilla · Charagua · Fortín Galpón · Miranda

ARARACA · Salar de Surire · Garci Mendoza · Betanzos · Villar · Copere · Monteagudo · Bahía Negra · Forte Coimbra · **MATO GROSSO DO SUL**

Buena Huara · Llica · Salar de Coipasa · Rio Mulatos · Chaqui · Azurduy · Vilacaya · Camiri · Aquidauana · Bonito

Mamiña · Co Caltama 5010 m · Yura · Villamontes · Fortín Teniente General Mendoza · Fortín Coronel Bogado · Puerto Mihanovich

Pozo Almonte · Chita · Salar de Uyuni · Vitichi · San Lucas · Boyuibe · General Eugenio A. Garay · Fortín Madrejón · Nioaque

Pica · Pintados · Pulacayo · Cotagaita · Camiri · Macdareti · Carandayti · Fortín Carlos Antonio López · Puerto Guarani · Jardim

Lagunas · Villa Martín · Atocha · Julaca · Ingre · **CHUQUISACA** · Fortín Infante Rivarola · Pôrto Murtinho · Maracaju

Collaguasi · Chiguana · San Cristóbal · Villa Abecia · Pilaya · **PARAGUAY** · Fortín Coronel Bogado · Fortín Hernandarias

HILE · Vol. Ollagüe 5869 m · Tupiza · Entre Rios · Villamontes · Sanandita · Puesto Estrella · Fortín Carlos Antonio López · Pôrto Murtinho

FAGASTA · Salar de Ascotán · San Pablo · Mojo · **TARIJA** · Fortín Infante Rivarola · Puerto Sastre

Vol. San Pedro 6154 m · Lequena · Co Bonete 5660 m · Villazón · Padcaya · Yacuba · Santa Maria · Mariscal Estigarribia

Toco · Conchi · Turi · Tarija · La Quiaca · Pocitos · La Esmeralda

Chuquicamata · Calama · Loa

5

E · 66° · F · 458 · 62° · G · 58° · H

0 · 100 · 200 · 300 · 400 kilometers

0 · 100 · 200 miles

Scale 1:7,000,000

Projection: Azimuthal Equal Area

South America

Southeast Brazil

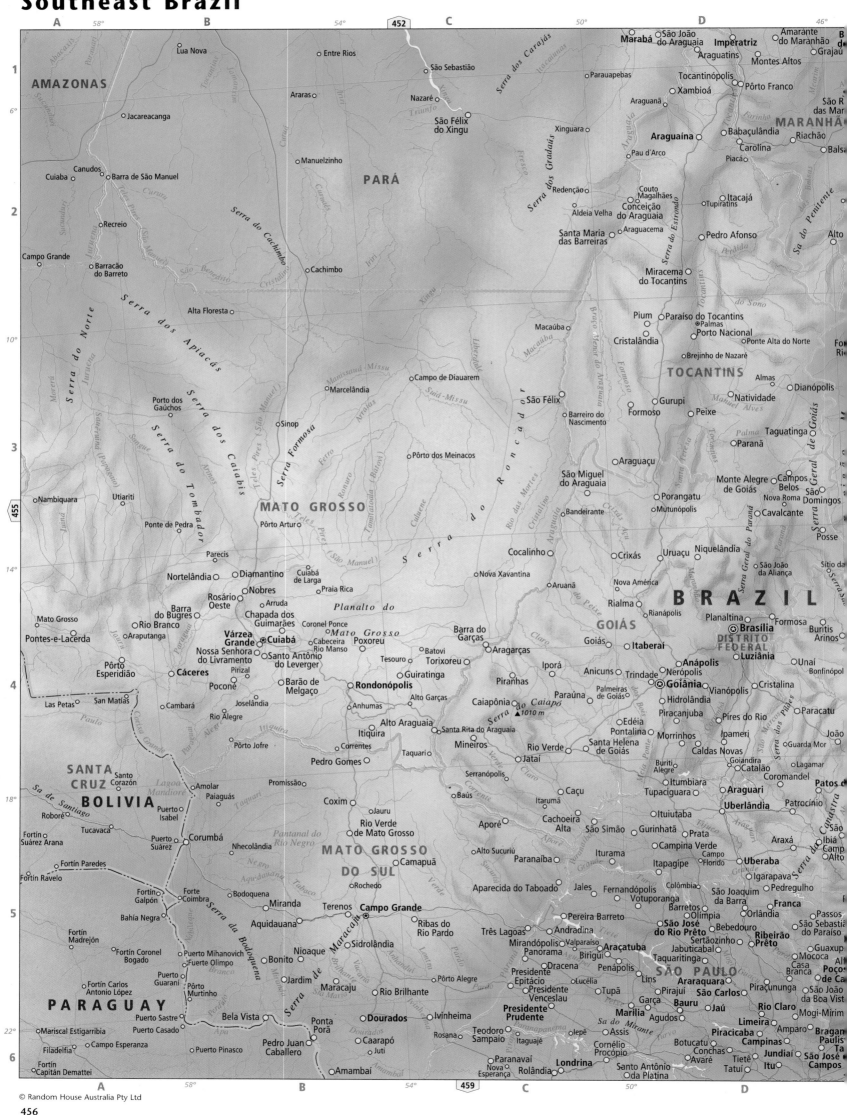

E 42° F 453 38° G 34° H

RIO GRANDE DO NORTE
Parnarama
Buriti Bravo
Novo Parnarama
Palmeirais
Colinas
São Miguel do Tapuio
Mombaça
Senador Pompeu
Solonópole
Apodi
Açu
Lajes
Cabo de São Roque
Natal
Tauá
Acopiara
Iguatu
Currais Novos
Caicó
Santa Cruz
São José de Mipibu
São João dos Patos
Valença do Piauí
Saboeiro
Icó
Sousa
Cangaretama
Floriano
Amarante
Picos
CEARÁ
Cajàzeiras
Pombal
Patos
Acari
Cuité
Parelhas
Guarabira
Santa Rita
Cabedelo
Jerumenha
Oeiras
Campos Sales
Crato
Juazeiro do Norte
Milagres
Conceição
PARAÍBA
Teixeira
São João do Cariri
Limoeiro
Carpina
João Pessoa
Bertolínia
Jaicós
Araripina
Exu
Sumé
Campina Grande
Timbaúba
Goiana
Paulista
Eliseu Martins
Simplício Mendes
Ouricuri
Salgueiro
Serra Talhada
Flores
Sertânia
Pesqueira
Caruaru
Jaboatão
Olinda
Recife
Cristino Castro
São João do Piauí
Afrânio
Parnamirim
Belo Jardim
Gravatá
Escada
Canto do Buriti
Paulistana
Cabrobó
Floresta
Ibimirim
PERNAMBUCO
Palmares
Barreiros
Caracol
Remanso
Santa Maria da Boa Vista
Belém de São Francisco
Inajá
Arcoverde
Garanhuns
Pilão Arcado
Petrolina
Curaçá
Chorrochó
Palmeira dos Indios
União dos Palmares
Redenção de Gurguéia
Juazeiro
Paulo Afonso
Santana do Ipanema
Atalaia
Rio Largo
Sento Sé
Uauá
Pão de Açúcar
ALAGOAS
Maceió
Raso da Catarina
Arapiraca
São Miguel dos Campos
Buritirama
Jeremoabo
Senhor do Bonfim
Monte Santo
Santana das Dores
Propriá
Coruripe
Xique-Xique
Campo Formoso
Euclides da Cunha
Nossa Senhora
SERGIPE
Simão Dias
Maruim
Laranjeiras
Ponta do Manguinho
Jucara
Irecê
Queimadas
Lagarto
Aracaju
Santo Inácio
Morro do Chapéu
Jacobina
Tucano
Nova Soure
Estância
Copixaba
Itabaianinha
Morpará
Ipupiara
BAHIA
Conceição do Coité
Serrinha
Esplanada
Ibotirama
Oliveira dos Brejinhos
Palmeiras
Lençóis
Mundo Novo
Riachão do Jacuípe
Ipirá
Inhambupe
Irará
Conde
Palame
Sitio do Mato
Ibitiara
Andaraí
Itaberaba
Feira de Santana
Alagoinhas
Bom Jesus da Lapa
Macaúbas
Itaetê
Juracі
Cachoeira
Santo Amaro
Maragogípe
Camaçari
Botuporã
Iramaia
Santo Antônio de Jesus
Nazaré
Salvador
Paramirim
Livramento do Brumado
Chapada de Maracás
Gandu
Valença
Caetité
Guanambi
Brumado
Jequié
Camamu
Palmas de Monte Alto
Aracatu
Anagé
Poções
Ipiaú
Maraú
Carinhanha
Urandi
Condeúba
Iguaí
Ubaitaba
Manga
Espinosa
Monte Azul
Itabuna
Vitória da Conquista
Arataca
Una
Ilhéus
Itapetinga
São João do Paraíso
Encruzilhada
Canavieiras
Rio Pardo de Minas
Porteirinha
Macarani
Belmonte
Januária
Janaúba
Pedra Azul
Jacinto
Salto da Divisa
Itapebi
Brasília de Minas
Barrocão
Francisco Sá
Salinas
Almenara
Jequitinhonha
Santa Cruz Cabrália
Mirabela
Itaobim
Pôrto Seguro
Coração de Jesus
Planalto
Grão Mogol
Itinga
Águas Formosas
Itanhém
Caraíva
Montes Claros
Virgem da Lapa
Caraí
Pavão
Mte Pascoal 536 m
Bocaiúva
do
Minas Novas
Prado
Alcobaça
Jequitaí
Carbonita
Capelinha
Carlos Chagas
Pta da Baleia
rapora
Teófilo Otoni
Nanuque
Caravelas
Diamantina
Brasil
Itamarandiba
Itambacuri
Mucuri
Arquipélago dos Abrolhos
Curvelo
2033 m P. de Itambé
Peçanha
Morro d'Anta
Serro
Guanhães
Nova Venécia
Conceição da Barra
Tarumirim
Governador Valadares
Conselheiro Pena
São Mateus
Lagoas
MINAS GERAIS
Ipatinga
ESPÍRITO SANTO
Linhares
Belo Horizonte
Santa Lagoa
Itabira
Coronel Fabriciano
Colatina
Sabará
Barra do Riacho
Contagem
Nova Lima
Caratinga
Ibiraçu
Aracruz
Itabirito
Ouro Prêto
Manhuaçu
2890 m
Cariacica
Serra
Conselheiro Lafaiete
Carangola
Muniz Freire
Vitória
Oliveira
Viçosa
Vila Velha
Carandaí
Tombos
Alegre
Guarapari
Barbacena
Ubá
Muriaé
Cachoeira do Itapemirim
Andrelândia
Cataguases
Itaperuna
Itapemirim
Santos Dumont
Leopoldina
São Fidélis
Sa. do Caparaó
Juiz de Fora
Além Paraíba
São João da Barra
Campos
Três Rios
RIO DE JANEIRO
Cabo de São Tomé
Lourenço
Nova Friburgo
Ilhas Negras
Volta Redonda
Teresópolis
Macaé
2797 m
Nova Iguaçu
Petrópolis
Barra Mansa
Duque de Caxias
Cabo Frio
Itaguaí
São Gonçalo
Niterói
I. Grande
Rio de Janeiro

PIAUÍ
Uruçuí
Santa Rita de Cássia
Barra
Represa de Sobradinho
Represa da Tabatinga
Desidério
Santana
Santa Maria da Vitória
Côcos
Cotegipe

ATLANTIC

OCEAN

1°
6°
2
10°
3
14°
4
18°
5
22°
6

E 42° F 38° G 34° H 30°

0 100 200 300 400 kilometers
0 100 200 miles
Scale 1:7,000,000
Projection: Azimuthal Equal Area

North Chile • North Argentina • Uruguay • South Paraguay

A 74° B 70° C 455 66° D 62°

BOLIVIA

POTOSÍ

TARIJA

JUJUY

SALTA

TUCUMÁN

CATAMARCA

SANTIAGO DEL ESTERO

LA RIOJA

ARGENTINA

CÓRDOBA

SAN JUAN

SAN LUIS

VALPARAÍSO

SANTIAGO

LIBERTADOR

MAULE

MENDOZA

LA PAMPA

BÍO BÍO

ARAUCANÍA

NEUQUÉN

RÍO NEGRO

COQUIMBO

ATACAMA

ANTOFAGASTA

PACIFIC OCEAN

Tropic of Capricorn

Bahía de Mejillones del Sur

Pta Tetas

Pta dos Reyes

Bahía Salada

Desierto de Atacama

Salar de Ascotán

Salar de Atacama

Salar de Arizaro

Salar de Calalaste

Selected place names:
Chiguana, San Cristóbal, Villamontes, Ollagüe, Vol. Ollagüe 5869 m, Co Bonete 5660 m, Tupiza, Fortín Infante Rivarola, Quillagua, Lequena, San Pablo, Mojo, Villazón, San Lorenzo, Tarija, Entre Ríos, Sanandita, Fortín Hernandarias, Tocopilla, Toco, Conchi, Turi, La Quiaca, Padcaya, Yacuiba, Santa María, La Esmeralda, María Elena, Chuquicamata, Vol. San Pedro 6154 m, Pocitos, Calama, Abra Pampa, San Ramón de la Nueva Orán, Bermejo, Tartagal, Pedro de Valdivia, Michilla, Vol. Licancábur 5930 m, San Pedro de Atacama, Co Zapaleri 5655 m, Humahuaca, Pichanal, Embarcación, Sierra Gorda, Carmen Alto, Toconao, Susques, Tilcara, La Estrella, Los Blancos, Ingeniero Guillermo N. Juárez, Mejillones, Baquedano, Domeyko, Tilomonte, San Salvador de Jujuy, San Pedro, Rivadavia, Antofagasta, La Negra, Augusta Victoria, Co Pular 6225 m, Co del Rincón 5594 m, San Antonio de los Cobres, Perico, General Martín Miguel de Güemes, Varillas, Escondida, Paso Socompa, Vol. Llullaillaco 6723 m, Nev. de Cachi 6720 m, Salta, Rosario de Lerma, Joaquín V. González, Nueva Pompeya, Paposo, Salinitas, Vol. Antofalla 6100 m, Cachi, Guachipas, Metán, Taltal, Altamira, Co Galán 6600 m, Cafayate, Trancas, Quebracho Coto, San José del Boquerón, Pampa de los Guanacos, El Salvador, Antofagasta de la Sierra, Santa María, Tafí Viejo, San Miguel de Tucumán, Las Cejas, Campo Gallo, Chañaral, Diego de Almagro, Inca de Oro, Sa Nevada 6400 m, Bella Vista, Monteros, Pozo Hondo, Patay, Tintina, Caldera, Algarrobo, Vol. Copiapó 6080 m, Ojos del Salado 6880 m, Fiambalá, Belén, Andalgalá, Concepción, Aguilares, Termas de Río Hondo, Otumpa, General Pinedo, Copiapó, Tierra Amarilla, Co Bonete 6872 m, Tinogasta, Copacabana, San Fernando del Valle de Catamarca, La Cocha, Santiago del Estero, La Banda, Fernández, Quimili, Totoral, Castilla, La Guardia, Las Juntas, Jagüé, Aimogasta, Las Cañas, Ciudad de Loreto, Añatuya, Colonia Dora, Carrizal Bajo, Miraflores, Co de Potro 5830 m, Famatina, Villa Mazán, Chumbicha, Frías, San Antonio, Los Telares, Pinto, Bandera, Huasco, Freirina, Vallenar, Mejicana 6250 m, Chilecito, Sa de Velasco, Villa Ojo de Agua, Argentina, Ceres, Sarco, El Tránsito, Domeyko, Co del Toro 6380 m, Famatina 6375 m, La Rioja, San Martín, Recreo, San Francisco del Chañar, Tostado, C. Bascuñán, Villa Unión, Guandacol, Patquía, Chamical, Quilino, Deán Funes, San José de la Dormida, San Cristóbal, Morteros, La Serena, Coquimbo, Rivadavia, Co Las Tórtolas 6332 m, Rodeo, San José de Jáchal, Agustín de Valle Fértil, Malanzán, Cruz del Eje, Capilla del Monte, Jesús María, Río Primero, Sunchales, Rafael, Andacollo, Co de Olivares 6282 m, Tucunuco, Chepes, Desiderio Tello, Chancaní, La Falda, Cosquín, Río Ceballos, Freyre, Ovalle, Punitaqui, Castaño Viejo, Talacasto, Mareyes, Mascasín, Alta Gracia, Salsacate, Córdoba, San Francisco, San Carlos Centro, Combarbalá, Barreal, San Juan, Caucete, Quines, Villa Dolores, Co Champaquí 2880 m, Oncativo, Oliva, Las Varillas, San Jorge, Maitencillo, Huentelauquén, Co Mercedario 6770 m, Pampa de las Salinas, Conlara, Villa María, Dalmacio Vélez Sarsfield, Bell Ville, Marcos Juárez, Huaso, Ollapel, Salamanca, Quilpué, Co Aconcagua 6960 m, Las Heras, Mendoza, Villa Valeria, La Toma, Río Cuarto, Sa del Morro 1727 m, La Laguna, La Ligua, La Calera, San Felipe, Godoy Cruz, Luján, Villa Nueva, San Luis, La Carlota, Viña del Mar, Quillota, Co Juncal 6060 m, Rivadavia, Las Catitas, La Paz, Beazley, Mercedes, Vicuña Mackenna, Arias, Valparaíso, San Antonio, Melipilla, Santiago, San Bernardo, Paine, Co Tupungato 6682 m, Tupungato, Tunuyán, San Carlos, Comandante Salas, Justo Daract, General Levalle, Laboulaye, Rufino, Navidad, Graneros, Vol. San José 5830 m, Vol. Maipú 5290 m, Venado Tuerto, Rengo, Rancagua, San Rafael, Monte Comán, Media Luna, Buena Esperanza, Villa Huidobro, Huinca Renancó, General Villegas, Pichilemu, San Fernando, Co Sosneado 5189 m, El Sosneado, General Alvear, Carmensa, Nueva Galia, Parera, Realicó, Intendente Alvear, Timote, Santa Cruz, Retén Llico, Vol. Tinguiririca 4300 m, Vol. Descabezado Grande 3830 m, Canalejas, Eduardo Castex, Quemú-Quemú, Meridiano, Rivadavia, Nueve De, Licantén, Vol. Peteroa 4090 m, Malargüe, Co Nevada 3810 m, General Pico, Pehuajó, Talca, San Clemente, Bardas Blancas, Victorica, Catriló, Tres Lomas, Dairea, San Javier, Linares, Campanario 4020 m, Santa Isabel, Telén, Salazar, Henderson, Chanco, Cauquenes, Co Payún 3680 m, Algarrobo del Águila, Toay, Santa Rosa, Maza, Salliqueló, Guamini, Quirihue, Parral, San Carlos, Longaví 3242 m, Vol. Domuyo 4709 m, Sa Chachahuén 2065 m, Limay Mahuida, Quehué, Macachín, Rivera, Carhué, Chillán, Tome, Recinto, Vol. Tromen 3980 m, Colorado, General Acha, Epu-pel, Puán, Pigüé, Talcahuano, Concepción, Lota, La Laja, Antuco, Vol. Copahue 2969 m, Loncopué, Sa de Auca Mahuida 2253 m, Catriel, Puelén, Darregueira, Bernasconi, Guatraché, Coronel S., Arauco, La Laja, Mulchén, Chihuido Medio 1494 m, Embalse Cerros Colorados, Gobernador Duval, Bahía Blanca, Los Angeles, Lebu, Cañete, Angol, Collipulli, Puelches, Cuchillo-Có, Sa de la Ventana 1243 m, Villa Iris, Purén, Victoria, Vol. Llaima 3124 m, Chihuido, Plaza Huincul, Cipolletti, Pichi Mahuida, Río Colorado, Médanos, Punta Alta, Puerto Saavedra, Carahue, Temuco, Zapala, Cutral-Có, Neuquén, General Roca, Choele Choel, Coronel D., Bahía Blanca, Major Buratovich, Nueva Imperial, Araucanía

A 74° B 70° C 460 66° D 62°

456

1

58°   F   54°   G   50°   H   1

Fortín Carlos Antonio López
Puerto Guarani
Pôrto Murtinho
Jardim   Maracaju
Rio Brilhante
MATO GROSSO DO SUL
Dourados
Puerto Sastre
Puerto Casado
Bela Vista
Ponta Porã
Caarapó

Mirandópolis   Valparaiso   **Araçatuba**
Panorama   Birigüi   Sertãozinho
Dracena   Jabuticabal
Presidente Epitácio   Penápolis   Taquaritinga
Presidente Venceslau   Tupã   Lins   Piraçununga
Tucélia   **Presidente Prudente**   Pirajuí   Garça   Bauru

São Sebastião do Paraíso
Guaxupé   Alfenas   Varginha
Ribeirão Prêto   **MINAS GERAIS**
Poços de Caldas   Três Corações
Casa Branca   São João da Boa Vista   Pouso Alegre
São Carlos   Mogi-Mirim   Itajubá   Cruzeiro
Araraquara   Limeira   **Amparo**
Rio Claro   **Piracicaba**   **Americana**   **Guaratinguetá**
Botucatu   **Campinas**   **Bragança Paulista**   **Taubaté**
SÃO PAULO   Jundiaí   **São José dos Campos**
Avaré   Tietê   Itu   **Sorocaba**   Santo André
Angatuba   Tatuí   **São Paulo**   Mogi das Cruzes
Itapetininga   Itapeva   **São Bernardo do Campo**
Capão Bonito   **Santos**   **Guarujá**   Caraguatatuba
São Vicente   I. de São Sebastião

PARANA
Umuarama   Goió-Erê   Campo Mourão
Maringá   Cianorte   **Apucarana**   **Londrina**
Paranavaí   Rolândia   Arapongas

Telêmaco Borba   Piraí do Sul
Pitanga   Reserva   Castro   Cêrro Azul
Guarapuava   **Ponta Grossa**
Irati   Palmeira   **Curitiba**
Prudentópolis   Ipiranga   Lapa   **Paranaguá**
Guaraqueçaba   I. do Cardoso
São José dos Pinhais   Guaratuba
Rio Negro   São Francisco do Sul
Mafra   **Joinville**

Asunción   **San Lorenzo**
Formosa   Villa Hayes
Clorinda   Espinillo   Coronel Oviedo
Paraguarí   Quiindy

Toledo   Cascavel
Foz do Iguaçu
Ciudad del Este   Capanema
Mangueirinha   União da Vitória
Clevelândia   Palmas   Canoinhas

2

22°

26°

SANTA CATARINA
Chapecó   Joaçaba   Ibirama   **Blumenau**
Rio Do Sul   Pôrto Belo   **Itajaí**
Curitibanos   Ituporanga   **São José**
Campos Novos   **Florianópolis**
Bom Retiro   Ilha de Sta Catarina

BRAZIL

RIO GRANDE DO SUL
Passo Fundo   Lajes   São Joaquim
Carazinho   Casca   Vacaria
Tapera   Soledade   Bom Jesus
Santa Cruz do Sul   Bento Gonçalves   Pta Imbituba
Lajeado   **Caxias do Sul**   Laguna
Garibaldi   **Criciúma**   C. de Sta Marta Grande
Novo Hamburgo   Araranguá
Montenegro   **São Leopoldo**   Tubarão   Jaguaruna
Canoas   Torres
Porto Alegre   Sao Francisco de Paula
Guaíba   Osório   Palmares do Sul
Barra do Ribeiro

3

30°

URUGUAY
Rivera
Tranqueras
Minas de Corrales   **Bagé**
Tacuarembó
Ansina
Melo
Vergara   **Pelotas**
Treinta-y-Tres   São José do Norte
José Pédro Varela   **Rio Grande**
Lascano   Santa Vitória do Palmar

Lagoa dos Patos
Camaquã   Mostardas
Boqueirão
Canguçu   São Lourenço do Sul
Piratini
Pinheiro Machado
Pedro Osório
Arroio Grande
Jaguarão

4

34°

Montevideo
Maldonado
Rocha   La Paloma
San Carlos

Buenos Aires   Avellaneda
Quilmes   La Plata   Magdalena
Tomás de Zamora

ATLANTIC

OCEAN

5

38°

Mar del Plata
C. Corrientes
Miramar
Necochea
Quequén

6

58°   F   54°   G   50°   H   46°   J

0   100   200   300   400   kilometers
0   100   200   miles
Projection: Azimuthal Equal Area

459

South Chile • South Argentina

458

B 74° **C** 70° **D** 66° **E** 62° **F**

ARAUCANIA
NEUQUÉN
RÍO NEGRO
BUENOS AIRES

Nueva Imperial · Curacautín · Vol. Llaima 3124 m · Las Lajas · Plaza Huincul · Cipolletti · Gobernador Duval · Bahía Blanca · Médanos · Coronel Dorrego · Tres Arroyos
Carahue · Temuco · Cutral-Có · Neuquén · General Roca · Pichi Mahuida · Río Colorado · Punta Alta · Oriente · Energía · Claromecó
Puerto Saavedra · Pitrufquén · Pucón · Zapala · Villa Regina · Chelforó · Lamarque · Choele Choel · Major Buratovich · Orense
Villarrica · Vol. Villarrica 2840 m · Picún Leufú · Colonia Josefa · Bahía Blanca · Península Verde
Queule · Lanco · Vol. Lanín 3776 m · Catan Lil · Junín de los Andes · La Esperanza · Santa Rosa · General Conesa · Villalonga · Bahía Unión
San José de la Mariquina · Panguipulli · RÍO NEGRO · Sierra Colorada · Cinco Chañares · San Antonio Oeste · Stroeder · Bahía Anegada
Valdivia · Riñihue · San Martín De los Andes · Co Azul 2480 m · Los Menucos · Valcheta · Aguada Cecilio · Viedma · Carmen De Patagones · Pta Rasa
Pta Galera · Paillaco · Lago Ranco · La Esperanza · Maquinchao · El Caín · Sierra Grande · La Loberia · Pta Bermeja
La Unión · Río Bueno · Ingeniero Jacobacci · Cona Niyeu · Golfo San Matías · Punta Pórfido
Osorno · Puyehue · Pilcaniyeu · Gastre · Gan Gan · Telsen · Puerto Lobos · Pta Norte · Punta Norte · Península Valdés
LOS LAGOS · Vol. Osorno 2652 m · Co Tronador 3554 m · San Carlos de Bariloche · Norquinco · **ARGENTINA** · Puerto Pirámides · Punta Delgada
Purranque · Vol. Huequi · L. Llanquihue · Ventisquero 2300 m · El Bolsón · Sa Huancache · Puerto Madryn · Pta Ninfas
Puerto Varas · Calbuco · Cochamó · Cholila · Gualjaina · Gaimán · Trelew · Pta Castro
Puerto Montt · Chacao · Minchinmávida 2470 m · Esquel · Chubut · Dolavón · Rawson
Maullín · Ancud · G. de Ancud · Vol. Huequi 1050 m · Chaitén · Vol. Futaleufú · Tecka · Las Plumas · Florentino Ameghino · Dos Pozos
Quemchi · Isla Grande de Chiloé · Castro · Corcovado 2300 m · Co Cónico 2270 m · Corcovado · Paso de Indios · C. Raso · Cabo Raso
Quellón · C. Quilán · Boca del Guafo · Golfo Corcovado · Palena · José de San Martín · El Sombrero · Camarones · Bahía Camarones · C. Dos Bahías
I. Guafo · Islas Guaitecas · L. Palena · Mte Melimoyu 2400 m · Co Steffen 2108 m · Nueva Lubecka · Sierra Cuadrada · Bahía Bustamante
I. Benjamín · Isla Magdalena · Puerto Cisnes · Buen Pasto · L. Colhué Huapi · Bahía Bustamante
I. James · Archipiélago de los Chonos · I. Melchor · Mte Macá 2960 m · Puerto Aisén · Alto Río Senguer · Facundo · Pico de Salamanca · Bahía Bustamante · Puerto Visser
I. Victoria · Bahía Darwin · Coihaique · Río Mayo · Sarmiento · Pampa del Castillo · Bahía Solano
Bahía Anna Pink · Vol. Hudson 2500 m · Balmaceda · **Comodoro Rivadavia** · Golfo de San Jorge
Chonos · Mte San Valentín 4058 m · L. Buenos Aires · Perito Moreno · Las Heras · Caleta Olivia · Bahía Langara
C. Raper · Península de Taitao · Chile Chico · Pampa del Castillo · Pico Truncado · Fitz Roy · Mazarredo · C. Tres Puntas
Península Tres Montes · L. General Carrera · Bajo Caracoles · Cerro Cojudo Blanco 1335 m · Las Martinetas · Antonio de Biedma · Cabo Blanco
Golfo de Penas · Co Arenales 3440 m · Cochrane · Meseta el Pedrero · Puerto Deseado
I. Campana · I. Prat · Mte San Lorenzo 3700 m · Tortel · Gran Altiplanicie Central · Tres Cerros · Florida Negra · Bahía Laura · Pta Medanosa
I. Patricio Lynch · I. Serrano · C. Mellizo Sur 3050 m · L. San Martín · Gobernador Gregores · El Salado · C. Dañoso
I. Esmeralda · Isla Wellington · Co Murallón 3600 m · **SANTA CRUZ** · Mte Fitz Roy 3375 m · Laguna Grande · Puerto San Julián · Pta Desengaño
I. Mornington · L. Viedma · Tres Lagos · Comandante Luis Piedrabuena · Puerto Santa Cruz · C. San Francisco de Paula
I. Madre de Dios · Charles Fuhr · El Calafate · Co Pináculo 2160 m · L. Argentino · Pta León · Bahía Grande
I. Duque de York · C. Santiago · Bahía Solvación · Puerto Coig · Gobernador Mayer · C. Buen Tiempo
I. Diego de Almagro · Esperanza · Puerto Natales · El Turbio · Bella Vista · Río Gallegos · Monte Dinero · Pta Dungeness
I. Ramírez · I. Contreras · **MAGALLANES** · Mte Burney 1750 m · Villa Tehuelche · Río Verde · Punta Delgada
I. Pacheco · Archipiélago de la Reina Adelaida · I. Manuel Rodríguez · Península Muñoz Gamero · Isla Riesco · Cerro Sombrero · Pta de Arenas
C. Pilar · I. Desolación · **Punta Arenas** · Península de Brunswick · Fuerte Bulnes · Porvenir · Bahía San Sebastián · San Sebastián
I. Santa Inés · Camerón · Isla Grande de Tierra del Fuego · Río Grande · C. Peñas
Clarence I. · Cap Arcena · Pico Nariz 822 m · **TIERRA DEL FUEGO** · Bahía Thetis · C. San Juan · San Juan de Salvamento
Península Brecknock · Mte Darwin 2488 m · Ushuaia · Puerto Harberton · Península Mitre · I. de los Estados
I. Stewart · Puerto Williams · I. Picton · I. Nueva
I. Londonderry · I. Hoste · I. Navarino · I. Lennox
Pen. Rous · Bahía Nassau · Islas Wollaston
Península Hardy · Isla Hermite · Cabo de Hornos (Cape Horn)

SOUTH ATLANTIC OCEAN

FALKLAND ISLANDS (U.K.)
West Falkland · King George Bay · Queen Charlotte Bay · Pebble I. · C. Dolphin · Mt Adam 700 m · Mt Usborne 705 m · Darwin · Stanley · Weddell I. · Port Stephens · Goose Green · Lively I. · Choiseul Sound · East Falkland · Bay of Harbours · C. Meredith · Falkland Sound

PATAGONIA

© Random House Australia Pty Ltd

kilometers 0 100 200 300 400
miles 0 100 200
Scale 1:7 000 000 · Projection: Azimuthal Equal Area

Islands around South America

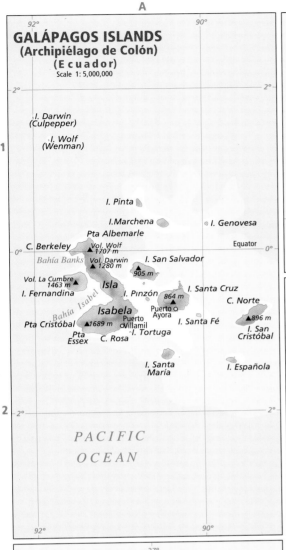

GALÁPAGOS ISLANDS
(Archipiélago de Colón)
(Ecuador)
Scale 1: 5,000,000

I. Darwin (Culpepper)
I. Wolf (Wenman)
I. Pinta
I. Marchena
Pta Albemarle
I. Genovesa
C. Berkeley
Vol. Wolf ▲1707 m
Equator
Bahía Banks
Vol. Darwin ▲1280 m
I. San Salvador
905 m
Vol. La Cumbre ▲1463 m
Isla
I. Pinzón
864 m
I. Santa Cruz
C. Norte
I. Fernandina
Isabela
Puerto Ayora
I. Santa Fé
▲896 m
Pta Cristóbal ▲1689 m
Puerto Villamil
I. San Cristóbal
Pta Essex
I. Tortuga
C. Rosa
I. Santa María
I. Española

PACIFIC OCEAN

SAN ANDRÉS
(Colombia)
Scale 1: 250,000

Pta Norte
Ensenada de Sardinata
San Andrés
Pta Paraíso
Bahía de San Andrés
Bahía Baja
Cayo Rocoso
La Loma
Cayo Córdoba
Caleta Schooner
Bahía Sonora
San Luís
Rada El Cove
El Cove
Pta Sur

CARIBBEAN SEA

PROVIDENCIA
(Colombia)
Scale 1: 200,000

I. Santa Catalina
Pta Bucanera
Santa Isabel
Bahía Catalina
San Felipe
Pueblo Viejo
Aguadulce
Providencia
Bogotá
Casabaja
La Paz
Aguamansa

CARIBBEAN SEA

EASTER ISLAND
(Chile)
Scale 1: 350,000

C. Norte
Pta San Juan
Pta Rosalia
Terevaka ▲608 m
C. O'Higgins
Vol. Katiki 390 m ▲
Motu Tautara
Vol. Puhi 470 m
270 m
Vol. Tangaroa
C. Roggewain
Pta Roa
Tuutapu 510 m
Pta Cuidado
Pta Baja
Hanga-Roa
Vaihu
Mataveri
Pta Redonda
Motu Iti
Motu Nui

PACIFIC OCEAN

RÓBINSON CRUSOE ISLAND
(Archipiélago Juan Fernández)
(Chile)
Scale 1: 250,000

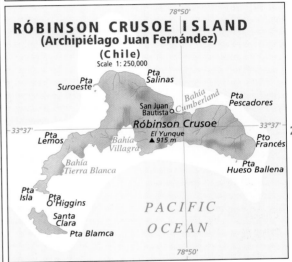

Pta Suroeste
Pta Salinas
Bahía Cumberland
Pta Pescadores
San Juan Bautista
Róbinson Crusoe
Pta Lemos
El Yunque ▲915 m
Pto Francés
Bahía Villagra
Bahía Tierra Blanca
Pta Isla
Pta O'Higgins
Pta Hueso Ballena
Santa Clara
Pta Blamca

PACIFIC OCEAN

SOUTH GEORGIA
(U.K.)
Scale 1: 3,000,000

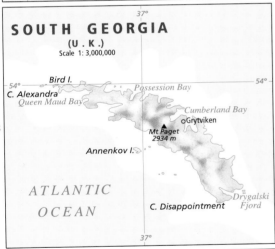

Bird I.
C. Alexandra
Possession Bay
Queen Maud Bay
Cumberland Bay
Grytviken
Mt Paget ▲2934 m
Annenkov I.
C. Disappointment
Drygalski Fjord

ATLANTIC OCEAN

ARUBA
(Netherlands)
Scale 1:1,000,000

CARIBBEAN SEA

Kudarebe
Alto Vista ▲71 m
Noord
Druif
Paradera
Oranjestad
Santa Cruz
Jamanota ▲188 m
Barcadera
Savaneta
Sint Nicolaas
Commanders Bay
Seroe Colorado
Pt Basora

CURAÇAO
(Netherlands Antilles)
Scale 1:1,000,000

Nordpunt
Westpunt
St Christoffelberg ▲372 m
Santa Cruz
Barber
Soto
CARIBBEAN SEA
Santa Martabaai
Bocht Van Hato
Sint Willebrordus
Bullenbaai
Julianadorp
Santa Catharina
Otrabanda
Emmastad
Willemstad
Nieuw Poort
Oostpunt

BONAIRE
(Netherlands Antilles)
Scale 1:1,000,000

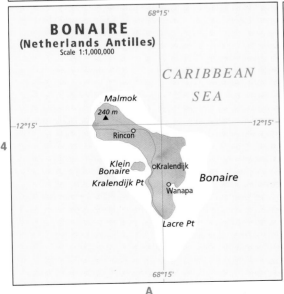

CARIBBEAN SEA

Malmok
240 m ▲
Rincon
Klein Bonaire
Kralendijk
Kralendijk Pt
Bonaire
Wanapa
Lacre Pt

TOBAGO
(Trinidad and Tobago)
Scale 1:1,000,000

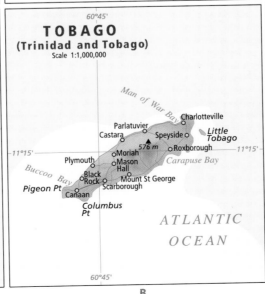

Man of War Bay
Charlotteville
Parlatuvier
Castara
Speyside
Moriah
576 m
Little Tobago
Plymouth
Roxborough
Carapuse Bay
Mason Hall
Buccoo Bay
Black Rock
Mount St George
Pigeon Pt
Scarborough
Cañaan
Columbus Pt

ATLANTIC OCEAN

TRINIDAD
(Trinidad and Tobago)
Scale 1: 2,000,000

ATLANTIC OCEAN

Chupara
Grande Rivière
Toco
Galera
Pta Peñas
Pt Blanchisseuse
Green Hill
El Cerro del Aripo 940 m ▲
Matelot
Redhead
Macuro
Corozal Pt
Chaguaramas
Northern Range
Salibea
Monos
Arima
Saline Bay
VENEZUELA
Port of Spain
Tunapuna
Sangre Grande
Chaguanas
Manzanilla Pt
Waterloo
Talparo
Cocos Bay
California
Biche
Flanagin Town
Tabaquite
Rio Claro
Guataro Pt
San Fernando
Princes Town
Saint Joseph
La Brea
St Marys
New Grant
Guayaguayare
Guapo Bay
Penal
Point Fortin
Basse Terre
304 m ▲
Galeota Pt
Icacos Pt
Bonasse
Siparia
Trinity Hills
Mayaro Bay
Fullarton
San Francique
Moruga
Erin Pt
Golfo de Paria
Caroni
Oropuche
Boca de la Serpiente
VENEZUELA

© Random House Australia Pty Ltd

South America

Polar Regions

The polar regions lie between 66° latitude and the North and South poles. The continent of Antarctica, which is 14 million sq km (5.5 million sq miles) in area, is almost completely enclosed within the Antarctic Circle (66°S) and the South Pole. Antarctica is surrounded by the only continuous seas circling Earth, and during winter the seas freeze around it, making the continent appear larger than it actually is. Various nations have laid claim to certain parts of Antarctica, several of which overlap. Most non-claimant countries—and the United Nations—do not recognize these claims.

The region between the Arctic Circle (66°N) and the North Pole includes the Arctic Ocean and the northern fringes of the Eurasian and North American landmasses. The arctic lands are shared by several countries: Canada, the USA, Russia, Finland, Sweden, and Norway.

Physiography

Eastern Antarctica was once part of the ancient supercontinent of Gondwana, while the Western Peninsula is an island chain related to the geologically younger Andean ranges. Floating ice shelves cover the seas around the land areas, giving the appearance of one large ice-covered continent. Volcanic chains, such as the Scotia Arc,

are found in the Antarctic Peninsula, and there are several active volcanoes. The highest point in Antarctica is Vinson Massif (5,140 m; 16,863 ft), while the average elevation of the continent exceeds 2,440 m (8,000 ft).

The Arctic Circle region encompasses the fringes of the North American, European, and Asian continents which surround the Arctic Ocean. The Arctic Ocean was formed when the Eurasian Plate moved towards the Pacific Plate, while the North American and Eurasian plates separated to form the Atlantic Ocean. The Arctic Ocean, reaching depths of 969 m (3,200 ft), is connected to the Atlantic and Pacific oceans by several straits through which its cold waters move southward.

Climate

Very cold climates prevail in the polar regions. Because of Earth's axial tilt, the polar regions receive the Sun's rays obliquely, so although during the summer months there is practically no darkness, there is nevertheless little solar radiation. During the long polar winter "nights," which also last for months, there is no net solar radiation at all to warm the land surface.

Snow reflects a large proportion of solar radiation back to space. This is particularly true of Antarctica, which is covered by extensive ice sheets. Temperatures within the Arctic Circle are higher than those of Antarctica because of the presence of a warming ocean. Within Antarctica, temperatures fall as low as –89.2°C (–128.6°F). In contrast, the lowest recorded temperature on the ice sheet of Greenland is –68°C (–90°F). Temperatures during summer in the Arctic Ocean, when parts of the floating ice melt, are around 0°C (32°F) and during winter, when larger areas are covered by ice, they fall to –34°C (–30°F).

The polar areas are characterized by cold air masses which blow toward warmer, temperate latitudes. In Antarctica, strong, chilly winds blow over the land surface. Winds blow continuously from west to east (the West Wind Drift) in the seas surrounding Antarctica; the seas are so often stormy that they have prevented explorers reaching the continent until relatively recently.

Winters within the Arctic Circle are windy, cold, and harsh; temperatures in northern Siberia can fall to –50°C (–122°F). During the arctic summer, temperatures in the southern margins average around 10°C (50°F), with some short spells up to 30°C (86°F). In Antarctica, only the northern part of the Antarctic Peninsula becomes warm (up to 15°C; 59°F), the temperatures of the interior remaining below freezing.

Flora and fauna

Marine life thrives in the nutrient-rich waters around Antarctica. Phytoplankton abound, and so do the tiny shrimp-like krill, which form part of an elaborate food chain that includes crustaceans, mollusks, fish, whales, porpoises, dolphins, and seals. Most of the fish are unique to the region. The ozone hole above the South Pole could adversely affect the phytoplakton of the Antarctic seas, which would disturb the food chain.

Around the Arctic lies the treeless tundra, south of which is boreal forest where firs, spruce, and larch grow. Lichens and mosses are common in the tundra; low-growing plants sprout in spring and blossom in summer.

There is marked contrast between the natural life of the Arctic Circle in summer and in winter. During summer there are large quantities of fish and whales in the sea, seals on the ice floes, and foxes, wolves, bears, caribou, and reindeer on land. There are also weasels, hares, and lemmings. Birds migrate to the Arctic during the summer in huge numbers; many birds and animals migrate to warmer lands and waters in winter.

Polar bears (left), and people fishing under the ice (above left) in Arctic Siberia. An iceberg towers over this group of Adélie penguins in Antarctica (top).

Antarctic scenes: a summer night at Cape Bird (above), a Weddell seal (above right), and penguins galore—a crowd scene (below right), an inquisitive-looking Gentoo penguin (below left), and an Emperor penguin group (left).

Natural resources

The world's largest deposits of ice are in Antarctica. A large quantity of fresh water is frozen in these, but this water cannot easily be exploited. Currently there is a concern that global warming could cause the ice sheets to melt, which would raise the levels of the world's oceans. Sea levels have risen in recent times but research indicates that the Antarctic ice sheets have not, to date, diminished in thickness.

As a large part of Antarctica was once part of Gondwana, minerals that occur in other parts of Gondwana, such as coal in Australia, might lie beneath the ice sheets. Likewise, because the Antarctic Peninsula can be considered an extension of the Andes, there is a possibility of metallic ore deposits being found in Antartica, as they have been in the Andes. In addition, the continental shelf around Antarctica could contain petroleum deposits. However, given the current state of technology, mining is not economically feasible in the harsh antarctic conditions.

International agreements which forbid mining and non-peaceful uses of Antarctica have been signed by claimant and non-claimant countries. These aim to ensure the conservation of its environment.

Human habitation

Antarctica is uninhabited, except for several scientific research stations. The nearest human habitations lie on the subantarctic islands of Macquarie, Crozet, South Georgia, and Kerguelen. There is now a small amount of tourism developing in the area, mainly in the Antarctic Peninsula; tourists make short, supervized trips ashore from small cruise vessels. There are also tourist flights over the Antarctic.

In contrast, the Arctic region has been inhabited for thousands of years by indigenous groups such as the Inuit (Eskimo) in Canada, the Saami (Lapps) in Scandinavia, and the Nanets and Yakuts of Russia. Relationships have recently been discovered between these now scattered peoples—there is evidence that some of these indigenous groups migrated from Asia to North America, across the Bering Strait.

As the Arctic is not conducive to agriculture, its inhabitants have to gather food, and their ability to succeed in this is determined primarily by environmental conditions. Saami who live in the traditional way herd reindeer, taking their herds to high ground to graze in summer, then moving to woodlands in low mountain territory in winter. Caribou are hunted by the Nanets and Yakuts in the Russian tundra during spring and summer and in the forests during winter; both animals and people need to migrate with the seasons to survive. In Canada, the Inuit hunt seals along the coast during winter and move inland to hunt caribou during summer.

Gazetteer

GAZETTEER

Abbreviations Used on Maps

Arch. Archipelago, Archipel, Archipiélago, Arquipélago
Arg. Argentina
Arm. Armenia
Aust. Australia
Azer. Azerbaijan

B. Bay, Baía, Baie, Bahía
B.-H. Bosnia and Herzegovina
Belg. Belgium

C.A.R. Central African Republic
C. Cape, Cabo, Cap, Capo
Co Cerro
Col. Colombia
Cord. Cordillera
Croat. Croatia
Cuch. Cuchillo
Czech Rep. Czech Republic

D.C. District of Columbia
Dem. Rep. of the Congo Democratic Republic of the Congo
Den. Denmark

E. East
Ecu. Ecuador
Emb. Embalse
Eq. Guinea Equatorial Guinea
Est. Estrecho

Fr. France

G. Gora
G. Gulf, Golfe, Golfo, Gulfo
G. Gunung
Germ. Germany

Harb. Harbor
Hung. Hungary

I. Island, Île, Ilha, Isla, Isola
Is Islands, Îles, Ilhas, Islas

Jez. Jezioro

K. Kolpos
Kep. Kepulauan

L. Lake, Lac, Lacul, Lago, Limni, Loch
Liech. Liechtenstein
Lux. Luxembourg

Mace. Macedonia
Mex. Mexico
Mt Mount, Mont
Mte Monte
Mti Monti
Mtn Mountain
Mts Mountains, Monts

N. North
N.Z. New Zealand
Neth. Netherlands
Nev. Nevado
Nor. Norway

P. Pic, Pico
P. Pulau
P.N.G. Papua New Guinea
Peg. Pegunungan
Pen. Peninsula, Péninsula, Péninsule
Pk Peak
Pk Puncak
Port. Portugal
Pt Point
Pta Ponta, Punta
Pte Pointe
Pto Porto, Pôrto, Puerto

R. River
Ra. Range
Rep. Republic
Res. Reservoir
Russ. Fed. Russian Federation

S. San
S. South
S.A. South Africa
Sa Serra
Sd Sound
Serr. Serranía
Slov. Slovenia
Sp. Spain
St Saint
Sta Santa
Ste Sainte
Sto Santo
Switz. Switzerland

Tel. Teluk
Tg Tanjong

U. Ujung
U.A.E. United Arab Emirates
U.K. United Kingdom
U.S., U.S.A. United States of America

Vol. Volcán

W. West

Yug. Yugoslavia

Foreign Geographical Terms

Açude *(Portuguese)* reservoir
Adası *(Turkish)* island
Adrar *(Berber)* mountains
Agios *(Greek)* saint
Akra *(Greek)* cape, point
Alpen *(German)* Alps
Alpi *(Italian)* Alps
Alta *(Spanish)* upper
Altiplanicie *(Spanish)* high plain, plateau
-älven *(Swedish)* river
Ao *(Thai)* bay
Archipel *(French)* archipelago
Archipiélago *(Spanish)* archipelago
Arquipélago *(Portuguese)* archipelago
Avtonomnaya Oblast' *(Russian)* autonomous region
Avtonomnyy Okrug *(Russian)* autonomous area

Bab *(Arabic)* strait
Bælt *(Danish)* strait
Bahía *(Spanish)* bay
Baḩr, Bahr *(Arabic)* lake, river, sea
Baía *(Portuguese)* bay
Baie *(French)* bay
Barajı *(Turkish)* dam
Barragem *(Portuguese)* reservoir
Bassin *(French)* basin
Beinn, Ben *(Gaelic)* mountain
Bjerg *(Danish)* hill, mountain
Bôca *(Portuguese)* river mouth
Boca *(Spanish)* river mouth
Bocht *(Dutch)* bay
Bodden *(German)* bay
Bogazi *(Turkish)* strait
Bögeni *(Kazakh)* reservoir
-bre/en *(Norwegian)* glacier
Bucht *(German)* bay
Bugt, -bugten *(Danish)* bay
Buḩayrat *(Arabic)* lake
Bukit *(Malay)* mountain
-bukten *(Swedish)* bay
Burnu, Burun *(Turkish)* cape, point
Buuraha *(Somali)* hill/s, mountain/s

Cabo *(Portuguese, Spanish)* cape
Canal *(Spanish)* channel
Cap *(French)* cape
Capo *(Italian)* cape
Cerro/s *(Spanish)* hill/s, peak/s
Chaîne *(French)* mountain range
Chapada *(Portuguese)* hills, upland/s
Chhâk *(Cambodian)* bay
Chott *(Arabic)* marsh, salt lake
Cima *(Italian)* mountain
Ciudad *(Spanish)* city
Co *(Tibetan)* lake
Colline *(Italian)* hill/s
Cordillera *(Spanish)* mountain range, mountain chain
Côte *(French)* coast, slope
Cù Lao *(Vietnamese)* island
Cuchilla *(Spanish)* mountain range

Dag/ı *(Turkish)* mountain
Daglar/ı *(Turkish)* mountains
-dake *(Japanese)* peak
Danau *(Indonesian)* lake
Dao *(Chinese)* island
Đao *(Vietnamese)* island
Daryācheh *(Persian)* lake
Dasht *(Persian)* desert
Denizi *(Turkish)* sea
Desierto *(Spanish)* desert
Détroit *(French)* strait
Djebel *(Arabic)* mountain, mountain range

-elva *(Norwegian)* river
Embalse *(Spanish)* reservoir
Ensenada *(Spanish)* bay
Erg *(Arabic)* sand dunes
Estrecho *(Spanish)* strait
Étang *(French)* lagoon, lake
ezers *(Latvian)* lake

Falaise *(French)* cliff
Feng *(Chinese)* peak
Fjeld *(Danish)* mountain
-fjell *(Norwegian)* mountain
-fjord/en *(Danish, Norwegian, Swedish)* fiord

Gang *(Chinese)* harbor
Gaoyuan *(Chinese)* plateau
Garet *(Arabic)* hill
Gebergte *(Dutch)* mountain chain, mountain range
-gebirge *(German)* mountain range
Ghubbat *(Arabic)* bay
Gjiri *(Albanian)* bay
Golfe *(French)* gulf
Golfo *(Italian, Portuguese)* gulf
Gölü *(Turkish)* lake
Gora *(Russian)* mountain
Góry *(Polish)* mountains
Gross/er *(German)* big
Gryada *(Russian)* ridge
Guba *(Russian)* bay, gulf
Gulfo *(Spanish)* gulf
Gunung *(Indonesian, Malay)* mountain

Haixia *(Chinese)* strait
-halvøya *(Norwegian)* peninsula
Har *(Hebrew)* mountain
Haut, Haute *(French)* high
Hawr *(Arabic)* lake
Häyk' *(Amharic)* lake
Helodrano *(Malagasy)* bay
Hohe *(German)* height
Hora *(Belorussian, Czech)* mountain
-horn *(German)* peak
Hory *(Czech)* mountains
Hsü *(Chinese)* island, islet
Hu *(Chinese)* lake

Île/s *(French)* island/s
Ilha/s *(Portuguese)* island/s
Ilheu *(Portuguese)* islet
Isla/s *(Spanish)* island/s
Isola, Isole *(Italian)* island/s

Jabal *(Arabic)* mountain, mountain range
Jarv *(Estonian)* lake
-järvi *(Finnish)* lake
Jazīrat, Jaza'īr *(Arabic)* island/s
Jazīreh *(Persian)* island
Jbel *(Arabic)* mountain
Jezioro *(Polish)* lake
-jima *(Japanese)* island
-joki *(Finnish)* river

Kalnas *(Lithuanian)* mountain
Kangri *(Tibetan)* mountain
Kap *(Danish, German)* cape
-kapp *(Norwegian)* cape
Kepi *(Albanian)* cape, point
Kepulauan *(Indonesian)* islands
Khalīj *(Arabic)* bay, gulf
Khao *(Thai)* peak
Khrebet *(Russian)* mountain range
Ko *(Thai)* island
Köli *(Kazakh)* lake
Kolpos *(Greek)* bay
Körfezi *(Turkish)* bay, gulf
Kray *(Russian)* territory
Kryazh *(Russian)* ridge
Kūh/hā *(Persian)* mountain/s
-kūl *(Tajik)* lake
Kyst *(Danish)* coast
Kyun *(Burmese)* island

Lac *(French)* lake
Lacul *(Romanian)* lake
Lago *(Italian, Portuguese, Spanish)* lake
Lagoa *(Portuguese)* lagoon, lake
Laht *(Estonian)* bay
Lich *(Armenian)* lake
Liedao *(Chinese)* archipelago, islands
Limni *(Greek)* lake
Ling *(Chinese)* mountain range
Loch, Lough *(Gaelic)* lake
Lohatanjona *(Malagasy)* point
Loi *(Burmese)* mountain
Loma *(Spanish)* hill

Mae Nam *(Thai)* river
-man *(Korean)* bay
Mar *(Spanish)* lake, sea
Maşabb *(Arabic)* river mouth
Massif *(French)* mountains, upland
Meer, -meer *(Dutch)* lake, sea
Mesa *(Spanish)* tableland
Meseta *(Spanish)* plateau, tableland
-misaki *(Japanese)* cape, point
Mont/s *(French)* mountain/s
Montagne/s *(French)* mountain/s
Monte *(Italian, Portuguese, Spanish)* mountain
Montes *(Spanish)* mountain
Monti *(Italian)* mountain/s
More *(Russian)* sea
Morne *(French)* mountain
Morro *(Portuguese)* hill
Munții *(Romanian)* mountains
Mys *(Russian)* cape, point

-nada *(Japanese)* gulf, sea
Nagor'ye *(Russian)* upland
Nevado *(Spanish)* snow-capped mountain
Nieuw *(Dutch)* new
Nisoi *(Greek)* islands
Nizmennost' *(Russian)* lowland
Nord *(French)* north
Norte *(Portuguese, Spanish)* north
Nos *(Bulgarian)* point
Nosy *(Malagasy)* island
Nur, Nuur *(Mongolian)* lake
Nuruu *(Mongolian)* mountain range

Ø, Øer *(Danish)* island/s
-ö, -ön *(Swedish)* island
Oblast' *(Russian)* province
Odde *(Danish)* cape, point
Oros *(Greek)* mountain
Ostrov/a *(Russian)* island/s
Oued *(Arabic)* river, watercourse
-øy, -øya *(Norwegian)* island
Ozero *(Russian)* lake

Pantanal *(Portuguese)* marsh, swamp
Pegunungan *(Indonesian)* island
Pelagos *(Greek)* sea
Pendi *(Chinese)* basin
Pertuis *(French)* strait
Phnum *(Cambodian)* mountain
Phou *(Laotian)* mountain
Pic *(French)* peak
Pico *(Spanish)* peak
Pik *(Russian)* peak
Piton *(French)* peak
Pivostriv *(Ukrainian)* peninsula
Piz, pizzo *(Italian)* peak
Planalto *(Portuguese)* plateau
Planina *(Bulgarian, Macedonian)* mountains
Plato *(Russian)* plateau
Ploskogor'ye *(Russian)* plateau, upland
Pointe *(French)* point
Poluostrov *(Russian)* peninsula
Ponta *(Portuguese)* point
Porthmos *(Greek)* strait
Porto, Pôrto *(Portuguese)* port
Proliv *(Russian)* strait
Puerto *(Spanish)* port
Pulau *(Indonesian, Malay)* island
Puncak *(Indonesian)* mountain
Punta *(Italian, Spanish)* point

Qārat *(Arabic)* hill
Qooriga *(Somali)* bay
Qundao *(Chinese)* archipelago, islands
Qurnat *(Arabic)* peak

Raas *(Somali)* cape, point
Ras, Ra's *(Arabic)* cape, point
Ravnina *(Russian)* plain
Represa *(Portuguese, Spanish)* reservoir
Réservoir *(French)* reservoir
Reshteh *(Persian)* mountain range
Respublika *(Russian)* republic
Respublikasi *(Uzbek)* republic
-retto *(Japanese)* island chain
Rio, Río *(Portuguese, Spanish)* river
Rivière *(French)* river
Rubha *(Gaelic)* cape, point
Rudohorie *(Slovak)* mountains

Sāgar/a *(Hindi)* lake
Şaḩrā' *(Arabic)* desert
-saki *(Japanese)* cape, point
Salar *(Spanish)* salt-flat, salt-pan
Salina/s *(Spanish)* salt-pan/s
Salto/s *(Portuguese, Spanish)* waterfall
-san *(Japanese, Korean)* mountain
San, Santa, Santo *(Spanish)* saint
-sanchi *(Japanese)* mountains
São *(Portuguese)* saint
Sarīr *(Arabic)* desert
Sebkha, Sebkhet *(Arabic)* salt-flat
See, -see *(German)* lake
Selat *(Indonesian)* strait
Serra *(Portuguese)* mountain range
Serranía *(Spanish)* mountain range
Shamo *(Chinese)* desert
Shan *(Chinese)* mountain/s
-shima *(Japanese)* island
-shotō *(Japanese)* islands
Shuiki *(Chinese)* reservoir
Sierra *(Spanish)* mountain range
Slieve *(Gaelic)* mountain
-spitze *(German)* peak
Steno *(Greek)* strait
Štít *(Slovak)* peak
Stretto *(Italian)* strait
Sud *(French)* south
Sul *(Portuguese)* south

Tanjona *(Malagasy)* cape
Tanjong *(Indonesian, Malay)* cape, point
Tao *(Chinese)* island
Tasek *(Malay)* lake
Tassili *(Berber)* plateau
Taungdan *(Burmese)* mountain range
Tekojärvi *(Finnish)* reservoir
Teluk *(Indonesian, Malay)* bay
Ténéré *(Berber)* desert
Tepe *(Turkish)* peak
Terara *(Amharic)* mountain
Tierra *(Spanish)* land
-to *(Japanese)* island

Ujung *(Indonesian)* cape, point
'Urūq *(Arabic)* dunes
Uul *(Mongolian)* mountain/s

väin *(Estonian)* channel, strait
-vatn *(Norwegian)* lake
-vesi *(Finnish)* lake, water
Voblasts' *(Belorussian)* province
Vodokhranilishche *(Russian)* reservoir
Vodoskhovyshche *(Ukrainian)* reservoir
Volcán *(Spanish)* volcano
Vozvyshennost' *(Russian)* plateau, upland
Vozyera *(Belorussian)* lake
Vrchovina *(Czech)* mountains

Wabē *(Amharic)* river, stream
Wādī *(Arabic)* watercourse
-wald *(German)* forest
Wan *(Chinese)* bay
-wan *(Japanese)* bay

Yam *(Hebrew)* lake, sea
Yang *(Chinese)* ocean
Yoma *(Burmese)* mountain range

-zaki *(Japanese)* cape, point
Zaliv *(Russian)* bay
Zangbo *(Tibetan)* river
Zatoka *(Polish)* bay, gulf
-zee *(Dutch)* sea
Zemlya *(Russian)* land
Zizhiqu *(Chinese)* autonomous region

Gazetteer

- The gazetteer contains the names shown on the continental and detailed regional maps at the end of each section.

- In the code given to locate a place, the **bold** number refers to the page on which the map is to be found, and the letter–number combination refers to the grid square formed by the lines of latitude and longitude on the map. Inset maps have their own letter–number combination.

- Where a name appears on more than one map, the gazetteer generally lists the largest scale map on which the name appears.

- Names that have a symbol (town or mountain peak) are given an area reference according to the location of the symbol. Names without a symbol are entered in the gazetteer according to the first letter of the name.

- Words in italics describe features in the gazetteer, e.g. *island*, *point* and *mountain peak*.

- All entries include the country or area in which the name is located.

- Features composed of a description and a proper name, e.g. Cape Hatteras, are positioned alphabetically by the proper name: Hatteras, Cape.

- Where a name contains a subordinate or alternative name in brackets on the map, the bracketed names are entered in the gazetteer with a cross-reference to the first name, eg. Peking *see* Beijing, China, **210** G5.

- Words abbreviated on the map, e.g. C. or I., are spelt out in the gazetteer. If the word is English, the description in italics is not included. For example, if I. (standing for island) is abbreviated on the map and spelt out in the gazetteer, *island* is not added. However, if Island is not in English, e.g. Isla, *island* is added.

- The location (ocean, area of a continent) is included before the area reference when a place is part of a country but not located within the country, e.g. Madeira, Portugal, Atlantic Ocean; and Ceuta, *enclave*, Spain, N.W. Africa.

A

A Cañiza, Spain, **292** C1
A Coruña, Spain, **292** C1
A Estrada, Spain, **292** C1
A Fonsagrada, Spain, **292** D1
A Guardia, Spain, **292** C2
A Gudiña, Spain, **292** D1
Aachen, Germany, **288** C3
Aalen, Germany, **288** E4
A'ali An Nīl, *state*, Sudan, **366** D2
Aapua, Sweden, **285** L3
Aarau, Switzerland, **291** J3
Aare, *river*, Switzerland, **291** J3
Aasleagh, Ireland, **309** C4
Aba, China, **215** G2
Aba, Democratic Republic of the Congo, **366** D4
Aba, Nigeria, **368** A1
Abacaxis, *river*, Brazil, **452** A4
Abaco, *island*, Bahamas, **428** F1
Ābādeh, Iran, **220** F2
Abadla, Algeria, **361** F2
Abaeté, *river*, Brazil, **456** D5
Abaetetuba, Brazil, **452** D3
Abag Qi, China, **210** F4
Abagaytuy, Russian Federation, **210** G2
Abaji, Nigeria, **365** F3
Abajo Peak, *mountain peak*, U.S.A., **423** J3
Abakaliki, Nigeria, **365** F3
Abakan, *river*, Russian Federation, **223** M2
Abakan, Russian Federation, **223** N2
Abala, Congo, **368** C3
Abala, Niger, **365** E2
Abalak, Niger, **365** E3/F1
Abalessa, Algeria, **361** G4
Abancay, Peru, **454** D3
Abarkūh, Iran, **220** F2
Abashiri, Japan, **209** J2
Abatskiy, Russian Federation, **223** J1
Abau, Papua New Guinea, **140** C5
Abay, Aqmola, Kazakhstan, **212** A2
Abay, Qaraghandy, Kazakhstan, **212** B2
Abaza, Russian Federation, **223** N2

Abba, Central African Republic, **368** C1
Abbeville, Alabama, U.S.A., **425** K4
Abbeville, France, **290** E1
Abbeville, Louisiana, U.S.A., **424** F5
Abbeville, South Carolina, U.S.A., **425** L2
Abbeyfeale, Ireland, **309** C5
Abbeyleix, Ireland, **309** E5
Abborrträsk, Sweden, **284** J4
Abbot Ice Shelf, Antarctica, **470** B6
Abbots Langley, England, U.K., **305** G3
Abbotsbury, England, U.K., **304** E4
Abbotsford, Canada, **412** H7
Abbott, U.S.A., **423** L3
Abbottābād, Pakistan, **218** C2
'Abd al Kūrī, *island*, Suquţrā (Socotra), Yemen, **373** B2
Abdelcader, Somalia, **367** F2
Abdulino, Russian Federation, **222** E2
Abéché, Chad, **366** B2
Abee, Canada, **413** N4
Abemama, *island*, Kiribati, **139** F4
Abengourou, Côte d'Ivoire, **364** D3
Åbenrå, Denmark, **286** D5
Abeokuta, Nigeria, **365** E3
Aberaeron, Wales, U.K., **304** C2
Aberchirder, Scotland, U.K., **308** G3
Aberdare, Wales, U.K., **304** D3
Aberdaron, Wales, U.K., **304** C2
Aberdeen, Idaho, U.S.A., **418** H5
Aberdeen, Mississippi, U.S.A., **425** H3
Aberdeen, Scotland, U.K., **308** G3
Aberdeen, South Africa, **370** D5
Aberdeen, South Dakota, U.S.A., **420** D3
Aberdeen, Washington, U.S.A., **418** C3
Aberdeen City, *local authority*, Scotland, U.K., **308** G3
Aberdeenshire, *local authority*, Scotland, U.K., **308** G3
Aberdyfi, Wales, U.K., **304** C2

Aberfeldy, Scotland, U.K., **308** F4
Aberfoyle, Scotland, U.K., **306** D1
Abergavenny, Wales, U.K., **304** E3
Abergele, Wales, U.K., **306** E4
Abernathy, U.S.A., **424** B3
Aberporth, Wales, U.K., **304** C2
Abersoch, Wales, U.K., **304** C2
Abert, Lake, U.S.A., **418** D5
Abertillery, Wales, U.K., **304** D3
Aberystwyth, Wales, U.K., **304** C2
Abhā, Saudi Arabia, **363** H5
Abhar, Iran, **222** D5
Abia, *state*, Nigeria, **365** F3
Abibe, Serranía de, *mountain range*, Colombia, **450** C2
Abide, Turkey, **297** G6
Abidjan, Côte d'Ivoire, **364** D3
Abilene, U.S.A., **424** C3
Abingdon, England, U.K., **305** F3
Abingdon, U.S.A., **421** N7
Abington, Scotland, U.K., **308** F5
Abiquiu, U.S.A., **423** K3
Abisko, Sweden, **284** J2
Abitibi, Lake, Canada, **415** Q7
Ābīy Ādī, Ethiopia, **367** E2
Abkhazia, *autonomous republic*, Georgia, **222** C4
Abnūb, Egypt, **363** F3
Abohar, India, **218** C3
Aboisso, Côte d'Ivoire, **364** D3
Abomey, Benin, **365** E3
Abong Mbang, Cameroon, **368** B2
Abongabong, Gunung, *mountain peak*, Indonesia, **200** B1
Abooso, Ghana, **364** D3
Aborlan, Philippines, **204** B4
Abou Deïa, Chad, **366** A2
Aboyne, Scotland, U.K., **308** G3
Abra Pampa, Argentina, **458** D2
Abra, *river*, Philippines, **204** C2
Abrantes, Portugal, **292** C3
Abrī, Sudan, **363** F4
Abriès, France, **291** H4
Abrolhos, Arquipélago dos, *islands*, Brazil, **457** F4
Abrud, Romania, **296** D2
Abruka, *island*, Estonia, **287** L3
Abruzzi, *autonomous region*, Italy, **295** D4

Absaroka Range, *mountain range*, U.S.A., **419** J4
Absarokee, U.S.A., **419** K4
Abu aḑ Ḑuhūr, Syria, **225** D2
Abū 'Arīsh, Saudi Arabia, **363** H5
Abu Dhabi *see* Abū Zaby, United Arab Emirates, **221** F4
Abū Dulayq, Sudan, **366** D1
Abū Durbah, Egypt, **225** B5
Abu Haggag, Egypt, **362** E2
Abū Ḥamad, Sudan, **363** F5
Abū Ḥammād, Egypt, **225** A4
Abū Kamāl, Syria, **363** H2
Abū Madd, Ra's, *point*, Saudi Arabia, **363** G4
Abū Maţāriq, Sudan, **366** C2
Abū Nujaym, Libya, **362** C2
Ābū Road, India, **218** C4
Abū Rubayq, Saudi Arabia, **363** G4
Abū Rudays, Egypt, **225** B5
Abū Rujmayn, Jabal, *mountain range*, Syria, **225** E2
Abu Shagara, Ras, *point*, Sudan, **363** G4
Abū Shanab, Sudan, **366** C2
Abu Simbel *see* Abū Sunbul, Egypt, **363** F4
Abū Sunbul (Abu Simbel), Egypt, **363** F4
Abū Zabad, Sudan, **366** C2
Abū Zaby (Abu Dhabi), United Arab Emirates, **221** F4
Abū Zanīmah, Egypt, **225** B5
Abu 'Ujaylah, Egypt, **225** C4
Abuja, Nigeria, **365** F3
Abulog, Philippines, **204** C2
Abumombazi, Democratic Republic of the Congo, **368** D2
Abunã, Brazil, **455** F2
Abunã, *river*, Bolivia/Brazil, **455** E2
Ābune Yosēf, *mountain peak*, Ethiopia, **367** E2
Aburo, *mountain peak*, Democratic Republic of the Congo, **366** D4
Ābuyē Mēda, *mountain peak*, Ethiopia, **367** E2
Åby, Sweden, **286** H3
Abyaḑ, Al Baḩr al (White Nile), *river*, Sudan, **366** D2
Abyaḑ, Sudan, **366** C2
Åbybro, Denmark, **286** D4

Abyei, Sudan, **366** C3
Åbyn, Sweden, **284** K4
Açailândia, Brazil, **452** D4
Acámbaro, Mexico, **431** E5
Acancéh, Mexico, **431** H4
Acandí, Colombia, **450** C2
Acaponeta, Mexico, **430** D4
Acapulco, Mexico, **431** F5
Acará, Brazil, **452** D3
Acará, *river*, Brazil, **452** D4
Acará-Mirim, *river*, Brazil, **452** D4
Acaraí, Serra, *mountain range*, Brazil, **452** B3
Acaraú, Brazil, **453** F4
Acaraú, *river*, Brazil, **453** F4
Acaray, Represa de, *reservoir*, Paraguay, **459** F2
Acari, Brazil, **453** G5
Acarigua, Venezuela, **451** E2
Acâș, Romania, **296** D2
Acatlán de Osorio, Mexico, **431** F5
Acayucan, Mexico, **431** G5
Acceglio, Italy, **294** A3
Accomac, U.S.A., **426** C6
Accra, Ghana, **364** D3
Aceh, *province*, Indonesia, **200** B1
Aceh, *river*, Indonesia, **200** A1
Achacachi, Bolivia, **455** E4
Achaguas, Venezuela, **451** E2
Achahoish, Scotland, U.K., **308** D5
Achalpur, India, **218** D5
Achahoish, Scotland, U.K., **308** D5
Acheng, China, **211** J3
Acheryok, *river*, Russian Federation, **285** U3
Acheux-en-Amiénois, France, **305** K4
Achill, Ireland, **309** C4
Achill Island, Ireland, **309** B4
Achiltibuie, Scotland, U.K., **308** D2
Achinsk, Russian Federation, **300** L4
Achit, Russian Federation, **222** F1
Achnasheen, Scotland, U.K., **308** D3
Achwa, *river*, Uganda, **369** F2
Acigöl, *lake*, Turkey, **297** G7
Acıpayam, Turkey, **297** G7
Acireale, Sicilia, Italy, **295** E7

Ackley, U.S.A., **420** G4
Acklins Island, Bahamas, **429** G2
Acle, England, U.K., **305** J2
Acme, U.S.A., **418** C2
Acomayo, Peru, **454** D3
Aconcagua, Cerro, *mountain peak*, Argentina, **458** B4
Acopiara, Brazil, **453** F5
Acora, Peru, **455** E4
Acoyapa, Nicaragua, **428** D5
Acquasparta, Italy, **294** D4
Acqui Terme, Italy, **294** B3
Acre, *river*, Brazil, **455** E2
Acre *see* 'Akko, Israel, **225** C3
Acre, *state*, Brazil, **455** E2
Acri, Italy, **295** F6
Actéon, Groupe, *islands*, French Polynesia, **137** H3
Acton Point, New Zealand, **133** E5
Acton, U.S.A., **419** K4
Actopan, Mexico, **431** F4
Açu, Brazil, **453** G4
Acurenam, Equatorial Guinea, **368** B2
Ad Dabbah, Sudan, **363** F5
Ad Dafīnah, Saudi Arabia, **363** H4
Ad Dahnā', *desert*, Saudi Arabia, **363** J3
Ad Dakhla, Western Sahara, **360** C4
Aḑ Ḑāli', Yemen, **220** D6
Ad Damazīn, Sudan, **366** D2
Ad Dāmir, Sudan, **363** F5
Ad Dammām, Saudi Arabia, **220** F3
Ad Dāmūr, Lebanon, **225** C3
Ad Darb, Saudi Arabia, **363** H5
Ad Dawādimī, Saudi Arabia, **363** H4
Ad Dawḩah (Doha), Qatar, **220** F3
Ad Dawqah, Saudi Arabia, **363** H5
Ad Dilam, Saudi Arabia, **220** E4
Ad Dir'īyah, Saudi Arabia, **220** E4
Ad Dīwānīyah, Iraq, **363** H2
Ad Du'ayn, Sudan, **366** C2
Ad Duwaym, Sudan, **366** D2
Ada, U.S.A., **424** D2
Ada, Yugoslavia, **296** C3
Adair, Cape, Canada, **411** M2
Adair, U.S.A., **420** F5
Adaja, *river*, Spain, **292** E2
Adak, Sweden, **284** J4
Adak Island, Aleutian Islands, U.S.A., **408** F3
Adam, Mount, *mountain peak*, Falkland Islands, **460** F4
Adamaoua, Massif de l', *mountain range*, Cameroon, **365** G3
Adamaoua, *province*, Cameroon, **365** G3
Adamausa, *state*, Nigeria, **365** G3
Adamawa, *state*, Nigeria, **365** G3
Adams, Mount, *mountain peak*, New Zealand, **133** E5
Adams, Mount, *mountain peak*, U.S.A., **418** D3
Adams, U.S.A., **420** D1
Adams Island, Auckland Islands, New Zealand, **132** J10
Adams Lake, Canada, **413** K6
Adam's Peak, *mountain peak*, Sri Lanka, **216** E5
Adamstown, Pitcairn Islands, **137** J3
'Adan (Aden), Yemen, **220** E6
Adana, *province*, Turkey, **225** C1
Adana, Turkey, **224** E5
Adang, Teluk, *bay*, Indonesia, **201** G3
Adapazarı, Turkey, **224** D4
Adare, Cape, Antarctica, **470** D8
Adare, Ireland, **309** D5
Adaut, Indonesia, **199** E5
Adaven, U.S.A., **422** F2
Aday, Kazakhstan, **222** G2
Adda, *river*, Italy, **294** B2
Adda, *river*, Sudan, **366** B3
Addis Ababa *see* Ādīs Ābeba, Ethiopia, **367** E3
Addlestone, England, U.K., **305** G3
Addu Atoll, Maldives, **216** C7
Adel, U.S.A., **425** L4
Adelaide, Australia, **135** H5
Adelaide River, Australia, **134** G1
Adelfia, Italy, **295** F5
Aden, Gulf of, Somalia/Yemen, **220** E6
Aden *see* 'Adan, Yemen, **220** E6
Aderbissinat, Niger, **365** F1
Adh Dhahībāt, Tunisia, **362** B2
Adi, Pulau, *island*, Indonesia, **199** F4
Ādī Ārk'ay, Ethiopia, **367** E2
Ādī Keyih, Eritrea, **367** E2
Ādī Kwala, Eritrea, **367** E2
Ādī Ugrī, Eritrea, **367** E2
Ādige, *river*, Italy, **294** C3
Adige, *state*, Italy, **294** C2
Ādīgrat, Ethiopia, **367** E2
Adıguzel Barajı, *dam*, Turkey, **297** G6
Ādilābād, India, **216** D2
Adilang, Uganda, **369** F2
Adin, U.S.A., **418** D6
Adīrī, Libya, **362** B3
Adirondack Mountains, *mountain range*, U.S.A., **426** C2
Ādīs Ābeba (Addis Ababa), Ethiopia, **367** E3
Ādīs 'Alem, Ethiopia, **367** E3
Ādīs Zemen, Ethiopia, **367** E2
Adıyaman, Turkey, **224** E5
Adjud, Romania, **296** F2
Admiralty Gulf, Australia, **134** E1
Admiralty Inlet, U.S.A., **418** C2
Admiralty Island, U.S.A., **412** B3
Admiralty Islands, Lord Howe Island, Australia, **135** U14
Admiralty Islands, Papua New Guinea, **140** B3
Ado-Ekiti, Nigeria, **365** F3
Adok, Sudan, **366** D3
Adonara, Pulau, *island*, Indonesia, **198** C5
Ādoni, India, **216** D3
Adoumandjali, Central African Republic, **368** C2
Adour, *river*, France, **290** D5
Adra, Spain, **293** F4
Adranga, Democratic Republic of the Congo, **369** F2
Adrano, Sicilia, Italy, **295** E7
Adrar, *administrative region*, Mauritania, **360** D4
Adrar, Algeria, **361** F3
Adrar, *mountain range*, Mauritania, **360** D4
Adré, Chad, **366** B2
Adria, Italy, **294** D3
Adrian, Michigan, U.S.A., **421** L5
Adrian, Texas, U.S.A., **423** M4
Adriatic Sea, Croatia/Italy, **294** D3
Adun Qulu, China, **210** G2
Adusa, Democratic Republic of the Congo, **369** E2
Adutiškis, Lithuania, **287** N5
Ādwa, Ethiopia, **367** E2
Adwāna, India, **218** B5
Adygeya, Respublika, *republic*, Russian Federation, **298** F4
Adzopé, Côte d'Ivoire, **364** D3
Aegean Sea, Greece/Turkey, **297** E6
Aegviidu, Estonia, **287** M3
Aeron, *river*, Wales, U.K., **304** C2
Afantou, Greece, **297** G7
Afféri, Côte d'Ivoire, **364** D3
Afghanistan, *country*, Asia, **196** H6
Afgooye, Somalia, **367** G4
'Afif, Saudi Arabia, **363** H4
Afikpo, Nigeria, **368** A1
Åfjord, Norway, **284** E5
Aflao, Ghana, **364** E3
Aflou, Algeria, **361** G2
Afmadow, Somalia, **369** H2
Afobaka, Suriname, **452** B2
Afognak Island, U.S.A., **410** D4
Afrânio, Brazil, **453** F5
Āfrēra Terara, *mountain peak*, Eritrea, **367** F2
Afrikanda, Russian Federation, **285** R3
'Afrīn, *river*, Syria/Turkey, **225** D1
'Afrīn, Syria, **225** D1
Afuá, Brazil, **452** C3
'Afula, Israel, **225** C3
Afyon, *province*, Turkey, **297** G6
Afyon, Turkey, **224** D5
Agadez, *department*, Niger, **365** F1
Agadez, Niger, **365** F1
Agadir, Morocco, **360** E2
Agalega Islands, Mauritius, **372** D3
Agana, Guam, **138** C3
Agapovka, Russian Federation, **222** F2
Agar, India, **218** C5
Āgaro, Ethiopia, **367** E3
Agartala, India, **219** G5
Agassiz Fracture Zone, *tectonic feature*, Pacific Ocean, **479** J7
Agate, U.S.A., **423** M2
Agathonisi, *island*, Dodekanisos, Greece, **297** F7
Agats, Indonesia, **199** G4
Agatti Island, India, **216** C4
Agawa, Canada, **421** L2
Agboville, Côte d'Ivoire, **364** D3
Agbulu, Philippines, **204** C2
Ağdam, Azerbaijan, **222** D5
Agde, Cap d', *cape*, France, **291** F5
Agde, France, **291** F5
Agen, France, **290** E4
Āgere Maryam, Ethiopia, **369** G1
Agger, Denmark, **286** D4
Aghla Mountain, *mountain peak*, Ireland, **309** D3
Aghor, Afganistan, **218** A4
Agia Marina, Dodekanisos, Greece, **297** F7
Agiabampo, Estero de, *inlet*, Mexico, **430** C3
Agighiol, Romania, **296** G3
Aginskiy Buryatskiy Avtonomnyy Okrug, *autonomous area*, Russian Federation, **210** F2
Aginskoye, Russian Federation, **210** F2
Agioi Theodoroi, Greece, **297** D7
Agiokampos, Greece, **297** D6
Agios Efstratios, *island*, Greece, **297** E6
Agios Georgios, *island*, Greece, **297** D7
Agios Ioannis, Akra, *point*, Kriti, Greece, **297** E8
Agios Nikolaos, Kriti, Greece, **297** E8
Agios Paraskevi, Greece, **297** F6
Agiou Orous, Kolpos, *bay*, Greece, **297** D5
Agira, Sicilia, Italy, **295** E7
Aglona, Latvia, **287** N4
Agnantero, Greece, **297** C6
Agness, U.S.A., **418** B5
Agnibilékrou, Côte d'Ivoire, **364** D3
Agnita, Romania, **296** E3
Agno, Philippines, **204** B2
Agnone, Italy, **295** E5
Agogo, Ghana, **364** D3
Agostinho, Brazil, **455** E2
Āgra, India, **218** D4
Agri, *river*, Italy, **295** F5
Ağri Dağı, *mountain peak*, Turkey, **224** F4
Agrigento, Sicilia, Italy, **295** D7
Agrihan, *island*, Northern Mariana Islands, **138** C3
Agrinio, Greece, **297** C6
Ağsu, Azerbaijan, **222** D4
Agua de Dios, Colombia, **450** C3
Agua Prieta, Mexico, **430** C2
Aguada Cecilio, Argentina, **460** E1
Aguadas, Colombia, **450** C3
Aguadilla, Puerto Rico, **427** C2
Aguadulce, Panama, **429** E5
Aguadulce, Providencia, Colombia, **461** C1
Aguamansa, Providencia, Colombia, **461** C1
Aguanaval, *river*, Mexico, **430** E3
Aguanus, *river*, Canada, **417** K4
Aguapeí, *river*, Brazil, **456** C5
Aguapey, *river*, Argentina, **459** F3
Aguaray-guazú, *river*, Paraguay, **459** E2
Águas Formosas, Brazil, **457** F4
Aguascalientes, Mexico, **430** E4
Aguascalientes, *state*, Mexico, **430** E4
Aguda, Punta, *point*, Islas Canarias, Spain, **373** B4
Agudos, Brazil, **459** H2
Águeda, Portugal, **292** C2
Águeda, *river*, Spain, **292** D2
Aguelhok, Mali, **361** G5
Agüenit, Western Sahara, **360** D4
Aguié, Niger, **365** F2
Aguila, U.S.A., **422** G5
Aguilar, Spain, **292** E4
Aguilar de Campóo, Spain, **292** E1
Aguilares, Argentina, **458** D3
Águilas, Spain, **293** G4
Agul, *river*, Russian Federation, **223** P1
Āgula'i, Ethiopia, **367** E2
Agulhas, Cape, South Africa, **370** D5
Agulhas Basin, *underwater feature*, Indian Ocean, **476** A8
Agulhas Negras, *mountain peak*, Brazil, **457** E6
Agulhas Plateau, *underwater feature*, Indian Ocean, **476** A7
Agung, Gunung, *mountain peak*, Indonesia, **201** F5
Agusan, *river*, Philippines, **204** D5
Ahar, Iran, **222** D5
Ahaura, New Zealand, **133** C6
Ahaus, Germany, **288** C2
Ahe, *island*, French Polynesia, **137** G2
Ahipara, New Zealand, **132** D2
Ahipara Bay, New Zealand, **132** D2
Ahititi, New Zealand, **132** E4
Ahlainen, Finland, **287** K2
Ahlat, Turkey, **363** H1
Ahmad Wāl, Pakistan, **218** A3
Ahmadābād, India, **218** C5
Ahmadnagar, India, **216** C2
Ahmadpur, India, **216** D2
Ahmadpur East, Pakistan, **218** B3
Ahmar Mountains, *mountain range*, Ethiopia, **367** F3
Aḩmed al Bāqir, Jabal, *mountain peak*, Jordan, **225** C5
Ahmetli, Turkey, **297** F6
Ahmovaara, Finland, **285** P5
Ahor, India, **218** C4
Ähtäri, Finland, **287** M1
Ahuachapán, El Salvador, **428** C4
Ahualulco, Mexico, **431** E4
Ahun, France, **290** F3
Ahuriri Point, New Zealand, **132** F4
Ahvāz, Iran, **220** E2
Ahvenanmaa (Åland), *island*, Finland, **287** J2
Ahvenanmaan Lääni (Åland), *province*, Finland, **287** J2
Ahvenselkä, Finland, **285** P3
Ai Yin Young, Vietnam, **203** E3
Aiambak, Papua New Guinea, **140** A4
Aiddejavrre, Norway, **285** L2
Aiduna, Indonesia, **199** F4
Aigina, Greece, **297** D7
Aigina, *island*, Greece, **297** D7
Aiginio, Greece, **297** D5
Aigio, Greece, **297** D6
Aigrettes, Pointe des, *point*, Réunion, **373** A1
Aiguá, Uruguay, **459** F5
Aiguillon, France, **290** E4
Ailao Shan, *mountain range*, China, **215** G5
Aileu, Indonesia, **198** D5
Ailigandí, Panama, **429** F5
Ailinglapalap, *island*, Marshall Islands, **139** E4
Ailly-le-Haut-Clocher, France, **305** J4
Ailly-sur-Noye, France, **305** K5
Ailsa Craig, *island*, Scotland, U.K., **308** D5
Aimogasta, Argentina, **458** C3
Ain, *river*, France, **291** G3
Aïn Beïda, Algeria, **361** H1
Aïn Ben Tili, Mauritania, **360** E3
Aïn Beni Mathar, Morocco, **361** F2
'Aïn Defla, Algeria, **361** G1
'Aïn Deheb, Algeria, **361** G2
'Aïn el Hadjel, Algeria, **361** G1
Aïn-M'Lila, Algeria, **361** H1
Aïn Oussera, Algeria, **293** J5
'Aïn Sefra, Algeria, **361** F2
'Aïn Temouchent, Algeria, **361** F1
Ainaži, Latvia, **287** M4
Ainsa, Spain, **293** H1
Ainsworth, U.S.A., **420** D4
Aipe, Colombia, **450** C3
Aiquile, Bolivia, **455** F5
Aïr, Massif de l', *mountain range*, Niger, **365** F1
Airaines, France, **290** E2
Airbangis, Indonesia, **200** B2
Airdrie, Canada, **413** M6
Airdrie, Scotland, U.K., **308** F5
Aire, *river*, France, **291** G2
Aire-sur-l'Adour, France, **290** D5
Airpanas, Indonesia, **198** D4
Airvault, France, **290** D3
Aisch, *river*, Germany, **288** E4
Aisén, *administrative region*, Chile, **460** C3
Aishalton, Guyana, **451** G3
Aisne, *river*, France, **291** F2
Aïssa, Djebel, *mountain peak*, Algeria, **361** F2
Aitana, *mountain peak*, Spain, **293** G3
Aitape, Papua New Guinea, **140** A3
Aitkin, U.S.A., **420** G2
Aitutaki, *island*, Cook Islands, **137** E2
Aiud, Romania, **296** D2
Aiviekste, *river*, Latvia, **287** N4
Aix-en-Provence, France, **291** G5
Aix-les-Bains, France, **291** G4
Āīzawl, India, **219** H5
Aizenay, France, **290** D3
Aizpute, Latvia, **287** K4
Aizu-Wakamatsu, Japan, **209** G3
Aj Bogd Uul, *mountain peak*, Mongolia, **213** G3
Ajā, Egypt, **225** A4
Ajaccio, Corse, France, **295** B5
Ajaccio, Golfe d', *gulf*, Corse, France, **295** B5
Ajaigarh, India, **218** E4
Ajalpán, Mexico, **431** F5
Ajanta, India, **218** C5
Ajanta Range, *mountain range*,

India, **218** C5
Ajaria, *autonomous republic*, Georgia, **222** C4
Ajaureforsen, Sweden, **284** G4
Ajax, Mount, *mountain peak*, New Zealand, **133** D6
Ajdābiyā, Libya, **362** D2
Ajdovščina, Slovenia, **294** D3
Ajmah, Jabal al, *plateau*, Egypt, **225** B5
Ajmer, India, **218** C4
Ajnala, India, **218** C3
Ajo, U.S.A., **422** G5
Ak Dağ, *mountain peak*, Turkey, **297** F6
Ak Dağlar, *mountain range*, Turkey, **297** G7
Ak-Dovurak, Russian Federation, **223** N2
Ak-Shyyrak, Kyrgyzstan, **223** K4
Akabira, Japan, **209** H2
Akabli, Algeria, **361** G3
Āk'ak'ī Besek'a, Ethiopia, **367** E3
Akalkot, India, **216** D2
Akanthou, Cyprus, **225** B2
Akaroa, New Zealand, **133** D6
Akaroa Harbour, New Zealand, **133** D6
Akatora, Chaine de l', *mountain range*, Benin, **364** E2
Akbou, Algeria, **361** G1
Akbulak, Kazakhstan, **223** J3
Akçakale, Turkey, **224** E5
Akçay, Turkey, **297** G7
Akdağ, *mountain peak*, Turkey, **297** G6
Akelamo, Indonesia, **199** E2
Akeld, England, U.K., **306** F2
Aken, Germany, **288** F3
Åkersberga, Sweden, **287** J3
Akershus, *county*, Norway, **286** E3
Aketi, Democratic Republic of the Congo, **368** D2
Akhalts'ikhe, Georgia, **222** C4
Akhisar, Turkey, **224** C5
Akhmīm, Egypt, **363** F3
Akhnūr, India, **218** C2
Akhtubinsk, Russian Federation, **222** D3
Aki, Japan, **208** F4
Akiaki, *island*, French Polynesia, **137** H2
Akiéni, Gabon, **368** B3
Akima, *river*, Russian Federation, **210** G1
Akima, Russian Federation, **210** F1
Akimiski Island, Canada, **415** P5
Akita, Japan, **209** H3
Akjoujt, Mauritania, **360** D5
Akka, Morocco, **360** E3
Akkajaure, *lake*, Sweden, **284** H3
Akkavare, *mountain peak*, Sweden, **284** H3
'Akko (Acre), Israel, **225** C3
Aklampa, Benin, **365** E3
Aklavik, Canada, **410** F3
Aknīste, Latvia, **287** M4
Akodia, India, **218** D5
Akoke, Sudan, **366** D3
Akola, India, **218** D5
Akom II, Cameroon, **368** B2
Akonolinga, Cameroon, **368** B2
Āk'ordat, Eritrea, **367** E1
Akören, Turkey, **363** F1
Akot, India, **218** D5
Akot, Sudan, **366** D3
Akoupé, Côte d'Ivoire, **364** D3
Akpatok Island, Canada, **411** N3
Akqi, China, **212** C4
Akra Lithino, Greece, **362** D2
Akranes, Iceland, **284** X7
Akrathos, Akra, *point*, Greece, **297** E5
Åkrehamn, Norway, **286** B3
Akrérèb, Niger, **365** F1
Åkrestrømmen, Norway, **286** E2
Akron, Colorado, U.S.A., **423** M1
Akron, Ohio, U.S.A., **421** N5
Akrotiri, Cyprus, **225** B2
Aksai Chin, *disputed region*, China/India, **218** D2
Aksakal, Turkey, **297** G5
Aksakovo, Bulgaria, **296** F4
Aksaray, Turkey, **224** D5
Aksay, Kazakhstan, **222** E2
Akşehir, Turkey, **224** D5
Akşehir Gölü, *lake*, Turkey, **363** F1
Akseki, Turkey, **363** F1
Aksha, Russian Federation, **210** F2
Aksu, China, **212** D4
Aksu, Kazakhstan, **222** E4
Āksum, Ethiopia, **367** E2
Aktash, Russian Federation, **223** M2
Aktau *see* Aqtaū, W. Kazakhstan, **222** E4
Aktaz, China, **212** E5
Akto, China, **212** B5
Aktyubinsk *see* Aqtöbe, Kazakhstan, **222** F2
Akūbū, Sudan, **366** D3
Akulivik, Canada, **415** Q1
Akure, Nigeria, **365** F3
Akureyri, Iceland, **284** Y7
Akutikha, Russian Federation, **223** L2
Akwa Ibon, *state*, Nigeria, **365** F4
Akwanga, Nigeria, **365** F3
Akxokesay, China, **213** F5
Akyab *see* Sittwe, Myanmar, **205** B3
Al Abyār, Libya, **362** D2
Al Ajfar, Saudi Arabia, **363** H3
Al Akhḑar, Saudi Arabia, **225** D5
Al 'Alamayn, Egypt, **362** E2
Al 'Amārah, Iraq, **363** J2
Al 'Aqabah, Jordan, **225** C5
Al 'Aqīq, Saudi Arabia, **363** H4
Al 'Arīsh, Egypt, **225** B4
Al Artāwīyah, Saudi Arabia, **363** J3
Al 'Azīzīyah, Libya, **362** B2
Al Bāb, Syria, **225** D1
Al Bad', Saudi Arabia, **225** C5
Al Badī', Saudi Arabia, **363** J4
Al Baḩr Al Aḩmar, *state*, Sudan, **363** F5
Al Balyanā, Egypt, **363** F3
Al Bardī, Libya, **362** E2
Al Barun, Sudan, **366** D2
Al Başrah (Basra), Iraq, **363** J2
Al Batrūn, Lebanon, **225** C2
Al Bauga, Sudan, **363** F5
Al Bawīţī, Egypt, **362** E3
Al Bayḑā', Libya, **362** D2
Al Bayḑā', Yemen, **220** E6
Al Bi'ār, Saudi Arabia, **363** G4
Al Bi'r, Saudi Arabia, **225** D5
Al Birk, Saudi Arabia, **363** H5
Al Biyāḑ, *desert*, Saudi Arabia, **220** E4
Al Buḩayrat, *state*, Sudan, **366** C3
Al Bukayrīyah, Saudi Arabia, **363** H3
Al Burayj, Syria, **225** D2
Al Burmah, Tunisia, **362** A2
Al Buşayyah, Iraq, **363** J2
Al Fāshir, Sudan, **366** C2
Al Fashn, Egypt, **363** F3
Al Fayyūm, Egypt, **363** F3
Al Fāzah, Yemen, **220** D6
Al Firdān, Egypt, **225** B4
Al Fujayrah, United Arab Emirates, **221** G3
Al Fūlah, Sudan, **366** C2
Al Fuqahā', Libya, **362** C3
Al Ghayḑah, Yemen, **220** F5
Al Ghurdaqah, Egypt, **363** F3
Al Ḩadīthah, Iraq, **363** H2
Al Ḩadīthah, Saudi Arabia, **225** D4
Al Ḩamdānīyah, Syria, **225** D2
Al Ḩamīdīyah, Syria, **225** C2
Al Ḩāmmah, Tunisia, **362** A2
Al Ḩammām, Egypt, **362** E2
Al Ḩammāmāt, Tunisia, **295** C7
Al Ḩamrāt, Syria, **225** D2
Al Ḩāmūl, Egypt, **225** A4
Al Ḩanākīyah, Saudi Arabia, **363** H4
Al Ḩasā, Jordan, **225** C4
Al Ḩasakah, Syria, **363** H1
Al Ḩawātah, Sudan, **366** D2
Al Ḩawjā', Saudi Arabia, **363** G3
Al Ḩawţah, Yemen, **220** E5
Al Ḩayz, Egypt, **362** E3
Al Ḩazm, Saudi Arabia, **225** D5
Al Ḩibāk, *desert*, Saudi Arabia, **220** F5
Al Hijaz, *desert*, Saudi Arabia, **363** G3
Al Ḩillah, Iraq, **363** H2
Al Ḩillah, Sudan, **366** C2
Al Hirmil, Lebanon, **225** D2
Al Ḩişn, Jordan, **225** C3
Al Hoceima, Morocco, **361** F1
Al Ḩudaydah, Yemen, **220** D6
Al Hufūf, Saudi Arabia, **220** E3
Al Ḩumayḑah, Saudi Arabia, **225** C5
Al Ḩumayshah, Yemen, **220** E6
Al Īsāwīyah, Saudi Arabia, **225** D4
Al Iskandarīya (Alexandria), Egypt, **363** E2
Al Ismā'īlīyah (Ismailia), Egypt, **225** B4
Al Jafr, Jordan, **225** D4
Al Jaghbūb, Libya, **362** D3
Al Jahrā', Kuwait, **363** J3
Al Jamm, Tunisia, **362** B1
Al Jawf, Libya, **362** D4
Al Jawf, Saudi Arabia, **363** G3
Al Jazīrah, *state*, Sudan, **366** D2
Al Jithāmīyah, Saudi Arabia, **363** H3
Al Jīzah, Egypt, **225** A5
Al Jubayl, Saudi Arabia, **220** E3
Al Jumūm, Saudi Arabia, **363** G4
Al Junaynah, Sudan, **366** B2
Al Kahfah, Saudi Arabia, **363** H3
Al Kāmil, Oman, **221** G4
Al Kāmilīn, Sudan, **366** D1
Al Karīb, Tunisia, **295** B7
Al Karak, Jordan, **225** C4
Al Karnak, Egypt, **363** F3
Al Kāẓimīyah, Iraq, **363** H2
Al Khābūrah, Oman, **221** G4
Al Khalil (Hebron), West Bank, **225** C4
Al Khandaq, Sudan, **363** F5
Al Khānkah, Egypt, **225** A4
Al Khārijah, Egypt, **363** F3
Al Kharfah, Saudi Arabia, **363** J4
Al Kharj, Saudi Arabia, **220** E4
Al Khartūm, *state*, Sudan, **366** D1
Al Kharţūm (Khartoum), Sudan, **366** D1
Al Kharţūm Baḩr (Khartoum North), Sudan, **366** D1
Al Khaşab, Oman, **221** G3
Al Khawsh, Saudi Arabia, **363** H5
Al Khufrah, Libya, **362** D4
Al Khums, Libya, **362** B2
Al Kidan, *desert*, Saudi Arabia, **221** F4
Al Kiswah, Syria, **225** D3
Al Kūfah, Iraq, **363** H2
Al Kuntillah, Egypt, **225** C5
Al Kūt, Iraq, **363** J2
Al Kuwayt (Kuwait), Kuwait, **363** J3
Al Lādhiqīyah, *district*, Syria, **225** C2
Al Lādhiqīyah (Latakia), Syria, **225** C2
Al Lagowa, Sudan, **366** C2
Al Līth, Saudi Arabia, **363** H4
Al Madāfi', *plateau*, Saudi Arabia, **225** D5
Al Madīnah (Medina), Saudi Arabia, **363** G4
Al Mafraq, Jordan, **225** D3
Al Maḩalla al Kubrá, Egypt, **225** A4
Al Mahrah, *mountain range*, Yemen, **220** F5
Al Majma'ah, Saudi Arabia, **363** J3
Al Manāmah, Bahrain, **220** F3
Al Manāqil, Sudan, **366** D2
Al Manşūrah, Egypt, **225** A4
Al Manzil, Jordan, **225** D4
Al Manzilah, Egypt, **225** A4
Al Ma'qil, Iraq, **363** J2
Al Marāwi'ah, Yemen, **220** D6
Al Māriyah, Oman, **220** F4
Al Marj, Libya, **362** D2
Al Mawşil (Mosul), Iraq, **363** H1
Al Mayādīn, Syria, **363** H2
Al Mazār, Jordan, **225** C4
Al Mazra'ah, Jordan, **225** C4
Al Metlaoui, Tunisia, **362** A2
Al Minyā, Egypt, **363** F3
Al Mismīyah, Syria, **225** D3
Al Mubarraz, Saudi Arabia, **220** E3
Al Mudawwarah, Jordan, **225** C5
Al Muglad, Sudan, **366** C2
Al Mukallā, Yemen, **220** E6
Al Mukhā, Yemen, **220** D6
Al Munastīr, Tunisia, **362** B1
Al Muqdādīyah, Iraq, **363** H2
Al Musayjīd, Saudi Arabia, **363** G4
Al Muwayh, Saudi Arabia, **363** H4
Al Qa'āmīyāt, *physical feature*, Saudi Arabia, **367** G1
Al Qa'āmīyāt, *region*, Saudi Arabia, **220** E5
Al Qaḑārif, *state*, Sudan, **366** E2
Al Qaḑārif, Sudan, **366** E2
Al Qaḑīmah, Saudi Arabia, **363** G4
Al Qadmūs, Syria, **225** D2
Al Qāhirah (Cairo), Egypt, **225** A4
Al Qaḩmah, Saudi Arabia, **363** H5
Al Qā'īyah, Saudi Arabia, **363** H4
Al Qalībah, Saudi Arabia, **225** D5
Al Qāmishlī, Syria, **363** H1
Al Qanţarah, Egypt, **225** B4
Al Qaryatayn, Syria, **225** D2
Al Qaşabāt, Libya, **362** B2
Al Qaşr, Egypt, **362** E3
Al Qaşrayn, Tunisia, **362** A1
Al Qaţrānah, Jordan, **225** D4
Al Qaţrūn, Libya, **362** B4
Al Quşaymah, Egypt, **225** C4
Al Quşayr, Egypt, **363** F3
Al Quţaynah, Sudan, **366** D2
Al Quţayfah, Syria, **225** D3
Al Qunayţirah, *district*, Syria, **225** C3
Al Qunayţirah, Syria, **225** C3
Al Qunfudhah, Saudi Arabia, **363** H5
Al Qurayyāt, Saudi Arabia, **225** D4
Al Quwayrah, Jordan, **225** C5
Al Ţawţah, Yemen, **220** E6
Al Ubayyiḑ (El Obeid), Sudan, **366** D2
Al 'Ulā, Saudi Arabia, **363** G3
Al 'Ulayyah, Saudi Arabia, **363** H5
Al 'Umarī, Jordan, **225** D4
Al 'Uqaylah, Libya, **362** C2
Al Uqşur (Luxor), Egypt, **363** F3
Al 'Urayq, *desert*, Saudi Arabia, **363** G3
Al Uthaylī, Saudi Arabia, **225** D5
Al 'Uthmānīyah, Saudi Arabia, **220** E3
Al 'Uwaynāt, E. Libya, **362** D4
Al 'Uwaynāt, W. Libya, **362** B3
Al 'Uwayqīlah, Saudi Arabia, **363** H2
Al 'Uyūn, N. Saudi Arabia, **363** H3
Al 'Uyūn, W. Saudi Arabia, **363** G4
Al Wīgh, Libya, **362** B4
Al Waḩdah, *state*, Sudan, **366** C3
Al Wajh, Saudi Arabia, **363** G3
Al Wāsiţah, Egypt, **225** A5
Al Waslātīyah, Tunisia, **295** B8
Al Wazz, Sudan, **366** D2
Al Yamāmah, Saudi Arabia, **220** E4
Ala-Vuokki, Finland, **285** P4
Alabama, *river*, U.S.A., **425** J4
Alabama, *state*, U.S.A., **425** J3
Alabaster, U.S.A., **425** J3
Alaçam Dağları, *mountain range*, Turkey, **297** G6
Alachua, U.S.A., **425** L5
Aladdin, U.S.A., **419** M4
Alaejos, Spain, **292** E2
Alagoas, *state*, Brazil, **457** G2
Alagoinhas, Brazil, **457** F3
Alahärmä, Finland, **285** L5
Alajärvi, Finland, **285** L5
Alajuela, Costa Rica, **428** D5
Alaköl', *lake*, Kazakhstan, **212** D3
Alakurtti, Russian Federation, **285** Q3
Alalau, *river*, Brazil, **451** G4
Alamagan, *island*, Northern Mariana Islands, **138** C3
Ālamat'ā, Ethiopia, **367** E2
Alamdo, China, **214** E3
Alamo, U.S.A., **422** F3
Alamo Lake, U.S.A., **422** G4
Alamogordo, U.S.A., **423** L5
Alamos, Mexico, **430** C3
Alamosa, U.S.A., **423** L3
Åland *see* Ahvenanmaa, *island*, Finland, **287** J2
Åland *see* Ahvenanmaan Lääni, *province*, Finland, **287** J2
Alantika, Monts, *mountain range*, Cameroon, **365** G3
Alanya (Coracesium), Turkey, **225** A1
Alapaha, U.S.A., **425** L4
Alapayevsk, Russian Federation, **222** G1
Alarcón, Embalse de, *reservoir*, Spain, **293** F3
Alarcón, Spain, **293** F3
Alaşehir, Turkey, **297** G6
Alaska, Gulf of, U.S.A., **410** E4
Alaska, *state*, U.S.A., **410** D3
Alaska Peninsula, U.S.A., **410** C4
Alaska Range, *mountain range*, U.S.A., **410** D3
Alassio, Italy, **294** B4
Älät, Azerbaijan, **222** D5
Alatri, Italy, **295** D5
Alatyr', Russian Federation, **222** D2
Alausí, Ecuador, **450** B5
Alavieska, Finland, **285** M4
Alavus, Finland, **287** L1
'Alawīyīn, Jibāl al, *mountain range*, Syria, **225** D2
Alay kyrka, *mountain range*, Kyrgyzstan/Tajikistan, **212** B5
'Ālayh, Lebanon, **225** C3
Alazeya, *river*, Russian Federation, **301** S2
Alba, Italy, **294** A3
Alba, Mount, *mountain peak*, New Zealand, **133** B7
Alba Iulia, Romania, **296** D3
Albacete, Spain, **293** G3
Ålbæk, Denmark, **286** E4
Alban, Canada, **421** N2
Albanel, Lac, *lake*, Canada, **416** E4
Albania, *country*, Europe, **282** F7
Albany, Australia, **134** D5
Albany, Kentucky, U.S.A., **425** K4
Albany, New York, U.S.A., **426** D3
Albany, New Zealand, **132** E3
Albany, Oregon, U.S.A., **418** C4
Albany, *river*, Canada, **415** N6
Albany, Texas, U.S.A., **424** C3
Albarracín, Spain, **293** G2

Apucarana, Brazil, **459** G2
Apucarana, Serra da, *mountain range*, Brazil, **459** G2
Apurímac, *river*, Peru, **454** D4
Aqaba, Gulf of, Red Sea, **225** C5
Aqadyr, Kazakhstan, **223** J3
Aqal, China, **212** C4
Aqbalyq, Kazakhstan, **212** C3
Āqchah, Afghanistan, **218** A1
'Aqdā, Iran, **220** F2
Aqitag, *mountain peak*, China, **213** F4
Aqköl, Kazakhstan, **223** J4
Aqmola, *province*, Kazakhstan, **212** A2
Aqmola *see* Astana, Kazakhstan, **223** J2
Aqqikkol Hu, *lake*, China, **212** F5
Aqshataū, Kazakhstan, **212** B3
Aqsorang Biigi, *mountain peak*, Kazakhstan, **212** B2
Aqsū, Aqmola, Kazakhstan, **223** J2
Aqsu, Kazakhstan, **212** C1
Aqsū, Pavlodar, Kazakhstan, **223** K2
Aqsū-Ayuly, Kazakhstan, **212** B2
Aqsūat, Central Shyghys Qazaqstan, Kazakhstan, **212** D3
Aqsūat, E. Shyghys Qazaqstan, Kazakhstan, **212** D2
Aqtasty, Kazakhstan, **223** K2
Aqtaū, E. Kazakhstan, **223** J2
Aqtaū (Aktau), W. Kazakhstan, **222** E4
Aqtöbe (Aktyubinsk), Kazakhstan, **222** F2
Aqtoghay, Pavlodar, Kazakhstan, **223** K2
Aqtoghay, Qaraghandy, Kazakhstan, **223** J2
Aqtoghay, Shyghys Qazaqstan, Kazakhstan, **212** C3
Aquidabán, *river*, Paraguay, **459** F2
Aquidauana, Brazil, **456** B5
Aquidauana, *river*, Brazil, **456** B5
Aquila, Mexico, **430** E5
Aquiles Serdán, Mexico, **430** D2
Aquiraz, Brazil, **453** F4
Aquitaine, *administrative region*, France, **290** D4
Aqyrap, Kazakhstan, **222** F2
Aqzhar, Kazakhstan, **223** L3
Ar-Asgat, Mongolia, **210** D2
Ar Horqin Qi, China, **211** H4
Ar Radīsīya Baḥrī, Egypt, **363** F4
Ar Rahad, Sudan, **366** D2
Ar Rāk, Suquṭrá (Socotra), Yemen, **373** B2
Ar Ramādī, Iraq, **363** H2
Ar Ramlah, Jordan, **225** D5
Ar Ramthā, Jordan, **225** D3
Ar Rank, Sudan, **366** D2
Ar Raqqa, *district*, Syria, **225** E2
Ar Raqqah, Syria, **363** G1
Ar Rass, Saudi Arabia, **363** H3
Ar Rastan, Syria, **225** D2
Ar Rawḑatayn, Kuwait, **363** J3
Ar Riyāḑ (Riyadh), Saudi Arabia, **220** E4
Ar Ru'āt, Sudan, **366** D2
Ar Rub' al Khālī, *desert*, Saudi Arabia, **220** E5
Ar Rubay'īyah, Saudi Arabia, **363** H3
Ar Ruṣayfah, Jordan, **225** D4
Ar Ruṣayriṣ, Sudan, **366** D2
Ar Ruṭbah, Iraq, **363** H2
Ar Ruwaydah, Saudi Arabia, **220** E4
Ar Ruways, Oman, **220** F4
'Arab, Baḥr al, *river*, Sudan, **366** C2
Arab, U.S.A., **425** J2
'Arab al Mulk, Syria, **225** C2
Arabelo, Venezuela, **451** F3

Arabian Basin, *underwater feature*, Indian Ocean, **476** D3
Arabian Peninsula, Asia, **194** F7
Arabian Sea, Indian Ocean, **194** H8
Arabopó, Venezuela, **451** G3
Araçá, *river*, Brazil, **451** F4
Aracaju, Brazil, **457** G3
Aracati, Brazil, **453** G4
Aracatu, Brazil, **457** F4
Araçatuba, Brazil, **456** C5
Aracena, Spain, **292** D4
Aracena, Sierra de, *mountain peak*, Spain, **292** D4
Aracena, Sierra de, *mountain range*, Spain, **292** D4
Aracruz, Brazil, **457** F5
'Arad, Israel, **225** C4
Arad, Romania, **296** C2
Arada, Chad, **366** B2
Aradan, Russian Federation, **213** G1
Arafura Sea, Australia/Indonesia, **138** B5
Aragarças, Brazil, **456** C4
Aragats Lerr, *mountain peak*, Armenia, **222** C4
Aragón, *autonomous community*, Spain, **293** G2
Aragón, *river*, Spain, **293** G1
Aragua de Barcelona, Venezuela, **451** F2
Araguacema, Brazil, **456** D2
Araguaçu, Brazil, **456** D3
Araguaia, *river*, Brazil, **456** D2
Araguaína, Brazil, **452** D5
Araguao, Boca, *bay*, Venezuela, **451** G2
Araguari, Brazil, **456** D5
Araguari, *river*, Amapá, Brazil, **452** C3
Araguari, *river*, Minas Gerais, Brazil, **456** D5
Araguatins, Brazil, **452** D4
Araioses, Brazil, **453** E4
Arak, Algeria, **361** G3
Arāk, Iran, **220** E2
Arak, Syria, **225** E2
Arakan, *state*, Myanmar, **205** B4
Arakan Yoma, *mountain range*, Myanmar, **205** B3
Aral, China, **212** D4
Aral Sea, Kazakhstan/Uzbekistan, **222** F3
Aralköl, Kazakhstan, **222** G2
Aralqi, China, **212** E5
Aral'sk, Kazakhstan, **222** G3
Aralsor Köli, *lake*, Kazakhstan, **222** D3
Aramberri, Mexico, **431** F3
Aramia, *river*, Papua New Guinea, **140** A4
Ārān, Iran, **220** F2
Aran Fawddwy, *mountain peak*, Wales, U.K., **304** D2
Aran Island, Ireland, **309** D2
Aran Islands, Ireland, **309** C4
Aranda de Duero, Spain, **293** F2
Aranđelovac, Yugoslavia, **296** C3
Aranjuez, Spain, **293** F2
Aranos, Namibia, **370** C3
Aranyaprathet, Thailand, **202** D3
Arao, Japan, **208** E4
Araouane, Mali, **361** F5
Arapahoe, U.S.A., **420** D5
Arapey Grande, *river*, Uruguay, **459** F4
Arapiraca, Brazil, **457** G2
Arapis, Akra, *point*, Greece, **297** E5
Arapkir, Turkey, **224** E5
Arapongas, Brazil, **459** G2
Araputanga, Brazil, **455** G4
'Ar'ar, Saudi Arabia, **363** H2
Araracuara, Colombia, **450** D4
Araranguá, Brazil, **459** H3
Araraquara, Brazil, **456** D5
Araras, Brazil, **452** B5

Araras, Serra das, *mountain range*, Brazil, **459** G2
Ararat, Australia, **135** J6
Ararat, Mount *see* Ağri Daği, *mountain peak*, Turkey, **224** F4
Arari, Brazil, **453** E4
Araria, India, **219** F4
Araripe, Chapada do, *mountain range*, Brazil, **453** F5
Araripina, Brazil, **453** F5
Aras, *river*, Armenia/Azerbaijan/Iran, **363** J1
Arataca, Brazil, **457** F4
Arataua, *mountain peak*, New Zealand, **132** E4
Aratika, *island*, French Polynesia, **137** G3
Aratika, New Zealand, **133** C6
Arauca, Colombia, **451** D2
Arauca, *river*, Venezuela, **451** E2
Araucanía, *administrative region*, Chile, **458** B6
Arauco, Chile, **458** B5
Arauco, Golfo de, *gulf*, Chile, **458** B5
Arauquita, Colombia, **450** D2
Arāvalli Range, *mountain range*, India, **218** C4
Arawa, Papua New Guinea, **140** E2
Araxá, Brazil, **456** D5
Araxos, Akra, *cape*, Greece, **297** C6
Ärba Minch', Ethiopia, **367** E3
Arbīl, Iraq, **363** H1
Arboga, Sweden, **286** G3
Arborfield, Canada, **414** C5
Arborg, Canada, **414** F6
Arbrå, Sweden, **286** H2
Arbroath, Scotland, U.K., **308** G4
Arcachon, Bassin d', *inlet*, France, **290** D4
Arcachon, France, **290** D4
Arcadia, Florida, U.S.A., **425** M6
Arcadia, Louisiana, U.S.A., **424** F3
Arcata, U.S.A., **418** B6
Arcelia, Mexico, **431** E5
Arch Cape, U.S.A., **418** C4
Archer City, U.S.A., **424** C3
Arcidosso, Italy, **294** C4
Arco, U.S.A., **418** H5
Arcos, Brazil, **456** E5
Arcos de la Frontera, Spain, **292** E4
Arcoverde, Brazil, **453** G5
Arctic Bay, Canada, **411** L2
Arctic Ocean, **471** C4
Arḑ aş Şawwān, *plain*, Jordan, **225** D4
Ardabīl, Iran, **222** D5
Ardakān, Iran, **221** F2
Ardal, Iran, **363** K2
Årdalstangen, Norway, **286** C2
Ardara, Ireland, **309** D3
Ardatov, Russian Federation, **298** F1
Ardbeg, Canada, **421** N3
Ardee, Ireland, **309** F4
Ardennes, *region*, Belgium/France, **280** E6
Ardentes, France, **290** E3
Ardgay, Scotland, U.K., **308** E3
Ardglass, Northern Ireland, U.K., **309** G3
Ardino, Bulgaria, **297** E5
Ardlussa, Scotland, U.K., **308** D4
Ardminish, Scotland, U.K., **308** D5
Ardmore, Ireland, **309** E6
Ardmore, U.S.A., **424** D2
Ardnamurchan, Point of, Scotland, U.K., **308** C4
Ardres, France, **305** J4
Ardrishaig, Orkney, Scotland, U.K., **308** D4
Ardrossan, Scotland, U.K., **308** E5

Ards, *district*, Northern Ireland, U.K., **309** G3
Ards Peninsula, Northern Ireland, U.K., **309** G3
Ardud, Romania, **296** D2
Ardvasar, Scotland, U.K., **308** D3
Åre, Sweden, **284** F5
Areavaara, Sweden, **285** L3
Arebi, Democratic Republic of the Congo, **369** E2
Arecibo, Puerto Rico, **427** C2
Areia Branca, Brazil, **453** G4
Arena, Point, U.S.A., **422** A2
Arena, Punta, *point*, Mexico, **430** C4
Arenales, Cerro, *mountain peak*, Chile, **460** C3
Arenas, Punta de, *point*, Argentina, **460** D4
Arenas de San Pedro, Spain, **292** E2
Arendal, Norway, **286** D3
Arendsee, Germany, **288** E2
Areopoli, Greece, **297** D7
Arequipa, Peru, **454** D4
Arere, Brazil, **452** C3
Arès, France, **290** D4
Arévalo, Spain, **292** E2
Arezzo, Italy, **294** C4
Arga, *river*, Spain, **293** G1
Argalasti, Greece, **297** D6
Argan, China, **212** F4
Argan, China, **223** M4
Argatay, Mongolia, **210** D3
Argens, *river*, France, **291** H5
Argenta, Italy, **294** C3
Argentan, France, **290** D2
Argentina, Argentina, **458** D3
Argentina, *country*, South America, **448** F7
Argentine Plain, *underwater feature*, Atlantic Ocean, **477** D8
Argentino, Lago, *lake*, Argentina, **460** C4
Argentino, *river*, Argentina, **460** C4
Argenton-sur-Creuse, France, **290** E3
Argeş, *river*, Romania, **296** E3
Arghandāb, *river*, Afghanistan, **218** A2
Arghastān, *river*, Afghanistan, **218** A3
Argolikos Kolpos, *bay*, Greece, **297** D7
Argopuro, Gunung, *mountain peak*, Indonesia, **201** F4
Argos, Greece, **297** D7
Argos Orestiko, Greece, **297** C5
Argostoli, Ionioi Nisoi, Greece, **297** C6
Argueil, France, **305** J5
Arguello, Point, U.S.A., **422** C4
Argun', *river*, Russian Federation, **211** H1
Argungu, Nigeria, **365** E2
Arguut, Mongolia, **213** J3
Argyle, Canada, **416** J8
Argyle, Lake, Australia, **134** F2
Argyll, *region*, Scotland, U.K., **308** D4
Argyll and Bute, *local authority*, Scotland, U.K., **308** D4
Arhangay, *province*, Mongolia, **213** J3
Århus, Denmark, **286** E4
Arhust, Mongolia, **210** D3
Ari Atoll, Maldives, **216** C5
Aria, *river*, Papua New Guinea, **140** C4
Ariamsvlei, Namibia, **370** C4
Ariano Irpino, Italy, **295** E5
Arias, Argentina, **458** D4
Ariaú, Brazil, **452** B4
Aribinda, Burkina Faso, **364** D2
Arica, Chile, **455** D5
Arica, Colombia, **450** D5
Arica, Peru, **450** C4

Arichat, Canada, **417** L7
Arid, Cape, Australia, **134** E5
Aride, *island*, Seychelles, **373** A2
Ariguani, *river*, Colombia, **450** C1
Arīhā (Jericho), West Bank, **225** C4
Ariki, New Zealand, **133** D5
Arilje, Yugoslavia, **296** C4
Arima, Trinidad, Trinidad and Tobago, **461** C4
Arimo, U.S.A., **419** H5
Arinos, Brazil, **456** D4
Arinos, *river*, Brazil, **456** B3
Ario de Rosales, Mexico, **430** E5
Aripuanã, Brazil, **455** G2
Aripuanã, *river*, Brazil, **455** G2
Ariquemes, Brazil, **455** F2
Arisaig, Scotland, U.K., **308** D4
Arisaig, Sound of, Scotland, U.K., **308** D4
Aristazabal Island, Canada, **412** D5
Aritzo, Sardegna, Italy, **295** B6
Ariza, Spain, **293** F2
Arizaro, Salar de, *salt-pan*, Argentina, **458** C2
Arizona, *state*, U.S.A., **423** H4
Ärjäng, Sweden, **286** F3
Arjeplog, Sweden, **284** H3
Arjona, Colombia, **450** C1
Arkadelphia, U.S.A., **424** F2
Arkanū, Jabal, *mountain peak*, Libya, **362** D4
Arkansas, *river*, U.S.A., **407** M5
Arkansas, *state*, U.S.A., **424** F2
Arkansas City, U.S.A., **420** E7
Arkatag Shan, *mountain range*, China, **212** F5
Arkhangel'sk, Russian Federation, **300** F3
Arkhangel'skaya Oblast', *province*, Russian Federation, **299** G2
Arkhangel'skoye, Russian Federation, **222** F2
Arkhara, Russian Federation, **211** K2
Arkhipovka, Russian Federation, **299** C5
Arklow, Ireland, **309** F5
Arkona, Kap, *cape*, Germany, **288** F1
Arkonam, India, **216** D3
Arkösund, Sweden, **287** H3
Arlan, *mountain peak*, Turkmenistan, **222** E5
Arlee, U.S.A., **418** G3
Arles, France, **291** G5
Arli, Burkina Faso, **364** E2
Arlington, Colorado, U.S.A., **423** M2
Arlington, Georgia, U.S.A., **425** K4
Arlington, Texas, U.S.A., **424** D3
Arlington, Virginia, U.S.A., **426** B5
Arlit, Niger, **361** H5
Arlon, Belgium, **288** B4
Armagh, *district*, Northern Ireland, U.K., **309** F3
Armagh, Northern Ireland, U.K., **309** F3
Armagnac, *region*, France, **290** E5
Armant, Egypt, **363** F3
Armathia, *island*, Greece, **297** F8
Armavir, Russian Federation, **222** C3
Armenia, Colombia, **450** C3
Armenia, *country*, Asia, **196** F5
Armero, Colombia, **450** C3
Armidale, Australia, **135** L5
Armour, U.S.A., **420** D4
Armoy, Northern Ireland, U.K., **309** F2
Armstrong, British Columbia, Canada, **413** K6
Armstrong, Ontario, Canada, **415** K6
Armstrong, U.S.A., **424** D6

Balifondo, Central African Republic, 368 D1
Balige, Indonesia, 200 B2
Baliguda, India, 219 E5
Balıkesir, *province*, Turkey, 297 F6
Balıkesir, Turkey, 297 F6
Balıklıçeşme, Turkey, 297 F5
Balikpapan, Indonesia, 201 G3
Balimbing, Indonesia, 200 D4
Balimo, Papua New Guinea, 140 A5
Balingasag, Philippines, 204 D4
Balingen, Germany, 288 D4
Balingoan, Philippines, 204 D4
Balintore, Scotland, U.K., 308 F3
Balj, *river*, Mongolia, 210 E2
Baljurashi, Saudi Arabia, 363 H5
Balkan Peninsula, Europe, 102 C4
Balkashīno, Kazakhstan, 223 H2
Balkon-Myl'k, Gora, *mountain peak*, Russian Federation, 285 T2
Ballālpur, India, 218 D6
Ballachulish, Scotland, U.K., 308 D4
Balladonia, Australia, 134 E5
Ballaghaderreen, Ireland, 309 D4
Ballangen, Norway, 284 H2
Ballantrae, Scotland, U.K., 308 D5
Ballarat, Australia, 135 J6
Ballard, Lake, Australia, 134 E4
Ballater, Scotland, U.K., 308 F3
Ballenas, Bahía, *bay*, Mexico, 430 B3
Balleny Islands, Antarctica, 470 E8
Ballina, Australia, 135 L4
Ballina, Ireland, 309 C3
Ballinafad, Ireland, 309 D3
Ballinalack, Ireland, 309 E4
Ballinamore, Ireland, 309 E3
Ballinasloe, Ireland, 309 D4
Ballindine, Ireland, 309 D4
Ballinger, U.S.A., 424 C4
Ballinluig, Scotland, U.K., 308 F4
Ballinrobe, Ireland, 309 C4
Ballon, Ireland, 309 F5
Ball's Pyramid, Lord Howe Island, Australia, 135 U14
Ballstad, Norway, 284 F2
Ballybay, Ireland, 309 F3
Ballybofey, Ireland, 309 E3
Ballybunnion, Ireland, 309 C5
Ballycanew, Ireland, 309 F5
Ballycastle, Ireland, 309 C3
Ballycastle, Northern Ireland, U.K., 309 F2
Ballyclare, Northern Ireland, U.K., 309 G3
Ballycroy, Ireland, 309 C3
Ballydesmond, Ireland, 309 C5
Ballyford Head, *point*, Ireland, 309 B4
Ballygar, Ireland, 309 D4
Ballygawley, Northern Ireland, U.K., 309 E3
Ballyhale, Ireland, 309 E5
Ballyheige, Ireland, 309 C5
Ballyheige Bay, Ireland, 309 B5
Ballyhoura Mountains, Ireland, 309 D5
Ballyjamesduff, Ireland, 309 E4
Ballykelly, Northern Ireland, U.K., 309 E2
Ballylynan, Ireland, 309 E5
Ballymacarbry, Ireland, 309 E5
Ballymahon, Ireland, 309 E4
Ballymena, *district*, Northern Ireland, U.K., 309 F3
Ballymena, Northern Ireland, U.K., 309 F3
Ballymoney, *district*, Northern Ireland, U.K., 309 F2
Ballymoney, Northern Ireland, U.K., 309 F2
Ballymote, Ireland, 309 D3

Ballymurphy, Ireland, 309 F5
Ballynahinch, Northern Ireland, U.K., 309 G3
Ballyragget, Ireland, 309 E5
Ballyshannon, Ireland, 309 D3
Ballyteige Bay, Ireland, 309 F5
Ballyvaughan, Ireland, 309 C4
Ballyvourney, Ireland, 309 C6
Balmaceda, Chile, 460 C2
Balmaceda, Sierra, *mountain range*, Argentina, 460 C4
Balmazújvaros, Hungary, 289 K5
Balmertown, Canada, 414 H6
Balmorhea, U.S.A., 423 M6
Balnakeil Bay, Scotland, U.K., 308 E2
Balnapaling, Scotland, U.K., 308 E3
Baloda Bāzār, India, 219 E5
Balombo, Angola, 368 B5
Balonne, *river*, Australia, 135 K4
Bālotra, India, 218 C4
Balqash, Kazakhstan, 212 B3
Balqash Köli, *lake*, Kazakhstan, 212 C3
Balquhidder, Scotland, U.K., 308 E4
Balranald, Australia, 135 J5
Balş, Romania, 296 E3
Balsas, Brazil, 452 D5
Balsas, das, *river*, Brazil, 456 D2
Balsas, Mexico, 431 F5
Balsas, *river*, Mexico, 431 F5
Balta, Ukraine, 296 G2
Balta Berilovac, Yugoslavia, 296 D4
Baltasound, Scotland, U.K., 308 L7
Bălţi, Moldova, 296 F2
Baltic Sea, Europe, 287 J4
Balţīm, Egypt, 225 A4
Baltimore, U.S.A., 426 B5
Baltinglass, Ireland, 309 F5
Baltiysk, Russian Federation, 287 J5
Baluchistān, *province*, Pakistan, 218 A3
Balud, Philippines, 204 C3
Bālurghāt, India, 219 G4
Balvatnet, *lake*, Norway, 284 G3
Balvi, Latvia, 287 N4
Balya, Turkey, 297 F6
Balykchy, Kyrgyzstan, 212 C4
Balyktyg-Khem, *river*, Russian Federation, 213 H2
Balyn, Ukraine, 296 F1
Balzar, Ecuador, 450 B4
Bam, Iran, 221 G3
Bama, China, 215 H4
Bamaga, Australia, 135 J1
Bamako, Mali, 364 C2
Bamba, Mali, 364 D1
Bambama, Congo, 368 B3
Bambamarca, Peru, 454 B2
Bambangando, Angola, 368 D6
Bambari, Central African Republic, 368 D1
Bamberg, Germany, 288 E4
Bamberg, U.S.A., 425 M3
Bambesa, Democratic Republic of the Congo, 369 E2
Bambey, Senegal, 364 A2
Bambili, Democratic Republic of the Congo, 369 E2
Bambio, Central African Republic, 368 C2
Bamboesberg, *mountain peak*, South Africa, 371 E5
Bambouti, Central African Republic, 369 E1
Bambudi, Ethiopia, 366 E2
Bambuí, Brazil, 456 E5
Bamburgh, England, U.K., 307 G2
Bamda, China, 215 F3
Bamenda, Cameroon, 368 B1
Bāmiān, Afghanistan, 218 A2
Bamiancheng, China, 211 H4

Bamingui, Central African Republic, 366 B3
Bamingui, *river*, Central African Republic, 366 A3
Bamingui-Bangoran, Central African Republic, 366 A3
Bâmnák, Cambodia, 203 E3
Bampton, Devon, England, U.K., 304 D4
Bampton, Oxfordshire, England, U.K., 305 F3
Bampūr, Iran, 221 H3
Bampūr, *river*, Iran, 221 G3
Bamy, Turkmenistan, 222 F5
Ban Ban, Laos, 203 D2
Ban Boun Tai, Laos, 202 D1
Ban Don, Ao, *bay*, Thailand, 202 C4
Ban Hangdon, Laos, 203 E3
Ban Hat Lek, Thailand, 203 D4
Ban Huai Yang, Thailand, 202 C4
Ban Khao Sai, Thailand, 202 D2
Ban Khok Kloi, Thailand, 202 C4
Ban Muong, Laos, 203 E2
Ban Na San, Thailand, 202 C4
Ban Nalè, Laos, 202 D2
Ban Nambak, Laos, 203 D1
Ban Napè, Laos, 203 E2
Ban Nongsim, Laos, 203 E3
Ban Pak Pat, Thailand, 202 D2
Ban Phai, Thailand, 203 D2
Ban Phon, Laos, 203 E3
Ban Phônkho, Laos, 203 E2
Ban Phu, Thailand, 202 D2
Ban Rai, Thailand, 202 C3
Ban Thabôk, Laos, 203 D2
Ban Vang-An, Laos, 203 D2
Banaadir, *administrative region*, Somalia, 367 G4
Banaba (Ocean), *island*, Kiribati, 139 F5
Banagher, Ireland, 309 E4
Banalia, Democratic Republic of the Congo, 369 E2
Banamba, Mali, 364 C2
Banana, Andaman and Nicobar Islands, India, 217 H5
Banarlı, Turkey, 297 F5
Banās, Ra's, *point*, Egypt, 363 G4
Banās, *river*, India, 218 D4
Banaue, Philippines, 204 C2
Banaz, Turkey, 297 G6
Banbar, China, 215 E3
Banbridge, *district*, Northern Ireland, U.K., 309 F3
Banbridge, Northern Ireland, U.K., 309 F3
Banbury, England, U.K., 305 F2
Banchory, Scotland, U.K., 308 G3
Bancroft, Canada, 416 C7
Bancroft, U.S.A., 420 E5
Banda, Cameroon, 365 G3
Banda, Democratic Republic of the Congo, 369 E2
Bānda, India, 218 E4
Banda Aceh, Indonesia, 200 A1
Banda Elat, Indonesia, 199 F4
Banda Sea, Indonesia, 198 D4
Bandahara, Gunung, *mountain peak*, Indonesia, 200 B2
Bandajuma, Sierra Leone, 364 B3
Bandar, Mozambique, 369 F6
Bandar-e 'Abbās, Iran, 221 G3
Bandar-e Anzalī, Iran, 222 D5
Bandar-e Khomeynī, Iran, 363 J2
Bandar-e Lengeh, Iran, 221 F3
Bandar Seri Begawan, Brunei, 201 F1
Bandar Sri Aman (Simanggang), Malaysia, 201 E2
Bandar Wanaag, Somalia, 367 F3
Bandarbeyla, Somalia, 367 H3
Bandarlampung, Indonesia, 200 D4
Bandeirante, Brazil, 456 C3
Bandera, Argentina, 458 D3
Bandera, U.S.A., 424 C5

Banderas, Mexico, 430 D2
Bāndhi, Pakistan, 218 B4
Bandiagara, Mali, 364 D2
Bāndīkŭi, India, 218 D4
Bandipura, India, 218 C2
Bandırma, Turkey, 297 F5
Bandon, Ireland, 309 D6
Bandon, *river*, Ireland, 309 D6
Bandon, U.S.A., 418 B5
Bandundu, *administrative region*, Democratic Republic of the Congo, 368 C3
Bandundu, Democratic Republic of the Congo, 368 C3
Bandung, Indonesia, 201 D4
Băneasa, Romania, 296 F3
Banes, Cuba, 429 G2
Banff, Canada, 413 M6
Banff, Scotland, U.K., 308 G3
Banfora, Burkina Faso, 364 D2
Banfu, China, 207 A4
Banga, Democratic Republic of the Congo, 368 D4
Bangalore, India, 216 D3
Bangangté, Cameroon, 368 B1
Bangassou, Central African Republic, 368 D2
Bangeta, Mount, *mountain peak*, Papua New Guinea, 140 B4
Banggai, Kepulauan, *islands*, Indonesia, 198 C3
Banggi, Pulau, *island*, Malaysia, 201 G1
Banghāzī, Libya, 362 D2
Banghiang, *river*, Laos, 203 E2
Bangka, Pulau, *island*, Sulawesi Utara, Indonesia, 198 D2
Bangka, Pulau, *island*, Sumatera Selatan, Indonesia, 200 D3
Bangka, Selat, *strait*, Indonesia, 200 D3
Bangkai, Tanjong, *point*, Indonesia, 201 E2
Bangkalan, Indonesia, 201 F4
Bangkaru, Pulau, *island*, Indonesia, 200 B2
Bangkinang, Indonesia, 200 C2
Bangko, Indonesia, 200 C3
Bangkok, Bight of, *bay*, Thailand, 202 D3
Bangkok *see* Krung Thep, Thailand, 202 D3
Bangladesh, *country*, Asia, 196 K7
Bangolo, Côte d'Ivoire, 364 C3
Bangor, Northern Ireland, U.K., 309 G3
Bangor, U.S.A., 426 F2
Bangor, Wales, U.K., 304 C1
Bangor Erris, Ireland, 309 C3
Bangs, Mount, *mountain peak*, U.S.A., 422 G3
Bangued, Philippines, 204 C2
Bangui, Central African Republic, 368 C2
Bangui, Philippines, 204 C2
Bangui-Motaba, Congo, 368 C2
Banguru, Democratic Republic of the Congo, 369 E2
Bangweulu, Lake, Zambia, 369 F5
Banhã, Egypt, 225 A4
Bani, Burkina Faso, 364 D2
Bani, Central African Republic, 366 B3
Bani Bangou, Niger, 365 E1
Banī Mazār, Egypt, 363 F3
Banī Suwayf, Egypt, 225 A5
Banī Thawr, Saudi Arabia, 363 H5
Banī Walīd, Libya, 362 B2
Bania, Central African Republic, 368 C2
Baniara, Papua New Guinea, 140 C5
Banija, *mountain range*, Bosnia and Herzegovina, 294 F3
Banikoara, Benin, 365 E2
Bāniyās, Al Qunayţirah, Syria, 225 C3

Bāniyās, Ţarţūs, Syria, 225 C2
Banja Luka, Bosnia and Herzegovina, 294 F3
Banjarmasin, Indonesia, 201 F3
Banjul, Gambia, 364 A2
Bānka, India, 219 F4
Bankass, Mali, 364 D2
Bankeryd, Sweden, 286 G4
Bankilaré, Niger, 364 E2
Banko, Guinea, 364 B2
Banks, Bahía, *bay*, Islas Galápagos (Galapagos Islands), Ecuador, 461 A1
Banks, U.S.A., 418 F4
Banks Island, British Columbia, Canada, 412 D5
Banks Island, Northwest Territories, Canada, 410 G2
Banks Islands, Vanuatu, 141 A2
Banks Lake, U.S.A., 418 E3
Banks Peninsula, New Zealand, 133 D6
Banksá Bystrica, Slovakia, 289 J4
Bānkura, India, 219 F5
Banli, China, 215 H5
Bann, *river*, Northern Ireland, U.K., 309 F2
Bannerman Town, Bahamas, 428 F1
Banning, U.S.A., 422 E5
Bannockburn, Scotland, U.K., 308 F4
Bannu, Pakistan, 218 B2
Banovići, Bosnia and Herzegovina, 294 G3
Banqiao, China, 215 H4
Bansko, Bulgaria, 296 D5
Banskobystrický, *administrative region*, Slovakia, 289 J4
Bānswāra, India, 218 C5
Bantayan, Philippines, 204 C4
Bantè, Benin, 365 E3
Banteer, Ireland, 309 D5
Bantry, Ireland, 309 C6
Bantry Bay, Ireland, 309 C6
Bāntva, India, 218 B5
Bantvāl, India, 216 C3
Banyalbufar, Spain, 293 J3
Banyo, Cameroon, 365 G3
Banyoles, Spain, 293 J1
Banyuwangi, Indonesia, 201 F5
Banz, Papua New Guinea, 140 B4
Banzare Coast, *region*, Antarctica, 470 F7
Banzart, Tunisia, 295 B7
Bảo Lộc, Vietnam, 203 E4
Baoan, China, 207 B3
Baode, China, 210 E5
Baodi, China, 210 G5
Baoding, China, 210 F5
Baoji, China, 215 H2
Baojing, China, 206 B2
Baolo, Solomon Islands, 141 A1
Baoqing, China, 211 L3
Baoro, Central African Republic, 368 C1
Baoshan, China, 215 F4
Baotou, China, 210 E4
Baoxia, China, 206 B1
Baoyi, China, 206 D1
Baoying, China, 206 D1
Bāp, India, 218 C4
Bapaume, France, 291 F1
Baqanas, Kazakhstan, 212 C3
Baqanas, *river*, Kazakhstan, 212 C3
Ba'qūbah, Iraq, 363 H2
Baquedano, Chile, 458 C2
Bar, Yugoslavia, 296 B4
Bar Harbor, U.S.A., 426 F2
Bar-le-Duc, France, 291 G2
Bar-sur-Aube, France, 291 G2
Bar-sur-Seine, France, 291 G2
Bara, Indonesia, 198 D3
Bara, Nigeria, 365 G2
Bāra Banki, India, 218 E4
Baraawe, Somalia, 367 F4
Barabinsk, Russian Federation, 223 K1
Barachois, Canada, 417 J5

Baracoa, Cuba, **429** G2
Baradero, Argentina, **459** E4
Baragua, Venezuela, **451** D1
Bārah, Sudan, **366** D2
Barahona, Dominican Republic, **429** H3
Barakī, Afganistan, **218** B2
Barakaldo, Spain, **293** F1
Bārākot, India, **219** F5
Baralzon Lake, Canada, **414** E2
Baram, *river*, Malaysia, **201** F2
Baram, Tanjong, *point*, Malaysia, **201** F1
Barama, *river*, Guyana, **451** G2
Baramanni, Guyana, **451** G2
Bārāmati, India, **216** C2
Bārāmūla, India, **218** C2
Baranavichy, Belarus, **298** C2
Baranoa, Colombia, **450** C1
Baranof, U.S.A., **412** B3
Baranof Island, U.S.A., **412** B3
Barão de Melgaço, Brazil, **456** B4
Baraolt, Romania, **296** E2
Barate, Indonesia, **198** C5
Baraya, Colombia, **450** C3
Barbacena, Brazil, **457** E5
Barbacoas, Colombia, **450** B4
Barbadillo, Spain, **292** E2
Barbados, *country*, Caribbean Sea, **427** E3
Barbar, Sudan, **363** F5
Barbas, Cabo, *cape*, Western Sahara, **360** C4
Barbastro, Spain, **293** H1
Barbate de Franco, Spain, **292** D4
Bărbătești, Romania, **296** D3
Barber, Curaçao, Netherlands Antilles, **461** C3
Barberton, South Africa, **371** F4
Barbezieux-Saint-Hilaire, France, **290** D4
Barbosa, Colombia, **450** D2
Barbuda, *island*, Antigua and Barbuda, **427** D2
Bârca, Romania, **296** D4
Barcadera, Aruba, **461** B3
Barcaldine, Australia, **135** K3
Barcarrota, Spain, **292** D3
Barcelona, Spain, **293** J2
Barcelona, Venezuela, **451** F1
Barcelonnette, France, **291** H4
Barcelos, Brazil, **451** F4
Barciany, Poland, **289** K1
Barcoo, *river*, Australia, **135** J3
Barcs, Hungary, **289** H5
Bärdä, Azerbaijan, **222** D4
Bardaï, Chad, **362** C4
Bardarban, Bangladesh, **219** H5
Bárðarbunga, *mountain peak*, Iceland, **284** Y7
Bardas Blancas, Argentina, **458** C5
Bardawīl, Sabkhat al, *lagoon*, Egypt, **225** B4
Barddhamān, India, **219** F5
Bardejov, Slovakia, **289** K4
Bardney, England, U.K., **305** G1
Bardsey Island, Wales, U.K., **304** C2
Bardsey Sound, Wales, U.K., **304** C2
Bardstown, U.S.A., **421** L7
Bareilly, India, **218** D3
Barentin, France, **290** E2
Barents Sea, Arctic Ocean, **300** E2
Barentsøya, *island*, Svalbard, **300** D2
Barentu, Eritrea, **367** E1
Barfleur, France, **305** F5
Barfleur, Pointe de, *point*, France, **290** D2
Barga, China, **214** B3
Barga, Italy, **294** C3
Bargaal, Somalia, **367** H2
Bargarh, India, **219** F5
Bargrennan, Scotland, U.K., **308** E5
Barham, England, U.K., **305** J3
Bari, *administrative region*, Somalia, **367** G3
Bari, Democratic Republic of the Congo, **368** C2
Bari, Italy, **295** F5
Bari Sādri, India, **218** C4
Barīdī, Ra's, *point*, Saudi Arabia, **363** G4
Barika, Algeria, **361** H1
Barṯkowṯ, Afghanistan, **218** B2
Barillas, Guatemala, **428** C4
Barinas, Venezuela, **451** D2
Baring, Cape, Canada, **410** H2
Baringa, Democratic Republic of the Congo, **368** D2
Bārīs, Egypt, **363** F4
Barisāl, Bangladesh, **214** D5
Barisan, Pegunungan, *mountain range*, Indonesia, **200** C3
Barito, *river*, Indonesia, **201** F3
Barkam, China, **215** G3
Barkava, Latvia, **287** N4
Barkerville, Canada, **412** J5
Bārkhān, Pakistan, **218** B3
Barki Saria, India, **219** F4
Barkley Sound, Canada, **412** G7
Barkly East, South Africa, **371** E5
Barkly Homestead Roadhouse, Australia, **135** H2
Barkly Tableland, *plateau*, Australia, **135** H2
Barkly West, South Africa, **370** D4
Barkol, China, **213** G4
Barkol Hu, *lake*, China, **213** G4
Barksdale, U.S.A., **424** B5
Barkway, England, U.K., **305** H3
Bârlad, Romania, **296** F2
Barlee, Lake, Australia, **134** D4
Barletta, Italy, **295** F5
Barley, England, U.K., **305** H2
Barlinek, Poland, **289** G2
Bārmer, India, **218** B4
Barmouth, Wales, U.K., **304** C2
Barmouth Bay, Wales, U.K., **304** C2
Barn, The, *mountain peak*, St Helena, **373** B3
Barn Long Point, St Helena, **373** B3
Barnagar, India, **218** C5
Barnard Castle, England, U.K., **307** G3
Barnaul, Russian Federation, **223** L2
Barnesville, U.S.A., **420** E2
Barnet, England, U.K., **305** G3
Barneville-Carteret, France, **290** D2
Barney, U.S.A., **425** L4
Barnhart, U.S.A., **424** B4
Barnoldswick, England, U.K., **306** F4
Barnsley, England, U.K., **307** G4
Barnstaple, England, U.K., **304** C3
Barnwell, U.S.A., **425** M3
Baro, *river*, Ethiopia, **366** D3
Baroda, India, **218** D4
Barques, Pointe Aux, *point*, U.S.A., **421** M3
Barquisimeto, Venezuela, **451** E1
Barra, Brazil, **457** E3
Barra, *island*, Scotland, U.K., **308** B4
Barra, Ponta da, *island*, Mozambique, **371** G3
Barra, Sound of, Scotland, U.K., **308** B3
Barra de Caratasca, Honduras, **428** E4
Barra de São Manuel, Brazil, **452** A5
Barra do Bugres, Brazil, **456** B4
Barra do Corda, Brazil, **452** E4
Barra do Cuanza, Angola, **368** B4
Barra do Dande, Angola, **368** B4
Barra do Garças, Brazil, **456** C4
Barra do Riacho, Brazil, **457** F5
Barra do Ribeiro, Brazil, **459** G4
Barra Falsa, Ponta da, *island*, Mozambique, **371** G3
Barra Mansa, Brazil, **457** E6
Barraca da Bôca, Brazil, **452** C3
Barracão do Barreto, Brazil, **455** G2
Barranca, Central Peru, **454** C3
Barranca, N. Peru, **454** C1
Barrancabermeja, Colombia, **450** C2
Barrancas, Colombia, **450** D1
Barrancas, Venezuela, **451** F2
Barrancos, Portugal, **292** D3
Barranqueras, Argentina, **459** E3
Barranquilla, Colombia, **450** C1
Barranquitas, Venezuela, **450** D2
Barras, Brazil, **453** E4
Barraute, Canada, **416** C5
Barrax, Spain, **293** F3
Barreal, Argentina, **458** C4
Barreiras, Brazil, **457** E3
Barreirinha, Brazil, **452** B4
Barreirinhas, Brazil, **453** E4
Barreiro do Nascimento, Brazil, **456** C3
Barreiros, Brazil, **457** G2
Barretos, Brazil, **456** D5
Barrhead, Canada, **413** M4
Barrhead, Scotland, U.K., **308** E5
Barrie, Canada, **421** P3
Barrier, Cape, New Zealand, **132** E3
Barrington, Mount, *mountain peak*, Australia, **135** L5
Barringun, Australia, **135** K4
Barrocão, Brazil, **457** E4
Barron, U.S.A., **420** H3
Barrow, Point, U.S.A., **410** D2
Barrow, U.S.A., **410** D2
Barrow-in-Furness, England, U.K., **306** E3
Barrow Island, Australia, **134** D3
Barry, Wales, U.K., **304** D3
Barrys Bay, Canada, **416** C7
Bârsana, Romania, **296** E2
Barsanikha, Russian Federation, **299** E3
Barshatas, Kazakhstan, **212** C2
Barshyn, Kazakhstan, **212** A2
Bārsi, India, **216** C2
Barstow, U.S.A., **422** E4
Bārta, Latvia, **287** K4
Bārta, *river*, Latvia/Lithuania, **287** K4
Barth, Germany, **288** F1
Bartica, Guyana, **451** G2
Bartle Frere, *mountain peak*, Australia, **135** K2
Bartlesville, U.S.A., **420** F7
Bartlett, U.S.A., **423** M3
Bartolomeu Dias, Mozambique, **371** G3
Barton, U.S.A., **426** D2
Barton-upon-Humber, England, U.K., **307** H4
Bartoszyce, Poland, **289** K1
Bartow, U.S.A., **425** M6
Baru, Irian Jaya, Indonesia, **199** F3
Baru, Maluku, Indonesia, **198** D2
Barú, Volcán, *mountain peak*, Panama, **429** E5
Barun, China, **213** H5
Barun-Torey, Ozero, *lake*, Russian Federation, **210** F2
Barung, Indonesia, **201** G2
Barus, Indonesia, **200** B2
Baruta, Venezuela, **451** E1
Baruth, Germany, **288** F2
Baruun-Urt, Mongolia, **210** F3
Baruunharaa, Mongolia, **210** D2
Baruunturuun, Mongolia, **213** G2
Barvas, Scotland, U.K., **308** C2
Barwāni, India, **218** C5
Barwon, *river*, Australia, **135** K4
Baryatino, Russian Federation, **299** E5
Barycz, *river*, Poland, **289** H3
Barysaw, Belarus, **299** B5
Barysh, Russian Federation, **222** D2
Bas-Zaïre, *province*, Democratic Republic of the Congo, **368** B4
Basail, Argentina, **459** E3
Bậsắk, *river*, Cambodia, **203** E4
Basakan, Gunung, *mountain peak*, Indonesia, **201** G2
Basāl, Pakistan, **218** C2
Basalt, U.S.A., **422** D2
Basalt Island, China, **207** C4
Basankusu, Democratic Republic of the Congo, **368** C2
Basarabeasca, Moldova, **296** G2
Basarabi, Romania, **296** G3
Baschurch, England, U.K., **304** E2
Basco, Philippines, **204** C1
Bascuñán, Cabo, *cape*, Chile, **458** B3
Basel, Switzerland, **291** H3
Bashi Channel, China, **206** E4
Bashkaus, *river*, Russian Federation, **212** F2
Bashkortostan, Respublika, *republic*, Russian Federation, **222** F1
Bāsht, Iran, **220** F2
Basi, India, **221** K3
Basia, India, **219** F5
Basilan Island, Philippines, **204** C5
Basildon, England, U.K., **305** H3
Basile, Pico, *mountain peak*, Equatorial Guinea, **368** A2
Basilicata, *autonomous region*, Italy, **295** E5
Basin, U.S.A., **419** K4
Basingstoke, England, U.K., **305** F3
Basirhat, India, **219** G5
Basīṭ, Ra's al, *cape*, Syria, **225** C2
Baška, Croatia, **294** E3
Başkale, Turkey, **224** F5
Baskatong, Réservoir, Canada, **416** D6
Baslow, England, U.K., **305** F1
Basoko, Democratic Republic of the Congo, **368** D2
Basora, Punt, *point*, Aruba, **461** B3
Basque, U.S.A., **418** F5
Basra *see* Al Başrah, Iraq, **363** J2
Bass Strait, Australia, **135** K6
Bassano, Canada, **413** N6
Bassano del Grappa, Italy, **294** C3
Bassar, Togo, **364** E3
Basse-Kotto, *prefecture*, Central African Republic, **366** B3
Basse-Normandie, *administrative region*, France, **290** D2
Basse-Terre, Guadeloupe, **427** D3
Basse Terre, Trinidad, Trinidad and Tobago, **461** C4
Bassein, Myanmar, **205** B4
Bassenthwaite Lake, England, U.K., **306** E3
Bassett, U.S.A., **420** D4
Basseterre, St Kitts and Nevis, **427** D2
Bassikounou, Mauritania, **364** C1
Bassila, Benin, **364** E3
Basso, *mountain peak*, Chad, **362** D5
Bastak, Iran, **221** F3
Bastelica, Corse, France, **295** B4
Bastī, India, **219** E4
Bastia, Corse, France, **294** B4
Bastogne, Belgium, **288** B4
Bastrop, Louisiana, U.S.A., **424** G3
Bastrop, Texas, U.S.A., **424** D4
Bat Khela, Pakistan, **218** B2
Bata, Equatorial Guinea, **368** A2
Batabanó, Cabo, *cape*, Cuba, **429** E2
Batabanó, Cuba, **429** E2
Batabanó, Golfo de, *gulf*, Cuba, **429** E2
Batac, Philippines, **204** C2
Batagol, Russian Federation, **213** J1
Batajnica, Yugoslavia, **296** C3
Batak, Bulgaria, **296** E5
Batakan, Indonesia, **201** F4
Batāla, India, **218** C3
Batalha, Portugal, **292** C3
Batama, Democratic Republic of the Congo, **369** E2
Batan Island, Philippines, **204** D3
Batan Islands, Philippines, **204** C1
Batang, China, **215** F3
Batanga, Gabon, **368** A3
Batangas, Philippines, **204** C3
Batas Island, Philippines, **204** B4
Batavia, U.S.A., **426** A3
Batchawana Bay, Canada, **421** L2
Bătdâmbâng, Cambodia, **203** D3
Batemans Bay, Australia, **135** L6
Batesburg, U.S.A., **425** M3
Batesland, U.S.A., **420** B4
Batesville, Arkansas, U.S.A., **424** G2
Batesville, Mississippi, U.S.A., **424** H2
Batesville, Texas, U.S.A., **424** C5
Batetskiy, Russian Federation, **299** C3
Bath, England, U.K., **304** E3
Bath, Maine, U.S.A., **426** F3
Bath, New York, U.S.A., **426** B3
Bath and North East Somerset, *unitary authority*, England, U.K., **304** E3
Batha, *prefecture*, Chad, **366** A2
Bathgate, Scotland, U.K., **308** F5
Bathurst, Australia, **135** K5
Bathurst, Canada, **416** J6
Bathurst, Cape, Canada, **410** F2
Bathurst Inlet, Canada, **410** J3
Bathurst Island, Australia, **134** F1
Bathurst Island, Canada, **411** J2
Batī, Ethiopia, **367** F2
Batı Menteşe Dağları, *mountain range*, Turkey, **297** F7
Bāṭin, Wādī al, *river*, Iraq/Kuwait/Saudi Arabia, **220** E3
Batkes, Indonesia, **199** E4
Batman, Turkey, **224** F5
Batna, Algeria, **361** H1
Baton Rouge, U.S.A., **424** G4
Batopilas, Mexico, **430** D3
Batouri, Cameroon, **368** B2
Batovi, Brazil, **456** C4
Batovi, *river*, *see* Tamitatoala, *river*, Brazil, **456** B3
Batrampur, India, **219** E4
Båtsfjord, Norway, **285** P1
Båtsjaur, Sweden, **284** H3
Båtskapp, *cape*, Norway, **285** Q1
Batteau, Canada, **417** P3
Batticaloa, Sri Lanka, **217** E5
Battipaglia, Italy, **295** E5
Battle, England, U.K., **305** H4
Battle, *river*, Canada, **413** P5
Battle Creek, U.S.A., **421** L4
Battle Mountain, U.S.A, **422** E1
Battleford, Canada, **413** Q5
Battonya, Hungary, **289** K5
Batu, Kepulauan, *islands*, Indonesia, **200** B3
Batu, *mountain peak*, Ethiopia, **367** E3
Batu, Tanjong, *point*, Indonesia, **201** G2
Batu Niah, Malaysia, **201** F2

Batu Pahat, Malaysia, **200** C2
Batu Puteh, Gunung, *mountain peak*, Malaysia, **200** C1
Batuberagam, Tanjong, *point*, Indonesia, **200** C4
Batuhitam, Tanjong, *point*, Indonesia, **198** C3
Batui, Indonesia, **198** C3
Batulaki, Philippines, **204** D5
Bat'umi, Georgia, **222** C4
Baturaja, Indonesia, **200** D4
Baturité, Brazil, **453** F4
Baturité, Serra de, *mountain range*, Brazil, **453** F4
Batyrevo, Russian Federation, **222** D1
Batz, Île de, *island*, France, **290** B2
Bau, Malaysia, **201** E2
Bauang, Philippines, **204** C2
Bauchi, Nigeria, **365** F2
Bauchi, *state*, Nigeria, **365** F2
Baudh, India, **219** F5
Baudó, Serranía de, *mountain range*, Colombia, **450** C2
Bauer Bay, Macquarie Island, **134** R11
Baugy, France, **290** F3
Baukau, Indonesia, **198** D5
Bauld, Cape, Canada, **417** P4
Baume-les-Dames, France, **291** H3
Baures, Bolivia, **455** F3
Bauru, Brazil, **459** H2
Baús, Brazil, **456** C5
Bauska, Latvia, **287** M4
Bautzen, Germany, **289** G3
Båven, *lake*, Sweden, **287** H3
Bavispe, *river*, Mexico, **430** C2
Bawal, Pulau, *island*, Indonesia, **201** E3
Bawang, Tanjong, *point*, Indonesia, **201** E3
Bawean, Pulau, *island*, Indonesia, **201** E4
Bawku, Ghana, **364** D2
Bawlf, Canada, **413** N5
Bawolung, China, **215** G3
Bawtry, England, U.K., **307** G4
Baxkorgan, China, **212** F5
Baxley, U.S.A., **425** L4
Baxoi, China, **215** F3
Bay, *administrative region*, Somalia, **369** H2
Bay Bulls, Canada, **417** Q6
Bay City, Michigan, U.S.A., **421** M4
Bay City, Texas, U.S.A., **424** E5
Bay Minette, U.S.A., **425** J4
Bay Roberts, Canada, **417** Q6
Bay-Soot, Russian Federation, **213** G2
Bay Springs, U.S.A., **425** H4
Bay View, New Zealand, **132** F4
Bayamo, Cuba, **429** F2
Bāyān, Band-e, *mountain range*, Afganistan, **218** A2
Bayan, Dornod, Mongolia, **210** F3
Bayan, Dornogovĭ, Mongolia, **210** E3
Bayan, Heilongjiang, China, **211** J3
Bayan, Hentiy, Mongolia, **210** E2
Bayan, Qinghai, China, **215** F2
Bayan Har, China, **210** F4
Bayan Har Shan, *mountain range*, China, **215** F2
Bayan-hushuu, Mongolia, **213** F2
Bayan Mod, China, **210** D4
Bayan Obo, China, **210** E4
Bayan-Ölgiy, *province*, Mongolia, **212** F2
Bayan-Ovoo, Govĭ-Altay, Mongolia, **213** G3
Bayan-Ovoo, Hentiy, Mongolia, **210** E2
Bayan Ovoo, Mongolia, **213** L2
Bayan Qagan, China, **210** F4
Bayan-Ulaan, Mongolia, **213** J3
Bayanauyl, Kazakhstan, **212** B2
Bayanbulag, N. Bayanhongor, Mongolia, **213** H3
Bayanbulag, S. Bayanhongor, Mongolia, **213** H3
Bayanbulak, China, **212** E4
Bayanga, Central African Republic, **368** C2
Bayanga-Didi, Central African Republic, **368** C1
Bayangol, Mongolia, **213** G3
Bayanhongor, Mongolia, **213** J3
Bayanhongor, *province*, Mongolia, **213** H3
Bayanhushuu, Mongolia, **213** H3
Bayansayr, Mongolia, **213** H3
Bayantsagaan, Mongolia, **213** J2
Bayard, U.S.A., **423** J5
Bayasgalant, Sühbaatar, Mongolia, **210** F3
Bayasgalant, Töv, Mongolia, **210** E3
Bayāzīyeh, Iran, **221** G2
Baybay, Philippines, **204** D4
Bayboro, U.S.A., **426** B7
Bayburt, Turkey, **224** F4
Baydhabo, Somalia, **369** H2
Baydrag, *river*, Mongolia, **213** H3
Bayeaux, France, **290** D2
Bayerischer Wald, *mountain range*, Germany, **288** F4
Bayern, *state*, Germany, **288** E4
Bayès, Cap, *cape*, New Caledonia, **141** A3
Bayghanīn, Kazakhstan, **222** F3
Bayḥān al Qişāb, Yemen, **220** E6
Bayındır, Turkey, **297** F6
Bayjī, Iraq, **363** H2
Baykal Ozero (Lake Baikal), *lake*, Russian Federation, **210** D1
Baykal'sk, Russian Federation, **210** D2
Baykurt, China, **212** B5
Bayonne, France, **290** D5
Bayovar, Peru, **454** B1
Bayqongyr, Qaraghandy, Kazakhstan, **222** H3
Bayqongyr, Qyzylorda, Kazakhstan, **222** G3
Bayramaly, Turkmenistan, **222** G5
Bayramiç, Turkey, **297** F6
Bayreuth, Germany, **288** E4
Bayrūt (Beirut), Lebanon, **225** C3
Bayshint, Mongolia, **210** D3
Baystonhill, England, U.K., **304** E2
Bayt al Faqīh, Yemen, **220** D6
Bayt Laḥm (Bethlehem), West Bank, **225** C4
Baytik Shan, *mountain range*, China/Mongolia, **213** F3
Baytown, U.S.A., **424** E5
Bayuda Desert, Sudan, **363** F5
Bayugan, Philippines, **204** D4
Bayunglincir, Indonesia, **200** C3
Bayyrqum, Kazakhstan, **222** H4
Baza, Spain, **293** F4
Bazardüzü Dağ, *mountain peak*, Azerbaijan, **222** D4
Bazaruto, Ilha do, *island*, Mozambique, **371** G3
Bazas, France, **290** D4
Bazdār, Pakistan, **218** A4
Bazhong, China, **215** H3
Baziaş, Romania, **296** C3
Bazmān, Iran, **221** H3
Bazmān, Kūh-e, *mountain peak*, Iran, **221** G3
Beachy Head, *point*, England, U.K., **305** H4
Beaconsfield, England, U.K., **305** G3
Beadnell Bay, England, U.K., **307** G2
Beagle Gulf, Australia, **134** F1
Beal, England, U.K., **307** G2
Bealanana, Madagascar, **372** B3
Beale, Cape, Canada, **412** G7
Bealeton, U.S.A., **426** B5
Beaminster, England, U.K., **304** E4
Bear Island, Ireland, **309** B6
Bear Lake, U.S.A., **419** J5
Bear Paw Mountain, *mountain peak*, U.S.A., **419** K2
Beardmore, Canada, **415** L7
Beardsley, U.S.A., **420** C6
Beardstown, U.S.A., **420** H5
Bearskin Lake, Canada, **414** J5
Beas de Segura, Spain, **293** F3
Beata, Cabo, *cape*, Dominican Republic, **429** H3
Beata Ridge, *underwater feature*, Caribbean Sea, **479** P3
Beatrice, U.S.A., **420** E5
Beattock, Scotland, U.K., **308** F5
Beatton, *river*, Canada, **412** J3
Beatty, Nevada, U.S.A, **422** E3
Beatty, Oregon, U.S.A., **418** D5
Beattyville, Canada, **416** C5
Beatys Butte, *mountain peak*, U.S.A., **418** E5
Beau Bassin, Mauritius, **373** C1
Beau Champ, Mauritius, **373** C1
Beaufort, Malaysia, **201** F1
Beaufort, U.S.A., **425** M3
Beaufort Sea, Arctic Ocean, **410** D2
Beaufort West, South Africa, **370** D5
Beaugency, France, **290** E3
Beauharnois, Canada, **416** E7
Beauly, Scotland, U.K., **308** E3
Beaumaris, Wales, U.K., **306** D4
Beaumetz-lès-Loges, France, **305** K4
Beaumont, Kansas, U.S.A., **420** E7
Beaumont, Mississippi, U.S.A., **425** H4
Beaumont, Texas, U.S.A., **424** E4
Beaune, France, **291** G3
Beaupré, Canada, **416** F6
Beaupréau, France, **290** D3
Beauséjour, Canada, **414** F6
Beauvais, France, **290** F2
Beauval, Canada, **413** R4
Beauval, France, **305** K4
Beaver, Wisconsin, U.S.A., **421** J3
Beaver, Utah, U.S.A., **422** G2
Beaver Creek, Canada, **410** E3
Beaver Dam, U.S.A., **421** J4
Beaver Falls, U.S.A., **421** N5
Beaver Island, U.S.A., **421** K3
Beaverhead Mountains, *mountain range*, U.S.A., **418** H4
Beaverhill Lake, Canada, **414** G4
Beaverlodge, Canada, **413** K4
Beāwar, India, **218** C4
Beazley, Argentina, **458** C4
Bebedouro, Brazil, **456** D5
Bebington, England, U.K., **306** E4
Béboto, Chad, **365** H3
Bebrene, Latvia, **287** N4
Beccles, England, U.K., **305** J2
Bečej, Yugoslavia, **296** C3
Becerreá, Spain, **292** D1
Béchar, Algeria, **361** F2
Beckley, U.S.A., **421** N7
Beclean, Romania, **296** E2
Bedale, England, U.K., **307** G3
Bédarieux, France, **291** F5
Beddgelert, Wales, U.K., **304** C1
Bedelē, Ethiopia, **367** E3
Bedēsa, Ethiopia, **367** F3
Bedford, England, U.K., **305** G2
Bedford, Indiana, U.S.A., **421** K6
Bedford, Kentucky, U.S.A., **421** L6
Bedford, Pennsylvania, U.S.A., **421** P6
Bedfordshire, *unitary authority*, England, U.K., **305** G2
Bedi Dat, Pakistan, **218** A4
Bedlington, England, U.K., **307** G2
Bedok, Singapore, **200** K7
Bedok Reservoir, Singapore, **200** K6
Bedourie, Australia, **135** H3
Beenoskee, *mountain peak*, Ireland, **309** B5
Be'ér Menuḥa, Israel, **225** C4
Be'ér Sheva' (Beersheba), Israel, **225** C4
Beersheba *see* Be'ér Sheva', Israel, **225** C4
Beeskow, Germany, **289** G2
Beeville, U.S.A., **424** D5
Befale, Democratic Republic of the Congo, **368** D2
Befandriana Avaratra, Madagascar, **372** B4
Befori, Democratic Republic of the Congo, **368** D2
Befotaka, Madagascar, **372** B5
Bega, Australia, **135** K6
Begejski Kanal, *canal*, Yugoslavia, **296** C3
Begunitsy, Russian Federation, **299** B3
Begusarai, India, **219** F4
Beh, *river*, Indonesia, **201** G5
Behbahān, Iran, **220** F2
Behleg, China, **213** F5
Behshahr, Iran, **222** E5
Bei, *river*, China, **206** C3
Bei Shan, *mountain range*, China, **213** G4
Bei'an, China, **211** J2
Beiarn, Norway, **284** G3
Beibu Wan, *bay*, China, **203** F1
Beicheng, China, **215** G4
Beichuan, China, **215** H3
Beida, *river*, China, **213** H4
Beidachi, China, **210** D5
Beidao, China, **215** H2
Beigi, Ethiopia, **366** D3
Beihai, China, **206** B4
Beijian Dao, *island*, China, **207** C5
Beijing (Peking), China, **210** G5
Beiliu, China, **206** B4
Beilu Heyan, China, **214** E2
Beipiao, China, **211** H4
Beira, Mozambique, **371** F2
Beiru, *river*, China, **206** C1
Beirut *see* Bayrūt, Lebanon, **225** C3
Beiseker, Canada, **413** N6
Beisfjord, Norway, **284** H2
Beishan, China, **213** H4
Beitbridge, Zimbabwe, **371** F3
Beiuş, Romania, **296** D2
Beixia, China, **207** B1
Beizha, China, **207** B3
Beizhen, China, **208** C2
Beja, *district*, Portugal, **292** C4
Beja, Portugal, **292** D3
Bejaïa, Algeria, **361** H1
Béjar, Spain, **292** E2
Bekan, Iran, **363** J1
Bekdash, Turkmenistan, **222** E4
Békés, Hungary, **289** K5
Békéscsaba, Hungary, **289** K5
Bekily, Madagascar, **372** B5
Bela, India, **219** E4
Bela, Pakistan, **218** A4
Bela Crkva, Yugoslavia, **296** C3
Bela Palanka, Yugoslavia, **296** D4
Bela Vista, Brazil, **456** B6
Bela Vista, Mozambique, **371** F4
Bélabo, Cameroon, **368** B2
Belaghash, Kazakhstan, **212** D2
Belamoty, Madagascar, **372** A5
Belanger, *river*, Canada, **414** F5
Belarus, *country*, Europe, **283** G5
Belawan, Indonesia, **200** B2
Belaya, Gora, *mountain peak*, Russian Federation, **301** U3
Bélbéji, Niger, **365** F2
Belbutte, Canada, **413** Q5
Belcher Islands, Canada, **415** P3
Belcherāgh, Afghanistan, **218** A2
Belchite, Spain, **293** G2
Belcoo, Northern Ireland, U.K., **309** E3
Belden, California, U.S.A., **422** C1
Belden, North Dakota, U.S.A., **420** B1
Belderg, Ireland, **309** C3
Belebelka, Russian Federation, **299** C4
Belebey, Russian Federation, **222** E2
Beledweyne, Somalia, **367** G4
Belefuanai, Liberia, **364** C3
Belel, Nigeria, **365** G3
Belém, Brazil, **452** D3
Belém de São Francisco, Brazil, **457** F2
Belén, Argentina, **458** C3
Belén, Colombia, **450** D2
Belen, Turkey, **225** B1
Belen, U.S.A., **423** K4
Belene, Bulgaria, **296** E4
Bélep, Île, *islands*, New Caledonia, **141** A3
Belev, Russian Federation, **299** F6
Bèlèya, Guinea, **364** B2
Belfast, *district*, Northern Ireland, U.K., **309** G3
Belfast, Northern Ireland, U.K., **309** G3
Belfast, U.S.A., **426** F2
Belfast Lough, *inlet*, Northern Ireland, U.K., **309** G3
Belfield, U.S.A., **420** B2
Bēlfodiyo, Ethiopia, **366** D2
Belford, England, U.K., **307** G2
Belfort, France, **291** H3
Belfry, U.S.A., **419** K4
Belgaum, India, **216** C3
Belgium, *country*, Europe, **282** E5
Belgorod, Russian Federation, **298** E2
Belgorodskaya Oblast', *province*, Russian Federation, **298** E2
Belgrade *see* Beograd, Yugoslavia, **296** C3
Belgrove, New Zealand, **133** D5
Belhaven, U.S.A., **426** B7
Beli, Nigeria, **365** G3
Beli Manastir, Croatia, **294** G3
Beli Timok, *river*, Yugoslavia, **296** D4
Belice, *river*, Sicilia, Italy, **295** D7
Belidzhi, Russian Federation, **222** D4
Belin-Béliet, France, **290** D4
Bélinga, Gabon, **368** B2
Belinyu, Indonesia, **200** D3
Belitsa, Belarus, **289** M2
Belitsa, Bulgaria, **296** D5
Belitung, Pulau, *island*, Indonesia, **201** D3
Belize, Angola, **368** B3
Belize, Belize, **428** C3
Belize, *country*, Central America, **409** Q7
Bélizon, French Guiana, **452** C2
Bell, *river*, Canada, **416** C5
Bell Island, Canada, **417** P4
Bell Rock, *island*, Scotland, U.K., **308** G4
Bell Ville, Argentina, **458** D4
Bella Coola, Canada, **412** F5
Bella Unión, Uruguay, **459** F4
Bella Vista, Corrientes, Argentina, **459** E3
Bella Vista, Santa Cruz, Argentina, **460** C4
Bella Vista, Tucumán, Argentina, **458** D3
Bellac, France, **290** E3
Bellary, India, **216** D3
Belle Fourche, *river*, U.S.A., **419** M4

Bolaiti, Democratic Republic of the Congo, 368 D3
Bolama, Guinea-Bissau, 364 A2
Bolān, *river*, Pakistan, 218 A3
Bolaños, Mexico, 430 E4
Bolbec, France, 290 E2
Boldeşti-Scăieni, Romania, 296 F3
Boldu, Romania, 296 F3
Bole, China, 212 D3
Bole, Ghana, 364 D3
Boleko, Democratic Republic of the Congo, 368 C3
Bolena, Democratic Republic of the Congo, 368 C2
Bolesławiec, Poland, 289 G3
Bolgatanga, Ghana, 364 D2
Bolhrad, Ukraine, 296 G3
Boli, China, 211 K3
Boli, Sudan, 366 C3
Bolia, Democratic Republic of the Congo, 368 C3
Boliden, Sweden, 284 K4
Bolinao, Philippines, 204 B2
Bolívar, Bolivia, 455 E3
Bolivar, Colombia, 450 C3
Bolivar, Missouri, U.S.A., 420 G7
Bolívar, Peru, 454 C2
Bolívar, Pico, *mountain peak*, Venezuela, 451 D2
Bolivar, Tennessee, U.S.A., 425 H2
Bolivia, *country*, South America, 449 F5
Boljevac, Yugoslavia, 296 C4
Bolkhov, Russian Federation, 299 F6
Bollnäs, Sweden, 286 H2
Bollons Island, Antipodes Islands, New Zealand, 133 P15
Bollstabruk, Sweden, 287 H1
Bollullos par del Condado, Spain, 292 D4
Bolobo, Democratic Republic of the Congo, 368 C3
Bologna, Italy, 294 C3
Bolognesi, Central Peru, 454 C2
Bolognesi, N. Peru, 454 D2
Bologovo, Russian Federation, 299 C4
Bologoye, Russian Federation, 299 E4
Bolomba, Democratic Republic of the Congo, 368 C2
Bolon', Ozero, *lake*, Russian Federation, 211 M2
Bolon', Russian Federation, 211 M2
Bolondo, Democratic Republic of the Congo, 368 C3
Bolong, Philippines, 204 C5
Bolotnoye, Russian Federation, 223 L1
Bolsena, Italy, 294 D4
Bolsena, Lago di, *lake*, Italy, 294 C4
Bol'shakovo, Russian Federation, 287 K5
Bol'shaya Belaya, *river*, Russian Federation, 210 C1
Bol'shaya Glushitsa, Russian Federation, 222 E2
Bol'shaya Kinel', *river*, Russian Federation, 222 E2
Bol'sherech'ye, Russian Federation, 223 J1
Bol'shevik, Ostrov, *island*, Russian Federation, 301 M2
Bol'shoy Begichev, Ostrov, *island*, Russian Federation, 301 N2
Bol'shoy Kavkaz (Caucasus), *mountain range*, Asia/Europe, 222 D4
Bol'shoy Lyakhovskiy, Ostrov, *island*, Russian Federation, 301 R2
Bol'shoy Uvat, Ozero, *lake*, Russian Federation, 223 H1
Bol'shoy Yenisey, *river*, Russian Federation, 223 P2

Bol'shoye Pole, Russian Federation, 299 B2
Bol'shoye Sorokino, Russian Federation, 223 H1
Bol'shoye Zaborov'ye, Russian Federation, 299 D3
Bolsover, England, U.K., 305 F1
Bolt Head, *point*, England, U.K., 304 D4
Bolton, England, U.K., 306 F4
Bolubolu, Papua New Guinea, 140 C5
Boluntay, China, 213 G5
Boluo, China, 203 G1
Bolva, *river*, Russian Federation, 299 E5
Bolvadin, Turkey, 363 F1
Bolyston, Canada, 417 L7
Bolzano, Italy, 294 C1
Bom Comércio, Brazil, 455 E2
Bom Jardim, Amazonas, Brazil, 455 E2
Bom Jardim, Pará, Brazil, 452 C4
Bom Jesus, Brazil, 459 G3
Bom Jesus da Lapa, Brazil, 457 E3
Bom Retiro, Brazil, 459 H3
Boma, Democratic Republic of the Congo, 368 B4
Bomassa, Congo, 368 C2
Bombala, Australia, 135 K6
Bombay *see* Mumbai, India, 216 C2
Bombay Beach, U.S.A., 422 F5
Bomboma, Democratic Republic of the Congo, 368 C2
Bomi, China, 215 E3
Bomili, Democratic Republic of the Congo, 369 E2
Bømlo, *island*, Norway, 286 B3
Bomongo, Democratic Republic of the Congo, 368 C2
Bomu, China, 215 E3
Bon, Cap, *cape*, Tunisia, 295 C7
Bon Air, U.S.A., 426 B6
Bonaire, *island*, Netherlands Antilles, 461 A4
Bonanza, Nicaragua, 428 D4
Bonao, Dominican Republic, 429 H3
Bonasse, Trinidad, Trinidad and Tobago, 461 C4
Bonaventure, Canada, 416 J5
Bonavista, Canada, 417 Q5
Bonavista Bay, Canada, 417 Q5
Bondo, Angola, 368 C6
Bondo, Democratic Republic of the Congo, 368 D2
Bondoukou, Côte d'Ivoire, 364 D3
Bondoukui, Burkina Faso, 364 D2
Bondowoso, Indonesia, 201 F4
Bondurant, U.S.A., 419 J5
Bone, Teluk, *bay*, Indonesia, 198 C3
Bonerate, Pulau, *island*, Indonesia, 198 C4
Bo'ness, Scotland, U.K., 308 F4
Bonete, Cerro, *mountain peak*, Argentina, 458 C3
Bonete, Cerro, *mountain peak*, Bolivia, 455 E5
Bonete, Spain, 293 G3
Bonfinópolis, Brazil, 456 D4
Bông Lông, Cambodia, 203 E3
Bonga, Ethiopia, 367 E3
Bongabong, Philippines, 204 C3
Bongandanga, Democratic Republic of the Congo, 368 D2
Bongo, Democratic Republic of the Congo, 368 D2
Bongor, Chad, 365 H2
Bongos, Massif des, *mountain range*, Central African Republic, 366 B3

Bongouanou, Côte d'Ivoire, 364 D3
Bonham, U.S.A., 424 D3
Bonifacio, Corse, France, 295 B5
Bonifacio, Strait of, Mediterranean, 280 E7
Bonifay, U.S.A., 425 K4
Bonin Trench, *underwater feature*, Pacific Ocean, 478 D3
Bonito, Brazil, 456 B5
Bonito, Pico, *mountain peak*, Honduras, 428 D4
Bonn, Germany, 288 C3
Bonners Ferry, U.S.A., 418 F2
Bonneville, France, 291 H3
Bonny, Bight of, *gulf*, Nigeria, 368 A2
Bonny, Nigeria, 368 A2
Bonnyrigg, Scotland, U.K., 308 F5
Bonnyville, Canada, 413 P4
Bono, U.S.A., 424 G2
Bonorva, Sardegna, Italy, 295 B5
Bonoua, Côte d'Ivoire, 364 D3
Bontang, Indonesia, 201 G2
Bontoc, Philippines, 204 C2
Bonyhád, Hungary, 289 J5
Boola, Guinea, 364 C3
Booligal, U.S.A., 425 H2
Bööntsagaan Nuur, *lake*, Mongolia, 213 H3
Boonville, U.S.A., 426 C3
Boorama, Somalia, 367 F3
Boosaaso, Somalia, 367 G2
Boothia, Gulf of, Canada, 411 K2
Boothia Peninsula, Canada, 411 K2
Bootle, England, U.K., 306 E4
Booué, Gabon, 368 B3
Boqueirão, Brazil, 459 G4
Boquete, Panama, 429 E5
Boquillas del Carmen, Mexico, 430 E2
Boquirão, Serra do, *mountain range*, Brazil, 459 F3
Bor, Czech Republic, 288 F4
Bor, Russian Federation, 299 E3
Bor, Sudan, 366 D3
Bor, Turkey, 224 D5
Bor, Yugoslavia, 296 D3
Bor-Üdzüür, Mongolia, 213 G3
Bora Bora, *island*, French Polynesia, 137 F2
Borah Peak, *mountain peak*, U.S.A., 418 H4
Boran, Kazakhstan, 212 E2
Borang, Tanjong, *point*, Indonesia, 199 F4
Borås, Sweden, 286 F4
Borāzjān, Iran, 220 F3
Borba, Brazil, 451 G5
Borborema, Planalto da, *plateau*, Brazil, 447 J4
Borchgrevink Coast, *region*, Antarctica, 470 D8
Bordeaux, France, 290 D4
Borden, Canada, 413 R5
Borden Island, Canada, 410 H2
Bordertown, Australia, 135 J6
Bordj Bou Arreridj, Algeria, 361 G1
Bordj Messouda, Algeria, 361 H2
Bordj Mokhtar, Algeria, 361 G4
Bordj Omar Driss, Algeria, 361 H3
Boré, Mali, 364 D1
Boreray, *island*, Scotland, U.K., 308 B3
Borgarfjörður, Iceland, 284 Z7
Borgarnes, Iceland, 284 X7
Borgefjellet, *mountain range*, Norway, 284 F4
Borger, U.S.A., 424 B2
Borgholm, Sweden, 287 H4
Borgo San Dalmazzo, France, 291 H4
Borgo San Lorenzo, Italy, 294 C4

Borgo Valsugara, Italy, 294 C2
Borgomanero, Italy, 294 B3
Borgund, Norway, 286 C2
Borhoyn Tal, Mongolia, 210 E4
Bori, India, 218 D5
Borisoglebsk, Russian Federation, 298 F2
Borisovo-Sudskoye, Russian Federation, 299 F3
Boriziny, Madagascar, 372 B4
Borja, Peru, 450 C5
Borja, Spain, 293 G2
Borken, Germany, 288 C3
Borkou, *physical feature*, Chad, 362 C5
Borkou-Ennedi-Tibesti, *prefecture*, Chad, 362 C5
Borkum, *island*, Germany, 288 C2
Borlänge, Sweden, 286 G2
Bormio, Italy, 294 C2
Borna, Germany, 288 F3
Borneo, *island*, Brunei/Indonesia/Malaysia, 201 F2
Bornholm, *island*, Denmark, 286 G5
Borno, *state*, Nigeria, 365 G2
Bornova, Turkey, 362 E1
Borodino, Russian Federation, 223 P1
Borodino, Ukraine, 296 G2
Borodinskoye, Russian Federation, 299 B2
Borohoro Shan, *mountain range*, China, 212 D3
Borok, Russian Federation, 299 C3
Boroko, Indonesia, 198 C2
Boromata, Central African Republic, 366 B2
Boromo, Burkina Faso, 364 D2
Borongan, Philippines, 204 D4
Boronów, Poland, 289 J3
Borotou, Côte d'Ivoire, 364 C3
Boroughbridge, England, U.K., 307 G3
Borovichi, Pskovskaya Oblast', Russian Federation, 299 B4
Borovichi, Novgorodskaya Oblast', Russian Federation, 299 D3
Borovoy, Russian Federation, 285 R4
Borovskoy, Kazakhstan, 222 G2
Borre, Denmark, 286 F5
Borrisokane, Ireland, 309 D5
Borrisoleigh, Ireland, 309 E5
Borroloola, Australia, 135 H2
Börrum, Sweden, 287 H3
Borşa, Romania, 296 E2
Borsec, Romania, 296 E2
Børselv, Norway, 285 M1
Borshchiv, Ukraine, 296 F1
Borshchovochnyy Khrebet, *mountain range*, Russian Federation, 211 G1
Borth, Wales, U.K., 304 C2
Börtnan, Sweden, 284 F5
Borūjerd, Iran, 220 E2
Borups Corners, Canada, 414 H7
Borve, Scotland, U.K., 308 C3
Boryslav, Ukraine, 289 L4
Borzya, Russian Federation, 210 G2
Bosa, Sardegna, Italy, 295 B5
Bosagha, Kazakhstan, 212 B3
Bosanska Dubica, Bosnia and Herzegovina, 294 F3
Bosanski Novi, Bosnia and Herzegovina, 294 F3
Bosanski Petrovac, Bosnia and Herzegovina, 294 F3
Bosavi, Mount, *mountain peak*, Papua New Guinea, 140 A4
Boscastle, England, U.K., 304 C4
Boscobel, U.S.A., 420 H4
Bose, China, 215 H5
Boshan, China, 211 G5
Bosherston, Wales, U.K., 304 C3
Bosilegrad, Yugoslavia, 296 D4
Bosilevad, Yugoslavia, 296 D4
Boskamp, Suriname, 452 B2

Boslanti, Suriname, 452 B2
Bosler, U.S.A., 419 M6
Bosna, *river*, Bosnia and Herzegovina, 294 G3
Bosnia and Herzegovina, *country*, Europe, 282 F7
Bosobolo, Democratic Republic of the Congo, 368 C2
Bosporus *see* Istanbul Boğazı, *strait*, Turkey, 297 G5
Bossembélé, Central African Republic, 368 C1
Bossentélé, Central African Republic, 368 C1
Bossier City, U.S.A., 424 F3
Bostan, China, 212 E5
Bostān, Pakistan, 218 A3
Bosten Hu, *lake*, China, 212 E4
Boston, England, U.K., 305 G2
Boston, U.S.A., 426 E3
Boston Bar, Canada, 412 J7
Boston Mountains, *mountain range*, U.S.A., 424 F2
Boston Spa, England, U.K., 307 G4
Bot Makak, Cameroon, 368 B2
Botād, India, 218 B5
Botany Bay, Australia, 135 L5
Boteå, Sweden, 287 H1
Boteka, Democratic Republic of the Congo, 368 C3
Botemola, Democratic Republic of the Congo, 368 C3
Botevgrad, Bulgaria, 296 D4
Bothel, England, U.K., 306 E3
Bothnia, Gulf of, Finland/Sweden, 287 J2
Boticas, Portugal, 292 D2
Botna, *river*, Moldova, 296 G2
Botngård, Norway, 284 D5
Boto-Pasi, Suriname, 452 B2
Botolan, Philippines, 204 C3
Botoşani, Romania, 296 F2
Botou, China, 210 G5
Botsmark, Sweden, 284 K4
Botswana, *country*, Africa, 359 H9
Botte Donato, Monte, *mountain peak*, Italy, 295 F6
Bottenviken Perämeri, *gulf*, Finland/Sweden, 285 L4
Bottineau, U.S.A., 420 C1
Bottrop, Germany, 288 C3
Botucatu, Brazil, 459 H2
Botuporã, Brazil, 457 E3
Bou Ismaïl, Algeria, 293 J4
Bou Izakarn, Morocco, 360 E3
Bou Kadir, Algeria, 293 H4
Bou Naceur, Jbel, *mountain peak*, Morocco, 361 F2
Bou Saâda, Algeria, 293 K5
Bouaflé, Côte d'Ivoire, 364 C3
Bouaké, Côte d'Ivoire, 364 C3
Bouandougou, Côte d'Ivoire, 364 C3
Bouar, Central African Republic, 368 C1
Bouârfa, Morocco, 361 F2
Bouble, *river*, France, 291 F3
Bouca, Central African Republic, 366 A3
Bouchegouf, Algeria, 295 A7
Boudenib, Morocco, 361 F2
Boudoua, Central African Republic, 368 C2
Bouenza, *administrative region*, Congo, 368 B3
Bougainville Island, Papua New Guinea, 140 E8
Boughessa, Mali, 361 G5
Bougouni, Mali, 364 C2
Bougtob, Algeria, 361 G2
Bougzoul, Algeria, 293 J5
Bouillon, Belgium, 288 B4
Bouira, Algeria, 293 J4
Boulder, Colorado, U.S.A., 423 L1
Boulder, Montana, U.S.A., 419 H3
Boulder, Utah, U.S.A., 423 H3
Boulder, Wyoming, U.S.A., 419 K5

Canguaretama, Brazil, **453** G5
Canguçu, Brazil, **459** G4
Canguçu, Serra do, *mountain range*, Brazil, **459** G4
Cangumbe, Angola, **368** C5
Cangwu, China, **206** B4
Cangxi, China, **215** H3
Cangyuan, China, **215** F5
Cangzhou, China, **210** G5
Caniapiscau, Lac, *lake*, Canada, **416** G2
Caniapiscau, *river*, Canada, **411** N4
Canicatti, Sicilia, Italy, **295** D7
Canigou, Pic du, *mountain peak*, France, **290** F5
Canindé, Ceará, Brazil, **453** F4
Canindé, Pará, Brazil, **452** D4
Canindé, *river*, Brazil, **453** E5
Canisp, *mountain peak*, Scotland, U.K., **308** D2
Cañitas de Felipe Pescador, Mexico, **430** E4
Cañizal, Spain, **292** E2
Canmore, Canada, **413** M6
Canna, *island*, Scotland, U.K., **308** C3
Cannanore, India, **216** C4
Cannanore Islands, India, **216** C4
Cannes, France, **291** H5
Cannington, England, U.K., **304** D3
Cannock, England, U.K., **304** E2
Cannon Beach, U.S.A., **418** C4
Cannoniers Point, Mauritius, **373** C1
Caño Macareo, *river*, Venezuela, **451** G2
Caño Manamo, *river*, Venezuela, **451** F2
Canoas, Brazil, **459** G3
Canoas, Peru, **450** B5
Canoas, *river*, Brazil, **459** G3
Canoe Lake, Canada, **413** Q4
Canoinhas, Brazil, **459** G3
Canon City, U.S.A., **423** L2
Canora, Canada, **414** C6
Canosa di Puglia, Italy, **295** F5
Canso, Canada, **417** L7
Canta, Peru, **454** C3
Cantabria, *autonomous community*, Spain, **293** F1
Cantábrica, Cordillera, *mountain range*, Spain, **292** D1
Cantagalo, Brazil, **451** G5
Cantalejo, Spain, **293** F2
Cantaura, Venezuela, **451** F2
Canterbury, England, U.K., **305** J3
Canterbury Bight, *bay*, New Zealand, **133** D6
Canterbury Plains, New Zealand, **133** C6
Cantiano, Italy, **294** D4
Cantilan, Philippines, **204** D4
Canto do Buriti, Brazil, **453** E5
Canton, Georgia, U.S.A., **425** K2
Canton, Illinois, U.S.A., **420** H5
Canton, Mississippi, U.S.A., **424** G3
Canton, New York, U.S.A., **426** C2
Canton, Ohio, U.S.A., **421** N5
Canton, Pennsylvania, U.S.A., **426** B4
Canton *see* Guangzhou, China, **207** A2
Canton, South Dakota, U.S.A., **420** E4
Cantu, *river*, Brazil, **459** G2
Cantwell, U.S.A., **410** E3
Canudos, Brazil, **452** A5
Cañuelas, Argentina, **459** E5
Canumã, N. Amazonas, Brazil, **452** A4
Canumã, S. Amazonas, Brazil, **455** G2
Canutama, Brazil, **455** F2
Canvey Island, England, U.K., **305** H3

Canwood, Canada, **413** R5
Cany-Barville, France, **290** E2
Canyon, U.S.A., **424** B2
Canyon Ferry Lake, U.S.A., **419** J3
Canyonville, U.S.A., **418** C5
Canzar, Angola, **368** D4
Cao Xian, China, **206** C1
Caojian, China, **215** F4
Caombo, Angola, **368** C4
Cap Aracena, Isla, *island*, Chile, **460** C5
Cap aux Meules, Canada, **417** L6
Cap-de-la-Madeleine, Canada, **416** E6
Cap-des-Rosiers, Canada, **417** J5
Cap-Haïtien, Haiti, **429** G3
Cap Sigli, Algeria, **361** G1
Capaccio, Italy, **295** E5
Capaia, Angola, **368** D4
Capanaparo, *river*, Venezuela, **451** E2
Capanema, Pará, Brazil, **452** D3
Capanema, Parana, Brazil, **459** G2
Capão Bonito, Brazil, **459** H2
Caparaó, Serra do, *mountain range*, Brazil, **457** F5
Caparo, *river*, Venezuela, **451** D2
Capas, Philippines, **204** C3
Cape Barren Island, Australia, **135** K7
Cape Basin, *underwater feature*, Atlantic Ocean, **477** H8
Cape Breton Island, Canada, **417** M7
Cape Charles, U.S.A., **426** C6
Cape Coast, Ghana, **364** D3
Cape Cod Bay, U.S.A., **426** E3
Cape Comorin, India, **216** D4
Cape Dorset, Canada, **411** M3
Cape Girardeau, U.S.A., **421** J7
Cape May Point, U.S.A., **426** C5
Cape North, Canada, **417** K6
Cape Race, Canada, **417** Q6
Cape St George, Canada, **417** M5
Cape Tormentine, Canada, **417** K6
Cape Town, South Africa, **370** C5
Cape Verde, *country*, Atlantic Ocean, **360** P8
Cape Verde Basin, *underwater feature*, Atlantic Ocean, **477** F4
Cape York Peninsula, Australia, **135** J1
Capel Curig, Wales, U.K., **304** D1
Capel St Mary, England, U.K., **305** J2
Capelinha, Brazil, **457** E4
Capenda-Camulemba, Angola, **368** C4
Capibara, Venezuela, **451** E3
Capilla del Monte, Argentina, **458** D4
Capim, *river*, Brazil, **452** D4
Čapljina, Bosnia and Herzegovina, **294** F4
Capinota, Bolivia, **455** E4
Capitan, U.S.A., **423** L5
Capitán Bado, Paraguay, **459** F2
Capitan Peak, *mountain peak*, U.S.A., **423** L5
Capitol, U.S.A., **419** M4
Capivari, *river*, Brazil, **457** F3
Capolo, Angola, **368** B5
Capotoan, Mount, *mountain peak*, Philippines, **204** D3
Cappoquin, Ireland, **309** E5
Capraia, Isola di, *island*, Italy, **294** B4
Capri, Isola di, *island*, Italy, **295** D5
Caprivi, *administrative region*, Namibia, **370** D2
Caprock, U.S.A., **423** M5

Captain Cook, Hawaiian Islands, U.S.A., **422** R10
Capua, Italy, **295** E5
Capucin Point, Seychelles, **373** A2
Caquetá, *river*, Colombia, **450** D4
Car, Slieve, *mountain peak*, Ireland, **309** C3
Car Nicobar Island, Andaman and Nicobar Islands, India, **217** G4
Caraşova, Romania, **296** C3
Carabaya, Cordillera de, *mountain range*, Peru, **454** D3
Caracal, Romania, **296** E3
Caracaraí, Brazil, **451** G4
Caracas, Venezuela, **451** E1
Caracol, Brazil, **457** E2
Caracollo, Bolivia, **455** E4
Caraga, Philippines, **204** D5
Caragh, Lough, *lake*, Ireland, **309** B5
Caraguatatuba, Brazil, **459** J2
Carahue, Chile, **458** B6
Caraí, Brazil, **457** F4
Caraíva, Brazil, **457** F4
Carajás, Serra dos, *mountain range*, Brazil, **453** F4
Caramat, Canada, **415** L7
Caranapatuba, Brazil, **455** F2
Carandaí, Brazil, **457** E5
Carandayti, Bolivia, **455** F5
Carangola, Brazil, **457** E5
Caransebeş, Romania, **296** D3
Carapuse Bay, Tobago, Trinidad and Tobago, **461** B4
Caraquet, Canada, **416** J6
Caráquez, Bahía de, *bay*, Ecuador, **450** B4
Caratinga, Brazil, **457** E5
Carauari, Brazil, **451** E5
Caravaca de la Cruz, Spain, **293** G3
Caravelas, Brazil, **457** F4
Caraz, Peru, **454** C2
Carazinho, Brazil, **459** G3
Carballo, Spain, **292** C1
Carbó, Mexico, **430** C2
Carbonara, Capo, *cape*, Italy, **295** B6
Carbondale, Colorado, U.S.A., **423** K2
Carbondale, Illinois, U.S.A., **421** J7
Carbondale, Pennsylvania, U.S.A., **426** C4
Carbonear, Canada, **417** Q6
Carboneras, Spain, **293** G4
Carboneras de Cuadazaón, Spain, **293** G3
Carbonia, Sardegna, Italy, **295** B6
Carbonita, Brazil, **457** E4
Carbonne, France, **290** E5
Carcajou, Canada, **413** L3
Carcassonne, France, **290** F5
Carcastillo, Spain, **293** G1
Carcross, Canada, **410** F3
Cardamom Hills, India, **216** D4
Cardel, Mexico, **431** F5
Cardeña, Spain, **292** E3
Cárdenas, Cuba, **429** E2
Cárdenas, San Luis Potosí, Mexico, **431** F4
Cárdenas, Tabasco, Mexico, **431** G5
Cardiel, Lago, *lake*, Argentina, **460** C3
Cardiff, *unitary authority*, Wales, U.K., **304** D3
Cardiff, Wales, U.K., **304** D3
Cardigan, Wales, U.K., **304** C2
Cardigan Bay, Wales, U.K., **304** C2
Cardona, Uruguay, **459** F4
Cardoso, Ilha do, *island*, Brazil, **459** H2
Cardrona, Mount, *mountain peak*, New Zealand, **133** B7
Cardston, Canada, **413** N7

Cardwell, Australia, **135** K2
Cardwell, U.S.A., **419** J4
Carei, Romania, **296** D2
Careiro, Brazil, **451** G5
Careme, Gunung, *mountain peak*, Indonesia, **201** E4
Carentan, France, **290** D2
Carey, Lake, Australia, **134** E4
Carey, U.S.A., **418** H5
Cargèse, Corse, France, **295** B4
Carhaix Plouguer, France, **290** C2
Carhué, Argentina, **458** D5
Cariacica, Brazil, **457** F5
Cariamanga, Ecuador, **450** B5
Cariango, Angola, **368** C5
Cariati, Italy, **295** F6
Caribou, *river*, Canada, **414** F2
Caribou, U.S.A., **426** F1
Caribou Lake, Canada, **415** K6
Caribou Mountains, *mountain range*, Canada, **413** L2
Carichic, Mexico, **430** D3
Carigara, Philippines, **204** D4
Cariñena, Spain, **293** G2
Carinhanha, Brazil, **457** E4
Caripe, Venezuela, **451** F1
Caripito, Venezuela, **451** F1
Cariré, Brazil, **453** F4
Caritianas, Brazil, **455** F2
Carleton Place, Canada, **416** C7
Carletonville, South Africa, **371** E4
Cârlibaba, Romania, **296** E2
Carlin, U.S.A., **422** E1
Carlingford, Ireland, **309** F3
Carlingford Lough, *inlet*, Northern Ireland, U.K., **309** F3
Carlinville, U.S.A., **420** J6
Carlisle, England, U.K., **306** F3
Carlisle, U.S.A., **426** B4
Carlos Casares, Argentina, **458** E5
Carlos Chagas, Brazil, **457** F4
Carlow, *county*, Ireland, **309** F5
Carlow, Ireland, **309** F5
Carloway, Scotland, U.K., **308** C2
Carlsbad, California, U.S.A., **422** E5
Carlsbad, New Mexico, U.S.A., **423** L5
Carlsberg Ridge, *underwater feature*, Indian Ocean, **476** C4
Carlton, U.S.A., **418** D2
Carluke, Scotland, U.K., **308** F5
Carlyle, Canada, **414** C7
Carlyle Lake, U.S.A., **421** J6
Carmacks, Canada, **410** F3
Carmagnola, Italy, **294** A3
Carman, Canada, **414** E7
Carmarthen, Wales, U.K., **304** C3
Carmarthen Bay, Wales, U.K., **304** C3
Carmarthenshire, *unitary authority*, Wales, U.K., **304** C3
Carmaux, France, **290** F4
Carmel Head, *point*, Wales, U.K., **306** D4
Carmelita, Guatemala, **428** C3
Carmelo, Uruguay, **459** F4
Carmen, Isla, *island*, Mexico, **430** C3
Carmen Alto, Chile, **458** C2
Carmen De Patagones, Argentina, **460** E1
Carmensa, Argentina, **458** C5
Carmona, Spain, **292** E4
Carmyllie, Scotland, U.K., **308** G4
Carn Eige, *mountain peak*, Scotland, U.K., **308** D3
Carnarvon, Australia, **134** C3
Carnarvon, South Africa, **370** D5
Carndonagh, Ireland, **309** E2
Carnduff, Canada, **414** D7
Carnegie, Lake, Australia, **134** E4
Carnegie Ridge, *underwater feature*, Pacific Ocean, **479** N4

Carnew, Ireland, **309** F5
Carney Island, Antarctica, **470** B7
Carnforth, England, U.K., **306** F3
Carnley Harbour, Auckland Islands, New Zealand, **132** J10
Carnlough, Northern Ireland, U.K., **309** G3
Carnot, Central African Republic, **368** C2
Carnoustie, Scotland, U.K., **308** G4
Carnsore Point, Ireland, **309** F5
Carnwath, Scotland, U.K., **308** F5
Caro, U.S.A., **421** M4
Carol City, U.S.A., **425** M7
Carolina, Brazil, **452** D5
Carolina, Puerto Rico, **427** C2
Caroline Cove, *bay*, Macquarie Island, **134** R11
Caroline Islands, Micronesia, **138** C4
Caroni, *river*, Trinidad, Trinidad and Tobago, **461** C4
Caroni, *river*, Venezuela, **451** F2
Carora, Venezuela, **451** D1
Carp, U.S.A., **422** F3
Carpathian Mountains, *mountain range*, Europe, **280** G6
Carpaţii Meridionali, *mountain range*, Romania, **280** G6
Carpentaria, Gulf of, Australia, **135** H1
Carpentras, France, **291** G4
Carpina, Brazil, **453** G5
Carr, U.S.A., **423** L1
Carra, Lough, *lake*, Ireland, **309** C4
Carrabelle, U.S.A., **425** K5
Carradale, Scotland, U.K., **308** D5
Carraipía, Colombia, **450** D1
Carrara, Italy, **294** C3
Carrauntoohil, *mountain peak*, Ireland, **309** C6
Carrbridge, Scotland, U.K., **308** F3
Carrickfergus, *district*, Northern Ireland, U.K., **309** G3
Carrickfergus, Northern Ireland, U.K., **309** G3
Carrickmacross, Ireland, **309** F4
Carrick-on-Shannon, Ireland, **309** D4
Carrick-on-Suir, Ireland, **309** E5
Carrigallen, Ireland, **309** E4
Carrigan Head, *point*, Ireland, **309** C3
Carrigtohill, Ireland, **309** D6
Carrillo, Mexico, **430** E3
Carrington, U.S.A., **420** D2
Carrizal, Colombia, **450** D1
Carrizal Bajo, Chile, **458** B3
Carrizo Springs, U.S.A., **424** C5
Carrizozo, U.S.A., **423** L5
Carroll, U.S.A., **420** F4
Carrollton, Georgia, U.S.A., **425** K3
Carrollton, Illinois, U.S.A., **420** H6
Carrollton, Missouri, U.S.A., **420** G6
Carrot, *river*, Canada, **414** B5
Carrowkeel, Ireland, **309** E2
Carrowmore Lake, Ireland, **309** C3
Carson, U.S.A., **420** C2
Carson City, U.S.A., **422** D2
Carstairs, Scotland, U.K., **308** F5
Cartagena, Colombia, **450** C1
Cartagena, Spain, **293** G4
Cartago, Colombia, **450** C3
Cartago, Costa Rica, **428** E5
Carter, U.S.A., **419** J3
Carterton, England, U.K., **305** F3
Carthage, Mississippi, U.S.A., **425** H3

Carthage, New York, U.S.A., **426** C2
Carthage, Texas, U.S.A., **424** E3
Carthage, Tunisia, **362** B1
Cartier, Canada, **421** N2
Cartier Islet, *island*, Ashmore and Cartier Islands, **134** P9
Cartmel, England, U.K., **306** F3
Cartwright, Canada, **417** N3
Caruaru, Brazil, **453** G5
Carúpano, Venezuela, **451** F1
Caruray, Philippines, **204** B4
Carutapera, Brazil, **452** E3
Carvalho, Brazil, **452** C4
Carvers, U.S.A., **422** E2
Carvoeiro, Brazil, **451** G4
Carvoeiro, Cabo, *cape*, Portugal, **292** C3
Casa Branca, Brazil, **456** D5
Casa Grande, U.S.A., **423** H5
Casa Piedra, U.S.A., **423** L7
Casabaja, Providencia, Colombia, **461** C1
Casablanca, Morocco, **360** E2
Casamance, *river*, Senegal, **364** A2
Casamassima, Italy, **295** F5
Casamozza, Corse, France, **294** B4
Casanare, *river*, Colombia, **451** D2
Casas Adobes, U.S.A., **423** H5
Casas del Puerto, Spain, **293** G3
Casas Grandes, Mexico, **430** D2
Casas Grandes, *river*, Mexico, **430** D2
Casas Ibáñez, Spain, **293** G3
Casca, Brazil, **459** G3
Cascade, Seychelles, **373** A2
Cascade, U.S.A., **420** H4
Cascade Bay, Norfolk Island, **135** T13
Cascade Point, New Zealand, **133** A6
Cascade Range, *mountain range*, U.S.A., **418** C6
Cascais, Portugal, **292** C3
Cascavel, Ceará, Brazil, **453** F4
Cascavel, Parana, Brazil, **459** G2
Caserta, Italy, **295** E5
Casey, *Australian research station*, Antarctica, **470** G7
Casey, Canada, **416** D6
Caseyr, Raas, *point*, Somalia, **367** H2
Cashel, Ireland, **309** E5
Cashel, Zimbabwe, **371** F2
Casigua, N. Venezuela, **450** D2
Casigua, W. Venezuela, **451** D1
Casilda, Argentina, **458** E4
Casino, Australia, **135** L4
Casinos, Spain, **293** G3
Casiquiare, *river*, Venezuela, **451** E3
Casma, Peru, **454** B2
Caspe, Spain, **293** G2
Casper, U.S.A., **419** L5
Caspian Depression *see* Prikaspiyskaya Nizmennost', *lowland*, Kazakhstan/Russian Federation, **222** D3
Caspian Sea, Asia/Europe, **222** E4
Cass City, U.S.A., **421** M4
Cass Lake, U.S.A., **420** F2
Cassacatiza, Mozambique, **369** F5
Cassai, Angola, **368** D5
Cassamba, Angola, **368** D5
Cassel, France, **305** K4
Cassiar, Canada, **412** E2
Cassiar Mountains, *mountain range*, Canada, **412** D2
Cassinga, Angola, **368** C6
Cassino, Italy, **295** D5
Cassley, *river*, Scotland, U.K., **308** E2
Cassoday, U.S.A., **420** E6
Cassongue, Angola, **368** B5
Castanhal, Brazil, **452** D3
Castanho, Brazil, **455** G2
Castaño, *river*, Argentina, **458** C4
Castaño Viejo, Argentina, **458** C4
Castara, Tobago, Trinidad and Tobago, **461** B4
Castelbuono, Sicilia, Italy, **295** E7
Casteljaloux, France, **290** E4
Castellane, France, **291** H5
Castelli, Buenos Aires, Argentina, **459** F5
Castelli, Chaco, Argentina, **458** E2
Castellnou de Bassella, Spain, **293** H1
Castelló de la Plana, Spain, **293** G2
Castelnau-Magnoac, France, **290** E5
Castelnaudary, France, **290** E5
Castelnovo ne'Monti, Italy, **294** C3
Castelo Branco, *district*, Portugal, **292** D2
Castelo Branco, Portugal, **292** D3
Castelo do Piauí, Brazil, **453** F4
Castelvetrano, Sicilia, Italy, **295** D7
Casterton, Australia, **135** J6
Castets, France, **290** D5
Castilla, Chile, **458** B3
Castilla, Peru, **454** B1
Castilla La Mancha, *autonomous community*, Spain, **293** F3
Castilla Y León, *autonomous community*, Spain, **292** E1
Castillo, Pampa del, *plain*, Argentina, **460** D3
Castillonnès, France, **290** E4
Castillos, Uruguay, **459** G5
Castle Carrock, England, U.K., **306** F3
Castle Cary, England, U.K., **304** E3
Castle Dale, U.S.A., **423** H2
Castle Dome Peak, *mountain peak*, U.S.A., **422** F5
Castle Donnington, England, U.K., **305** F2
Castle Douglas, Scotland, U.K., **308** F6
Castle Rock, Colorado, U.S.A., **423** L2
Castle Rock, Washington, U.S.A., **418** C3
Castle Rock Point, St Helena, **373** B3
Castlebar, Ireland, **309** C4
Castlebay, Scotland, U.K., **308** B4
Castlebellingham, Ireland, **309** F4
Castleblayney, Ireland, **309** F3
Castlebridge, Ireland, **309** F5
Castlecomer, Ireland, **309** E5
Castleconnell, Ireland, **309** D5
Castlederg, Northern Ireland, U.K., **309** E3
Castledermot, Ireland, **309** F5
Castleford, England, U.K., **307** G4
Castlegar, Canada, **413** L7
Castlegregory, Ireland, **309** B5
Castleisland, Ireland, **309** C5
Castlemaine, Ireland, **309** C5
Castlemartyr, Ireland, **309** D6
Castlepoint, New Zealand, **133** F5
Castlepollard, Ireland, **309** E4
Castlereagh, *district*, Northern Ireland, U.K., **309** G3
Castleton, England, U.K., **307** H3
Castletown, Ireland, **309** E5
Castletown, Isle of Man, **306** D3
Castletown, Scotland, U.K., **308** F2
Castletown Bearhaven, Ireland, **309** C6
Castlewellan, Northern Ireland, U.K., **309** G3
Castlewood, U.S.A., **420** E3
Castor, Canada, **413** P5
Castor, *river*, Canada, **415** Q5
Castor, U.S.A., **424** F3
Castres, France, **290** F5
Castries, St Lucia, **427** D3
Castro, Brazil, **459** G2
Castro, Chile, **460** C2
Castro, Punta, *point*, Argentina, **460** E2
Castro Marim, Portugal, **292** D4
Castro-Urdiales, Spain, **293** F1
Castro Verde, Portugal, **292** C4
Castrovillari, Italy, **295** F6
Castrovirreyna, Peru, **454** C3
Castuera, Spain, **292** E3
Casuarito, Colombia, **451** E3
Caswell Sound, New Zealand, **133** A7
Cat Island, Bahamas, **428** G1
Cat Lake, Canada, **414** J6
Cat Lake, *lake*, Canada, **414** J6
Catabola, Angola, **368** C5
Catacaos, Peru, **454** B1
Catacocha, Ecuador, **450** B5
Cataguases, Brazil, **457** E5
Catahoula Lake, U.S.A., **424** F4
Catalão, Brazil, **456** D5
Çatalca, Turkey, **297** G5
Catalina, Bahía, *bay*, Providencia, Colombia, **461** C1
Catalina, U.S.A., **423** H5
Cataluña, *autonomous community*, Spain, **293** H2
Catamarca, *province*, Argentina, **458** C3
Catan Lil, Argentina, **460** C1
Catandica, Mozambique, **371** F2
Catanduanes Island, Philippines, **204** D3
Catania, Golfo di, *gulf*, Sicilia, Italy, **295** E7
Catania, Sicilia, Italy, **295** E7
Catanzaro, Italy, **295** F6
Catarina, Raso da, *mountain range*, Brazil, **457** F2
Catarina, U.S.A., **424** C5
Catarman, Philippines, **204** D3
Catarroja, Spain, **293** G3
Catatumbo, *river*, Venezuela, **450** D2
Cataxa, Mozambique, **369** F6
Catbalogan, Philippines, **204** D4
Catedral, Cerro, *mountain peak*, Uruguay, **459** F5
Cateel, Philippines, **204** D5
Caterham, England, U.K., **305** G3
Catete, Angola, **368** B4
Cathedral Mountain, *mountain peak*, U.S.A., **423** M6
Catherine Point, Ascension, **373** A3
Cathlamet, U.S.A., **418** C3
Catia La Mar, Venezuela, **451** E1
Catió, Guinea-Bissau, **364** A2
Catnip Mountain, *mountain peak*, U.S.A., **418** E6
Catoche, Cabo, *cape*, Mexico, **431** J4
Catorce, Mexico, **431** E4
Catoute, *mountain peak*, Spain, **292** D1
Catriel, Argentina, **458** C5
Catriló, Argentina, **458** D5
Catrimani, Brazil, **451** G4
Catrimani, *river*, Brazil, **451** F4
Catskill, U.S.A., **426** D3
Catskill Mountains, *mountain range*, U.S.A., **426** C3
Catterick, England, U.K., **307** G3
Catuane, Mozambique, **371** F4
Cauaxi, *river*, Brazil, **452** D4
Cauayan, Luzon Island, Philippines, **204** C2
Cauayan, Negros Island, Philippines, **204** C4
Cauca, *river*, Colombia, **450** C2
Caucaia, Brazil, **453** F4
Caucasia, Colombia, **450** C2
Caucasus *see* Bol'shoy Kavkaz, *mountain range*, Asia/Europe, **222** D4
Caucete, Argentina, **458** C4
Caungula, Angola, **368** C4
Cauquenes, Chile, **458** B5
Caura, *river*, Venezuela, **451** F2
Caures, *river*, Brazil, **451** F4
Causapscal, Canada, **416** H5
Căuşeni, Moldova, **296** G2
Caussade, France, **290** E4
Cautário, *river*, Brazil, **455** F3
Cauto, *river*, Cuba, **429** F2
Cavalcante, Brazil, **456** D3
Cavalier, U.S.A., **420** E1
Cavalla, *river*, Liberia, **364** C3
Cavalli Islands, New Zealand, **132** D2
Cavallo, Île, *island*, Corse, France, **295** B5
Cavally, *river*, Côte d'Ivoire, **364** C3
Cavan, *county*, Ireland, **309** E4
Cavan, Ireland, **309** E4
Cavarzere, Italy, **294** D3
Çavdarhisar, Turkey, **297** G6
Cave, New Zealand, **133** C7
Cave City, U.S.A., **424** G2
Cavern Peak, *mountain peak*, Auckland Islands, New Zealand, **132** J10
Caviana, Ilha, *island*, Brazil, **452** C3
Cavinas, Bolivia, **455** E3
Cavnic, Romania, **296** D2
Cawdor, Scotland, U.K., **308** F3
Cawston, England, U.K., **305** J2
Caxias, Brazil, **453** E4
Caxias do Sul, Brazil, **459** G3
Caxito, Angola, **368** B4
Çay, Turkey, **224** D5
Cayambe, Ecuador, **450** B4
Cayambe, Volcán, *mountain peak*, Ecuador, **450** C4
Cayenne, French Guiana, **452** C2
Cayman Brac, *island*, Cayman Islands, **429** F3
Cayman Islands, *U.K. dependency*, Caribbean Sea, **409** Q7
Cayman Trench, *underwater feature*, Caribbean Sea, **479** N3
Caynabo, Somalia, **367** G3
Cayuga Lake, U.S.A., **426** B3
Cazalla de la Sierra, Spain, **292** E4
Căzăneşti, Romania, **296** F3
Cazaux et de Sanguinet, Étang de, *lake*, France, **290** D4
Čazma, Croatia, **294** F3
Cazombo, Angola, **368** D5
Cazorla, Spain, **293** F4
Cazula, Mozambique, **369** F6
Cea, *river*, Spain, **292** E1
Ceará, *state*, Brazil, **453** F4
Ceara Plain, *underwater feature*, Atlantic Ocean, **477** E6
Cébaco, Isla de, *island*, Panama, **429** E6
Ceballos, Mexico, **430** D3
Cebolla, U.S.A., **423** K3
Cebollati, *river*, Uruguay, **459** F4
Cebu, *island*, Philippines, **204** C4
Cebu, Philippines, **204** C4
Ceccano, Italy, **295** D5
Cece, Hungary, **289** J5
Cecina, Italy, **294** C4
Cedar, *river*, Iowa, U.S.A., **420** G4
Cedar, *river*, North Dakota, U.S.A., **420** B2
Cedar City, U.S.A., **422** G3
Cedar Grove, U.S.A., **421** N6
Cedar Key, U.S.A., **425** L5
Cedar Lake, Canada, **414** D5
Cedar Rapids, U.S.A., **420** H5
Cedartown, U.S.A., **425** K2
Cedarvale, U.S.A., **423** L4
Cedros, Isla, *island*, Mexico, **430** B2
Cedros Trench, *underwater feature*, Pacific Ocean, **479** L3
Ceduna, Australia, **134** G5
Cedynia, Poland, **289** G2
Cée, Spain, **292** C1
Ceel Gaal, Bari, Somalia, **367** H2
Ceel Gaal, Woqooyi Galbeed, Somalia, **367** F2
Ceelbuur, Somalia, **367** G4
Ceerigaabo, Somalia, **367** G2
Cefalù, Sicilia, Italy, **295** D6
Cega, *river*, Spain, **292** E2
Cegléd, Hungary, **289** J5
Cehegin, Spain, **293** G3
Ceheng, China, **215** H4
Cehu Silvaniei, Romania, **296** D2
Celaya, Mexico, **431** E4
Celbridge, Ireland, **309** F4
Celebes Basin, *underwater feature*, South China Sea, **478** C4
Celebes Sea, Indonesia/ Philippines, **198** C2
Celebes *see* Sulawesi, *island*, Indonesia, **198** B3
Celendín, Peru, **454** C2
Celina, U.S.A., **425** K1
Celje, Slovenia, **294** E2
Celle, Germany, **288** E2
Celny, Russian Federation, **211** M2
Celorico da Beira, Portugal, **292** D2
Celyn, Llyn, *lake*, Wales, U.K., **304** D2
Cenajo, Embalse del, *reservoir*, Spain, **293** G3
Cenderawasih, Teluk, *bay*, Indonesia, **199** F3
Centenary, Zimbabwe, **371** F2
Center, Colorado, U.S.A., **423** L3
Center, Texas, U.S.A., **424** E4
Centerville, Iowa, U.S.A., **420** G5
Centerville, South Dakota, U.S.A., **420** E4
Centinela, Picacho del, *mountain peak*, Mexico, **430** E2
Cento, Italy, **294** C3
Central, *administrative region*, Ghana, **364** D3
Central, *administrative region*, Malawi, **369** F5
Central, Cordillera, *mountain range*, Bolivia, **447** F5
Central, Cordillera, *mountain range*, Panama, **429** E5
Central, *district*, Botswana, **370** D3
Central, *province*, Kenya, **369** G3
Central, *province*, Papua New Guinea, **140** B5
Central, *province*, Zambia, **369** E5
Central African Republic, *country*, Africa, **358** G6
Central Brāhui Range, *mountain range*, Pakistan, **218** A3
Central Butte, Canada, **413** R6
Central City, U.S.A., **421** K7
Central Makrān Range, *mountain range*, Pakistan, **221** H3
Central Pacific Basin, *underwater feature*, Pacific Ocean, **478** F4
Central Patricia, Canada, **414** J6
Central Range, *mountain range*, Papua New Guinea, **140** A4
Centralia, Illinois, U.S.A., **421** J6
Centralia, Washington, U.S.A., **418** C3

Cleopatra Needle, *mountain peak*, Philippines, **204** B4
Cléres, France, **305** J5
Clermont, Australia, **135** K3
Clermont, France, **305** K5
Clermont-Ferrand, France, **291** F4
Clervaux, Luxembourg, **291** H1
Clevedon, England, U.K., **304** E3
Cleveland, Georgia, U.S.A., **425** L2
Cleveland, Mississippi, U.S.A., **424** G3
Cleveland, Ohio, U.S.A., **421** N5
Cleveland, Tennessee, U.S.A., **425** K2
Cleveland, Texas, U.S.A., **424** E4
Cleveland Hills, England, U.K., **307** G3
Clevelândia, Brazil, **459** G3
Clevelândia do Norte, Brazil, **452** C2
Cleveleys, England, U.K., **306** E4
Clew Bay, Ireland, **309** C4
Clewiston, U.S.A., **425** M6
Clifden, Ireland, **309** B4
Cliffdell, U.S.A., **418** D3
Cliffe, England, U.K., **305** H3
Cliffony, Ireland, **309** D3
Clifford Bay, New Zealand, **133** E5
Clifton, U.S.A., **423** J5
Clifton Forge, U.S.A., **421** P7
Climax, Canada, **413** Q7
Climax, Colorado, U.S.A., **423** K2
Climax, Minnesota, U.S.A., **420** E2
Cline, U.S.A., **424** B5
Clinton, British Columbia, Canada, **412** J6
Clinton, Iowa, U.S.A., **420** H5
Clinton, Massachusetts, U.S.A., **426** E3
Clinton, Mississippi, U.S.A., **424** G3
Clinton, Missouri, U.S.A., **420** G6
Clinton, Montana, U.S.A., **418** H3
Clinton, North Carolina, U.S.A., **425** N2
Clinton, Oklahoma, U.S.A., **424** C2
Clinton, Ontario, Canada, **421** N4
Clinton, South Carolina, U.S.A., **425** M2
Clipperton Fracture Zone, *tectonic feature*, Pacific Ocean, **479** J4
Clitheroe, England, U.K., **306** F4
Cliza, Bolivia, **455** F4
Clo-oose, Canada, **412** G7
Clogh, Northern Ireland, U.K., **309** F3
Clogheen, Ireland, **309** D5
Clogher Head, *point*, Ireland, **309** F4
Clonakilty, Ireland, **309** D6
Clonakilty Bay, Ireland, **309** D6
Clonbern, Ireland, **309** D4
Cloncurry, Australia, **135** J3
Clones, Ireland, **309** E3
Clonmel, Ireland, **309** E5
Clonroche, Ireland, **309** F5
Cloonbannin, Ireland, **309** C5
Cloppenburg, Germany, **288** D2
Cloquet, U.S.A., **420** G2
Cloridorme, Canada, **416** J5
Clorinda, Argentina, **459** F2
Cloud Peak, *mountain peak*, U.S.A., **419** L4
Clova, Scotland, U.K., **308** F4
Cloverdale, U.S.A., **422** B2
Clovis, U.S.A., **423** M4
Cluanie, Loch, *lake*, Scotland, U.K., **308** D3
Cluff Lake, Canada, **413** Q2
Cluj-Napoca, Romania, **296** D2
Clun, England, U.K., **304** D2

Cluny, France, **291** G3
Clutha, *river*, New Zealand, **133** B7
Clydach, Wales, U.K., **304** D3
Clyde, *river*, Scotland, U.K., **308** F5
Clyde Park, U.S.A., **419** J4
Clyde River, Canada, **411** N2
Clydebank, Scotland, U.K., **308** E5
Clydevale, New Zealand, **133** B8
Clyro, Wales, U.K., **304** D2
Cnoc Moy, Scotland, U.K., **308** D5
Coahuila, *state*, Mexico, **430** E3
Coal, *river*, Canada, **412** E1
Coal River, Canada, **412** F2
Coaldale, U.S.A., **422** E2
Coalgate, U.S.A., **424** D2
Coalinga, U.S.A., **422** C3
Coalville, England, U.K., **305** F2
Coari, Brazil, **451** F5
Coari, Lago de, *lake*, Brazil, **451** F5
Coari, *river*, Brazil, **451** F5
Coast, *province*, Kenya, **369** G3
Coast Mountains, *mountain range*, Canada, **412** C2
Coast Range, *mountain range*, U.S.A., **406** L5
Coatbridge, Scotland, U.K., **308** E5
Coats Island, Canada, **411** L3
Coats Land, *region*, Antarctica, **470** C4
Coatzacoalcos, Mexico, **431** G5
Cobadin, Romania, **296** G3
Cobán, Guatemala, **428** C4
Cobar, Australia, **135** K5
Cobequid Mountains, *mountain range*, Canada, **417** J7
Cobh, Ireland, **309** D6
Cobham, *river*, Canada, **414** G5
Cobija, Bolivia, **455** E3
Cobleskill, U.S.A., **426** C3
Cobourg Peninsula, Australia, **134** G1
Cobram, Australia, **135** K6
Cóbuè, Mozambique, **369** F5
Coburg, Germany, **288** E3
Coburg Island, Canada, **411** M2
Coca, Pizzo di, *mountain peak*, Italy, **294** B2
Cocachacra, Peru, **454** D4
Cocalinho, Brazil, **456** C4
Cochabamba, Bolivia, **455** E4
Cochabamba, *department*, Bolivia, **455** E4
Cochamó, Chile, **460** C1
Cochem, Germany, **288** C3
Cochin, Canada, **413** Q5
Cochin *see* Kochi, India, **216** D4
Cochise, U.S.A., **423** J5
Cochrane, Alberta, Canada, **413** M6
Cochrane, Chile, **460** C3
Cochrane, Ontario, Canada, **415** P7
Cockburn, Canal, *channel*, Chile, **460** C5
Cockburn, Cape, Australia, **199** F5
Cockburn Harbour, Turks and Caicos Islands, **429** H2
Cockburn Town, Bahamas, **428** G1
Cockburnspath, Scotland, U.K., **308** G5
Cockerham, England, U.K., **306** F4
Cockermouth, England, U.K., **306** E3
Coclé del Norte, Panama, **429** E5
Coco, Punta, *point*, Colombia, **450** B3
Coco, *river*, Honduras/Nicaragua, **428** D4
Coco Channel, Andaman and Nicobar Islands, India, **217** H3
Cocorná, Colombia, **450** C2
Côcos, Brazil, **457** E4

Cocos Bay, Trinidad, Trinidad and Tobago, **461** C4
Cocos (Keeling) Islands, *Australian territory*, Indian Ocean, **134** Q10
Cocos Ridge, *underwater feature*, Pacific Ocean, **479** N4
Cocula, Mexico, **430** E4
Cod, Cape, U.S.A., **426** E3
Cod Island, Canada, **411** N4
Codajás, Brazil, **451** F5
Coddington, England, U.K., **305** G1
Codera, Cabo, *cape*, Venezuela, **451** E1
Codfish Island, New Zealand, **133** A8
Codigoro, Italy, **294** D3
Codlea, Romania, **296** E3
Codó, Brazil, **453** E4
Codrington, Antigua and Barbuda, **427** D2
Codrington, Mount, *mountain peak*, Antarctica, **470** F4
Codsall, England, U.K., **304** E2
Cody, U.S.A., **419** K4
Coe, Glen, *valley*, Scotland, U.K., **308** D4
Coen, Australia, **135** J1
Coeroeni, *river*, Suriname, **452** B2
Coesfeld, Germany, **288** C3
Coetivy Island, Seychelles, **372** D2
Coeur d'Alene, U.S.A., **418** F3
Coeur d'Alene Lake, U.S.A., **418** F3
Coffee Bay, South Africa, **371** E5
Coffeeville, U.S.A., **425** H4
Coffeyville, U.S.A., **420** F7
Coffs Harbour, Australia, **135** L5
Cofrentes, Spain, **293** G3
Cogealac, Romania, **296** G3
Coggeshall, England, U.K., **305** H3
Cognac, France, **290** D4
Cogo, Equatorial Guinea, **368** A2
Cohagen, U.S.A., **419** L3
Coiba, Isla de, *island*, Panama, **429** E6
Coig, *river*, Argentina, **460** C4
Coigeach, Rubha, *point*, Scotland, U.K., **308** D2
Coihaique, Chile, **460** C2
Coimbatore, India, **216** D4
Coimbra, *district*, Portugal, **292** C2
Coimbra, Portugal, **292** C2
Coin, Spain, **292** E4
Coipasa, Lago de, *lake*, Bolivia, **455** E5
Coipasa, Salar de, *salt-pan*, Bolivia, **455** E5
Cojudo Blanco, Cerro, *mountain peak*, Argentina, **460** D3
Cojutepeque, El Salvador, **428** C4
Colac, Australia, **135** J6
Colac Bay, New Zealand, **133** A8
Colares, Brazil, **452** D3
Colatina, Brazil, **457** F5
Colby, U.S.A., **420** C6
Colchester, England, U.K., **305** J3
Cold Lake, Canada, **413** P4
Cold Lake, *lake*, Canada, **413** Q4
Cold Springs, U.S.A., **422** E2
Coldstream, Canada, **413** K6
Coldwater, Kansas, U.S.A., **420** D7
Coldwater, Michigan, U.S.A., **421** L5
Coldwater, Missouri, U.S.A., **420** H7
Colebrook, U.S.A., **426** E2
Coleford, England, U.K., **304** E3
Coleman, U.S.A., **424** C4
Çölemerik, Turkey, **224** F5

Colemon, U.S.A., **421** L4
Coleraine, *district*, Northern Ireland, U.K., **309** F2
Coleraine, Northern Ireland, U.K., **309** F2
Coleridge, Lake, New Zealand, **133** C6
Coles, Punta, *point*, Peru, **454** D4
Colesberg, South Africa, **370** E5
Colfax, California, U.S.A., **422** C2
Colfax, Louisiana, U.S.A., **424** F4
Colfax, Washington, U.S.A., **418** F3
Colhué Huapi, Lago, *lake*, Argentina, **460** D2
Colico, Italy, **294** B2
Colima, Mexico, **430** E5
Colima, *state*, Mexico, **430** D5
Colinas, Brazil, **453** E5
Coll, *island*, Scotland, U.K., **308** C4
Collaguasi, Chile, **455** E5
College Station, U.S.A., **424** D4
Collie, Australia, **134** D5
Collier Bay, Australia, **134** E2
Collingwood, Canada, **421** N3
Collingwood, New Zealand, **133** D5
Collins, Iowa, U.S.A., **420** G5
Collins, Mississippi, U.S.A., **425** H4
Collipulli, Chile, **458** B5
Collooney, Ireland, **309** D3
Colmar, France, **291** H2
Colmenar, France, **290** E5
Colmonell, Scotland, U.K., **308** E5
Coln, *river*, England, U.K., **305** F3
Colne, England, U.K., **306** F4
Colne, *river*, England, U.K., **305** H3
Cologne *see* Köln, Germany, **288** C3
Colômbia, Brazil, **456** D5
Colombia, Colombia, **450** C3
Colombia, *country*, South America, **449** E3
Colombo, Sri Lanka, **216** D5
Colome, U.S.A., **420** D4
Colomiers, France, **290** E5
Colón, Buenos Aires, Argentina, **458** E4
Colón, Cuba, **429** E2
Colón, Entre Rios, Argentina, **459** E4
Colón, Panama, **429** F5
Colonel Hill, Bahamas, **429** G2
Colonia del Sacramento, Uruguay, **459** F5
Colonia Dora, Argentina, **458** D3
Colonia Josefa, Argentina, **460** E1
Colonia Lavalleja, Uruguay, **459** F4
Colonia Vicente Guerrero, Mexico, **430** A2
Colonsay, *island*, Scotland, U.K., **308** C4
Colorado, *river*, Argentina, **460** E1
Colorado, *river*, Brazil, **455** F3
Colorado, *river*, Mexico/U.S.A., **407** M5
Colorado, *state*, U.S.A., **423** K2
Colorado City, Colorado, U.S.A., **422** G3
Colorado City, Texas, U.S.A., **424** B3
Colorado Desert, U.S.A., **422** E5
Colorado do Oeste, Brazil, **455** G3
Colorado Plateau, U.S.A., **423** H3
Colorado Springs, U.S.A., **423** L2
Colotlán, Mexico, **430** E4
Colquechaca, Bolivia, **455** E5
Colquiri, Bolivia, **455** E4

Colquitt, U.S.A., **425** K4
Colsterworth, England, U.K., **305** G2
Colstrip, U.S.A., **419** L4
Coltishall, England, U.K., **305** J2
Colton, U.S.A., **423** H2
Columbia, District of, *district*, U.S.A., **421** Q6
Columbia, Kentucky, U.S.A., **421** L7
Columbia, Louisiana, U.S.A., **424** F3
Columbia, Mississippi, U.S.A., **424** H4
Columbia, Missouri, U.S.A., **420** G6
Columbia, Mount, *mountain peak*, Canada, **413** L5
Columbia, North Carolina, U.S.A., **426** B7
Columbia, *river*, Canada/U.S.A., **406** L4
Columbia, South Carolina, U.S.A., **425** M3
Columbia, Tennessee, U.S.A., **425** J2
Columbia Basin, U.S.A., **406** M4
Columbia City, U.S.A., **421** L5
Columbia Falls, U.S.A., **418** G2
Columbia Mountains, *mountain range*, Canada, **412** J5
Columbia Plateau, U.S.A., **418** E4
Columbiana, U.S.A., **425** J3
Columbine, Cape, South Africa, **370** C5
Columbus, Georgia, U.S.A., **425** K3
Columbus, Indiana, U.S.A., **421** L6
Columbus, Iowa, U.S.A., **421** J4
Columbus, Mississippi, U.S.A., **425** H3
Columbus, Nebraska, U.S.A., **420** E5
Columbus, New Mexico, U.S.A., **423** K6
Columbus, Ohio, U.S.A., **421** M6
Columbus, Texas, U.S.A., **424** D5
Columbus Point, Tobago, Trinidad and Tobago, **461** B4
Colville, Cape, New Zealand, **132** E3
Colville, *river*, U.S.A., **410** D3
Colville, U.S.A., **418** F2
Colville Lake, Canada, **410** G3
Colwyn Bay, Wales, U.K., **306** E4
Colyford, England, U.K., **304** D4
Comacchio, Italy, **294** D3
Comallo, *river*, Argentina, **460** C1
Coman, Mount, *mountain peak*, Antarctica, **470** B5
Comanche, Oklahoma, U.S.A., **424** D2
Comanche, Texas, U.S.A., **424** C4
Comandante Salas, Argentina, **458** C4
Comăneşti, Romania, **296** F2
Comarapa, Bolivia, **455** F4
Comarnic, Romania, **296** E3
Comas, Peru, **454** C3
Comayagua, Honduras, **428** D4
Combarbalá, Chile, **458** B4
Combe Martin, England, U.K., **304** C3
Comber, Northern Ireland, U.K., **309** G3
Combermere Bay, Myanmar, **205** B4
Comendador, Dominican Republic, **429** H3
Comeragh Mountains, *mountain range*, Ireland, **309** E5
Comfort, U.S.A., **424** C5
Comfort Bight, Canada, **417** P3
Comino, Capo, *cape*, Sardegna, Italy, **295** B5

Comitán de Domínguez, Mexico, **431** G5
Commanda, Canada, **421** P3
Commandante Luis Piedrabuena, Argentina, **460** D3
Commanders Bay, Aruba, Netherlands, **461** B3
Commerce, U.S.A., **424** E3
Committee Bay, Canada, **411** L3
Como, Italy, **294** B3
Como, Lago di, *lake*, Italy, **294** B3
Comodoro Rivadavia, Argentina, **460** D2
Comoé, *river*, Côte d'Ivoire, **364** D3
Comondú, Mexico, **430** C3
Comoros, *country*, Indian Ocean, **359** K8
Comox, Canada, **412** G7
Compiègne, France, **291** F2
Comprida, Ilha, *island*, Brazil, **459** H2
Comrat, Moldova, **296** G2
Comrie, Scotland, U.K., **308** F4
Côn Sơn, Vietnam, **203** E4
Cona, China, **214** D4
Cona Niyeu, Argentina, **460** D1
Conakry, Guinea, **364** B3
Concarneau, France, **290** C3
Conceição, Brazil, **453** F5
Conceição da Barra, Brazil, **457** F5
Conceição do Araguaia, Brazil, **456** D2
Conceição do Coité, Brazil, **457** F3
Concepción, Argentina, **458** D3
Concepción, Beni, Bolivia, **455** E3
Concepción, Canal, *channel*, Chile, **460** B4
Concepción, Chile, **458** B5
Concepción, Paraguay, **459** F2
Concepción, Santa Cruz, Bolivia, **455** F4
Concepción del Uruguay, Argentina, **459** E4
Conception Bay, Canada, **417** Q6
Concession, Zimbabwe, **371** F2
Conchas, Brazil, **459** H2
Conches-en-Ouche, France, **290** E2
Conchi, Chile, **458** C2
Concho, U.S.A., **423** J4
Conchos, *river*, Mexico, **430** D3
Concord, California, U.S.A., **422** B3
Concord, New Hampshire, U.S.A., **426** E3
Concord, North Carolina, U.S.A., **425** M2
Concordia, Argentina, **459** E4
Concordia, Peru, **450** C5
Conde, Brazil, **457** G3
Condega, Nicaragua, **428** D4
Condeúba, Brazil, **457** F4
Condom, France, **290** E5
Condon, U.S.A., **418** D4
Cóndor, Cordillera del, *mountain range*, Peru/Ecuador, **450** B5
Conecuh, *river*, U.S.A., **425** J4
Conegliano, Italy, **294** D3
Conejos, Mexico, **430** E3
Confolens, France, **290** E3
Confuso, *river*, Paraguay, **459** E2
Cong, Ireland, **309** C4
Congaz, Moldova, **296** G2
Conghua, China, **207** B1
Congjiang, China, **206** B3
Congleton, England, U.K., **304** E1
Congo, *country*, Africa, **359** G6
Congo, *river*, Congo, **357** G7
Congo Basin, Africa, **357** G6
Congress, U.S.A., **422** G4
Cónico, Cerro, *mountain peak*, Argentina, **460** C2
Coningsby, England, U.K., **307** H4
Coniston, England, U.K., **306** E3
Coniston Water, *lake*, England, U.K., **306** E3
Conklin, Canada, **413** P4
Conlara, Argentina, **458** D4
Conn, Lough, *lake*, Ireland, **309** C3
Connah's Quay, Wales, U.K., **304** D1
Connaught, *province*, Ireland, **309** C4
Conneaut, U.S.A., **421** N5
Connecticut, *river*, U.S.A., **426** D3
Connecticut, *state*, U.S.A., **426** D4
Connell, U.S.A., **418** E3
Connemara, *region*, Ireland, **309** C4
Conon Bridge, Scotland, U.K., **308** E3
Conroe, Lake, U.S.A., **424** E4
Conroe, U.S.A., **424** E4
Conselheiro Lafaiete, Brazil, **457** E5
Conselheiro Pena, Brazil, **457** F5
Consett, England, U.K., **307** G3
Consort, Canada, **413** P5
Constância dos Baetas, Brazil, **455** F2
Constanța, Romania, **296** G3
Constantine, Algeria, **361** H1
Consuegra, Spain, **293** F3
Consul, Canada, **413** Q7
Contact, U.S.A., **418** G6
Contagem, Brazil, **457** E5
Contamaná, Peru, **454** C2
Contas, de, *river*, Brazil, **457** F3
Contreras, Embalse de, *reservoir*, Spain, **293** G3
Contreras, Isla, *island*, Chile, **460** B4
Contres, France, **290** E3
Contrexéville, France, **291** G2
Contumazá, Peru, **454** B2
Contwoyto Lake, Canada, **410** H3
Conty, France, **305** K5
Conway, Arkansas, U.S.A., **424** F2
Conway, New Hampshire, U.S.A., **426** E3
Conway, South Carolina, U.S.A., **425** N3
Conwy, *unitary authority*, Wales, U.K., **304** D1
Conwy, Wales, U.K., **306** E4
Conwy Bay, Wales, U.K., **306** D4
Coober Pedy, Australia, **135** G4
Cook, Bahía, *bay*, Chile, **460** C5
Cook, Cape, Canada, **412** E6
Cook, Mount, *mountain peak*, Antarctica, **470** F4
Cook, Mount, *mountain peak*, New Zealand, **129** F6
Cook Islands, *New Zealand territory*, Pacific Ocean, **131** J3
Cook Strait, New Zealand, **133** E5
Cookeville, U.S.A., **425** K1
Cooking Lake, Canada, **413** N5
Cookstown, *district*, Northern Ireland, U.K., **309** F3
Cookstown, Northern Ireland, U.K., **309** F3
Cooktown, Australia, **135** K2
Coolangatta, Australia, **135** L4
Coolgardie, Australia, **134** E5
Coolidge, U.S.A., **423** H5
Cooma, Australia, **135** K6
Coon Rapids, U.S.A., **420** G3
Coonabarabran, Australia, **135** K5
Coonamble, Australia, **135** K5
Coondapoor, India, **216** C3
Coonoor, India, **216** D4
Cooper, *river*, Australia, **135** H4
Cooper's Town, Bahamas, **428** F1
Cooperstown, U.S.A., **420** D2
Coos Bay, U.S.A., **418** B5
Cootehill, Ireland, **309** E3
Copacabana, Argentina, **458** C3
Copahue, Volcán, *mountain peak*, Chile, **458** B5
Copala, Mexico, **431** F5
Cope, U.S.A., **423** M2
Copeland, U.S.A., **420** C7
Copemish, U.S.A., **421** L3
Copenhagen *see* København, Denmark, **286** F5
Copere, Bolivia, **455** F5
Copiapó, Chile, **458** B3
Copiapó, *river*, Chile, **458** B3
Copiapó, Volcán, *mountain peak*, Chile, **458** C3
Copixaba, Brazil, **457** E3
Copper Harbor, U.S.A., **421** K2
Copperas Cove, U.S.A., **424** D4
Copperbelt, *province*, Zambia, **369** E5
Copplestone, England, U.K., **304** D4
Coqên, China, **214** C3
Coquille, U.S.A., **418** B5
Coquimbo, *administrative region*, Chile, **458** B4
Coquimbo, Chile, **458** B3
Corabia, Romania, **296** E4
Coração de Jesus, Brazil, **457** E4
Coracesium *see* Alanya, Turkey, **225** A1
Coracora, Peru, **454** D4
Coral, Cape, U.S.A., **425** M6
Coral Bay, Australia, **134** C3
Coral Gables, U.S.A., **425** M7
Coral Harbour, Canada, **411** L3
Coral Sea, Pacific Ocean, **135** K1
Coral Sea Basin, *underwater feature*, Pacific Ocean, **478** D5
Coral Sea Islands, *Australian territory*, Pacific Ocean, **135** L2
Corantijn, *river*, Suriname, **452** B2
Corbett, Argentina, **458** E5
Corbie, France, **290** F2
Corbigny, France, **291** F3
Corbin, U.S.A., **421** L7
Corbridge, England, U.K., **306** F3
Corby, England, U.K., **305** G2
Corbyvale, New Zealand, **133** D5
Corcovado, Argentina, **460** C2
Corcovado, Golfo, *gulf*, Chile, **460** C2
Corcovado, Volcán, *mountain peak*, Chile, **460** C2
Cordele, U.S.A., **425** L4
Cordell, U.S.A., **424** C2
Cordes-sur-Ciel, France, **290** E4
Córdoba, Argentina, **458** D4
Córdoba, Cayo, *island*, San Andrés, Colombia, **461** B1
Córdoba, Durango, Mexico, **430** E3
Córdoba, *province*, Argentina, **458** D4
Córdoba, Sierras de, *mountain range*, Argentina, **447** F7
Córdoba, Spain, **292** E4
Córdoba, Veracruz, Mexico, **431** F5
Córdova, Peru, **454** C4
Cordova, U.S.A., **410** E3
Coreaú, Brazil, **453** F4
Corfe Castle, England, U.K., **304** E4
Corfu *see* Kerkyra, *island*, Ionioi Nisoi, Greece, **297** B6
Coria, Spain, **292** D2
Corigliano Calabro, Italy, **295** F6
Corinth, Kentucky, U.S.A., **421** L6
Corinth, Mississippi, U.S.A., **425** H2
Corinth *see* Korinthos, Greece, **297** D7
Corinthian Head, *point*, Heard and McDonald Islands, **134** S12
Corinto, Brazil, **457** E5
Corixa Grande, *river*, Bolivia/Brazil, **455** G4
Cork, *county*, Ireland, **309** C6
Cork, Ireland, **309** D6
Cork Harbour, Ireland, **309** D6
Corleone, Sicilia, Italy, **295** D7
Corleto Perticara, Italy, **295** F5
Çorlu, Turkey, **297** F5
Cormontibo, French Guiana, **452** B2
Cormorant Lake, Canada, **414** D4
Cornélio Procópio, Brazil, **459** G2
Corneliskondre, Suriname, **452** B2
Cornell, U.S.A., **420** H3
Corner Brook, Canada, **417** M5
Cornes, Pointe aux, *point*, Rodrigues, **373** B1
Cornești, Moldova, **296** F2
Corning, California, U.S.A., **422** B2
Corning, Iowa, U.S.A., **420** F5
Corning, New York, U.S.A., **426** B3
Cornudas, U.S.A., **423** L6
Cornwall, Canada, **416** D7
Cornwall, *unitary authority*, England, U.K., **304** C4
Coro, Venezuela, **451** E1
Coroatá, Brazil, **453** E4
Corocoro, Bolivia, **455** E4
Coroico, Bolivia, **455** E4
Coromandel, Brazil, **456** D5
Coromandel Range, *mountain range*, New Zealand, **132** E3
Coron, Philippines, **204** C3
Coron Island, Philippines, **204** C4
Corona, U.S.A., **423** L4
Coronach, Canada, **413** S7
Coronado, Bahía de, *bay*, Costa Rica, **428** D5
Coronation, Canada, **413** P5
Coronation Gulf, Canada, **410** H3
Coronda, Argentina, **458** E4
Coronel Dorrego, Argentina, **458** E6
Coronel Fabriciano, Brazil, **457** E5
Coronel Oviedo, Paraguay, **459** F2
Coronel Ponce, Brazil, **456** B4
Coronel Pringles, Argentina, **458** E5
Coronel Sapucaia, Brazil, **459** F2
Coronel Suárez, Argentina, **458** E5
Coronel Vidal, Argentina, **459** F5
Coropuna, Nevado, *mountain peak*, Peru, **454** D4
Çorovodë, Albania, **297** C5
Corozal, Belize, **428** C3
Corozal Point, Trinidad, Trinidad and Tobago, **461** C4
Corpus Christi, U.S.A., **424** D6
Corque, Bolivia, **455** E5
Corral, U.S.A., **418** G5
Corralejo, Islas Canarias, Spain, **373** B4
Corrales, Spain, **292** E2
Corraun Peninsula, Ireland, **309** B4
Corrente, Brazil, **457** E3
Corrente, *river*, Bahia, Brazil, **457** E3
Corrente, *river*, Goiás, Brazil, **456** C5
Correntes, Brazil, **456** B4
Correntina, Brazil, **457** E3
Corrib, Lough, *lake*, Ireland, **309** C4
Corrientes, Argentina, **459** E3
Corrientes, Cabo, *cape*, Argentina, **459** F6
Corrientes, Cabo, *cape*, Colombia, **450** C3
Corrientes, Cabo, *cape*, Cuba, **428** D2
Corrientes, Cabo, *cape*, Mexico, **430** D4
Corrientes, *province*, Argentina, **459** E3
Corrientes, *river*, Argentina, **459** E3
Corrigan, U.S.A., **424** E4
Corrigin, Australia, **134** D5
Corris, Wales, U.K., **304** D2
Corriverton, Guyana, **451** H3
Corrofin, Ireland, **309** C5
Corse, *administrative region*, France, **295** B4
Corse, Cap, *cape*, Corse, France, **294** B4
Corse (Corsica), *island*, France, **295** B4
Corsham, England, U.K., **304** E3
Corsica *see* Corse, *island*, France, **295** B4
Corsica, U.S.A., **420** D4
Corsicana, U.S.A., **424** D3
Corte, Corse, France, **295** B4
Cortegana, Spain, **292** D4
Cortez, U.S.A., **423** J3
Cortina d'Ampezzo, Italy, **294** D2
Cortland, U.S.A., **426** B3
Corton, England, U.K., **305** J2
Cortona, Italy, **294** D4
Coruche, Portugal, **292** C3
Çoruh Nehri, *river*, Turkey, **224** F4
Çorum, Turkey, **224** D4
Corumbá, Brazil, **456** B5
Corumbá, *river*, Brazil, **456** D4
Corund, Romania, **296** E2
Coruripe, Brazil, **457** G3
Corvallis, U.S.A., **418** C4
Corvette, Lac de la, *lake*, Canada, **416** D3
Corvo, *island*, Azores, Portugal, **360** L6
Corwen, Wales, U.K., **304** D2
Cosalá, Mexico, **430** D3
Cosapa, Bolivia, **455** E5
Coscaya, Chile, **455** E5
Cosenza, Italy, **295** F6
Coshocton, U.S.A., **421** N5
Cosigüina, Punta, *point*, Nicaragua, **428** C4
Cosmoledo Group, *islands*, Seychelles, **372** B2
Cosne-sur-Loire, France, **291** F3
Cosquín, Argentina, **458** D4
Costa Blanca, *coastal area*, Spain, **293** G3
Costa Brava, *coastal area*, Spain, **293** J2
Costa Daurada, *coastal area*, Spain, **293** H2
Costa de Cantabria, *coastal area*, Spain, **293** F1
Costa de la Luz, *coastal area*, Spain, **292** D4
Costa de Sol, *coastal area*, Spain, **292** E4
Costa del Azahar, *coastal area*, Spain, **293** H3
Costa Marques, Brazil, **455** F3
Costa Rica, *country*, Central America, **409** Q8
Costa Rica, Mexico, **430** D3
Costa Vasca, *coastal area*, Spain, **293** F1
Costa Verde, *central area*, Spain, **292** D1
Costelloe, Ireland, **309** C4
Costești, Moldova, **296** F2
Costești, Romania, **296** E3
Cotabato, Philippines, **204** D5
Cotagaita, Bolivia, **455** F5
Côte d'Azur, *coastal area*, France, **291** H5
Côte d'Ivoire, *country*, Africa, **358** E6
Côte d'Or, *region*, France, **291** G3
Coteau, U.S.A., **419** N2

C6
Cunene, *river*, Angola, **368** B6
Cuneo, Italy, **294** A3
Cunnamulla, Australia, **135** K4
Cupar, Scotland, U.K., **308** F4
Cupcina, Moldova, **296** F1
Cupica, Colombia, **450** C2
Cupica, Golfo de, *gulf*, Colombia, **450** B2
Ćuprija, Yugoslavia, **296** C4
Curaçá, Brazil, **457** F2
Curaçao, *island*, Netherlands Antilles, **461** C3
Curacautín, Chile, **458** B6
Curacó, *river*, Argentina, **458** D6
Curaray, *river*, Ecuador/Peru, **450** C4
Curaumilla, Punta, *point*, Chile, **458** B4
Curepipe, Mauritius, **373** C1
Curicó, Chile, **458** B5
Curicuriari, *river*, Brazil, **451** E4
Curieuse, *island*, Seychelles, **373** A2
Curimatá, Brazil, **457** E3
Curimataú, *river*, Brazil, **453** G5
Curitiba, Brazil, **459** H2
Curitibanos, Brazil, **459** G3
Curlew, U.S.A., **418** E2
Curoca, *river*, Angola, **368** B6
Currais Novos, Brazil, **453** G5
Curral Velho, Cape Verde, **360** Q8
Curralinho, Brazil, **452** D3
Currant, U.S.A., **422** F2
Currie, Australia, **135** J6
Currie, U.S.A., **422** F1
Currituck, U.S.A., **426** C6
Curtea de Argeş, Romania, **296** E3
Curtici, Romania, **296** C2
Curtis Island, Australia, **135** L3
Curtis Island, Kermadec Islands, New Zealand, **132** L12
Curuá, Amapá, *river*, Brazil, **452** B3
Curuá, Ilha, *island*, Brazil, **452** C3
Curuá, Pará, *river*, Brazil, **452** B5
Curuá Una, *river*, Brazil, **452** B4
Curuaés, *river*, Brazil, **452** B5
Curuçá, Brazil, **452** D3
Curuçá, *river*, Brazil, **450** D5
Curumu, Brazil, **452** C3
Curupira, Serra, *mountain range*, Brazil/Venezuela, **451** F4
Cururu, Brazil, **456** B2
Cururu, *river*, Brazil, **452** B5
Cururupu, Brazil, **453** E3
Curuzú Cuatiá, Argentina, **459** E3
Curvelo, Brazil, **457** E5
Cushendall, Northern Ireland, U.K., **309** F2
Cushendun, Northern Ireland, U.K., **309** F2
Cushing, Mount, *mountain peak*, Canada, **412** F3
Cushing, U.S.A., **424** D2
Cusseta, U.S.A., **425** K3
Custer, Montana, U.S.A., **419** L3
Custer, South Dakota, U.S.A., **420** B4
Cut Bank, U.S.A., **418** H2
Cut Knife, Canada, **413** Q5
Cutato, *river*, Angola, **368** C5
Cutler Ridge, U.S.A., **425** M7
Cutra, Lough, *lake*, Ireland, **309** D4
Cutral-Có, Argentina, **458** C6
Cuttack, India, **219** F5
Cuvelai, Angola, **368** C6
Cuveşdia, Romania, **296** C3
Cuvette, *administrative region*, Congo, **368** C3
Cuxhaven, Germany, **288** D2
Cuya, Chile, **455** D5
Cuyabeno, Ecuador, **450** C4
Cuyo Islands, Philippines, **204** C4
Cuyuni, *river*, Guyana, **451** G2
Cuza Vodă, Romania, **296** F3
Cuzco, Peru, **454** D3
Čvrsnica, *mountain peak*, Bosnia and Herzegovina, **294** F4
Cwmbran, Wales, U.K., **304** D3
Cyangugu, Rwanda, **369** E3
Cyclades *see* Kyklades, *islands*, Greece, **297** E7
Cynthia, Canada, **413** M5
Cynwyl Elfed, Wales, U.K., **304** C3
Cypress Hills, Canada, **419** J2
Cyprus, *country*, Asia, **196** E6
Czaplinek, Poland, **289** H2
Czar, Canada, **413** P5
Czarnków, Poland, **289** H2
Czech Republic, *country*, Europe, **282** F6
Czersk, Poland, **289** H2
Częstochowa, Poland, **289** J3
Człopa, Poland, **289** H2
Człuchów, Poland, **289** H2
Czyżew-Osada, Poland, **289** L2

D

Đà, *river*, Vietnam, **203** E1
Da Hinggan Ling, *mountain range*, China, **211** G3
Da Juh, China, **213** G5
Đà Lạt, Vietnam, **203** F4
Đà Nẵng, Vietnam, **203** F2
Da Qaidam, China, **213** G5
Da Xian, China, **215** H3
Da'an, China, **211** J3
Daanbantayan, Philippines, **204** C4
Daba Shan, *mountain range*, China, **206** B1
Ḑab'ah, Jordan, **225** C4
Dabajuro, Venezuela, **451** D1
Dabakala, Côte d'Ivoire, **364** D3
Dabas, Hungary, **289** J5
Dabat, Ethiopia, **367** E2
Dabatou, Guinea, **364** B2
Dabbāgh, Jabal, *mountain peak*, Saudi Arabia, **225** C6
Dabeiba, Colombia, **450** C2
Daborow, Somalia, **367** G3
Dabou, Côte d'Ivoire, **364** D3
Dabra, India, **218** D4
Dąbrowa Górnicza, Poland, **289** J3
Dăbuleni, Romania, **296** E4
Dacca *see* Dhaka, Bangladesh, **214** D5
Dachang, China, **215** H4
Dachau, Germany, **288** E4
Dacre, New Zealand, **133** B8
Dadale, Solomon Islands, **141** A1
Dadanawa, Guyana, **451** G3
Dade City, U.S.A., **425** L5
Dādhar, Pakistan, **218** A3
Dadi, Tanjong, *point*, Indonesia, **199** E3
Dadiangas *see* General Santos, Philippines, **204** D5
Dādra and Nagar Haveli, *union territory*, India, **218** C6
Dādri, *river*, India, **218** D4
Dādu, Pakistan, **218** A4
Dăeni, Romania, **296** G3
Daet, Philippines, **204** C3
Dafang, China, **215** H4
Dafdaf, Jabal, *mountain peak*, Saudi Arabia, **225** C5
Dafeng, China, **206** E1
Dafla Hills, India, **214** E4
Daga Medo, Ethiopia, **367** F3
Dagali, Norway, **286** D2
Dagana, Senegal, **364** A1
Dagang, China, **207** A3
Dagda, Latvia, **287** N4
Dagestan, Respublika, *republic*, Russian Federation, **222** D4
Daglung, China, **214** D3
Dagu, China, **210** G5
Dagua, Papua New Guinea, **140** A3
Daguan, China, **215** G4
Dagupan, Philippines, **204** C2
Dagur, China, **213** G5
Dagzê, China, **214** D3
Dagzhuka, China, **214** D3
Dahlak Archipelago, *islands*, Eritrea, **367** F1
Dahlenburg, Germany, **288** E2
Dahme, Germany, **288** F3
Dāhod, India, **218** C5
Dahongliutan, China, **218** D1
Dahūk, Iraq, **363** H1
Dai Xian, China, **210** F5
Dai Yue Shan (Lantau Island), *island*, China, **207** B4
Dailekh, Nepal, **219** E3
Daimiel, Spain, **293** F3
Dainkog, China, **215** F2
Daiqin Tal, China, **211** H3
Daireaux, Argentina, **458** E5
Dairyland, U.S.A., **420** G2
Daiyun Shan, *mountain range*, China, **206** D3
Dājal, Pakistan, **218** B3
Dajiang, *river*, China, **207** C3
Đak Pé, Vietnam, **203** E3
Dakar, Senegal, **364** A2
Dakhlet Nouâdhibou, *administrative region*, Mauritania, **360** C4
Daki Takwas, Nigeria, **365** F2
Dakingari, Nigeria, **365** E2
Dako, Gunung, *mountain peak*, Indonesia, **198** C2
Dākor, India, **218** C5
Dakoro, Niger, **365** F2
Đakovica, Yugoslavia, **296** C4
Đakovo, Croatia, **294** G3
Dala, Angola, **368** D5
Dalaba, Guinea, **364** B2
Dalaguete, Philippines, **204** C4
Dalai Nur, China, **210** G4
Dalakhay, Russian Federation, **213** J2
Ḑalal, Jabal, *mountain peak*, Egypt, **225** B5
Dalaman, Turkey, **297** G7
Dalan, China, **207** D2
Dalandzadgad, Mongolia, **210** D4
Dalang, China, **207** B3
Dalap-Uliga-Darrit, Marshall Islands, **139** F4
Dalay, Mongolia, **213** J4
Dālbandin, Pakistan, **221** H3
Dalbeattie, Scotland, U.K., **308** F6
Dalby, Australia, **135** L4
Dale, Norway, **286** B2
Dale, U.S.A., **418** E4
Dale Hollow Lake, U.S.A., **425** K1
Dalen, Norway, **286** D3
Daletme, Myanmar, **205** B3
Dalfors, Sweden, **286** G2
Dalhart, U.S.A., **423** M3
Dalhousie, Canada, **416** H5
Dali, China, **205** D2
Dali, Shaanxi, China, **206** B1
Dali, Yunnan, China, **215** G4
Dalian, China, **211** H5
Daliang, China, **213** J5
Dalías, Spain, **293** F4
Dalin, China, **211** H4
Daliuhao, China, **210** F4
Dalkeith, Scotland, U.K., **308** F5
Dallas, U.S.A., **424** D3
Dalmacija, *region*, Croatia, **294** E3
Dalmacio Vélez Sarsfield, Argentina, **458** D4
Dalmally, Scotland, U.K., **308** E4
Dalmellington, Scotland, U.K., **308** E5
Dal'negorsk, Russian Federation, **301** Q5
Dal'nerechensk, Russian Federation, **211** L3
Dal'noye, Kazakhstan, **222** H2
Daloa, Côte d'Ivoire, **364** C3
Dalqū, Sudan, **363** F4
Dalrymple, Lake, Australia, **135** K3
Dalrymple, Scotland, U.K., **308** E5
Dalsbruk, Finland, **287** L2
Dalston, England, U.K., **306** F3
Dāltenganj, India, **214** C4
Dalton, Canada, **421** L1
Dalton, Georgia, U.S.A., **425** K2
Dalton, Nebraska, U.S.A., **420** B5
Dalton-in-Furness, England, U.K., **306** E3
Dalvík, Iceland, **284** Y7
Dalwhinnie, Scotland, U.K., **308** E4
Daly, *river*, Australia, **134** G1
Daly Bay, Canada, **411** L3
Daly Waters, Australia, **134** G2
Dam, *river*, China, **214** E2
Đầm Hà, Vietnam, **203** E1
Damān, India, **218** C5
Daman and Diu, *union territory*, India, **218**, B5
Damanhūr, Egypt, **363** F2
Damar, Kepulauan, *islands*, Indonesia, **199** E4
Damara, Central African Republic, **368** C2
Damasak, Nigeria, **365** G2
Damascus *see* Dimashq, Syria, **225** D3
Damaturu, Nigeria, **365** G2
Damāvand, Qolleh-ye, *mountain peak*, Iran, **222** E5
Damba, Angola, **368** C4
Dambatta, Nigeria, **365** F2
Damboa, Nigeria, **365** G2
Dame-Marie, Haiti, **429** G3
Dāmghān, Iran, **222** E5
Dămieneşti, Romania, **296** F2
Damietta *see* Dumyāţ, Egypt, **225** A4
Daming, China, **210** F5
Damoh, India, **218** D5
Damongo, Ghana, **364** D3
Dampelas, Tanjong, *point*, Indonesia, **198** B2
Dampier, Australia, **134** D3
Dampier, Selat, *strait*, Indonesia, **199** E3
Damqawt, Yemen, **220** F5
Damxoi, China, **214** D3
Damxung, China, **214** D3
Dan-Gulbi, Nigeria, **365** F2
Dan Oever, Netherlands, **288** B2
Dan Xian, China, **203** F2
Ḑānā, Jordan, **225** C4
Danakil Depression, Ethiopia, **367** F2
Danakil Desert, Ethiopia, **367** F2
Danané, Côte d'Ivoire, **364** C3
Dananhu, China, **213** G4
Danao, Philippines, **204** D4
Dānāpur, India, **219** F4
Danba, China, **215** G3
Danby Lake, U.S.A., **422** F4
Dand, Afghanistan, **218** A3
Dande, Ethiopia, **369** G2
Dandeli, India, **216** C3
Dandong, China, **211** J4
Daneborg, Greenland, **411** T2
Daneti, Romania, **296** E4
Danfeng, China, **206** B1
Dang, *river*, China, **213** G5
Dangan Dao, *island*, China, **207** C4
Dangan Liedao, *islands*, China, **207** C4
Dangchang, China, **215** H2
Dange, Angola, **368** C4
Dange, Nigeria, **365** F2
Danger Point, South Africa, **370** C5
Danghe Nanshan, *mountain range*, China, **213** G5
Dangila, Ethiopia, **367** E2
Dângrek, Chuŏr Phnum, *mountain range*, Cambodia/Thailand, **203** D3
Dangriga, Belize, **428** C3
Dangshan, China, **206** D1
Dangtu, China, **206** D2
Dangur, Ethiopia, **366** E2
Daniel, U.S.A., **419** J5
Daniel's Harbour, Canada, **417** N4
Danilovgrad, Yugoslavia, **296** B4
Daning, China, **210** E5
Danjiangkou, China, **206** B1
Dānkojaure, *lake*, Sweden, **284** G4
Dankov, Russian Federation, **299** G6
Dankova, Pik, *mountain peak*, Kyrgyzstan, **212** C4
Danlí, Honduras, **428** D4
Dannenberg (Elbe), Germany, **288** E2
Dano, Burkina Faso, **364** D2
Dañoso, Cabo, *cape*, Argentina, **460** D3
Danot, Ethiopia, **367** G3
Danshui, China, **207** C3
Dansville, U.S.A., **426** B3
Danube, *river*, Europe, **288** E4; *see also* Donau, *river*, Austria, **289** F4; Donau, *river*, Germany, **288** E4; Duna, *river*, Hungary, **289** J5; Dunărea, *river*, Romania, **296** D4
Danubyu, Myanmar, **205** B4
Danville, Illinois, U.S.A., **421** J5
Danville, Kentucky, U.S.A., **421** L7
Danville, Virginia, U.S.A., **421** P7
Dao Xian, China, **206** B3
Daojiao, China, **207** B2
Daotanghe, China, **213** J5
Daoukro, Côte d'Ivoire, **364** D3
Daozhen, China, **215** H3
Dapa, Philippines, **204** D4
Dapaong, Togo, **364** E2
Dapitan, Philippines, **204** C4
Dāpoli, India, **216** C2
Dapp, Canada, **413** N4
Daqing, China, **211** J3
Daquan, China, **213** G4
Daquanwan, China, **213** G4
Dar es Salaam, Tanzania, **369** G4
Dar'ā, *district*, Syria, **225** D3
Dara, Senegal, **364** A1
Dar'ā, Syria, **225** D3
Dārāb, Iran, **221** F3
Darabani, Romania, **296** F1
Darasun, Russian Federation, **210** F2
Đaravica, *mountain peak*, Yugoslavia, **296** C4
Darāw, Egypt, **363** F4
Darazo, Nigeria, **365** G2
Darbhanga, India, **219** F4
Darby, U.S.A., **418** G3
D'arcy, Cape, Antarctica, **470** G7
Darende, Turkey, **224** E5
Darfo Boario Terme, Italy, **291** K4
Dārfūr, *physical feature*, Sudan, **366** B2
Dargaville, New Zealand, **132** D2
Darhan, Bulgan, Mongolia, **213** J2
Darhan, Selenge, Mongolia, **210** D2
Darhan Muminggan Lianheqi, China, **210** E4
Darién, Golfo del, *gulf*, Colombia, **450** C2
Darién, Serrania del, *mountain range*, Panama, **450** B2
Darien, U.S.A., **425** M4
Darío, Nicaragua, **428** D4
Darīya, Kazakhstan, **223** J3

Der-Chantecoq, Lac du, *lake*, France, 291 G2
Dera Bugti, Pakistan, 218 B3
Dera Ghāzi Khān, Pakistan, 218 B3
Dera Ismāīl Khān, Pakistan, 218 B3
Derbent, Russian Federation, 222 D4
Derbent, Turkey, 297 G6
Derbent, Uzbekistan, 222 H5
Derbissaka, Central African Republic, 368 D1
Derbur, China, 211 H2
Derby, Australia, 134 E2
Derby, England, U.K., 305 F2
Derby City, *unitary authority*, England, U.K., 305 F2
Derbyshire, *unitary authority*, England, U.K., 305 F1
Déréssa, Chad, 366 B2
Derg, Lough, *lake*, Clare/Galway, Ireland, 309 D5
Derg, Lough, *lake*, Donegal, Ireland, 309 D3
Derg, *river*, Northern Ireland, U.K., 309 E3
Dergachi, Russian Federation, 222 D2
DeRidder, U.S.A., 424 F4
Dermott, U.S.A., 424 B3
Dernberg, Cape, Namibia, 370 B4
Dêrong, China, 215 F3
Déroute, Passage de la, *strait*, Channel Islands/France, 290 C2
Derre, Mozambique, 369 G6
Derri, Somalia, 367 G4
Derry, U.S.A., 426 E3
Derryveagh Mountains, Ireland, 309 D3
Dersingham, England, U.K., 305 H2
Derst, China, 210 F4
Derudeb, Sudan, 363 G5
Derval, France, 290 D3
Derventa, Bosnia and Herzegovina, 294 F3
Derwent, Canada, 413 P5
Derwent, *river*, England, U.K., 307 H4
Derwent Reservoir, England, U.K., 306 F3
Derwent Water, *lake*, England, U.K., 306 E3
Derzhavīnsk, Kazakhstan, 222 H2
Des Lacs, U.S.A., 420 C1
Des Moines, Iowa, U.S.A., 420 G5
Des Moines, New Mexico, U.S.A., 423 M3
Des Moines, *river*, U.S.A., 420 G5
Des Monts, Pointe, Canada, 416 H5
Desaguadero, Peru, 455 E4
Desaguadero, *river*, Argentina, 458 C4
Desaguadero, *river*, Bolivia, 455 E4
Descabezado Grande, Volcán, *mountain peak*, Chile, 458 B5
Descartes, France, 290 E3
Deschambault Lake, Canada, 414 C4
Deschutes, *river*, U.S.A., 418 D4
Desē, Ethiopia, 367 E2
Deseado, *river*, Argentina, 460 D3
Desengaño, Punta, *point*, Argentina, 460 D3
Desert Center, U.S.A., 422 F5
Desert Peak, *mountain peak*, U.S.A., 422 G1
Deserta Grande, *island*, Madeira, Portugal, 373 C3
Desertas, Ilhas, *islands*, Madeira, Portugal, 373 C3
Deshnoke, India, 218 C4

Desiderio Tello, Argentina, 458 C4
Deskati, Greece, 297 C6
Desmaraisville, Canada, 416 D5
Desmochado, Paraguay, 459 E3
Desna, *river*, Russian Federation/Ukraine, 298 D2
Desolación, Isla, *island*, Chile, 460 B4
Desolation Point, Philippines, 204 D4
Despotovac, Yugoslavia, 296 C3
Dessau, Germany, 288 F3
Destoya Peak, *mountain peak*, U.S.A., 422 E2
Desvres, France, 305 J4
Deta, Romania, 296 C3
Dete, Zimbabwe, 371 E2
Detmold, Germany, 288 D3
Detour, Point, U.S.A., 421 K3
Detroit, Michigan, U.S.A., 421 M4
Detroit, Texas, U.S.A., 424 E3
Detroit Lakes, U.S.A., 420 F2
Deutsche Bucht, *bay*, Germany, 288 C1
Deva, Romania, 296 D3
Develi, Turkey, 363 G1
Devgarh, India, 218 C4
Devīkot, India, 218 B4
Devil River Peak, *mountain peak*, New Zealand, 133 D5
Devils Lake, *lake*, U.S.A., 420 D2
Devils Lake, U.S.A., 420 D1
Devilsbit Mountain, *mountain peak*, Ireland, 309 E5
Devin, Bulgaria, 297 E5
Devli, India, 218 C4
Devnya, Bulgaria, 296 F4
Devon, *unitary authority*, England, U.K., 304 D4
Devon, U.S.A., 419 J2
Devon Island, Canada, 411 K2
Devonport, Australia, 135 K7
Dewa, Tanjong, *point*, Indonesia, 200 A2
Dewās, India, 218 D5
Dewsbury, England, U.K., 307 G4
Dexter, Maine, U.S.A., 426 F2
Dexter, Missouri, U.S.A., 420 J7
Deyang, China, 215 H3
Deyhūk, Iran, 221 G2
Deyyer, Iran, 220 F3
Dezfūl, Iran, 220 E2
Dezhou, China, 210 G5
Dhahab, Egypt, 225 C5
Dhahabān, Saudi Arabia, 363 G4
Dhahran *see* Aẓ Ẓahrān, Saudi Arabia, 220 E3
Dhaka (Dacca), Bangladesh, 214 D5
Dhaka, *division*, Bangladesh, 214 D4
Dhali, Cyprus, 225 B2
Dhamār, Yemen, 220 D6
Dhamtari, India, 219 E5
Dhānāna, India, 218 B4
Dhanbād, India, 219 F5
Dhandhuka, India, 218 B5
Dharampur, India, 218 C5
Dharmjaygarh, India, 219 E5
Dhārwād, India, 216 C3
Dhasa, India, 218 B5
Dhaulagiri, *mountain peak*, Nepal, 219 E3
Dhībān, Jordan, 225 C4
Dhrāngadhra, India, 218 B5
Dhrol, India, 218 B5
Dhubāb, Yemen, 220 D6
Dhuburi, India, 219 G4
Dhule, India, 218 C5
Dhūma, India, 218 D5
Dhuudo, Raas, *point*, Somalia, 367 H3
Dhuudo, Somalia, 367 H3
Dhuusamarreeb, Somalia, 367 G3
Di Linh, Vietnam, 203 F4
Dia, *island*, Greece, 297 E8
Diable, Pointe du, *point*, Rodrigues, 373 B1

Diablo Range, *mountain range*, U.S.A., 422 C3
Diablotin, Morne, *mountain peak*, Dominica, 427 D3
Diaca, Mozambique, 369 H5
Diafarabé, Mali, 364 C2
Dialafara, Mali, 364 B2
Dialakoto, Senegal, 364 B2
Diamante, Argentina, 458 E4
Diamante, *river*, Argentina, 458 C5
Diamantina, Brazil, 457 E5
Diamantina, Chapada, *mountain range*, Brazil, 457 E3
Diamantina, *river*, Australia, 135 J3
Diamantina Fracture Zone, *tectonic feature*, Indian Ocean, 476 F7
Diamantino, Brazil, 456 B4
Diamond Harbour, India, 219 G5
Diamond Head, *point*, Hawaiian Islands, U.S.A., 422 R9
Diamond Islands, Coral Sea Islands, 135 L2
Diamond Lake, U.S.A., 418 C5
Diamounguel, Senegal, 364 B1
Diana's Peak, *mountain peak*, St Helena, 373 B3
Dianbai, China, 206 B4
Diandioumé, Mali, 364 C1
Dianjiang, China, 215 H3
Dianópolis, Brazil, 456 D3
Dianra, Côte d'Ivoire, 364 C3
Diapaga, Burkina Faso, 365 E2
Diaz Point, Namibia, 370 B4
Dibaya, Democratic Republic of the Congo, 368 D4
Dibaya-Lubwe, Democratic Republic of the Congo, 368 C3
Dibrugarh, India, 219 H4
Dibs, Sudan, 366 B2
Dibsī Faraj, Syria, 225 E2
Dick, Mount, *mountain peak*, New Zealand, 132 J10
Dickens, U.S.A., 424 B3
Dickinson, U.S.A., 420 B2
Dickson, U.S.A., 425 J1
Dicle (Tigris), *river*, Turkey, 224 F5
Didcot, England, U.K., 305 F3
Didiéni, Mali, 364 C2
Didsbury, Canada, 413 M6
Dīdwāna, India, 218 C4
Didy, Madagascar, 372 B4
Didymoteicho, Greece, 297 F5
Die, France, 291 G4
Diébougou, Burkina Faso, 364 D2
Diecke, Guinea, 364 C3
Diefenbaker, Lake, Canada, 413 R6
Diego de Almagro, Chile, 458 B3
Diego de Almagro, Isla, *island*, Chile, 460 B4
Diéma, Mali, 364 C2
Diembéreng, Senegal, 364 A2
Dienvidsusēja, *river*, Latvia, 287 M4
Diepholz, Germany, 288 D2
Dieppe, France, 290 E2
Dietrich, U.S.A., 418 G5
Dieuze, France, 291 H2
Dif, Kenya, 367 F4
Diffa, *department*, Niger, 365 G1
Diffa, Niger, 365 G2
Digba, Democratic Republic of the Congo, 369 D2
Digby, Canada, 416 J7
Digermulen, Norway, 284 G2
Dīglūr, India, 216 D2
Digne-les-Bains, France, 291 H4
Digoin, France, 291 F3
Digos, Philippines, 204 D5
Digri, Pakistan, 218 B4
Digue, La, *island*, Seychelles, 373 A2
Digul, *river*, Indonesia, 199 G4

Diinsoor, Somalia, 369 H2
Dijlah (Tigris), *river*, Iraq, 363 J2
Dijon, France, 291 G3
Dikanäs, Sweden, 284 H4
Dikhil, Djibouti, 367 F2
Dikili, Turkey, 297 F6
Dikimdya, Russian Federation, 301 P4
Dikirnis, Egypt, 225 A4
Dikodougou, Côte d'Ivoire, 364 C3
Diksmuide, Belgium, 288 A3
Dikwa, Nigeria, 365 G2
Dīla, Ethiopia, 367 E3
Dili, Democratic Republic of the Congo, 369 E2
Dili, Indonesia, 198 D5
Dilley, U.S.A., 424 C5
Dilling, Sudan, 366 C2
Dillingen an der Donau, Germany, 288 E4
Dillingham, U.S.A., 410 D4
Dillon, Montana, U.S.A., 418 H4
Dillon, South Carolina, U.S.A., 425 N2
Dilolo, Democratic Republic of the Congo, 368 D5
Dimāpur, India, 219 H4
Dimashq, *district*, Syria, 225 D3
Dimashq (Damascus), Syria, 225 D3
Dimbelenge, Democratic Republic of the Congo, 368 D4
Dimbokro, Côte d'Ivoire, 364 D3
Dimitrovgrad, Bulgaria, 296 E4
Dimitrovgrad, Russian Federation, 222 D2
Dimitrovgrad, Yugoslavia, 296 D4
Dīmona, Israel, 225 C4
Dinājpur, Bangladesh, 219 G4
Dinagat Island, Philippines, 204 D4
Dinan, France, 290 C2
Dinant, Belgium, 288 B3
Dinar, Turkey, 297 H6
Dinara, *mountain peak*, Croatia, 294 F3
Dinara, *mountain range*, Croatia, 294 F4
Dinard, France, 290 C2
Dinde, Angola, 368 B5
Dinder, *river*, Ethiopia/Sudan, 366 D2
Dindigul, India, 216 D4
Dindima, Nigeria, 365 G2
Dindori, India, 219 E5
Dinga, Democratic Republic of the Congo, 368 C4
Dinga, N. Pakistan, 218 C2
Dinga, S. Pakistan, 218 A4
Dingalan Bay, Philippines, 204 C3
Dingbian, China, 210 D5
Dinge, Angola, 368 B4
Dinggyê, China, 214 C3
Dingle, Ireland, 309 B5
Dingle Bay, Ireland, 309 B6
Dingnan, China, 206 C3
Dingtao, China, 206 C1
Dinguiraye, Guinea, 364 B2
Dingwall, Scotland, U.K., 308 E3
Dingxi, China, 215 H2
Dingxing, China, 210 F5
Dingyuan, China, 206 D1
Dingzhou, China, 210 F5
Dingzikou, China, 213 G5
Dīnhāta, India, 219 G4
Dinorwic, Canada, 414 H7
Dioïla, Mali, 364 C2
Diou, France, 291 F3
Diouloulou, Senegal, 364 A2
Dioumara, Mali, 364 C2
Dioundiou, Niger, 365 E2
Diourbel, Senegal, 364 A2
Diphu, India, 219 H4
Diplo, Pakistan, 218 B4
Dipolog, Philippines, 204 C4

Dīr, Pakistan, 218 B2
Diré, Mali, 364 D1
Dirē Dawa, Ethiopia, 367 F3
Direction, Cape, Australia, 135 J1
Direction Island, Cocos (Keeling) Islands, 134 Q10
Dirico, Angola, 370 D2
Dirj, Libya, 362 B2
Dirk Hartog Island, Australia, 134 C4
Dirkou, Niger, 362 B5
Dirranbandi, Australia, 135 K4
Dirs, Saudi Arabia, 363 H5
Dīsa, India, 218 C4
Disappointment, Cape, South Georgia, 461 A3
Disappointment, Cape, U.S.A., 418 B3
Disappointment, Lake, Australia, 134 E3
Disappointment Island, Auckland Islands, New Zealand, 132 J10
Discovery Bay, Australia, 135 H6
Disko *see* Qeqertarsuaq, *island*, Greenland, 411 P2
Disley, Canada, 413 S6
Dispur, India, 219 G4
Diss, England, U.K., 305 J2
Distington, England, U.K., 306 E3
Distrito Federal, *federal district*, Brazil, 456 D4
Distrito Federal, *federal district*, Mexico, 431 F5
Ditrău, Romania, 296 E2
Dittaino, *river*, Sicilia, Italy, 295 E7
Diu, India, 218 B5
Diuta Point, Philippines, 204 D4
Dīvān Derrah, Iran, 222 D5
Divénié, Congo, 368 B3
Divelva, *river*, Norway/Sweden, 284 J2
Divinhe, Mozambique, 371 F3
Divinópolis, Brazil, 457 E5
Divnogorsk, Russian Federation, 223 N1
Divo, Côte d'Ivoire, 364 C3
Divriği, Turkey, 363 G1
Dixie, U.S.A., 418 G4
Dixmont, U.S.A., 426 F2
Dixon, California, U.S.A., 422 C2
Dixon, Illinois, U.S.A., 421 J5
Dixon, Montana, U.S.A., 418 G3
Dixon Entrance, *channel*, Canada/U.S.A., 412 C4
Dixons Mills, U.S.A., 425 J3
Dixonville, Canada, 413 L3
Diyarbakır, Turkey, 224 F5
Dja, *river*, Cameroon, 368 B2
Djado, Niger, 362 B4
Djado, Plateau du, *plateau*, Niger, 362 B4
Djamaa, Algeria, 361 H2
Djambala, Congo, 368 B3
Djampie, Democratic Republic of the Congo, 368 C3
Djanet, Algeria, 362 A4
Djébrène, Chad, 366 A2
Djédaa, Chad, 366 A2
Djelfa, Algeria, 361 G2
Djéma, Central African Republic, 369 E1
Djenné, Mali, 364 D2
Djibo, Burkina Faso, 364 D2
Djibouti, *country*, Africa, 196 F8
Djibouti, Djibouti, 367 F2
Djiguéni, Mauritania, 364 C1
Djoemoe, Suriname, 452 B2
Djohong, Cameroon, 365 G3
Djolu, Democratic Republic of the Congo, 368 D2
Djougou, Benin, 365 E3
Djoum, Cameroon, 368 B2
Djoumboli, Cameroon, 365 G3
Djourab, Erg du, *desert*, Chad, 362 C5
Djúpivogur, Iceland, 284 Z7

Djupvik, Norway, **284** K2
Djurås, Sweden, **286** G2
Dmitriyevka, Kazakhstan, **222** H2
Dmitriyevskoye, Russian Federation, **299** G4
Dmitrov, Russian Federation, **299** F4
Dnepr, *river*, Russian Federation, **299** C5
Dnestrovsc, Moldova, **296** G2
Dnipropetrovs'k, Ukraine, **298** E3
Dnister, *river*, Moldova/ Ukraine, **298** C3
Dnistrovs'kyy Lyman, *lake*, Ukraine, **296** H2
Dno, Russian Federation, **299** C4
Do Gonbardān, Iran, **220** F2
Đô Lương, Vietnam, **203** E2
Do Rūd, Iran, **220** E2
Doaktown, Canada, **416** H6
Đoan Hùng, Vietnam, **203** E1
Doany, Madagascar, **372** B3
Doba, Chad, **365** H3
Dobbiaco, Italy, **294** D2
Dobbs, Cape, Canada, **411** L3
Dobele, Latvia, **287** L4
Döbeln, Germany, **288** F3
Doberai, Jazirah, *peninsula*, Indonesia, **195** Q10
Döbern, Germany, **289** G3
Dobiegniew, Poland, **289** G2
Dobo, Indonesia, **199** F4
Doboj, Bosnia and Herzegovina, **294** G3
Dobre Miasto, Poland, **289** K2
Dobrich, Bulgaria, **296** F4
Dobro Polje, Bosnia and Herzegovina, **294** G4
Dobrodzień, Poland, **289** J3
Dobrovăţ, Romania, **296** F2
Dobrovelychkivka, Ukraine, **296** H1
Dobrovol'sk, Russian Federation, **287** L5
Dobruchi, Russian Federation, **299** A3
Dobzha, China, **214** D3
Doce, *river*, Brazil, **457** F5
Docking, England, U.K., **305** H2
Doctor Arroyo, Mexico, **431** E4
Doda, India, **218** C2
Dodecanese *see* Dodekanisos, *islands*, Greece, **297** F7
Dodekanisos (Dodecanese), *islands*, Greece, **297** F7
Dodge City, U.S.A., **420** C7
Dodgeville, U.S.A., **420** H4
Dodman Point, England, U.K., **304** C4
Dodoma, *administrative region*, Tanzania, **369** G4
Dodoma, Tanzania, **369** G4
Dodson, U.S.A., **419** K2
Doetinchem, Netherlands, **288** C3
Dog Creek, Canada, **412** H6
Dog Island, U.S.A., **425** K5
Dog Lake, Canada, **415** K7
Dogai Coring, *lake*, China, **214** D2
Doğanbey, Aydin, Turkey, **297** F7
Doğanbey, İzmir, Turkey, **297** F6
Dōgo, *island*, Japan, **208** F3
Dogondoutchi, Niger, **365** E2
Dogoumbo, Chad, **365** H2
Doğu Menteşe Dağları, *mountain range*, Turkey, **297** G7
Doğubayazıt, Turkey, **224** F5
Do'gyaling, China, **214** D3
Doha *see* Ad Dawḩah, Qatar, **220** F2
Dohazar, Bangladesh, **219** H5
Doilungdêqên, China, **214** D3
Dokka, Norway, **286** E2
Dokshytsy, Belarus, **287** N5
Dolak, Pulau, *island*, Indonesia, **199** G4

Dolavón, Argentina, **460** E2
Dolbeau, Canada, **416** E5
Dolbenmaen, Wales, U.K., **304** C2
Dolce, Cape, U.S.A., **426** C5
Doldrums Fracture Zone, *tectonic feature*, Atlantic Ocean, **477** D5
Dole, France, **291** G3
Dolgellau, Wales, U.K., **304** D2
Dolianova, Sardegna, Italy, **295** B6
Dolit, Indonesia, **198** D3
Doljevac, Yugoslavia, **296** C4
Dolný Kubín, Slovakia, **289** J4
Dolo Odo, Ethiopia, **369** H2
Dolomiti, *mountain range*, Italy, **294** C2
Doloon, Mongolia, **210** D3
Dolores, Argentina, **459** F5
Dolores, Guatemala, **428** C3
Dolores, Uruguay, **459** E4
Dolphin, Cape, Falkland Islands, **460** F4
Dolphin and Union Strait, Canada, **410** G2
Dolphin Head, *point*, Namibia, **370** B4
Dolyna, Ukraine, **289** L4
Dom, Gunung, *mountain peak*, Indonesia, **199** G3
Dom Pedrito, Brazil, **459** F4
Dom Pedro, Brazil, **453** E4
Domanivka, Ukraine, **296** H2
Domar, China, **214** B2
Domaradz, Poland, **289** L4
Domažlice, Czech Republic, **288** F4
Domba, China, **215** E2
Dombarovskiy, Russian Federation, **222** F2
Dombås, Norway, **286** D1
Dombe, Mozambique, **371** F2
Dombóvár, Hungary, **289** H5
Dome Creek, Canada, **412** J5
Domett, Mount, *mountain peak*, New Zealand, **133** D5
Domeyko, Antofagasta, Chile, **458** C2
Domeyko, Atacama, Chile, **458** B3
Domeyko, Cordillera, *mountain range*, Chile, **458** C2
Domfront, France, **290** D2
Dominica, *country*, Caribbean Sea, **427** D3
Dominica Passage, Caribbean Sea, **427** D3
Dominical, Costa Rica, **428** E5
Dominican Republic, *country*, Caribbean Sea, **409** R7
Dominion, Cape, Canada, **411** M3
Dömitz, Germany, **288** E2
Domneşti, Romania, **296** E3
Domo, Ethiopia, **367** G3
Domodedovo, Russian Federation, **299** F5
Domodossola, Italy, **294** B2
Domokos, Greece, **297** D6
Domoni, Comoros, **372** A3
Dompu, Indonesia, **201** G5
Domuyo, Volcán, *mountain peak*, Argentina, **458** B5
Domžale, Slovenia, **294** E2
Don, Mexico, **430** C3
Don, *river*, France, **290** D3
Don, *river*, Russian Federation, **298** F3
Don, *river*, Scotland, U.K., **308** F3
Donaghmore, Northern Ireland, U.K., **306** B3
Donaldson, U.S.A., **420** E1
Donaldsonville, U.S.A., **424** G4
Donard, Slieve, *mountain peak*, Northern Ireland, U.K., **309** G3
Donau (Danube), *river*, Austria, **289** F4
Donau (Danube), *river*, Germany, **288** E4
Donaueschingen, Germany, **288** D5

Donauwörth, Germany, **288** E4
Doncaster, England, U.K., **307** G4
Dondo, Angola, **368** B4
Dondo, Mozambique, **371** F2
Dondra Head, Sri Lanka, **217** E5
Donduşeni, Moldova, **296** F1
Donegal, *county*, Ireland, **309** D3
Donegal, Ireland, **309** D3
Donegal Bay, Ireland, **309** D3
Donegal Point, Ireland, **309** C5
Donets'k, Ukraine, **298** E3
Dong, *river*, N. China, **213** J4
Dong, *river*, S. China, **207** C2
Đông Hà, Vietnam, **203** E2
Đông Hôi, Vietnam, **203** E2
Đông Nai, *river*, Vietnam, **203** E4
Dong Ujimqin Qi, China, **210** G3
Donga, Nigeria, **365** G3
Dong'an, Heilongjiang, China, **211** L3
Dong'an, Hunan, China, **206** B3
Dongarra, Australia, **134** C4
Dongchuan, China, **215** G4
Dongco, China, **214** C2
Dongfang, China, **203** F2
Dongfanghong, China, **211** L3
Dongfeng, Guangdong, China, **207** A3
Dongfeng, Jilin, China, **211** J4
Donggala, Indonesia, **198** B3
Donggou, China, **208** D3
Dongguan, China, **207** B2
Donghai Dao, *island*, China, **203** F1
Dongjiangkou, China, **206** B1
Dongkou, China, **206** B3
Donglan, China, **215** H4
Dongning, China, **211** K3
Dongnyi, China, **215** G3
Dongo, Angola, **368** C5
Dongo, Democratic Republic of the Congo, **368** C2
Dongou, Congo, **368** C2
Dongping, China, **203** G1
Dongping, Guangdong, China, **206** C4
Dongping, Shandong, China, **206** D1
Dongsanjia, China, **211** J3
Dongshan, China, **206** B4
Dongshan Dao, *island*, China, **206** D4
Dongsheng, China, **210** E5
Dongtai, China, **206** E1
Dongting Hu, *lake*, China, **206** C2
Dongyang, China, **206** E2
Dongying, China, **211** G5
Dongzhi, China, **206** D2
Donji Milanovac, Yugoslavia, **296** F3
Donji Mu, Croatia, **294** F4
Donji Srb, Croatia, **294** E3
Dønna, *island*, Norway, **284** E4
Donna, U.S.A., **424** C6
Donnelly, Canada, **413** L4
Donon, *mountain peak*, France, **291** H2
Donostia-San Sebastián, Spain, **293** F1
Donoughmore, Ireland, **309** D6
Donskoy, Russian Federation, **299** G6
Donsol, Philippines, **204** C3
Donxing, China, **208** E1
Dooagh, Ireland, **309** B4
Doon, Loch, *lake*, Scotland, U.K., **308** E5
Doon, *river*, Scotland, U.K., **308** E5
Doonbeg, Ireland, **309** C5
Doonbeg, *river*, Ireland, **309** C5
Dora, Lake, Australia, **134** E3
Dorchester, England, U.K., **304** E4
Dordabis, Namibia, **370** C3

Dordogne, *river*, France, **290** D4
Dordrecht, Netherlands, **288** B3
Dore, Monts, *mountain range*, France, **290** F4
Doré Lake, Canada, **413** R4
Dores, Scotland, U.K., **308** E3
Dori, Burkina Faso, **364** D2
Dorking, England, U.K., **305** G3
Dormaa Ahenkro, Ghana, **364** D3
Dormans, France, **291** F2
Dornie, Scotland, U.K., **308** D3
Dornoch Firth, *river mouth*, Scotland, U.K., **308** E3
Dornod, *province*, Mongolia, **210** F3
Dornogovĭ, *province*, Mongolia, **210** E3
Doro, Mali, **364** D1
Dorobanţu, Romania, **296** F3
Dorobino, Russian Federation, **299** F6
Dorogobuzh, Russian Federation, **299** D5
Dorohoi, Romania, **296** F2
Dorokhovo, Russian Federation, **299** F5
Dorolemo, Indonesia, **199** E2
Dorotea, Sweden, **284** H4
Dorre Island, Australia, **134** C4
Dorsale, *mountain range*, Tunisia, **362** A1
Dorset, *unitary authority*, England, U.K., **304** E4
Dortmund, Germany, **288** C3
Dorum, Germany, **288** D2
Doruma, Democratic Republic of the Congo, **369** E2
Dos Bahías, Cabo, *cape*, Argentina, **460** E2
dos Bois, *river*, Brazil, **456** D4
Dos de Mayo, Peru, **454** C2
Dos Pozos, Argentina, **460** E2
Dosi, Indonesia, **199** E2
Dospat, Bulgaria, **297** E5
Dosquet, Canada, **416** F6
Dosso, *department*, Niger, **365** E2
Dosso, Niger, **365** E2
Dossor, Kazakhstan, **222** E3
Dostyq, Kazakhstan, **212** D3
Dothan, U.S.A., **425** K4
Douai, France, **291** F1
Douala, Cameroon, **368** A2
Douarnenez, France, **290** B2
Double Cone, *mountain peak*, New Zealand, **133** B7
Double Mer, *river*, Canada, **417** M2
Doubs, *river*, France, **291** G3
Doubtful Sound, New Zealand, **133** A7
Doubtless Bay, New Zealand, **132** D2
Doudeville, France, **305** H5
Douentza, Mali, **364** D2
Douéoulou, New Caledonia, **141** A3
Doughboy Bay, New Zealand, **133** A8
Douglas, Alaska, U.S.A., **412** B2
Douglas, Arizona, U.S.A., **423** J6
Douglas, Georgia, U.S.A., **425** L4
Douglas, Isle of Man, **306** D3
Douglas, North Dakota, U.S.A., **420** C2
Douglas, Scotland, U.K., **308** F5
Douglas, South Africa, **370** D4
Douglas, Wyoming, U.S.A., **419** M5
Douglas City, U.S.A., **422** B1
Douglas Lake, Canada, **412** J6
Douglass, U.S.A., **420** E7
Doullens, France, **290** F1
Doumen, China, **207** A4
Dounreay, Scotland, U.K., **308** F2
Dourados, Brazil, **456** B6
Dourados, *river*, Brazil, **456** B6
Dourados, Serra dos, *mountain range*, Brazil, **459** G2

D5
Dourbali, Chad, **365** H2
Douro, *river*, Portugal, **292** D2
Douze, *river*, France, **290** E5
Dove, *river*, England, U.K., **305** F1
Dover, Delaware, U.S.A., **426** C5
Dover, England, U.K., **305** J3
Dover, New Hampshire, U.S.A., **426** E3
Dover, New Jersey, U.S.A., **426** C4
Dover, Strait of, France/U.K., **305** J4
Dovey, *river*, Wales, U.K., **304** D2
Dovre, Norway, **286** D2
Dowi, Tanjong, *point*, Indonesia, **200** B2
Dowlat Yār, Afghanistan, **218** A2
Dowlatābād, Afghanistan, **218** A1
Down, *district*, Northern Ireland, U.K., **309** G3
Downey, U.S.A., **419** H5
Downham Market, England, U.K., **305** H2
Downpatrick, Northern Ireland, U.K., **309** G3
Downpatrick Head, *point*, Ireland, **309** C3
Downs, U.S.A., **420** D6
Downton, England, U.K., **305** F4
Dowshī, Afghanistan, **218** B2
Dowsk, Belarus, **299** C6
Doyleville, U.S.A., **423** K2
Dōzen, *island*, Japan, **208** F3
Drâa, Hamada du, *plateau*, Algeria, **360** E3
Drac, *river*, France, **291** G4
Dracena, Brazil, **456** C5
Dragalina, Romania, **296** F3
Drăgăşani, Romania, **296** E3
Drăgăneşti-Olt, Romania, **296** E3
Drăgăneşti-Vlaşca, Romania, **296** E3
Dragón, Bocas del, *bay*, Trinidad and Tobago, **451** G1
Dragón, Bocas del, *strait*, Trinidad and Tobago/ Venezuela, **427** D4
Dragonada, *island*, Greece, **297** F8
Draguignan, France, **291** H5
Drăguşeni, Romania, **296** F2
Drahichyn, Belarus, **289** M2
Drake, U.S.A., **420** C2
Drake Passage, *strait*, Antarctica, **477** C9
Drakensberg, *mountain range*, South Africa, **357** H10
Drama, Greece, **297** E5
Drammen, Norway, **286** E3
Drangedal, Norway, **286** D3
Draper, U.S.A., **420** C4
Draperstown, Northern Ireland, U.K., **306** B3
Drava, *river*, Croatia/Hungary/ Slovenia, **294** F2
Dravograd, Slovenia, **294** E2
Drawa, *river*, Poland, **289** G2
Drawsko, Jezioro, *lake*, Poland, **289** G2
Drayton, U.S.A., **420** E1
Drayton Valley, Canada, **413** M5
Dreikikir, Papua New Guinea, **140** A3
Dremsel, Mount, *mountain peak*, Papua New Guinea, **140** B3
Drenthe, *province*, Netherlands, **288** C2
Drepano, Akra, *point*, Greece, **297** D6
Dresden, Germany, **288** F3
Dretun', Belarus, **299** B5
Dreux, France, **290** E2
Drevsjø, Norway, **286** F2
Drewsey, U.S.A., **418** E5
Dreyers Rock, New Zealand, **133** E5

Dzhangala, Kazakhstan, **222** E3
Dzhankel'dy, Uzbekistan, **222** G4
Dzhankoy, Ukraine, **298** D3
Dzhebel, Turkmenistan, **222** E5
Dzhugdzhur, Khrebet, *mountain range*, Russian Federation, **301** Q4
Dzhuryn, Ukraine, **296** G1
Działdowo, Poland, **289** K2
Dzibalchén, Mexico, **431** H5
Dzilam De Bravo, Mexico, **431** H4
Dzioua, Algeria, **361** H2
Dzisna, Belarus, **287** N5
Dzisna, *river*, Belarus/ Lithuania, **287** N5
Dzivin, Belarus, **289** M3
Dzöölön, Mongolia, **213** H2
Dzüünbayan, Mongolia, **210** E3
Dzüünbulag, Mongolia, **210** F3
Dzüünharaa, Mongolia, **210** D2
Dzuunmod, Dzavhan, Mongolia, **213** H2
Dzuunmod, Töv, Mongolia, **210** D3
Dzüyl, Mongolia, **213** G3
Dźwierzuty, Poland, **289** K2
Dzyarechyn, Belarus, **289** M2
Dzyarzhynskaya, Hora, *mountain peak*, Belarus, **298** C2
Dzyatlava, Belarus, **289** M2

E

Ea H'leo, Vietnam, **203** F3
Eads, U.S.A., **423** M2
Eagar, U.S.A., **423** J4
Eagle, *river*, Canada, **417** M3
Eagle, U.S.A., **423** K2
Eagle Butte, U.S.A., **420** C3
Eagle Lake, California, U.S.A., **422** C1
Eagle Lake, *lake*, U.S.A., **426** F1
Eagle Lake, Maine, U.S.A., **426** F1
Eagle Pass, U.S.A., **424** B5
Eagle River, U.S.A., **421** J3
Ealing, England, U.K., **305** G3
Ear Falls, Canada, **414** H6
Earith, England, U.K., **305** H2
Earl Shilton, England, U.K., **305** F2
Earlton, Canada, **421** P2
Earnslaw, Mount, *mountain peak*, New Zealand, **133** B7
Earth, U.S.A., **423** M4
Easebourne, England, U.K., **305** G4
Easington, England, U.K., **307** J4
Easingwold, England, U.K., **307** G3
Easley, U.S.A., **425** L2
East Angus, Canada, **416** F7
East Antarctica, *region*, Antarctica, **470** E5
East Aurora, U.S.A., **426** A3
East Ayrshire, *local authority*, Scotland, U.K., **308** E5
East Bay, Papua New Guinea, **140** B4
East Bay, U.S.A., **425** H5
East Braintree, Canada, **414** G7
East Cape, New Zealand, **132** G3
East Caroline Basin, *underwater feature*, Pacific Ocean, **478** D4
East Dereham, England, U.K., **305** H2
East Dunbartonshire, *local authority*, Scotland, U.K., **308** E5
East Falkland, *island*, Falkland Islands, **460** G4
East Glacier Park, U.S.A., **418** H2

East Grand Forks, U.S.A., **420** E2
East Grinstead, England, U.K., **305** G3
East Hampton, U.S.A., **426** D4
East Harling, England, U.K., **305** H2
East Indian Ridge, *underwater feature*, Indian Ocean, **476** F6
East Islet, *island*, Ashmore and Cartier Islands, **134** P9
East Jordan, U.S.A., **421** L3
East Kilbride, Scotland, U.K., **308** E5
East Linton, Scotland, U.K., **308** G5
East Liverpool, U.S.A., **421** N5
East Loch Tarbert, *inlet*, Scotland, U.K., **308** C3
East London, South Africa, **371** E5
East Lothian, *local authority*, Scotland, U.K., **308** G4
East Malling, England, U.K., **305** H3
East Mariana Basin, *underwater feature*, Pacific Ocean, **478** E4
East New Britain, *province*, Papua New Guinea, **140** D4
East Pacific Rise, *underwater feature*, Pacific Ocean, **479** L7
East Point, Canada, **417** L6
East Point, Lord Howe Island, Australia, **135** U14
East Point, Tristan da Cunha, **373** C2
East Point, U.S.A., **425** K3
East Poplar, Canada, **413** S7
East Renfrewshire, *local authority*, Scotland, U.K., **308** E5
East Riding of Yorkshire, *unitary authority*, England, U.K., **307** H4
East St Louis, U.S.A., **420** H6
East Sepik, *province*, Papua New Guinea, **140** A3
East Sussex, *unitary authority*, England, U.K., **305** H4
East Tasman Plateau, *underwater feature*, Pacific Ocean, **478** E7
East Wittering, England, U.K., **305** G4
Eastbourne, England, U.K., **305** H4
Eastend, Canada, **413** Q7
Easter Fracture Zone, *tectonic feature*, Pacific Ocean, **479** K6
Easter Island see Pascua, Isla, *island*, Chile, Pacific Ocean, **461** B2
Eastern, *administrative region*, Ghana, **364** D3
Eastern, *province*, Kenya, **369** G2
Eastern, *province*, Sierra Leone, **364** B3
Eastern, *province*, Zambia, **369** F5
Eastern Cape, *province*, South Africa, **371** E5
Eastern Desert see Sharqīyah, Aş-Şahrā' ash, *desert*, Egypt, **225** A5
Eastern Ghats, *mountain range*, India, **216** D3
Eastern Group, *islands*, Bounty Islands, New Zealand, **133** N14
Eastern Group see Lau Group, *islands*, Fiji, **141** A4
Eastern Highlands, *province*, Papua New Guinea, **140** B4
Eastland, U.S.A., **424** C3
Eastleigh, England, U.K., **305** F4
Eastmain, Canada, **415** Q5
Eastmain, *river*, Canada, **416** C3
Eastman, U.S.A., **425** L3
Easton, England, U.K., **304** E4

Eastry, England, U.K., **305** J3
Eastwood, England, U.K., **305** F1
Eaton Socon, England, U.K., **305** G2
Eatonton, U.S.A., **425** L3
Eau Claire, Lac à l', *lake*, Canada, **415** Q3
Eau Claire, U.S.A., **420** H3
Eauripik, *island*, Micronesia, **138** C4
Eban, Nigeria, **365** E3
Ebano, Mexico, **431** F4
Ebbw Vale, Wales, U.K., **304** D3
Ebebiyin, Equatorial Guinea, **368** B2
Ebeltoft, Denmark, **286** E4
Eberbach, Germany, **288** D4
Eberswalde-Finow, Germany, **289** F2
Ebetsu, Japan, **209** H2
Ebian, China, **215** G3
Ebino, Japan, **208** E4
Ebinur Hu, *lake*, China, **212** D3
Ebolowa, Cameroon, **368** B2
Ebon, *island*, Marshall Islands, **139** E4
Ebony, Namibia, **370** C3
Ebro, *river*, Spain, **280** D7
Ebruchorr, Gora, *mountain peak*, Russian Federation, **285** R3
Ecclefechan, Scotland, U.K., **308** F5
Eccleshall, England, U.K., **304** E2
Eceabat, Turkey, **297** F5
Echinos, Greece, **297** E5
Echt, Netherlands, **288** B3
Echuca, Australia, **135** J6
Écija, Spain, **292** E4
Eckenförde, Germany, **288** D1
Eckington, England, U.K., **304** E2
Écommoy, France, **290** E3
Ecuador, *country*, South America, **449** E4
Écueillé, France, **290** E3
Ēd, Eritrea, **367** F2
Ed, Sweden, **286** E3
Edam, Canada, **413** Q5
Edam, Netherlands, **288** B2
Eday, *island*, Orkney, Scotland, U.K., **308** G1
Ede, Nigeria, **365** E3
Ede Point, Canada, **411** J2
Edéa, Cameroon, **368** A2
Edehon Lake, Canada, **414** F1
Edéia, Brazil, **456** D4
Eden, Australia, **135** K6
Eden, Canada, **414** E6
Eden, *river*, England, U.K., **306** F3
Eden, Texas, U.S.A., **424** C4
Eden, Wyoming, U.S.A., **419** K5
Edenbridge, England, U.K., **305** H3
Edendale, New Zealand, **133** B8
Edenderry, Ireland, **309** E4
Edenton, U.S.A., **426** B6
Eder, *river*, Germany, **288** D3
Edessa, Greece, **297** D5
Edgartown, U.S.A., **426** E4
Edgeley, U.S.A., **420** D2
Edgemont, U.S.A., **420** B4
Edgeøya, *island*, Svalbard, **300** D2
Edgerton, Canada, **413** P5
Edgeworthstown, Ireland, **309** E4
Edina, U.S.A., **420** G5
Edinboro, U.S.A., **421** N5
Edinburgh, Scotland, U.K., **308** F5
Edinburgh, Tristan da Cunha, **373** C2
Edinburgh City, *local authority*, Scotland, U.K., **308** F5
Edineţ, Moldova, **296** F1

Edirne, *province*, Turkey, **297** F5
Edirne, Turkey, **224** C4
Edjeleh, Algeria, **361** H3
Edlingham, England, U.K., **307** G2
Edmond, Kansas, U.S.A., **420** D6
Edmond, Oklahoma, U.S.A., **424** D2
Edmonton, Canada, **413** N5
Edmund Lake, Canada, **414** H4
Edmundston, Canada, **416** G6
Edna, U.S.A., **424** D5
Edo, *state*, Nigeria, **365** F3
Edolo, Italy, **294** C2
Edremit, Turkey, **297** F6
Edremit Körfezi, *bay*, Turkey, **297** F6
Edsbro, Sweden, **287** J3
Edsbyn, Sweden, **286** G2
Edson, Canada, **413** L5
Eduardo Castex, Argentina, **458** D5
Edward VII Land, *region*, Antarctica, **470** C7
Edwards Plateau, U.S.A., **424** B4
Edzo, Canada, **410** H3
Edzouga, Congo, **368** B3
Efate (Vaté), *island*, Vanuatu, **141** A2
Effie, U.S.A., **420** G2
Effingham, U.S.A., **421** J6
Effon-Alaiye, Nigeria, **365** E3
Eforie, Romania, **296** G3
Eg, Mongolia, **210** E2
Egadi, Isole, *islands*, Sicilia, Italy, **295** D7
Egan Range, *mountain range*, U.S.A., **422** F2
Eganville, Canada, **416** C7
Eger, Hungary, **289** K5
Egeria Point, Christmas Island, **134** N8
Egersund, Norway, **286** C3
Egg Island, St Helena, **373** B3
Eggedal, Norway, **286** D2
Eggenfelden, Germany, **288** F4
Egilsstaðir, Iceland, **284** Z7
Egindibulaq, Kazakhstan, **212** C2
Egiyn, *river*, Mongolia, **213** J2
Égletons, France, **290** F4
Eglinton, Northern Ireland, U.K., **309** E2
Eglwys Fach, Wales, U.K., **304** D2
Egmont, Mount (Mount Taranaki), *mountain peak*, New Zealand, **132** E4
Egremont, Canada, **413** N4
Egremont, England, U.K., **306** E3
Eğrigöz Dağı, *mountain range*, Turkey, **297** G6
Egton, England, U.K., **307** H3
Egtved, Denmark, **286** D5
Egypt, *country*, Africa, **358** H4
Eiao, *island*, French Polynesia, **137** G1
Eide, Norway, **284** C5
Eidfjord, Norway, **286** C2
Eidsdal, Norway, **286** C1
Eidsvåg, Norway, **286** D1
Eifel, *mountain range*, Germany, **288** C3
Eigg, *island*, Scotland, U.K., **308** C4
Eight Degree Channel, India/ Maldives, **216** C5
Eights Coast, *region*, Antarctica, **470** B6
Eighty Mile Beach, Australia, **134** E2
Eikefjord, Norway, **286** B2
Eiken, Norway, **286** C3
Eilenburg, Germany, **288** F3
Eiler Rasmussen, Kap, *cape*, Greenland, **411** S1
Eilerts de Haan Gebergte, *mountain range*, Suriname, **452** B2
Eilsleben, Germany, **288** E2

Eina, Norway, **286** E2
Einasleigh, Australia, **135** J2
Einasleigh, *river*, Australia, **135** J2
Einbeck, Germany, **288** D3
Eindhoven, Netherlands, **288** B3
Eirunepé, Brazil, **455** E2
Eisenach, Germany, **288** E3
Eisenstadt, Austria, **289** H5
Eisfeld, Germany, **288** E3
Eišiškės, Lithuania, **287** M5
Eitel, Mount, *mountain peak*, Macquarie Island, **134** R11
Eivinvik, Norway, **286** B2
Eivissa (Ibiza), *island*, Islas Baleares, Spain, **293** H3
Eivissa (Ibiza), Islas Baleares, Spain, **293** H3
Ejea de los Caballeros, Spain, **293** G1
Ejeda, Madagascar, **372** A5
Ejido Insurgentes, Mexico, **430** C3
Ejin Horo Qi, China, **210** E5
Ejin Qi, China, **213** J4
Ejura, Ghana, **364** D3
Ejutla, Mexico, **431** F5
Ekalaka, U.S.A., **419** M4
Ekenäs, Sweden, **286** F3
Ekerem, Turkmenistan, **222** E5
Eket, Nigeria, **368** A2
Eketahuna, New Zealand, **132** E5
Ekibastuz, Kazakhstan, **223** K2
Ekombe, Democratic Republic of the Congo, **368** D2
Ekouamou, Congo, **368** C2
Ekshärad, Sweden, **286** F2
Eksjö, Sweden, **286** G4
Ekuku, Democratic Republic of the Congo, **368** D3
Ekwan, *river*, Canada, **415** M5
El Aaiún (Laâyoune), Western Sahara, **360** D3
El Aargub, Western Sahara, **360** C4
El Abiodh Sidi Cheikh, Algeria, **361** G2
El Adeb Larache, Algeria, **361** H3
El Affroun, Algeria, **293** J4
El Alia, Algeria, **361** H2
El Aouinet, Algeria, **295** A8
El Arco, Mexico, **430** B2
El Banco, Colombia, **450** D2
El Barco de Ávila, Spain, **292** E2
El Baúl, Venezuela, **451** E2
El Bayadh, Algeria, **361** G2
El Bolsón, Argentina, **460** C1
El Burgo de Osma, Spain, **293** F2
El Cabaco, Spain, **292** D2
El Caín, Argentina, **460** D1
El Cajon, U.S.A., **422** E5
El Calafate, Argentina, **460** C4
El Callao, Venezuela, **451** G2
El Campo, U.S.A., **424** D5
El Carmen, Bolivia, **455** F3
El Carmen de Bolívar, Colombia, **450** C2
El Centro, U.S.A., **422** F5
El Cerro, Bolivia, **455** G4
El Cerro del Aripo, *mountain peak*, Trinidad, Trinidad and Tobago, **461** C4
El Cerron, Cerro, *mountain peak*, Venezuela, **451** D1
El Chaparro, Venezuela, **451** F2
El Cocuy, Colombia, **450** D2
El Cove, San Andrés, Colombia, **461** B1
El Cuervo, Mexico, **430** D2
El Cuyo, Mexico, **431** J4
El Desemboque, Mexico, **430** B2
El Difícil, Colombia, **450** C2
El Diviso, Colombia, **450** B4
El Djenoun, Garet, *mountain peak*, Algeria, **361** H4
El Dorado, Arkansas, U.S.A., **424** F3
El Dorado, Kansas, U.S.A., **420** E7
El Dorado, Mexico, **430** D3

El Dorado, Venezuela, **451** G2
El Dorado Springs, U.S.A., **420** G7
El Eglab, *mountain range*, Algeria, **361** E3
El Encanto, Colombia, **450** D4
El Escorial, Spain, **292** E2
El Estor, Guatemala, **428** C4
El Eulma, Algeria, **361** H1
El Fahs, Tunisia, **295** B7
El Fud, Ethiopia, **367** F3
El Fuerte, Mexico, **430** C3
El Goléa, Algeria, **361** G2
El Golfo de Santa Clara, Mexico, **430** B2
El Grado, Spain, **293** H1
El Hadjar, Algeria, **361** H1
El Hank, *mountain range*, Mauritania, **360** E4
El Haouaria, Tunisia, **295** C7
El Harrach, Algeria, **293** J4
El Homr, Algeria, **361** G3
El Jadida, Morocco, **360** E2
El Jaralito, Mexico, **430** D3
El Jicaral, Nicaragua, **428** D4
El Kala, Algeria, **295** B7
El Kef, Tunisia, **295** B7
El Kelaa des Srarhna, Morocco, **360** E2
Ēl Kerē, Ethiopia, **367** F3
Ēl Lēh, Ethiopia, **369** G2
El Limón, Mexico, **431** F4
El Meghaïer, Algeria, **361** H2
El Miamo, Venezuela, **451** G2
El Mojar, Bolivia, **455** F3
El Molinillo, Spain, **292** E3
El Nido, Philippines, **204** B4
El Oasis, Islas Canarias, Spain, **373** B4
El Obeid *see* Al Ubayyiḍ, Sudan, **366** D2
El Oro, Mexico, **430** E3
El Oued, Algeria, **361** H2
El Palmar, Venezuela, **451** G2
El Palmito, Mexico, **430** D3
El Pao, E. Venezuela, **451** F2
El Pao, N. Venezuela, **451** E2
El Paso, U.S.A., **423** K6
El Pensamiento, Bolivia, **455** G4
El Perú, Bolivia, **455** E3
El Portugués, Peru, **454** B2
El Porvenir, Mexico, **430** D2
El Porvenir, Panama, **429** F5
El Potosí, Mexico, **431** E3
El Progreso, Guatemala, **428** C4
El Progreso, Honduras, **428** D4
El Puente, Bolivia, **455** F4
El Puerto de Santa Maria, Spain, **292** D4
El Real, Panama, **429** F5
El Reno, U.S.A., **424** D2
El Rocío, Spain, **292** D4
El Ronquillo, Spain, **292** D4
El Rosario de Arriba, Mexico, **430** B2
El Salado, Argentina, **460** D3
El Salado, Mexico, **431** E3
El Salto, Mexico, **430** D4
El Salvador, Chile, **458** C3
El Salvador, *country*, Central America, **409** P7
El Salvador, Mexico, **431** E3
El Salvador, Philippines, **204** D4
El Seibo, Dominican Republic, **429** H3
El Soberbio, Argentina, **459** F3
El Socorro, Mexico, **430** B2
El Sombrero, Argentina, **460** D2
El Sombrero, Venezuela, **451** E2
El Sosneado, Argentina, **458** C5
El Sueco, Mexico, **430** D2
El Teleno, *mountain peak*, Spain, **292** D1
El Tigre, Venezuela, **451** F2
El Tocuyo, Venezuela, **451** E2
El Tofo, Chile, **458** B3
El Toro, *mountain peak*, Islas Baleares, Spain, **293** K2
El Toro, Venezuela, **451** G2
El Tránsito, Chile, **458** B3
El Trébol, Argentina, **458** E4
El Triunfo, Mexico, **430** C4
El Turbio, Argentina, **460** C4
El Valle, Colombia, **450** C2
El Vigía, Venezuela, **450** D2
El Wak, Kenya, **369** H2
El Yunque, *mountain peak*, Róbinson Crusoe Island, Archipiélago Juan Fernández, Chile, **461** C2
Ela, Tanjong, *point*, Indonesia, **198** D5
Elafonisos, *island*, Greece, **297** D7
Elafonisou, Steno, *strait*, Greece, **297** D7
Elasa, *island*, Greece, **297** F8
Elassona, Greece, **297** D6
Elat, Israel, **225** C5
Elazığ, Turkey, **224** E5
Elba, Alabama, U.S.A., **425** J4
Elba, Idaho, U.S.A., **418** H5
Elba, Isola d', *island*, Italy, **294** B4
El'ban, Russian Federation, **211** M2
Elbasan, Albania, **297** C5
Elbe, *river*, Germany, **280** F5
Elbe *see* Labe, *river*, Czech Republic, **289** G3
Elbert, Mount, *mountain peak*, U.S.A., **423** K2
Elberton, U.S.A., **425** L2
Elbeuf, France, **290** E2
Elbistan, Turkey, **224** E5
Elbląg, Poland, **289** J1
Elbow, Canada, **413** R6
Elbow Lake, U.S.A., **420** F3
El'brus, Gora, *mountain peak*, Russian Federation, **222** C4
Elburz Mountains *see* Alborz, Reshteh-ye Kūhhā-ye, *mountain range*, Iran, **222** E5
Elche, Spain, **293** G3
Elche de la Sierra, Spain, **293** F3
Elda, Spain, **293** G3
Elder, Mount, *mountain peak*, Macquarie Island, **134** R11
Eldon, U.S.A., **420** G6
Eldorado, Argentina, **459** F3
Eldorado, Illinois, U.S.A., **421** J7
Eldorado, Texas, U.S.A., **424** B4
Eldoret, Kenya, **369** G2
Elea, Cape, Cyprus, **225** C2
Elefsina, Greece, **297** D6
Eleja, Latvia, **287** L4
Elektrostal', Russian Federation, **299** G5
Elemi Triangle, Kenya, **367** D3
Elena, Bulgaria, **296** E4
Elephant Butte Reservoir, U.S.A., **423** K5
Elephant Island, Antarctica, **470** A3
Eleuthera Island, Bahamas, **428** F1
Elfin Cove, U.S.A., **412** A2
Elgå, Norway, **286** E1
Elgin, Illinois, U.S.A., **421** J4
Elgin, Nebraska, U.S.A., **420** D5
Elgin, Nevada, U.S.A., **422** F3
Elgin, North Dakota, U.S.A., **420** C2
Elgin, Oregon, U.S.A., **418** F4
Elgin, Scotland, U.K., **308** F3
Elgin, Texas, U.S.A., **424** D4
Elgol, Scotland, U.K., **308** C3
Elgon, *mountain peak*, Uganda, **369** F2
Elgoras, Gora, *mountain peak*, Russian Federation, **285** Q2
Eliase, Indonesia, **199** E5
Elida, U.S.A., **423** M5
Elie, Scotland, U.K., **308** G4
Elie de Beaumont, *mountain peak*, New Zealand, **133** C6
Elifaz, Israel, **225** C5
Elila, Democratic Republic of the Congo, **369** E3
Elimäki, Finland, **287** N2
Elin Pelin, Bulgaria, **296** D4
Eling, England, U.K., **305** F4
Elipa, Democratic Republic of the Congo, **368** D3
Eliseu Martins, Brazil, **453** E5
Elista, Russian Federation, **222** C3
Elizabeth, U.S.A., **426** C4
Elizabeth Bay, Namibia, **370** B4
Elizabeth City, U.S.A., **426** B6
Elizabethton, U.S.A., **421** M7
Elizabethtown, Kentucky, U.S.A., **421** L7
Elizabethtown, South Carolina, U.S.A., **425** N2
Elizaveta, Moldova, **296** G2
Ełk, Poland, **289** L2
Elk, *river*, U.S.A., **421** N6
Elk City, Idaho, U.S.A., **418** G4
Elk City, Oklahoma, U.S.A., **424** C2
Elk Grove, U.S.A., **422** C2
Elk Lake, Canada, **421** N2
Elk Mountain, *mountain peak*, U.S.A., **418** F4
Elk Mountain, U.S.A., **419** L6
Elk Point, Canada, **413** P5
Elk River, U.S.A., **420** G3
Elk Springs, U.S.A., **423** J1
Elkhart, U.S.A., **421** L5
Elkhorn, Canada, **414** D7
Elkhovo, Bulgaria, **296** F4
Elkins, Mount, *mountain peak*, Antarctica, **470** F4
Elkins, New Mexico, U.S.A., **423** L5
Elkins, West Virginia, U.S.A., **421** P6
Elkland, U.S.A., **426** B4
Elko, Canada, **413** M7
Elko, U.S.A, **422** F1
Elkton, U.S.A., **421** P6
Ellef Ringnes Island, Canada, **411** J2
Ellen, Mount, *mountain peak*, U.S.A., **423** H3
Ellendale, U.S.A., **420** D2
Ellensburg, U.S.A., **418** D3
Ellesmere, England, U.K., **304** E2
Ellesmere, Lake, New Zealand, **133** D6
Ellesmere Island, Canada, **411** L2
Ellesmere Port, England, U.K., **306** F4
Ellijay, U.S.A., **425** K2
Elliot, South Africa, **371** E5
Elliot Lake, Canada, **421** M2
Elliott, Australia, **134** G2
Elliott Knob, *mountain peak*, U.S.A, **421** P6
Ellisras, South Africa, **371** E3
Elliston, Australia, **135** G5
Ellon, Scotland, U.K., **308** G3
Ellsworth, Kansas, U.S.A., **420** D6
Ellsworth, Iowa, U.S.A., **420** G3
Ellsworth, Maine, U.S.A., **426** F2
Ellsworth Land, *region*, Antarctica, **470** B6
Ellsworth Mountains, *mountain range*, Antarctica, **470** C5
Ellwangen (Jagst), Germany, **288** E4
Elma, U.S.A., **418** C3
Elmalı, Turkey, **297** G7
Elmhurst, U.S.A., **421** K5
Elmira, Canada, **417** K6
Elmira, U.S.A., **426** B3
Elmshorn, Germany, **288** D2
Elorza, Venezuela, **451** E2
Eloy, U.S.A., **423** H5
Elphinstone, Canada, **414** D6
Elsas, Canada, **415** N7
Elsen Nur, *lake*, China, **214** E2
Elsfjord, Norway, **284** F3
Elsie, U.S.A., **420** C5
Elsterwerda, Germany, **288** F3
Elstow, Canada, **413** R6
Eltanin Fracture Zone, *tectonic feature*, Pacific Ocean, **479** J8
Elton, England, U.K., **305** G2
Eluru, India, **217** E2
Elva, Estonia, **287** N3
Elva, Slieve, *mountain peak*, Ireland, **309** C4
Elvanfoot, Scotland, U.K., **308** F5
Elvas, Portugal, **292** D3
Elven, France, **290** C3
Elverum, Norway, **286** E2
Elwell, Lake, U.S.A., **419** J2
Ely, England, U.K., **305** H2
Ely, Minnesota, U.S.A., **420** H2
Ely, Nevada, U.S.A, **422** F2
Elyria, U.S.A., **421** M5
Elze, Germany, **288** D2
Emådalen, Sweden, **286** G2
Emajõgi, *river*, Estonia, **287** N3
Emām, Iran, **222** F5
Emāmshahr, Iran, **222** F5
Emba, Kazakhstan, **222** F3
Embaluh, *river*, Indonesia/Malaysia, **201** F2
Embar, Canada, **416** J3
Embarcación, Argentina, **458** D2
Embleton, England, U.K., **307** G2
Embondo, Democratic Republic of the Congo, **368** C2
Embrun, Canada, **416** D7
Embu, Kenya, **369** G3
Emden, Germany, **288** C2
Emei, China, **215** G3
Emerald, Australia, **135** K3
Emery, U.S.A., **423** H2
Emet, Turkey, **297** G6
Emeti, Papua New Guinea, **140** A4
Emigrant, U.S.A., **419** J4
Emilia Romagna, *autonomous region*, Italy, **294** C3
Emiliano Zapata, Mexico, **431** H5
Emin, China, **212** D3
Emine, Nos, *point*, Bulgaria, **296** F4
Emissi, Tarso, *mountain peak*, Chad, **362** C4
Emlichheim, Germany, **288** C2
Emmaboda, Sweden, **286** G4
Emmastad, Curaçao, Netherlands Antilles, **461** C3
Emmaste, Estonia, **287** L3
Emmen, Netherlands, **288** C2
Emmetsburg, U.S.A., **420** F4
Emmett, U.S.A., **418** F5
Emmiganūru, India, **216** D3
Emory Peak, *mountain peak*, U.S.A., **423** M7
Empalme, Mexico, **430** C2
Empangeni, South Africa, **371** F4
Empedrado, Argentina, **459** E3
Emperor Seamounts, *underwater feature*, Pacific Ocean, **478** F1
Emperor Trough, *underwater feature*, Pacific Ocean, **478** F1
Empoli, Italy, **294** C4
Emporia, Kansas, U.S.A., **420** E6
Emporia, Virginia, U.S.A., **426** B6
Emporium, U.S.A., **426** A4
Empress Mine, Zimbabwe, **371** E2
Ems, *river*, Germany, **288** C2
Enånger, Sweden, **287** H2
Enarotali, Indonesia, **199** G3
Encantadas, Serra das, *mountain range*, Brazil, **459** G4
Encarnación, Paraguay, **459** F3
Encinal, U.S.A., **424** C5
Encinitas, U.S.A., **422** E5
Encino, New Mexico, U.S.A., **423** L4
Encino, Texas, U.S.A., **424** C6
Encontrados, Venezuela, **450** D2
Encounter Bay, Australia, **128** C5
Encruzilhada, Brazil, **457** F4
Encruzilhada do Sul, Brazil, **459** G4
Encs, Hungary, **289** K4
Ende, Indonesia, **198** C5
Endeavour, Canada, **414** C5
Enderbury, *island*, Kiribati, **139** G5
Enderby Island, Auckland Islands, New Zealand, **132** J10
Enderby Land, *region*, Antarctica, **470** F4
Enderby Plain, *underwater feature*, Indian Ocean, **476** B8
Endicott, New York, U.S.A., **426** B3
Endicott, Washington, U.S.A., **418** F3
Energía, Argentina, **459** E6
Enewetak, *island*, Marshall Islands, **138** E3
Enez, Turkey, **297** F5
Enfida, Tunisia, **295** C7
Enfield, Connecticut, U.S.A., **426** D4
Enfield, England, U.K., **305** G3
Enfield, North Carolina, U.S.A., **426** B6
Enga, *province*, Papua New Guinea, **140** A4
Engan, Norway, **284** D5
Engaño, Cabo, *cape*, Dominican Republic, **429** H3
Engaño, Cape, Philippines, **204** C2
Engaru, Japan, **209** H1
Engel's, Russian Federation, **222** D2
Engen, Canada, **412** G4
Enggano, Pulau, *island*, Indonesia, **200** C4
England, *administrative division*, U.K., **304** E2
Englee, Canada, **417** N4
Englehart, Canada, **421** P2
Englewood, Colorado, U.S.A., **423** L2
Englewood, Kansas, U.S.A., **420** D7
English Bay, Ascension, **373** A3
English Channel, France/U.K., **304** D5
English Coast, *region*, Antarctica, **470** B5
English River, Canada, **414** J7
Engozero, Ozero, *lake*, Russian Federation, **285** R4
Engozero, Russian Federation, **285** R4
Engure, Latvia, **287** L4
Engures ezers, *lake*, Latvia, **287** L4
Enid, U.S.A., **420** E7
Enköping, Sweden, **287** H3
Enmore, Guyana, **451** H2
Enna, Sicilia, Italy, **295** E7
Ennadai, Canada, **414** D1
Ennadai Lake, Canada, **414** D1
Ennedi, *mountain range*, Chad, **362** D5
Ennell, Lough, *lake*, Ireland, **309** E4
Enning, U.S.A., **420** B3
Ennis, Ireland, **309** D5
Ennis, Montana, U.S.A., **419** J4
Ennis, Texas, U.S.A., **424** D3
Enniscorthy, Ireland, **309** F5
Enniskean, Ireland, **309** D6
Enniskerry, Ireland, **309** F4
Enniskillen, Northern Ireland, U.K., **309** E3
Ennistimon, Ireland, **309** C5
Eno, Finland, **285** Q5
Enochs, U.S.A., **423** M5
Enonkoski, Finland, **287** P1
Enontekiö, Finland, **285** L2
Enping, China, **206** C4
Enschede, Netherlands, **288** C2
Ensenada, Mexico, **430** A2
Enshi, China, **206** B2
Entebbe, Uganda, **369** F2
Entente, *island*, French Polynesia, **137** G2
Enterprise, Alabama, U.S.A., **425** K4
Enterprise, Canada, **413** L1
Enterprise, Oregon, U.S.A., **418** F4
Enterprise, Utah, U.S.A., **422** G3

GAZETTEER

Entiat, U.S.A., **418** D3
Entrance, Canada, **413** L5
Entre Ríos, Bolivia, **455** F5
Entre Rios, Brazil, **452** B4
Entre Ríos, *province*, Argentina, **459** E4
Entrepeñas, Embalse de, *reservoir*, Spain, **293** F2
Entwistle, Canada, **413** M5
Enugu, Nigeria, **365** F3
Enugu, *state*, Nigeria, **365** F3
Enumclaw, U.S.A., **418** C3
Envermeu, France, **305** J5
Envigado, Colombia, **450** C2
Envira, Brazil, **455** D2
Enyamba, Democratic Republic of The Congo, **368** D3
Enyellé, Congo, **368** C2
Enys, Mount, *mountain peak*, New Zealand, **133** C6
Eolie o Lipari, Isole, *islands*, Italy, **295** E6
Epéna, Congo, **368** C2
Épernay, France, **291** F2
Ephrata, Pennsylvania, U.S.A., **426** B4
Ephrata, Washington, U.S.A., **418** E3
Epi, *island*, Vanuatu, **141** A2
Épinal, France, **291** H2
Epira, Guyana, **451** H3
Episkopi, Cyprus, **225** B2
Episkopi Bay, Cyprus, **225** B2
Epping, England, U.K., **305** H3
Epsom, England, U.K., **305** G3
Epu-pel, Argentina, **458** D5
Epworth, England, U.K., **307** H4
Equateur, *administrative region*, Democratic Republic of the Congo, **368** C2
Equatorial Guinea, *country*, Africa, **359** F6
Equeipa, Venezuela, **451** F3
Er Rachidia, Morocco, **361** F2
Era, *river*, Papua New Guinea, **140** B4
Erave, Papua New Guinea, **140** A4
Erba, Jabal, *mountain peak*, Sudan, **363** G4
Érd, Hungary, **289** J5
Erdaohezi, China, **211** K3
Erdek, Turkey, **297** F5
Erdemli, Turkey, **225** C1
Erdenet, Bulgan, Mongolia, **213** J2
Erdenet, Hövsgöl, Mongolia, **213** H2
Erdenetsogt, Bayanhongor, Mongolia, **213** J3
Erdenetsogt, Ömnögovĭ, Mongolia, **210** D4
Erding, Germany, **288** E4
Erechim, Brazil, **459** G3
Ereentsav, Mongolia, **210** F2
Ereğli, Turkey, **224** D5
Ereikoussa, *island*, Ionioi Nisoi, Greece, **297** B6
Erenhot, China, **210** E4
Eretria, Greece, **297** D6
Ereymentaū, Kazakhstan, **223** J2
Erezée, Belgium, **288** B3
Erfjord, Norway, **286** C3
Erfoud, Morocco, **361** F2
Erfurt, Germany, **288** E3
Ergani, Turkey, **363** G1
Ergel, Mongolia, **210** E4
Ergene, *river*, Turkey, **297** F5
Ērgļi, Latvia, **287** M4
Ergun, *river*, China, **211** H1
Erick, U.S.A., **424** C2
Erickson, Canada, **414** E6
Ericson, U.S.A., **420** D5
Erie, Lake, Canada/U.S.A., **421** N5
Erie, U.S.A., **421** N4
Erîgât, *desert*, Mali, **361** E4
Eriksdale, Canada, **414** E6
Erillas, *mountain peak*, Spain, **292** E3
Erimo, Japan, **209** H2
Erimo-misaki, *point*, Japan, **209** H2
Erin Point, Trinidad, Trinidad and Tobago, **461** C4
Eringsboda, Sweden, **286** G4
Eriskay, *island*, Scotland, U.K., **308** B3
Eritrea, *country*, Africa, **358** J5
Erkowit, Sudan, **363** G5
Erlangen, Germany, **288** E4
Erldunda, Australia, **134** G4
Erlongshan, China, **211** L3
Ermelo, South Africa, **371** F4
Ermenek, Turkey, **363** F1
Ermioni, Greece, **297** D7
Ermoupoli, Kyklades, Greece, **297** E7
Erndtebrück, Germany, **288** D3
Ernée, France, **290** D2
Ernei, Romania, **296** E2
Ernstbrunn, Austria, **289** H4
Erode, India, **216** D4
Eromanga, Australia, **135** J4
Erongo, *administrative region*, Namibia, **370** B3
Erongo, *mountain peak*, Namibia, **370** C3
Errego, Mozambique, **369** G6
Errigal Mountain, *mountain peak*, Ireland, **309** D2
Erris Head, *point*, Ireland, **309** B3
Errol, U.S.A., **426** E2
Erromango, *island*, Vanuatu, **141** A3
Ersekë, Albania, **297** C5
Ershiwuzhan, China, **211** H1
Ershizhan, China, **211** J1
Erskine, U.S.A., **420** E2
Ertai, China, **212** F3
Ertis, Kazakhstan, **223** K2
Ertis, *river*, Kazakhstan, **223** K2
Ertvågøy, *island*, Norway, **284** D5
Eruki, Mount, *mountain peak*, Papua New Guinea, **140** B4
Erval, Brazil, **459** G4
Erwood, Canada, **414** C5
Erythres, Greece, **297** D6
Eryuan, China, **215** F4
Erzgebirge, *mountain range*, Germany, **288** F3
Erzhan, China, **211** J2
Erzin, Russian Federation, **213** G2
Erzincan, Turkey, **224** E5
Erzurum, Turkey, **224** F5
Eržvilkas, Lithuania, **287** L5
Esa'ala, Papua New Guinea, **140** C5
Esashi, N. Hokkaidō, Japan, **209** H1
Esashi, S. Hokkaidō, Japan, **209** H2
Esbjerg, Denmark, **286** D5
Escada, Brazil, **453** G5
Escalada, Spain, **293** F1
Escalante, U.S.A., **423** H3
Escalaplano, Sardegna, Italy, **295** B6
Escalón, Mexico, **430** D3
Escanaba, U.S.A., **421** K3
Eschede, Germany, **288** E2
Escocesa, Bahía, *bay*, Dominican Republic, **429** H3
Escoma, Bolivia, **455** E4
Escondida, Chile, **458** C2
Escondido, U.S.A., **422** E5
Escuinapa, Mexico, **430** D4
Escuintla, Guatemala, **428** C4
Eséka, Cameroon, **368** B2
Eşen, Turkey, **297** G7
Esens, Germany, **288** C2
Eşfahān, Iran, **220** F2
Esfandak, Iran, **221** H3
Esfarāyen, Iran, **222** F5
Esha Ness, *point*, Shetland, Scotland, U.K., **308** K7
Esigodini, Zimbabwe, **371** E3
Esik, Kazakhstan, **212** C4
Esil, Kazakhstan, **222** H2
Esil, *river*, Kazakhstan, **223** H2
Eskdale, *valley*, Scotland, U.K., **308** G5
Eskdalemuir, Scotland, U.K., **308** F5
Eske, Lough, *lake*, Ireland, **309** D3
Esker, Canada, **416** H3
Eskilstuna, Sweden, **286** H3
Eskişehir, Turkey, **224** D5
Esla, *river*, Spain, **292** E1
Eslöv, Sweden, **286** F5
Eşme, Turkey, **297** G6
Esmeralda, Cuba, **429** F2
Esmeralda, Isla, *island*, Chile, **460** B3
Esmeraldas, Ecuador, **450** B4
Espakeh, Iran, **221** H3
Espalion, France, **290** F4
Espanola, Canada, **421** N2
Española, Isla, *island*, Islas Galápagos (Galapagos Islands), Ecuador, **461** A2
Espanola, U.S.A., **423** K3
Esperance, Australia, **134** E5
Esperantinópolis, Brazil, **453** E4
Esperanza, *Argentinian research station*, Antarctica, **470** A4
Esperanza, Mexico, **430** C3
Esperanza, Peru, **454** D2
Esperanza, Santa Cruz, Argentina, **460** C4
Esperanza, Santa Fé, Argentina, **458** E4
Espichel, Cabo, *cape*, Portugal, **292** C3
Espiel, Spain, **292** E3
Espigão, Serra do, *mountain range*, Brazil, **459** G3
Espigão Mestre, *mountain range*, Brazil, **456** E3
Espinhaço, Serra do, *mountain range*, Brazil, **447** H6
Espinilho, Serra do, *mountain range*, Brazil, **459** F3
Espinillo, Argentina, **459** E2
Espinosa, Brazil, **457** E4
Espírito Santo, *state*, Brazil, **457** F5
Espíritu Santo, *island*, Vanuatu, **141** A2
Esplanada, Brazil, **457** G3
Espoo, Finland, **287** M2
Espungabera, Mozambique, **371** F3
Esquel, Argentina, **460** C2
Esquina, Argentina, **459** E4
Esrange, Sweden, **284** K3
Essaouira, Morocco, **360** E2
Essen, Germany, **288** C3
Essequibo, *river*, Guyana, **451** G3
Essex, California, U.S.A., **422** F4
Essex, Montana, U.S.A., **418** H2
Essex, Punta, *point*, Islas Galápagos (Galapagos Islands), Ecuador, **461** A2
Essex, *unitary authority*, England, U.K., **305** H3
Est, Pointe de l', *point*, Canada, **417** L5
Est, *province*, Cameroon, **368** B2
Estaca de Bares, Punta da, *point*, Spain, **292** D1
Estacado, Llano, *plain*, U.S.A., **423** M4
Estados, Isla, de los, *island*, Argentina, **460** E5
Estagel, France, **290** F5
Estaires, France, **305** K4
Estância, Brazil, **457** G3
Estats, Pic d', France/Spain, **293** H1
Estcourt, South Africa, **371** E4
Esteban Rams, Argentina, **458** E3
Estelí, Nicaragua, **428** D4
Estella, Spain, **293** F1
Estepa, Spain, **292** E4
Estépar, Spain, **293** F1
Estepona, Spain, **292** E4
Esterhazy, Canada, **414** C6
Estevan, Canada, **414** C7
Estevan Point, Canada, **412** F7
Estherville, U.S.A., **420** F4
Estill, U.S.A., **425** M3
Estissac, France, **291** F2
Estiva, *river*, Brazil, **453** E5
Eston, Canada, **413** Q6
Estonia, *country*, Europe, **282** G4
Estrées-St-Denis, France, **305** K5
Estrela, Serra da, *mountain range*, Portugal, **292** C2
Estremoz, Portugal, **292** D3
Estrondo, Serra do, *mountain range*, Brazil, **452** D5
Estuaire, *province*, Gabon, **368** A2
Esztergom, Hungary, **289** J5
Etah, India, **218** D4
Etampes, France, **290** F2
Étaples, France, **290** E1
Etāwah, India, **218** D4
Etelä-Suomen Lääni, *province*, Finland, **287** M2
Ethelbert, Canada, **414** D6
Ethiopa, *country*, Africa, **358** J6
Ethiopian Highlands, *mountain range*, Ethiopa, **356** J5
Ethridge, U.S.A., **419** H2
Etive, Loch, *inlet*, Scotland, U.K., **308** D4
Etna, Monte, *mountain peak*, Sicilia, Italy, **295** E7
Etne, Norway, **286** B3
Eton, Canada, **421** L2
Etoumbi, Congo, **368** B2
Étretat, France, **305** H5
Etropole, Bulgaria, **296** E4
Ettelbruck, Luxembourg, **291** H2
Ettington, England, U.K., **305** F2
Etwall, England, U.K., **305** F2
Etzatlan, Mexico, **430** D4
Eu, France, **305** J4
'Eua, *island*, Tonga, **141** B4
'Eua Iki, *island*, Tonga, **141** B4
Euakafa, *island*, Vava'u Group, Tonga, **141** B3
Euboea *see* Evvoia, *island*, Greece, **297** E6
Eucla, Australia, **134** F5
Euclides da Cunha, Brazil, **457** F3
Eufaula, U.S.A., **425** K4
Eufaula Lake, U.S.A., **424** E2
Eugene, U.S.A., **418** C4
Eugenia, Punta, *point*, Mexico, **430** A3
Eunice, Louisiana, U.S.A., **424** F4
Eunice, New Mexico, U.S.A., **423** M5
Eupen, Belgium, **288** B3
Euphrates, *river*, Asia, **194** F6; *see also* Euphrates, *river*, Iraq, **363** H2; Fırat, *river*, Turkey, **224** E5; Firat Nehri, *river*, Syria, **363** G1
Eupora, U.S.A., **425** H3
Eura, Finland, **287** L2
Eurajoki, Finland, **287** K2
Eureka, California, U.S.A., **422** A1
Eureka, Canada, **411** L1
Eureka, Montana, U.S.A., **418** G2
Eureka, Nevada, U.S.A, **422** F2
Eureka, Utah, U.S.A., **423** G2
Eureka, Washington, U.S.A., **418** E3
Europa, Île, *island*, Réunion, **371** H3
Europa, Picos de, *mountain peak*, Spain, **292** E1
Eustis, U.S.A., **425** M5
Eutaw, U.S.A., **425** J3
Eutin, Germany, **288** E1
Eutsuk Lake, Canada, **412** F5
Evanger, Norway, **286** C2
Evans, Lac, *lake*, Canada, **416** C4
Evans, Mount, *mountain peak*, U.S.A., **418** H3
Evans Peninsula, Antarctica, **470** A6
Evans Strait, Canada, **411** L3
Evanston, Illinois, U.S.A., **421** K4
Evanston, Wyoming, U.S.A., **419** J6
Evansville, Canada, **421** M3
Evansville, Illinois, U.S.A., **420** J6
Evansville, Indiana, U.S.A., **421** K7
Evaro, U.S.A., **418** G3
Evaton, South Africa, **371** E4
Evaz, Iran, **220** F3
Everest, Mount, *mountain peak*, China, **214** C3
Everett, U.S.A., **418** C3
Evergreen, U.S.A., **425** J4
Evesham, England, U.K., **305** F2
Evijärvi, Finland, **285** L5
Evijärvi, *lake*, Finland, **285** L5
Evinayong, Equatorial Guinea, **368** B2
Evje, Norway, **286** C3
Évora, *district*, Portugal, **292** D3
Évora, Portugal, **292** D3
Evoron, Ozero, *lake*, Russian Federation, **211** M2
Évreux, France, **290** E2
Évry, France, **290** F2
Evvoia (Euboea), *island*, Greece, **297** E6
Ewan, U.S.A., **418** F3
Ewango, Nigeria, **365** F3
Ewaso Ngiro, *river*, Kenya, **369** G2
Ewe, Loch, *inlet*, Scotland, U.K., **308** D3
Ewo, Congo, **368** B3
Exaltación, Bolivia, **455** F3
Exe, *river*, England, U.K., **304** D4
Executive Committee Range, *mountain range*, Antarctica, **470** C7
Exeter, Canada, **421** N4
Exeter, England, U.K., **304** D4
Exminster, England, U.K., **304** D4
Exmoor, *moorland*, England, U.K., **304** D3
Exmore, U.S.A., **426** C6
Exmouth, Australia, **134** C3
Exmouth, England, U.K., **304** D4
Exmouth Gulf, Australia, **134** C3
Exmouth Plateau, *underwater feature*, Indian Ocean, **476** G6
Extremadura, *district*, Spain, **292** D3
Extrême-Nord, *province*, Cameroon, **365** G2
Exu, Brazil, **453** F5
Eyasi, Lake, Tanzania, **369** F3
Eye, Cambridgeshire, England, U.K., **305** G2
Eye, Suffolk, England, U.K., **305** J2
Eye Peninsula, Scotland, U.K., **308** C2
Eyemouth, Scotland, U.K., **308** G5
Eyl, Somalia, **367** G3
Eymet, France, **290** E4
Eynsham, England, U.K., **305** F3
Eyre North, Lake, Australia, **135** H4
Eyre Peninsula, Australia, **135** H5
Eyre South, Lake, Australia, **135** H4
Eyreton, New Zealand, **133** D6
Eysturoy, *island*, Faeroe Islands, **302** D1
Eyumojok, Cameroon, **368** A1
Ezequiel Ramos Mexia, Embalse, *reservoir*, Argentina, **460** D1
Ezere, Latvia, **287** L4
Ezernieki, Latvia, **287** N4
Ezhou, China, **206** C2
Ezine, Turkey, **297** F6

F

Faadhippolhu Atoll, Maldives, **216** C5
Faafxadhuun, Somalia, **369** H2
Faaite, *island*, French Polynesia, **137** G2
Fabens, U.S.A., **423** K6
Fåberg, Norway, **286** E2
Fabiuola, *river*, Spain, **292** D3
Fåborg, Denmark, **286** E5
Fabriano, Italy, **294** D4
Facatativá, Colombia, **450** C3
Fachi, Niger, **365** G1
Facundo, Argentina, **460** C2
Fada, Chad, **362** D5
Fada N'Gourma, Burkina Faso, **364** E2
Faddeyevskiy, Ostrov, *island*, Russian Federation, **301** R2
Faenza, Italy, **294** C3
Faeroe-Iceland Ridge, *underwater feature*, Atlantic Ocean, **477** G1
Faeroe Islands, *Danish territory*, Atlantic Ocean, **302** C2
Fagamalo, Samoa, **141** B1
Făgăraș, Romania, **296** E3
Fagatogo, American Samoa, **141** B2
Fågelberget, Sweden, **284** G4
Fagernes, Oppland, Norway, **286** D2
Fagernes, Troms, Norway, **284** J2
Fagersta, Sweden, **286** G3
Făget, Romania, **296** D3
Faggo, Nigeria, **365** G2
Fagnano, Lago, *lake*, Argentina, **460** D5
Faguibine, Lac, *lake*, Mali, **364** D1
Fagurhólsmýri, Iceland, **284** Y8
Faial, *island*, Azores, Portugal, **360** M7
Faial, Madeira, Portugal, **373** C3
Fā'id, Egypt, **225** B4
Fair Head, *point*, Northern Ireland, U.K., **309** F2
Fairbank, U.S.A., **423** H6
Fairbanks, U.S.A., **410** E3
Fairfax, U.S.A., **420** D4
Fairfield, California, U.S.A., **422** C2
Fairfield, Idaho, U.S.A., **418** G5
Fairfield, Illinois, U.S.A., **421** J6
Fairfield, Iowa, U.S.A., **420** H5
Fairfield, Montana, U.S.A., **419** J3
Fairfield, North Dakota, U.S.A., **420** B2
Fairfield, Texas, U.S.A., **424** D4
Fairford, Canada, **414** E6
Fairlie, New Zealand, **133** C7
Fairlight, Canada, **414** D7
Fairlight, England, U.K., **305** H4
Fairmont, Nebraska, U.S.A., **420** E5
Fairmont, West Virginia, U.S.A., **421** N6
Fairplay, U.S.A., **423** L2
Fairview, Canada, **413** K3
Fairview, U.S.A., **425** J2
Fairweather, Mount, *mountain peak*, U.S.A., **412** A2
Fais, *island*, Micronesia, **138** C4
Faisalābād, Pakistan, **218** C3
Faither, The, *point*, Shetland, Scotland, U.K., **308** K7
Faizābād, India, **219** E4
Fajaghalia, Solomon Islands, **141** A1
Fajardo, Puerto Rico, **427** C2
Fakahina, *island*, French Polynesia, **137** H2
Fakaofo, *island*, Tokelau, **139** G5

Fakarava, *island*, French Polynesia, **137** G2
Fakenham, England, U.K., **305** H2
Fakfak, Indonesia, **199** F3
Fakiya, Bulgaria, **296** F4
Fakse Bugt, *bay*, Denmark, **286** F5
Faku, China, **211** H4
Falaba, Sierra Leone, **364** B3
Falaise, France, **290** D2
Falcon Lake, Canada, **414** G7
Falcone, Capo del, *cape*, Sardegna, Italy, **295** A5
Fălciu, Romania, **296** G2
Faleasi'u, Samoa, **141** B1
Falelatai, Samoa, **141** B1
Falelima, Samoa, **141** B1
Fălești, Moldova, **296** F2
Faleula, Samoa, **141** B1
Falfurrias, U.S.A., **424** C6
Falkenberg, Sweden, **286** F4
Falkirk, *local authority*, Scotland, U.K., **308** F5
Falkirk, Scotland, U.K., **308** F5
Falkland, Scotland, U.K., **308** F4
Falkland Escarpment, *underwater feature*, Atlantic Ocean, **477** D9
Falkland Islands, *U.K. dependency*, Atlantic Ocean, **460** F4
Falkland Plateau, *underwater feature*, Atlantic Ocean, **477** D9
Falkland Sound, Falkland Islands, **460** F4
Falkonera, *island*, Greece, **297** D7
Falköping, Sweden, **286** F3
Fall, *river*, U.S.A., **420** F7
Fall City, U.S.A., **418** D3
Fall River, U.S.A., **426** E4
Fallon, Montana, U.S.A., **419** M3
Fallon, Nevada, U.S.A., **422** D2
Falls City, U.S.A., **420** F5
Falls Lake Reservoir, U.S.A., **421** P7
Fallsville, U.S.A., **424** F2
Falmouth, England, U.K., **304** B4
Falmouth, Jamaica, **429** F3
Falmouth Bay, England, U.K., **304** B4
False Bay, South Africa, **370** C5
False Point, India, **219** F5
Falster, *island*, Denmark, **286** E5
Fălticeni, Romania, **296** F2
Falun, Sweden, **286** G2
Famagusta *see* Ammochostos, Cyprus, **225** B2
Famatina, Argentina, **458** C3
Famatina, *mountain peak*, Argentina, **458** C3
Famatina, Sierra de, *mountain range*, Argentina, **458** C3
Fan Si Pan, *mountain peak*, Vietnam, **203** D1
Fana, Mali, **364** C2
Fanad Head, *point*, Ireland, **309** E2
Fanandrana, Madagascar, **372** B4
Fanārah, Egypt, **225** B4
Fanchang, China, **206** D2
Fandriana, Madagascar, **372** B5
Fang, Thailand, **202** C2
Fang-liao, Taiwan, **206** E4
Fang Xian, China, **206** B1
Fangak, *river*, Sudan, **366** D3
Fangak, Sudan, **366** D3
Fangatau, *island*, French Polynesia, **137** G2
Fangataufa, *island*, French Polynesia, **137** H3
Fangcheng, China, **206** C1
Fangzheng, China, **211** K3
Fanjiatun, China, **211** J4
Fanli, China, **206** B1
Fanling, China, **207** C4

Fannich, Loch, *lake*, Scotland, U.K., **308** D3
Fanø, *island*, Denmark, **286** D5
Fano, Italy, **294** D4
Fanshan, China, **206** E3
Fanshi, China, **210** F5
Fara in Sabina, Italy, **295** D4
Faradje, Democratic Republic of the Congo, **369** E2
Farafangana, Madagascar, **372** B5
Farafenni, Gambia, **364** A2
Farāh, Afghanistan, **221** H2
Farallon de Pajaros, *island*, Northern Mariana Islands, **138** C2
Faranah, Guinea, **364** B2
Farasān, Jazā'ir, *islands*, Saudi Arabia, **220** D5
Faraulep, *island*, Micronesia, **138** C4
Fareham, England, U.K., **305** F4
Farewell, Cape, New Zealand, **132** D5
Farewell Spit, New Zealand, **132** D5
Fargo, Georgia, U.S.A., **425** L4
Fargo, North Dakota, U.S.A., **420** E2
Farīdkot, India, **218** C3
Farīdpur, Bangladesh, **219** G5
Färila, Sweden, **286** G2
Faringdon, England, U.K., **305** F3
Farinha, *river*, Brazil, **452** D5
Färiskür, Egypt, **225** A4
Farmington, Georgia, U.S.A., **425** L3
Farmington, Illinois, U.S.A., **420** H5
Farmington, Maine, U.S.A., **426** E2
Farmington, New Mexico, U.S.A., **423** J3
Farmville, North Carolina, U.S.A., **426** B7
Farmville, Virginia, U.S.A., **421** P7
Farnborough, England, U.K., **305** G3
Farndon, England, U.K., **304** E1
Farnham, England, U.K., **305** G3
Faro, Brazil, **452** B4
Faro, Canada, **410** F3
Faro, *district*, Portugal, **292** C4
Fårö, *island*, Sweden, **287** J3
Faro, *mountain peak*, Spain, **292** D1
Faro, Portugal, **292** D4
Fårösund, Sweden, **287** J4
Farquhar Group, *islands*, Seychelles, **372** C3
Farrukhābād, India, **218** D4
Farsala, Greece, **297** D6
Farson, U.S.A., **419** K5
Farsund, Norway, **286** C3
Fartak, Ra's, *cape*, Yemen, **220** F5
Fartura, Serra da, *mountain range*, Brazil, **459** G3
Farwell Island, Antarctica, **470** B5
Fasā, Iran, **220** F3
Fasano, Italy, **295** F5
Fáskrúðsfjörður, Iceland, **284** Z7
Fataki, Democratic Republic of the Congo, **369** F2
Fatehābād, India, **218** C3
Fatehpur, India, **218** E4
Fatehpur, Pakistan, **218** B3
Fatick, Senegal, **364** A2
Fátima, Portugal, **292** C3
Fatu Hiva, *island*, French Polynesia, **137** H2
Fatunda, Democratic Republic of the Congo, **368** C3
Fauquembergues, France, **305** K4
Fauquier, Canada, **413** K7
Făurei, Romania, **296** F3
Fauske, Norway, **284** G3
Faust, Canada, **413** M4
Fauville-en-Caux, France, **305** H5

Faversham, England, U.K., **305** H3
Fawcett, Canada, **413** M4
Fawley, England, U.K., **305** F4
Fawnie Nose, *mountain peak*, Canada, **412** G5
Faxaflói, *bay*, Iceland, **284** W7
Faxälven, *river*, Sweden, **284** H5
Faya-Largeau, Chad, **362** C5
Fayaoué, New Caledonia, **141** A3
Fayette, Alabama, U.S.A., **425** J3
Fayette, Mississippi, U.S.A., **424** G4
Fayetteville, Arkansas, U.S.A., **424** E1
Fayetteville, North Carolina, U.S.A., **425** N2
Fayetteville, Tennessee, U.S.A., **425** J2
Fdérik, Mauritania, **360** D4
Feale, *river*, Ireland, **309** C5
Featherville, U.S.A., **418** G5
Fécamp, France, **290** E2
Federación, Argentina, **459** F4
Federal, Argentina, **459** E4
Federal Capital Territory, *state*, Nigeria, **365** F3
Fedje, Norway, **286** B2
Fedorovka, Kazakhstan, **222** G2
Fedyukovo, Russian Federation, **299** E5
Feeagh, Lough, *lake*, Ireland, **309** C4
Fehérgyarmat, Hungary, **289** L5
Fehmarn, *island*, Germany, **288** E1
Fei Xian, China, **208** B4
Feijó, Brazil, **455** D2
Feilding, New Zealand, **132** E5
Feira de Santana, Brazil, **457** F3
Feldbach, Austria, **289** G5
Feldkirch, Austria, **288** D5
Feletoa, Vava'u Group, Tonga, **141** B3
Feliciano, *river*, Argentina, **459** E4
Felicité, *island*, Seychelles, **373** A2
Felidu Atoll, Maldives, **216** C6
Felipe Carrillo Puerto, Mexico, **431** H5
Félix U. Gómez, Mexico, **430** D2
Felixlândia, Brazil, **457** E5
Felixstowe, England, U.K., **305** J3
Feltre, Italy, **294** C2
Femund, *lake*, Norway, **286** E1
Fence Lake, U.S.A., **423** J4
Fenelon Falls, Canada, **416** B7
Fener Burnu, *point*, Turkey, **224** E4
Fenestrelle, Italy, **294** A3
Feng-kang, Taiwan, **206** E4
Feng-lin, Taiwan, **206** E4
Feng-shan, Taiwan, **206** E4
Feng Xian, Shaanxi, China, **215** H2
Feng Xian, Shandong, China, **206** D1
Feng-yüan, Taiwan, **206** E3
Fengari, *mountain peak*, Greece, **297** E5
Fengcheng, Gansu, China, **213** J5
Fengcheng, Jiangxi, China, **206** C2
Fengcheng, Liaoning, China, **211** J4
Fengdu, China, **215** H3
Fenggang, China, **215** H4
Fenghua, China, **206** E2
Fenghuang, Guangdong, China, **206** D4
Fenghuang, Hunan, China, **206** B3
Fengjie, China, **206** B2
Fengning, China, **210** G4
Fengqiu, China, **206** C1
Fengshan, China, **215** F4
Fengshun, China, **206** D4

Fengtai, China, **206** D1
Fengxian, China, **206** E2
Fengxiang, China, **215** H2
Fengxin, China, **206** C2
Fengyang, China, **206** D1
Fengyi, China, **215** H3
Fengzhen, China, **210** F4
Feni, Bangladesh, **219** G5
Feni Islands, Papua New Guinea, **140** D4
Fennimore, U.S.A., **420** H4
Fenoarivo Atsinanana, Madagascar, **372** B4
Fens, The, *region*, England, U.K., **305** G2
Fenyang, China, **210** E5
Feodosiya, Ukraine, **298** E3
Feolin Ferry, Scotland, U.K., **308** C5
Fer, Cap de, *cape*, Algeria, **361** H1
Ferapontovo, Russian Federation, **299** G3
Ferdinand, U.S.A., **421** K6
Ferdows, Iran, **221** G2
Fère-Champenoise, France, **291** F2
Fère-en-Tardenois, France, **291** F2
Feres, Greece, **297** F5
Fergus Falls, U.S.A., **420** E2
Fergusson Island, Papua New Guinea, **140** C5
Feriana, Tunisia, **362** A2
Ferkessédougou, Côte d'Ivoire, **364** C3
Fermanagh, *district*, Northern Ireland, U.K., **309** E3
Fermo, Italy, **294** D4
Fermoselle, Spain, **292** D2
Fermoy, Ireland, **309** D5
Fernández, Argentina, **458** D3
Fernandina, Isla, *island*, Islas Galápagos (Galapagos Islands), Ecuador, **461** A2
Fernandina Beach, U.S.A., **425** M4
Fernandópolis, Brazil, **456** C5
Ferndale, U.S.A., **418** C2
Ferndown, England, U.K., **305** F4
Fernie, Canada, **413** M7
Fernley, U.S.A., **422** D2
Ferns, Ireland, **309** F5
Ferrara, Italy, **294** C3
Ferreira do Alentejo, Portugal, **292** C3
Ferreira Gomes, Brazil, **452** C3
Ferreñafe, Peru, **454** B2
Ferriday, U.S.A., **424** G4
Ferro, Ilhéu de, *island*, Madeira, Portugal, **373** C3
Ferro, *river*, Brazil, **456** B3
Ferrol, Spain, **292** C1
Ferryhill, England, U.K., **307** G3
Ferryland, Canada, **417** Q6
Fès, Morocco, **361** F2
Feshi, Democratic Republic of the Congo, **368** C4
Fessenden, U.S.A., **420** D2
Festvåg, Norway, **284** G3
Fété Bowé, Senegal, **364** B2
Fetești, Romania, **296** F3
Fethard, Ireland, **309** E5
Fethiye, Turkey, **297** G7
Fethiye Körfezi, *bay*, Turkey, **297** G7
Fetisovo, Kazakhstan, **222** E4
Fetlar, *island*, Shetland, Scotland, U.K., **308** L7
Fettercairn, Scotland, U.K., **308** G4
Feuilles, Rivière aux, *river*, Canada, **411** M4
Feurs, France, **291** G4
Fevral'sk, Russian Federation, **211** K1
Feyzābād, Afghanistan, **218** B1
Ffestiniog, Wales, U.K., **304** D2
Fiambalá, Argentina, **458** C3
Fian, Ghana, **364** D2
Fianarantsoa, Madagascar, **372** B5

Fianarantsoa, *province*, Madagascar, **372** B5
Fianga, Chad, **365** H3
Fichē, Ethiopia, **367** E3
Fichtelgebirge, *mountain range*, Germany, **288** E4
Fidenza, Italy, **294** C3
Field, Canada, **421** N2
Fieni, Romania, **296** E3
Fier, Albania, **297** B5
Fierras, *mountain peak*, Sweden, **284** H3
Fife, *local authority*, Scotland, U.K., **308** F4
Fife Ness, *point*, Scotland, U.K., **308** G4
Figari, Capo, *cape*, Sardegna, Italy, **295** B5
Figari, Corse, France, **295** B5
Figeac, France, **290** F4
Figeholm, Sweden, **286** H4
Figueira da Foz, Portugal, **292** C2
Figueres, Spain, **293** J1
Figuig, Morocco, **361** F2
Figuil, Cameroon, **365** G3
Fiji, *country*, Pacific Ocean, **131** G3
Fiji Plateau, *underwater feature*, Pacific Ocean, **478** F6
Filabres, Sierra de los, *mountain range*, Spain, **293** F4
Filabusi, Zimbabwe, **371** E3
Filadelfia, Costa Rica, **428** D5
Filadelfia, Paraguay, **459** E2
Fil'akovo, Slovakia, **289** J4
Filamana, Mali, **364** C2
Filchner Ice Shelf, Antarctica, **470** C4
Filer, U.S.A., **418** G5
Filey, England, U.K., **307** H3
Filey Head, *point*, England, U.K., **307** H3
Filiaşi, Romania, **296** D3
Filiates, Greece, **297** C6
Filiatra, Greece, **297** C7
Filicudi, Isola, *island*, Italy, **295** E6
Filingué, Niger, **365** E2
Filippiada, Greece, **297** C6
Filipstad, Sweden, **286** G3
Fillmore, Canada, **414** C7
Fillmore, U.S.A., **422** G2
Filton, England, U.K., **304** E3
Filtu, Ethiopia, **367** F3
Fimbulheimen, *mountain range*, Antarctica, **470** D3
Fimbulisen, *ice shelf*, Antarctica, **470** D3
Finale Ligure, Italy, **294** B3
Finby, Finland, **287** K2
Findhorn, Scotland, U.K., **308** F3
Findlay, U.S.A., **421** M5
Findon, England, U.K., **305** G4
Fingal, U.S.A., **420** E2
Fingoè, Mozambique, **369** F6
Finke, *river*, Australia, **135** G4
Finland, *country*, Europe, **282** G3
Finland, Gulf of, Estonia/ Finland/Russian Federation, **287** M3
Finlay, *river*, Canada, **412** G3
Finley, U.S.A., **420** E2
Finn, *river*, Ireland, **309** D3
Finnmark, *county*, Norway, **285** M1
Finnsnes, Norway, **284** J2
Finnvollheia, *mountain peak*, Norway, **284** E4
Finschhafen, Papua New Guinea, **140** B4
Finsteraarhorn, *mountain peak*, Switzerland, **291** J3
Finsterwalde, Germany, **288** F3
Fintona, Northern Ireland, U.K., **309** E3
Fintown, Ireland, **309** D3
Fionn Loch, *lake*, Scotland, U.K., **308** D3
Fionnphort, Scotland, U.K., **308** C4
Fiora, *river*, Italy, **294** C4
Fırat (Euphrates), *river*, Turkey, **224** E5
Firat Nehri (Euphrates), *river*, Syria, **363** G1
Fire River, Canada, **415** N7
Firebag, *river*, Canada, **413** P3
Firenze (Florence), Italy, **294** C4
Firesteel, U.S.A., **420** C3
Firmat, Argentina, **458** E4
Fīrozābād, India, **218** D4
Fīrozpur, India, **218** C3
Firsovo, Russian Federation, **211** G1
Fīrūz Kūh, Iran, **220** F1
Fīrūzābād, Iran, **220** F3
Fisher Strait, Canada, **411** L3
Fishguard, Wales, U.K., **304** C3
Fishguard Bay, Wales, U.K., **304** B2
Fishtoft, England, U.K., **305** H2
Fiskebøl, Norway, **284** G2
Fisterra, Cabo, *cape*, Spain, **292** C1
Fisterra, Spain, **292** C1
Fitful Head, *point*, Scotland, U.K., **308** K8
Fito, Mount, *mountain peak*, Samoa, **141** B1
Fitz Roy, Argentina, **460** D3
Fitz Roy, Monte, *mountain peak*, Argentina, **460** C3
Fitzcarrald, Peru, **454** D3
Fitzgerald, U.S.A., **425** L4
Fitzroy, *river*, Australia, **134** F2
Fitzroy Crossing, Australia, **134** F2
Fiuggi, Italy, **295** D5
Five Sisters, *mountain peak*, Scotland, U.K., **308** D3
Fivemiletown, Northern Ireland, U.K., **309** E3
Fizi, Democratic Republic of the Congo, **369** E3
Fjærland, Norway, **286** C2
Fjällbacka, Sweden, **286** E3
Fjellerup, Denmark, **286** E4
Fjerritslev, Denmark, **286** D4
Flå, Norway, **286** D2
Fladdabister, Shetland, Scotland, U.K., **308** K7
Flagstaff, U.S.A., **423** H4
Flagstaff Bay, St Helena, **373** B3
Flagstaff Lake, U.S.A., **426** E2
Flakstad, Norway, **284** F2
Flamanville, France, **305** F5
Flamborough, England, U.K., **307** H3
Flamborough Head, *point*, England, U.K., **307** H3
Fläming, *mountain range*, Germany, **288** F2
Flaming Gorge Reservoir, U.S.A., **419** K6
Flamingo, U.S.A., **425** M7
Flanagin Town, Trinidad, Trinidad and Tobago, **461** C4
Flannan Isles, *islands*, Scotland, U.K., **308** B2
Flasher, U.S.A., **420** C2
Flåsjön, *lake*, Sweden, **284** G4
Flat Island, Mauritius, **373** C1
Flat Top Butte, *mountain peak*, U.S.A., **420** B2
Flatbush, Canada, **413** M4
Flathead, *river*, U.S.A., **418** H3
Flathead Lake, U.S.A., **418** G3
Flattery, Cape, Australia, **135** K1
Flattery, Cape, U.S.A., **418** B2
Flaxton, U.S.A., **419** N2
Fleet, England, U.K., **305** G3
Fleetwood, England, U.K., **306** E4
Flekkefjord, Norway, **286** C3
Flen, Sweden, **286** H3
Flensburg, Germany, **288** D1
Flers, France, **290** D2
Flesberg, Norway, **286** D3
Flesherton, Canada, **421** N3
Fletcher, Mount, *mountain peak*, Macquarie Island, **134** R11
Flevøland, *province*, Netherlands, **288** B2
Flimby, England, U.K., **306** E3
Flin Flon, Canada, **414** D4
Flinders, *river*, Australia, **135** J2
Flinders Bay, Australia, **134** C6
Flinders Island, Australia, **135** K7
Flinders Ranges, *mountain range*, Australia, **135** H5
Flint, *island*, Kiribati, **139** J6
Flint, *river*, U.S.A., **421** M4
Flint, U.S.A., **421** M4
Flint, Wales, U.K., **304** D1
Flintshire, *unitary authority*, Wales, U.K., **304** D1
Flisa, Norway, **286** F2
Flisa, *river*, Norway, **286** E2
Flixecourt, France, **290** F2
Floby, Sweden, **286** F3
Flora, Illinois, U.S.A., **421** J6
Flora, Oregon, U.S.A., **418** F4
Florac, France, **291** F4
Floral City, U.S.A., **425** L5
Florence, Alabama, U.S.A., **425** J2
Florence, Arizona, U.S.A., **423** H5
Florence, Kansas, U.S.A., **420** E6
Florence, Pennsylvania, U.S.A., **421** N5
Florence *see* Firenze, Italy, **294** C4
Florence, South Carolina, U.S.A., **425** N2
Florencia, Colombia, **450** C4
Florentino Ameghino, Argentina, **460** E2
Florentino Ameghino, Embalse, *reservoir*, Argentina, **460** D2
Flores, Brazil, **453** G5
Flores, Das, *river*, Brazil, **453** E4
Flores, Guatemala, **428** C3
Flores, *island*, Azores, Portugal, **360** L7
Flores, *island*, Indonesia, **198** C5
Flores do Piauí, Brazil, **453** E5
Flores Island, Canada, **412** F7
Flores Sea, Indonesia, **198** B4
Floresta, Brazil, **453** F5
Floreşti, Moldova, **296** G2
Floresville, U.S.A., **424** C5
Floriano, Brazil, **453** E5
Floriano Peixoto, Brazil, **455** E2
Florianópolis, Brazil, **459** H3
Florida, Bolivia, **455** F5
Florida, *state*, U.S.A., **425** L5
Florida, Straits of, Atlantic Ocean/Gulf of Mexico, **425** N7
Florida, Uruguay, **459** F5
Florida Bay, U.S.A., **425** M7
Florida City, U.S.A., **425** M7
Florida Islands, Solomon Islands, **141** A1
Florida Keys, *islands*, U.S.A., **424** M7
Florida Negra, Argentina, **460** D3
Floridablanca, Colombia, **450** D2
Floridia, Sicilia, Italy, **295** E7
Florien, U.S.A., **424** F4
Florina, Greece, **297** C5
Flornes, Norway, **284** E5
Florø, Norway, **286** B2
Flotta, *island*, Orkney, Scotland, U.K., **308** F2
Floydada, U.S.A., **424** B3
Fluk, Indonesia, **198** D3
Fluvià, *river*, Spain, **293** J1
Fly, *river*, Papua New Guinea, **140** A4
Flying Fish Cove, *bay*, Christmas Island, **134** N8
Foča, Bosnia and Herzegovina, **294** G4
Foça, Turkey, **297** F6
Fochabers, Scotland, U.K., **308** F3
Focşani, Romania, **296** F3
Fodé, Central African Republic, **368** D1
Fofoa, *island*, Vava'u Group, Tonga, **141** B3
Fogang, China, **207** B1
Foggaret ez Zoua, Algeria, **361** G3
Foggia, Italy, **295** E5
Fogo, Canada, **417** P5
Fogo, *island*, Cape Verde, **360** Q9
Fogo Island, Canada, **417** Q5
Föhr, *island*, Germany, **288** D1
Fóia, *mountain peak*, Portugal, **292** C4
Foinaven, Scotland, U.K., **308** E2
Foix, France, **290** E5
Fokino, Russian Federation, **299** E6
Fokku, Nigeria, **365** E2
Folda, *fiord*, Norway, **284** G3
Folegandros, *island*, Kyklades, Greece, **297** E7
Foley, U.S.A., **425** J4
Foleyet, Canada, **421** M1
Foligno, Italy, **294** D4
Folkestone, England, U.K., **305** J3
Folkingham, England, U.K., **305** G2
Folldal, Norway, **286** E1
Föllinge, Sweden, **284** G5
Follonica, Italy, **294** C4
Fomboni, Comoros, **372** A3
Fond du Lac, Canada, **413** R2
Fond du Lac, *lake*, Canada, **413** R2
Fond du Lac, *river*, Canada, **413** S2
Fond Du Lac, U.S.A., **421** J4
Fonda, Iowa, U.S.A., **420** F4
Fonda, North Dakota, U.S.A., **420** D1
Fondi, Italy, **295** D5
Fonggang, China, **207** C3
Fonseca, Golfo de, *gulf*, Nicaragua, **428** C4
Fontaine-le-Dun, France, **305** H5
Fontainebleau, France, **290** F2
Fonte Boa, Brazil, **451** E5
Fontenay-le-Comte, France, **290** D3
Fontur, *point*, Iceland, **284** Z6
Fonuakula, Niue, **132** M13
Fonualei, *island*, Tonga, **136** D2
Fonua'one'one, *island*, Vava'u Group, Tonga, **141** B3
Fonyód, Hungary, **289** H5
Foping, China, **215** H2
Forari, Vanuatu, **141** A2
Forbes, Australia, **135** K5
Forbes, Mount, *mountain peak*, New Zealand, **133** A7
Forbesganj, India, **219** F4
Forchheim, Germany, **288** E4
Ford, Cape, Australia, **134** F1
Førde, Hordaland, Norway, **286** B3
Førde, Sogn og Fjordane, Norway, **286** B2
Fordham, England, U.K., **305** H2
Fordingbridge, England, U.K., **305** F4
Fordon, Poland, **289** J2
Fordville, U.S.A., **420** E1
Fordyce, U.S.A., **424** F3
Forécariah, Guinea, **364** B3
Forel, Mont, *mountain peak*, Greenland, **411** R3
Foreland Point, England, U.K., **304** E4
Forelshogna, *mountain peak*, Norway, **284** E5
Forest, Canada, **421** M4
Forest, U.S.A., **425** H3
Forest Lake, U.S.A., **420** G3
Forestdale, Canada, **412** F4
Forestgrove, U.S.A., **419** K3
Forestville, Canada, **416** G5
Forez, Monts du, *mountain range*, France, **291** F4
Forfar, Scotland, U.K., **308** G4
Forges-les-Eaux, France, **290** E2
Forks, U.S.A., **418** B3
Forli, Italy, **294** D3
Formby, England, U.K., **306** E4
Formentera, *island*, Islas Baleares, Spain, **293** H3
Formentor, Cabo de, *cape*, Islas Baleares, Spain, **293** J3
Formerie, France, **305** J5
Formiga, Brazil, **456** E5
Formosa, Argentina, **459** E3
Formosa, Brazil, **456** D4
Formosa, *province*, Argentina, **459** E2
Formosa do Rio Prêto, Brazil, **456** E3
Formoso, Brazil, **456** D3
Formoso, *river*, Bahia, Brazil, **457** E4
Formoso, *river*, Tocantins, Brazil, **456** D3
Forpost-Kargat, Russian Federation, **223** L1
Forres, Scotland, U.K., **308** F3
Forrest City, U.S.A., **424** G2
Forsayth, Australia, **135** J2
Forshaga, Sweden, **286** F3
Forsinard, Scotland, U.K., **308** F2
Forsnes, Norway, **284** D5
Forssa, Finland, **287** L2
Forst, Germany, **289** G3
Forster, Australia, **135** L5
Forsyth, Georgia, U.S.A., **425** L3
Forsyth, Missouri, U.S.A., **420** G7
Forsyth, Montana, U.S.A., **419** L3
Forsythe, Canada, **416** C5
Fort Abbās, Pakistan, **218** C3
Fort Albany, Canada, **415** P5
Fort Alexander, Canada, **414** F6
Fort Assiniboine, Canada, **413** M4
Fort Augustus, Scotland, U.K., **308** E3
Fort Beaufort, South Africa, **371** E5
Fort Benton, U.S.A., **419** J3
Fort Black, Canada, **413** R4
Fort Bragg, U.S.A., **422** B2
Fort Chipewyan, Canada, **413** P2
Fort Collins, U.S.A., **423** L1
Fort Davis, U.S.A., **423** M6
Fort-de-France, Martinique, **427** D3
Fort Dodge, U.S.A., **420** F4
Fort Fitzgerald, Canada, **413** P2
Fort Frances, Canada, **414** H7
Fort Good Hope, Canada, **410** G3
Fort Lauderdale, U.S.A., **425** M6
Fort Liard, Canada, **412** H1
Fort Liberté, Haiti, **429** H3
Fort MacKay, Canada, **413** P3
Fort Macleod, Canada, **413** N7
Fort McMurray, Canada, **413** P3
Fort McPherson, Canada, **410** F3
Fort Madison, U.S.A., **420** H5
Fort-Mahon-Plage, France, **305** J4
Fort Morgan, U.S.A., **423** M1
Fort Myers, U.S.A., **425** M6
Fort Nelson, Canada, **412** H2
Fort Nelson, *river*, Canada, **412** H2
Fort Payne, U.S.A., **425** K2
Fort Peck, U.S.A., **419** L2
Fort Peck Lake, U.S.A., **419** L3
Fort Pierce, U.S.A., **425** M6
Fort Portal, Uganda, **369** F2
Fort Providence, Canada, **413** L1
Fort Qu'Appelle, Canada, **414** C6
Fort Resolution, Canada, **413**

N1
Fort Rixon, Zimbabwe, **371** E2
Fort Rock, U.S.A., **418** D5
Fort St James, Canada, **412** G4
Fort St John, Canada, **412** J3
Fort Severn, Canada, **415** L3
Fort-Shevchenko, Kazakhstan, **222** E4
Fort Simpson, Canada, **410** G3
Fort Smith, Canada, **413** P1
Fort Smith, U.S.A., **424** E2
Fort Stockton, U.S.A., **423** M6
Fort Summer, U.S.A., **423** L4
Fort Thomas, U.S.A., **423** J5
Fort Valley, U.S.A., **425** L3
Fort Vermilion, Canada, **413** M2
Fort Walton Beach, U.S.A., **425** J4
Fort Wayne, U.S.A., **421** L5
Fort Wellington, Guyana, **451** H2
Fort William, Scotland, U.K., **308** D4
Fort Worth, U.S.A., **424** D3
Fort Yukon, U.S.A., **410** E3
Fortaleza, Bolivia, **455** E3
Fortaleza, Brazil, **453** F4
Forte Coimbra, Brazil, **455** H5
Forteaux, Canada, **417** N4
Fortescue, *river*, Australia, **134** D3
Forth, Firth of, *river mouth*, Scotland, U.K., **308** G4
Forth, *river*, Scotland, U.K., **308** E4
Fortín Ávalos Sánchez, Paraguay, **459** E2
Fortín Capitán Demattei, Paraguay, **458** E2
Fortín Capitán Escobar, Paraguay, **458** E2
Fortín Carlos Antonio López, Paraguay, **455** G5
Fortín Coronel Bogado, Paraguay, **455** G5
Fortín Falcón, Paraguay, **459** E2
Fortín Galpón, Paraguay, **455** G5
Fortín Hernandarias, Paraguay, **458** E1
Fortín Infante Rivarola, Paraguay, **455** F5
Fortín Lavalle, Argentina, **459** E2
Fortín Madrejón, Paraguay, **455** G5
Fortín Paredes, Bolivia, **455** G5
Fortín Pilcomayo, Argentina, **458** E2
Fortín Presidente Ayala, Paraguay, **459** E2
Fortín Ravelo, Bolivia, **455** G5
Fortín Suárez Arana, Bolivia, **455** G5
Fortín Teniente General Mendoza, Paraguay, **455** G5
Fortrose, New Zealand, **133** B8
Fortrose, Scotland, U.K., **308** E3
Fortuna, California, U.S.A., **418** B6
Fortuna, North Dakota, U.S.A., **419** N2
Fortuna, Spain, **293** G3
Fortune, Canada, **417** P6
Fortune Bay, Canada, **417** P6
Fortuneswell, England, U.K., **304** E4
Forty Fours, The, *islands*, Chatham Islands, New Zealand, **133** Q16
Forvik, Norway, **284** F4
Foshan, China, **206** C4
Foso, Ghana, **364** D3
Fossano, Italy, **294** A3
Fossbakken, Norway, **284** J2
Fossombrone, Italy, **294** D4
Foster Bugt, *bay*, Greenland, **411** S2
Fotadrevo, Madagascar, **372** A5
Fotokol, Cameroon, **365** G2
Fougamou, Gabon, **368** B3
Fougères, France, **290** D2
Foul Bay, Egypt, **363** G4
Foula, *island*, Shetland, Scotland, U.K., **308** J7
Foulenzem, Gabon, **368** A3
Foulness Point, England, U.K., **305** H3
Foulwind, Cape, New Zealand, **133** C5
Foum Zguid, Morocco, **360** E3
Foumban, Cameroon, **368** B1
Fountain, U.S.A., **423** L2
Four Corners, U.S.A., **419** M4
Fourchu, Canada, **417** L7
Fournaise, Piton de la, *mountain peak*, Réunion, **373** A1
Fournier, Cape, Chatham Islands, New Zealand, **133** Q16
Fournoi, *island*, Dodekanisos, Greece, **297** F7
Fouta Djalon, *mountain range*, Guinea, **364** B2
Foveaux Strait, New Zealand, **133** A8
Fowler, Colorado, U.S.A., **423** L2
Fowler, Indiana, U.S.A., **421** K5
Fowlers Bay, Australia, **134** G5
Fox, *river*, Canada, **413** N3
Fox Creek, Canada, **413** L4
Fox Glacier, New Zealand, **133** C6
Fox Lake, Canada, **413** M2
Fox Mine, Canada, **414** D3
Fox Mountain, *mountain peak*, U.S.A., **418** E6
Fox Peak, *mountain peak*, New Zealand, **133** C6
Fox Valley, Canada, **413** Q6
Foxdale, Isle of Man, **306** D3
Foxe Basin, Canada, **411** M3
Foxe Channel, Canada, **411** L3
Foxe Peninsula, Canada, **411** M3
Foxen, *lake*, Sweden, **286** E3
Foxford, Ireland, **309** C4
Foxton, New Zealand, **132** E5
Foxwarren, Canada, **414** D6
Foyle, Lough, *inlet*, Northern Ireland, U.K., **309** F2
Foynes, Ireland, **309** C5
Foz do Cunene, Angola, **370** B2
Foz do Iguaçu, Brazil, **459** F2
Foz do Jordão, Brazil, **454** D2
Fraga, Spain, **293** H2
Frailes, Sierra de los, *mountain range*, Mexico, **430** D4
Frakes, Mount, *mountain peak*, Antarctica, **470** C6
Fram Peak, *mountain peak*, Antarctica, **470** F4
Framlingham, England, U.K., **305** J2
Franca, Brazil, **456** D5
Francavilla Fontana, Italy, **295** F5
France, *country*, Europe, **282** D6
France, Île de, *island*, Greenland, **411** T2
Francés, Puerto, *harbor*, Róbinson Crusoe Island, Archipiélago Juan Fernández, Chile, **461** C2
Franceville, Gabon, **368** B3
Franche-Comtè, *administrative region*, France, **291** G3
Francisco de Orellana, Peru, **450** D5
Francisco Escárcega, Mexico, **431** H5
Francisco Madero, Mexico, **430** E3
Francisco Sá, Brazil, **457** E4
Francistown, Botswana, **371** E3
Francois Lake, Canada, **412** F5
Frankfort, U.S.A., **421** L6
Frankfurt (Oder), Germany, **289** G2
Frankfurt am Main, Germany, **288** D3
Frankische Alb, *mountain range*, Germany, **288** E4
Franklin, Indiana, U.S.A., **421** K6
Franklin, Mount, *mountain peak*, New Zealand, **133** D6
Franklin, North Carolina, U.S.A., **425** L2
Franklin, Pennsylvania, U.S.A., **421** P5
Franklin, Virginia, U.S.A., **426** B6
Franklin, West Virginia, U.S.A., **421** P6
Franklin D. Roosevelt Lake, U.S.A., **418** E2
Franklin Mountains, *mountain range*, Canada, **410** G3
Frannie, U.S.A., **419** K4
Fränsta, Sweden, **286** H1
Frantsa-Iosifa, Zemlya, *islands*, Russian Federation, **300** F2
Franz Joseph Glacier, New Zealand, **133** C6
Frasca, Capo della, *cape*, Italy, **295** B6
Frascati, Italy, **295** D5
Fraser, *river*, Canada, **406** L3
Fraser, U.S.A., **423** L2
Fraser Island, Australia, **135** L4
Fraser Lake, Canada, **412** G4
Fraserburg, South Africa, **370** D5
Fraserdale, Canada, **415** P7
Frasertown, New Zealand, **132** F4
Frătești, Romania, **296** E4
Fray Bentos, Uruguay, **459** E4
Frazee, U.S.A., **420** F2
Frederic, U.S.A., **420** G3
Fredericia, Denmark, **286** D5
Frederick, Maryland, U.S.A., **426** B5
Frederick, Oklahoma, U.S.A., **424** C2
Frederick, South Dakota, U.S.A., **420** D3
Fredericksburg, Texas, U.S.A., **424** C4
Fredericksburg, Virginia, U.S.A., **426** B5
Fredericktown, U.S.A., **420** H7
Fredericton, Canada, **416** H7
Frederikshavn, Denmark, **286** E4
Frederiksted, U.S. Virgin Islands, **427** C2
Fredonia, Arizona, U.S.A., **422** G3
Fredonia, North Dakota, U.S.A., **420** D2
Fredrika, Sweden, **284** J4
Fredriksberg, Sweden, **286** G2
Fredrikstad, Norway, **286** E3
Free State, *province*, South Africa, **371** E4
Freels, Cape, Canada, **417** Q5
Freeman, U.S.A., **420** E4
Freemont Mountains, *mountain range*, U.S.A., **418** D5
Freeport, Bahamas, **428** F1
Freeport, Florida, U.S.A., **425** J4
Freeport, Illinois, U.S.A., **421** J4
Freeport, Texas, U.S.A., **424** E5
Freer, U.S.A., **424** C6
Freetown, Sierra Leone, **364** B3
Fregenal de la Sierra, Spain, **292** D3
Freiberg, Germany, **288** F3
Freiburg im Breisgau, Germany, **288** C4
Freirina, Chile, **458** B3
Freising, Germany, **288** E4
Freistadt, Austria, **289** G4
Fréjus, France, **291** H5
Fremont, Michigan, U.S.A., **421** L4
Fremont, Nebraska, U.S.A., **420** E5
French Guiana, *French department*, South America, **452** C2
French Polynesia, *French territory*, Pacific Ocean, **131** K3
French Southern and Antarctic Islands, *French territory*, Indian Ocean, **104** C13
Frenchglen, U.S.A., **418** E5
Frenchpark, Ireland, **309** D4
Frenda, Algeria, **361** G1
Fresco, Côte d'Ivoire, **364** C3
Fresco, *river*, Brazil, **452** C5
Fresnillo, Mexico, **430** E4
Fresno, U.S.A., **422** D3
Fresno Alhándiga, Spain, **292** E2
Fressingfield, England, U.K., **305** J2
Fresvik, Norway, **286** C2
Fréteval, France, **290** E3
Freudenstadt, Germany, **288** D4
Frévent, France, **290** F1
Freycinet Peninsula, Australia, **135** K7
Freyre, Argentina, **458** D4
Freyung, Germany, **288** F4
Fria, Cape, Namibia, **370** B2
Fria, Guinea, **364** B2
Friant, U.S.A., **422** D3
Frías, Argentina, **458** D3
Fribourg, Switzerland, **291** H3
Fridaythorpe, England, U.K., **307** H3
Friedberg, Austria, **289** H5
Friedrichshafen, Germany, **288** D5
Friesach, Austria, **289** G5
Friesland, *province*, Netherlands, **288** B2
Friesoythe, Germany, **288** C2
Frigate, *island*, Seychelles, **373** A2
Frinton-on-Sea, England, U.K., **305** J3
Frio, *river*, U.S.A., **424** C5
Friockheim, Scotland, U.K., **308** G4
Friona, U.S.A., **423** M4
Frisa, Loch, *lake*, Scotland, U.K., **308** C4
Frisco City, U.S.A., **425** J4
Frisco Peak, *mountain peak*, U.S.A., **422** G2
Fritsla, Sweden, **286** F4
Fritzlar, Germany, **288** D3
Friuli-Venezia Giulia, *autonomous region*, Italy, **294** D2
Friville-Escarbotin, France, **305** J4
Friza, Proliv, *strait*, Russian Federation, **209** K1
Frobisher Bay, Canada, **411** N3
Frobisher Lake, Canada, **413** Q3
Frohavet, *bay*, Norway, **284** D5
Froid, U.S.A., **419** M2
Froissy, France, **305** K5
Frome, England, U.K., **304** E3
Frome, Lake, Australia, **135** H5
Front Royal, U.S.A., **426** A5
Frontera, Islas Canarias, Spain, **373** A4
Frontera, Mexico, **431** G5
Fronteras, Mexico, **430** C2
Frontier, Canada, **413** Q7
Frosinone, Italy, **295** D5
Frøya, *island*, Norway, **284** D5
Fruges, France, **305** K4
Fruita, U.S.A., **423** J2
Frunzivka, Ukraine, **296** G2
Fruška Gora, *mountain range*, Yugoslavia, **296** B3
Frutigen, Switzerland, **291** H3
Fu Xian, China, **210** E5
Fua'amotu, Tongatapu Group, Tonga, **141** B4
Fu'an, China, **206** D3
Fuding, China, **206** E3
Fuencaliente, Islas Canarias, Spain, **373** A4
Fuencaliente, Punta de, *point*, Islas Canarias, Spain, **373** A4
Fuengirola, Spain, **292** E4
Fuente de Cantos, Spain, **292** D3
Fuente el Fresno, Spain, **293** F3
Fuente Obejuna, Spain, **292** E3
Fuentesaúco, Spain, **292** E2
Fuento-Álamo, Spain, **293** G4
Fuerte Bulnes, Chile, **460** C4
Fuerte Olimpo, Paraguay, **456** B5
Fuerteventura, *island*, Islas Canarias, Spain, **373** B4
Fuglafjørður, Faeroe Islands, **302** D1
Fugong, China, **215** F4
Fugou, China, **206** C1
Fugu, China, **210** E5
Fuguo, China, **211** G5
Fuhai, China, **212** E3
Fuhe, China, **207** B2
Fuji, Dome, *ice dome*, Antarctica, **470** E4
Fuji, Japan, **209** G4
Fuji-san, *mountain peak*, Japan, **209** G4
Fujian, *province*, China, **206** D3
Fujieda, Japan, **209** G4
Fujin, China, **211** L3
Fukagawa, Japan, **209** H2
Fukang, China, **212** E3
Fukave, *island*, Tonga, **141** B4
Fukeshan, China, **211** H1
Fukuchiyama, Japan, **208** F4
Fukui, Japan, **209** G3
Fukuoka, Japan, **208** E4
Fukushima, Japan, **209** H3
Fukuyama, Japan, **208** F4
Fulacunda, Guinea-Bissau, **364** A2
Fulaga, *island*, Fiji, **141** A4
Fulda, Germany, **288** D3
Fulda, *river*, Germany, **288** D3
Fulham, England, U.K., **305** G3
Fuling, China, **215** H3
Fullarton, Trinidad, Trinidad and Tobago, **461** C4
Fulleborn, Papua New Guinea, **140** C4
Fulton, U.S.A., **420** H6
Fulunäs, Sweden, **286** F2
Fumel, France, **290** E4
Funafuti, Tuvalu, **139** F5
Funan, China, **206** C1
Funäsdalen, Sweden, **286** F1
Funchal, Madeira, Portugal, **373** C3
Fundación, Colombia, **450** C1
Fundão, Portugal, **292** D2
Fundición, Mexico, **430** C3
Fundulea, Romania, **296** F3
Fundy, Bay of, Canada, **416** H7
Funhalouro, Mozambique, **371** F3
Funing, China, **206** D1
Funtua, Nigeria, **365** F2
Funzie, Scotland, U.K., **308** L7
Fuping, Hebei, China, **210** F5
Fuping, Shaanxi, China, **206** B1
Fuqing, China, **206** D3
Furancungo, Mozambique, **369** F5
Furao, China, **211** K2
Furneaux Group, *islands*, Australia, **135** K6
Furong, *river*, China, **215** H3
Furqlus, Syria, **225** D2
Fürstenau, Germany, **288** C2
Fürstenberg, Germany, **288** F2
Fürth, Germany, **288** E4
Furudal, Sweden, **286** G2
Furukawa, Japan, **209** H3
Fusa, Norway, **286** B2
Fusagasugá, Colombia, **450** C3
Fusha, China, **207** A3
Fushun, Liaoning, China, **211** H4
Fushun, Sichuan, China, **215** H3
Fusong, China, **211** J4
Füssen, Germany, **288** E5
Fusui, China, **215** H5
Futaleufú, Chile, **460** C2
Futian, China, **207** B2
Futog, Yugoslavia, **296** B3
Futuna, *island*, Vanuatu, **141** A3
Futuna, *island*, Wallis and Futuna, **139** G6
Fuxin, China, **211** H4

Glåma, *river*, Norway, **286** E2
Glamis, Scotland, U.K., **308** F4
Glåmos, Norway, **286** E1
Glan, Philippines, **204** D5
Glanaruddery Mountains, Ireland, **309** C5
Glanton, England, U.K., **307** G2
Glarner Alpen, *mountain range*, Switzerland, **291** J3
Glarus, Switzerland, **291** J3
Glasbury, Wales, U.K., **304** D2
Glasgow, Kentucky, U.S.A., **421** L7
Glasgow, Montana, U.S.A., **419** L2
Glasgow, Scotland, U.K., **308** E5
Glasgow, Virginia, U.S.A., **421** P7
Glasgow City, *local authority*, Scotland, U.K., **308** E5
Glaslyn, Canada, **413** Q5
Glass Butte, *mountain peak*, U.S.A., **418** D5
Glassboro, U.S.A., **426** C5
Glastonbury, England, U.K., **304** E3
Glazov, Russian Federation, **300** G4
Gleisdorf, Austria, **289** G5
Glen Canyon, *gorge*, U.S.A., **423** H3
Glen Cove, U.S.A., **426** D4
Glen Falls, U.S.A., **426** D3
Glen Innes, Australia, **135** L4
Glen Ullin, U.S.A., **419** P3
Glenavy, New Zealand, **133** C7
Glenbarr, Scotland, U.K., **308** D5
Glencross, U.S.A., **420** C3
Glendale, Arizona, U.S.A., **423** G5
Glendale, California, U.S.A., **422** D4
Glendambo, Australia, **135** H5
Glendive, U.S.A., **419** M3
Glendo, U.S.A., **419** M5
Glendon, Canada, **413** P4
Gleneagles, Scotland, U.K., **308** F4
Glenelg, *river*, Australia, **135** J6
Glenfield, U.S.A., **420** D2
Glenfinnan, Scotland, U.K., **308** D4
Glengad Head, *point*, Ireland, **309** E2
Glengarriff, Ireland, **309** C6
Glenluce, Scotland, U.K., **308** E6
Glennallen, U.S.A., **410** E3
Glennamaddy, Ireland, **309** D4
Glennville, U.S.A., **425** M4
Glenorchy, New Zealand, **133** B7
Glenrock, U.S.A., **419** M5
Glenrothes, Scotland, U.K., **308** F4
Glenties, Ireland, **309** D3
Glentworth, Canada, **413** R7
Glenville, U.S.A., **425** K3
Glenwood, Arkansas, U.S.A., **424** F2
Glenwood, Iowa, U.S.A., **420** F5
Glenwood, Minnesota, U.S.A., **420** F3
Glenwood, New Mexico, U.S.A., **423** J5
Glenwood Springs, U.S.A., **423** K2
Glide, U.S.A., **418** C5
Glina, Croatia, **294** F3
Glinojeck, Poland, **289** K2
Glinton, England, U.K., **305** G2
Glittertind, *mountain peak*, Norway, **286** D2
Gliwice, Poland, **289** J3
Globe, U.S.A., **423** H5
Glodeanu-Sărat, Romania, **296** F3
Glodeni, Moldova, **296** F2
Głogów, Poland, **289** H3
Glomfjord, Norway, **284** F3
Glommersträsk, Sweden, **284** J4
Glonn, *river*, Germany, **288** E4

Glorieuses, Îles, *islands*, Réunion, **372** B3
Glossop, England, U.K., **307** G4
Gloucester, England, U.K., **304** E3
Gloucester, Papua New Guinea, **140** C4
Gloucester, U.S.A., **426** E3
Gloucestershire, *unitary authority*, England, U.K., **304** E3
Glover Island, Canada, **417** N5
Głubczyce, Poland, **289** H3
Glübokoe, Kazakhstan, **223** L2
Gmünd, Austria, **289** G4
Gmunden, Austria, **289** F5
Gniew, Poland, **289** J2
Gniewkowo, Poland, **289** J2
Gniezno, Poland, **289** H2
Gnjilane, Yugoslavia, **296** C4
Goa, *state*, India, **216** C3
Goålpära, India, **219** G4
Goaso, Ghana, **364** D3
Goat Fell, *mountain peak*, Scotland, U.K., **308** D5
Goba, Ethiopia, **367** F3
Gobabis, Namibia, **370** C3
Gobernador Duval, Argentina, **460** D1
Gobernador Gregores, Argentina, **460** C3
Gobernador Mayer, Argentina, **460** C4
Gobi, China, **213** H5
Gobi, *desert*, Mongolia, **195** M5
Gobowen, England, U.K., **304** D2
Gochas, Namibia, **370** C3
Godalming, England, U.K., **305** G3
Godavari, *river*, India, **216** D2
Godbout, Canada, **416** H5
Godda, India, **219** F4
Godë, Ethiopia, **367** F3
Godech, Bulgaria, **296** D4
Godere, Ethiopia, **367** F3
Goderich, Canada, **421** N4
Goderville, France, **305** H5
Godhra, India, **218** C5
Godinlabe, Somalia, **367** G3
Godmanchester, England, U.K., **305** G2
Gödöllő, Hungary, **289** J5
Godoy Cruz, Argentina, **458** C4
Gods, *river*, Canada, **414** H3
Gods Lake, Canada, **414** G4
Gods Lake, *lake*, Canada, **414** G4
Godthåb *see* Nuuk, Greenland, **411** P3
Goe, Papua New Guinea, **140** A5
Goéland, Lac au, *lake*, Canada, **416** C5
Goes, Netherlands, **288** A3
Goffs, U.S.A., **422** F4
Gogland, Ostrov, *island*, Russian Federation, **287** N2
Gogounou, Benin, **365** E2
Gogrial, Sudan, **366** C3
Gohad, India, **218** D4
Goiana, Brazil, **453** G5
Goiandira, Brazil, **456** D5
Goiânia, Brazil, **456** D4
Goiás, Brazil, **456** C4
Goiás, *state*, Brazil, **456** C4
Goio-Erê, Brazil, **459** G2
Góis, Portugal, **292** C2
Gojra, Pakistan, **218** C3
Gökçeada, *island*, Turkey, **297** E5
Göksun, Turkey, **224** E5
Gokwe, Zimbabwe, **371** E2
Gol, Norway, **286** D2
Gola, India, **218** E3
Goläghät, India, **219** H4
Golan, *region*, Syria, **225** C3
Gölbaşı, Turkey, **363** G1
Golbembal, Nigeria, **365** G3
Golconda, U.S.A., **422** E1
Gölcük, Kocaeli, Turkey, **297** G5
Gölcük, Turkey, **297** F6
Gold Beach, U.S.A., **418** B5

Gold Bridge, Canada, **412** H6
Gold Coast, Australia, **135** L4
Gold Coast, *coastal area*, Ghana/Togo, **364** D4
Gold River, Canada, **412** F7
Gołdap, Poland, **289** L1
Golden, Canada, **413** L6
Golden Bay, New Zealand, **132** D5
Golden Meadow, U.S.A., **424** G5
Goldendale, U.S.A., **418** D4
Goldfield, U.S.A., **422** E3
Goldsboro, U.S.A., **425** N2
Goldsmith, U.S.A., **423** M6
Goldthwaite, U.S.A., **424** C4
Goldyrevskiy, Russian Federation, **222** F1
Goleniów, Poland, **289** G2
Goleta, U.S.A., **422** D4
Golets Skalistyy, Gora, *mountain peak*, Russian Federation, **301** Q4
Golfo Aranci, Sardegna, Italy, **295** B5
Gölgeli Dağları, *mountain range*, Turkey, **297** G7
Goliad, U.S.A., **424** D5
Gölmarmara, Turkey, **297** F6
Golmud, China, **213** G5
Golnik, Slovenia, **294** E2
Golo, *river*, Corse, France, **294** B4
Golo Island, Philippines, **204** C3
Golovnino, Russian Federation, **209** J2
Golpäyegän, Iran, **220** F2
Gölpazarı, Turkey, **297** H5
Golspie, Scotland, U.K., **308** F3
Golungo Alto, Angola, **368** B4
Golyam Perelik, *mountain peak*, Bulgaria, **297** E5
Gölyazı, Turkey, **297** G5
Golyshmanovo, Russian Federation, **223** H1
Goma, Democratic Republic of the Congo, **369** E3
Gomati, *river*, India, **219** E4
Gombe, Nigeria, **365** G2
Gombi, Nigeria, **365** G2
Gombrani Island, Rodrigues, **373** B1
Gomera, *island*, Islas Canarias, Spain, **373** A4
Gómez Farías, Mexico, **430** D2
Gómez Palacio, Mexico, **430** E3
Gomo, China, **219** F2
Gomorovichi, Russian Federation, **299** E2
Gonaïves, Haiti, **429** G3
Gonâve, Golfe de la, *gulf*, Haiti, **429** G3
Gonâve, Île de la, *island*, Haiti, **429** G3
Gonbad-e Qābūs, Iran, **222** F5
Gonda, India, **219** E4
Gondal, India, **218** B5
Gonder, Ethiopia, **367** E2
Gondia, India, **218** E5
Gönen, *river*, Turkey, **297** F5
Gönen, Turkey, **297** F5
Gonfreville-L'Orcher, France, **290** E2
Gong Xian, China, **206** C1
Gong'an, China, **206** C2
Gongbo'gyamba, China, **214** E3
Gongcheng, China, **206** B3
Gonggar, China, **214** D3
Gonghe, China, **213** J5
Gonghui, China, **210** F4
Gongliu, China, **223** L4
Gongming, China, **207** B3
Gongpoquan, China, **213** H4
Gongzhuling, China, **211** J4
Goniri, Nigeria, **365** G2
Gonzaga, Philippines, **204** C2
Gonzales, California, U.S.A., **422** C3
Gonzales, Texas, U.S.A., **424** D5
González, Mexico, **431** F4
Goobies, Canada, **417** P6
Good Hope, Cape of, South Africa, **370** C5

Good Hope Lake, Canada, **412** E2
Goodenough Island, Papua New Guinea, **140** C5
Goodeve, Canada, **414** C6
Gooding, U.S.A., **418** G5
Goodland, U.S.A., **420** C6
Goodlands, Mauritius, **373** C1
Goodrich, U.S.A., **420** C2
Goodsoil, Canada, **413** Q4
Goodwick, Wales, U.K., **304** C2
Goodwin, U.S.A., **420** E3
Goole, England, U.K., **307** H4
Goomalling, Australia, **134** D5
Goondiwindi, Australia, **135** L4
Goose Green, Falkland Islands, **460** E4
Goose Lake, U.S.A., **418** D6
Gopalganj, India, **219** F4
Góra, near Płock, Poland, **289** K2
Góra, Poland, **289** H3
Gora, Russian Federation, **299** G2
Gorakhpur, India, **219** E4
Goram, Tanjong, *point*, Indonesia, **198** C4
Goras, India, **218** D4
Goražde, Bosnia and Herzegovina, **294** G4
Gorbitsa, Russian Federation, **211** G1
Gorda, Punta, *point*, Chile, **454** D5
Gördalen, Sweden, **286** F2
Gördes, Turkey, **297** G6
Gordil, Central African Republic, **366** B3
Gordon, Lake, Australia, **135** J7
Gordon, Scotland, U.K., **308** G5
Gordon, U.S.A., **420** B4
Gordondale, Canada, **413** K4
Gordonsville, U.S.A., **426** A5
Goré, Chad, **365** H3
Gorê, Ethiopia, **366** E3
Gore, New Zealand, **133** B8
Gore Mountain, *mountain peak*, U.S.A., **426** E2
Gorebridge, Scotland, U.K., **308** F5
Gorel'de, Turkmenistan, **222** G4
Gorey, Ireland, **309** F5
Gorgal, *administrative region*, Mauritania, **364** B1
Gorge Creek, New Zealand, **133** B7
Gorgona, Isola di, *island*, Italy, **294** B4
Gorgora, Ethiopia, **367** E2
Gorgova, Romania, **296** G3
Gorham, U.S.A., **426** E2
Gorinchem, Netherlands, **288** B3
Goris, Armenia, **363** J1
Goritsy, Russian Federation, **299** F4
Gorizia, Italy, **294** D3
Gorlice, Poland, **289** K4
Görlitz, Germany, **289** G3
Gorlovo, Russian Federation, **299** G6
Gorm, Loch, *lake*, Scotland, U.K., **308** C5
Gorna Oryakhovitsa, Bulgaria, **296** E4
Gorna Dŭbnik, Bulgaria, **296** E4
Gornji Milanovac, Yugoslavia, **296** C3
Gorno Altaysk, Russian Federation, **223** M2
Gornozavodsk, Russian Federation, **209** H1
Gornyak, Russian Federation, **223** L2
Gorodishche, Russian Federation, **299** B3
Gorogoro, Indonesia, **198** D3
Goroka, Papua New Guinea, **140** B4
Gorom-Gorom, Burkina Faso, **364** D2
Gorong, Kepulauan, *islands*, Indonesia, **199** E4

Gorongosa, Mozambique, **371** F2
Gorongosa, Serra da, *mountain range*, Mozambique, **371** F2
Gorontalo, Indonesia, **198** C2
Gort, Ireland, **309** D4
Gortahork, Ireland, **309** D2
Gorumna Island, Ireland, **309** C4
Görvik, Sweden, **284** G5
Goryachegorsk, Russian Federation, **223** M1
Goryachinsk, Russian Federation, **210** E1
Gorzów Wielkopolski, Poland, **289** G2
Gosberton, England, U.K., **305** G2
Gosfield, England, U.K., **305** H3
Gosford, Australia, **135** L5
Gosforth, Cumbria, England, U.K., **306** E3
Gosforth, Tyne and Wear, England, U.K., **307** G2
Goshogawara, Japan, **209** H2
Goslar, Germany, **288** E3
Gospić, Croatia, **294** E3
Gosport, England, U.K., **305** F4
Gossen, *island*, Norway, **286** C1
Gossi, Mali, **364** D1
Gostivar, Macedonia, **296** C5
Gostyń, Poland, **289** H3
Gostynin, Poland, **289** J2
Gota, Ethiopia, **367** F3
Göteborg (Gothenburg), Sweden, **286** E4
Göteborg Och Bohus, *county*, Sweden, **286** E3
Götene, Sweden, **286** F3
Goth Ämri, Pakistan, **218** A4
Gotha, Germany, **288** E3
Gothem, Sweden, **287** J4
Gothenburg *see* Göteborg, Sweden, **286** E4
Gothenburg, U.S.A., **420** C5
Gothèye, Niger, **365** E2
Gotland, *county*, Sweden, **287** J4
Gotland, *island*, Sweden, **287** J4
Gotō-rettō, *islands*, Japan, **208** E4
Gotowasi, Indonesia, **199** E2
Gotse Delchev, Bulgaria, **297** D5
Gotska Sandön, *island*, Sweden, **287** J3
Göttingen, Germany, **288** D3
Gouda, Netherlands, **288** B3
Goudiri, Senegal, **364** B2
Goudoumaria, Niger, **365** G2
Gouéké, Guinea, **364** C3
Gouin, Réservoir, Canada, **416** D5
Goulais River, Canada, **421** L2
Goulburn, Australia, **135** K5
Goulburn Islands, Australia, **134** G1
Gould, U.S.A., **423** K1
Gould Coast, *region*, Antarctica, **470** D6
Goulfey, Cameroon, **365** G2
Goumbou, Mali, **364** C2
Goundam, Mali, **364** D1
Goundi, Chad, **365** H3
Gourcy, Burkina Faso, **364** D2
Gourdon, Cape, Papua New Guinea, **140** B4
Gourdon, France, **290** E4
Gouré, Niger, **365** G2
Gourin, France, **290** C2
Gourma-Rharous, Mali, **364** D1
Gournay-en-Bray, France, **305** J5
Gouro, Chad, **362** C5
Gouverneur, U.S.A., **426** C2
Gouzon, France, **290** F3
Governador Valadares, Brazil, **457** F5
Governor's Harbour, Bahamas, **428** F1
Govĭ-Altay, *province*, Mongolia, **213** G3

Hyesan, North Korea, **208** E2
Hyrynsalmi, Finland, **285** P4
Hysham, U.S.A., **419** L3
Hythe, Canada, **413** K4
Hythe, Hampshire, England, U.K., **305** F4
Hythe, Kent, England, U.K., **305** J3
Hytölä, Finland, **287** N1
Hyvinkää, Finland, **287** M2

I

I-lan, Taiwan, **206** E3
I-n-Amenas, Algeria, **361** H3
I-n-Amguel, Algeria, **361** H4
I-n-Belbel, Algeria, **361** G3
I-n-Eker, Algeria, **361** H4
I-n-Guezzam, Algeria, **361** H5
I-n-Salah, Algeria, **361** G3
I-n-Tebezas, Mali, **365** E1
Iacobeni, Romania, **296** E2
Iaçu, Brazil, **457** F3
Ialomiţa, *river*, Romania, **296** F3
Ialoveni, Moldova, **296** G2
Ianca, Romania, **296** F3
Iargara, Moldova, **296** G2
Iaşi, Romania, **296** F2
Iauaretê, Brazil, **451** E4
Iba, Philippines, **204** B3
Ibadan, Nigeria, **365** E3
Ibagué, Colombia, **450** C3
Ibar, *river*, Yugoslavia, **296** C4
Ibarra, Ecuador, **450** B4
Ibarreta, Argentina, **459** E2
Ibb, Yemen, **220** D6
Ibba, Sudan, **369** E2
Iberá, Esteros del, *marshes*, Argentina, **459** E3
Iberia, Peru, **454** C1
Iberian Peninsula, Portugal/Spain, **280** D7
Iberville, Lac d', *lake*, Canada, **416** E2
Ibestad, Norway, **284** H2
Ibeto, Nigeria, **365** F2
Ibi, Nigeria, **365** F3
Ibiá, Brazil, **456** D5
Ibiapaba, Serra da, *mountain range*, Brazil, **453** F4
Ibicuí, *river*, Brazil, **459** F3
Ibimirim, Brazil, **453** G5
Ibinty, *mountain peak*, Madagascar, **372** C5
Ibiraçu, Brazil, **457** F5
Ibirama, Brazil, **459** H3
Ibirapuita, *river*, Brazil, **459** F4
Ibitiara, Brazil, **457** E3
Ibiza, *mountain peak*, Spain, **292** E2
Ibiza *see* Eivissa, *island*, Islas Baleares, Spain, **293** H3
Ibiza *see* Eivissa, Islas Baleares, Spain, **293** H3
Ibotirama, Brazil, **457** E3
Iboundji, Mont, *mountain peak*, Gabon, **368** B3
Ibrā', Oman, **221** G4
'Ibrī, Oman, **221** G4
Ibstock, England, U.K., **305** F2
Ica, Peru, **454** C4
Ica, Punta, *point*, Peru, **454** C4
Içá, *river*, Brazil, **451** E5
Icacos Point, Trinidad, Trinidad and Tobago, **461** C4
Içana, Brazil, **451** E4
Içana, *river*, Brazil, **451** E4
Icatu, Brazil, **453** E4
İçel, *province*, Turkey, **225** B1
İçel (Mersin), Turkey, **363** F1
Iceland, *country*, Europe, **282** C3
Icha, *river*, Russian Federation, **223** K1
Ichalkaranji, India, **216** C2
Ichilo, *river*, Bolivia, **455** F4
Ichinoseki, Japan, **209** H3
Ich'ŏn, South Korea, **208** D3
Icklingham, England, U.K., **305** H2
İçmeler, Turkey, **297** G7
Icó, Brazil, **453** F5
Icod de Los Vinos, Islas Canarias, Spain, **373** A4
Ida Grove, U.S.A., **420** F4
Idabel, U.S.A., **424** E3
Idaburn, New Zealand, **133** B7
Idah, Nigeria, **365** F3
Idaho, *state*, U.S.A., **418** G4
Idaho Falls, U.S.A., **419** H5
Idalia, U.S.A., **423** M2
Idar-Oberstein, Germany, **288** C4
'Idd al Ghanam, Sudan, **366** B2
Idel', Russian Federation, **285** S4
Ideles, Algeria, **361** H4
Ider, Mongolia, **213** H2
Ider, *river*, Mongolia, **213** H2
Idfū, Egypt, **363** F4
Idiofa, Democratic Republic of the Congo, **368** C4
Idivuoma, Sweden, **285** L2
Idlib, *district*, Syria, **225** D1
Idlib, Syria, **225** D2
Idre, Sweden, **286** F2
Idrija, Slovenia, **294** D3
Idrinskoye, Russian Federation, **223** N2
Iecava, Latvia, **287** M4
Iepê, Brazil, **459** G2
Ieper (Ypres), Belgium, **288** A3
Ierapetra, Kriti, Greece, **297** E8
Ierissou, Kolpos, *bay*, Greece, **297** D5
Iernut, Romania, **296** E2
Ifakara, Tanzania, **369** G4
Ifalik, *island*, Micronesia, **138** C4
Ifanadiana, Madagascar, **372** B5
Ife, Nigeria, **365** E3
Iferouâne, Niger, **361** H5
Ifetesene, *mountain peak*, Algeria, **361** G3
Ifjord, Norway, **285** N1
Igabi, Nigeria, **365** F2
Igal, Hungary, **289** H5
Igalula, Tanzania, **369** F4
Iganga, Uganda, **369** F2
Igarapava, Brazil, **456** D5
Igarapé-Açu, Brazil, **452** D3
Igarapé Grande, Brazil, **453** E4
Igarka, Russian Federation, **300** K3
Igboho, Nigeria, **365** E3
Iggesund, Sweden, **287** H2
Iglesias, Sardegna, Italy, **295** B6
Igloolik, Canada, **411** L3
Ignace, Canada, **414** J7
Ignacio Zaragoza, Mexico, **430** D2
Ignalina, Lithuania, **287** N5
Ignatovo, Russian Federation, **299** F2
İğneada, Turkey, **296** F5
İğneada Burnu, *cape*, Turkey, **296** G5
Igombe, *river*, Tanzania, **369** F3
Igoumenitsa, Greece, **297** C6
Igra, Russian Federation, **222** E1
Igrim, Russian Federation, **300** H3
Iguaçu, *river*, Brazil, **459** G2
Iguaçu, Saltos do, *waterfall*, Argentina/Brazil, **459** F2
Iguaí, Brazil, **457** F4
Iguaje, Mesa de, *plateau*, Colombia, **450** D4
Iguala, Mexico, **431** F5
Igualada, Spain, **293** H2
Iguape, Brazil, **459** H2
Iguatemi, Brazil, **459** F2
Iguatemi, *river*, Brazil, **459** F2
Iguatu, Brazil, **453** F5
Iguéla, Gabon, **368** A3
Iguidi, Erg, *desert*, Algeria/Mauritania, **360** E3
Igunga, Tanzania, **369** F3
Iharaña, Madagascar, **372** B3
Ihbulag, Mongolia, **210** D4
Ihiala, Nigeria, **365** F3
Ihnāsiyat al Madīnah, Egypt, **225** A5
Ihosy, Madagascar, **372** B5
Ihsuuj, Mongolia, **210** D2
Iida, Japan, **209** G4
Iidaan, Somalia, **367** G3
Iijärvi, *lake*, Finland, **285** N2
Iijoki, *river*, Finland, **285** N4
Iisaku, Estonia, **287** N3
Iisalmi, Finland, **285** N5
Ijebu-Ode, Nigeria, **365** E3
Ijill, Kediet, *mountain peak*, Mauritania, **360** D4
Ijsselmeer, *lake*, Netherlands, **288** B2
Ijui, Brazil, **459** G3
Ijuí, *river*, Brazil, **459** F3
Ikahavo, *mountain peak*, Madagascar, **372** B4
Ikalamavony, Madagascar, **372** B5
Ikali, Democratic Republic of the Congo, **368** D3
Ikamatua, New Zealand, **133** C6
Ikanda, Democratic Republic of the Congo, **368** D3
Ikare, Nigeria, **365** F3
Ikaria, *island*, Dodekanisos, Greece, **297** F7
Ikawai, New Zealand, **133** C7
Ikeda, Japan, **209** H2
Ikeja, Nigeria, **365** E3
Ikela, Democratic Republic of the Congo, **368** D3
Ikey, Russian Federation, **223** Q2
Ikhtiman, Bulgaria, **296** D4
Ikhwān, Al (The Brothers), *islands*, Suquţrá (Socotra), Yemen, **373** B2
Ikire, Nigeria, **365** E3
Ikohahoene, Adrar, *mountain peak*, Algeria, **361** H3
Ikom, Nigeria, **365** F3
Ikongo, Madagascar, **372** B5
Ikorodu, Nigeria, **365** E3
Ikot Ekpene, Nigeria, **368** A1
Ikungu, Tanzania, **369** F4
Ila-Orangun, Nigeria, **365** E3
Ilagan, Philippines, **204** C2
Īlām, Iran, **220** E2
Iława, Poland, **289** J2
Ilchester, England, U.K., **304** E4
Ile, *river*, Kazakhstan, **223** K4
Île-à-la-Crosse, Canada, **413** R4
Île-à-la-Crosse, Lac, *lake*, Canada, **413** R4
Île-de-France, *administrative region*, France, **291** F2
Ilebo, Democratic Republic of the Congo, **368** D3
Ileksa, *river*, Russian Federation, **285** T5
Ileret, Kenya, **369** G2
Ilesha, Nigeria, **365** E3
Ilfracombe, England, U.K., **304** C3
Ilgaz, Turkey, **224** D4
Ilgın, Turkey, **363** F1
Ilha Grande, Brazil, **451** F4
Ilhéus, Brazil, **457** F4
Ili, *river*, China, **212** D4
Ilia, Romania, **296** D3
Iliamna Lake, U.S.A., **410** D3
Ilidža, Bosnia and Herzegovina, **294** G4
Iligan, Philippines, **204** D4
Iligan Bay, Philippines, **204** C4
Ilin Island, Philippines, **204** C3
Il'ino, Russian Federation, **299** C5
Il'inskoye, Russian Federation, **299** G4
Ilirska Bistrica, Slovenia, **294** E3
Il'ka, Russian Federation, **210** E2
Ilkeston, England, U.K., **305** F2
Ilkley, England, U.K., **307** G4
Illampu, Nevado de, *mountain peak*, Bolivia, **455** E4
Illapel, Chile, **458** B4
Iller, *river*, Germany, **288** E4
Illichivs'k, Ukraine, **296** H2
Illimani, Nevado, *mountain peak*, Bolivia, **455** E4
Illinois, *river*, U.S.A., **420** H6
Illinois, *state*, U.S.A., **421** J5
Illizi, Algeria, **361** H3
Illorsuit, Greenland, **411** P2
Illulissat, Greenland, **411** P3
Ilmajoki, Finland, **285** L5
Il'men', Ozero, *lake*, Russian Federation, **299** C3
Ilminster, England, U.K., **304** E4
Ilo, Peru, **454** D4
Iloc Island, Philippines, **204** B4
Iloilo, Philippines, **204** C4
Ilomantsi, Finland, **285** Q5
Ilorin, Nigeria, **365** E3
Iłowa, Poland, **289** G3
Ilūkste, Latvia, **287** N5
Ilva Mare, Romania, **296** E2
Ilwaco, U.S.A., **418** C3
Il'ya, Belarus, **287** N5
Imabari, Japan, **208** F4
Imala, Mozambique, **369** G5
Imandra, Ozero *lake*, Russian Federation, **285** R3
Imanombo, Madagascar, **372** B5
Imari, Japan, **208** E4
Imarssuak Seachannel, *underwater feature*, Atlantic Ocean, **477** E2
Imata, Peru, **454** D4
Imataca, Serranía de, *mountain range*, Venezuela, **451** G2
Imatra, Finland, **287** P2
Imbituba, Punta, *point*, Brazil, **459** H3
Imi-n-Tanoute, Morocco, **360** E2
Imlay, U.S.A., **422** D1
Immingham, England, U.K., **307** H4
Immokalee, U.S.A., **425** M6
Imo, *state*, Nigeria, **365** F3
Imola, Italy, **294** C3
Imonda, Papua New Guinea, **140** A3
Imperatriz, Brazil, **452** D4
Imperia, Italy, **294** B4
Imperial, Peru, **454** C3
Imperial, U.S.A., **420** C5
Impfondo, Congo, **368** C2
Imphāl, India, **214** E4
Imralı Adası, *island*, Turkey, **297** G5
Imroz, Turkey, **297** E5
Imtān, Syria, **225** D3
Imuris, Mexico, **430** C2
Imuruan Bay, Philippines, **204** B4
Ina, Japan, **209** G4
Inaccessible Island, Tristan da Cunha, **373** C2
Inajá, Brazil, **453** G5
Inambari, Peru, **455** E3
Inambari, *river*, Peru, **455** D3
Inangahua, New Zealand, **133** C5
Inanwatan, Indonesia, **199** F3
Iñapari, Peru, **455** E3
Inari, Finland, **285** N2
Inarijärvi, *lake*, Finland, **285** N2
Inauini, *river*, Brazil, **455** E2
Inca, Spain, **293** J3
Inca de Oro, Chile, **458** C3
İnce Burnu, *point*, Turkey, **297** F5
İncekum Burnu, *point*, Turkey, **225** C1
Inch, Kerry, Ireland, **309** C5
Inch, Wexford, Ireland, **309** F5
Inchard, Loch, *inlet*, Scotland, U.K., **308** D2
Inchiri, *administrative region*, Mauritania, **360** C5
Inch'ŏn, South Korea, **208** D3
Incudine, Monte, *mountain peak*, Corse, France, **295** B5
Inčukalns, Latvia, **287** M4
Inda Silasē, Ethiopia, **367** E2
Indaiá, *river*, Brazil, **456** E5
Indal, Sweden, **287** H1
Indalsälven, *river*, Sweden, **284** G5
Indaw, Myanmar, **205** C3
Indé, Mexico, **430** D3
Independenţa, near Galati, Romania, **296** F3
Independenţa, Romania, **296** G4
Independence, Kansas, U.S.A., **420** F7
Independence, Minnesota, U.S.A., **420** G2
Independence, Missouri, U.S.A., **420** F6
Independence Mountains, *mountain range*, U.S.A., **422** E1
Independencia, Bahía de la, *bay*, Peru, **454** C4
India, Bassas da, *islands*, Réunion, **371** G3
India, *country*, Asia, **196** J8
Indian Cabins, Canada, **413** L2
Indian Head, Canada, **414** C6
Indian Lake, U.S.A., **426** C3
Indian Ocean, **476** C6
Indian Springs, U.S.A., **422** F3
Indian Wells, U.S.A., **423** H4
Indiana, *state*, U.S.A., **421** K5
Indiana, U.S.A., **421** P5
Indianapolis, U.S.A., **421** K6
Indianola, Iowa, U.S.A., **420** G5
Indianola, Mississippi, U.S.A., **424** G3
Indigirka, *river*, Russian Federation, **301** R3
Inđija, Yugoslavia, **296** C3
Indio, U.S.A., **422** E5
Indo-China Peninsula, Asia, **195** L8
Indo-Gangetic Plain, India/Pakistan, **194** J7
Indomed Fracture Zone, *tectonic feature*, Indian Ocean, **476** B7
Indonesia, *country*, Asia, **197** N10
Indore, India, **218** C5
Indragiri, *river*, Indonesia, **200** C3
Indramayu, Indonesia, **201** E4
Indravati, *river*, India, **216** E2
Indre Arna, Norway, **286** B2
Indre Billefjord, Norway, **285** M1
Indre, *river*, France, **290** E3
Indura, Belarus, **289** L2
Indus, *river*, Asia, **218** A4
Indus Fan, *underwater feature*, Indian Ocean, **476** D3
İnebolu, Turkey, **224** D4
İnegöl, Turkey, **297** G5
Ineu, Romania, **296** C2
Infanta, Philippines, **204** C3
Infante Dom Henrique, São Tomé and Príncipe, **373** C4
Infiernillo, Presa del, *dam*, Mexico, **430** E5
Ingal, Niger, **365** F1
Ingaly, Russian Federation, **223** J1
Ingatestone, England, U.K., **305** H3
Ingende, Democratic Republic of the Congo, **368** C3
Ingeniero Guillermo N. Juárez, Argentina, **458** E2
Ingeniero Jacobacci, Argentina, **460** D1
Ingenio, Islas Canarias, Spain, **373** B4
Ingettolgoy, Mongolia, **210** D2
Ingham, Australia, **135** K2
Ingleborough, *mountain peak*, England, U.K., **306** F3
Ingleton, England, U.K., **306** F3
Inglewood, U.S.A., **422** D5
Inglis, Canada, **414** D6
Ingoda, *river*, Russian Federation, **210** F2
Ingoldmells, England, U.K., **305** H1
Ingolstadt, Germany, **288** E4
Ingomar, U.S.A., **419** L3

Itapagipe, Brazil, **456** D5
Itapebi, Brazil, **457** F4
Itapecuru-Mirim, Brazil, **453** E4
Itapemirim, Brazil, **457** F5
Itaperuna, Brazil, **457** F5
Itapetinga, Brazil, **457** F4
Itapetininga, Brazil, **459** H2
Itapeva, Brazil, **459** H2
Itapicuru, *river*, Bahia, Brazil, **457** F3
Itapicuru, *river*, Maranhão, Brazil, **453** E4
Itapicuru, Serra do, *mountain range*, Brazil, **452** E5
Itapipoca, Brazil, **453** F4
Itapiranga, Brazil, **451** G5
Itaqui, Brazil, **459** F3
Itararé, Brazil, **459** H2
Itararé, *river*, Brazil, **459** H2
Itārsi, India, **218** D5
Itarumã, Brazil, **456** C5
Itatupã, Brazil, **452** C3
Ite, Peru, **454** D4
Itea, Greece, **297** D6
Itebero, Democratic Republic of the Congo, **369** E3
Ithaca, U.S.A., **426** B3
Ithaki, Ionioi Nisoi, Greece, **297** C6
Ithaki, *island*, Ionioi Nisoi, Greece, **297** C6
Ithrīyat, Jabal, *mountain range*, Jordan, **225** D4
Itimbiri, *river*, Democratic Republic of the Congo, **368** D2
Itinga, Brazil, **457** F4
Itiquira, Brazil, **456** B4
Itiquira, *river*, Brazil, **456** B4
Itoko, Democratic Republic of the Congo, **368** D3
Ittiri, Sardegna, Italy, **295** B5
Ittoqqortoormiit, Greenland, **411** S2
Itu, Brazil, **459** H2
Ituango, Colombia, **450** C2
Ituí, *river*, Brazil, **454** D1
Ituiutaba, Brazil, **456** D5
Itula, Democratic Republic of the Congo, **369** E3
Itumbiara, Brazil, **456** D5
Ituni, Guyana, **451** G3
Itupiranga, Brazil, **452** D4
Ituporanga, Brazil, **459** H3
Iturama, Brazil, **456** C5
Iturbe, Paraguay, **459** F3
Iturup, *island*, Kuril'skiye Ostrova, Russian Federation, **209** J1
Iturup, Ostrov, *island*, Russian Federation, **301** R5
Ituxi, *river*, Brazil, **455** E2
Ituzaingó, Argentina, **459** F3
Itzehoe, Germany, **288** D2
Iul'tin, Russian Federation, **301** V3
Iutica, Brazil, **451** E4
Iva, Samoa, **141** B1
Ivai, *river*, Brazil, **459** G2
Ivakoany, *mountain peak*, Madagascar, **372** B5
Ivalo, Finland, **285** N2
Ivalojoki, *river*, Finland, **285** N2
Ivanec, Croatia, **294** F2
Ivangorod, Russian Federation, **299** B3
Ivangrad, Yugoslavia, **296** B4
Ivanhoe, Australia, **135** J5
Ivanhoe, U.S.A., **420** E3
Ivanić Grad, Croatia, **294** F3
Ivanivka, Ukraine, **296** H2
Ivanjica, Yugoslavia, **296** C4
Ivanjska, Bosnia and Herzegovina, **294** F3
Ivankovtsy, Russian Federation, **211** L2
Ivano-Frankivs'k, Ukraine, **298** B3
Ivano-Frankivs'ka Oblast', *province*, Ukraine, **296** D1
Ivanova, Russian Federation, **299** C4
Ivanovka, Russian Federation,

211 G2
Ivanovo, Russian Federation, **300** F4
Ivatsevichy, Belarus, **289** M2
Ivaylovgrad, Bulgaria, **297** F5
Ivdel', Russian Federation, **300** H3
Iveşti, near Bârlad, Romania, **296** F2
Iveşti, Romania, **296** F3
Ivindo, *river*, Gabon, **368** B3
Ivinheima, Brazil, **459** G2
Ivinheima, *river*, Brazil, **456** C6
Ivittuut, Greenland, **411** Q3
Ivohibe, Madagascar, **372** B5
Ivory Coast, *coastal area*, Côte d'Ivoire, **364** C4
Ivrea, Italy, **294** A3
İvrindi, Turkey, **297** F6
Ivujivik, Canada, **411** M3
Ivybridge, England, U.K., **304** D4
Ivydale, U.S.A., **421** N6
Iwaki, Japan, **209** H3
Iwakuni, Japan, **208** F4
Iwamizawa, Japan, **209** H2
Iwanai, Japan, **209** H2
Iwo, Nigeria, **365** E3
Iwon, North Korea, **208** E2
Iwye, Belarus, **289** M2
Ixiamas, Bolivia, **455** E3
Iximiquilpán, Mexico, **431** F4
Ixtlán de Juárez, Mexico, **431** F5
Ixtlán del Río, Mexico, **430** D4
Ixworth, England, U.K., **305** H2
Iyevlevo, Russian Federation, **222** H1
Iza, *river*, Romania, **296** E2
Īzad Khvāst, Iran, **220** F2
Izazi, Tanzania, **369** G4
Izberbash, Russian Federation, **222** D4
Izbica, Poland, **289** H1
Izborsk, Russian Federation, **299** A4
Izhevsk, Russian Federation, **222** E1
Izhma, *river*, Russian Federation, **281** K3
Izmayil, Ukraine, **296** G3
İzmir, *province*, Turkey, **297** F6
İzmir, Turkey, **297** F6
İzmit *see* Kocaeli, Turkey, **297** G5
Iznájar, Embalse de, *reservoir*, Spain, **292** E4
İznik, Turkey, **297** G5
İznik Gölü, *lake*, Turkey, **297** G5
Iznoski, Russian Federation, **299** E5
Izra', Syria, **225** D3
Izsák, Hungary, **289** J5
Izu-Shotō, *islands*, Japan, **209** G4
Izuhara, Japan, **208** E4
Izumi, Japan, **208** E4
Izumo, Japan, **208** F4

J

J.A.D. Jensen Nunatakker, *mountain peak*, Greenland, **411** Q3
Jaakonvaara, Finland, **285** Q5
Jaala, Finland, **287** N2
Jabalpur, India, **218** D5
Jabbūl, Sabkhat al, *lake*, Syria, **225** D1
Jabiru, Australia, **134** G1
Jablah, Syria, **225** C2
Jablanica, Bosnia and Herzegovina, **294** F4
Jablanica, *mountain range*, Albania/Macedonia, **297** C5
Jabłonowo-Pomorskie, Poland, **289** J2

Jaboatão, Brazil, **453** G5
Jabukovac, Yugoslavia, **296** D3
Jabung, Tanjong, *point*, Indonesia, **200** D3
Jabuticabal, Brazil, **456** D5
Jaca, Spain, **293** G1
Jacaré, *river*, Brazil, **457** F3
Jacareacanga, Brazil, **452** B5
Jacareí, Brazil, **459** J2
Jáchal, *river*, Argentina, **458** C4
Jacinto, Brazil, **457** F4
Jaciparaná, Brazil, **455** F2
Jaciparaná, *river*, Brazil, **455** F2
Jack Creek, U.S.A., **418** F6
Jackhead, Canada, **414** F6
Jackman, U.S.A., **426** E2
Jacksboro, U.S.A., **424** C3
Jackson, Alabama, U.S.A., **425** J4
Jackson, California, U.S.A., **422** C2
Jackson, Cape, New Zealand, **133** E5
Jackson, Michigan, U.S.A., **421** L4
Jackson, Minnesota, U.S.A., **420** F4
Jackson, Mississippi, U.S.A., **424** G3
Jackson, Montana, U.S.A., **418** H4
Jackson, Ohio, U.S.A., **421** M6
Jackson, Tennessee, U.S.A., **425** H2
Jackson, Wyoming, U.S.A., **419** J5
Jackson Bay, New Zealand, **133** B6
Jackson Lake, U.S.A., **419** J5
Jacksonboro, U.S.A., **425** M3
Jacksons, New Zealand, **133** C6
Jacksonville, Arkansas, U.S.A., **424** F2
Jacksonville, Florida, U.S.A., **425** M4
Jacksonville, Illinois, U.S.A., **420** H6
Jacksonville, North Carolina, U.S.A., **425** P2
Jacksonville, Texas, U.S.A., **424** E4
Jacksonville Beach, U.S.A., **425** M4
Jäckvik, Sweden, **284** H3
Jacmel, Haiti, **429** G3
Jaco, Mexico, **430** E3
Jacobābād, Pakistan, **218** B3
Jacobina, Brazil, **457** F3
Jacquemart Island, Auckland Islands, New Zealand, **132** K11
Jacques-Cartier, Détroit de, *strait*, Canada, **417** J4
Jacquet River, Canada, **416** H6
Jacui, *river*, Brazil, **459** G3
Jacuípe, *river*, Brazil, **457** F3
Jacundá, Brazil, **452** D4
Jacundá, *river*, Brazil, **452** C4
Jacupiranga, Brazil, **459** H2
Jacura, Venezuela, **451** E1
Jadū, Libya, **362** B2
Jaén, Peru, **454** B1
Jaén, Spain, **293** F4
Jaffa, Cape, Australia, **135** H6
Jaffna, Sri Lanka, **216** E4
Jaffray, Canada, **413** M7
Jafr, Qā' al, *salt-pan*, Jordan, **225** D4
Jagdalpur, India, **217** E2
Jagdaqi, China, **211** J2
Jagersfontein, South Africa, **370** E4
Jaggang, China, **214** A2
Jagodina, Yugoslavia, **296** C4
Jagraon, India, **218** C3
Jagtiāl, India, **216** D2
Jaguarão, Brazil, **459** G4
Jaguarão, *river*, Brazil, **459** G4
Jaguari, Brazil, **459** F3
Jaguari, *river*, Brazil, **459** F3
Jaguaribe, Brazil, **453** F4

Jaguaruna, Brazil, **459** H3
Jagüé, Argentina, **458** C3
Jagüey Grande, Cuba, **429** E2
Jahānābād, India, **219** F4
Jahāzpur, India, **218** C4
Jahrom, Iran, **220** F3
Jaicós, Brazil, **453** F5
Jaipur, India, **218** C4
Jais, India, **219** E4
Jaisalmer, India, **218** B4
Jājapur, India, **219** F5
Jajce, Bosnia and Herzegovina, **294** F3
Jakarta, Indonesia, **201** D4
Jakarta Raya, *autonomous district*, Indonesia, **200** D4
Jakes Corner, Canada, **412** C1
Jakobābād *see* Jacobābād
Jakupica, *mountain range*, Macedonia, **297** C5
Jal, U.S.A., **423** M5
Jalai Nur, China, **210** G2
Jalaid Qi, China, **211** H3
Jalal-Abad, Kyrgyzstan, **212** B4
Jalālah al Baḥrīyah, Jabal al, *mountain range*, Egypt, **225** A5
Jalālah al Qiblīyah, Jabal al, *mountain range*, Egypt, **225** A5
Jalālābād, Afghanistan, **218** B2
Jalapa Enríquez, Mexico, **431** F5
Jalapa, Guatemala, **428** C4
Jalapa, Nicaragua, **428** D4
Jālaun, India, **218** D4
Jales, Brazil, **456** C5
Jaleshwar, India, **219** F5
Jaleswar, Nepal, **219** F4
Jālgaon, India, **218** C5
Jalingo, Nigeria, **365** G3
Jalisco, *state*, Mexico, **430** D4
Jālna, India, **218** C6
Jalor, India, **218** C4
Jalostotitlán, Mexico, **430** E4
Jalpāiguri, India, **219** G4
Jalpa, Mexico, **430** E4
Jalpan, Mexico, **431** F4
Jālū, Libya, **362** D3
Jaluit, *island*, Marshall Islands, **139** F4
Jamaame, Somalia, **369** H3
Jamaica, *country*, Caribbean Sea, **409** R7
Jamaica Channel, Haiti/Jamaica, **429** G3
Jamālpur, Bangladesh, **214** D4
Jamanota, *mountain peak*, Aruba, **461** B3
Jamanxin, *river*, Brazil, **452** B5
Jamari, *river*, Brazil, **455** F2
Jambi, Indonesia, **200** C3
Jambi, *province*, Indonesia, **200** C3
Jamboaye, *river*, Indonesia, **200** B1
Jambongan, Pulau, *island*, Malaysia, **201** G1
Jambuair, Tanjong, *point*, Indonesia, **200** B1
James, Isla, *island*, Chile, **460** B2
James, *river*, U.S.A., **420** D2
James Bay, Canada, **415** P5
Jamesābād, Pakistan, **218** B4
Jamestown, New York, U.S.A., **421** P4
Jamestown, North Dakota, U.S.A., **420** D2
Jamestown, St Helena, **373** B3
Jamkhandi, India, **216** C2
Jammerbugten, *bay*, Denmark, **286** D4
Jammu, India, **218** C2
Jammu and Kashmīr, *state*, India, **218** C2
Jāmnagar, India, **218** B5
Jāmpur, Pakistan, **218** B3
Jämsä, Finland, **287** M2
Jamsah, Egypt, **363** F3
Jamshedpur, India, **219** F5
Jamtari, Nigeria, **365** G3
Jämtland, *county*, Sweden, **284** F5
Jamūi, India, **219** F4

Jan Mayen, *Norwegian dependency*, Greenland Sea, **471** D8
Jan Mayen Ridge, *underwater feature*, Atlantic Ocean, **477** G1
Janāb Kurdufān, *state*, Sudan, **366** D2
Janaúba, Brazil, **457** E4
Janaucu, Ilha, *island*, Brazil, **452** C3
Jand, Pakistan, **218** B2
Jandaq, Iran, **221** F2
Jandia, Punta de, *point*, Islas Canarias, Spain, **373** B4
Jane Peak, *mountain peak*, New Zealand, **133** B7
Janesville, U.S.A., **421** J4
Jangeru, Indonesia, **201** G3
Jangipur, India, **219** F4
Janin, West Bank, **225** C3
Janja, Bosnia and Herzegovina, **296** B3
Janjina, Croatia, **294** F4
Janos, Mexico, **430** C2
Jánoshalma, Hungary, **289** J5
Jánosháza, Hungary, **289** H5
Janów Lubelski, Poland, **289** L3
Janów Podlaski, Poland, **289** L2
Jänsmässholmen, Sweden, **284** F5
Januária, Brazil, **457** E4
Janūb Dārfūr, *state*, Sudan, **366** B2
Janzé, France, **290** D3
Japan, *country*, Asia, **197** Q6
Japan Basin, *underwater feature*, Sea of Japan, **478** C2
Japan Trench, *underwater feature*, Pacific Ocean, **478** D2
Japurá, Brazil, **451** E4
Japura, Indonesia, **200** C3
Japurá, *river*, Brazil, **451** F5
Jaqué, Panama, **429** F6
Jaques Cartier, Mont, *mountain peak*, Canada, **416** J5
Jaraguá do Sul, Brazil, **459** H3
Jaraicejo, Spain, **292** E3
Jarama, *river*, Spain, **293** F2
Jarandilla de la Vera, Spain, **292** E2
Jarash, Jordan, **225** C3
Jarauçu, *river*, Brazil, **452** C4
Jarbah, Jazīrat, *island*, Tunisia, **361** J2
Jardim, Brazil, **456** B5
Jardines de la Reina, Archipiélago de los, *islands*, Cuba, **429** F2
Jargalang, China, **211** H4
Jargalant, Arhangay, Mongolia, **213** J3
Jargalant, Govĭ-Altay, Mongolia, **213** H3
Jargalant, Töv, Mongolia, **210** D2
Jargalthaan, Mongolia, **210** E3
Jargeau, France, **290** F3
Jari, *river*, Brazil, **452** C3
Jarīd, Shaṭṭ al, *lake*, Tunisia, **361** H2
Jarjīs, Tunisia, **362** B2
Järna, Kopparberg, Sweden, **286** G2
Järna, Stockholm, Sweden, **287** H3
Jarny, France, **291** G2
Jarocin, Poland, **289** H3
Jarod, India, **218** D5
Jarosław, Poland, **289** L4
Jarrāhi, *river*, Iran, **220** E2
Jarrell, U.S.A., **424** D4
Jartai, China, **210** D5
Jaru, Brazil, **455** F3
Jarud Qi, China, **211** H3
Järva-Jaani, Estonia, **287** M3
Järvenpää, Finland, **287** M2
Jarvis Island, *U.S. territory*, Pacific Ocean, **131** J2
Järvsö, Sweden, **286** H2
Jashpurnagar, India, **219** F5

Jašiūnai, Lithuania, **287** M5
Jāsk, Iran, **221** G3
Jasło, Poland, **289** K4
Jasper, Alabama, U.S.A., **425** J3
Jasper, Arkansas, U.S.A., **424** F2
Jasper, Canada, **413** K5
Jasper, Florida, U.S.A., **425** L4
Jasper, Georgia, U.S.A., **425** K2
Jasper, Indiana, U.S.A., **421** K6
Jasper, Texas, U.S.A., **424** F4
Jastrebarsko, Croatia, **294** E3
Jastrowie, Poland, **289** H2
Jastrzebie Zdroj, Poland, **289** J4
Jászárokszállás, Hungary, **289** J5
Jászberény, Hungary, **289** J5
Jataí, Brazil, **456** C4
Jatapu, *river*, Brazil, **451** G4
Jāti, Pakistan, **218** B4
Jatiluhur, Danau, *lake*, Indonesia, **201** D4
Jaú, Brazil, **459** H2
Jáua, Meseta del Cerro, *mountain range*, Venezuela, **451** F3
Jauaperi, *river*, Brazil, **451** G4
Jauja, Peru, **454** C3
Jaunjelgava, Latvia, **287** M4
Jaunpiebalga, Latvia, **287** N4
Jaunpils, Latvia, **287** L4
Jaunpur, India, **219** E4
Jauru, Brazil, **456** B5
Jauru, *river*, Brazil, **456** A4
Javādi Hills, India, **216** D3
Java *see* Jawa, *island*, Indonesia, **201** E5
Java Sea, Indonesia, **201** F4
Java Trench, *underwater feature*, Indian Ocean, **476** F4
Javalambre, *mountain peak*, Spain, **293** G2
Javarthushuu, Mongolia, **210** F2
Jávea, Spain, **293** H3
Javořice, *mountain peak*, Czech Republic, **289** G4
Jävre, Sweden, **284** K4
Javron, France, **290** D2
Jawa (Java), *island*, Indonesia, **201** E5
Jawa Barat, *province*, Indonesia, **201** D4
Jawa Tengah, *province*, Indonesia, **201** E4
Jawa Timur, *province*, Indonesia, **201** E5
Jawabarat, *province*, Indonesia, **201** D4
Jawand, Afghanistan, **218** A2
Jawbān Bayk, Syria, **225** D1
Jawhar, Somalia, **367** G4
Jawor, Poland, **289** H3
Jay Em, U.S.A., **419** M5
Jaya, Puncak, *mountain peak*, Indonesia, **199** G4
Jayanca, Peru, **454** B2
Jayapura, Indonesia, **199** H3
Jayawijaya, Pegunungan, *mountain range*, Indonesia, **199** G4
Jaynagar, India, **219** F4
Jaypur, India, **217** E2
Jayrūd, Syria, **225** D3
Jazīreh-ye Forūr, Iran, **221** F3
Jeanerette, U.S.A., **424** G5
Jebba, Nigeria, **365** E3
Jebel, Romania, **296** C3
Jedburgh, Scotland, U.K., **308** G5
Jedda *see* Jiddah, Saudi Arabia, **363** G4
Jeddito, U.S.A., **423** H4
Jędrzejów, Poland, **289** K3
Jedwabne, Poland, **289** L2
Jefferson, Mount, *mountain peak*, Nevada, U.S.A., **422** E2
Jefferson, Mount, *mountain peak*, Oregon, U.S.A., **418** D4
Jefferson, U.S.A., **424** E3
Jefferson City, Missouri, U.S.A., **420** G6
Jefferson City, Tennessee, U.S.A., **425** L1
Jeffrey City, U.S.A., **419** L5
Jeffrey's Bay, South Africa, **370** D5
Jeffryes, Mount, *mountain peak*, Macquarie Island, **134** R11
Jega, Nigeria, **365** E2
Jejuí Guazú, *river*, Paraguay, **459** F2
Jēkabpils, Latvia, **287** M4
Jektvik, Norway, **284** F3
Jeldesa, Ethiopia, **367** F3
Jelenia Góra, Poland, **289** G3
Jelgava, Latvia, **287** L4
Jeli, Malaysia, **200** C1
Jellicoe, Canada, **415** L7
Jemaluang, Malaysia, **200** C2
Jember, Indonesia, **201** F5
Jeminay, China, **212** E3
Jempang, Danau, *lake*, Indonesia, **201** F3
Jena, Germany, **288** E3
Jendouba, Tunisia, **295** B7
Jenner, Canada, **413** P6
Jennings, U.S.A., **424** F4
Jenpeg, Canada, **414** E4
Jensen, U.S.A., **423** J1
Jepara, Indonesia, **201** E4
Jepua, Finland, **285** L5
Jequié, Brazil, **457** F3
Jequitaí, Brazil, **457** E4
Jequitinhonha, Brazil, **457** F4
Jequitinhonha, *river*, Brazil, **457** F4
Jerada, Morocco, **361** F2
Jerbar, Sudan, **369** F1
Jérémie, Haiti, **429** G3
Jeremoabo, Brazil, **457** F3
Jerez de García Salinas, Mexico, **430** E4
Jeréz de la Frontera, Spain, **292** D4
Jergucat, Albania, **297** C6
Jericho *see* Arīḩā, West Bank, **25**, C4
Jerilderie, Australia, **135** K6
Jerome, U.S.A., **418** G5
Jerramungup, Australia, **134** D5
Jersey, *island*, Channel Islands, **290** C2
Jersey City, U.S.A., **426** C4
Jersey Shore, U.S.A., **426** B4
Jerseyville, U.S.A., **420** H6
Jerumenha, Brazil, **453** E5
Jerusalem *see* Yerushalayim, Israel, **225** C4
Jesi, Italy, **294** D4
Jessen, Germany, **288** F3
Jessheim, Norway, **286** E2
Jessore, Bangladesh, **214** D5
Jesup, U.S.A., **425** M4
Jesús María, Argentina, **458** D4
Jesús María, Boca de, *river mouth*, Mexico, **431** F3
Jetait, Canada, **414** D3
Jetmore, U.S.A., **420** D6
Jetpur, India, **218** B5
Jever, Germany, **288** C2
Jeziorak, Jeziora, *lake*, Poland, **289** J2
Jha Jha, India, **219** F4
Jhābua, India, **218** C5
Jhal, Pakistan, **218** A3
Jhang Sadr, Pakistan, **218** C3
Jhānsi, India, **218** D4
Jhārsuguda, India, **219** F5
Jhatpat, Pakistan, **218** B3
Jhelum, Pakistan, **218** C2
Jhelum, *river*, Pakistan, **218** C2
Jhenida, Bangladesh, **214** D5
Jhumri Tilaiyā, India, **219** F4
Ji Xian, Shanxi, China, **210** E5
Ji Xian, Tianjin Shi, China, **210** G4
Jia Xian, China, **210** E5
Jiaganj-Azimganj, India, **219** G4
Jiahe, Guangdong, China, **207** A2
Jiahe, Hunan, China, **206** C3
Jialing, *river*, China, **215** H3
Jiamusi, China, **211** K3
Ji'an, Jiangxi, China, **206** C3
Ji'an, Jilin, China, **211** J4
Jianchuan, China, **215** F4
Jiande, China, **206** D2
Jiang'an, China, **215** H3
Jiange, China, **215** H2
Jianggao, China, **207** A2
Jianghua, China, **206** B3
Jiangjin, China, **215** H3
Jiangjunmiao, China, **212** F3
Jiangle, China, **206** D3
Jiangling, China, **206** C2
Jiangluo, China, **215** H2
Jiangmen, China, **206** C4
Jiangsu, *province*, China, **206** D1
Jiangxi, *province*, China, **206** C3
Jiangxigou, China, **213** J5
Jiangyin, China, **206** E2
Jiangyou, China, **215** H3
Jianhu, China, **206** D1
Jianli, China, **206** C2
Jianning, China, **206** D3
Jian'ou, China, **206** D3
Jianquanzi, China, **213** H4
Jianshi, China, **206** B2
Jianshui, China, **215** G5
Jianyang, Fujian, China, **206** D3
Jianyang, Sichuan, China, **215** H3
Jiaocheng, China, **210** F5
Jiaohe, Hebei, China, **210** G5
Jiaohe, Jilin, China, **211** J4
Jiaojiang, China, **206** E2
Jiaokou, China, **210** E5
Jiaoling, China, **206** D3
Jiaonan, China, **211** G6
Jiaozhou, China, **211** H5
Jiaozuo, China, **206** C1
Jiasa, China, **215** G4
Jiashan, Anhui, China, **206** D1
Jiashan, Zhejiang, China, **206** E2
Jiashi, China, **212** C5
Jiawang, China, **206** D1
Jiaxing, China, **206** E2
Jiayin, China, **211** K2
Jiayuguan, China, **213** H5
Jiazi, China, **206** D4
Jibou, Romania, **296** D2
Jiddah (Jedda), Saudi Arabia, **363** G4
Jiddat al Ḩarāsīs, *desert*, Oman, **221** G5
Jiddī, Jabal al, *mountain peak*, Egypt, **225** B4
Jiekkevarre, *mountain peak*, Norway, **284** J2
Jieshi Wan, *bay*, China, **206** C4
Jieshou, China, **206** C1
Liešjavrre, *lake*, Norway, **285** M2
Jiexiu, China, **210** E5
Jieyang, China, **206** D4
Jieznas, Lithuania, **287** M5
Jigawa, *state*, Nigeria, **365** F2
Jigzhi, China, **215** G2
Jihlava, Czech Republic, **289** G4
Jihlava, *river*, Czech Republic, **289** G4
Jihoceský, *administrative region*, Czech Republic, **289** F4
Jihomoravský, *administrative region*, Czech Republic, **289** G4
Jijel, Algeria, **361** H1
Jijiga, Ethiopia, **367** F3
Jilf al Kabūr, Haḑabat al, *plain*, Egypt, **362** E4
Jili Hu, *lake*, China, **212** E3
Jilib, Somalia, **369** H2
Jilin, China, **211** J4
Jilin, *province*, China, **211** J4
Jiloca, *river*, Spain, **293** G2
Jilong, China, **207** D3
Jīma, Ethiopia, **367** E3
Jimaní, Haiti, **429** H3
Jimbolia, Romania, **296** C3
Jimena de la Frontera, Spain, **292** E4
Jiménez, Mexico, **430** D3
Jimenez, Philippines, **204** C4
Jimo, China, **211** H5
Jimsar, China, **212** F3
Jimulco, *mountain peak*, Mexico, **430** E3
Jinan, China, **210** G5
Jinchai, China, **206** B3
Jinchang, China, **213** J5
Jincheng, China, **206** C1
Jinchuan, China, **215** G3
Jīnd, India, **218** D3
Jindřichuv Hradec, Czech Republic, **289** G4
Jing Xian, Anhui, China, **206** D2
Jing Xian, Hunan, China, **206** B3
Jingbian, China, **210** E5
Jingchuan, China, **215** H2
Jingde, China, **206** D2
Jingdezhen, China, **206** D2
Jinggu, China, **215** G5
Jinghai, Guangdong, China, **206** D4
Jinghai, Tianjin Shi, China, **210** G5
Jinghe, China, **212** D3
Jinghong, China, **215** G5
Jingmen, China, **206** C2
Jingning, China, **215** H2
Jingshan, China, **206** C2
Jingtai, China, **210** D5
Jingxi, China, **215** H5
Jingyu, China, **211** J4
Jingyuan, China, **210** D5
Jingzhi, China, **211** G5
Jinhua, China, **206** D2
Jining, Nei Mongol Zizhiqu, China, **210** F4
Jining, Shandong, China, **206** D1
Jinja, Uganda, **369** F2
Jinjiang, Fujian, China, **206** D3
Jinjiang, Yunnan, China, **215** G4
Jinjuling, China, **207** B3
Jinka, Ethiopia, **369** G1
Jinkouhe, China, **215** G3
Jinkuang, China, **215** G3
Jinmen Dao, *island*, Taiwan, **206** D3
Jinotega, Nicaragua, **428** D4
Jinotepe, Nicaragua, **428** D5
Jinsha, China, **215** H4
Jinsha (Yangtze), *river*, China, **215** F3
Jinshantun, China, **211** K3
Jinshi, China, **206** B2
Jinta, China, **213** H5
Jintan, China, **206** D2
Jintang, China, **215** H3
Jinxi, Jiangshi, China, **206** D3
Jinxi, Liaoning, China, **211** H4
Jinxiang, China, **206** D1
Jinzhou, S. Liaoning, China, **211** H5
Jinzhou, W. Liaoning, China, **211** H4
Jipijapa, Ecuador, **450** B4
Jirin Gol, China, **210** G3
Jirjā, Egypt, **363** F3
Jirriiban, Somalia, **367** G3
Jishan, China, **206** B1
Jishou, China, **206** B2
Jisr ash Shughūr, Syria, **225** D2
Jitra, Malaysia, **200** C1
Jiu, *river*, Romania, **296** D3
Jiu'ao Dao, *island*, China, **207** B4
Jiucai Ling, *mountain peak*, China, **206** B3
Jiudengkou, China, **210** D5
Jiufo, China, **207** B2
Jiuhe, China, **207** D2
Jiujiang, China, **206** C2
Jiuling Shan, *mountain range*, China, **206** C2
Jiulong, China, **215** G3
Jiulong (Kowloon), China, **207** C4
Jiuquan, China, **213** H5
Jiutai, China, **211** J3
Jiuyuhang, China, **206** D2
Jiuzhan, Heilongjiang, China, **211** J2
Jiuzhan, Jilin, China, **211** J4
Jiuzhou, China, **215** H4
Jīwani, Pakistan, **221** H3
Jiwen, China, **211** H2
Jixi, Anhui, China, **206** D2
Jixi, Heilongjiang, China, **211** K3
Jixian, China, **211** K3
Jīzān, Saudi Arabia, **363** H5
Jizzakh, Uzbekistan, **222** H4
Joaçaba, Brazil, **459** G3
Joal-Fadiout, Senegal, **364** A2
João Pessoa, Brazil, **453** G5
João Pinheiro, Brazil, **456** D4
Joaquín V. González, Argentina, **458** D2
Jobat, India, **218** C5
Jock, Sweden, **285** L3
Jódar, Spain, **293** F4
Jodhpur, India, **218** C4
Joensuu, Finland, **287** P1
Jōetsu, Japan, **209** G3
Jofane, Mozambique, **371** F3
Jogbani, India, **219** F4
Jogbura, Nepal, **218** E3
Jõgeva, Estonia, **287** N3
Jogues, Canada, **415** N7
Johannesburg, South Africa, **371** E4
Johannesburg, U.S.A., **422** E4
John Day, *river*, U.S.A., **418** D4
John o'Groats, Scotland, U.K., **308** F2
Johnson, Pico de, *mountain peak*, Mexico, **430** B2
Johnson City, Kansas, U.S.A., **423** N3
Johnson City, Tennessee, U.S.A., **421** M7
Johnsons Crossing, Canada, **412** C1
Johnston, Wales, U.K., **304** B3
Johnston Atoll, *U.S. territory*, Pacific Ocean, **139** H3
Johnstone, Scotland, U.K., **308** E5
Johnstown, Ireland, **309** E5
Johor, Selat, *strait*, Malaysia/Singapore, **200** J6
Johor, *state*, Malaysia, **200** C2
Johor Baharu, Malaysia, **200** C2
Jõhvi, Estonia, **287** N3
Joigny, France, **291** F3
Joinville, Brazil, **459** H3
Joinville, France, **291** G2
Jokkmokk, Sweden, **284** J3
Jökulsá á Brú, *river*, Iceland, **284** Z7
Jolfā, Iran, **222** D5
Joliet, U.S.A., **421** J5
Joliette, Canada, **416** E6
Jolo, Philippines, **204** C5
Jolo Island, Philippines, **204** C5
Jombo, *river*, Angola, **368** C5
Jomppala, Finland, **285** N2
Jonava, Lithuania, **287** M5
Jondal, Norway, **286** C2
Jonê, China, **215** G2
Jones, Cape, Canada, **411** K3
Jones Sound, Canada, **411** L2
Jonesboro, Arkansas, U.S.A., **424** G2
Jonesboro, Louisiana, U.S.A., **424** F3
Jonesville, U.S.A., **425** M2
Joniškis, Lithuania, **287** L4
Jönköping, *county*, Sweden, **286** F4
Jönköping, Sweden, **286** G4
Jonquière, Canada, **416** F5
Joplin, Missouri, U.S.A., **420** F7
Joplin, Montana, U.S.A., **419** J2
Jora, India, **218** D4
Jordan, *country*, Asia, **196** E7
Jordan, *river*, Israel/Jordan, **225** C4
Jordan, U.S.A., **419** L3
Jordan Valley, U.S.A., **418** F5
Jordão, *river*, Brazil, **459** G2
Jordet, Norway, **286** F2
Jorhāt, India, **219** H4
Jormlien, Sweden, **284** G4
Jörn, Sweden, **284** K4
Joroinen, Finland, **287** N1

K

Kalbarri, Australia, **134** C4
Kale, Denizli, Turkey, **297** G7
Kale, Hatay, Turkey, **225** C1
Kalegauk Island, Myanmar, **202** C3
Kalehe, Democratic Republic of the Congo, **369** E3
Kalema, Democratic Republic of the Congo, **368** D3
Kalemie, Democratic Republic of the Congo, **369** E4
Kalemyo, Myanmar, **205** B3
Kalevala, Russian Federation, **285** Q4
Kalewa, Myanmar, **205** B3
Kálfafellsstaður, Iceland, **284** Z7
Kalga, Russian Federation, **211** G2
Kalgoorlie-Boulder, Australia, **134** E5
Kaliakra, Nos, *point*, Bulgaria, **298** C4
Kalibo, Philippines, **204** C4
Kalima, Democratic Republic of the Congo, **369** E3
Kalimantan Barat, *province*, Indonesia, **201** E3
Kalimantan Selatan, *province*, Indonesia, **201** F3
Kalimantan Tengah, *province*, Indonesia, **201** F3
Kalimantan Timur, *province*, Indonesia, **201** F2
Kālimpang, India, **219** G4
Kalinga, India, **219** F5
Kaliningrad, Russian Federation, **298** B2
Kaliningradskaya Oblast', *province*, Russian Federation, **287** K5
Kālinjra, India, **218** C5
Kalis, Somalia, **367** G3
Kalispell, U.S.A., **418** G2
Kalisz, Poland, **289** J3
Kalisz Pomorski, Poland, **289** G2
Kaliua, Tanzania, **369** F4
Kalix, Sweden, **285** L4
Kalkan, Turkey, **297** G7
Kalkarindji, Australia, **134** G2
Kalkaska, U.S.A., **421** L3
Kalkfeld, Namibia, **370** C3
Kall, Sweden, **284** F5
Kallavesi, *lake*, Finland, **285** N5
Kallislahti, Finland, **287** P2
Kallsjön, *lake*, Sweden, **284** F5
Kalmar, *county*, Sweden, **286** G4
Kalmar, Sweden, **286** H4
Kalmykiya, Respublika, *republic*, Russian Federation, **222** D3
Kálna nad Hronom, Slovakia, **289** J4
Kalnciems, Latvia, **287** L4
Kalocsa, Hungary, **289** J5
Kalole, Democratic Republic of the Congo, **369** E3
Kalomo, Zambia, **369** E6
Kaloniya, Belarus, **289** M2
Kalpa, India, **218** D3
Kalpeni Island, India, **216** C4
Kālpi, India, **218** D4
Kalpin, China, **212** C4
Kaltanėnai, Lithuania, **287** M5
Kālu Khuhar, Pakistan, **218** A4
Kaluga, Russian Federation, **299** F5
Kalulushi, Zambia, **369** E5
Kalumburu, Australia, **134** F1
Kalundborg, Denmark, **286** E5
Kalūr Kot, Pakistan, **218** B2
Kalutara, Sri Lanka, **216** D5
Kaluzhskaya Oblast', *province*, Russian Federation, **299** E5
Kalvarija, Lithuania, **287** L5
Kälviä, Finland, **285** L5
Kalvola, Finland, **287** M2
Kalvträsk, Sweden, **284** J4
Kalwapur, Nepal, **218** E3
Kalyān, India, **216** C2
Kalyāndrug, India, **216** D3
Kalyazin, Russian Federation, **299** F4
Kalymnos, Dodekanisos, Greece, **297** F7
Kalymnos, *island*, Dodekanisos, Greece, **297** F7
Kama, Democratic Republic of the Congo, **369** E3
Kama, Myanmar, **205** B4
Kamaishi, Japan, **209** H3
Kamal, Chad, **362** C4
Kamālia, Pakistan, **218** C3
Kaman, Turkey, **363** F1
Kamande, Democratic Republic of the Congo, **369** E3
Kamanjab, Namibia, **370** B2
Kamanyola, Democratic Republic of the Congo, **369** E3
Kamaron, Sierra Leone, **364** B3
Kamativi, Zimbabwe, **371** E2
Kambalda, Australia, **134** E5
Kambia, Sierra Leone, **364** B3
Kambove, Democratic Republic of the Congo, **369** E5
Kambuno, Gunung, *mountain peak*, Indonesia, **198** B3
Kamchatka, Poluostrov, *peninsula*, Russian Federation, **301** S4
Kamen, Bulgaria, **296** E4
Kamen'-na-Obi, Russian Federation, **223** L2
Kamena Vourla, Greece, **297** D6
Kamende, Democratic Republic of the Congo, **368** D4
Kamenica, Bosnia and Herzegovina, **294** G3
Kamenka, Kazakhstan, **222** E2
Kamenka, Russian Federation, **298** F2
Kamennogorsk, Russian Federation, **299** B2
Kamennoye, Ozero, *lake*, Russian Federation, **285** Q4
Kameno, Bulgaria, **296** F4
Kamensk-Ural'skiy, Russian Federation, **222** G1
Kamenz, Germany, **289** G3
Kameshnaya, Russian Federation, **299** G2
Kamień Pomorski, Poland, **289** G2
Kamieńsk, Poland, **289** J3
Kamin'-Kashyrs'kyy, Ukraine, **289** M3
Kamina, Democratic Republic of the Congo, **368** D4
Kamina, Togo, **364** E3
Kamloops, Canada, **412** J6
Kamnik, Slovenia, **294** E2
Kamoa Mountains, Guyana, **451** G4
Kampa, Teluk, *bay*, Indonesia, **200** D3
Kampala, Uganda, **369** F2
Kampar, Malaysia, **200** C1
Kampene, Democratic Republic of the Congo, **369** E3
Kamphaeng, Khao, *mountain peak*, Thailand, **202** C3
Kamphaeng Phet, Thailand, **202** C2
Kâmpóng Cham, Cambodia, **203** E4
Kâmpóng Chhnăng, Cambodia, **203** E3
Kâmpóng Khleăng, Cambodia, **203** E3
Kâmpóng Saôm, Cambodia, **203** D4
Kâmpóng Saôm, Chhâk, *bay*, Cambodia, **203** D4
Kâmpóng Spoe, Cambodia, **203** E4
Kâmpóng Thum, Cambodia, **203** E3
Kâmpôt, Cambodia, **203** E4
Kampti, Burkina Faso, **364** D2
Kampung, *river*, Indonesia, **199** G4
Kamrau, Teluk, *bay*, Indonesia, **199** F3
Kamsar, Guinea, **364** B2
Kamsuuma, Somalia, **369** H2
Kāmthi, India, **218** D5
Kamui-dake, *mountain peak*, Japan, **209** H2
Kamui-misaki, *point*, Japan, **209** H2
Kamuli, Uganda, **369** F2
Kamundan, *river*, Indonesia, **199** F3
Kamyanets, Belarus, **289** L2
Kam''yanets'-Podil's'kyy, Ukraine, **298** C3
Kam''yans'ke, Ukraine, **296** G3
Kamyanyuki, Belarus, **289** L2
Kāmyārān, Iran, **220** E2
Kamyen', Belarus, **299** B5
Kamyshet, Russian Federation, **223** P1
Kamyshin, Russian Federation, **222** D2
Kan, Myanmar, **205** B3
Kana, *river*, Zimbabwe, **371** E2
Kanaaupscow, *river*, Canada, **416** D2
Kanab, U.S.A., **422** G3
Kanaga Island, Aleutian Islands, U.S.A., **408** F3
Kanairiktok, *river*, Canada, **417** K2
Kanā'is, Ra's al, *point*, Egypt, **362** E2
Kanallaki, Greece, **297** C6
Kananga, Democratic Republic of the Congo, **368** D4
Kanāsar, India, **218** B4
Kanash, Russian Federation, **222** D1
Kanazawa, Japan, **209** G3
Kanbalu, Myanmar, **205** B3
Kanchenjunga, *mountain peak*, India, **214** D4
Kānchipuram, India, **216** D3
Kandalaksha, Russian Federation, **285** R3
Kandalakshskiy Zaliv, *bay*, Russian Federation, **285** R3
Kandi, Benin, **365** E2
Kandi, Tanjong, *point*, Indonesia, **198** C2
Kandila, Greece, **297** C6
Kandıra, Turkey, **297** H5
Kandkhot, Pakistan, **218** B3
Kāndla, India, **218** B5
Kandreho, Madagascar, **372** B4
Kandrian, Papua New Guinea, **140** C4
Kandukūr, India, **216** D3
Kandy, Sri Lanka, **217** E5
Kane Basin, Greenland, **411** N2
Kane Fracture Zone, *tectonic feature*, Atlantic Ocean, **477** D4
Kanem, *prefecture*, Chad, **365** H1
Kaneohe, Hawaiian Islands, U.S.A., **422** R9
Kanepi, Estonia, **287** N4
Kanevka, Russian Federation, **285** U3
Kang, Botswana, **370** D3
Kangaatsiaq, Greenland, **411** P3
Kangaba, Mali, **364** C2
Kangal, Turkey, **363** G1
Kangar, Malaysia, **200** C1
Kangaroo Island, Australia, **135** H6
Kangaruma, Guyana, **451** G3
Kangaslampi, Finland, **287** P1
Kangasniemi, Finland, **287** N2
Kangbao, China, **210** F4
Kangding, China, **215** G3
Kangdong, North Korea, **208** D3
Kangean, Kepulauan, *islands*, Indonesia, **201** F4
Kangeeak Point, Canada, **411** N3
Kangen, *river*, Sudan, **366** D3
Kangeq, *cape*, Greenland, **411** Q3
Kangerlussuaq, *bay*, Greenland, **411** R3
Kangerlussuaq, Greenland, **411** P3
Kangertittivag, *bay*, Greenland, **411** S2
Kangetet, Kenya, **369** G2
Kanggye, North Korea, **208** D2
Kangikajik, *cape*, Greenland, **411** S2
Kangilinnguit, Greenland, **411** Q3
Kangiqsualujjuaq, Canada, **411** N4
Kangiqsujuaq, Canada, **411** M3
Kangirsuk, Canada, **411** M3
Kangiwa, Nigeria, **365** E2
Kangmar, S. Xizang Zizhiqu, China, **214** D3
Kangmar, W. Xizang Zizhiqu, China, **214** C3
Kangnŭng, South Korea, **208** E3
Kango, Gabon, **368** B2
Kangosjärvi, Finland, **285** L3
Kangping, China, **211** H4
Kangra, India, **218** D2
Kangrinboqê Feng, *mountain peak*, China, **218** E3
Kangro, China, **214** C2
Kangtog, China, **214** C2
Kangyidaung, Myanmar, **205** B4
Kani, Côte d'Ivoire, **364** C3
Kani, Myanmar, **205** B3
Kaniama, Democratic Republic of the Congo, **368** D4
Kanibongan, Malaysia, **201** G1
Kaniet Islands, Papua New Guinea, **140** B3
Kanigiri, India, **216** D3
Kanin Nos, Mys, *point*, Russian Federation, **300** F3
Kaniwāra, India, **218** D5
Kanjiža, Yugoslavia, **296** C2
Kankaanpää, Finland, **287** L2
Kankakee, *river*, U.S.A., **421** J5
Kankakee, U.S.A., **421** K5
Kankan, Guinea, **364** C2
Kānker, India, **219** E5
Kankesanturai, Sri Lanka, **216** E4
Kannapolis, U.S.A., **425** M2
Kannauj, India, **218** D4
Kanniyākumāri, India, **216** D4
Kannod, India, **218** D5
Kannus, Finland, **285** L5
Kano, Nigeria, **365** F2
Kano, *state*, Nigeria, **365** F2
Kanoya, Japan, **208** E5
Kanozero, Ozero, *lake*, Russian Federation, **285** S3
Kanpur, India, **218** E4
Kansas, *river*, U.S.A., **420** E6
Kansas, *state*, U.S.A., **420** D6
Kansas City, U.S.A., **420** F6
Kansk, Russian Federation, **300** L4
Kantala, Finland, **287** N1
Kantang, Thailand, **202** C5
Kantanos, Kriti, Greece, **297** D8
Kantchari, Burkina Faso, **364** E2
Kanté, Togo, **364** E3
Kantegir, *river*, Russian Federation, **213** F1
Kānthi, India, **219** F5
Kanton, *island*, Kiribati, **139** G5
Kanuku Mountains, *mountain range*, Brazil/Guyana, **451** G3
Kanus, Namibia, **370** C4
Kānwat, India, **218** C4
Kanye, Botswana, **370** E4
Kao, *island*, Tonga, **136** D2
Kao-hsiung, Taiwan, **206** E4
Kaolack, Senegal, **364** A2
Kaolinovo, Bulgaria, **296** F4
Kaoma, Zambia, **368** D5
Kaouadja, Central African Republic, **366** B3
Kapa, *island*, Vava'u Group, Tonga, **141** B3
Kapaa, Kauai, Hawaiian Islands, U.S.A., **422** R9
Kapaau, Hawaii, Hawaiian Islands, U.S.A., **422** R9
Kapalatmada, Gunung, *mountain peak*, Indonesia, **198** D3
Kapanga, Democratic Republic of the Congo, **368** D4
Kapatu, Zambia, **369** F4
Kapellskär, Sweden, **287** J3
Kapenguria, Kenya, **369** G2
Kapingamarangi Atoll, *island*, Micronesia, **138** D4
Kapiri Mposhi, Zambia, **369** E5
Kapisillit, Greenland, **411** P3
Kapiskau, *river*, Canada, **415** N5
Kapit, Malaysia, **201** F2
Kapiti Island, New Zealand, **133** E5
Kaplice, Czech Republic, **289** G4
Kapoeta, Sudan, **369** F2
Kaposvár, Hungary, **294** F2
Kapp Norvegia, *cape*, Antarctica, **470** C3
Kappelshamn, Sweden, **287** J4
Kapsabet, Kenya, **369** G2
Kapsan, North Korea, **208** E2
Kaptiau, Indonesia, **199** G3
Kaptyrevo, Russian Federation, **223** N2
Kapuas, *river*, Kalimantan Barat, Indonesia, **201** E2
Kapuas, *river*, Kalimantan Tengah, Indonesia, **201** F3
Kapuskasing, Canada, **415** N7
Kapuskasing, *river*, Canada, **415** N7
Kapustnoye, Russian Federation, **285** S3
Kaputir, Kenya, **369** G2
Kapuvár, Hungary, **289** H5
Kara, Togo, **364** E3
Kara-Balta, Kyrgyzstan, **223** J4
Kara-Köl, Kyrgyzstan, **223** J4
Kara K'orē, Ethiopia, **367** E2
Kara-Su, Kyrgyzstan, **223** J4
Karaart, Tajikistan, **223** J5
Karabash, Russian Federation, **222** G1
Karabiğa, Turkey, **297** F5
Karabük, Turkey, **224** D4
Karaburun, Turkey, **297** F6
Karacabey, Turkey, **297** G5
Karacaköy, Turkey, **297** G5
Karaçal Tepe, *mountain peak*, Turkey, **224** D5
Karacasu, Turkey, **297** G7
Karachayevo-Cherkesskaya, Respublika, *republic*, Russian Federation, **222** C4
Karāchi, Pakistan, **218** A4
Karād, India, **216** C2
Karaganda *see* Qaraghandy, Kazakhstan, **212** B2
Karaginskiy, Ostrov, *island*, Russian Federation, **301** T4
Karagwe, Tanzania, **369** F3
Karahisar, Turkey, **297** G7
Karaidel', Russian Federation, **222** F1
Kāraikkudi, India, **216** D4
Karakol, Kyrgyzstan, **223** K4
Karaj, Iran, **220** F1
Karajül, China, **212** C4
Karak, Malaysia, **200** C2
Karakalpakiya, Uzbekistan, **222** F4
Karakax, *river*, China, **212** C5
Karaki, China, **212** D5
Karakoçan, Turkey, **224** F5
Karakoram Range, *mountain range*, Asia, **212** B5
Karaköse, Turkey, **224** F5
Karal, Chad, **365** G2
Karaman, *province*, Turkey, **225** B1
Karaman, Turkey, **224** D5
Karamay, China, **212** E3
Karamea, New Zealand, **133** D5
Karamea Bight, *bay*, New Zealand, **133** C5
Karamu, New Zealand, **132** E3
Karamyshevo, Russian Federation, **299** B4
Kāranja, India, **218** D5
Karanji, India, **218** D5
Karanjia, India, **219** F5
Karapelit, Bulgaria, **296** F4

Kebock Head, *cape*, Scotland, U.K., **308** C2
K'ebrī Dehar, Ethiopia, **367** F3
Kecel, Hungary, **289** J5
K'ech'a Terara, *mountain peak*, Ethiopia, **367** E3
Kechika, *river*, Canada, **412** F2
Kecskemét, Hungary, **289** J5
Kedah, *state*, Malaysia, **200** C1
Kėdainiai, Lithuania, **287** L5
Kédédéssé, Chad, **365** H2
Kediri, Indonesia, **201** F4
Kedong, China, **211** J2
Kédougou, Senegal, **364** B2
Kedrovyy, Russian Federation, **223** K1
Kędzierzyn-Koźle, Poland, **289** J3
Keele Peak, *mountain peak*, Canada, **410** G3
Keeling Islands *see* Cocos Islands, *Australian territory*, Indian Ocean, **134** Q10
Keen, Mount, *mountain peak*, Scotland, U.K., **308** G4
Keene, U.S.A., **426** D3
Keetmanshoop, Namibia, **370** C4
Keewatin, Canada, **414** G7
Kefallonia, *island*, Ionioi Nisoi, Greece, **297** C6
Kefalos, Dodekanisos, Greece, **297** F7
Kefamenanu, Indonesia, **198** D5
Keffi, Nigeria, **365** F3
Keg River, Canada, **413** L3
Kegaska, Canada, **417** L4
Kegen, Kazakhstan, **223** K4
Kegul'ta, Russian Federation, **222** C3
Kegworth, England, U.K., **305** F2
Keheili, Sudan, **366** D1
Kehra, Estonia, **287** M3
Keighley, England, U.K., **307** G4
Keila, Estonia, **287** M3
Keimoes, South Africa, **370** D4
Ķeipene, Latvia, **287** M4
Kéita, Bahr, *river*, Chad, **366** A3
Keïta, Niger, **365** F2
Keitele, Finland, **285** N5
Keitele, *lake*, Finland, **285** M5
Keith, Australia, **135** J6
Keith, Cape, Australia, **199** E6
Keith, Scotland, U.K., **308** G3
Kejaman, Malaysia, **201** F2
Kekaha, Hawaiian Islands, U.S.A., **422** R9
Kekerengu, New Zealand, **133** E6
Kékes, *mountain peak*, Hungary, **289** K5
Kekri, India, **218** C4
K'elafo, Ethiopia, **367** F3
Kelamet, Eritrea, **367** E1
Kelan, China, **210** E5
Kelang, Malaysia, **200** C2
Kelankylä, Finland, **285** N4
Kelantan, *state*, Malaysia, **200** C1
Keleft, Turkmenistan, **218** A1
Keles, Turkey, **297** G6
Kelfield, Canada, **413** Q6
Kelheim, Germany, **288** E4
Kelimutu, Gunung, *mountain peak*, Indonesia, **198** C5
Keling, Indonesia, **201** E4
Kéllé, Congo, **368** B3
Kelliher, Canada, **414** C6
Kelliher, U.S.A., **420** F2
Kellogg, U.S.A., **418** F3
Kelloselkä, Finland, **285** P3
Kells, Kilkenny, Ireland, **309** E5
Kells, Meath, Ireland, **309** F4
Kelmė, Lithuania, **287** L5
Kel'mentsi, Ukraine, **296** F1
Kélo, Chad, **365** H3
Kelowna, Canada, **413** K7
Kelsey Bay, Canada, **412** G6
Kelso, Scotland, U.K., **308** G5
Kelso, U.S.A., **418** C3
Keluang, Tanjong, *point*, Indonesia, **201** E3
Kelume, Indonesia, **200** D3
Kelvedon, England, U.K., **305** H3
Kelwood, Canada, **414** E6
Kem', *river*, Russian Federation, **285** R4
Kem', Russian Federation, **285** S4
Kemal, Gunung, *mountain peak*, Indonesia, **201** G2
Kemalpaşa, Turkey, **297** F6
Kemano, Canada, **412** F5
Kemba, Central African Republic, **368** D2
Kembangjanggut, Indonesia, **201** G2
Kembé, Central African Republic, **368** D2
Kembolcha, Ethiopia, **220** C6
Kembolcha, Ethiopia, **367** E2
Kemer, Turkey, **297** G7
Kemer Barajı, *dam*, Turkey, **297** G7
Kemerovo, Russian Federation, **223** M1
Kemerovskaya Oblast', *province*, Russian Federation, **223** M1
Kemi, Finland, **285** M4
Kemihaara, *river*, Finland, **285** P3
Kemijärvi, Finland, **285** N3
Kemijärvi, *lake*, Finland, **285** N3
Kemijoki, *river*, Finland, **285** M3
Keminmaa, Finland, **285** M4
Kemmerer, U.S.A., **419** J6
Kemnath, Germany, **288** E4
Kemnay, Scotland, U.K., **308** G3
Kémo, *prefecture*, Central African Republic, **368** C1
Kemp, Lake, U.S.A., **424** C3
Kemp Land, *region*, Antarctica, **470** F4
Kempele, Finland, **285** M4
Kemps Bay, Bahamas, **428** F1
Kempsey, Australia, **135** L5
Kempsey, England, U.K., **304** E2
Kempston, England, U.K., **305** G2
Kempt, Lac, *lake*, Canada, **416** D6
Kempten (Allgäu), Germany, **288** E5
Kemptville, Canada, **416** D7
Kenai, U.S.A., **410** D3
Kenansville, U.S.A., **425** M6
Kenaston, Canada, **413** R6
Kendal, England, U.K., **306** F3
Kendall, Mount, *mountain peak*, New Zealand, **133** D5
Kendallville, U.S.A., **421** L5
Kendari, Indonesia, **198** C3
Kendawangan, Indonesia, **201** E3
Kendégué, Chad, **366** A2
Kendrāpara, India, **219** F5
Kendrick, U.S.A., **418** F3
Kenedy, U.S.A., **424** D5
Kenema, Sierra Leone, **364** B3
Kenes, Kazakhstan, **223** J4
Keng Hkam, Myanmar, **205** C3
Keng Lon, Myanmar, **205** C3
Keng Tawng, Myanmar, **205** C3
Keng Tung, Myanmar, **205** C3
Kenga, *river*, Russian Federation, **223** L1
Kenge, Democratic Republic of the Congo, **368** C3
Kenhardt, South Africa, **370** D4
Kenilworth, England, U.K., **305** F2
Kénitra, Morocco, **360** E2
Kenmare, *inlet*, Ireland, **309** B6
Kenmare, Ireland, **309** C6
Kenmore, Scotland, U.K., **308** F4
Kenna, U.S.A., **423** M5
Kennebec, *river*, U.S.A., **426** F2
Kennebunk, U.S.A., **426** E3
Kennet, *river*, England, U.K., **305** F3
Kennett, U.S.A., **424** G1
Kennewick, U.S.A., **418** E3
Kenogami Lake, Canada, **421** N1
Kenora, Canada, **414** G7
Kenosee Lake, Canada, **414** C7
Kenosha, U.S.A., **421** K4
Kenozero, Ozero, *lake*, Russian Federation, **299** G1
Kent, *unitary authority*, England, U.K., **305** H3
Kent, Oregon, U.S.A., **418** D4
Kent, Texas, U.S.A., **423** L6
Kent Peninsula, Canada, **410** J3
Kentland, U.S.A., **421** K5
Kentozero, Russian Federation, **285** Q4
Kentriki Makedonia, *administrative region*, Greece, **297** D5
Kentucky, *river*, U.S.A., **421** M7
Kentucky, *state*, U.S.A., **421** L7
Kentucky Lake, U.S.A., **425** J1
Kentville, Canada, **417** J7
Kentwood, U.S.A., **424** G4
Kenya, *country*, Africa, **359** J6
Kenya, Mount *see* Kirinyaga, *mountain peak*, Kenya, **357** J7
Kenyir, Tasek, *lake*, Malaysia, **200** C1
Keonjhar, India, **219** F5
Kepa, Russian Federation, **285** R4
Kepahiang, Indonesia, **200** C3
Kepanjen, Indonesia, **201** F5
Kępno, Poland, **289** J3
Kepros, Akra, *point*, Greece, **297** E6
Kepsut, Turkey, **297** G6
Kerala, *state*, India, **216** C4
Keram, *river*, Papua New Guinea, **140** B4
Kerang, Australia, **135** J6
Keratea, Greece, **297** D7
Kerch, Ukraine, **298** E3
Kerema, Papua New Guinea, **140** B4
Keremeos, Canada, **412** K7
Kerempe Burnu, *cape*, Turkey, **224** D4
Keren, Eritrea, **367** E1
Kerend, Iran, **363** J2
Keret', Ozero, *lake*, Russian Federation, **285** R4
Keret', Russian Federation, **285** R3
Kerguélen, Îles de, *islands*, French Southern and Antarctic Islands, **104** E13
Kerguelen Plateau, *underwater feature*, Indian Ocean, **476** D8
Kericho, Kenya, **369** G3
Kerihun, Gunung, *mountain peak*, Indonesia, **201** F2
Kerikeri, New Zealand, **132** D2
Kerinci, Danau, *lake*, Indonesia, **200** C3
Kerinci, Gunung, *mountain peak*, Indonesia, **200** C3
Kerkhoven, U.S.A., **420** F3
Kerki, Turkmenistan, **222** H5
Kerkinitis, Limni, *lake*, Greece, **297** D5
Kerkyra (Corfu), *island*, Ionioi Nisoi, Greece, **297** B6
Kermadec Islands, New Zealand, **132** L12
Kermadec Trench, *underwater feature*, Pacific Ocean, **478** G7
Kermān, Iran, **221** G2
Kermānshāh, Iran, **220** E2
Kermit, U.S.A., **423** M6
Kern, *river*, U.S.A., **422** D3
Keros, *island*, Kyklades, Greece, **297** E7
Kérou, Benin, **365** E2
Kérouané, Guinea, **364** C3
Kerrobert, Canada, **413** Q6
Kerrville, U.S.A., **424** C4
Kerry, *county*, Ireland, **309** C5
Kerry Head, *point*, Ireland, **309** B5
Kershaw, U.S.A., **425** M2
Kersley, Canada, **412** H5
Kertamulia, Indonesia, **201** E3
Kerulen (Herlen), *river*, Mongolia, **210** F3
Keryneia, Cyprus, **225** B2
Kerzaz, Algeria, **361** F3
Kesagami Lake, Canada, **415** P6
Keşan, Turkey, **297** F5
Kesennuma, Japan, **209** H3
Keshan, China, **211** J2
Keshod, India, **218** B5
Keskikylä, Finland, **285** M4
Keskin, Turkey, **363** F1
Kes'ma, Russian Federation, **299** F3
Kesova Gora, Russian Federation, **299** F4
Kessingland, England, U.K., **305** J2
Kesten'ga, Russian Federation, **285** Q4
Kestilä, Finland, **285** N4
Keswick, England, U.K., **306** E3
Keszthely, Hungary, **289** H5
Ket', *river*, Russian Federation, **300** K4
Keta, Ghana, **364** E3
Ketapang, Jawa Timur, Indonesia, **201** F4
Ketapang, Kalimantan Barat, Indonesia, **201** E3
Ketaun, Indonesia, **200** C3
Ketchikan, U.S.A., **412** D4
Keti Bandar, Pakistan, **218** A4
Kętrzyn, Poland, **289** K1
Ketta, Congo, **368** C2
Kétté, Cameroon, **368** B2
Kettering, England, U.K., **305** G2
Kettering, U.S.A., **421** L6
Kettle, *river*, Canada/U.S.A., **413** K7
Kettle Falls, U.S.A., **418** E2
Keuka Lake, U.S.A., **426** B3
Keur Momar Sar, Senegal, **364** A1
Keuruu, Finland, **287** M1
Keweigek, Guyana, **451** G3
Key, Lough, *lake*, Ireland, **309** D3
Key Lake Mine, Canada, **413** S3
Key Largo, U.S.A., **425** M7
Key West, U.S.A., **425** M7
Keyala, Sudan, **369** F2
Keyes, U.S.A., **420** B7
Keyihe, China, **211** H2
Keymer, England, U.K., **305** G4
Keynsham, England, U.K., **304** E3
Keyser, U.S.A., **421** P6
Kezi, Zimbabwe, **371** E3
Kežmarok, Slovakia, **289** K4
Kgalagadi, *district*, Botswana, **370** D3
Kgatleng, *district*, Botswana, **371** E3
Khabarovsk, Russian Federation, **301** Q5
Khabarovskiy Kray, *territory*, Russian Federation, **211** L2
Khadama, Russian Federation, **223** P2
Khadzhybeys'kyy Lyman, *lake*, Ukraine, **296** H2
Khagaria, India, **219** F4
Khairāgarh, India, **218** E5
Khairpur, Pakistan, **218** B4
Khakasiya, Respublika, *republic*, Russian Federation, **223** M2
Khallikot, India, **219** F6
Khalopyenichy, Belarus, **299** B5
Khalūf, Oman, **221** G4
Kham-Syra, *river*, Russian Federation, **223** P2
Kham Ta Kla, Thailand, **203** D2
Khamar-Daban, Khrebet, *mountain range*, Russian Federation, **213** J2
Khamaria, India, **218** E5
Khambhāliya, India, **218** B5
Khambhāt, Gulf of, India, **218**, B5
Khambhāt, India, **218** C5
Khāmgaon, India, **218** D5
Khamīs Mushayţ, Saudi Arabia, **363** H5
Khammam, India, **216** E2
Khamr, Yemen, **220** D5
Khān az Zābīb, Jordan, **225** D4
Khān Shaykhūn, Syria, **225** D2
Khan Tängiri Shyngy, *mountain peak*, Kazakhstan/Kyrgyzstan, **212** D4
Khān Yūnus, Gaza Strip, **225** B4
Khānābād, Afghanistan, **218** B1
Khanāşir, Syria, **225** D2
Khandagayty, Russian Federation, **213** F2
Khandāla, India, **218** D6
Khandwa, India, **218** D5
Khandyga, Russian Federation, **301** Q3
Khānewāl, Pakistan, **218** B3
Khanka, Ozero, *lake*, Russian Federation, **211** L3
Khanna, India, **218** D3
Khānpur, Pakistan, **218** B3
Khansiir, Raas, *point*, Somalia, **367** G2
Khantaū, Kazakhstan, **223** J4
Khapalu, Pakistan, **218** D2
Kharabali, Russian Federation, **222** D3
Kharagpur, India, **219** F5
Kharagun, Russian Federation, **210** E2
Khārān, Pakistan, **218** A3
Kharanor, Russian Federation, **210** G2
Kharbara, India, **218** C3
Kharg Island *see* Khārk, Jazīreh-ye, *island*, Iran, **220** E3
Khargon, India, **218** C5
Khāriān, Pakistan, **218** C2
Khariār, India, **219** E5
Kharīm, Jabal, *mountain peak*, Egypt, **225** B4
Khārk, Jazīreh-ye (Kharg Island), *island*, Iran, **220** E3
Kharkiv, Ukraine, **298** E3
Kharlamovskaya, Russian Federation, **299** F3
Kharlovka, *river*, Russian Federation, **285** T2
Kharlovka, Russian Federation, **285** T2
Kharmanli, Bulgaria, **296** E5
Kharovsk, Russian Federation, **299** H3
Khartoum *see* Al Kharţūm, Sudan, **366** D1
Khartoum North *see* Al Kharţūm Baḩr, Sudan, **366** D1
Khasan, Russian Federation, **211** K4
Khasavyurt, Russian Federation, **222** D4
Khāsh, Iran, **221** H3
Khashm al Qirbah, Sudan, **366** E2
Khaskovo, *administrative region*, Bulgaria, **296** E4
Khaskovo, Bulgaria, **296** E5
Khatanga, Russian Federation, **301** M2
Khautavaara, Russian Federation, **299** D2
Khavast, Uzbekistan, **223** H4
Khāvda, India, **218** B5
Khaybar, Saudi Arabia, **363** H5
Khè, Phou, *mountain peak*, Laos, **203** D2
Khela, India, **218** E3
Khemarat, Thailand, **203** E2
Khemis Miliana, Algeria, **293** J4
Khemisset, Morocco, **361** E2
Khenchela, Algeria, **361** H1
Khenifra, Morocco, **361** E2
Khenjān, Afghanistan, **218** B2
Kherālu, India, **218** C5

Khersan, *river*, Iran, **220** E2
Kherson, Ukraine, **298** D3
Kherwāra, India, **218** C5
Kheta, *river*, Russian Federation, **300** L2
Khetolambina, Russian Federation, **285** R3
Khewra, Pakistan, **218** C2
Khilok, Russian Federation, **210** E2
Khimki, Russian Federation, **299** F5
Khipro, Pakistan, **218** B4
Khisarya, Bulgaria, **296** E4
Khislavichi, Russian Federation, **299** D5
Khlong Khlung, Thailand, **202** C2
Khmelita, Russian Federation, **299** D5
Khmel'nyts'kyy, Ukraine, **298** C3
Khnâchîch, El, *mountain range*, Mali, **361** F4
Khogali, Sudan, **366** C3
Khok Samrong, Thailand, **202** D3
Kholm, Russian Federation, **299** C4
Kholm-Zhirkovskiy, Russian Federation, **299** D5
Kholof Harar, Kenya, **369** H2
Khomas, *administrative region*, Namibia, **370** C3
Khomeyn, Iran, **220** F2
Khomeynīshahr, Iran, **220** F2
Khon Kaen, Thailand, **203** D2
Khonuu, Russian Federation, **301** R3
Khôr 'Angar, Djibouti, **367** F2
Khor, *river*, Russian Federation, **211** M3
Khor, Russian Federation, **211** L3
Khorat *see* Nakhon Ratchasima, Thailand, **202** D3
Khorinsk, Russian Federation, **210** E1
Khorixas, Namibia, **370** B3
Khorog, Tajikistan, **223** J5
Khorramābād, Iran, **220** E2
Khost, Pakistan, **218** A3
Khouribga, Morocco, **360** E2
Khovu-Aksy, Russian Federation, **213** G2
Khowst, Afghanistan, **218** B2
Khreum, Myanmar, **205** B3
Khuchinarai, Thailand, **203** E2
Khuff, Saudi Arabia, **363** H4
Khujand, Tajikistan, **223** H4
Khŭjayli, Uzbekistan, **222** F4
Khukhan, Thailand, **203** D3
Khulayş, Saudi Arabia, **363** G4
Khulna, Bangladesh, **219** G5
Khulna, *division*, Bangladesh, **219** G5
Khunti, India, **219** F5
Khuriyā Muriyā, Jazā'ir (Kuria Muria Islands), *islands*, Oman, **221** G5
Khurja, India, **218** D3
Khushāb, Pakistan, **218** C2
Khust, Ukraine, **296** D1
Khuwayy, Sudan, **366** C2
Khuzdār, Pakistan, **218** A4
Khvalovo, Russian Federation, **299** D3
Khvor, Iran, **221** G2
Khvormūj, Iran, **220** F3
Khvoy, Iran, **363** J1
Khvoynaya, Russian Federation, **299** E3
Khwae Noi, *river*, Thailand, **202** C3
Khyriv, Ukraine, **289** L4
Kičevo, Macedonia, **297** C5
Kia, Solomon Islands, **141** A1
Kiama, Australia, **135** L5
Kiamba, Philippines, **204** D5
Kiambi, Democratic Republic of the Congo, **369** E4
Kiantajärvi, *lake*, Finland, **285** P4

Kibaha, Tanzania, **369** G4
Kibangou, Congo, **368** B3
Kibawe, Philippines, **204** D5
Kibaya, Tanzania, **369** G4
Kibiti, Tanzania, **369** G4
Kiboga, Uganda, **369** F2
Kibombo, Democratic Republic of the Congo, **369** E3
Kibondo, Tanzania, **369** F3
Kibre Mengist, Ethiopia, **367** E3
Kidal, *administrative region*, Mali, **361** G5
Kidal, Mali, **361** G5
Kidapawan, Philippines, **204** D5
Kidderminster, England, U.K., **304** E2
Kidira, Senegal, **364** B2
Kidlington, England, U.K., **305** F3
Kidnappers, Cape, New Zealand, **132** F4
Kidsgrove, England, U.K., **304** E1
Kidurong, Tanjong, *point*, Malaysia, **201** F2
Kidwelly, Wales, U.K., **304** C3
Kiekinkoski, Finland, **285** Q4
Kiel, Germany, **288** E1
Kiel, U.S.A., **421** J4
Kielce, Poland, **289** K3
Kielder Water, *lake*, England, U.K., **306** F2
Kieler Bucht, *bay*, Germany, **288** E1
Kiến ửớc, Vietnam, **203** E4
Kienge, Democratic Republic of the Congo, **369** E5
Kieta, Papua New Guinea, **140** E8
Kiev *see* Kyyiv, Ukraine, **298** D2
Kiffa, Mauritania, **364** B1
Kifino Selo, Bosnia and Herzegovina, **294** G4
Kifisia, Greece, **297** D6
Kifisos, *river*, Greece, **297** D6
Kifrī, Iraq, **363** H2
Kigali, Rwanda, **369** F3
Kignan, Mali, **364** C2
Kigoma, *administrative region*, Tanzania, **369** F3
Kigoma, Tanzania, **369** E3
Kihelkonna, *island*, Estonia, **287** L3
Kihikihi, New Zealand, **132** E4
Kihlanki, Finland, **285** L3
Kihniö, Finland, **287** L1
Kihnu, *island*, Estonia, **287** L3
Kii Landing, Hawaiian Islands, U.S.A., **422** Q9
Kiik, Kazakhstan, **223** J3
Kiiminki, Finland, **285** M4
Kiistala, Finland, **285** M3
Kika, Russian Federation, **210** D1
Kikinda, Yugoslavia, **296** C3
Kikki, Pakistan, **221** H3
Kikondja, Democratic Republic of the Congo, **369** E4
Kikori, Papua New Guinea, **140** B4
Kikori, *river*, Papua New Guinea, **140** A4
Kikwit, Democratic Republic of the Congo, **368** C4
Kil, Sweden, **286** F3
Kilafors, Sweden, **286** H2
Kilauea, Hawaiian Islands, U.S.A., **422** R9
Kilauea Crater, Hawaiian Islands, U.S.A., **422** R10
Kilboghamn, Norway, **284** F3
Kilbotn, Norway, **284** H2
Kilchu, North Korea, **208** E2
Kilcormac, Ireland, **309** E4
Kilcullen, Ireland, **309** F4
Kildare, *county*, Ireland, **309** F4
Kildare, Ireland, **309** F4
Kil'din Ostrov, *island*, Russian Federation, **285** S2
Kil'dinstroy, Russian Federation, **285** R2
Kilembe, Democratic Republic of the Congo, **368** C4

Kilfinan, Scotland, U.K., **308** D5
Kilgore, Nebraska, U.S.A., **420** C4
Kilgore, Texas, U.S.A., **424** E3
Kilham, England, U.K., **306** F2
Kili, *island*, Marshall Islands, **139** E4
Kiliba, Democratic Republic of the Congo, **369** E3
Kilifi, Kenya, **369** G3
Kilimanjaro, *administrative region*, Tanzania, **369** G3
Kilimanjaro, *mountain peak*, Tanzania, **357** J7
Kilindoni, Tanzania, **369** G4
Kilingi-Nõmme, Estonia, **287** M3
Kilis, Turkey, **224** E5
Kiliya, Ukraine, **296** G3
Kilkee, Ireland, **309** C5
Kilkeel, Northern Ireland, U.K., **309** F3
Kilkenny, *county*, Ireland, **309** E5
Kilkenny, Ireland, **309** E5
Kilkhampton, England, U.K., **304** C4
Kilkis, Greece, **297** D5
Killala Bay, Ireland, **309** C3
Killala, Ireland, **309** C3
Killaloe, Ireland, **309** D5
Killaly, Canada, **414** C6
Killarney, Canada, **421** N2
Killarney, Ireland, **309** C5
Killary Harbour, Ireland, **309** B4
Killdeer, Canada, **413** R7
Killdeer, U.S.A., **420** B2
Killeen, U.S.A., **424** D4
Killenaule, Ireland, **309** E5
Killiecrankie, Scotland, U.K., **308** F4
Killimor, Ireland, **309** D4
Killin, Scotland, U.K., **308** E4
Killingi, Sweden, **284** K3
Killinick, Ireland, **309** F5
Killiniq, Canada, **411** N3
Killorglin, Ireland, **309** C5
Killybegs, Ireland, **309** D3
Kilmacrenan, Ireland, **309** E2
Kilmaine, Ireland, **309** C4
Kilmallock, Ireland, **309** D5
Kilmaluag, Scotland, U.K., **308** C3
Kilmarnock, Scotland, U.K., **308** E5
Kilmartin, Scotland, U.K., **308** D4
Kilmelford, Scotland, U.K., **308** D4
Kil'mez', *river*, Russian Federation, **222** E1
Kil'mez', Russian Federation, **222** E1
Kilmore Quay, Ireland, **309** F5
Kilmuckridge, Ireland, **309** F5
Kilosa, Tanzania, **369** G4
Kilrea, Northern Ireland, U.K., **309** F3
Kilrush, Ireland, **309** C5
Kilsyth, Scotland, U.K., **308** E5
Kiltamagh, Ireland, **309** D4
Kilttān Island, India, **216** C4
Kiltullagh, Ireland, **309** D4
Kilvakkala, Finland, **287** L2
Kilwa, Democratic Republic of the Congo, **369** E4
Kilwa Kivinje, Tanzania, **369** G4
Kilwa Masoko, Tanzania, **369** G4
Kilwinning, Scotland, U.K., **308** E5
Kilwo, Indonesia, **199** E3
Kim, Chad, **365** H3
Kim, U.S.A., **423** M3
Kimaan, Indonesia, **199** G4
Kimambi, Tanzania, **369** G4
Kimasozero, Russian Federation, **285** Q4
Kimba, Congo, **368** B3
Kimball, Nebraska, U.S.A., **419** N6
Kimball, South Dakota, U.S.A., **420** D4

Kimbe, Papua New Guinea, **140** C4
Kimberley, South Africa, **370** D4
Kimberley Plateau, Australia, **128** B3
Kimberly, U.S.A., **418** E4
Kimch'aek, North Korea, **208** E2
Kimch'ŏn, South Korea, **208** E3
Kimito, Finland, **287** L2
Kimje, South Korea, **208** D4
Kimmirut, Canada, **411** N3
Kimolos, *island*, Kyklades, Greece, **297** E7
Kimongo, Congo, **368** B3
Kimovaara, Russian Federation, **285** Q5
Kimovsk, Russian Federation, **299** G6
Kimparana, Mali, **364** D2
Kimpese, Democratic Republic of the Congo, **368** B4
Kimry, Russian Federation, **299** F4
Kimvula, Democratic Republic of the Congo, **368** C4
Kin-u, Myanmar, **205** B3
Kinabalu, Gunung, *mountain peak*, Malaysia, **201** G1
Kinabatangan, *river*, Malaysia, **201** G1
Kinango, Kenya, **369** G3
Kinaros, *island*, Kyklades, Greece, **297** F7
Kinbasket Lake, Canada, **413** K5
Kinbrace, Scotland, U.K., **308** F2
Kincardine, Canada, **421** N3
Kincraig, Scotland, U.K., **308** F3
Kinda, Democratic Republic of the Congo, **368** C4
Kinder, U.S.A., **424** F4
Kindersley, Canada, **413** Q6
Kindia, Guinea, **364** B2
Kindu, Democratic Republic of the Congo, **369** E3
Kinelakhti, Russian Federation, **299** D2
Kineshma, Russian Federation, **300** F4
King City, U.S.A., **422** C3
King George Bay, Falkland Islands, **460** F4
King George Islands, Canada, **415** Q3
King Island *see* Kadan Kyun, *island*, Myanmar, **202** C3
King Island, Australia, **135** J6
King Leopold and Queen Astrid Coast, *region*, Antarctica, **470** G5
King Leopold Ranges, *mountain range*, Australia, **134** E2
King Mountain, *mountain peak*, Canada, **412** E2
King Peak, *mountain peak*, U.S.A., **422** A1
King Point, Lord Howe Island, Australia, **135** U14
King Sound, Australia, **134** E2
King William Island, Canada, **411** K3
King William's Town, South Africa, **371** E5
Kingaroy, Australia, **135** L4
Kingisepp, Russian Federation, **299** B3
Kingman, Arizona, U.S.A., **422** F4
Kingman, Kansas, U.S.A., **420** D7
Kingman Reef, *U.S. territory*, Pacific Ocean, **139** H4
King's Lynn, England, U.K., **305** H2
Kings Peak, *mountain peak*, U.S.A., **423** H1
King's Worthy, England, U.K., **305** F3
Kingsbridge, England, U.K., **304** D4
Kingsclere, England, U.K., **305** F3
Kingscote, Australia, **135** H6
Kingscourt, Ireland, **309** F4

Kingsland, U.S.A., **425** M4
Kingsnorth, England, U.K., **305** H3
Kingsport, U.S.A., **421** M7
Kingsteignton, England, U.K., **304** D4
Kingston, Canada, **416** C7
Kingston, Jamaica, **429** F3
Kingston, New Mexico, U.S.A., **423** K5
Kingston, New York, U.S.A., **426** D4
Kingston, New Zealand, **133** B7
Kingston, Norfolk Island, **135** T13
Kingston Southeast, Australia, **135** H6
Kingston upon Hull, England, U.K., **307** H4
Kingston upon Hull, *unitary authority*, England, U.K., **307** H4
Kingston upon Thames, England, U.K., **305** G3
Kingstown, St Vincent and the Grenadines, **427** D3
Kingsville, U.S.A., **424** D6
Kingswood, England, U.K., **304** E3
Kington, England, U.K., **304** D2
Kingulube, Democratic Republic of the Congo, **369** E3
Kingungi, Democratic Republic of the Congo, **368** C4
Kingussie, Scotland, U.K., **308** E3
Kingwood, U.S.A., **424** E4
Kınık, Turkey, **297** F6
Kinkala, Congo, **368** B3
Kinkosi, Democratic Republic of the Congo, **368** C4
Kinloch, New Zealand, **132** E4
Kinloch, Scotland, U.K., **308** C3
Kinloch Rannoch, Scotland, U.K., **308** E4
Kinlochewe, Scotland, U.K., **308** D3
Kinlochleven, Scotland, U.K., **308** E4
Kinloss, Scotland, U.K., **308** F3
Kinna, Sweden, **286** F4
Kinnegad, Ireland, **309** E4
Kinneret, Yam, *lake*, Israel, **225** C3
Kinniyai, Sri Lanka, **217** E4
Kinnula, Finland, **285** M5
Kinohaku, New Zealand, **132** E4
Kinoosao, Canada, **414** C3
Kinross, Scotland, U.K., **308** F4
Kinsale, Ireland, **309** D6
Kinshasa, *administrative region*, Democratic Republic of the Congo, **368** C3
Kinshasa, Democratic Republic of the Congo, **368** C3
Kinsley, U.S.A., **420** D7
Kinston, Alabama, U.S.A., **425** J4
Kinston, North Carolina, U.S.A., **426** B7
Kintampo, Ghana, **364** D3
Kintap, Indonesia, **201** F3
Kintinian, Guinea, **364** C2
Kintore, Scotland, U.K., **308** G3
Kintyre, Mull of, *point*, Scotland, U.K., **308** D5
Kintyre, *peninsula*, Scotland, U.K., **308** D5
Kinvarra, Ireland, **309** D4
Kinyangiri, Tanzania, **369** F3
Kinyeti, *mountain peak*, Sudan, **369** F2
Kiowa, U.S.A., **420** D7
Kipawa, Lac, *lake*, Canada, **416** B6
Kipembawe, Tanzania, **369** F4
Kipili, Tanzania, **369** F4
Kipinä, Finland, **285** N4
Kipushi, Democratic Republic of the Congo, **369** E5
Kipushia, Democratic Republic of the Congo, **369** E5
Kır Klar Tepe, *mountain peak*,

Lac La Biche, Canada, **413** P4
Lac la Hache, Canada, **412** J6
Lac-Saguay, Canada, **416** D6
Lacanau, Étang de, *lake*, France, **290** D4
Lacanau, France, **290** D4
Lacaune, France, **290** F5
Laccadive Islands *see* Lakshadweep Islands, India, Indian Ocean, **216** B4
Lacha, Ozero, *lake*, Russian Federation, **299** G2
Lachung, India, **219** G4
Läckö, Sweden, **286** F3
Laclede, U.S.A., **418** F2
Lacombe, Canada, **413** N5
Laconi, Sardegna, Italy, **295** B6
Laconia, U.S.A., **426** E3
Lacre Punt, *point*, Bonaire, Netherlands Antilles, **461** A4
Lada, *river*, Russian Federation, **299** D3
Ladákh Range, *mountain range*, India, **218** D2
Ladismith, South Africa, **370** D5
Ladispoli, Italy, **295** D5
Lādnūn, India, **218** C4
Ladozhskoye Ozero, *lake*, Russian Federation, **299** C2
Ladrillero, Golfo, *gulf*, Chile, **460** B3
Ladron Peak, *mountain peak*, U.S.A., **423** K4
Ladushkin, Russian Federation, **287** K5
Ladva, Russian Federation, **299** E2
Ladvozero, Russian Federation, **285** P4
Lady Barron, Australia, **135** K7
Ladybank, Scotland, U.K., **308** F4
Ladysmith, Canada, **412** H7
Ladysmith, South Africa, **371** E4
Ladysmith, U.S.A., **420** H3
Ladyzhyn, Ukraine, **296** G1
Ladyzhynka, Ukraine, **296** H1
Lae, Papua New Guinea, **140** B4
Lærdalsøyri, Norway, **286** C2
Læsø, *island*, Denmark, **286** E4
Lævvajok, Norway, **285** N2
Lafayette, Indiana, U.S.A., **421** K5
Lafayette, Louisiana, U.S.A., **424** G4
Lafia, Nigeria, **365** F3
Lafiagi, Nigeria, **365** F3
Lagamar, Brazil, **456** D5
Lagan', Russian Federation, **222** D3
Lagan, Sweden, **286** F4
Lagarto, Brazil, **457** G3
Lagbar, Senegal, **364** B1
Lågen, *river*, Norway, **286** D2
Lagg, Scotland, U.K., **308** D5
Laggan, Loch, *lake*, Scotland, U.K., **308** E4
Laggan, Scotland, U.K., **308** E3
Laghouat, Algeria, **361** G2
Lagkadas, Greece, **297** D5
Lago Agrio, Ecuador, **450** C4
Lago Ranco, Chile, **460** C1
Lagoa Santa, Brazil, **457** E5
Lagoa Vermelha, Brazil, **459** G3
Lagonegro, Italy, **295** E5
Lagong, Pulau, *island*, Indonesia, **201** E2
Lagonoy, Philippines, **204** C3
Lagonoy Gulf, Philippines, **204** C3
Lagos, Nigeria, **365** E3
Lagos, Portugal, **292** C4
Lagos, *state*, Nigeria, **365** E3
Lagos de Moreno, Mexico, **430** E4
Lagosa, Tanzania, **369** E4
Lagrange, Australia, **134** E2
Lagrasse, France, **290** F5
Lagrave, Mont, *mountain peak*, Mauritus, **373** C1
Lagrave, Pointe, *point*, Mauritius, **373** C1

Laguiole, France, **290** F4
Laguna, Brazil, **459** H3
Laguna, Ilha da, *island*, Brazil, **452** C3
Laguna, U.S.A., **423** K4
Laguna de Perlas, Nicaragua, **428** E4
Laguna Grande, Argentina, **460** C3
Laguna Madre, *bay*, U.S.A., **424** D6
Lagunas, Chile, **455** E5
Lagunas, Peru, **450** C5
Lagunillas, Bolivia, **455** F5
Lagunillas, Venezuela, **450** D1
Laha, China, **211** J2
Lahad Datu, Malaysia, **201** G1
Lahaina, Hawaiian Islands, U.S.A., **422** R9
Lahat, Indonesia, **200** C3
Lahe, Myanmar, **205** B2
Lahewa, Indonesia, **200** B2
Laḥij, Yemen, **220** D6
Lahn, *river*, Germany, **288** D3
Laholm, Sweden, **286** F4
Laholmsbukten, *bay*, Sweden, **286** F4
Lahore, Pakistan, **218** C3
Lahr, Germany, **288** C4
Lahri, Pakistan, **218** B3
Lāhrūd, Iran, **222** D5
Lahti, Finland, **287** M2
Laï, Chad, **365** H3
Lai Châu, Vietnam, **203** D1
Lai-hka, Myanmar, **205** C3
Laiagam, Papua New Guinea, **140** A4
Lai'an, China, **206** D1
Laifeng, China, **206** B2
L'Aigle, France, **290** E2
Laihia, Finland, **287** L1
Laingsburg, South Africa, **370** D5
Lainio, Sweden, **285** L3
Lainioälven, *river*, Sweden, **284** K2
Lair, Scotland, U.K., **308** D3
Lairg, Scotland, U.K., **308** E2
Lais, Indonesia, **200** C3
Laisamis, Kenya, **369** G2
Laissac, France, **291** F4
Laisvall, Sweden, **284** H3
Laitila, Finland, **287** K2
Laiwu, China, **210** G5
Laiwui, Indonesia, **198** D3
Laixi, China, **211** H5
Laiyang, China, **211** H5
Laiyuan, China, **210** F5
Laizhou, China, **211** G5
Laizhou Wan, *bay*, China, **211** G5
Laja, Laguna de, *lake*, Chile, **458** B5
Lajeado, Brazil, **459** G3
Lajes, Rio Grande da Norte, Brazil, **453** G4
Lajes, Santa Catarina, Brazil, **459** G3
Lajkovac, Yugoslavia, **296** C3
Lakamané, Mali, **364** C2
Lakatoro, Vanuatu, **141** A2
Lakaträsk, Sweden, **284** K3
Lake, U.S.A., **419** J4
Lake Alma, Canada, **419** M2
Lake Argyle Village, Australia, **134** F2
Lake Cargelligo, Australia, **135** K5
Lake Charles, U.S.A., **424** F4
Lake City, Florida, U.S.A., **425** L4
Lake City, South Carolina, U.S.A., **425** N3
Lake District, *region*, England, U.K., **306** E3
Lake Elwell, U.S.A., **413** P7
Lake George, U.S.A., **420** F2
Lake Havasu City, U.S.A., **422** F4
Lake Hawea, New Zealand, **133** B7
Lake Jackson, U.S.A., **424** E5
Lake King, Australia, **134** D5

Lake Koocanusa, U.S.A., **413** M7
Lake Louise, Canada, **413** L6
Lake McConaughy, U.S.A., **420** C5
Lake Mills, U.S.A., **420** G4
Lake Preston, U.S.A., **420** E3
Lake Providence, U.S.A., **424** G3
Lake View, U.S.A., **420** F4
Lake Village, U.S.A., **424** G3
Lake Wales, U.S.A., **425** M6
Lakeba, *island*, Fiji, **141** A4
Lakeba Passage, *strait*, Fiji, **141** A4
Lakeland, Australia, **135** J2
Lakeland, Florida, U.S.A., **425** M5
Lakeland, South Carolina, U.S.A., **425** L4
Lakenheath, England, U.K., **305** H2
Lakepa, Niue, **132** M13
Lakeport, U.S.A., **422** B2
Lakes Entrance, Australia, **135** K6
Lakeside, California, U.S.A., **418** B5
Lakeside, Virginia, U.S.A., **426** B6
Laketown, U.S.A., **419** J6
Lakeview, U.S.A., **418** D5
Lakewood, Colorado, U.S.A., **423** L2
Lakewood, New Jersey, U.S.A., **426** C4
Lakewood, New Mexico, U.S.A., **423** L5
Lakhdaria, Algeria, **293** J4
Lakhīmpur, India, **218** E4
Lakhnādon, India, **218** D5
Lakhpat, India, **218** B5
Laki, *mountain peak*, Iceland, **284** Y7
Lakki, Pakistan, **218** B2
Lakonikos Kolpos, *bay*, Greece, **297** D7
Lakota, Côte d'Ivoire, **364** C3
Laksefjorden, *fiord*, Norway, **285** N1
Lakselv, Norway, **285** M1
Lakshadweep, *union territory*, India, **216** C4
Lakshadweep Islands (Laccadive Islands), India, Indian Ocean, **216** B4
Laktaši, Bosnia and Herzegovina, **294** F3
Lakuramau, Papua New Guinea, **140** C3
Lalang, *river*, Indonesia, **200** D3
Lalapansi, Zimbabwe, **371** F2
Lalapaşa, Turkey, **296** F5
Lalara, Gabon, **368** B2
Lālī, Iran, **220** E2
Lāliān, Pakistan, **218** C3
Lalibela, Ethiopia, **367** E2
Laliki, Indonesia, **198** D4
Lalin, China, **211** J3
Lalín, Spain, **292** C1
Lalinda, Vanuatu, **141** A2
Lalitpur, India, **218** D4
Lalomanu, Samoa, **141** B1
Lālsot, India, **218** D4
Lam Pao Reservoir, Thailand, **203** D2
Lamag, Malaysia, **201** G1
Lamakera, Indonesia, **198** C5
Lamap, Vanuatu, **141** A2
Lamar, Colorado, U.S.A., **423** M2
Lamar, Missouri, U.S.A., **420** F7
Lamarque, Argentina, **460** E1
Lamastre, France, **291** G4
Lamballe, France, **290** C2
Lambaréné, Gabon, **368** B3
Lambay Island, Ireland, **309** G4
Lambayeque, Peru, **454** B2
Lamberts Bay, South Africa, **370** C5
Lambeth, Canada, **421** N4
Lambeth Bluff, *point*, Heard and McDonald Islands, **134** S12

Lambi, Solomon Islands, **141** A1
Lambourn, England, U.K., **305** F3
Lame Deer, U.S.A., **419** L4
Lamego, Portugal, **292** D2
Lamesa, U.S.A., **424** B3
L'Ametlla de Mar, Spain, **293** H2
Lamia, Greece, **297** D6
Lamigan Point, Philippines, **204** D5
Lamitan, Philippines, **204** C5
Lamlash, Scotland, U.K., **308** D5
Lamma Island *see* Pok Liu Chau, *island*, China, **207** C4
Lammermoor Range, *mountain range*, New Zealand, **133** B7
Lammi, Finland, **287** M2
Lamon Bay, Philippines, **204** C3
Lamont, Canada, **413** N5
Lamont, U.S.A., **419** L5
Lamotrek, *island*, Micronesia, **138** C4
Lampang, Thailand, **202** C2
Lampasas, U.S.A., **424** C4
Lampazos de Naranjo, Mexico, **431** E3
Lampedusa, Isola di, *island*, Isole Pelagie, Italy, **295** D8
Lampeter, Wales, U.K., **304** C2
Lamphun, Thailand, **202** C2
Lampung, *province*, Indonesia, **200** D4
Lamu, Kenya, **369** H3
Lan Hsü, *island*, Taiwan, **206** E4
Lanai, *island*, Hawaiian Islands, U.S.A., **422** R9
Lanai City, Hawaiian Islands, U.S.A., **422** R9
Lanao, Lake, Philippines, **204** C5
Lancang (Mekong), *river*, China, **215** F3
Lancashire, *unitary authority*, England, U.K., **306** F4
Lancaster, California, U.S.A., **422** D4
Lancaster, Canada, **416** D7
Lancaster, England, U.K., **306** F3
Lancaster, Minnesota, U.S.A., **420** E1
Lancaster, New Hampshire, U.S.A., **426** E2
Lancaster, Ohio, U.S.A., **421** M6
Lancaster, Pennsylvania, U.S.A., **426** B4
Lancaster, South Carolina, U.S.A., **425** M2
Lancaster, Wisconsin, U.S.A., **420** H4
Lancaster Sound, Canada, **411** L2
Lance Creek, U.S.A., **419** M5
Lancer, Canada, **413** Q6
Lanciano, Italy, **295** E4
Lanco, Chile, **460** C1
Lancun, China, **211** H5
Landau an der Isar, Germany, **288** F4
Landau in der Pfalz, Germany, **288** D4
Landeck, Austria, **288** E5
Lander, U.S.A., **419** K5
Landes, *region*, France, **290** D4
Landete, Spain, **293** G3
Landfall Island, Andaman and Nicobar Islands, India, **217** H3
Landis, Canada, **413** Q5
Landön, Sweden, **284** G5
Land's End, *point*, England, U.K., **304** B4
Landsberg am Lech, Germany, **288** E4
Landshut an der Isar, Germany, **294** D1
Landskrona, Sweden, **286** F5
Lanesborough, Ireland, **309** E4
Lang, Canada, **419** M2
Lang Shan, *mountain range*, China, **210** D4
Lạng Sơn, Vietnam, **203** E1

Lang Suan, Thailand, **202** C4
Långå, Sweden, **286** F1
Langar, Afghanistan, **218** C1
Langara, Bahía, *bay*, Argentina, **460** D3
Langavat, Loch, *lake*, Scotland, U.K., **308** C2
Langdon, U.S.A., **420** D1
Langdon Point, Macquarie Island, **134** R11
Langeais, France, **290** E3
Langenburg, Canada, **414** D6
Langenthal, Switzerland, **291** H3
Langeoog, *island*, Germany, **288** C2
Langepas, Russian Federation, **300** J3
Langevin, Réunion, **373** A1
Langfang, China, **210** G5
Langgapayung, Indonesia, **200** B2
Langgar, China, **214** E3
Langham, Canada, **413** R5
Langholm, Scotland, U.K., **308** F5
Langholt, Iceland, **284** Y8
Langjökull, *ice cap*, Iceland, **284** X7
Langkawi, Pulau, *island*, Malaysia, **200** B1
Langkon, Malaysia, **201** G1
Langlade, Canada, **416** D5
Langley, Canada, **412** H7
Langlois, U.S.A., **418** B5
Langon, France, **290** D4
Langøya, *island*, Norway, **284** G2
Langport, England, U.K., **304** E3
Langreo, Spain, **292** E1
Langres, France, **291** G3
Langres, Plateau de, *plateau*, France, **291** G3
Langru, China, **212** C5
Langruth, Canada, **414** E6
Langsa, Indonesia, **200** B1
Långseleän, *river*, Sweden, **284** G4
Langshan, China, **210** D4
Langstrand, Norway, **285** L1
Langtang, Nigeria, **365** F3
Langting, India, **214** E4
Langtoft, England, U.K., **307** H3
Långträsk, Sweden, **284** K4
Langtry, U.S.A., **423** N7
Languedoc, *region*, France, **290** F5
Languedoc-Roussillon, *administrative region*, France, **291** F5
Långvattnet, Sweden, **284** H4
Langwang, China, **207** A3
Langwathby, England, U.K., **306** F3
Langxi, China, **206** D2
Langzhong, China, **215** H3
Lanhe, China, **207** A3
Laniel, Canada, **421** P2
Łanięta, Poland, **289** J2
Lanigan, Canada, **413** S6
Lanin, Volcán, *mountain peak*, Argentina, **460** C1
Lanivet, England, U.K., **304** C4
Länkäran, Azerbaijan, **222** D5
Länkipohja, Finland, **287** M2
Lanlacuni Bajo, Peru, **454** D3
Lannavaara, Sweden, **285** L2
Lannilis, France, **290** B2
Lannion, France, **290** C2
Lansdowne House, Canada, **415** L5
L'Anse aux Meadows, Canada, **417** P4
Lansford, U.S.A., **420** C1
Lanshan, China, **213** J5
Lansing, U.S.A., **421** L4
Länsi-Suomen Lääni, *province*, Finland, **285** L5
Lansjärv, Sweden, **285** L3
Lanslebourg-Mont-Cenis, France, **291** H4
Lantang, China, **207** D2
Lantau Island *see* Dai Yue Shan,

island, China, **207** B4
Lantian, Guangdong, China, **207** C1
Lantian, Shaanxi, China, **206** B1
Lantry, U.S.A., **420** C3
Lanusei, Sardegna, Italy, **295** B6
Lanxi, Anhui, China, **211** J3
Lanxi, Heilongjiang, China, **206** D2
Lanzarote, *island*, Islas Canarias, Spain, **373** B4
Lanzhou, China, **213** J5
Laoag, Philippines, **204** C2
Laobie Shan, *mountain range*, China, **215** F5
Laoha, *river*, China, **211** H4
Laoheishan, China, **211** K4
Laohekou, China, **206** B1
Laois, *county*, Ireland, **309** E5
Laon, France, **291** F2
Laos, *country*, Asia, **197** M8
Lapa, Brazil, **459** H2
Lapachito, Argentina, **459** E3
Lapai, Nigeria, **365** F3
Lapalisse, France, **291** F3
Lapi, Indonesia, **198** D2
Lapinlahti, Finland, **285** N5
Lapithos, Cyprus, **225** B2
Laplace, U.S.A., **424** G4
Lappajärvi, *lake*, Finland, **285** L5
Läppe, Sweden, **286** G3
Lappeenranta, Finland, **287** P2
Lappin Lääni, *province*, Finland, **285** M3
Lappland, *region*, Finland/ Russian Federation/Sweden, **284** K3
Lappohja, Finland, **287** L3
Lappoluobbal, Norway, **285** L2
Lâpseki, Turkey, **297** F5
Laptev Log, Russian Federation, **223** L2
Laptevo, Russian Federation, **299** B4
Laptevykh, More, *sea*, Russian Federation, **301** N2
Lapu, China, **207** B2
Lapu-Lapu, Philippines, **204** C4
Lapua, Finland, **285** L5
Lapväärtti, Finland, **287** K1
L'Aquila, Italy, **295** D4
Lār, Iran, **221** F3
Larache, Morocco, **361** E1
Laramie, U.S.A., **419** M6
Laramie Mountains, *mountain range*, U.S.A., **419** M5
Laranjal, Brazil, **452** B2
Laranjeiras, Brazil, **457** G3
Laranjeiras do Sul, Brazil, **459** G2
Laranjinha, *river*, Brazil, **459** G2
Larantuka, Indonesia, **198** C5
Larba, Algeria, **361** G1
Laredo, U.S.A., **424** C6
Largo, Cayo, *island*, Cuba, **429** E2
Largo, U.S.A., **425** L6
Largs, Scotland, U.K., **308** E5
Larino, Italy, **295** E5
Larionovo, Russian Federation, **299** G3
Larisa, Greece, **297** D6
Lārkāna, Pakistan, **218** B4
Larkhall, Scotland, U.K., **308** F5
Larmor, France, **290** C3
Larnaka, Cyprus, **225** B2
Larne, *district*, Northern Ireland, U.K., **309** F3
Larne, Northern Ireland, U.K., **309** G3
Larne Lough, *inlet*, Northern Ireland, U.K., **309** G3
Larned, U.S.A., **420** D6
Laro, Cameroon, **365** G3
Larouco, Serra do, *mountain peak*, Portugal, **292** D2
Larrimah, Australia, **134** G2
Lars Christensen Coast, *region*, Antarctica, **470** F4
Larsen Ice Shelf, Antarctica, **470** B4

Larsen Sound, Canada, **411** K2
Laru Mat, Tanjong, *point*, Indonesia, **199** E4
Laruns, France, **290** D5
Larvik, Norway, **286** D3
Las Animas, U.S.A., **423** M2
Las Cañas, Argentina, **458** D3
Las Casitas, Islas Canarias, Spain, **373** A4
Las Catitas, Argentina, **458** C4
Las Cejas, Argentina, **458** D3
Las Cruces, U.S.A., **423** K5
Las Flores, Argentina, **459** E5
Las Galletas, Islas Canarias, Spain, **373** A4
Las Heras, Mendoza, Argentina, **458** C4
Las Heras, Santa Cruz, Argentina, **460** D3
Las Herreras, Mexico, **430** D3
Las Juntas, Chile, **458** C3
Las Lajas, Argentina, **460** C1
Las Lajitas, Venezuela, **451** F2
Las Lomas, Peru, **454** B1
Las Lomitas, Argentina, **458** E2
Las Martinetas, Argentina, **460** D3
Las Mercedes, Venezuela, **451** E2
Las Minas, Cerro, *mountain peak*, Honduras, **428** C4
Las Negras, Spain, **293** F4
Las Palmas de Gran Canaria, Islas Canarias, Spain, **373** B4
Las Petas, Bolivia, **455** G4
Las Piedras, Uruguay, **459** F5
Las Plumas, Argentina, **460** D2
Las Tablas, Panama, **429** E6
Las Tres Vírgenes, Volcán, *mountain peak*, Mexico, **430** B3
Las Trincheras, Venezuela, **451** F2
Las Tunas, Cuba, **429** F2
Las Varas, Mexico, **430** D4
Las Varillas, Argentina, **458** D4
Las Vegas, Nevada, U.S.A., **422** F3
Las Vegas, New Mexico, U.S.A., **423** L4
Lasanga Island, Papua New Guinea, **140** B4
Lascano, Uruguay, **459** F4
Lāsh-e Joveyn, Afghanistan, **221** H2
Lashio, Myanmar, **205** C3
Lashio, Myanmar, **215** F5
Łask, Poland, **289** J3
Lasoni, Tanjong, *point*, Indonesia, **198** C3
Lasqoray, Somalia, **367** G2
Lassen Peak, *mountain peak*, U.S.A., **422** C1
Lassiter Coast, *region*, Antarctica, **470** B4
Last Chance, U.S.A., **423** M2
Last Mountain Lake, Canada, **413** S6
Lastoursville, Gabon, **368** B3
Lastovo, *island*, Croatia, **294** F4
Lastovski Kanal, *channel*, Croatia, **294** F4
Latacunga, Ecuador, **450** B4
Lataday Island, Antarctica, **470** B5
Latakia *see* Al Lādhiqīyah, Syria, **225** C2
Lätäseno, *river*, Finland/ Sweden, **285** L2
Latdalam, Indonesia, **199** E4
Late, *island*, Tonga, **136** D2
Lätehär, India, **219** F5
Laterza, Italy, **295** F5
Latheron, Scotland, U.K., **308** F2
Lathrop, U.S.A., **420** F6
Latikberg, Sweden, **284** H4
Latina, Italy, **295** D5
Latulipe, Canada, **421** P2
Lātūr, India, **216** D2
Latvia, *country*, Europe, **282** G4

Lau (Eastern) Group, *islands*, Fiji, **141** A4
Laudal, Norway, **286** C3
Lauder, Scotland, U.K., **308** G5
Lauenburg (Elbe), Germany, **288** E2
Lauker, Sweden, **284** J4
Lauksletta, Norway, **284** K1
Laukuva, Lithuania, **287** L5
Lauli'i, Samoa, **141** B1
Launceston, Australia, **135** K7
Launceston, England, U.K., **304** C4
Launggyaung, Myanmar, **205** C2
Lauragh, Ireland, **309** C6
Laurel, Mississippi, U.S.A., **425** H4
Laurel, Montana, U.S.A., **419** K4
Laurel, Nebraska, U.S.A., **420** E4
Laurencekirk, Scotland, U.K., **308** G4
Laurens, U.S.A., **425** L2
Laurens Peninsula, Heard and McDonald Islands, **134** S12
Laurentian Fan, *underwater feature*, Atlantic Ocean, **477** D3
Laurentian Mountains, *mountain range*, Canada, **416** E5
Lauria, Italy, **295** E5
Laurier, Canada, **414** E6
Lauriston, New Zealand, **133** C6
Lausanne, Switzerland, **291** H3
Laut, Pulau, *island*, Indonesia, **201** G3
Laut, Selat, *strait*, Indonesia, **201** F4
Lautaporras, Finland, **287** L2
Lautem, Indonesia, **198** D5
Lautoka, Fiji, **141** A4
Laval, Canada, **416** E7
Laval, France, **290** D2
Lāvān, Jazīreh-ye, *island*, Iran, **220** F3
Lavanggu, Solomon Islands, **141** A1
Lavapié, Punta, *point*, Chile, **458** A5
Lavassaare, Estonia, **287** M3
Lavenham, England, U.K., **305** H2
Laverton, Australia, **134** E4
Lavia, Finland, **287** L2
Lavik, Norway, **286** B2
Lavina, U.S.A., **419** K3
Lavras, Brazil, **457** E5
Lavras do Sul, Brazil, **459** G4
Lavrio, Greece, **297** E7
Lavumisa, Swaziland, **371** F4
Law, Dome, *ice dome*, Antarctica, **470** F7
Lawa, Myanmar, **205** C2
Lawagamau, *river*, Canada, **415** Q6
Lawdar, Yemen, **220** E6
Lawers, Ben, *mountain peak*, Scotland, U.K., **308** E4
Lawford, England, U.K., **305** J3
Lawit, Gunung, *mountain peak*, Indonesia, **201** F2
Lawit, Gunung, *mountain peak*, Malaysia, **200** C1
Lawksawk, Myanmar, **205** C3
Lawra, Ghana, **364** D2
Lawrence, Kansas, U.S.A., **420** F6
Lawrence, Massachusetts, U.S.A., **426** E3
Lawrence, New Zealand, **133** B7
Lawrenceburg, U.S.A., **425** J2
Lawton, U.S.A., **424** C2
Lawu, Gunung, *mountain peak*, Indonesia, **201** E4
Lawz, Jabal al, *mountain peak*, Saudi Arabia, **225** C5
Laxå, Sweden, **286** G3
Laxey, Isle of Man, **306** D3
Laxford Bridge, Scotland, U.K., **308** D2
Laxo, Shetland, Scotland, U.K.,

308 K7
Lay, U.S.A., **423** K1
Layar, Tanjong, *point*, Indonesia, **201** G4
Laylá, Saudi Arabia, **363** J4
Laysan, *island*, Hawaiian Islands, U.S.A., **139** G2
Laytonville, U.S.A., **422** B2
Lazare, Pointe, *point*, Seychelles, **373** A2
Lazarevac, Yugoslavia, **296** C3
Lázaro Cárdenas, Mexico, **430** E5
Lazdijai, Lithuania, **287** L5
Lazio, *autonomous region*, Italy, **295** D5
Lazo, Russian Federation, **211** L4
Lazu, Romania, **296** F3
Le Blanc, France, **290** E3
Le Caylar, France, **291** F5
Le Conquet, France, **290** B2
Le Creusot, France, **291** G3
Le Croisic, France, **290** C3
Le Crotoy, France, **305** J4
Le Donjon, France, **291** F3
Le Dorat, France, **290** E3
Le Faouët, France, **290** C2
Le Havre, France, **290** E2
Le Lamentin, Martinique, **427** D3
Le Lion-d'Angers, France, **290** D3
Le Lude, France, **290** E3
Le Maire, Estrecho de, *strait*, Argentina, **460** E5
Le Mans, France, **290** E2
Le Mars, U.S.A., **420** E4
Le Mont-Saint-Michel, France, **290** D2
Le Petit-Quevilly, France, **305** J5
Le Port, Réunion, **373** A1
Le Portel, France, **305** J4
Le Puy-en-Velay, France, **291** F4
Le Riviere, Réunion, **373** A1
Le Tampon, Réunion, **373** A1
Le Teil, France, **291** G4
Le Touquet-Paris-Plage, France, **305** J4
Le Tréport, France, **290** E1
Le Verdon-sur-Mer, France, **290** D4
Leša, Poland, **289** G3
Leżajsk, Poland, **289** L3
Lead, U.S.A., **420** B3
Leadenham, England, U.K., **305** G1
Leader, Canada, **413** Q6
Leadore, U.S.A., **418** H4
Leadville, U.S.A., **423** K2
Leaf Rapids, Canada, **414** E3
League, Slieve, *mountain peak*, Ireland, **309** D3
Leakey, U.S.A., **424** C5
Leamington, Canada, **421** M4
Leandro N. Alem, Argentina, **459** F3
Leane, Lough, *lake*, Ireland, **309** C5
Leanja, Madagascar, **372** B4
Leap, Ireland, **309** C6
Leasingham, England, U.K., **307** H4
Leatherhead, England, U.K., **305** G3
Leavenworth, U.S.A., **420** F6
Łeba, Poland, **289** H1
Lebak, Philippines, **204** D5
Lébamba, Gabon, **368** B3
Lebane, Yugoslavia, **296** C4
Lebanon, *country*, Asia, **225** C3
Lebanon, Indiana, U.S.A., **421** K5
Lebanon, Missouri, U.S.A., **420** G7
Lebanon, New Hampshire, U.S.A., **426** D3
Lebanon, Oregon, U.S.A., **418** C4
Lebanon, South Dakota, U.S.A., **420** D3
Lebanon, Tennessee, U.S.A., **425** J1
Lebanon, Virginia, U.S.A., **421** M7

Lebap, Turkmenistan, **222** G4
Lebo, Democratic Republic of the Congo, **368** D2
Lębork, Poland, **289** H1
Lebowakgomo, South Africa, **371** E3
Lebrija, Spain, **292** D4
Łebsko, Jezioro, *lake*, Poland, **289** H1
Lebu, Chile, **458** B5
Lebyazh'e, Kazakhstan, **212** C2
Lecce, Italy, **295** G5
Lecco, Italy, **294** B3
Lechaina, Greece, **297** C7
Lechang, China, **206** C3
Lechinţa, Romania, **296** E2
Lechlade, England, U.K., **305** F3
Lechtaler Alpen, *mountain range*, Austria, **288** E5
Lēči, Latvia, **287** K4
Leck, Germany, **288** D1
Lecompte, U.S.A., **424** F4
Łęczna, Poland, **289** L3
Łęczyca, Poland, **289** J2
Ledang, Gunung, *mountain peak*, Malaysia, **200** C2
Ledbury, England, U.K., **304** E2
Ledesma, Spain, **292** E2
Ledmore, Scotland, U.K., **308** E2
Ledmozero, Russian Federation, **285** R4
Ledu, China, **213** J5
Leduc, Canada, **413** N5
Lee Vining, U.S.A., **422** D3
Leech, *river*, U.S.A., **420** F3
Leech Lake, U.S.A., **420** F2
Leeds, England, U.K., **307** G4
Leeds, U.S.A., **425** J3
Leedstown, England, U.K., **304** B4
Leek, England, U.K., **304** E1
Leeming Bar, England, U.K., **307** G3
Leer, Germany, **288** C2
Leesburg, Florida, U.S.A., **425** M5
Leesburg, Virginia, U.S.A., **426** B5
Leesi, Estonia, **287** M3
Leesville, U.S.A., **424** F4
Leeuwarden, Netherlands, **288** B2
Leeuwin, Cape, Australia, **134** D5
Leeville, U.S.A., **424** G5
Leeward Island, Antipodes Islands, New Zealand, **133** P15
Leeward Islands, Caribbean Sea, **427** C2
Lefaga, Samoa, **141** B1
Lefka, Cyprus, **225** B2
Lefkada, Ionioi Nisoi, Greece, **297** C6
Lefkada, *island*, Ionioi Nisoi, Greece, **297** C6
Lefkimmi, Ionioi Nisoi, Greece, **297** C6
Lefkoniko, Cyprus, **225** B2
Lefkosia (Nicosia), Cyprus, **225** B2
Lefroy, Lake, Australia, **134** E5
Leganés, Spain, **293** F2
Legaspi, Philippines, **204** C3
Legé, France, **290** D3
Leggett, U.S.A., **424** E4
Legnica, Poland, **289** H3
Leguga, Democratic Republic of the Congo, **368** E2
Leh, India, **218** D2
Lehliu Gară, Romania, **296** F3
Lehman, U.S.A., **423** M5
Lehrte, Germany, **288** D2
Lehua, *island*, Hawaiian Islands, U.S.A., **422** Q9
Lehututu, Botswana, **370** D3
Lei, *river*, China, **206** C3
Leiah, Pakistan, **218** B3
Leibnitz, Austria, **289** G5
Leicester, England, U.K., **305** F2
Leicester City, *unitary authority*, England, U.K., **305** F2

Ligui, Mexico, **430** C3
Liguria, *autonomous region*, Italy, **294** B3
Ligurian Sea, Italy, **294** B4
Liha Point, Niue, **132** M13
Lihehe, Tanzania, **369** G5
Lihir Group, *islands*, Papua New Guinea, **140** D3
Lihir Islands, Lihir Group, Papua New Guinea, **140** D3
Lihue, Hawaiian Islands, U.S.A., **422** R9
Lihue, *island*, Hawaiian Islands, U.S.A., **139** J2
Lihula, Estonia, **287** L3
Lijiang, China, **215** G4
Lik, *river*, Laos, **202** D2
Likasi, Democratic Republic of the Congo, **369** E5
Likati, Democratic Republic of the Congo, **368** D2
Likhachevo, Russian Federation, **299** F3
Likhoslavl', Russian Federation, **299** E4
Likiep, *island*, Marshall Islands, **139** E4
Likoto, Democratic Republic of the Congo, **368** D3
Likouala, *administrative region*, Congo, **368** C2
Liku, Niue, **132** M13
L'Île-Rousse, Corse, France, **294** B4
Lilienthal, Germany, **288** D2
Lilin, China, **207** C3
Liling, China, **206** C3
Lilla Edet, Sweden, **286** F3
Lille, France, **291** F1
Lillebonne, France, **305** H5
Lillehammer, Norway, **286** E2
Lillers, France, **305** K4
Lillesand, Norway, **286** D3
Lilleshall, England, U.K., **304** E2
Lillestrøm, Norway, **286** E3
Lillhärdal, Sweden, **286** G2
Lillögda, Sweden, **284** H4
Lillooet, Canada, **412** J6
Lilongwe, Malawi, **369** F5
Liloy, Philippines, **204** C4
Lily Lake, Canada, **412** G5
Lima, Montana, U.S.A., **418** H4
Lima, Ohio, U.S.A., **421** L5
Lima, Peru, **454** C3
Lima, *river*, Portugal, **292** C2
Lima, Sweden, **286** F2
Liman, Gunung, *mountain peak*, Indonesia, **201** E4
Limanowa, Poland, **289** K4
Limassol *see* Lemesos, Cyprus, **225** B2
Limavady, *district*, Northern Ireland, U.K., **309** F3
Limavady, Northern Ireland, U.K., **309** F2
Limay, *river*, Argentina, **460** C1
Limay Mahuida, Argentina, **458** C5
Limbani, Peru, **455** E4
Limbaži, Latvia, **287** M4
Limbe, Cameroon, **368** A2
Limboto, Danau, *lake*, Indonesia, **198** C2
Limburg, *province*, Belgium, **288** B3
Limburg, *province*, Netherlands, **288** B3
Limburg an der Lahn, Germany, **288** D3
Lime Acres, South Africa, **370** D4
Lime Springs, U.S.A., **420** G4
Limeira, Brazil, **459** H2
Limerick, *county*, Ireland, **309** D5
Limerick, Ireland, **309** D5
Limestone, U.S.A., **426** G1
Limfjorden, *strait*, Denmark, **286** D4
Liminka, Finland, **285** M4
Limmared, Sweden, **286** F4
Limmen Bight, *bay*, Australia, **135** H1

Limni, Voreioi Sporades, Greece, **297** D6
Limnos, *island*, Greece, **297** E6
Limoeiro, Brazil, **453** G5
Limoges, France, **290** E4
Limón, Honduras, **428** D4
Limon, Mont, *mountain peak*, Rodrigues, **373** B1
Limon, U.S.A., **423** M2
Limoquije, Bolivia, **455** F4
Limousin, *administrative region*, France, **290** E4
Limpopo, *river*, Southern Africa, **357** H9
Limufuafua Point, Niue, **132** M13
Linakhamari, Russian Federation, **285** Q2
Lin'an, China, **206** D2
Linao Point, Philippines, **204** C5
Linapacan Island, Philippines, **204** B4
Linard, Piz, *mountain peak*, Switzerland, **291** K3
Linares, Chile, **458** B5
Linares, Mexico, **431** F3
Linares, Spain, **293** F3
Linaria, Greece, **297** E6
Linas, Monte, *mountain peak*, Sardegna, Italy, **295** B6
Lincang, China, **215** G5
Lincoln, Argentina, **458** E5
Lincoln, England, U.K., **305** G1
Lincoln, Illinois, U.S.A., **421** J5
Lincoln, Kansas, U.S.A., **420** D6
Lincoln, Maine, U.S.A., **426** F2
Lincoln, Montana, U.S.A., **418** H3
Lincoln, Nebraska, U.S.A., **420** E5
Lincoln, New Mexico, U.S.A., **423** L5
Lincoln City, U.S.A., **418** C4
Lincoln Sea, Canada/Greenland, **411** N1
Lincolnshire, *unitary authority*, England, U.K., **307** H4
Lincolnshire Wolds, *region*, England, U.K., **307** H4
Lind, U.S.A., **418** E3
Linden, Guyana, **451** G2
Linden, U.S.A., **425** J3
Lindesberg, Sweden, **286** G3
Lindi, *administrative region*, Tanzania, **369** G4
Lindi, Tanzania, **369** G4
Lindian, China, **211** J3
Lindisfarne, England, U.K., **307** G2
Lindos, Dodekanisos, Greece, **297** G7
Lindozero, Russian Federation, **285** R5
Lindsay, Canada, **416** B7
Lindsay, Montana, U.S.A., **419** M3
Lindsay, Oklahoma, U.S.A., **424** D2
Lindsborg, U.S.A., **420** E6
Line Islands, Kiribati, **139** J4
Linfen, China, **210** E5
Linganamakki Reservoir, India, **216** C3
Lingayen, Philippines, **204** C3
Lingayen Gulf, Philippines, **204** C2
Lingbao, China, **206** B1
Lingbi, China, **206** D1
Lingen, Germany, **288** C2
Lingfield, England, U.K., **305** G3
Lingga, Kepulauan, *islands*, Indonesia, **200** D3
Lingga, Pulau, *island*, Indonesia, **200** D3
Lingkabau, Malaysia, **201** G1
Lingle, U.S.A., **419** M5
Lingomo, Democratic Republic of the Congo, **368** D2
Lingqiu, China, **210** F5
Lingshan, China, **206** B4
Lingshi, China, **210** E5
Lingshui, China, **203** F2
Lingtai, China, **215** H2

Linguère, Senegal, **364** A1
Lingwu, China, **210** D5
Lingyuan, China, **211** G4
Linhai, Heilongjiang, China, **211** J2
Linhai, Zhejiang, China, **206** E2
Linhares, Brazil, **457** F5
Linhe, China, **210** D4
Linjiang, Gonsu, China, **215** H2
Linjiang, Jilin, China, **211** J4
Linköping, Sweden, **286** G3
Linkou, China, **211** K3
Linkuva, Lithuania, **287** L4
Linnhe, Loch, *inlet*, Scotland, U.K., **308** D4
Linosa, Isola di, *island*, Isole Pelagie, Italy, **295** D8
Linova, Belarus, **289** M2
Linping, China, **206** E2
Linqing, China, **210** F5
Linqu, China, **208** B3
Linquan, China, **206** C1
Lins, Brazil, **456** D5
Linsell, Sweden, **286** F1
Linshu, China, **206** D1
Linshui, China, **215** H3
Linta, *river*, Madagascar, **372** A5
Lintan, China, **215** G2
Lintao, China, **215** G2
Linton, Indiana, U.S.A., **421** K6
Linton, North Dakota, U.S.A., **420** C2
Lintong, China, **206** B1
Linxi, Hebei, China, **211** G5
Linxi, Nei Mongol Zizhiqu, China, **211** G4
Linxia, China, **215** G2
Linyanti, *river*, Botswana/ Namibia, **370** D2
Linyi, Shanxi, China, **206** B1
Linyi, S. Shandong, China, **206** D1
Linyi, N. Shandong, China, **210** G5
Linyou, China, **215** H2
Linz, Austria, **289** G4
Linze, China, **213** J5
Lioboml', Ukraine, **289** M3
Lion, Golfe du, *gulf*, France, **291** F5
Lioua, Chad, **365** G2
Liouesso, Congo, **368** C2
Lipa, Philippines, **204** C3
Lipany, Slovakia, **289** K4
Lipari, Isola, *island*, Italy, **295** E6
Lipari, Italy, **295** E6
Lipcani, Moldova, **296** F1
Liperi, Finland, **285** P5
Lipetsk, Russian Federation, **298** E2
Lipetskaya Oblast', *province*, Russian Federation, **299** G6
Liphook, England, U.K., **305** G3
Lipiany, Poland, **289** G2
Lipin Bor, Russian Federation, **299** F2
Liping, China, **206** B3
Lipki, Russian Federation, **299** F6
Lipljan, Yugoslavia, **296** C4
Lipnica, Poland, **289** J2
Lipno, Poland, **289** J2
Lipobane, Ponta, *point*, Mozambique, **369** G6
Lipova, Romania, **296** C2
Lippe, *river*, Germany, **288** C3
Lipsk, Poland, **289** L2
Liptougou, Burkina Faso, **364** E2
Liptovský Mikuláš, Slovakia, **289** J4
Lipu, China, **206** B3
Lira, Uganda, **369** F2
Liranga, Congo, **368** C3
Lircay, Peru, **454** C3
Liria, Sudan, **369** F2
Lisala, Democratic Republic of the Congo, **368** D2
Lisbellaw, Northern Ireland, U.K., **309** E3
Lisboa, *district*, Portugal, **292** C3

Lisboa (Lisbon), Portugal, **292** C3
Lisbon *see* Lisboa, Portugal, **292** C3
Lisbon, U.S.A., **421** N5
Lisburne, Cape, U.S.A., **410** C3
Lisburn, *district*, Northern Ireland, U.K., **309** G3
Lisburn, Northern Ireland, U.K., **309** F3
Liscannor Bay, Ireland, **309** C5
Lisco, U.S.A., **420** B5
Lisdoonvarna, Ireland, **309** C4
Lishi, China, **210** E5
Lishu, China, **211** J4
Lishui, China, **206** D2
Lisianski, *island*, Hawaiian Islands, U.S.A., **139** G2
Lisieux, France, **290** E2
Liskeard, England, U.K., **304** C4
Liski, Russian Federation, **298** E2
Lismore, Australia, **135** L4
Lismore, Ireland, **309** E5
Lisnaskea, Northern Ireland, U.K., **309** E3
Liss, England, U.K., **305** G3
Lister, Mount, *mountain peak*, Antarctica, **470** D7
Listowel, Ireland, **309** C5
Lit, Sweden, **284** G5
Litang, Guangxi Zhuangzu Zizhiqu, China, **206** B4
Litang, Sichuan, China, **215** G3
Līṭānī, *river*, Lebanon, **225** C3
Litani, *river*, Suriname, **452** B2
Litchfield, Illinois, U.S.A., **421** J6
Litchfield, Nebraska, U.S.A., **420** D5
Lithakia, Ionioi Nisoi, Greece, **297** C7
Lithgow, Australia, **135** L5
Lithino, Akra, *point*, Kriti, Greece, **297** E8
Lithuania, *country*, Europe, **282** G4
Litovko, Russian Federation, **211** L2
Little Aden, Yemen, **220** D6
Little Andaman, *island*, Andaman and Nicobar Islands, India, **217** H4
Little Cayman, *island*, Cayman Islands, **429** E3
Little Coco Island, Myanmar, **217** H3
Little Colorado, *river*, U.S.A., **423** H4
Little Current, Canada, **421** N3
Little Falls, Minnesota, U.S.A., **420** F3
Little Falls, New York, U.S.A., **426** C3
Little Fort, Canada, **412** J6
Little Grand Rapids, Canada, **414** G5
Little Inagua Island, Bahamas, **429** G2
Little Kanawha, *river*, U.S.A., **421** N6
Little Lake, U.S.A., **422** E4
Little Mecatina, *river*, Canada, **417** L3
Little Minch, The, *strait*, Scotland, U.K., **308** B3
Little Missouri, *river*, U.S.A., **420** B2
Little Nicobar, *island*, Andaman and Nicobar Islands, India, **217** H5
Little Oakley, England, U.K., **305** J3
Little Ouse, *river*, England, U.K., **305** H2
Little Quill Lake, Canada, **414** B6
Little Rock, U.S.A., **424** F2
Little Sachigo Lake, Canada, **414** H4
Little Sioux, *river*, U.S.A., **420** E4
Little Smoky, Canada, **413** L4

Little Smoky, *river*, Canada, **413** K4
Little Tobago, *island*, Tobago, Trinidad and Tobago, **461** B4
Little Wabash, *river*, U.S.A., **421** J6
Littleborough, England, U.K., **306** F4
Littlefield, Arizona, U.S.A., **422** G3
Littlefield, Texas, U.S.A., **423** M5
Littlehampton, England, U.K., **305** G4
Littlemore, England, U.K., **305** F3
Littleport, England, U.K., **305** H2
Littoral, *province*, Cameroon, **368** A2
Litunde, Mozambique, **369** G5
Liu, *river*, China, **214** E3
Liuba, Gansu, China, **213** J5
Liuba, Shaanxi, China, **215** H2
Liucheng, China, **206** B3
Liuhe, China, **211** J4
Liuhu, China, **211** H3
Liujiang, China, **206** B3
Liulin, China, **210** E5
Liupanshui, China, **215** H4
Liushuquan, China, **213** G4
Liuxi, *river*, China, **207** A2
Liuxihe Reservoir, China, **207** B1
Liuyang, China, **206** C2
Liuyuan, China, **213** G4
Liuzhou, China, **206** B3
Livada, Romania, **296** D2
Livadiya, Russian Federation, **211** L4
Līvāni, Latvia, **287** N4
Livanovka, Kazakhstan, **222** G2
Live Oak, U.S.A., **425** L4
Lively Island, Falkland Islands, **460** F4
Livermore, Mount, *mountain peak*, U.S.A., **423** L6
Liverpool, Canada, **417** J7
Liverpool, England, U.K., **306** F4
Liverpool Bay, England, U.K., **306** E4
Livingston, Guatemala, **428** C4
Livingston, Lake, U.S.A., **424** E4
Livingston, Montana, U.S.A., **419** J4
Livingston, Texas, U.S.A., **424** E4
Livingstone, Zambia, **371** E2
Livingstonia, Malawi, **369** F5
Livno, Bosnia and Herzegovina, **294** F4
Livo, Finland, **285** N4
Livonia, U.S.A., **421** M4
Livorno, Italy, **294** C3
Livramento do Brumado, Brazil, **457** F3
Liwale, Tanzania, **369** G4
Lixi, China, **215** G4
Lixouri, Ionioi Nisoi, Greece, **297** C6
Liyang, China, **206** D2
Lizard, England, U.K., **304** B5
Lizard Point, England, U.K., **304** B5
Lizotte, Canada, **416** E5
Iizuka, Japan, **208** E4
Ljig, Yugoslavia, **296** C3
Ljubljana, Slovenia, **294** E2
Ljubovija, Yugoslavia, **296** B3
Ljugarn, Sweden, **287** J4
Ljungan, *river*, Sweden, **287** H1
Ljungby, Sweden, **286** F4
Ljungdalen, Sweden, **284** F5
Ljusdal, Sweden, **286** H2
Ljusnan, *river*, Sweden, **286** G2
Ljustorp, Sweden, **287** H1
Llagostera, Spain, **293** J2
Llaima, Volcán, *mountain peak*, Chile, **458** B6
Llanaelhaearn, Wales, U.K., **304** C2
Llanarth, Wales, U.K., **304** C2

Lopatka, Mys, *cape*, Russian Federation, **301** S4
Lopatyn, Ukraine, **289** M3
Lopez, Cap, *cape*, Gabon, **368** A3
Lopez, U.S.A., **426** B4
Lopez Point, U.S.A., **422** B3
Lopori, *river*, Democratic Republic of the Congo, **368** D2
Lopphavet, *channel*, Norway, **284** K1
Loppi, Finland, **287** M2
Lopshen'ga, Russian Federation, **285** T4
Lora del Río, Spain, **292** E4
Lorain, U.S.A., **421** M5
Loralai, Pakistan, **218** B3
Lorca, Spain, **293** G4
Lord Howe Island, Australia, **135** U14
Lord Howe Rise, *underwater feature*, Pacific Ocean, **478** E6
Lordsburg, U.S.A., **423** J5
Lore, Indonesia, **198** D5
Lorella, U.S.A., **418** D5
Lorengau, Papua New Guinea, **140** B3
Loreto, Bolivia, **455** F4
Loreto, Brazil, **452** E5
Loreto, Italy, **294** D4
Loreto, Mexico, **430** C3
Loreto, Philippines, **204** D4
Lorica, Colombia, **450** C2
Lorient, France, **290** C3
Loring, U.S.A., **419** L2
Loris, U.S.A., **425** N2
Lorn, Firth of, *river mouth*, Scotland, U.K., **308** D4
Lorraine, *administrative region*, France, **291** G2
Lorris, France, **290** F3
Lorzot, Tunisia, **361** J2
Los, Sweden, **286** G2
Los Alamos, U.S.A., **423** K4
Los Amores, Argentina, **459** E3
Los Angeles, Chile, **458** B5
Los Angeles, U.S.A., **422** D4
Los Banos, U.S.A., **422** C3
Los Blancos, Argentina, **458** D2
Los Cristianos, Islas Canarias, Spain, **373** A4
Los Cusis, Bolivia, **455** F4
Los Llanos de Aridane, Islas Canarias, Spain, **373** A4
Los Lunas, U.S.A., **423** K4
Los Menucos, Argentina, **460** D1
Los Mochis, Mexico, **430** C3
Los Molinos, Islas Canarias, Spain, **373** B4
Los Navalmorales, Spain, **292** E3
Los Palacios, Cuba, **428** E2
Los Palos, Indonesia, **198** D5
Los Pocitos, Mexico, **430** C2
Los Rosas, Argentina, **458** E4
Los Taques, Venezuela, **451** D1
Los Telares, Argentina, **458** D3
Los Teques, Venezuela, **451** E1
Los Vilos, Chile, **458** B4
Los Yébenes, Spain, **293** F3
Lošinj, *island*, Croatia, **294** E3
Los'mino, Russian Federation, **299** E5
Losombo, Democratic Republic of the Congo, **368** C2
Lossiemouth, Scotland, U.K., **308** F3
Lost Hills, U.S.A., **422** D4
Lostwithiel, England, U.K., **304** C4
Losuia, Papua New Guinea, **140** C5
Lot, *river*, France, **290** E4
Lota, Chile, **458** B5
Løten, Norway, **286** E2
Loto, Democratic Republic of the Congo, **368** D3
Lotofaga, Samoa, **141** B1
Lot's Wife, *mountain peak*, St Helena, **373** B3
Lotta, *river*, Russian Federation, **285** P2
Lotuke, *mountain peak*, Sudan, **369** F2
Louang Namtha, Laos, **202** D1
Louangphrabang, Laos, **202** D2
Loubomo, Congo, **368** B3
Loudéac, France, **290** C2
Loudi, China, **206** B3
Loudima, Congo, **368** B3
Loué, France, **290** D3
Loue, *river*, France, **288** B5
Louga, Senegal, **364** A1
Loughborough, England, U.K., **305** F2
Loughrea, Ireland, **309** D4
Loughton, England, U.K., **305** H3
Louhans, France, **291** G3
Louis-XIV, Pointe, *point*, Canada, **415** Q4
Louis Trichardt, South Africa, **371** E3
Louisburgh, Ireland, **309** C4
Louisiade Archipelago, Papua New Guinea, **140** D5
Louisiana, *state*, U.S.A., **424** F4
Louisville, Kentucky, U.S.A., **421** L6
Louisville, Mississippi, U.S.A., **425** H3
Louisville Ridge, *underwater feature*, Pacific Ocean, **478** G7
Loukhi, Russian Federation, **285** R3
Loukoléla, Congo, **368** C3
Loukouo, Congo, **368** B3
Loulé, Portugal, **292** C4
Loum, Cameroon, **368** A2
Loup, *river*, U.S.A., **420** D5
Lour-Escale, Senegal, **364** B2
Lourdes, Canada, **417** M5
Lourdes, France, **290** D5
Lourenço, Brazil, **452** C2
Louth, *county*, Ireland, **309** F4
Louth, England, U.K., **307** H4
Loutra Aidipsou, Greece, **297** D6
Loutraki, Greece, **297** D7
Louviers, France, **290** E2
Lövånger, Sweden, **284** K4
Lovat', *river*, Russian Federation, **299** C4
Lövberga, Sweden, **284** G5
Lovech, *administrative region*, Bulgaria, **296** E4
Lovech, Bulgaria, **296** E4
Loveland, U.S.A., **423** L1
Lovell, U.S.A., **419** K4
Lovelock, U.S.A., **422** D1
Lovere, Italy, **294** C3
Loviisa, Finland, **287** N2
Lovington, U.S.A., **423** M5
Lövnäs, Kopperberg, Sweden, **286** F2
Lövnäs, Norbotten, Sweden, **284** H3
Lovozero, Ozero, *lake*, Russian Federation, **285** S3
Lovozero, Russian Federation, **285** S2
Lovrin, Romania, **296** C3
Lövstabruk, Sweden, **287** H2
Lóvua, Lunda Norte, Angola, **368** D4
Lóvua, Moxico, Angola, **368** D5
Low, Canada, **416** D7
Low, Cape, Canada, **411** L3
Lowa, Democratic Republic of the Congo, **369** E3
Lowa, *river*, Democratic Republic of the Congo, **369** E3
Lowell, U.S.A., **418** G3
Löwenberg, Germany, **288** F2
Lower Arrow Lake, Canada, **413** K7
Lower Hutt, New Zealand, **133** E5
Lower Lake, U.S.A., **422** B2
Lower Lough Erne, *lake*, Northern Ireland, U.K., **309** E3
Lower Peirce Reservoir, Singapore, **200** K6
Lower Red Lake, U.S.A., **420** F2
Lowestoft, England, U.K., **305** J2
Łowicz, Poland, **289** J2
Lowman, U.S.A., **418** G4
Lowrah, *river*, Afghanistan, **218** A3
Lowther, Canada, **415** N7
Lowville, U.S.A., **426** C3
Loxton, South Africa, **370** D5
Loxur, China, **215** G2
Loyal, Ben, *mountain peak*, Scotland, U.K., **308** E2
Loyal Valley, U.S.A., **424** C4
Loyalty Islands *see* Loyauté, Îles, *islands*, New Caledonia, **141** A3
Loyauté, Îles (Loyalty Islands), New Caledonia, **141** A3
Loymola, Russian Federation, **299** C2
Loyne, Loch, Scotland, U.K., **308** D3
Lozère, Mont, *mountain peak*, France, **291** F4
Loznica, Yugoslavia, **296** B3
Loznitsa, Bulgaria, **296** F4
Lozoyuela, Spain, **293** F2
Lučenec, Slovakia, **289** J4
Lua Nova, Brazil, **452** B4
Luacano, Angola, **368** D5
Lualuba, *river*, Democratic Republic of the Congo, **369** E2
Luama, *river*, Democratic Republic of the Congo, **369** E3
Luampa, *river*, Zambia, **368** D5
Luan Xian, China, **211** G5
Lu'an, China, **206** D2
Luan, China, **210** G4
Luanchuan, China, **206** B1
Luanda, Angola, **368** B4
Luanda, *province*, Angola, **368** B4
Luando, Angola, **368** C5
Luando, *river*, Angola, **368** C5
Luanguinga, *river*, Angola, **368** D5
Luangwa, *river*, Zambia, **369** F5
Luangwa, Zambia, **371** F2
Luanjing, China, **210** D5
Luanshya, Zambia, **369** E5
Luanza, Democratic Republic of the Congo, **369** E4
Luapula, *province*, Zambia, **369** E5
Luar, Danau, *lake*, Indonesia, **201** F2
Luar *see* Horsburgh Island, Cocos (Keeling) Islands, **134** Q10
Luarca, Spain, **292** D1
Luashi, Democratic Republic of the Congo, **368** D5
Luau, Angola, **368** D5
Lubāna, Latvia, **287** N4
Lubāns, *lake*, Latvia, **287** N4
Luba, Equatorial Guinea, **368** A2
Lubaczów, Poland, **289** L3
Lubalo, Angola, **368** C4
Lubango, Angola, **368** B5
Lubang Islands, Philippines, **204** B3
Lubao, Democratic Republic of the Congo, **369** E4
Lubartów, Poland, **289** L3
Lubawa, Poland, **289** J2
Lübben, Germany, **289** F3
Lubbock, U.S.A., **424** B3
Lübeck, Germany, **288** E2
Lübecker Bucht, *bay*, Germany, **288** E1
Lubefu, Democratic Republic of the Congo, **368** D3
Lubefu, *river*, Democratic Republic of the Congo, **368** D3
Lubero, Democratic Republic of the Congo, **369** E3
Lubin, Poland, **289** H3
Lublin, Poland, **289** L3
Lubliniec, Poland, **289** J3
Lubnān, Jabal, *mountain range*, Lebanon, **225** C3
Lubny, Ukraine, **298** D3
Lubsko, Poland, **289** G3
Lubuagan, Philippines, **204** C2
Lubudi, Democratic Republic of the Congo, **369** E4
Lubumbashi, Democratic Republic of the Congo, **369** E5
Lubungu, Zambia, **369** E5
Lubutu, Democratic Republic of the Congo, **369** E3
Łuby, Poland, **289** J2
Lucala, Angola, **368** C4
Lucan, Ireland, **309** F4
Lücaoshan, China, **213** G5
Lucapa, Angola, **368** D4
Lucca, Italy, **294** C4
Lucélia, Brazil, **456** C5
Lucena, Philippines, **204** C3
Lucena, Spain, **292** E4
Lucera, Italy, **295** E5
Lucerna, Peru, **455** E3
Luchang, China, **215** G4
Lüchow, Germany, **288** E2
Luchuan, China, **206** B4
Lucie, *river*, Suriname, **452** B2
Lucile, U.S.A., **418** F4
Lucira, Angola, **368** B5
Luckau, Germany, **288** F3
Luckeesarai, India, **219** F4
Luckenwalde, Germany, **288** F2
Lucknow, India, **218** E4
Luçon, France, **290** D3
Lucrecia, Cabo, *cape*, Cuba, **429** G2
Lucusse, Angola, **368** D5
Luda Kamchiya, *river*, Bulgaria, **296** F4
Ludden, U.S.A., **420** D2
Lüderitz, Namibia, **370** C4
Lüderitz Bay, Namibia, **370** B4
Ludhiāna, India, **218** C3
Ludian, China, **215** G4
Ludington, U.S.A., **421** K4
Ludlow, California, U.S.A., **422** E4
Ludlow, Colorado, U.S.A., **423** L3
Ludlow, England, U.K., **304** E2
Ludlow, Vermont, U.S.A., **426** D3
Ludowici, U.S.A., **425** M4
Luduş, Romania, **296** E2
Ludvika, Sweden, **286** G2
Ludwigsburg, Germany, **288** D4
Ludwigshafen am Rhein, Germany, **288** D4
Ludwigslust, Germany, **288** E2
Ludza, Latvia, **287** N4
Luebo, Democratic Republic of the Congo, **368** D4
Lueki, Democratic Republic of the Congo, **369** E3
Luena, Angola, **368** C5
Luepa, Venezuela, **451** G3
Lüeyang, China, **215** H2
Lufeng, China, **206** C4
Lufkin, U.S.A., **424** E4
Luga, *river*, Russian Federation, **299** B3
Luga, Russian Federation, **299** B3
Lugait, Philippines, **204** D4
Lugano, Switzerland, **291** J3
Luganville, Vanuatu, **141** A2
Lugela, Mozambique, **369** G6
Lughaye, Somalia, **367** F2
Lugnaquillia, *mountain peak*, Ireland, **309** F5
Lugo, Italy, **294** C3
Lugo, Spain, **292** D1
Lugoj, Romania, **296** C3
Lugovoy, Kazakhstan, **223** J4
Lugu, China, **214** C2
Luhačovice, Czech Republic, **289** H4
Luhans'k, Ukraine, **298** E3
Luhombero, Tanzania, **369** G4
Luhuo, China, **215** G3
Lui, Ben, *mountain peak*, Scotland, U.K., **308** E4
Luia, *river*, Mozambique, **369** F6
Luiana, Angola, **370** D2
Luikonlahti, Finland, **285** P5
Luing, *island*, Scotland, U.K., **308** D4
Luís Correia, Brazil, **453** F4
Luitpold Coast, *region*, Antarctica, **470** C4
Luiza, Democratic Republic of the Congo, **368** D4
Luján, Argentina, **458** C4
Lujiang, China, **206** D2
Lukachek, Russian Federation, **211** L1
Lukala, Democratic Republic of the Congo, **368** B4
Lukavac, Bosnia and Herzegovina, **294** G3
Lukengo, Democratic Republic of the Congo, **369** E4
Lukeville, U.S.A., **422** G6
Lukhovitsy, Russian Federation, **299** G5
Lŭki, Bulgaria, **296** E5
Lukolela, Democratic Republic of the Congo, **368** C3
Lukovit, Bulgaria, **296** E4
Lukovnikovo, Russian Federation, **299** E4
Łuków, Poland, **289** L3
Lukula, Democratic Republic of the Congo, **368** B4
Lukulu, Zambia, **368** D5
Lukumburu, Tanzania, **369** G4
Lukunor, *island*, Micronesia, **138** D4
Lukwasa, India, **218** D4
Luleå, Sweden, **285** L4
Luleälven, *river*, Sweden, **284** K4
Lüleburgaz, Turkey, **297** F5
Luliang, China, **215** G4
Lüliang Shan, *mountain range*, China, **210** E5
Lulimba, Democratic Republic of the Congo, **369** E3
Luling, U.S.A., **424** D5
Lulonga, Democratic Republic of the Congo, **368** C2
Lulua, *river*, Democratic Republic of the Congo, **368** D4
Lülung, China, **214** C3
Luma, American Samoa, **141** B2
Lumbala Kaquengue, Angola, **368** D5
Lumbala N'guimbo, Angola, **368** D5
Lumberton, Mississippi, U.S.A., **425** H4
Lumberton, North Carolina, U.S.A., **425** N2
Lumbrales, Spain, **292** D2
Lumbrera, Argentina, **458** D2
Lumbres, France, **305** K4
Lumding, India, **219** H4
Lumecha, Tanzania, **369** G5
Lumimba, Zambia, **369** F5
Lumo, *island*, Micronesia, **138** C4
Lumphăt, Cambodia, **203** E3
Lumsden, Canada, **413** S6
Lumsden, New Zealand, **133** B7
Lumut, Gunung, *mountain peak*, Indonesia, **201** F3
Lumut, Tanjong, *point*, Indonesia, **200** D3
Lün, Mongolia, **210** D3
Lunan Bay, Scotland, U.K., **308** G4
Lund, Sweden, **286** F5
Lunda Norte, *province*, Angola, **368** C4
Lunda Sul, *province*, Angola, **368** D5
Lundazi, Zambia, **369** F5
Lunde, Sweden, **287** H1
Lundy, *island*, England, U.K., **304** C3
Lune, *river*, England, U.K., **306** F3
Lüneburg, Germany, **288** E2
Lunenburg, Canada, **417** J7
Lunéville, France, **291** H2
Lung Kwu Tan, China, **207** B4

Murcia, *autonomous community*, Spain, **293** G4
Murcia, Spain, **293** G4
Murdo, U.S.A., **420** C4
Murdochville, Canada, **416** J5
Mureck, Austria, **289** G5
Mureș, *river*, Romania, **296** D2
Muret, France, **290** E5
Murewa, Zimbabwe, **371** F2
Murfreesboro, North Carolina, U.S.A., **426** B6
Murfreesboro, Tennessee, U.S.A., **425** J2
Murgeni, Romania, **296** G2
Murgha Kibzai, Pakistan, **218** B3
Murghob, Tajikistan, **223** J5
Murgon, Australia, **135** L4
Muria, Gunung, *mountain peak*, Indonesia, **201** E4
Muriaé, Brazil, **457** E5
Muriege, Angola, **368** D4
Murilo, *island*, Micronesia, **138** D4
Müritz, *lake*, Germany, **288** F2
Muriwai, New Zealand, **132** F4
Murjek, Sweden, **284** K3
Murmansk, Russian Federation, **285** R2
Murmanskaya Oblast', *province*, Russian Federation, **285** Q2
Murmashi, Russian Federation, **285** R2
Murole, Finland, **287** M2
Murom, Russian Federation, **298** F1
Murongo, Tanzania, **369** F3
Muroran, Japan, **209** H2
Muroto, Japan, **208** F4
Muroto-zaki, *point*, Japan, **208** F4
Murovani Kurylivtsi, Ukraine, **296** F1
Murphy, U.S.A., **425** K2
Murrat al Kubrā, Al Buḩayrat al, *lake*, Egypt, **225** B4
Murray, Iowa, U.S.A., **420** G5
Murray, Kentucky, U.S.A., **421** J7
Murray, Lake, Papua New Guinea, **140** A4
Murray, Lake, U.S.A., **425** M2
Murray, Mount, *mountain peak*, Canada, **412** E1
Murray, *river*, Australia, **135** J6
Murray Bridge, Australia, **135** H6
Murray Fracture Ridge, *underwater feature*, Pacific Ocean, **479** H3
Murray Hill, *mountain peak*, Christmas Island, **134** N8
Murraysburg, South Africa, **370** D5
Murrayville, U.S.A., **420** H6
Murro di Porco, Capo, *cape*, Sicilia, Italy, **295** E7
Murroogh, Ireland, **309** C4
Murrupula, Mozambique, **369** G6
Murska Sobota, Slovenia, **294** F2
Murtle Lake, Canada, **412** K5
Murtovaara, Finland, **285** P4
Murud, Gunung, *mountain peak*, Malaysia, **201** F2
Murud, India, **216** C2
Murupara, New Zealand, **132** F4
Mururoa, *island*, French Polynesia, **137** H3
Murwāra, India, **218** E5
Murwillumbah, Australia, **135** L4
Murygino, Russian Federation, **299** D5
Murzuq, Şaḩrā', *desert*, Libya, **362** B4
Murzuq, Libya, **362** B3
Mürzzuschlag, Austria, **289** G5
Muş, Turkey, **224** F5
Mūsā, Jabal (Mount Sinai), *mountain peak*, Egypt, **225** B5

Mūša, *river*, Lithuania, **287** L4
Musa Ālī Terara, Ethiopia, **220** D6
Musa Ālī Terara, *mountain peak*, Ethiopia, **367** F2
Mūsa Khel Bāzār, Pakistan, **218** B3
Mūsá Qal'eh, Afghanistan, **218** A2
Musadi, Democratic Republic of the Congo, **368** D3
Musala, *mountain peak*, Bulgaria, **296** D4
Musala, Pulau, *island*, Indonesia, **200** B2
Musan, North Korea, **208** E2
Muscat *see* Masqaṭ, Oman, **221** G4
Musgrave Harbour, Canada, **417** Q5
Musgrave Ranges, *mountain range*, Australia, **134** G4
Musgravetown, Canada, **417** Q5
Musheramore, *mountain peak*, Ireland, **309** D5
Mushie, Democratic Republic of the Congo, **368** C3
Mushu, *island*, Papua New Guinea, **140** A3
Musi, *river*, Indonesia, **200** D3
Muskeg, *river*, Canada, **412** H1
Muskegon, *river*, U.S.A., **421** L4
Muskegon, U.S.A., **421** K4
Muskogee, U.S.A., **424** E2
Muskrat Dam, Canada, **414** J5
Muskwa, *river*, Canada, **412** H2
Muslimīyah, Syria, **225** D1
Musoma, Tanzania, **369** F3
Musombe, Tanzania, **369** F4
Musquaro, Lac, *lake*, Canada, **417** L4
Musquodoboit Harbour, Canada, **417** K7
Mussau Island, Papua New Guinea, **140** C3
Musselburgh, Scotland, U.K., **308** F5
Musselshell, U.S.A., **419** K3
Mussende, Angola, **368** C5
Mussidan, France, **290** E4
Musswellbrook, Australia, **135** L5
Mustafakemalpaşa, *river*, Turkey, **297** G6
Mustafakemalpaşa, Turkey, **297** G6
Mustahīl, Ethiopia, **367** F3
Musters, Lago, *lake*, Argentina, **460** D2
Mustjala, Estonia, **287** L3
Mustla, Estonia, **287** M3
Mustvee, Estonia, **287** N3
Muszyna, Poland, **289** K4
Mūṭ, Egypt, **362** E3
Mut, Turkey, **225** B1
Mutalau, Niue, **132** M13
Mutare, Zimbabwe, **371** F2
Mutis, Gunung, *mountain peak*, Indonesia, **198** D5
Mutoko, Zimbabwe, **371** F2
Mutorashanga, Zimbabwe, **369** F6
Mutshatsha, Democratic Republic of the Congo, **368** D5
Mutsu, Japan, **209** H2
Mutton Bay, Canada, **417** M4
Mutton Bird Island, Lord Howe Island, Australia, **135** U14
Muttonbird (Titi) Islands, New Zealand, **133** A8
Muttukūru, India, **216** E3
Mutuali, Mozambique, **369** G5
Mutum, Brazil, **455** G2
Mutum Biyu, Nigeria, **365** G3
Mutunópolis, Brazil, **456** D3
Mutur, Sri Lanka, **217** E4
Muurasjärvi, Finland, **285** M5
Muurola, Finland, **285** M3
Muxaluando, Angola, **368** B4
Muxima, Angola, **368** B4
Muyezerskiy, Russian Federation, **285** R5

Muyinga, Burundi, **369** F3
Muyumba, Democratic Republic of the Congo, **369** E4
Muzaffargarh, Pakistan, **218** B3
Muzaffarnagar, India, **218** D3
Muzaffarpur, India, **219** F4
Muzillac, France, **290** C3
Muztag, China, **219** F1
Muztag, *mountain peak*, China, **212** E5
Muztagata, *mountain peak*, China, **212** B5
Mvangan, Cameroon, **368** B2
Mvolo, Sudan, **369** E1
Mvomero, Tanzania, **369** G4
Mvouti, Congo, **368** B3
Mvuma, Zimbabwe, **371** F2
Mwali (Mohéli), *island*, Comoros, **372** A3
Mwanza, *administrative region*, Tanzania, **369** F3
Mwanza, Democratic Republic of the Congo, **369** E4
Mwanza, Tanzania, **369** F3
Mweelrea, *mountain peak*, Ireland, **309** C4
Mweka, Democratic Republic of the Congo, **368** D4
Mwenda, Zambia, **369** E5
Mwene-Ditu, Democratic Republic of the Congo, **368** D4
Mwenezi, Zimbabwe, **371** F3
Mwenga, Democratic Republic of the Congo, **369** E3
Mweru, Lake, Democratic Republic of the Congo/ Tanzania, **369** E4
Mwimba, Democratic Republic of the Congo, **368** D4
Mwinilunga, Zambia, **368** D5
Mỹ Tho, Vietnam, **203** E4
Myadzyel, Belarus, **287** N5
Myagostrov, Ostrov, *island*, Russian Federation, **285** T4
Myājlār, India, **218** B4
Myakka City, U.S.A., **425** L6
Myaksa, Russian Federation, **299** G3
Myanmar (Burma), *country*, Asia, **197** L7
Myaungmya, Myanmar, **205** B4
Mybster, Scotland, U.K., **308** F2
Myckelgensjö, Sweden, **284** H5
Myingyan, Myanmar, **205** B3
Myinmoletkat Taung, *mountain peak*, Myanmar, **202** C3
Myitkyinā, Myanmar, **205** C2
Myittha, Myanmar, **205** C3
Mykolayiv, Ukraine, **298** D3
Mykolayivs'ka Oblast', *province*, Ukraine, **296** H2
Mykonos, *island*, Kyklades, Greece, **297** E7
Mykonos, Kyklades, Greece, **297** E7
Myla, Russian Federation, **213** J2
Mymensingh, Bangladesh, **214** D4
Mynämäki, Finland, **287** K2
Mynaral, Kazakhstan, **212** B3
Myohaung, Myanmar, **205** B3
Myory, Belarus, **287** N5
Myotha, Myanmar, **205** B3
Mýrdalsjökull, *ice cap*, Iceland, **284** Y7
Myre, Norway, **284** G2
Myrheden, Sweden, **284** K4
Mýri, Iceland, **284** Y7
Myrina, Greece, **297** E6
Myrtle Beach, U.S.A., **425** N3
Myrtle Creek, U.S.A., **418** C5
Myrtle Point, U.S.A., **418** B5
Myrtou, Cyprus, **225** B2
Myrviken, Sweden, **284** G5
Mysen, Norway, **286** E3
Myshkin, Russian Federation, **299** G4
Myślenice, Poland, **289** J4
Myślibórz, Poland, **289** G2
Mysore, India, **216** D3
Mytilini, Greece, **297** F6

Mytishchi, Russian Federation, **299** F5
Mzimba, Malawi, **369** F5
Mzuzu, Malawi, **369** F5

N

Nà Hang, Vietnam, **203** E1
Na-lang, Myanmar, **205** C3
Naalehu, Hawaiian Islands, U.S.A., **422** R10
Naama, Algeria, **361** F2
Naantali, Finland, **287** L2
Naarva, Finland, **285** Q5
Naas, Ireland, **309** F4
Naasa, Finland, **284** K5
Nababiep, South Africa, **370** C4
Nabas, Philippines, **204** C4
Naberera, Tanzania, **369** G3
Naberezhnyye Chelny, Russian Federation, **222** E1
Nābha, India, **218** D3
Nabī Shu'ayb, Jabal an, *mountain peak*, Yemen, **220** D5
Nabileque, *river*, Brazil, **456** B5
Nabire, Indonesia, **199** F3
Nabolo, Ghana, **364** D2
Nabouwalu, Fiji, **141** A4
Nabq, Egypt, **225** C5
Nabua, Philippines, **204** C3
Nābul, Tunisia, **362** B1
Nābulus, West Bank, **225** C3
Nacala, Mozambique, **372** A3
Nacaome, Honduras, **428** D4
Nacaroa, Mozambique, **369** G5
Nachen, China, **206** B4
Nachingwea, Tanzania, **369** G5
Nāchna, India, **218** B4
Náchod, Czech Republic, **289** H3
Nachuge, Andaman and Nicobar Islands, India, **217** H4
Nacogdoches, U.S.A., **424** E4
Nacozari de García, Mexico, **430** C2
Nadi, Fiji, **141** A4
Nădlac, Romania, **296** C2
Nador, Morocco, **361** F1
Nadporozh'ye, Russian Federation, **299** G3
Nadvirna, Ukraine, **296** E1
Nadvoitsy, Russian Federation, **285** S5
Nadym, Russian Federation, **300** J3
Nærbø, Norway, **286** B3
Næstved, Denmark, **286** E5
Nafpaktos, Greece, **297** C6
Nafplio, Greece, **297** D7
Nafūsah, Jabal, *mountain range*, Libya, **362** B2
Nagina, India, **218** D3
Naga, Philippines, **204** C3
Nagaj, India, **216** C2
Nāgāland, *state*, India, **219** H4
Nagano, Japan, **209** G3
Nagaoka, Japan, **209** G3
Nagaon, India, **219** H4
Nagar, India, **218** D4
Nagarjuna Sāgar, *reservoir*, India, **216** D2
Nagasaki, Japan, **208** E4
Nāgaur, India, **218** C4
Nagda, India, **218** C5
Nāgercoil, India, **216** D4
Naggen, Sweden, **286** H1
Nagichot, Sudan, **369** F2
Nagles Mountains, Ireland, **309** D5
Nago, Japan, **209** P8
Nāgod, India, **218** E4
Nagorno-Karabakh, *autonomous region*, Azerbaijan, **222** D5
Nagor'ye, Russian Federation, **299** G4
Nagoya, Japan, **209** G4

Nāgpur, India, **218** D5
Nagqu, China, **214** E3
Nagyatád, Hungary, **289** H5
Nagyhalász, Hungary, **289** K4
Nagykálló, Hungary, **289** K5
Nagykanizsa, Hungary, **289** H5
Nagykáta, Hungary, **289** J5
Nagykőrös, Hungary, **296** B2
Nagza, China, **213** H5
Naha, Japan, **209** N8
Nahariyya, Israel, **225** C3
Nahe, *river*, Germany, **288** C4
N'Ahnet, Adrar, *mountain range*, Algeria, **361** G3
Nahrīn, Afghanistan, **218** B1
Nahuel Huapi, Lago, *lake*, Argentina, **460** C1
Nahuo, China, **206** B4
Naica, Mexico, **430** D3
Naidăş, Romania, **296** C3
Naij Tal, China, **214** E2
Naila, Germany, **288** E3
Nailsworth, England, U.K., **304** E3
Naiman Qi, China, **211** H4
Nain, Canada, **411** N4
Nā'īn, Iran, **220** F2
Nainpur, India, **218** E5
Nainwa, India, **218** C4
Naiopué, Mozambique, **369** G6
Nairai, *island*, Fiji, **141** A4
Nairn, Scotland, U.K., **308** F3
Nairobi, Kenya, **369** G3
Naissaar, *island*, Estonia, **287** M3
Naivasha, Kenya, **369** G3
Naj' Ḩammādī, Egypt, **363** F3
Najac, France, **290** F4
Najafābād, Iran, **220** F2
Nájera, Spain, **293** F1
Najībābād, India, **218** D3
Najin, North Korea, **208** E2
n'Ajjer, Tassili, *plateau*, Algeria, **361** H3
Najrān, Saudi Arabia, **363** H5
Naju, South Korea, **208** D4
Nakasongola, Uganda, **369** F2
Nakatsugawa, Japan, **209** G4
Nakfa, Eritrea, **220** C5
Nakhodka, Russian Federation, **211** L4
Nakhon Nayok, Thailand, **202** D3
Nakhon Phanom, Thailand, **203** E2
Nakhon Ratchasima (Khorat), Thailand, **202** D3
Nakhon Sawan, Thailand, **202** D3
Nakhon Si Thammarat, Thailand, **202** C4
Nakhtarāna, India, **218** B5
Nakina, British Columbia, Canada, **412** C2
Nakina, Ontario, Canada, **415** L6
Nakło nad Notecią, Poland, **289** H2
Nakodar, India, **218** C3
Nakonde, Zambia, **369** F4
Nakskov, Denmark, **286** E5
Näkten, *lake*, Sweden, **286** G1
Nakuru, Kenya, **369** G3
Nakusp, Canada, **413** L6
Nāl, Pakistan, **218** A4
Nalao, China, **215** H4
Nalayh, Mongolia, **210** D3
Nal'chik, Russian Federation, **222** C4
Naliya, India, **218** B5
Näljänkä, Finland, **285** P4
Nālūt, Libya, **362** B2
Nam Co, *lake*, China, **214** D3
Nam Định, Vietnam, **203** E1
Nam Ngum Reservoir, Laos, **203** D2
Nam Pawn, *river*, Myanmar, **205** C4
Nam Phong, Thailand, **203** D2
Namacunde, Angola, **368** C6
Namacurra, Mozambique, **371** G2
Namai, Nepal, **219** E4

Nok Kundi, Pakistan, **221** H3
Nokh, India, **218** C4
Nokha, India, **218** C4
Nokia, Finland, **287** L2
Nokou, Chad, **365** G2
Nokuku, Vanuatu, **141** A2
Nola, Central African Republic, **368** C2
Nom, China, **213** G4
Nome, Alaska, U.S.A., **410** C3
Nome, Texas, U.S.A., **424** E4
Nong Bua, Thailand, **202** D3
Nong Bua Lamphu, Thailand, **203** D2
Nong Khai, Thailand, **203** D2
Nong'an, China, **211** J3
Nonoava, Mexico, **430** D3
Nonouti, *island*, Kiribati, **139** F5
Nonthaburi, Thailand, **202** D3
Nontron, France, **290** E4
Noonan, U.S.A., **419** N2
Noondie, Lake, Australia, **134** D4
Noord, Aruba, **461** B3
Noord-Brabant, *province*, Netherlands, **288** B3
Noord-Holland, *province*, Netherlands, **288** B2
Noormarkku, Finland, **287** K2
Noosa Heads, Australia, **135** L4
Nootka, Canada, **412** F7
Nootka Island, Canada, **412** F7
Nóqui, Angola, **368** B4
Nora, *river*, Russian Federation, **211** K1
Nora, Sweden, **286** G3
Norala, Philippines, **204** D5
Norcia, Italy, **294** D4
Nord, Greenland, **411** T1
Nord, *province*, Cameroon, **365** G3
Nord-Kivu, *administrative region*, Democratic Republic of the Congo, **369** E3
Nord-Ouest, *province*, Cameroon, **365** G3
Nord-Pas-de-Calais, *administrative region*, France, **290** E1
Nørd-Trøndelag, *county*, Norway, **284** E4
Nordaustlandet, *island*, Svalbard, **300** C1
Nordberg, Norway, **286** D2
Nordegg, Canada, **413** L5
Norden, Germany, **288** C2
Nordenham, Germany, **288** D2
Nordenshel'da, Arkhipelag, *islands*, Russian Federation, **300** L2
Norderney, *island*, Germany, **288** C2
Nordfjordeid, Norway, **286** C2
Nordfold, Norway, **284** G3
Nordhausen, Germany, **288** E3
Nordhorn, Germany, **288** C2
Nordkapp, *cape*, Norway, **285** M1
Nordkinnhalvøya, *peninsula*, Norway, **285** P1
Nordkjosbotn, Norway, **284** J2
Nordkvaløy, *island*, Norway, **284** J1
Nordland, *county*, Norway, **284** F3
Nordli, Norway, **284** F4
Nördlingen, Germany, **288** E4
Nordmaling, Sweden, **284** J5
Nordmela, Norway, **284** G2
Nordmøre, *island*, Norway, **284** C5
Nordøyane, *island*, Norway, **286** B1
Nordoyar, *islands*, Faeroe Islands, **302** D1
Nordpunt, *point*, Curaçao, Netherlands Antilles, **461** C3
Nordrhein-Westfalen, *state*, Germany, **288** C3
Nore, Norway, **286** D2
Noresund, Norway, **286** D2
Norfolk, Nebraska, U.S.A., **420** E4

Norfolk, *unitary authority*, England, U.K., **305** H2
Norfolk, Virginia, U.S.A., **426** B6
Norfolk Broads, *region*, England, U.K., **305** J2
Norfolk Island, *Australian territory*, Pacific Ocean, **135** T13
Norfolk Ridge, *underwater feature*, Pacific Ocean, **478** F6
Noril'sk, Russian Federation, **300** K3
Noring, Gunung, *mountain peak*, Malaysia, **200** C1
Norma, U.S.A., **420** C1
Norman, Lake, U.S.A., **425** M2
Norman, *river*, Australia, **135** J2
Norman, U.S.A., **424** D2
Norman Inlet, *bay*, Auckland Islands, New Zealand, **132** J10
Norman Wells, Canada, **410** G3
Normanby Island, Papua New Guinea, **140** D4
Normandia, Brazil, **451** G3
Normanton, Australia, **135** J2
Normétal, Canada, **416** B5
Norquay, Canada, **414** D2
Norquinco, Argentina, **460** C1
Norr-dellen, *lake*, Sweden, **286** H2
Norra Bergnäs, Sweden, **284** J3
Norra Storfjället, *mountain peak*, Sweden, **284** G4
Norråker, Sweden, **284** G4
Norrbotten, *county*, Sweden, **284** J3
Nørre Nebel, Denmark, **286** D5
Norrent-Fontès, France, **305** K4
Nørresundby, Denmark, **286** D4
Norris, U.S.A., **419** J4
Norrköping, Sweden, **286** H3
Norrtälje, Sweden, **287** J3
Norseman, Australia, **134** E5
Norsjö, *lake*, Norway, **286** D3
Norsjö, Sweden, **284** J4
Norsk, Russian Federation, **211** K1
Norske Øer, *islands*, Greenland, **411** T2
Norte, Cabo, *cape*, Brazil, **452** D3
Norte, Cabo, *cape*, Isla de Pascua (Easter Island), Chile, **461** B2
Norte, Cabo, *cape*, Islas Galápagos (Galapagos Islands), Ecuador, **461** A2
Norte, Canal do, *channel*, Brazil, **452** C3
Norte, Punta, *point*, Argentina, **460** E1
Norte, Punta, *point*, San Andrés, Colombia, **461** B1
Norte, Serra do, *mountain range*, Brazil, **455** G3
Norte del Cabo San Antonio, Punta, *point*, Argentina, **459** F5
Nortelândia, Brazil, **456** B4
North, Cape, Canada, **417** L6
North, U.S.A., **425** M3
North Adams, U.S.A., **426** D3
North Andaman, *island*, Andaman and Nicobar Islands, India, **217** H3
North Augusta, U.S.A., **425** M3
North Australian Basin, *underwater feature*, Indian Ocean, **476** G5
North Ayrshire, *local authority*, Scotland, U.K., **308** E5
North Battleford, Canada, **413** Q5
North Bay, Canada, **421** P2
North Bend, U.S.A., **418** B5
North Berwick, Scotland, U.K., **308** G4
North Cape, Antipodes Islands, New Zealand, **133** P15
North Cape, Canada, **417** K6
North Cape, New Zealand, **132** D2

North Carolina, *state*, U.S.A., **425** M2
North Channel, Canada, **421** M2
North Channel, Northern Ireland, U.K., **308** D5
North Dakota, *state*, U.S.A., **420** C2
North Down, *district*, Northern Ireland, U.K., **309** G3
North Downs, *region*, England, U.K., **305** H3
North East, *district*, Botswana, **371** E3
North East, U.S.A., **421** P4
North East Bay, Ascension, **373** A3
North East Harbour, Campbell Island, New Zealand, **132** K11
North East Island, Snares Islands, New Zealand, **132** H9
North East Lincolnshire, *unitary authority*, England, U.K., **307** H4
North East Point, Christmas Island, **134** N8
North-Eastern, *province*, Kenya, **369** G2
North Esk, *river*, Scotland, U.K., **308** G4
North European Plain, Europe, **280** F5
North Fiji Basin, *underwater feature*, Pacific Ocean, **478** F5
North Foreland, *cape*, England, U.K., **305** J3
North Fork, Idaho, U.S.A., **418** H4
North Fork, Nevada, U.S.A., **418** G6
North Grimston, England, U.K., **307** H3
North Head, Canada, **426** G2
North Head, *point*, Lord Howe Island, Australia, **135** U14
North Head, *point*, Macquarie Island, **134** R11
North Head, *point*, New Zealand, **132** D3
North Head, U.S.A., **416** H7
North Horr, Kenya, **369** G2
North Hykeham, England, U.K., **305** G1
North Island, New Zealand, **132** D3
North Island, Seychelles, **373** A2
North Keeling Island, Cocos (Keeling) Islands, **134** Q10
North Knife, *river*, Canada, **414** F2
North Knife Lake, Canada, **414** F2
North Korea, *country*, Asia, **197** P5
North Lakhimpur, India, **219** H4
North Lanarkshire, *local authority*, Scotland, U.K., **308** F5
North Lincolnshire, *unitary authority*, England, U.K., **307** H4
North Little Rock, U.S.A., **424** F2
North Loup, *river*, U.S.A., **420** C4
North Moose Lake, Canada, **414** D4
North Platte, *river*, U.S.A., **419** L5
North Platte, U.S.A., **420** C5
North Point, Ascension, **373** A3
North Point, Seychelles, **373** A2
North Point, U.S.A., **421** M3
North Port, U.S.A., **425** L6
North Powder, U.S.A., **418** F4
North Promontory, *point*, Snares Islands, New Zealand, **132** H9
North Rona, *island*, Scotland, U.K., **308** D1
North Ronaldsay, *island*, Orkney, Scotland, U.K., **308** G1
North Saskatchewan, *river*,

Canada, **413** R5
North Sea, Europe, **280** E4
North Seal, *river*, Canada, **414** D2
North Shields, England, U.K., **307** G3
North Solomons, *province*, Papua New Guinea, **140** E2
North Somercotes, England, U.K., **307** J4
North Somerset, *unitary authority*, England, U.K., **304** E3
North Sound, The, Orkney, Scotland, U.K., **308** G1
North Spirit Lake, Canada, **414** H5
North Star, Canada, **413** L3
North Stradbroke Island, Australia, **135** L4
North Sunderland, England, U.K., **307** G2
North Taranaki Bight, *bay*, New Zealand, **132** D4
North Tidworth, England, U.K., **305** F3
North Twin Island, Canada, **415** Q5
North Tyne, *river*, England, U.K., **306** F2
North Uist, *island*, Scotland, U.K., **308** B3
North Wabasca Lake, Canada, **413** M3
North Walsham, England, U.K., **305** J2
North West, *province*, South Africa, **370** D4
North West Cape, Auckland Islands, New Zealand, **132** J10
North West Cape, Australia, **134** C3
North-West Frontier Province, *province*, Pakistan, **218** B2
North West Highlands, *mountain range*, Scotland, U.K., **308** D3
North West Point, Christmas Island, **134** N8
North-Western, *province*, Zambia, **368** D5
North Wildwood, U.S.A., **426** C5
North Woodstock, U.S.A., **426** E2
North York Moors, *moorland*, England, U.K., **307** H3
North Yorkshire, *unitary authority*, England, U.K., **307** G3
Northallerton, England, U.K., **307** G3
Northam, Australia, **134** D5
Northampton, Australia, **134** C4
Northampton, England, U.K., **305** G2
Northampton, U.S.A., **426** D3
Northamptonshire, *unitary authority*, England, U.K., **305** F2
Northeast Point, Bahamas, **429** G2
Northeast Providence Channel, Bahamas, **428** F1
Northeim, Germany, **288** D3
Northern, *administrative region*, Ghana, **364** D3
Northern, *administrative region*, Malawi, **369** F5
Northern, *province*, Sierra Leone, **364** B3
Northern, *province*, Zambia, **369** F5
Northern Cape, *province*, South Africa, **370** C4
Northern Cook Islands, Cook Islands, **139** H5
Northern Indian Lake, Canada, **414** F3
Northern Ireland, *administrative division*, U.K., **309** E3
Northern Mariana Islands, *U.S. territory*, Pacific Ocean, **138** C3

Northern Peninsula, Canada, **417** N4
Northern (Oro), *province*, Papua New Guinea, **140** C5
Northern Province, *province*, South Africa, **371** E3
Northern Range, *mountain range*, Trinidad, Trinidad and Tobago, **461** C4
Northern Territory, *territory*, Australia, **134** G2
Northfield, U.S.A., **420** G3
Northton, Scotland, U.K., **308** B3
Northville, U.S.A., **416** D8
Northwest Atlantic Mid-Ocean Canyon, *underwater feature*, Atlantic Ocean, **477** D2
Northwest Bay, Seychelles, **373** A2
Northwest Pacific Basin, *underwater feature*, Pacific Ocean, **478** E2
Northwest Providence Channel, Bahamas, **428** F1
Northwest Territories, *territory*, Canada, **410** G3
Northwich, England, U.K., **306** F4
Northwood, U.S.A., **420** E2
Norton, England, U.K., **307** H3
Norton, U.S.A., **420** D6
Norton Fitzwarren, England, U.K., **304** D3
Norton Sound, U.S.A., **410** C3
Norwalk, U.S.A., **421** M5
Norway, *country*, Europe, **282** E3
Norway House, Canada, **414** F5
Norwegian Bay, Canada, **411** K2
Norwegian Sea, Atlantic Ocean, **280** D2
Norwich, England, U.K., **305** J2
Norwood, U.S.A., **420** G3
Noshiro, Japan, **209** H2
Noṣratābād, Iran, **221** G3
Noss, Isle of, *island*, Scotland, U.K., **308** K7
Nossa Senhora das Dores, Brazil, **457** G3
Nossa Senhora do Livramento, Brazil, **456** B4
Nossebro, Sweden, **286** F3
Nossombougou, Mali, **364** C2
Nosy Bé, *island*, Madagascar, **372** B3
Nosy-Varika, Madagascar, **372** B5
Nota, *river*, Russian Federation, **285** P3
Notch Peak, *mountain peak*, U.S.A., **422** G2
Notio Aigaio, *administrative region*, Greece, **297** E7
Notio Steno Kerkyras, *channel*, Greece, **297** C6
Notodden, Norway, **286** D3
Notre Dame, Monts, *mountain range*, Canada, **416** F7
Notre Dame Bay, Canada, **417** P5
Notre-Dame-de-la-Salette, Canada, **426** C2
Notre-Dame-du-Nord, Canada, **416** B6
Notsé, Togo, **364** E3
Nottaway, *river*, Canada, **416** B4
Nottingham, England, U.K., **305** F2
Nottingham City, *unitary authority*, England, U.K., **305** F2
Nottingham Island, Canada, **411** M3
Nottinghamshire, *unitary authority*, England, U.K., **305** F1
Nottoway, *river*, U.S.A., **426** A6
Nouâdhibou, Mauritania, **360** C4
Nouâdhibou, Râs, *cape*, Western Sahara, **360** C4

Obispos, Venezuela, **451** D2
Obluch'ye, Russian Federation, **211** K2
Obninsk, Russian Federation, **299** F5
Obo, Central African Republic, **369** E1
Obo, China, **213** J5
Obock, Djibouti, **367** F2
Obokote, Democratic Republic of the Congo, **369** E3
Obol', Belarus, **299** B5
Obol', *river*, Belarus, **299** B5
Oborniki, Poland, **289** H2
Obouya, Congo, **368** C3
Obrenovac, Yugoslavia, **296** C3
O'Brien, U.S.A., **418** C5
Obrochishte, Bulgaria, **296** F4
Obrovac, Croatia, **294** E3
Obskaya Guba, *gulf*, Russian Federation, **300** J3
Obuasi, Ghana, **364** D3
Obytichna Kosa, *physical feature*, Ukraine, **298** E3
Ocala, U.S.A., **425** L5
Ocaña, Andalucía, Spain, **293** F4
Ocaña, Castilla la Mancha, Spain, **293** F3
Ocaña, Colombia, **450** D2
Ocate, U.S.A., **423** L3
Occidental, Cordillera, *mountain range*, Chile/Peru, **447** E5
Occidental, Cordillera, *mountain range*, Colombia, **447** E3
Ocean *see* Banaba, *island*, Kiribati, **139** F5
Ocean Beach, New Zealand, **132** E2
Ocean City, Maryland, U.S.A., **426** C5
Ocean City, New Jersey, U.S.A., **426** C5
Ocean Springs, U.S.A., **425** H4
Oceanographer Fracture Zone, *tectonic feature*, Atlantic Ocean, **477** D3
Oceanside, U.S.A., **422** E5
Ochil Hills, Scotland, U.K., **308** F4
Ocho Rios, Jamaica, **429** F3
Ochopee, U.S.A., **425** M7
Ochthonia, Greece, **297** E6
Ocilla, U.S.A., **425** L4
Ockelbo, Sweden, **287** H2
Ocmulgee, *river*, U.S.A., **425** L3
Ocna Sibiului, Romania, **296** E3
Ocnița, Moldova, **296** F1
Ococingo, Mexico, **431** G5
Oconee, Lake, U.S.A., **425** L3
Ocotal, Nicaragua, **428** D4
Ocotepeque, Honduras, **428** C4
Ocotillo Wells, U.S.A., **422** E5
Ocotlán, Mexico, **430** E4
Ocracoke, U.S.A., **426** C7
Ocreza, *river*, Portugal, **292** D3
Octavia, U.S.A., **424** E2
Octeville, France, **305** F5
Oda, Ghana, **364** D3
Oda, Jabal, *mountain peak*, Sudan, **363** G4
Ōda, Japan, **208** F4
Oda, Ras, *point*, Egypt, **363** G4
ūdáðahraun, *lava field*, Iceland, **284** Y7
Ōdate, Japan, **209** H2
Odawara, Japan, **209** G4
Odda, Norway, **286** C2
Odeceixe, Portugal, **292** C4
Odemira, Portugal, **292** C4
Ödemiş, Turkey, **224** C5
Ōdèngk, Cambodia, **203** E4
Odensbacken, Sweden, **286** G3
Odense, Denmark, **286** E5
Oder *see* Odra, *river*, Germany/ Poland, **280** F5
Oderhaff, *lake*, Germany, **289** G2
Odesa (Odessa), Ukraine, **298** D3
Ödeshög, Sweden, **286** G3

Odes'ka Oblast', *province*, Ukraine, **296** G2
Odessa *see* Odesa, Ukraine, **298** D3
Odessa, U.S.A., **423** M6
Odienné, Côte d'Ivoire, **364** C3
Odintsovo, Russian Federation, **299** F5
Odobești, Romania, **296** F3
O'Donnell, U.S.A., **424** B3
Odorheiu Secuiesc, Romania, **296** E2
Odoyev, Russian Federation, **299** F6
Odra (Oder), *river*, Germany/ Poland, **280** F5
Odrzywół, Poland, **289** K3
Odžaci, Yugoslavia, **296** B3
Odžak, Bosnia and Herzegovina, **294** G3
Oebisfelde, Germany, **288** E2
Oeiras, Brazil, **453** E5
Oeno Island, Pitcairn Islands, **137** H3
Ofaqim, Israel, **225** C4
Offa, Nigeria, **365** E3
Offaly, *county*, Ireland, **309** E4
Offenbach am Main, Germany, **288** D3
Offenburg, Germany, **288** C4
Offranville, France, **305** J5
Ofidoussa, *island*, Kyklades, Greece, **297** E7
Ofu, *island*, American Samoa, **141** B2
Ofu, *island*, Vava'u Group, Tonga, **141** B3
Ōfunato, Japan, **209** H3
Ogachi, Japan, **209** H3
Ogaden, *region*, Ethiopia, **367** F3
Ogallala, U.S.A., **420** C5
Ogan, *river*, Indonesia, **200** D3
Ogasawara-shotō, *islands*, Japan, **138** B2
Ogbomosho, Nigeria, **365** E3
Ogden, U.S.A., **420** F4
Ogeechee, *river*, U.S.A., **425** L3
Ogema, Canada, **419** M2
Ogilvie Mountains, *mountain range*, Canada, **410** F3
Oglala, U.S.A., **420** B4
Ognon, *river*, France, **291** G3
Ogoamas, Gunung, *mountain peak*, Indonesia, **198** C2
Ogoja, Nigeria, **365** F3
Ogoki, Canada, **415** M6
Ogoki, *river*, Canada, **415** L6
Ogoki Reservoir, Canada, **415** K6
Ogooué, *river*, Gabon, **368** A3
Ogooué-Ivindo, *province*, Gabon, **368** B2
Ogooué-Lolo, *province*, Gabon, **368** B3
Ogooué-Maritime, *province*, Gabon, **368** A3
Ogorelyshi, Russian Federation, **285** S5
Ogre, Latvia, **287** M4
Ogulin, Croatia, **294** E3
Ogun, *state*, Nigeria, **365** E3
Ogurjaly, *island*, Turkmenistan, **222** E5
Ohakune, New Zealand, **132** E4
Ohanet, Algeria, **361** H3
Ohangwena, *administrative region*, Namibia, **370** C2
Ohau, Lake, New Zealand, **133** B7
Ohau, New Zealand, **132** E5
Ohaupo, New Zealand, **132** E3
O'Higgins, Cabo, *cape*, Isla de Pascua (Easter Island), Chile, **461** B2
O'Higgins, Lago, *lake*, Chile, **460** B3
O'Higgins, Punta, *point*, Róbinson Crusoe Island, Archipiélago Juan Fernández, Chile, **461** C2
Ohio, *river*, U.S.A., **407** Q5
Ohio, *state*, U.S.A., **421** M5

'Ohonua, Tongatapu Group, Tonga, **141** B4
Ohře, *river*, Czech Republic, **289** F3
Ohrid, Lake *see* Ohridsko Jezero, *lake*, Macedonia, **297** C5
Ohrid, Macedonia, **297** C5
Ohridsko Jezero (Lake Ohrid), *lake*, Macedonia, **297** C5
Ohura, New Zealand, **132** E4
Oiapoque, Brazil, **452** C2
Oijärvi, Finland, **285** N4
Oil City, U.S.A., **421** P5
Oir, Beinn an, *mountain peak*, Scotland, U.K., **308** C5
Oise, *river*, France, **291** F2
Oisemont, France, **305** J5
Ōita, Japan, **208** E4
Oiti Oros, *mountain peak*, Greece, **297** D6
Öje, Sweden, **286** F2
Ojibwa, U.S.A., **420** H3
Ojinaga, Mexico, **430** D2
Ojo de Laguna, Mexico, **430** D2
Ojos del Salado, *mountain peak*, Argentina/Chile, **458** C3
Ōjung, Sweden, **286** G2
Ok Tedi, Papua New Guinea, **140** A4
Oka, *river*, Russian Federation, **299** F5
Okaba, Indonesia, **199** G5
Okahandja, Namibia, **370** C3
Okaihau, New Zealand, **132** D2
Okak Islands, Canada, **411** N4
Okakarara, Namibia, **370** C3
Okanagan Lake, Canada, **418** E2
Okaputa, Namibia, **370** C3
Okāra, Pakistan, **218** C3
Okarito Lagoon, *bay*, New Zealand, **133** B6
Okaukuejo, Namibia, **370** C2
Okavango, *administrative region*, Namibia, **370** C2
Okavango, *river*, Southern Africa, **357** G8
Okavango Delta, Botswana, **370** D2
Okawa Point, Chatham Islands, New Zealand, **133** Q16
Okaya, Japan, **209** G3
Okayama, Japan, **208** F4
Okazize, Namibia, **370** C3
Okeechobee, Lake, U.S.A., **425** M6
Okeechobee, U.S.A., **425** M6
Okehampton, England, U.K., **304** C4
Okemah, U.S.A., **424** D2
Okha, Russian Federation, **301** R4
Okhaldhungā, Nepal, **219** F4
Okhotsk, Russian Federation, **301** R4
Okhotsk, Sea of *see* Okhotskoye More, *sea*, Russian Federation, **301** R4
Okhotskoye More (Sea of Okhotsk), *sea*, Russian Federation, **301** R4
Okhtan-Yarvi, Ozero, *lake*, Russian Federation, **285** Q4
Oki-shotō, *islands*, Japan, **208** F3
Okinawa, Japan, **209** N8
Okinawa-jima, *island*, Japan, **209** P8
Okinawa-shotō, *islands*, Japan, **209** N8
Okino-Tori-shima, *island*, Japan, **138** B2
Okinoerabu-jima, *island*, Japan, **209** P8
Okiore, New Zealand, **132** F4
Oklahoma, *state*, U.S.A., **424** C2
Oklahoma City, U.S.A., **424** D2
Okmulgee, U.S.A., **424** E2
Okondja, Gabon, **368** B3
Okotoks, Canada, **413** M6
Okoyo, Congo, **368** C3

Okpo, Myanmar, **205** B4
Okreek, U.S.A., **420** C4
Oksbøl, Denmark, **286** D5
Øksfjord, Norway, **285** L1
Oktyabr'sk, Kazakhstan, **222** F3
Oktyabr'skiy, Russian Federation, **222** E2
Oktyabr'skoy Revolyutsii, Ostrov, *island*, Russian Federation, **300** L2
Okučani, Croatia, **294** F3
Okulovka, Russian Federation, **299** D3
Okurcalar, Turkey, **225** A1
Okushiri-tō, *island*, Japan, **209** G2
Okuta, Nigeria, **365** E3
Ola, U.S.A., **418** F4
ūlafsfjörður, Iceland, **284** Y6
Olaine, Latvia, **287** L4
Olal, Vanuatu, **141** A2
Olanchito, Honduras, **428** D4
Öland, *island*, Sweden, **287** H4
Olanga, *river*, Finland/Russian Federation, **285** Q3
Olathe, U.S.A., **420** F6
Olavarría, Argentina, **459** E5
Olbia, Sardegna, Italy, **295** B5
Old Crow, Canada, **410** F3
Old Faithful, U.S.A., **419** J4
Old Forge, U.S.A., **426** C3
Old Head of Kinsale, *point*, Ireland, **309** D6
Old Leake, England, U.K., **305** H1
Old Orchard Beach, U.S.A., **426** E3
Old Town, U.S.A., **426** F2
Old Wives Lake, Canada, **413** R6
Oldcastle, Ireland, **309** E4
Oldenburg in Holstein, Germany, **288** E1
Olderfjord, Norway, **285** M1
Oldervik, Norway, **284** J2
Oldham, England, U.K., **306** F4
Oldmeldrum, Scotland, U.K., **308** G3
Olds, Canada, **413** M6
Öldziyt, Arhangay, Mongolia, **213** J2
Öldziyt, Dorngovĭ, Mongolia, **210** L3
Olean, U.S.A., **426** A3
Olecko, Poland, **289** L1
Olekminsk, Russian Federation, **301** P3
Oleksandriya, Ukraine, **298** D3
Olenegorsk, Russian Federation, **285** R2
Olenek, *river*, Russian Federation, **301** N3
Olenino, Russian Federation, **299** D4
Olenitsa, Russian Federation, **285** S3
Oleniy, Ostrov, *island*, Russian Federation, **285** S4
Olen'ya Rechka, Russian Federation, **213** G1
Oléron, Île d', *island*, France, **290** D4
Oles'ko, Ukraine, **289** M4
Oleśnica, Poland, **289** H3
Olesno, Poland, **289** J3
Ølfjellet, *mountain peak*, Norway, **284** G3
Olga, Mount *see* Katatjuta, *mountain peak*, Australia, **134** G4
Ol'ga, Russian Federation, **211** L4
Ol'ginsk, Russian Federation, **211** L1
Ölgiy, Mongolia, **212** F2
Ølgod, Denmark, **286** D5
Olhava, Finland, **285** M4
Olib, *island*, Croatia, **294** E3
Olímpia, Brazil, **456** D5
Olinalá, Mexico, **431** F5
Olinda, Brazil, **453** G5
Olinga, Mozambique, **369** G6
Olingskog, Sweden, **286** G2
Oliva, Argentina, **458** D4

Oliva, Cordillera de, *mountain range*, Argentina/Chile, **458** C3
Oliva, Spain, **293** G3
Olivares, Cerro de, *mountain peak*, Argentina/Chile, **458** C4
Olivares de Júcar, Spain, **293** F3
Olive, U.S.A., **419** M4
Olive Hill, U.S.A., **421** M6
Oliveira, Brazil, **457** E5
Oliveira dos Brejinhos, Brazil, **457** E3
Olivenza, Spain, **292** D3
Oliver, Canada, **413** K7
Oliver Lake, Canada, **414** C3
Ölkeyek, *river*, Kazakhstan, **222** G3
Ol'khon, Ostrov, *island*, Russian Federation, **210** D1
Olkusz, Poland, **289** J3
Ollagüe, Chile, **455** E5
Ollagüe, Volcán, *mountain peak*, Bolivia/Chile, **455** E5
Ollita, Cordillera de, *mountain range*, Argentina/Chile, **458** B4
Ollombo, Congo, **368** C3
Olmedo, Spain, **292** E2
Olmillos de Sasamon, Spain, **293** F1
Olmos, Peru, **454** B1
Olney, England, U.K., **305** G2
Olney, U.S.A., **421** J6
Olofström, Sweden, **286** G4
Olomane, *river*, Canada, **417** L4
Olomouc, Czech Republic, **289** H4
Olonets, Russian Federation, **299** D2
Olongapo, Philippines, **204** C3
Olonzac, France, **290** F5
Oloron-Sainte-Marie, France, **290** D5
Olosega, *island*, American Samoa, **141** B2
Olot, Spain, **293** J1
Olovo, Bosnia and Herzegovina, **294** G3
Olovyannaya, Russian Federation, **210** F2
Olpe, Germany, **288** C3
Ol'sha, Russian Federation, **299** C5
Olsztyn, Poland, **289** K2
Olsztynek, Poland, **289** K2
Olt, *river*, Romania, **296** E3
Olten, Switzerland, **291** H3
Oltenița, Romania, **296** F3
Oltina, Romania, **296** F3
Olton, U.S.A., **424** A2
Olutlanga Island, Philippines, **204** C5
Olympia, U.S.A., **418** C3
Olympic Mountains, *mountain range*, U.S.A., **418** C3
Olympos, *mountain peak*, Cyprus, **225** B2
Olympos, Oros (Mount Olympus), *mountain peak*, Greece, **280** G7
Olympus, Mount, *mountain peak*, U.S.A., **418** C3
Olympus, Mount *see* Olympos Oros, *mountain peak*, Greece, **280** G7
Olyutorskiy, Mys, *cape*, Russian Federation, **301** U4
Om', *river*, Russian Federation, **223** L1
Om Hájer, Eritrea, **367** E2
Oma, China, **219** E2
Ōma, Japan, **209** H2
Oma, Russian Federation, **300** F3
Ōmagari, Japan, **209** H3
Omagh, *district*, Northern Ireland, U.K., **309** E3
Omagh, Northern Ireland, U.K., **309** E3
Omaguas, Peru, **450** D5
Omaha, U.S.A., **420** F5
Omaheke, *administrative region*, Namibia, **370** C3

Omak, U.S.A., **418** E2
Omakau, New Zealand, **133** B7
Omakere, New Zealand, **132** F5
Oman, *country*, Asia, **196** G8
Oman, Gulf of, Arabian Peninsula/Iran, **221** G4
Omarama, New Zealand, **133** B7
Omaruru, Namibia, **370** C3
Omate, Peru, **454** D4
Ombalantu, Namibia, **370** B2
Ombella-Mpoko, *prefecture*, Central African Republic, **368** C1
Ombersley, England, U.K., **304** E2
Ombo, *island*, Norway, **286** B3
Omboué, Gabon, **368** A3
Ombu, China, **214** C3
Omdurman *see* Umm Durmān, Sudan, **366** D1
Ometepec, Mexico, **431** F5
Omineca, *river*, Canada, **412** G4
Omineca Mountains, *mountain range*, Canada, **412** F3
Omiš, Croatia, **294** F4
Ömnögovĭ, *province*, Mongolia, **213** J4
Omo, *river*, Ethiopia, **367** E3
Omoku, Nigeria, **365** F3
Omolon, *river*, Russian Federation, **301** S3
Ömossa, Finland, **287** K1
Omsk, Russian Federation, **223** J2
Omskaya Oblast', *province*, Russian Federation, **223** J1
Omsukchan, Russian Federation, **301** S3
Ōmura, Japan, **208** E4
Omurtag, Bulgaria, **296** F4
Omusati, *administrative region*, Namibia, **370** B2
Ōmuta, Japan, **208** E4
Omutinskiy, Russian Federation, **222** H1
Ona, *river*, Russian Federation, **212** F2
Onalaska, U.S.A., **420** H4
Onaping Lake, U.S.A., **421** N2
Onavas, Mexico, **430** C2
Onaway, U.S.A., **421** L3
Oncativo, Argentina, **458** D4
Onchan, Isle of Man, **306** D3
Oncócua, Angola, **368** B6
Ondangwa, Namibia, **370** C2
Ondava, *river*, Slovakia, **289** K4
Onder, India, **218** D4
Ondjiva, Angola, **368** C6
Ondo, Nigeria, **365** E3
Ondo, *state*, Nigeria, **365** E3
Öndörhaan, Mongolia, **210** E3
Öndörhushuu, Mongolia, **210** F3
Ondozero, Ozero, *lake*, Russian Federation, **285** R5
One and Half Degree Channel, Maldives, **216** C6
100 Mile House, Canada, **412** J6
Onega, *river*, Russian Federation, **281** H3
Oneida, U.S.A., **426** C3
Oneida Lake, U.S.A., **426** B3
O'Neill, U.S.A., **420** D4
Onekotan, Ostrov, *island*, Russian Federation, **301** S5
Oneonta, Alabama, U.S.A., **425** J3
Oneonta, New York, U.S.A., **426** C3
Onești, Romania, **296** F2
Onetar, Vanuatu, **141** A2
Onevai, *island*, Tonga, **141** B4
Onezhskaya Guba, *bay*, Russian Federation, **285** S4
Onezhskiy Poluostrov, *peninsula*, Russian Federation, **285** T4
Onezhskoye Ozero, *lake*, Russian Federation, **299** E2
Onga, Gabon, **368** B3
Ongandjera, Namibia, **370** B2
Onggunoi, Indonesia, **198** D2
Ongi, Mongolia, **213** J3
Ongiyn, *river*, Mongolia, **213** J3
Ongjin, North Korea, **208** D3
Ongniud Qi, China, **211** G4
Ongole, India, **216** E3
Ongon, Mongolia, **213** J3
Onguday, Russian Federation, **212** E2
Onida, U.S.A., **420** C3
Onitsha, Nigeria, **365** F3
Ono, *island*, Fiji, **141** A4
Ōnojō, Japan, **208** E4
Onokhoy, Russian Federation, **210** E2
Onon, *river*, Mongolia, **210** E2
Onor, China, **211** H2
Onotoa, *island*, Kiribati, **139** F5
Ons, Illa de, *island*, Spain, **292** C1
Onseepkans, South Africa, **370** C4
Onslow, Australia, **134** D3
Onslow Bay, U.S.A., **425** P2
Ontario, Lake, Canada/U.S.A., **416** B8
Ontario, *province*, Canada, **415** K6
Ontario, U.S.A., **418** F4
Ontonagon, U.S.A., **421** J2
Ontong Java, *island*, Solomon Islands, **138** E5
Ontur, Spain, **293** G3
Onverwacht, Suriname, **452** B2
Onycha, U.S.A., **425** J4
Oodnadatta, Australia, **135** H4
Oodweyne, Somalia, **367** G3
Oologah Lake, U.S.A., **420** F7
Oost-Vaanderen, *province*, Belgium, **288** A3
Oostende, Belgium, **288** A3
Oostpunt, *point*, Curaçao, Netherlands Antilles, **461** C3
Ootsa Lake, Canada, **412** F5
Opal, U.S.A., **419** J6
Opala, Democratic Republic of the Congo, **368** D3
Opari, Sudan, **369** F2
Opasatika, Canada, **415** N7
Opatija, Croatia, **294** E3
Opatów, Poland, **289** K3
Opava, Czech Republic, **289** H4
Opelika, U.S.A., **425** K3
Opelousas, U.S.A., **424** F4
Opheim, U.S.A., **419** L2
Ophir, Gunung, *mountain peak*, Indonesia, **200** C2
Opienge, Democratic Republic of the Congo, **369** E2
Opinaca, Réservoir, Canada, **416** C3
Opobo, Nigeria, **368** A2
Opochka, Russian Federation, **299** B4
Opoczno, Poland, **289** K3
Opole, Poland, **289** H3
Opole Lubelskie, Poland, **289** K3
Opotiki, New Zealand, **132** F4
Opp, U.S.A., **425** J4
Oppdal, Norway, **286** D1
Oppland, *county*, Norway, **286** D2
Opsa, Belarus, **287** N5
Opua, New Zealand, **132** E2
Opunake, New Zealand, **132** D4
Opuwo, Namibia, **370** B2
Oq-Suu, *river*, Tajikistan, **223** J5
Oracle, U.S.A., **423** H5
Oradea, Romania, **296** C2
Orahov Do, Bosnia and Herzegovina, **294** F4
Orahovac, Yugoslavia, **296** C4
Orahovica, Croatia, **294** F3
Orai, India, **218** D4
Oral, Kazakhstan, **222** E2
Oran, Algeria, **361** F1
Orange, Australia, **135** K5
Orange, Cabo, *cape*, Brazil, **452** C2
Orange, France, **291** G4
Orange, Louisiana, U.S.A., **424** F4
Orange, *river*, Namibia/South Africa, **370** C4
Orange, Virginia, U.S.A., **426** A5
Orange Walk, Belize, **428** C3
Orangeburg, U.S.A., **425** M3
Orangerie Bay, Papua New Guinea, **140** C5
Orango, *island*, Guinea-Bissau, **364** A2
Oranienburg, Germany, **288** F2
Oranje Gebergte, *mountain range*, Suriname, **452** B2
Oranjemund, Namibia, **370** C4
Oranjestad, Aruba, **461** B3
Oranmore, Ireland, **309** D4
Oransbari, Indonesia, **199** F3
Orap, Vanuatu, **141** A2
Orapa, Botswana, **371** E3
Orăștie, Romania, **296** D3
Orava, *river*, Slovakia, **289** J4
Oravița, Romania, **296** C3
Orawia, New Zealand, **133** A8
Orbec, France, **290** E2
Orbetello, Italy, **295** C4
ūrbigo, *river*, Spain, **292** E1
Orbost, Australia, **135** K6
Orcadas, *Argentinian research station*, Antarctica, **470** B3
Orchard, Idaho, U.S.A., **418** G5
Orchard, Nebraska, U.S.A., **420** D4
Orcotuna, Peru, **454** C3
Ord, *river*, Australia, **134** F2
Orderville, U.S.A., **422** G3
Ordes, Spain, **292** C1
Ordu, Turkey, **224** E4
Ordway, U.S.A., **423** M2
Orealla, Guyana, **451** H3
Orebić, Croatia, **294** F4
Örebro, *county*, Sweden, **286** G3
Örebro, Sweden, **286** G3
Oredezh, *river*, Russian Federation, **299** C3
Oredezh, Russian Federation, **299** C3
Oregon, *state*, U.S.A., **418** D4
Oregon, U.S.A., **421** J4
Oregon City, U.S.A., **418** C4
Oregon Inlet, U.S.A., **426** C7
Orekhovo-Zuyevo, Russian Federation, **299** G5
Orel, Russian Federation, **298** E2
Orellana, N. Peru, **454** B1
Orellana, on Ucayali, *river*, Peru, **454** C2
Ören, Turkey, **297** F7
Orenburg, Russian Federation, **222** F2
Orenburgskaya Oblast', *province*, Russian Federation, **222** E2
Orense, Argentina, **459** E6
Orepuki, New Zealand, **133** A8
Orere, New Zealand, **132** E3
Orestiada, Greece, **297** F5
Oreti, *river*, New Zealand, **133** B7
Orford, England, U.K., **305** J2
Orford Ness, *spit*, England, U.K., **305** J2
Organ, U.S.A., **423** K5
Organabo, French Guiana, **452** C2
Orgaz, Spain, **293** F3
Orgil, Mongolia, **213** H2
Orgiva, Spain, **293** F4
Örgön, Mongolia, **213** J3
Orhaneli, Turkey, **297** G6
Orhei, Moldova, **296** G2
Orhon, *river*, Mongolia, **210** D2
Orhontuul, Mongolia, **210** D2
Orhy, Pic d', *mountain peak*, France/Spain, **293** G1
Orick, U.S.A., **418** B6
Oriental, Cordillera, *mountain range*, Bolivia, **447** F5
Oriental, Cordillera, *mountain range*, Colombia, **447** E3
Oriente, Argentina, **458** E6
Orihuela, Spain, **293** G3
Orillia, Canada, **421** P3
Orimattila, Finland, **287** M2
Orin, U.S.A., **419** M5
Orinduik, Guyana, **451** G3
Orinoco, *river*, Venezuela, **447** F3
Oriomo, Papua New Guinea, **140** A5
Orissa, *state*, India, **217** E2
Orissaare, Estonia, **287** L3
Oristano, Golfo di, *gulf*, Italy, **295** A6
Oristano, Sardegna, Italy, **295** B6
Orivesi, *lake*, Finland, **287** P1
Oriximina, Brazil, **452** B3
Orizaba, Mexico, **431** F5
Orizaba, Pico de *see* Citlaltepetl, Volcán, *mountain peak*, Mexico, **431** F5
Orkanger, Norway, **284** D5
Örkelljunga, Sweden, **286** F4
Orkla, *river*, Norway, **284** D5
Orkney, *local authority*, Scotland, U.K., **308** F1
Orkney Islands, Scotland, U.K., **308** F1
Orla, U.S.A., **423** M6
Orlândia, Brazil, **456** D5
Orlando, U.S.A., **425** M5
Orléans, France, **290** E3
Orleans, U.S.A., **426** F4
Orlické hory, *mountain range*, Czech Republic, **289** H3
Orlik, Russian Federation, **213** H1
Orlovka, Russian Federation, **223** K1
Orlovskaya Oblast', *province*, Russian Federation, **299** E6
Ormāra, Pakistan, **221** H3
Ormea, Italy, **294** A3
Ormoc, Philippines, **204** D4
Ormond Beach, U.S.A., **425** M5
Ormskirk, England, U.K., **306** F4
Ormylia, Greece, **297** D5
Ørnes, Norway, **284** F3
Orneta, Poland, **289** K1
Ornö, *island*, Sweden, **287** J3
Örnsköldsvik, Sweden, **284** J5
Oro *see* Northern, *province*, Papua New Guinea, **140** C5
Orobie, Alpi, *mountain range*, Italy, **294** B3
Orocué, Colombia, **450** D2
Orodara, Burkina Faso, **364** D2
Orofino, U.S.A., **418** F3
Orog Nuur, *lake*, Mongolia, **213** H3
Orogrande, U.S.A., **423** K5
Oromocto, Canada, **416** H7
Oron, Israel, **225** C4
Oron, Nigeria, **368** A2
Oron, *river*, Jordan, **225** C4
Orona, *island*, Kiribati, **139** G5
Oroquieta, Philippines, **204** C4
Orós, Açude, *reservoir*, Brazil, **453** F5
Orosei, Golfo di, *gulf*, Sardegna, Italy, **295** B5
Orosei, Sardegna, Italy, **295** B5
Orosháza, Hungary, **289** K5
Orovada, U.S.A., **418** F6
Oroville, Lake, U.S.A., **422** C2
Oroville, U.S.A., **422** C2
Orpesa, Spain, **293** H2
Orphir, Orkney, Scotland, U.K., **308** F2
Orqen Zizhiqi, China, **211** H2
Orqohan, China, **211** H2
Orr, Mount, *mountain peak*, New Zealand, **133** C7
Orrin, *river*, Scotland, U.K., **308** E3
Orsa, Sweden, **286** G2
Orsha, Belarus, **299** C5
Örsjö, Sweden, **286** G4
Orsk, Russian Federation, **222** F2
Orșova, Romania, **296** D3
Ørsta, Norway, **286** C1
Ørsted, Denmark, **286** E4
Örsundsbro, Sweden, **287** H3
Orta, Lago d', *lake*, Italy, **294** B3
Orta Nova, Italy, **295** E5
Ortaca, Turkey, **297** G7
Orte, Italy, **295** D4
Ortegal, Cabo, *cape*, Spain, **292** C1
Orthez, France, **290** D5
Ortigueira, Spain, **292** D1
Orting, U.S.A., **418** C3
Ortiz, Mexico, **430** C2
Ortiz, Venezuela, **451** E2
Ortoire, *river*, Trinidad, Trinidad and Tobago, **461** C4
Orton, England, U.K., **306** F3
Ortón, *river*, Bolivia, **455** E3
Ortona, Italy, **295** E4
Ortonville, U.S.A., **420** E3
Örträsk, Sweden, **284** J4
Orulgan, Khrebet, *mountain range*, Russian Federation, **301** P3
Orūmīyeh, Daryācheh-ye, *lake*, Iran, **363** J1
Orūmīyeh (Urmia), Iran, **363** H1
Oruro, Bolivia, **455** E4
Oruro, *department*, Bolivia, **455** E5
Orust, *island*, Sweden, **286** E3
Orvieto, Italy, **294** C4
Orville Coast, *region*, Antarctica, **470** B5
Orwell, U.S.A., **421** N5
Oryakhovo, Bulgaria, **296** D4
Orynyn, Ukraine, **296** F1
Orzysz, Poland, **289** K2
Os, Norway, **286** E1
Osa, Península de, Costa Rica, **428** E5
Osa, Russian Federation, **222** F1
Osage, U.S.A., **420** G4
Ōsaka, Japan, **209** F4
Osakarovka, Kazakhstan, **212** B2
Osawatomie, U.S.A., **420** F6
Osby, Sweden, **286** G4
Oscar, French Guiana, **452** C2
Osceola, U.S.A., **420** E5
Oschiri, Sardegna, Italy, **295** B5
Oscoda, U.S.A., **421** M3
Osečina, Yugoslavia, **296** B3
Osen, Norway, **284** E4
Osera, Spain, **293** G2
Osh, Kyrgyzstan, **223** J4
Oshakati, Namibia, **370** C2
Oshamambe, Japan, **209** H2
Oshana, *administrative region*, Namibia, **370** C2
Oshawa, Canada, **421** P4
Oshikango, Namibia, **370** C2
Oshikoto, *administrative region*, Namibia, **370** C2
Oshkosh, Nebraska, U.S.A., **420** B5
Oshkosh, Wisconsin, U.S.A., **421** J3
Oshogbo, Nigeria, **365** E3
Oshwe, Democratic Republic of the Congo, **368** C3
Osiān, India, **218** C4
Osie, Poland, **289** J2
Osijek, Croatia, **294** G3
Oskaloosa, U.S.A., **420** G5
Oskarshamn, Sweden, **286** H4
Oskarström, Sweden, **286** F4
Oskélanéo, Canada, **416** D5
Öskemen, Kazakhstan, **212** D2
Oslo, *county*, Norway, **286** E3
Oslo, Norway, **286** E3
Oslofjorden, *fiord*, Norway, **286** E3
Osmānābād, India, **216** D2
Osmaniye, Turkey, **224** E5
Os'mino, Russian Federation, **299** B3
Osnabrück, Germany, **288** D2
Oso, U.S.A., **418** D2
Osogovske Planine, Bulgaria/Macedonia, **296** D4
Osório, Brazil, **459** G3
Osorno, Chile, **460** C1
Osorno, Volcán, *mountain peak*, Chile, **460** C1
Osoyoos, Canada, **413** K7

Ossa, Mount, *mountain peak*, Australia, **135** K7
Ossa, *mountain peak*, Portugal, **292** D3
Ossa de Montiel, Spain, **293** F3
Ossabaw Island, U.S.A., **425** M4
Osse, *river*, France, **290** E5
Ossima, Papua New Guinea, **140** A3
Ossjøen, *lake*, Norway, **286** E2
Östansjö, Sweden, **284** J4
Ostashkov, Russian Federation, **299** D4
Östavall, Sweden, **286** G1
Østby, Norway, **284** E5
Oster, *river*, Russian Federation, **299** D6
Øster Vrå, Denmark, **286** E4
Osterburg, Germany, **288** E2
Österbybruk, Sweden, **287** H2
Österbymo, Sweden, **286** G4
Österdalälven, *river*, Sweden, **286** F2
Østerdalen, *valley*, Norway, **286** F2
Österfärnebo, Sweden, **287** H2
Östergötland, *county*, Sweden, **286** G3
Östersund, Sweden, **284** G5
Østfold, *county*, Norway, **286** E3
Ostfriesische Inseln, *islands*, Germany, **288** C2
Östhammar, Sweden, **287** J2
Ostiglia, Italy, **294** C3
Ostrava, Czech Republic, **289** J4
Ostrogozhsk, Russian Federation, **298** E2
Ostróda, Poland, **289** K2
Ostrołęka, Poland, **289** K2
Ostrov, Pskovskaya Oblast', Russian Federation, **299** B4
Ostrov, Vologodskaya Oblast', Russian Federation, **299** F3
Ostrów Mazowiecka, Poland, **289** K2
Ostrów Wielkopolski, Poland, **289** H3
Ostrowiec Świętokrzyski, Poland, **289** K3
Ostrzeszów, Poland, **289** J3
Osttirol, *region*, Austria, **288** F5
Ostuni, Italy, **295** F5
Osům, *river*, Bulgaria, **296** E4
Ōsumi-shotō, *islands*, Japan, **208** E5
Osun, *state*, Nigeria, **365** E3
Osuna, Spain, **292** E4
Oswego, U.S.A., **426** B3
Oswestry, England, U.K., **304** D2
Oświęcim, Poland, **289** J3
Otago Peninsula, New Zealand, **133** C7
Otaika, New Zealand, **132** E2
Otaki, New Zealand, **133** E5
Otakiri, New Zealand, **132** F3
Otar, Kazakhstan, **212** B4
Otaru, Japan, **209** H2
Otavalo, Ecuador, **450** B4
Otavi, Namibia, **370** C2
Otelnuk, Lac, *lake*, Canada, **416** G1
Oţelu Roşu, Romania, **296** D3
Otematata, New Zealand, **133** C7
Otepää, Estonia, **287** N3
Othello, U.S.A., **418** E3
Othonoi, *island*, Ionioi Nisoi, Greece, **297** B6
Oti, *river*, Togo, **364** E2
Otish, Monts, *mountain range*, Canada, **416** F3
Otjiwarongo, Namibia, **370** C3
Otjozondjupa, *administrative region*, Namibia, **370** C2
Otley, England, U.K., **307** G4
Otnes, Norway, **286** E2
Otog Qi, China, **210** E5
Otog Qianqi, China, **210** D5
Otorohanga, New Zealand, **132** E4

Otorokua Point, New Zealand, **133** B6
Otra, *river*, Norway, **286** C3
Otrabanda, Curaçao, Netherlands Antilles, **461** C3
Otranto, Italy, **295** G5
Otranto, Strait of, Albania/Italy, **280** F7
Otsego, U.S.A., **421** L4
Otta, Norway, **286** D2
Otta, *river*, Norway, **286** C1
Ottawa, Canada, **416** D7
Ottawa, *river*, Canada, **416** C6
Ottawa, U.S.A., **420** F6
Ottawa Islands, Canada, **415** P2
Ottenby, Sweden, **286** H4
Otterburn, England, U.K., **306** F2
Otterndorf, Germany, **288** D2
Otterøy, Norway, **284** E4
Otterup, Denmark, **286** E5
Ottery, *river*, England, U.K., **304** C4
Otukpa, Nigeria, **365** F3
Otumpa, Argentina, **458** D3
Oturkpo, Nigeria, **365** F3
Otuzco, Peru, **454** B2
Otway, Bahía, *bay*, Chile, **460** B4
Otway, Cape, Australia, **135** J6
Otyniya, Ukraine, **296** E1
Ötztaler Alpen, *mountain range*, Austria, **288** E5
Ou, *river*, China, **206** E2
Ōu-sanmyaku, *mountain range*, Japan, **209** H2
Ouachita, Lake, U.S.A., **424** F2
Ouachita, *river*, U.S.A., **424** F3
Ouachita Mountains, *mountain range*, U.S.A., **424** F2
Ouadane, Mauritania, **360** D4
Ouadda, Central African Republic, **366** B3
Ouaddaï, *prefecture*, Chad, **366** B2
Ouagadougou, Burkina Faso, **364** D2
Ouahigouya, Burkina Faso, **364** D2
Ouaka, *prefecture*, Central African Republic, **368** D1
Oualâta, Mauritania, **364** C1
Ouallam, Niger, **365** E2
Ouanary, French Guiana, **452** C2
Ouanda Djallé, Central African Republic, **366** B3
Ouandago, Central African Republic, **366** A3
Ouando, Central African Republic, **369** E1
Ouango, Central African Republic, **368** D2
Ouangolodougou, Côte d'Ivoire, **364** C3
Ouaqui, French Guiana, **452** C2
Ouargaye, Burkina Faso, **364** E2
Ouargla, Algeria, **361** H2
Ouarkziz, Jebel, *mountain range*, Algeria/Morocco, **360** E3
Ouarzazate, Morocco, **360** E2
Oudtshoorn, South Africa, **370** D5
Oued Rhiou, Algeria, **293** H5
Ouégoa, New Caledonia, **141** A3
Ouéléssébougou, Mali, **364** C2
Ouessa, Burkina Faso, **364** D2
Ouessant, Île d', *island*, France, **290** B2
Ouésso, Congo, **368** C2
Ouest, *province*, Cameroon, **368** B1
Oughter, Lough, *lake*, Ireland, **309** E3
Oughterard, Ireland, **309** C4
Ouham, *prefecture*, Central African Republic, **365** H3
Ouham-Pendé, *prefecture*, Central African Republic, **365** H3
Ouidah, Benin, **365** E3

Oujda, Morocco, **361** F2
Oujeft, Mauritania, **360** D5
Oulad Teïma, Morocco, **360** E2
Oulainen, Finland, **285** M4
Ould Yenjé, Mauritania, **364** B1
Ouled Djellal, Algeria, **361** H2
Oulton Broad, England, U.K., **305** J2
Oulu, Finland, **285** M4
Oulujärvi, *lake*, Finland, **285** N4
Oulujoki, *river*, Finland, **285** M4
Oulun Lääni, *province*, Finland, **285** N4
Oulx, Italy, **294** A3
Oum-Chalouba, Chad, **366** B1
Oum el Bouaghi, Algeria, **361** H1
Oum-Hadjer, Chad, **366** A2
Oumm ed Droûs Guebli, Sebkhet, *salt-pan*, Mauritania, **360** D4
Oumm ed Droûs Telli, Sebkhet, *salt-pan*, Mauritania, **360** D4
Ounane, Djebel, *mountain peak*, Algeria, **361** H3
Ounara, Morocco, **360** E2
Ounasjoki, *river*, Finland, **285** M3
Oundle, England, U.K., **305** G2
Oungre, Canada, **414** C7
Ounianga Kébir, Chad, **362** D5
Ounianga Sérir, Chad, **362** D5
Oupu, China, **211** J1
Ouray, U.S.A., **423** K2
Ourém, Brazil, **452** D3
Ourense, Spain, **292** D1
Ouricuri, Brazil, **453** F5
Ouro Prêto, Brazil, **457** E5
Ourville-en-Caux, France, **305** H5
Ouse, *river*, E. Sussex, England, U.K., **305** H4
Ouse, *river*, Yorkshire, England, U.K., **307** H4
Outakoski, Finland, **285** N2
Outaouais, Rivière des, *river*, Canada, **416** B6
Outardes Quatre, Réservoir, Canada, **416** G4
Outer Hebrides, *islands*, Scotland, U.K., **308** B3
Outjo, Namibia, **370** C3
Outokumpu, Finland, **285** P5
Outram, New Zealand, **133** C7
Ouvéa, *island*, New Caledonia, **141** A3
Ouyen, Australia, **135** J6
Ovacık, Turkey, **363** G1
Ovada, Italy, **294** B3
Ovaka, *island*, Vava'u Group, Tonga, **141** B3
Ovalau, *island*, Fiji, **141** A4
Ovalle, Chile, **458** B4
Ovan, Gabon, **368** B2
Ovando, U.S.A., **418** H3
Ovar, Portugal, **292** C2
Oveng, Cameroon, **368** B2
Overbister, Orkney, Scotland, U.K., **308** G1
Överijssel, *province*, Netherlands, **288** C2
Överkalix, Sweden, **285** L3
Overland Park, U.S.A., **420** F6
Overlander Roadhouse, Australia, **134** C4
Overton, U.S.A., **422** F3
Overton, Wales, U.K., **304** E2
Övertorneå, Sweden, **285** L3
Överturingen, Sweden, **286** G1
Överum, Sweden, **286** H4
Övgödiy, Mongolia, **213** H2
Ovidiopol', Ukraine, **296** H2
Ovidiu, Romania, **296** G3
Oviedo, Spain, **292** E1
Ovino, Russian Federation, **299** D3
Oviši, Latvia, **287** K4
Ovoot, Mongolia, **210** F3
Övör-Ereen, Mongolia, **210** F2
Övre Soppero, Sweden, **284** K2
Övt, Mongolia, **213** J3

Owaka, New Zealand, **133** B8
Owando, Congo, **368** C3
Owase, Japan, **209** G4
Owase-zaki, *point*, Japan, **209** G4
Owego, U.S.A., **426** B3
Owel, Lough, *lake*, Ireland, **309** E4
Owen, Mount, *mountain peak*, New Zealand, **133** D5
Owen Fracture Zone, *tectonic feature*, Indian Ocean, **476** C4
Owen Head, *point*, New Zealand, **133** B8
Owen Sound, Canada, **421** N3
Owen Stanley Range, *mountain range*, Papua New Guinea, **128** D2
Owenga, Chatham Islands, New Zealand, **133** Q16
Owens, U.S.A., **426** B5
Owens Lake, U.S.A., **422** E3
Owensboro, U.S.A., **421** K7
Owerri, Nigeria, **368** A1
Owl, *river*, Alberta, Canada, **413** P4
Owl, *river*, Manitoba, Canada, **414** H3
Owo, Nigeria, **365** F3
Owosso, U.S.A., **421** L4
Owyhee, Lake, U.S.A., **418** F5
Owyhee, *river*, U.S.A., **418** F5
Owyhee, U.S.A., **418** F6
Oxapampa, Peru, **454** C3
Oxbow, Canada, **414** C7
Oxelösund, Sweden, **287** H3
Oxford, Canada, **417** K7
Oxford, England, U.K., **305** F3
Oxford, Mississippi, U.S.A., **425** H2
Oxford, Nebraska, U.S.A., **420** D5
Oxford, New Zealand, **133** D6
Oxford, North Carolina, U.S.A., **421** P7
Oxford Lake, Canada, **414** G4
Oxfordshire, *unitary authority*, England, U.K., **305** F3
Oxnard, U.S.A., **422** D4
Oxted, England, U.K., **305** H3
Oxylithos, Greece, **297** E6
Oyama, Japan, **209** G3
Oyapok, Baie d', *bay*, French Guiana, **452** C2
Oyapok, *river*, French Guiana, **452** C2
Oyat', *river*, Russian Federation, **299** E2
Øye, Norway, **286** D2
Oyem, Gabon, **368** B2
Oyen, Canada, **413** P6
Øyeren, *lake*, Norway, **286** E3
Oykel, *river*, Scotland, U.K., **308** E3
Oykel Bridge, Scotland, U.K., **308** E3
Oyo, Congo, **368** C3
Oyo, Nigeria, **365** E3
Oyo, *state*, Nigeria, **365** E3
Oyón, Peru, **454** C3
Oyster Island, Myanmar, **205** B4
Oysterville, U.S.A., **418** B3
Oytal, Kazakhstan, **223** J4
Oytal, Kyrgyzstan, **223** J4
Oytograk, China, **212** D5
Oyyl, Kazakhstan, **222** E3
Oyyl, *river*, Kazakhstan, **222** E3
Ozamiz, Philippines, **204** C4
Ozark Plateau, U.S.A., **424** E1
Ozarks, Lake of the, U.S.A., **420** G6
Ozbaşı, Turkey, **297** F7
üzd, Hungary, **289** K4
Özen, Kazakhstan, **222** E4
Ozernoy, Mys, *cape*, Russian Federation, **301** T4
Ozersk, Russian Federation, **287** L5
Ozery, Russian Federation, **299** G5
Özgön, Kyrgyzstan, **223** J4
Ozhukarai, India, **216** D3
Ozieri, Sardegna, Italy, **295** B5

Ozimek, Poland, **289** J3
Ozinki, Russian Federation, **222** D2
Ozizweni, South Africa, **371** F4
Ozona, U.S.A., **424** B4
Ozuluama, Mexico, **431** F4

P

Pa, *river*, China, **207** A1
Pa-an, Myanmar, **205** C4
Paamiut, Greenland, **411** Q3
Paarl, South Africa, **370** C5
Paavola, Finland, **285** M4
Pabbay, *island*, Central Western Isles, Scotland, U.K., **308** B3
Pabbay, *island*, S. Western Isles, Scotland, U.K., **308** B4
Pabianice, Poland, **289** J3
Pābna, Bangladesh, **214** D5
Pabradė, Lithuania, **287** M5
Pacaás Novos, Serra dos, *mountain range*, Brazil, **455** F3
Pacaraima, Serra, *mountain range*, Brazil/Venezuela, **447** F3
Pacasmayo, Peru, **454** B2
Pacheco, Isla, *island*, Chile, **460** B4
Pachino, Sicilia, Italy, **295** E7
Pachitea, *river*, Peru, **454** C2
Pachmarhi, India, **218** D5
Pachuca, Mexico, **431** F4
Pacific Antarctic Ridge, *underwater feature*, Pacific Ocean, **478** G8
Pacific Ocean, **478** F4
Pacific Ranges, *mountain range*, Canada, **412** F6
Pacitan, Indonesia, **201** E5
Packwood, U.S.A., **418** D3
Pacov, Czech Republic, **289** G4
Pacoval, Brazil, **452** B4
Pacoval, *river*, Brazil, **452** B4
Padam, India, **218** D2
Padamarang, Pulau, *island*, Indonesia, **198** C4
Padang, Indonesia, **200** C3
Padang, Pulau, *island*, Indonesia, **200** C2
Padangsidempuan, Indonesia, **200** B2
Padangtikar, Pulau, *island*, Indonesia, **201** E3
Padany, Russian Federation, **285** R5
Padasjoki, Finland, **287** M2
Padauari, Pico, *mountain peak*, Brazil, **451** F4
Padauari, *river*, Brazil, **451** F4
Padcaya, Bolivia, **455** F5
Paddle Prairie, Canada, **413** L3
Paderborn, Germany, **288** D3
Padilla, Bolivia, **455** F5
Padina, Romania, **296** F3
Padova, Italy, **294** C3
Padrão, Ponta do, *point*, Angola, **368** B4
Padre Island, U.S.A., **424** D6
Padrón, Spain, **292** C1
Padstow, England, U.K., **304** C4
Padsvillye, Belarus, **287** N5
Paducah, Kentucky, U.S.A., **421** J7
Paducah, Texas, U.S.A., **424** B2
Paektu-san, *mountain peak*, North Korea, **208** F1
Paeroa, *mountain peak*, New Zealand, **132** F4
Paeroa, New Zealand, **132** E3
Pafos, Cyprus, **225** B2
Pafuri, Mozambique, **371** F3
Pag, Croatia, **294** E3
Pag, *island*, Croatia, **294** E3
Paga, Indonesia, **198** C5
Paga Conta, Brazil, **452** B4

Pagadian, Philippines, **204** C5
Pagai Selatan, Pulau, *island*, Indonesia, **200** B3
Pagai Utara, Pulau, *island*, Indonesia, **200** B3
Pagan, *island*, Northern Mariana Islands, **138** C3
Pagan, Myanmar, **205** B3
Pagaralam, Indonesia, **200** C4
Pagasitikos Kolpos, *bay*, Greece, **297** D6
Pagatan, Indonesia, **201** F3
Page, U.S.A., **423** H3
Pagėgiai, Lithuania, **287** K5
Paget, Mount, *mountain peak*, South Georgia, **461** A3
Pago Pago, American Samoa, **141** B2
Pagoda Peak, *mountain peak*, U.S.A., **423** K1
Pagon, Gunung, *mountain peak*, Brunei, **201** F1
Pagri, China, **214** D4
Pahala, Hawaiian Islands, U.S.A., **422** R10
Pahang, *river*, Malaysia, **200** C2
Pahang, *state*, Malaysia, **200** C2
Pahlāgaon, Andaman and Nicobar Islands, India, **217** H3
Pahoa, Hawaiian Islands, U.S.A., **422** R10
Pahute Peak, *mountain peak*, U.S.A., **418** E6
Paiaguás, Brazil, **456** B5
Paide, Estonia, **287** M3
Paige, U.S.A., **424** D4
Paignton, England, U.K., **304** D4
Paihia, New Zealand, **132** E2
Päijänne, *lake*, Finland, **287** M2
Pail, Pakistan, **218** C2
Pailĭn, Cambodia, **203** D3
Paillaco, Chile, **460** C1
Pailolo Channel, Hawaiian Islands, U.S.A., **422** R9
Paimio, Finland, **287** L2
Paimpol, France, **290** C2
Painan, Indonesia, **200** C3
Paine, Chile, **458** B4
Painswick, England, U.K., **304** E3
Painted Desert, U.S.A., **423** H3
Paintsville, U.S.A., **421** M7
País Vasco, *autonomous community*, Spain, **293** F1
Paisley, Scotland, U.K., **308** E5
Paisley, U.S.A., **418** D5
Paita, Peru, **454** B1
Paitan, China, **207** B2
Paitan, Teluk, *bay*, Malaysia, **201** G1
Paittasjärvi, Sweden, **285** L2
Pajala, Sweden, **285** L3
Paján, Ecuador, **450** B4
Pájara, Islas Canarias, Spain, **373** B4
Pajares, Spain, **292** E1
Pajeú, *river*, Brazil, **453** G5
Pak Khat, Thailand, **203** D2
Pak Tam Chung, China, **207** C4
Pak Thong Chai, Thailand, **202** D3
Pakaraima Mountains, *mountain range*, Guyana, **451** G3
Pakaur, India, **219** F4
Pakch'ŏn, North Korea, **208** D3
Paki, Nigeria, **365** F2
Pakistan, *country*, Asia, **196** H7
Pakokku, Myanmar, **205** B3
Pakotai, New Zealand, **132** D2
Pakrac, Croatia, **294** F3
Paks, Hungary, **289** J5
Pakuli, Indonesia, **198** B3
Pakuratahi, New Zealand, **133** E5
Pakxé, Laos, **203** E3
Pala, Chad, **365** G3
Pala, U.S.A., **422** E5
Palacios, U.S.A., **424** D5
Palafrugell, Spain, **293** J2
Palaiochora, Kriti, Greece, **297** D8
Palairos, Greece, **297** C6
Palaiseau, France, **290** F2
Pālakollu, India, **217** E2
Palamas, Greece, **297** D6
Palame, Brazil, **457** G3
Palamós, Spain, **293** J2
Palampur, India, **218** D2
Palanan Point, Philippines, **204** C2
Palanga, Lithuania, **287** K5
Palangkaraya, Indonesia, **201** F3
Pālanpur, India, **218** C4
Palapye, Botswana, **371** E3
Palatka, U.S.A., **425** M5
Palau, *country*, Pacific Ocean, **130** C1
Palau, Sardegna, Italy, **295** B5
Palau Islands, Palau, **138** B4
Palaui Island, Philippines, **204** C2
Palaw, Myanmar, **202** C3
Palawan, *island*, Philippines, **204** B4
Palawan Passage, Philippines, **204** B4
Palawan Trough, *underwater feature*, South China Sea, **478** B4
Palayankottai, India, **216** D4
Paldiski, Estonia, **287** M3
Pale, Bosnia and Herzegovina, **294** G4
Paleleh, Pegunungan, *mountain range*, Indonesia, **198** C2
Palembang, *river*, Indonesia, **200** D3
Palen Lake, U.S.A., **422** F5
Palena, Chile, **460** C2
Palena, Lago, *lake*, Chile, **460** C2
Palencia, Spain, **292** E1
Palenque, Panama, **429** F5
Palermo, Sicilia, Italy, **295** D6
Palestine, Lake, U.S.A., **424** E3
Palestine, U.S.A., **424** E4
Paletwa, Myanmar, **205** B3
Pālghāt, India, **216** D4
Palgrave Point, Namibia, **370** B3
Pāli, India, **218** C4
Paliki, Russian Federation, **299** E6
Palikir, Micronesia, **138** D4
Palinuro, Italy, **295** E5
Paliouri, Akra, *point*, Greece, **297** D6
Palisade, U.S.A., **420** C5
Pālitāna, India, **218** B5
Pāliyād, India, **218** B5
Palk Strait, India/Sri Lanka, **216** D4
Palkino, Russian Federation, **299** B4
Palkonda, India, **217** E2
Pālkonda Range, *mountain range*, India, **216** D3
Pallas Grean, Ireland, **309** D5
Pallastunturi, *mountain peak*, Finland, **285** M2
Pallës, Bishti i, *point*, Albania, **297** B5
Pallisa, Uganda, **369** F2
Palliser, Cape, New Zealand, **133** E5
Palliser Bay, New Zealand, **133** E5
Pallu, India, **218** C3
Palm Bay, U.S.A., **425** M6
Palm Beach, U.S.A., **425** M6
Palm-Mar, Islas Canarias, Spain, **373** A4
Palm Springs, U.S.A., **422** E5
Palma, Mozambique, **369** H5
Palma, *river*, Brazil, **456** D3
Palma de Mallorca, Spain, **293** J3
Palma del Río, Spain, **292** E4
Palma Soriano, Cuba, **429** F2
Palmaner, India, **216** D3
Palmares, Acre, Brazil, **455** E3
Palmares, Pernambuco, Brazil, **457** G2
Palmares do Sul, Brazil, **459** G4
Palmarito, Venezuela, **451** D2
Palmas, Cape, Liberia, **364** C4
Palmas, Santa Catarina, Brazil, **459** G3
Palmas, Tocantins, Brazil, **456** D3
Palmas de Monte Alto, Brazil, **457** E4
Palmdale, U.S.A., **422** D4
Palmeira, Brazil, **459** H2
Palmeira das Missões, Brazil, **459** G3
Palmeira dos Indios, Brazil, **457** G2
Palmeirais, Brazil, **453** E4
Palmeiras, Brazil, **457** F3
Palmeiras de Goiás, Brazil, **456** D4
Palmeiras do Javari, Brazil, **450** D5
Palmeirinhas, Ponta das, *point*, Angola, **368** B4
Palmer, *U.S. research station*, Antarctica, **470** A4
Palmer, U.S.A., **410** E3
Palmer Land, *region*, Antarctica, **470** B4
Palmerston, Australia, **134** G1
Palmerston, *island*, Cook Islands, **137** E2
Palmerston, New Zealand, **133** C7
Palmerston North, New Zealand, **132** E5
Palmi, Italy, **295** E6
Palmillas, Mexico, **431** F4
Palmira, Colombia, **450** C3
Palmyra *see* Tadmur, Syria, **225** E2
Palmyra Atoll, *U.S. territory*, Pacific Ocean, **131** J1
Palmyras Point, India, **219** F5
Palo de las Letras, Colombia, **450** C2
Palo Santo, Argentina, **459** E2
Paloh, Indonesia, **201** E2
Paloich, Sudan, **366** D2
Palojärvi, Finland, **285** L2
Palojoensuu, Finland, **285** L2
Paloma, Punta, *point*, Islas Canarias, Spain, **373** B4
Palomani, *mountain peak*, Bolivia/Peru, **455** E4
Palomar Mountain, *mountain peak*, U.S.A., **422** E5
Palopo, Indonesia, **198** C3
Palos, Cabo de, *cape*, Spain, **293** G4
Palpa, Peru, **454** C4
Palpetu, Tanjong, *point*, Indonesia, **198** D3
Palu, Indonesia, **198** B3
Paluan, Philippines, **204** C3
Paluwat, *island*, Micronesia, **138** C4
Pamanukan, Indonesia, **201** D4
Pamar, Colombia, **450** D4
Pamdai, Indonesia, **199** G3
Pamekasan, Indonesia, **201** F4
Pāmgarh, India, **219** E5
Pamiers, France, **290** E5
Pamirs, *mountain range*, China/Tajikistan, **212** B5
Pamlico Sound, U.S.A., **426** B7
Pampa, U.S.A., **424** B2
Pampa Aullagas, Bolivia, **455** E5
Pampa de los Guanacos, Argentina, **458** E3
Pampa del Castillo, Argentina, **460** D2
Pampa Grande, Bolivia, **455** F4
Pampachiri, Peru, **454** D4
Pampas, Peru, **454** C3
Pampas, *plain*, Argentina, **447** F7
Pamplemousses, Mauritius, **373** C1
Pamplona, Colombia, **450** D2
Pamplona, Spain, **293** G1
Pampur, India, **218** C2
Pamukan, Teluk, *bay*, Indonesia, **201** G3
Pamukçu, Turkey, **297** F6
Pan, Phou, *mountain peak*, Laos, **203** E1
Pan Xian, China, **215** H4
Pana, Gabon, **368** B3
Pana, *river*, Russian Federation, **285** S3
Pana, U.S.A., **421** J6
Panabá, Mexico, **431** H4
Panaca, U.S.A., **422** F3
Panagtaran Point, Philippines, **204** B4
Panagyurishte, Bulgaria, **296** E4
Panaitan, Pulau, *island*, Indonesia, **200** D4
Panaji, India, **216** C3
Panama, *country*, Central America, **409** Q8
Panamá, Golfo de, *gulf*, Panama, **429** F6
Panamá, Panama, **429** F5
Panama Basin, *underwater feature*, Pacific Ocean, **479** N4
Panama Canal, Panama, **429** E5
Panama City, U.S.A., **425** K4
Panamint Range, *mountain range*, U.S.A., **422** E3
Panamint Springs, U.S.A., **422** E3
Panao, Peru, **454** C2
Panarea, Isola, *island*, Italy, **295** E6
Panay, *island*, Philippines, **204** C4
Panay Gulf, Philippines, **204** C4
Pančevo, Yugoslavia, **296** C3
Panciu, Romania, **296** F3
Pâncota, Romania, **296** C2
Panda, Mozambique, **371** F3
Pandan Reservoir, Singapore, **200** J7
Pandanan Island, Philippines, **204** B4
Pandegelang, Indonesia, **200** D4
Pandėlys, Lithuania, **287** M4
Pandharpur, India, **216** C2
Pāndhurna, India, **218** D5
Pando, *department*, Bolivia, **455** E3
Pandu, Democratic Republic of the Congo, **368** C2
Pandu, India, **219** G4
Panevėžys, Lithuania, **287** M5
Pang, Thailand, **202** C2
Pāng-yāng, Myanmar, **205** C3
Panga, Democratic Republic of the Congo, **369** E2
Pangai, Tongatapu Group, Tonga, **141** B4
Pangaimotu, *island*, Vava'u Group, Tonga, **141** B3
Pangani, Tanzania, **369** G4
Panganuran, Philippines, **204** C4
Pangeo, Indonesia, **199** E2
Pangi, Democratic Republic of The Congo, **369** E3
Pangkalanbrandan, Indonesia, **200** B1
Pangkalanbuun, Indonesia, **201** E3
Pangkalpinang, Indonesia, **200** D3
Pangman, Canada, **419** M2
Pangnao, Loi, *mountain peak*, Myanmar, **205** D3
Pangnirtung, Canada, **411** N3
Pangu, China, **211** H1
Panguipulli, Chile, **460** C1
Panguipulli, Lago, *lake*, Chile, **460** C1
Panguitch, U.S.A., **422** G3
Panguna, Papua New Guinea, **140** E2
Paniai, Danau, *lake*, Indonesia, **199** F3
Panié, Mont, *mountain peak*, New Caledonia, **141** A3
Pānīpat, India, **218** D3
Panj, *river*, Afghanistan/Tajikistan, **223** J5
Panjāb, Afghanistan, **218** A2
Panjakent, Tajikistan, **222** H5
Panjang, Pulau, *island*, Indonesia, **201** E2
Panjang *see* West Island, Cocos (Keeling) Islands, **134** Q10
Panjgūr, Pakistan, **221** H3
Panjshīr, *river*, Afghanistan, **218** B2
Pankakoski, Finland, **285** Q5
Pankshin, Nigeria, **365** F3
Panna, India, **218** E4
Pannawonica, Australia, **134** D3
Panngi, Vanuatu, **141** A2
Pano Lefkara, Cyprus, **225** B2
Panorama, Brazil, **456** C5
Panozero, Russian Federation, **285** R4
Panshan, China, **211** H4
Panshi, China, **211** J4
Päntäne, Finland, **287** L1
Pantar, Pulau, *island*, Indonesia, **198** D4
Pantelleria, Isola di, *island*, Sicilia, Italy, **295** D7
Pantemakassar, Indonesia, **198** D5
Pantha, Myanmar, **205** B3
Panti, Indonesia, **200** C2
Pantoja, Peru, **450** C4
Pánuco, Mexico, **431** F4
Pánuco, *river*, Mexico, **431** F4
Panychevo, Russian Federation, **223** L1
Panyu (Shiqiao), China, **207** A3
Panzhihua, China, **215** G4
Panzi, Democratic Republic of the Congo, **368** C4
Panzós, Guatemala, **428** C4
Pão de Açúcar, Brazil, **457** G2
Paola, Italy, **295** F6
Paoli, U.S.A., **421** K6
Paoziyan, China, **211** J4
Pápa, Hungary, **289** H5
Papa Playa, Peru, **454** C2
Papa Stour, *island*, Shetland, Scotland, U.K., **308** K7
Papa Westray, *island*, Orkney, Scotland, U.K., **308** G1
Papagaio *see* Sauêruiná, *river*, Brazil, **455** G3
Papakai, New Zealand, **132** E4
Papakura, New Zealand, **132** E3
Papamoa, New Zealand, **132** F3
Papantla de Olarte, Mexico, **431** F4
Paparoa, New Zealand, **132** E3
Papatoetoe, New Zealand, **132** E3
Papeete, French Polynesia, **137** G2
Papenburg, Germany, **288** C2
Papilys, Lithuania, **287** M4
Papisoi, Tanjong, *point*, Indonesia, **199** F4
Paporotno, Russian Federation, **299** C3
Paposo, Chile, **458** B2
Pāppadāhāndi, India, **217** E2
Paps, The, *mountain peak*, Ireland, **309** C5
Papua, Gulf of, Papua New Guinea, **140** B5
Papua New Guinea, *country*, Pacific Ocean, **130** D2
Papun, Myanmar, **205** C4
Par, England, U.K., **304** C4
Pará, *river*, Brazil, **452** C3
Pará, *state*, Brazil, **452** C4
Pará de Minas, Brazil, **457** E5
Paraburdoo, Australia, **134** D3
Paracas, Península de, Peru, **454** C3
Paracatu, Brazil, **456** D4
Paracatu, *river*, Brazil, **456** E4
Paracel Islands *see* Xisha Qundao, *sovereignty disputed*, South China Sea, **203** G4
Parachute, U.S.A., **423** J2
Paraćin, Yugoslavia, **296** C4
Paracuru, Brazil, **453** F4
Paradera, Aruba, **461** B3

Paradise, California, U.S.A., **422** C2
Paradise, Guyana, **451** H3
Paradise, Montana, U.S.A., **418** G3
Paradise Valley, U.S.A., **418** F6
Paradwip, India, **219** F5
Paragould, U.S.A., **424** G1
Paraguá, *river*, Bolivia, **455** G4
Paragua, *river*, Venezuela, **451** F3
Paraguaçu, *river*, Brazil, **457** F3
Paraguai, *river*, Brazil, **456** B4
Paraguaipoa, Venezuela, **450** D1
Paraguaná, Peninsula de, Venezuela, **451** E1
Paraguarí, Paraguay, **459** F2
Paraguay, *country*, South America, **449** F6
Paraguay, *river*, South America, **447** G6
Paraiba, *river*, Paraíba, Brazil, **457** G2
Paraíba, *river*, Rio de Janeiro, Brazil, **457** E5
Paraíba, *state*, Brazil, **457** G2
Parainen, Finland, **287** L2
Paraíso, Mexico, **431** G5
Paraiso, Punta, *point*, San Andrés, Colombia, **461** B1
Paraíso do Tocantins, Brazil, **456** D3
Parakou, Benin, **365** E3
Paramaribo, Suriname, **452** B2
Paramillo, *mountain peak*, Colombia, **450** C2
Paramirim, Brazil, **457** E3
Paramirim, *river*, Brazil, **457** E3
Paramushir, Ostrov, *island*, Russian Federation, **301** S4
Paramythia, Greece, **297** C6
Paraná, Argentina, **458** E4
Paranã, Brazil, **456** D3
Paranã, *river*, Brazil, **456** D4
Paraná, *river*, South America, **447** G6
Parana, *state*, Brazil, **459** G2
Paranaguá, Brazil, **459** H2
Paranaíba, Brazil, **456** C5
Paranaíba, *river*, Brazil, **456** C5
Paranapanema, *river*, Brazil, **459** G2
Paranapiacaba, Serra, *mountain range*, Brazil, **459** H2
Paranavaí, Brazil, **459** G2
Parang, Philippines, **204** D5
Parangtritis, Indonesia, **201** E5
Parapara Peak, *mountain peak*, New Zealand, **133** D5
Paraso, Solomon Islands, **141** A1
Paraspori, Akra, *point*, Dodekanisos, Greece, **297** F8
Paratwādā, India, **218** D5
Parauapebas, Brazil, **452** D5
Parauari, *river*, Brazil, **452** A4
Paraúna, Brazil, **456** C4
Paray-le-Monial, France, **291** G3
Parazinho, Brazil, **453** G4
Parbhani, India, **216** D2
Parbig, *river*, Russian Federation, **223** L1
Parc, Pointe du, *point*, Réunion, **373** A1
Parchel, Punta del, *point*, Islas Canarias, Spain, **373** A4
Parchim, Germany, **288** E2
Parczew, Poland, **289** L3
Parding, China, **214** D2
Pardo, *river*, Bahia, Brazil, **457** F4
Pardo, *river*, Mato Grosso do Sul, Brazil, **456** C5
Pardo, *river*, São Paulo, Brazil, **456** D5
Pardoo Roadhouse, Australia, **134** D3
Pardubice, Czech Republic, **289** G3
Parecis, Brazil, **456** B4
Parecis, Chapada dos, *mountain range*, Brazil, **455** F3
Parelhas, Brazil, **453** G5
Parent, Canada, **416** D6
Pareora, New Zealand, **133** C7
Parepare, Indonesia, **198** B3
Parera, Argentina, **458** D5
Parga, Greece, **297** C6
Pargo, Ponta do, *point*, Madeira, Portugal, **373** C3
Parguaza, Sierra de, *mountain range*, Venezuela, **451** E2
Parguaza, Venezuela, **451** E2
Paria, Golfo de, *gulf*, Trinidad and Tobago, Venezuela, **427** D4
Paria, Península de, Venezuela, **451** F1
Paria, U.S.A., **423** H3
Pariaguán, Venezuela, **451** F2
Parigi, Indonesia, **198** C3
Parika, Guyana, **451** G2
Parima, *river*, Brazil, **451** F3
Parima, Serra, *mountain range*, Brazil, **451** F3
Pariñas, Punta, *point*, Peru, **454** B1
Parincea, Romania, **296** F2
Parintins, Brazil, **452** B4
Paris, France, **290** F2
Paris, Kentucky, U.S.A., **421** L6
Paris, Tennessee, U.S.A., **425** H1
Paris, Texas, U.S.A., **424** E3
Parita, Panama, **450** B2
Pārīz, Iran, **221** G3
Park Falls, U.S.A., **420** H3
Park Rapids, U.S.A., **420** F2
Park Valley, U.S.A., **418** H6
Parkano, Finland, **287** L1
Parker, U.S.A., **422** F4
Parkersburg, U.S.A., **421** N6
Parkes, Australia, **135** K5
Parkland, Canada, **413** N6
Parkston, U.S.A., **420** E4
Parlākimidi, India, **217** F2
Parlatuvier, Tobago, Trinidad and Tobago, **461** B4
Parli, India, **216** D2
Parma, Italy, **294** C3
Parmana, Venezuela, **451** F2
Parnaíba, Brazil, **453** F4
Parnaíba, *river*, Brazil, **453** E4
Parnamirim, Brazil, **453** F5
Parnarama, Brazil, **453** E4
Parnassos, *mountain peak*, Greece, **297** D6
Parnon Oros, *mountain range*, Greece, **297** D7
Pärnu, Estonia, **287** M3
Pärnu, *river*, Estonia, **287** M3
Pärnu-Jaagupi, Estonia, **287** M3
Pärnu laht, *bay*, Estonia, **287** M3
Paro, Bhutan, **219** G4
Pārola, India, **218** C5
Paroo, *river*, Australia, **135** J4
Paros, *island*, Kyklades, Greece, **297** E7
Paros, Kyklades, Greece, **297** E7
Parowan, U.S.A., **422** G3
Parpaillon, *mountain range*, France, **291** H4
Parral, Chile, **458** B5
Parras de la Fuente, Mexico, **430** E3
Parrita, Costa Rica, **428** D5
Parrsboro, Canada, **417** J7
Parry, Cape, Canada, **410** G2
Parry, Kap, *cape*, Greenland, **411** M2
Parry Bay, Canada, **411** L3
Parry Islands, Canada, **410** J2
Parry Sound, Canada, **421** N3
Parseierspitze, *mountain peak*, Austria, **288** E5
Parsęta, *river*, Poland, **289** H2
Parshall, U.S.A., **420** B2
Parsons, U.S.A., **420** F7
Partanna, Sicilia, Italy, **295** D7
Pårtefjällen, *mountain peak*, Sweden, **284** H3
Parthenay, France, **290** D3
Partizansk, Russian Federation, **211** L4
Partizánske, Slovakia, **289** J4
Partney, England, U.K., **305** H1
Partry, Ireland, **309** C4
Partry Mountains, *mountain range*, Ireland, **309** C4
Paru, *river*, Brazil, **452** C3
Paru de Este, *river*, Brazil, **452** B3
Paru de Oeste, *river*, Brazil, **452** B3
Parvatsar, India, **218** C4
Paryang, China, **219** E3
Pas-en-Artois, France, **305** K4
Pasadena, California, U.S.A., **422** D4
Pasadena, Texas, U.S.A., **424** E5
Paşalimanı Adası, *island*, Turkey, **297** F5
Pasapuat, Indonesia, **200** C3
Paşayiğit, Turkey, **297** F5
Pascagoula, U.S.A., **425** H4
Paşcani, Romania, **296** F2
Pasco, U.S.A., **418** E3
Pascoal, Monte, *mountain peak*, Brazil, **457** F4
Pascua, Isla de (Easter Island), *island*, Chile, Pacific Ocean, **461** B2
Pasewalk, Germany, **289** G2
Pasfield Lake, Canada, **414** B2
Pasha, *river*, Russian Federation, **299** D2
Pasha, Russian Federation, **299** D2
Pāsighāt, India, **219** H3
Pasir Panjang, Singapore, **200** J7
Pasir Puteh, Malaysia, **200** C1
Pasir Ris, Singapore, **200** K6
Pasirpengarayan, Indonesia, **200** C2
Påskallavik, Sweden, **286** H4
Pasłęk, Poland, **289** J1
Pasley, Cape, Australia, **128** B5
Pasni, Pakistan, **221** H3
Paso Caballos, Guatemala, **428** C3
Paso de Indios, Argentina, **460** D2
Paso de los Libres, Argentina, **459** F3
Paso de los Toros, Uruguay, **459** F4
Paso de Patria, Paraguay, **459** E3
Paso Socompa, Chile, **458** C2
Pasrūr, Pakistan, **218** C2
Passage Point, Canada, **410** H2
Passau, Germany, **288** F4
Passero, Capo, *cape*, Sicilia, Italy, **295** E7
Passi, Philippines, **204** C4
Passo Fundo, Brazil, **459** G3
Passos, Brazil, **456** D5
Pastavy, Belarus, **287** N5
Pastaza, *river*, Peru, **450** C5
Pasto, Colombia, **450** C4
Pastos Bons, Brazil, **453** E5
Pasu, India, **212** B5
Pasu, Pakistan, **218** C1
Pasuruan, Indonesia, **201** F4
Pasvalys, Lithuania, **287** M4
Pasvikelva, *river*, Norway, **285** P2
Pásztó, Hungary, **289** J5
Pata, Central African Republic, **366** B3
Pata, Senegal, **364** B2
Patagonia, U.S.A., **423** H6
Patah, Gunung, *mountain peak*, Indonesia, **200** C4
Patamea, Samoa, **141** B1
Pātan, Gujarat, India, **218** C5
Pātan, Madhya Pradesh, India, **218** D5
Pātan, Nepal, **219** F4
Patani, Indonesia, **199** E2
Patay, Argentina, **458** D3
Patay, France, **290** E2
Patchway, England, U.K., **304** E3
Patea, New Zealand, **132** E4
Patea, *river*, New Zealand, **132** E4
Pategi, Nigeria, **365** F3
Pateley Bridge, England, U.K., **307** G3
Paterno, Sicilia, Italy, **295** E7
Paterson, U.S.A., **426** C4
Pathfinder Reservoir, U.S.A., **419** L5
Pathiu, Thailand, **202** C4
Patía, *river*, Colombia, **450** B4
Patiāla, India, **218** D3
Patience, French Guiana, **452** C2
Patikul, Philippines, **204** C5
Patmos, *island*, Dodekanisos, Greece, **297** F7
Patna, India, **219** F4
Patnos, Turkey, **363** H1
Patoka Lake, U.S.A., **421** K6
Patos, Albania, **297** B5
Patos, Brazil, **453** G5
Patos, Lagoa dos, *lagoon*, Brazil, **459** G4
Patos de Minas, Brazil, **456** D5
Patquía, Argentina, **458** C4
Patra, Greece, **297** C6
Patricio Lynch, Isla, *island*, Chile, **460** B3
Patrington, England, U.K., **307** H4
Patrocínio, Brazil, **456** D5
Pattani, Thailand, **202** D5
Pattaya, Thailand, **202** D3
Patten, U.S.A., **426** F1
Patterdale, England, U.K., **306** F3
Patti, Sicilia, Italy, **295** E6
Pattisson, Cape, Chatham Islands, New Zealand, **133** Q16
Pattoki, Pakistan, **218** C3
Patton Escarpment, *underwater feature*, Pacific Ocean, **479** K2
Patuākhāli, Bangladesh, **214** D5
Patuca, Punta, *point*, Honduras, **428** D4
Patuca, *river*, Honduras, **428** D4
Patūr, India, **218** D5
Patzcuaro, Mexico, **430** E5
Pau, France, **290** D5
Paucarbamba, Peru, **454** C3
Paucartambo, Peru, **454** D3
Pauillac, France, **290** D4
Pauini, Brazil, **455** E2
Pauini, *river*, Brazil, **455** E2
Pauk, Myanmar, **205** B3
Pauksa Taung, *mountain peak*, Myanmar, **205** B4
Paulatuk, Canada, **410** G3
Paulden, U.S.A., **422** G4
Paulista, Brazil, **453** G5
Paulistana, Brazil, **457** F2
Paulo Afonso, Brazil, **457** F2
Paulo, *river*, Bolivia, **455** G4
Pauls Valley, U.S.A., **424** D2
Păunești, Romania, **296** F2
Paungbyin, Myanmar, **205** B2
Paungde, Myanmar, **205** B4
Paup, Papua New Guinea, **140** A3
Paurī, India, **218** D4
Pauri, India, **218** D3
Pauto, *river*, Colombia, **450** D3
Pauträsk, Sweden, **284** H4
Pāvagada, India, **216** D3
Pavão, Brazil, **457** F4
Pavia, Italy, **294** B3
Pavilion, Canada, **412** J6
Pavilly, France, **305** H5
Pāvilosta, Latvia, **287** K4
Pavlikeni, Bulgaria, **296** E4
Pavlodar, Kazakhstan, **223** K2
Pavlodar, *province*, Kazakhstan, **212** C2
Pavlogradka, Russian Federation, **223** J2
Pavlohrad, Ukraine, **298** E3
Pavlovac, Croatia, **294** F3
Pavlovo, Russian Federation, **298** F1
Pavlovsk, Russian Federation, **223** L2
Pavlovskaya, Russian Federation, **298** E3
Pavón, Colombia, **450** D3
Pavullo nel Frignano, Italy, **294** C3
Pawan, *river*, Indonesia, **201** E3
Pawhuska, U.S.A., **420** E7
Pawnee, *river*, U.S.A., **420** C6
Paximadia, *island*, Greece, **297** E8
Paxoi, *island*, Ionioi Nisoi, Greece, **297** B6
Pay, Russian Federation, **299** E2
Paya Lebar, Singapore, **200** K6
Payagyi, Myanmar, **205** C4
Payakumbuh, Indonesia, **200** C3
Payne, Lac, *lake*, Canada, **415** S2
Paynes Creek, U.S.A., **422** C1
Paynton, Canada, **413** Q5
Payong, Tanjong, *point*, Malaysia, **201** F2
Pays de la Loire, *administrative region*, France, **290** D3
Paysandú, Uruguay, **459** E4
Payson, U.S.A., **423** H4
Payún, Cerro, *mountain peak*, Argentina, **458** C5
Payung, Indonesia, **200** D3
Paz de Ariporo, Colombia, **450** D3
Paz de Río, Colombia, **450** D2
Pazardzhik, Bulgaria, **296** E4
Pazarlar, Turkey, **297** G6
Pazaryeri, Turkey, **297** G6
Pazin, Croatia, **294** D3
Pea, Tongatapu Group, Tonga, **141** B4
Peace, *river*, Canada, **413** L3
Peace Point, Canada, **413** N2
Peace River, Canada, **413** L3
Peacehaven, England, U.K., **305** G4
Peach Springs, U.S.A., **422** G4
Peak, The, *mountain peak*, Ascension, **373** A3
Peal de Becerro, Spain, **293** F4
Peale, Mount, *mountain peak*, U.S.A., **423** J2
Pearce, U.S.A., **423** J6
Pearl, *river*, U.S.A., **424** G4
Pearl *see* Zhu, *river*, China, **207** B2
Pearl City, Hawaiian Islands, U.S.A., **422** R9
Pearl Harbor, Hawaiian Islands, U.S.A., **422** R9
Pearsall, U.S.A., **424** C5
Pearson, U.S.A., **425** L4
Peary Channel, Canada, **411** J2
Peary Land, *region*, Greenland, **411** R1
Peawanuck, Canada, **415** M4
Pebane, Mozambique, **369** G6
Pebas, Peru, **450** D5
Pebble Island, Falkland Islands, **460** F4
Peć, Yugoslavia, **296** C4
Peçanha, Brazil, **457** E5
Peças, Ilha das, *island*, Brazil, **459** H2
Pechenga, *river*, Russian Federation, **285** Q2
Pechenga, Russian Federation, **285** Q2
Pechenicheno, Russian Federation, **299** D5
Pechenizhyn, Ukraine, **296** E1
Pechora, *river*, Russian Federation, **300** G3
Pechora, Russian Federation, **300** G3
Pechory, Russian Federation, **299** A4
Peck, U.S.A., **421** M4
Pecka, Yugoslavia, **296** B3
Pecos, *river*, U.S.A., **423** L4
Pecos, U.S.A., **423** M6

Pécs, Hungary, **289** J5
Pedasí, Panama, **429** E6
Pedder, Lake, Australia, **135** J7
Pededze, *river*, Estonia/Latvia, **287** N4
Pedernales, Dominican Republic, **429** H3
Pedernales, Mexico, **430** D2
Pedhoulas, Cyprus, **225** B2
Pediva, Angola, **368** B6
Pedra Azul, Brazil, **457** F4
Pedra Lume, Cape Verde, **360** Q8
Pedras Negras, Brazil, **455** F3
Pedraza La Vieja, Venezuela, **450** D2
Pedregal, Venezuela, **451** D1
Pedregulho, Brazil, **456** D5
Pedreiras, Brazil, **453** E4
Pedrero, Meseta el, *plateau*, Argentina, **460** D3
Pedriceña, Mexico, **430** E3
Pedro Afonso, Brazil, **456** D2
Pedro Chico, Colombia, **450** D4
Pedro de Valdivia, Chile, **458** C2
Pedro Gomes, Brazil, **456** B4
Pedro Juan Caballero, Paraguay, **459** F2
Pedro Osorio, Brazil, **459** G4
Pedro II, Brazil, **453** F4
Peebles, Canada, **414** C6
Peebles, Scotland, U.K., **308** F5
Peekskill, U.S.A., **426** D4
Peel, Isle of Man, **306** D3
Peel, *river*, Canada, **410** F3
Peel Sound, Canada, **411** K2
Peene, *river*, Germany, **288** F2
Peenemünde, Germany, **289** G1
Peerless, U.S.A., **413** S7
Peetz, U.S.A., **423** M1
Pegasus Bay, New Zealand, **133** D6
Pegnitz, Germany, **288** E4
Pego, Spain, **293** G3
Pegu, *division*, Myanmar, **205** C4
Pegu, Myanmar, **205** C4
Pegu Yoma, *mountain range*, Myanmar, **205** B4
Pegwell Bay, England, U.K., **305** J3
Pehlivanköy, Turkey, **297** F5
Pehuajó, Argentina, **458** E5
Peipohja, Finland, **287** L2
Peipsi Järv, *lake*, Estonia, **287** N3
Peiraias (Piraeus), Greece, **297** D7
Peitz, Germany, **289** G3
Peixe, Brazil, **456** D3
Peixe, do, *river*, Brazil, **456** C4
Peixe, *river*, Brazil, **456** C6
Pejirá, Sierra de, *mountain range*, Venezuela, **450** D2
Pekalongan, Indonesia, **201** E4
Pekan, Malaysia, **200** C2
Pekanbaru, Indonesia, **200** C2
Peking *see* Beijing, China, **210** G5
Peklino, Russian Federation, **299** D6
Peksha, *river*, Russian Federation, **299** G4
Pelabuhanratu, Indonesia, **200** D4
Pelabuhanratu, Teluk, *bay*, Indonesia, **200** D4
Pelagie, Isole, *islands*, Sicilia, Italy, **295** D8
Pelawanbesar, Indonesia, **201** G2
Pelée, Montagne, *mountain peak*, Martinique, **427** D3
Pelee Island, Canada, **421** M5
Peleng, Pulau, *island*, Indonesia, **198** C3
Peleng, Selat, *strait*, Indonesia, **198** C3
Pelhřimov, Czech Republic, **289** G4
Pelican Mountains, *mountain range*, Canada, **413** M4
Pelican Rapids, Canada, **414** D5
Peligro, Punta del, *point*, Islas Canarias, Spain, **373** A4
Pelkosenniemi, Finland, **285** N3
Pell City, U.S.A., **425** J3
Pellegrini, Lago, *lake*, Argentina, **460** D1
Pello, Finland, **285** M3
Pellworm, *island*, Germany, **288** D1
Pelly, *river*, Canada, **410** F3
Pelly Bay, Canada, **411** L3
Pelly Crossing, Canada, **410** F3
Pelona Mountain, *mountain peak*, U.S.A., **423** J5
Peloponnisos, *administrative region*, Greece, **297** C7
Peloritani, Monti, *mountain range*, Sicilia, Italy, **295** E7
Pelotas, Brazil, **459** G4
Peltovuoma, Finland, **285** M2
Pemali, Tanjong, *point*, Indonesia, **198** C4
Pemangkat, Indonesia, **201** E2
Pematangsiantar, Indonesia, **200** B2
Pemba, Baía de, *bay*, Mozambique, **369** H5
Pemba, Mozambique, **369** H5
Pemba Island, Tanzania, **369** G4
Pemberton, Canada, **412** H6
Pembine, U.S.A., **421** K3
Pembre, Indonesia, **199** G4
Pembrey, Wales, U.K., **304** C3
Pembroke, Canada, **416** C7
Pembroke, Wales, U.K., **304** C3
Pembroke Dock, Wales, U.K., **304** C3
Pembrokeshire, *unitary authority*, Wales, U.K., **304** B3
Pen-y-ghent, *mountain peak*, England, U.K., **306** F3
Peña de Francia, *mountain peak*, Spain, **292** D2
Peña Nevada, Cerro, *mountain peak*, Mexico, **431** F4
Penafiel, Portugal, **292** C2
Peñafiel, Spain, **292** E2
Penal, Trinidad, Trinidad and Tobago, **461** C4
Penalva, Brazil, **452** E4
Penamacor, Portugal, **292** D2
Penang *see* Pinang, Pulau, *island*, Malaysia, **200** B1
Penanjung, Teluk, *bay*, Indonesia, **201** E4
Penápolis, Brazil, **456** C5
Peñaranda de Bracamonte, Spain, **292** E2
Peñarroya, *mountain peak*, Spain, **293** G2
Penarth, Wales, U.K., **304** D3
Peñas, Cabo, *cape*, Argentina, **460** D4
Peñas, Cabo de, *cape*, Spain, **292** E1
Penas, Golfo de, *gulf*, Chile, **460** B3
Peñas, Punta, *point*, Venezuela, **461** C4
Pend Oreille Lake, U.S.A., **418** F2
Pendang, Indonesia, **201** F3
Pendleton, U.S.A., **418** E4
Pendroy, U.S.A., **418** H2
Peneda, *mountain peak*, Portugal, **292** C2
Penetanguishene, Canada, **421** P3
P'eng-hu Lieh-tao (Pescadores), *island*, Taiwan, **206** D4
P'eng-hu Tao, *island*, Taiwan, **206** D4
Peng Xian, China, **215** G3
Penganga, *river*, India, **218** D5
Penge, Democratic Republic of the Congo, **368** D4
Penglai, China, **211** H5
Pengshui, China, **206** B2
Pengxi, China, **215** H3
Peniche, Portugal, **292** C3
Penicuik, Scotland, U.K., **308** F5
Peninga, Russian Federation, **285** R5
Penitente, Serra do, *mountain range*, Brazil, **456** D2
Penkridge, England, U.K., **304** E2
Penmarch, France, **290** B3
Penmarc'h, Pointe de, *point*, France, **290** B3
Penn Yan, U.S.A., **426** B3
Pennell Coast, *region*, Antarctica, **470** D8
Pennine, Alpi, *mountain range*, Italy, **294** A3
Pennines, *mountain range*, England, U.K., **306** F3
Pennsylvania, *state*, U.S.A., **426** B4
Pennycutaway, *river*, Canada, **414** H3
Pennyghael, Scotland, U.K., **308** C4
Peno, Russian Federation, **299** D4
Penobscot, *river*, U.S.A., **426** F1
Penong, Australia, **134** G5
Penonomé, Panama, **429** E5
Penrhyn *see* Tongareva, *island*, Cook Islands, **139** J5
Penrith, England, U.K., **306** F3
Penryn, England, U.K., **304** B4
Pensacola, U.S.A., **425** J4
Pensacola Mountains, *mountain range*, Antarctica, **470** C5
Pentecost, *island*, Vanuatu, **141** A2
Penticton, Canada, **413** K7
Pentire Point, England, U.K., **304** B4
Pentland Firth, *strait*, Orkney, Scotland, U.K., **308** F2
Pentland Hills, Scotland, U.K., **308** F5
Penukonda, India, **216** D3
Penyagolosa, *mountain peak*, Spain, **293** G2
Penybont, Wales, U.K., **304** D2
Penybontfawr, Wales, U.K., **304** D2
Penygadair, *mountain peak*, Wales, U.K., **304** D2
Penza, Russian Federation, **298** G2
Penzance, England, U.K., **304** B4
Penzberg, Germany, **288** E5
Penzenskaya Oblast', *province*, Russian Federation, **298** F2
Peoria, U.S.A., **421** J5
Pepacton Reservoir, U.S.A., **426** C3
Pepe, Pointe, *point*, France, **290** C3
Pepeekeo, Hawaiian Islands, U.S.A., **422** R10
Pepepe, New Zealand, **132** E3
Peperi-Guaçu, *river*, Argentina/Brazil, **459** G3
Pëqin, Albania, **297** B5
Pér, Hungary, **289** H5
Perä-Posio, Finland, **285** N3
Perabumulih, Indonesia, **200** D3
Perak, *river*, Malaysia, **200** C1
Perak, *state*, Malaysia, **200** C1
Perama, Kriti, Greece, **297** E8
Perambalūr, India, **216** D4
Peranka, Finland, **285** P4
Percé, Canada, **417** J5
Percival Lakes, Australia, **134** F3
Perdida, *river*, Brazil, **456** D2
Perdido, Monte, *mountain peak*, Spain, **293** H1
Perdido, *river*, Argentina, **460** D2
Perdido, *river*, Brazil, **456** B5
Perdika, Greece, **297** C6
Perechyn, Ukraine, **289** L4
Perehins'ke, Ukraine, **289** M4
Pereira, Colombia, **450** C3
Pereira Barreto, Brazil, **456** C5
Peremyshl', Russian Federation, **299** F5
Perené, Peru, **454** C3
Pereslavl' Zalesskiy, Russian Federation, **299** G4
Pereyaslavka, Russian Federation, **211** L3
Perez, U.S.A., **418** D6
Pergamino, Argentina, **458** E4
Pergola, Italy, **294** D4
Perham, U.S.A., **420** F2
Perho, Finland, **285** M5
Perhonjoki, *river*, Finland, **285** L5
Péribonca, Lac, *lake*, Canada, **416** F4
Péribonca, *river*, Canada, **416** F4
Perico, Argentina, **458** D2
Perico, U.S.A., **423** M3
Pericos, Mexico, **430** D3
Périers, France, **290** D2
Perigoso, Canal, *channel*, Brazil, **452** D3
Périgueux, France, **290** E4
Peristera, *island*, Greece, **297** E6
Perito Moreno, Argentina, **460** C3
Peritoró, Brazil, **453** E4
Perleberg, Germany, **288** E2
Perlis, *state*, Malaysia, **200** B1
Perm', Russian Federation, **300** G4
Perma, U.S.A., **418** G3
Përmet, Albania, **297** C5
Permskaya Oblast', *province*, Russian Federation, **222** F1
Pernambuco, *state*, Brazil, **457** G2
Pernambuco Plain, *underwater feature*, Atlantic Ocean, **477** F6
Pernik, Bulgaria, **296** D4
Perniö, Finland, **287** L2
Péronne, France, **291** F2
Perote, Mexico, **431** F5
Perpignan, France, **291** F5
Perranporth, England, U.K., **304** B4
Perrault Falls, Canada, **414** H6
Perros-Guirec, France, **290** C2
Perry, Florida, U.S.A., **425** L4
Perry, Georgia, U.S.A., **425** L3
Perry, Iowa, U.S.A., **420** F5
Perry, Oklahoma, U.S.A., **424** D1
Perryton, U.S.A., **420** C7
Perryvale, Canada, **413** N4
Perryville, U.S.A., **420** J7
Persåsen, Sweden, **286** G1
Perseverance Harbour, Campbell Island, New Zealand, **132** K11
Perseverancia, Bolivia, **455** F4
Pershore, England, U.K., **304** E2
Persian Gulf, Asia, **220** E3
Pertandangan, Tanjong, *point*, Indonesia, **200** C2
Perth, Australia, **134** D5
Perth, Canada, **416** C7
Perth, Scotland, U.K., **308** F4
Perth and Kinross, *local authority*, Scotland, U.K., **308** F4
Perth-Andover, Canada, **416** H6
Perth Basin, *underwater feature*, Indian Ocean, **476** G6
Pertusato, Cap, *cape*, Corse, France, **295** B5
Peru, *country*, South America, **449** E4
Peru Basin, *underwater feature*, Pacific Ocean, **479** M5
Peru-Chile Trench, *underwater feature*, Pacific Ocean, **479** N5
Perugia, Italy, **294** D4
Perugorria, Argentina, **459** E3
Peruíbe, Brazil, **459** H2
Perušić, Croatia, **294** E3
Pervomays'k, Ukraine, **296** H1
Pervomayskiy, Russian Federation, **210** F2
Pervomayskoye, Russian Federation, **299** B2
Pervoural'sk, Russian Federation, **222** F1
Pesagi, Gunung, *mountain peak*, Indonesia, **200** D4
Pesaro, Italy, **294** D4
Pescadores, Punta, *point*, Róbinson Crusoe Island, Archipiélago Juan Fernández, Chile, **461** C2
Pescadores *see* P'eng-hu Lieh-tao, *island*, Taiwan, **206** D4
Pescara, Italy, **295** E4
Peschanoye, Russian Federation, **285** S5
Peschici, Italy, **295** F5
Pesek, Pulau, *island*, Singapore, **200** J7
Pesek Kechil, Pulau, *island*, Singapore, **200** J7
Peshāwar, Pakistan, **218** B2
Peshkopi, Albania, **297** C5
Peshtera, Bulgaria, **296** E4
Pesochnya, Russian Federation, **299** D6
Pesqueira, Brazil, **453** G5
Pessac, France, **290** D4
Pestovo, Russian Federation, **299** E3
Petacalco, Bahía de, *bay*, Mexico, **430** E5
Petäiskylä, Finland, **285** P5
Petäjävesi, Finland, **287** M1
Petalidi, Greece, **297** C7
Petaluma, U.S.A., **422** B2
Pétange, Luxembourg, **291** G2
Petare, Venezuela, **451** E1
Petatlan, Mexico, **431** E5
Petauke, Zambia, **369** F5
Petawawa, Canada, **416** C7
Petén Itzá, Lago, *lake*, Guatemala, **428** C3
Petenwell Lake, U.S.A., **420** H3
Peter I Øy, *Norwegian dependency*, Antarctica, **470** A6
Peter Pond Lake, Canada, **413** Q4
Peterbell, Canada, **415** N7
Peterborough, Australia, **135** H5
Peterborough, Canada, **416** B7
Peterborough, England, U.K., **305** G2
Peterborough, *unitary authority*, England, U.K., **305** G2
Peterculter, Scotland, U.K., **308** G3
Peterlee, England, U.K., **307** G3
Petermanns Bjerg, *mountain peak*, Greenland, **411** S2
Peteroa, Volcán, *mountain peak*, Chile, **458** B5
Peter's Mine, Guyana, **451** G2
Petersburg, U.S.A., **426** B6
Petersfield, England, U.K., **305** G3
Petisikapau Lake, Canada, **416** H2
Petit Goâve, Haiti, **429** G3
Petite Rivière Noire, Piton de la, *mountain peak*, Mauritius, **373** C1
Petitot, *river*, Canada, **412** J2
Petkula, Finland, **285** N3
Peto, Mexico, **431** H4
Petolahti, Finland, **287** K1
Petoskey, U.S.A., **421** L3
Petre Bay, Chatham Islands, New Zealand, **133** Q16
Petrich, Bulgaria, **297** D5
Petrila, Romania, **296** D3
Petrivka, Ukraine, **296** H2
Petrodvorets, Russian Federation, **299** B3
Petrolina, Brazil, **457** F2
Petropavl, Kazakhstan, **223** H2
Petropavlovka, Russian Federation, **210** D2

Petropavlovsk-Kamchatskiy, Russian Federation, **301** S4
Petrópolis, Brazil, **457** E6
Petroşani, Romania, **296** D3
Petrovichi, Russian Federation, **299** D6
Petrovka, Russian Federation, **223** L2
Petrovo, Russian Federation, **299** E3
Petrovsk Zabaykal'skiy, Russian Federation, **210** E2
Petrovskoye, Russian Federation, **299** G4
Petrozavodsk, Russian Federation, **299** E2
Petruşeni, Moldova, **296** F2
Pettigo, Northern Ireland, U.K., **309** E3
Petukhovo, Russian Federation, **222** H1
Petushki, Russian Federation, **299** G5
Petworth, England, U.K., **305** G4
Peureulak, Indonesia, **200** B1
Pevek, Russian Federation, **301** U3
Pewsey, England, U.K., **305** F3
Pézenas, France, **291** F5
Pezinok, Slovakia, **289** H4
Pezu, Pakistan, **218** B2
Pfaffenhofen an der Ilm, Germany, **288** E4
Pforzheim, Germany, **288** D4
Phalaborwa, South Africa, **371** F3
Phālia, Pakistan, **218** C2
Phalodi, India, **218** C4
Phalsund, India, **218** B4
Phan Rang, Vietnam, **203** F4
Phan Thiết, Vietnam, **203** F4
Phang Khon, Thailand, **203** D2
Phangan, Ko, *island*, Thailand, **202** D4
Phangnga, Thailand, **202** C4
Pharr, U.S.A., **424** C6
Phayao, Thailand, **202** C2
Phenix City, U.S.A., **425** K3
Phet Buri Reservoir, Thailand, **202** C3
Phetchabun, Thailand, **202** D2
Phetchaburi, Thailand, **202** C3
Phiamay, Phou, *mountain peak*, Laos, **203** E3
Phichit, Thailand, **202** D2
Phidim, Nepal, **219** F4
Philadelphia, Mississippi, U.S.A., **425** H3
Philadelphia, Pennsylvania, U.S.A., **426** C4
Philip, U.S.A., **420** C3
Philip Island, Norfolk Island, **135** T13
Philippeville, Belgium, **288** B3
Philippine Sea, Philippines, **204** D2
Philippine Trench, *underwater feature*, Pacific Ocean, **478** C3
Philippines, *country*, Asia, **197** P8
Philipsburg, Montana, U.S.A., **418** H3
Philipsburg, Pennsylvania, U.S.A., **421** P5
Philipsburg, St Maarten, Netherlands Antilles, **427** D2
Philipstown, South Africa, **370** D5
Phillip Island, Australia, **135** J6
Phillips, U.S.A., **420** H3
Phillipsburg, Kansas, U.S.A., **420** D6
Phillipsburg, Pennsylvania, U.S.A., **426** C4
Philomath, U.S.A., **418** C4
Philpots Island, Canada, **411** M2
Phimai, Thailand, **203** D3
Phitsanulok, Thailand, **202** D2
Phnom Penh *see* Phnum Pénh, Cambodia, **203** E4
Phnum Pénh (Phnom Penh), Cambodia, **203** E4
Phoenix *see* Rawaki, *island*, Kiribati, **139** G5
Phoenix, U.S.A., **423** G5
Phoenix Islands, Kiribati, **139** G5
Phon, Thailand, **203** D3
Phôngsali, Laos, **202** D1
Photharam, Thailand, **202** C3
Phra Nakhon Si Ayutthaya, Thailand, **202** D3
Phra Thong, Ko, *island*, Thailand, **202** C4
Phrae, Thailand, **202** D2
Phsar Réam, Cambodia, **203** D4
Phú Nhơn, Vietnam, **203** F3
Phú Quô'c, Đao, *island*, Vietnam, **203** D4
Phú Thọ, Vietnam, **203** E1
Phuket, Ko, *island*, Thailand, **202** C4
Phuket, Thailand, **202** C5
Phulabāni, India, **219** F5
Phumĭ Banam, Cambodia, **203** E4
Phumĭ Bântéay Chhmar, Cambodia, **203** D3
Phumĭ Chrăng Khpós, Cambodia, **203** D4
Phumĭ Krêk, Cambodia, **203** E4
Phumĭ Mlu Prey, Cambodia, **203** E3
Phumĭ Moŭng, Cambodia, **203** D3
Phumĭ Phsa Rômeás, Cambodia, **203** E3
Phumĭ Prâmaôy, Cambodia, **203** D3
Phumĭ Prêk Preăh, Cambodia, **203** E3
Phumĭ Prey Chruk, Cambodia, **203** D3
Phumĭ Sâmraông, E. Cambodia, **203** E3
Phumĭ Sâmraông, W. Cambodia, **203** D3
Phumĭ Véal Rénh, Cambodia, **203** D4
Phuthaditjhaba, South Africa, **371** E4
Pi Xian, Jiangsu, China, **206** D1
Pi Xian, Sichuan, China, **215** G3
Piacá, Brazil, **452** D5
Piacenza, Italy, **294** B3
Piadena, Italy, **294** C3
Piana-Mwanga, Democratic Republic of the Congo, **369** E4
Pianguan, China, **210** E5
Pianosa, Isola, Adriatic Sea, *island*, Italy, **295** E4
Pianosa, Isola, Tyrrhenian Sea, *island*, Italy, **294** C4
Piaski, Poland, **289** L3
Piatra, near Bals, Romania, **296** E3
Piatra, Romania, **296** E4
Piatra Neamţ, Romania, **296** F2
Piauí, *river*, Brazil, **457** E2
Piauí, *state*, Brazil, **453** E5
Piave, *river*, Italy, **294** D2
Piazza Armerina, Sicilia, Italy, **295** E7
Pibor Post, Sudan, **366** D3
Pica, Chile, **455** E5
Picardie, *administrative region*, France, **290** E2
Picayune, U.S.A., **425** H4
Picentini, Monti, *mountain peak*, Italy, **295** E5
Picháchic, Mexico, **430** D2
Pichanal, Argentina, **458** D2
Pichhor, India, **218** D4
Pichi Mahuida, Argentina, **460** E1
Pichilemu, Chile, **458** B5
Pichilingue, Mexico, **430** C3
Pichucalo, Mexico, **431** G5
Pickering, England, U.K., **307** H3
Pickle Lake, Canada, **414** J6
Pico, *island*, Azores, Portugal, **360** M7
Pico de Salamanca, Argentina, **460** D2
Pico Truncado, Argentina, **460** D3
Picos, Brazil, **453** F5
Picota, Peru, **454** C2
Picton, Canada, **416** C8
Picton, Isla, *island*, Chile, **460** D5
Picton, New Zealand, **133** D5
Picton, U.S.A., **426** B2
Picún Leufú, Argentina, **460** D1
Picún Leufú, *river*, Argentina, **460** C1
Pidārak, Pakistan, **221** H3
Pidi, Democratic Republic of the Congo, **369** E4
Pidurutalagata, *mountain peak*, Sri Lanka, **217** E5
Pie Town, U.S.A., **423** J4
Piedmont, Alabama, U.S.A., **425** K3
Piedmont, South Dakota, U.S.A., **420** B3
Piedrabuena, Spain, **292** E3
Piedrahita, Spain, **292** E2
Piedras, de las, *river*, Peru, **454** D3
Piedras Negras, Coahuila, Mexico, **431** E2
Piedras Negras, Veracruz, Mexico, **431** F5
Pieksämäki, Finland, **287** N1
Pielavesi, Finland, **285** N5
Pielinen, *lake*, Finland, **285** P5
Piemonte, *autonomous region*, Italy, **294** A3
Pieniężno, Poland, **289** K1
Pierce, U.S.A., **418** G3
Pierceland, Canada, **410** J4
Pierowall, Orkney, Scotland, U.K., **308** F1
Pierre, U.S.A., **420** C3
Pierrelatte, France, **291** G4
Pierreville, Canada, **416** E6
Pierrot Island, Rodrigues, **373** B1
Pierson, Canada, **414** D7
Piet Retief, South Africa, **371** F4
Pietarsaari, Finland, **285** L5
Pietermaritzburg, South Africa, **371** F4
Pietersburg, South Africa, **371** E3
Pieve di Cadore, Italy, **294** D2
Pigeon, *river*, Canada, **414** F5
Pigeon Point, Tobago, Trinidad and Tobago, **461** B4
Pigüé, Argentina, **458** D5
Pihāni, India, **218** E4
Pihlajavesi, Finland, **287** M1
Pihtipudas, Finland, **285** M5
Piippola, Finland, **285** N4
Pijijiapan, Mexico, **431** G6
Pikalevo, Russian Federation, **299** E3
Pikangikum, Canada, **414** H6
Piketberg, South Africa, **370** C5
Pikeville, U.S.A., **421** M7
Pikine, Senegal, **364** A2
Pikit, Philippines, **204** D5
Pikou, China, **211** H5
Pikounda, Congo, **368** C2
Pikwitonei, Canada, **414** F4
Pila, Argentina, **459** E5
Piła, Poland, **289** H2
Pilagá, *river*, Argentina, **459** E2
Pilão Arcado, Brazil, **457** E2
Pilar, Argentina, **459** E5
Pilar, Cabo, *cape*, Chile, **460** B4
Pilar, Paraguay, **459** E3
Pilaya, *river*, Bolivia, **455** F5
Pilbara, *region*, Australia, **134** D3
Pilcaniyeu, Argentina, **460** C1
Pilcomayo, *river*, Argentina/Bolivia/Paraguay, **455** F5
Pīleru, India, **216** D3
Pili, Philippines, **204** C3
Pīlībhīt, India, **218** D3
Pilica, *river*, Poland, **289** K3
Pillar Bay, Ascension, **373** A3
Pillcopata, Peru, **454** D3
Pilões, Serra dos, *mountain range*, Brazil, **456** D4
Pilón, Cuba, **429** F3
Pilot Mound, Canada, **414** E7
Pilot Rock, U.S.A., **418** E4
Pilsen *see* Plzeň, Czech Republic, **288** F4
Pilzno, Poland, **289** K4
Pima, U.S.A., **423** J5
Pimenta Bueno, Brazil, **455** G3
Pimperne, England, U.K., **304** E4
Pimpri-Chinchwad, India, **216** C2
Pináculo, Cerro, *mountain peak*, Argentina, **460** C4
Pinamalayan, Philippines, **204** C3
Pinang (Penang), Pulau, *island*, Malaysia, **200** B1
Pinang, *state*, Malaysia, **200** B1
Pinangah, Malaysia, **201** G1
Pinar del Río, Cuba, **428** E2
Pınarhisar, Turkey, **297** F5
Piñas, Ecuador, **450** B5
Pinatubo, Mount, *mountain peak*, Philippines, **204** C3
Pinchbeck, England, U.K., **305** G2
Pincher Creek, Canada, **413** N7
Pindaré, *river*, Brazil, **452** D4
Pindaré-Mirim, Brazil, **452** E4
Pindi Gheb, Pakistan, **218** C2
Pindobal, Brazil, **452** D4
Pindos Oros (Pindus Mountains), *mountain range*, Albania, **297** C5
Pindushi, Russian Federation, **285** S5
Pindwāra, India, **218** C4
Pine, Cape, Canada, **417** Q6
Pine, U.S.A., **423** H4
Pine Bluff, U.S.A., **424** F2
Pine Creek, Australia, **134** G1
Pine Dock, Canada, **414** F6
Pine Hills, U.S.A., **425** M5
Pine Point, Canada, **413** M1
Pine Ridge, U.S.A., **420** B4
Pine River, Canada, **414** D6
Pine Springs, U.S.A., **423** L6
Pinedale, Arizona, U.S.A., **423** H4
Pinedale, Wyoming, U.S.A., **419** K5
Pinehouse Lake, Canada, **413** R4
Pinehouse Lake, *lake*, Canada, **413** R4
Pineimuta, *river*, Canada, **415** K5
Pineios, *river*, Greece, **297** D6
Pinerolo, Italy, **294** A3
Pines, Isle of *see* Pins, Île des, *island*, New Caledonia, **141** A3
Pinetop-Lakeside, U.S.A., **423** J4
Pineville, U.S.A., **424** F4
Pinewood, Canada, **414** G7
Piney, France, **291** G2
Ping, Mae Nam, *river*, Thailand, **202** C2
P'ing-tung, Taiwan, **206** E4
Ping'an, China, **207** C2
Pingchang, China, **215** H3
Pingdi, China, **207** C3
Pingdingshan, China, **206** C1
Pingdu, China, **211** G5
Pingelap, *island*, Micronesia, **138** E4
Pingguo, China, **215** H5
Pinghai, China, **207** D3
Pinghe, China, **206** D3
Pinghu, Guangdong, China, **207** C3
Pinghu, Zhejiang, China, **206** E2
Pingjiang, China, **206** C2
Pingle, China, **206** B3
Pingli, China, **206** B1
Pingliang, China, **215** H2
Pingling, China, **207** C1
Pingluo, China, **210** D5
Pingquan, China, **211** G4
Pingree, U.S.A., **420** D2
Pingsha, China, **206** C4
Pingshan, China, **207** C3
Pingtan, Fujian, China, **206** D3
Pingtan, Guangdong, China, **207** D2
Pingwu, China, **215** H2
Pingxiang, Guangxi Zhuangzu Zizhiqu, China, **215** H5
Pingxiang, Jiangxi, China, **206** C3
Pingxiang, Vietnam, **203** E1
Pingyang, China, **206** E3
Pingyao, China, **210** F5
Pingyi, China, **206** D1
Pingyin, China, **210** G5
Pingyuanjie, China, **215** G5
Pingzhuang, China, **211** G4
Pinheiro, Brazil, **452** E4
Pinheiro Machado, Brazil, **459** G4
Pinhel, Portugal, **292** D2
Pinhoe, England, U.K., **304** D4
Pini, Pulau, *island*, Indonesia, **200** B2
Pinjarra, Australia, **134** D5
Pink, *river*, Canada, **414** B3
Pink Mountain, Canada, **412** H3
Pinlebu, Myanmar, **205** B2
Pinnacle, *mountain peak*, New Zealand, **133** D5
Pinnes, Akra, *point*, Greece, **297** E5
Pinoso, Spain, **293** G3
Pins, Île des (Isle of Pines), *island*, New Caledonia, **141** A3
Pinsk, Belarus, **298** C2
Pinta, Isla, *island*, Islas Galápagos (Galapagos Islands), Ecuador, **461** A1
Pintados, Chile, **455** E5
Pintamo, Finland, **285** N4
Pintatu, Indonesia, **198** D2
Pinto, Argentina, **458** D3
Pintuyan, Philippines, **204** D4
Pınzón, Isla, *island*, Islas Galápagos (Galapagos Islands), Ecuador, **461** A2
Piombino, Italy, **294** C4
Pioneer Fracture Zone, *tectonic feature*, Pacific Ocean, **479** H2
Pioner, Ostrov, *island*, Russian Federation, **300** K2
Pionerskiy, Russian Federation, **287** K5
Piopio, New Zealand, **132** E4
Piotrków Trybunalski, Poland, **289** J3
Piperi, *island*, Greece, **297** E6
Pipestone, Canada, **414** D7
Pipestone, *river*, Canada, **413** R3
Pipestone, U.S.A., **420** E3
Pipili, India, **219** F5
Pipiriki, New Zealand, **132** E4
Pipmuacan, Réservoir, Canada, **416** F5
Pipri, India, **219** E4
Piquiri, *river*, Brazil, **459** G2
Pīr Panjāl Range, *mountain range*, India, **218** C2
Piracanjuba, Brazil, **456** D4
Piracicaba, Brazil, **459** H2
Piracicaba, *river*, Brazil, **459** H2
Piraçununga, Brazil, **456** D5
Piracuruca, Brazil, **453** F4
Piraeus *see* Peiraias, Greece, **297** D7
Piraí do Sul, Brazil, **459** H2
Pirajuí, Brazil, **456** D5
Pirané, Argentina, **459** E2
Piranhas, Brazil, **456** C4
Piranhas, *river*, Brazil, **453** G5
Pirapó, *river*, Brazil, **459** G2
Pirapora, Brazil, **457** E4
Piratini, Brazil, **459** G4
Piratini, *river*, Brazil, **459** G4
Piray, *river*, Bolivia, **455** F4
Piray Guazu, *river*, Argentina, **459** F3
Pires do Rio, Brazil, **456** D4

Pontyberem, Wales, U.K., **304** C3
Pontypridd, Wales, U.K., **304** D3
Ponui Island, New Zealand, **132** E3
Ponya, *river*, Belarus, **287** N5
Ponza, Isola di, *island*, Italy, **295** D5
Pool, *administrative region*, Congo, **368** B3
Poole, England, U.K., **305** E4
Poole, *unitary authority*, England, U.K., **304** E4
Poole Bay, England, U.K., **305** F4
Poolewe, Scotland, U.K., **308** D3
Pooley Bridge, England, U.K., **306** F3
Poopó, Lago, *lake*, Bolivia, **455** E5
Poor Knights Islands, New Zealand, **132** E2
Popa, Mount, *mountain peak*, Myanmar, **205** B3
Popayán, Colombia, **450** C3
Pope, Latvia, **287** K4
Poperinge, Belgium, **305** K4
Poplar, *river*, Canada, **414** F5
Poplar Bluff, U.S.A., **420** H7
Poplar Creek, Canada, **413** L6
Poplar Hill, Canada, **414** G5
Poplarfield, Canada, **414** F6
Poplarville, U.S.A., **425** H4
Popocatépetl, Volcán, *mountain peak*, Mexico, **431** F5
Popokabaka, Democratic Republic of the Congo, **368** C4
Popoli, Italy, **295** D4
Popondetta, Papua New Guinea, **140** C5
Popov Porog, Russian Federation, **285** R5
Popovo, Bulgaria, **296** F4
Poprad, Slovakia, **289** K4
Porangahau, New Zealand, **132** F5
Porangatu, Brazil, **456** D3
Porazava, Belarus, **289** M2
Porbandar, India, **218** B5
Porcher Island, Canada, **412** D5
Porcuna, Spain, **292** E4
Porcupine, Cape, Canada, **417** N3
Porcupine, *river*, Canada/U.S.A., **406** J2
Porcupine Plain, *underwater feature*, Atlantic Ocean, **477** F2
Pordenone, Italy, **294** D3
Pore, Colombia, **450** D3
Poreč, Croatia, **294** D3
Porech'ye, Moskovskaya Oblast', Russian Federation, **299** E5
Porech'ye, Tverskaya Oblast', Russian Federation, **299** F3
Poretskoye, Russian Federation, **298** G1
Pórfido, Punta, *point*, Argentina, **460** E1
Porgera, Papua New Guinea, **140** A4
Pori, Finland, **287** K2
Porirua, New Zealand, **133** E5
Porjus, Sweden, **284** J3
Porkhov, Russian Federation, **299** B4
Porlamar, Venezuela, **451** F1
Porlock, England, U.K., **304** D3
Pormpuraaw, Australia, **135** J1
Pornic, France, **290** C3
Poronaysk, Russian Federation, **301** R5
Poros, Greece, **297** D7
Porosozero, Russian Federation, **285** R5
Porpoise Bay, Antarctica, **470** F7
Porpoise Point, Ascension, **373** A3
Porquerolles, Île de, *island*,

France, **291** H5
Porquis Junction, Canada, **415** P7
Porsangen, *bay*, Norway, **285** M1
Porsgrunn, Norway, **286** D3
Port-à-Piment, Haiti, **429** G3
Port Alberni, Canada, **412** G7
Port Alfred, South Africa, **371** E5
Port Alice, Canada, **412** F6
Port Angeles, U.S.A., **418** C2
Port Antonio, Jamaica, **429** F3
Port Arthur, Australia, **135** K7
Port Arthur, U.S.A., **424** F5
Port Askaig, Scotland, U.K., **308** C5
Port-au-Prince, Haiti, **429** G3
Port Augusta, Australia, **135** H5
Port Austin, U.S.A., **421** M4
Port aux Choix, Canada, **417** N4
Port Barre, U.S.A., **424** G4
Port Beaufort, South Africa, **370** D5
Port Bell, Uganda, **369** F2
Port Blair, Andaman and Nicobar Islands, India, **217** H4
Port Burwell, Canada, **421** N4
Port Canning, India, **219** G5
Port Chalmers, New Zealand, **133** C7
Port Charlotte, U.S.A., **425** L6
Port Clinton, U.S.A., **421** M5
Port Colborne, Canada, **421** P4
Port-de-Paix, Haiti, **429** G3
Port Dickson, Malaysia, **200** C2
Port Dover, Canada, **421** N4
Port Elgin, Canada, **421** N3
Port Elizabeth, South Africa, **370** E5
Port Ellen, Scotland, U.K., **308** C5
Port Erin, Isle of Man, **306** D3
Port Fitzroy, New Zealand, **132** E3
Port-Gentil, Gabon, **368** A3
Port Gibson, U.S.A., **424** G4
Port Glasgow, Scotland, U.K., **308** E5
Port Harcourt, Nigeria, **368** A2
Port Hardy, Canada, **412** F6
Port Hawkesbury, Canada, **417** L7
Port Hedland, Australia, **134** D3
Port Hood, Canada, **417** L6
Port Hope, Canada, **416** B8
Port Hope, U.S.A., **426** A3
Port Hope Simpson, Canada, **417** N3
Port Howe, Bahamas, **428** G1
Port Huron, U.S.A., **421** M4
Port Isaac Bay, England, U.K., **304** B4
Port Isabel, U.S.A., **424** D6
Port Kaituma, Guyana, **451** G2
Port Laoise, Ireland, **309** E4
Port Lavaca, U.S.A., **424** D5
Port Lincoln, Australia, **135** H5
Port Logan, Scotland, U.K., **308** E6
Port Loko, Sierra Leone, **364** B3
Port Louis, Mauritius, **373** C1
Port Macquarie, Australia, **135** L5
Port Mathurin, Rodrigues, **373** B1
Port-Menier, Canada, **417** J5
Port Moresby, Papua New Guinea, **140** B5
Port Nelson, Bahamas, **428** G2
Port Nolloth, South Africa, **370** C4
Port O'Connor, U.S.A., **424** D5
Port of Ness, Scotland, U.K., **308** C2
Port of Spain, Trinidad, Trinidad and Tobago, **461** C4
Port Orford, U.S.A., **418** B5
Port Pegasus, *bay*, New Zealand, **133** A8
Port Phillip Bay, Australia, **135** J6
Port Pirie, Australia, **135** H5

Port Puponga, New Zealand, **132** D5
Port Renfrew, Canada, **412** G7
Port Ross, *bay*, Auckland Islands, New Zealand, **132** J10
Port Said *see* Būr Sa'īd, Egypt, **225** B4
Port St Joe, U.S.A., **425** K5
Port St Johns, South Africa, **371** E5
Port St Mary, Isle of Man, **306** D3
Port Severn, Canada, **421** P3
Port Shepstone, South Africa, **371** F5
Port Stanley, Canada, **421** N4
Port Stephens, Falkland Islands, **460** F4
Port Sudan *see* Būr Sūdān, Sudan, **363** G5
Port Sulphur, U.S.A., **425** H5
Port Talbot, Wales, U.K., **304** D3
Port-Vendres, France, **291** F5
Port-Vila, Vanuatu, **141** A2
Port-Vladimir, Russian Federation, **285** R2
Port Waikato, New Zealand, **132** E3
Port Wakefield, Australia, **135** H5
Port William, Scotland, U.K., **308** E6
Portadown, Northern Ireland, U.K., **309** F3
Portaferry, Northern Ireland, U.K., **309** G3
Portage, U.S.A., **421** J4
Portage la Prairie, Canada, **414** E7
Portalegre, *district*, Portugal, **292** D3
Portalegre, Portugal, **292** D3
Portales, U.S.A., **423** M4
Portarlington, Ireland, **309** E4
Portavogie, Northern Ireland, U.K., **309** G3
Portchester, England, U.K., **305** F4
Porteirinha, Brazil, **457** E4
Portel, Brazil, **452** C3
Portel, Portugal, **292** D3
Porteño, *river*, Argentina, **459** E2
Porterville, South Africa, **370** C5
Porterville, U.S.A., **422** D3
Porth, Wales, U.K., **304** D3
Porthcawl, Wales, U.K., **304** D3
Porthleven, England, U.K., **304** B4
Porthmadog, Wales, U.K., **304** C2
Portimão, Portugal, **292** C4
Portimo, Finland, **285** N3
Portishead, England, U.K., **304** E3
Portknockie, Scotland, U.K., **308** G3
Portland, Australia, **135** J6
Portland, Indiana, U.S.A., **421** L5
Portland, Maine, U.S.A., **426** E3
Portland, Oregon, U.S.A., **418** C4
Portland Island, New Zealand, **132** F4
Portland Point, Ascension, **373** A3
Portland Point, Jamaica, **429** F3
Portland Roads, Australia, **135** J1
Portlaw, Ireland, **309** E5
Portlethen, Scotland, U.K., **308** G3
Portmagee, Ireland, **309** B6
Portnacroish, Scotland, U.K., **308** D4
Portnaguran, Scotland, U.K., **308** C2
Portnahaven, Scotland, U.K., **308** C5
Pôrto, Brazil, **453** E4
Porto, *district*, Portugal, **292** C2

Porto, Golfe de, *gulf*, Corse, France, **295** B4
Porto, Portugal, **292** C2
Pôrto Acre, Brazil, **455** E2
Pôrto Alegre, Amazonas, Brazil, **455** E2
Pôrto Alegre, Mato Grosso do Sul, Brazil, **456** C5
Pôrto Alegre, Pará, Brazil, **452** C4
Porto Alegre, Rio Grande do Sul, Brazil, **459** G4
Porto Alegre, São Tomé and Príncipe, **373** C4
Porto Amboim, Angola, **368** B5
Pôrto Artur, Brazil, **456** B3
Pôrto Belo, Brazil, **459** H3
Porto Cristo, Islas Baleares, Spain, **293** J3
Pôrto de Moz, Brazil, **452** C3
Porto dos Gaúchos, Brazil, **456** B3
Pôrto dos Meinacos, Brazil, **456** C3
Porto Empedocle, Sicilia, Italy, **295** D7
Pôrto Esperidião, Brazil, **455** G4
Pôrto Franco, Brazil, **452** D5
Pôrto Grande, Brazil, **452** C3
Porto Inglês, Cape Verde, **360** Q8
Pôrto Jofre, Brazil, **456** B4
Porto Moniz, Madeira, Portugal, **373** C3
Pôrto Murtinho, Brazil, **456** B5
Porto Nacional, Brazil, **456** D3
Porto-Novo, Benin, **365** E3
Porto Novo, Cape Verde, **360** P8
Porto Recanati, Italy, **294** D4
Pôrto Santana, Brazil, **452** C3
Porto Santo, *island*, Madeira, Portugal, **373** C3
Porto Santo, Madeira, Portugal, **373** C3
Pôrto Seguro, Brazil, **457** F4
Porto Tolle, Italy, **294** D3
Porto Torres, Sardegna, Italy, **295** B5
Porto-Vecchio, Corse, France, **295** B5
Pôrto Velho, Brazil, **455** F2
Porto Walter, Brazil, **454** D2
Portobelo, Panama, **429** F5
Portoferraio, Italy, **294** C4
Portofino, Italy, **294** B3
Portogruaro, Italy, **294** D3
Portoviejo, Ecuador, **450** B4
Portpatrick, Scotland, U.K., **308** D6
Portreath, England, U.K., **304** B4
Portree, Scotland, U.K., **308** C3
Portrush, Northern Ireland, U.K., **309** F2
Portsalon, Ireland, **309** E2
Portsmouth, Dominica, **427** D3
Portsmouth, England, U.K., **305** F4
Portsmouth, New Hampshire, U.S.A., **426** E3
Portsmouth, Ohio, U.S.A., **421** M6
Portsmouth, Virginia, U.S.A., **426** B6
Portsmouth City, *unitary authority*, England, U.K., **305** F4
Portsmouth Island, U.S.A., **426** B7
Portsoy, Scotland, U.K., **308** G3
Portstewart, Northern Ireland, U.K., **309** F2
Porttipahdan tekojärvi, *lake*, Finland, **285** M2
Portugal, *country*, Europe, **282** D8
Portuguesa, *river*, Venezuela, **451** E2
Portumna, Ireland, **309** D4
Porvenir, Chile, **460** C4
Porvoo, Finland, **287** M2

Por'ya Guba, Russian Federation, **285** R3
Porzuna, Spain, **292** E3
Posadas, Argentina, **459** F3
Posarae, Solomon Islands, **141** A1
Posen, U.S.A., **421** M3
Posevnaya, Russian Federation, **223** L2
Poshekhon'ye, Russian Federation, **299** G3
Posht-e Bādām, Iran, **221** G2
Posio, Finland, **285** P3
Poso, Danau, *lake*, Indonesia, **198** C3
Poso, Indonesia, **198** C3
Poso, Teluk, *bay*, Indonesia, **198** C3
Posŏng, South Korea, **208** D4
Pospelikha, Russian Federation, **223** L2
Posse, Brazil, **456** D4
Possession Bay, South Georgia, **461** A3
Post, U.S.A., **424** B3
Post Falls, U.S.A., **418** F3
Postmasburg, South Africa, **370** D4
Postojna, Slovenia, **294** E3
Postville, U.S.A., **420** H4
Posušje, Croatia, **294** F4
Poteau, U.S.A., **424** E2
Poteet, U.S.A., **424** C5
Potenza, Italy, **295** E5
Poth, U.S.A., **424** C5
P'ot'i, Georgia, **222** C4
Potiskum, Nigeria, **365** G2
Potok, Croatia, **294** F3
Potomac, *river*, U.S.A., **426** B5
Potosí, Bolivia, **455** F5
Potosí, *department*, Bolivia, **455** E5
Potosí, Nicaragua, **428** D4
Potosi, U.S.A., **420** H7
Potro, Cerro de, *mountain peak*, Chile, **458** C3
Potsdam, Germany, **288** F2
Potsdam, U.S.A., **426** C2
Potters Bar, England, U.K., **305** G3
Pottstown, U.S.A., **426** C4
Pottsville, U.S.A., **426** B4
Pottuvil, Sri Lanka, **217** E5
Potwar Plateau, Pakistan, **218** C2
Pouce Coupe, Canada, **412** J4
Pouch Cove, Canada, **417** Q6
Pouembout, New Caledonia, **141** A3
Poughkeepsie, U.S.A., **426** D4
Poukawa, New Zealand, **132** F4
Poulton-le-Fylde, England, U.K., **306** F4
Poum, New Caledonia, **141** A3
Pouso Alegre, Brazil, **456** E6
Poutasi, Samoa, **141** B1
Poŭthĭsăt, Cambodia, **203** D3
Povenets, Russian Federation, **285** S5
Povenetskiy Zaliv, *bay*, Russian Federation, **285** S5
Poverty Bay, New Zealand, **132** F4
Póvoa de Varzim, Portugal, **292** C2
Povoação, Azores, Portugal, **360** M7
Povorot, Russian Federation, **210** D2
Povungnituk, Rivière de, *river*, Canada, **415** R1
Povungnituk Bay, Canada, **415** Q2
Powder, *river*, U.S.A., **419** L5
Powder River, U.S.A., **419** L5
Powderhorn, U.S.A., **423** K2
Powell, Lake, U.S.A., **423** H3
Powell, U.S.A., **419** K4
Powell Point, St Helena, **373** B3
Powell River, Canada, **412** G7
Power, U.S.A., **419** J3
Powers, U.S.A., **421** K3

Puerto Isabel, Bolivia, **455** H5
Puerto Jesús, Costa Rica, **428** D5
Puerto La Concordia, Colombia, **450** D3
Puerto la Cruz, Venezuela, **451** F1
Puerto Leguízamo, Colombia, **450** C4
Puerto Lempira, Honduras, **428** E4
Puerto Libertad, Mexico, **430** B2
Puerto Limón, Costa Rica, **429** E5
Puerto Lobos, Argentina, **460** E2
Puerto López, Colombia, **450** D3
Puerto Lumbreras, Spain, **293** G4
Puerto Madryn, Argentina, **460** E2
Puerto Maldonado, Peru, **455** E3
Puerto Mamoré, Bolivia, **455** F4
Puerto Márquez, Bolivia, **455** E4
Puerto Mihanovich, Paraguay, **455** H5
Puerto Miraña, Colombia, **451** D4
Puerto Miranda, Venezuela, **451** E2
Puerto Montt, Chile, **460** C1
Puerto Morin, Peru, **454** B2
Puerto Natales, Chile, **460** C4
Puerto Nuevo, Colombia, **451** E3
Puerto Obaldía, Panama, **429** F5
Puerto Ocopa, Peru, **454** C3
Puerto Ordaz, Venezuela, **451** F2
Puerto Padre, Cuba, **429** F2
Puerto Páez, Venezuela, **451** E2
Puerto Pardo, Peru, **450** C5
Puerto Peñasco, Mexico, **430** B2
Puerto Pinasco, Paraguay, **459** F2
Puerto Piràmides, Argentina, **460** E2
Puerto Plata, Dominican Republic, **429** H3
Puerto Portillo, Peru, **454** D2
Puerto Princesa, Philippines, **204** B4
Puerto Rey, Colombia, **450** C2
Puerto Rico, Argentina, **459** F3
Puerto Rico, Bolivia, **455** E3
Puerto Rico, *U.S. territory*, Caribbean Sea, **427** C2
Puerto Rico Trench, *underwater feature*, Caribbean Sea, **479** P3
Puerto Rondón, Colombia, **450** D2
Puerto Saavedra, Chile, **460** C1
Puerto San Jose, Guatemala, **428** C4
Puerto San Julián, Argentina, **460** D3
Puerto Santa Cruz, Argentina, **460** D4
Puerto Sastre, Paraguay, **456** A5
Puerto Saucedo, Bolivia, **455** F3
Puerto Siles, Bolivia, **455** F3
Puerto Suárez, Bolivia, **455** H5
Puerto Supe, Peru, **454** C3
Puerto Tahuantinsuyo, Peru, **455** D3
Puerto Tejada, Colombia, **450** C3
Puerto Tunigrama, Peru, **450** C5
Puerto Vallarta, Mexico, **430** D4
Puerto Varas, Chile, **460** C1
Puerto Victoria, Peru, **454** C2
Puerto Villamil, Islas Galápagos (Galapagos Islands), Ecuador, **461** A2
Puerto Villazón, Bolivia, **455** G3
Puerto Visser, Argentina, **460** D2
Puerto Williams, Chile, **460** D5
Puertollano, Spain, **292** E3
Puesto Estrella, Paraguay, **455** F5

Pugachev, Russian Federation, **222** D2
Puge, China, **215** G4
Puget Sound, U.S.A., **418** C3
Puglia, *autonomous region*, Italy, **295** F5
Puhi, Volcán, *mountain peak*, Isla de Pascua (Easter Island), Chile, **461** B2
Puhos, Finland, **285** N4
Pui O Wan, *bay*, China, **207** B4
Puig-reig, Spain, **293** H1
Puigcerdà, Spain, **293** H1
Pujehun, Sierra Leone, **364** B3
Pukaki, Lake, New Zealand, **133** B6
Pukapuka, *island*, Cook Islands, **139** H6
Pukapuka, *island*, French Polynesia, **137** H2
Pukarua, *island*, French Polynesia, **137** H2
Pukatawagan, Canada, **414** D4
Pukch'ŏng, North Korea, **208** E2
Pukë, Albania, **296** B4
Pukekura, New Zealand, **133** C6
Pukeuri, New Zealand, **133** C7
Pukhnovo, Russian Federation, **299** C5
Pukuatu, Tanjong, *point*, Indonesia, **198** C5
Pula, Croatia, **294** D3
Pula, Sardegna, Italy, **295** B6
Pulacayo, Bolivia, **455** E5
Pulai, Indonesia, **201** G2
Pulanduta Point, Philippines, **204** C4
Pulangpisau, Indonesia, **201** F3
Pular, Cerro, *mountain peak*, Chile, **458** C2
Pulaski, New York, U.S.A., **426** B3
Pulaski, Tennessee, U.S.A., **425** J2
Pulaski, Wisconsin, U.S.A., **421** J3
Pulau, *river*, Indonesia, **199** G4
Puławy, Poland, **289** K3
Pulborough, England, U.K., **305** G4
Pulicat Lake, India, **216** E3
Pulkkila, Finland, **285** M4
Pulo Anna, *island*, Palau, **138** B4
Pulo Pandang, *island*, Cocos (Keeling) Islands, **134** Q10
Pulog, Mount, *mountain peak*, Philippines, **204** C2
Pulozero, Russian Federation, **285** R2
Pulsujärvi, Sweden, **284** K2
Pułtusk, Poland, **289** K2
Pulu, China, **212** D5
Pulusuk, *island*, Micronesia, **138** C4
Pumasillo, Cerro, *mountain peak*, Peru, **454** D3
Pummanki, Russian Federation, **285** Q2
Pumpėnai, Lithuania, **287** M5
Pumpsaint, Wales, U.K., **304** D2
Puná, Isla, *island*, Ecuador, **450** B5
Punakaiki, New Zealand, **133** C6
Punàkha, Bhutan, **214** D4
Punalur, India, **216** D4
Punata, Bolivia, **455** F4
Pūndri, India, **218** D3
Pune, India, **216** C2
Pungești, Romania, **296** F2
Punggol, *river*, Singapore, **200** K6
Punggol, Singapore, **200** K6
Punggol, Tanjong, *point*, Singapore, **200** K6
P'ungsan, North Korea, **208** E2
Punia, Democratic Republic of the Congo, **369** E3
Punitaqui, Chile, **458** B4
Punjab, *province*, Pakistan, **218** B3
Punjab, *state*, India, **218** C3

Punkaharju, Finland, **287** P2
Punkalaidun, Finland, **287** L2
Punkin Centre, U.S.A., **423** M2
Puno, Peru, **455** D4
Punta, Cerro de, *mountain peak*, Puerto Rico, **427** C2
Punta Alta, Argentina, **460** E1
Punta Arenas, Chile, **460** C4
Punta Banda, Cabo, *cape*, Mexico, **430** A2
Punta Delgada, Argentina, **460** E2
Punta Delgada, Chile, **460** D4
Punta Gorda, Bahía de, *bay*, Costa Rica, **428** E5
Punta Gorda, Belize, **428** C3
Punta Gorda, Nicaragua, **428** E5
Punta Gorda, *river*, Nicaragua, **428** D5
Punta Norte, Argentina, **460** E2
Punta Prieta, Mexico, **430** B2
Puntagorda, Islas Canarias, Spain, **373** A4
Puntarenas, Costa Rica, **428** D5
Punto Fijo, Venezuela, **451** D1
Puokio, Finland, **285** N4
Puolanka, Finland, **285** N4
Puoltikasvaara, Sweden, **284** K3
Puottaure, Sweden, **284** K3
Puqi, China, **206** C2
Puquio, Peru, **454** C4
Puquios, Chile, **458** C3
Puracé, Volcán, *mountain peak*, Colombia, **450** C3
Pūranpur, India, **218** E3
Purari, *river*, Papua New Guinea, **140** B4
Purcell, U.S.A., **424** D2
Purcell Mountains, *mountain range*, Canada, **413** L6
Purekkari neem, *point*, Estonia, **287** M3
Purén, Chile, **458** B6
Purgatoire, *river*, U.S.A., **423** M3
Puri, India, **219** F6
Purificación, Mexico, **430** D5
Purna, India, **218** D6
Purnach, *river*, Russian Federation, **285** U3
Pūrnia, India, **219** F4
Purranque, Chile, **460** C1
Puruarán, Mexico, **431** E5
Purukcahu, Indonesia, **201** F3
Puruliya, India, **219** F5
Purus, *river*, Brazil, **451** F5
Puruvesi, *lake*, Finland, **287** P1
Pŭrvomay, Bulgaria, **296** E4
Purwakarta, Indonesia, **201** D4
Purwokerto, Indonesia, **201** E4
Pusad, India, **218** D6
Pusan, South Korea, **208** E4
Pushkin, Russian Federation, **299** C3
Pushlakhta, Russian Federation, **285** T4
Pushnoy, Russian Federation, **285** S4
Püspökladány, Hungary, **289** K5
Pustaya Guba, Russian Federation, **285** R3
Pustoshka, Russian Federation, **299** B4
Pu'tai, Taiwan, **206** E4
Putao, Myanmar, **205** C2
Putaruru, New Zealand, **132** E4
Putia, Indonesia, **198** D3
Putian, China, **206** D3
Putina, Peru, **455** E4
Puting, Tanjong, *point*, Indonesia, **201** E3
Putla, Mexico, **431** F5
Putlitz, Germany, **288** F2
Putnam, U.S.A., **424** C2
Putorana, Plato, *mountain range*, Russian Federation, **300** L3
Putorino, New Zealand, **132** F4
Putre, Chile, **455** E5
Puttalam, Sri Lanka, **216** D4
Puttalam Lagoon, Sri Lanka, **216** D4
Puttgarden, Germany, **288** E1

Puttūr, India, **216** C3
Putumayo, *river*, Colombia/Peru, **450** C4
Putus, Tanjong, *point*, Indonesia, **201** E3
Putussibau, Indonesia, **201** F2
Putyla, Ukraine, **296** E2
Puukkokumpu, Finland, **285** M4
Puula, *lake*, Finland, **287** N2
Puumala, Finland, **287** P2
Puuwai, Hawaiian Islands, U.S.A., **422** Q9
Puvirnituq, Canada, **415** R1
Puyang, China, **206** C1
Puyehue, Chile, **460** C1
Puyo, Ecuador, **450** C4
Puysegur Point, New Zealand, **133** A8
Pwani, *administrative region*, Tanzania, **369** G4
Pweto, Democratic Republic of the Congo, **369** E4
Pwllheli, Wales, U.K., **304** C2
Pyal'ma, Russian Federation, **285** S5
Pyamalaw, *river*, Myanmar, **205** B4
Pyaozero, Ozero, *lake*, Russian Federation, **285** Q3
Pyapon, Myanmar, **205** B4
Pyasinskiy Zaliv, *bay*, Russian Federation, **300** J2
Pyatigorsk, Russian Federation, **222** C4
Pyawbwe, Myanmar, **205** C3
Pyè (Prome), Myanmar, **205** B4
Pyhäjärvi, Finland, **285** N5
Pyhäjoki, Finland, **285** M4
Pyhäjoki, *river*, Finland, **285** M4
Pyhältö, Finland, **287** N2
Pyhäntä, Finland, **285** N4
Pyhäranta, Finland, **287** K2
Pyhäselkä, Finland, **287** Q1
Pyhäselkä, *lake*, Finland, **287** P1
Pyhätunturi, *mountain peak*, Finland, **285** N3
Pyinmana, Myanmar, **205** C4
Pyle, Wales, U.K., **304** D3
Pylkönmäki, Finland, **285** M5
Pylos, Greece, **297** C7
Pymatuning Reservoir, U.S.A., **421** N5
Pyramid Island, Chatham Islands, New Zealand, **133** Q16
Pyramid Lake, U.S.A., **422** D1
Pyramid Point, Ascension, **373** A3
Pyrenees, *mountain range*, Andorra/France/Spain, **280** D7
Pyrgetos, Greece, **297** D6
Pyrgi, Greece, **297** E6
Pyrgos, Greece, **297** C7
Pyrzyce, Poland, **289** G2
Pyshna, Belarus, **299** B5
Pyttegga, *mountain peak*, Norway, **286** C1
Pyu, Myanmar, **205** C4
Pyuntaza, Myanmar, **205** C4
Pyzdry, Poland, **289** H2

Q

Qaanaaq (Thule), Greenland, **411** N2
Qabanbay, Kazakhstan, **212** D3
Qabātiyah, West Bank, **225** C3

Qābis, Tunisia, **362** B2
Qāḍub, Suquṭrá (Socotra), Yemen, **373** B2
Qā'en, Iran, **221** G2
Qagan, China, **211** G2
Qagan Nur, China, **210** F4
Qagan Nur, *lake*, China, **210** F4
Qagan Teg, China, **210** F4
Qagca, China, **215** F2
Qaidam Pendi, *basin*, China, **213** G5
Qakar, China, **212** D5
Qala'an Naḥl, Sudan, **366** D2
Qalāt, Afghanistan, **218** A2
Qal'at al Ḥiṣn, Syria, **225** D2
Qal'at Bīshah, Saudi Arabia, **363** H5
Qal'at Ṣāliḥ, Iraq, **363** J2
Qalba Zhotasy, *mountain range*, Kazakhstan, **212** D2
Qal'eh Shahr, Afghanistan, **218** A2
Qal'eh-ye Now, Afghanistan, **221** H2
Qal'eh-ye Sarkārī, Afghanistan, **218** A2
Qallābāt, Sudan, **366** E2
Qalyūb, Egypt, **225** A4
Qamalung, China, **215** F2
Qamar, Ghubbat al, *bay*, Oman/Yemen, **220** F5
Qamdo, China, **215** F3
Qamīnis, Libya, **362** C2
Qandahār, Afghanistan, **218** A3
Qandala, Somalia, **367** G2
Qanshenggel, Kazakhstan, **212** B3
Qapqal, China, **212** D4
Qapshaghay, Kazakhstan, **212** C4
Qapshaghay Bögeni, *reservoir*, Kazakhstan, **212** C3
Qaqortoq, Greenland, **411** Q3
Qarabas, Kazakhstan, **212** B2
Qaraböget, Kazakhstan, **212** A3
Qarabulaq, Almaty, Kazakhstan, **212** C3
Qarabulaq, Shyghys Qazaqstan, Kazakhstan, **212** E3
Qarabulaq, Yuzhnyy Qazaqstan, Kazakhstan, **223** H4
Qarabutaq, Kazakhstan, **222** G3
Qaraghandy, *province*, Kazakhstan, **212** B2
Qaraghandy (Karaganda), Kazakhstan, **212** B2
Qaraghayly, Kazakhstan, **212** B2
Qārah, Egypt, **362** E3
Qarak, China, **212** C5
Qarakūl, *lake*, Tajikistan, **212** B5
Qaraqamys, Kazakhstan, **222** E3
Qarasor Köli, Kazakhstan, **212** B2
Qaratal, *river*, Kazakhstan, **212** C3
Qaratöbe, Kazakhstan, **222** E3
Qaraūyl, Kazakhstan, **212** C2
Qarazhal, Kazakhstan, **212** A2
Qardho, Somalia, **367** G3
Qarqan, *river*, China, **212** E5
Qarqaraly, Kazakhstan, **212** B2
Qarqi, Central Xinjiang Uygur Zizhiqu, China, **212** E4
Qarqi, W. Xinjiang Uygur Zizhiqu, China, **212** D4
Qarsan, China, **211** H3
Qarshi, Uzbekistan, **222** H5
Qarṭabā, Lebanon, **225** C2
Qaryat al Qaddāḥīyah, Libya, **362** C2
Qasigiannguit (Christianshåb), Greenland, **411** P3
Qaskeleng, Kazakhstan, **212** C4
Qaṣr Ḥamām, Saudi Arabia, **363** J4
Qaṣr al Farāfirah, Egypt, **362** E3
Qaṭanā, Syria, **225** D3
Qaṭānan, Ra's, *point*, Suquṭrá (Socotra), Yemen, **373** B2

Rāichūr, India, **216** D2
Raiganj, India, **219** G4
Raigarh, India, **219** E5
Rainbow Lake, Canada, **413** K2
Rainer, Mount, *mountain peak*, U.S.A., **418** D3
Rainier, U.S.A., **418** C3
Rainy Lake, Canada/U.S.A., **420** G1
Rainy River, Canada, **414** G7
Raippaluoto (Vallgrund), *island*, Finland, **284** K5
Raipur, India, **219** E5
Raisen, India, **218** D5
Raisio, Finland, **287** L2
Raith, Canada, **414** K7
Raivavae, *island*, French Polynesia, **137** G3
Rāj-Nāndgaon, India, **219** E5
Raja-Jooseppi, Finland, **285** P2
Rajagangapur, India, **219** F5
Rājahmundry, India, **217** E2
Rajala, Finland, **285** N3
Rajang, *river*, Malaysia, **201** F2
Rājanpur, Pakistan, **218** B3
Rājapālaiyam, India, **216** D4
Rājapur, India, **216** C2
Rājasthān, *state*, India, **218** C4
Rajauli, India, **219** F4
Rājgarh, E. Central Rājasthān, India, **218** D4
Rājgarh, N. Rājasthān, India, **218** C3
Rājkot, India, **218** B5
Rājpīpla, India, **218** C5
Rājpur, India, **218** D5
Rājsamand, India, **218** C4
Rajshahi, Bangladesh, **214** D4
Rajshahi, *division*, Bangladesh, **214** D4
Raka, China, **214** C3
Rakahanga, *island*, Cook Islands, **139** H5
Rakai, Uganda, **369** F3
Rakaia, New Zealand, **133** D6
Rakaw, Belarus, **287** N6
Rakhiv, Ukraine, **296** E1
Rakhmet, Kazakhstan, **222** H3
Rakhni, Pakistan, **218** B3
Rakhyūt, Oman, **220** F5
Rakiraki, Fiji, **141** A4
Rakkestad, Norway, **286** E3
Rakovník, Czech Republic, **288** F4
Rakovski, Bulgaria, **296** E4
Rakvere, Estonia, **287** N3
Raleigh, North Carolina, U.S.A., **425** N2
Raleigh, North Dakota, U.S.A., **420** C2
Ralston, Canada, **413** P6
Ralston, U.S.A., **419** K4
Ramādah, Tunisia, **362** B2
Ramalho, Serra do, *mountain range*, Brazil, **457** E4
Rāmanāthapuram, India, **216** D4
Rāmānuj Ganj, India, **219** E5
Rambouillet, France, **290** E2
Rāmdevra, India, **218** B4
Rāmechhāp, Nepal, **219** F4
Ramena, Madagascar, **372** B3
Rameshki, Russian Federation, **299** F4
Ramgarh, Bihār, India, **219** F5
Rāmgarh, Rājasthān, India, **218** B4
Rāmhormoz, Iran, **363** J2
Ramírez, Isla, *island*, Chile, **460** B4
Ramla, Israel, **225** C4
Ramlu, *mountain peak*, Eritrea/ Ethiopia, **367** F2
Ramm, Jabal, *mountain peak*, Jordan, **225** C5
Ramm, Jordan, **225** C5
Rāmnagar, India, **218** D3
Ramnäs, Sweden, **286** H3
Ramni, Belarus, **299** C5
Râmnicu Sărat, Romania, **296** F3
Râmnicu Vâlcea, Romania, **296** E3
Ramor, Lough, *lake*, Ireland, **309** F4
Ramore, Canada, **415** P7
Ramotswa, Botswana, **371** E3
Rāmpur, Gujarat, India, **218** B5
Rāmpur, Himāchal Pradesh, India, **218** D3
Rampūr, Orissa, India, **217** F1
Rāmpur, Uttar Pradesh, India, **218** D3
Rāmpur Hāt, India, **219** F4
Rāmpura, India, **218** C4
Rampside, England, U.K., **306** E3
Ramree Island, Myanmar, **205** B4
Ramsele, Sweden, **284** H5
Ramsey, Canada, **421** M2
Ramsey, England, U.K., **305** G2
Ramsey, Isle of Man, **306** D3
Ramsey Bay, Isle of Man, **306** D3
Ramsey Island, Wales, U.K., **304** B3
Ramsgate, England, U.K., **305** J3
Ramsjö, Sweden, **286** G1
Ramu, Bangladesh, **214** E5
Ramu, *river*, Papua New Guinea, **140** B4
Ramundberget, Sweden, **284** F5
Ramvik, Sweden, **287** H1
Ramygala, Lithuania, **287** M5
Rana Pratap Sāgar, *lake*, India, **218** C4
Ranakah, Gunung, *mountain peak*, Indonesia, **198** C5
Ranau, Danau, *lake*, Indonesia, **200** C4
Rānāvāv, India, **218** B5
Ranbausawa, Tanjong, *point*, Indonesia, **199** F3
Rancagua, Chile, **458** B5
Ranchester, U.S.A., **419** L4
Rānchī, India, **219** F5
Rancho Cordova, U.S.A., **422** C2
Ranco, Lago, *lake*, Chile, **460** C1
Randado, U.S.A., **424** C6
Randalstown, Northern Ireland, U.K., **309** F3
Randazzo, Sicilia, Italy, **295** E7
Rånddalen, Sweden, **286** F1
Randers, Denmark, **286** E4
Randijaure, *lake*, Sweden, **284** J3
Randolph, Nebraska, U.S.A., **420** E4
Randolph, Vermont, U.S.A., **426** D3
Råneå, Sweden, **285** L4
Ranérou, Senegal, **364** B1
Ranfurly, New Zealand, **133** C7
Rangae, Thailand, **202** D5
Rangamati, Bangladesh, **214** E5
Rangatira Island, Chatham Islands, New Zealand, **133** Q16
Rangaunu Bay, New Zealand, **132** D2
Rangeley, U.S.A., **426** E2
Rangely, U.S.A., **423** J1
Rangia, India, **219** G4
Rangipo, New Zealand, **132** E4
Rangiriri, New Zealand, **132** E3
Rangiroa, *island*, French Polynesia, **137** G2
Rangitaiki, *river*, New Zealand, **132** F4
Rangitata, New Zealand, **133** C7
Rangiuru, New Zealand, **132** F3
Rangoon *see* Yangon, Myanmar, **205** C4
Rangpur, Bangladesh, **214** D4
Rangsang, Pulau, *island*, Indonesia, **200** C2
Rānībennur, India, **216** C3
Raniganj, India, **219** F5
Rānīpur, Pakistan, **218** B4
Rankin, U.S.A., **423** N6
Rankin Inlet, Canada, **411** K3
Rannoch, Loch, *lake*, Scotland, U.K., **308** E4
Rannoch Moor, *moorland*, Scotland, U.K., **308** E4
Rano, Nigeria, **365** F2
Ranobe, *river*, Madagascar, **372** A4
Ranohira, Madagascar, **372** B5
Ranomena, Madagascar, **372** B5
Ranong, Thailand, **202** C4
Ransarn, *lake*, Sweden, **284** G4
Ransiki, Indonesia, **199** F3
Rantajärvi, Sweden, **285** L3
Rantasalmi, Finland, **287** P1
Rantau, Indonesia, **201** F3
Rantekombola, Gunung, *mountain peak*, Indonesia, **198** C3
Rantepao, Indonesia, **198** B3
Rantoul, U.S.A., **421** J5
Rantsila, Finland, **285** M4
Ranua, Finland, **285** N4
Raoping, China, **206** D4
Raoui, Erg er, *desert*, Algeria, **361** F3
Raoul Island, Kermadec Islands, New Zealand, **132** L12
Rapa, *island*, French Polynesia, **137** G3
Rāpar, India, **218** B5
Rapahoe, New Zealand, **133** C6
Rapallo, Italy, **294** B3
Rapel, *river*, Chile, **458** B4
Raper, Cabo, *cape*, Chile, **460** B3
Raper, Cape, Canada, **411** N3
Raphoe, Ireland, **309** E3
Rapid City, U.S.A., **420** B3
Rapide Blanc, Canada, **416** E6
Räpina, Estonia, **287** N3
Rapla, Estonia, **287** M3
Rappahannock, *river*, U.S.A., **426** B5
Rapu Rapu Island, Philippines, **204** D3
Raroia, *island*, French Polynesia, **137** G2
Rarotonga, *island*, Cook Islands, **137** F3
Ra's Ajdīr, Tunisia, **362** B2
Ra's an Naqb, Jordan, **225** C5
Ra's at Tin, Libya, **224** B6
Ras Dashen Terara, *mountain peak*, Ethiopia, **367** E2
Râs el Mâ, Mali, **364** D1
Ra's Ghārib, Egypt, **363** F3
Ra's Matārimah, Egypt, **225** B5
Ra's Sudr, Egypt, **225** B5
Ra's Tannūrah, Saudi Arabia, **220** E3
Raša, Croatia, **294** E3
Rasa, Punta, *point*, Argentina, **460** E1
Rasa Island, Philippines, **204** B4
Râşcani, Moldova, **296** F2
Raseiniai, Lithuania, **287** L5
Rashād, Sudan, **366** D2
Rashaant, Bayan-Ölgiy, Mongolia, **213** F3
Rashaant, Dundgovĭ, Mongolia, **210** D3
Rashm, Iran, **221** F1
Rasht, Iran, **222** D5
Rasi Salai, Thailand, **203** E3
Rāsk, Iran, **221** H3
Raška, Yugoslavia, **296** C4
Råsken, *river*, Norway, **286** C2
Râşnov, Romania, **296** E3
Raso, Cabo, *cape*, Argentina, **460** E2
Rastede, Germany, **288** D2
Rastegai'sa, *mountain peak*, Norway, **285** N2
Råstojaure, *lake*, Sweden, **284** K2
Rasu, Monte, *mountain peak*, Sardegna, Italy, **295** B5
Rasūl, Pakistan, **218** C2
Rat Islands, United States of America, **301** U4
Rata, New Zealand, **132** E5
Rata, Tanjong, *point*, Indonesia, **200** D4
Rätan, Sweden, **286** G1
Ratanpur, India, **219** E5
Ratchaburi, Thailand, **202** C3
Rāth, India, **218** D4
Rath Luirc, Ireland, **309** D5
Rathangan, Ireland, **309** E4
Rathbun Lake, U.S.A., **420** G5
Rathdowney, Ireland, **309** E5
Rathdrum, Ireland, **309** F5
Rathenow, Germany, **288** F2
Rathfriland, Northern Ireland, U.K., **309** F3
Rathkeale, Ireland, **309** D5
Rathlin Island, Northern Ireland, U.K., **309** F2
Rathvilly, Ireland, **309** F5
Rathwell, Canada, **414** E7
Rätische Alpen, *mountain range*, Switzerland, **291** J3
Ratlām, India, **218** C5
Ratnāgiri, India, **216** C2
Ratne, Ukraine, **289** M3
Ratodero, Pakistan, **218** B4
Raton, U.S.A., **423** L3
Rättvik, Sweden, **286** G2
Ratz, Mount, *mountain peak*, Canada, **412** C3
Raub, Malaysia, **200** C2
Raub, U.S.A., **420** B2
Rauch, Argentina, **459** E5
Raufarhöfn, Iceland, **284** Z6
Raukumara Range, *mountain range*, New Zealand, **132** F4
Rauland, Norway, **286** D3
Rauma, Finland, **287** K2
Rauma, *river*, Norway, **286** D1
Raunds, England, U.K., **305** G2
Raung, Gunung, *mountain peak*, Indonesia, **201** F5
Raurkela, India, **219** F5
Răut, *river*, Moldova, **296** G2
Rautavaara, Finland, **285** P5
Rautjärvi, Finland, **287** P2
Rava-Rus'ka, Ukraine, **289** L3
Ravalli, U.S.A., **418** G3
Rāvar, Iran, **221** G2
Ravelo, Bolivia, **455** F5
Ravendale, U.S.A., **422** C1
Ravenglass, England, U.K., **306** E3
Ravenna, Italy, **294** D3
Ravensburg, Germany, **288** D5
Ravenshoe, Australia, **135** K2
Ravensthorpe, Australia, **134** E5
Ravenswood, U.S.A., **421** N6
Rāvi, *river*, India/Pakistan, **218** C3
Rawa Mazowiecka, Poland, **289** K3
Rawaki (Phoenix), *island*, Kiribati, **139** G5
Rāwalpindi, Pakistan, **218** C2
Rawāndūz, Iraq, **363** H1
Rawarra, *river*, Indonesia, **199** F3
Rawas, Indonesia, **199** F3
Rāwatsār, India, **218** C3
Rawḩah, Saudi Arabia, **363** H5
Rawicz, Poland, **289** H3
Rawlins, U.S.A., **419** L6
Rawson, Argentina, **460** E2
Rawtenstall, England, U.K., **306** F4
Rawu, China, **215** F3
Ray, Cape, Canada, **417** M6
Ray, U.S.A., **420** B1
Raya, Gunung, *mountain peak*, Indonesia, **201** F3
Raya, Tanjong, *point*, Aceh, Indonesia, **200** B2
Raya, Tanjong, *point*, Sumatera Selatan, Indonesia, **200** D3
Raychikhinsk, Russian Federation, **211** K2
Raydah, Yemen, **220** D5
Rayleigh, England, U.K., **305** H3
Raymond, Canada, **413** N7
Raymond, U.S.A., **418** C3
Raymondville, U.S.A., **424** D6
Raymore, Canada, **414** B6
Raynesford, U.S.A., **419** J3
Rayong, Thailand, **202** D3
Raystown Lake, U.S.A., **426** A4
Raz, Pointe du, *point*, France, **290** B3
Ražanj, Yugoslavia, **296** C4
Razelm, Lacul, *lake*, Romania, **296** G3
Razgrad, Bulgaria, **296** F4
Razim, Lacul, *lagoon*, Romania, **298** C4
Razlog, Bulgaria, **296** D5
Razmak, Pakistan, **218** B2
Ré, Île de, *island*, France, **290** D3
Reading, England, U.K., **305** G3
Reading, U.S.A., **426** C4
Reading, *unitary authority*, England, U.K., **305** G3
Readstown, U.S.A., **420** H4
Real, Cordillera, *mountain range*, Bolivia, **455** E4
Realicó, Argentina, **458** D5
Reao, *island*, French Polynesia, **137** H2
Rebbenesøy, *island*, Norway, **284** H1
Rebecca, Lake, Australia, **134** E5
Reboly, Russian Federation, **285** Q5
Rebordelo, Portugal, **292** D2
Rebun-tō, *island*, Japan, **209** H1
Recess, Ireland, **309** C4
Rechane, Russian Federation, **299** C4
Recherche, Archipelago of, *islands*, Australia, **134** E5
Recife, Brazil, **453** G5
Recife, Cape, South Africa, **371** E5
Récifs, Île aux, *island*, Seychelles, **373** A2
Recinto, Chile, **458** B5
Recklinghausen, Germany, **288** C3
Reconquista, Argentina, **459** E3
Recreio, Brazil, **455** G2
Recreo, Argentina, **458** D3
Red, *river*, Minnesota, U.S.A., **420** E2
Red, *river*, Oklahoma, U.S.A., **424** C2
Red Bank, New Jersey, U.S.A., **426** C4
Red Bank, Tennessee, U.S.A., **425** K2
Red Bay, Canada, **417** N4
Red Bluff, U.S.A., **422** B1
Red Cloud, U.S.A., **420** D5
Red Deer, Canada, **413** N5
Red Deer, *river*, Alberta, Canada, **413** N6
Red Deer, *river*, Saskatchewan, Canada, **414** C5
Red Deer Lake, Canada, **414** D5
Red Elm, U.S.A., **420** C3
Red Indian Lake, Canada, **417** N5
Red Lake, Canada, **414** H6
Red Lake Road, Canada, **414** H7
Red Lodge, U.S.A., **419** K4
Red Rock, British Columbia, Canada, **412** H5
Red Rock, Ontario, Canada, **421** J1
Red Sea, Africa/Asia, **220** C4
Red Sucker Lake, Canada, **414** G4
Red Wing, U.S.A., **420** G3
Redang, Pulau, *island*, Malaysia, **200** C1
Redbird, U.S.A., **419** M5
Redcar, England, U.K., **307** G3
Redcar and Cleveland, *unitary authority*, England, U.K., **307** G3
Redcliff, Canada, **413** P6
Redcliff, Zimbabwe, **371** E2
Redding, California, U.S.A., **422** B1
Redding, Iowa, U.S.A., **420** F5
Redditch, England, U.K., **305** F2
Redditt, Canada, **414** G7
Rede, *river*, England, U.K., **306** F2

Redenção, Brazil, **452** C5
Redenção de Gurguéia, Brazil, **457** E2
Redeyef, Tunisia, **361** H2
Redfield, New York, U.S.A., **426** C3
Redfield, South Dakota, U.S.A., **420** D3
Redhead, Trinidad, Trinidad and Tobago, **461** C4
Redhill, England, U.K., **305** G3
Rédics, Hungary, **289** H5
Redkino, Russian Federation, **299** F4
Redland, Orkney, Scotland, U.K., **308** F1
Redlynch, England, U.K., **305** F4
Redmond, U.S.A., **418** D4
Redon, France, **290** C3
Redonda, *island*, Antigua and Barbuda, **427** D2
Redonda, Punta, *point*, Isla de Pascua (Easter Island), Chile, **461** B2
Redondo, Portugal, **292** D3
Redruth, England, U.K., **304** B4
Redstone, Canada, **412** H5
Redwood City, U.S.A., **422** B3
Redwood Valley, U.S.A., **422** B2
Red'ya, *river*, Russian Federation, **299** C4
Ree, Lough, *lake*, Ireland, **309** E4
Reed City, U.S.A., **421** L4
Reedpoint, U.S.A., **419** K4
Reedsburg, U.S.A., **420** H4
Reedsport, U.S.A., **418** B5
Reedville, U.S.A., **426** B6
Reefton, New Zealand, **133** C6
Reform, U.S.A., **425** J3
Regeb, Sudan, **366** B2
Regen, Germany, **288** F4
Regen, *river*, Germany, **288** F4
Regensburg, Germany, **288** F4
Regent, U.S.A., **420** B2
Reggane, Algeria, **361** G3
Reggane, Sebkha, *lake*, Algeria, **361** F3
Reggio di Calabria, Italy, **295** E6
Reggio nell' Emilia, Italy, **294** C3
Reghin, Romania, **296** E2
Regina, Brazil, **452** C2
Regina, Canada, **414** B6
Régina, French Guiana, **452** C2
Regina, U.S.A., **423** K3
Regna, Sweden, **286** G3
Reharaka, Madagascar, **372** A4
Rehli, India, **218** D5
Rehoboth, Namibia, **370** C3
Rehovot, Israel, **225** C4
Reichenau, Switzerland, **291** J3
Reichenbach, Germany, **288** F3
Reidsville, U.S.A., **421** P7
Reigate, England, U.K., **305** G3
Reigh, Rubha, *point*, Scotland, U.K., **308** C3
Reilly Hill, U.S.A., **420** B5
Reims, France, **291** G2
Reina Adelaida, Archipiélago de la, *islands*, Chile, **460** B4
Reinbek, Germany, **288** E2
Reindeer, *river*, Canada, **414** C4
Reindeer Lake, Canada, **414** C3
Reinga, Cape, New Zealand, **132** D2
Reinosa, Spain, **292** E1
Reinøy, *island*, Norway, **284** J2
Reinsfjell, *mountain peak*, Norway, **284** E5
Reisaelva, *river*, Norway, **284** K2
Reisjärvi, Finland, **285** M5
Reisseck, *mountain peak*, Austria, **294** D2
Reisterstown, U.S.A., **426** B5
Reitoru, *island*, French Polynesia, **137** G2
Rejunya, Venezuela, **451** F3
Rekovac, Yugoslavia, **296** C4
Relizane, Algeria, **361** G1
Rémalard, France, **290** E2
Remanso, Brazil, **457** E2
Rembang, Indonesia, **201** E4
Remennikovo, Russian Federation, **299** B4
Rémire, French Guiana, **452** C2
Remiremont, France, **291** H2
Remo, *mountain peak*, Italy, **295** D4
Rempang, Pulau, *island*, Indonesia, **200** C2
Remscheld, Germany, **288** C3
Rena, Norway, **286** E2
Renam, Myanmar, **205** C2
Rencēni, Latvia, **287** M4
Rend Lake, U.S.A., **421** J6
Renda, Latvia, **287** L4
Rendova, *island*, Solomon Islands, **141** A1
Rendsburg, Germany, **288** D1
Renfrew, Canada, **416** C7
Renfrewshire, *local authority*, Scotland, U.K., **308** E5
Rengat, Indonesia, **200** C3
Rengo, Chile, **458** B5
Renhua, China, **206** C3
Reni, Ukraine, **296** G3
Renmark, Australia, **135** J5
Rennebu, Norway, **286** D1
Rennell, *island*, Solomon Islands, **141** A1
Rennes, France, **290** D2
Rennie, Canada, **414** G7
Reno, U.S.A., **422** D2
Renovo, U.S.A., **426** B4
Renqiu, China, **210** G5
Renshan, China, **207** D3
Renshou, China, **215** H3
Rensjön, Sweden, **284** J2
Renwer, Canada, **414** D5
Réo, Burkina Faso, **364** D2
Reo, Indonesia, **198** C5
Répcelak, Hungary, **289** H5
Repetek, Turkmenistan, **222** G5
Republic, U.S.A., **418** E2
Repulse Bay, Canada, **411** L3
Repvåg, Norway, **285** M1
Requena, Peru, **454** D1
Requena, Spain, **293** G3
Réquista, France, **290** F4
Rere, Solomon Islands, **141** A1
Resang, Tanjong, *point*, Malaysia, **200** C2
Resen, Macedonia, **297** C5
Reserva, Brazil, **459** G2
Reserve, Canada, **414** C5
Reserve, U.S.A., **419** M2
Resistencia, Argentina, **459** E3
Reşiţa, Romania, **296** C3
Resko, Poland, **289** G2
Resolute, Canada, **411** K2
Resolution Island, Canada, **411** N4
Resolution Island, New Zealand, **133** A7
Resseta, *river*, Russian Federation, **299** E6
Restigouche, *river*, Canada, **416** H6
Restinga, Punta, *point*, Islas Canarias, Spain, **373** A4
Retalhuleu, Guatemala, **428** C4
Reteag, Romania, **296** E2
Retén Llico, Chile, **458** B5
Retford, England, U.K., **307** H4
Rethel, France, **291** G2
Rethymno, Kriti, Greece, **297** E8
Retz, Austria, **289** G4
Réunion, *French department*, Indian Ocean, **373** A1
Reus, Spain, **293** H2
Reutlingen, Germany, **288** D4
Revda, Russian Federation, **285** S3
Revelstoke, Canada, **413** K6
Reventazón, Peru, **454** B2
Revermont, *region*, France, **291** G3
Revillagigedo, Islas, *islands*, Mexico, **409** M7
Revivim, Israel, **225** C4
Revúboè, *river*, Mozambique, **369** F6
Revúca, Slovakia, **289** K4
Rewa, India, **219** E4
Rewāri, India, **218** D3
Rexburg, U.S.A., **419** J5
Rexford, U.S.A., **418** G2
Rey, Isla del, *island*, Panama, **429** F5
Rey Bouba, Cameroon, **365** G3
Reyes, Bolivia, **455** E4
Reyes, Point, U.S.A., **422** B3
Reyes, Punta dos, *point*, Chile, **458** B2
Reyhanlı, Turkey, **225** D1
Reykhólar, Iceland, **284** X7
Reykjanes Ridge, *underwater feature*, Atlantic Ocean, **477** E2
Reykjavík, Iceland, **284** X7
Reynosa, Mexico, **431** F3
Rēzekne, Latvia, **287** N4
Rezina, Moldova, **296** G2
Rgotina, Yugoslavia, **296** D3
Rhayader, Wales, U.K., **304** D2
Rhein, *river*, Austria, **291** J3
Rhein, *river*, Germany, **288** C3
Rhein, *river*, Switzerland, **291** J3
Rheine, Germany, **288** C2
Rheinland-Pfalz, *state*, Germany, **288** C3
Rheinwaldhorn, *mountain peak*, Switzerland, **291** J3
Rhiconich, Scotland, U.K., **308** E2
Rhin, *river*, France, **291** H3
Rhine, *river*, Europe, **280** E5; *see also* Rhein, *river*, Austria, **291** J3; Rhein, *river*, Germany, **288** C3; Rhein, *river*, Switzerland, **291** J3; Rhin, *river*, France, **291** H3
Rhinelander, U.S.A., **421** J3
Rhino Camp, Uganda, **369** F2
Rhinow, Germany, **288** F2
Rhir, Cap, *cape*, Morocco, **360** D2
Rho, Italy, **294** B3
Rhode Island, *state*, U.S.A., **426** E4
Rhodes *see* Rodos, *island*, Dodekanisos, Greece, **297** G7
Rhododendron, U.S.A., **418** D4
Rhondda, Wales, U.K., **304** D3
Rhondda Cynon Taff, *unitary authority*, Wales, U.K., **304** D3
Rhône, *river*, France/Germany/Switzerland, **280** E7
Rhône-Alpes, *administrative region*, France, **291** G4
Rhosllanerchrugog, Wales, U.K., **304** D1
Rhossili, Wales, U.K., **304** C3
Rhum, *island*, Scotland, U.K., **308** C4
Rhyl, Wales, U.K., **306** E4
Riaba, Equatorial Guinea, **368** A2
Riachão, Brazil, **452** D5
Riachão das Neves, Brazil, **457** E3
Riachão do Jacuípe, Brazil, **457** F3
Riacho de Santana, Brazil, **457** E3
Rialma, Brazil, **456** D4
Rianápolis, Brazil, **456** D4
Riang, India, **219** H4
Riaño, Spain, **292** E1
Riánsares, *river*, Spain, **293** F3
Riau, Kepulauan, *islands*, Indonesia, **200** D2
Riau, *province*, Indonesia, **200** C2
Ribadeo, Spain, **292** D1
Ribadesella, Spain, **292** E1
Ribas do Rio Pardo, Brazil, **456** C5
Ribáué, Mozambique, **369** G5
Ribe, Denmark, **286** D5
Ribeira, *river*, Brazil, **459** H2
Ribeira Brava, Madeira, Portugal, **373** C3
Ribeirão Prêto, Brazil, **456** D5
Ribera, Sicilia, Italy, **295** D7
Ribérac, France, **290** E4
Riberalta, Bolivia, **455** E3
Ribnica, Slovenia, **294** E3
Ribnitz-Damgarten, Germany, **288** F1
Ricardo Flores Magón, Mexico, **430** D2
Rice, California, U.S.A., **422** F4
Rice, Washington, U.S.A., **418** E2
Rice Lake, Canada, **416** B7
Riceboro, U.S.A., **425** M4
Rich Hill, U.S.A., **420** F6
Richard Toll, Senegal, **364** A1
Richards Bay, South Africa, **371** F4
Richardson, *river*, Canada, **413** P2
Richardton, U.S.A., **420** B2
Richdale, Canada, **413** P6
Richey, U.S.A., **419** M3
Richfield, Idaho, U.S.A., **418** G5
Richfield, Utah, U.S.A., **423** G2
Richibucto, Canada, **416** J6
Richland Center, U.S.A., **420** H4
Richland Springs, U.S.A., **424** C4
Richmond, Australia, **135** J3
Richmond, England, U.K., **307** G3
Richmond, Indiana, U.S.A., **421** L6
Richmond, Kentucky, U.S.A., **421** L7
Richmond, Mount, *mountain peak*, New Zealand, **133** D5
Richmond, New Zealand, **133** D5
Richmond, South Africa, **370** D5
Richmond, Virginia, U.S.A., **426** B6
Richmond Hill, U.S.A., **425** M4
Richmond Range, *mountain range*, New Zealand, **133** D5
Ricobayo, Embalse de, *reservoir*, Spain, **292** E2
Riddle, U.S.A., **418** F5
Ridgecrest, U.S.A., **422** E4
Ridgeview, U.S.A., **420** C3
Ridgway, U.S.A., **423** K2
Riedenburg, Germany, **288** E4
Riedlingen, Germany, **288** D4
Riepentjåkkå, *mountain peak*, Sweden, **284** H3
Riesa, Germany, **288** F3
Riesco, Isla, *island*, Chile, **460** C4
Rietavas, Lithuania, **287** K5
Rieti, Italy, **295** D4
Riez, France, **291** H5
Rifle, U.S.A., **423** K2
Rifstangi, *point*, Iceland, **284** Y6
Rift Valley, *province*, Kenya, **369** G2
Rig-Rig, Chad, **365** G2
Riga, Gulf of, Estonia/Latvia, **287** L4
Rīga, Latvia, **287** M4
Rigby, U.S.A., **419** J5
Rigestān, *region*, Afganistan, **218** A3
Riggins, U.S.A., **418** F4
Riguldi, Estonia, **287** L3
Riihimäki, Finland, **287** M2
Riiser-Larsenhalvøya, *peninsula*, Antarctica, **470** E3
Riisipere, Estonia, **287** M3
Rijau, Nigeria, **365** F2
Rijeka, Croatia, **294** E3
Riksgränsen, Sweden, **284** J2
Riley, U.S.A., **418** E5
Rimatara, *island*, French Polynesia, **137** F3
Rimavská Sobota, Slovakia, **289** K4
Rimbo, Sweden, **287** J3
Rimforsa, Sweden, **286** G3
Rimini, Italy, **294** D3
Rimouski, Canada, **416** G5
Rinbung, China, **214** D3
Rinca, Pulau, *island*, Indonesia, **198** B5
Rincon, Bonaire, Netherlands Antilles, **461** A4
Rincón, Cerro del, *mountain peak*, Argentina/Chile, **458** C2
Rincon, U.S.A., **423** K5
Rinda, China, **215** G3
Rindal, Norway, **284** D5
Rindü, China, **214** D3
Rineia, *island*, Kyklades, Greece, **297** E7
Ringarum, Sweden, **286** H3
Ringas, India, **218** C4
Ringdove, Vanuatu, **141** A2
Ringgi, Solomon Islands, **141** A1
Ringim, Nigeria, **365** F2
Ringkøbing, Denmark, **286** D4
Ringling, U.S.A., **419** J3
Ringsted, Denmark, **286** E5
Ringvassøy, *island*, Norway, **284** J2
Ringwood, England, U.K., **305** F4
Riñihue, Chile, **460** C1
Rinjani, Gunung, *mountain peak*, Indonesia, **201** G5
Rintala, Russian Federation, **299** B2
Rinteln, Germany, **288** D2
Rio, Greece, **297** C6
Rio Alegre, Brazil, **456** B4
Rio Blanco, U.S.A., **423** K2
Rio Branco, Acre, Brazil, **455** E2
Rio Branco, Mato Grosso, Brazil, **455** G4
Rio Branco do Sul, Brazil, **459** H2
Río Bravo, Mexico, **431** F3
Rio Brilhante, Brazil, **456** B5
Río Bueno, Chile, **460** C1
Río Caribe, Venezuela, **451** F1
Río Ceballos, Argentina, **458** D4
Rio Claro, Brazil, **459** H2
Rio Claro, Trinidad, Trinidad and Tobago, **461** C4
Río Colorado, Argentina, **460** E1
Río Cuarto, Argentina, **458** D4
Rio de Janeiro, Brazil, **457** E6
Rio de Janeiro, *state*, Brazil, **457** E5
Río de Jesús, Panama, **429** E6
Rio Do Ouro, São Tomé and Príncipe, **373** C4
Rio Do Sul, Brazil, **459** H3
Río Frío, Costa Rica, **428** E5
Río Gallegos, Argentina, **460** D4
Río Grande, Argentina, **460** D4
Rio Grande, Brazil, **459** G4
Río Grande, Mexico, **430** E4
Rio Grande City, U.S.A., **424** C6
Rio Grande do Norte, *state*, Brazil, **453** G4
Rio Grande do Sul, *state*, Brazil, **459** G3
Rio Grande Rise, *underwater feature*, Atlantic Ocean, **477** E8
Río Lagartos, Mexico, **431** H4
Rio Largo, Brazil, **457** G2
Rio Maior, Portugal, **292** C3
Río Mayo, Argentina, **460** C2
Río Mulatos, Bolivia, **455** E5
Rio Negro, Brazil, **459** H3
Rio Negro, Pantanal do, *swamp*, Brazil, **456** B5
Río Negro, *province*, Argentina, **460** D1
Río Negro, Represa del, *reservoir*, Uruguay, **459** F4
Rio Pardo, Brazil, **459** G4
Rio Pardo de Minas, Brazil, **457** E4
Rio Primero, Argentina, **458** D4
Río Tigre, Ecuador, **450** C5
Rio Tuba, Philippines, **204** B4
Rio Verde, Brazil, **456** C4
Río Verde, Chile, **460** C4
Río Verde, Mexico, **431** F4
Rio Verde de Mato Grosso, Brazil, **456** B5

St Simons Island, U.S.A., **425** M4
St Stephen, Canada, **416** H7
St Stephen, U.S.A., **425** N3
St Theresa Point, Canada, **414** G5
St Thomas, Canada, **421** N4
St Thomas, U.S.A., **420** E1
Saint-Tropez, France, **291** H5
Saint-Vaast-la-Hougue, France, **290** D2
Saint-Valéry-en-Caux, France, **290** E2
Saint-Valéry-sur-Somme, France, **290** E1
Saint-Vallier, France, **291** G3
St Vincent, Gulf, Australia, **135** H5
St Vincent and the Grenadines, *country*, Caribbean Sea, **409** S7
St Vincent Passage, Caribbean Sea, **427** D3
Saint-Vivien-de-Médoc, France, **290** D4
St Walburg, Canada, **413** Q5
St Xavier, U.S.A., **419** L4
Saint-Yrieix-la-Perche, France, **290** E4
Sainte-Adresse, France, **305** H5
Sainte-Anne, Lac, *lake*, Canada, **416** H4
Ste-Agathe-des-Monts, Canada, **416** D6
Sainte-Énimie, France, **291** F4
Sainte-Marie, Martinique, **427** D3
Sainte-Marie, Réunion, **373** A1
Sainte-Mère-Église, France, **305** F5
Sainte-Rose, Guadeloupe, **427** D2
Sainte-Rose, Réunion, **373** A1
Ste-Rose-du-Lac, Canada, **414** E6
Sainte-Suzanne, Réunion, **373** A1
Saintes, France, **290** D4
Saintes-Maries-de-la-Mer, France, **291** G5
Saintfield, Northern Ireland, U.K., **309** G3
Sāipal, *mountain peak*, Nepal, **219** E3
Saipan, *island*, Northern Mariana Islands, **138** C3
Saipan, Northern Mariana Islands, **138** C3
Sajam, Indonesia, **199** F3
Sajama, Bolivia, **455** E5
Sajama, Nevado, *mountain peak*, Bolivia, **455** E5
Sājir, Ra's, *cape*, Oman, **220** F5
Sājūr, *river*, Syria/Turkey, **225** D1
Saka, Ethiopia, **367** E3
Sakākah, Saudi Arabia, **363** H3
Sakakawea, Lake, U.S.A., **420** C2
Sakami, Lac, *lake*, Canada, **416** C3
Sakami, *river*, Canada, **416** D3
Sakaraha, Madagascar, **372** A5
Sakassou, Côte d'Ivoire, **364** C3
Sakata, Japan, **209** G3
Saketa, Indonesia, **198** D3
Sakété, Benin, **365** E3
Sakha, Respublika, *republic*, Russian Federation, **301** P3
Sakhalin, Ostrov, *island*, Russian Federation, **301** R4
Sakht-Sar, Iran, **222** E5
Şäki, Azerbaijan, **222** D4
Saki, Nigeria, **365** E3
Šakiai, Lithuania, **287** L5
Sakishima-shotō, *islands*, Japan, **209** M8
Sakleshpur, India, **216** C3
Sakmara, *river*, Russian Federation, **222** F2
Sakon Nakhon, Thailand, **203** E2
Sakra, Pulau, *island*, Singapore, **200** J7
Sakrivier, South Africa, **370** D5
Sakura, Japan, **209** H4
Säkylä, Finland, **287** L2
Sal, *island*, Cape Verde, **360** Q8
Sal Rei, Cape Verde, **360** Q8
Šal'a, Slovakia, **289** H4
Sala, Sweden, **286** H3
Sala y Gómez, *Chilean dependency*, Pacific Ocean, **105** P11
Salacgrīva, Latvia, **287** M4
Salada, Bahía, *bay*, Chile, **458** B3
Saladas, Argentina, **459** E3
Saladillo, Argentina, **459** E5
Saladillo, *river*, Córdoba, Argentina, **458** D4
Saladillo, *river*, Santa Fé, Argentina, **459** E4
Saladillo, *river*, Santiago del Estero, Argentina, **458** D3
Salado, *river*, Buenos Aires, Argentina, **459** E5
Salado, *river*, Formosa, Argentina, **459** E2
Salado, *river*, Mexico, **431** E3
Salado, *river*, Rio Nego, Argentina, **460** E1
Salado, *river*, Santiago del Estero, Argentina, **458** D3
Saladougou, Guinea, **364** C2
Salaga, Ghana, **364** D3
Sala'ilua, Samoa, **141** B1
Salal, Chad, **365** H2
Şalālah, Oman, **221** F5
Salālah, Sudan, **363** G4
Salamá, Guatemala, **428** C4
Salamanca, Chile, **458** B4
Salamanca, Mexico, **431** E4
Salamanca, Spain, **292** E2
Salamat, *prefecture*, Chad, **366** B2
Salamaua, Papua New Guinea, **140** B4
Salamina, Colombia, **450** C3
Salamīyah, Syria, **225** D2
Salamo, Papua New Guinea, **140** C5
Salani, Samoa, **141** B1
Salantai, Lithuania, **287** K4
Salas, Spain, **292** D1
Salas de los Infantes, Spain, **293** F1
Salatiga, Indonesia, **201** E4
Sălătrucu, Romania, **296** E3
Salau, France, **290** E5
Salavat, Russian Federation, **222** F2
Salawati, Pulau, *island*, Indonesia, **199** E3
Salāya, India, **218** B5
Salazar, Argentina, **458** D5
Salazie, Réunion, **373** A1
Salbris, France, **290** F3
Salcea, Romania, **296** F2
Šalčininkai, Lithuania, **287** M5
Salcombe, England, U.K., **304** D4
Sălcuța, Romania, **296** D3
Salda Gölü, *lake*, Turkey, **297** G7
Saldaña, Colombia, **450** C3
Saldanha, South Africa, **370** C5
Saldungaray, Argentina, **458** E6
Saldus, Latvia, **287** L4
Sale, Australia, **135** K6
Sale, England, U.K., **306** F4
Salehurst, England, U.K., **305** H4
Salekhard, Russian Federation, **300** H3
Salelologa, Samoa, **141** B1
Salem, Illinois, U.S.A., **421** J6
Salem, India, **216** D4
Salem, Missouri, U.S.A., **420** H7
Salem, Ohio, U.S.A., **421** N5
Salem, Oregon, U.S.A., **418** C4
Salem, South Dakota, U.S.A., **420** E4
Salemi, Sicilia, Italy, **295** D7
Salen, Scotland, U.K., **308** D4
Sälen, Sweden, **286** F2
Salernes, France, **291** H5
Salerno, Golfo di, *gulf*, Italy, **295** E5
Salerno, Italy, **295** E5
Salford, England, U.K., **306** F4
Salgado, *river*, Brazil, **453** F5
Salgótarján, Hungary, **289** J4
Salgueiro, Brazil, **453** F5
Salibea, Trinidad, Trinidad and Tobago, **461** C4
Salida, U.S.A., **423** L2
Salihli, Turkey, **297** G6
Salihorsk, Belarus, **298** C2
Salima, Malawi, **369** F5
Salina, Arizona, U.S.A., **423** J3
Salina, Isola, *island*, Italy, **295** E6
Salina, Kansas, U.S.A., **420** E6
Salina, Utah, U.S.A., **423** H2
Salina Cruz, Mexico, **431** G5
Salinas, Brazil, **457** E4
Salinas, Cabo de, *cape*, Islas Baleares, Spain, **293** J3
Salinas, Ecuador, **450** B5
Salinas, Pampa de la, *plain*, Argentina, **458** C4
Salinas, Punta, *point*, Dominican Republic, **429** H3
Salinas, Punta, *point*, Róbinson Crusoe Island, Archipiélago Juan Fernández, Chile, **461** C2
Salinas, U.S.A., **422** C3
Salinas de Garci Mendoza, Bolivia, **455** E5
Salinas de Hidalgo, Mexico, **430** E4
Salinas ó Lachay, Punta, *point*, Peru, **454** B3
Salinas Peak, *mountain peak*, U.S.A., **423** K5
Saline Bay, Trinidad, Trinidad and Tobago, **461** C4
Saline Lake, U.S.A., **424** F4
Salinitas, Chile, **458** B2
Salinópolis, Brazil, **452** D3
Salisbury, England, U.K., **305** F3
Salisbury, Maryland, U.S.A., **426** C5
Salisbury, North Carolina, U.S.A., **425** M2
Salisbury Island, Canada, **411** M3
Salisbury Plain, England, U.K., **305** E3
Sălişte, Romania, **296** D3
Salitre, *river*, Brazil, **457** F3
Şalkhad, Syria, **225** D3
Salla, Finland, **285** P3
Salliqueló, Argentina, **458** D5
Sallisaw, U.S.A., **424** E2
Salluit, Canada, **411** M3
Sallūm, Sudan, **363** G5
Sally's Cove, Canada, **417** N5
Salmās, Iran, **224** F5
Salmi, Russian Federation, **299** C2
Salmi, Sweden, **284** K2
Salmon, *river*, U.S.A., **418** F4
Salmon, U.S.A., **418** H4
Salmon Arm, Canada, **413** K6
Salmon Peak, *mountain peak*, U.S.A., **424** B5
Salmon River Mountains, *mountain range*, U.S.A., **418** F4
Salo, Finland, **287** L2
Saloinen, Finland, **285** M4
Salonica *see* Thessaloniki, Greece, **297** D5
Salonta, Romania, **296** C2
Salor, *river*, Spain, **292** D3
Salsacate, Argentina, **458** D4
Sal'sk, Russian Federation, **298** F3
Salso, *river*, Sicilia, Italy, **295** D7
Salsomaggiore Terme, Italy, **294** B3
Salt, *river*, U.S.A., **423** H5
Salt Basin, U.S.A., **423** L6
Salt Flat, U.S.A., **423** L6
Salt Lake City, U.S.A., **423** H1
Salta, Argentina, **458** D2
Salta, *province*, Argentina, **458** D2
Saltash, England, U.K., **304** C4
Saltburn-by-the-Sea, England, U.K., **307** H3
Saltcoats, Scotland, U.K., **308** E5
Saltee Islands, Ireland, **309** F5
Saltillo, Mexico, **431** E3
Salto, Argentina, **459** E5
Salto, *river*, Italy, **295** D4
Salto, Uruguay, **459** F4
Salto da Divisa, Brazil, **457** F4
Salto del Guairá, Paraguay, **459** F2
Salto Santiago, Represa de, *reservoir*, Brazil, **459** G2
Salton Sea, *lake*, U.S.A., **422** E5
Saltpond, Ghana, **364** D3
Saltvik, Finland, **287** K2
Saluafata, Samoa, **141** B1
Saluda, U.S.A., **425** M3
Salūm, Khalīj as, *gulf*, Egypt/Libya, **362** E2
Sālūmbar, India, **218** C4
Saluzzo, Italy, **294** A3
Salvacion, Philippines, **204** D4
Salvador, Brazil, **457** F3
Salvaterra, Brazil, **452** D3
Salvatierra, Mexico, **431** E4
Salviac, France, **290** E4
Salween, *river*, Asia, **195** L7; *see also* Nu, *river*, China, **215** F3; Thanlwin, *river*, Myanmar, **205** C4
Salyan, Azerbaijan, **222** D5
Salzburg, Austria, **288** F5
Salzburg, *state*, Austria, **288** F5
Salzgitter, Germany, **288** E2
Salzkammergut, *region*, Austria, **289** F5
Salzwedel, Germany, **288** E2
Sām, India, **218** B4
Sam A Tsuen, China, **207** C3
Sam Rayburn Reservoir, U.S.A., **424** E4
Sầm Sơn, Vietnam, **203** E2
Samagaltay, Russian Federation, **223** N2
Samaipata, Bolivia, **455** F5
Samal Island, Philippines, **204** D5
Samalaeulu, Samoa, **141** B1
Samālūţ, Egypt, **363** F3
Samaná, Bahía de, *bay*, Dominican Republic, **429** H3
Samandağı, Turkey, **225** C1
Samangān, Afghanistan, **218** B2
Samar, *island*, Philippines, **204** D4
Samara, Russian Federation, **222** E2
Samarai, Papua New Guinea, **140** C5
Samariapo, Venezuela, **451** E3
Samarinda, Indonesia, **201** G3
Samarqand, Uzbekistan, **222** H5
Sāmarrā', Iraq, **363** H2
Samarskaya Oblast', *province*, Russian Federation, **222** D2
Samasodu, Solomon Islands, **141** A1
Samastīpur, India, **219** F4
Samatait, Samoa, **141** B1
Samatau, Samoa, **141** B1
Samba, Democratic Republic of the Congo, **369** E3
Samba Cajú, Angola, **368** C4
Sambaliung, Pegunungan, *mountain range*, Indonesia, **201** G2
Sambalpur, India, **219** F5
Sambar, Tanjong, *point*, Indonesia, **201** E3
Sambas, Indonesia, **201** E2
Sambau, Indonesia, **200** D3
Sambava, Madagascar, **372** C3
Sāmbhar, India, **218** C4
Sambir, Ukraine, **289** L4
Sambito, *river*, Brazil, **453** F5
Sambo, Angola, **368** C5
Samborombón, Bahía, *bay*, Argentina, **459** F5
Sambre, *river*, France, **291** F1
Sambro, Canada, **417** K7
Samch'ŏk, South Korea, **208** E3
Samdari, India, **218** C4
Same, Tanzania, **369** G3
Samer, France, **305** J4
Samfya, Zambia, **369** E5
Samḩah, *island*, Suquţrá (Socotra), Yemen, **373** B2
Sami, India, **218** B5
Samia, Tanjong, *point*, Indonesia, **198** C2
Samijiyŏn, North Korea, **211** K4
Samka, Myanmar, **205** C3
Samnū, Libya, **362** B3
Samoa, *country*, Pacific Ocean, **131** H3
Samobor, Croatia, **294** E3
Samokov, Bulgaria, **296** D4
Šamorín, Slovakia, **289** H4
Samos, Dodekanisos, Greece, **297** F7
Samos, *island*, Dodekanisos, Greece, **297** F7
Samosir, Pulau, *island*, Indonesia, **200** B2
Samothraki, *island*, Greece, **297** E5
Sampit, Indonesia, **201** F3
Sampit, *river*, Indonesia, **201** F3
Sampit, Teluk, *bay*, Indonesia, **201** F3
Sampun, Papua New Guinea, **140** D4
Sampwe, Democratic Republic of the Congo, **369** E4
Samsang, China, **214** B3
Samsø Bælt, *strait*, Denmark, **286** E5
Samsu, North Korea, **208** E2
Samsun, Turkey, **224** E4
Samucumbi, Angola, **368** C5
Samui, Ko, *island*, Thailand, **202** D4
Samut Prakan, Thailand, **202** D3
Samut Sakhon, Thailand, **202** D3
Samut Songkhram, Thailand, **202** D3
San, Mali, **364** D2
San, *river*, Cambodia, **203** E3
San Agustín, Argentina, **459** E5
San Agustín de Valle Fértil, Argentina, **458** C4
San Ambrosio, Isla, *island*, Chile, **449** E6
San Andreas, U.S.A., **422** C2
San Andrés, Bahía de, *bay*, San Andrés, Colombia, **461** B1
San Andrés, Bolivia, **455** F4
San Andrés, *island*, Colombia, Caribbean Sea, **461** B1
San Andres, Philippines, **204** C3
San Andrés, San Andrés, Colombia, **461** B1
San Andrés Tuxtla, Mexico, **431** G5
San Angelo, U.S.A., **424** B4
San Antonio, Belize, **428** C3
San Antonio, Bolivia, **455** F4
San Antonio, Cabo, *cape*, Cuba, **428** D2
San Antonio, Catamarca, Argentina, **458** D3
San Antonio, Chile, **458** B4
San Antonio, Mount, *mountain peak*, U.S.A., **422** E4
San Antonio, San Luis, Argentina, **458** C4
San Antonio, U.S.A., **424** C5
San Antonio, Venezuela, **451** E3
San Antonio Abad, Islas Baleares, Spain, **293** H3
San Antonio Bay, Philippines, **204** B4
San Antonio de Caparo, Venezuela, **450** D2
San Antonio de los Cobres, Argentina, **458** C2
San Antonio de Tamanaco, Venezuela, **451** E2

San Antonio Oeste, Argentina, **460** E1
San Ardo, U.S.A., **422** C3
San Augustin, Cape, Philippines, **204** D5
San Bartolo, Mexico, **431** E4
San Bartolomeo in Galdo, Italy, **295** E5
San Benedetto del Tronto, Italy, **294** D4
San Bernando, Argentina, **458** E3
San Bernardino, U.S.A., **422** E4
San Bernardino Mountains, *mountain range*, U.S.A., **422** E4
San Bernardo, Chile, **458** B4
San Bernardo, Mexico, **430** D3
San Blás, Archipiélago, *islands*, Panama, **429** F5
San Blas, Nayarit, Mexico, **430** D4
San Blas, Sinaloa, Mexico, **430** C3
San Borja, Bolivia, **455** E4
San Buenaventura, Mexico, **430** E3
San Camilo, Argentina, **458** E2
San Carlos, Argentina, **458** C4
San Carlos, Bolivia, **455** F4
San Carlos, Chile, **458** B5
San Carlos, Luzon Island, Philippines, **204** C3
San Carlos, Mexico, **431** F3
San Carlos, N. Venezuela, **451** E2
San Carlos, Negros Island, Philippines, **204** C4
San Carlos, Nicaragua, **428** D5
San Carlos, *river*, Paraguay, **459** E2
San Carlos, S. Venezuela, **451** E4
San Carlos, Uruguay, **459** F5
San Carlos, U.S.A., **423** H5
San Carlos Centro, Argentina, **458** E4
San Carlos de Bariloche, Argentina, **460** C1
San Carlos de Bolívar, Argentina, **458** E4
San Carlos del Zulia, Venezuela, **450** D2
San Ciro de Acosta, Mexico, **431** F4
San Clemente, Chile, **458** B5
San Clemente, *island*, U.S.A., **422** D5
San Clemente, Spain, **293** F3
San Clemente, U.S.A., **422** E5
San Cristóbal, Argentina, **458** E4
San Cristóbal, Bolivia, **455** E5
San Cristóbal, Dominican Republic, **429** H3
San Cristóbal, Isla, *island*, Islas Galápagos (Galapagos Islands), Ecuador, **461** A2
San Cristóbal, Venezuela, **450** D2
San Cristóbal de las Casas, Mexico, **431** G5
San Diego, California, U.S.A., **422** E5
San Diego, Texas, U.S.A., **424** C6
San Dimas, Mexico, **430** D3
San Donà di Piave, Italy, **294** D3
San Estanislao, Paraguay, **459** F2
San Esteban de Gormaz, Spain, **293** F2
San Felipe, Baja California, Mexico, **430** B2
San Felipe, Chile, **458** B4
San Felipe, Guanajuato, Mexico, **431** E4
San Felipe, Providencia, Colombia, **461** C1
San Felipe, Venezuela, **451** E1
San Felipe de Jesús, Mexico, **430** D3
San Feliu de Guíxols, Spain, **293** J2

San Félix, Isla, *island*, Chile, **449** D6
San Fernando, Argentina, **459** E5
San Fernando, Central Luzon Island, Philippines, **204** C3
San Fernando, Chile, **458** B5
San Fernando, Mexico, **431** F3
San Fernando, N. Luzon Island, Philippines, **204** C2
San Fernando, Spain, **292** D4
San Fernando, Trinidad, Trinidad and Tobago, **461** C4
San Fernando de Apure, Venezuela, **451** E3
San Fernando de Atabapo, Venezuela, **451** E3
San Fernando del Valle de Catamarca, Argentina, **458** D3
San Fidel, U.S.A., **423** K4
San Francique, Trinidad, Trinidad and Tobago, **461** C4
San Francisco, Argentina, **458** D4
San Francisco, Cabo de, *cape*, Ecuador, **450** B4
San Francisco, Mexico, **430** B2
San Francisco, Panama, **429** E5
San Francisco, Philippines, **204** C3
San Francisco, U.S.A., **422** B3
San Francisco de Macorís, Dominican Republic, **429** H3
San Francisco de Paula, Cabo, *cape*, Argentina, **460** D3
San Francisco del Chañar, Argentina, **458** D3
San Francisco del Oro, Mexico, **430** D3
San Gabriel, Ecuador, **450** C4
San Germán, Puerto Rico, **427** C2
San Gil, Colombia, **450** D2
San Hipólito, Punta, *point*, Mexico, **430** B3
San Ignacio, Belize, **428** C3
San Ignacio, Beni, Bolivia, **455** F4
San Ignacio, Paraguay, **459** F3
San Ignacio, Peru, **454** B1
San Ignacio, Santa Cruz, Bolivia, **455** G4
San Ildefonso, Cape, Philippines, **204** C2
San Javier, Bolivia, **455** F4
San Javier, Chile, **458** B5
San Javier, Misiones, Argentina, **459** F3
San Javier, Santa Fé, Argentina, **459** E4
San Javier, Spain, **293** G4
San Jerónimo, Serranía de, *mountain range*, Colombia, **450** C2
San Joaquin, *river*, U.S.A., **422** C3
San Joaquin Valley, U.S.A., **422** C3
San Jorge, Argentina, **458** E4
San Jorge, Golfo de, *gulf*, Argentina, **460** C3
San Jorge, Golfo de, *gulf*, Spain, **293** H2
San Jorge, *river*, Colombia, **450** C2
San José, Costa Rica, **428** D5
San José, Golfo, *gulf*, Argentina, **460** E2
San José, Isla, *island*, Mexico, **430** C3
San José, Isla, *island*, Panama, **429** F5
San Jose, Luzon Island, Philippines, **204** C3
San Jose, Mindoro Island, Philippines, **204** C3
San Jose, Panay Island, Philippines, **204** C4
San José, Spain, **293** F4
San Jose, U.S.A., **422** C3
San José, Volcán, *mountain peak*, Chile, **458** B4
San José de Amacuro,

Venezuela, **451** G2
San José de Chiquitos, Bolivia, **455** G4
San José de Dimas, Mexico, **430** C2
San José de Feliciano, Argentina, **459** E4
San José de Gracia, Baja California Sur, Mexico, **430** B3
San José de Gracia, Sinaloa, Mexico, **430** D3
San José de Guanipa, Venezuela, **451** F2
San José de Jáchal, Argentina, **458** C4
San José de la Dormida, Argentina, **458** D4
San José de la Mariquina, Chile, **460** C1
San José de Mayo, Uruguay, **459** F5
San José de Ocuné, Colombia, **451** D3
San José de Quero, Peru, **454** C3
San José de Raíces, Mexico, **431** E3
San Jose del Boqueron, Argentina, **458** D3
San José del Cabo, Mexico, **430** C4
San José del Guaviare, Colombia, **450** D3
San José del Progreso, Mexico, **431** F5
San Jose Island, U.S.A., **424** D6
San Juan, Argentina, **458** C4
San Juan, Cabo, *cape*, Argentina, **460** E5
San Juan, Cabo, *cape*, Equatorial Guinea, **368** A2
San Juan, Dominican Republic, **429** H3
San Juan, Peru, **454** C4
San Juan, Pico, *mountain peak*, Cuba, **429** E2
San Juan, *province*, Argentina, **458** C4
San Juan, Puerto Rico, **427** C2
San Juan, Punta, *point*, Isla de Pascua (Easter Island), Chile, **461** B2
San Juan, *river*, Costa Rica/Nicaragua, **428** D5
San Juan, U.S.A., **423** H3
San Juan, Venezuela, **451** F3
San Juan Bautista, Islas Baleares, Spain, **293** H3
San Juan Bautista, Paraguay, **459** F3
San Juan Bautista, Róbinson Crusoe Island, Archipiélago Juan Fernández, Chile, **461** C2
San Juan Bautista Tuxtepec, Mexico, **431** F5
San Juan de Guadalupe, Mexico, **430** E3
San Juan de los Cayos, Venezuela, **451** E1
San Juan de los Morros, Venezuela, **451** E2
San Juan de Salvamento, Argentina, **460** E5
San Juan del Norte, Nicaragua, **428** E5
San Juan del Río, Durango, Mexico, **430** D3
San Juan del Río, Queretaro, Mexico, **431** F4
San Juan del Sur, Nicaragua, **428** D5
San Juan Mountains, *mountain range*, U.S.A., **423** K3
San Juancito, Honduras, **428** D4
San Juanico, Punta, *point*, Mexico, **430** B3
San Justo, Argentina, **458** E4
San Lázaro, Cabo, *cape*, Mexico, **430** B3
San Lorenzo, Argentina, **458** E4
San Lorenzo, Beni, Bolivia, **455** F4

San Lorenzo, Ecuador, **450** B4
San Lorenzo, Monte, *mountain peak*, Chile, **460** C3
San Lorenzo, *mountain peak*, Spain, **293** F1
San Lorenzo, Paraguay, **459** F2
San Lorenzo, Peru, **455** E3
San Lorenzo, Tarija, Bolivia, **455** F5
San Lucas, Baja California Sur, Mexico, **430** B3
San Lucas, Bolivia, **455** F5
San Lucas, Cabo, *cape*, Mexico, **430** C4
San Lucas, S. Baja California Sur, Mexico, **430** C4
San Lucas Ojitlán, Mexico, **431** F5
San Luis, Argentina, **458** C4
San Luis, Guatemala, **428** C3
San Luis, Lago de, *lake*, Bolivia, **455** F3
San Luis, Mexico, **430** D3
San Luis, *province*, Argentina, **458** C4
San Luís, San Andrés, Colombia, **461** B1
San Luis, Sierra de, *mountain range*, Argentina, **458** D4
San Luis de la Paz, Mexico, **431** E4
San Luis del Palmar, Argentina, **459** E3
San Luis Obispo, U.S.A., **422** C4
San Luis Potosí, Mexico, **431** E4
San Luis Potosí, *state*, Mexico, **431** E4
San Luis Río Colorado, Mexico, **430** B1
San Luisito, Mexico, **430** B2
San Marco, Capo, *cape*, Italy, **295** D7
San Marcos, Guatemala, **428** C4
San Marcos, Mexico, **431** F5
San Marcos, U.S.A., **424** D5
San Marino, *country*, Europe, **282** F7
San Marino, San Marino, **294** D4
San Martín, Argentina, **458** D3
San Martin, Cape, U.S.A., **422** B4
San Martín, Colombia, **450** D3
San Martin, Lago, *lake*, Argentina, **460** C3
San Martín, *river*, Bolivia, **455** F4
San Martín De Los Andes, Argentina, **460** C1
San Martín de Valdeiglesias, Spain, **292** E2
San Mateo, U.S.A., **422** B3
San Matías, Bolivia, **455** G4
San Matías, Golfo, *gulf*, Argentina, **460** E1
San Mauricio, Venezuela, **451** E2
San Miguel, Bolivia, **455** G4
San Miguel, El Salvador, **428** C4
San Miguel, *island*, U.S.A., **422** C4
San Miguel, Panama, **429** F5
San Miguel, Peru, **454** D3
San Miguel, *river*, Bolivia, **455** F4
San Miguel, *river*, Colombia/Ecuador, **450** C4
San Miguel, *river*, Mexico, **430** C2
San Miguel Bay, Philippines, **204** C3
San Miguel de Huachi, Bolivia, **455** E4
San Miguel de Tucumán, Argentina, **458** D3
San Miguel del Monte, Argentina, **459** E5
San Miguelito, Bolivia, **455** E3
San Miguelito, Panama, **429** F5
San Millán, *mountain peak*, Spain, **293** F1
San Nicolás, Bahía, *bay*, Peru, **454** C4

San Nicolas, *island*, U.S.A., **422** C5
San Nicolás de los Arroyos, Argentina, **459** E4
San Nicolás de Tolentino, Islas Canarias, Spain, **373** B4
San Pablo, Beni, Bolivia, **455** F4
San Pablo, Philippines, **204** C3
San Pablo, Potosí, Bolivia, **455** E5
San Patricio, U.S.A., **423** L5
San Pedro, Bolivia, **455** F4
San Pedro, Buenos Aires, Argentina, **459** E4
San-Pédro, Côte d'Ivoire, **364** C4
San Pedro, Jujuy, Argentina, **458** D2
San Pedro, Mexico, **430** C4
San Pedro, Misiones, Argentina, **459** F3
San Pedro, Paraguay, **459** F2
San Pedro, *river*, Cuba, **429** F2
San Pedro *see* Bulalacao, Philippines, **204** C3
San Pedro, Sierra de, *mountain range*, Spain, **292** D3
San Pedro, Volcán, *mountain peak*, Chile, **458** C1
San Pedro de Arimena, Colombia, **450** D3
San Pedro de Atacama, Chile, **458** C2
San Pedro de Las Bocas, Venezuela, **451** F2
San Pedro de las Colonias, Mexico, **430** D3
San Pedro de Macorís, Dominican Republic, **429** H3
San Pedro Sula, Honduras, **428** D4
San Pedro Tapanatepec, Mexico, **431** F5
San Pedro Totalapan, Mexico, **431** F5
San Pietro, Isola di, *island*, Italy, **295** A6
San Quintín, Mexico, **430** B2
San Rafael, Argentina, **458** C5
San Rafael, Bolivia, **455** G4
San Rafael, Cerro, *mountain peak*, Paraguay, **459** F3
San Rafael, Venezuela, **450** D1
San Rafael Knob, *mountain peak*, U.S.A., **423** H2
San Ramón, Beni, Bolivia, **455** F3
San Ramón, Santa Cruz, Bolivia, **455** F4
San Ramón de la Nueva Orán, Argentina, **458** D2
San Remigio, Philippines, **204** C4
San Remo, Italy, **294** A4
San Román, Cabo, *cape*, Venezuela, **451** D1
San Roque, Argentina, **459** E3
San Saba, U.S.A., **424** C4
San Salvador, Argentina, **459** E4
San Salvador, El Salvador, **428** C4
San Salvador, Isla, *island*, Islas Galápagos (Galapagos Islands), Ecuador, **461** A1
San Salvador, *island*, Bahamas, **428** G2
San Salvador de Jujuy, Argentina, **458** D2
San Sebastián, Argentina, **460** D4
San Sebastián, Bahía, *gulf*, Argentina, **460** D4
San Sebastián de la Gomera, Islas Canarias, Spain, **373** A4
San Severo, Italy, **295** E5
San Telmo, Mexico, **430** A2
San Telmo, Punta, *point*, Mexico, **430** D5
San Tin, China, **207** C4
San Valentín, Monte, *mountain peak*, Chile, **460** C3
San Vicente, El Salvador, **428** C4

San Vicente, Mexico, **430** A2
San Vicente de Cañete, Peru, **454** C3
San Vicente de Toranzo, Spain, **293** F1
San Vicente del Caguán, Colombia, **450** C3
San Vincenzo, Italy, **294** C4
San Vito, Capo, *cape*, Sicilia, Italy, **295** D6
San Ysidro, U.S.A., **423** K4
Şan'ā', Yemen, **220** D5
Sanaag, *administrative region*, Somalia, **367** G2
SANAE IV, *South African research station*, Antarctica, **470** D3
Sanaga, *river*, Cameroon, **368** B2
Sanaigmore, Scotland, U.K., **308** C5
Sanana, Pulau, *island*, Indonesia, **198** D3
Sanandaj, Iran, **222** D5
Sanandita, Bolivia, **455** F5
Sanāw, Yemen, **220** F5
Sanchahe, China, **211** J3
Sanchakou, China, **212** C5
Sanchidrián, Spain, **292** E2
Sānchor, India, **218** B4
Sanchursk, Russian Federation, **222** D1
Sanco Point, Philippines, **204** D4
Sancti Spíritus, Cuba, **429** F2
Sand, Hedmark, Norway, **286** E2
Sand, Rogaland, Norway, **286** C3
Sand Hill, *river*, Canada, **417** N3
Sand Hills, U.S.A., **420** B4
Sand Springs, Montana, U.S.A., **419** L3
Sand Springs, Oklahoma, U.S.A., **424** D1
Sandai, Indonesia, **201** E3
Sandakan, Malaysia, **201** G1
Sândăn, Cambodia, **203** E3
Sandane, Norway, **286** C2
Sandanski, Bulgaria, **297** D5
Sandaré, Mali, **364** B2
Sandarne, Sweden, **287** H2
Sanday, *island*, Orkney, Scotland, U.K., **308** G1
Sanday Sound, Orkney, Scotland, U.K., **308** G1
Sandbach, England, U.K., **304** E1
Sandbukta, Norway, **284** K2
Sanddøla, *river*, Norway, **284** F4
Sande, Sogn og Fjordane, Norway, **286** B2
Sande, Vestfold, Norway, **286** E3
Sandefjord, Norway, **286** E3
Sandell Bay, Macquarie Island, **134** R11
Sanders, U.S.A., **423** J4
Sanderson, U.S.A., **423** M6
Sandfire Roadhouse, Australia, **134** E2
Sandgerði, Iceland, **284** X7
Sandhead, Scotland, U.K., **308** E6
Sandhurst, England, U.K., **305** G3
Sandia, Peru, **455** E4
Sandıklı, Turkey, **297** H6
Sandīla, India, **218** E4
Sanding, Pulau, *island*, Indonesia, **200** C3
Sandlake, U.S.A., **418** C4
Sandnäset, Sweden, **284** H5
Sandnes, Norway, **286** B3
Sandness, Shetland, Scotland, U.K., **308** K7
Sandnessjøen, Norway, **284** F4
Sandoa, Democratic Republic of the Congo, **368** D4
Sandomierz, Poland, **289** K3
Sândominic, Romania, **296** E2
Sandön, *island*, Sweden, **285** L4

Sandoná, Colombia, **450** C4
Sandovo, Russian Federation, **299** F3
Sandow, Mount, *mountain peak*, Antarctica, **470** G5
Sandown, England, U.K., **305** F4
Sandoy, *island*, Faeroe Islands, **302** D2
Sandplace, England, U.K., **304** C4
Sandpoint, U.S.A., **418** F2
Sandray, *island*, Scotland, U.K., **308** B4
Sandsend, England, U.K., **307** H3
Sandspit, Canada, **412** D5
Sandstone, U.S.A., **420** G2
Sandu, China, **206** C3
Sandusky, Michigan, U.S.A., **421** M4
Sandusky, Ohio, U.S.A., **421** M5
Sandusky, *river*, U.S.A., **421** M5
Sandverhaar, Namibia, **370** C4
Sandvik, Sweden, **287** H4
Sandvika, Norway, **284** F5
Sandviken, Sweden, **287** H2
Sandwich, England, U.K., **305** J3
Sandwich Bay, Canada, **417** N3
Sandwich Bay, Namibia, **370** B3
Sandwick, Scotland, U.K., **308** K7
Sandy, England, U.K., **305** G2
Sandy, U.S.A., **418** C4
Sandy Bay, Macquarie Island, **134** R11
Sandy Bay, St Helena, **373** B3
Sandy Cape, Australia, **135** L3
Sandy Lake, Australia, **134** E2
Sandy Lake, *lake*, Canada, **414** H5
Sandy Lake, Newfoundland, Canada, **417** N5
Sandy Lake, Ontario, Canada, **414** H5
Sandy Point, Tristan da Cunha, **373** C2
Sandykgachy, Turkmenistan, **222** G5
Sanford, Florida, U.S.A., **425** M5
Sanford, Maine, U.S.A., **426** E3
Sanford, North Carolina, U.S.A., **425** N2
Sang, Loi, *mountain peak*, Myanmar, **205** C3
Sangān, Kūh-e, *mountain peak*, Afghanistan, **221** H2
Sangar, Russian Federation, **301** P3
Sangay, Volcán, *mountain peak*, Ecuador, **450** B4
Sângeorgiu de Pădure, Romania, **296** E2
Sângeorz-Băi, Romania, **296** E2
Sanger, U.S.A., **422** D3
Sângerei, Moldova, **296** G2
Sangerhausen, Germany, **288** E3
Sanggarpar, China, **215** G2
Sanggau, Indonesia, **201** E2
Sangha, *administrative region*, Congo, **368** C2
Sangha, Burkina Faso, **364** E2
Sangha-Mbaéré, *prefecture*, Central African Republic, **368** C2
Sānghar, Pakistan, **218** B4
Sangihe, Pulau, *island*, Indonesia, **198** D2
Sanginkylä, Finland, **285** N4
Sangis, Sweden, **285** L4
Sangiyn Dalay, Mongolia, **213** H3
Sangkha, Thailand, **203** D3
Sāngli, India, **216** C2
Sangmélima, Cameroon, **368** B2
Sango, Zimbabwe, **371** F3
Sāngola, India, **216** C2
Sangonera, *river*, Spain, **293** G4
Sangre de Cristo Mountains, *mountain range*, U.S.A., **423** L2

Sangre Grande, Trinidad, Trinidad and Tobago, **461** C4
Sangri, China, **214** D3
Sangruma, China, **215** F2
Sangrūr, India, **218** C3
Sangsang, China, **214** C3
Sangue, *river*, Brazil, **455** H3
Sangwali, Namibia, **370** D2
Sangzhi, China, **206** B2
Sanibel Island, U.S.A., **425** L6
Sanje, Tanzania, **369** G4
Sanjiachang, China, **215** G4
Sanjiao, China, **207** A3
Sanjō, Japan, **209** G3
Sankarankovil, India, **216** D4
Sankt Gallen, Switzerland, **291** J3
Sankt Peter-Ording, Germany, **288** D1
Sankt-Peterburg (St Petersburg), Russian Federation, **299** C3
Sanlúcar de Barrameda, Spain, **292** D4
Sanluri, Sardegna, Italy, **295** B6
Sanmen Dao, *island*, China, **207** D4
Sanmen Wan, *bay*, China, **206** E2
Sanmenxia, China, **206** B1
Sanming, China, **206** D3
Sänna, Sweden, **286** G3
Sannār, Sudan, **366** D2
Sânnicolau Mare, Romania, **296** C2
Sanniki, Poland, **289** J2
Sanniquellie, Liberia, **364** C3
Sanok, Poland, **289** L4
Sanquhar, Scotland, U.K., **308** F5
Sansepolcro, Italy, **294** D4
Sansha Wan, *bay*, China, **206** D3
Sanski Most, Bosnia and Herzegovina, **294** F3
Sansui, China, **206** B3
Sansuri, *mountain peak*, North Korea, **211** H4
Sant' Antioco, Isola di, *island*, Sardegna, Italy, **295** B6
Sant' Antioco, Sardegna, Italy, **295** B6
Sant' Arcangelo, Italy, **295** F5
Sant' Eufemia, Golfo di, *gulf*, Italy, **295** E6
Sant Mateu, Spain, **293** H2
Santa Ana, Beni, Bolivia, **455** F3
Santa Ana, Ecuador, **450** B4
Santa Ana, El Salvador, **428** C4
Santa Ana, La Paz, Bolivia, **455** E4
Santa Ana, Mexico, **430** C2
Santa Anna, U.S.A., **422** D5
Santa Anna, U.S.A., **424** C4
Santa Bárbara, Colombia, **450** C3
Santa Bárbara, Honduras, **428** C4
Santa Bárbara, Mexico, **430** D3
Santa Barbara, *mountain peak*, Spain, **293** F4
Santa Barbara, U.S.A., **422** D4
Santa Catalina, Isla, *island*, Providencia, Colombia, **461** C1
Santa Catalina, *island*, U.S.A., **422** D5
Santa Catalina, Panama, **429** E5
Santa Catalina, Philippines, **204** C4
Santa Catarina, Baja California, Mexico, **430** B2
Santa Catarina, Ilha de, *island*, Brazil, **459** H3
Santa Catarina, Nuevo Leon, Mexico, **431** E3
Santa Catarina, *state*, Brazil, **459** G3
Santa Caterina, São Tomé and Príncipe, **373** C4

Santa Catharina, Curaçao, Netherlands Antilles, **461** C3
Santa Clara, Colombia, **451** E5
Santa Clara, Cuba, **429** F2
Santa Clara, *island*, Róbinson Crusoe Island, Archipiélago Juan Fernández, Chile, **461** C2
Santa Clara, Mexico, **430** D2
Santa Clarita, U.S.A., **422** D4
Santa Clotilde, Peru, **450** D5
Santa Coloma de Gramanet, Spain, **293** J2
Santa Cristina, Italy, **294** C2
Santa Croce Camerina, Sicilia, Italy, **295** E7
Santa Cruz, Aruba, **461** B3
Santa Cruz, Bolivia, **455** F4
Santa Cruz, Chile, **458** B5
Santa Cruz, Curaçao, Netherlands Antilles, **461** C3
Santa Cruz, *department*, Bolivia, **455** F5
Santa Cruz, Isla, *island*, Islas Galápagos (Galapagos Islands), Ecuador, **461** A2
Santa Cruz, *island*, U.S.A., **422** C4
Santa Cruz, Luzon Island, Philippines, **204** C3
Santa Cruz, Madeira, Portugal, **373** C3
Santa Cruz, Marinduque Island, Philippines, **204** C3
Santa Cruz, Mexico, **430** C2
Santa Cruz, Pará, Brazil, **452** C4
Santa Cruz, *province*, Argentina, **460** C3
Santa Cruz, Rio Grande do Norte, Brazil, **453** F5
Santa Cruz, *river*, Argentina, **460** D4
Santa Cruz, São Tomé and Príncipe, **373** C4
Santa Cruz, U.S.A., **422** B3
Santa Cruz Cabrália, Brazil, **457** F4
Santa Cruz de la Palma, Islas Canarias, Spain, **373** A4
Santa Cruz de Moya, Spain, **293** G3
Santa Cruz de Mudela, Spain, **293** F3
Santa Cruz de Tenerife, Islas Canarias, Spain, **373** A4
Santa Cruz del Sur, Cuba, **429** F2
Santa Cruz do Sul, Brazil, **459** G3
Santa Cruz Islands, Solomon Islands, **138** E6
Santa da Boa Vista, Brazil, **459** G4
Santa Elena, Argentina, **459** E4
Santa Elena, Bahía de, *bay*, Ecuador, **450** B4
Santa Elena, Cabo, *cape*, Costa Rica, **428** D5
Santa Elena, Ecuador, **450** B5
Santa Elena de Uairén, Venezuela, **451** G3
Santa Eufemia, Spain, **292** E3
Santa Eugenia, Spain, **292** C1
Santa Fe, Argentina, **458** E4
Santa Fé, Isla, *island*, Islas Galápagos (Galapagos Islands), Ecuador, **461** A2
Santa Fé, *province*, Argentina, **458** E3
Santa Fe, U.S.A., **423** L4
Santa Helena, Brazil, **452** E4
Santa Helena de Goiás, Brazil, **456** C4
Santa Inés, Isla, *island*, Chile, **460** B4
Santa Isabel, Argentina, **458** C5
Santa Isabel, Brazil, **455** G3
Santa Isabel, *island*, Solomon Islands, **141** A1
Santa Isabel, Providencia, Colombia, **461** C1
Santa Lucia, Argentina, **459** E3
Santa Lucía, Ecuador, **450** B4
Santa Lucia Cotzumalguapa, Guatemala, **428** C4

Santa Lucia Range, *mountain range*, U.S.A., **422** C3
Santa Luzia, Brazil, **452** E4
Santa Luzia, Portugal, **292** C4
Santa Mare, Romania, **296** F2
Santa Margarita, Isla, *island*, Mexico, **430** B3
Santa Maria, Amazonas, Brazil, **452** A3
Santa María, Bahía de, *bay*, Mexico, **430** C3
Santa María, Cabo de, *cape*, Mozambique, **371** F4
Santa Maria, Cabo de, *cape*, Portugal, **292** D4
Santa María, Catamarca, Argentina, **458** C3
Santa María, Isla, *island*, Islas Galápagos (Galapagos Islands), Ecuador, **461** A2
Santa Maria, *island*, Azores, Portugal, **360** M7
Santa Maria (Gaua), *island*, Vanuatu, **141** A2
Santa María, Peru, **450** C4
Santa Maria, Rio Grande do Sul, Brazil, **459** G3
Santa Maria, *river*, Mato Grosso do Sul, Brazil, **456** B5
Santa Maria, *river*, Rio Grande do Sul, Brazil, **459** F4
Santa María, Salta, Argentina, **458** D2
Santa Maria, U.S.A., **422** C4
Santa Maria da Boa Vista, Brazil, **453** F5
Santa Maria da Vitória, Brazil, **457** E3
Santa Maria das Barreiras, Brazil, **452** D5
Santa María de Ipire, Venezuela, **451** F2
Santa María de Nanay, Peru, **450** D5
Santa Maria del Río, Mexico, **431** E4
Santa Maria di Leuca, Capo, *cape*, Italy, **295** G6
Santa Maria, Cabo de, *point*, Angola, **368** B5
Santa Marta, Colombia, **450** C1
Santa Marta, Spain, **292** D3
Santa Marta Grande, Cabo de, *cape*, Brazil, **459** H3
Santa Martabaai, *bay*, Curaçao, Netherlands Antilles, **461** C3
Santa Monica, U.S.A., **422** C4
Santa Paula, U.S.A., **422** D4
Santa Quitéria, Brazil, **453** F4
Santa Rita, Brazil, **453** G5
Santa Rita, Colombia, **450** D4
Santa Rita, Venezuela, **450** D1
Santa Rita de Cássia, Brazil, **457** E3
Santa Rita de Sihuas, Peru, **454** D4
Santa Rita do Araguaia, Brazil, **456** C4
Santa Rosa, Acre, Brazil, **454** D2
Santa Rosa, Argentina, **460** D1
Santa Rosa, California, U.S.A., **422** B2
Santa Rosa, Ecuador, **450** B5
Santa Rosa, *island*, U.S.A., **422** C5
Santa Rosa, Mexico, **431** H5
Santa Rosa, N. Beni, Bolivia, **455** F3
Santa Rosa, New Mexico, U.S.A., **423** L4
Santa Rosa, Peru, **454** D4
Santa Rosa, Rio Grande do Sul, Brazil, **459** F3
Santa Rosa, S. Beni, Bolivia, **455** E4
Santa Rosa de Copán, Honduras, **428** C4
Santa Rosa de la Roca, Bolivia, **455** F4
Santa Rosa Range, *mountain range*, U.S.A., **418** F6
Santa Rosalía, Mexico, **430** B3

Santa Sylvina, Argentina, **458** E3
Santa Tecla *see* Nueva San Salvador, El Salvador, **428** C4
Santa Teresa, *river*, Brazil, **456** D3
Santa Teresa Gallura, Sardegna, Italy, **295** B5
Santa Victoria, Sierra, *mountain range*, Argentina, **458** D2
Santa Vitória do Palmar, Brazil, **459** G4
Santa, Peru, **454** B2
Santa, *river*, Peru, **454** B2
Santa, U.S.A., **418** F3
Santai, Sichuan, China, **215** H3
Santai, Xinjiang Uygur Zizhiqu, China, **212** D3
Santalpur, India, **218** B5
Santana, Brazil, **457** E3
Santana, Coxilha de, *mountain range*, Brazil/Uruguay, **459** F4
Santana, Madeira, Portugal, **373** C3
Santana do Ipanema, Brazil, **457** G2
Santander, Colombia, **450** C3
Santander, Philippines, **204** C4
Santander, Spain, **293** F1
Santander Jiménez, Mexico, **431** F3
Santanghu, China, **213** G3
Santanyí, Islas Baleares, Spain, **293** J3
Santarém, Brazil, **452** B4
Santarém, *district*, Portugal, **292** C3
Santarém, Portugal, **292** C3
Santee, *river*, U.S.A., **425** N3
Santiago, *administrative region*, Chile, **458** B4
Santiago, Brazil, **459** F3
Santiago, Cabo, *cape*, Chile, **460** B4
Santiago, Chile, **458** B4
Santiago, Dominican Republic, **429** H3
Santiago, Mexico, **430** C4
Santiago, Panama, **429** E5
Santiago, Philippines, **204** C2
Santiago, *river*, Peru, **450** C5
Santiago, Sierra de, *mountain range*, Bolivia, **455** G4
Santiago Astata, Mexico, **431** G6
Santiago de Cao, Peru, **454** B2
Santiago de Chocorvos, Peru, **454** C3
Santiago de Chuco, Peru, **454** B2
Santiago de Compostela, Spain, **292** C1
Santiago de Cuba, Cuba, **429** G2
Santiago del Estero, Argentina, **458** D3
Santiago del Estero, *province*, Argentina, **458** D3
Santiago do Cacém, Portugal, **292** C3
Santiago Ixcuintla, Mexico, **430** D4
Santiago Papasquiaro, Mexico, **430** D3
Santiago Peak, *mountain peak*, U.S.A., **423** M7
Santiago Pinotepa Nacional, Mexico, **431** F5
Santigi, Tanjong, *point*, Indonesia, **198** C3
Säntis, *mountain peak*, Switzerland, **291** J3
Santo Amaro, Brazil, **457** F3
Santo André, Brazil, **459** H2
Santo Angelo, Brazil, **459** F3
Santo Antão, *island*, Cape Verde, **360** Q8
Santo António, São Tomé and Príncipe, **373** C4
Santo António da Platina, Brazil, **459** G2
Santo António de Jesus, Brazil, **457** F3

Santo Antônio do Içá, Brazil, **451** E5
Santo Antônio do Leverger, Brazil, **456** B4
Santo Corazón, Bolivia, **455** G4
Santo Domingo, Baja California, Mexico, **430** A2
Santo Domingo, Baja California Sur, Mexico, **430** B3
Santo Domingo, Dominican Republic, **429** H3
Santo Domingo, Nicaragua, **428** D4
Santo Domingo, Peru, **455** E3
Santo Domingo de los Colorados, Ecuador, **450** B4
Santo Estêvão, *river*, Portugal, **292** C3
Santo Inácio, Brazil, **457** E3
Santo Stefano di Camastra, Sicilia, Italy, **295** E6
Santo Tomás, Baja California, Mexico, **430** A2
Santo Tomás, Chihuahua, Mexico, **430** D2
Santo Tomás, Peru, **454** D4
Santo Tomé, Argentina, **459** E3
Santorini *see* Thira, *island*, Kyklades, Greece, **297** E7
Santos, Brazil, **459** H2
Santos Dumont, Brazil, **457** E5
Sanxiang, China, **207** A4
Sanya, China, **203** F2
Sanyati, *river*, Zimbabwe, **371** E2
Sanying, China, **210** D5
Sanyuan, China, **206** B1
Sanza Pombo, Angola, **368** C4
Sanzao, China, **207** A4
Sanzao Dao, *island*, China, **207** A4
Sanzhan, China, **211** J2
São Benedito, Brazil, **453** F4
São Benedito, *river*, Brazil, **456** B2
São Bento, Amazonas, Brazil, **455** F2
São Bento, Maranhão, Brazil, **453** E4
São Bento do Norte, Brazil, **453** G4
São Bernardo, Brazil, **453** E4
São Bernardo do Campo, Brazil, **459** H2
São Borja, Brazil, **459** F3
Sao Carlos, Santa Catarina, Brazil, **459** G3
São Carlos, São Paulo, Brazil, **459** H2
São Desidério, Brazil, **457** E3
São Domingos, Brazil, **456** D3
São Domingos, Serra, *mountain range*, Brazil, **456** D4
São Félix, Brazil, **456** C3
São Félix do Xingu, Brazil, **452** C5
São Fidélis, Brazil, **457** F5
São Francisco, Brazil, **457** E4
São Francisco, *river*, Brazil, **457** F2
São Francisco de Assis, Brazil, **459** F3
Sao Francisco de Paula, Brazil, **459** G3
São Francisco do Sul, Brazil, **459** H3
São Gabriel, Brazil, **459** F4
São Gabriel da Cachoeira, Brazil, **451** E4
São Gonçalo, Brazil, **457** E6
São Gonçalo do Amarante, Brazil, **453** F4
São Gotardo, Brazil, **456** D5
São João da Aliança, Brazil, **456** D4
São João da Barra, Brazil, **457** F5
São João da Boa Vista, Brazil, **456** D5
São João da Madeira, Portugal, **292** C2
São João do Araguaia, Brazil, **452** D4

São João do Cariri, Brazil, **453** G5
São João do Paraíso, Brazil, **457** E4
São João do Piauí, Brazil, **453** E5
São João dos Patos, Brazil, **453** E5
São Joaquim, Pará, Brazil, **452** D4
São Joaquim, Santa Catarina, Brazil, **459** G3
São Joaquim da Barra, Brazil, **456** D5
São Jorge, *island*, Azores, Portugal, **360** M7
São José, Amazonas, Brazil, **451** E4
São José, Baía de, *bay*, Brazil, **453** E4
São José, Santa Catarina, Brazil, **459** H3
São José de Mipibu, Brazil, **453** G5
São José do Norte, Brazil, **459** G4
São José do Rio Prêto, Brazil, **456** D5
São Jose dos Campos, Brazil, **456** E6
São José dos Pinhais, Brazil, **459** H2
São Leopoldo, Brazil, **459** G3
São Lourenço, Brazil, **457** E6
São Lourenço, Ponta de, *point*, Madeira, Portugal, **373** C3
São Lourenço do Sul, Brazil, **459** G4
São Luís, Brazil, **453** E4
São Luís, Ilha de, *island*, Brazil, **453** E4
São Luis Gonzaga, Brazil, **459** F3
São Mamede, *mountain peak*, Portugal, **292** D3
São Manuel *see* Teles Pires, *river*, Brazil, **452** B5
São Marcos, Baía de, *bay*, Brazil, **453** E4
São Marcos, *river*, Brazil, **456** D4
São Mateus, Brazil, **457** F5
São Miguel, *island*, Azores, Portugal, **360** M7
São Miguel, *river*, Brazil, **455** F3
São Miguel do Araguaia, Brazil, **456** C3
São Miguel do Guamá, Brazil, **452** D3
São Miguel do Tapuio, Brazil, **453** F4
São Miguel dos Campos, Brazil, **457** G2
São Nicolau, *island*, Cape Verde, **360** P8
São Paulo, Brazil, **459** H2
São Paulo, *state*, Brazil, **459** H2
São Paulo de Olivença, Brazil, **451** E5
São Pedro, Brazil, **451** G5
São Pedro, *river*, Brazil, **453** F5
São Pedro do Sul, Portugal, **292** C2
São Raimundo das Mangabeiras, Brazil, **452** E5
São Raimundo Nonato, Brazil, **457** E2
São Romão, Amazonas, Brazil, **455** E1
São Romão, Minas Gerais, Brazil, **457** E4
São Roque, Cabo de, *cape*, Brazil, **453** G4
São Sebastião, Ilha de, *island*, Brazil, **459** J2
São Sebastião, Pará, Brazil, **452** C4
São Sebastião, Rondônia, Brazil, **455** G2
São Sebastiao da Boa Vista, Brazil, **452** D3
São Sebastião do Paraíso,

Brazil, **456** D5
São Sepé, Brazil, **459** G4
São Simão, Brazil, **456** C5
São Tiago, *island*, Cape Verde, **360** Q8
São Tomé, Cabo de, *cape*, Brazil, **457** F5
São Tomé, *island*, São Tomé and Príncipe, **373** C4
São Tomé, Pico de, *mountain peak*, São Tomé and Príncipe, **373** C4
São Tomé, São Tomé and Príncipe, **373** C4
São Tomé and Príncipe, *country*, Atlantic Ocean, **359** F6
São Vicente, Brazil, **459** H2
São Vicente, Cabo de, *cape*, Portugal, **292** C4
São Vicente, *island*, Cape Verde, **360** P8
São Vicente, Madeira, Portugal, **373** C3
Saona, Isla, *island*, Dominican Republic, **429** H3
Saône, *river*, France, **291** G3
Sapanca, Turkey, **297** H5
Sapanda, Papua New Guinea, **140** B4
Sapele, Nigeria, **365** F3
Sapello, U.S.A., **423** L4
Sapelo Island, U.S.A., **425** M4
Sapernoye, Russian Federation, **299** C2
Sapes, Greece, **297** E5
Saposoa, Peru, **454** C2
Sapphire Mountains, *mountain range*, U.S.A., **418** E4
Sappho, U.S.A., **418** B2
Sapporo, Japan, **209** H2
Sapri, Italy, **295** E5
Sapucaia, Brazil, **452** B4
Sapulpa, U.S.A., **424** D1
Sapulut, Malaysia, **201** G1
Saqqez, Iran, **222** D5
Sar Bisheh, Iran, **221** G2
Šar Planina, *mountain range*, Macedonia/Yugoslavia, **296** C4
Sara, Philippines, **204** C4
Sarāb, Iran, **363** J1
Saraburi, Thailand, **202** D3
Saraby, Norway, **285** L1
Saragosa, U.S.A., **423** M6
Saraguro, Ecuador, **450** B5
Saraipāli, India, **219** E5
Säräisniemi, Finland, **285** N4
Sarajärvi, Finland, **285** N4
Sarajevo, Bosnia and Herzegovina, **294** G4
Saraktash, Russian Federation, **222** F2
Saramati, *mountain peak*, Myanmar, **205** B2
Saran, Gunung, *mountain peak*, Indonesia, **201** E3
Saranac Lake, U.S.A., **426** C2
Sarandë, Albania, **297** C6
Sarandi, Brazil, **459** G3
Sarandí del Yí, Uruguay, **459** F4
Sarandi Grande, Uruguay, **459** F4
Sarangani Islands, Philippines, **204** D5
Sārangarh, India, **219** E5
Sārangpur, India, **218** D5
Saransk, Russian Federation, **298** G2
Sarapul, Russian Federation, **222** E1
Sarasota, U.S.A., **425** L6
Sarata, Ukraine, **296** G2
Saratoga, U.S.A., **419** L6
Saratok, Malaysia, **201** E2
Saratov, Russian Federation, **222** D2
Saratovskaya Oblast', *province*, Russian Federation, **222** D2
Sarāvān, Iran, **221** H3
Saravan, Laos, **203** E3
Sarawak, *state*, Malaysia, **201** F2

Saray, Turkey, **297** F5
Saraya, Senegal, **364** B2
Sarāyā, Syria, **225** C2
Sarayakpınar, Turkey, **296** F5
Sarayköy, Turkey, **297** G7
Sarayönü, Turkey, **224** D5
Sarbāz, Iran, **221** H3
Sárbogárd, Hungary, **289** J5
Sarco, Chile, **458** B3
Sardārpur, India, **218** C5
Sardārshahr, India, **218** C3
Sardegna, *autonomous region*, Italy, **295** B5
Sardegna (Sardinia), *island*, Italy, **295** C5
Sardinata, Colombia, **450** D2
Sardinata, Ensenada de, *bay*, San Andrés, Colombia, **461** B1
Sardinia *see* Sardegna, *island*, Italy, **295** C5
Sardis Lake, U.S.A., **425** H2
Sar-e Pol, Afghanistan, **218** A1
Sargent, U.S.A., **420** D5
Sargodha, Pakistan, **218** C2
Sarh, Chad, **366** A3
Sarhro, Jebel, *mountain range*, Morocco, **360** D2
Sārī, Iran, **222** E5
Saria, *island*, Dodekanisos, Greece, **297** F8
Sarichioi, Romania, **296** G3
Sarigan, *island*, Northern Mariana Islands, **138** C3
Sarıgöl, Turkey, **297** G6
Sarıkaya, Turkey, **363** G1
Sarikei, Malaysia, **201** E2
Sarıkemer, Turkey, **297** F7
Sarıköy, Turkey, **297** F5
Sarimbun Reservoir, Singapore, **200** J6
Sarina, Australia, **135** K3
Sariñena, Spain, **293** G2
Sariwon, North Korea, **208** D3
Sarıyer, Turkey, **297** G5
Sarıyer, Turkey, **297** G5
Sark, *Guernsey dependency*, English Channel, **290** C2
Sarkāri Tala, India, **218** B4
Särkijärvi, Finland, **285** L3
Särkisalmi, Finland, **287** P2
Şarkışla, Turkey, **363** G1
Şarköy, Turkey, **297** F5
Sărmaşu, Romania, **296** E2
Sarmi, Indonesia, **199** G3
Sarmiento, Argentina, **460** D2
Särna, Sweden, **286** F2
Sarnen, Switzerland, **291** J3
Sarnia, Canada, **421** M4
Sarny, Ukraine, **298** C2
Särö, Sweden, **286** E4
Saros Körfezi, *bay*, Turkey, **297** F5
Sárospatak, Hungary, **289** K4
Sarowbī, Afghanistan, **218** B2
Sarpsborg, Norway, **286** E3
Sarqan, Kazakhstan, **212** D3
Sarre, England, U.K., **305** J3
Sarre, England, U.K., **305** J3
Sarrebourg, France, **291** H2
Sarriá, Spain, **292** D1
Sarroch, Sardegna, Italy, **295** B6
Sartène, Corse, France, **295** B5
Sarthe, *river*, France, **290** D3
Saru, *river*, Japan, **209** H2
Saruhanlı, Turkey, **297** F5
Sárvár, Hungary, **289** H5
Sarvestān, Iran, **220** F3
Sárvíz, *river*, Hungary, **294** G2
Särvsjö, Sweden, **286** F1
Sary-Tash, Kyrgyzstan, **212** B5
Saryesik-Atyraū Qumy, *desert*, Kazakhstan, **212** B3
Saryözek, Kazakhstan, **212** C3
Saryqopa Köli, *lake*, Kazakhstan, **222** G2
Saryshagan, Kazakhstan, **212** B3
Sarysu, *river*, Kazakhstan, **212** A2
Sarzhal, Kazakhstan, **212** C2
Sasak, Indonesia, **200** B3
Sasamungga, Solomon Islands, **141** A1

Sasar, Tanjong, *point*, Indonesia, 198 C5
Sasarām, India, 219 E4
Sasebo, Japan, 208 E4
Saser Kangri, *mountain peak*, India, 218 D2
Saskatchewan, *province*, Canada, 413 R4
Saskatchewan, *river*, Canada, 413 S5
Saskatoon, Canada, 413 R5
Saslaya, Cerro, *mountain peak*, Nicaragua, 428 D4
Sasolburg, South Africa, 371 E4
Sasovo, Russian Federation, 298 F2
Sassandra, Côte d'Ivoire, 364 C4
Sassari, Sardegna, Italy, 295 B5
Sassnitz, Germany, 288 F1
Sasstown, Liberia, 364 C4
Sasyk, Ozero, *lake*, Ukraine, 296 G3
Sasyqköl, *lake*, Kazakhstan, 212 D3
Sata-misaki, *point*, Japan, 208 E5
Satāna, India, 218 C5
Satanta, U.S.A., 420 C7
Satapuala, Samoa, 141 B1
Sātāra, India, 216 C2
Sataua, Samoa, 141 B1
Satawal, *island*, Micronesia, 138 C4
Sātbaev, Kazakhstan, 222 H3
Säter, Sweden, 286 G2
Satipo, Peru, 454 C3
Sātmala Hills, India, 218 C5
Satna, India, 218 E4
Sátoraljaújhely, Hungary, 289 K4
Sātpura Range, *mountain range*, India, 218 C5
Satrokala, Madagascar, 372 B5
Satti, India, 218 D2
Sattūr, India, 216 D4
Satu Mare, Romania, 296 D2
Satun, Thailand, 202 D5
Satupa'itea, Samoa, 141 B1
Sauce, Argentina, 459 E4
Saucillo, Mexico, 430 D2
Sauda, Norway, 286 C3
Saūdakent, Kazakhstan, 223 H4
Saudi Arabia, *country*, Asia, 196 F7
Sauêruiná, (Papagaio), *river*, Brazil, 455 G3
Saugstad, Mount, *mountain peak*, Canada, 412 F5
Saül, French Guiana, 452 C2
Sauldre, *river*, France, 290 E3
Saulgau, Germany, 288 D4
Saulieu, France, 291 G3
Saulkrasti, Latvia, 287 M4
Sault Ste Marie, Canada, 421 L2
Sault Ste Marie, U.S.A., 421 L2
Saumlaki, Indonesia, 199 E4
Saumur, France, 290 D3
Saunders, Cape, Australia, 129 G6
Saundersfoot, Wales, U.K., 304 C3
Saurimo, Angola, 368 D4
Sauvo, Finland, 287 L2
Sauzé-Vaussais, France, 290 E3
Savá, Honduras, 428 D4
Sava, *river*, Europe, 280 F6
Savage, U.S.A., 419 M3
Savageton, U.S.A., 419 M5
Savai'i, *island*, Samoa, 141 B1
Savalou, Benin, 365 E3
Savaneta, Aruba, 461 B3
Savanna-la-Mar, Jamaica, 429 F3
Savannah, Georgia, U.S.A., 425 M3
Savannah, Missouri, U.S.A., 420 F6
Savannah, *river*, U.S.A., 425 M3
Savannah, Tennessee, U.S.A., 425 H2
Savannakhét, Laos, 203 E2
Savant Lake, Canada, 414 J6
Sāvantvādi, India, 216 C3
Sävar, Sweden, 284 K5
Savaştepe, Turkey, 297 F6
Savè, Benin, 365 E3
Save, *river*, Mozambique, 371 F3
Sāveh, Iran, 220 F2
Savelugu, Ghana, 364 D3
Savenay, France, 290 D3
Săveni, Romania, 296 F2
Saverdun, France, 290 E5
Savikylä, Finland, 285 P5
Savissivik, Denmark, 411 N2
Savitaipale, Finland, 287 N2
Šavnik, Yugoslavia, 296 B4
Savona, Canada, 412 J6
Savona, Italy, 294 B3
Savonlinna, Finland, 287 P2
Savonranta, Finland, 287 P1
Savran', Ukraine, 296 H1
Sävsjö, Sweden, 286 G4
Savu Sea, Indonesia, 198 C5
Savukoski, Finland, 285 P3
Savusavu, Fiji, 141 A4
Savuti, Botswana, 370 D2
Saw, Myanmar, 205 B3
Sawākin, Sudan, 363 G5
Sawan, Myanmar, 205 C2
Sawankhalok, Thailand, 202 C2
Sawatch Range, *mountain range*, U.S.A., 423 K2
Sawbill, Canada, 416 H3
Sawdā', Jabal, *mountain peak*, Saudi Arabia, 363 H5
Sawdā', Qurnat as, *mountain peak*, Lebanon, 225 D2
Sawdirī, Sudan, 366 C2
Sawel Mountain, *mountain peak*, Northern Ireland, U.K., 306 A3
Sawi, Ao, *bay*, Thailand, 202 C4
Şawqirah, Ghubbat, *bay*, Oman, 221 G5
Sawston, England, U.K., 305 H2
Sawtell, Australia, 135 L5
Sawu, *island*, Indonesia, 134 E1
Sawu, Pulau, *island*, Indonesia, 198 C5
Saxilby, England, U.K., 305 G1
Saxmundham, England, U.K., 305 J2
Saxnäs, Sweden, 284 G4
Say, Niger, 365 E2
Sayán, Peru, 454 C3
Sayaq, Kazakhstan, 212 C3
Sayaxché, Guatemala, 428 C3
Şaydā (Sidon), Lebanon, 225 C3
Sayghān, Afghanistan, 218 A2
Sayḩūt, Yemen, 220 F5
Saylac, Somalia, 367 F2
Säyneinen, Finland, 285 P5
Saynshand, Dornogovĭ, Mongolia, 210 E3
Saynshand, Ömnögovĭ, Mongolia, 213 J4
Sayn-Ust, Mongolia, 213 G3
Sayötesh, Kazakhstan, 222 E4
Sayqal, Baḩr, *lake*, Syria, 225 D3
Sayram Hu, *lake*, China, 212 D3
Sayre, U.S.A., 424 C2
Sayula, Mexico, 430 E5
Sayula de Alemán, Mexico, 431 G5
Sayward, Canada, 412 G6
Saywūn, Yemen, 220 E5
Sazan, *island*, Albania, 297 B5
Sazonovo, Russian Federation, 299 E3
Sbaa, Algeria, 361 F3
Sbega, Russian Federation, 211 G1
Sbeïtla, Tunisia, 362 A1
Scafell Pike, *mountain peak*, England, U.K., 306 E3
Scalasaig, Scotland, U.K., 308 C4
Scalby, England, U.K., 307 H3
Scalloway, Shetland, Scotland, U.K., 308 K7
Scalp, *mountain peak*, Ireland, 309 D5
Scalpay, *island*, Scotland, U.K., 308 C3
Scammon Bay, U.S.A., 410 C3
Scandia, Canada, 413 N6
Scandinavia, *region*, Europe, 280 F3
Scansano, Italy, 294 C4
Scanzano, Italy, 295 F5
Scapa Flow, *bay*, Orkney, Scotland, U.K., 308 F2
Scarba, *island*, Scotland, U.K., 308 D4
Scarborough, England, U.K., 307 H3
Scarborough, Tobago, Trinidad and Tobago, 461 B4
Scargill, New Zealand, 133 D6
Scarp, *island*, Scotland, U.K., 308 B2
Scarth, Canada, 414 D7
Schaffhausen, Switzerland, 291 J3
Schärding, Austria, 294 D1
Schefferville, Canada, 416 H2
Scheibbs, Austria, 289 G5
Schelde, *river*, Belgium, 288 A3
Schell Creek Range, *mountain range*, U.S.A., 422 F2
Schenectady, U.S.A., 426 C3
Scheveningen, Netherlands, 288 B2
Schiermonnikoog, Netherlands, 288 C2
Schitu Duca, Romania, 296 F2
Schleiden, Germany, 288 C3
Schleswig, Germany, 288 D1
Schleswig-Holstein, *state*, Germany, 288 D1
Schongau, Germany, 288 E5
Schooner, Caleta, *bay*, San Andrés, Colombia, 461 B1
Schouten Islands, Papua New Guinea, 140 B3
Schrader, Mount, *mountain peak*, Papua New Guinea, 140 B4
Schroffenstein, *mountain peak*, Namibia, 370 C4
Schulenburg, U.S.A., 424 D5
Schuler, Canada, 413 P6
Schurz, U.S.A., 422 D2
Schuyler, U.S.A., 420 E5
Schwabach, Germany, 288 E4
Schwäbisch Hall, Germany, 288 D4
Schwäbische Alb, *mountain range*, Germany, 288 D4
Schwaner, Pegunungan, *mountain range*, Indonesia, 201 E3
Schwarzwald, *mountain range*, Germany, 280 E6
Schwaz, Austria, 288 E5
Schwedt, Germany, 289 G2
Schweinfurt, Germany, 288 E3
Schwerin, Germany, 288 E2
Schweriner See, *lake*, Germany, 288 E2
Schwyz, Switzerland, 291 J3
Sciacca, Sicilia, Italy, 295 D7
Scilly, Isles of, England, U.K., 304 A5
Scioto, *river*, U.S.A., 421 M5
Scobey, U.S.A., 419 M2
Scole, England, U.K., 305 J2
Scotch Corner, England, U.K., 307 G3
Scotland, *administrative division*, U.K., 308 D3
Scotland Neck, U.S.A., 426 B6
Scott, Cape, Canada, 412 E6
Scott Base, *New Zealand research station*, Antarctica, 470 D7
Scott City, U.S.A., 420 C6
Scott Coast, *region*, Antarctica, 470 D7
Scott Lake, Canada, 413 S2
Scottburgh, South Africa, 371 F5
Scottish Borders, *local authority*, Scotland, U.K., 308 F5
Scottsbluff, U.S.A., 419 N6
Scottsboro, U.S.A., 425 J2
Scottsburg, U.S.A., 421 L6
Scottsdale, Australia, 135 K7
Scottsdale, U.S.A., 423 H5
Scourie, Scotland, U.K., 308 D2
Scousburgh, Scotland, U.K., 308 K8
Scrabster, Scotland, U.K., 308 F2
Scranton, North Dakota, U.S.A., 420 B2
Scranton, Pennsylvania, U.S.A., 426 C4
Scunthorpe, England, U.K., 307 H4
Seaford, England, U.K., 305 H4
Seaford, U.S.A., 426 C5
Seagraves, U.S.A., 423 M5
Seal, Cape, South Africa, 370 D5
Seal, *river*, Canada, 414 F2
Seal Bay, Tristan da Cunha, 373 C2
Seal Cove, Canada, 426 G2
Seal Cove, U.S.A., 416 H7
Seamer, England, U.K., 307 H3
Searchlight, U.S.A., 422 F4
Searcy, U.S.A., 424 G2
Seascale, England, U.K., 306 E3
Seaside, U.S.A., 418 C4
Seaton, England, U.K., 304 D4
Seattle, U.S.A., 418 C3
Seaward Kaikoura Range, *mountain range*, New Zealand, 133 D6
Sebago Lake, U.S.A., 426 E3
Sebakor, Teluk, *bay*, Indonesia, 199 F3
Sebangka, Pulau, *island*, Indonesia, 200 D2
Sebastían Vizcaíno, Bahía, *bay*, Mexico, 430 B2
Sebatik, Pulau, *island*, Indonesia/Malaysia, 201 G1
Sebayan, Gunung, *mountain peak*, Indonesia, 201 E3
Sebba, Burkina Faso, 364 E2
Sebdou, Algeria, 361 F2
Sébékoro, Mali, 364 C2
Seberida, Indonesia, 200 C3
Sebeș, Romania, 296 D3
Sebezh, Russian Federation, 299 B4
Sebina, Botswana, 371 E3
Sebiș, Romania, 296 D2
Sebring, U.S.A., 425 M6
Sebuku, Pulau, *island*, Indonesia, 201 G3
Sechelt, Canada, 412 H7
Sechura, Bahía de, *bay*, Peru, 454 B1
Sechura, Desierto de, *desert*, Peru, 454 B2
Sechura, Peru, 454 B1
Secondigny, France, 290 D3
Secretary Island, New Zealand, 133 A7
Secunderābād, India, 216 D2
Sécure, *river*, Bolivia, 455 F4
Seda, Lithuania, 287 L4
Seda, *river*, Latvia, 287 M4
Seda, *river*, Portugal, 292 D3
Sedalia, U.S.A., 420 G6
Sedan, France, 291 G2
Sedaung Taung, *mountain peak*, Myanmar, 202 C3
Sedbergh, England, U.K., 306 F3
Seddon, Kap, *cape*, Greenland, 411 N2
Seddon, New Zealand, 133 E5
Sede Boqer, Israel, 225 C4
Sedeh, Iran, 221 G2
Sedel'nikovo, Russian Federation, 223 K1
Sederot, Israel, 225 C4
Sedgewick, Canada, 413 P5
Sédhiou, Senegal, 364 A2
Sedoa, Indonesia, 198 C3
Sedom, Israel, 225 C4
Sedrata, Algeria, 295 A7
Sedro Woolley, U.S.A., 418 C2
Sędziszów Małopolski, Poland, 289 K3
Seeheim, Namibia, 370 C4
Seeley Lake, U.S.A., 418 H3
Seelig, Mount, *mountain peak*, Antarctica, 470 C6
Seelow, Germany, 289 G2
Seely, U.S.A., 419 M4
Sées, France, 290 E2
Seesen, Germany, 288 E3
Sefadu, Sierra Leone, 364 B3
Seferihisar, Turkey, 297 F6
Sefophe, Botswana, 371 E3
Ségala, Mali, 364 B2
Segamat, Malaysia, 200 C2
Segarcea, Romania, 296 D3
Ségbana, Benin, 365 E2
Seget, Indonesia, 199 E3
Segezha, Russian Federation, 285 S5
Seglvik, Norway, 284 K1
Segorbe, Spain, 293 G3
Ségou, *administrative region*, Mali, 364 C2
Ségou, Mali, 364 C2
Segovia, Colombia, 450 C2
Segovia, Spain, 292 E2
Segozero, Ozero, *lake*, Russian Federation, 285 R5
Segre, *river*, Spain, 293 H2
Seguam Island, Aleutian Islands, U.S.A., 408 F3
Séguédine, Niger, 362 B4
Séguéla, Côte d'Ivoire, 364 C3
Séguélon, Côte d'Ivoire, 364 C3
Seguin, U.S.A., 424 D5
Segundo, *river*, Argentina, 458 D4
Segura, Portugal, 292 D3
Segura, *river*, Spain, 293 F3
Sehithwa, Botswana, 370 D3
Sehore, India, 218 D5
Sehulea, Papua New Guinea, 140 C5
Sehwān, Pakistan, 218 A4
Seibert, U.S.A., 423 M2
Seiland, *island*, Norway, 285 L1
Seiling, U.S.A., 424 C1
Seille, *river*, France, 291 G3
Seinäjoki, Finland, 287 L1
Seine, Baie de la, *bay*, France, 290 D2
Seine, *river*, France, 280 E6
Seini, Romania, 296 D2
Sejny, Poland, 289 L1
Sekayu, Indonesia, 200 C3
Sekondi, Ghana, 364 D4
Sekseūil, Kazakhstan, 222 G3
Sela Dingay, Ethiopia, 367 E3
Selah, U.S.A., 418 D3
Selangor, *state*, Malaysia, 200 C2
Selaphum, Thailand, 203 D2
Selatan, Tanjong, *point*, Indonesia, 201 F4
Selattyn, England, U.K., 304 D2
Selayar, Pulau, *island*, Indonesia, 198 B4
Selayar, Selat, *strait*, Indonesia, 198 B4
Selbekken, Norway, 284 D5
Selbu, Norway, 284 E5
Selby, England, U.K., 307 G4
Selby, U.S.A., 420 C3
Selçuk, Turkey, 297 F7
Sele, *river*, Italy, 295 E5
Selebi Phikwe, Botswana, 371 E3
Selemdzha, *river*, Russian Federation, 301 Q4
Selendi, Turkey, 297 G6
Selenduma, Russian Federation, 210 D2
Selenge, Democratic Republic of the Congo, 368 C3
Selenge, Mongolia, 213 J2
Selenge, *province*, Mongolia, 210 D2
Selenge, *river*, Mongolia, 210 D2
Selenginsk, Russian Federation, 210 D1

Selenicë, Albania, **297** B5
Sélestat, France, **291** H2
Seletar, Pulau, *island*, Singapore, **200** K6
Seletar Reservoir, Singapore, **200** J6
Selfridge, U.S.A., **420** C2
Sel'ga, Russian Federation, **285** R5
Sel'gon, Russian Federation, **211** L2
Sélibabi, Mauritania, **364** B1
Seliger, Ozero, *lake*, Russian Federation, **299** D4
Seligman, U.S.A., **422** G4
Selimiye, Turkey, **297** F7
Selizharovo, Russian Federation, **299** D4
Selkirk, Canada, **414** F6
Selkirk, Scotland, U.K., **308** G5
Selkirk Mountains, *mountain range*, Canada, **413** K6
Selle, Pic de la, *mountain peak*, Haiti, **429** G3
Selles-sur-Cher, France, **290** E3
Sellindge, England, U.K., **305** J3
Sells, U.S.A., **423** H6
Selma, Alabama, U.S.A., **425** J3
Selma, California, U.S.A., **422** D3
Selmer, U.S.A., **425** H2
Selo, Russian Federation, **299** G2
Selong, Indonesia, **201** G5
Selsey, England, U.K., **305** G4
Sel'tso, Russian Federation, **299** E6
Selty, Russian Federation, **222** E1
Selvas, *region*, Brazil, **446** F4
Selwyn Lake, Canada, **414** B1
Selwyn Mountains, *mountain range*, Canada, **410** F3
Selyatyn, Ukraine, **296** E2
Selz, U.S.A., **420** D2
Sem, Norway, **286** E3
Sem Tripa, Brazil, **452** C4
Semara, Western Sahara, **360** D3
Semarang, Indonesia, **201** E4
Semaras, Indonesia, **201** G3
Sematan, Malaysia, **201** E2
Semayang, Danau, *lake*, Indonesia, **201** G3
Sembawang, Singapore, **200** J6
Sembé, Congo, **368** B2
Sembulu, Danau, *lake*, Indonesia, **201** F3
Semendua, Democratic Republic of the Congo, **368** C3
Semeru, Gunung, *mountain peak*, Indonesia, **201** F5
Semey, Kazakhstan, **212** D2
Seminoe Reservoir, U.S.A., **419** L5
Seminole, U.S.A., **423** M5
Semiozer'ye, Russian Federation, **210** E2
Semirara Islands, Philippines, **204** C4
Semlevo, Russian Federation, **299** E5
Semnān, Iran, **220** F1
Semois, Belgium, **288** B4
Semois, *river*, Belgium, **291** G2
Semporna, Malaysia, **201** G1
Semuda, Indonesia, **201** F3
Sên, *river*, Cambodia, **203** E3
Sena, Bolivia, **455** E3
Seňa, Slovakia, **289** K4
Sena Madureira, Brazil, **455** E2
Senador Pompeu, Brazil, **453** F4
Senanayake Samudra, *lake*, Sri Lanka, **217** E5
Senanga, Zambia, **368** D6
Sendai, Honshū, Japan, **209** H3
Sendai, Kyūshū, Japan, **208** E5
Senebui, Tanjong, *point*, Indonesia, **200** C2
Senec, Slovakia, **289** H4
Seneca, Oregon, U.S.A., **418** E4
Seneca, South Dakota, U.S.A., **420** D3

Seneca Lake, U.S.A., **426** B3
Senegal, *country*, Africa, **358** D5
Sénégal, *river*, Senegal, **364** B1
Senftenberg, Germany, **289** G3
Senga Hill, Zambia, **369** F4
Sengerema, Tanzania, **369** F3
Senguerr, *river*, Argentina, **460** C2
Senhor do Bonfim, Brazil, **457** F3
Senigallia, Italy, **294** D4
Senirkent, Turkey, **363** F1
Senj, Croatia, **294** E3
Senj, Mongolia, **210** E3
Senja, *island*, Norway, **284** H2
Senjitu, China, **210** G4
Senlin Shan, *mountain peak*, China, **211** K4
Senlis, France, **290** F2
Sennen, England, U.K., **304** B4
Senneterre, Canada, **416** C5
Sennybridge, Wales, U.K., **304** D3
Senoia, U.S.A., **425** K3
Senokos, Bulgaria, **296** G4
Senorbì, Sardegna, Italy, **295** B6
Sens, France, **291** F2
Sensuntepeque, El Salvador, **428** C4
Senta, Yugoslavia, **296** C3
Sentani, Danau, *lake*, Indonesia, **199** H3
Sentarum, Danau, *lake*, Indonesia, **201** E2
Sentinel, U.S.A., **422** G5
Sento Sé, Brazil, **457** F2
Sentosa, *island*, Singapore, **200** J7
Senyavin Islands, Micronesia, **138** D4
Seoni, India, **218** D5
Seoul *see* Sŏul, South Korea, **208** D3
Separation Point, Canada, **417** N3
Separation Point, New Zealand, **133** D5
Sepasu, Indonesia, **201** G2
Sepi, Solomon Islands, **141** A1
Sepik, *river*, Papua New Guinea, **140** A4
Sept-Îles, Canada, **416** H4
Septemvri, Bulgaria, **296** E4
Sequim, U.S.A., **418** C2
Seram, India, **216** D2
Seram, Pulau, *island*, Indonesia, **199** E3
Serang, Indonesia, **200** D4
Serangoon, Pulau, *island*, Singapore, **200** K6
Serangoon, *river*, Singapore, **200** K6
Serangoon, Singapore, **200** K6
Serangoon Harbour, Singapore, **200** K6
Serasan, Pulau, *island*, Indonesia, **201** E2
Serasan, Selat, *strait*, Indonesia/Malaysia, **201** E2
Seraya, Pulau, *island*, Singapore, **200** J7
Şerbăneşti, Romania, **296** E3
Serbia *see* Srbija, *republic*, Yugoslavia, **296** C4
Sêrca, China, **215** E3
Serdo, Ethiopia, **367** F2
Serebryansk, Kazakhstan, **212** D2
Serebryannye Prudy, Russian Federation, **299** G5
Sered', Slovakia, **289** H4
Seredka, Russian Federation, **299** B3
Seredžius, Lithuania, **287** L5
Seremban, Malaysia, **200** C2
Serempaka, Gunung, *mountain peak*, Indonesia, **201** F3
Serenje, Zambia, **369** F5
Serere, Uganda, **369** F2
Sergelen, Dornod, Mongolia, **210** F2
Sergelen, Sühbaatar, Mongolia, **210** E3

Sergeyevka, Russian Federation, **211** L4
Sergipe, *state*, Brazil, **457** G3
Sergiyev Posad, Russian Federation, **299** G4
Sergiyevo, Russian Federation, **285** T5
Sergozero, Ozero, *lake*, Russian Federation, **285** T3
Serh, China, **213** H5
Sérifontaine, France, **305** J5
Serifos, *island*, Kyklades, Greece, **297** E7
Serik, Turkey, **363** F1
-Sermata, Kepulauan, *islands*, Indonesia, **199** E5
Sermiligaaq, Greenland, **411** R3
Seroe Colorado, Aruba, **461** B3
Seronga, Botswana, **370** D2
Serov, Russian Federation, **300** H4
Serowe, Botswana, **371** E3
Serpa, Portugal, **292** D4
Serpiente, Boca de la, *strait*, Trinidad and Tobago/Venezuela, **461** C4
Serpukhov, Russian Federation, **299** F5
Serra, Brazil, **457** F5
Serra do Navio, Brazil, **452** C3
Serra Formosa, Brazil, **456** B3
Serra San Bruno, Italy, **295** F6
Serra Talhada, Brazil, **453** F5
Serrano, Isla, *island*, Chile, **460** B3
Serranópolis, Brazil, **456** C5
Serre, *river*, France, **291** F2
Serres, France, **291** G4
Serres, Greece, **297** D5
Serrezuela, Argentina, **458** D4
Serrinha, Brazil, **457** F3
Sêrro, Brazil, **457** E5
Serrota, *mountain peak*, Spain, **292** E2
Sertânia, Brazil, **453** G5
Sertãozinho, Brazil, **456** D5
Sêrtar, China, **215** G2
Sertung, Pulau, *island*, Indonesia, **200** D4
Serui, Indonesia, **199** G3
Serule, Botswana, **371** E3
Seruyan, *river*, Indonesia, **201** F3
Servia, Greece, **297** D5
Seryshevo, Russian Federation, **211** K2
Sesayap, Indonesia, **201** G2
Sese Islands, Uganda, **369** F3
Sesepe, Indonesia, **198** D3
Sesfontein, Namibia, **370** B2
Sesheke, Zambia, **370** D2
Seskarö, *island*, Sweden, **285** L4
Sessa, Angola, **368** D5
Sessa Aurunca, Italy, **295** D5
Sestri Levante, Italy, **294** B3
Šėta, Lithuania, **287** M5
Sète, France, **291** F5
Sete Lagoas, Brazil, **457** E5
Setermoen, Norway, **284** J2
Setesdal, *valley*, Norway, **286** C3
Sétif, Algeria, **361** H1
Settat, Morocco, **360** E2
Setté Cama, Gabon, **368** A3
Settle, England, U.K., **306** F3
Setúbal, Baía de, *bay*, Portugal, **292** C3
Setúbal, *district*, Portugal, **292** C3
Setúbal, Portugal, **292** C3
Seui, Sardegna, Italy, **295** B6
Seul, Lac, *lake*, Canada, **414** H6
Sevana Lich, *lake*, Armenia, **222** D4
Sevastopol', Ukraine, **298** D4
Seven Persons, Canada, **413** P7
Seven Sisters Peaks, *mountain peak*, Canada, **412** E4
Sevenoaks, England, U.K., **305** H3
Severn, *river*, Canada, **415** K4

Severn, *river*, Wales, U.K., **304** D2
Severn Lake, Canada, **414** J4
Severnaya Osetiya-Alaniya, Respublika, *republic*, Russian Federation, **222** C4
Severnaya Zemlya, *islands*, Russian Federation, **301** M1
Severnoye, Novosibirskaya Oblast', Russian Federation, **223** K1
Severnoye, Orenburgskaya Oblast', Russian Federation, **222** E2
Severnyye Uvaly, *mountain range*, Russian Federation, **300** F4
Severobaykal'sk, Russian Federation, **301** M4
Severočeský, *administrative region*, Czech Republic, **289** F3
Severodvinsk, Russian Federation, **300** F3
Severomoravský, *administrative region*, Czech Republic, **289** H4
Severomorsk, Russian Federation, **285** R2
Severo-Sibirskaya Nizmennost', Russian Federation, **300** K2
Severo-Yeniseyskiy, Russian Federation, **300** L3
Severo-Zadonsk, Russian Federation, **299** G5
Severy, U.S.A., **420** E7
Sevettijärvi, Finland, **285** P2
Sevi, Russian Federation, **213** G1
Sevier, *river*, U.S.A., **422** G2
Sevier Desert, U.S.A., **422** G2
Sevier Lake, U.S.A., **422** G2
Sevilla, Colombia, **450** C3
Sevilla, Spain, **292** E4
Sevlievo, Bulgaria, **296** E4
Sevnica, Slovenia, **294** E2
Sèvre Niortaise, *river*, France, **290** D3
Sevryukovo, Russian Federation, **299** F5
Seward, U.S.A., **410** E3
Seward Peninsula, Canada, **410** C3
Sexsmith, Canada, **413** K4
Seybaplaya, Mexico, **431** H5
Seychelles, *country*, Indian Ocean, **359** L7
Seychellois, Morne, *mountain peak*, Seychelles, **373** A2
Seydişehir, Turkey, **363** F1
Seyðisfjörður, Iceland, **284** Z7
Seymour, U.S.A., **421** L6
Seymour, Australia, **135** K6
Seymour, U.S.A., **424** C3
Seyssel, France, **291** G4
Sežana, Slovenia, **294** D3
Sézanne, France, **291** F2
Sezze, Italy, **295** D5
Sfakia, Kriti, Greece, **297** E8
Sfântu Gheorghe, Central Romania, **296** E3
Sfântu Gheorghe, E. Romania, **296** G3
Sfax, Tunisia, **362** B2
Sgurr Mor, *mountain peak*, Scotland, U.K., **308** D3
Sha, *river*, China, **206** D3
Sha Tau Kok *see* Shatoujiao, China, **207** C3
Sha Tin, China, **207** C4
Sha Xian, China, **206** D3
Shaanxi, *province*, China, **210** E5
Shaba, *administrative region*, Democratic Republic of the Congo, **369** E4
Shabaqua Corners, Canada, **414** K7
Shabeellaha Dhexe, *administrative region*, Somalia, **367** G4
Shabeellaha Hoose,

administrative region, Somalia, **367** F4
Shabeelle, *river*, Somalia, **367** F4
Shabelē, Wabē, *river*, Ethiopia, **367** F3
Shabla, Bulgaria, **296** G4
Shabla, Nos, *point*, Bulgaria, **296** G4
Shabogamo Lake, Canada, **416** H3
Shabunda, Democratic Republic of the Congo, **369** E3
Shache, China, **212** C5
Shackleton Coast, *region*, Antarctica, **470** D6
Shackleton Ice Shelf, Antarctica, **470** G6
Shackleton Range, *mountain range*, Antarctica, **470** C4
Shadehill, U.S.A., **420** B3
Shadrinsk, Russian Federation, **222** G1
Shadwān, Jazīrat, *island*, Egypt, **363** F3
Shaftesbury, England, U.K., **304** E3
Shag Point, New Zealand, **133** C7
Shagamu, *river*, Canada, **415** L4
Shagari, Nigeria, **365** F2
Shaghan, Kazakhstan, **212** C2
Shaghan, *river*, Kazakhstan, **212** C2
Shāh, *river*, Iran, **222** D5
Shah Alam, Malaysia, **200** C2
Shāhāda, India, **218** C5
Shahany, Ozero, *lake*, Ukraine, **296** H3
Shahbā', Syria, **225** D3
Shāhbandar, Pakistan, **218** A4
Shahdol, India, **219** E5
Shahe, Guangdong, China, **207** A2
Shahe, Hebei, China, **210** F5
Shāhganj, India, **219** E4
Shaḥḥāt, Libya, **362** D2
Shāhjahānpur, India, **218** D4
Shāhpur, India, **216** D2
Shāhpur Chākar, Pakistan, **218** B4
Shāhpura, Madhya Pradesh, India, **218** E5
Shāhpura, N. Rājasthān, India, **218** C4
Shāhpura, S. Rājasthān, India, **218** C4
Shahrak, Afghanistan, **218** A2
Shahr-e Kord, Iran, **220** F2
Shajing, northeast of Yonghan, Guangdong, China, **207** C1
Shajing, southeast of Taiping, Guangdong, China, **207** B3
Shaka, Ras, *point*, Kenya, **369** H3
Shakhovskaya, Russian Federation, **299** E4
Shakhtinsk, Kazakhstan, **212** B2
Shakhty, Russian Federation, **298** F3
Shakhun'ya, Russian Federation, **300** F4
Shakopee, U.S.A., **420** G3
Shalday, Kazakhstan, **212** C2
Shallotte, U.S.A., **425** N3
Shalqar, Kazakhstan, **222** F3
Shal'skiy, Russian Federation, **299** E2
Shaluli Shan, *mountain range*, China, **215** F3
Shalya, Russian Federation, **222** F1
Shām, Bādiyat ash (Syrian Desert), *desert*, Asia, **225** D3
Shām, Jabal ash, *mountain peak*, Oman, **221** G4
Sham Tseng, China, **207** C4
Shamāl Baḥr al Ghazal, *state*, Sudan, **366** C3
Shamāl Dārfūr, *state*, Sudan, **362** D5
Shamāl Kurdufān, *state*, Sudan, **366** C1

Show Low, U.S.A., **423** H4
Shoyna, Russian Federation, **300** F3
Shreveport, U.S.A., **424** F3
Shrewsbury, England, U.K., **304** E2
Shri Mohangarh, India, **218** B4
Shrivenham, England, U.K., **305** F3
Shropshire, *unitary authority*, England, U.K., **304** E2
Shū, Kazakhstan, **212** B4
Shu, *river*, China, **206** D1
Shū, *river*, Kazakhstan, **223** H4
Shu'ab, Ra's, *point*, Suquṭrá (Socotra), Yemen, **373** B2
Shuajingsi, China, **215** G3
Shuangcheng, China, **211** J3
Shuangfeng, China, **206** C3
Shuangjiang, China, **215** F5
Shuangliao, China, **211** H4
Shuangliao, South Korea, **211** H4
Shuangyashan, China, **211** K3
Shubarqudyq, Kazakhstan, **222** F3
Shubrā al Khaymah, Egypt, **225** A4
Shucheng, China, **206** D2
Shuitou, China, **207** B1
Shujālpur, India, **218** D5
Shūl, *river*, Iran, **220** F2
Shulan, China, **211** J3
Shule, China, **212** C5
Shule, *river*, China, **213** H5
Shule Nanshan, *mountain range*, China, **213** H5
Shūlgareh, Afghanistan, **218** A1
Shulu, China, **210** F5
Shumen, Bulgaria, **296** F4
Shumerlya, Russian Federation, **222** D1
Shumikha, Russian Federation, **222** G1
Shumilina, Belarus, **299** B5
Shunchang, China, **206** D3
Shunde, China, **206** C4
Shun'ga, Russian Federation, **285** S5
Shungnak, U.S.A., **410** D3
Shūr-e Gaz, Iran, **221** G3
Shūrāb, Iran, **221** G2
Shurugwi, Zimbabwe, **371** E2
Shūsf, Iran, **221** H2
Shūsh, Iran, **220** E2
Shūshtar, Iran, **220** E2
Shuswap Lake, Canada, **413** K6
Shuwak, Sudan, **366** E2
Shuya, *river*, Russian Federation, **299** D2
Shuya, Russian Federation, **299** E2
Shuyang, China, **206** D1
Shuyeretskoye, Russian Federation, **285** S4
Shwebo, Myanmar, **205** B3
Shyghanaq, Kazakhstan, **212** B3
Shyghys Qazaqstan, *province*, Kazakhstan, **212** D2
Shymkent, Kazakhstan, **223** H4
Shyngghyrlaū, *river*, Kazakhstan, **222** E2
Shyok, India, **218** D2
Shyryayeve, Ukraine, **296** H2
Si Sa Ket, Thailand, **203** E3
Si Xian, China, **206** D1
Siāhān Range, *mountain range*, Pakistan, **221** H3
Siālkot, Pakistan, **218** C2
Sialum, Papua New Guinea, **140** B4
Sianów, Poland, **289** H1
Siapa, *river*, Venezuela, **451** E4
Siargao Island, Philippines, **204** D4
Siasi, Philippines, **204** C5
Siassi, Papua New Guinea, **140** B4
Siatista, Greece, **297** C5
Siatlai, Myanmar, **205** B3
Siaton, Philippines, **204** C4
Siau, Pulau, *island*, Indonesia, **198** D2
Šiaulėnai, Lithuania, **287** L5
Šiauliai, Lithuania, **287** L5
Sibari, Italy, **295** F6
Sibati, China, **212** F3
Sibayak, Gunung, *mountain peak*, Indonesia, **200** B2
Sibbald, Canada, **413** P6
Šibenik, Croatia, **294** E4
Siber', *region*, Russian Federation, **195** N3
Siberia *see* Siber', *region*, Russian Federation, **195** N3
Siberimanua, Indonesia, **200** B3
Siberut, Pulau, *island*, Indonesia, **200** B3
Siberut, Selat, *strait*, Indonesia, **200** B3
Sibi, Pakistan, **218** A3
Sibiti, Congo, **368** B3
Sibiu, Romania, **296** E3
Sible Hedingham, England, U.K., **305** H3
Sibolga, Indonesia, **200** B2
Siborongborong, Indonesia, **200** B2
Sibsāgar, India, **219** H4
Sibsey, England, U.K., **307** J4
Sibu, Malaysia, **201** E2
Sibuco, Philippines, **204** C5
Sibut, Central African Republic, **368** C1
Sibutu Group, *islands*, Philippines, **204** B5
Sibutu Island, Philippines, **204** B5
Sibuyan Island, Philippines, **204** C3
Sicamous, Canada, **413** K6
Sicapoo, Mount, *mountain peak*, Philippines, **204** C2
Sichuan, *province*, China, **215** G3
Sichuan Pendi, *basin*, China, **215** H3
Sicié, Cap, *cape*, France, **291** G5
Sicilia, *autonomous region*, Italy, **295** D7
Sicilia (Sicily), *island*, Italy, **295** E7
Sicily *see* Sicilia, *island*, Italy, E7
Sicily, Strait of, Italy, **295** C7
Sicuani, Peru, **454** D4
Šid, Yugoslavia, **296** B3
Sidaouet, Niger, **365** F1
Sidbury, England, U.K., **304** D4
Siddhapur, India, **218** C5
Siddipet, India, **216** D2
Sidéradougou, Burkina Faso, **364** D2
Siderno, Italy, **295** F6
Sideros, Akra, *point*, Kriti, Greece, **297** F8
Sidhi, India, **219** E4
Sidi Ali, Algeria, **361** G1
Sīdī Barrānī, Egypt, **362** E2
Sidi Bel Abbès, Algeria, **361** F1
Sidi Bou Zid, Tunisia, **362** A2
Sidi el Hani, Sebkhet de, *salt-pan*, Tunisia, **295** C8
Sidi Ifni, Morocco, **360** D3
Sidi Kacem, Morocco, **361** E2
Sidi Khaled, Algeria, **361** G2
Sidi Lakhdar, Algeria, **293** H4
Sidi Okba, Algeria, **361** H2
Sīdī Sālim, Egypt, **225** A4
Sidikalang, Indonesia, **200** B2
Sidirokastra, Greece, **297** D5
Sidlaw Hills, Scotland, U.K., **308** F4
Sidley, Mount, *mountain peak*, Antarctica, **470** C6
Sidmouth, England, U.K., **304** D4
Sidney, Canada, **412** H7
Sidney, Iowa, U.S.A., **420** F5
Sidney, Montana, U.S.A., **419** M3
Sidney, Nebraska, U.S.A., **420** B5
Sidney Lanier, Lake, U.S.A., **425** L2
Sido, Mali, **364** C2
Sidon *see* Ṣaydā, Lebanon, **225** C3
Sidorovo, Russian Federation, **299** G4
Sidrolândia, Brazil, **456** B5
Siedlce, Poland, **289** L2
Siegen, Germany, **288** D3
Sielkentjahke, *mountain peak*, Sweden, **284** G4
Siembra, Indonesia, **199** F3
Siemens, Cape, Papua New Guinea, **140** C3
Siemiatycze, Poland, **289** L2
Siĕmréab, Cambodia, **203** D3
Siena, Italy, **294** C4
Sieppijärvi, Finland, **285** M3
Sieradz, Poland, **289** J3
Sierpc, Poland, **289** J2
Sierra, Punta, *point*, Argentina, **460** E1
Sierra Blanca, U.S.A., **423** L6
Sierra Colorada, Argentina, **460** D1
Sierra Gorda, Chile, **458** C2
Sierra Grande, Argentina, **460** E1
Sierra Leone, *country*, Africa, **358** D6
Sierra Leone Basin, *underwater feature*, Atlantic Ocean, **477** F5
Sierra Mojada, Mexico, **430** E3
Sierra Vista, U.S.A., **423** H6
Sierraville, U.S.A., **422** C2
Sierre, Switzerland, **291** H3
Şieu, Romania, **296** E2
Sievi, Finland, **285** M5
Sifnos, *island*, Kyklades, Greece, **297** E7
Sig, Algeria, **293** G5
Sig, Russian Federation, **285** S4
Sigatoka, Fiji, **141** A4
Sigean, France, **291** F5
Sigenti, Indonesia, **198** C2
Sigep, Tanjong, *point*, Indonesia, **200** B3
Sighetu Marmației, Romania, **296** D2
Sighișoara, Romania, **296** E2
Sigli, Indonesia, **200** B1
Siglufjörður, Iceland, **284** Y6
Signal de Botrange, *mountain peak*, Belgium, **288** C3
Signy, *U.K. research station*, Antarctica, **470** A3
Sigri, Greece, **297** E6
Siguatepeque, Honduras, **428** D4
Sigüenza, Spain, **293** F2
Sigüés, Spain, **293** G1
Siguiri, Guinea, **364** C2
Sigulda, Latvia, **287** M4
Sihong, China, **206** D1
Sihora, India, **218** E5
Sihuas, Peru, **454** C2
Sihui, China, **206** C4
Siikainen, Finland, **287** K2
Siikajoki, *river*, Finland, **285** M4
Siilinjärvi, Finland, **285** N5
Siirt, Turkey, **224** F5
Siivikko, Finland, **285** N4
Sikaiana, *island*, Solomon Islands, **141** A1
Sikanni Chief, Canada, **412** H3
Sīkar, India, **218** C4
Sikasso, *administrative region*, Mali, **364** C2
Sikasso, Mali, **364** C2
Sikaw, Myanmar, **205** C3
Sikea, Greece, **297** D5
Sikes, U.S.A., **424** F3
Sikeston, U.S.A., **421** J7
Sikhote-Alin', *mountain range*, Russian Federation, **211** L3
Sikinos, *island*, Kyklades, Greece, **297** E7
Sikkim, *state*, India, **219** G4
Siktyakh, Russian Federation, **301** P3
Sil, *river*, Spain, **292** D1
Sila, La, *mountain range*, Italy, **295** F6
Silandro Schlandres, Italy, **294** C2
Silay, Philippines, **204** C4
Silba, *island*, Croatia, **294** E3
Silchar, India, **219** H4
Silet, Algeria, **361** G4
Siletz, U.S.A., **418** C4
Silhouette, *island*, Seychelles, **373** A2
Silifke, Turkey, **225** B1
Silin, China, **215** H5
Siling Co, *lake*, China, **214** D3
Silíqua, Sardegna, Italy, **295** B6
Silistră, Bulgaria, **298** C4
Silivri, Turkey, **297** G5
Siljan, *lake*, Sweden, **286** G2
Silkeborg, Denmark, **286** D4
Sillamäe, Estonia, **287** N3
Sillé-le-Guillaume, France, **290** D2
Sillon de Talbert, *point*, France, **290** C2
Silloth, England, U.K., **306** E3
Silsbee, U.S.A., **424** E4
Şiluko, Nigeria, **365** F3
Šilutė, Lithuania, **287** K5
Silvassa, India, **218** C5
Silver Bay, U.S.A., **420** H2
Silver City, Idaho, U.S.A., **418** F5
Silver City, New Mexico, U.S.A., **423** J5
Silver Dollar, Canada, **414** J7
Silver Lake, U.S.A., **418** D5
Silverdale, New Zealand, **132** E3
Silverstone, England, U.K., **305** F2
Silverton, Colorado, U.S.A., **423** K3
Silverton, England, U.K., **304** D4
Silverton, Oregon, U.S.A., **418** C4
Silverton, Texas, U.S.A., **424** B2
Silves, Brazil, **451** G5
Silvituc, Mexico, **431** H5
Silvrettagruppe, *mountain range*, Austria/Switzerland, **291** J3
Sima, China, **207** C3
Simanggang *see* Bandar Sri Aman, Malaysia, **201** E2
Simao, China, **215** G5
Simão Dias, Brazil, **457** G3
Simara, Nepal, **219** F4
Simaria Ghāt, India, **219** F4
Simav, Turkey, **297** G6
Simav Dağları, *mountain range*, Turkey, **297** G6
Simba, Democratic Republic of the Congo, **368** D2
Simbai, Papua New Guinea, **140** B4
Simbu, *province*, Papua New Guinea, **140** B4
Simcoe, Canada, **421** N4
Simcoe, Lake, Canada, **421** P3
Simdega, India, **219** F5
Simēn, *mountain range*, Ethiopia, **367** E2
Simeria, Romania, **296** D3
Simeulue, Pulau, *island*, Indonesia, **200** B2
Simferopol', Ukraine, **298** D4
Simga, India, **219** E5
Simi Valley, U.S.A., **422** D4
Simití, Colombia, **450** D2
Simla, U.S.A., **423** L2
Simleu Silvaniei, Romania, **296** D2
Simms, U.S.A., **419** J3
Simnas, Lithuania, **287** L5
Simo, Finland, **285** M4
Simojärvi, *lake*, Finland, **285** N3
Simojoki, *river*, Finland, **285** M4
Simplício Mendes, Brazil, **453** F5
Simpson, Canada, **413** S6
Simpson, Mount, *mountain peak*, Papua New Guinea, **140** C5
Simpson Desert, Australia, **128** C4
Simrishamn, Sweden, **286** G5
Simushir, Ostrov, *island*, Russian Federation, **301** S5
Sīnā' (Sinai), *peninsula*, Egypt, **225** B4
Sina Dhaqa, Somalia, **367** G3
Sinabang, Indonesia, **200** B2
Sinai, Mount *see* Mūsā, Jabal, *mountain peak*, Egypt, **225** B5
Sinai *see* Sīnā', *peninsula*, Egypt, **225** B4
Sinaia, Romania, **296** E3
Sinaloa, *state*, Mexico, **430** C3
Sinalunga, Italy, **294** C4
Sinarades, Greece, **297** B6
Sīnāwin, Libya, **362** B2
Sinbaungwe, Myanmar, **205** B4
Sinbo, Myanmar, **205** C2
Sinbyugyun, Myanmar, **205** B3
Şinca Nouă, Romania, **296** E3
Sincé, Colombia, **450** C2
Sincelejo, Colombia, **450** C2
Sinch'ŏn, North Korea, **208** D3
Sinclair, Lake, U.S.A., **425** L3
Sinclair, U.S.A., **419** L6
Sinclair Mills, Canada, **412** J4
Sinclair's Bay, Scotland, U.K., **308** F2
Sind, *river*, India, **218** D4
Sindangan, Philippines, **204** C4
Sindangbarang, Indonesia, **201** D4
Sindara, Gabon, **368** B3
Sindari, India, **218** B4
Sindh, *province*, Pakistan, **218** B4
Sindhnūr, India, **216** D3
Sindi, Estonia, **287** M3
Sındırgı, Turkey, **297** G6
Sindri, India, **219** F5
Sinegor'ye, Russian Federation, **301** S3
Sinendé, Benin, **365** E2
Sines, Portugal, **292** C4
Sinewit, Mount, *mountain peak*, Papua New Guinea, **140** D4
Sinfra, Côte d'Ivoire, **364** C3
Sing Buri, Thailand, **202** D3
Singapore, *country*, Asia, **197** M9
Singapore, Singapore, **200** K7
Singapore, Straits of, Indonesia/Singapore, **200** K7
Singaraja, Indonesia, **201** F5
Singarāyakonda, India, **216** E3
Singida, *administrative region*, Tanzania, **369** F4
Singida, Tanzania, **369** F3
Singkang, Indonesia, **198** C4
Singkarak, Danau, *lake*, Indonesia, **200** B3
Singkawang, Indonesia, **201** E2
Singkep, Pulau, *island*, Indonesia, **200** D3
Singleton, Australia, **135** L5
Singoli, India, **218** C4
Singsås, Norway, **284** E5
Siniscola, Sardegna, Italy, **295** B5
Sinj, Croatia, **294** F4
Sinjah, Sudan, **366** D2
Sinjai, Indonesia, **198** C4
Sinjār, Iraq, **363** H1
Sinkan, Myanmar, **205** C2
Sinkāt, Sudan, **363** G5
Sinko, Guinea, **364** C3
Sinn Bishr, Jabal, *mountain peak*, Egypt, **225** B5
Sinnamary, French Guiana, **452** C2
Sinnār, *state*, Sudan, **366** D2
Sinni, *river*, Italy, **295** F5
Sinoie, Lacul, *lake*, Romania, **296** G3
Sinop, Brazil, **456** B3
Sinop, Turkey, **224** E4
Sinp'o, North Korea, **208** E2
Sint Nicolaas, Aruba, **461** B3
Sint Willebrordus, Curaçao, Netherlands Antilles, **461** C3

Snowflake, U.S.A., **423** H4
Snowtown, Australia, **135** H5
Snowy Mountains, *mountain range*, Australia, **135** K6
Snug Corner, Bahamas, **429** G2
Snyatyn, Ukraine, **296** E1
Snyder, Colorado, U.S.A., **423** M1
Snyder, Oklahoma, U.S.A., **424** C2
Snyder, Texas, U.S.A., **424** B3
Soacha, Colombia, **450** C3
Soai Dao, Phu, *mountain peak*, Laos, **202** D2
Soalala, Madagascar, **372** B4
Soamanonga, Madagascar, **372** A5
Soanierana-Ivongo, Madagascar, **372** B4
Soap Lake, U.S.A., **418** E3
Sobāt, *river*, Sudan, **366** D3
Soběslav, Czech Republic, **289** G4
Sobradinho, Represa de, *reservoir*, Brazil, **457** E3
Sobral, Brazil, **453** F4
Sobrance, Slovakia, **289** L4
Sóc Trăng, Vietnam, **203** E4
Sočanica, Yugoslavia, **296** C4
Sochaczew, Poland, **289** K2
Sochi, Russian Federation, **224** E4
Sochos, Greece, **297** D5
Société, Archipel de la, *islands*, French Polynesia, **137** F2
Socorro, Colombia, **450** D2
Socorro, U.S.A., **423** K4
Socotra *see* Suquṭrá, *island*, Yemen, **373** B2
Soda Creek, Canada, **412** H5
Soda Springs, U.S.A., **419** J5
Sodankylä, Finland, **285** N3
Söderhamn, Sweden, **287** H2
Söderköping, Sweden, **286** H3
Sodermanland, *county*, Sweden, **287** H3
Södertälje, Sweden, **287** H3
Sodo, Ethiopia, **367** E3
Södra Kvarken, *strait*, Finland/ Sweden, **287** J2
Södra Vallgrund, Finland, **284** K5
Soe, Indonesia, **198** D5
Soekmekaar, South Africa, **371** E3
Soela väin, *strait*, Estonia, **287** L3
Soest, Germany, **288** D3
Soeurs, Les, *islands*, Seychelles, **373** A2
Sofades, Greece, **297** D6
Sofala, Mozambique, **371** F3
Sofala, *province*, Mozambique, **371** F2
Sofia *see* Sofiya, Bulgaria, **296** D4
Sofiko, Greece, **297** D7
Sofiya, *administrative region*, Bulgaria, **296** D4
Sofiya (Sofia), Bulgaria, **296** D4
Sofiysk, E. Khabarovskiy Kray, Russian Federation, **211** M2
Sofiysk, *river*, Russian Federation, **211** L1
Sofiysk, W. Khabarovskiy Kray, Russian Federation, **211** L1
Sofporog, Russian Federation, **285** Q4
Sōfu-gan, *island*, Japan, **138** C2
Sog Xian, China, **214** E3
Sogamoso, Colombia, **450** D3
Sogda, Russian Federation, **211** L2
Sogn og Fjordane, *county*, Norway, **286** C2
Søgne, Norway, **286** C3
Sognefjorden, *fiord*, Norway, **286** B2
Sogo Nur, *lake*, China, **213** J4
Sogod, Philippines, **204** D4
Sŏgwip'o, South Korea, **208** D4
Soham, England, U.K., **305** H2
Sohano, Papua New Guinea, **140** E2
Sohela, India, **219** E5
Soi Dao Tai, Khao, *mountain peak*, Thailand, **202** D3
Soignies, Belgium, **288** B3
Soila, China, **215** F3
Soini, Finland, **285** M5
Sointula, Canada, **412** F6
Soira, *mountain peak*, Eritrea, **367** E2
Soissons, France, **291** F2
Sojat, India, **218** C4
Sokal', Ukraine, **289** M3
Sokch'o, South Korea, **208** E3
Söke, Turkey, **297** F7
Sokhondo, Gora, *mountain peak*, Russian Federation, **210** E2
Sokhumi, Georgia, **222** C4
Sokna, Norway, **286** D2
Soko Banja, Yugoslavia, **296** C4
Sokodé, Togo, **364** E3
Sokolac, Bosnia and Herzegovina, **294** G4
Sokółka, Poland, **289** L2
Sokolo, Mali, **364** C2
Sokołów-Podlaski, Poland, **289** L2
Sokoły, Poland, **289** L2
Sokosti, *mountain peak*, Finland, **285** P2
Sokoto, Nigeria, **365** F2
Sokoto, *state*, Nigeria, **365** F2
Sokyryany, Ukraine, **296** F1
Sol'-Iletsk, Russian Federation, **222** F2
Sola, Vanuatu, **141** A2
Solan, India, **218** D3
Solander Island (Hautere), New Zealand, **133** A8
Solano, Bahía, *bay*, Argentina, **460** D2
Solano, U.S.A., **423** L4
Solāpur, India, **216** C2
Solberg, Sweden, **284** H5
Solca, Romania, **296** E2
Soldăneşti, Moldova, **296** G2
Soldier Summit, U.S.A., **423** H2
Soledad, Colombia, **450** C1
Soledad, U.S.A., **422** C3
Soledad, Venezuela, **451** F2
Soledad de Doblado, Mexico, **431** F5
Soledade, Brazil, **459** G3
Solenzara, Corse, France, **295** B5
Solheim, Norway, **286** B2
Solihull, England, U.K., **305** F2
Solikamsk, Russian Federation, **300** G4
Solimões, *river*, Brazil, **451** F5
Solingen, Germany, **288** C3
Solitary, Mount, *mountain peak*, New Zealand, **133** A7
Sollefteå, Sweden, **284** H5
Sollentuna, Sweden, **287** H3
Sóller, Spain, **293** J3
Solnechnogorsk, Russian Federation, **299** F4
Solo, *river*, Indonesia, **201** E4
Solo *see* Surakarta, Indonesia, **201** E4
Solok, Indonesia, **200** C3
Sololá, Guatemala, **428** C4
Solomon, *river*, U.S.A., **420** D6
Solomon, U.S.A., **423** J5
Solomon Islands, *country*, Pacific Ocean, **131** F2
Solomon Sea, Papua New Guinea/Solomon Islands, **128** E2
Solon, China, **211** H3
Solon Springs, U.S.A., **420** H2
Soloneshnoye, Russian Federation, **223** L2
Solonópole, Brazil, **453** F4
Solor, Kepulauan, *islands*, Indonesia, **198** C5
Solothurn, Switzerland, **291** H3
Solotvyn, Ukraine, **296** E1
Solovetskiye Ostrova, *island*, Russian Federation, **285** S4
Solsem, Norway, **284** E4
Solsona, Spain, **293** H2
Solt, Hungary, **289** J5
Šolta, *island*, Croatia, **294** F4
Soltau, Germany, **288** D2
Sol'tsy, Russian Federation, **299** C3
Solvacion, Bahía, *bay*, Chile, **460** B4
Sölvesborg, Sweden, **286** G4
Solway Firth, *river mouth*, Scotland, U.K., **308** F6
Solwezi, Zambia, **369** E5
Soma, Turkey, **297** F6
Somali Basin, *underwater feature*, Indian Ocean, **476** C4
Somalia, *country*, Africa, **358** K6
Somanya, Ghana, **364** D3
Sombo, Angola, **368** D4
Sombor, Yugoslavia, **296** B3
Sombrerete, Mexico, **430** E4
Sombrero Channel, Andaman and Nicobar Islands, India, **217** H5
Şomcuta Mare, Romania, **296** D2
Somers, U.S.A., **418** G2
Somerset, *unitary authority*, England, U.K., **304** E3
Somerset, U.S.A., **421** L7
Somerset East, South Africa, **370** E5
Somerset Island, Canada, **411** K2
Somerton, England, U.K., **304** E3
Somerville, New Jersey, U.S.A., **426** C4
Somerville, Texas, U.S.A., **424** D4
Somes Bar, U.S.A., **418** C6
Somino, Russian Federation, **299** E3
Somme, *river*, France, **290** E1
Sommen, *lake*, Sweden, **286** G4
Sommières, France, **291** G5
Sømna, *island*, Norway, **284** E4
Somotillo, Nicaragua, **428** D4
Somoto, Nicaragua, **428** D4
Sompeta, India, **217** F2
Somuncurá, Meseta de, *plateau*, Argentina, **460** D1
So'n, Cù Lao, *island*, Vietnam, **203** E4
Son, *river*, India, **219** E4
Sơn Hạ, Vietnam, **203** F3
Sơn La, Vietnam, **203** D1
Sơn Tây, Vietnam, **203** E1
Soná, Panama, **429** E5
Sŏnch'ŏn, North Korea, **208** D3
Sønderborg, Denmark, **286** D5
Sondrio, Italy, **294** B2
Sonepur, India, **219** E5
Song, Malaysia, **201** F2
Sông ũốc, Vietnam, **203** E4
Song Xian, China, **206** B1
Songbai, China, **206** C3
Songe, Norway, **286** D3
Songea, Tanzania, **369** G5
Songeons, France, **305** J5
Songgang, China, **207** B3
Songhua, *river*, China, **211** K3
Songjiang, China, **206** E2
Songkhla, Thailand, **202** D5
Songling, China, **211** H2
Songming, China, **215** G4
Songmushan, China, **207** B3
Songnim, North Korea, **208** D3
Songo, Angola, **368** B4
Songo, Mozambique, **369** F6
Songpan, China, **215** G2
Songsak, India, **219** G4
Songxi, China, **206** D3
Songzi, China, **206** B2
Sonid Youqi, China, **210** F4
Sonid Zuoqi, China, **210** F4
Sonīpat, India, **218** D3
Sonkajärvi, Finland, **285** N5
Sonkovo, Russian Federation, **299** F4
Sonmiāni Bay, Pakistan, **218** A4
Sonmiāni, Pakistan, **218** A4
Sono, do, *river*, Brazil, **456** D3
Sonoita, U.S.A., **423** H6
Sonoma, U.S.A., **422** B2
Sonora, Bahía, *bay*, San Andrés, Colombia, **461** B1
Sonora, California, U.S.A., **422** C3
Sonora, *river*, Mexico, **430** C2
Sonora, *state*, Mexico, **430** B2
Sonora, Texas, U.S.A., **424** B4
Sonoran Desert, U.S.A., **422** F5
Sonostrov, Russian Federation, **285** S3
Sonoyta, Mexico, **430** B2
Sonskiy, Russian Federation, **223** N2
Sonsón, Colombia, **450** C3
Sonsonate, El Salvador, **428** C4
Sonsorol, *island*, Palau, **138** B4
Sooke, Canada, **412** H7
Sop Huai, Thailand, **202** C2
Sopachuy, Bolivia, **455** F5
Sopki, Russian Federation, **299** C4
Sopokha, Russian Federation, **285** S5
Sopot, Bulgaria, **296** E4
Sopot, Poland, **289** J1
Sopot, Yugoslavia, **296** C3
Sopron, Hungary, **289** H5
Sor, *river*, Portugal, **292** C3
Sör-dellen, *lake*, Sweden, **287** H2
Sør-Flatanger, Norway, **284** E4
Sør-Rondane, *mountain range*, Antarctica, **470** E3
Sør-Trøndelag, *county*, Norway, **284** E5
Sora, Italy, **295** D5
Sorāh, Pakistan, **218** B4
Söråker, Sweden, **287** H1
Sorang, Kazakhstan, **212** B2
Sorata, Bolivia, **455** E4
Sorbe, *river*, Spain, **293** F2
Sørbovag, Norway, **286** B2
Sörbygden, Sweden, **286** H1
Sorel, Canada, **416** E6
Sorell, Australia, **135** K7
Sorgono, Sardegna, Italy, **295** B5
Soria, Spain, **293** F2
Sørli, Norway, **284** F4
Soro, India, **219** F5
Soro, Pakistan, **218** A3
Soroca, Moldova, **296** G1
Sorocaba, Brazil, **459** H2
Sorochinsk, Russian Federation, **222** E2
Sorok, Russian Federation, **213** J1
Sorokino, Russian Federation, **299** B4
Sorol, *island*, Micronesia, **138** C4
Sorong, Indonesia, **199** E3
Sorot', *river*, Russian Federation, **299** B4
Soroti, Uganda, **369** F2
Sørøya, *island*, Norway, **285** L1
Sørøysundet, *channel*, Norway, **285** L1
Sørreisa, Norway, **284** J2
Sorrento, Italy, **295** E5
Sorsatunturi, *mountain peak*, Finland, **285** P3
Sorsele, Sweden, **284** H4
Sorsogon, Philippines, **204** D3
Sortavala, Russian Federation, **299** C2
Sortland, Norway, **284** G2
Sørvågen, Norway, **284** F3
Sørvika, Norway, **286** E1
Sosanpal, India, **217** E2
Sösdala, Sweden, **286** F4
Sösjöfjällen, *mountain peak*, Sweden, **284** F5
Sosneado, Cerro, *mountain peak*, Argentina, **458** C5
Sosnovets, Russian Federation, **285** S4
Sosnovyy, Russian Federation, **285** R3
Sosnovyy Bor, Russian Federation, **299** B3
Sosnowiec, Poland, **289** J3
Sospel, France, **291** H5
Sotkamo, Finland, **285** P4
Soto, Curaçao, Netherlands Antilles, **461** C3
Soto La Marina, Mexico, **431** F4
Sotomayor, Colombia, **450** C4
Sotra, *island*, Norway, **286** B2
Sotteville-lès-Rouen, France, **305** J5
Sotuf, Adrar, *mountain range*, Western Sahara, **360** C4
Sotuta, Mexico, **431** H4
Souanké, Congo, **368** B2
Soubré, Côte d'Ivoire, **364** C3
Souda, Kriti, Greece, **297** E8
Soufli, Greece, **297** F5
Soufrière, *mountain peak*, St Vincent and the Grenadines, **427** D3
Sougéta, Guinea, **364** B2
Sougueur, Algeria, **361** G1
Souillac, France, **290** E4
Souillac, Mauritius, **373** C1
Souk Ahras, Algeria, **361** H1
Souk-el-Arba-du-Rharb, Morocco, **361** E2
Sŏul (Seoul), South Korea, **208** D3
Sour el Ghozlane, Algeria, **293** J4
Soure, Brazil, **452** D3
Souris, Canada, **414** D7
Sousa, Brazil, **453** F5
Sousse, Tunisia, **362** B1
South Africa, *country*, **359** H9
South Andaman, *island*, Andaman and Nicobar Islands, India, **217** H4
South Australia, *state*, Australia, **134** G4
South Australian Basin, *underwater feature*, Indian Ocean, **476** H7
South Ayrshire, *local authority*, Scotland, U.K., **308** E5
South Baldy, *mountain peak*, U.S.A., **423** K5
South Bay, Canada, **414** H6
South Bend, Indiana, U.S.A., **421** K5
South Bend, Washington, U.S.A., **418** C3
South Boston, U.S.A., **421** P7
South Bruny Island, Australia, **135** K7
South Cape, New Zealand, **133** A8
South Carolina, *state*, U.S.A., **424** M2
South Cave, England, U.K., **307** H4
South China Basin, *underwater feature*, South China Sea, **478** B3
South China Sea, China/ Philippines/Vietnam, **195** N8
South Dakota, *state*, U.S.A., **420** C3
South Downs, *region*, England, U.K., **305** G4
South East, *district*, Botswana, **371** E3
South East Bay, Ascension, **373** A3
South East Cape, Australia, **135** K7
South East Harbour, Campbell Island, New Zealand, **132** K11
South East Head, *point*, Ascension, **373** A3
South Elmsall, England, U.K., **307** G4
South Fork, U.S.A., **423** K3
South Georgia, *island*, South Georgia and South Sandwich Islands, **449** J9
South Georgia and South Sandwich Islands, *U.K. dependency*, Atlantic Ocean, **449** J9
South Georgia Ridge,

Starke, U.S.A., **425** L5
Starkville, U.S.A., **425** H3
Starnberger See, *lake*, Germany, **288** E5
Staro Oryakhovo, Bulgaria, **296** F4
Starosel'ye, Russian Federation, **299** F6
Start Bay, England, U.K., **304** D4
Start Point, England, U.K., **304** D4
Startup, U.S.A., **418** D3
Staryy Oskol, Russian Federation, **298** E2
Staryy Sambir, Ukraine, **289** L4
Staryya Darohi, Belarus, **299** B6
Staszów, Poland, **289** K3
Statesboro, U.S.A., **425** M3
Statesville, U.S.A., **425** M2
Staunton, U.S.A., **421** P6
Stavanger, Norway, **286** B3
Stavaträsk, Sweden, **284** K4
Staveley, England, U.K., **305** F1
Staveley, New Zealand, **133** C6
Stavely, Canada, **413** N6
Stavropol', Russian Federation, **298** F3
Stavropol'skiy Kray, *territory*, Russian Federation, **298** F3
Stavros, Greece, **297** D5
Stawell, Australia, **135** J6
Stawiski, Poland, **289** L2
Stawiszyn, Poland, **289** J3
Steamboat, U.S.A., **418** C5
Steamboat Canyon, U.S.A., **423** J4
Steamboat Mountain, *mountain peak*, U.S.A., **419** K6
Steamboat Springs, U.S.A., **423** K1
Steele, U.S.A., **420** C2
Steels Point, Norfolk Island, **135** T13
Steen River, Canada, **413** L2
Steens Mountain, *mountain range*, U.S.A., **418** E5
Steenvoorde, France, **305** K4
Steenwijk, Netherlands, **288** C2
Steep Point, Australia, **134** C4
Ştefan Vodă, Moldova, **296** G2
Stefansson Island, Canada, **410** J2
Steffen, Cerro, *mountain peak*, Argentina, **460** C2
Stege, Denmark, **286** F5
Steiermark, *state*, Austria, **289** G5
Steinbach, Canada, **414** F7
Steine, Norway, **284** G2
Steinfort, Luxembourg, **291** G2
Steinhatchee, U.S.A., **425** L5
Steinhausen, Namibia, **370** C3
Steinkjer, Norway, **284** E5
Steinkopf, South Africa, **370** C4
Stellarton, Canada, **417** K7
Stellenbosch, South Africa, **370** C5
Stenay, France, **291** G2
Stendal, Germany, **288** E2
Stende, Latvia, **287** L4
Steneby, Sweden, **286** F3
Stenness, Loch of, *lake*, Orkney, Scotland, U.K., **308** F1
Stenstorp, Sweden, **286** F3
Stenudden, Sweden, **284** H3
Stenungsund, Sweden, **286** E3
Stephens, Cape, New Zealand, **133** D5
Stephens Lake, Canada, **414** G3
Stephenville, Canada, **417** M5
Stephenville, U.S.A., **424** C3
Stepojevac, Yugoslavia, **296** C3
Sterea Ellas, *administrative region*, Greece, **297** E6
Sterling, Colorado, U.S.A., **423** M1
Sterling, Illinois, U.S.A., **420** J5
Sterling, Nebraska, U.S.A., **420** E5
Sterling City, U.S.A., **424** B4
Sterling Heights, U.S.A., **421** M4
Sterlitamak, Russian Federation, **222** F2
Sternes, Kriti, Greece, **297** E8
Stettler, Canada, **413** N5
Steubenville, U.S.A., **421** N5
Stevenage, England, U.K., **305** G3
Stevens Point, U.S.A., **421** J3
Stevenson, Mount, *mountain peak*, New Zealand, **133** C6
Stevenson, U.S.A., **425** K2
Stewart, Canada, **412** E4
Stewart, Isla, *island*, Chile, **460** C5
Stewart Island, New Zealand, **133** B8
Stewarts Point, U.S.A., **422** B2
Steyr, Austria, **289** G4
Stibb Cross, England, U.K., **304** C4
Stickney, U.S.A., **420** D4
Stikine, *river*, Canada, **412** D3
Stikine Plateau, Canada, **412** D2
Stillington, England, U.K., **307** G3
Stillwater, Nevada, U.S.A., **422** D2
Stillwater, New Zealand, **133** C6
Stillwater, Oklahoma, U.S.A., **424** D1
Stillwater Range, *mountain range*, U.S.A., **422** D2
Stilo, Italy, **295** F6
Stilton, England, U.K., **305** G2
Štimlje, Yugoslavia, **296** C4
Stintino, Sardegna, Italy, **295** B5
Štip, Macedonia, **297** D5
Stirling, *local authority*, Scotland, U.K., **308** E4
Stirling, Scotland, U.K., **308** F4
Stjernøya, *island*, Norway, **285** L1
Stjørdalshalsen, Norway, **284** E5
Stockerau, Austria, **289** H4
Stockholm, *county*, Sweden, **287** H3
Stockholm, Sweden, **287** J3
Stockport, England, U.K., **306** F4
Stockton, California, U.S.A., **422** C3
Stockton, Kansas, U.S.A., **420** D6
Stockton Lake, U.S.A., **420** G7
Stockton Plateau, U.S.A., **423** M6
Stockton-on-Tees, England, U.K., **307** G3
Stockton-on-Tees, *unitary authority*, England, U.K., **307** G3
Stoczek Łukowski, Poland, **289** K3
Stod, Czech Republic, **288** F4
Stöde, Sweden, **286** H1
Stødi, Norway, **284** G3
Stœng Trêng, Cambodia, **203** E3
Stoer, Point of, Scotland, U.K., **308** D2
Stoke-on-Trent, England, U.K., **304** E1
Stoke-on-Trent, *unitary authority*, England, U.K., **304** E1
Stokes, Bahía, *bay*, Chile, **460** C5
Stokes, Mount, *mountain peak*, New Zealand, **133** E5
Stokesay, England, U.K., **304** E2
Stokesley, England, U.K., **307** G3
Stokksnes, *point*, Iceland, **284** Z7
Stolac, Bosnia and Herzegovina, **294** G4
Stoltenhoff Island, Tristan da Cunha, **373** C2
Ston, Croatia, **294** F4
Stone, Gloucestershire, England, U.K., **304** E3
Stone, Staffordshire, England, U.K., **304** E2
Stonecliffe, Canada, **416** C6
Stoneham, U.S.A., **423** M1
Stonehaven, Scotland, U.K., **308** G4
Stonewall, U.S.A., **423** L3
Stony Lake, Canada, **414** E2
Stony Plain, Canada, **413** M5
Stony Rapids, Canada, **413** S2
Stonyhill Point, Tristan da Cunha, **373** C2
Stör, *river*, Germany, **288** D2
Storå, Sweden, **286** G3
Stora Blåsjön, Sweden, **284** G4
Stora Lulevatten, *lake*, Sweden, **284** J3
Stora Sjöfallet, *lake*, Sweden, **284** H3
Storavan, *lake*, Sweden, **284** J4
Storby, Finland, **287** J2
Stord, *island*, Norway, **286** B3
Stordal, Norway, **284** E5
Store Bælt, *strait*, Denmark, **286** E5
Store Koldewey, *island*, Greenland, **411** T2
Store Sølnkletten, *mountain peak*, Norway, **286** E2
Støren, Norway, **284** E5
Storfjordbotn, Norway, **285** N1
Storfors, Sweden, **286** G3
Storforshei, Norway, **284** G3
Storjord, Norway, **284** G3
Storkow, Germany, **289** F2
Storlien, Sweden, **284** F5
Storm Lake, U.S.A., **420** F4
Stornoway, Scotland, U.K., **308** C2
Storozhynets', Ukraine, **296** E1
Storr, The, *mountain peak*, Scotland, U.K., **308** C3
Storsätern, Sweden, **286** F1
Storsjön, *lake*, near Ljungdalen, Sweden, **284** F5
Storsjön, *lake*, by Östersund, Sweden, **284** G5
Storsteinfjellet, *mountain peak*, Norway, **284** H2
Storthoaks, Canada, **414** D7
Storuman, *lake*, Sweden, **284** H4
Storuman, Sweden, **284** H4
Storvätteshågna, *mountain peak*, Sweden, **286** F1
Storvik, Sweden, **286** H2
Story, U.S.A., **419** L4
Stoughton, U.S.A., **421** J4
Stour, *river*, England, U.K., **305** F2
Stourbridge, England, U.K., **304** E2
Stourport-on-Severn, England, U.K., **304** E2
Stout Lake, Canada, **414** G5
Støvring, Denmark, **286** D4
Stow, Scotland, U.K., **308** G5
Stowmarket, England, U.K., **305** H2
Stow-on-the-Wold, England, U.K., **305** F3
Stoyba, Russian Federation, **211** K1
Strabane, *district*, Northern Ireland, U.K., **309** E3
Strabane, Northern Ireland, U.K., **309** E3
Stradbally, Ireland, **309** E4
Stradbroke, England, U.K., **305** J2
Stradella, Italy, **294** B3
Stradishall, England, U.K., **305** H2
Stradsett, England, U.K., **305** H2
Strahan, Australia, **135** K7
Strakonice, Czech Republic, **289** F4
Straldzha, Bulgaria, **296** F4
Stralki, Belarus, **287** P5
Stralsund, Germany, **288** F1
Strand, South Africa, **370** C5
Stranda, Norway, **286** C1
Strangford, Northern Ireland, U.K., **309** G3
Strangford Lough, *inlet*, Northern Ireland, U.K., **309** G3
Strängnäs, Sweden, **287** H3
Stranorlar, Ireland, **309** E3
Stranraer, Scotland, U.K., **308** D6
Strasbourg, Canada, **413** S6
Strasbourg, France, **291** H2
Strasburg, U.S.A., **420** C2
Strășeni, Moldova, **296** G2
Straßwalchen, Austria, **288** F5
Stratford, Canada, **421** N4
Stratford, New Zealand, **132** E4
Stratford, U.S.A., **423** M3
Stratford-upon-Avon, England, U.K., **305** F2
Strathaven, Scotland, U.K., **308** E5
Strathcona, Mount, *mountain peak*, Antarctica, **470** G5
Strathdon, Scotland, U.K., **308** F3
Strathmore, Canada, **413** N6
Strathnaver, Canada, **412** H5
Strathspey, *valley*, Scotland, U.K., **308** F3
Strathy, Scotland, U.K., **308** E2
Strathy Point, Scotland, U.K., **308** E2
Strathyre, Scotland, U.K., **308** E4
Stratton, England, U.K., **304** C4
Stratton, U.S.A., **426** E2
Stratton Mountain, *mountain peak*, U.S.A., **426** D3
Straubing, Germany, **288** F4
Straumen, Norway, **284** E5
Straumnes, *point*, Iceland, **284** W6
Strawberry, U.S.A., **422** C2
Streaky Bay, Australia, **134** G5
Streatley, England, U.K., **305** F3
Středočeský, *administrative region*, Czech Republic, **289** G4
Street, England, U.K., **304** E3
Strehaia, Romania, **296** D3
Strel'na, *river*, Russian Federation, **285** T3
Strel'na, Russian Federation, **285** U3
Strenči, Latvia, **287** M4
Stretham, England, U.K., **305** H2
Strevell, U.S.A., **418** H5
Streymoy, *island*, Faeroe Islands, **302** D1
Stříbo, Czech Republic, **291** L4
Stříbro, Czech Republic, **288** F4
Strichen, Scotland, U.K., **308** G3
Strickland, *river*, Papua New Guinea, **140** A4
Strimonikos Kolpos, *bay*, Greece, **297** D5
Stroeder, Argentina, **460** E1
Strofades, *island*, Ionioi Nisoi, Greece, **297** C7
Strokestown, Ireland, **309** D4
Stromboli, Isola, *island*, Italy, **295** E6
Stromeferry, Scotland, U.K., **308** D3
Stromness, Orkney, Scotland, U.K., **308** F2
Strömsbruk, Sweden, **287** H2
Stromsburg, U.S.A., **420** E5
Strömsnäsbruk, Sweden, **286** F4
Strömstad, Sweden, **286** E3
Strömsund, Sweden, **284** G5
Strong, Mount, *mountain peak*, Papua New Guinea, **140** B4
Stronsay, *island*, Orkney, Scotland, U.K., **308** G1
Stronsay Firth, *channel*, Orkney, Scotland, U.K., **308** G1
Strontian, Scotland, U.K., **308** D4
Stroud, England, U.K., **304** E3
Stroudsburg, U.S.A., **426** C4
Struer, Denmark, **286** D4
Struga, Macedonia, **297** C5
Strumble Head, *point*, Wales, U.K., **304** B2
Strumica, Macedonia, **297** D5
Stryker, U.S.A., **418** G2
Stryukove, Ukraine, **296** H2
Stryy, Ukraine, **289** L4
Strzegom, Poland, **289** H3
Strzelce Opolskie, Poland, **289** J3
Strzelecki Desert, Australia, **135** H4
Strzelin, Poland, **289** H3
Strzelno, Poland, **289** J2
Stuart, Florida, U.S.A., **425** M6
Stuart, Nebraska, U.S.A., **420** D4
Stubaier Alpen, *mountain range*, Austria, **288** E5
Stubbington, England, U.K., **305** F4
Stuben, Austria, **288** E5
Studley, England, U.K., **305** F2
Study Butte, U.S.A., **423** M7
Stugudal, Norway, **284** E5
Stugun, Sweden, **284** G5
Stupino, Russian Federation, **299** G5
Sturgeon, Point, U.S.A., **421** K3
Sturgeon Bay, U.S.A., **421** K3
Sturgeon Falls, Canada, **421** P2
Sturgeon Lake, Canada, **414** J6
Sturgis, U.S.A., **420** B3
Sturminster Newton, England, U.K., **304** E4
Štúrovo, Slovakia, **289** J5
Sturt, *river*, Australia, **134** F2
Stutterheim, South Africa, **371** E5
Stuttgart, Germany, **288** D4
Stuttgart, U.S.A., **424** G2
Stykkishólmur, Iceland, **284** X7
Stylida, Greece, **297** D6
Suaçuí Grande, *river*, Brazil, **457** E5
Suai, Indonesia, **198** D5
Suana, Democratic Republic of the Congo, **368** D4
Su'ao, Taiwan, **206** E3
Subang, Indonesia, **201** D4
Subay', 'Urūq, *desert*, Saudi Arabia, **363** H4
Subei, China, **213** G5
Subi, Pulau, *island*, Indonesia, **201** E2
Subi Besar, Pulau, *island*, Indonesia, **201** E2
Subiaco, Italy, **295** D5
Subotica, Yugoslavia, **296** B2
Subrag, China, **211** G3
Success, Canada, **413** Q6
Suceava, Romania, **296** F2
Sučevići, Croatia, **294** F3
Sucevița, Romania, **296** E2
Suchary, Belarus, **299** C6
Suchorze, Poland, **289** H1
Suchowola, Poland, **289** L2
Suck, *river*, Ireland, **309** D4
Sucre, Bolivia, **455** F5
Sucre, Colombia, **450** C2
Sucuaro, Colombia, **451** E3
Sucunduri, *river*, Brazil, **455** G1
Sucuriú, *river*, Brazil, **456** C5
Sud, *province*, Cameroon, **365** G4
Sud-Kivu, *administrative region*, Democratic Republic of the Congo, **369** E3
Sud Ouest, Pointe, *point*, Mauritius, **373** C1
Sud-Ouest, *province*, Cameroon, **368** A2
Suda, *river*, Russian Federation, **299** F3
Sudan, *country*, Africa, **358** H5
Sudbury, Canada, **421** N2
Sudbury, England, U.K., **305** H2
Suddie, Guyana, **451** G2
Sudety, *mountain range*, Czech Republic/Poland, **289** G3
Sudimir, Russian Federation, **299** E6
Sudok, Sweden, **284** K3
Suðureyri, Iceland, **284** X6

Tatarbunary, Ukraine, **296** G3
Tatarka, Belarus, **299** B6
Tatarsk, Russian Federation, **223** K1
Tatarskiy Proliv, *strait*, Russian Federation, **301** R4
Tatarstan, Respublika, *republic*, Russian Federation, **222** D1
Tatau, Malaysia, **201** F2
Taṭāwin, Tunisia, **362** B2
Tateyama, Japan, **209** G4
Tathlina Lake, Canada, **413** L1
Tathlīth, Saudi Arabia, **363** H5
Tatla Lake, Canada, **412** G6
Tatlow, Mount, *mountain peak*, Canada, **412** H6
Tatnam, Cape, Canada, **414** J3
Tatrang, China, **212** E5
Tatuí, Brazil, **459** H2
Tatum, U.S.A., **423** M5
Tatvan, Turkey, **224** F5
Tau, *island*, American Samoa, **141** B2
Tau, Norway, **286** B3
Tauá, Brazil, **453** F4
Tauariá, Brazil, **455** F1
Taubaté, Brazil, **456** E6
Taukihepa *see* Big South Cape Island, New Zealand, **133** A8
Taula, *island*, Vava'u Group, Tonga, **141** B3
Taunga, *island*, Vava'u Group, Tonga, **141** B3
Taungdwingyi, Myanmar, **205** B3
Taunggyi, Myanmar, **205** C3
Taungtha, Myanmar, **205** B3
Taungup, Myanmar, **205** B4
Taunton, England, U.K., **304** D3
Taunton, U.S.A., **426** E4
Taunus, *mountain range*, Germany, **288** C3
Taupeka Point, Chatham Islands, New Zealand, **133** Q16
Taupiri, New Zealand, **132** E3
Taupo, Lake, New Zealand, **132** F4
Taupo, New Zealand, **132** F4
Taūqum, *desert*, Kazakhstan, **212** B3
Tauragė, Lithuania, **287** L5
Tauranga, New Zealand, **132** F3
Taureau, Réservoir, Canada, **416** E6
Tauri, *river*, Papua New Guinea, **140** B4
Tauroa Peninsula, New Zealand, **132** D2
Taurus Mountains *see* Toros Dağları, *mountain range*, Turkey, **224** D5
Taūshyq, Kazakhstan, **222** E4
Tauu Islands, Papua New Guinea, **138** D5
Tavan Bogd Uul, *mountain peak*, Mongolia, **212** F2
Tavanbulag, Mongolia, **213** J3
Tavas, Turkey, **297** G7
Tavda, Russian Federation, **222** H1
Tavelsjö, Sweden, **284** K4
Taverham, England, U.K., **305** J2
Taveuni, *island*, Fiji, **141** A4
Tavin, Dundgovĭ, Mongolia, **210** D3
Tavin, Selenge, Mongolia, **210** D2
Tavira, Portugal, **292** D4
Tavistock, England, U.K., **304** C4
Tavolara, Isola, *island*, Sardegna, Italy, **295** B5
Tavoy (Dawei), Myanmar, **202** C3
Tavoy Island *see* Mali Kyun, *island*, Myanmar, **202** C3
Tavoy Point, Myanmar, **202** C3
Tavrichanka, Russian Federation, **211** K4
Tavricheskoye, Russian

Federation, **223** J2
Tavşanlı, Turkey, **297** G6
Tavy, *river*, England, U.K., **304** C4
Taw, *river*, England, U.K., **304** D4
Tawa Reservoir, India, **218** D5
Tawaeli, Indonesia, **198** B3
Tawakoni, Lake, U.S.A., **424** E3
Tawas City, U.S.A., **421** M3
Tawau, Malaysia, **201** G1
Tawhiuau, *mountain peak*, New Zealand, **132** F4
Tawitawi Island, Philippines, **204** B5
Ṭawkar, Sudan, **363** G5
Tawsar, Tunisia, **361** H2
Taxco de Alarcón, Mexico, **431** F5
Taxkorgan, China, **212** B5
Tay, *river*, Scotland, U.K., **308** F4
Tây Ninh, Vietnam, **203** E4
Tayabas Bay, Philippines, **204** C3
Taybola, Russian Federation, **285** R2
Tayeeglow, Somalia, **367** F4
Tayga, Russian Federation, **223** M1
Taygan, Mongolia, **213** H3
Tayinloan, Scotland, U.K., **308** D5
Taylor, Canada, **412** J3
Taylor, Mount, *mountain peak*, U.S.A., **423** K4
Taylor, Nebraska, U.S.A., **420** D5
Taylor, Texas, U.S.A., **424** D4
Taylors, U.S.A., **425** L2
Taymā', Saudi Arabia, **363** G3
Taymyr, Ozero, *lake*, Russian Federation, **301** M2
Taymyr, Poluostrov, *peninsula*, Russian Federation, **300** K2
Taynuilt, Scotland, U.K., **308** D4
Taypaq, Kazakhstan, **222** E3
Tayport, Scotland, U.K., **308** G4
Tayshet, Russian Federation, **300** L4
Taytay, Philippines, **204** B4
Tayuan, China, **211** J2
Ṭayyebāt, Iran, **221** H2
Ṭayyib al Ism, Saudi Arabia, **225** C5
Taz, *river*, Russian Federation, **300** K3
Taza, Morocco, **361** F2
Tazin Lake, Canada, **413** Q2
Tāzirbū, Libya, **362** D3
Tazlău, Romania, **296** F2
Tazungdām, Myanmar, **205** C1
T'bilisi, Georgia, **222** C4
Tchad, Lac, *lake*, Chad, **365** G2
Tchamba, Togo, **364** E3
Tchaourou, Benin, **365** E3
Tchibanga, Gabon, **368** B3
Tchin-Tabaradene, Niger, **365** F1
Tchindjenje, Angola, **368** B5
Tcholliré, Cameroon, **365** G3
Tczew, Poland, **289** J1
Té, *river*, Cambodia, **203** E3
Te Anau, Lake, New Zealand, **133** A7
Te Anau, New Zealand, **133** A7
Te Araroa, New Zealand, **132** G3
Te Kaha, New Zealand, **132** F3
Te Kao, New Zealand, **132** D2
Te Kapu, *mountain peak*, New Zealand, **132** F4
Te Karaka, New Zealand, **132** F4
Te Kaukau Point (Mungaroa), New Zealand, **133** E5
Te Kuiti, New Zealand, **132** E4
Te Mapou, *mountain peak*, New Zealand, **132** F4
Te One, Chatham Islands, New Zealand, **133** Q16
Te Paki, *mountain peak*, New Zealand, **132** D2

Te Pohue, New Zealand, **132** F4
Te Puninga, New Zealand, **132** E3
Te Raupua, *mountain peak*, New Zealand, **132** D2
Te Te Re, Solomon Islands, **141** A1
Te Teko, New Zealand, **132** F4
Te Waewae Bay, New Zealand, **133** A8
Te Whanga Lagoon, *bay*, Chatham Islands, New Zealand, **133** Q16
Teacapán, Mexico, **430** D4
Teapa, Mexico, **431** G5
Teare, Mount, *mountain peak*, Canada, **412** J5
Teba, Indonesia, **199** G3
Tebay, England, U.K., **306** F3
Tébessa, Algeria, **361** H1
Tebicuary, *river*, Paraguay, **459** F3
Tebingtinggi, Indonesia, **200** B2
Tebingtinggi, Pulau, *island*, Indonesia, **200** C2
Tecate, Mexico, **430** A1
Techiman, Ghana, **364** D3
Techirghiol, Romania, **296** G3
Techniti Limni Kremaston, *reservoir*, Greece, **297** C6
Tecka, Argentina, **460** C2
Tecka, *river*, Argentina, **460** C2
Tecolutla, Mexico, **431** F4
Tecomán, Mexico, **430** E5
Tecoripa, Mexico, **430** C2
Tecpán de Galeana, Mexico, **431** E5
Tecuci, Romania, **296** F3
Tecumseh, U.S.A., **420** E5
Ted Ceidaar Dabole, Somalia, **367** F4
Teel, Mongolia, **213** J2
Teeli, Russian Federation, **223** N2
Tees Bay, England, U.K., **307** G3
Teesdale, *region*, England, U.K., **306** F3
Tefé, Brazil, **451** F5
Tefé, Lago de, *lake*, Brazil, **451** F5
Tefé, *river*, Brazil, **451** F5
Tefedest, *mountain range*, Algeria, **361** H4
Tefenni, Turkey, **297** G7
Tegal, Indonesia, **201** E4
Tegernsee, Germany, **288** E5
Tegid, Llyn, *lake*, Wales, U.K., **304** D2
Tegina, Nigeria, **365** F2
Tegucigalpa, Honduras, **428** D4
Teguidda-n-Tessoumt, Niger, **365** F1
Teguise, Islas Canarias, Spain, **373** B4
Teheran *see* Tehrān, Iran, **220** F1
Téhini, Côte d'Ivoire, **364** D3
Tehrān (Teheran), Iran, **220** F1
Tehri, India, **218** D3
Tehuacán, Mexico, **431** F5
Tehuantepec, Golfo de, *gulf*, Mexico, **431** G6
Tehuantepec, Istmo de, *isthmus*, Mexico, **431** G5
Tehuitzingo, Mexico, **431** F5
Tehumardi, Estonia, **287** L3
Teide, Pico de, *mountain peak*, Islas Canarias, Spain, **373** A4
Teifi, *river*, Wales, U.K., **304** C2
Teignmouth, England, U.K., **304** D4
Teisko, Finland, **287** L2
Teiuș, Romania, **296** D2
Teixeira, Brazil, **453** G5
Tejen, Turkmenistan, **222** G5
Tejo, *river*, Portugal, **292** C3
Tekapo, Lake, New Zealand, **133** C6
Tekapo, New Zealand, **133** C7
Tekax, Mexico, **431** H4
Tekeli, Kazakhstan, **212** C3
Tekes, China, **212** D4

Tekes, *river*, China/Kazakhstan, **212** D4
Tekirdağ, *province*, Turkey, **297** F5
Tekirdağ, Turkey, **297** F5
Teku, Indonesia, **198** C3
Tel Aviv-Yafo, Israel, **225** C3
Tela, Honduras, **428** D4
Télagh, Algeria, **361** F2
Télataï, Mali, **365** E1
Telč, Czech Republic, **289** G4
Telchac Puerto, Mexico, **431** H4
Telciu, Romania, **296** E2
Telde, Islas Canarias, Spain, **373** B4
Tele, *river*, Democratic Republic of the Congo, **368** D2
Telefomin, Papua New Guinea, **140** A4
Telegraph Creek, Canada, **412** D3
Telêmaco Borba, Brazil, **459** G2
Telemark, *county*, Norway, **286** C3
Telemba, Russian Federation, **210** F1
Télemsès, Niger, **365** E1
Telén, Argentina, **458** D5
Telenești, Moldova, **296** G2
Teleorman, *river*, Romania, **296** E3
Telerhteba, Djebel, *mountain peak*, Algeria, **361** H4
Teles Pires (São Manuel), *river*, Brazil, **452** B5
Telescope Peak, *mountain peak*, U.S.A., **422** E3
Telford, England, U.K., **304** E2
Telford and Wrekin, *unitary authority*, England, U.K., **304** E2
Telica, Nicaragua, **428** D4
Teljo, Jabal, *mountain peak*, Sudan, **366** C2
Telkwa, Canada, **412** F4
Telmen Nuur, *lake*, Mongolia, **213** H2
Telok Blangah, Singapore, **200** J7
Teloloapan, Mexico, **431** F5
Telsen, Argentina, **460** D2
Telšiai, Lithuania, **287** L5
Telukbatang, Indonesia, **201** E3
Telukdalam, Indonesia, **200** B2
Telupid, Malaysia, **201** G1
Tema, Ghana, **364** E3
Temagami, Canada, **421** P2
Temagami, Lake, Canada, **421** N2
Tematangi, *island*, French Polynesia, **137** G3
Temax, Mexico, **431** H4
Tembagapura, Indonesia, **199** G4
Tembesi, *river*, Indonesia, **200** C3
Tembhurni, India, **216** C2
Tembilahan, Indonesia, **200** C3
Tembisa, South Africa, **371** E4
Tembito, Indonesia, **198** C2
Tembleque, Spain, **293** F3
Tembo, Democratic Republic of the Congo, **368** C4
Tembo Aluma, Angola, **368** C4
Temecula, U.S.A., **422** E5
Téméra, Mali, **364** D1
Temerin, Yugoslavia, **296** B3
Temerloh, Malaysia, **200** C2
Temirtaū, Kazakhstan, **212** B2
Témiscaming, Canada, **416** B6
Temoe, *island*, French Polynesia, **137** H3
Temora, Australia, **135** K5
Temósachic, Mexico, **430** D2
Tempe, Danau, *lake*, Indonesia, **198** B4
Tempe, U.S.A., **423** H5
Tempio Pausania, Sardegna, Italy, **295** B5
Temple, U.S.A., **424** D4
Temple Bar, Wales, U.K., **304** C2
Temple Ewell, England, U.K.,

305 J3
Temple Sowerby, England, U.K., **306** F3
Templemore, Ireland, **309** E5
Templeton, Wales, U.K., **304** C3
Templetouhy, Ireland, **309** E5
Templin, Germany, **288** F2
Tempoal, Mexico, **431** F4
Tempué, Angola, **368** C5
Temska, Yugoslavia, **296** D4
Temuco, Chile, **460** C1
Temuka, New Zealand, **133** C7
Ten Degree Channel, Andaman and Nicobar Islands, India, **217** G4
Ten Sleep, U.S.A., **419** L4
Ten Thousand Islands, U.S.A., **425** M7
Tena, Ecuador, **450** C4
Tenāli, India, **216** E2
Tenamatua, Gunung, *mountain peak*, Indonesia, **198** C3
Tenasserim, *division*, Myanmar, **202** C3
Tenbury Wells, England, U.K., **304** E2
Tenby, Wales, U.K., **304** C3
Tendaho, Ethiopia, **367** F2
Tende, France, **291** H4
Tendô, Japan, **209** H3
Tendoy, U.S.A., **418** H4
Tendrara, Morocco, **361** F2
Ténenkou, Mali, **364** C2
Tenerife, *island*, Islas Canarias, Spain, **373** A4
Ténès, Algeria, **361** G1
Teng Xian, China, **206** B4
Tengchong, China, **215** F4
Tengeh Reservoir, Singapore, **200** J6
Tengiz Köli, *lake*, Kazakhstan, **223** J2
Tengréla, Côte d'Ivoire, **364** C2
Tenhola, Finland, **287** L2
Tenja, Croatia, **294** G3
Tenke, Democratic Republic of the Congo, **369** E5
Tenkiller Ferry Lake, U.S.A., **424** E2
Tenkodogo, Burkina Faso, **364** D2
Tenmarou, Vanuatu, **141** A2
Tenna, *river*, Italy, **294** D4
Tennant Creek, Australia, **134** G2
Tennessee, *river*, U.S.A., **425** H2
Tennessee, *state*, U.S.A., **425** J2
Tennevoll, Norway, **284** H2
Tenniöjoki, *river*, Finland/Russian Federation, **285** P3
Tenojoki, *river*, Finland, **285** N2
Tenosique de Pino Suárez, Mexico, **431** H5
Tenryū, *river*, Japan, **209** G4
Tensed, U.S.A., **418** F3
Tenstrike, U.S.A., **420** F2
Tenterden, England, U.K., **305** H3
Tenterfield, Australia, **135** L4
Tentolomatinan, Gunung, *mountain peak*, Indonesia, **198** C2
Tentudia, *mountain peak*, Spain, **292** D3
Teodoro Sampaio, Brazil, **459** G2
Teófilo Otoni, Brazil, **457** F4
Teopisca, Mexico, **431** G5
Tepa, Indonesia, **199** E4
Tepa Point, Niue, **132** M13
Tepasto, Finland, **285** M3
Tepatitlán, Mexico, **430** E4
Tepehuanes, Mexico, **430** D3
Tepelenë, Albania, **297** B5
Tepequém, Brazil, **451** G3
Tepequém, Serra, *mountain range*, Brazil, **451** G3
Tepic, Mexico, **430** D4
Teploye, Russian Federation, **299** F6
Tepoto, *island*, French Polynesia, **137** G2

Tepsa, Finland, **285** M3
Téra, Niger, **364** E2
Tera, *river*, Spain, **292** D1
Tera Nova Bay, *Italian research station*, Antarctica, **470** D7
Teraina, *island*, Kiribati, **139** H4
Teramo, Italy, **294** D4
Teratyn, Poland, **289** L3
Terceira, *island*, Azores, Portugal, **360** M7
Teregova, Romania, **296** D3
Terengganu, *state*, Malaysia, **200** C1
Terenos, Brazil, **456** B5
Teresina, Brazil, **453** E4
Teresópolis, Brazil, **457** E6
Terespol, Poland, **289** L2
Terevaka, *mountain peak*, Isla de Pascua (Easter Island), Chile, **461** B2
Terevinto, Bolivia, **455** F4
Tergun Daba Shan, *mountain range*, China, **213** G5
Teriberka, *river*, Russian Federation, **285** S2
Teriberka, Russian Federation, **285** S2
Teriberskiy, Mys, *cape*, Russian Federation, **285** S2
Terlingua, U.S.A., **423** M7
Termas de Río Hondo, Argentina, **458** D3
Terminillo, Monte, *mountain peak*, Italy, **295** D4
Términos, Laguna de, *lagoon*, Mexico, **431** H5
Termit-Kaoboul, Niger, **365** G1
Termiz, Uzbekistan, **218** A1
Termoli, Italy, **295** E5
Tern, *island*, Hawaiian Islands, U.S.A., **139** H2
Ternate, Indonesia, **198** D2
Terneuzen, Netherlands, **288** A3
Terney, Russian Federation, **209** G1
Terni, Italy, **295** D4
Ternivka, Ukraine, **296** G1
Ternopil', Ukraine, **298** C3
Terpeniya, Mys, *cape*, Russian Federation, **301** R5
Terra Firma, South Africa, **370** D4
Terrace, Canada, **412** E4
Terrace Bay, Canada, **415** L7
Terracina, Italy, **295** D5
Terråk, Norway, **284** F4
Terralba, Sardegna, Italy, **295** B6
Terrassa, Spain, **293** H2
Terre Adélie, *region*, Antarctica, **470** E7
Terre Haute, U.S.A., **421** K6
Terrebonne Bay, U.S.A., **424** G5
Terreton, U.S.A., **418** H5
Terrington St Clement, England, U.K., **305** H2
Terry, Mississippi, U.S.A., **424** G3
Terry, Montana, U.S.A., **419** M3
Terschelling, *island*, Netherlands, **288** B2
Tertenia, Sardegna, Italy, **295** B6
Teruel, Spain, **293** G2
Tervel, Bulgaria, **296** F4
Tērvete, Latvia, **287** L4
Tervo, Finland, **285** N5
Tervola, Finland, **285** M3
Tešanj, Bosnia and Herzegovina, **294** F3
Teseney, Eritrea, **367** E1
Teshig, Mongolia, **213** J2
Teshikaga, Japan, **209** J2
Teshio, *river*, Japan, **209** H1
Teskey Ala-Too, *mountain range*, Kyrgyzstan, **212** C4
Teslin, Canada, **412** C1
Teslin Lake, Canada, **412** C1
Tesouro, Brazil, **456** C4
Tesovo Netyl'skiy, Russian Federation, **299** C3
Tessalit, Mali, **361** G4
Tessaoua, Niger, **365** F2
Tessin, Germany, **288** F1
Test, *river*, England, U.K., **305** F3
Tét, Hungary, **289** H5
Tetas, Punta, *point*, Chile, **458** B2
Tetbury, England, U.K., **304** E3
Tete, Mozambique, **369** F6
Tete, *province*, Mozambique, **369** F6
Tête Jaune Cache, Canada, **413** K5
Tetepare, *island*, Solomon Islands, **141** A1
Tetere, Solomon Islands, **141** A1
Teteven, Bulgaria, **296** E4
Tetiaroa, *island*, French Polynesia, **137** G2
Tetney, England, U.K., **307** H4
Teton, U.S.A., **419** J5
Tetonia, U.S.A., **419** J5
Tetouan (Tetuán), Morocco, **361** E1
Tetovo, Macedonia, **296** C4
Tetrino, Russian Federation, **285** U3
Tetuán *see* Tetouan, Morocco, **361** E1
Teuco, *river*, Argentina, **458** E2
Teulada, Capo, *cape*, Italy, **295** B6
Teulada, Sardegna, Italy, **295** B6
Teulon, Canada, **414** F6
Teutoburger Wald, *mountain range*, Germany, **288** C2
Teuva, Finland, **287** K1
Teverya, Israel, **225** C3
Teviotdale, *valley*, Scotland, U.K., **308** G5
Tevriz, Russian Federation, **223** J1
Tewkesbury, England, U.K., **304** E3
Têwo, China, **215** G2
Texarkana, U.S.A., **424** E3
Texas, Australia, **135** L4
Texas, *state*, U.S.A., **423** M5
Texas City, U.S.A., **424** E5
Texas Creek, U.S.A., **423** L2
Texel, *island*, Netherlands, **288** B2
Texhoma, U.S.A., **420** C7
Texoma, Lake, U.S.A., **424** D2
Teyateyaneng, Lesotho, **371** E4
Teziutlan, Mexico, **431** F5
Tezpur, India, **219** H4
Tha-anne, *river*, Canada, **414** E1
Tha Song Yang, Thailand, **202** C2
Tha Tum, Thailand, **203** D3
Thabana-Ntlenyana, *mountain peak*, Lesotho, **371** E4
Thabazimbi, South Africa, **371** E3
Thabong, South Africa, **371** E4
Thabt, Jabal ath, *mountain peak*, Egypt, **225** C5
Thagaya, Myanmar, **205** C4
Thái Nguyên, Vietnam, **203** E1
Thailand, *country*, Asia, **197** L8
Thailand, Gulf of, South East Asia, **202** D4
Thal, Pakistan, **218** B2
Thale, Germany, **288** E3
Thamarīt, Oman, **367** H1
Thame, England, U.K., **305** G3
Thames, Firth of, *bay*, New Zealand, **132** E3
Thames, New Zealand, **132** E3
Thames, *river*, Canada, **421** N4
Thames, *river*, England, U.K., **305** H3
Than Kyun, *island*, Myanmar, **202** C4
Thāna Ghāzi, India, **218** D4
Thāne, India, **216** C2
Thānesar, India, **218** D3
Thanh Hóa, Vietnam, **203** E2
Thánh Lang Xã, Vietnam, **203** E2
Thanh Phố Hồ Chí Minh (Saigon), Vietnam, **203** E4
Thanjāvur, India, **216** D4
Thanlwin (Salween), *river*, Myanmar, **205** C1
Thāno Būla Khān, Pakistan, **218** A4
Thap Sakae, Thailand, **202** C4
Thar Desert, India/Pakistan, **218** B4
Thargomindah, Australia, **135** J4
Tharthār, Buḩayrat ath, *lake*, Iraq, **363** H2
Tharwānīyah, Oman, **221** F4
Thasos, Greece, **297** E5
Thasos, *island*, Greece, **297** E5
Thatcham, England, U.K., **305** F3
Thaton, Myanmar, **205** C4
Thatta, Pakistan, **218** A4
Thau, Bassin de, *lake*, France, **291** F5
Thaxted, England, U.K., **305** H3
The Dalles, U.S.A., **418** D4
The Forks, New Zealand, **133** C6
The Hague *see* 's-Gravenhage, Netherlands, **288** B2
The Pas, Canada, **414** D5
The Valley, Anguilla, **427** D2
Thedford, U.S.A., **420** C5
Theinkun, Myanmar, **202** C4
Thekulthili Lake, Canada, **413** P1
Thelon, *river*, Canada, **410** J3
Theniet el Had, Algeria, **361** G1
Thenon, France, **290** E4
Theodore, Canada, **414** C6
Theodore Roosevelt, *river*, Brazil, **455** G2
Theodore Roosevelt Lake, U.S.A., **423** H5
Thermaïkos Kolpos, *bay*, Greece, **297** D5
Thermo, Greece, **297** C6
Thermopolis, U.S.A., **419** K5
Thesiger Bay, Canada, **410** G2
Thessalia, *administrative region*, Greece, **297** D6
Thessalon, Canada, **421** M2
Thessaloniki (Salonica), Greece, **297** D5
Thet, *river*, England, U.K., **305** H2
Thetford, England, U.K., **305** H2
Thetford Mines, Canada, **416** F6
Thibodaux, U.S.A., **424** G5
Thief River Falls, U.S.A., **420** E1
Thiene, Italy, **294** C3
Thiers, France, **291** F4
Thiès, Senegal, **364** A2
Thika, Kenya, **369** G3
Thimphu, Bhutan, **205** A2
Thio, New Caledonia, **141** A3
Thionville, France, **291** H2
Thira (Santorini), *island*, Kyklades, Greece, **297** E7
Thirsk, England, U.K., **307** G3
Thiruvananthapuram (Trivandrum), India, **216** D4
Thiruvattiyur, India, **216** E3
Thisted, Denmark, **286** D4
Thisvi, Greece, **297** D6
Thiva, Greece, **297** D6
Thiviers, France, **290** E4
Þjórsá, *river*, Iceland, **284** Y7
Thlewiaza, *river*, Canada, **414** F1
Thohoyandou, South Africa, **371** F3
Thới Bình, Vietnam, **203** E4
Thomas, U.S.A., **421** P6
Thomaston, Alabama, U.S.A., **425** J3
Thomaston, Georgia, U.S.A., **425** K3
Thomastown, Ireland, **309** E5
Thomasville, Alabama, U.S.A., **425** J4
Thomasville, Georgia, U.S.A., **425** K4
Thompson, Canada, **414** F4
Thompson Falls, U.S.A., **418** G3
Thompson Peak, *mountain peak*, U.S.A., **418** C6
Thompson Point, Canada, **414** H2
Thomson, *river*, Australia, **135** J3
Thomson, U.S.A., **425** L3
Thoreau, U.S.A., **423** J4
Þorlákshöfn, Iceland, **284** X8
Thornaby on Tees, England, U.K., **307** G3
Thornbury, England, U.K., **304** E3
Thorne, England, U.K., **307** H4
Thornhill, Scotland, U.K., **308** F5
Thornton, England, U.K., **306** F4
Thornton, U.S.A., **418** F3
Thorsby, Canada, **413** M5
Thorshavnheiane, *mountain range*, Antarctica, **470** E3
Thouars, France, **290** D3
Thouet, *river*, France, **290** D3
Thousand Springs, U.S.A., **418** G6
Thrakiko Pelagos, *sea*, Greece, **297** E5
Thrapston, England, U.K., **305** G2
Three Forks, U.S.A., **419** J4
Three King Islands, New Zealand, **132** D2
Three Points, Cape, Ghana, **364** D4
Three Rivers, Michigan, U.S.A., **421** L5
Three Rivers, Texas, U.S.A., **424** C5
Three Sisters, *mountain peak*, U.S.A., **418** D4
Throckmorton, U.S.A., **424** C3
Thu, Cù Lao, *island*, Vietnam, **203** F4
Thủ Dầu Một, Vietnam, **203** E4
Thul, Pakistan, **218** B3
Thule *see* Qaanaag, Greenland, **411** N2
Thun, Switzerland, **291** H3
Thunder Bay, Canada, **421** J1
Thuner See, *lake*, Switzerland, **291** H3
Thung Chang, Thailand, **202** D2
Thung Song, Thailand, **202** C4
Thüringen, *state*, Germany, **288** E3
Thüringer Wald, *mountain range*, Germany, **288** E3
Thurles, Ireland, **309** E5
Thurrock, *unitary authority*, England, U.K., **305** H3
Thursby, England, U.K., **306** E3
Thursday Island, Australia, **140** A5
Thurso, *river*, Scotland, U.K., **308** F2
Thurso, Scotland, U.K., **308** F2
Thurston Island, Antarctica, **470** B6
Thwaite, England, U.K., **306** F3
Thyborøn, Denmark, **286** D4
Ti-n-Aguelhaj, Mali, **364** D1
Ti-n-Bessaïs, Sebkhet, *salt-pan*, Mauritania, **360** E4
Ti-n-Essako, Mali, **361** G5
Ti-n-Zaouâtene, Mali, **361** G5
Ti-Tree, Australia, **134** G3
Tian Shan, *mountain range*, China/Kyrgyzstan, **212** C4
Tiancang, China, **213** H4
Tianchang, China, **206** D1
Tiancheng, China, **213** H5
Tiandeng, China, **215** H5
Tian'e, China, **215** H4
Tianguá, Brazil, **453** F4
Tianjin, China, **210** G5
Tianjun, China, **213** H5
Tianlin, China, **215** H4
Tianmen, China, **206** C2
Tianqiaoling, China, **211** K4
Tianquan, China, **215** G3
Tianshui, China, **215** H2
Tianshuibu, China, **210** D5
Tianshuihai, China, **218** D2
Tianshuijing, China, **213** G4
Tiantai, China, **206** E2
Tiantangwei, China, **207** C3
Tianxin, China, **207** A4
Tianyang, China, **215** H5
Tianzhu, China, **206** B3
Tianzhuangtai, China, **211** H4
Tiaret, Algeria, **293** H5
Tías, Islas Canarias, Spain, **373** B4
Tias, Punta, *point*, Islas Canarias, Spain, **373** B4
Tiassalé, Côte d'Ivoire, **364** D3
Ti'avea, Samoa, **141** B1
Tibaji, *river*, Brazil, **459** G2
Ţibana, Romania, **296** F2
Tibati, Cameroon, **365** G3
Tibba, Pakistan, **218** B3
Tibé, Pic de, *mountain peak*, Guinea, **364** C3
Tibesti, *mountain range*, Chad, **362** C4
Tibesti, Sarīr, *desert*, Libya, **362** C4
Tibet, Plateau of *see* Qingzang Gaoyuan, *plateau*, China, **214** C2
Tibet *see* Xizang Zizhiqu, *autonomous region*, China, **214** C2
Tibiao, Philippines, **204** C4
Tibo, Democratic Republic of the Congo, **369** E2
Tibooburra, Australia, **135** J4
Tibro, Sweden, **286** G3
Tiburon, Haiti, **429** G3
Tiburón, Isla, *island*, Mexico, **430** B2
Ticao Island, Philippines, **204** C3
Ticehurst, England, U.K., **305** H3
Tîchît, Mauritania, **360** E5
Tichla, Western Sahara, **360** D4
Ticonderoga, U.S.A., **426** D3
Ticul, Mexico, **431** H4
Tidaholm, Sweden, **286** G3
Tidarméné, Mali, **365** E1
Tiddim, Myanmar, **205** B3
Tidikelt, Plaine du, *plain*, Algeria, **361** G3
Tidjikja, Mauritania, **360** D5
Tiechang, Guangdong, China, **207** B2
Tiechang, Jilin, China, **211** J4
Tiedra, Spain, **292** E2
Tiefa, China, **211** H4
Tiefencastel, Switzerland, **291** J3
Tieli, China, **211** K3
Tieling, China, **211** H4
Tielongtan, China, **218** D2
Tienen, Belgium, **288** B3
Tierp, Sweden, **287** H2
Tierra Amarilla, Chile, **458** B3
Tierra Amarilla, U.S.A., **423** K3
Tierra Blanca, Bahía, *bay*, Róbinson Crusoe Island, Archipiélago Juan Fernández, Chile, **461** C2
Tierra Blanca, Mexico, **431** F5
Tierra Colorada, Mexico, **431** F5
Tierra de Campos, *region*, Spain, **292** E2
Tierra del Fuego, Isla Grande de, *island*, Chile/Argentina, **460** C4
Tierra del Fuego, *province*, Argentina, **460** D4
Tierralta, Colombia, **450** C2
Tiétar, *river*, Spain, **292** E2
Tietê, Brazil, **459** H2
Tieté, *river*, Brazil, **456** C5
Tifariti, Western Sahara, **360** D3
Tiffin, U.S.A., **421** M5
Tifton, U.S.A., **425** L4
Tifu, Indonesia, **198** D3
Tiger, U.S.A., **418** F2
Tigharry, Scotland, U.K., **308** B3
Tighina, Moldova, **296** G2
Tighnabruaich, Scotland, U.K.,

308 D5
Tignère, Cameroon, **365** G3
Tignish, Canada, **417** J6
Tigre, Cerro del, *mountain peak*, Mexico, **431** F4
Tigre, *river*, Peru, **450** C5
Tigre, *river*, Venezuela, **451** F2
Tigris, *river*, Asia, **194** F6; *see also* Dicle, *river*, Turkey, **224** F5; Dijlah, *river*, Iraq, **363** J2
Tiguent, Mauritania, **364** A1
Tiguidit, Falaise de, *escarpment*, Niger, **365** F1
Tihoi, New Zealand, **132** E4
Tiistenjoki, Finland, **287** L1
Tijāra, India, **218** D4
Tiji, Libya, **362** B2
Tijola, Spain, **293** F4
Tijuana, Mexico, **430** A1
Tijuco, *river*, Brazil, **456** D5
Tika, Canada, **416** J4
Tikanlik, China, **212** E4
Tikehau, *island*, French Polynesia, **137** G2
Tikei, *island*, French Polynesia, **137** G2
Tikem, Chad, **365** H3
Tikhvin, Russian Federation, **299** D3
Tikhvinskaya Gryada, *mountain range*, Russian Federation, **299** D3
Tikitiki, New Zealand, **132** G3
Tikokino, New Zealand, **132** F4
Tikopia, *island*, Solomon Islands, **139** E6
Tikota, India, **216** C2
Tikrīt, Iraq, **363** H2
Tiksha, Russian Federation, **285** R4
Tiksheozero, Ozero *lake*, Russian Federation, **285** R3
Tiksi, Russian Federation, **301** P2
Tiladummati Atoll, Maldives, **216** C5
Tilburg, Netherlands, **288** B3
Tilbury, England, U.K., **305** H3
Tilcara, Argentina, **458** D2
Tilehurst, England, U.K., **305** F3
Till, *river*, England, U.K., **306** F2
Tillabéri, *department*, Niger, **364** E2
Tillabéri, Niger, **365** E2
Tillamook, U.S.A., **418** C4
Tilley, Canada, **413** P6
Tillia, Niger, **365** E1
Tillman, U.S.A., **425** M3
Tillyfourie, Scotland, U.K., **308** G3
Tiloa, Niger, **365** E1
Tilomonte, Chile, **458** C2
Tilos, *island*, Dodekanisos, Greece, **297** F7
Tilrhemt, Algeria, **361** G2
Ţimā, Egypt, **363** F3
Timah, Bukit, *mountain peak*, Singapore, **200** J6
Timanskiy Kryazh, *mountain range*, Russian Federation, **300** G3
Timaru, New Zealand, **133** C7
Timashevsk, Russian Federation, **298** E3
Timbaúba, Brazil, **453** G5
Timbedgha, Mauritania, **364** C1
Timber Creek, Australia, **134** G2
Timbue, Ponta, *cape*, Mozambique, **371** G2
Timbun Mata, Pulau, *island*, Malaysia, **201** G1
Timétrine, Mali, **361** F5
Timia, Niger, **361** H5
Timimoun, Algeria, **361** G3
Timirist, Râs, *cape*, Mauritania, **360** C5
Timiș, *river*, Romania, **296** D3
Timișoara, Romania, **296** C3
Timmiarmiut, Greenland, **411** Q3
Timmins, Canada, **421** N1
Timmoudi, Algeria, **361** F3
Timms Hill, *mountain peak*, U.S.A., **420** H3
Timoforo, *river*, Indonesia, **199** F3
Timokhino, Russian Federation, **299** F3
Timolin, Ireland, **309** F5
Timon, Brazil, **453** E4
Timor, *island*, Indonesia, **198** D5
Timor Sea, Australia/Indonesia, **128** A3
Timor Timur, *province*, Indonesia, **198** D5
Timoshino, Russian Federation, **299** F2
Timote, Argentina, **458** D5
Timpas, U.S.A., **423** M3
Timrå, Sweden, **287** H1
Timūrni, India, **218** D5
Tin, Ra's at, *point*, Libya, **362** D2
Tinabogan, Indonesia, **198** C2
Tinaco, Venezuela, **451** E2
Ţīnah, Khalīj aţ, *bay*, Egypt, **225** B4
Tinaja, Punta, *point*, Peru, **454** C4
Tinajo, Islas Canarias, Spain, **373** B4
Tinambac, Philippines, **204** C3
Tinchebray, France, **290** D2
Tindouf, Algeria, **360** E3
Tinfouchy, Algeria, **361** E3
Ting, *river*, China, **206** D3
Tinggoa, Solomon Islands, **141** A1
Tingo María, Peru, **454** C2
Tingri, China, **214** C3
Tingstäde, Sweden, **287** J4
Tinguiririca, Volcán, *mountain peak*, Chile, **458** B5
Tingvoll, Norway, **284** D5
Tinian, *island*, Northern Mariana Islands, **138** C3
Tinjar, *river*, Malaysia, **201** F2
Tinniswood, Mount, *mountain peak*, Canada, **412** H6
Tinnoset, Norway, **286** D3
Tinogasta, Argentina, **458** C3
Tinombo, Indonesia, **198** C2
Tinos, *island*, Kyklades, Greece, **297** E7
Tinos, Kyklades, Greece, **297** E7
Tinrhert, Plateau du, *mountain range*, Algeria, **361** H3
Tinsukia, India, **219** H4
Tintagel, England, U.K., **304** C4
Tîntâne, Mauritania, **364** B1
Tintang, Indonesia, **201** G2
Tintina, Argentina, **458** D3
Tioman, Pulau, *island*, Malaysia, **200** D2
Tiong Bahru, Singapore, **200** J7
Tipasa, Algeria, **361** G1
Tipitapa, Nicaragua, **428** D4
Tipperary, *county*, Ireland, **309** D5
Tipperary, Ireland, **309** D5
Tipton, Mount, *mountain peak*, U.S.A., **422** F4
Tipton, U.S.A., **420** H5
Tiptree, England, U.K., **305** H3
Tiptūr, India, **216** D3
Tipuani, Bolivia, **455** E4
Tiquicheo, Mexico, **431** E5
Tiquié, *river*, Brazil, **451** E4
Tiquina, Bolivia, **455** E4
Tiracambu, Serra do, *mountain range*, Brazil, **452** D4
Tīrān, Jazīrat, *island*, Saudi Arabia, **225** C6
Tirana *see* Tiranë, Albania, **297** B5
Tiranë (Tirana), Albania, **297** B5
Tirano, Italy, **294** C2
Tiraspol, Moldova, **296** G2
Tiraumea, New Zealand, **132** F5
Tirebolu, Turkey, **224** E4
Tiree, *island*, Scotland, U.K., **308** B4
Tirga Mór, *mountain peak*, Scotland, U.K., **308** C3
Tiris Zemmour, *administrative region*, Mauritania, **360** D4
Tirol, *state*, Austria, **288** E5
Tiroungoulou, Central African Republic, **366** B3
Tirstrup, Denmark, **286** E4
Tirua Point, New Zealand, **132** E4
Tiruchchirāppalli, India, **216** D4
Tirunelveli, India, **216** D4
Tiruntán, Peru, **454** C2
Tirupati, India, **216** D3
Tiruppur, India, **216** D4
Tiruvannāmalai, India, **216** D3
Tisaiyānvilai, India, **216** D4
Tisbury, England, U.K., **304** E3
Tisdale, Canada, **414** B5
Tisgui-Remz, Morocco, **360** E3
Tishomingo, U.S.A., **424** D2
Ţisīyah, Syria, **225** D3
Tiškovka, Ukraine, **296** H1
Tissemsilt, Algeria, **361** G1
Tisza, *river*, Europe, **280** G6
Tiszaföldvár, Hungary, **289** K5
Tiszafüred, Hungary, **289** K5
Tiszaújváros, Hungary, **289** K5
Tiszavasvári, Hungary, **289** K5
Titaguas, Spain, **293** G3
Titao, Burkina Faso, **364** D2
Titel, Yugoslavia, **296** C3
Titi Islands *see* Muttonbird Islands, New Zealand, **133** A8
Titicaca, Lago, *lake*, Bolivia/Peru, **455** E4
Titlāgarh, India, **219** E5
Titlis, *mountain peak*, Switzerland, **291** J3
Titran, Norway, **284** D5
Tittmoning, Germany, **288** F4
Titu, Romania, **296** E3
Titusville, U.S.A., **425** M5
Tivari, India, **218** C4
Tivat, Yugoslavia, **296** B4
Tiverton, England, U.K., **304** D4
Tivoli, Italy, **295** D5
Tivoli, U.S.A., **424** D5
Tiwanacu, Bolivia, **455** E4
Tixkokob, Mexico, **431** H4
Tixtla, Mexico, **431** F5
Tiyās, Syria, **225** D2
Tizi Ouzou, Algeria, **361** G1
Tizimín, Mexico, **431** H4
Tiznit, Morocco, **360** E3
Tjaktjajaure, *lake*, Sweden, **284** H3
Tjåmotis, Sweden, **284** J3
Tjeggelvas, *lake*, Sweden, **284** H3
Tjentište, Bosnia and Herzegovina, **294** G4
Tjörn, *island*, Sweden, **286** E4
Tjøtta, Norway, **284** F4
Tlacolula de Matamoros, Mexico, **431** F5
Tlacotalpan, Mexico, **431** G5
Tlalnepantla, Mexico, **431** F5
Tlaltenango, Mexico, **430** E4
Tlapa de Comonfort, Mexico, **431** F5
Tlaxcala, Mexico, **431** F5
Tlaxcala, *state*, Mexico, **431** F5
Tlaxiaco, Mexico, **431** F5
Tlemcen, Algeria, **361** F2
Tlokweng, Botswana, **371** E3
Tlumach, Ukraine, **296** E1
Tmassah, Libya, **362** C3
Tmeïmîchât, Mauritania, **360** D4
Toa Payoh, Singapore, **200** K6
Toad River, Canada, **412** G2
Toamasina, Madagascar, **372** B4
Toamasina, *province*, Madagascar, **372** B4
Toay, Argentina, **458** D5
Toba, China, **215** F3
Toba, *mountain peak*, China, **215** E3
Toba Danau, *lake*, Indonesia, **200** B2
Toba Kākar Range, *mountain range*, Pakistan, **218** A3
Toba Tek Singh, Pakistan, **218** C3
Tobago, *island*, Trinidad and Tobago, **461** B4
Tobarra, Spain, **293** G3
Tobelo, Indonesia, **198** D2
Tobercurry, Ireland, **309** D3
Tobermory, Canada, **421** N3
Tobermory, Scotland, U.K., **308** C4
Tobi, *island*, Palau, **138** B4
Tobin, Mount, *mountain peak*, U.S.A., **422** E1
Tobin Lake, Canada, **414** C5
Tobin Lake, *lake*, Canada, **414** C5
Toboali, Indonesia, **200** D3
Toboli, Indonesia, **198** C3
Tobol'sk, Russian Federation, **223** H1
Tobyl, Kazakhstan, **222** G2
Tocantinópolis, Brazil, **452** D5
Tocantins, *river*, E. Pará, Brazil, **452** D4
Tocantins, *river*, W. Pará, Brazil, **452** B4
Tocantins, *state*, Brazil, **456** D3
Töcksfors, Sweden, **286** E3
Toco, Chile, **458** C2
Toco, Trinidad, Trinidad and Tobago, **461** C4
Toconao, Chile, **458** C2
Tocopilla, Chile, **458** B2
Tocuyo, *river*, Venezuela, **451** E1
Toda Rāisingh, India, **218** C4
Todal, Norway, **286** D1
Toddington, England, U.K., **305** F3
Todenyang, Kenya, **366** E4
Todi, Italy, **294** D4
Todos Santos, Bolivia, **455** F4
Todos Santos, Mexico, **430** C4
Toe Head, *point*, Ireland, **309** C6
Toetoes Bay, New Zealand, **133** B8
Tofield, Canada, **413** N5
Tofino, Canada, **412** G7
Toft, Shetland, Scotland, U.K., **308** K7
Tofte, U.S.A., **420** H2
Toftlund, Denmark, **286** D5
Tofua, *island*, Tonga, **136** D2
Togdheer, *administrative region*, Somalia, **367** G3
Togiak, U.S.A., **410** C4
Togian, Kepulauan, *islands*, Indonesia, **198** C3
Togo, *country*, Africa, **358** F6
Togo, U.S.A., **420** G2
Tögöl, Mongolia, **213** H2
Tögrög, Govĭ-Altay, Mongolia, **213** G3
Tögrög, Hovd, Mongolia, **213** G3
Togtoh, China, **210** E4
Toguchin, Russian Federation, **223** L1
Tohatchi, U.S.A., **423** J4
Toholampi, Finland, **285** M5
Töhöm, Mongolia, **210** E3
Toivala, Finland, **285** N5
Tok, *river*, Russian Federation, **222** F2
Tok, U.S.A., **410** E3
Tokaj, Hungary, **289** K4
Tōkamachi, Japan, **209** G3
Tokara-rettō, *islands*, Japan, **208** E5
Tokarahi, New Zealand, **133** C7
Tokari, Russian Federation, **299** E2
Tokat, Turkey, **224** E4
Tokelau, *New Zealand territory*, Pacific Ocean, **131** H2
Tokirima, New Zealand, **132** E4
Tokmak, Kyrgyzstan, **212** B4
Tokomaru Bay, New Zealand, **132** G4
Tokoroa, New Zealand, **132** E4
Tokouno, Guinea, **364** C3
Toksovo, Russian Federation, **299** C2
Toksun, China, **212** F4
Toktogul, Kyrgyzstan, **212** B4
Toktomush, Tajikistan, **223** J5
Toku, *island*, Tonga, **136** D2
Tokuno-shima, *island*, Japan, **209** P8
Tokushima, Japan, **208** F4
Tokuyama, Japan, **208** E4
Tōkyō, Japan, **209** G4
Tokzār, Afghanistan, **218** A2
Tolaga Bay, New Zealand, **132** G4
Tôlañaro, Madagascar, **372** B6
Tolbo, Mongolia, **212** F2
Tolé, Panama, **429** E5
Töle Bī, Kazakhstan, **212** B4
Toledo, Brazil, **459** G2
Toledo, Iowa, U.S.A., **420** G5
Toledo, Montes de, *mountain range*, Spain, **292** E3
Toledo, Ohio, U.S.A., **421** M5
Toledo, Oregon, U.S.A., **418** C4
Toledo, Philippines, **204** C4
Toledo, Spain, **292** E3
Toledo, Washington, U.S.A., **418** C3
Toledo Bend Reservoir, U.S.A., **424** E4
Tolga, Norway, **286** E1
Toli, China, **212** D3
Toliara, Madagascar, **372** A5
Toliara, *province*, Madagascar, **372** A5
Tolitoli, Indonesia, **198** C2
Tolkmicko, Poland, **289** J1
Tollesbury, England, U.K., **305** H3
Tolmachevo, Russian Federation, **299** B3
Tolmezzo, Italy, **294** D2
Tolmin, Slovenia, **294** D2
Tolna, Hungary, **289** J5
Tolo, Democratic Republic of the Congo, **368** C3
Tolo, Teluk, *bay*, Indonesia, **198** C3
Tolong Bay, Philippines, **204** C4
Tolsta Head, *cape*, Scotland, U.K., **308** C2
Tolstoy, Mys, *cape*, Russian Federation, **301** S4
Tolú, Colombia, **450** C2
Toluca, Mexico, **431** F5
Tolvayarvi, Russian Federation, **285** Q5
Tolvuya, Russian Federation, **285** S5
Tol'yatti, Russian Federation, **222** D2
Tom Burke, South Africa, **371** E3
Tom Price, Australia, **134** D3
Tom Price, Mount, *mountain peak*, Australia, **134** D3
Toma, Burkina Faso, **364** D2
Tomah, U.S.A., **420** H4
Tomakomai, Japan, **209** H2
Tomanivi, *mountain peak*, Fiji, **141** A4
Tomar, Kazakhstan, **212** B3
Tomar, Portugal, **292** C3
Tomarza, Turkey, **363** G1
Tomás Barron, Bolivia, **455** E4
Tomás Garrido, Mexico, **431** H5
Tomás Gomensoro, Uruguay, **459** F4
Tomaszów Lubelski, Poland, **289** L3
Tomaszów Mazowiecki, Poland, **289** K3
Tomatin, Scotland, U.K., **308** F3
Tomatlán, Mexico, **430** D5
Tombador, Serra do, *mountain range*, Brazil, **456** B3
Tombigbee, *river*, U.S.A., **425** H4
Tomboco, Angola, **368** B4
Tombos, Brazil, **457** E5
Tombouctou, *administrative region*, Mali, **364** D1
Tombouctou, Mali, **364** D1
Tombstone, U.S.A., **423** J6
Tombua, Angola, **368** B6

Tres Lomas, Argentina, **458** D5
Tres Mapajos, Bolivia, **455** F3
Tres Marías, Islas, *islands*, Mexico, **430** D4
Três Marias, Represa, *reservoir*, Brazil, **457** E5
Tres Montes, Península, Chile, **460** B3
Tres Picos, Cerro, *mountain peak*, Argentina, **458** E6
Tres Picos, Mexico, **431** G6
Tres Piedras, U.S.A., **423** L3
Três Pontas, Brazil, **456** E5
Tres Puntas, Cabo, *cape*, Argentina, **460** E3
Três Rios, Brazil, **457** E6
Tres Valles, Mexico, **431** F5
Tresfjord, Norway, **286** C1
Tretten, Norway, **286** E2
Treviglio, Italy, **294** B3
Treviso, Italy, **294** D3
Trevose Head, *point*, England, U.K., **304** B4
Trévoux, France, **291** G4
Trgovište, Yugoslavia, **296** D4
Tria Nisia, *island*, Kyklades, Greece, **297** F7
Tribal Areas, *province*, Pakistan, **218** B2
Tribune, U.S.A., **420** C6
Tricase, Italy, **295** G6
Trichonida, Limni, *lake*, Greece, **297** C6
Trichūr, India, **216** D4
Trier, Germany, **288** C4
Trieste, Golfo di, *gulf*, Italy, **294** D3
Trieste, Italy, **294** D3
Triglav, *mountain peak*, Slovenia, **294** D2
Trigno, *river*, Italy, **295** E5
Trikala, Greece, **297** C6
Trikomo, Cyprus, **225** B2
Trikora, Puncak, *mountain peak*, Indonesia, **199** G4
Trilj, Croatia, **294** F4
Trim, Ireland, **309** F4
Trimdon, England, U.K., **307** G3
Trincomalee, Sri Lanka, **217** E4
Trindade, Brazil, **456** D4
Trindade, *island*, Brazil, Atlantic Ocean, **105** T10
Tring, England, U.K., **305** G3
Trinidad, Bolivia, **455** F4
Trinidad, California, U.S.A., **418** B6
Trinidad, Colombia, **450** D3
Trinidad, Colorado, U.S.A., **423** L3
Trinidad, Cuba, **429** F2
Trinidad, Golfo, *gulf*, Chile, **460** B3
Trinidad, *island*, Trinidad and Tobago, **461** C4
Trinidad, Uruguay, **459** F4
Trinidad and Tobago, *country*, Caribbean Sea, **409** S7
Trinity, *river*, U.S.A., **424** E4
Trinity Bay, Canada, **417** Q6
Trinity Hills, *mountain peak*, Trinidad, Trinidad and Tobago, **461** C4
Trino, Italy, **294** B3
Triolet, Mauritius, **373** C1
Tripa, *river*, Indonesia, **200** B1
Tripoli, Greece, **297** D7
Tripoli *see* Ţarābulus, Lebanon, **225** C2
Tripoli *see* Ţarābulus, Libya, **362** B2
Tripura, *state*, India, **219** G5
Tristan da Cunha, *island*, St Helena, **373** C2
Tristan da Cunha, *St Helena dependency*, Atlantic Ocean, **359** D10
Triunfo, *river*, Brazil, **452** C5
Trivandrum *see* Thiruvananthapuram, India, **216** D4
Trivento, Italy, **295** E5
Trnava, Slovakia, **289** H4
Trnavský, *administrative region*, Slovakia, **289** H4
Trobriand Islands, Papua New Guinea, **140** C5
Troebratskiy, Kazakhstan, **222** H2
Trofors, Norway, **284** F4
Trogir, Croatia, **294** F4
Troglav, *mountain peak*, Bosnia and Herzegovina, **294** F4
Troia, Italy, **295** E5
Trois Bassins, Réunion, **373** A1
Trois Fourches, Cap des, *cape*, Morocco, **293** F5
Trois-Pistoles, Canada, **416** G5
Trois-Rivières, Canada, **416** E6
Troisdorf, Germany, **288** C3
Troitsk, Russian Federation, **222** G2
Troitskoye, Russian Federation, **211** M2
Trollhättan, Sweden, **286** F3
Trombetas, *river*, Brazil, **452** B3
Tromelin Île, *island*, Réunion, **372** C4
Tromen, Volcán, *mountain peak*, Argentina, **458** B5
Troms, *county*, Norway, **284** J2
Tromsø, Norway, **284** J2
Tromvik, Norway, **284** J2
Tron, *mountain peak*, Norway, **286** E1
Tronador, Cerro, *mountain peak*, Chile, **460** C1
Trondheim, Norway, **284** E5
Trönninge, Sweden, **286** F4
Troodos, Cyprus, **225** B2
Troodos Mountains, *mountain range*, Cyprus, **225** B2
Troon, Scotland, U.K., **308** E5
Tropaia, Greece, **297** C7
Tropeiros, Serra dos, *mountain range*, Brazil, **457** E4
Trostan, *mountain peak*, Northern Ireland, U.K., **309** F2
Trou d'Eau Dolce, Mauritius, **373** C1
Trout Creek, Canada, **416** B7
Trout Creek, U.S.A., **418** G3
Trout Lake, Canada, **413** L6
Trout Lake, *lake*, Northwest Territories, Canada, **412** J1
Trout Lake, *lake*, Ontario, Canada, **414** H6
Trout Lake, U.S.A., **418** D4
Trouville-sur-Mer, France, **290** E2
Trowbridge, England, U.K., **304** E3
Troy, Alabama, U.S.A., **425** K4
Troy, Montana, U.S.A., **418** G2
Troy, New York, U.S.A., **426** D3
Troy Peak, *mountain peak*, U.S.A., **422** F2
Troyan, Bulgaria, **296** E4
Troyanka, Ukraine, **296** H1
Troyes, France, **291** G2
Troyits'ke, Ukraine, **296** H2
Trstenik, Yugoslavia, **296** C4
Trsteno, Croatia, **294** F4
Truckee, U.S.A., **422** C2
Trujillo, Honduras, **428** D4
Trujillo, Peru, **454** B2
Trujillo, Spain, **292** E3
Trujillo, Venezuela, **451** D2
Trumann, U.S.A., **424** G2
Trumbull, Mount, *mountain peak*, U.S.A., **422** G3
Trŭn, Bulgaria, **296** D4
Truro, Canada, **417** K7
Truro, England, U.K., **304** B4
Trus Madi, Gunung, *mountain peak*, Malaysia, **201** G1
Truşeşti, Romania, **296** F2
Truskmore, *mountain peak*, Ireland, **309** D3
Trutch, Canada, **412** H3
Truth or Consequences, U.S.A., **423** K5
Trutnov, Czech Republic, **289** G3
Truyère, *river*, France, **290** F4
Trwyn Cilan, *point*, Wales, U.K., **304** C2
Tryavna, Bulgaria, **296** E4
Tryon, U.S.A., **420** C5
Trysilelva, *river*, Norway, **286** E2
Tryškiai, Lithuania, **287** L4
Tržac, Bosnia and Herzegovina, **294** E3
Trzcianka, Poland, **289** H2
Trzciel, Poland, **289** G2
Trzebnica, Poland, **289** H3
Tsagaan-Olom, Mongolia, **213** H3
Tsagaan Ovoo, Mongolia, **213** J3
Tsagaanchuluut, Mongolia, **213** H3
Tsagaandörvölj, Mongolia, **210** E3
Tsagaannuur, Bayan-Ölgiy, Mongolia, **212** F2
Tsagaannuur, Dornod, Mongolia, **211** G3
Tsagan Aman, Russian Federation, **222** D3
Tsakir, Russian Federation, **213** J2
Tsåktso, *mountain peak*, Sweden, **284** K2
Tsaratanana, Madagascar, **372** B4
Tsaris Mountains, Namibia, **370** C3
Tsebrykove, Ukraine, **296** H2
Tseel, Mongolia, **213** G3
Tsengel, Mongolia, **213** J2
Tsentral'nyy, Russian Federation, **223** M1
Tses, Namibia, **370** C4
Tsetseng, Botswana, **370** D3
Tsetserleg, Mongolia, **213** J3
Tsévié, Togo, **364** E3
Tshabong, Botswana, **370** D4
Tshane, Botswana, **370** D3
Tshela, Democratic Republic of the Congo, **368** B3
Tshibala, Democratic Republic of the Congo, **368** D4
Tshibwika, Democratic Republic of the Congo, **368** D4
Tshikapa, Democratic Republic of the Congo, **368** D4
Tshilenge, Democratic Republic of the Congo, **368** D4
Tshimbalanga, Democratic Republic of the Congo, **368** D4
Tshimbo, Democratic Republic of the Congo, **369** E4
Tshimbulu, Democratic Republic of the Congo, **368** D4
Tshinsenda, Democratic Republic of the Congo, **369** E5
Tshokwane, South Africa, **371** F3
Tshootsha, Botswana, **370** D3
Tsiigehtchic, Canada, **410** F3
Tsimlyanskoye Vodokhranilishche, *reservoir*, Russian Federation, **222** C3
Tsineng, South Africa, **370** D4
Tsiombe, Madagascar, **372** B6
Tsiribihina, *river*, Madagascar, **372** A4
Tsiribihina, Tanjona, *cape*, Madagascar, **372** A4
Tsiroanomandidy, Madagascar, **372** B4
Tsivil'sk, Russian Federation, **222** D1
Tsolo, South Africa, **371** E5
Tsoohor, Mongolia, **210** D4
Tsuchiura, Japan, **209** H3
Tsuen Wan, China, **207** C4
Tsumeb, Namibia, **370** C2
Tsumis Park, Namibia, **370** C3
Tsumkwe, Namibia, **370** D2
Tsuruga, Japan, **209** G4
Tsuruoka, Japan, **209** G3
Tsushima, *island*, Japan, **208** E4
Tsuyama, Japan, **208** F4
Tu, *river*, Myanmar, **205** C3
Tuai, New Zealand, **132** F4
Tuakau, New Zealand, **132** E3
Tuam, Ireland, **309** D4
Tuamarina, New Zealand, **133** D5
Tuamotu, Archipel des, *islands*, French Polynesia, **137** G2
Tuan, Tanjong, *point*, Malaysia, **200** C2
Tuâ'n Giáo, Vietnam, **203** D1
Tuangku, Pulau, *island*, Indonesia, **200** B2
Tu'anuku, Vava'u Group, Tonga, **141** B3
Tuao, Philippines, **204** C2
Tuaran, Malaysia, **201** G1
Tuas, Singapore, **200** J7
Tuba City, U.S.A., **423** H3
Tuban, Indonesia, **201** F4
Tubarão, Brazil, **459** H3
Ţubarjal, Saudi Arabia, **225** E4
Ţūbās, West Bank, **225** C3
Tübingen, Germany, **288** D4
Tubmanburg, Liberia, **364** B3
Tubou, Fiji, **141** A4
Tubruq, Libya, **362** D2
Tubuai, Îles *see* Australes, Îles, *islands*, French Polynesia, **137** F3
Tubuai, *island*, French Polynesia, **137** G3
Tucano, Brazil, **457** F3
Tucavaca, Bolivia, **455** G5
Tuchan, France, **290** F5
Tuchola, Poland, **289** H2
Tucson, U.S.A., **423** H5
Tucumán, *province*, Argentina, **458** D3
Tucumcari, U.S.A., **423** M4
Tucunuco, Argentina, **458** C4
Tucupita, Venezuela, **451** F2
Tucuruí, Brazil, **452** D4
Tucuruí, Represa de, *reservoir*, Brazil, **452** D4
Tudela, Spain, **293** G1
Tudor Vladimirescu, Romania, **296** F3
Tudu, Estonia, **287** N3
Tudun Wada, Nigeria, **365** F2
Tuekta, Russian Federation, **223** M2
Tuen Mun, China, **207** B4
Tueré, *river*, Brazil, **452** C4
Tufi, Papua New Guinea, **140** C5
Tufts Plain, *underwater feature*, Pacific Ocean, **479** J1
Tugozvonovo, Russian Federation, **223** L2
Tuguegarao, Philippines, **204** C2
Tugulym, Russian Federation, **222** G1
Tugutuy, Russian Federation, **210** D1
Tuhkakylä, Finland, **285** P4
Tuhua, *mountain peak*, New Zealand, **132** E4
Tuhua, New Zealand, **132** E4
Tuhua *see* Mayor Island, New Zealand, **133** F3
Tui, Spain, **292** C1
Tuiguang, China, **207** A2
Tuineje, Islas Canarias, Spain, **373** B4
Tuira, *river*, Panama, **429** F5
Tuirc, Beinn an, *mountain peak*, Scotland, U.K., **308** D5
Tukangbesi, Kepulauan, *islands*, Indonesia, **198** D4
Tukayel, Ethiopia, **367** G3
Tukhkala, Russian Federation, **285** Q4
Tukosmera, Mont, *mountain peak*, Vanuatu, **141** A3
Tūkrah, Libya, **362** D2
Tuktoyaktuk, Canada, **410** F3
Tukums, Latvia, **287** L4
Tukuyu, Tanzania, **369** F4
Tula, American Samoa, **141** B2
Tula, Mexico, **431** F4
Tula, Russian Federation, **299** F5
Tulaghi, Solomon Islands, **141** A1
Tulangbawang, *river*, Indonesia, **200** D4
Tulare, U.S.A., **420** D3
Tularosa, U.S.A., **423** K5
Tulcán, Ecuador, **450** C4
Tulcea, Romania, **296** G3
Tul'chyn, Ukraine, **296** G1
Tule, Venezuela, **450** D1
Tulghes, Romania, **296** E2
Tuli, Zimbabwe, **371** E3
Tulia, U.S.A., **424** B2
Tulihe, China, **211** H2
Tulita, Canada, **410** G3
Ţūlkarm, West Bank, **225** C3
Tulla, Ireland, **309** D5
Tullahoma, U.S.A., **425** J2
Tullamore, Ireland, **309** E4
Tulle, France, **290** E4
Tulln, Austria, **289** H4
Tullos, U.S.A., **424** F4
Tullow, Ireland, **309** F5
Tully, Australia, **135** K2
Tulnici, Romania, **296** F3
Tuloma, *river*, Russian Federation, **285** R2
Tulos, Ozero, *lake*, Russian Federation, **285** Q5
Tulos, Russian Federation, **285** Q5
Tulppio, Finland, **285** P3
Tulsa, U.S.A., **424** E1
Tul'skaya Oblast', *province*, Russian Federation, **299** F6
Tuluá, Colombia, **450** C3
Tuluceşti, Romania, **296** G3
Tuma, Russian Federation, **298** F1
Tumaco, Colombia, **450** B4
Tumaco, Ensenada de, *bay*, Colombia, **450** B4
Tumannyy, Russian Federation, **285** S2
Tumatumari, Guyana, **451** G3
Tumba, Democratic Republic of the Congo, **368** D3
Tumba, Lac, *lake*, Democratic Republic of the Congo, **368** C3
Tumba, Sweden, **287** H3
Tumbangsamba, Indonesia, **201** F3
Tumbes, Peru, **450** B5
Tumby Bay, Australia, **135** H5
Tumcha, *river*, Russian Federation, **285** Q3
Tumd Youqi, China, **210** E4
Tumd Zuoqi, China, **210** E4
Tumen, China, **208** E2
Tumen, *river*, China/North Korea, **211** K4
Tumeremo, Venezuela, **451** G2
Tumkūr, India, **216** D3
Tumpu, Gunung, *mountain peak*, Indonesia, **198** C3
Tumu, Ghana, **364** D2
Tumucumaque Serra, *mountain range*, Brazil, **452** B2
Tumureng, Guyana, **451** G2
Tuna, India, **218** B5
Tunapuna, Trinidad, Trinidad and Tobago, **461** C4
Tunceli, Turkey, **363** G1
Tunchang, China, **203** F2
Tunduru, Tanzania, **369** G5
Tundzha, *river*, Bulgaria, **296** E4
Tunga, Nigeria, **365** F3
Tungabhadra Reservoir, India, **216** C3
Tungaru, Sudan, **366** D2
Tungawan, Philippines, **204** C5
Tungokochen, Russian Federation, **210** F1
Tungozero, Russian Federation, **285** Q4
Tünhel, Mongolia, **210** D2
Tuni, India, **217** E2
Tunis, Golfe de, *gulf*, Tunisia, **362** B1
Tūnis, Tunisia, **362** B1
Tunisia, *country*, Africa, **358** F3

Ulan-Ude, Russian Federation, **210** D2
Ulan Ul Hu, *lake*, China, **214** D2
Ulanbel, Kazakhstan, **223** J4
Ulanhot, China, **211** H3
Ulantolgoy, Mongolia, **223** N3
Ulaş, Turkey, **297** F5
Ulawa, *island*, Solomon Islands, **141** A1
Ulawun, Mount, *mountain peak*, Papua New Guinea, **140** C4
Ulbanep, Mount, *mountain peak*, Papua New Guinea, **140** A3
Ulbster, Scotland, U.K., **308** F2
Ulchin, South Korea, **208** E3
Ulcinj, Yugoslavia, **296** B5
Uldz, Mongolia, **210** E2
Uldz, *river*, Mongolia, **210** F2
Ulety, Russian Federation, **210** F2
Ulfborg, Denmark, **286** D4
Ulhāsnagar, India, **216** C2
Uliastay, Mongolia, **213** H3
Ulithi, *island*, Micronesia, **138** B3
Ülken Borsyq Qumy, *desert*, Kazakhstan, **222** F3
Ülken Vladīmīrovka, Kazakhstan, **212** C2
Ülkennaryn, Kazakhstan, **212** E2
Ulla, Belarus, **299** B5
Ulla, *river*, Spain, **292** C1
Ullånger, Sweden, **287** J1
Ullapool, Scotland, U.K., **308** D3
Ullared, Sweden, **286** F4
Ullatti, Sweden, **284** K3
Ullava, Finland, **285** L5
Ullfors, Sweden, **287** H2
Ullswater, *lake*, England, U.K., **306** F3
Ullŭngdo, *island*, South Korea, **208** E3
Ulm, Germany, **288** D4
Ul'ma, *river*, Russian Federation, **211** K2
Ulmeni, near Baia Mare, Romania, **296** D2
Ulmeni, Romania, **296** F3
Ulog, Bosnia and Herzegovina, **294** G4
Ulongwe, Mozambique, **369** F5
Ulricehamn, Sweden, **286** F4
Ulsan, South Korea, **208** E4
Ulsberg, Norway, **286** D1
Ulsta, Shetland, Scotland, U.K., **308** K7
Ulu, Indonesia, **198** D2
Ulubat Gölü, *lake*, Turkey, **297** G5
Uluçinar, Turkey, **225** C1
Ulugan Bay, Philippines, **204** B4
Uluqqat, China, **212** B5
Ulundi, South Africa, **371** F4
Ulungur, *river*, China, **212** E3
Ulungur Hu, *lake*, China, **212** E3
Uluriyskiy Golets, Gora, *mountain peak*, Russian Federation, **210** E2
Uluru (Ayers Rock), *mountain peak*, Australia, **128** C4
Ulva, *island*, Scotland, U.K., **308** C4
Ulverston, England, U.K., **306** E3
Ulvik, Norway, **286** C2
Ul'yanovka, Ukraine, **296** H1
Ul'yanovsk, Russian Federation, **222** D2
Ul'yanovskaya Oblast', *province*, Russian Federation, **222** D2
Ül'yanovskţy, Kazakhstan, **212** B2
Ulysses, U.S.A., **420** C7
Umag, Croatia, **294** D3
Umán, Mexico, **431** H4
Uman', Ukraine, **298** D3
Umaria, India, **218** E5
Umarkot, India, **219** E6
Umarkot, Pakistan, **218** B4

Umba, *river*, Russian Federation, **285** S3
Umba, Russian Federation, **285** S3
Umboi Island, Papua New Guinea, **140** B4
Umbozero, Ozero, *lake*, Russian Federation, **285** S3
Umbria, *autonomous state*, Italy, **294** D4
Umbukul, Papua New Guinea, **140** C3
Umbulan Gayohpecoh, Indonesia, **200** D3
Umeå, Sweden, **284** K5
Umeälven, *river*, Sweden, **284** J4
Umfreville Lake, Canada, **414** G6
Umiat, U.S.A., **410** D3
Umlazi, South Africa, **371** F4
Umm ad Daraj, Jabal, *mountain peak*, Jordan, **225** C3
Umm Bel, Sudan, **366** C2
Umm Durmān (Omdurman), Sudan, **366** D1
Umm Kaddādah, Sudan, **366** C2
Umm Lajj, Saudi Arabia, **363** G3
Umm Ruwābah, Sudan, **366** D2
Umm Sa'ad, Libya, **362** E2
Umm Şawwānah, Jabal, *mountain peak*, Jordan, **225** C4
Umm Sayyālah, Sudan, **366** D2
Umm Shawmar, Jabal, *mountain peak*, Egypt, **225** B5
Umm 'Umayd, Ra's, *mountain peak*, Egypt, **225** B6
Umm Urūmah, *island*, Saudi Arabia, **363** G3
Umnak Island, Aleutian Islands, U.S.A., **408** G3
Umpilua, Mozambique, **369** G5
Umpulo, Angola, **368** C5
Umred, India, **218** D5
Umtata, South Africa, **371** E5
Umuahia, Nigeria, **368** A1
Umuarama, Brazil, **459** G2
Umuna, *island*, Vava'u Group, Tonga, **141** B3
Umurbey, Turkey, **297** F5
Umzinto, South Africa, **371** F5
Una, Brazil, **457** F4
Una, India, **218** B5
Una, Mount, *mountain peak*, New Zealand, **133** D6
Una, *river*, Bosnia and Herzegovina, **294** F3
Una, Russian Federation, **285** U4
Unaðsdalur, Iceland, **284** X6
Unaí, Brazil, **456** D4
Unaja, Finland, **287** K2
Unalaska Island, Aleutian Islands, U.S.A., **408** G3
Unango, Mozambique, **369** G5
Unapool, Scotland, U.K., **308** D2
Unari, Finland, **285** M3
Unari, *lake*, Finland, **285** M3
'Unayzah, Jordan, **225** C4
'Unayzah, Saudi Arabia, **363** H3
Uncia, Bolivia, **455** E5
Uncompahgre Plateau, U.S.A., **423** J2
Undersåker, Sweden, **284** F5
Underwood, U.S.A., **420** C2
Unduksa, Russian Federation, **285** S4
Unea Island, Papua New Guinea, **140** C4
Unecha, Russian Federation, **298** D2
Unezhma, Russian Federation, **285** T5
Ungana Bay, Kenya, **369** H3
Ungava, Péninsule d', *peninsula*, Canada, **411** M3
Ungheni, Moldova, **296** F2
União, Brazil, **453** E4
União da Vitória, Brazil, **459** G3
União dos Palmares, Brazil, **457** G2

Unichowo, Poland, **289** H1
Unije, *island*, Croatia, **294** E3
Unini, Peru, **454** C3
Unini, *river*, Brazil, **451** F4
Unión, Bahía, *bay*, Argentina, **460** E1
Union, Missouri, U.S.A., **420** H6
Union, Oregon, U.S.A., **418** F4
Unión, Paraguay, **459** F2
Union City, Pennsylvania, U.S.A., **421** P5
Union City, Tennessee, U.S.A., **425** H1
Union Creek, U.S.A., **418** C5
Union Springs, U.S.A., **425** K3
Uniontown, U.S.A., **421** P6
Unionville, U.S.A., **420** G5
United Arab Emirates, *country*, Asia, **196** G7
United Kingdom, *country*, Europe, **282** C4
United States of America, *country*, North America, **409** M5
Unitsa, Russian Federation, **285** S5
Unity, Canada, **413** Q5
Unity, U.S.A., **418** E4
University Park, U.S.A., **423** K5
Unnão, India, **218** E4
Unpongkor, Vanuatu, **141** A3
Unquera, Spain, **292** E1
Unst, *island*, Shetland, Scotland, U.K., **308** L7
Unturán, Sierra de, *mountain range*, Venezuela, **451** F3
Unuli Horog, China, **214** D2
Upata, Venezuela, **451** F2
Upavon, England, U.K., **305** F3
Upernavik, Greenland, **411** P2
Upía, *river*, Colombia, **450** D3
Upington, South Africa, **370** D4
Upleta, India, **218** B5
Uplyme, England, U.K., **304** E4
Upoloksha, Russian Federation, **285** Q3
Upolu, *island*, Samoa, **141** B1
Upper Arrow Lake, Canada, **413** K6
Upper East, *administrative region*, Ghana, **364** D2
Upper Fraser, Canada, **412** H4
Upper Hutt, New Zealand, **133** E5
Upper Klamath Lake, U.S.A., **418** D5
Upper Lough Erne, *lake*, Northern Ireland, U.K., **309** E3
Upper Peirce Reservoir, Singapore, **200** J6
Upper Red Lake, U.S.A., **420** F1
Upper Sandusky, U.S.A., **421** M5
Upper West, *administrative region*, Ghana, **364** D2
Uppingham, England, U.K., **305** G2
Upplands-Väsby, Sweden, **287** H3
Uppsala, county, Sweden, **287** H3
Upsala, Canada, **414** J7
Upshi, India, **218** D2
Upton, U.S.A., **419** M4
Upton upon Severn, England, U.K., **304** E2
'Uqayribāt, Syria, **225** D2
Urabá, Golfo de, *gulf*, Colombia, **450** C2
Urad Houqi, China, **210** D4
Urad Qianqi, China, **210** E4
Urad Zhongqi, China, **210** E4
Urakawa, Japan, **209** H2
Ural, *river*, Russian Federation, **222** E2
Ural Mountains *see* Ural'skiy Khrebet, *mountain range*, Russian Federation, **194** G4
Ural'skiy Khrebet (Ural Mountains), *mountain range*, Russian Federation, **194** G4
Urambo, Tanzania, **369** F4

Urandi, Brazil, **457** E4
Uraricoera, Brazil, **451** G3
Uraricoera, *river*, Brazil, **451** F3
Urawa, Japan, **209** G4
'Urayf an Nāqah, Jabal, *mountain peak*, Egypt, **225** C4
Urbana, U.S.A., **421** J5
Urbano Santos, Brazil, **453** E4
Urbino, Italy, **294** D4
Urbión, Sierra de, *mountain peak*, Spain, **293** F1
Urçay, France, **290** F3
Urcel, France, **291** F2
Urcos, Peru, **454** D3
Urdgol, Mongolia, **213** G3
Urdos, France, **290** D5
Urdzhar, Kazakhstan, **223** L3
Ure, *river*, England, U.K., **307** G3
Urengoy, Russian Federation, **300** J3
'Urf, Jabal al, *mountain peak*, Egypt, **225** B6
Urfa, Turkey, **224** E5
Urganch, Uzbekistan, **222** G4
Urho, China, **212** E3
Uriah, Mount, *mountain peak*, New Zealand, **133** C6
Uribia, Colombia, **450** D1
Urie, *river*, Scotland, U.K., **308** G3
Uril, Russian Federation, **211** K2
Ürṭṭskţy, Kazakhstan, **222** H2
Urjala, Finland, **287** L2
Urla, Turkey, **297** F6
Urlingford, Ireland, **309** E5
Ürmā aş Şughrá, Syria, **225** D1
Urmi, *river*, Russian Federation, **211** L2
Urmia *see* Orūmīyeh, Iran, **363** H1
Uromi, Nigeria, **365** F3
Uroševac, Yugoslavia, **296** C4
Urosozero, Russian Federation, **285** S5
Ŭroteppa, Tajikistan, **223** H5
Urov, *river*, Russian Federation, **211** H1
Urt, Mongolia, **213** J4
Urt Moron, China, **213** G5
Uruáchic, Mexico, **430** C3
Uruaçu, Brazil, **456** D4
Uruapan, Mexico, **430** E5
Uruará, *river*, Brazil, **452** C4
Urubamba, Cordillera, *mountain range*, Peru, **454** D3
Urubamba, *river*, Peru, **454** D3
Urubu, *river*, Brazil, **451** G5
Urucará, Brazil, **451** H5
Uruçuí, Brazil, **453** E5
Uruçuí, Serra do, *mountain range*, Brazil, **453** E5
Uruçui Prêto, *river*, Brazil, **453** E5
Urucuia, *river*, Brazil, **456** E4
Urucurituba, Brazil, **451** H5
Uruguai, *river*, Brazil, **459** G3
Uruguaiana, Brazil, **459** F3
Uruguay, *country*, South America, **449** G7
Uruguay, *river*, South America, **447** G6
Ürümqi, China, **212** E4
Urung, Indonesia, **199** E3
Urup, *island*, Kuril'skiye Ostrova, Russian Federation, **209** K1
Urup, Ostrov, *island*, Russian Federation, **301** S5
Uryumkan, *river*, Russian Federation, **211** G2
Urziceni, Romania, **296** F3
Us, *river*, Russian Federation, **213** G2
Usa, Japan, **208** E4
Usa, *river*, Russian Federation, **300** G3
Usadishche, Russian Federation, **299** D3
Uşak, *province*, Turkey, **297** G6
Uşak, Turkey, **297** G6
Usakos, Namibia, **370** C3

Usborne, Mount, *mountain peak*, Falkland Islands, **460** F4
Ušće, Yugoslavia, **296** C4
Usedom, Germany, **289** F2
'Usfān, Saudi Arabia, **363** G4
Usha, *river*, Belarus, **299** B6
Ushachy, Belarus, **299** B5
Ushakovskoye, Russian Federation, **301** V2
'Ushayrah, Saudi Arabia, **363** H4
Üshtöbe, Kazakhstan, **223** K3
Ushuaia, Argentina, **460** D5
Ushumun, Russian Federation, **211** J1
Usino, Papua New Guinea, **140** B4
Usinsk, Russian Federation, **300** G3
Usk, *river*, Wales, U.K., **304** D3
Usk, Wales, U.K., **304** E3
Uslar, Germany, **288** D3
Usmas ezers, *lake*, Latvia, **287** K4
Usogorsk, Russian Federation, **300** F3
Usol'ye-Sibirskoye, Russian Federation, **301** M4
Ussel, France, **290** F4
Ussuriysk, Russian Federation, **211** K4
Ust'-Barguzin, Russian Federation, **210** E1
Ust'-Chorna, Ukraine, **296** D1
Ust'-Dolyssy, Russian Federation, **299** B4
Ust'-Ilim'sk, Russian Federation, **301** M4
Ust'-Ishim, Russian Federation, **223** J1
Ust'-Kamchatsk, Russian Federation, **301** T4
Ust'-Kan, Russian Federation, **212** E2
Ust'-Koksa, Russian Federation, **212** E2
Ust'-Kut, Russian Federation, **301** M4
Ust'-Luga, Russian Federation, **299** B3
Ust'-Nera, Russian Federation, **301** R3
Ust'-Ordynskiy Buryatskiy Avtonomnyy Okrug, *autonomous area*, Russian Federation, **210** D1
Ust'-Ordynskiy, Russian Federation, **210** D1
Ust'-Reka, Russian Federation, **299** F2
Ust'-Tsil'ma, Russian Federation, **300** G3
Ust'-Tygda, Russian Federation, **211** J1
Ust'-Umal'ta, Russian Federation, **211** L2
Ust'-Undurga, Russian Federation, **211** G1
Ústí nad Labem, Czech Republic, **289** G3
Ustica, Isola di, *island*, Sicilia, Italy, **295** D6
Ustka, Poland, **289** H1
Ustrem, Bulgaria, **296** F4
Ustronie Morskie, Poland, **289** G1
Ustrzyki Dolne, Poland, **289** L4
Ust'ye, *river*, Russian Federation, **299** G4
Ust'ye, Russian Federation, **299** G3
Ustyurt, Plato, *plateau*, Kazakhstan/Uzbekistan, **222** F4
Ustyuzhna, Russian Federation, **299** F3
Usu, China, **212** E3
Usulután, El Salvador, **428** C4
Usumacinta, Mexico, **431** H5
Usvyaty, Russian Federation, **299** C5
Uta, Indonesia, **199** G4

Vatra Dornei, Romania, **296** E2
Vatra Moldoviţei, Romania, **296** E2
Vättern, *lake*, Sweden, **286** G3
Vattholma, Sweden, **287** H2
Vatulele, *island*, Fiji, **141** A4
Vaucouleurs, France, **291** G2
Vaughn, Montana, U.S.A., **419** J3
Vaughn, New Mexico, U.S.A., **423** L4
Vaupés, *river*, Colombia, **450** D4
Vauxhall, Canada, **413** N6
Vavatenina, Madagascar, **372** B4
Vava'u Group, *islands*, Tonga, **141** B3
Vavenby, Canada, **412** K6
Vavuniya, Sri Lanka, **216** E4
Vawkavysk, Belarus, **289** M2
Vawkavyskaye wzvyshsha, *mountain range*, Belarus, **289** M2
Växjö, Sweden, **286** G4
Vaygach, Ostrov, *island*, Russian Federation, **300** H2
Vechta, Germany, **288** D2
Vecinos, Spain, **292** E2
Vecpiebalga, Latvia, **287** M4
Veddige, Sweden, **286** F4
Vedea, *river*, Romania, **296** E3
Vedea, Romania, **296** E4
Vedel, Kap, *cape*, Greenland, **411** S3
Vedevåg, Sweden, **286** G3
Vedia, Argentina, **458** E5
Veeate, *island*, Vava'u Group, Tonga, **141** B3
Veendam, Netherlands, **288** C2
Vega, *island*, Norway, **284** E4
Vegadeo, Spain, **292** D1
Veglie, Italy, **295** F5
Vegreville, Canada, **413** N5
Veidnes, Norway, **285** N1
Veinticinco de Mayo, Argentina, **459** E5
Veiros, Brazil, **452** C4
Vejen, Denmark, **286** D5
Vejer de la Frontera, Spain, **292** E4
Vejle, Denmark, **286** D5
Vekshino, Russian Federation, **299** C4
Vela, Cabo de la, *cape*, Colombia, **450** D1
Velasco, Sierra de, *mountain range*, Argentina, **458** C3
Velay, Monts du, *mountain range*, France, **291** F4
Velebit, *mountain range*, Croatia, **294** E3
Velenje, Slovenia, **294** E2
Veles, Macedonia, **297** C5
Vélez, Colombia, **450** D2
Vélez-Málaga, Spain, **292** E4
Vélez Rubio, Spain, **293** F4
Velhas, das, *river*, Brazil, **457** E5
Velika Gorica, Croatia, **294** F3
Velika Hlusha, Ukraine, **289** M3
Velika Kapela, *mountain range*, Croatia, **294** E3
Velika Kladuša, Bosnia and Herzegovina, **294** E3
Velika Kruša, Yugoslavia, **296** C4
Velika Plana, Yugoslavia, **296** C3
Velikaya, *river*, Russian Federation, **299** B4
Velikaya Guba, Russian Federation, **285** S5
Velikaya Kema, Russian Federation, **209** G1
Veliki Kanal, *canal*, Yugoslavia, **296** B3
Velikiye Luki, Russian Federation, **299** C4
Veliko Tŭrnovo, Bulgaria, **296** E4
Vélingara, N. Senegal, **364** B2
Vélingara, S. Senegal, **364** B2
Velingrad, Bulgaria, **296** D4
Velizh, Russian Federation, **299** C5
Velká Bíteš, Czech Republic, **289** H4
Vel'ké Kapusany, Slovakia, **289** L4
Velké Meziříčí, Czech Republic, **289** G4
Vel'ký Meder, Slovakia, **289** H5
Vella Lavella, *island*, Solomon Islands, **141** A2
Velletri, Italy, **295** D5
Vellinge, Sweden, **286** F5
Vellore, India, **216** D3
Velopoula, *island*, Greece, **297** D7
Vel'sk, Russian Federation, **300** F3
Velva, U.S.A., **420** C1
Velyka Mykhaylivka, Ukraine, **296** G2
Velyki Mosty, Ukraine, **289** M3
Velykodolyns'ke, Ukraine, **296** H2
Vema Fracture Zone, *tectonic features*, Atlantic Ocean, **477** D4
Vemb, Denmark, **286** D4
Vemhån, Sweden, **286** G1
Vena, Sweden, **286** H4
Venaco, Corse, France, **295** B4
Venado Tuerto, Argentina, **458** D4
Venceslau Bras, Brazil, **459** H2
Vendas Novas, Portugal, **292** C3
Vendinga, Russian Federation, **300** F3
Vendôme, France, **290** E3
Veneguera, Islas Canarias, Spain, **373** B4
Veneto, *autonomous region*, Italy, **294** C3
Venev, Russian Federation, **299** G5
Venezia, Golfo di, *gulf*, Italy, **294** D3
Venezia (Venice), Italy, **294** D3
Venezuela, *country*, South America, **449** F3
Venezuela, Golfo de, *gulf*, Venezuela, **450** D1
Vengurla, India, **216** C3
Venice, Florida, U.S.A., **425** L6
Venice, Louisiana, U.S.A., **425** H5
Venice *see* Venezia, Italy, **294** D3
Venjan, Sweden, **286** F2
Venkatāpuram, India, **216** E2
Venlo, Netherlands, **288** C3
Venta, *river*, Latvia/Lithuania, **287** K4
Venta de Baños, Spain, **292** E2
Ventana, Sierra de la, *mountain range*, Argentina, **458** D5
Ventisquero, *mountain peak*, Argentina, **460** C1
Ventnor, England, U.K., **305** F4
Ventotene, Isola, *island*, Italy, **295** D5
Ventoux, Mont, *mountain peak*, France, **291** G4
Ventspils, Latvia, **287** K4
Ventuari, *river*, Venezuela, **451** E3
Ventura, U.S.A., **422** D4
Vepsovskaya Vozvyshennost', *mountain range*, Russian Federation, **299** E2
Vera, Argentina, **459** E3
Vera, Spain, **293** G4
Vera Cruz, Brazil, **455** E2
Veracruz, Mexico, **431** F5
Veracruz, *state*, Mexico, **431** F4
Verāval, India, **218** B5
Vercelli, Italy, **294** B3
Verdalsøra, Norway, **284** E5
Verde, Peninsula, Argentina, **460** F1
Verde, *river*, Argentina, **460** E1
Verde, *river*, Goiás, Brazil, **456** C4
Verde, *river*, Mato Grosso do Sul, Brazil, **456** C5
Verde, *river*, Paraguay, **459** E2
Verde, *river*, U.S.A., **423** H4
Verde Grande, *river*, Brazil, **457** E4
Verden (Aller), Germany, **288** D2
Verdigre, U.S.A., **420** D4
Verdun, France, **291** G2
Vereeniging, South Africa, **371** E4
Veregin, Canada, **414** C6
Verga, Cap, *cape*, Guinea, **364** A2
Verga, Islas Canarias, Spain, **373** B4
Vergara, Uruguay, **459** G4
Vergennes, U.S.A., **426** D2
Vergt, France, **290** E4
Verín, Spain, **292** D2
Verkhnetulomskiy, Russian Federation, **285** Q2
Verkhnetulomskoye Vodokhranilishche, *lake*, Russian Federation, **285** P2
Verkhneye Kuyto, Ozero, *lake*, Russian Federation, **285** Q4
Verkhniy Kuzhebar, Russian Federation, **223** N2
Verkhniy Ufaley, Russian Federation, **222** G1
Verkhoyansk, Russian Federation, **301** Q3
Verkhoyanskiy Khrebet, *mountain range*, Russian Federation, **301** P3
Vermilion, Canada, **413** P5
Vermilion, *river*, Canada, **421** N2
Vermilion Bay, Canada, **414** H7
Vermilion Lake, U.S.A., **420** G1
Vermilion Range, *mountain range*, U.S.A., **420** H2
Vermillion, U.S.A., **420** E4
Vermont, *state*, U.S.A., **426** D2
Vernadsky, *Ukrainian research station*, Antarctica, **470** A4
Vernal, U.S.A., **423** J1
Vernantes, France, **290** E3
Vernár, Slovakia, **289** K4
Verner, Canada, **421** N2
Vernon, Alabama, U.S.A., **425** H3
Vernon, Canada, **413** K6
Vernon, France, **290** E2
Vernon, Texas, U.S.A., **424** C2
Vernon, Utah, U.S.A., **422** G1
Vero Beach, U.S.A., **425** M6
Veroia, Greece, **297** D5
Verona, Italy, **294** C3
Verónica, Argentina, **459** F5
Versailles, U.S.A., **421** L6
Vert, Cap, *cape*, Senegal, **364** A2
Vertientes, Cuba, **429** F2
Vertou, France, **290** D3
Vervins, France, **291** F2
Verwood, Canada, **413** S7
Vesanto, Finland, **285** N5
Veselovskoye, Russian Federation, **223** K2
Vesle, *river*, France, **291** F2
Vesoul, France, **291** H3
Vest-Agder, *county*, Norway, **286** C3
Vestbygd, Norway, **286** C3
Vesterålen, *islands*, Norway, **284** G2
Vesterø Havn, Denmark, **286** E4
Vestfjorden, *fiord*, Norway, **284** F3
Vestfold, *county*, Norway, **286** D3
Vestre Gausdal, Norway, **286** E2
Vestvågøy, *island*, Norway, **284** F2
Vesuvio, *mountain peak*, Italy, **295** E5
Ves'yegonsk, Russian Federation, **299** F3
Veszprém, Hungary, **289** H5
Vetal, U.S.A., **420** C4
Veteli, Finland, **285** L5
Vetlanda, Sweden, **286** G4
Vetovo, Bulgaria, **296** F4
Vetralla, Italy, **295** D4
Vetrenyy Poyas, Kryazh, *mountain range*, Russian Federation, **285** S5
Vetsikko, Finland, **285** N2
Veurne, Belgium, **290** F1
Vézère, *river*, France, **290** E4
Vị Thanh, Vietnam, **203** E4
Viacha, Bolivia, **455** E4
Viana, Angola, **368** B4
Viana, Brazil, **453** E4
Viana do Castelo, *district*, Portugal, **292** C2
Viana do Castelo, Portugal, **292** C2
Viangchan (Vientiane), Laos, **203** D2
Viangphoukha, Laos, **202** D1
Vianópolis, Brazil, **456** D4
Viareggio, Italy, **294** C4
Vibo Valentia, Italy, **295** F6
Viborg, Denmark, **286** D4
Vic, Spain, **293** J2
Vice Comodoro Marambio, *Argentinian research station*, Antarctica, **470** A4
Vicenza, Italy, **294** C3
Vichada, *river*, Colombia, **451** E3
Vichy, France, **291** F3
Vici, U.S.A., **424** C1
Vicksburg, U.S.A., **424** G3
Viçosa, Brazil, **457** E5
Victor, Mount, *mountain peak*, Antarctica, **470** E4
Victor, U.S.A., **419** J5
Victor Harbor, Australia, **135** H6
Victoria, Argentina, **459** E4
Victoria, Canada, **412** H7
Victoria, Chile, **458** B6
Victoria, Isla, *island*, Chile, **460** B2
Victoria, Lake, Tanzania/Uganda, **369** F3
Victoria, Malaysia, **201** F1
Victoria, Mount, *mountain peak*, Myanmar, **205** B3
Victoria, Mount, *mountain peak*, New Zealand, **133** D6
Victoria, Mount, *mountain peak*, Papua New Guinea, **140** B5
Victoria, *river*, Australia, **134** G2
Victoria, Romania, **296** E3
Victoria, Seychelles, **373** A2
Victoria, Sierra de la, *mountain range*, Argentina, **459** F2
Victoria, *state*, Australia, **135** J6
Victoria, U.S.A., **424** D5
Victoria Falls, Zimbabwe, **371** E2
Victoria Island, Canada, **410** H2
Victoria Lake, Canada, **417** N5
Victoria Land, *region*, Antarctica, **470** E7
Victoria Peak, *mountain peak*, Belize, **428** C3
Victoria Peak, *mountain peak*, Philippines, **204** B4
Victoria Peak, *mountain peak*, U.S.A., **423** L6
Victoria Point, Macquarie Island, **134** R11
Victoria River Wayside Inn, Australia, **134** G2
Victoria West, South Africa, **370** D5
Victoriaville, Canada, **416** F6
Victorica, Argentina, **458** D5
Victorville, U.S.A., **422** E4
Victory, Mount, *mountain peak*, Papua New Guinea, **140** C5
Vicuña Mackenna, Argentina, **458** D4
Vida, U.S.A., **418** C4
Vidal, U.S.A., **422** F4
Vidalia, U.S.A., **425** L3
Vidamlya, Belarus, **289** L2
Videbæk, Denmark, **286** D4
Videle, Romania, **296** E3
Vidigueira, Portugal, **292** D3
Vidin, Bulgaria, **296** D4
Vidio, Cabo, *cape*, Spain, **292** D1
Vidlin, Shetland, Scotland, U.K., **308** K7
Vidlitsa, Russian Federation, **299** D2
Vidsel, Sweden, **284** K4
Viduklė, Lithuania, **287** L5
Viduša, *mountain range*, Bosnia and Herzegovina, **294** G4
Vidzy, Belarus, **287** N5
Viedma, Argentina, **460** E1
Viedma, Lago, *lake*, Argentina, **460** C3
Vieja, Sierra, *mountain range*, U.S.A., **423** L6
Viekšniai, Lithuania, **287** L4
Vienna *see* Wien, Austria, **289** H4
Vienne, France, **291** G4
Vienne, *river*, France, **290** E3
Vientiane *see* Viangchan, Laos, **203** D2
Viento, Cordillera del, *mountain range*, Argentina, **458** B5
Vieremä, Finland, **285** N5
Vierwaldstätter See, *lake*, Switzerland, **291** J3
Vierzon, France, **290** F3
Viesīte, Latvia, **287** M4
Vieste, Italy, **295** F5
Việt Tri, Vietnam, **203** E1
Vietas, Sweden, **284** J3
Vietnam, *country*, Asia, **197** M8
Vieux Fort, St Lucia, **427** D3
Vif, France, **291** G4
Viga, Philippines, **204** D3
Vigan, Philippines, **204** C2
Vigia, Brazil, **452** D3
Vigía Chico, Mexico, **431** J5
Vignacourt, France, **305** K4
Vignemale, *mountain peak*, France/Spain, **293** G1
Vignola, Italy, **294** C3
Vigo, Spain, **292** C1
Vihanti, Finland, **285** M4
Vihāri, Pakistan, **218** C3
Vihiers, France, **290** D3
Vihtari, Finland, **287** P1
Vihti, Finland, **287** M2
Viiala, Finland, **287** L2
Viipustunturit, *mountain peak*, Finland, **285** M2
Viitasaari, Finland, **285** M5
Viitna, Estonia, **287** N3
Vijāpur, India, **218** C5
Vijayawāda, India, **216** E2
Vík, Iceland, **284** Y8
Vik, Norway, **284** F4
Vika, Sweden, **286** G2
Vikajärvi, Finland, **285** N3
Vikanes, Norway, **286** B2
Vikārābād, India, **216** D2
Vikeke, Indonesia, **198** D5
Vikersund, Norway, **286** E3
Vikhren, *mountain peak*, Macedonia, **297** D5
Viking, Canada, **413** P5
Vikna, *island*, Norway, **284** E4
Vikran, Norway, **284** J2
Viksjö, Sweden, **287** H1
Viksøyri, Norway, **286** C2
Vila Bittencourt, Brazil, **451** E4
Vila da Ribeira Brava, Cape Verde, **360** Q8
Vila de Sena, Mozambique, **371** G2
Vila do Bispo, Portugal, **292** C4
Vila Franca de Xira, Portugal, **292** C3
Vila Nova, Brazil, **452** B4
Vila Real, *district*, Portugal, **292** D2
Vila Real, Portugal, **292** D2
Vila Velha, Amapá, Brazil, **452** C2
Vila Velha, Espíritu Santo, Brazil, **457** F5

Vilacaya, Bolivia, **455** F5
Vilaine, *river*, France, **290** D2
Viļaka, Latvia, **287** N4
Vilakalaka, Vanuatu, **141** A2
Vilaller, Spain, **293** H1
Vilanandro, Tanjona, *cape*, Madagascar, **372** A4
Vilanculos, Mozambique, **371** G3
Viļāni, Latvia, **287** N4
Vilanova i la Geltrú, Spain, **293** H2
Vilar Formoso, Portugal, **292** D2
Vilātikkulam, India, **216** D4
Vilcabamba, Cordillera, *mountain range*, Peru, **454** D3
Vilhelmina, Sweden, **284** H4
Vilhena, Brazil, **455** G3
Viliya, *river*, Belarus, **298** C2
Viljandi, Estonia, **287** M3
Vilkaviškis, Lithuania, **287** L5
Vilkija, Lithuania, **287** L5
Villa Abecia, Bolivia, **455** F5
Villa Ahumada, Mexico, **430** D2
Villa Ángela, Argentina, **458** E3
Villa Berthet, Argentina, **458** E3
Villa Constitución, Argentina, **458** E4
Villa de Alvarez, Mexico, **430** E5
Villa de Cos, Mexico, **430** E4
Villa de Tamazulapan, Mexico, **431** F5
Villa del Rosario, Argentina, **458** D4
Villa Dolores, Argentina, **458** D4
Villa Flores, Mexico, **431** G5
Villa Florida, Paraguay, **459** F3
Villa Gesell, Argentina, **459** F5
Villa Hayes, Paraguay, **459** F2
Villa Huidobro, Argentina, **458** D5
Villa Iris, Argentina, **458** D6
Villa Juárez, Mexico, **431** E3
Villa María, Argentina, **458** D4
Villa Martín, Bolivia, **455** E5
Villa Mazán, Argentina, **458** C3
Villa Nueva, Argentina, **458** C4
Villa Ocampo, Argentina, **459** E3
Villa Ocampo, Mexico, **430** D3
Villa Ojo de Agua, Argentina, **458** D3
Villa Oropeza, Bolivia, **455** F5
Villa Regina, Argentina, **460** D1
Villa San José, Argentina, **459** E4
Villa Tehuelche, Chile, **460** C4
Villa Unión, Argentina, **458** C3
Villa Unión, Durango, Mexico, **430** D4
Villa Unión, Sinaloa, Mexico, **430** D4
Villa Valeria, Argentina, **458** D5
Villa Viscarra, Bolivia, **455** F4
Villablino, Spain, **292** D1
Villacarrillo, Spain, **293** F3
Villacastin, Spain, **292** E2
Villach, Austria, **289** F5
Villada, Spain, **292** E1
Villagarcía de Arousa, Spain, **292** C1
Villagra, Bahía, *bay*, Róbinson Crusoe Island, Archipiélago Juan Fernández, Chile, **461** C2
Villagrán, Mexico, **431** F3
Villaguay, Argentina, **459** E4
Villahermosa, Mexico, **431** G5
Villahermosa, Spain, **293** F3
Villahoz, Spain, **293** F1
Villajoyosa, Spain, **293** G3
Villalba, Spain, **292** D1
Villaldama, Mexico, **431** E3
Villalonga, Argentina, **460** E1
Villalpando, Spain, **292** E2
Villamalea, Spain, **293** G3
Villamartín, Spain, **292** E4
Villamontes, Bolivia, **455** F5
Villandraut, France, **290** D4
Villano, Ecuador, **450** C4
Villanueva, Colombia, **450** D1
Villanueva, Mexico, **430** E4
Villanueva de Córdoba, Spain, **292** E3
Villanueva de la Serena, Spain, **292** E3
Villanueva del Fresno, Spain, **292** D3
Villány, Hungary, **289** J6
Villapalacios, Spain, **293** F3
Villar, Bolivia, **455** F5
Villarrica, Chile, **460** C1
Villarrica, Lago, *lake*, Chile, **460** C1
Villarrica, Paraguay, **459** F2
Villarrica, Volcán, *mountain peak*, Chile, **460** C1
Villarrobledo, Spain, **293** F3
Villasis, Philippines, **204** C3
Villavicencio, Colombia, **450** D3
Villazón, Bolivia, **455** F6
Ville-Marie, Canada, **416** B6
Villedieu-les-Poêles, France, **290** D2
Villefranche-de-Rouergue, France, **290** F4
Villefranche-sur-Saône, France, **291** G3
Villemontel, Canada, **416** B5
Villena, Spain, **293** G3
Villeneuve-sur-Lot, France, **290** E4
Villers-Bocage, France, **290** D2
Villers-Bretonneux, France, **305** K5
Villeurbanne, France, **291** G4
Villingen-Schwenningen, Germany, **288** D4
Villisca, U.S.A., **420** F5
Vilnius, Lithuania, **287** M5
Vilppula, Finland, **287** M2
Vils, *river*, Germany, **288** E4
Vilsbiburg, Germany, **288** F4
Vilshofen, Germany, **288** F4
Vilusi, Yugoslavia, **294** G4
Vilyeyka, Belarus, **287** N5
Vilyuy, Russian Federation, **301** P3
Vimianzo, Spain, **292** C1
Vimieiro, Portugal, **292** D3
Vimmerby, Sweden, **286** G4
Vimoutiers, France, **290** E2
Viña del Mar, Chile, **458** B4
Vinanivao, Madagascar, **372** C4
Vinaròs, Spain, **293** H2
Vincennes, U.S.A., **421** K6
Vincennes Bay, Antarctica, **470** G6
Vindelälven, *river*, Sweden, **284** H3
Vindeln, Sweden, **284** J4
Vindhya Range, *mountain range*, India, **194** J7
Vineland, U.S.A., **426** C5
Vinga, Romania, **296** C2
Vingåker, Sweden, **286** G3
Vinh, Vietnam, **203** E2
Vĩnh Long, Vietnam, **203** E4
Vinica, Macedonia, **296** D5
Vinita, U.S.A., **420** F7
Vinje, Norway, **286** C2
Vinkovci, Croatia, **294** G3
Vinnitsy, Russian Federation, **299** E2
Vinnyts'ka Oblast', *province*, Ukraine, **296** G1
Vinnytsya, Ukraine, **298** C3
Vinson Massif, *mountain peak*, Antarctica, **470** C5
Vinstra, Norway, **286** D2
Vinsulla, Canada, **412** J6
Vinza, Congo, **368** B3
Vinzili, Russian Federation, **222** H1
Vipiteno, Italy, **294** C2
Virac, Philippines, **204** D3
Viramgām, India, **218** C5
Virandozero, Russian Federation, **285** S4
Viranşehir, Turkey, **224** E5
Virden, Canada, **414** D7
Vire, France, **290** D2
Virei, Angola, **368** B6
Vireši, Latvia, **287** N4
Virgem da Lapa, Brazil, **457** E4
Virgin Islands, *U.K. dependency*, Caribbean Sea, **409** S7
Virgin Islands, *U.S. territory*, Caribbean Sea, **409** S7
Virginia, Ireland, **309** E4
Virginia, South Africa, **371** E4
Virginia, *state*, U.S.A., **421** P7
Virginia, U.S.A., **420** G2
Virginia Beach, U.S.A., **426** B6
Virginia City, U.S.A., **422** D2
Virihaure, *lake*, Sweden, **284** H3
Virma, Russian Federation, **285** S4
Virolanti, Finland, **287** N2
Viroqua, U.S.A., **420** H4
Virovitica, Croatia, **294** F3
Virserum, Sweden, **286** G4
Virtaniemi, Finland, **285** P2
Virtsu, Estonia, **287** L3
Virttaa, Finland, **287** L2
Virú, Peru, **454** B2
Vis, *island*, Croatia, **294** F4
Visaginas, Lithuania, **287** N5
Visale, Solomon Islands, **141** A1
Visalia, U.S.A., **422** D3
Visayan Sea, Philippines, **204** C4
Visby, Sweden, **287** J4
Viscount, Canada, **413** S6
Viscount Melville Sound, Canada, **410** H2
Višegrad, Bosnia and Herzegovina, **296** B4
Viseu, Brazil, **452** D3
Viseu, *district*, Portugal, **292** D2
Viseu, Portugal, **292** D2
Vişeu de Sus, Romania, **296** E2
Vishākhapatnam, India, **217** E2
Vishnevaya, Russian Federation, **299** F5
Vishnevka, Kazakhstan, **223** J2
Vislanda, Sweden, **286** G4
Visoko, Bosnia and Herzegovina, **294** G4
Vissefjärda, Sweden, **286** G4
Visso, Italy, **294** D4
Vit, *river*, Bulgaria, **296** E4
Viterbo, Italy, **295** D4
Viti Levu, *island*, Fiji, **141** A4
Vitichi, Bolivia, **455** F5
Vitigudino, Spain, **292** D2
Vitina, Bosnia and Herzegovina, **294** F4
Vitis, Austria, **289** G4
Vítor, Peru, **454** D4
Vitória, Espírito Santo, Brazil, **457** F5
Vitória, Pará, Brazil, **452** C4
Vitória da Conquista, Brazil, **457** F4
Vitória do Mearim, Brazil, **453** E4
Vitoria-Gasteiz, Spain, **293** F1
Vitorog, *mountain peak*, Bosnia and Herzegovina, **294** F3
Vitré, France, **290** D2
Vitry-le-François, France, **291** G2
Vitsyebsk, Belarus, **299** C5
Vitsyebskaya Voblasts', *province*, Belarus, **287** N5
Vittangi, Sweden, **284** K3
Vitteaux, France, **291** G3
Vittoria, Sicilia, Italy, **295** E7
Vityaz Trench, *underwater feature*, Pacific Ocean, **478** F5
Vivarais, Monts du, *mountain range*, France, **291** G4
Viveiro, Spain, **292** D1
Vivian, Canada, **414** F7
Vivian, U.S.A., **420** C4
Viviers, France, **291** G4
Vivigani, Papua New Guinea, **140** C5
Vivo, South Africa, **371** E3
Vivonne, France, **290** E3
Vizcaíno, Sierra, *mountain range*, Mexico, **430** B3
Vize, Turkey, **297** F5
Vizianagaram, India, **217** E2
Vižinada, Croatia, **294** D3
Viziru, Romania, **296** F3
Vizzini, Sicilia, Italy, **295** E7
Vjosë, *river*, Albania, **297** B5
Vlaams Brabant, *province*, Belgium, **288** B3
Vlădeasa, *mountain peak*, Romania, **296** D2
Vladičin Han, Yugoslavia, **296** C4
Vladikavkaz, Russian Federation, **222** C4
Vladimir, Russian Federation, **298** F1
Vladimirci, Yugoslavia, **296** B3
Vladimirovo, Bulgaria, **296** D4
Vladimirskaya Oblast', *province*, Russian Federation, **299** G4
Vladivostok, Russian Federation, **211** K4
Vladychnoye, Russian Federation, **299** G3
Vlasenica, Bosnia and Herzegovina, **294** G3
Vlašić, *mountain peak*, Bosnia and Herzegovina, **294** F3
Vlasotince, Yugoslavia, **296** D4
Vlieland, *island*, Netherlands, **288** B2
Vlissingen, Netherlands, **288** A3
Vlorë, Albania, **297** B5
Vltava, *river*, Czech Republic, **289** G4
Voćin, Croatia, **294** F3
Vöcklabruck, Austria, **288** F4
Vodla, *river*, Russian Federation, **299** F2
Vodlozero, Ozero, *lake*, Russian Federation, **285** T5
Vogel, Cape, Papua New Guinea, **140** C5
Vogelsberg, *mountain peak*, Germany, **288** D3
Voghera, Italy, **294** B3
Voh, New Caledonia, **141** A3
Vohilava, Madagascar, **372** B5
Vohimena, Tanjona, *cape*, Madagascar, **372** A6
Vohipeno, Madagascar, **372** B5
Vohitrandriana, Madagascar, **372** B5
Võhma, Estonia, **287** M3
Võhma, Saaremaa Island, Estonia, **287** L3
Voi, Kenya, **369** G3
Void-Vacon, France, **291** G2
Voineasa, Romania, **296** D3
Voinjama, Liberia, **364** C3
Voiron, France, **291** G4
Voitila, Finland, **287** M2
Vojakkala, Finland, **287** M2
Vojmån, Sweden, **284** H4
Vojmsjön, *lake*, Sweden, **284** G4
Vojnić, Croatia, **294** E3
Vojvodina, *province*, Yugoslavia, **296** B3
Voknavolok, Russian Federation, **285** Q4
Voko, Cameroon, **365** G3
Volary, Czech Republic, **289** F4
Volborg, U.S.A., **419** M4
Volcán, Panama, **429** E5
Volchikha, Russian Federation, **223** L2
Volch'ya, *river*, Russian Federation, **299** B2
Volda, Norway, **286** C1
Volendam, Netherlands, **288** B2
Volga, *river*, Russian Federation, **281** H4
Volga, Russian Federation, **222** D1
Volga-Baltiyskiy Kanal, *canal*, Russian Federation, **299** F2
Volgino, Russian Federation, **299** D3
Volgodonsk, Russian Federation, **298** F3
Volgograd (Stalingrad), Russian Federation, **298** F3
Volgogradskaya Oblast', *province*, Russian Federation, **298** F3
Volgogradskoye Vodokhranilishche, *reservoir*, Russian Federation, **298** G3
Völkermarkt, Austria, **289** G5
Volkhov, *river*, Russian Federation, **299** C3
Volkhov, Russian Federation, **299** D3
Volksrust, South Africa, **371** E4
Volna, Gora, *mountain peak*, Russian Federation, **301** S3
Voloddymr-Volyns'kyy, Ukraine, **289** M3
Volodino, Russian Federation, **223** L1
Vologda, Russian Federation, **299** G3
Vologodskaya Oblast', *province*, Russian Federation, **299** F2
Volokolamsk, Russian Federation, **299** E4
Voloma, Russian Federation, **285** Q5
Volos, Greece, **297** D6
Volosovo, Russian Federation, **299** B3
Volot, Russian Federation, **299** C4
Volovets', Ukraine, **289** L4
Volovo, Russian Federation, **299** F6
Volta, *administrative region*, Ghana, **364** E3
Volta, Lake, Ghana, **364** D3
Volta Noire, *river*, Burkina Faso, **364** D2
Volta Redonda, Brazil, **457** E6
Volterra, Italy, **294** C4
Volturino, Monte, *mountain peak*, Italy, **295** E5
Volturno, *river*, Italy, **295** E5
Volvi, Limni, *lake*, Greece, **297** D5
Volyns'ka Oblast', *province*, Ukraine, **289** M3
Volzhskiy, Russian Federation, **298** F3
Vondrozo, Madagascar, **372** B5
Von'ga, Russian Federation, **285** S4
Vonitsa, Greece, **297** C6
Võnnu, Estonia, **287** N3
Vop', *river*, Russian Federation, **299** D5
Vopnafjörður, Iceland, **284** Z7
Voranava, Belarus, **287** M5
Vorarlberg, *state*, Austria, **288** D5
Vordingborg, Denmark, **286** E5
Voreio Aigaio, *administrative region*, Greece, **297** E6
Voreioi Sporades, *islands*, Greece, **297** D6
Voreios Evvoikos Kolpos, *bay*, Greece, **297** D6
Vorenzha, Russian Federation, **285** S5
Vorga, Russian Federation, **299** D6
Vorkuta, Russian Federation, **300** H3
Vormsi, *island*, Estonia, **287** L3
Vorob'yevo, Russian Federation, **223** K1
Vorokhta, Ukraine, **296** E1
Voronezh, Russian Federation, **298** E2
Voronezhskaya Oblast', *province*, Russian Federation, **222** B2
Voronovo, Belarus, **289** M1
Voron'ya, *river*, Russian Federation, **285** S2
Vorozhgora, Russian Federation, **285** S5
Võrtsjärv, *lake*, Estonia, **287** M3
Võru, Estonia, **287** N4
Vorzogory, Russian Federation, **285** T5

Wangmo, China, **215** H4
Wangniudun, China, **207** B2
Wangou, China, **211** J4
Wangqi, China, **211** J4
Wangqing, China, **211** K4
Wanham, Canada, **413** K4
Wanie-Rukula, Democratic Republic of the Congo, **369** E2
Wanlaweyn, Somalia, **367** F4
Wanning, China, **203** F2
Wanpan Yang, *bay*, China, **206** E2
Wanqingsha, China, **207** B3
Wanshan Qundao, *islands*, China, **207** B5
Wantage, England, U.K., **305** F3
Wanup, Canada, **421** N2
Wanyuan, China, **206** A1
Wanzai, Guangdong, China, **207** B4
Wanzai, Jiangxi, China, **206** C2
Wanzleben, Germany, **288** E2
Wapakoneta, U.S.A., **421** L5
Wapato, U.S.A., **418** D3
Wapawekka Lake, Canada, **413** S4
Wapekeka, Canada, **415** K5
Wapella, Canada, **414** D6
Wapoga, *river*, Indonesia, **199** G3
Wapsipinicon, *river*, U.S.A., **420** H4
Warab, *state*, Sudan, **366** C3
Warab, Sudan, **366** C3
Warangal, India, **216** D2
Wararisbari, Tanjong, *point*, Indonesia, **199** G3
Warboys, England, U.K., **305** G2
Warburg, Canada, **413** M5
Warburg, Germany, **288** D3
Warburton, *river*, Australia, **135** H4
Ward Hunt, Cape, Papua New Guinea, **140** C5
Wardha, India, **218** D5
Ware, Canada, **412** G3
Wareham, England, U.K., **304** E4
Warialda, Australia, **135** L4
Warizhên, China, **215** G3
Wark, England, U.K., **306** F2
Warka, Poland, **289** K3
Warkworth, England, U.K., **307** G2
Warkworth, New Zealand, **132** E3
Warlingham, England, U.K., **305** G3
Warm Springs, Nevada, U.S.A., **422** E2
Warm Springs, Oregon, U.S.A., **418** D4
Warmandi, Indonesia, **199** F3
Warmbad, Namibia, **370** C4
Warmbad, South Africa, **371** E3
Warmington, England, U.K., **305** F2
Warminster, England, U.K., **304** E3
Warnemünde, Germany, **288** F2
Warner, Canada, **413** N7
Warner, U.S.A., **420** D3
Warner Robins, U.S.A., **425** L3
Warnes, Bolivia, **455** F4
Waropen, Teluk, *bay*, Indonesia, **199** G3
Warora, India, **218** D5
Warracknabeal, Australia, **135** J6
Warrego, *river*, Australia, **135** K4
Warren, Arkansas, U.S.A., **424** F3
Warren, Michigan, U.S.A., **421** M4
Warren, Minnesota, U.S.A., **420** E1
Warren, Montana, U.S.A., **419** K4
Warren, Ohio, U.S.A., **421** N5
Warren, Pennsylvania, U.S.A., **421** P5
Warren Landing, Canada, **414**

F5
Warrensburg, Missouri, U.S.A., **420** G6
Warrensburg, New York, U.S.A., **426** D3
Warrenton, Oregon, U.S.A., **418** C3
Warrenton, South Africa, **370** D4
Warrenton, Virginia, U.S.A., **426** B5
Warri, Nigeria, **365** F3
Warrington, England, U.K., **306** F4
Warrington, *unitary authority*, England, U.K., **306** F4
Warrington, U.S.A., **425** J4
Warrnambool, Australia, **135** J6
Warroad, U.S.A., **420** F1
Warsaw, Indiana, U.S.A., **421** L5
Warsaw, New York, U.S.A., **421** P4
Warsaw see Warszawa, Poland, **289** K2
Warshiikh, Somalia, **367** G4
Warslow, England, U.K., **305** F1
Warsop, England, U.K., **305** F1
Warszawa (Warsaw), Poland, **289** K2
Warta, *river*, Poland, **280** F5
Warud, India, **218** D5
Waruta, *river*, Indonesia, **199** G3
Warwick, Australia, **135** L4
Warwick, England, U.K., **305** F2
Warwickshire, *unitary authority*, England, U.K., **305** F2
Warzhong, China, **215** G3
Wasatch Range, *mountain range*, U.S.A., **423** H2
Wasby, Lake, Australia, **135** J4
Waseca, U.S.A., **420** G3
Wash, The, *bay*, England, U.K., **305** H2
Washakie Needles, *mountain peak*, U.S.A., **419** K5
Washburn, U.S.A., **420** H2
Wāshīm, India, **218** D5
Washington, England, U.K., **307** G3
Washington, Indiana, U.S.A., **421** K6
Washington, Iowa, U.S.A., **420** H5
Washington, Kansas, U.S.A., **420** E6
Washington, Missouri, U.S.A., **420** H6
Washington, Mount, *mountain peak*, U.S.A., **426** E2
Washington, North Carolina, U.S.A., **426** B7
Washington, Pennsylvania, U.S.A., **421** N5
Washington, *state*, U.S.A., **418** D3
Washington, Utah, U.S.A., **422** G3
Washington Court House, U.S.A., **421** M6
Washington D.C., U.S.A., **426** B5
Washita, *river*, U.S.A., **424** C2
Wasile, Indonesia, **198** D2
Waskaganish, Canada, **415** Q6
Waskaiowaka Lake, Canada, **414** F3
Waskesiu Lake, Canada, **413** R5
Waskish, U.S.A., **420** F1
Waspán, Nicaragua, **428** D4
Wassadou, Senegal, **364** B2
Wasserkuppe, *mountain peak*, Germany, **288** D3
Wast Water, *lake*, England, U.K., **306** E3
Wasta, U.S.A., **420** B3
Wasu, Papua New Guinea, **140** B4
Wasua, Papua New Guinea, **140** A5
Watam, Indonesia, **199** E2
Watam, Papua New Guinea, **140** B3

Watauga, U.S.A., **420** C3
Watchet, England, U.K., **304** D3
Water Valley, U.S.A., **424** B4
Waterbury, U.S.A., **426** D4
Waterford, *county*, Ireland, **309** E5
Waterford, Ireland, **309** E5
Waterford Harbour, Ireland, **309** E6
Watergate Bay, England, U.K., **304** B4
Watergrasshill, Ireland, **309** D5
Waterloo, Belgium, **288** B3
Waterloo, Canada, **421** N4
Waterloo, Trinidad, Trinidad and Tobago, **461** C4
Waterloo, U.S.A., **420** G4
Waterloo Lake, Canada, **413** Q2
Waterlooville, England, U.K., **305** F4
Watersmeet, U.S.A., **421** J2
Watertown, New York, U.S.A., **426** C3
Watertown, South Dakota, U.S.A., **420** E3
Waterville, U.S.A., **426** F2
Watford, England, U.K., **305** G3
Watford City, U.S.A., **420** B2
Wa'th, Sudan, **366** D3
Wathaman, *river*, Canada, **414** B3
Watino, Canada, **413** L4
Watlington, England, U.K., **305** F3
Watmuri, Indonesia, **199** E4
Watonga, U.S.A., **424** C2
Watrous, Canada, **413** S6
Watrous, U.S.A., **423** L2
Watsa, Democratic Republic of the Congo, **369** E2
Watseka, U.S.A., **421** K5
Watsi Kengo, Democratic Republic of the Congo, **368** D3
Watson, Canada, **414** B5
Watson Lake, Canada, **412** E1
Watsonville, U.S.A., **422** C3
Watten, Loch, *lake*, Scotland, U.K., **308** F2
Watten, Scotland, U.K., **308** F2
Watton, England, U.K., **305** H2
Watts Bar Lake, U.S.A., **425** K2
Wattwil, Switzerland, **291** J3
Watubela, Kepulauan, *islands*, Indonesia, **199** E4
Watunea, Indonesia, **198** C4
Watzmann, *mountain peak*, Germany, **288** F5
Wau, Papua New Guinea, **140** B4
Waubay, U.S.A., **420** E3
Waubun, U.S.A., **420** F2
Wauchope, Canada, **414** D7
Wauchula, U.S.A., **425** M6
Waukegan, U.S.A., **421** K4
Waukesha, U.S.A., **421** K4
Wauneta, U.S.A., **420** C5
Waupaca, U.S.A., **421** J3
Waupun, U.S.A., **421** J4
Waurika, U.S.A., **424** D2
Wausau, U.S.A., **421** J3
Wautoma, U.S.A., **421** J3
Waverly, Tennessee, U.S.A., **425** J1
Waverly, Virginia, U.S.A., **426** B6
Wavre, Belgium, **288** B3
Wāw, Sudan, **366** C3
Wāw al Kabīr, Libya, **362** C3
Wawa, Canada, **421** L2
Wawa, Nigeria, **365** E3
Wawanesa, Canada, **414** E7
Wawoi, *river*, Papua New Guinea, **140** A4
Waxahachie, U.S.A., **424** D3
Waya, *island*, Fiji, **141** A4
Wayabula, Indonesia, **199** E2
Waycross, U.S.A., **425** L4
Wayne, U.S.A., **420** E4
Waynesboro, Alabama, U.S.A., **425** H4
Waynesboro, Georgia, U.S.A., **425** L3

Waynesboro, Pennsylvania, U.S.A., **426** B5
Waynesboro, Tennessee, U.S.A., **425** J2
Waynoka, U.S.A., **420** D7
Waza, Cameroon, **365** G2
Wazīrābād, Pakistan, **218** C2
Wda, *river*, Poland, **289** J2
Wdzydze, Jezioro, *lake*, Poland, **289** H1
Wé, New Caledonia, **141** A3
We, Pulau, *island*, Indonesia, **200** A1
Weagamow Lake, Canada, **414** J5
Weagamow Lake, *lake*, Canada, **414** J5
Weald, The, *region*, England, U.K., **305** H3
Weatherford, Oklahoma, U.S.A., **424** C2
Weatherford, Texas, U.S.A., **424** D3
Weaverham, England, U.K., **304** E1
Weaverville, U.S.A., **422** B1
Webb, Canada, **413** Q6
Webequie, Canada, **415** L5
Webster, Iowa, U.S.A., **420** G3
Webster, North Dakota, U.S.A., **420** D1
Webster, South Dakota, U.S.A., **420** E3
Webster City, U.S.A., **420** G4
Webster Spring, U.S.A., **421** N6
Weda, Teluk, *bay*, Indonesia, **199** E2
Wedau, Papua New Guinea, **140** C5
Weddell Island, Falkland Islands, **460** E4
Weddell Sea, Antarctica, **470** B4
Wedmore, England, U.K., **304** E3
Weduar, Tanjong, *point*, Indonesia, **199** F4
Wedza, Zimbabwe, **371** F2
Wee Waa, Australia, **135** K5
Weed, U.S.A., **418** C6
Weedon Bec, England, U.K., **305** F2
Węgorzewo, Poland, **289** K1
Węgrów, Poland, **289** K2
Wei, *river*, Henan, China, **210** F5
Wei, *river*, Shaanxi, China, **206** B1
Weichang, China, **210** G4
Weiden in der Oberpfalz, Germany, **288** F4
Weifang, China, **211** G5
Weihai, China, **211** H5
Weihe, China, **211** K3
Weimar, Germany, **288** E3
Weinan, China, **206** B1
Weiner Neustadt, Austria, **289** H5
Weining, China, **215** H4
Weipa, Australia, **135** J1
Weishan, China, **215** G4
Weishi, China, **206** C1
Weiss Lake, U.S.A., **425** K2
Weißenburg in Bayern, Germany, **288** E4
Weitchpec, U.S.A., **418** C6
Weitra, Austria, **289** G4
Weixi, China, **215** F4
Weiya, China, **213** G4
Weizhou Dao, *island*, China, **203** F1
Wejherowo, Poland, **289** J1
Wekakura Point, New Zealand, **133** C5
Wekusko Lake, Canada, **414** E4
Welch, Texas, U.S.A., **423** M5
Welch, West Virginia, U.S.A., **421** N7
Weldiya, Ethiopia, **367** E2
Weldon, U.S.A., **422** D4
Welel, Tulu, *mountain peak*, Ethiopia, **366** D3
Welk'it'ē, Ethiopia, **367** E3
Welkom, South Africa, **371** E4
Welland, *river*, England, U.K.,

305 G2
Wellawaya, Sri Lanka, **217** E5
Wellesbourne, England, U.K., **305** F2
Wellesley Islands, Australia, **135** H2
Wellfleet, U.S.A., **420** C5
Wellingborough, England, U.K., **305** G2
Wellington, Colorado, U.S.A., **423** L1
Wellington, England, U.K., **304** E2
Wellington, Isla, *island*, Chile, **460** B3
Wellington, Kansas, U.S.A., **420** E7
Wellington, New Zealand, **133** E5
Wellington, Ohio, U.S.A., **421** M5
Wellington, Texas, U.S.A., **424** B2
Wellington Bridge, Ireland, **309** F5
Wellman, U.S.A., **420** H5
Wells, Canada, **412** J3
Wells, England, U.K., **304** E3
Wells, Lake, Australia, **134** E4
Wells, U.S.A., **422** F1
Wells next the Sea, England, U.K., **305** H2
Wellsboro, U.S.A., **426** B4
Wellsford, New Zealand, **132** E3
Wellston, U.S.A., **421** M6
Wellsville, U.S.A., **426** B3
Wels, Austria, **289** G4
Welsford, Canada, **416** H7
Welshpool, Wales, U.K., **304** D2
Welwyn, Canada, **414** D6
Welwyn Garden City, England, U.K., **305** G3
Wem, England, U.K., **304** E2
Wema, Democratic Republic of the Congo, **368** D3
Wembley, Canada, **413** K4
Wemindji see Nouveau-Comptoir, Canada, **416**, B3
Wen Xian, China, **215** H2
Wenatchee, U.S.A., **418** D3
Wenchang, China, **203** F2
Wencheng, China, **206** E2
Wenchi, Ghana, **364** D3
Wenchuan, China, **215** G3
Wendell, U.S.A., **418** G5
Wenden, U.S.A., **422** G5
Wendeng, China, **211** H5
Wendens Ambo, England, U.K., **305** H3
Wendover, England, U.K., **305** G3
Wendover, U.S.A., **422** F1
Wenfengzhen, China, **215** H2
Wenjiang, China, **215** G3
Wenling, China, **206** E2
Wenman see Wolf, Isla, *island*, Islas Galápagos (Galapagos Islands), Ecuador, **461** A1
Wenquan, Guangdong, China, **207** B1
Wenquan, Qinghai, China, **214** D2
Wenquan, Xinjiang Uygur Zizhiqu, China, **212** D3
Wenshan, China, **215** H5
Wensum, *river*, England, U.K., **305** H2
Wentworth, Australia, **135** J5
Wenxi, China, **206** B1
Wenzhou, China, **206** E2
Werda, Botswana, **370** D4
Werdēr, Ethiopia, **367** G3
Werfen, Austria, **288** F5
Werota, Ethiopia, **367** E2
Werta, *river*, Germany, **288** E4
Wertheim, Germany, **288** D4
Wesel, Germany, **288** C3
Weser, *river*, Germany, **288** D2
Wesley, U.S.A., **426** G2
Wesleyville, Canada, **417** Q5
Wessel, Cape, Australia, **135** H1
Wessel Islands, Australia, **135** H1
Wessington Springs, U.S.A., **420**